COLLINS

PAPERBACK
DICTIONARY
AND
THESAURUS

COLLINS

PAPERBACK
DICTIONARY
AND
THESAURUS

HarperCollins*Publishers*

First Published 1994
Reprinted 1996, 1997
Latest reprint 1997
4 5 6 7 8 9
© HarperCollins Publishers 1994
PO Box, Glasgow G4 0NB

ISBN 0 00 470513 - 0

EDITORIAL STAFF

Senior Editor
Lorna Knight

Editorial Assistance
Anne Young

A catalogue record for this book is
available from the British Library.

Entered words that we have reason to believe constitute trademarks
have been designated as such. However, neither the presence nor
absence of such designation should be regarded as affecting the legal
status of any trademark.

Computer typeset by Barbers Ltd.
Wrotham, England

Printed and bound in Great Britain by
Caledonian International Book Manufacturing Ltd,
Glasgow, G64

CONTENTS

FOREWORD

Collins Paperback Dictionary and Thesaurus provides two kinds of language help, arranged on the same page for quick and easy reference. In the top section of each page, you will find a dictionary text which gives help with spellings and meanings, while the lower section of each page provides a thesaurus with a choice of synonyms.

The dictionary entries are simply and clearly laid out, to enable you to check spelling, meaning, and grammatical function at a glance. If you then look at the lower half of the page, you will find, for many of the words covered by the dictionary, lists of synonyms. These synonym lists offer you a choice of alternative words to use in place of the one you have in mind.

Suppose, for instance, you want to find another word for *difficult*. Perhaps you have used it already, or perhaps you feel that it is not quite suited to the tone or context of what you want to write or say.

The entry for *difficult* in the thesaurus section of the page provides you with a choice of words, suited to all occasions, that can be used in its place. So from the many alternatives given, you could, for example, substitute: an *onerous* task; *trying* circumstances; an *obstreperous* customer.

Because the two texts are arranged in parallel format, you can refer from dictionary to thesaurus entries and then back again with ease. All the information on any one word in all its aspects is contained at one place.

Collins Paperback Dictionary and Thesaurus is thus a uniquely helpful book, providing spelling, meaning, and a wide choice of alternative words all together at one place. The convenience of the matching text makes it an invaluable reference book for many occasions, and an ideal companion for everyone who wants to increase their command of English.

HOW THE DICTIONARY ENTRIES ARE ARRANGED

Irregular Parts

or confusing forms of verbs, nouns, and
adjectives shown, e.g.

> **abut** *v.* **abutting, abutted.**
> **benefit** ... *–v.* **-fiting, -fited.**
> **ability** *n., pl.* **-ties.**
> **husky** *adj.* **huskier, huskiest.**

Meanings

separated by semicolons, e.g.

> **advance** *v.* go or bring forward; propose;
> further (a cause); lend (a sum of money).

Phrases and Idioms

included after the headword meanings, e.g.

> **hand** *n.* ... *–v.* pass or give.
> **–hand in glove** in close association.
> **–hands down** easily.

Related Words

shown in the headword paragraph, e.g.

> **hard** *adj.* ... **–harden** *–v.* **–hardness**
> *–n.* **–hardship** *–n.* suffering; ...

Note: where the sense of a related word
is not given it may be understood from
the meaning of the headword or of
another related word.

Compounds

made up of the headword and another
word shown in alphabetical order
towards the end of the headword
paragraph, e.g.

> **head** *n.* ... **–headache** *n.*
> continuous pain ... **–headboard**
> *n.* ... **–headway** *n.* progress.
> **–headwind** *n.* ...

Phrasal Verbs

shown towards the end of the headword
paragraph, e.g.

> **have** *v.* ... **–have on** *v. Informal*
> trick or tease. **–have up** *v.* bring
> to trial.

HOW THE DICTIONARY ENTRIES ARE ARRANGED

Main Entry Words

printed in large bold type, e.g.
abbey
All main entry words, including
abbreviations, foreign words, and
combining forms, in one
alphabetical sequence, e.g.
heyday
Hg
HGV
hiatus

Variant Spellings

shown in full, e.g.
racket, racquet
or by bracketing an optional letter, e.g.
abridg(e)ment
Note: -ize, -ization spellings are used
but -ise, -isation are equally acceptable.

Pronunciations

given for words that are difficult or
confusing by respelling, with the stressed
syllable in bold type, e.g.
acerbic [ass-**sir**-bik]

Parts of Speech

shown as an abbreviation, e.g.
ablaze *adj.*
When a word can be used as more than
one part of speech, the change of part of
speech is shown after a dash, e.g.
absent *adj.* not present; ... *–v.*
keep (oneself) away.
Parts of speech combined for some
words, e.g.
alone *adj., adv.* without anyone or
anything else.

Cross References

shown in small capital letters, e.g.
aether *n.* same as ETHER.

HOW THE THESAURUS ENTRIES ARE ARRANGED

1. Under each main entry word, the synonyms are arranged alphabetically. When a word has distinctly separate meanings, separate numbered lists are given for the different senses.

2. Where it is desirable to distinguish between different parts of speech, labels have been added as follows: *n.* (noun), *v.* (verb), *adj.* (adjective), *adv.* (adverb), *pron.* (pronoun), *conj.* (conjunction), *prep.* (preposition), *interj.* (interjection). See entries for *living, local*.

3. Usually the synonyms for a particular part of speech are grouped together. Thus, in the entry *catch* synonyms for all the verb senses are given first, followed by synonyms for all the noun senses. Sometimes, however, noun and verb functions are very closely associated in specific meanings, and where this is the case the synonyms are grouped by meanings.

4. When a headword has more than one meaning *and* can function as more than one part of speech, a new part-of-speech function is shown by a large swung dash (~), as in the entry for *glance* or *grasp*.

5. Much-used phrases appear as main entries; for instance, *abide by* comes after *abide*. Expressions such as *de luxe* or *en route* are also given as main entries within the alphabetical listing. Short idiomatic phrases are entered under their key word and are to be found either at the end of the entry or immediately following the sense with which they are associated. Thus, the phrase *by heart* appears as sense 4 of the entry *heart*, since the synonyms in sense 3 most closely approximate to the meaning of the phrase.

6. Plural forms that have a distinctly separate meaning, such as *provisions*, are entered at their own alphabetical position, while those with a less distinct difference, such as *scraps*, are given as a separate sense under the singular form, e.g. *scrap* . . . 3. *Plural* . . .

7. A label in brackets applies only to the synonym preceding it while one which is not bracketed relates to the whole of that particular sense. Labels have been abbreviated when a readily understandable shortened form exists, such as *Sl.* (Slang), *Inf.* (Informal), and *Fig.* (Figurative).

8. The small swung dash symbol (~) is used to show that a word has been broken merely because it happens to fall at the end of a line, while the conventional sign (-) is used to distinguish a word which is always written with a hyphen, as in the entry for *airy*.

airy 1. blowy, breezy, draughty, fresh, gusty, light, lofty, open, spacious, uncluttered, well-ventilated, windy 2. animated, blithe, buoy~ant, cheerful, cheery, debonair, gay, happy, high-spirited, jaunty, light, light-hearted, lively, merry, nonchalant

ABBREVIATIONS USED IN THE TEXT

AD	anno Domini	**Lit.**	Literary
adj.	adjective	**masc.**	masculine
adv.	adverb	**Med.**	Medical
Anat.	Anatomy	**Meteorol.**	Meteorology
Archit.	Architecture	**Mil.**	Military
Astrol.	Astrology	**N**	North
Aust.	Australia(n)	**n.**	noun
BC	before Christ	**Naut.**	Nautical
Biol.	Biology	**NZ**	New Zealand
Bot.	Botany	**Obs.**	Obsolete
Brit.	Britain, British	**Offens.**	Offensive
Canad.	Canadian	**orig.**	originally
Chem.	Chemistry	**Pathol.**	Pathology
C of E	Church of England	**Photog.**	Photography
conj.	conjunction	**pl.**	plural
det.	determiner	**pl. n.**	plural noun
E	East	**prep.**	preposition
e.g.	for example	**pron.**	pronoun
esp.	especially	**Psychol.**	Psychology
etc.	etcetera	**®**	Trademark
fem.	feminine	**RC**	Roman Catholic
Fig.	Figurative	**S**	South
foll.	followed	**S Afr.**	South Africa(n)
Geog.	Geography	**Scot.**	Scottish
Geom.	Geometry	**sing.**	singular
Gram.	Grammar	**Sl.**	Slang
Hist.	History	**US**	United States
Inf.	Informal	**usu.**	usually
interj.	interjection	**v.**	verb
kg.	kilogram(s)	**W**	West
km.	kilometre(s)	**Zool.**	Zoology
lb(s)	pound(s)		

A

a *det.* indefinite article, used before a noun being mentioned for the first time.

a priori [eh pry-or-rye] *adj.* involving reasoning from cause to effect.

AA Alcoholics Anonymous; Automobile Association.

aardvark *n.* S African anteater with long ears and snout.

AB able-bodied seaman.

aback *adv.* —**taken aback** startled or disconcerted.

abacus [**ab**-a-cuss] *n.* beads on a wire frame, used for doing calculations.

abalone [ab-a-**lone**-ee] *n.* edible shellfish yielding mother-of-pearl.

abandon *v.* desert or leave (one's wife, children, etc.); give up (hope etc.) altogether. —*n.* freedom from inhibition. —**abandoned** *adj.* deserted; uninhibited. —**abandonment** *n.*

abase *v.* humiliate, degrade (oneself). —**abasement** *n.*

abashed *adj.* embarrassed and ashamed.

abate *v.* diminish in strength. —**abatement** *n.*

abattoir [**ab**-a-twahr] *n.* slaughterhouse.

abbess *n.* nun in charge of a convent.

abbey *n.* dwelling place of, or a church belonging to, a community of monks or nuns.

abbot *n.* head of an abbey of monks.

abbr., abbrev. abbreviation.

abbreviate *v.* shorten (a word) by omitting some letters. —**abbreviation** *n.* shortened form of a word or words.

ABC *n.* alphabet; rudiments of a subject.

abdicate *v.* give up (the throne or a responsibility). —**abdication** *n.*

abdomen *n.* part of the body containing the stomach and intestines. —**abdominal** *adj.*

abduct *v.* carry off, kidnap. —**abduction** *n.* —**abductor** *n.*

Aberdeen Angus *n.* breed of cattle, orig. Scottish.

aberration *n.* deviation from what is normal; mental lapse. —**aberrant** *adj.* showing aberration. —**aberrance** *n.*

abet *v.* **abetting, abetted.** assist or encourage in wrongdoing. —**abettor** *n.*

abeyance *n.* state of not being in use.

abhor *v.* **-horring, -horred.** dislike strongly. —**abhorrence** *n.* —**abhorrent** *adj.* hateful, loathsome.

abide *v.* endure, put up with; *Obs.* stay or dwell, e.g. *abide with me.* —**abide by** *v.* obey (the law, rules, etc.). —**abiding** *adj.* lasting.

ability *n.*, *pl.* **-ties.** competence, power; talent.

abject *adj.* utterly miserable; lacking all self-respect. —**abjectly** *adv.* —**abjectness** *n.*

abjure *v.* deny or renounce on oath. —**abjuration** *n.*

ablative [**ab**-lat-iv] *n.* case of nouns in Latin and

THESAURUS

abandon *v.* 1. desert, forsake, jilt, leave, leave behind 2. evacuate, quit, vacate, withdraw from ~*n.* 3. careless freedom, dash, recklessness, unrestraint, wantonness, wild impulse, wildness

abandonment dereliction, desertion, forsaking, jilting, leaving

abbey cloister, convent, friary, monastery, nunnery, priory

abdicate abandon, abjure, abnegate, cede, forgo, give up, quit, relinquish, renounce, resign, retire, surrender, vacate, waive, yield

abduct carry off, kidnap, make off with, run away with, run off with, seize, snatch (*Sl.*)

abhor abominate, detest, hate, loathe, shrink from, shudder at

abhorrent abominable, detestable, disgusting, distasteful, hated, hateful, horrible, horrid, loathsome, odious, offensive, repulsive

abide 1. accept, bear, brook, endure, put up with, stand, submit to, suffer, tolerate 2. continue, endure, last, persist, remain, survive

abide by 1. agree to, conform to, follow, obey, observe, submit to 2. carry out, discharge, fulfil, hold to, keep to, stand by

ability aptitude, capability, capacity, competence, competency, expertise, expertness, facility, faculty, flair, force, gift, knack, power, proficiency, skill, talent

abject 1. base, cringing, despicable, dishonourable, fawning, grovelling, ignominious, low, mean, servile, slavish, submissive, vile, worthless 2. deplorable, forlorn, hopeless, miserable, outcast, pitiable, wretched

ablaze afire, alight, blazing, burning, fiery, flaming, ignited, lighted, on fire

DICTIONARY

other languages, indicating source, agent, or instrument of action.

ablaze *adj.* burning fiercely.

able *adj.* capable, competent. —**ably** *adv.* —**able-bodied** *adj.* strong and healthy.

ablutions *pl. n.* act of washing.

abnegate *v.* give up, renounce. —**abnegation** *n.*

abnormal *adj.* not normal or usual. —**abnormally** *adv.* —**abnormality** *n.*

aboard *adv., prep.* on, in, onto, or into a ship, train, or aircraft.

abode *n.* home, dwelling.

abolish *v.* do away with. —**abolition** *n.* —**abolitionist** *n.* person who wishes to do away with something, esp. slavery.

abominate *v.* detest or hate. —**abominable** *adj.* detestable, very bad. —**abominably** *adv.* —**abomination** *n.* —**abominable snowman** large apelike creature said to inhabit the Himalayas.

aborigine [ab-or-rij-in-ee], **aboriginal** *n.* original inhabitant of a country or region, esp. (A-) Australia. —**aboriginal** *adj.*

abort *v.* terminate (a pregnancy) prematurely; give birth to a dead fetus; end prematurely and unsuccessfully. —**abortion** *n.* operation to terminate a pregnancy; *Informal* something grotesque. —**abortionist** *n.* person who performs abortions, esp. illegally. —**abortive** *adj.* unsuccessful.

abound *v.* be plentiful; overflow. —**abounding** *adj.*

about *prep.* concerning, on the subject of; in or near a place. —*adv.* nearly, approximately; nearby. —**about to** intending to; on the point of, e.g. *about to give up hope*. —**about turn** *v.* (*US* **about face**) *Mil.* turn to face the opposite direction. —**about-turn** *n.* (*US* **about-face**) turn to the opposite direction; complete change of attitude.

above *adv., prep.* over or higher than; greater than; superior to. —**above board** in the open, without dishonesty.

abracadabra *n.* supposedly magic word.

abrade *v.* rub or scrape away.

abrasion *n.* scraped area on the skin. —**abrasive** *adj.* harsh and annoying in manner; causing

THESAURUS

able accomplished, adept, adequate, capable, clever, competent, effective, efficient, experienced, expert, fit, fitted, gifted, masterly, powerful, practised, proficient, qualified, skilful, skilled, strong, talented

able-bodied firm, fit, hale, hardy, healthy, hearty, lusty, powerful, robust, sound, staunch, stout, strapping, strong, sturdy, vigorous

abnormal atypical, curious, deviant, eccentric, exceptional, extraordinary, irregular, odd, peculiar, queer, singular, strange, uncommon, untypical, unusual, weird

abnormality bizarreness, deformity, deviation, eccentricity, exception, flaw, irregularity, oddity, peculiarity, singularity, strangeness, uncommonness, unexpectedness, unnaturalness, unusualness, weirdness

abolish annul, blot out, cancel, destroy, do away with, eliminate, end, eradicate, expunge, extinguish, extirpate, invalidate, nullify, obliterate, overthrow, overturn, put an end to, quash, rescind, revoke, stamp out, subvert, suppress, terminate, void, wipe out

abolition cancellation, destruction, elimination, end, ending, eradication, extermination, extinction, extirpation, obliteration, overthrow, overturning, revocation, stamping out, subversion, suppression, termination, wiping out

abominable base, contemptible, despicable, detestable, disgusting, execrable, foul, hateful, heinous, hellish, horrible, horrid, loathsome,

obnoxious, odious, repellent, repugnant, repulsive, revolting, terrible, vile

abominate abhor, detest, hate, loathe, shudder at

abomination antipathy, aversion, detestation, disgust, distaste, hate, hatred, repugnance, revulsion

abound be plentiful, crowd, flourish, increase, luxuriate, overflow, proliferate, swarm, swell, teem, thrive

abounding abundant, bountiful, copious, full, lavish, luxuriant, overflowing, plenteous, plentiful, profuse, prolific, rich, teeming

about *prep.* 1. as regards, concerned with, concerning, dealing with, on, re, referring to, regarding, relative to 2. adjacent, beside, close to, near, nearby 3. around, encircling, on all sides, round, surrounding 4. all over, over, through, throughout ~*adv.* 5. almost, approaching, approximately, around, close to, more or less, nearing, nearly, roughly

above *prep.* beyond, exceeding, higher than, on top of, over, upon

abrade erase, erode, file, grind, rub off, scour, scrape away, scrape out, wear away, wear down, wear off

abrasive annoying, biting, caustic, cutting, galling, grating, hurtful, irritating, nasty, rough, sharp, unpleasant

DICTIONARY

abrasion. —*n.* substance for cleaning or polishing by rubbing.

abreast *adj.* side by side. —**abreast of** up to date with.

abridge *v.* shorten by using fewer words. —**abridg(e)ment** *n.*

abroad *adv.* to or in a foreign country; at large.

abrogate *v.* cancel (a law or agreement) formally. —**abrogation** *n.*

abrupt *adj.* sudden, unexpected; blunt and rude. —**abruptly** *adv.* —**abruptness** *n.*

abscess *n.* inflamed swelling containing pus.

abscond *v.* leave secretly.

abseil [ab-sale] *v.* descend a vertical cliff by using a rope fixed at a higher point.

absent *adj.* not present; lacking; inattentive. —*v.* keep (oneself) away. —**absently** *adv.* —**absence** *n.* being away; lack. —**absentee** *n.* person who should be present but is not. —**absenteeism** *n.* persistent absence from work or school. —**absent-minded** *adj.* inattentive or forgetful. —**absent-mindedly** *adv.*

absinth(e) *n.* potent green aniseed-flavoured liqueur.

absolute *adj.* complete, perfect; not limited, unconditional; pure, e.g. *absolute alcohol.* —**absolutely** *adv.* completely. —*interj.* certainly, yes. —**absolutism** *n.* government by a ruler with unrestricted power.

absolve *v.* declare to be free from blame or sin. —**absolution** *n.*

absorb *v.* soak up (a liquid); take in; engage the interest of (someone). —**absorption** *n.* —**absorbent** *adj.* able to absorb liquid. —**absorbency** *n.*

abstain *v.* choose to refrain; choose not to vote. —**abstainer** *n.* —**abstention** *n.* abstaining, esp. from voting. —**abstinence** *n.* abstaining, esp. from drinking alcohol. —**abstinent** *adj.*

abstemious [ab-**steem**-ee-uss] *adj.* sparing in the consumption of food or alcohol. —**abstemiously** *adv.* —**abstemiousness** *n.*

abstract *adj.* existing as a quality or idea rather than a material object; theoretical; (of art) using patterns of shapes and colours rather than realistic likenesses. —*n.* summary; abstract work of art; abstract word or idea. —*v.* remove; summarize. —**abstracted** *adj.* preoccupied. —**abstraction** *n.*

THESAURUS

abreast *au fait,* conversant, familiar, informed, in touch, knowledgeable

abridge abbreviate, compress, condense, contract, curtail, cut, cut down, diminish, epitomize, lessen, précis, reduce, shorten, summarize, trim

abroad beyond the sea, in foreign lands, out of the country, overseas

abrupt blunt, brisk, brusque, curt, direct, gruff, impolite, rough, rude, short, terse, uncivil, ungracious

absence 1. absenteeism, truancy 2. default, defect, deficiency, lack, need, omission, privation, want

absent 1. away, elsewhere, gone, lacking, missing, not present, out, truant, unavailable, wanting 2. absent-minded, abstracted, day-dreaming, distracted, dreamy, empty, faraway, heedless, inattentive, musing, oblivious, preoccupied, unaware, unconscious, unheeding, unthinking, vacant, vague

absent-minded abstracted, bemused, distracted, dreaming, dreamy, engrossed, faraway, forgetful, heedless, oblivious, preoccupied, unaware, unthinking

absolute 1. complete, downright, entire, out-and-out, outright, perfect, pure, sheer, thorough, total, unqualified, utter 2. categorical, certain, decided, definite, exact, genuine, positive, precise, sure, unequivocal 3. auto-

cratic, despotic, dictatorial, full, sovereign, supreme, unbounded, unconditional, unlimited, unqualified, unquestionable, unrestrained, unrestricted

absolutely 1. completely, entirely, fully, perfectly, purely, thoroughly, totally, utterly, wholly 2. categorically, certainly, decidedly, decisively, definitely, exactly, genuinely, infallibly, positively, precisely, surely, truly

absolution deliverance, discharge, forgiveness, freeing, indulgence, liberation, mercy, pardon, release, remission, setting free

absolve acquit, clear, deliver, discharge, excuse, exonerate, forgive, free, let off, loose, pardon, release, remit, set free

absorb 1. consume, devour, digest, drink in, exhaust, imbibe, receive, soak up, suck up, take in 2. captivate, engage, engross, fascinate, fill, fill up, fix, hold, immerse, occupy, preoccupy, rivet

abstain avoid, cease, desist, forbear, forgo, give up, keep from, refrain, refuse, renounce, shun, stop, withhold

abstention abstaining, abstinence, avoidance, forbearance, refraining, refusal, self-control, self-denial

abstinence abstemiousness, forbearance, moderation, self-denial, self-restraint, soberness, sobriety, temperance

DICTIONARY

abstruse *adj.* not easy to understand.

absurd *adj.* incongruous or ridiculous. —**absurdly** *adv.* —**absurdity** *n.*

abundant *adj.* plentiful. —**abundantly** *adv.* —**abundance** *n.*

abuse *v.* use wrongly; ill-treat violently; speak harshly and rudely to. —*n.* harsh and vulgar comments; violent ill-treatment; wrong use. —**abusive** *adj.* —**abusively** *adv.* —**abusiveness** *n.*

abut *v.* **abutting, abutted.** adjoin, border on. —**abutment** *n.* end support of a bridge or arch.

abysmal *adj. Informal* extremely bad, awful. —**abysmally** *adv.*

abyss *n.* very deep hole or chasm.

a/c account.

AC alternating current.

acacia [a-**kay**-sha] *n.* tree or shrub with yellow or white flowers.

academy *n., pl.* **-mies.** society to advance arts or sciences; institution for specialized training; *Scot.* secondary school. —**academic** *adj.* of an academy or university; of theoretical interest only. —*n.* lecturer or researcher at a university. —**academically** *adv.* —**academician** *n.* member of an academy.

acanthus *n.* prickly plant; ornamental carving in the shape of an acanthus leaf.

ACAS Advisory Conciliation and Arbitration Service.

accede *v.* consent or agree (to); take up (an office or position).

accelerate *v.* (cause to) move faster. —**acceleration** *n.* —**accelerator** *n.* pedal in a motor vehicle to increase speed.

accent *n.* distinctive style of pronunciation of a local, national, or social group; stress on a sylla-

---

THESAURUS

abstinent abstaining, abstemious, continent, forbearing, moderate, sober, temperate

abstract *adj.* 1. abstruse, complex, conceptual, deep, general, occult, philosophical, profound, separate, subtle, theoretical, unpractical, unrealistic ~*n.* 2. digest, epitome, essence, outline, précis, recapitulation, résumé, summary, synopsis ~*v.* 3. abridge, condense, digest, epitomize, outline, précis, shorten, summarize 4. detach, extract, isolate, remove, separate, steal, take away, withdraw

abstraction 1. absent-mindedness, inattention, preoccupation, remoteness 2. concept, generality, idea, notion, theorem, theory, thought

abstruse abstract, complex, dark, deep, mysterious, obscure, perplexing, profound, recondite, vague

absurd crazy, farcical, foolish, idiotic, illogical, irrational, laughable, ludicrous, nonsensical, preposterous, ridiculous, senseless, silly, stupid

absurdity craziness, folly, foolishness, idiocy, incongruity, irrationality, joke, ludicrousness, nonsense, senselessness, silliness, stupidity

abundance affluence, bounty, fullness, plenteousness, plenty, profusion

abundant ample, bountiful, copious, exuberant, filled, full, lavish, luxuriant, overflowing, plenteous, plentiful, profuse, rich, teeming

abuse *v.* 1. damage, exploit, harm, hurt, ill-treat, injure, maltreat, mar, misapply, misuse, oppress, spoil, wrong 2. curse, defame, disparage, insult, libel, malign, revile, scold, slander, smear, swear at, traduce, upbraid, vilify, vituperate ~*n.* 3. damage, exploitation, harm,

hurt, ill-treatment, imposition, maltreatment, misapplication, misuse, oppression, spoiling, wrong 4. blame, calumniation, castigation, censure, cursing, defamation, disparagement, insults, invective, libel, reproach, revilement, scolding, slander, swearing, tirade, traducement, upbraiding, vilification, vituperation

abusive 1. censorious, disparaging, insulting, libellous, maligning, offensive, opprobrious, reproachful, reviling, rude, scathing, scolding, slanderous, traducing, upbraiding, vilifying, vituperative 2. brutal, cruel, destructive, harmful, hurtful, injurious, rough

abyss abysm, chasm, gulf, pit, void

academic *adj.* 1. bookish, erudite, highbrow, learned, lettered, literary, scholarly, scholastic, school, studious 2. conjectural, impractical, notional, speculative, theoretical ~*n.* 3. academician, don, fellow, lecturer, master, professor, pupil, scholar, scholastic, schoolman, student, tutor

accede 1. accept, acquiesce, admit, agree, assent, comply, concede, concur, consent, endorse, grant, yield 2. assume, attain, come to, enter upon, inherit, succeed, succeed to (*as heir*)

accelerate expedite, forward, further, hasten, hurry, pick up speed, precipitate, quicken, speed, speed up, spur

acceleration expedition, hastening, hurrying, quickening, speeding up, spurring, stimulation

accent *n.* 1. beat, emphasis, force, rhythm, stress 2. inflection, intonation, modulation, pronunciation, tone ~*v.* 3. accentuate, stress, underline, underscore

DICTIONARY

ble or musical note; mark over a letter to show how it is pronounced. —v. place emphasis on.

accentuate v. stress, emphasize. —**accentuation** n.

accept v. receive willingly; consider to be true; agree to. —**acceptance** n. —**acceptable** adj. satisfactory; tolerable. —**acceptably** adv. —**acceptability** n.

access n. means of or right to approach or enter. —v. obtain (data) from a computer. —**accessible** adj. easy to approach or enter. —**accessibility** n.

accession n. taking up of an office or position.

accessory n., pl. -ries. supplementary part or object; person involved in a crime although not present when it is committed.

accident n. mishap, usu. one causing injury or death; event happening by chance. —**accidental** adj. happening by accident. —n. Music symbol

indicating that a sharp, flat, or natural note is not a part of the key signature. —**accidentally** adv.

acclaim v. applaud, praise. —n. applause. —**acclamation** n.

acclimatize v. adapt to a new climate or environment. —**acclimatization** n.

accolade n. award, honour, or praise; award of knighthood.

accommodate v. provide with lodgings; oblige, do a favour for; have room for; adapt or adjust (to something). —**accommodating** adj. obliging. —**accommodation** n. house or room for living in.

accompany v. -nying, -nied. go along with; occur with; provide a musical accompaniment for. —**accompaniment** n. something that accompanies; Music supporting part that goes with a solo. —**accompanist** n.

THESAURUS

accept 1. obtain, receive, secure, take 2. accede, acknowledge, acquiesce, admit, adopt, affirm, agree to, approve, believe, concur with, consent to, cooperate with, recognize, swallow (Inf.) 3. defer to, put up with, stand, submit to, suffer, take, yield to 4. acknowledge, admit, assume, take on, undertake

acceptable 1. agreeable, gratifying, pleasant, pleasing, welcome 2. adequate, admissible, all right, fair, moderate, passable, satisfactory, so-so (Inf.), tolerable

acceptance 1. obtaining, receipt, securing, taking 2. accession, acknowledgment, acquiescence, admission, adoption, affirmation, agreement, approbation, approval, assent, belief, compliance, concession, concurrence, consent, cooperation, permission, recognition, stamp or seal of approval 3. deference, standing, submission 4. acknowledgment, admission, assumption, undertaking

access admission, admittance, course, door, entrance, entrée, entry, key, path, road

accessibility 1. approachability, nearness, obtainability, possibility, readiness 2. exposedness, openness, susceptibility

accessible 1. achievable, at hand, attainable, available, handy, near, nearby, obtainable, on hand, possible, reachable, ready 2. exposed, liable, open, subject, susceptible, vulnerable, wide-open

accessory 1. abettor, accomplice, assistant, associate (in crime), colleague, confederate, helper, partner 2. addition, adjunct, adornment, aid, appendage, attachment, component, convenience, decoration, extension, extra, frill, help, supplement

accident 1. calamity, casualty, chance, collision, crash, disaster, misadventure, mischance, misfortune, mishap, pile-up 2. chance, fate, fortune, hazard, luck

accidental casual, chance, fortuitous, haphazard, incidental, random, uncertain, unexpected, unforeseen, unintended, unintentional, unplanned, unpremeditated, unwitting

accidentally by accident, by chance, by mistake, fortuitously, haphazardly, inadvertently, incidentally, randomly, undesignedly, unintentionally

acclaim 1. v. applaud, approve, celebrate, cheer, clap, commend, exalt, extol, hail, honour, laud, praise, salute, welcome 2. n. acclamation, applause, approbation, approval, celebration, commendation, exaltation, honour, plaudits, praise, welcome

acclimatization adaptation, adjustment, naturalization

acclimatize accommodate, accustom, adapt, adjust, become seasoned to, get used to, inure, naturalize

accommodate 1. billet, board, cater for, harbour, house, lodge, put up, quarter, shelter 2. aid, assist, furnish, help, oblige, provide, serve, supply 3. comply, compose, conform, fit, harmonize, modify, reconcile, settle

accommodating complaisant, considerate, cooperative, friendly, helpful, hospitable, kind, obliging, polite, unselfish, willing

accommodation board, digs (Inf.), harbouring, house, housing, lodging(s), quartering, quarters, shelter, sheltering

accompany attend, conduct, convoy, escort, go with, usher

DICTIONARY

accomplice *n.* person who helps another to commit a crime.

accomplish *v.* manage to do; finish. —**accomplished** *adj.* expert, proficient. —**accomplishment** *n.* personal ability or skill; completion.

accord *n.* agreement, harmony. —*v.* fit in with.

accordance *n.* —**in accordance with** in conformity with.

according *adv.* —**according to** as stated by; in conformity with. —**accordingly** *adv.* in an appropriate manner; consequently.

accordion *n.* portable musical instrument played by moving the two sides apart and together, and pressing a keyboard or buttons to produce the notes. —**accordionist** *n.*

accost *v.* approach and speak to.

account *n.* report, description; importance, value; person's money held in a bank; record of money received and paid out with the resulting balance; business arrangement making credit available. —*v.* judge to be. —**on account of** because of. —**accountable** *adj.* responsible to someone or for something. —**accountability** *n.*

accounting *n.* skill or practice of maintaining and auditing business accounts. —**accountant** *n.* person who maintains and audits business accounts. —**accountancy** *n.*

accoutrements [ak-**koo**-trem-ments] *pl. n.* clothing and equipment.

accredited *adj.* authorized, officially recognized.

accretion [ak-**kree**-shun] *n.* gradual growth; something added.

accrue *v.* -cruing, -crued. increase gradually. —**accrual** *n.*

accumulate *v.* gather together in increasing quantity. —**accumulation** *n.* —**accumulative** *adj.* —**accumulator** *n.* rechargeable electric battery.

accurate *adj.* exact, correct. —**accurately** *adv.* —**accuracy** *n.*

THESAURUS

accompanying added, additional, attached, attendant, connected, fellow, joint, related, supplementary

accomplice accessory, ally, assistant, associate, collaborator, colleague, confederate, helper, henchman, partner

accomplish achieve, attain, bring off (*Inf.*), carry out, complete, conclude, do, effect, execute, finish, fulfil, manage, perform, produce, realize

accomplished adept, cultivated, expert, gifted, masterly, polished, practised, proficient, skilful, skilled, talented

accomplishment 1. achievement, bringing about, carrying out, completion, conclusion, doing, effecting, execution, finishing, fulfilment, performance, production, realization 2. ability, achievement, art, attainment, proficiency, skill, talent

accordingly as a result, consequently, ergo, hence, in consequence, so, therefore, thus

according to 1. as believed by, as maintained by, as stated by, in the light of, on the authority of 2. after, after the manner of, in accordance with, in conformity with, in harmony with, in keeping with, in line with, in step with, in the manner of

account *n.* 1. chronicle, description, history, narration, narrative, recital, record, relation, report, statement, story, tale, version 2. *Commerce* balance, bill, book, books, charge, inventory, invoice, ledger, reckoning, register, score, statement, tally ~*v.* 3. assess, believe, calculate, consider, count, deem, esteem, estimate, hold, judge, rate, reckon, regard, think, value

accountability answerability, liability, responsibility

accountable amenable, answerable, charged with, liable, obliged, responsible

accredited appointed, certified, commissioned, endorsed, guaranteed, licensed, official, recognized, sanctioned, vouched for

accumulate accrue, amass, build up, collect, gather, grow, hoard, increase, pile up, stockpile, store

accumulation aggregation, build-up, collection, gathering, heap, hoard, increase, mass, pile, stack, stock, stockpile, store

accuracy carefulness, correctness, exactitude, faithfulness, faultlessness, niceness, nicety, precision, strictness, truth, truthfulness, veracity

accurate close, correct, exact, faithful, faultless, just, meticulous, nice, precise, proper, regular, right, scrupulous, strict, true, truthful, unerring

accurately correctly, exactly, faithfully, faultlessly, justly, meticulously, nicely, precisely, properly, regularly, rightly, scrupulously, strictly, truly, truthfully, unerringly

accursed bedevilled, bewitched, condemned, cursed, damned, doomed, hopeless, ill-fated, ill-omened, luckless, ruined, undone, unfortunate, wretched

accusation allegation, attribution, charge, complaint, imputation, incrimination, indictment, recrimination

DICTIONARY

accursed *adj.* under a curse; detestable.

accusative *n.* grammatical case indicating the direct object.

accuse *v.* charge with wrongdoing; blame. —**accused** *n.*, *adj.* —**accuser** *n.* —**accusing** *adj.* —**accusation** *n.* —**accusatory** *adj.*

accustom *v.* make used to. —**accustomed** *adj.* usual; used (to); in the habit (of).

ace *n.* playing card with one spot on it; *Informal* expert; *Tennis* unreturnable serve. —*adj. Informal* excellent.

acerbic [ass-**sir**-bik] *adj.* harsh or bitter. —**acerbity** *n.*

acetate [**ass**-it-tate] *n. Chem.* salt or ester of acetic acid; (also **acetate rayon**) synthetic textile fibre.

acetic [ass-**see**-tik] *adj.* of or involving vinegar. —**acetic acid** colourless liquid used to make vinegar.

acetone [**ass**-it-tone] *n.* colourless liquid used as a solvent.

acetylene [ass-**set**-ill-een] *n.* colourless flammable gas used in welding metals.

ache *n.* dull continuous pain. —*v.* be in or cause continuous pain.

achieve *v.* gain by hard work or ability. —**achievement** *n.* something accomplished.

Achilles heel [ak-**kill**-eez] *n.* small but fatal weakness. —**Achilles tendon** *n.* cord connecting the calf to the heelbone.

achromatic *adj.* colourless; *Music* with no sharps or flats.

acid *n. Chem.* one of a class of compounds, corrosive and sour when dissolved in water, that combine with a base to form a salt; *Slang* LSD. —*adj.* containing acid; sour-tasting; sharp or sour in manner. —**acidic** *adj.* —**acidify** *v.* —**acidity** *n.* —**acidulous** *adj.* sharp; caustic. —**Acid (House)** *n.* type of funk-based electronically edited disco music with hypnotic sound effects. —**acid rain** rain containing acid from atmospheric pollution. —**acid test** conclusive test of value.

acknowledge *v.* admit, recognize; indicate recognition of (a person); say one has received. —**acknowledg(e)ment** *n.*

acme [**ak**-mee] *n.* highest point of achievement or excellence.

acne [**ak**-nee] *n.* pimply skin disease.

acolyte *n.* follower or attendant; *Christianity* person who assists a priest.

aconite *n.* poisonous plant with hoodlike flowers; poison obtained from this plant.

acorn *n.* nut of the oak tree.

acoustic *adj.* of sound and hearing. —**acoustics** *n.* science of sounds. —*pl.* features of a room or building determining how sound is heard within it. —**acoustically** *adv.*

acquaint *v.* make familiar, inform. —**acquainted** *adj.* —**acquaintance** *n.* person known; personal knowledge.

THESAURUS

accuse blame, censure, charge, impute, incriminate, indict, recriminate, tax

accustom acclimatize, adapt, familiarize, habituate, inure, season, train

accustomed 1. acclimatized, adapted, familiar, given to, habituated, in the habit of, inured, seasoned, trained, used 2. common, conventional, customary, established, everyday, expected, habitual, normal, ordinary, regular, routine, set

ace adept, champion, dab hand (*Inf.*), expert, genius, master, star, virtuoso, winner, wizard

ache *v.* hurt, pain, smart, suffer, throb, twinge

achieve accomplish, attain, bring about, carry out, complete, do, earn, effect, execute, finish, fulfil, gain, get, obtain, perform, procure, reach, win

achievement accomplishment, attainment, completion, execution, fulfilment, performance, production, realization

acid acrid, biting, pungent, sharp, sour, tart

acidity acridity, bitterness, pungency, sharpness, sourness, tartness

acknowledge 1. accept, acquiesce, admit, allow, concede, confess, declare, grant, own, profess, recognize, yield 2. answer, notice, react to, recognize, reply to, respond to, return

acknowledgment 1. acceptance, acquiescence, admission, allowing, confession, yielding 2. answer, appreciation, credit, gratitude, reaction, recognition, reply, response, return, thanks

acquaint announce, apprise, disclose, divulge, enlighten, inform, let (someone) know, notify, reveal, tell

acquaintance associate, colleague, contact

acquainted apprised of, *au fait*, aware of, cognizant of, conscious of, conversant with, familiar with, informed of, in on, privy to, versed in

acquiesce accept, agree, assent, bow to, comply, concur, conform, consent, give in, go along with, submit, yield

acquiescence acceptance, agreement, assent, compliance, concurrence, conformity, consent, giving in, submission, yielding

DICTIONARY

acquiesce [ak-wee-**ess**] *v.* accept without complaining. —**acquiescence** *n.* —**acquiescent** *adj.*

acquire *v.* gain, get. —**acquirement** *n.* —**acquisition** *n.* act of getting; thing acquired. —**acquisitive** *adj.* eager to gain material possessions. —**acquisitiveness** *n.*

acquit *v.* -**quitting,** -**quitted.** declare innocent; conduct (oneself) in a particular way. —**acquittal** *n.*

acre *n.* measure of land, 4840 square yards. —**acreage** [**ake**-er-rij] *n.* land area in acres.

acrid [ak-rid] *adj.* pungent, bitter. —**acridity** *n.*

acrimony [ak-rim-mon-ee] *n.* bitterness of speech or manner. —**acrimonious** *adj.*

acrobat *n.* person skilled in gymnastic feats requiring agility and balance. —**acrobatic** *adj.* —**acrobatics** *pl. n.* acrobatic feats.

acronym *n.* word formed from the initial letters of other words, such as NATO.

acropolis [a-**crop**-pol-liss] *n.* citadel of an ancient Greek city.

across *adv., prep.* from side to side (of); on or to the other side (of).

acrostic *n.* word puzzle in which the first or last letters of each line spell a word or saying.

acrylic *n., adj.* (synthetic fibre, paint, etc.) made from acrylic acid. —**acrylic acid** strong-smelling corrosive liquid.

act *n.* thing done; law or decree; section of a play or opera; one of several short performances in a show; pretended attitude. —*v.* do something; behave in a particular way; perform in a play, film, etc. —**act of God** unpredictable natural event. —**acting** *n.* art of an actor. —*adj.* temporarily performing the duties of. —**actor, actress** *n.* person who acts in a play, film, etc.

actinium *n.* radioactive chemical element.

action *n.* process of doing; thing done; operating mechanism; lawsuit; minor battle. —**actionable** *adj.* giving grounds for a lawsuit. —**action replay** rerun of an event on a television tape.

active *adj.* moving, working; busy, energetic; *Grammar* (of a verb) in a form indicating that the subject is performing the action, e.g. *threw* in *Kim threw the ball.* —**actively** *adv.* —**activity** *n.* active behaviour; leisure pursuit. —**activate** *v.* make active. —**activation** *n.* —**activator** *n.* —**activist** *n.* person who works energetically to achieve political or social goals. —**activism** *n.*

THESAURUS

acquire amass, attain, buy, collect, earn, gain, gather, get, obtain, pick up, procure, realize, receive, secure, win

acquisition buy, gain, possession, prize, property, purchase

acquisitive avaricious, avid, greedy, predatory, rapacious

acquit absolve, clear, deliver, discharge, exculpate, exonerate, free, fulfil, liberate, release, relieve, vindicate

acquittal absolution, clearance, discharge, exculpation, exoneration, liberation, release, relief, vindication

acrimonious astringent, bitter, caustic, censorious, cutting, irascible, mordant, petulant, pungent, rancorous, sarcastic, severe, sharp, spiteful, tart, testy, trenchant

acrimony asperity, astringency, bitterness, ill will, mordancy, peevishness, rancour, sarcasm, spleen, tartness, virulence

act *n.* 1. action, blow, deed, doing, execution, exertion, exploit, feat, operation, performance, step, stroke, undertaking 2. bill, decree, edict, enactment, law, measure, ordinance, resolution, statute 3. performance, routine, show, sketch, turn ~*v.* 4. acquit, bear, behave, carry, carry out, comport, conduct, do, enact, execute, exert, function, go about, make, move, operate, perform, react, serve, strike, take ef-fect, undertake, work 5. affect, counterfeit, feign, imitate, perform, pose, posture, pretend, put on, seem 6. act out, characterize, enact, impersonate, mime, mimic, perform, personate, personify, play, play *or* take the part of, portray, represent

acting 1. *adj.* interim, *pro tem*, provisional, substitute, surrogate, temporary 2. *n.* dramatics, impersonation, performance, performing, portrayal, portraying

action 1. accomplishment, achievement, act, deed, feat, move, operation, performance, step, stroke, undertaking 2. battle, combat, conflict, fighting, warfare 3. case, cause, lawsuit, litigation, proceeding, prosecution, suit

active 1. acting, astir, at work, doing, functioning, in action, in force, in operation, live, moving, operative, running, working 2. bustling, busy, engaged, full, involved, occupied, on the go (*Inf.*), on the move 3. alert, animated, diligent, energetic, industrious, lively, nimble, on the go (*Inf.*), quick, spirited, sprightly, spry, vibrant, vigorous, vital, vivacious

activity 1. action, animation, bustle, exertion, hurly-burly, hustle, labour, life, liveliness, motion, movement, stir, work 2. hobby, interest, job, labour, occupation, pastime, project, pursuit, scheme, task, undertaking, venture, work

DICTIONARY

actual *adj.* existing in reality. —**actually** *adv.* really, indeed. —**actuality** *n.*

actuary *n., pl.* **-aries.** statistician who calculates insurance risks. —**actuarial** *adj.*

actuate *v.* activate (a device). —**actuation** *n.*

acuity [ak-kew-it-ee] *n.* keenness of vision or thought.

acumen [ak-yew-men] *n.* ability to make good judgments.

acupuncture *n.* medical treatment involving the insertion of needles at various points on the body. —**acupuncturist** *n.*

acute *adj.* keen, shrewd; sharp, sensitive; severe; (of an angle) less than 90°. —*n.* accent (´) over a letter to indicate the quality or length of its sound, as in café. —**acutely** *adv.* —**acuteness** *n.*

AD anno Domini.

ad *n. Informal* advertisement.

adage [ad-ij] *n.* wise saying, proverb.

adagio [ad-dah-]-yo] *Music* slowly and gracefully.

adamant *adj.* inflexibly determined. —**adamantly** *adv.*

Adam's apple *n.* projecting lump of thyroid cartilage at the front of the throat.

adapt *v.* alter for new use or new conditions. —**adaptable** *adj.* —**adaptability** *n.* —**adaptation** *n.* adapting; thing produced by adapting something. —**adaptor, -er** *n.* device for connecting several electrical appliances to a single socket.

add *v.* combine (numbers or quantities); join (to something); say further.

addendum *n., pl.* **-da.** an addition; appendix to a book etc.

adder *n.* small poisonous snake.

addict *n.* person who is unable to stop taking drugs; *Informal* person devoted to something. —**addicted** *adj.* —**addiction** *n.* —**addictive** *adj.* causing addiction.

addition *n.* adding; thing added. —**in addition** besides, as well. —**additional** *adj.* —**additionally** *adv.* —**additive** *n.* something added, esp. to foodstuffs.

addle *v.* make rotten or muddled.

address *n.* place where a person lives; direction on a letter; location; formal public speech. —*v.* mark the destination, as on an envelope; speak to; give attention to (a problem, task, etc.). —**addressee** *n.* person addressed.

THESAURUS

actor actress, dramatic artist, leading man, performer, play-actor, player, Thespian, tragedian, trouper

actress actor, dramatic artist, leading lady, performer, play-actor, player, starlet, Thespian, trouper

actual absolute, categorical, certain, definite, factual, indisputable, indubitable, physical, positive, real, substantial, tangible, undeniable, unquestionable

actually as a matter of fact, de facto, essentially, indeed, in fact, in reality, in truth, literally, really, truly

acute 1. clever, discerning, discriminating, incisive, intuitive, keen, observant, perceptive, perspicacious, sharp, smart, subtle 2. needle-shaped, pointed, sharp, sharpened

acuteness cleverness, discernment, discrimination, intuitiveness, keenness, perception, perceptiveness, perspicacity, sharpness, smartness, subtlety

adamant determined, firm, fixed, immovable, inexorable, inflexible, insistent, intransigent, obdurate, resolute, rigid, set, stiff, stubborn, unbending, uncompromising, unrelenting, unshakable, unyielding

adapt accommodate, adjust, alter, apply, change, comply, conform, fit, habituate, make,

match, modify, prepare, qualify, remodel, shape, suit, tailor

adaptability changeability, compliancy, flexibility, malleability, pliancy, resilience, versatility

adaptable adjustable, compliant, easy-going, flexible, malleable, modifiable, plastic, pliant, resilient, versatile

adaptation adjustment, alteration, change, conversion, modification, refitting, shift, transformation, variation, version

add 1. amplify, append, attach, augment, enlarge by, include, increase by, supplement 2. add up, compute, count up, reckon, sum up, total, tot up

addendum addition, adjunct, affix, appendage, appendix, attachment, augmentation, extension, postscript, supplement

addict dope-fiend (*Sl.*), junkie (*Sl.*), user (*Inf.*)

addicted dedicated, dependent, devoted, hooked (*Sl.*), obsessed, prone

addiction craving, dependence, habit, obsession

addition 1. adding, adjoining, affixing, amplification, attachment, augmentation, enlargement, extension, inclusion 2. addendum, adjunct, appendage, appendix, extension, extra, gain, increase, increment, supplement

additional added, extra, fresh, further, more, new, other, spare, supplementary

DICTIONARY

adduce *v.* cite as proof.

adenoids [ad-in-oidz] *pl. n.* mass of tissue at the back of the nose. —**adenoidal** *adj.* having a nasal voice caused by swollen adenoids.

adept *adj., n.* very skilful (person).

adequate *adj.* sufficient, enough; not outstanding. —**adequately** *adv.* —**adequacy** *n.*

adhere *v.* stick to; be devoted to. —**adherence** *n.* —**adherent** *n.* devotee, follower. —**adhesion** *n.* adhering; abnormal sticking together of parts of the body, as after surgery.

adhesive *adj.* able to stick to things. —*n.* substance used to stick things together.

ad hoc *adj., adv.* for a particular occasion only.

adieu [a-dew] *interj.* farewell, goodbye.

ad infinitum *adv. Latin* endlessly.

adipose *adj.* of fat, fatty.

adj. adjective.

adjacent *adj.* near or next to; having a common boundary; *Geom.* (of a side in a right-angled triangle) lying between a specified angle and the right angle.

adjective *n.* word that adds information about a noun or pronoun. —**adjectival** *adj.*

adjoin *v.* be next to. —**adjoining** *adj.*

adjourn *v.* close (a court) at the end of a session; postpone temporarily; *Informal* go elsewhere. —**adjournment** *n.*

adjudge *v.* declare (to be).

adjudicate *v.* decide on (a dispute); judge (a competition). —**adjudication** *n.* —**adjudicator** *n.*

adjunct *n.* subordinate or additional person or thing.

adjure *v.* command to do; appeal earnestly.

adjust *v.* alter slightly so as to be suitable; adapt to new conditions. —**adjustable** *adj.* —**adjuster** *n.* —**adjustment** *n.*

adjutant [aj-oo-tant] *n.* army officer in charge of routine administration.

ad-lib *v.* **-libbing, -libbed.** improvise a speech etc. without preparation. —*n.* improvised remark.

admin *n. Informal* administration.

administer *v.* manage (business affairs); dispense (justice); give (medicine or treatment).

administrate *v.* manage (an organization). —**administration** *n.* —**administrative** *adj.* —**administrator** *n.*

THESAURUS

address *n.* 1. abode, domicile, dwelling, home, house, location, lodging, place, residence 2. direction, inscription, superscription 3. discourse, disquisition, dissertation, harangue, lecture, oration, sermon, speech, talk ~*v.* 4. apostrophize, greet, hail, invoke, salute, speak to, talk to 5. discourse, give a speech, give a talk, harangue, lecture, orate, sermonize, speak, talk

adept able, accomplished, adroit, dexterous, expert, practised, proficient, skilful, skilled, versed

adequacy competence, fairness, satisfactoriness, sufficiency, tolerability

adequate capable, competent, enough, fair, passable, satisfactory, sufficient, suitable, tolerable

adhere attach, cement, cling, fasten, fix, glue, glue on, hold fast, paste, stick, stick fast

adherent admirer, advocate, devotee, disciple, fan, follower, hanger-on, partisan, supporter, upholder, votary

adhesive 1. *adj.* clinging, gummy, holding, sticking, sticky, tacky, tenacious 2. *n.* glue, gum, paste

adieu farewell, goodbye, parting, valediction

adjacent adjoining, alongside, beside, bordering, close, near, neighbouring, next door, touching

adjoining adjacent, bordering, connecting, contiguous, joined, joining, near, neighbouring, next door, touching

adjourn defer, delay, discontinue, interrupt, postpone, prorogue, put off, recess, stay, suspend

adjournment deferment, delay, discontinuation, interruption, recess, stay, suspension

adjudicate adjudge, arbitrate, decide, determine, judge, referee, settle, umpire

adjudication arbitration, decision, determination, finding, judgment, pronouncement, ruling, settlement, verdict

adjust adapt, alter, arrange, compose, dispose, fit, fix, harmonize, make conform, measure, modify, order, reconcile, redress, regulate, remodel, set, settle, suit

adjustable flexible, malleable, modifiable, movable, tractable

adjustment adaptation, alteration, arrangement, arranging, fitting, fixing, modification, ordering, rectification, redress, regulation, remodelling, setting, tuning

ad-lib *v.* extemporize, improvise, make up, speak extemporaneously, speak impromptu, speak off the cuff

administer conduct, control, direct, govern, manage, oversee, run, superintend, supervise

administration conduct, control, direction, execution, government, management, overse-

DICTIONARY

admiral *n.* highest naval rank. —**Admiralty** *n.* (formerly) the government department in charge of the Royal Navy.

admire *v.* regard with esteem and approval. —**admirable** *adj.* —**admirably** *adv.* —**admiration** *n.* —**admirer** *n.* —**admiring** *adj.* —**admiringly** *adv.*

admissible *adj.* allowed to be brought in as evidence in court. —**admissibility** *n.*

admission *n.* permission to enter; entrance fee; confession.

admit *v.* -**mitting**, -**mitted**. confess, acknowledge; concede the truth of; allow in. —**admittance** *n.* permission to enter. —**admittedly** *adv.* it must be agreed (that).

admixture *n.* mixture; ingredient.

admonish *v.* reprove sternly. —**admonition** *n.* —**admonitory** *adj.*

ad nauseam [ad naw-zee-am] *adv. Latin* to a boring or sickening extent.

ado *n.* fuss, trouble.

adobe [ad-oh-bee] *n.* sun-dried brick.

adolescence *n.* period between puberty and adulthood. —**adolescent** *n., adj.* (person) between puberty and adulthood.

adopt *v.* take (someone else's child) as one's own; take up (a plan or principle). —**adoption** *n.* —**adoptive** *adj.* related by adoption.

adore *v.* love intensely; worship. —**adorable** *adj.* —**adoration** *n.* —**adoring** *adj.* —**adoringly** *adv.*

adorn *v.* decorate, embellish. —**adornment** *n.*

ADP automatic data processing.

adrenal [ad-reen-al] *adj.* near the kidney. —**adrenal glands** *pl. n.* glands covering the top of the kidneys.

adrenalin(e) *n.* hormone secreted by the adrenal glands in response to stress.

adrift *adj., adv.* drifting; without clear purpose.

adroit *adj.* quick and skilful. —**adroitly** *adv.* —**adroitness** *n.*

adsorb *v.* (of a gas or vapour) condense and form a thin film on a surface. —**adsorbent** *adj.* —**adsorption** *n.*

adulation *n.* uncritical admiration.

THESAURUS

ing, performance, provision, running, superintendence, supervision

administrative executive, governmental, management, managerial, organizational, regulatory, supervisory

admirable commendable, estimable, excellent, exquisite, fine, laudable, meritorious, praiseworthy, rare, superior, valuable, wonderful, worthy

admiration adoration, affection, amazement, appreciation, approval, astonishment, delight, esteem, pleasure, praise, regard, respect, surprise, wonder

admire adore, appreciate, approve, esteem, idolize, look up to, praise, prize, respect, think highly of, value, worship

admirer 1. beau, boyfriend, lover, suitor, sweetheart, wooer 2. devotee, disciple, enthusiast, fan, follower, partisan, supporter, worshipper

admissible acceptable, allowable, allowed, passable, permissible, permitted, tolerable, tolerated

admission 1. access, entrance, entrée, entry, initiation, introduction 2. acknowledgment, allowance, avowal, concession, confession, declaration, disclosure, divulgence, profession, revelation

admit 1. allow, allow to enter, give access, initiate, introduce, let in, receive, take in 2. acknowledge, affirm, avow, concede, confess, declare, disclose, divulge, profess, reveal 3. agree, allow, grant, let, permit, recognize

adolescence boyhood, girlhood, minority, teens, youth

adolescent 1. *adj.* boyish, girlish, growing, immature, juvenile, puerile, teenage, young, youthful 2. *n.* juvenile, minor, teenager, youngster, youth

adopt 1. accept, appropriate, approve, assume, choose, embrace, endorse, espouse, follow, maintain, ratify, select, support, take on, take over, take up 2. foster, take in

adoption 1. acceptance, approbation, appropriation, approval, assumption, choice, embracing, endorsement, espousal, ratification, support, taking on, taking over, taking up 2. adopting, fosterage, fostering, taking in

adore admire, cherish, dote on, esteem, exalt, glorify, honour, idolize, love, revere, reverence, venerate, worship

adorn beautify, deck, decorate, embellish, enhance, enrich, garnish, grace, ornament, trim

adornment decoration, embellishment, frill, frippery, ornament, trimming

adrift float, drifting, unanchored, unmoored

adulation blandishment, fawning, fulsome praise, servile flattery, sycophancy, worship

adult 1. *adj.* full grown, fully developed, fully grown, grown-up, mature, of age, ripe 2. *n.* grown or grown-up person (man or woman), grown-up

DICTIONARY

adult *adj.* fully grown, mature. —*n.* adult person or animal. —**adulthood** *n.*

adulterate *v.* make impure by addition. —**adulteration** *n.*

adultery *n., pl.* **-teries.** sexual unfaithfulness of a husband or wife. —**adulterer, adulteress** *n.* —**adulterous** *adj.*

adumbrate *v.* give a faint indication of. —**adumbration** *n.*

adv. adverb.

advance *v.* go or bring forward; propose; further (a cause); lend (a sum of money). —*n.* forward movement; improvement; loan. —*pl.* approaches to a person with the hope of starting a romantic or sexual relationship. —*adj.* previous. —**in advance** ahead. —**advanced** *adj.* at a late stage in development; not elementary. —**advancement** *n.* promotion.

advantage *n.* more favourable position or state; benefit or profit; *Tennis* point scored after deuce. —**take advantage of** use (an opportunity); use (a person) unfairly. —**advantageous** *adj.* —**advantageously** *adv.*

advent *n.* arrival; (A-) season of four weeks before Christmas. —**Adventist** *n.* member of a Christian sect that believes in the imminent return of Christ.

adventitious *adj.* added or appearing accidentally.

adventure *n.* exciting and risky undertaking or exploit. —**adventurer, adventuress** *n.* person who seeks adventures; person who unscrupulously seeks money or power. —**adventurous** *adj.*

adverb *n.* word that adds information about a verb, adjective, or other adverb. —**adverbial** *adj.* —**adverbially** *adv.*

adversary [ad-verse-er-ree] *n., pl.* **-saries.** opponent or enemy.

adverse *adj.* antagonistic or hostile; unfavourable. —**adversely** *adv.* —**adversity** *n.* affliction or hardship.

advert *n. Informal* advertisement.

advertise *v.* present or praise (goods or services) to the public in order to encourage sales; make (a vacancy, event, etc.) known publicly. —**advertisement** *n.* public announcement to sell goods or publicize an event. —**advertiser** *n.* —**advertising** *adj., n.*

advice *n.* recommendation as to what to do. —**advise** *v.* offer advice to; notify (someone). —**adviser, -or** *n.* —**advisable** *adj.* prudent, sensible. —**advisability** *n.* —**advisory** *adj.* giving advice. —**advised** *adj.* considered, thought-out, e.g. *ill-advised.* —**advisedly** *adv.* deliberately.

THESAURUS

advance *v.* 1. accelerate, bring forward, bring up, come forward, elevate, go ahead, go forward, go on, hasten, move onward, move up, press on, proceed, progress, promote, send forward, send up, speed, upgrade 2. adduce, allege, cite, offer, present, proffer, propose, put forward, submit, suggest 3. lend, pay beforehand, raise (*price*), supply on credit ~*n.* 4. advancement, amelioration, betterment, breakthrough, furtherance, gain, growth, improvement, progress, promotion, step 5. appreciation, credit, deposit, down payment, increase (*in price*), loan, prepayment, retainer, rise (*in price*) 6. **advances** approach, approaches, moves, overtures, proposals, proposition ~*adj.* 7. beforehand, early, foremost, forward, in front, leading, previous, prior

advanced avant-garde, extreme, forward, higher, late, leading, precocious, progressive

advancement advance, amelioration, betterment, gain, growth, improvement, preferment, progress, promotion, rise

advantage aid, ascendancy, asset, assistance, avail, benefit, blessing, boon, convenience, edge, gain, good, help, interest, lead, profit, service, start, superiority, sway, upper hand, use, utility, welfare

advantageous 1. dominant, favourable, superior 2. beneficial, convenient, helpful, profitable, useful, valuable, worthwhile

adventure chance, contingency, enterprise, experience, exploit, hazard, incident, occurrence, risk, speculation, undertaking, venture

adventurer daredevil, hero, heroine, swashbuckler, traveller, venturer, wanderer

adventurous adventuresome, audacious, bold, dangerous, daredevil, daring, enterprising, foolhardy, hazardous, headstrong, intrepid, rash, reckless, risky

adverse conflicting, contrary, detrimental, disadvantageous, hostile, inexpedient, inopportune, negative, opposing, opposite, reluctant, repugnant, unfavourable, unfortunate, unfriendly, unlucky, unpropitious, unwilling

adversity affliction, bad luck, calamity, disaster, distress, hardship, hard times, ill-fortune, ill-luck, misery, misfortune, mishap, reverse, sorrow, suffering, trial, trouble, woe

advertise advise, announce, declare, display, inform, make known, notify, praise, proclaim, promote, promulgate, publicize, publish, puff, tout

advertisement ad (*Inf.*), advert (*Inf.*), announcement, bill, blurb, circular, commercial,

DICTIONARY

advocaat *n.* liqueur with a raw egg base.

advocate *v.* propose or recommend. —*n.* person who publicly supports a cause; *Scot.* barrister. —**advocacy** *n.*

adze *n.* tool with an arched blade set at right angles to the handle.

aegis [ee-jiss] *n.* sponsorship, protection.

aeolian harp [ee-**oh**-lee-an] *n.* musical instrument that produces sounds when the wind passes over its strings.

aeon [ee-on] *n.* immeasurably long period of time.

aerate *v.* put gas into (a liquid), as when making a fizzy drink. —**aeration** *n.*

aerial *adj.* in, from, or operating in the air; relating to aircraft. —*n.* metal pole or wire for receiving or transmitting radio or TV signals.

aerie *n.* same as EYRIE.

aerobatics *pl. n.* stunt flying. —**aerobatic** *adj.*

aerobics *pl. n.* exercises designed to increase the amount of oxygen in the blood. —**aerobic** *adj.*

aerodrome *n.* small airport.

aerodynamics *pl. n.* (study of) air flow, esp. around moving solid objects. —**aerodynamic** *adj.*

aerofoil *n.* part of an aircraft, such as the wing, designed to give lift.

aerogram *n.* airmail letter on a single sheet of paper that seals to form an envelope.

aeronautics *n.* study or practice of aircraft flight. —**aeronautical** *adj.*

aeroplane *n.* powered flying vehicle with fixed wings.

aerosol *n.* pressurized can from which a substance can be dispensed as a fine spray.

aerospace *n.* earth's atmosphere and space beyond.

aesthetic [iss-**thet**-ik] *adj.* relating to the appreciation of art and beauty. —**aesthetics** *n.* study of art, beauty, and good taste. —**aesthetically** *adv.* —**aesthete** [eess-theet] *n.* person who has or affects an extravagant love of art. —**aestheticism** *n.*

aether *n.* same as ETHER.

aetiology [ee-tee-**ol**-a-jee] *n.* same as ETIOLOGY.

afar *adv.* from or at a great distance.

affable *adj.* friendly and easy to talk to. —**affably** *adv.* —**affability** *n.*

affair *n.* thing to be done or attended to; event or happening; sexual relationship outside marriage. —*pl.* personal or business interests; matters of public interest.

affect[1] *v.* act on, influence; move (someone) emotionally. —**affecting** *adj.* moving the feelings. —**affection** *n.* fondness or love. —**affectionate** *adj.* loving. —**affectionately** *adv.*

affect[2] *v.* put on a show of; wear or use by preference. —**affectation** *n.* show, pretence. —**affected** *adj.* full of affectation; pretended.

THESAURUS

display, notice, placard, poster, promotion, publicity, puff

advice admonition, caution, counsel, guidance, help, injunction, opinion, recommendation, suggestion, view

advisable apt, desirable, expedient, fit, fitting, judicious, politic, profitable, proper, prudent, seemly, sensible, sound, suitable, wise

advise admonish, caution, commend, counsel, enjoin, recommend, suggest, urge

adviser aide, authority, coach, confidant, consultant, counsel, counsellor, guide, helper, lawyer, mentor, right-hand man, solicitor, teacher, tutor

advisory advising, consultative, counselling, helping, recommending

advocate 1. *v.* advise, argue for, campaign for, champion, defend, encourage, favour, plead for, press for, promote, propose, recommend, speak for, support, uphold, urge 2. *n.* backer, campaigner, champion, counsellor, defender, promoter, proposer, speaker, spokesman, supporter, upholder

affable amiable, benevolent, benign, civil, con-

genial, cordial, courteous, friendly, genial, good-humoured, good-natured, kindly, mild, obliging, pleasant, sociable, urbane

affair 1. activity, business, circumstance, concern, episode, event, happening, incident, interest, matter, occurrence, proceeding, project, question, subject, transaction, undertaking 2. amour, intrigue, liaison, relationship, romance

affect 1. act on, alter, bear upon, change, concern, influence, interest, involve, modify, regard, relate to, sway, transform 2. assume, contrive, feign, imitate, pretend, sham, simulate

affectation appearance, artificiality, façade, false display, insincerity, mannerism, pose, pretence, pretentiousness, sham, show, simulation

affected artificial, assumed, conceited, contrived, counterfeit, feigned, insincere, mannered, precious, pretended, pretentious, put-on, sham, simulated, stiff, studied, unnatural

affecting moving, pitiable, pitiful, poignant, sad, saddening, touching

DICTIONARY

affianced [af-**fie**-anst] *adj. Old-fashioned* engaged to be married.

affidavit [af-fid-**dave**-it] *n.* written statement made on oath.

affiliate *v.* (of a group) link up with a larger group. —**affiliation** *n.*

affinity *n., pl.* **-ties.** close connection or liking; close resemblance; chemical attraction.

affirm *v.* assert, declare; uphold or confirm (an idea or belief). —**affirmation** *n.* —**affirmative** *n., adj.* (word or phrase) indicating agreement.

affix *v.* attach or fasten. —*n.* word or syllable added to a word to change its meaning.

afflict *v.* give pain or grief to. —**affliction** *n.*

affluent *adj.* wealthy. —**affluence** *n.* wealth.

afford *v.* have enough money to buy; be able to spare (the time etc.); give or supply. —**affordable** *adj.*

afforest *v.* plant trees on. —**afforestation** *n.*

affray *n.* noisy fight, brawl.

affront *v., n.* insult.

Afghan hound *n.* large slim dog with long silky hair.

afield *adv., adj.* —**far afield** far away.

aflame *adv., adj.* burning.

afloat *adv., adj.* floating; at sea.

afoot *adv., adj.* happening, in operation.

aforesaid *adj.* referred to previously.

aforethought *adj.* premeditated, e.g. *with malice aforethought.*

Afr. Africa(n).

afraid *adj.* frightened; regretful.

afresh *adv.* again, anew.

African *adj.* of Africa. —*n.* person from Africa. —**African lily** S African plant with funnel-shaped flowers. —**African violet** house plant with pink or purple flowers and hairy leaves.

Afrikaans *n.* language used in S Africa, related to Dutch.

Afrikaner *n.* White S African whose mother tongue is Afrikaans.

Afro *n., pl.* **-ros.** frizzy bushy hair style.

Afro- *combining form* African, e.g. *Afro-Caribbean.*

aft *adv.* at or towards the rear of a ship or aircraft.

after *prep.* following in time or place; in pursuit of; in imitation of. —*conj.* at a later time than. —*adv.* at a later time. —**afters** *pl. n.* dessert.

afterbirth *n.* material expelled from the womb after childbirth.

aftercare *n.* support given to a person discharged from a hospital or prison; regular care required to keep something in good condition.

aftereffect *n.* effect occurring some time after its cause.

afterglow *n.* glow left after a source of light has gone; pleasant feeling left after an enjoyable experience.

afterlife *n.* life after death.

aftermath *n.* aftereffects collectively.

afternoon *n.* time between noon and evening.

aftershave *n.* lotion applied to the face after shaving.

afterthought *n.* idea occurring later; something added later.

afterward(s) *adv.* later.

Ag *Chem.* silver.

again *adv.* once more; in addition.

against *prep.* in opposition or contrast to; in contact with; in readiness for.

THESAURUS

affection attachment, care, desire, feeling, fondness, friendliness, good will, inclination, kindness, liking, love, tenderness, warmth

affectionate attached, caring, devoted, doting, fond, friendly, kind, loving, tender, warm, warm-hearted

affinity analogy, closeness, compatibility, connection, correspondence, kinship, likeness, relation, relationship, resemblance, similarity

affirm assert, attest, aver, avouch, avow, certify, confirm, declare, maintain, state, swear, testify

affirmation assertion, averment, avouchment, avowal, confirmation, declaration, oath, pronouncement, ratification, statement, testimony

affirmative agreeing, approving, assenting, concurring, confirming, consenting, positive

afflict burden, distress, grieve, harass, hurt, oppress, pain, plague, trouble, try, wound

affluence abundance, fortune, opulence, plenty, profusion, prosperity, riches, wealth

affluent moneyed, opulent, prosperous, rich, wealthy, well-off, well-to-do

afford bear, spare, stand, sustain

afraid alarmed, anxious, apprehensive, cowardly, faint-hearted, fearful, frightened, intimidated, nervous, scared, timid, timorous

afresh again, anew, newly, once again, once more, over again

after afterwards, behind, below, following, later, subsequently, succeeding, thereafter

again 1. afresh, anew, another time, once more

DICTIONARY

agape *adj.* (of the mouth) wide open; (of a person) very surprised.

agaric *n.* fungus with gills on the underside of the cap, such as a mushroom.

agate [ag-git] *n.* semiprecious form of quartz with striped colouring.

age *n.* length of time a person or thing has existed; time of life; latter part of human life; period of history; long time. —*v.* ag-(e)ing, aged. make or grow old. —**aged** [ay-jid] *adj.* old; [rhymes with **raged**] having the age of. —**ag(e) ing** *n., adj.* —**ageless** *adj.* apparently never growing old; timeless. —**age-old** *adj.* very old.

agenda *n.* list of things to be dealt with, esp. at a meeting.

agent *n.* person acting on behalf of another; person or thing producing an effect. —**agency** *n.* organization providing a service; business or function of an agent; *Old-fashioned* power or action by which something happens.

agent provocateur [azh-on prov-vok-at-**tur**] *n., pl.* **agents provocateurs** [azh-on prov-vok-at-**tur**]. person employed by the authorities to tempt people to commit illegal acts and so be discredited or punished.

agglomerate *v.* gather into a mass. —*n.* confused mass; rock consisting of fused volcanic fragments. —*adj.* formed into a mass. —**agglomeration** *n.*

agglutinate *v.* stick with or as if with glue. —**agglutination** *n.* —**agglutinative** *adj.*

aggrandize *v.* make greater in size, power, or rank. —**aggrandizement** *n.*

aggravate *v.* make worse; *Informal* annoy. —**aggravating** *adj.* —**aggravation** *n.*

aggregate *v.* gather into a mass. —*adj.* gathered into a mass; total or final. —*n.* total; rock consisting of a mixture of minerals; sand or gravel used to make concrete. —**aggregation** *n.*

aggression *n.* unprovoked attack; hostile behaviour. —**aggressive** *adj.* showing aggression; forceful. —**aggressively** *adv.* —**aggressiveness** *n.* —**aggressor** *n.*

aggrieved *adj.* upset and angry.

aggro *n. Slang* aggression.

aghast *adj.* amazed or shocked.

agile *adj.* nimble, quick-moving; mentally quick. —**agilely** *adv.* —**agility** *n.*

agitate *v.* disturb or excite; stir or shake (a liquid); stir up public opinion for or against something. —**agitation** *n.* —**agitator** *n.*

aglow *adj.* glowing.

AGM annual general meeting.

THESAURUS

2. also, besides, furthermore, in addition, moreover, on the contrary, on the other hand

against 1. counter, hostile to, in contrast to, in defiance of, in opposition to, in the face of, opposed to, opposing, resisting, versus 2. abutting, close up to, facing, fronting, in contact with, on, opposite to, touching, upon

age *n.* 1. date, day(s), duration, epoch, era, generation, lifetime, period, span, time 2. advancing years, decline (*of life*), majority, maturity, old age, senescence, senility, seniority ~*v.* 3. decline, deteriorate, grow old, mature, mellow, ripen

aged age-old, ancient, antiquated, antique, elderly, getting on, grey, hoary, old, senescent, superannuated

agency bureau, business, department, office, organization

agent 1. advocate, deputy, emissary, envoy, factor, go-between, negotiator, rep (*Inf.*), representative, substitute, surrogate 2. agency, cause, force, instrument, means, power, vehicle

aggravate 1. exacerbate, exaggerate, heighten, increase, inflame, intensify, magnify, make worse, worsen 2. *Inf.* annoy, exasperate, get on one's nerves (*Inf.*), irk, irritate, needle (*Inf.*), nettle, pester, provoke, tease, vex

aggression assault, attack, encroachment, injury, invasion, offence, offensive, onslaught, raid

aggressive belligerent, destructive, hostile, offensive, pugnacious, quarrelsome

aghast amazed, appalled, astonished, astounded, awestruck, confounded, horrified, horrorstruck, shocked, startled, stunned

agile active, acute, alert, brisk, clever, lithe, lively, nimble, quick, sharp, sprightly, spry, supple, swift

agitate 1. beat, convulse, disturb, rock, rouse, shake, stir, toss 2. alarm, arouse, confuse, disquiet, distract, disturb, excite, ferment, fluster, incite, inflame, perturb, rouse, trouble, upset, work up, worry

agitation 1. convulsion, disturbance, rocking, shake, shaking, stir, stirring, tossing, turbulence 2. alarm, arousal, clamour, commotion, confusion, discomposure, disquiet, distraction, disturbance, excitement, ferment, flurry, fluster, incitement, outcry, stimulation, trouble, tumult, turmoil, upset, worry

agitator demagogue, firebrand, inciter, rabblerouser, revolutionary, troublemaker

DICTIONARY

agnostic *n.* person who believes that it is impossible to know whether God exists. —*adj.* of agnostics. —**agnosticism** *n.*

ago *adv.* in the past.

agog *adj.* eager or curious.

agony *n., pl.* -**nies.** extreme physical or mental pain. —**agonize** *v.* (cause to) suffer agony; worry greatly. —**agonizing** *adj.* —**agony aunt** woman who gives advice in an agony column. —**agony column** newspaper or magazine feature offering advice on personal problems.

agoraphobia *n.* fear of open spaces. —**agoraphobic** *n., adj.*

agrarian *adj.* of land or agriculture. —**agrarianism** *n.*

agree *v.* **agreeing, agreed.** be of the same opinion; consent; reach a joint decision; be consistent; (foll. by *with*) be suitable to one's health or digestion. —**agreeable** *adj.* willing; pleasant. —**agreeably** *adv.* —**agreement** *n.* agreeing; contract.

agriculture *n.* raising of crops and livestock. —**agricultural** *adj.* —**agriculturist** *n.*

agronomy [ag-**ron**-om-mee] *n.* science of soil management and crop production. —**agronomist** *n.*

aground *adv.* onto the bottom of shallow water.

ague [**aig**-yew] *n.* periodic fever with shivering.

ahead *adv.* in front; forwards.

ahoy *interj.* shout used at sea to attract attention.

AI artificial insemination; artificial intelligence.

AID artificial insemination by donor.

aid *v., n.* help, support.

aide *n.* assistant.

aide-de-camp [aid-de-kom] *n., pl.* **aides-de-camp** [aid-de-kom]. military officer serving as personal assistant to a senior.

AIDS acquired immunodeficiency syndrome, a viral disease that destroys the body's ability to fight infection.

AIH artificial insemination by husband.

ail *v.* trouble, afflict; be ill. —**ailing** *adj.* sickly. —**ailment** *n.* illness.

aileron [**ale**-er-on] *n.* movable flap on an aircraft wing which controls rolling.

aim *v.* point (a weapon or missile) or direct (a blow or remark) at a target; propose or intend. —*n.* aiming; intention, purpose. —**aimless** *adj.* without purpose. —**aimlessly** *adv.*

ain't *Not standard* am not; is not; are not; has not; have not.

air *n.* mixture of gases forming the earth's atmosphere; space above the ground; sky; breeze; tune; quality or manner. —*pl.* affected manners. —*v.* expose to air to dry or ventilate; make

---

THESAURUS

agog avid, curious, eager, enthralled, enthusiastic, excited, expectant, impatient, in suspense, keen

agony affliction, anguish, distress, misery, pain, pangs, suffering, throes, torment, torture, woe

agree 1. accede, acquiesce, admit, allow, assent, be of the same mind, comply, concede, concur, consent, engage, grant, permit, see eye to eye, settle 2. accord, answer, chime, coincide, conform, correspond, fit, get on (together), harmonize, match, square, suit, tally

agreeable 1. acceptable, delightful, enjoyable, gratifying, pleasant, pleasing, pleasurable, satisfying, to one's liking, to one's taste 2. acquiescent, amenable, approving, complying, concurring, consenting, in accord, responsive, sympathetic, well-disposed, willing

agreement 1. accord, accordance, agreeing, compatibility, compliance, concert, concord, concurrence, conformity, congruity, consistency, correspondence, harmony, similarity, union 2. arrangement, bargain, compact, contract, covenant, deal (*Inf.*), pact, settlement, treaty, understanding

agriculture culture, farming, husbandry, tillage

aground ashore, beached, foundered, grounded, high and dry, on the rocks, stranded, stuck

ahead along, at an advantage, at the head, before, forwards, in advance, in front, in the foreground, in the lead, leading, on, onwards, winning

aid 1. *v.* abet, assist, befriend, encourage, favour, help, promote, relieve, second, serve, subsidize, succour, support, sustain 2. *n.* assistance, benefit, encouragement, favour, help, relief, service, succour, support

aide aide-de-camp, assistant, helper, second, supporter

aim 1. *v.* aspire, attempt, design, direct, endeavour, intend, level, mean, plan, point, propose, purpose, resolve, seek, set one's sights on, sight, strive, take aim (at), train, try, want, wish 2. *n.* ambition, aspiration, course, design, desire, direction, end, goal, intent, intention, mark, object, objective, plan, purpose, scheme, target, wish

aimless chance, erratic, haphazard, pointless, purposeless, random, stray, undirected, unguided, unpredictable, wayward

DICTIONARY

known publicly. —**on the air** in the act of broadcasting on radio or television. —**airy** adj. well-ventilated; jaunty, nonchalant. —**airily** adv. —**airiness** n. —**airless** adj. stuffy. —**airing** n. exposure to air for drying or ventilation; exposure to public debate. —**air base** centre from which military aircraft operate. —**airborne** adj. carried by air; (of aircraft) in flight. —**air brake** brake worked by compressed air. —**airbrush** n. atomizer spraying paint by compressed air. —**air conditioning** system that controls the temperature and humidity of the air in a building. —**air conditioner** —**aircraft** n. any machine that flies, such as an aeroplane. —**aircraft carrier** warship from which aircraft operate. —**airfield** n. place where aircraft can land and take off. —**air force** branch of the armed forces responsible for air warfare. —**air gun** gun discharged by the force of compressed air. —**air hostess** stewardess on an aircraft. —**air letter** air-mail letter, aerogram. —**airlift** n. transport of troops or cargo by aircraft when other routes are blocked. —v. transport by airlift. —**airline** n. company providing scheduled flights for passengers and cargo. —**airliner** n. large passenger aircraft. —**airlock** n. air bubble obstructing the flow of liquid in a pipe; airtight chamber. —**air mail** system of sending mail by aircraft; mail sent in this way. —**airman** n. member of the air force. —**airplay** n. broadcast performances (of a record) on radio. —**airport** n. airfield for civilian aircraft, with facilities for aircraft maintenance and passengers. —**air raid** attack by aircraft. —**airship** n. lighter-than-air flying machine with means of propulsion. —**airsick** adj. nauseated from travelling in an aircraft. —**airspace** n. atmosphere above a country, regarded as its territory. —**airstrip** n. strip of ground where aircraft can take off and land. —**airtight** adj. not allowing the passage of air. —**airworthy** adj. (of aircraft) fit to fly. —**airworthiness** n.

Airedale n. large rough-coated terrier dog.

aisle [rhymes with **mile**] n. passageway separating seating areas in a church, theatre, etc., or row of shelves in a supermarket.

ajar adj., adv. (of a door) partly open.

akimbo adv. —**with arms akimbo** with hands on hips and elbows outwards.

akin adj. similar, related.

Al Chem. aluminium.

alabaster n. soft white translucent stone.

à la carte adj., adv. (of a menu) having dishes individually priced.

alack interj. Obs. cry of grief or sorrow.

alacrity n. speed, eagerness.

à la mode adj. fashionable.

alarm n. sudden fear caused by awareness of danger; warning sound; device that gives this; alarm clock. —v. frighten. —**alarming** adj. —**alarmist** n. person who alarms others needlessly. —**alarm clock** clock which sounds at a set time to wake someone up.

alas adv. unfortunately, regrettably.

albatross n. large sea bird with very long wings.

albeit conj. although.

albino n., pl. -**nos**. person or animal with white skin and hair and pink eyes. —**albinism** n.

album n. book with blank pages for keeping photographs or stamps in; long-playing record.

albumen n. egg white.

THESAURUS

air n. 1. atmosphere, heavens, sky 2. blast, breath, breeze, draught, puff, waft, whiff, wind, zephyr 3. ambience, appearance, atmosphere, aura, bearing, character, demeanour, effect, feeling, flavour, impression, look, manner, mood, quality, style, tone 4. aria, lay, melody, song, tune ~v. 5. aerate, expose, freshen, ventilate 6. circulate, communicate, declare, disclose, display, disseminate, divulge, exhibit, expose, express, give vent to, make known, make public, proclaim, publicize, reveal, tell, utter, ventilate, voice

airiness 1. breeziness, freshness, lightness, openness, windiness 2. animation, blitheness, breeziness, buoyancy, gaiety, happiness, high spirits, jauntiness, light-heartedness

airing 1. aeration, drying, freshening, ventilation 2. circulation, display, dissemination, exposure, expression, publicity, utterance, vent, ventilation

airless breathless, close, heavy, muggy, oppressive, stale, stifling, stuffy, suffocating, sultry, unventilated

airs affectation, affectedness, haughtiness, hauteur, pretensions, superciliousness

airy 1. blowy, breezy, draughty, fresh, gusty, light, lofty, open, spacious, uncluttered, well-ventilated, windy 2. animated, blithe, buoyant, cheerful, cheery, debonair, gay, happy, high-spirited, jaunty, light, light-hearted, lively, merry, nonchalant

alarm v. 1. distress, frighten, panic, scare, startle, terrify, unnerve ~n. 2. anxiety, dismay, distress, fear, fright, panic, scare, terror, unease 3. alarm-bell, alert, bell, danger signal, distress signal, siren, warning

alarming dismaying, distressing, disturbing, frightening, scaring, shocking, startling, terrifying

DICTIONARY

albumin, albumen *n.* protein found in blood plasma, egg white, milk, and muscle. —**albuminous** *adj.*

alchemy *n.* medieval form of chemistry concerned with trying to turn base metals into gold and to find the elixir of life. —**alchemist** *n.*

alcohol *n.* colourless flammable liquid present in intoxicating drinks; intoxicating drinks generally. —**alcoholic** *adj.* of alcohol. —*n.* person addicted to alcohol. —**alcoholism** *n.* addiction to alcohol.

alcove *n.* recess in the wall of a room.

aldehyde *n.* one of a group of chemical compounds derived from alcohol by oxidation.

alder *n.* tree related to the birch.

alderman *n.* formerly, senior member of a local council.

ale *n.* kind of beer.

aleatory *adj.* dependent on chance.

alert *adj.* watchful, attentive. —*n.* warning of danger. —*v.* warn of danger; make (someone) aware of (a fact). —**on the alert** watchful. —**alertness** *n.*

alfalfa *n.* kind of plant used as fodder.

alfresco *adv., adj.* in the open air.

algae [al-jee] *pl. n.* plants which live in or near water and have no true stems, leaves, or roots.

algebra *n.* branch of mathematics using symbols to represent numbers. —**algebraic** *adj.*

ALGOL *n. Computers* computer programming language designed for mathematical and scientific purposes.

algorithm *n.* logical arithmetical or computational procedure for solving a problem.

alias *adv.* also known as, e.g. *William Bonney, alias Billy the Kid.* —*n.* false name.

alibi *n.* plea of being somewhere else when a crime was committed; *Informal* excuse.

alien *adj.* foreign; repugnant (to); from another world. —*n.* foreigner; being from another world. —**alienable** *adj. Law* able to be transferred to another owner. —**alienate** *v.* cause to become hostile. —**alienation** *n.*

alight[1] *v.* step out of (a vehicle); land.

alight[2] *adj.* burning; lit up.

align [a-**line**] *v.* place in a line; make or bring (a person or group) into agreement with the policy of another. —**alignment** *n.*

alike *adj.* like, similar. —*adv.* in the same way.

alimentary *adj.* of nutrition. —**alimentary canal** food passage in the body.

alimony *n.* allowance paid under a court order to a separated or divorced spouse.

A-line *adj.* (of a skirt) slightly flared.

aliquot *adj.* of or denoting an exact divisor of a number. —*n.* exact divisor.

alive *adj.* living, in existence; lively. —**alive to** aware of. —**alive with** swarming with.

alkali [**alk**-a-lie] *n.* substance which combines with acid and neutralizes it to form a salt. —**alkaline** *adj.* —**alkalinity** *n.* —**alkaloid** *n.* any of a group of organic compounds containing nitrogen.

all *adj.* whole quantity or number (of). —*adv.* wholly, entirely; (in the score of games) each. —*n.* whole; everything, everyone. —**all in** *adj.* exhausted; (of wrestling) with no style prohibited. —*adv.* with all expenses included. —**all right** *adj.* adequate, satisfactory; unharmed. —*interj.* expression of approval or agreement. —**allrounder** *n.* person with ability in many fields.

THESAURUS

alcoholic *n.* boozer (*Inf.*), dipsomaniac, drunk, drunkard, hard drinker, inebriate, soak (*Inf.*), sot, sponge (*Inf.*), toper, wino (*Inf.*)

alert 1. *adj.* agile, attentive, brisk, careful, heedful, lively, nimble, observant, on guard, on the ball (*Inf.*), perceptive, quick, ready, spirited, sprightly, vigilant, wary, watchful, wideawake 2. *n.* alarm, signal, siren, warning 3. *v.* alarm, forewarn, inform, notify, signal, warn

alias 1. *adv.* also called, also known as, otherwise, otherwise known as 2. *n.* assumed name, *nom de guerre*, nom de plume, pen name, pseudonym, stage name

alibi defence, explanation, plea

alien 1. *adj.* adverse, exotic, foreign, inappropriate, incompatible, not native, opposed, outlandish, remote, repugnant, separated, strange, unfamiliar 2. *n.* foreigner, outsider, stranger

alight[1] *v.* come down, descend, disembark, dismount, get down, get off, land, light, perch, settle, touch down

alight[2] *adj.* ablaze, aflame, blazing, burning, fiery, flaming, flaring, lighted, lit, on fire

alike analogous, corresponding, equal, equivalent, even, identical, parallel, similar, the same, uniform

alive 1. animate, breathing, having life, living, subsisting 2. active, existent, existing, extant, functioning, in existence, in force, operative 3. active, alert, animated, awake, brisk, cheerful, eager, energetic, full of life, lively, quick, spirited, sprightly, spry, vigorous, vital, vivacious

all *adj.* 1. every bit of, the complete, the entire, the sum of, the total of, the whole of 2. each,

DICTIONARY

Allah *n.* name of God in Islam.

allay *v.* reduce (fear or anger) or relieve (pain or grief).

allege *v.* state without proof. **—alleged** *adj.* **—allegedly** *adv.* **—allegation** *n.* thing alleged.

allegiance *n.* loyalty to a person, country, or cause.

allegory *n., pl.* **-ries.** story with an underlying meaning as well as the literal one. **—allegorical** *adj.* **—allegorically** *adv.* **—allegorize** *v.*

allegretto *Music* fairly quickly or briskly.

allegro *Music* in a brisk lively manner.

allergy *n., pl.* **-gies.** extreme sensitivity to a substance, which causes the body to react to any contact with it. **—allergic** *adj.* having or caused by an allergy; *Informal* having an aversion (to), e.g. *allergic to work.* **—allergen** [al-ler-jen] *n.* substance capable of causing an allergic reaction.

alleviate *v.* lessen (pain or suffering). **—alleviation** *n.*

alley *n.* narrow street or path; long narrow enclosure in which tenpin bowling or skittles is played.

alliance *n.* state of being allied; formal union or association between countries or groups for a shared purpose.

alligator *n.* reptile of the crocodile family, found in the southern U.S. and China.

alliteration *n.* use of the same sound at the start of consecutive words. **—alliterative** *adj.*

allocate *v.* allot or assign. **—allocation** *n.*

allot *v.* **-lotting, -lotted.** assign as a share or for a particular purpose. **—allotment** *n.* distribution; portion allotted; small piece of public land rented to grow vegetables on.

allotrope *n.* any of two or more physical forms in which an element can exist. **—allotropic** *adj.*

allow *v.* permit; acknowledge (a point or claim); set aside. **—allow for** take into account. **—allowable** *adj.* **—allowance** *n.* amount of money given at regular intervals; amount permitted. **—make allowances for** be lenient towards (someone) because he or she has special problems; take into account.

alloy *n.* mixture of two or more metals. *—v.* mix (metals).

allspice *n.* spice made from the berries of a tropical American tree.

allude *v.* (foll. by *to*) refer indirectly to. **—allusion** *n.* indirect reference. **—allusive** *adj.*

allure *v.* entice or attract. *—n.* attractiveness. **—allurement** *n.* **—alluring** *adj.*

alluvium *n.* fertile soil deposited by flowing water. **—alluvial** *adj.*

ally *n., pl.* **-lies.** country or person having an agreement to support another. *—v.* **-lying, -lied.** **—ally oneself with** join as an ally. **—allied** *adj.*

alma mater *n.* one's former school, university, or college.

almanac *n.* yearly calendar with detailed information on anniversaries, phases of the moon, etc.

almighty *adj.* having absolute power; *Informal* very great. *—n.* **—the Almighty** God.

THESAURUS

each and every, every, every one of, every single 3. complete, entire, full, greatest, perfect, total, utter ~*n.* 4. aggregate, entirety, everything, sum, sum total, total, total amount, totality, whole ~*adv.* 5. altogether, completely, entirely, fully, totally, utterly, wholly

allergic affected by, sensitive, susceptible

alley alleyway, backstreet, lane, passage, passageway, pathway, walk

alliance affinity, agreement, association, coalition, combination, confederation, federation, league, marriage, pact, treaty, union

allied affiliated, associated, bound, combined, confederate, connected, in league, joined, kindred, married, related, unified, united, wed

allot allocate, apportion, assign, budget, designate, earmark, set aside, share out

allotment 1. allocation, grant, lot, measure, portion, quota, ration, share, stint 2. kitchen garden, patch, plot, tract

allow 1. acknowledge, acquiesce, admit, concede, confess, grant, own 2. approve, authorize, endure, let, permit, sanction, stand, suffer, tolerate

allowance 1. allocation, amount, grant, lot, measure, pension, portion, quota, ration, share, stint, stipend, subsidy 2. concession, deduction, discount, rebate, reduction

allow for arrange for, consider, foresee, make allowances for, plan for, provide for, take into account

all right *adj.* acceptable, adequate, fair, O.K. (*Inf.*), passable, satisfactory

allusion glance, hint, indirect reference, innuendo, intimation, mention, suggestion

ally accessory, accomplice, associate, collaborator, colleague, confederate, friend, helper, partner

almighty absolute, all-powerful, omnipotent, supreme

DICTIONARY

almond *n.* edible oval-shaped nut which grows on a small tree.

almoner *n.* formerly, a hospital social worker.

almost *adv.* very nearly.

alms [ahmz] *pl. n. Old-fashioned* gifts to the poor. —**almshouse** *n.* formerly, a house financed by charity, offering accommodation to the poor.

aloe *n.* plant with fleshy spiny leaves. —*pl.* bitter drug made from aloe leaves.

aloft *adv.* in the air; in a ship's rigging.

alone *adj., adv.* without anyone or anything else.

along *prep.* over part or all the length of. —*adv.* forward; in company with others, e.g. *come along for the ride.* —**alongside** *adv., prep.* beside.

aloof *adj.* distant or haughty in manner. —**aloofness** *n.*

alopecia [al-loh-**pee**-sha] *n.* loss of hair.

aloud *adv.* in an audible voice.

alpaca *n.* Peruvian llama; its wool; cloth made from this.

alpenstock *n.* iron-tipped staff used by climbers.

alphabet *n.* set of letters used in writing a language. —**alphabetical** *adj.* in the conventional order of the letters of an alphabet. —**alphabetically** *adv.* —**alphabetize** *v.* put in alphabetical order. —**alphabetization** *n.*

alpine *adj.* of high mountains; (**A-**) of the Alps, a high mountain range in S central Europe. —*n.* mountain plant.

already *adv.* before this time; sooner than expected.

Alsatian *n.* large wolflike dog.

also *adv.* in addition; too. —**also-ran** *n.* loser in a race, competition, or election.

altar *n.* raised structure on which sacrifices are offered and religious rites are performed; table used for Communion in Christian churches. —**altarpiece** *n.* work of art above and behind the altar in some Christian churches.

alter *v.* make or become different. —**alteration** *n.*

alter ego *n.* second self; very close friend.

altercation *n.* heated argument.

alternate *v.* (cause to) occur by turns. —*adj.* occurring by turns; every second one of a series, e.g. *alternate Fridays.* —**alternately** *adv.* —**alternation** *n.* —**alternative** *n.* one of two choices. —*adj.* able to be done or used instead of something else; (of medicine, lifestyle, etc.) not conventional. —**alternatively** *adv.* —**alternator** *n.* electric generator for producing alternating current. —**alternating current** electric current that reverses direction at frequent regular intervals.

although *conj.* despite the fact that.

altimeter [al-**tim**-it-er] *n.* instrument that measures altitude.

altitude *n.* height above sea level.

alto *n., pl.* **-tos.** *Music* short for CONTRALTO; (singer with) the highest adult male voice; instrument with the second-highest pitch in its group.

altogether *adv.* entirely; on the whole; in total.

altruism *n.* unselfish concern for the welfare of others. —**altruist** *n.* —**altruistic** *adj.* —**altruistically** *adv.*

THESAURUS

almost about, all but, approximately, as good as, close to, just about, nearly, not quite, practically, virtually

alone abandoned, apart, deserted, desolate, detached, forsaken, isolated, lonely, lonesome, only, separate, single, sole, solitary, unaccompanied, unaided, unassisted, unattended, uncombined, unescorted

aloud audibly, clearly, distinctly, intelligibly, out loud, plainly

already as of now, at present, before now, by now, by that time, by then, by this time, even now, previously

also additionally, along with, and, as well, as well as, besides, further, furthermore, in addition, including, into the bargain, moreover, on top of that, plus, to boot, too

alter adapt, adjust, amend, change, convert, modify, recast, reform, remodel, reshape, revise, shift, transform, turn, vary

alteration amendment, change, difference, diversification, metamorphosis, modification, revision, shift, transformation, variance, variation

alternate 1. *v.* act reciprocally, follow in turn, interchange, intersperse, oscillate, rotate, substitute, take turns, vary 2. *adj.* alternating, every other, every second

alternative *n.* choice, option, other (*of two*), preference, recourse, selection, substitute

alternatively if not, instead, on the other hand, or, otherwise

although albeit, despite the fact that, even if, even supposing, even though, notwithstanding, though, while

altogether 1. absolutely, completely, entirely, fully, perfectly, quite, thoroughly, totally, utterly, wholly 2. all in all, all things considered, as a whole, collectively, generally, in general, *in toto*, on the whole 3. all told, in all, taken together

DICTIONARY

aluminium n. light nonrusting silvery-white metal.

alumnus [al-**lumm**-nuss] n., pl. -**ni** [-nie]. US graduate of a college. —**alumna** [al-**lumm**-na] n. fem., pl. -**nae** [-nee].

always adv. at all times; for ever.

alyssum n. garden plant with small yellow or white flowers.

a.m. before noon.

AM amplitude modulation.

am v. see BE.

amalgam n. blend or combination; alloy of mercury and another metal.

amalgamate v. combine or unite. —**amalgamation** n.

amanuensis [am-man-yew-en-siss] n., pl. -**ses** [-seez]. person who writes from dictation.

amaranth n. imaginary flower that never fades; lily-like plant with red, green, or purple flowers.

amaryllis n. lily-like plant with large red or white flowers.

amass v. collect or accumulate.

amateur n. person who engages in a sport or activity as a pastime rather than as a profession; person unskilled in something. —adj. not professional. —**amateurish** adj. lacking skill. —**amateurishly** adv.

amatory adj. relating to romantic or sexual love.

amaze v. surprise greatly, astound. —**amazing** adj. —**amazingly** adv. —**amazement** n.

Amazon n. legendary female warrior; tall strong woman. —**Amazonian** adj.

ambassador n. senior diplomat who represents his or her country in another country. —**ambassadorial** adj. —**ambassadorship** n.

amber n. yellowish translucent fossil resin. —adj. brownish-yellow.

ambergris [am-ber-greece] n. waxy substance secreted by the sperm whale, used in making perfumes.

ambidextrous adj. able to use both hands with equal ease.

ambience n. atmosphere of a place.

ambient adj. surrounding.

ambiguous adj. having more than one possible meaning; uncertain. —**ambiguously** adv. —**ambiguity** n.

ambit n. limits or boundary.

ambition n. desire for success; something so desired, goal. —**ambitious** adj. —**ambitiously** adv. —**ambitiousness** n.

ambivalence [am-**biv**-a-lenss] n. state of feeling two conflicting emotions at the same time. —**ambivalent** adj. —**ambivalently** adv.

amble v. walk at a leisurely pace. —n. leisurely walk or pace.

ambrosia n. Myth food of the gods; anything delightful to taste or smell. —**ambrosial** adj.

ambulance n. motor vehicle designed to carry the sick or injured.

ambush n. act of waiting in a concealed position to make an attack; attack from a concealed position. —v. attack from a concealed position.

ameliorate [am-**meal**-yor-rate] v. make (something) better. —**amelioration** n. —**ameliorative** adj.

amen interj. so be it: used at the end of a prayer.

amenable adj. likely or willing to cooperate. —**amenability** n.

amend v. correct or improve (something). —**amendment** n.

THESAURUS

always consistently, continually, ever, evermore, every time, forever, in perpetuum, invariably, perpetually, repeatedly, unceasingly, without exception

amass accumulate, aggregate, assemble, collect, compile, garner, gather, heap up, hoard, pile up, rake up, scrape together

amateur dabbler, dilettante, layman, nonprofessional

amaze alarm, astonish, astound, bewilder, bowl over (Inf.), daze, shock, stagger, startle, stun, stupefy, surprise

amazement astonishment, bewilderment, confusion, marvel, perplexity, shock, surprise, wonder

ambassador agent, consul, deputy, diplomat,

emissary, envoy, legate, minister, plenipotentiary, representative

ambiguous doubtful, dubious, equivocal, inconclusive, indefinite, indeterminate, obscure, puzzling, uncertain, unclear, vague

ambition 1. aspiration, desire, drive, eagerness, enterprise, longing, striving, yearning, zeal 2. aim, aspiration, desire, dream, end, goal, hope, intent, objective, purpose, wish

ambitious aspiring, avid, desirous, driving, eager, enterprising, hopeful, intent, purposeful, striving, zealous

ambush n. cover, hiding, hiding place, lying in wait, retreat, shelter, trap

amenable acquiescent, agreeable, open, persuadable, responsive, susceptible, tractable

DICTIONARY

amends *pl. n.* —**make amends for** compensate for.

amenity *n., pl.* **-ties.** useful or enjoyable facility.

American *adj.* of the United States of America or the American continent. —*n.* American person. —**Americanism** *n.* expression or custom peculiar to Americans.

amethyst [am-myth-ist] *n.* bluish-violet variety of quartz used as a gemstone.

amiable *adj.* friendly, pleasant-natured. —**amiably** *adv.* —**amiability** *n.*

amicable *adj.* friendly. —**amicably** *adv.* —**amicability** *n.*

amid, amidst *prep.* in the middle of, among. —**amidship(s)** *adv.* at or towards the middle of a ship.

amino acid [am-mean-oh] *n.* organic compound found in protein.

amiss *adv.* wrongly, badly. —*adj.* wrong, faulty. —**take something amiss** be offended by something.

amity *n.* friendship.

ammeter *n.* instrument for measuring electric current.

ammonia *n.* pungent alkaline gas containing hydrogen and nitrogen; solution of this in water.

ammonite *n.* fossilized spiral shell of an extinct sea creature.

ammunition *n.* any projectile that can be fired from or as a weapon; facts that can be used in an argument.

amnesia *n.* loss of memory. —**amnesiac** *adj., n.*

amnesty *n., pl.* **-ties.** general pardon for offences against a government.

amniocentesis *n., pl.* **-ses.** removal of amniotic fluid to test for possible abnormalities in a fetus.

amniotic fluid *n.* fluid surrounding a fetus in the womb.

amoeba [am-mee-ba] *n., pl.* **-bae, -bas.** microscopic single-celled animal able to change its shape.

amok *adv.* —**run amok** run about in a violent frenzy.

among, amongst *prep.* in the midst of; in the group or number of; to each of, e.g. *divide it among yourselves.*

amoral [aim-mor-ral] *adj.* without moral standards. —**amorality** *n.*

amorous *adj.* feeling, showing, or relating to sexual love. —**amorously** *adv.* —**amorousness** *n.*

amorphous *adj.* without distinct shape.

amortize *v.* pay off (a debt) gradually by periodic transfers to a sinking fund. —**amortization** *n.*

amount *n.* extent or quantity. —*v.* (foll. by *to*) be equal or add up to.

amour *n.* (illicit) love affair.

amp *n.* ampere; *Informal* amplifier.

ampere [am-pair] *n.* unit of electric current.

ampersand *n.* the character (&), meaning *and.*

amphetamine [am-fet-am-in] *n.* drug used as a stimulant.

amphibian *n.* animal that lives on land but breeds in water; vehicle that can travel both on land and water. —**amphibious** *adj.* living or operating both on land and in water.

amphitheatre *n.* open oval or circular building with tiers of seats rising round an arena.

amphora *n., pl.* **-phorae, -phoras.** two-handled ancient Greek or Roman jar.

THESAURUS

amend alter, ameliorate, better, change, correct, enhance, fix, improve, mend, modify, rectify, reform, remedy, repair, revise

amendment 1. alteration, amelioration, change, correction, improvement, modification, reform, remedy, repair, revision 2. addendum, addition, adjunct, alteration, attachment, clarification

amenity advantage, comfort, convenience, facility, service

amiable affable, agreeable, benign, charming, cheerful, engaging, friendly, genial, kind, kindly, lovable, obliging, pleasant, pleasing, sociable, winsome

amid amidst, among, amongst, in the middle of, in the midst of, in the thick of, surrounded by

ammunition armaments, explosives, munitions, powder, rounds, shot and shell

among, amongst 1. amid, in association with, in the middle of, in the midst of, midst, with 2. between, to each of 3. in the company of, in the group of, in the number of, out of

amount 1. expanse, extent, magnitude, mass, measure, number, quantity, supply, volume 2. addition, aggregate, extent, sum total, total, whole

amount to add up to, aggregate, become, come to, develop into, equal, grow, mean, purport, total

ample abounding, abundant, big, bountiful, broad, capacious, commodious, copious, expansive, extensive, full, generous, great, large, lavish, liberal, plenteous, plentiful, plenty, profuse, rich, roomy, spacious, substantial, wide

DICTIONARY

ample *adj.* more than sufficient; large. **—amply** *adv.*

amplify *v.* **-fying, -fied.** increase the strength of (a current or sound signal); explain in more detail; increase the size or effect of. **—amplification** *n.* **—amplifier** *n.* device used to amplify a current or sound signal.

amplitude *n.* greatness of extent; breadth or scope. **—amplitude modulation** method of sending information by varying the size of the peaks and troughs of the carrier wave to suit the input signal.

ampoule *n.* small sealed glass vessel containing liquid for injection.

amputate *v.* cut off (a limb etc.) for medical reasons. **—amputation** *n.*

amuck *adv.* same as AMOK.

amulet *n.* something carried or worn as a charm against evil.

amuse *v.* entertain or divert; cause to laugh or smile. **—amusing** *adj.* **—amusement** *n.* state of being amused; something that amuses.

an *det.* form of A used before vowels, and sometimes before *h*, e.g. *an hour.*

anabolic steroid *n.* synthetic steroid hormone used by athletes to stimulate muscle growth.

anachronism [an-**nak**-kron-iz-zum] *n.* person or thing placed in the wrong historical period or seeming to belong to another time. **—anachronistic** *adj.*

anaconda *n.* large S American snake which kills by constriction.

anaemia [an-**neem**-ee-a] *n.* deficiency in the number of red blood cells. **—anaemic** *adj.* having anaemia; pale and sickly; lacking vitality.

anaesthetic [an-niss-**thet**-ik] *n., adj.* (substance) causing loss of sensation. **—anaesthesia** [an-niss-**theez**-ee-a] *n.* loss of sensation. **—anaes-**

thetist [an-**neess**-thet-ist] *n.* doctor trained to administer anaesthetics. **—anaesthetize** *v.*

anagram *n.* word or phrase made by rearranging the letters of another word or phrase.

anal [**ain**-al] *adj.* of the anus.

analgesic [an-nal-**jeez**-ik] *n., adj.* (drug) relieving pain. **—analgesia** *n.* absence of pain.

analogy [an-**nal**-a-jee] *n., pl.* **-gies.** similarity in some respects; comparison made to show such a similarity. **—analogical** *adj.* **—analogically** *adv.* **—analogize** *v.* use or show analogy. **—analogue** [**an**-nal-log] *n.* something that is analogous to something else. **—analogous** [an-**nal**-log-uss] *adj.* similar in some respects.

analysis [an-**nal**-liss-iss] *n., pl.* **-ses** [-seez]. separation of a whole into its components for study and interpretation; psychoanalysis. **—analyse** [**an**-nal-lize] *v.* make an analysis of (something); psychoanalyse. **—analyst** [**an**-nal-list] *n.* person skilled in analysis. **—analytic(al)** [an-nal-**lit**-tik(-al)] *adj.* **—analytically** *adv.*

anarchy [**an**-ark-ee] *n.* lawlessness and disorder; lack of government in a state. **—anarchic(al)** *adj.* **—anarchism** *n.* doctrine advocating the abolition of government. **—anarchist** *n.* person who believes in anarchism. **—anarchistic** *adj.*

anathema [an-**nath**-im-a] *n.* detested person or thing. **—anathematize** *v.* curse (a person or thing).

anatomy *n., pl.* **-mies.** science of the structure of the body; physical structure; person's body, e.g. *a delicate part of his anatomy;* detailed analysis. **—anatomical** *adj.* **—anatomically** *adv.* **—anatomist** *n.* expert in anatomy.

ancestor *n.* person from whom one is descended; forerunner. **—ancestral** *adj.* **—ancestry** *n.* lineage or descent.

anchor *n.* heavy hooked device attached to a boat by a cable and dropped overboard to fasten the ship to the sea bottom. **—** *v.* fasten with or as

THESAURUS

amuse beguile, charm, cheer, divert, enliven, entertain, occupy, please, recreate, regale

amusement 1. cheer, delight, diversion, enjoyment, entertainment, fun, gratification, interest, laughter, merriment, mirth, pleasure, recreation, sport **2.** distraction, diversion, entertainment, game, hobby, joke, lark, pastime, prank, recreation, sport

amusing charming, cheerful, comical, delightful, diverting, droll, enjoyable, entertaining, funny, humorous, interesting, jocular, laughable, lively, merry, pleasant, pleasing, witty

analyse 1. estimate, evaluate, examine, investigate, judge, test **2.** break down, consider, dissect, dissolve, divide, resolve, separate, study

analysis 1. breakdown, dissection, dissolution, division, enquiry, examination, investigation, scrutiny, separation, sifting, test **2.** estimation, evaluation, opinion, study

analytic, analytical diagnostic, discrete, dissecting, inquiring, investigative, logical, organized, problem-solving, questioning, rational, searching, studious, systematic, testing

anarchist insurgent, nihilist, rebel, revolutionary, terrorist

anatomy dissection, division, enquiry, examination, investigation, study

ancestor forebear, forefather, precursor, progenitor

DICTIONARY

if with an anchor. —**anchorage** n. place where boats can be anchored. —**anchorman** n. broadcaster in a central studio who links up and presents items from outside camera units and other studios; last person to compete in a relay team.

anchorite n. religious recluse.

anchovy [**an**-chov-ee] n., pl. **-vies.** small strong-tasting fish.

ancient adj. dating from very long ago; very old. —n. person who lived long ago.

ancillary adj. auxiliary, supplementary; subsidiary.

and conj. in addition to; as a consequence; then, afterwards.

andante [an-**dan**-tay] Music moderately slowly.

andiron n. iron stand for supporting logs in a fireplace.

androgynous adj. having both male and female characteristics.

android n. robot resembling a human.

anecdote n. short amusing account of an incident. —**anecdotal** adj.

anemometer n. instrument for recording wind speed.

anemone [an-**nem**-on-ee] n. plant with large white, purple, or red flowers.

aneroid barometer n. device for measuring air pressure, consisting of a partially evacuated chamber in which variations in pressure cause a pointer on the lid to move.

aneurysm, aneurism [**an**-new-riz-zum] n. permanent swelling of a blood vessel.

anew adv. once more; in a different way.

angel n. spiritual being believed to be an attendant or messenger of God; very kind person. —**angelic** adj. —**angelically** adv.

angelica [an-**jell**-ik-a] n. aromatic plant; its candied stalks, used in cookery.

Angelus [an-**jell**-uss] n. in the Roman Catholic Church, prayers recited in the morning, at midday, and in the evening; bell signalling the times of these prayers.

anger n. fierce displeasure; extreme annoyance; rage, wrath. —v. make (someone) angry. —**angry** adj. full of anger; inflamed, e.g. an angry wound. —**angrily** adv.

angina (pectoris) [an-**jine**-a] n. heart disorder causing sudden severe chest pains.

angle[1] n. space between or shape formed by two lines or surfaces that meet; divergence between these, measured in degrees; corner; point of view. —v. bend or place (something) at an angle.

angle[2] v. fish with a hook and line; try to get by hinting. —**angler** n. —**angling** n.

Anglican n., adj. (member) of the Church of England. —**Anglicanism** n.

anglicize v. make English in outlook, form, etc. —**Anglicism** n. expression or custom peculiar to the English.

Anglo- combining form English or British, e.g. Anglo-French.

Anglo-Saxon n. member of any of the W Germanic tribes which settled in England from the fifth century AD; language of the Anglo-Saxons. —adj. of the Anglo-Saxons or their language.

angora n. variety of goat, cat, or rabbit with long silky hair; hair of the angora goat or rabbit; cloth made from this hair.

Angostura Bitters pl. n. ® bitter tonic, used as a flavouring in alcoholic drinks.

angstrom n. unit of length used to measure wavelengths.

THESAURUS

ancient aged, antediluvian, antiquated, antique, archaic, early, hoary, old, olden, old-fashioned, out-of-date, superannuated, time-worn

and along with, also, as well as, furthermore, in addition to, including, moreover, plus, together with

anecdote reminiscence, short story, sketch, story, tale, yarn

angel 1. archangel, cherub, divine messenger, guardian spirit, seraph 2. darling, dear, dream, gem, ideal, jewel, paragon, saint

angelic celestial, cherubic, ethereal, heavenly, seraphic

anger 1. n. annoyance, displeasure, exasperation, fury, ill humour, ill temper, indignation, ire, irritability, irritation, outrage, passion, pique, rage, resentment, spleen, temper, vexation, wrath 2. v. affront, annoy, displease, enrage, exasperate, excite, gall, incense, infuriate, irritate, madden, nettle, offend, outrage, pique, provoke, rile, vex

angle n. 1. bend, corner, crook, crotch, cusp, edge, elbow, intersection, knee, nook, point 2. approach, aspect, outlook, perspective, point of view, position, side, slant, standpoint, viewpoint ~v. 3. cast, fish

angry annoyed, choleric, displeased, enraged, exasperated, furious, heated, hot, ill-tempered, incensed, indignant, infuriated, irascible, irate, ireful, irritable, irritated, nettled, outraged, passionate, piqued, provoked, raging, resentful, wrathful

DICTIONARY

anguish *n.* great mental or physical pain. **—anguished** *adj.*

angular *adj.* (of a person) lean and bony; having angles; measured by an angle. **—angularity** *n.*

anhydrous *adj. Chem.* containing no water.

aniline *n.* colourless oily liquid obtained from coal tar and used for making dyes, plastics, and explosives.

animadversion *n.* criticism or censure.

animal *n.* living creature having specialized sense organs and the power of voluntary motion, esp. one other than a human being; quadruped. **—***adj.* of animals; sensual, physical. **—animalcule** *n.* microscopic animal.

animate *v.* give life to; enliven; motivate; make a cartoon film of. **—***adj.* having life. **—animated** *adj.* **—animation** *n.* life, vigour; technique of making cartoon films. **—animator** *n.*

animism *n.* belief that natural objects possess souls. **—animist** *n., adj.* **—animistic** *adj.*

animosity *n., pl.* **-ties.** hostility, hatred.

animus *n.* hatred, animosity.

anion [an-eye-on] *n.* ion with negative charge.

anise [an-niss] *n.* plant with liquorice-flavoured seeds.

aniseed *n.* liquorice-flavoured seeds of the anise.

ankle *n.* joint between the foot and leg. **—anklet** *n.* ornamental chain worn round the ankle.

annals *pl. n.* yearly records of events. **—annalist** *n.*

anneal *v.* toughen (metal or glass) by heating and slow cooling.

annelid *n.* worm with a segmented body, such as an earthworm.

annex *v.* seize (territory); take (something) without permission; join or add (something) to something larger. **—annexation** *n.*

annexe *n.* extension to a building; nearby building used as an extension.

annihilate *v.* destroy utterly. **—annihilation** *n.*

anniversary *n., pl.* **-ries.** date on which something occurred in a previous year; celebration of this.

anno Domini *adv. Latin* (indicating years numbered from the supposed year of the birth of Christ) in the year of our Lord.

annotate *v.* add notes to (a written work). **—annotation** *n.*

announce *v.* make known publicly; proclaim. **—announcement** *n.* **—announcer** *n.* person who introduces radio or television programmes.

annoy *v.* irritate or displease. **—annoyance** *n.*

annual *adj.* happening once a year; lasting for a year. **—***n.* plant that completes its life-cycle in a year; book published each year. **—annually** *adv.*

annuity *n., pl.* **-ties.** fixed sum paid every year.

annul *v.* **-nulling, -nulled.** make (something, esp. a marriage) invalid. **—annulment** *n.*

annular [an-new-lar] *adj.* ring-shaped.

Annunciation *n. Christianity* angel Gabriel's announcement to the Virgin Mary of her conception of Christ.

anode *n. Electricity* positive electrode in a battery, valve, etc. **—anodize** *v.* coat (metal) with a protective oxide film by electrolysis.

anodyne *n.* something that relieves pain or distress. **—***adj.* relieving pain or distress.

anoint *v.* smear with oil as a sign of consecration.

anomaly [an-nom-a-lee] *n., pl.* **-lies.** something that deviates from the normal, irregularity. **—anomalous** *adj.*

THESAURUS

animal 1. *n.* beast, brute, creature 2. *adj.* bestial, bodily, brutish, carnal, fleshly, gross, physical, sensual

animate activate, embolden, encourage, enliven, excite, fire, impel, incite, inspire, invigorate, kindle, move, quicken, revive, rouse, spark, spur, stimulate, stir, urge

animosity animus, antagonism, antipathy, bad blood, bitterness, enmity, hate, hatred, hostility, ill will, malice, rancour, resentment

annals accounts, archives, chronicles, history, journals, memorials, records, registers

annihilate abolish, destroy, eradicate, exterminate, extinguish, obliterate, wipe out

announce advertise, broadcast, declare, disclose, give out, intimate, make known, proclaim, promulgate, publish, report, reveal, tell

announcement advertisement, broadcast, bulletin, communiqué, declaration, disclosure, intimation, proclamation, publication, report, statement

annoy anger, bedevil, bore, bother, displease, disturb, exasperate, harass, harry, irk, irritate, madden, molest, needle (*Inf.*), nettle, pester, plague, provoke, rile, ruffle, tease, trouble, vex

annoyance anger, bother, displeasure, disturbance, exasperation, irritation, nuisance, provocation, trouble, vexation

annual once a year, yearlong, yearly

annually by the year, each year, every year, once a year, per annum, per year, year after year, yearly

anomalous abnormal, eccentric, exceptional,

DICTIONARY

anon *adv. Obs.* in a short time, soon.

anon. anonymous.

anonymous *adj.* by someone whose name is not known; having no known name. —**anonymously** *adv.* —**anonymity** *n.*

anorak *n.* waterproof hooded jacket.

anorexia (nervosa) *n.* psychological disorder characterized by fear of becoming fat and refusal to eat. —**anorexic** *adj., n.*

another *det.* one more; a different one.

answer *n.* reply to a question, request, letter, etc.; solution to a problem; reaction or response. —*v.* give an answer (to); respond or react; be responsible to (a person). —**answerable** *adj.* (foll. by *for* or *to*) responsible for or accountable to. —**answering machine** device for answering a telephone automatically and recording messages.

ant *n.* small insect living in highly organized colonies. —**anteater** *n.* mammal which feeds on ants by means of a long sticky tongue. —**ant hill** mound built by ants around their nest.

antagonist *n.* opponent or adversary. —**antagonism** *n.* open opposition or hostility. —**antagonistic** *adj.* —**antagonize** *v.* arouse hostility in, annoy.

Antarctic *n.* —**the Antarctic** area around the South Pole. —*adj.* of this region.

ante *n.* player's stake in poker. —*v.* **-teing, -ted** *or* **-teed.** place (one's stake) in poker.

ante- *prefix* before in time or position, e.g. *antedate; antechamber.*

antecedent *n.* thing coming before something else. —*adj.* preceding, prior.

antedate *v.* precede in time.

antediluvian *adj.* of the time before the biblical Flood; old-fashioned.

antelope *n.* deer-like mammal with long legs and horns.

antenatal *adj.* during pregnancy, before birth.

antenna *n., pl.* **-nae.** insect's feeler; (*pl.* **-nas.**) aerial.

anterior *adj.* to the front; earlier.

anteroom *n.* small room leading into a larger one, often used as a waiting room.

anthem *n.* song of loyalty, esp. to a country; piece of music for a choir, usu. set to words from the Bible.

anther *n.* part of a flower's stamen containing pollen.

anthology *n., pl.* **-gies.** collection of poems or other literary pieces by various authors. —**anthologist** *n.*

anthracite *n.* hard coal burning slowly with little smoke or flame but intense heat.

anthrax *n.* dangerous disease of cattle and sheep, communicable to humans.

anthropoid *adj.* like a human. —*n.* ape, such as a chimpanzee, resembling a human.

anthropology *n.* study of human origins, institutions, and beliefs. —**anthropological** *adj.* —**anthropologist** *n.*

anthropomorphic *adj.* attributing human form or personality to a god, animal, or object. —**anthropomorphism** *n.*

anti- *prefix* against, opposed to, e.g. *anti-war;* opposite to, e.g. *anticlimax;* counteracting, e.g. *antifreeze.*

anti-aircraft *adj.* for defence against aircraft attack.

antibiotic *n.* chemical substance capable of destroying bacteria. —*adj.* of antibiotics.

antibody *n., pl.* **-bodies.** protein produced in the blood, which destroys bacteria.

anticipate *v.* foresee and act in advance of; look forward to; expect. —**anticipation** *n.* —**anticipatory** *adj.*

THESAURUS

incongruous, inconsistent, irregular, odd, peculiar, rare, unusual

anomaly abnormality, departure, eccentricity, exception, incongruity, inconsistency, irregularity, oddity, peculiarity, rarity

anonymous incognito, nameless, unacknowledged, unidentified, unknown, unnamed, unsigned

answer 1. *n.* acknowledgment, defence, explanation, reaction, refutation, rejoinder, reply, report, response, retort, return, riposte 2. *v.* acknowledge, explain, react, rejoin, reply, resolve, respond, retort, return, solve

answerable accountable, chargeable, liable, responsible, subject, to blame

antagonism antipathy, conflict, contention, discord, dissension, friction, hostility, rivalry

antagonist adversary, competitor, contender, enemy, foe, opponent, opposer, rival

antagonize alienate, anger, annoy, disaffect, estrange, insult, irritate, offend, repel

anthem canticle, chant, chorale, hymn, psalm

anticipate 1. await, count upon, expect, forecast, foresee, foretell, hope for, look for, predict 2. antedate, forestall, intercept, prevent

anticipation awaiting, expectancy, expectation, foresight, foretaste, forethought, hope, premonition

anticlimax bathos, disappointment, letdown

DICTIONARY

anticlimax *n.* disappointing conclusion to a series of events.

anticlockwise *adv., adj.* in the opposite direction to the rotation of the hands of a clock.

antics *pl. n.* absurd acts or postures.

anticyclone *n.* area of moving air of high pressure in which the winds rotate outwards.

antidote *n.* substance that counteracts a poison.

antifreeze *n.* liquid added to water to lower its freezing point, used in car radiators.

antigen [an-tee-jen] *n.* substance, usu. a toxin, causing the blood to produce antibodies.

antihero *n., pl.* **-roes.** central character in a book, film, etc. who lacks the traditional heroic virtues.

antihistamine *n.* drug used to treat allergies.

antimacassar *n.* cloth put over a chair-back to prevent soiling.

antimony [an-tim-mon-ee] *n.* brittle silvery-white metallic element.

antipathy [an-tip-a-thee] *n.* dislike, hostility. —**antipathetic** *adj.*

antiperspirant *n.* substance used to reduce or prevent sweating.

antiphon *n.* hymn sung in alternate parts by two groups of singers. —**antiphonal** *adj.*

antipodes [an-tip-pod-deez] *pl. n.* any two places diametrically opposite one another on the earth's surface. —**the Antipodes** Australia and New Zealand. —**antipodean** *adj.*

antipyretic *adj.* reducing fever. —*n.* drug that reduces fever.

antique *n.* object of an earlier period, valued for its beauty, workmanship, or age. —*adj.* made in an earlier period; old-fashioned. —**antiquary, antiquarian** *n.* student or collector of antiques or ancient works of art. —**antiquated** *adj.* out-of-date. —**antiquity** *n.* great age; ancient times; object dating from ancient times.

antiracism *n.* policy of challenging racism and promoting racial tolerance.

antirrhinum *n.* two-lipped flower of various colours.

anti-Semitism *n.* prejudice against Jews. —**anti-Semitic** *adj.*

antiseptic *adj.* preventing infection by killing germs. —*n.* antiseptic substance.

antisocial *adj.* avoiding the company of other people; (of behaviour) harmful to society.

antistatic *adj.* reducing the effects of static electricity.

antithesis [an-tith-iss-iss] *n., pl.* **-ses** [-seez]. exact opposite; placing together of contrasting ideas or words to produce an effect of balance. —**antithetical** *adj.*

antitoxin *n.* (serum containing) an antibody that acts against a toxin.

antler *n.* branching horn of male deer.

antonym *n.* word that means the opposite of another.

anus [ain-uss] *n.* opening at the end of the alimentary canal, through which faeces are discharged.

anvil *n.* heavy iron block on which a smith hammers metal into shape.

anxiety *n., pl.* **-ties.** state of being anxious.

anxious *adj.* worried and tense; intensely desiring. —**anxiously** *adv.*

any *det.* one or some, no matter which, e.g. *take any clothes you want.* —*adv.* at all, e.g. *it isn't any worse.* —**anybody** *pron.* anyone. —**anyhow** *adv.* anyway. —**anyone** *pron.* any person; person of any importance. —**anything** *pron.* —**anyway** *adv.* at any rate, nevertheless; in any manner. —**anywhere** *adv.* in, at, or to any place.

Anzac *n.* (in World War 1) a soldier serving with the Australian and New Zealand Army Corps.

AOB (on the agenda for a meeting) any other business.

aorta [eh-or-ta] *n., pl.* **-tas, -tae.** main artery of the body, carrying oxygen-rich blood from the heart. —**aortal** *adj.*

THESAURUS

antipathy antagonism, aversion, bad blood, disgust, dislike, distaste, enmity, hatred, hostility, ill will, loathing, rancour, repugnance

antique *adj.* 1. aged, ancient, elderly, old 2. archaic, obsolete, old-fashioned, outdated ~*n.* 3. bygone, heirloom, object of virtu, relic

antiquity 1. age, ancientness, elderliness, old age, oldness 2. ancient times, distant past, olden days

antiseptic 1. *adj.* aseptic, clean, hygienic, pure, sanitary, sterile, unpolluted 2. *n.* bactericide, disinfectant, germicide, purifier

antisocial alienated, misanthropic, reserved, retiring, unfriendly, unsociable, withdrawn

anxiety apprehension, care, concern, disquiet, distress, misgiving, nervousness, restlessness, solicitude, suspense, tension, unease, uneasiness, worry

anxious apprehensive, careful, concerned, distressed, disturbed, fearful, fretful, in suspense, nervous, restless, solicitous, tense, troubled, uneasy, watchful, worried

DICTIONARY

apace *adv. Lit.* swiftly.

apart *adv.* to or in pieces; to or at a distance; individual, distinct.

apartheid *n.* official government policy of racial segregation in S Africa.

apartment *n.* room in a building; *US* flat.

apathy *n.* lack of interest or enthusiasm. —**apathetic** *adj.* —**apathetically** *adv.*

ape *n.* tailless monkey such as the chimpanzee or gorilla; stupid, clumsy, or ugly man. —*v.* imitate. —**apish** *adj.*

aperient [ap-**peer**-ee-ent] *adj.* mildly laxative. —*n.* mild laxative.

aperitif [ap-per-rit-**teef**] *n.* alcoholic drink taken before a meal.

aperture *n.* opening or hole.

APEX Advance Purchase Excursion: reduced fare for journeys booked a specified period in advance.

apex *n.* highest point.

aphasia *n.* disorder of the central nervous system that affects the ability to speak and understand words.

aphid [**eh**-fid], **aphis** [**eh**-fiss] *n.* small insect which sucks the sap from plants.

aphorism *n.* short wise saying. —**aphoristic** *adj.*

aphrodisiac [af-roh-**diz**-zee-ak] *adj.* arousing sexual desire. —*n.* aphrodisiac substance.

apiary [**ape**-yar-ee] *n., pl.* **-ries.** place where bees are kept. —**apiarist** *n.* beekeeper. —**apiculture** *n.* breeding and care of bees.

apiece *adv.* each, e.g. *they were given two apples apiece.*

aplomb [ap-**plom**] *n.* calm self-possession.

apocalypse *n.* end of the world; event of great destruction. —**the Apocalypse** book of Revelation, last book of the New Testament. —**apocalyptic** *adj.*

Apocrypha [ap-**pok**-rif-fa] *pl. n.* **the Apocrypha.**

collective name for the 14 books of the Old Testament which are not accepted as part of the Hebrew scriptures. —**apocryphal** *adj.* (of a story) of questionable authenticity.

apogee [**ap**-oh-jee] *n.* point of the moon's or a satellite's orbit farthest from the earth; highest point.

apology *n., pl.* **-gies.** expression of regret for wrongdoing; (foll. by *for*) poor example of; formal written defence of a cause. —**apologetic** *adj.* making an apology. —**apologetically** *adv.* —**apologetics** *n.* branch of theology concerned with the reasoned defence of Christianity. —**apologist** *n.* person who formally defends a cause. —**apologize** *v.* make an apology.

apophthegm [**ap**-poth-em] *n.* short wise saying.

apoplexy *n. Med.* stroke. —**apoplectic** *adj.* of apoplexy; *Informal* furious.

apostasy [ap-**poss**-stass-ee] *n., pl.* **-sies.** abandonment of one's religious faith or other belief. —**apostate** [ap-**poss**-state] *n., adj.*

a posteriori [eh poss-steer-ee-**or**-rye] *adj. Logic* involving reasoning from effect to cause.

Apostle *n.* one of the twelve disciples chosen by Christ to preach the Gospel; (**a-**) ardent supporter of a cause or movement. —**apostolic** *adj.*

apostrophe [ap-**poss**-trof-fee] *n.* punctuation mark (') showing the omission of a letter or letters in a word, as in *don't*, or forming the possessive, as in *Jill's car*; digression from a speech to address an imaginary or absent person or thing. —**apostrophize** *v.* address an apostrophe to.

apothecary *n., pl.* **-caries.** *Obs.* chemist.

apotheosis [ap-poth-ee-oh-siss] *n., pl.* **-ses** [-seez]. elevation to the rank of a god; perfect example.

appal *v.* **-palling, -palled.** dismay, terrify. —**appalling** *adj.* dreadful, terrible.

THESAURUS

apart 1. afar, alone, aside, away, cut off, distant, distinct, divorced, excluded, independent, isolated, separate, singly, to itself, to oneself, to one side 2. asunder, in bits, in pieces, into parts, to bits, to pieces

apartment accommodation, compartment, quarters, room, rooms, suite

apathetic cool, emotionless, impassive, insensible, passive, stoic, stoical, torpid, unconcerned, unemotional, unfeeling, uninterested, unmoved, unresponsive

apathy coolness, impassivity, indifference, insensibility, listlessness, passiveness, passiv-

ity, stoicism, torpor, unconcern, unfeelingness, unresponsiveness

apiece each, for each, from each, individually, respectively, separately, severally, to each

aplomb balance, calmness, composure, coolness, equanimity, poise, self-assurance, self-confidence, stability

apologetic contrite, penitent, sorry

apologize ask forgiveness, beg pardon, express regret, say sorry

apology confession, defence, excuse, extenuation, vindication

appal alarm, astound, daunt, dismay, harrow,

DICTIONARY

apparatus *n.* equipment for a particular purpose.

apparel [ap-**par**-rel] *n. Old-fashioned* clothing.

apparent *adj.* readily seen, obvious; seeming as opposed to real. —**apparently** *adv.*

apparition *n.* ghost or ghost-like figure.

appeal *v.* make an earnest request; be attractive; request a review of a lower court's decision by a higher court. —*n.* earnest request; attractiveness; request for a review of a lower court's decision by a higher court. —**appealing** *adj.*

appear *v.* become visible or present; seem; be seen in public. —**appearance** *n.* an appearing; outward aspect.

appease *v.* pacify (a person) by yielding to his or her demands; satisfy or relieve (a feeling). —**appeasement** *n.*

appellant *n.* person who makes an appeal to a higher court.

appellation *n.* name, title.

append *v.* join on, add. —**appendage** *n.* thing joined on or added.

appendicitis *n.* inflammation of the appendix.

appendix *n., pl.* -**dixes,** -**dices.** separate additional material at the end of a book; *Anat.* short closed tube attached to the large intestine.

appertain *v.* (foll. by *to*) belong to; be connected with.

appetite *n.* desire or inclination, esp. for food or drink. —**appetizer** *n.* thing eaten or drunk to increase the appetite. —**appetizing** *adj.* stimulating the appetite. —**appetizingly** *adv.*

applaud *v.* show approval of by clapping one's hands; approve strongly. —**applause** *n.* approval shown by clapping one's hands.

apple *n.* round firm fleshy fruit that grows on trees. —**apple-pie order** *Informal* perfect order.

appliance *n.* device with a specific function.

appliqué [ap-**plee**-kay] *n.* kind of decoration in which one material is cut out and attached to another.

THESAURUS

horrify, outrage, petrify, scare, shock, terrify, unnerve

appalling alarming, astounding, awful, daunt~ ing, dire, dreadful, fearful, frightful, ghastly, grim, harrowing, hideous, horrible, horrid, horrifying, intimidating, petrifying, scaring, shocking, terrible, terrifying

apparatus appliance, device, equipment, gear, implements, machine, machinery, materials, means, mechanism, outfit, tackle, tools, uten~ sils

apparent clear, conspicuous, discernible, dis~ tinct, evident, indubitable, manifest, marked, obvious, open, overt, patent, plain, under~ standable, unmistakable, visible

apparently it appears that, it seems that, on the face of it, ostensibly, outwardly, seemingly, superficially

apparition chimera, ghost, phantom, spectre, spirit, spook (*Inf.*), visitant, wraith

appeal *n.* 1. entreaty, invocation, petition, plea, prayer, request, suit, supplication 2. allure, attraction, beauty, charm, fascination, inter~ estingness, pleasingness ~*v.* 3. adjure, apply, ask, beg, beseech, call, call upon, entreat, implore, petition, plead, pray, refer, request, solicit, sue, supplicate 4. allure, attract, charm, engage, entice, fascinate, interest, in~ vite, please, tempt

appear 1. arise, arrive, attend, be present, come forth, come into sight, come out, come to light, develop, emerge, issue, loom, materialize, oc~ cur, surface, turn out, turn up 2. look (like *or* as if), occur, seem, strike one as 3. be appar~

ent, be clear, be evident, be obvious, be plain 4. act, enter, perform, play, play a part, take part

appearance 1. advent, arrival, debut, emer~ gence, introduction, presence 2. air, aspect, bearing, demeanour, expression, face, figure, form, image, look, looks, manner 3. front, guise, image, impression, outward show, pre~ tence

appendix addition, adjunct, postscript, sup~ plement

appetite craving, demand, desire, hunger, lik~ ing, longing, passion, relish, stomach, taste, zeal, zest

appetizing delicious, inviting, mouthwatering, palatable, savoury

applaud approve, cheer, clap, commend, eulo~ gize, extol, laud, praise

applause acclamation, approval, cheering, cheers, hand-clapping, laudation, ovation, plaudit, praise

appliance apparatus, device, gadget, imple~ ment, instrument, machine, mechanism, tool

applicable apposite, appropriate, apt, fit, fit~ ting, germane, pertinent, relevant, suitable, useful

applicant candidate, inquirer, petitioner, suit~ or, suppliant

application 1. appeal, claim, inquiry, petition, request, requisition, suit 2. assiduity, atten~ tiveness, commitment, dedication, diligence, effort, hard work, industry, perseverance, study

DICTIONARY

apply v. -**plying**, -**plied**. make a formal request; put to practical use; put onto a surface; be relevant or appropriate. —**apply oneself** concentrate one's efforts. —**applicable** adj. relevant. —**applicably** adv. —**applicability** n. —**applicant** n. person who applies for something. —**application** n. formal request; act of applying something to a particular use; act of putting something onto a surface. —**applied** adj. (of a skill, science, etc.) put to practical use.

appoint v. assign to a job or position; fix or decide, e.g. *appoint a time;* equip or furnish. —**appointment** n. arrangement to meet a person; act of placing someone in a job; the job itself. —*pl.* fixtures or fittings.

apportion v. divide out in shares. —**apportionment** n.

apposite adj. suitable, apt. —**appositeness** n. —**apposition** n. grammatical construction in which two nouns or phrases referring to the same thing are placed one after another without a conjunction, as in *my son the doctor.*

appraise v. estimate the value or quality of. —**appraisal** n.

appreciate v. be grateful for; value highly; be aware of and understand; rise in value. —**appreciable** adj. enough to be noticed. —**appreciably** adv. —**appreciation** n. act of appreciating. —**appreciative** adj. feeling or showing appreciation.

apprehend v. seize, arrest; understand. —**apprehension** n. dread, anxiety; arrest; understanding. —**apprehensive** adj. fearful or anxious.

apprentice n. someone working for a skilled person for a fixed period in order to learn his or her trade. —v. take or place (someone) as an apprentice. —**apprenticeship** n.

apprise v. make aware (of).

appro n. —**on appro** *Informal* on approval.

approach v. come near or nearer (to); make a proposal or suggestion to; begin to deal with (a matter). —n. approaching or means of approaching; approximation. —**approachable** adj. —**approachability** n.

THESAURUS

apply 1. bring into play, bring to bear, carry out, employ, engage, execute, exercise, practise, put to use, use, utilize 2. appertain, be applicable, be appropriate, bear upon, be fitting, be relevant, fit, pertain, refer, relate, suit 3. anoint, bring into contact with, cover with, lay on, paint, place, put on, smear, spread on, touch to 4. claim, inquire, make application, petition, put in, request, requisition, solicit, sue 5. **apply oneself** be diligent, be industrious, commit, concentrate, dedicate, devote, direct, give, pay attention, persevere, study, try, work hard

appoint 1. allot, arrange, assign, choose, decide, designate, determine, establish, fix, set, settle 2. assign, choose, commission, delegate, elect, install, name, nominate, select

appointment 1. arrangement, assignation, consultation, date, engagement, interview, meeting, rendezvous, session, tryst (*Archaic*) 2. assignment, job, office, place, position, post, situation

apportion allocate, allot, assign, deal, dispense, distribute, divide, dole out, measure out, mete out, share

apportionment allocation, allotment, assignment, dealing out, distribution, division

apposite appertaining, applicable, appropriate, apropos, apt, befitting, germane, pertinent, proper, relevant, suitable, suited, to the point, to the purpose

appreciate 1. be appreciative, be grateful for, be indebted, be obliged, be thankful for, give thanks for 2. acknowledge, be alive to, know,

perceive, realize, recognize, take account of, understand 3. esteem, like, prize, rate highly, regard, relish, respect, savour, treasure, value 4. gain, grow, improve, increase, inflate, rise

appreciation 1. acknowledgment, gratefulness, gratitude, indebtedness, obligation, thanks 2. admiration, assessment, awareness, cognizance, enjoyment, esteem, knowledge, liking, perception, realization, recognition, regard, relish, respect, sensitivity, sympathy, valuation 3. gain, growth, improvement, increase, rise 4. notice, praise, review, tribute

appreciative 1. beholden, grateful, indebted, obliged, thankful 2. admiring, aware, cognizant, conscious, enthusiastic, mindful, perceptive, pleased, respectful, responsive, sensitive, sympathetic, understanding

apprehend 1. arrest, capture, catch, pinch (*Inf.*), run in (*Sl.*), seize, take, take prisoner 2. appreciate, comprehend, conceive, grasp, know, perceive, realize, recognize, think, understand

apprehension 1. alarm, anxiety, concern, disquiet, doubt, dread, fear, foreboding, misgiving, mistrust, unease, uneasiness, worry 2. arrest, capture, seizure 3. awareness, comprehension, grasp, intellect, intelligence, ken, knowledge, perception

apprehensive afraid, alarmed, anxious, concerned, fearful, foreboding, mistrustful, uneasy, worried

apprentice beginner, learner, novice, pupil, student

approach v. 1. advance, catch up, come close,

DICTIONARY

approbation *n.* approval.

appropriate *adj.* suitable, fitting. —*v.* take for oneself; put aside for a particular purpose. —**appropriately** *adv.* —**appropriateness** *n.* —**appropriation** *n.*

approve *v.* consider good or right; authorize, agree to. —**approval** *n.* favourable opinion; consent. —**on approval** (of goods) with an option to be returned without payment if unsatisfactory.

approx. approximate(ly).

approximate *adj.* almost but not quite exact. —*v.* come close to; be almost the same as. —**approximately** *adv.* —**approximation** *n.*

appurtenance *n.* minor or additional feature.

Apr. April.

après-ski [ap-ray-**skee**] *n.* social activities after a day's skiing.

apricot *n.* yellowish-orange juicy fruit like a small peach. —*adj.* yellowish-orange.

April *n.* fourth month of the year. —**April fool** victim of a practical joke played on April 1 (**April Fools' Day**).

apron *n.* garment worn over the front of the body to protect the clothes; part of a stage in front of the curtain; area at an airport or hangar for manoeuvring and loading aircraft.

apropos [ap-prop-**poh**] *adj., adv.* appropriate-(ly). —**apropos of** with regard to.

apse *n.* arched or domed recess, esp. in a church.

apt *adj.* suitable; having a specified tendency; quick to learn. —**aptly** *adv.* —**aptness** *n.* —**aptitude** *n.* natural ability.

aqua vitae [ak-wa vee-tie] *n. Obs.* brandy.

aqualung *n.* mouthpiece attached to air cylinders, worn for underwater swimming.

aquamarine *n.* greenish-blue gemstone. —*adj.* greenish-blue.

aquaplane *n.* board on which a person stands to be towed by a motorboat. —*v.* ride on an aquaplane; (of a motor vehicle) skim uncontrollably on a thin film of water.

aquarium *n., pl.* **aquariums, aquaria.** tank in which fish and other underwater creatures are kept; building containing such tanks.

aquatic *adj.* living in or near water; done in or on water. —**aquatics** *pl. n.* water sports.

THESAURUS

come near, come to, draw near, gain on, meet, move towards, near, push forward, reach 2. appeal to, apply to, make advances to, make a proposal to, make overtures to, sound out ~*n.* 3. access, advance, advent, arrival, avenue, coming, drawing near, entrance, nearing, passage, road, way 4. approximation, likeness, semblance 5. *Often plural* advance, appeal, application, invitation, offer, overture, proposal, proposition 6. attitude, course, manner, means, method, mode, procedure, style, technique, way

appropriate *adj.* 1. apposite, apropos, apt, becoming, befitting, belonging, congruous, correct, felicitous, fit, fitting, opportune, pertinent, proper, relevant, right, seemly, suitable, to the point, to the purpose, well-suited, well-timed ~*v.* 2. annex, arrogate, assume, commandeer, confiscate, expropriate, impound, seize, take, take over, take possession of, usurp 3. embezzle, filch, misappropriate, pilfer, pocket, steal

approval 1. acquiescence, agreement, assent, authorization, blessing, compliance, confirmation, consent, countenance, endorsement, leave, licence, mandate, O.K. (*Inf.*), permission, sanction, the go-ahead (*Inf.*), the green light (*Inf.*) 2. acclaim, admiration, applause, appreciation, approbation, commendation, esteem, favour, good opinion, liking, praise, regard, respect

approve 1. acclaim, admire, applaud, appreciate, be pleased with, commend, esteem, favour, have a good opinion of, like, praise, regard highly, respect, think highly of 2. accede to, accept, advocate, agree to, allow, assent to, authorize, bless, concur in, confirm, consent to, countenance, endorse, give the go-ahead (*Inf.*), give the green light (*Inf.*), go along with, mandate, O.K. (*Inf.*), pass, permit, ratify, recommend, uphold

approximate *adj.* 1. close, near 2. estimated, inexact, loose, rough ~*v.* 3. approach, border on, come close, come near, resemble, touch, verge on

approximately about, almost, around, circa (*used with dates*), close to, generally, just about, loosely, more or less, nearly, not far off, relatively, roughly

approximation conjecture, estimate, estimation, guess, guesswork, rough calculation, rough idea

apron pinafore, pinny (*Inf.*)

apt 1. applicable, apposite, appropriate, befitting, correct, fit, fitting, germane, pertinent, proper, relevant, seemly, suitable, to the point, to the purpose 2. disposed, given, inclined, liable, likely, of a mind, prone, ready 3. astute, bright, clever, expert, gifted, ingenious, intelligent, prompt, quick, sharp, skilful, smart, talented, teachable

DICTIONARY

aquatint *n.* print like a watercolour, produced by etching copper.

aqueduct *n.* structure carrying water across a valley or river.

aqueous *adj.* of, like, or containing water.

aquiline *adj.* of or like an eagle; (of a nose) curved like an eagle's beak.

Ar *Chem.* argon.

Arab *n.* member of a Semitic people originally from Arabia. —*adj.* of the Arabs. —**Arabic** *n.* language of the Arabs. —*adj.* of Arabic, Arabs, or Arabia.

arabesque [ar-ab-**besk**] *n.* ballet position in which one leg is raised behind and the arms are extended; elaborate ornamental design.

arable *adj.* suitable for growing crops on.

arachnid [ar-**rak**-nid] *n.* eight-legged invertebrate, such as a spider, scorpion, tick, or mite.

Aran *adj.* (of sweaters etc.) knitted in a complicated pattern traditional to the Aran Islands, usu. with natural unbleached wool.

arbiter *n.* person empowered to judge in a dispute; person with influential opinions about something. —**arbitrary** *adj.* based on personal choice or chance, rather than reason. —**arbitrarily** *adv.* —**arbitrate** *v.* settle (a dispute) by arbitration. —**arbitration** *n.* hearing and settling of a dispute by an impartial referee chosen by both sides. —**arbitrator** *n.*

arboreal [ahr-**bore**-ee-al] *adj.* of or living in trees.

arboretum [ahr-bore-ee-tum] *n., pl.* **-ta.** place where rare trees or shrubs are cultivated.

arboriculture *n.* cultivation of trees or shrubs.

arbour *n.* glade sheltered by trees.

arc *n.* part of a circle or other curve; luminous discharge of electricity across a small gap between two electrodes. —*v.* form an arc. —**arc welding** welding in which the heat is generated by an electric arc.

arcade *n.* row of arches on pillars; covered passageway, usu. lined with shops; set of arches.

arcane *adj.* mysterious and secret.

arch[1] *n.* curved structure supporting a bridge or roof; something curved; curved lower part of the foot. —*v.* (cause to) form an arch. —**archway** *n.* passageway under an arch.

arch[2] *adj.* superior, knowing; coyly playful. —**archly** *adv.* —**archness** *n.*

arch- *combining form* chief, principal, e.g. archenemy.

archaeology *n.* study of ancient cultures from their physical remains. —**archaeological** *adj.* —**archaeologist** *n.*

archaic [ark-**kay**-ik] *adj.* ancient; out-of-date. —**archaically** *adv.* —**archaism** [ark-kay-iz-zum] *n.* archaic word or phrase.

archangel [ark-ain-jell] *n.* chief angel.

archbishop *n.* chief bishop.

archdeacon *n.* priest ranking just below a bishop. —**archdeaconry** *n.*

archdiocese *n.* diocese of an archbishop.

archery *n.* art or sport of shooting with a bow and arrow. —**archer** *n.*

archetype [ark-ee-type] *n.* original model; perfect specimen. —**archetypal** *adj.*

archiepiscopal *adj.* of an archbishop.

archipelago [ark-ee-pel-a-go] *n., pl.* **-gos.** group of islands; sea full of small islands. —**archipelagic** *adj.*

architect *n.* person qualified to design and supervise the construction of buildings. —**architecture** *n.* designing and construction of buildings; style of building. —**architectural** *adj.*

architrave *n.* *Archit.* beam that rests on columns; moulding round a doorway or window.

archive [ark-ive] *n.* (often *pl.*) collection of records or documents; place where these are

---

THESAURUS

arable fertile, fruitful, ploughable, productive, tillable

arbiter adjudicator, arbitrator, judge, referee, umpire

arbitrary capricious, erratic, fanciful, inconsistent, optional, personal, random, subjective, unreasonable, whimsical, wilful

arbitrate adjudge, adjudicate, decide, determine, judge, referee, settle, umpire

arbitration adjudication, decision, judgment, settlement

arbitrator adjudicator, arbiter, judge, referee, umpire

arc arch, bend, bow, crescent, curve, half-moon

arch[1] archway, curve, dome, span, vault

arch[2] 1. accomplished, chief, consummate, expert, finished, first, foremost, greatest, highest, leading, main, major, master, preeminent, primary, principal, superior, top 2. artful, frolicsome, knowing, mischievous, pert, playful, roguish, saucy, sly, waggish, wily

archetype classic, form, ideal, model, original, pattern, prototype, standard

architect designer, master builder, planner

architecture building, construction, design, planning

archives annals, chronicles, documents, papers, records, registers, rolls

DICTIONARY

kept. —**archival** *adj.* —**archivist** [ark-iv-ist] *n.* person in charge of archives.

Arctic *n.* —**the Arctic.** area around the North Pole. —*adj.* of this region; (a-) *Informal* very cold.

ardent *adj.* passionate; eager, zealous. —**ardently** *adv.* —**ardency** *n.* —**ardour** *n.* passion; enthusiasm, zeal.

arduous *adj.* hard to accomplish, strenuous. —**arduously** *adv.* —**arduousness** *n.*

are *v.* see BE.

area *n.* part or region; size of a two-dimensional surface; subject field; small sunken yard giving access to a basement.

arena *n.* seated enclosure for sports events; area of a Roman amphitheatre where gladiators fought; sphere of intense activity.

aren't are not.

areola *n., pl.* **-lae, -las.** small circular area, such as the coloured ring around the human nipple.

argon *n.* inert gas found in the air.

argot [ahr-go] *n.* slang or jargon.

argue *v.* **-guing, -gued.** quarrel, dispute; try to prove by giving reasons; debate. —**arguable** *adj.* —**arguably** *adv.* —**argument** *n.* quarrel; discussion; point presented for or against something.

—**argumentation** *n.* process of reasoning methodically. —**argumentative** *adj.* given to arguing.

argy-bargy *n., pl.* **-bargies.** *Informal* squabbling argument.

aria [ah-ree-a] *n.* elaborate song for solo voice, esp. one from an opera.

arid *adj.* parched, dry; uninteresting. —**aridity** *n.*

aright *adv.* rightly.

arise *v.* **arising, arose, arisen.** come about; get up; come into notice.

aristocracy *n., pl.* **-cies.** highest social class; government by this class. —**aristocrat** *n.* member of the aristocracy. —**aristocratic** *adj.* —**aristocratically** *adv.*

arithmetic *n.* calculation by or of numbers. —**arithmetic(al)** *adj.* —**arithmetically** *adv.* —**arithmetician** *n.*

ark *n. Bible* boat built by Noah, which survived the Flood; (A-) *Judaism* chest containing the writings of Jewish Law.

arm[1] *n.* upper limb from the shoulder to the wrist; sleeve of a garment; side of a chair. —**armful** *n.* as much as an arm can hold. —**armlet** *n.* band worn round the arm. —**armchair** *n.* upholstered chair with side supports for the arms. —**armhole** *n.* opening in a garment

THESAURUS

arctic 1. far-northern, polar 2. cold, freezing, frosty, frozen, gelid, glacial, icy

ardent avid, eager, enthusiastic, fervent, fiery, hot, impassioned, intense, keen, passionate, spirited, vehement, warm, zealous

ardour avidity, eagerness, enthusiasm, feeling, fervour, fire, heat, intensity, keenness, passion, spirit, vehemence, warmth, zeal

arduous burdensome, difficult, exhausting, fatiguing, hard, harsh, heavy, onerous, painful, punishing, rigorous, severe, steep, strenuous, taxing, tiring, tough, troublesome

area 1. district, locality, neighbourhood, patch, plot, realm, region, sector, sphere, stretch, territory, tract, zone 2. part, portion, section, sector 3. sunken space, yard

arena 1. amphitheatre, field, ground, park (*Inf.*), ring, stadium, stage 2. battleground, domain, field, lists, province, realm, scene, scope, sphere, territory, theatre

argue 1. altercate, bandy words, bicker, disagree, dispute, fall out (*Inf.*), feud, fight, have an argument, quarrel, squabble, wrangle 2. assert, claim, contend, controvert, debate, discuss, dispute, expostulate, hold, maintain, plead, question, reason, remonstrate 3. demonstrate, evince, exhibit, imply, indicate, point to, show, suggest

argument 1. altercation, barney (*Inf.*), clash, controversy, difference of opinion, disagreement, dispute, feud, fight, quarrel, row, squabble, wrangle 2. assertion, claim, contention, debate, discussion, dispute, plea, pleading, remonstrance, remonstration 3. case, defence, dialectic, ground(s), logic, polemic, reason, reasoning

argumentative belligerent, combative, contrary, opinionated, quarrelsome

arid barren, desert, dried up, dry, parched, sterile, waterless

arise 1. appear, begin, come to light, commence, crop up (*Inf.*), emanate, emerge, ensue, follow, happen, issue, occur, originate, proceed, result, set in, spring, start, stem 2. ascend, climb, lift, mount, move upward, rise, soar, tower

aristocracy elite, gentry, *haut monde*, nobility, noblesse (*Literary*), patricians, peerage, upper class

aristocrat grandee, lady, lord, noble, nobleman, patrician, peer

aristocratic blue-blooded, elite, gentlemanly, highborn, lordly, noble, patrician, titled, upper-class, well-born

DICTIONARY

through which the arm passes. —**armpit** n. hollow under the arm at the shoulder.

arm² v. supply with weapons; prepare (a bomb etc.) for use. —**arms** pl. n. weapons; military exploits; heraldic emblem. —**armament** n. military weapons; preparation for war.

armada n. large number of warships.

armadillo n., pl. -**los**. small S American mammal covered in strong bony plates.

Armageddon n. Bible final battle between good and evil at the end of the world; catastrophic conflict.

armature n. revolving structure in an electric motor or generator, wound with coils carrying the current.

armistice [arm-miss-stiss] n. suspension of fighting.

armour n. metal clothing formerly worn to protect the body in battle; metal plating of tanks, warships, etc. —**armorial** adj. relating to heraldry. —**armourer** n. maker, repairer, or keeper of arms or armour. —**armoury** n. place where weapons are stored.

army n., pl. -**mies**. military force that fights on land; great number.

aroma n. pleasant smell. —**aromatic** adj.

aromatheraphy n. massage with fragrant oils to relieve tension.

arose v. past tense of ARISE.

around prep., adv. on all sides (of); from place to place (in); somewhere in or near; approximately.

arouse v. awaken; stimulate, make active.

arpeggio [arp-**pej**-ee-oh] n., pl. -**gios**. Music notes of a chord played or sung in quick succession.

arr. arranged (by); arrival; arrive(d).

arraign [ar-**rain**] v. indict (a person) on a charge; accuse. —**arraignment** n.

arrange v. put in order; agree; plan; adapt (music) for performance in a certain way. —**arrangement** n.

arrant adj. utter, downright.

arras n. tapestry wall-hanging.

array n. impressive display or collection; orderly arrangement, esp. of troops; Poetic rich clothing. —v. arrange in order; dress in rich clothing.

arrears pl. n. money owed. —**in arrears** late in paying a debt.

arrest v. take (a person) into custody; stop the movement or development of; catch and hold (the attention). —n. act of taking a person into custody; slowing or stopping. —**arresting** adj. attracting attention, striking.

arrive v. reach a place or destination; happen, come; Informal be born; Informal attain success.

THESAURUS

arm¹ n. appendage, limb, upper limb

arm² v. 1. Esp. with weapons array, deck out, equip, furnish, issue with, outfit, provide, rig, supply 2. mobilize, muster forces, prepare for war, take up arms

armada fleet, flotilla, navy, squadron

armaments arms, guns, munitions, ordnance, weapons

arms 1. armaments, firearms, guns, ordnance, weaponry, weapons 2. blazonry, crest, escutcheon, heraldry, insignia

army 1. armed force, land forces, legions, military, soldiers, soldiery, troops 2. Fig. array, horde, host, multitude, pack, swarm, throng, vast number

aroma bouquet, fragrance, odour, perfume, redolence, savour, scent, smell

aromatic balmy, fragrant, perfumed, pungent, redolent, savoury, spicy

around prep. 1. about, encircling, enclosing, on all sides of, surrounding 2. about, approximately, circa (used with dates), roughly ~adv. 3. about, all over, everywhere, here and there, in all directions, on all sides, throughout, to and fro 4. at hand, close, close at hand, close by, near, nearby, nigh (Archaic or dialect)

arouse agitate, awaken, call forth, enliven, excite, foster, goad, incite, inflame, instigate, kindle, move, provoke, quicken, rouse, sharpen, spark, spur, stimulate, stir up, summon up, waken, wake up, warm, whet, whip up

arrange 1. array, class, dispose, file, form, group, line up, marshal, order, organize, position, range, rank, set out, sort 2. adjust, agree to, come to terms, compromise, construct, contrive, determine, devise, plan, prepare, schedule, settle 3. adapt, instrument, orchestrate, score

arrangement 1. array, classification, design, display, disposition, form, line-up, order, organization, rank, setup (Inf.), structure, system 2. adaptation, instrumentation, interpretation, orchestration, score, version

array arrangement, collection, display, disposition, exhibition, formation, line-up, marshalling, muster, order, parade, show, supply

arrest 1. v. apprehend, capture, catch, detain, lay hold of, run in (Sl.), seize, take, take into custody, take prisoner 2. n. apprehension, capture, cop (Sl.), detention, seizure

arrival advent, appearance, entrance, occurrence, taking place

DICTIONARY

—**arrival** *n.* arriving; person or thing that has just arrived.

arrogant *adj.* proud and overbearing. —**arrogantly** *adv.* —**arrogance** *n.*

arrogate *v.* claim or seize without justification.

arrow *n.* pointed shaft shot from a bow; arrow-shaped sign or symbol used to show direction. —**arrowhead** *n.* pointed tip of an arrow.

arrowroot *n.* nutritious starch obtained from the root of a W Indian plant.

arse *n. Taboo* buttocks or anus. —**arsehole** *Taboo n.* anus; stupid or annoying person.

arsenal *n.* place where arms and ammunition are made or stored.

arsenic *n.* toxic grey element; highly poisonous compound of this. —**arsenical** *adj.*

arson *n.* crime of intentionally setting property on fire. —**arsonist** *n.*

art *n.* creation of works of beauty, esp. paintings or sculpture; works of art collectively; skill. —*pl.* nonscientific branches of knowledge. —**artful** *adj.* cunning, wily. —**artfully** *adv.* —**artfulness** *n.* —**artist** *n.* person who produces works of art, esp. paintings or sculpture; person skilled at something; artiste. —**artiste** *n.* professional entertainer such as a singer or dancer. —**artistic** *adj.* —**artistically** *adv.* —**artistry** *n.* artistic skill. —**artless** *adj.* free from deceit or cunning; natural, unpretentious. —**artlessly** *adv.* —**artlessness** *n.* —**arty** *adj. Informal* having an affected interest in art.

artefact, artifact *n.* something made by man.

arteriosclerosis [art-ear-ee-oh-skler-**oh**-siss] *n.* hardening of the arteries.

artery *n., pl.* **-teries.** one of the tubes carrying blood from the heart; major road or means of communication. —**arterial** *adj.* of an artery; (of a route) major.

artesian well [art-**teez**-yan] *n.* well bored vertically so that the water is forced to the surface by natural pressure.

Artex *n.* ® textured plaster-like covering for ceilings and walls.

arthritis *n.* painful inflammation of a joint or joints. —**arthritic** *adj., n.*

arthropod *n.* animal, such as a spider or insect, with jointed limbs and a segmented body.

artichoke *n.* thistle-like plant with a flower cooked as a vegetable. —**Jerusalem artichoke** plant with edible potato-like roots.

article *n.* item or object; written piece in a magazine or newspaper; clause in a document; *Grammar* any of the words *the, a,* or *an.* —*v.* bind by a contract as an apprentice.

articulate *adj.* able to express oneself clearly and coherently; *Zool.* having joints; (of speech) clear, distinct. —*v.* speak or say clearly and coherently. —**articulately** *adv.* —**articulated** *adj.* jointed. —**articulated lorry** large lorry in two separate sections joined by a pivoted bar. —**articulation** *n.*

artifice *n.* clever trick; cleverness, skill. —**artificer** [art-**tiff**-iss-er] *n.* craftsman. —**artificial** *adj.* man-made, not occurring naturally; made in imitation of something natural; not sincere. —**artificial insemination** introduction of semen into the womb by means other than sexual intercourse. —**artificial intelligence** branch of computer science aiming to produce machines which can imitate intelligent human behaviour. —**artificial respiration** method of restarting a person's breathing after it has stopped. —**artificially** *adv.* —**artificiality** *n.*

THESAURUS

arrive appear, befall, come, enter, get to, happen, occur, reach, show up (*Inf.*), take place, turn up

arrogance bluster, conceit, hauteur, insolence, loftiness, lordliness, pomposity, pompousness, presumption, pretentiousness, pride, scornfulness, superciliousness, swagger

arrogant assuming, blustering, conceited, contemptuous, disdainful, haughty, high-handed, imperious, insolent, lordly, overbearing, pompous, presumptuous, pretentious, proud, scornful, supercilious

arrow 1. bolt, dart, flight, quarrel, reed (*Archaic*), shaft (*Archaic*) 2. indicator, pointer

arsenal ammunition dump, armoury, arms depot, magazine, ordnance depot, stock, stockpile, store, storehouse, supply

art adroitness, aptitude, artistry, craft, crafts-manship, dexterity, expertise, facility, ingenuity, knack, knowledge, mastery, method, profession, skill, trade, virtuosity

artful adept, adroit, clever, crafty, cunning, deceitful, designing, dexterous, ingenious, intriguing, masterly, politic, proficient, resourceful, sharp, shrewd, skilful, sly, smart, subtle, tricky, wily

article 1. commodity, item, object, piece, substance, thing, unit 2. composition, discourse, essay, feature, item, paper, piece, story, treatise

articulate 1. *adj.* clear, coherent, comprehensible, eloquent, expressive, fluent, intelligible, lucid, meaningful, vocal 2. *v.* enunciate, express, pronounce, say, speak, state, talk, utter, voice

artificial 1. man-made, manufactured, plastic,

DICTIONARY

artillery *n.* large-calibre guns; branch of the army who use these.

artisan *n.* skilled worker, craftsman.

arum lily [**air**-rum] *n.* plant with a white funnel-shaped leaf surrounding a spike of flowers.

As *Chem.* arsenic.

as *conj.* while, when; in the way that; that which, e.g. *do as you are told;* since, seeing that; for instance. —*adv., conj.* used to indicate amount or extent in comparisons, e.g. *he is as tall as you.* —*prep.* in the role of, being, e.g. *as a mother, I am concerned.*

asafoetida *n.* strong-smelling plant resin used as a spice in Eastern cookery.

a.s.a.p. as soon as possible.

asbestos *n.* fibrous mineral which does not burn. —**asbestosis** *n.* lung disease caused by inhalation of asbestos fibre.

ascend *v.* go or move up. —**ascension** *n.* ascending. —**ascent** *n.* ascending; upward slope. —**ascendant** *adj.* dominant or influential. —*n.* —**in the ascendant** increasing in power or influence. —**ascendancy** *n.* condition of being dominant.

ascertain *v.* find out definitely. —**ascertainable** *adj.* —**ascertainment** *n.*

ascetic [ass-**set**-tik] *n.* person who abstains from worldly pleasures and comforts. —*adj.* abstaining from worldly pleasures and comforts. —**ascetically** *adv.* —**asceticism** *n.*

ascorbic acid [ass-**core**-bik] *n.* vitamin C.

ascribe *v.* attribute, as to a particular origin. —**ascribable** *adj.* —**ascription** *n.*

aseptic [eh-**sep**-tik] *adj.* germ-free. —**asepsis** [eh-**sep**-siss] *n.* aseptic condition.

asexual [eh-**sex**-yewal] *adj.* without sex. —**asexually** *adv.*

ash[1] *n.* powdery substance left when something is burnt. —*pl.* remains after burning, esp. of a human body after cremation. —**the Ashes** cricket trophy competed for in test matches by England and Australia. —**ashen** *adj.* pale with shock. —**Ash Wednesday** first day of Lent. —**ashtray** *n.* receptacle for tobacco ash and cigarette butts.

ash[2] *n.* tree with grey bark.

ashamed *adj.* feeling shame.

ashlar *n.* square block of hewn stone used in building.

ashore *adv.* towards or on land.

ashram *n.* religious retreat where a Hindu holy man lives.

Asian *adj.* of the continent of Asia or any of its peoples or languages. —*n.* person from Asia or a descendant of one. —**Asiatic** *adj.*

aside *adv.* to one side; out of other people's hearing, e.g. *he took me aside to tell me his plans.* —*n.* remark not meant to be heard by everyone present.

asinine [**ass**-in-nine] *adj.* stupid, idiotic. —**asininity** *n.*

ask *v.* say or write (something) in a form that

THESAURUS

synthetic 2. bogus, counterfeit, ersatz, fake, imitation, mock, sham, simulated, specious, spurious

artisan artificer, craftsman, mechanic, skilled workman, technician

artistic aesthetic, beautiful, creative, cultivated, cultured, decorative, elegant, exquisite, graceful, imaginative, refined, sensitive, stylish

as *conj.* 1. at the time that, during the time that, just as, when, while 2. in the manner that, in the way that, like 3. that which, what 4. because, considering that, seeing that, since 5. in the same manner with, in the same way that, like 6. for instance, like, such as ~*prep.* 7. being, in the character of, in the role of, under the name of

ascend climb, float up, fly up, go up, lift off, mount, move up, rise, scale, slope upwards, soar, take off, tower

ascent 1. climb, climbing, mounting, rise, ris-

ing, scaling, upward movement 2. gradient, incline, ramp, rise, upward slope

ascertain confirm, determine, discover, establish, find out, fix, identify, learn, make certain, settle, verify

ascribe assign, attribute, charge, credit, impute, put down, refer, set down

ashamed bashful, blushing, crestfallen, discomfited, distressed, embarrassed, guilty, humiliated, mortified, prudish, reluctant, remorseful, shamefaced, sheepish, shy, sorry

ashore aground, landwards, on dry land, on land, on the beach, on the shore, shorewards, to the shore

aside alone, alongside, apart, away, beside, in reserve, on one side, out of mind, privately, separately, to one side, to the side

ask 1. inquire, interrogate, query, question, quiz 2. appeal, apply, beg, beseech, claim, crave, demand, entreat, implore, petition, plead, pray, request, seek, solicit, sue, supplicate 3. bid, invite, summon

DICTIONARY

requires an answer; make a request or demand; invite.

askance [ass-**kanss**] *adv.* —**look askance at** look at with an oblique glance; regard with suspicion.

askew *adv., adj.* to one side, crooked.

aslant *adv., prep.* at a slant (to), slanting (across).

asleep *adj.* sleeping; (of limbs) numb.

asp *n.* small venomous snake.

asparagus *n.* plant whose shoots are cooked as a vegetable.

aspect *n.* feature or element; appearance or look; position facing a particular direction.

aspen *n.* kind of poplar tree.

asperity [ass-**per**-rit-ee] *n.* roughness of temper.

aspersion *n.* —**cast aspersions on** make derogatory remarks about.

asphalt *n.* black hard tarlike substance used for road surfaces etc. —*v.* cover with asphalt.

asphodel *n.* plant with clusters of yellow or white flowers.

asphyxia [ass-**fix**-ee-a] *n.* suffocation. —**asphyxiate** *v.* suffocate. —**asphyxiation** *n.*

aspic *n.* savoury jelly used to coat meat, eggs, fish, etc.

aspidistra *n.* plant with long tapered leaves.

aspirate *Phonetics* —*v.* pronounce with an *h* sound. —*n.* *h* sound.

aspire *v.* (foll. by *to*) yearn (for), hope (to do or

be). —**aspirant** *n.* person who aspires. —**aspiration** *n.* strong desire or aim.

aspirin *n.* drug used to relieve pain and fever; tablet of this.

ass *n.* donkey; stupid person.

assagai *n.* same as ASSEGAI.

assail *v.* attack violently. —**assailant** *n.*

assassin *n.* person who murders a prominent person. —**assassinate** *v.* murder (a prominent person). —**assassination** *n.*

assault *n.* violent attack. —*v.* attack violently. —**assault course** series of obstacles used in military training.

assay *n.* analysis of a substance, esp. a metal, to ascertain its purity. —*v.* make such an analysis.

assegai *n.* slender spear used in S Africa.

assemble *v.* collect or congregate; put together the parts of (a machine). —**assemblage** *n.* collection or group; assembling. —**assembly** *n.* assembling; assembled group. —**assembly line** sequence of machines and workers in a factory assembling a product.

assent *n.* agreement or consent. —*v.* agree or consent.

assert *v.* declare forcefully; insist upon (one's rights etc.). —**assert oneself** put oneself forward forcefully. —**assertion** *n.* —**assertive** *adj.* —**assertively** *adv.*

assess *v.* judge the worth or importance of; estimate the value of (income or property) for

THESAURUS

asleep dead to the world (*Inf.*), dormant, dozing, sleeping, slumbering

aspect 1. air, appearance, attitude, bearing, condition, countenance, demeanour, expression, look, manner 2. angle, facet, feature, side

aspiration aim, ambition, dream, endeavour, goal, hope, longing, object, objective, wish, yearning

aspire aim, crave, desire, dream, hanker, hope, long, pursue, seek, wish

ass 1. donkey 2. blockhead, dolt, dope (*Sl.*), dunce, fool, halfwit, idiot, jackass, nincompoop, nitwit, numskull, simpleton

assassin executioner, hatchet man (*Sl.*), hit man (*Sl.*), killer, murderer

assassinate eliminate (*Sl.*), hit (*U.S. sl.*), kill, liquidate, murder, slay

assault 1. *n.* aggression, attack, charge, invasion, offensive, storm, storming, strike 2. *v.* attack, charge, invade, lay into, set about, set upon, storm

assemble 1. accumulate, amass, bring together, call together, collect, come together, congre-

gate, convene, convoke, flock, forgather, gather, marshal, meet, muster, rally, summon 2. connect, construct, erect, fabricate, fit together, join, make, piece together, set up

assembly 1. accumulation, aggregation, body, collection, company, conference, congregation, council, crowd, diet, flock, gathering, group, mass, meeting, rally, throng 2. construction, erection, fabrication, manufacture

assent 1. *v.* accede, accept, acquiesce, agree, allow, approve, comply, concur, consent, grant, permit 2. *n.* acceptance, accord, acquiescence, agreement, approval, consent, permission, sanction

assert affirm, allege, avow, contend, declare, maintain, profess, state, swear

assess 1. compute, determine, estimate, evaluate, fix, gauge, judge, rate, value, weigh 2. fix, impose, levy, rate, tax, value

assessment 1. determination, estimate, judgment, rating, valuation 2. charge, demand, duty, evaluation, impost, levy, rate, rating, tax, taxation, toll

DICTIONARY

taxation purposes. —**assessment** *n.* —**assessor** *n.*

asset *n.* valuable or useful person or thing. —*pl.* property that a person or firm can sell, esp. to pay debts.

asseverate *v.* declare solemnly. —**asseveration** *n.*

assiduous *adj.* diligent and persevering. —**assiduously** *adv.* —**assiduity** *n.*

assign *v.* appoint (someone) to a job or task; allot (a task); attribute. —**assignation** [ass-sig-nay-shun] *n.* assigning; secret arrangement to meet. —**assignment** *n.* assigning; task assigned.

assimilate *v.* learn and understand (information); absorb or be absorbed or incorporated. —**assimilable** *adj.* —**assimilation** *n.*

assist *v.* give help or support. —**assistance** *n.* —**assistant** *n.* helper. —*adj.* junior or deputy.

assizes *pl. n.* court sessions formerly held in each county of England and Wales.

associate *v.* connect in the mind; mix socially. —*n.* partner in business; friend or companion. —*adj.* having partial rights or subordinate status, e.g. *associate member.* —**association** *n.* associating; society or club.

assonance *n.* rhyming of vowel sounds but not consonants, as in *time* and *light.* —**assonant** *adj.*

assorted *adj.* consisting of various types mixed together. —**assortment** *n.* assorted mixture.

assuage [ass-**wage**] *v.* relieve (pain, grief, thirst, etc.).

assume *v.* take to be true without proof; pretend, e.g. *I assumed indifference;* take upon oneself, e.g. *he assumed command.* —**assumption** *n.* assuming; thing assumed. —**assumptive** *adj.*

assure *v.* promise or guarantee; convince; make (something) certain; insure against loss of life. —**assured** *adj.* confident; certain to happen. —**assuredly** *adv.* definitely. —**assurance** *n.* assuring or being assured.

aster *n.* plant with daisy-like flowers.

asterisk *n.* star-shaped symbol (*) used in printing to indicate a footnote etc. —*v.* mark with an asterisk.

astern *adv.* at or towards the stern of a ship; backwards.

asteroid *n.* any of the small planets that orbit the sun between Mars and Jupiter.

asthma [ass-ma] *n.* illness causing difficulty in breathing. —**asthmatic** *adj., n.*

THESAURUS

asset 1. advantage, aid, benefit, blessing, boon, help, resource, service 2. *Plural* capital, estate, funds, goods, holdings, means, money, possessions, property, reserves, resources, valuables, wealth

assign 1. appoint, choose, name, nominate, select 2. allocate, allot, consign, give, grant

assignment appointment, charge, commission, duty, job, mission, position, post, responsibility, task

assist aid, back, boost, collaborate, cooperate, expedite, facilitate, further, help, reinforce, second, serve, succour, support, sustain, work for, work with

assistance aid, backing, boost, collaboration, cooperation, furtherance, help, helping hand, reinforcement, relief, service, succour, support

assistant accessory, accomplice, aide, ally, associate, auxiliary, backer, collaborator, colleague, helper, helpmate, henchman, partner

associate 1. *v.* affiliate, ally, combine, connect, couple, join, league, link, mix, pair, relate, unite, yoke 2. *n.* ally, colleague, companion, comrade, co-worker, follower, friend, mate, partner

association 1. alliance, band, clique, club, company, confederacy, confederation, cooperative, corporation, federation, fraternity, group,

league, partnership, society, syndicate, union 2. blend, bond, combination, concomitance, connection, correlation, identification, mixture, pairing, relation, tie, union

assorted different, diverse, diversified, heterogeneous, mixed, motley, sundry, varied, various

assortment array, choice, collection, diversity, hotchpotch, jumble, medley, *mélange,* miscellany, mishmash, mixture, selection, variety

assume 1. accept, believe, expect, fancy, imagine, presuppose, suppose, surmise, suspect, take for granted, think 2. affect, feign, imitate, impersonate, mimic, put on, sham, simulate 3. accept, enter upon, put on, set about, shoulder, take on, take over, take responsibility for, take up, undertake

assumption belief, conjecture, inference, premise, premiss, presumption, surmise

assurance 1. affirmation, declaration, guarantee, oath, pledge, promise, vow, word, word of honour 2. aggressiveness, assuredness, boldness, certainty, confidence, conviction, coolness, courage, faith, firmness, nerve, poise, self-confidence, sureness

assure 1. convince, embolden, encourage, hearten, persuade, reassure, soothe 2. guarantee, pledge, promise, swear, vow 3. make certain, make sure, seal, secure

DICTIONARY

astigmatism [eh-**stig**-mat-tiz-zum] *n.* inability of a lens, esp. of the eye, to focus properly. —**astigmatic** *adj.*

astir *adj.* out of bed; in motion.

astonish *v.* surprise greatly. —**astonishment** *n.*

astound *v.* overwhelm with amazement. —**astounding** *adj.*

astrakhan *n.* dark curly fleece of lambs from Astrakhan in the U.S.S.R.; fabric resembling this.

astral *adj.* of stars; of the spirit world.

astray *adv.* off the right path.

astride *adv., prep.* with a leg on either side (of).

astringent *adj.* severe or harsh; causing contraction of body tissue; checking the flow of blood from a cut. —*n.* astringent substance. —**astringency** *n.*

astrolabe *n.* instrument formerly used to measure the altitude of stars and planets.

astrology *n.* study of the alleged influence of the stars, planets, and moon on human affairs. —**astrologer** *n.* —**astrological** *adj.*

astronaut *n.* person trained for travelling in space.

astronautics *n.* science and technology of space flight. —**astronautical** *adj.*

astronomy *n.* scientific study of heavenly bodies. —**astronomer** *n.* —**astronomical** *adj.* of astronomy; very large. —**astronomically** *adv.*

astrophysics *n.* science of the physical and chemical properties of stars, planets, etc. —**astrophysical** *adj.* —**astrophysicist** *n.*

astute *adj.* perceptive or shrewd. —**astutely** *adv.* —**astuteness** *n.*

asunder *adv.* into parts or pieces.

asylum *n.* refuge or sanctuary; old name for a mental hospital.

asymmetry *n.* lack of symmetry. —**asymmetric(al)** *adj.*

asymptote [**ass**-im-tote] *n.* straight line closely approached by but never met by a curve.

at *prep.* indicating position in space or time; towards; engaged in; in exchange for, e.g. *it's selling at two pounds;* indicating the cause of an emotion, e.g. *shocked at his rudeness.*

atavism [**at**-a-viz-zum] *n.* recurrence of a trait present in distant ancestors. —**atavistic** *adj.*

ataxia *n.* lack of muscular coordination. —**ataxic** *adj.*

ate *v.* past tense of EAT.

atheism [**aith**-ee-iz-zum] *n.* belief that there is no God. —**atheist** *n.* —**atheistic(al)** *adj.*

atherosclerosis *n., pl.* -ses. disease in which deposits of fat cause the walls of the arteries to thicken.

athlete *n.* person trained in or good at athletics. —**athletic** *adj.* physically fit or strong; of an athlete or athletics. —**athletics** *pl. n.* track and field sports such as running, jumping, throwing, etc. —**athletically** *adv.* —**athleticism** *n.*

athwart *prep.* across. —*adv.* transversely.

atlas *n.* book of maps.

atmosphere *n.* mass of gases surrounding a heavenly body, esp. the earth; prevailing tone or mood (of a place etc.); unit of pressure. —**atmospheric** *adj.* —**atmospherics** *pl. n.* radio interference due to electrical disturbance in the atmosphere.

atoll *n.* ring-shaped coral island enclosing a lagoon.

atom *n.* smallest unit of matter which can take part in a chemical reaction; very small amount. —**atomic** *adj* of atoms; of or using atomic bombs or atomic energy. —**atom(ic) bomb** bomb in which the energy is provided by nuclear fission. —**atomic energy** nuclear energy. —**atomic number** number of protons in the nucleus of an atom. —**atomic weight** ratio of the mass per atom of an element to one twelfth of the mass of a carbon atom. —**atomize** *v.* reduce to atoms or small particles. —**atomizer** *n.* device for discharging a liquid in a fine spray.

THESAURUS

astonish amaze, astound, bewilder, confound, daze, stagger, stupefy, surprise

astonishment amazement, awe, bewilderment, stupefaction, surprise, wonder

astute adroit, artful, bright, calculating, canny, clever, crafty, cunning, intelligent, keen, knowing, perceptive, sagacious, sharp, shrewd, sly, subtle, wily

asylum harbour, haven, refuge, retreat, safety, sanctuary, shelter

atheism disbelief, godlessness, irreligion, paganism, scepticism, unbelief

atheist disbeliever, pagan, sceptic, unbeliever

athlete competitor, contender, contestant, games player, runner, sportsman

athletic 1. *adj.* able-bodied, active, energetic, fit, muscular, powerful, robust, strapping, strong, sturdy, vigorous 2. *pl. n.* contests, exercises, gymnastics, races, sports

atmosphere 1. air, heavens, sky 2. air, aura, character, climate, feel, feeling, flavour, mood, quality, spirit, surroundings, tone

atom fragment, grain, iota, jot, mite, molecule, morsel, particle, scrap, shred, speck, spot, tittle, trace, whit

DICTIONARY

atonal [eh-**tone**-al] *adj.* (of music) not written in an established key. —**atonality** *n.*

atone *v.* make amends (for sin or wrongdoing). —**atonement** *n.*

atop *prep.* on top of.

atrium *n., pl.* **atria.** main courtyard of an ancient Roman house; central hall extending through several storeys of a modern building.

atrocious *adj.* extremely cruel or wicked; horrifying or shocking; *Informal* very bad. —**atrociously** *adv.* —**atrocity** *n.* wickedness; act of cruelty.

atrophy [at-trof-fee] *n., pl.* **-phies.** wasting away of an organ or part. —*v.* **-phying, -phied.** (cause to) waste away.

attach *v.* join, fasten, or connect; attribute or ascribe, e.g. *he attaches great importance to his looks.* —**attached** *adj.* (foll. by *to*) fond of. —**attachment** *n.*

attaché [at-**tash**-shay] *n.* specialist attached to a diplomatic mission. —**attaché case** flat rectangular briefcase for papers.

attack *v.* launch a physical assault (against); criticize; set about (a job or problem) with vigour; affect adversely. —*n.* act of attacking; sudden bout of illness. —**attacker** *n.*

attain *v.* achieve or accomplish (a task or aim); reach. —**attainment** *n.* accomplishment. —**attainable** *adj.* —**attainability** *n.*

attar *n.* fragrant oil made from roses.

attempt *v.* try, make an effort. —*n.* effort or endeavour.

attend *v.* be present at; look after; pay attention; accompany; apply oneself (to). —**attendance** *n.* attending; number attending. —**attendant** *n.* person who assists, guides, or provides a service. —*adj.* accompanying. —**attention** *n.* concentrated direction of the mind; consideration; care; alert position in military drill. —**attentive** *adj.* giving attention; considerately helpful. —**attentively** *adv.* —**attentiveness** *n.*

attenuate *v.* weaken; make or become thin. —**attenuation** *n.*

attest *v.* affirm the truth of, be proof of. —**attestation** *n.*

attic *n.* space or room within the roof of a house.

attire *n.* fine or formal clothes. —*v.* clothe.

attitude *n.* way of thinking and behaving; posture of the body.

attorney *n.* person legally appointed to act for another; *US* lawyer.

THESAURUS

atrocious barbaric, brutal, cruel, fiendish, infamous, infernal, inhuman, monstrous, ruthless, savage, vicious, wicked

atrocity abomination, barbarity, brutality, crime, cruelty, enormity, evil, horror, outrage, villainy

attach add, adhere, bind, connect, couple, fasten, fix, join, link, secure, stick, tie, unite

attached affectionate towards, devoted, fond of, possessive

attachment bond, clamp, connection, connector, coupling, fastening, joint, junction, link, tie

attack *n.* 1. assault, charge, foray, incursion, inroad, invasion, offensive, onset, onslaught, raid, rush, strike 2. abuse, censure, criticism, denigration 3. access, bout, convulsion, fit, paroxysm, seizure, spasm, spell, stroke ~*v.* 4. assault, charge, fall upon, invade, raid, rush, set about, set upon, storm 5. abuse, blame, censure, criticize, impugn, malign, revile, vilify

attain accomplish, achieve, arrive at, bring off, complete, earn, fulfil, gain, get, grasp, reach, realize, secure, win

attempt 1. *n.* attack, bid, crack (*Inf.*), endeavour, go, shot (*Inf.*), try, undertaking, venture 2. *v.* endeavour, essay, experiment, seek, strive, tackle, take on, try, undertake, venture

attend 1. appear, be at, be here, be present, be there, frequent, go to, haunt, show oneself, show up (*Inf.*), turn up, visit 2. hear, heed, listen, look on, mark, mind, note, notice, observe, pay attention, pay heed, regard, watch 3. *With* **to** apply oneself to, concentrate on, devote oneself to, look after, see to, tale care of 4. accompany, escort, guard, squire, usher

attendance audience, crowd, gate, house, number present, turnout

attendant aide, assistant, auxiliary, companion, escort, flunky, follower, guard, guide, helper, servant, steward, usher, waiter

attention 1. concentration, consideration, heed, mind, scrutiny, thinking, thought, thoughtfulness 2. consideration, notice, recognition, regard 3. care, concern, looking after, ministration, treatment

attentive alert, careful, concentrating, heedful, mindful, observant, regardful, studious, watchful

attic garret, loft

attitude 1. approach, frame of mind, mood, opinion, outlook, position, posture, stance, standing, view 2. air, aspect, bearing, carriage, condition, demeanour, manner, pose, position, posture, stance

DICTIONARY

attract v. arouse the interest or admiration of; draw (something) closer by exerting a force on it. —**attraction** n. power to attract; something that attracts. —**attractive** adj. —**attractively** adv. —**attractiveness** n.

attribute v. (usu. foll. by *to*) regard as belonging to or produced by. —n. quality or feature representative of a person or thing. —**attributable** adj. —**attribution** n. —**attributive** adj. Grammar (of an adjective) preceding the noun modified.

attrition n. constant wearing down to weaken or destroy, e.g. *war of attrition*.

attune v. adjust or accustom (a person or thing).

atypical [eh-**tip**-ik-al] adj. not typical.

Au Chem. gold.

aubergine [**oh**-bur-zheen] n. dark purple tropical vegetable.

aubrietia [aw-**bree**-sha] n. trailing plant with purple flowers.

auburn adj., n. (of hair) reddish-brown.

auction n. public sale in which articles are sold to the highest bidder. —v. sell by auction. —**auctioneer** n. person who conducts an auction.

audacious adj. recklessly bold or daring; impudent. —**audaciously** adv. —**audacity** n.

audible adj. loud enough to hear. —**audibly** adv. —**audibility** n.

audience n. group of spectators or listeners; formal interview.

audio adj. of sound or hearing; of or for the transmission or reproduction of sound. —**audiotypist** n. typist trained to type from a dictating machine. —**audiovisual** adj. (esp. of teaching aids) involving both sight and hearing.

audit n. official examination of business accounts. —v. examine (business accounts) officially. —**auditor** n.

audition n. test of a performer's ability for a particular role or job. —v. test or be tested in an audition.

auditorium n., pl. -**toriums**, -**toria**. area of a concert hall or theatre where the audience sits.

auditory adj. of or relating to hearing.

au fait [oh **fay**] adj. French fully informed; expert.

Aug. August.

auger n. carpenter's tool for boring holes.

aught pron. Old-fashioned anything.

augment v. increase or enlarge. —**augmentation** n.

au gratin [oh **grat**-tan] adj. covered and cooked with breadcrumbs and sometimes cheese.

augur v. be a sign of (future events). —**augury** n. foretelling of the future; omen.

august adj. dignified and imposing.

August n. eighth month of the year.

auk n. northern sea bird with short wings and black-and-white plumage.

aunt n. father's or mother's sister; uncle's wife. —**auntie**, **aunty** n. Informal aunt. —**Aunt Sally** figure used in fairgrounds as a target; target of abuse or criticism.

au pair n. young foreign woman who does housework in return for board and lodging.

aura n. distinctive air or quality of a person or thing.

aural adj. of or using the ears or hearing. —**aurally** adv.

aureole, **aureola** n. halo.

au revoir [oh rev-**vwahr**] interj. French goodbye.

auricle n. upper chamber of the heart; outer part of the ear. —**auricular** adj.

aurochs n., pl. **aurochs**. recently extinct European wild ox.

aurora n., pl. -**ras**, -**rae**. bands of light sometimes seen in the sky in polar regions. —**aurora australis** aurora seen near the South Pole.

THESAURUS

attract allure, charm, decoy, draw, enchant, endear, engage, entice, incline, interest, invite, lure, tempt

attraction allure, charm, draw, enticement, fascination, interest, lure, magnetism

attractive agreeable, appealing, beautiful, captivating, charming, engaging, fair, fetching, good-looking, gorgeous, handsome, interesting, inviting, lovely, magnetic, pleasing, pretty, seductive, tempting

attribute 1. v. apply, assign, blame, charge, lay at the door of, refer 2. n. aspect, characteristic, facet, feature, indication, mark, note, point,

property, quality, quirk, sign, symbol, trait, virtue

audacious adventurous, bold, brave, courageous, daredevil, daring, fearless, intrepid, rash, reckless, risky

audacity 1. adventurousness, boldness, bravery, courage, daring, nerve, rashness, recklessness 2. cheek, defiance, effrontery, impertinence, impudence, insolence, nerve

audible clear, discernible, distinct

audience 1. congregation, crowd, gathering, house, listeners, viewers 2. consultation, hearing, interview, reception

DICTIONARY

—**aurora borealis** aurora seen near the North Pole.

auscultation *n.* listening to the internal sounds of the body, usu. with a stethoscope, to help with diagnosis.

auspices [aw-spiss-siz] *pl. n.* —**under the auspices of** with the support and approval of.

auspicious *adj.* showing signs of future success, favourable. —**auspiciously** *adv.*

Aussie *n., adj. Informal* Australian.

austere *adj.* stern or severe; ascetic; severely simple or plain. —**austerely** *adv.* —**austerity** *n.*

Australasian *n., adj.* (person) from Australia, New Zealand, and neighbouring islands.

Australian *n., adj.* (person) from Australia.

autarchy [aw-tar-kee] *n.* absolute power or autocracy.

autarky [aw-tar-kee] *n.* policy of economic self-sufficiency.

authentic *adj.* known to be real, genuine. —**authentically** *adv.* —**authenticity** *n.* —**authenticate** *v.* establish as genuine. —**authentication** *n.*

author *n.* writer of a book etc.; originator or creator. —**authoress** *n. fem.* —**authorship** *n.*

authority *n., pl.* -**ties.** power to command or control others; (often *pl.*) person or group having this power; expert in a particular field. —**authoritarian** *n., adj.* (person) insisting on strict obedience to authority. —**authoritative** *adj.* recognized as being reliable, e.g. *the authoritative book on Shakespeare;* possessing authority. —**authoritatively** *adv.* —**authorize** *v.*

give authority to; give permission for. —**authorization** *n.*

autism *n. Psychiatry* disorder, usu. of children, characterized by lack of response to people and limited ability to communicate. —**autistic** *adj.*

auto- *combining form* self-, e.g. *autobiography.*

autobiography *n., pl.* -**phies.** account of a person's life written by that person. —**autobiographical** *adj.* —**autobiographically** *adv.*

autocrat *n.* absolute ruler; dictatorial person. —**autocratic** *adj.* —**autocratically** *adv.* —**autocracy** *n.* government by an autocrat.

autocross *n.* motor-racing over a rough course.

Autocue *n.* ® electronic television prompting device displaying a speaker's script, unseen by the audience.

autogiro, autogyro *n., pl.* -**ros.** self-propelled aircraft resembling a helicopter but with an unpowered rotor.

autograph *n.* handwritten signature of a (famous) person. — *v.* write one's signature on or in.

automat *n. US* vending machine.

automate *v.* make (a manufacturing process) automatic.

automatic *adj.* (of a device) operating mechanically by itself; (of a process) performed by automatic equipment; done without conscious thought; (of a firearm) self-loading. —*n.* self-loading firearm. —**automatically** *adv.* —**automation** *n.* use of automatic devices in industrial production. —**automaton** *n.* robot; person who acts mechanically.

automobile *n. US* motor car.

THESAURUS

auspicious bright, encouraging, favourable, fortunate, happy, hopeful, lucky, propitious, rosy

austere 1. cold, forbidding, grave, grim, hard, serious, severe, solemn, stern, stiff 2. abstemious, abstinent, puritanical, sober, solemn, Spartan

austerity 1. coldness, harshness, inflexibility, rigour, solemnity, sternness 2. economy, rigidity, self-denial

authentic actual, authoritative, faithful, genuine, real, reliable, true, valid

authenticity actuality, genuineness, truth, truthfulness, validity

author composer, creator, father, founder, inventor, maker, mover, originator, parent, planner, producer, writer

authoritarian autocratic, despotic, dictatorial, disciplinarian, doctrinaire, domineering, harsh, imperious, rigid, severe, strict, tyrannical

authority 1. charge, command, control, domination, dominion, force, government, influence, might, power, prerogative, right, rule, strength, supremacy, sway, weight 2. authorization, licence, permission, permit, sanction, warrant 3. arbiter, expert, master, professional, scholar, specialist, textbook

authorize 1. empower, enable, entitle, give authority 2. allow, approve, confirm, countenance, give leave, license, permit, ratify, sanction, warrant

autocracy absolutism, despotism, dictatorship, tyranny

automatic 1. mechanical, push-button, robot, self-activating, self-propelling, self-regulating 2. habitual, mechanical, perfunctory, routine, unconscious

autonomous free, independent, self-governing, sovereign

DICTIONARY

autonomy *n.* self-government. —**autonomous** *adj.*

autopsy *n., pl.* **-sies.** examination of a corpse to determine the cause of death.

autosuggestion *n.* process in which a person unconsciously influences his or her own behaviour or beliefs.

autumn *n.* season between summer and winter. —**autumnal** *adj.* —**autumnally** *adv.*

auxiliary *adj.* secondary or supplementary; supporting. —*n., pl.* **-ries.** person or thing that supplements or supports. —**auxiliary verb** verb used to form the tense, voice, or mood of another, such as *will* in *I will go.*

avail *v.* be of use or advantage (to). —*n.* use or advantage (esp. in **to no avail**). —**avail oneself of** make use of.

available *adj.* obtainable or accessible. —**availability** *n.*

avalanche *n.* mass of snow or ice falling down a mountain; sudden overwhelming quantity of anything.

avant-garde [av-ong-**gard**] *n.* group of innovators, esp. in the arts. —*adj.* innovative and progressive.

avarice [av-a-riss] *n.* greed for wealth. —**avaricious** *adj.*

avast *interj. Naut.* stop.

avatar *n. Hinduism* appearance of a god in animal or human form.

Ave. Avenue.

avenge *v.* take revenge in retaliation for (harm done) or on behalf of (a person harmed). —**avenger** *n.*

avenue *n.* wide street; road between two rows of trees; way of approach.

aver [av-**vur**] *v.* **averring, averred.** state to be true. —**averment** *n.*

average *n.* typical or normal amount or quality; result obtained by adding quantities together and dividing the total by the number of quantities. —*adj.* usual or typical; calculated as an average. —*v.* calculate the average of; amount to as an average.

averse *adj.* (usu. foll. by *to*) disinclined or unwilling. —**aversion** *n.* strong dislike; person or thing disliked.

avert *v.* turn away; ward off.

aviary *n., pl.* **aviaries.** large cage or enclosure for birds.

aviation *n.* art of flying aircraft. —**aviator** *n.*

avid *adj.* keen or enthusiastic; greedy (for). —**avidly** *adv.* —**avidity** *n.*

avocado *n., pl.* **-dos.** pear-shaped tropical fruit with a leathery green skin and yellowish-green flesh.

avocation *n. Old-fashioned* occupation; hobby.

avocet *n.* long-legged wading bird with a long slender upward-curving bill.

avoid *v.* keep away from; refrain from; prevent from happening. —**avoidable** *adj.* —**avoidance** *n.*

avoirdupois [av-er-de-**poise**] *n.* system of weights based on pounds and ounces.

avow *v.* state or affirm; admit openly. —**avowal** *n.* —**avowed** *adj.* —**avowedly** *adv.*

avuncular *adj.* friendly, helpful, and caring towards someone younger.

await *v.* wait for; be in store for.

awake *v.* **awaking, awoke, awoken.** emerge or rouse from sleep; (cause to) become alert. —*adj.* not sleeping; alert.

THESAURUS

auxiliary accessory, aiding, ancillary, assisting, helping, reserve, secondary, subsidiary, substitute, supplementary

available accessible, applicable, at hand, free, handy, obtainable, on hand, on tap, ready, to hand, vacant

avalanche 1. landslide, landslip, snow-slide, snow-slip 2. barrage, deluge, flood, inundation, torrent

avaricious close-fisted, covetous, grasping, greedy, mean, miserly, parsimonious, penurious, stingy

avenge punish, repay, requite, retaliate, revenge, take satisfaction for, take vengeance

avenue access, approach, boulevard, channel, course, drive, entrance, entry, pass, path, road, route, street, way

average *n.* 1. mean, medium, midpoint, norm,

normal, par, rule, run, standard ~*adj.* 2. fair, general, indifferent, mediocre, middling, moderate, normal, not bad, ordinary, regular, so-so (*Inf.*), standard, tolerable, typical 3. intermediate, mean, median, medium, middle

averse disinclined, hostile, ill-disposed, loath, opposed, reluctant, unfavourable, unwilling

aviator aeronaut, airman, flier, pilot

avid ardent, devoted, eager, enthusiastic, fanatical, fervent, intense, keen, passionate, zealous

avoid avert, bypass, circumvent, dodge, elude, escape, evade, keep away from, prevent, shirk, shun, sidestep, steer clear of

await 1. anticipate, expect, look for, stay for, wait for 2. attend, be in readiness for, be in store for, be ready for, wait for

awake alert, alive, aroused, attentive, aware,

43

DICTIONARY

awaken v. awake.

award v. give (something, such as a prize) formally. —n. something awarded, such as a prize.

aware adj. having knowledge, informed. —**awareness** n.

awash adv. washed over by water.

away adv. from a place, e.g. go away; to another place, e.g. put that gun away; out of existence, e.g. fade away; continuously, e.g. laughing away. —adj. not present; distant, e.g. two miles away; Sport played on an opponent's ground.

awe n. wonder and respect mixed with dread. —v. fill with awe. —**awesome** adj. inspiring awe. —**awestruck** adj. filled with awe.

awful adj. very bad or unpleasant; Obs. inspiring awe; Informal very great. —**awfully** adv. in an unpleasant way; Informal very.

awhile adv. for a time.

awkward adj. clumsy or ungainly; difficult to use or handle; inconvenient; embarrassed. —**awkwardly** adv. —**awkwardness** n.

awl n. pointed tool for piercing wood, leather, etc.

awning n. canvas roof supported by a frame to give protection against the weather.

awoke v. past tense of AWAKE. —**awoken** v. past participle of AWAKE.

AWOL adj. Mil. absent without leave.

awry [a-rye] adv., adj. with a twist to one side, askew; amiss.

axe n. tool with a sharp blade for felling trees or chopping wood; Informal dismissal from employment etc. —v. Informal dismiss (employees), restrict (expenditure), or terminate (a project).

axil n. angle where the stalk of a leaf joins a stem.

axiom n. generally accepted principle; self-evident statement. —**axiomatic** adj. containing axioms; self-evident.

axis n., pl. **axes.** (imaginary) line round which a body can rotate or about which an object or geometrical figure is symmetrical; one of two fixed lines on a graph, against which quantities

---

THESAURUS

conscious, not sleeping, observant, on guard, on the alert, on the lookout, vigilant, wakeful, waking, watchful, wide-awake

awaken activate, alert, arouse, awake, call forth, excite, incite, kindle, provoke, revive, rouse, stimulate, stir up, wake

award 1 v. accord, allot, apportion, assign, bestow, confer, decree, endow, gift, give, grant, render 2. n. decoration, gift, grant, prize, trophy

aware alive to, apprised, attentive, cognizant, conscious, conversant, familiar, knowing, mindful, sensible, wise (Inf.)

awareness appreciation, attention, consciousness, familiarity, knowledge, mindfulness, perception, realization, recognition, understanding

away adv. 1. abroad, elsewhere, from here, from home, hence, off 2. apart, at a distance, far, remote 3. aside, out of the way, to one side ~adj. 4. abroad, elsewhere, gone, not here, not present, not there, out

awesome alarming, amazing, astonishing, awe-inspiring, awful, breathtaking, daunting, dreadful, fearful, fearsome, formidable, frightening, horrible, horrifying, imposing, impressive, intimidating, magnificent, majestic, overwhelming, redoubtable, shocking, solemn, stunning, stupefying, terrible, terrifying, wonderful, wondrous

awful alarming, appalling, deplorable, dire, distressing, dreadful, fearful, frightful, ghastly,

gruesome, hideous, horrible, nasty, shocking, terrible, ugly, unpleasant

awfully badly, disgracefully, disreputably, dreadfully, unforgivably, unpleasantly, wickedly, woefully, wretchedly

awkward 1. artless, blundering, bungling, clownish, clumsy, coarse, gauche, gawky, graceless, ham-fisted, inelegant, inept, inexpert, lumbering, maladroit, oafish, rude, stiff, uncoordinated, uncouth, ungainly, ungraceful, unpolished, unrefined, unskilful, unskilled 2. cumbersome, difficult, inconvenient, troublesome, unhandy, unmanageable, unwieldy

awkwardness 1. clumsiness, coarseness, gaucheness, gaucherie, gawkiness, gracelessness, inelegance, ineptness, inexpertness, maladroitness, oafishness, rudeness, stiffness, uncoordination, uncouthness, ungainliness 2. cumbersomeness, difficulty, inconvenience, troublesomeness, unwieldiness 3. delicacy, embarrassment, inconvenience

axe n. 1. chopper, hatchet 2. **the axe** Inf. cancellation, cutback, discharge, dismissal, termination, the boot (Sl.), the chop (Sl.), the sack (Inf.), wind-up

axiom adage, aphorism, dictum, fundamental, maxim, postulate, precept, principle, truism

axiomatic 1. accepted, assumed, fundamental, given, granted, manifest, self-evident, understood, unquestioned 2. aphoristic, pithy, terse

axis axle, centre line, pivot, shaft, spindle

DICTIONARY

or positions are measured. —**axial** *adj.* —**axially** *adv.*

axle *n.* shaft on which a wheel or pair of wheels turn.

axolotl *n.* aquatic salamander of central America.

ayatollah *adj.* Islamic religious leader in Iran.

ay(e) *interj.* yes. —*n.* affirmative vote or voter.

azalea [az-**zale**-ya] *n.* garden shrub grown for its showy flowers.

azimuth *n.* arc of the sky between the zenith and the horizon; horizontal angle of a bearing measured clockwise from the north.

Aztec *n., adj.* (person) of the Indian race ruling Mexico before the Spanish conquest in the 16th century.

azure *adj., n.* (of) the colour of a clear blue sky.

THESAURUS

axle axis, pin, pivot, rod, shaft, spindle

B

BA Bachelor of Arts.

baa v. **baaing, baaed.** make the cry of a sheep. —n. cry made by a sheep.

babble v. talk excitedly or foolishly; (of streams) make a low murmuring sound. —n. incoherent or foolish talk.

babe n. baby.

babel [**babe**-el] n. confused mixture of noises or voices.

baboon n. large monkey with a pointed face and a long tail.

baby n., pl. **-bies.** very young child or animal; Slang sweetheart. —adj. comparatively small of its type. —**babyish** adj. —**baby-sit** v. take care of a child while the parents are out. —**baby-sitter** n.

baccarat [**back**-a-rah] n. card game involving gambling.

bacchanalia pl. n. drunken revelry or orgy.

bachelor n. unmarried man; person who holds the lowest university degree.

bacillus [bass-**ill**-luss] n., pl. **-li** [-lie]. rod-shaped bacterium.

back n. rear part of the human body, from the neck to the pelvis; part or side of an object opposite the front; part of anything less often seen or used; Ball games defensive player or position. —v. (cause to) move backwards; provide money for (a person or enterprise); bet on the success of; (foll. by onto) have the back facing towards. —adj. situated behind; owing from an earlier date. —adv. at, to, or towards the rear; to or towards the original starting point or condition. —**backer** n. person who gives financial support. —**backing** n. support; musical accompaniment for a pop singer. —**backward** adj. directed towards the rear; retarded in physical, material, or intellectual development. —**back-**

wardness n. —**backwards** adv. towards the rear; with the back foremost; in the reverse of the usual direction. —**backbencher** n. Brit., Aust., & NZ Member of Parliament who does not hold office in the government or opposition. —**backbiting** n. spiteful talk about an absent person. —**backbone** n. spinal column. —**backchat** n. Informal answering back, esp. impudently. —**backcloth, backdrop** n. painted curtain at the back of a stage set. —**backdate** v. make (a document) effective from an earlier date. —**backfire** v. (of a plan) fail to have the desired effect; (of an engine) make a loud noise like an explosion. —**background** n. person's social class, education, or experience; events or circumstances that help to explain something; space behind the chief figures in a picture. —**backhanded** adj. sarcastic, e.g. a backhanded compliment. —**backhander** n. Slang bribe. —**backlash** n. sudden and adverse reaction. —**backlog** n. accumulation of things to be dealt with. —**backpack** n. rucksack. —**backside** n. Informal buttocks. —**backslide** v. relapse into former bad habits. —**backslider** n. —**backstage** adv., adj. behind the stage in a theatre. —**backstroke** n. swimming stroke performed on the back. —**backtrack** v. return by the same route by which one has come; retract or reverse one's opinion or policy. —**back up** v. support. —**backup** n. support or reinforcement; reserve or substitute. —**backwash** n. water washed backwards by the motion of a boat; repercussion. —**backwater** n. isolated or backward place or condition. —**backwoods** pl. n. remote sparsely populated area.

backgammon n. game played with counters and dice.

THESAURUS

baby 1. n. babe, bairn (Scot.), child, infant, newborn child 2. adj. diminutive, dwarf, little, midget, mini, miniature, minute, pygmy, small, tiny, wee

babyish baby, infantile, juvenile, namby-pamby, puerile, silly, soft (Inf.), spoiled

back v. 1. abet, advocate, assist, champion, countenance, encourage, endorse, favour, finance, sanction, second, side with, sponsor, subsidize, support, sustain, underwrite 2. backtrack, go back, regress, retire, retreat, reverse, turn tail, withdraw ~n. 3. backside, end, far end, hind part, hindquarters, posterior, rear, reverse, stern, tail end ~adj. 4. end, hind, hindmost, posterior, rear, tail

backbone Medical spinal column, spine, vertebrae, vertebral column

backer advocate, angel (Inf.), benefactor, patron, promoter, second, sponsor, subscriber, supporter, underwriter, well-wisher

backfire boomerang, disappoint, fail, flop, miscarry, rebound, recoil

background breeding, circumstances, credentials, culture, education, environment, experience, history, qualifications, tradition, upbringing

backing accompaniment, advocacy, aid, assistance, encouragement, endorsement, funds, grant, moral support, patronage, sponsorship,

DICTIONARY

bacon *n.* salted or smoked pig meat.

bacteria *pl. n., sing.* **-rium.** large group of microorganisms, many of which cause disease. —**bacterial** *adj.* —**bacteriology** *n.* study of bacteria. —**bacteriologist** *n.*

bad *adj.* **worse, worst.** of poor quality; lacking skill or talent; harmful; immoral or evil; naughty or mischievous; rotten or decayed; severe or unpleasant. —**badly** *adv.* —**badness** *n.*

bade *v.* a past tense of BID.

badge *n.* emblem worn to show membership, rank, etc.

badger *n.* nocturnal burrowing mammal with a black and white head. —*v.* pester or harass.

badinage [**bad**-in-nahzh] *n.* playful and witty conversation.

badminton *n.* game played with a racket and shuttlecock, which is hit over a high net.

baffle *v.* perplex or puzzle. —**bafflement** *n.*

bag *n.* flexible container with an opening at one end; handbag; *Offens.* ugly or bad-tempered woman. —*pl. Informal* (foll. by *of*) lots (of). —*v.* **bagging, bagged.** put into a bag; (cause to) bulge; capture or kill. —**baggy** *adj.* (of clothes) hanging loosely.

bagatelle *n.* something of little value; board game in which balls are struck into holes.

baggage *n.* suitcases packed for a journey.

bagpipes *pl. n.* musical wind instrument with reed pipes and an inflatable bag.

bail¹ *n. Law* money deposited with a court as security for a person's reappearance in court. —*v.* pay bail for (a person).

bail², **bale** *v.* (foll. by *out*) remove (water) from (a boat). —**bail out, bale out** *v. Informal* help (a person or organization) out of a predicament; make an emergency parachute jump from an aircraft.

bail³ *n. Cricket* either of two wooden bars across the tops of the stumps.

bailey *n.* outermost wall or court of a castle.

bailiff *n.* sheriff's officer who serves writs and summonses; landlord's agent.

bairn *n. Scot.* child.

bait *n.* piece of food on a hook or in a trap to attract fish or animals. —*v.* put a piece of food on or in (a hook or trap); persecute or tease.

baize *n.* woollen fabric used to cover billiard and card tables.

bake *v.* cook by dry heat as in an oven; make or become hardened by heat. —**baker** *n.* person whose business is to make or sell bread, cakes, etc. —**baker's dozen** thirteen. —**bakery** *n., pl.* **-eries.** place where bread, cakes, etc. are baked

THESAURUS

subsidy, support

backlash backfire, boomerang, counteraction, reaction, recoil, repercussion, resentment, response, retaliation

backlog excess, hoard, reserve, reserves, resources, stock, supply

backslider recidivist, turncoat

back up aid, assist, bolster, confirm, corroborate, reinforce, stand by, support

backward *adj.* 1. bashful, diffident, hesitating, late, reluctant, shy, sluggish, unwilling 2. behind, behindhand, dense, dull, retarded, slow, stupid, subnormal, undeveloped

backwards *adv.* aback, behind, in reverse, rearward

bacteria bacilli, germs, microorganisms

bad 1. defective, deficient, faulty, imperfect, inadequate, incorrect, inferior, poor, substandard, unsatisfactory 2. damaging, dangerous, detrimental, harmful, hurtful, injurious, ruinous, unhealthy 3. base, corrupt, criminal, delinquent, evil, immoral, mean, sinful, vile, villainous, wicked, wrong 4. naughty, unruly 5. decayed, mouldy, off, putrid, rancid, rotten, sour, spoiled 6. adverse, discouraged, discouraging, distressing, gloomy, grim, melancholy, troubled, unfortunate, unpleasant

badge brand, device, emblem, mark, sign, token

badger bully, chivvy, goad, harass, harry, hound, importune, nag, pester, plague, torment

badinage banter, chaff, drollery, mockery, persiflage, pleasantry, raillery, repartee, teasing, waggery, wordplay

badly 1. carelessly, defectively, faultily, imperfectly, inadequately, incorrectly, ineptly, poorly, shoddily, wrong, wrongly 2. criminally, evilly, immorally, improperly, naughtily, shamefully, unethically, wickedly

bag *v.* acquire, capture, catch, gain, get, kill, land, shoot, take, trap

baggage bags, belongings, equipment, gear, luggage, suitcases, things

baggy billowing, bulging, droopy, floppy, ill-fitting, loose, oversize, roomy, sagging, seated, slack

bail¹ *n.* bond, guarantee, guaranty, pledge, security, surety, warranty

bail², **bale** *v.* dip, drain off, ladle, scoop

bait 1. *n.* allurement, attraction, bribe, decoy, enticement, inducement, lure, snare, temptation 2. *v.* irritate, needle (*Inf.*), persecute, provoke, tease, torment

DICTIONARY

or sold. —**baking powder** powdered mixture used in baking instead of yeast.

Balaclava (helmet) *n.* close-fitting woollen hood that covers the ears and neck.

balalaika *n.* guitar-like musical instrument with a triangular body.

balance *n.* state in which a weight or amount is evenly distributed; pair of scales; difference between the credits and debits of an account; amount that remains. —*v.* remain steady; weigh on a balance; consider or compare; equalize in weight, amount, etc.

balcony *n., pl.* **-nies.** platform on the outside of a building with a rail along the outer edge; upper tier of seats in a theatre or cinema.

bald *adj.* having little or no hair on the scalp; (of a tyre) having a worn tread; without unnecessary words. —**balding** *adj.* becoming bald. —**baldness** *n.*

balderdash *n.* stupid talk.

bale¹ *n.* large bundle of hay or goods tightly bound together. —*v.* make or put into bales.

bale² *v.* same as BAIL².

baleful *adj.* vindictive or menacing. —**balefully** *adv.*

balk, baulk *v.* be reluctant to (do something); thwart or hinder.

ball¹ *n.* round or nearly round object, esp. one used in games; single delivery of the ball in a game. —*pl. Taboo slang* testicles; nonsense. —*v.* form into a ball. —**ball bearings** steel balls between moving parts of a machine to reduce friction. —**ball cock** device with a floating ball and a valve for regulating the flow of water. —**ballpoint (pen)** pen with a tiny ball bearing as a writing point.

ball² *n.* formal social function for dancing. —**ballroom** *n.*

ballad *n.* narrative poem or song; slow sentimental song.

ballast *n.* substance, such as sand, used to stabilize a ship when it is not carrying cargo.

ballet *n.* classical style of expressive dancing based on conventional steps; theatrical performance of this. —**ballerina** *n.* female ballet dancer.

ballistics *n.* study of the flight of projectiles, such as bullets. —**ballistic missile** missile guided automatically in flight but which falls freely at its target.

balloon *n.* inflatable rubber bag used as a plaything; large bag inflated with air or gas, designed to carry passengers in a basket underneath. —*v.* inflate or be inflated. —**balloonist** *n.*

ballot *n.* method of voting secretly; actual vote or paper indicating a person's choice. —*v.* **-loting, -loted.** vote or ask for a vote from. —**ballot box.**

ballyhoo *n.* exaggerated fuss.

balm *n.* aromatic substance used for healing and soothing; anything that comforts or soothes.

balmy *adj.* **balmier, balmiest.** (of weather) mild and pleasant; same as BARMY.

baloney *n. Informal* nonsense.

balsa [bawl-sa] *n.* tropical American tree that yields light wood.

balsam *n.* soothing ointment; flowering plant.

baluster *n.* set of posts supporting a rail. —**balustrade** *n.* ornamental rail supported by balusters.

bamboo *n.* tall treelike tropical grass with hollow stems.

bamboozle *v. Informal* cheat or mislead; confuse, puzzle.

ban *v.* **banning, banned.** prohibit or forbid officially. —*n.* official prohibition.

banal [ban-nahl] *adj.* ordinary and unoriginal. —**banality** *n.*

banana *n.* yellow crescent-shaped fruit.

band¹ *n.* group of musicians playing together;

THESAURUS

balance *v.* 1. level, match, poise, stabilize, steady 2. adjust, compensate for, counteract, counterbalance, equalize, equate, make up for, neutralize, offset ~*n.* 3. correspondence, equilibrium, equipoise, equity, equivalence, evenness, parity, symmetry 4. difference, remainder, residue, rest, surplus

balcony 1. terrace, veranda 2. gallery, gods, upper circle

bald baldheaded, depilated, hairless

balk 1. demur, evade, flinch, hesitate, jib, recoil, refuse, resist, shirk 2. baffle, bar, check, defeat, hinder, obstruct, prevent, thwart

ball globe, orb, pellet, sphere, spheroid

ballast balance, equilibrium, sandbag, stabilizer, weight

ballot election, poll, polling, vote, voting

ballyhoo babble, commotion, fuss, hubbub, hue and cry, hullabaloo, noise, racket, to-do

ban 1. *v.* banish, debar, disallow, exclude, forbid, outlaw, prohibit, proscribe, restrict, suppress 2. *n.* boycott, censorship, embargo, prohibition, proscription, restriction, suppression, taboo

banal commonplace, everyday, hackneyed, humdrum, old hat, ordinary, pedestrian, platitudinous, stale, stereotyped, stock, threadbare, tired, trite, vapid

DICTIONARY

group of people having a common purpose. —**bandsman** n. —**bandstand** n. roofed outdoor platform for a band. —**band together** v. unite.

band² n. strip of material, used to hold objects together; *Physics* range of frequencies or wavelengths between two limits.

bandage n. piece of material used to cover a wound. —v. cover with a bandage.

bandan(n)a n. large brightly coloured handkerchief.

b. and b., B and B bed and breakfast.

bandit n. robber, esp. a member of an armed gang. —**banditry** n.

bandoleer, bandolier n. shoulder belt for holding cartridges.

bandwagon n. —**climb, jump on the bandwagon** join a party or movement that seems assured of success.

bandy adj. **-dier, -diest.** having legs curved outwards at the knees. —v. **-dying, -died.** exchange (words) in a heated manner; circulate (a name, rumour, etc.).

bane n. person or thing that causes misery or distress. —**baneful** adj.

bang n. short loud explosive noise; hard blow or loud knock. —v. hit or knock, esp. with a loud noise; close (a door) noisily. —adv. with a sudden impact; precisely.

banger n. *Slang* sausage; *Informal* old decrepit car; firework that explodes loudly.

bangle n. bracelet worn round the arm or the ankle.

banish v. send (someone) into exile; dismiss from one's thoughts. —**banishment** n.

banisters pl. n. railing supported by posts on a staircase.

banjo n., pl. **-jos, -joes.** guitar-like musical instrument with a circular body.

bank¹ n. institution offering services, such as the safekeeping and lending of money; any supply, store, or reserve. —v. deposit (cash or cheques) in a bank. —**banker** n. —**banking** n. —**banknote** n. piece of paper money. —**bank on** v. rely on.

bank² n. raised mass, esp. of earth; sloping ground at the side of a river. —v. form into a bank; cause (an aircraft) or (of an aircraft) to tip to one side on turning.

bank³ n. row of switches, keys, etc. on a machine.

bankrupt n. person declared by a court to be unable to pay his or her debts. —adj. financially ruined. —v. make bankrupt. —**bankruptcy** n.

banner n. long strip of cloth displaying a slogan, advertisement, etc.; placard carried in a demonstration or procession.

bannisters pl. n. same as BANISTERS.

banns pl. n. public declaration, esp. in a church, of an intended marriage.

banquet n. elaborate formal dinner.

banshee n. (in Irish folklore) female spirit whose wailing warns of impending death.

bantam n. small chicken. —**bantamweight** n. boxer weighing up to 118lb (professional) or 54 kg (amateur).

THESAURUS

band¹ 1. assembly, association, body, clique, club, company, coterie, crew (*Inf.*), gang, horde, party, society, troop 2. ensemble, group, orchestra

band² bandage, belt, bond, chain, cord, fetter, ribbon, shackle, strap, strip, tie

bandage 1. n. compress, dressing, gauze, plaster 2. v. bind, cover, dress, swathe

bandit brigand, crook, desperado, freebooter, gangster, gunman, hijacker, marauder, outlaw, pirate, robber, thief

bang n. 1. boom, burst, clang, clap, clash, detonation, explosion, peal, pop, report, shot, slam, thud, thump 2. blow, box, bump, cuff, hit, knock, punch, smack, stroke, wallop (*Inf.*), whack ~v. 3. bash (*Inf.*), beat, bump, clatter, crash, hammer, knock, pound, rap, slam, strike, thump

banish deport, drive away, eject, evict, exclude, exile, expel, ostracize, outlaw, shut out, transport

banishment deportation, exile, proscription

banisters balusters, balustrade, handrail, rail, railing

bank¹ 1. n. depository, fund, hoard, repository, reserve, savings, stock, store, storehouse 2. v. deal with, deposit, keep, save

bank² n. 1. embankment, heap, mass, mound, pile, ridge 2. brink, edge, margin, shore, side ~v. 3. amass, heap, mass, mound, pile, stack 4. camber, cant, incline, pitch, slant, slope, tilt, tip

bank³ n. array, file, group, line, rank, row, sequence, series, succession, tier, train

bankrupt broke (*Inf.*), destitute, exhausted, failed, impoverished, insolvent, lacking, ruined, spent

banner burgee, colours, ensign, flag, pennant, standard, streamer

banquet dinner, feast, meal, repast, revel, treat

DICTIONARY

banter v. tease jokingly. —n. teasing or joking conversation.

Bantu n. group of languages of Africa; *Offens.* Black speaker of a Bantu language.

banyan n. Indian tree whose branches grow down into the soil forming additional trunks.

baptism n. Christian religious ceremony in which a person is immersed in or sprinkled with water as a sign of purification and acceptance into the Church. —**baptismal** adj. —**baptize** v. perform baptism on.

Baptist n. member of a Protestant denomination that believes in adult baptism by immersion.

bar[1] n. rigid length of metal, wood, etc.; solid, usu. rectangular block, of any material; counter or room where drinks are served; heating element in an electric fire; *Music* group of beats repeated throughout a piece of music. —v. **barring, barred.** secure with a bar; ban or forbid; obstruct. —prep. (*also* **barring**) except for. —**the Bar** barristers collectively. —**barman, barmaid** n.

bar[2] n. unit of atmospheric pressure.

barb n. point facing in the opposite direction to the main point of a fish-hook etc.; cutting remark. —**barbed** adj. —**barbed wire** strong wire with protruding sharp points.

barbarian n. member of a primitive or uncivilized people. —**barbaric** adj. cruel or brutal. —**barbarism** n. condition of being backward or ignorant. —**barbarity** n. state of being barbaric or barbarous; vicious act. —**barbarous** adj. uncivilized; brutal or cruel.

barbecue n. grill on which food is cooked over hot charcoal, usu. outdoors; outdoor party at which barbecued food is served. —v. cook (food) on a barbecue.

barber n. person who cuts men's hair.

barbiturate n. drug used as a sedative.

bard n. *Lit.* poet. —**the Bard** William Shakespeare.

bare adj. unclothed; without the natural or usual covering; unembellished, simple; just sufficient. —v. uncover. —**barely** adv. only just. —**bareness** n. —**bareback** adj., adv. (of horse-riding) without a saddle. —**barefaced** adj. shameless or impudent.

bargain n. agreement establishing what each party will give, receive, or perform in a transaction; something bought or offered at a low price. —v. negotiate the terms of an agreement. —**bargain for** v. anticipate or take into account.

barge n. flat-bottomed boat used to transport freight. —v. *Informal* push violently. —**bargee** n. person in charge of a barge. —**barge in, into** v. interrupt rudely.

baritone n. (singer with) the second lowest adult male voice.

barium [bare-ee-um] n. soft white metallic element.

bark[1] n. loud harsh cry of a dog. —v. (of a dog) make its typical cry; shout in an angry tone.

bark[2] n. tough outer layer of a tree.

barley n. tall grasslike plant cultivated for grain.

barmy adj. -**mier, -miest.** *Slang* insane.

barn n. large building on a farm used for storing grain.

barnacle n. shellfish that lives attached to objects under water.

barney n. *Informal* noisy fight or argument.

barometer n. instrument for measuring atmospheric pressure. —**barometric** adj.

baron n. member of the lowest rank of nobility;

THESAURUS

baptism christening

bar n. 1. batten, crosspiece, paling, pole, rail, rod, shaft, stake, stick 2. canteen, counter, inn, lounge, pub (*Inf.*), public house, saloon, tavern ~v. 3. barricade, bolt, fasten, latch, lock, secure 4. ban, exclude, forbid, hinder, keep out, obstruct, prevent, prohibit, restrain

barbarian n. 1. hooligan, lout, ruffian, savage, vandal 2. bigot, boor, ignoramus, illiterate, lowbrow, philistine

barbaric brutal, cruel, primitive, rude, uncivilized, wild

barbarism coarseness, crudity, savagery, uncivilizedness

bare 1. denuded, exposed, naked, nude, peeled, shorn, stripped, unclad, unclothed, uncovered, undressed 2. barren, blank, empty, lacking, mean, open, poor, scanty, scarce, simple,

unembellished, unfurnished, vacant, void, wanting

barely almost, hardly, just, only just, scarcely

bargain n. 1. agreement, business, compact, contract, negotiation, pact, pledge, promise, stipulation, transaction, treaty, understanding 2. (cheap) purchase, discount, giveaway, good buy, good deal, good value, reduction, snip (*Inf.*) ~v. 3. agree, contract, covenant, promise, stipulate, transact

barge canal boat, flatboat, lighter

bark[1] n./v. bay, growl, howl, snarl, woof, yap, yelp

bark[2] n. casing, cortex (*Anat., bot.*), covering, crust, husk, rind, skin

barmy *Also* **balmy** crazy, daft, foolish, idiotic, insane, loony (*Sl.*), nuts (*Sl.*), nutty (*Sl.*), odd, silly, stupid

DICTIONARY

powerful businessman. —**baroness** *fem. n.* —**baronial** *adj.*

baronet *n.* commoner who holds the lowest hereditary British title. —**baronetcy** *n.*

baroque [bar-**rock**] *n.* highly ornate style of art and architecture from the late 16th to the early 18th century. —*adj.* extremely complicated, rich, and elaborate.

barque [**bark**] *n.* sailing ship, esp. one with three masts.

barrack *v.* criticize loudly or shout against (a team or speaker).

barracks *pl. n.* building used to accommodate military personnel.

barracuda [bar-rack-**kew**-da] *n.* predatory tropical sea fish.

barrage [**bar**-rahzh] *n.* continuous delivery of questions, complaints, etc.; continuous artillery fire; artificial barrier across a river.

barrel *n.* cylindrical container with rounded sides and flat ends; tube in a firearm through which the bullet is fired. —**barrel organ** musical instrument played by turning a handle.

barren *adj.* (of land) unable to support the growth of crops, fruit, etc.; (of a woman or female animal) incapable of producing offspring. —**barrenness** *n.*

barricade *n.* barrier, esp. one erected hastily for defence. —*v.* erect a barricade across (an entrance).

barrier *n.* anything that prevents access or progress.

barrister *n.* lawyer qualified to plead in a higher court.

barrow¹ *n.* wheelbarrow; movable stall, used esp. by street vendors.

barrow² *n.* mound of earth placed over a prehistoric tomb.

barter *v.* trade (goods) in exchange for other goods. —*n.* trade by the exchange of goods.

basalt [**bass**-awlt] *n.* dark volcanic rock. —**basaltic** *adj.*

bascule *n.* drawbridge that operates by a counterbalanced weight.

base¹ *n.* bottom or supporting part of anything; fundamental part; centre of operations, organization, or supply; starting point. —*v.* (foll. by *on* or *upon*) use as a basis (for). —**baseless** *adj.* —**basement** *n.* partly or wholly underground storey of a building.

base² *adj.* dishonourable or immoral; of inferior quality. —**basely** *adv.* —**baseness** *n.*

baseball *n.* American team game played with a bat and ball; ball used for this.

bash *Informal* —*v.* hit violently or forcefully. —*n.* heavy blow.

bashful *adj.* shy or modest. —**bashfully** *adv.* —**bashfulness** *n.*

basic *adj.* of or forming a base or basis; elementary or simple. —**basics** *pl. n.* fundamental principles, facts, etc. —**basically** *adv.*

BASIC *n.* computer programming language that uses common English words.

basil *n.* aromatic herb used in cooking.

basilica *n.* rectangular church with a rounded end and two aisles.

basilisk *n.* legendary serpent said to kill by its breath or glance.

basin *n.* round open container; sink for washing the hands and face; sheltered area of water where boats may be moored; catchment area of a particular river.

THESAURUS

barrage battery, bombardment, gunfire, salvo, shelling, volley

barren 1. childless, infecund, infertile, sterile, unprolific 2. arid, desert, desolate, dry, empty, unfruitful, unproductive, waste

barrier 1. bar, barricade, blockade, boundary, ditch, fence, obstacle, obstruction, railing, rampart, stop, wall 2. difficulty, drawback, hindrance, impediment, limitation, obstacle, restriction, stumbling block

barter bargain, exchange, haggle, sell, swap, trade, traffic

base *n.* 1. bed, bottom, foot, foundation, groundwork, pedestal, rest, stand, support 2. basis, core, essence, essential, fundamental, heart, key, origin, principle, root, source 3. camp, centre, headquarters, home, post, settlement, starting point, station ~*v.* 4. build,

construct, depend, derive, establish, found, ground, hinge, locate, station

baseless groundless, unfounded, unjustified, unsubstantiated, unsupported

bashful blushing, coy, diffident, modest, nervous, reserved, retiring, self-conscious, sheepish, shrinking, shy, timid, timorous

basic central, elementary, essential, fundamental, indispensable, intrinsic, key, necessary, primary, underlying, vital

basics brass tacks (*Inf.*), core, essentials, facts, hard facts, nitty-gritty (*Sl.*), practicalities, principles, rudiments

basis base, bottom, footing, foundation, ground, groundwork, support

DICTIONARY

basis *n., pl.* **-ses.** fundamental principles etc. from which something is started or developed.

bask *v.* lie in or be exposed to (pleasant warmth).

basket *n.* container made of interwoven strips of wood or cane. —**basketwork** *n.*

basketball *n.* team game similar to netball; ball used for this.

Basque *n., adj.* (member or language) of a people living in the W Pyrenees in France and Spain.

bas-relief *n.* sculpture in which the figures stand out slightly from the background.

bass¹ [base] *n.* (singer with) the lowest adult male voice. —*adj.* of the lowest range of musical notes.

bass² *n.* edible sea fish.

basset hound *n.* smooth-haired dog with short legs and long ears.

bassoon *n.* large woodwind instrument.

bastard *n.* person born of parents not married to each other; *Offens.* obnoxious or despicable person. —**bastardize** *v.* debase or corrupt. —**bastardy** *n.*

baste¹ *v.* moisten (meat) during cooking with hot fat.

baste² *v.* sew with loose temporary stitches.

bastion *n.* projecting part of a fortification; thing or person regarded as defending a principle.

bat¹ *n.* any of various types of club used to hit the ball in certain sports. —*v.* **batting, batted.** strike with or as if with a bat. —**batsman** *n. Cricket* person who bats or specializes in batting.

bat² *n.* nocturnal mouselike flying animal.

batch *n.* group of people or things dealt with at the same time.

bated *adj.* —**with bated breath** in suspense or fear.

bath *n.* large container in which to wash the body; act of washing in such a container. —*pl.*

public swimming pool. —*v.* wash in a bath. —**bathroom** *n.* room with a bath, sink, and usu. a toilet.

Bath chair *n.* wheelchair for an invalid.

bathe *v.* swim in open water; apply liquid to (the skin or a wound) in order to cleanse or soothe; (foll. by *in*) fill (with), e.g. *bathed in sunlight.* —**bather** *n.*

bathos [bay-thoss] *n.* sudden change in speech or writing from a serious subject to a trivial one.

bathyscaph(e) *n.* deep-sea diving vessel for observation.

batik [bat-teek] *n.* process of printing fabric using wax to cover areas not to be dyed; fabric printed in this way.

batman *n.* officer's servant in the armed forces.

baton *n.* thin stick used by the conductor of an orchestra; short bar transferred in a relay race; policeman's truncheon.

battalion *n.* army unit consisting of three or more companies.

batten¹ *n.* strip of wood fixed to something, esp. to hold it in place. —**batten down** *v.* secure with a batten.

batten² —**batten on** *v.* thrive at the expense of (someone else).

batter¹ *v.* hit repeatedly. —**battering ram** large beam used to break down fortifications.

batter² *n.* mixture of flour, eggs, and milk, used in cooking.

battery *n., pl.* **-teries.** device that produces electricity in a torch, radio, etc.; group of heavy guns operating as a single unit; series of cages for intensive rearing of poultry.

battle *n.* fight between large armed forces; conflict or struggle. —*v.* struggle. —**battle-axe** *n. Informal* domineering woman; large heavy axe.

battlement *n.* wall with gaps for shooting through.

battleship *n.* heavily armoured warship.

batty *adj.* **-tier, -tiest.** *Slang* crazy; eccentric.

THESAURUS

bass deep, deep-toned, grave, low, low-pitched, resonant, sonorous

bastard *n.* illegitimate (child), love child, natural child

bastion bulwark, citadel, defence, fortress, prop, rock, stronghold, support

bat bang, hit, rap, smack, strike, swat, thump, wallop (*Inf.*), whack

batch accumulation, amount, collection, crowd, group, lot, pack, set

bath 1. *n.* ablution, douche, shower, soak, tub,

wash 2. *v.* bathe, clean, scrub down, soak, soap, sponge, tub, wash

bathe *v.* 1. cleanse, immerse, moisten, rinse, soak, steep, wash, wet 2. dip, swim

baton club, mace, rod, staff, stick, truncheon, wand

batten down board up, cover up, fasten down, fix, nail down, secure

batten on fatten, flourish, gain, grow, increase, prosper, thrive, wax

batter assault, beat, belabour, break, buffet, lash, pelt, pound, smash, smite, thrash

DICTIONARY

bauble *n.* trinket of little value.

baulk *v.* same as BALK.

bauxite *n.* claylike substance from which aluminium is obtained.

bawdy *adj.* **bawdier, bawdiest.** (of writing etc.) containing humorous references to sex. —**bawdiness** *n.*

bawl *v.* shout or weep noisily.

bay¹ *n.* wide curving coastline.

bay² *n.* recess in a wall; area in which vehicles may park or unload.

bay³ *v.* (of a hound or wolf) howl in deep prolonged tones.

bay⁴ *n.* Mediterranean laurel tree. —**bay leaf** dried leaf of a laurel, used in cooking.

bay⁵ *adj., n.* reddish-brown (horse).

bayonet *n.* sharp blade that can be fixed to the end of a rifle. —*v.* **-neting, -neted.** stab with a bayonet.

bazaar *n.* sale in aid of charity; market area, esp. in Eastern countries.

bazooka *n.* rocket launcher that fires a projectile capable of piercing armour.

BBC British Broadcasting Corporation.

BC before Christ.

BCG antituberculosis vaccine.

be *v. present sing. 1st person* **am;** *2nd person* **are;** *3rd person* **is.** *present pl.* **are.** *past sing. 1st person* **was;** *2nd person* **were;** *3rd person* **was.** *past pl.* **were.** *present participle* **being.** *past participle* **been.** exist or live; used as a linking between the subject of a sentence and its complement, e.g. *John is a musician;* forms the progressive present tense, e.g. *the man is running;* forms the passive voice of all transitive verbs, e.g. *a good film is being shown on television tonight.*

beach *n.* area of sand or pebbles on a shore. —*v.* run or haul (a boat) onto a beach. —**beachhead** *n.* beach captured by an attacking army on which troops can be landed.

beacon *n.* fire or light on a hill or tower, used as a warning.

bead *n.* small ball of plastic etc., pierced for threading on a string to form a necklace etc.; small drop of moisture. —**beaded** *adj.* —**beading** *n.* strip of moulding used for edging furniture. —**beady** *adj.* small, round, and glittering, e.g. *beady eyes.*

beagle *n.* small hunting dog with short legs and drooping ears.

beak¹ *n.* projecting horny jaws of a bird; *Slang* nose. —**beaky** *adj.*

beak² *n. Slang* judge, magistrate, or headmaster.

beaker *n.* large drinking cup; lipped glass container used in laboratories.

beam *n.* long thick piece of wood, metal, etc., used in building; ray of light; broad smile; narrow flow of electromagnetic radiation or particles. —*v.* smile broadly; divert or aim (a radio signal, light, etc.) in a certain direction.

bean *n.* seed or pod of various plants, eaten as a vegetable or used to make coffee etc.

bear¹ *v.* **bearing, bore, borne.** support or hold up; (**born** in passive use) give birth to; produce as by natural growth; tolerate or endure; hold in the mind; show or be marked with; move in a specified direction. —**bearable** *adj.* —**bearer** *n.* —**bear out** *v.* show to be truthful.

bear² *n.* large heavy mammal with a long shaggy coat. —**bearskin** *n.* tall fur helmet worn by some British soldiers.

THESAURUS

battle action, attack, combat, conflict, encounter, engagement, fight, fray, hostilities, skirmish, struggle, war, warfare

batty barmy (*Sl.*), bats (*Sl.*), bonkers (*Sl.*), cracked (*Sl.*), crackers (*Sl.*), crazy, dotty (*Sl.*), eccentric, insane, loony (*Sl.*), mad, nuts (*Sl.*), nutty (*Sl.*), odd, peculiar, potty (*Inf.*), touched

bay¹ cove, gulf, inlet, sound

bay² alcove, niche, nook, opening, recess

bay³ bark, bell, clamour, cry, growl, howl, yelp

bazaar 1. exchange, market, marketplace, mart 2. bring-and-buy, fair, fête

be be alive, breathe, exist, inhabit, live

beach coast, sands, seashore, seaside, shingle, shore, strand, water's edge

beacon beam, bonfire, flare, lighthouse, sign, signal, watchtower

bead blob, bubble, dot, drop, droplet, globule, pill

beak 1. bill, neb (*Archaic or dialect*), nib 2. nose, proboscis, snout

beam *n.* 1. girder, joist, plank, rafter, spar, support, timber 2. gleam, glimmer, glint, glow, radiation, ray, shaft, streak, stream ~*v.* 3. grin, laugh, smile

bear 1. bring, carry, convey, move, take, tote, transport 2. allow, endure, permit, put up with (*Inf.*), stomach, suffer, tolerate, undergo 3. beget, breed, bring forth, generate, give birth to, produce, yield

bearable endurable, supportable, sustainable, tolerable

bearer carrier, conveyor, messenger, porter, runner, servant

DICTIONARY

beard *n.* hair growing on the lower parts of a man's face. —**bearded** *adj.*

bearing *n.* relevance (to); person's general social conduct; part of a machine that supports another part, esp. one that reduces friction. —*pl.* sense of one's own relative position.

beast *n.* large wild animal; brutal or uncivilized person. —**beastly** *adj.* unpleasant or disagreeable.

beat *v.* **beating, beat; beaten** *or* **beat.** hit hard and repeatedly; throb rhythmically; stir or mix vigorously; overcome or defeat. —*n.* regular throb; assigned route, as of a policeman; basic rhythmic unit in a piece of music. —**beater** *n.*

beatify [bee-at-if-fie] *v.* **-fying, -fied.** *RC Church* declare (a dead person) to be among the blessed in heaven. —**beatific** *adj.* displaying great happiness. —**beatification** *n.* —**beatitude** *n.* supreme blessedness.

beau [boh] *n., pl.* **beaus, beaux.** dandy.

Beaufort scale *n.* scale for measuring the speed of wind.

beauty *n., pl.* **-ties.** combination of all the qualities of a person or thing that delight the senses and mind; very attractive woman; *Informal* something outstanding of its kind. —**beautiful** *adj.* possessing beauty; very pleasant. —**beautifully** *adv.* —**beautify** *v.* make or become beautiful. —**beautification** *n.* —**beautician** *n.* person whose profession is to give beauty treatments.

beaver *n.* amphibious rodent with a big flat tail. —**beaver away** *v.* work industriously.

becalmed *adj.* (of a sailing ship) motionless through lack of wind.

became *v.* past tense of BECOME.

because *conj.* on account of the fact that. —**because of** on account of.

beck[1] *n.* —**at someone's beck and call** subject to someone's slightest whim.

beck[2] *n.* N *English* stream.

beckon *v.* summon with a gesture.

become *v.* **-coming, -came, -come.** come to be; (foll. by *of*) happen to; suit. —**becoming** *adj.* attractive or pleasing; appropriate or proper.

bed *n.* piece of furniture on which to sleep; garden plot; bottom of a river, lake, or sea; layer of rock. —*v.* **bedding, bedded.** have sexual intercourse with. —**bedding** *n.* sheets and covers that are used on a bed. —**bed down** *v.* go to or put into a place to sleep or rest. —**bedpan** *n.* shallow bowl used as a toilet by bedridden people. —**bedridden** *adj.* confined to bed because of illness or old age. —**bedrock** *n.* solid rock beneath the surface soil; basic facts or principles. —**bedroom** *n.* —**bedsit(ter)** *n.* furnished sitting room with a bed.

THESAURUS

bearing 1. air, aspect, attitude, behaviour, carriage, demeanour, deportment, manner, mien, posture 2. connection, import, pertinence, relation, relevance

bear out confirm, endorse, justify, prove, support, uphold, vindicate

beast 1. animal, brute, creature 2. barbarian, brute, fiend, monster, ogre, sadist, savage, swine

beastly awful, disagreeable, foul, mean, nasty, unpleasant

beat *v.* 1. bang, batter, break, buffet, cane, cudgel, drub, flog, hit, knock, lash, maul, pound, punch, strike, thrash, whip 2. conquer, defeat, excel, outdo, outrun, overcome, subdue, surpass, vanquish ~*n.* 3. flutter, palpitation, pulsation, pulse, throb 4. accent, cadence, measure, metre, rhythm, stress, time 5. circuit, course, path, rounds, route, way

beaten 1. cowed, defeated, disheartened, frustrated, overcome, overwhelmed, thwarted, vanquished 2. blended, foamy, frothy, mixed, stirred, whipped, whisked

beautiful appealing, attractive, charming, comely, delightful, exquisite, fair, fine, good-looking, gorgeous, graceful, handsome, lovely, pleasing, radiant, stunning (*Inf.*)

beautify adorn, bedeck, deck, decorate, embellish, enhance, garnish, grace

beauty 1. attractiveness, bloom, charm, elegance, fairness, glamour, grace, handsomeness, loveliness, pulchritude, seemliness 2. belle, charmer, cracker (*Sl.*), good-looker, stunner (*Inf.*), Venus

becalmed settled, still, stranded

because as, by reason of, in that, on account of, owing to, since, thanks to

beckon bid, gesticulate, gesture, motion, nod, signal, summon, wave at

become 1. alter to, be transformed into, change into, come to be, evolve into, grow into, mature into, ripen into 2. embellish, enhance, fit, flatter, grace, harmonize, ornament, set off, suit

becoming attractive, comely, flattering, graceful, neat, pretty, tasteful

bed 1. bedstead, berth, bunk, cot, couch, divan, pallet 2. area, border, garden, patch, plot, row, strip

bedevil afflict, annoy, distress, fret, frustrate, harass, irk, irritate, pester, plague, torment, trouble, vex, worry

DICTIONARY

bedevil [bid-**dev**-ill] v. **-illing, -illed.** harass or torment.

bedlam n. noisy confused situation.

bedraggled adj. untidy, wet, or dirty.

bee n. insect that makes wax and honey. —**beehive** n. structure in which bees live. —**beeswax** n. wax secreted by bees, used in polishes etc.

beech n. European tree with a smooth greyish bark.

beef n. flesh of a cow, bull, or ox. —v. Informal complain. —**beefy** adj. like beef; Informal strong and muscular; Informal fleshy, obese. —**beefburger** n. flat grilled or fried cake of minced beef. —**beefeater** n. yeoman warder at the Tower of London.

been v. past participle of BE.

beep n. high-pitched sound, like that of a car horn. —v. (cause to) make this noise.

beer n. alcoholic drink brewed from malt and hops. —**beery** adj.

beet n. plant with an edible root and leaves. —**beetroot** n. type of beet plant with a dark red root.

beetle n. insect with a hard wing cover on its back. —v. Informal scuttle or scurry.

befall v. Old-fashioned happen to (someone).

befit v. be appropriate or suitable for. —**befitting** adj.

before conj. earlier than the time when; rather than. —prep. preceding in space or time; in the presence of; in preference to. —adv. at an earlier time, previously; in front. —**beforehand** adv. in advance.

befriend v. be a friend to.

beg v. **begging, begged.** solicit (for money or food), esp. in the street; ask formally or humbly. —**beggar** n. —**beggarly** adj.

began v. past tense of BEGIN.

beget v. **-getting; -got** or **-gat; -gotten** or **-got.** cause or create; father.

begin v. **-ginning, -gan, -gun.** start; bring or come into being. —**beginner** n. person who has just started learning to do something. —**beginning** n.

begonia n. tropical plant with waxy flowers.

begrudge v. grudge.

beguile [big-**gile**] v. cheat or mislead; charm or amuse. —**beguiling** adj.

begun v. past participle of BEGIN.

behalf n. —**on behalf of** in the interest of or for the benefit of.

behave v. act or function in a particular way; conduct (oneself) properly. —**behaviour** n.

behead v. remove the head from.

beheld v. past of BEHOLD.

behest n. order or earnest request.

behind prep. at the back of; responsible for or causing; supporting. —adv. in or to a position further back; remaining after someone's departure; in arrears. —n. Informal buttocks. —**behindhand** adj., adv. in arrears; late.

behold v. Old-fashioned look (at). —**beholder** n.

THESAURUS

bedridden confined, incapacitated, laid up (Inf.)

bedrock bed, bottom, foundation, rock bottom, substratum

befitting appropriate, becoming, fit, fitting, right, seemly, suitable

before 1. adv. ahead, earlier, formerly, in advance, in front, previously, sooner 2. prep. earlier than, in advance of, in front of, in the presence of, preceding, prior to

beforehand before now, earlier, in advance, previously, sooner

befriend advise, aid, assist, back, benefit, favour, help, patronize, side with, stand by, succour, support, sustain, uphold, welcome

beg 1. beseech, crave, desire, entreat, implore, importune, petition, plead, pray, request, solicit, supplicate 2. cadge, call for alms, sponge on

beggar cadger, mendicant, scrounger (Inf.), sponger (Inf.), supplicant, tramp, vagrant

begin commence, embark on, initiate, instigate, institute, prepare, set about, set on foot, start

beginner amateur, apprentice, fledgling, freshman, greenhorn (Inf.), initiate, learner, neophyte, novice, recruit, starter, student, tenderfoot, trainee, tyro

beginning birth, commencement, inauguration, inception, initiation, onset, opening, origin, outset, preface, prelude, rise, rudiments, source, start, starting point

begrudge be jealous, envy, grudge, resent

behave 1. act, function, operate, perform, run, work 2. act correctly, conduct oneself properly, mind one's manners

behaviour 1. actions, bearing, carriage, conduct, demeanour, deportment, manner, manners, ways 2. action, operation, performance

behind prep. 1. after, at the back of, at the rear of, following, later than 2. at the bottom of, causing, initiating, instigating, responsible for 3. backing, for, in agreement, on the side of, supporting ~adv. 4. after, afterwards, follow-

DICTIONARY

beholden *adj.* indebted or obliged.

behove *v. Old-fashioned* be necessary or fitting for.

beige *adj.* pale brown.

being *v.* present participle of BE. —*n.* existence; something that exists or is thought to exist; human being, person.

belabour *v.* attack verbally or physically.

belated *adj.* late or too late. —**belatedly** *adv.*

belch *v.* expel wind from the stomach noisily through the mouth; expel or be expelled forcefully, e.g. *smoke belched from the factory.* —*n.* act of belching.

beleaguered *adj.* besieged; surrounded or beset.

belfry *n., pl.* -**fries.** part of a tower where bells are hung.

belie *v.* show to be untrue.

belief *n.* principle etc. accepted as true; opinion; religious faith. —**believe** *v.* accept as true or real; (foll. by *in*) be convinced of the truth or existence of; think, assume, or suppose. —**believable** *adj.* —**believer** *n.*

Belisha beacon [bill-**lee**-sha] *n.* flashing orange globe mounted on a post, marking a pedestrian crossing.

belittle *v.* treat as having little value or importance.

bell *n.* hollow, usu. metal, cup-shaped instrument that emits a ringing sound when struck; device that rings or buzzes as a signal.

belladonna *n.* (drug obtained from) deadly nightshade.

belle *n.* beautiful woman.

bellicose *adj.* warlike and aggressive.

belligerent *adj.* hostile and aggressive; engaged in war. —*n.* person or country engaged in war. —**belligerence** *n.*

bellow *v.* make a low deep cry like that of a bull; shout in a loud deep voice. —*n.* loud deep roar.

bellows *pl. n.* instrument for pumping a stream of air into something.

belly *n., pl.* -**lies.** part of the body of a vertebrate which contains the intestines; stomach; front, lower, or inner part of something. —*v.* -**lying,** -**lied.** (cause to) swell out. —**bellyful** *n. Slang* more than one can tolerate.

belong *v.* (foll. by *to*) be the property of; (foll. by *to*) be a part of; have a proper or usual place. —**belongings** *pl. n.* personal possessions.

beloved *adj.* dearly loved. —*n.* person dearly loved.

below *prep., adv.* at or to a position lower than, under.

belt *n.* band of cloth, leather, etc., worn usu. around the waist; circular strip of rubber that drives moving parts in a machine; area where a specific thing is found. —*v.* fasten with a belt; *Slang* hit very hard; *Slang* move very fast.

bemoan *v.* express sorrow or dissatisfaction about.

bemused *adj.* puzzled or confused.

bench *n.* long seat; long narrow work table; judge or magistrate sitting in court. —**bench mark** mark on a fixed object, used as a reference point in surveying; criterion by which to measure something.

THESAURUS

ing, in the wake (of), next, subsequently 5. behindhand, in arrears, in debt, overdue

behold consider, contemplate, discern, eye, look at, observe, regard, scan, view, watch, witness

being 1. actuality, existence, life, living, reality 2. animal, beast, body, creature, human being, individual, living thing, mortal, thing

belated delayed, late, overdue, tardy

beleaguered beset, besieged, bothered, harassed, nagged, persecuted, plagued, put upon, set upon, vexed

belief 1. admission, assurance, confidence, conviction, credit, feeling, impression, judgment, notion, opinion, persuasion, reliance, theory, trust, view 2. credence, credo, creed, doctrine, dogma, faith, ideology, principles, tenet

believe 1. accept, be certain of, be convinced of, count on, credit, depend on, have faith in, hold, place confidence in, swear by, trust 2. assume, consider, gather, guess, imagine,

judge, postulate, presume, reckon, speculate, suppose, think

believer adherent, convert, devotee, disciple, follower, proselyte, supporter

bellow bawl, call, clamour, cry, howl, roar, scream, shout, shriek, yell

belong 1. *With* **to** be at the disposal of, be held by, be owned by, be the property of 2. *With* **to** be allied to, be a member of, be associated with, be included in 3. attach to, be connected with, be part of, fit, go with

belongings effects, gear, goods, personal property, possessions, things

beloved adored, cherished, darling, dear, dearest, loved, precious, sweet

below *prep./adv.* beneath, down, lower, under, underneath

belt band, girdle, girth, sash, waistband

bemused bewildered, confused, dazed, fuddled,

DICTIONARY

bend *v.* **bending, bent.** (cause to) form a curve; (often foll. by *down* etc.) incline the body. —*n.* curved part. —**bendy** *adj.*

beneath *adv., prep.* below; not worthy of.

Benedictine *n., adj.* (monk or nun) of the order of Saint Benedict.

benediction *n.* prayer for divine blessing.

benefit *n.* something helpful, beneficial, or advantageous; payment made by a government to a poor, ill, or unemployed person. —*v.* **-fiting, -fited.** do or receive good. —**beneficial** *adj.* advantageous. —**beneficiary** *n.* person who gains or benefits. —**benefactor, benefactress** *n.* someone who supports a person or institution by giving money. —**benefaction** *n.* —**beneficent** [bin-**eff**-iss-ent] *adj.* charitable or generous. —**beneficence** *n.*

benevolent *adj.* kind and helpful. —**benevolently** *adv.* —**benevolence** *n.*

benighted *adj.* ignorant or uncultured.

benign [bin-**nine**] *adj.* showing kindliness; (of a tumour) not malignant. —**benignly** *adv.*

bent *v.* past of BEND. —*adj. Slang* dishonest; *Slang* homosexual. —*n.* personal inclination or aptitude. —**bent on** determined to pursue (a course of action).

benzene *n.* flammable poisonous liquid used as a solvent, fuel, etc.

bequeath *v.* dispose of (property) as in a will. —**bequest** *n.* legal gift of money or property by someone who has died.

berate *v.* scold harshly.

bereaved *adj.* having recently lost someone close through death. —**bereavement** *n.*

bereft *adj.* (foll. by *of*) deprived.

beret [ber-**ray**] *n.* round flat close-fitting brimless cap.

bergamot *n.* small Asian tree with sour pear-shaped fruit.

beriberi *n.* tropical disease caused by vitamin B deficiency.

berk *n.* stupid person.

berry *n., pl.* **-ries.** small soft stoneless fruit.

berserk *adj.* —**go berserk** become violent or destructive.

berth *n.* bunk in a ship or train; place assigned to a ship at a mooring. —*v.* dock (a vessel).

beryl *n.* hard transparent mineral.

beseech *v.* **-seeching, -sought** *or* **-seeched.** ask (someone) earnestly.

beset *v.* trouble or harass constantly.

beside *prep.* at, by, or to the side of; as compared with. —**beside oneself** overwhelmed or overwrought. —**besides** *adv., prep.* in addition.

besiege *v.* surround with military forces; overwhelm, as with requests.

besom *n.* broom made of twigs.

besotted *adj.* infatuated.

besought *v.* past of BESEECH.

bespeak *v.* indicate or suggest. —**bespoke** *adj.*

THESAURUS

muddled, perplexed, puzzled, stunned, stupefied, tipsy

bench 1. form, pew, seat, settle 2. counter, table, workbench, worktable 3. court, courtroom, judge, judges, judiciary, magistrate, magistrates

bend 1. *v.* bow, buckle, contort, curve, diverge, flex, incline, lean, stoop, swerve, turn, twist, veer, warp 2. *n.* angle, arc, bow, corner, crook, curve, hook, loop, turn, twist

beneath 1. *adv., prep.* below, in a lower place, underneath 2. *prep.* below, inferior to, less than, lower than, unbefitting, underneath, unworthy of

beneficial advantageous, favourable, healthful, helpful, useful, valuable, wholesome

benefit 1. *n.* advantage, aid, asset, blessing, boon, favour, gain, good, help, interest, profit, use 2. *v.* advance, aid, assist, avail, better, enhance, further, improve, profit, promote, serve

bent *adj.* 1. angled, arched, bowed, crooked, curved, hunched, twisted 2. *With* **on** determined, inclined, insistent, resolved, set ~*n.* 3.

ability, aptitude, flair, forte, inclination, penchant, proclivity, propensity, talent

bequest dower, endowment, estate, gift, heritage, inheritance, legacy, settlement, trust

bereavement death, deprivation, loss

berserk crazy, frenzied, insane, mad, manic, rabid, raging, violent, wild

berth *n.* 1. bed, billet, bunk 2. anchorage, dock, harbour, haven, pier, port, quay, wharf

beseech ask, beg, crave, entreat, implore, importune, petition, plead, pray, solicit, sue, supplicate

beside abreast of, adjacent to, alongside, at the side of, close to, near, nearby, neighbouring, next door to, next to, overlooking

besides *adv.* also, as well, further, furthermore, in addition, moreover, otherwise, too, what's more

besiege beleaguer, beset, blockade, encircle, encompass, hedge in, hem in, lay siege to, shut in, surround

besotted doting, hypnotized, infatuated, smitten, spellbound

DICTIONARY

(of clothes) made to the customer's specifications.

best *adj.* most excellent of a particular group etc. —*adv.* in a manner surpassing all others. —*n.* most outstanding or excellent person, thing, or group in a category. —**best man** groom's attendant at a wedding. —**best seller** book or other product that has sold in great numbers.

bestial *adj.* brutal or savage; of or like a beast. —**bestiality** *n.*

bestir *v.* cause (oneself) to become active.

bestow *v.* present (a gift) or confer (an honour). —**bestowal** *n.*

bestride *v.* have or put a leg on either side of.

bet *n.* agreement that money will be paid to someone who correctly predicts the outcome of an event; stake risked. —*v.* **betting, bet** *or* **betted.** make or place (a bet); *Informal* predict.

betel [bee-tl] *n.* Asian climbing plant, the leaves and nuts of which can be chewed.

bête noire [bet nwahr] *n., pl.* **bêtes noires.** person or thing that one particularly dislikes.

betide *v.* happen (to).

betoken *v.* indicate or signify.

betray *v.* hand over or expose (one's nation etc.) treacherously to an enemy; disclose (a secret or confidence) treacherously; reveal unintentionally. —**betrayal** *n.* —**betrayer** *n.*

betrothed *adj.* engaged to be married. —**betrothal** *n.*

better *adj.* more excellent than others; improved or fully recovered in health. —*adv.* in a more excellent manner; in or to a greater degree. —*pl. n.* one's superiors. —*v.* improve upon.

between *prep.* at a point intermediate to two other points in space, time, etc.; indicating a linked relation or comparison; indicating alternatives. —*adv.* between one specified thing and another.

betwixt *prep., adv. Old-fashioned* between.

bevel *n.* slanting edge. —*v.* **-elling, -elled.** cut a bevel on (a piece of timber etc.).

beverage *n.* drink.

bevy *n., pl.* **bevies.** flock or group.

bewail *v.* express great sorrow over.

beware *v.* be on one's guard (against).

bewilder *v.* confuse utterly. —**bewildering** *adj.* —**bewilderment** *n.*

bewitch *v.* attract and fascinate; cast a spell over. —**bewitching** *adj.*

beyond *prep.* at or to a point on the other side of; outside the limits or scope of. —*adv.* at or to the far side of something.

bi- *combining form* twice or two, e.g. *bifocal.*

THESAURUS

best *adj.* 1. chief, finest, first, first-class, first-rate, foremost, highest, leading, outstanding, perfect, pre-eminent, superlative, supreme, unsurpassed 2. greatest, largest, most ~*adv.* 3. advantageously, excellently, most fortunately 4. extremely, greatly, most deeply, most fully, most highly ~*n.* 5. choice, cream, elite, finest, first, flower, pick, prime, top

bestial animal, beastly, brutal, brutish, carnal, depraved, gross, inhuman, low, savage, sensual, sordid, vile

bestow accord, allot, award, commit, confer, donate, entrust, give, grant, impart, lavish, present

bet 1. *n.* ante, gamble, hazard, pledge, risk, speculation, stake, venture, wager 2. *v.* chance, gamble, hazard, pledge, risk, speculate, stake, venture, wager

betray 1. be disloyal break with, double-cross (*Inf.*), inform on *or* against, sell out (*Inf.*) 2. disclose, divulge, evince, expose, give away, lay bare, let slip, reveal, show, tell, tell on, uncover, unmask

betrayal 1. disloyalty, double-cross (*Inf.*), double-dealing, duplicity, falseness, perfidy, sell-out (*Inf.*), treachery, treason, trickery 2. disclosure, revelation, telling

better *adj.* 1. bigger, excelling, finer, fitter, greater, higher quality, larger, preferable, superior, surpassing, worthier 2. cured, fitter, healthier, improving, more healthy, on the mend (*Inf.*), progressing, recovering, stronger, well ~*adv.* 3. in a more excellent manner, in a superior way, to a greater degree

between amidst, among, halfway, in the middle of, mid

beverage draught, drink, liquid, liquor, refreshment

bevy covey, flight, flock, group

bewail cry over, deplore, grieve for, lament, moan, mourn, regret, repent, rue, wail

beware avoid, be careful (cautious, wary), guard against, heed, look out, mind, shun, steer clear of, take heed, watch out

bewilder bemuse, confound, confuse, daze, mix up, mystify, perplex, puzzle

bewitch allure, attract, beguile, charm, enchant, entrance, fascinate, spellbind

beyond above, apart from, at a distance, away from, before, farther, out of range, out of reach, over, past, remote

DICTIONARY

biannual *adj.* occurring twice a year. —**biannually** *adv.*

bias *n.* mental tendency, esp. prejudice; diagonal cut across the weave of a fabric; *Bowls* weight on one side of a bowl that causes it to run in a curve. —*v.* **-asing, -ased** *or* **-assing, -assed.** cause to have a bias. —**bias(s)ed** *adj.*

bib *n.* piece of cloth or plastic worn under a child's chin to protect his or her clothes when eating; upper front part of dungarees etc.

Bible *n.* sacred writings of the Christian and Jewish religions; (**b-**) book regarded as authoritative. —**biblical** *adj.*

bibliography *n., pl.* **-phies.** list of books on a subject; list of sources used in a book etc. —**bibliographer** *n.*

bibliophile *n.* person who collects or is fond of books.

bibulous *adj.* addicted to alcohol.

bicarbonate *n.* salt of carbonic acid. —**bicarbonate of soda** powder used in baking or as medicine.

bicentenary *n., pl.* **-naries.** 200th anniversary.

biceps *n.* large muscle in the upper arm.

bicker *v.* argue over petty matters.

bicycle *n.* vehicle with two wheels, one behind the other, pedalled by the rider.

bid *v.* **bidding, bade, bidden.** offer (a sum of money) in an attempt to buy something (*past* **bid**); say (a greeting etc.); command. —*n.* offer of a sum of money; attempt. —**bidder** *n.* —**biddable** *adj.* obedient. —**bidding** *n.* command.

bide *v.* —**bide one's time** wait patiently for an opportunity.

bidet [bee-day] *n.* low basin for washing the genital area.

biennial *adj.* occurring every two years. —*n.* plant that completes its life cycle in two years.

bier *n.* stand on which a coffin rests before burial.

bifocals *pl. n.* pair of spectacles with each lens in two parts, the upper for distance and the lower for reading.

big *adj.* **bigger, biggest.** of considerable size, height, number, or capacity; important through having wealth etc.; elder; generous, magnanimous. —*adv.* on a grand scale. —**bighead** *n. Informal* conceited person. —**big-headed** *adj.* —**big shot, bigwig** *n. Informal* important person.

bigamy *n.* crime of marrying a person while still legally married to someone else. —**bigamist** *n.* —**bigamous** *adj.*

bigot *n.* person who is intolerant, esp. regarding religion or race. —**bigoted** *adj.* —**bigotry** *n.*

bijou [bee-zhoo] *adj.* small but tasteful.

bike *n. Informal* bicycle or motorcycle.

bikini *n.* woman's brief two-piece swimming costume.

bilateral *adj.* affecting or undertaken by two parties.

bilberry *n.* bluish-black edible berry.

bile *n.* bitter yellow fluid secreted by the liver. —**bilious** *adj.* sick, nauseous.

bilge *n.* ship's bottom, where dirty water collects; *Informal* nonsense.

bilingual *adj.* involving or using two languages.

bill[1] *n.* statement of money owed for goods or services supplied; draft of a proposed new law; poster; *US* piece of paper money; list of events, such as a theatre programme. —*v.* send or present a bill to; advertise by posters.

bill[2] *n.* bird's beak.

billabong *n. Aust.* stagnant pool in an intermittent stream.

billet *n.* civilian accommodation for a soldier. —*v.* **-leting, -leted.** assign a lodging to (a soldier).

THESAURUS

bias favouritism, inclination, leaning, narrow-mindedness, one-sidedness, partiality, prejudice, proneness, propensity, tendency, turn, unfairness

biased distorted, one-sided, partial, prejudiced, slanted, swayed, twisted, warped, weighted

bicker argue, disagree, dispute, fight, quarrel, squabble

bid *v.* 1. offer, proffer, propose, submit, tender 2. call, greet, say, tell, wish 3. ask, call, charge, command, desire, direct, enjoin, instruct, invite, require, solicit, summon, tell ~*n.* 4. offer, price, proposal, proposition, sum, tender 5. attempt, effort, try, venture

bidding behest, call, charge, command, demand, invitation, order, request, summons

big 1. bulky, burly, colossal, enormous, extensive, gigantic, great, huge, hulking, immense, large, mammoth, massive, prodigious, sizable, spacious, substantial, vast, voluminous 2. eminent, important, leading, main, powerful, principal, prominent, serious, significant, valuable, weighty 3. generous, gracious, heroic, magnanimous, noble, princely

bill[1] *n.* 1. account, charges, invoice, reckoning, score, statement, tally 2. advertisement, broadsheet, circular, handbill, handout, leaflet, notice, placard, playbill, poster 3. meas-

DICTIONARY

billet-doux [bill-ee-**doo**] *n., pl.* **billets-doux.** love letter.

billhook *n.* tool with a hooked blade, used for chopping etc.

billiards *n.* game played on a table with balls and a cue.

billion *n.* one thousand million; (formerly) one million million. —**billionth** *adj.*

billow *n.* large sea wave. —*v.* rise up or swell out.

billy, billycan *n., pl.* **-lies** *or* **-lycans.** metal can or pot for cooking on a camp fire.

bimbo *n. Slang* attractive but empty-headed young woman.

bin *n.* container for rubbish or for storing grain, coal, etc.

binary [**bine**-a-ree] *adj.* composed of two parts; *Maths, computers* of or expressed in a counting system with only two digits, 0 and 1.

bind *v.* **binding, bound.** make or become secure with or as if with a rope; place (someone) under obligation; enclose and fasten (the pages of a book) between covers. —*n. Informal* annoying situation. —**binder** *n.* firm cover for holding loose sheets of paper together. —**binding** *n.* book cover; strip of cloth used as edging. —**bindweed** *n.* plant that twines around a support.

binge *n. Informal* bout of excessive eating or drinking.

bingo *n.* gambling game in which numbers are called out and covered by the players on their individual cards.

binoculars *pl. n.* telescope made for both eyes.

binomial *n., adj.* (mathematical expression) consisting of two terms.

bio- *combining form* life or living organisms, e.g. *biology.*

biochemistry *n.* study of the chemistry of living things. —**biochemist** *n.*

biodegradable *adj.* capable of being decomposed by natural means.

biography *n., pl.* **-phies.** account of a person's life by another. —**biographical** *adj.* —**biographer** *n.*

biology *n.* study of living organisms. —**biological** *adj.* —**biologist** *n.*

bionic *adj.* having a part of the body that is operated electronically.

biopsy *n., pl.* **-sies.** examination of tissue from a living body.

biped [**bye**-ped] *n.* animal with two feet.

biplane *n.* aeroplane with two sets of wings.

birch *n.* tree with thin peeling bark; birch rod or twigs used, esp. formerly, for flogging offenders.

bird *n.* creature with feathers and wings, the female of which lays eggs; *Slang* young woman.

birdie *n. Golf* score of one stroke under par for a hole.

biretta *n.* stiff square cap worn by the Catholic clergy.

Biro *n.* ® ballpoint pen.

birth *n.* childbirth; act of being born; ancestry. —**give birth to** *v.* bear (offspring). —**birth control** any method of contraception. —**birthday** *n.* anniversary of the day of one's birth. —**birthmark** *n.* blemish on the skin formed before birth. —**birthright** *n.* privileges or possessions that someone is entitled to as soon as he or she is born.

biscuit *n.* small flat sweet or plain cake.

bisect *v.* divide into two equal parts.

bisexual *adj.* sexually attracted to both men and women. —**bisexuality** *n.*

bishop *n.* clergyman who governs a diocese; piece at chess. —**bishopric** *n.* diocese or office of a bishop.

bismuth *n.* pinkish-white metallic element.

bison *n., pl.* **-son.** large hairy animal of the cattle family.

bistro *n., pl.* **-tros.** small restaurant.

bit[1] *n.* small piece, portion, or quantity. —**a bit** rather, somewhat. —**bit by bit** gradually.

bit[2] *n.* metal mouthpiece on a bridle; cutting or drilling part of a tool.

THESAURUS

ure, projected law, proposal ~*v.* 4. charge, debit, figure, invoice

bill[2] beak, mandible

billet 1. *n.* accommodation, barracks, lodging, quarters 2. *v.* accommodate, berth, quarter, station

billow 1. *n.* breaker, surge, swell, tide, wave 2. *v.* balloon, puff up, rise up, roll, surge, swell

bind *v.* 1. attach, fasten, glue, hitch, lash, paste, rope, secure, stick, strap, tie, tie up 2. compel, constrain, force, necessitate, oblige

birth 1. childbirth, delivery, nativity, parturition 2. ancestry, background, blood, breeding, descent, genealogy, line, lineage, nobility, pedigree, race, stock, strain

bisect cut in half, cut in two, divide in two, halve

bit[1] chip, crumb, fragment, grain, iota, jot, mite, morsel, part, piece, scrap, slice, speck, tittle, whit

bit[2] brake, check, curb, restraint, snaffle

DICTIONARY

bit³ *v.* past tense of BITE.

bit⁴ *n.* smallest unit of information held in a computer's memory, either 0 or 1.

bitch *n.* female dog, fox, or wolf; *Offens.* spiteful woman. —*v. Informal* complain or grumble. —**bitchy** *adj.* —**bitchiness** *n.*

bite *v.* **biting, bit, bitten.** cut off, puncture, or tear as with the teeth or fangs; take firm hold of or act effectively upon. —*n.* act of biting; wound or sting inflicted by biting; snack. —**biter** *n.* —**biting** *adj.* piercing or keen; sarcastic.

bitter *adj.* having a sharp unpleasant taste; showing or caused by hostility or resentment; extremely cold. —*n.* beer with a slightly bitter taste. —*pl.* bitter-tasting alcoholic drink. —**bitterly** *adv.* —**bitterness** *n.*

bittern *n.* wading bird like a heron.

bitumen *n.* black sticky substance obtained from tar or petrol.

bivalve *n.* marine mollusc with a double shell.

bivouac *n.* temporary camp in the open air. —*v.* **-acking, -acked.** camp in a bivouac.

bizarre *adj.* odd or unusual.

blab *v.* **blabbing, blabbed.** reveal (secrets) indiscreetly; chatter thoughtlessly.

black *adj.* of the darkest colour, like jet or coal; (**B-**) dark-skinned; without hope; angry or resentful, e.g. *black looks;* unpleasant in a macabre manner, e.g. *black comedy.* —*n.* darkest colour; (**B-**) member of a dark-skinned race, esp. a Negro; complete darkness. —*v.* make black; (of

trade unionists) boycott (goods or people). —**blackness** *n.* —**blacken** *v.* make or become black; defame or slander. —**blackball** *v.* exclude from a group. —**blackbird** *n.* common European thrush. —**blackboard** *n.* hard black surface used for writing on with chalk. —**blackguard** [blaggard] *n.* unprincipled person. —**blackhead** *n.* small black spot on the skin. —**blackleg** *n.* person who continues to work during a strike. —**blacklist** *n.* list of people or organizations considered untrustworthy etc. —**blackmail** *n.* act of attempting to extort money by threats. —*v.* (attempt to) obtain money by blackmail. —**black magic** magic used for evil purposes. —**black market** illegal trade in goods or currencies. —**black out** *v.* extinguish (lights); lose consciousness or memory temporarily. —**blackout** *n.* extinguishing of all light as a precaution against an air attack; momentary loss of consciousness or memory. —**black sheep** person who is regarded as a disgrace by his or her family. —**blacksmith** *n.* person who works iron with a furnace, anvil, etc. —**black spot** place on a road where accidents frequently occur.

bladder *n.* sac in the body where urine is held; hollow bag which may be filled with air or liquid.

blade *n.* cutting edge of a weapon or tool; thin flattish part of a propeller, oar, etc.; leaf of grass.

blame *n.* responsibility for something that is wrong. —*v.* consider (someone) responsible for. —**blameless** *adj.* —**blameworthy** *adj.* deserving blame.

THESAURUS

bite *v.* 1. chew, clamp, crunch, crush, cut, gnaw, grip, hold, nibble, nip, pierce, pinch, rend, seize, snap, tear, wound ~*n.* 2. itch, nip, pinch, prick, sting, tooth marks, wound 3. food, light meal, morsel, mouthful, piece, snack

bitter 1. acid, acrid, astringent, sharp, sour, tart, unsweetened, vinegary 2. hostile, morose, rancorous, resentful, sore, sour, sullen

bitterness 1. acerbity, acidity, sharpness, sourness, tartness 2. grudge, hostility, pique, rancour, resentment

bizarre curious, eccentric, extraordinary, fantastic, freakish, grotesque, ludicrous, odd, offbeat, outlandish, outré, peculiar, queer, strange, unusual, weird

black *adj.* 1. dark, dusky, ebony, inky, jet, murky, sable, starless, swarthy 2. *Fig.* depressing, dismal, distressing, doleful, foreboding, funereal, gloomy, hopeless, lugubrious, mournful, ominous, sad, sombre ~*v.* 3. ban, bar, blacklist, boycott

blacken 1. befoul, cloud, darken, make black,

smudge, soil 2. calumniate, decry, defame, defile, denigrate, dishonour, malign, slander, smear, smirch, stain, sully, taint, tarnish, traduce, vilify

blackguard bounder (*Brit. inf.*), miscreant, rascal, rogue, scoundrel, swine, villain, wretch

black magic necromancy, sorcery, voodoo, witchcraft, wizardry

blackmail *n.* bribe, exaction, extortion, hush money (*Sl.*), intimidation, protection (*Inf.*), ransom

blackness darkness, duskiness, gloom, murkiness

blackout *n.* coma, faint, oblivion, swoon, unconsciousness

black sheep disgrace, ne'er-do-well, outcast, prodigal, renegade, reprobate, wastrel

blame 1. *n.* culpability, fault, guilt, incrimination, liability onus, responsibility 2. *v.* accuse, admonish, censure, charge, chide, condemn, criticize, disapprove, find fault with, hold responsible, reprehend, reproach, reprove, tax, upbraid

DICTIONARY

blanch v. become pale; prepare (vegetables etc.) by plunging them in boiling water.

blancmange [blam-**monzh**] n. jelly-like dessert made with milk.

bland adj. dull and uninteresting. —**blandly** adv.

blandishments pl. n. persuasive flattery.

blank adj. not written on; showing no interest, feeling, or understanding. —n. empty space; cartridge containing no bullet. —**blankly** adv. —**blank verse** unrhymed verse.

blanket n. thick covering for a bed; concealing cover, as of snow. —v. cover as with a blanket.

blare v. sound loudly and harshly. —n. loud harsh noise.

blarney n. flattering talk.

blasé [**blah**-zay] adj. indifferent or bored through familiarity.

blaspheme v. speak disrespectfully of (God or sacred things). —**blasphemy** n. —**blasphemous** adj. —**blasphemer** n.

blast n. explosion; sudden strong gust of air or wind; sudden loud sound, as of a trumpet. —v. blow up (a rock etc.) with explosives. —**blastoff** n. launching of a rocket.

blatant [**blay**-tant] adj. glaringly obvious. —**blatantly** adv.

blaze[1] n. strong fire or flame; very bright light. —v. burn or shine brightly.

blaze[2] n. mark made on a tree to indicate a route.

blazer n. lightweight jacket, esp. in the colours of a school etc.

blazon v. proclaim publicly.

bleach v. make or become white or colourless. —n. bleaching agent.

bleak adj. exposed and barren; offering little hope.

bleary adj. -rier, -riest. with eyes dimmed, as by tears or tiredness. —**blearily** adv.

bleat v., n. (utter) the plaintive cry of a sheep, goat, or calf.

bleed v. **bleeding, bled.** lose blood; draw blood from (a person or animal); *Informal* obtain money by extortion.

bleep n. short high-pitched sound made by an electrical device. —v. make a bleeping sound. —**bleeper** n.

blemish n. defect or stain. —v. spoil or tarnish.

blench v. shy away, as in fear.

blend v. mix or mingle (components); look good together. —n. mixture. —**blender** n. kitchen appliance for mixing food or liquid at high speed.

bless v. make holy by means of a religious rite; call upon God to protect; endow with health, talent, etc. —**blessed** adj. holy. —**blessing** n. prayer for God's favour; happy event.

THESAURUS

blameless above suspicion, clean, faultless, guiltless, innocent, in the clear, irreproachable, perfect, stainless, unblemished, upright, virtuous

bland boring, dull, flat, humdrum, insipid, tasteless, tedious, uninteresting, vapid, weak

blank adj. 1. bare, clean, clear, empty, plain, spotless, unfilled, unmarked, void, white 2. at a loss, bewildered, confounded, confused, nonplussed, uncomprehending ~n. 3. emptiness, empty space, gap, nothingness, space, vacancy, vacuum, void

blanket n. 1. cover, coverlet, rug 2. carpet, cloak, coat, coating, covering, envelope, film, layer, mantle, sheet, wrapper, wrapping ~v. 3. cloak, cloud, coat, conceal, cover, hide, mask, obscure

blare blast, boom, clang, honk, hoot, peal, resound, roar, trumpet

blaspheme curse, damn, desecrate, execrate, profane, swear

blasphemous godless, impious, profane, sacrilegious, ungodly

blasphemy cursing, desecration, execration, impiety, impiousness, profaneness, profanity, sacrilege, swearing

blast n./v. 1. blare, blow, clang, honk, peal, scream, toot, wail ~n. 2. bang, blow-up, burst, crash, explosion, outburst, salvo, volley ~v. 3. blow up, break up, burst, demolish, destroy, explode, ruin, shatter

blatant brazen, conspicuous, flagrant, glaring, naked, obvious, ostentatious, outright, overt, prominent, sheer

blaze n. 1. bonfire, conflagration, fire, flame, flames 2. beam, brilliance, flare, flash, glare, gleam, glitter, glow, light, radiance ~v. 3. beam, burn, fire, flame, flare, flash, glare, gleam, glow, shine

bleak 1. bare, barren, chilly, cold, desolate, exposed, gaunt, open, raw, windswept, windy 2. cheerless, depressing, dismal, dreary, gloomy, grim, hopeless, joyless, sombre, unpromising

blemish n. blot, blotch, blur, defect, disfigurement, disgrace, dishonour, fault, flaw, imperfection, mark, smudge, speck, spot, stain, taint

blend v. 1. coalesce, combine, compound, fuse, intermix, merge, mingle, mix, unite 2. complement, fit, go well, go with, harmonize, suit ~n.

DICTIONARY

blether *Scot.* —*v.* speak at length, esp. foolishly. —*n.* foolish or babbling talk.

blew *v.* past tense of BLOW.

blight *n.* withering plant disease; person or thing that spoils or prevents growth. —*v.* frustrate or disappoint.

blighter *n. Informal* irritating person.

blimp *n.* small airship.

blind *adj.* unable to see; unable or unwilling to understand; not determined by reason, e.g. *blind hatred.* —*v.* deprive of sight; deprive of good sense, reason, or judgment. —*n.* covering for a window; something that serves to conceal the truth. —**blindly** *adv.* —**blindness** *n.* —**blindfold** *v.* prevent (a person) from seeing by covering the eyes. —*n.* piece of cloth used to cover the eyes.

blink *v.* close and immediately reopen (the eyes); shine intermittently. —*n.* act of blinking. —**on the blink** *Slang* not working properly. —**blinkers** *pl. n.* leather flaps on a horse's bridle to prevent sideways vision.

blip *n.* small light which flashes on and off regularly on equipment such as a radar screen.

bliss *n.* perfect happiness. —**blissful** *adj.* —**blissfully** *adv.*

blister *n.* small bubble on the skin; swelling, as on a painted surface. —*v.* (cause to) have blisters. —**blistering** *adj.* (of weather) very hot; (of criticism) extremely harsh.

blithe *adj.* casual and indifferent. —**blithely** *adv.*

blitz *n.* violent and sustained attack by aircraft; intensive attack or concerted effort. —*v.* attack suddenly and intensively.

blizzard *n.* blinding storm of wind and snow.

bloated *adj.* swollen up with liquid or gas.

bloater *n.* salted smoked herring.

blob *n.* soft mass or drop.

bloc *n.* people or countries combined by a common interest.

block *n.* large solid piece of wood, stone, etc.; large building of offices, flats, etc.; group of buildings enclosed by intersecting streets; obstruction or hindrance; *Slang* person's head. —*v.* obstruct or impede by introducing an obstacle. —**blockage** *n.* —**blockhead** *n.* stupid person. —**block letter** plain capital letter.

blockade *n.* action that prevents goods from reaching a place. —*v.* impose a blockade on.

bloke *n. Informal* man.

blonde, (*masc.*) **blond** *adj., n.* fair-haired (person).

blood *n.* red fluid that flows around the body; race or ancestry. —**in cold blood** done deliber-

THESAURUS

3. alloy, amalgam, composite, compound, concoction, fusion, mix, mixture, synthesis, union

bless 1. consecrate, dedicate, exalt, extol, glorify, hallow, magnify, ordain, praise, sanctify, thank 2. bestow, endow, favour, give, grace, grant, provide

blessed adored, beatified, divine, hallowed, holy, revered, sacred, sanctified

blessing 1. benediction, benison, consecration, dedication, grace, invocation, thanksgiving 2. advantage, benefit, boon, bounty, favour, gain, gift, godsend, good fortune, help, kindness, profit, service, windfall

blight 1. *n.* canker, decay, disease, fungus, infestation, mildew, pest, rot 2. *v.* annihilate, crush, dash, disappoint, frustrate, mar, nullify, ruin, spoil, wreck

blind *adj.* 1. eyeless, sightless, unseeing, unsighted, visionless 2. *Fig.* careless, heedless, ignorant, inattentive, inconsiderate, indifferent, insensitive, neglectful, oblivious, prejudiced, thoughtless, unaware of, unconscious of, uncritical, undiscerning, unmindful of, unobservant, unreasoning 3. hasty, impetuous, irrational, mindless, rash, reckless, senseless, unthinking, violent, wild ~*n.* 4. camouflage, cloak, cover, façade, feint, front, mask, screen, smoke screen

blindly aimlessly, at random, confusedly, frantically, indiscriminately, instinctively, madly, purposelessly, wildly

bliss beatitude, blessedness, ecstasy, euphoria, happiness, heaven, joy, paradise, rapture

blissful delighted, ecstatic, elated, enchanted, euphoric, happy, joyful, rapturous

blister abscess, boil, canker, carbuncle, cyst, pimple, sore, swelling, ulcer

blithe buoyant, carefree, casual, cheerful, cheery, debonair, gay, happy, indifferent, jaunty, light-hearted, merry, mirthful, sprightly, sunny, vivacious

blizzard blast, gale, snowstorm, squall, storm, tempest

block *n.* 1. bar, brick, cake, chunk, cube, hunk, ingot, lump, mass, piece, square 2. bar, barrier, blockage, hindrance, impediment, jam, obstacle, obstruction, stoppage ~*v.* 3. choke, clog, close, obstruct, plug, stop up 4. bar, check, deter, halt, hinder, impede, obstruct, stop

blockade barrier, closure, hindrance, impediment, obstacle, obstruction, restriction, siege, stoppage

DICTIONARY

ately. —**bloodless** adj. —**bloody** adj. covered with blood; marked by much killing. —adj., adv. Slang extreme or extremely. —v. stain with blood. —**bloody-minded** adj. deliberately unhelpful. —**blood bath** massacre. —**bloodhound** n. large dog used for tracking. —**bloodshed** n. slaughter or killing. —**bloodshot** adj. (of eyes) inflamed. —**blood sport** sport involving the killing of animals. —**bloodstream** n. flow of blood round the body. —**bloodsucker** n. animal that sucks blood; Informal person who extorts money from other people. —**bloodthirsty** adj. taking pleasure in violence.

bloom n. blossom on a flowering plant; youthful or healthy glow. —v. bear flowers; be in a healthy glowing condition.

bloomer n. Informal stupid mistake.

bloomers pl. n. woman's baggy knickers.

blossom n. flowers of a plant. —v. (of plants) flower; come to a promising stage.

blot n. spot or stain; something that spoils or stains. —v. **blotting, blotted.** cause a blemish in or on; soak up (ink) by using blotting paper. —**blotter** n. —**blot out** v. darken or hide completely. —**blotting paper** soft absorbent paper for soaking up ink.

blotch n. discoloured area or stain. —**blotchy** adj.

blotto adj. Slang extremely drunk.

blouse n. woman's shirtlike garment.

blow[1] v. **blowing, blew, blown.** (of air, the wind, etc.) move; move or be carried as if by the wind; expel (air etc.) through the mouth or nose; cause (a musical instrument) to sound by forcing air into it; burn out (a fuse etc.); Slang spend (money) freely. —**blower** n. —**blowy** adj. windy. —**blow-dry** v. style (the hair) with a hand-held dryer. —**blowout** n. sudden loss of air in a tyre; escape of oil or gas from a well; Slang filling meal. —**blow up** v. explode; fill with air; Informal enlarge (a photograph); Informal lose one's temper.

blow[2] n. hard hit; sudden setback; attacking action.

blown v. past participle of BLOW.

blowzy, blowsy adj. fat, untidy, and red-faced.

blubber v. sob without restraint. —n. fat of whales, seals, etc.

bludgeon n. short thick club. —v. hit with a bludgeon; force or bully.

blue n. colour of a clear unclouded sky. —pl. feeling of depression; sad slow music like jazz. —adj. **bluer, bluest.** of the colour blue; depressed; pornographic. —**out of the blue** unexpectedly. —**bluish** adj. —**bluebell** n. flower with blue bell-shaped flowers. —**bluebottle** n. large fly with a dark-blue body. —**blue-collar** adj. denoting manual industrial workers. —**blueprint** n. photographic print of a plan; description of how a plan is expected to work.

bluff[1] v. pretend to be confident in order to influence (someone). —n. act of bluffing.

THESAURUS

blood 1. gore, lifeblood, vital fluid 2. ancestry, birth, descent, extraction, family, kindred, kinship, lineage, race, relations

bloodshed blood bath, butchery, carnage, gore, killing, massacre, murder, slaughter

bloodthirsty brutal, cruel, ferocious, inhuman, ruthless, savage, vicious, warlike

bloody 1. bleeding, blood-soaked, bloodstained, raw 2. cruel, ferocious, fierce, savage

bloom n. 1. blossom, blossoming, bud, flower 2. Fig. beauty, flush, freshness, glow, health, heyday, lustre, perfection, prime, radiance, rosiness ~v. 3. blossom, blow, bud, burgeon, open, sprout

blossom n. 1. bloom, bud, flower, flowers ~v. 2. bloom, burgeon, flower 3. Fig. bloom, develop, flourish, grow, mature, progress, prosper, thrive

blot n. 1. mark, patch, smear, smudge, speck, splodge, spot 2. blemish, blur, defect, disgrace, fault, flaw, spot, stain, taint

blow[1] v. 1. blast, breathe, exhale, fan, pant, puff, waft 2. flow, rush, stream, whirl 3. bear, buffet, drive, fling, flutter, sweep, waft 4. pipe, play, sound, trumpet, vibrate

blow[2] n. 1. bang, buffet, knock, punch, rap, smack, stroke, thump, wallop (Inf.), whack 2. Fig. bombshell, calamity, catastrophe, disappointment, disaster, jolt, misfortune, reverse, setback, shock, upset

blow up 1. distend, enlarge, expand, fill, inflate, swell 2. blast, bomb, burst, detonate, explode, go off, rupture, shatter 3. enlarge, enlarge on, exaggerate, heighten, magnify, overstate

blue 1. azure, cobalt, navy, sapphire, ultramarine 2. Fig. dejected, depressed, despondent, dismal, downcast, down-hearted, fed up, gloomy, glum, low, melancholy, sad, unhappy

blueprint design, draft, layout, outline, pattern, pilot scheme, plan, project, prototype, scheme, sketch

bluff 1. v. deceive, delude, fake, feign, humbug, lie, mislead, pretend, sham 2. n. bluster, boast, deceit, deception, fake, feint, fraud, humbug, idle boast, lie, mere show, pretence, sham, show, subterfuge

DICTIONARY

bluff² n. steep cliff or bank. —adj. good-naturedly frank and hearty.

blunder n. clumsy mistake. —v. make a blunder; act clumsily.

blunderbuss n. obsolete gun with a wide muzzle.

blunt adj. lacking sharpness; (of people, speech, etc.) straightforward or uncomplicated. —v. make less sharp. —**bluntly** adv.

blur v. **blurring, blurred.** make or become vague or less distinct. —n. something vague, hazy, or indistinct. —**blurry** adj.

blurb n. promotional description, as on the jacket of a book.

blurt v. (foll. by out) utter suddenly and involuntarily.

blush v. become red in the face, esp. from embarrassment or shame. —n. reddening of the face.

bluster v. speak loudly or in a bullying way. —n. empty threats or protests. —**blustery** adj. (of weather) rough and windy.

BMA British Medical Association.

BO Informal body odour.

boa constrictor n. large snake that kills its prey by crushing.

boar n. uncastrated male pig; wild pig.

board n. long flat piece of wood; smaller flat piece of rigid material for a specific purpose, e.g. ironing board; group of people who administer a company, trust, etc.; meals provided for money. —v. go aboard (a train, aeroplane, etc.); cover with boards; receive meals and lodgings in return for money. —**on board** on or in a ship, aeroplane, etc. —**boarder** n. pupil who lives at school during the school term. —**boarding house** private house that provides meals and accom-

modation for paying guests. —**boardroom** n. room where the board of a company meets.

boast v. speak too proudly about one's talents, etc.; possess (something to be proud of). —n. boasting statement. —**boastful** adj.

boat n. small vehicle for travelling across water. —**boater** n. flat straw hat. —**boating** n. —**boatswain, bo's'n, bosun** [boh-sn] n. ship's officer in charge of the equipment.

bob¹ v. **bobbing, bobbed.** move up and down repeatedly. —n. short abrupt movement.

bob² n. hair style in which the hair is cut level with the chin. —v. **bobbing, bobbed.** cut (the hair) in a bob.

bobbin n. reel on which thread is wound.

bobble n. small ball of material, usu. for decoration.

bobby n., pl. **-bies.** Informal policeman.

bobsleigh n. sledge used for racing. —v. ride on a bobsleigh.

bode v. be an omen of (good or ill).

bodice n. upper part of a dress.

bodkin n. blunt large-eyed needle.

body n., pl. **bodies.** entire physical structure of an animal or human; trunk or torso; corpse; main part of anything; group regarded as a single entity. —**bodily** adj. relating to the body. —adv. by taking hold of the body. —**bodyguard** n. person or group of people employed to protect someone. —**bodywork** n. outer shell of a motor vehicle.

Boer n. descendant of the Dutch settlers in S Africa.

boffin n. Informal scientist.

bog n. wet spongy ground; Slang toilet. —**boggy** adj. —**bog down** v. **bogging, bogged.** impede physically or mentally.

THESAURUS

blunder 1. n. error, fault, mistake, oversight, slip 2. v. botch, bungle, err

blunt 1. dull, rounded, unsharpened 2. Fig. bluff, brusque, forthright, frank, impolite, outspoken, plain-spoken, rude, tactless, trenchant, uncivil

blur v. 1. befog, cloud, darken, dim, fog, make hazy, mask, obscure, soften 2. blot, smear, smudge, spot, stain ~n. 3. blear, confusion, dimness, fog, haze, indistinctness, obscurity

blush colour, crimson, flush, redden, turn red

bluster 1. v. boast, brag, bulldoze, bully, domineer, hector, rant, roar, storm, swagger, swell, vaunt 2. n. bombast, bragging, bravado, crowing, swagger

board n. 1. panel, plank, slat, timber 2. daily meals, food, meals, provisions 3. committee,

conclave, council, directorate, directors, panel, trustees ~v. 4. embark, embus, enplane, enter, entrain, mount 5. accommodate, feed, house, lodge, put up, quarter, room

boast v. 1. bluster, brag, crow, exaggerate, puff, strut, swagger, talk big (Sl.), vaunt 2. be proud of, exhibit, flatter oneself, possess, show off ~n. 3. avowal, brag, swank (Inf.), vaunt

boastful cocky, conceited, crowing, egotistical, puffed-up, swaggering, (Inf.), swollen-headed, vainglorious

body 1. build, figure, form, frame, physique, shape, torso, trunk 2. cadaver, carcass, corpse, dead body, remains 3. bulk, essence, main part, mass, material, matter, substance 4. association, band, collection, company, con~

DICTIONARY

bogey *n.* something that worries or annoys; *Golf* standard score for a hole or course.

boggle *v.* be surprised, confused, or alarmed.

bogus [boh-guss] *adj.* not genuine.

bogy *n., pl.* **-gies.** same as BOGEY.

bohemian *n., adj.* (person) leading an unconventional life.

boil[1] *v.* (cause to) change from a liquid to a vapour so quickly that bubbles are formed; cook by the process of boiling. —*n.* state or action of boiling. —**boiler** *n.* piece of equipment which provides hot water.

boil[2] *n.* red pus-filled swelling on the skin.

boisterous *adj.* noisy and lively. —**boisterously** *adv.*

bold *adj.* confident and fearless; immodest or impudent. —**boldly** *adv.* —**boldness** *n.*

bole *n.* tree trunk.

bolero *n., pl.* **-ros.** short open jacket; traditional Spanish dance.

bollard *n.* short thick post used to prevent the passage of motor vehicles.

boloney *n.* same as BALONEY.

Bolshevik *n.* Russian Communist; *Offens.* political radical. —**bolshie, bolshy** *adj. Informal* difficult or rebellious.

bolster *v.* support or strengthen. —*n.* long narrow pillow.

bolt *n.* metal pin which screws into a nut; sliding metal bar for fastening a door etc.; flash (of lightning). —*v.* fasten with a bolt; eat hurriedly; run away suddenly. —**bolt upright** stiff and rigid. —**bolt hole** place of escape.

bomb *n.* container fitted with explosive material; *Slang* large amount of money. —*v.* attack with bombs; move very quickly. —**the bomb** nuclear bomb. —**bomber** *n.* aircraft that drops bombs; person who throws or puts a bomb in a particular place. —**bombard** *v.* attack with heavy gunfire or bombs; attack verbally, esp. with questions. —**bombardment** *n.* —**bombshell** *n.* shocking or unwelcome surprise.

bombastic *adj.* using pompous language.

bona fide [bone-a fide-ee] *adj.* real or genuine.

bonanza *n.* sudden good luck or wealth.

bond *n.* something that binds or fastens; feeling of friendship etc., that unites two people or a group of people; written or spoken agreement; *Finance* certificate of debt issued to raise funds. —*pl.* something that restrains or imprisons. —*v.* bind. —**bonded** *adj.*

bondage *n.* slavery.

bone *n.* any of the hard parts in the body that form the skeleton. —*v.* remove the bones from (meat for cooking etc.). —**boneless** *adj.* —**bony** *adj.* having many bones; thin or emaciated. —**bone-dry** *adj.* completely dry. —**bone-idle** *adj.* extremely lazy.

bonfire *n.* large outdoor fire.

bongo *n., pl.* **-gos, -goes.** small drum played with the fingers.

bonhomie [bon-om-ee] *n.* happy friendliness.

bonk *Informal* —*v.* have sex with; hit. —**bonking** *n.*

bonnet *n.* metal cover over a vehicle's engine; hat which ties under the chin.

bonny *adj.* **-nier, -niest.** *Scot.* beautiful.

THESAURUS

gress, corporation, society 5. crowd, horde, majority, mass, mob, multitude, throng

bog fen, marsh, mire, morass, peat bog, quagmire, slough, swamp

bogey bugbear, nightmare, worry

bogus artificial, counterfeit, dummy, fake, false, forged, fraudulent, imitation, sham, spurious

bohemian avant-garde, eccentric, exotic, left bank, nonconformist, offbeat, unconventional, unorthodox

boil agitate, bubble, churn, effervesce, fizz, foam, froth, seethe

boisterous bouncy, clamorous, impetuous, loud, noisy, riotous, rollicking, rowdy, rumbustious, unrestrained, unruly, uproarious, vociferous, wild

bold adventurous, audacious, brave, confident, courageous, daring, dauntless, enterprising, fearless, gallant, heroic, intrepid, valiant

bolt *n.* 1. bar, catch, latch, lock 2. peg, pin, rivet, rod ~*v.* 3. bar, fasten, latch, lock, secure 4. cram, devour, gobble, gorge, gulp, guzzle, stuff, wolf 5. abscond, bound, dash, escape, flee, fly, hurtle, jump, leap, run, rush, spring, sprint

bomb 1. *n.* bombshell, charge, device, explosive, grenade, mine, missile, projectile, rocket, shell, torpedo 2. *v.* attack, blow up, bombard, destroy, shell, strafe, torpedo

bona fide authentic, genuine, lawful, legal, legitimate, real, true

bond *n.* 1. band, binding, chain, cord, fastening, fetter, link, shackle, tie 2. affinity, attachment, connection, link, relation, tie, union 3. compact, contract, covenant, guarantee, obligation, pledge, promise, word ~*v.* 4. bind, connect, fasten, fix together, fuse, glue, gum, paste

DICTIONARY

bonsai *n., pl.* **-sai.** ornamental miniature tree or shrub.

bonus *n.* something given, paid, or received above what is due or expected.

boo *interj.* shout of disapproval. —*v.* **booing, booed.** shout 'boo' to show disapproval.

boob *Slang* —*n.* foolish mistake; female breast.

booby *n., pl.* **-bies.** foolish person. —**booby prize** prize given for the lowest score in a competition. —**booby trap** hidden bomb primed to be set off by an unsuspecting victim.

boogie *v. Informal* dance quickly to pop music.

book *n.* number of printed pages bound together between covers; written work; number of tickets, stamps, etc. fastened together. —*v.* reserve (a place, passage, etc.) in advance; record the name of (a person) in a book or on a list. —**booklet** *n.* thin book with paper covers. —**book-keeping** *n.* systematic recording of business transactions. —**bookmaker** *n.* person whose occupation is taking bets. —**bookworm** *n.* person devoted to reading.

boom[1] *v.* make a loud deep echoing sound; prosper vigorously and rapidly. —*n.* loud deep echoing sound; rapid increase.

boom[2] *n.* pole to which the foot of a sail is attached; pole carrying an overhead microphone.

boomerang *n.* curved wooden missile which returns to the thrower. —*v.* (of a plan) recoil unexpectedly.

boon *n.* something helpful or beneficial.

boor *n.* rude or insensitive person. —**boorish** *adj.*

boost *n.* encouragement or help; increase. —*v.*

improve; increase. —**booster** *n.* small additional injection of a vaccine.

boot[1] *n.* shoe that covers the whole foot and the lower part of the leg; space in a car for luggage; *Informal* kick. —*v. Informal* kick. —**bootee** *n.* baby's soft shoe.

boot[2] *n.* —**to boot** in addition.

booth *n.* small partly enclosed cubicle; stall where goods are sold.

bootleg *v.* **-legging, -legged.** make, carry, or sell (illicit goods). —*adj.* produced, distributed, or sold illicitly. —**bootlegger** *n.*

booty *n., pl.* **-ties.** valuable articles obtained as plunder.

booze *v., n. Informal* (consume) alcoholic drink. —**boozy** *adj.* —**boozer** *n. Informal* person who is fond of drinking; *Informal* pub. —**booze-up** *n. Informal* drinking spree.

bop *v.* **bopping, bopped.** *Informal* dance to pop music.

borax *n.* white mineral used in making glass.

border *n.* dividing line between regions; band around or along the edge of something. —*v.* provide with a border; be nearly the same as, e.g. *his stupidity borders on madness.*

bore[1] *v.* make (a hole) with a drill etc. —*n.* (diameter of the) hollow of a gun barrel.

bore[2] *v.* make weary by being dull or repetitious. —*n.* dull or repetitious person or thing. —**boredom** *n.*

bore[3] *n.* tidal wave in a narrow estuary.

bore[4] *v.* past tense of BEAR[1].

born *v.* a past participle of BEAR[1]. —*adj.* possessing certain qualities from birth, e.g. *a born musician.*

THESAURUS

bonus benefit, bounty, commission, dividend, extra, gift, gratuity, hand-out, prize, reward

book 1. *n.* manual, publication, roll, textbook, tome, tract, volume, work 2. *v.* arrange for, bill, charter, engage, line up, make reservations, organize, reserve, schedule

boom *v.* 1. bang, blast, crash, explode, resound, reverberate, roar, roll, rumble, thunder 2. develop, expand, flourish, gain, grow, increase, intensify, prosper, spurt, succeed, swell, thrive ~*n.* 3. bang, blast, burst, clap, crash, explosion, roar, rumble, thunder 4. advance, development, expansion, gain, growth, improvement, increase, spurt, upsurge

boon advantage, benefaction, benefit, blessing, favour, gift, grant, present, windfall

boost *n.* 1. encouragement, help, improvement, praise, promotion 2. addition, expansion, improvement, increase, increment, jump, rise

~*v.* 3. advance, advertise, assist, encourage, foster, further, improve, inspire, plug (*Inf.*), praise, promote, support, sustain

boot *v. Inf.* dismiss, eject, expel, kick out, oust, sack (*Inf.*), throw out

border 1. bound, boundary, bounds, brim, brink, confine, confines, edge, hem, limit, limits, lip, margin, rim, skirt, verge 2. borderline, boundary, frontier, line, march

bore[1] 1. *v.* drill, mine, penetrate, pierce, sink, tunnel 2. *n.* borehole, calibre, drill hole, hole, shaft, tunnel

bore[2] 1. *v.* be tedious, bother, exhaust, fatigue, pall on, tire, trouble, vex, wear out, weary, worry 2. *n.* bother, drag (*Sl.*), dull person, nuisance, pain (*Inf.*), pest, tiresome person

boredom apathy, dullness, ennui, flatness, monotony, sameness, tedium, tediousness, weariness

DICTIONARY

borne *v.* a past participle of BEAR¹.

boron *n.* chemical element used in hardening steel.

borough *n.* town or district with its own council.

borrow *v.* obtain (something) temporarily; adopt (ideas etc.) from another source. **—borrower** *n.*

borstal *n.* prison for young criminals.

borzoi *n.* tall dog with a long silky coat.

bosh *n. Informal* empty talk, nonsense.

bosom *n.* chest of a person, esp. the female breasts. **—**adj. very dear, e.g. *a bosom friend.*

boss¹ *n.* person in charge of or employing others. **—**v. **—boss around, about** be domineering towards. **—bossy** *adj.*

boss² *n.* raised knob or stud.

botany *n.* study of plants. **—botanic(al)** *adj.* **—botanist** *n.*

botch *v.* spoil through clumsiness. **—**n. (also **botch-up**) badly done piece of work.

both *det.* two considered together.

bother *v.* give annoyance or trouble to; pester; take the time or trouble. **—**n. trouble, fuss, or difficulty. **—bothersome** *adj.*

bottle *n.* container for holding liquids. **—**v. put in a bottle. **—bottleneck** *n.* narrow stretch of road where traffic is held up. **—bottle up** *v.* restrain (powerful emotion).

bottom *n.* lowest, deepest, or farthest removed part of a thing; buttocks. **—**adj. lowest or last. **—bottomless** *adj.*

botulism *n.* severe food poisoning.

boudoir [boo-dwahr] *n.* woman's bedroom or private sitting room.

bougainvillea *n.* climbing plant with red or purple flowers.

bough *n.* large branch of a tree.

bought *v.* past of BUY.

boulder *n.* large rounded rock.

boulevard *n.* wide road.

bounce *v.* (of a ball etc.) rebound from an impact; *Slang* (of a cheque) be returned uncashed owing to a lack of funds in the account. **—**n. act of rebounding; springiness; *Informal* vitality or vigour. **—bouncer** *n.* person employed at a disco etc. to remove unwanted people. **—bouncing** *adj.* vigorous and robust.

bound¹ *v.* past of BIND. **—**adj. destined or certain; compelled or obliged.

bound² *v.* move forwards by jumps. **—**n. jump upwards or forwards.

bound³ *v.* form a boundary of. **—**pl. n. limit, e.g. *his ignorance knows no bounds.* **—boundary** *n.* dividing line that indicates the farthest limit.

bound⁴ *adj.* going or intending to go towards, e.g. *homeward bound.*

bounty *n., pl.* **-ties.** generosity; generous gift or reward. **—bountiful, bounteous** *adj.*

bouquet *n.* bunch of flowers; aroma of wine.

THESAURUS

borrow 1. take on loan, use temporarily 2. acquire, adopt, appropriate, copy, imitate, obtain, pilfer, pirate, simulate, steal, take, use, usurp

bosom 1. *n.* breast, bust, chest 2. *adj.* boon, cherished, close, intimate, very dear

boss¹ chief, director, employer, executive, foreman, gaffer (*Inf.*), governor (*Inf.*), head, leader, manager, master, overseer, owner, supervisor

boss² knob, nub, nubble, point, protuberance, stud, tip

botch *v.* blunder, bungle, cobble, fumble, mar, mend, mess, muff, patch, spoil

bother 1. *v.* alarm, annoy, concern, dismay, distress, disturb, harass, inconvenience, irritate, molest, nag, pester, plague, put out, trouble, upset, vex, worry 2. *n.* annoyance, bustle, difficulty, flurry, fuss, inconvenience, irritation, nuisance, pest, problem, strain, trouble, vexation, worry

bottom *n.* 1. base, basis, bed, deepest part, depths, floor, foot, foundation, groundwork, lowest part, pedestal, support 2. lower side, sole, underneath, underside ~*adj.* 3. base, basement, basic, fundamental, ground, last, lowest, undermost

bounce *v.* 1. bound, bump, jump, leap, rebound, recoil, ricochet, spring, thump ~*n.* 2. bound, elasticity, give, rebound, recoil, resilience, spring, springiness 3. animation, dynamism, energy, go (*Inf.*), life, liveliness, pep, vigour, vitality, vivacity, zip (*Inf.*)

bound¹ *adj.* 1. certain, destined, doomed, fated, sure 2. compelled, constrained, forced, obligated, obliged, pledged, required

bound² *v./n.* bounce, caper, frisk, gambol, hurdle, jump, leap, pounce, prance, skip, spring, vault

bound³ *n. Usually plural* border, boundary, confine, edge, extremity, fringe, limit, line, march, margin, rim, verge

boundary barrier, border, borderline, bounds, brink, confines, edge, extremity, fringe, frontier, limits, margin, precinct

bountiful beneficent, generous, liberal, munificent, open-handed, princely, unstinting

DICTIONARY

bourbon [**bur**-bn] *n. US* whiskey made from maize.

bourgeois [**boor**-zhwah] *adj., n. Offens.* middle-class (person).

bout *n.* period of activity or illness; boxing or wrestling match.

boutique *n.* small clothes shop.

bovine *adj.* relating to cattle; rather slow and stupid.

bow¹ *v.* lower (one's head) or bend (one's knee or body) as a sign of respect or shame; comply or accept. —*n.* movement made when bowing.

bow² *n.* knot with two loops and loose ends; weapon for shooting arrows; long stick stretched with horsehair for playing stringed instruments. —**bow-legged** *adj.* bandy.

bow³ *n.* front end of a ship.

bowdlerize *v.* remove words regarded as indecent from (a play etc.). —**bowdlerization** *n.*

bowel *n.* intestine, esp. the large intestine. —*pl.* innermost part.

bower *n.* shady leafy shelter.

bowl¹ *n.* round container with an open top; hollow part of an object.

bowl² *n.* large heavy ball. —*pl.* game played on smooth grass with wooden bowls. —*v. Cricket* send (a ball) towards the batsman. —**bowler** *n.* —**bowling** *n.* game in which bowls are rolled at a group of pins.

bowler *n.* stiff felt hat with a rounded crown.

box¹ *n.* container with a flat base and sides; separate compartment in a theatre, stable, etc.; *Informal* television. —*v.* put into a box. —**box office** place where theatre or cinema tickets are sold.

box² *v.* fight (an opponent) in a boxing match. —**boxer** *n.* man who participates in the sport of boxing; medium-sized dog similar to a bulldog. —**boxing** *n.* sport of fighting with the fists.

box³ *n.* evergreen tree with shiny leaves.

boy *n.* male child. —**boyish** *adj.* —**boyhood** *n.* —**boyfriend** *n.* woman's male companion.

boycott *v.* refuse to deal with or engage in. —*n.* instance of boycotting.

Br *Chem.* bromine.

bra *n.* woman's undergarment for supporting the breasts.

brace *n.* object fastened to something to straighten or support it; pair, esp. of game birds. —*pl.* straps worn over the shoulders to hold up trousers. —*v.* steady or prepare (oneself) for something unpleasant; strengthen or fit with a brace. —**bracing** *adj.* refreshing and invigorating.

bracelet *n.* ornamental chain for the wrist.

bracken *n.* large fern.

bracket *n.* pair of characters used to enclose a section of writing; group falling within certain defined limits; support fixed to a wall. —*v.* **-eting, -eted.** put in brackets; class together.

brackish *adj.* (of water) slightly salty.

bract *n.* leaf at the base of a flower.

brad *n.* small tapered nail. —**bradawl** *n.* small boring tool.

brag *v.* **bragging, bragged.** speak arrogantly and boastfully. —**braggart** *n.*

Brahman, Brahmin *n.* member of the highest Hindu caste.

braid *v.* interweave (hair, thread, etc.). —*n.* length of hair, etc. that has been braided; narrow ornamental tape of woven silk etc.

Braille *n.* system of writing for the blind, consisting of raised dots interpreted by touch.

brain *n.* soft mass of nervous tissue in the head; intellectual ability. —*v.* hit (someone) hard on the head. —**brainless** *adj.* stupid. —**brainy** *adj. Informal* clever. —**brainchild** *n.* idea produced by creative thought. —**brainwash** *v.* force (a person) to change his or her beliefs, esp. by methods based on isolation, pain, sleeplessness, etc. —**brainwave** *n.* sudden idea.

THESAURUS

bout competition, contest, encounter, engagement, fight, match, set-to

bow *v.* 1. bend, droop, genuflect, incline, make obeisance, nod, stoop 2. accept, comply, concede, defer, give in, relent, submit, surrender, yield ~*n.* 3. bending, bob, genuflexion, inclination, nod, obeisance

bowl basin, deep dish, vessel

box¹ carton, case, chest, container, pack, package, trunk

box² *v.* exchange blows, fight, spar

boxer fighter, prizefighter, pugilist, sparrer, sparring partner

boy fellow, junior, lad, schoolboy, stripling, youngster, youth

boycott ban, bar, black, blackball, blacklist, exclude, outlaw, prohibit, proscribe, refuse, reject, spurn

boyfriend admirer, date, follower, lover, man, steady, suitor, swain

bracing brisk, cool, crisp, energizing, exhilarating, fresh, invigorating, lively, refreshing, stimulating, tonic, vigorous

brainless foolish, idiotic, inept, mindless, senseless, stupid, thoughtless, unintelligent, witless

DICTIONARY

braise *v.* stew slowly in a covered pan.

brake *n.* device for slowing or stopping a vehicle. —*v.* slow down or stop by using a brake.

bramble *n.* prickly shrub that produces blackberries.

bran *n.* husks of cereal grain.

branch *n.* secondary stem of a tree; offshoot or subsidiary part of something larger or more complex. —*v.* (of stems, roots, etc.) grow and diverge (from another part). —**branch out** *v.* expand one's interests.

brand *n.* particular product; particular kind or variety; identifying mark burnt onto the skin of an animal. —*v.* mark with a brand; denounce or stigmatize. —**brand-new** *adj.* absolutely new.

brandish *v.* wave (a weapon etc.) in a threatening way.

brandy *n., pl.* **-dies.** alcoholic spirit distilled from wine.

brash *adj.* self-confident and aggressive. —**brashness** *n.*

brass *n.* alloy of copper and zinc; group of wind instruments made of brass; *Informal* money. —**brassy** *adj.* like brass, esp. in colour; insolent or brazen.

brassiere *n.* bra.

brat *n.* unruly child.

bravado *n.* showy display of self-confidence.

brave *adj.* having or showing courage, resolution, and daring. —*n.* North American Indian warrior. —*v.* confront with resolution or courage. —**bravery** *n.*

brawl *n.* rough fight. —*v.* fight noisily.

brawn *n.* physical strength; pressed meat from the head of a pig or calf. —**brawny** *adj.*

bray *v.* (of a donkey) utter its loud harsh sound. —*n.* donkey's loud harsh sound.

brazen *adj.* shameless and bold. —**brazenly** *adv.*

brazier [bray-zee-er] *n.* container for burning charcoal or coal.

breach *n.* breaking or violation of a promise etc.; gap or break. —*v.* break (a promise etc.); make a gap in.

bread *n.* food made of baked flour and water; *Slang* money. —**breadwinner** *n.* person whose earnings support a family.

breadth *n.* extent of something from side to side.

break *v.* **breaking, broke, broken.** separate or become separated into two or more pieces; damage or become damaged so as to be inoperative; fail to observe (an agreement etc.); disclose or be disclosed, e.g. *he broke the news;* bring or come to an end, e.g. *the good weather broke at last;* weaken or be weakened, as in spirit; cut through or penetrate; improve on or surpass, e.g. *break a record;* (of the male voice) become permanently deeper at puberty. —*n.* act or result of breaking; gap or interruption in continuity; *Informal* fortunate opportunity. —**break even** *v.* make neither a profit nor a loss. —**breakable** *adj.* —**breakage** *n.* —**breaker** *n.* large wave. —**break down** *v.* cease to function; yield to strong emotion; analyse. —**breakdown** *n.* act or instance of breaking down; nervous breakdown; analysis. —**break-in** *n.* illegal entering of a building, esp. by thieves. —**breakneck** *adj.* fast and dangerous. —**break off** *v.* sever or detach; end (a relationship etc.). —**break out** *v.* begin or arise suddenly. —**breakthrough** *n.* important development or discovery. —**break up** *v.* (cause to) separate; (of a relationship) come to

---

THESAURUS

brake 1. *n.* check, constraint, control, curb, rein, restraint 2. *v.* check, decelerate, halt, moderate, reduce speed, slacken, slow, stop

branch 1. arm, bough, limb, offshoot, prong, ramification, shoot, spray, sprig 2. chapter, department, division, local office, office, part, section, subdivision, subsection, wing

brand *n.* 1. cast, class, grade, kind, make, quality, sort, species, type, variety ~*v.* 2. burn, burn in, label, mark, scar, stamp 3. denounce, disgrace, expose, mark, stigmatize

brandish display, exhibit, flourish, raise, shake, swing, wield

bravado bluster, boastfulness, bombast, brag, swagger

brave bold, courageous, daring, fearless, gallant, heroic, intrepid, plucky, resolute, valiant

bravery boldness, courage, daring, fortitude, gallantry, grit, guts (*Inf.*), hardiness, heroism, intrepidity, mettle, pluck, pluckiness, spirit, valour

brawl 1. *n.* argument, battle, broil, clash, disorder, dispute, fight, fracas, fray, free-for-all (*Inf.*), quarrel, row (*Inf.*), rumpus, scrap (*Inf.*), uproar, wrangle 2. *v.* battle, dispute, fight, quarrel, row (*Inf.*), scrap (*Inf.*), scuffle, wrangle, wrestle

breach 1. break, chasm, cleft, crack, fissure, gap, hole, opening, rent, rift, rupture, split 2. infringement, offence, transgression, trespass, violation

bread diet, fare, food, nourishment, nutriment, provisions, subsistence, sustenance, viands, victuals

breadth latitude, span, spread, wideness, width

DICTIONARY

an end; (of a school) close for the holidays.
—**breakwater** n. wall that extends into the sea to
protect a harbour or beach from the force of
waves.

breakfast v., n. (eat) the first meal of the day.

bream n. freshwater silvery fish.

breast n. either of the two soft fleshy milk-
secreting glands on a woman's chest; chest. —v.
meet at breast level, e.g. *she breasted the finishing line.* —**breaststroke** n. swimming stroke
performed on the front.

breath n. taking in and letting out of air during
breathing; air taken in and let out during breathing. —**breathless** adj. —**breathtaking** adj. causing awe or excitement. —**breathe** v. take in
oxygen and give out carbon dioxide; whisper.
—**breather** n. *Informal* short rest. —**breathing** n.

Breathalyzer n. ® device for estimating the
amount of alcohol in the breath. —**breathalyze**
v.

bred v. past of BREED.

breech n. buttocks; part of a firearm behind the
barrel. —**breech delivery** birth of baby with the
feet or buttocks appearing first.

breeches pl. n. trousers extending to just below
the knee.

breed v. **breeding, bred.** produce new or improved strains of (domestic animals or plants);
bear (offspring); produce or be produced, e.g.
breed trouble. —n. group of animals etc. within a
species; kind or sort. —**breeder** n. —**breeding** n.
result of good upbringing or training.

breeze n. gentle wind. —v. move quickly or
casually. —**breezy** adj. windy; casual or carefree.

brethren pl. n. *Old-fashioned* (used in religious
contexts) brothers.

breve n. long musical note.

breviary n., pl. -**aries.** book of prayers to be
recited daily by a Roman Catholic priest.

brevity n. shortness.

brew v. make (beer, ale, etc.) by steeping,
boiling, and fermentation; prepare (a drink) by
infusing; be impending or forming. —n. beverage produced by brewing. —**brewer** n. —**brewery** n. company that brews beer etc.; place
where beer etc. is brewed.

THESAURUS

break v. 1. batter, burst, crack, crash, demolish,
destroy, divide, fracture, fragment, part, rend,
separate, shatter, shiver, smash, snap, splinter, split, tear 2. breach, disobey, disregard,
infringe, transgress, violate 3. demoralize, dispirit, enfeeble, impair, incapacitate, subdue,
tame, undermine, weaken 4. *Of a record, etc.*
beat, better, cap (*Inf.*), exceed, excel, go
beyond, outdo, outstrip, surpass, top 5. appear, burst out, be disclosed, emerge, erupt,
happen, occur ~n. 6. breach, cleft, crack, division, fissure, fracture, gap, gash, hole, opening, rent, rift, rupture, split, tear 7. breather
(*Inf.*), halt, interlude, intermission, interruption, interval, let-up (*Inf.*), lull, pause, recess,
respite, rest, suspension

breakdown 1. collapse, disintegration, disruption, failure, stoppage 2. analysis, detailed
list, diagnosis, dissection, itemization

break-in burglary, invasion, robbery

break off 1. detach, divide, part, pull off, separate, sever, snap off, splinter 2. cease, desist,
discontinue, end, finish, halt, pause, stop,
suspend, terminate

break out appear, arise, begin, commence,
emerge, happen, occur, set in, spring up, start

breakthrough advance, development, discovery,
find, gain, improvement, invention, leap, progress

break up adjourn, disband, dismantle, disperse,
disrupt, dissolve, divide, divorce, end, part,

scatter, separate, sever, split, stop, suspend,
terminate

breath air, exhalation, gasp, gulp, inhalation,
pant, respiration, wheeze

breathe 1. draw in, gasp, gulp, inhale and
exhale, pant, puff, respire, wheeze 2. articulate, express, murmur, say, sigh, utter, voice,
whisper

breathless exhausted, gasping, gulping, out of
breath, panting, spent, wheezing, winded

breathtaking amazing, astonishing, awe-
inspiring, awesome, exciting, impressive,
magnificent, moving, overwhelming, stunning
(*Inf.*), thrilling

breed 1. v. bear, beget, bring forth, engender,
generate, hatch, multiply, originate, procreate,
produce, propagate, reproduce 2. n. brand,
class, extraction, family, ilk, kind, line, lineage pedigree, progeny, race, sort, species,
stamp, stock, strain, type, variety

breeding civility, conduct, courtesy, cultivation, culture, gentility, manners, polish, refinement, urbanity

breeze air, draught, flurry, gust, light wind, puff
of air, waft, whiff, zephyr

brevity 1. conciseness, crispness, curtness,
economy, pithiness, succinctness, terseness 2.
ephemerality, impermanence, shortness, transience, transitoriness

brew v. 1. boil, ferment, infuse (*tea*), make
(*beer*), seethe, soak, steep, stew 2. breed, con-

DICTIONARY

briar *n.* wild rose with long thorny stems.

bribe *n.* anything offered or given to someone to gain favour, influence, etc. —*v.* give (someone) a bribe. —**bribery** *n.*

bric-a-brac *n.* miscellaneous small ornamental objects.

brick *n.* (rectangular block of) baked clay used in building. —*v.* build, enclose, or fill with bricks. —**bricklayer** *n.* person who builds with bricks.

bride *n.* woman who has just been or is about to be married. —**bridal** *adj.* —**bridegroom** *n.* man who has just been or is about to be married. —**bridesmaid** *n.* girl who attends a bride at her wedding.

bridge[1] *n.* structure for crossing a river etc.; platform from which a ship is steered or controlled; upper part of the nose; piece of wood supporting the strings of a violin etc. —*v.* build or form a bridge over (something). —**bridgehead** *n.* fortified position at the end of a bridge nearest the enemy.

bridge[2] *n.* card game based on whist.

bridle *n.* headgear for controlling a horse. —*v.* put a bridle on (a horse); restrain. —**bridle path** path suitable for riding horses.

brief *adj.* short in duration. —*n.* condensed statement or written synopsis; set of instructions.

—*pl.* men's or women's underpants. —*v.* give information and instructions to (a person). —**briefly** *adv.* —**briefcase** *n.* small flat case for carrying papers, books, etc.

brier *n.* same as BRIAR.

brig *n.* two-masted square-rigged ship.

brigade *n.* army unit smaller than a division; group of people organized for a certain task. —**brigadier** *n.* high-ranking army officer.

brigand *n.* bandit.

brigantine *n.* two-masted sailing ship.

bright *adj.* emitting or reflecting much light; (of colours) intense; clever. —**brightly** *adv.* —**brightness** *n.* —**brighten** *v.*

brilliant *adj.* shining with light; splendid; extremely clever. —**brilliance, brilliancy** *n.*

brim *n.* projecting edge of a hat; upper rim of a cup etc. —*v.* **brimming, brimmed.** be full to the brim.

brimstone *n. Obs.* sulphur.

brindled *adj.* brown streaked with another colour.

brine *n.* salt water. —**briny** *adj.* very salty. —**the briny** *Informal* the sea.

bring *v.* **bringing, brought.** carry, convey, or take to a designated place or person; cause to

---

THESAURUS

coct, contrive, develop, devise, excite, foment, form, gather, hatch, plan, plot, project, scheme, start, stir up

bribe 1. *n.* allurement, enticement, graft, hush money (*Sl.*), incentive, inducement, pay-off (*Inf.*) 2. *v.* buy off, corrupt, get at, grease the palm *or* hand of (*Sl.*), influence by gifts, lure, pay off (*Inf.*), reward, square, suborn

bribery buying off, corruption, graft, inducement

bridge 1. *n.* arch, flyover, overpass, span, viaduct 2. *v.* arch over, attach, bind, connect, couple, cross, cross over, extend across, go over, join, link, reach across, span, traverse, unite

bridle *v.* check, constrain, control, curb, govern, master, moderate, repress, restrain, subdue

brief *adj.* 1. compressed, concise, crisp, curt, laconic, limited, pithy, short, succinct, terse, thumbnail, to the point 2. fast, fleeting little, momentary, quick, short, short-lived, swift, transitory ~*n.* 3. abstract, digest, epitome, outline, précis, sketch, summary, synopsis ~*v.* 4. advise, explain, fill in (*Inf.*), instruct, prepare, prime

briefly concisely, cursorily, curtly, hastily, hurriedly, in brief, in outline, in passing, momentarily, precisely, quickly, shortly

bright 1. beaming, blazing, brilliant, effulgent, flashing, gleaming, glistening, glittering, glowing, illuminated, intense, luminous, radiant, resplendent, shining, sparkling, twinkling, vivid 2. acute, astute, aware, brilliant, clear-headed, clever, ingenious, intelligent, inventive, keen, quick, quick-witted, sharp, smart, wide-awake

brighten clear up, enliven, gleam, glow, illuminate, lighten, light up, make brighter, shine

brilliance, brilliancy 1. blaze, brightness, dazzle, gleam, glitter, intensity, radiance, sheen, sparkle, vividness 2. aptitude, braininess, cleverness, distinction, excellence, genius, giftedness, greatness, talent, wisdom 3. éclat, glamour, grandeur, magnificence, splendour

brilliant 1. ablaze, bright, dazzling, glittering, glossy, intense, luminous, radiant, refulgent, scintillating, shining, sparkling, vivid 2. celebrated, eminent, exceptional, famous, glorious, magnificent, outstanding, splendid, superb 3. accomplished, acute, astute, brainy, clever, discerning, expert, gifted, intellectual, intelligent, penetrating, profound, quick, talented

brim border, brink, circumference, edge, lip, margin, rim, skirt, verge

DICTIONARY

happen; *Law* put forward (charges) officially. **—bring about** *v.* cause to happen. **—bring off** *v.* succeed in achieving. **—bring out** *v.* publish or have (a book) published; reveal or cause to be seen. **—bring up** *v.* rear (a child); mention; vomit (food).

brink *n.* edge of a steep place.

brisk *adj.* lively and quick. **—briskly** *adv.*

brisket *n.* beef from the breast of a cow.

bristle *n.* short stiff hair. *—v.* (cause to) stand up like bristles; show anger. **—bristly** *adj.*

Brit *n. Informal* British person.

brittle *adj.* hard but easily broken. **—brittleness** *n.*

broach *v.* introduce (a topic) for discussion; open (a bottle or barrel).

broad *adj.* having great breadth or width; not detailed; extensive, e.g. *broad support;* vulgar or coarse; strongly marked, e.g. *a broad Yorkshire accent.* **—broadly** *adv.* **—broaden** *v.* **—broad bean** thick flat edible bean. **—broad-minded** *adj.* tolerant. **—broadside** *n.* strong verbal or written attack; *Naval* firing of all the guns on one side of a ship at once.

broadcast *v.* transmit (a programme or an-

nouncement) on radio or television; make widely known. *—n.* programme or announcement on radio or television. **—broadcaster** *n.* **—broadcasting** *n.*

brocade *n.* rich woven fabric with a raised design.

broccoli *n.* type of cabbage with greenish flower heads.

brochure *n.* booklet that contains information about a product or service.

brogue[1] *n.* sturdy walking shoe.

brogue[2] *n.* strong accent, esp. Irish.

broil *v.* grill.

broke *v.* past tense of BREAK. *—adj. Informal* having no money.

broken *v.* past participle of BREAK. *—adj.* fractured or smashed; (of the speech of a foreigner) imperfectly spoken, e.g. *broken English.* **—brokenhearted** *adj.* overwhelmed by grief.

broker *n.* agent who buys or sells shares, securities, etc.

brolly *n., pl.* **-lies.** *Informal* umbrella.

bromide *n.* chemical compound used in medicine and photography.

bromine *n.* toxic liquid element.

THESAURUS

bring 1. accompany, bear, carry, conduct, convey, deliver, escort, fetch, gather, guide, import, lead, take, transfer, transport, usher 2. cause, contribute to, create, effect, engender, inflict, occasion, produce, result in, wreak

bring about accomplish, achieve, cause, compass, create, effect, make happen, manage, occasion, produce, realize

bring off accomplish, achieve, carry out, discharge, execute, perform, pull off, succeed

bring up develop, educate, form, nurture, raise, rear, support, teach, train

brink border, brim, edge, fringe, frontier, limit, margin, point, rim, skirt

brisk active, agile, alert, bustling, busy, energetic, lively, nimble, quick, speedy, spry, vigorous, vivacious

briskly actively, efficiently, energetically, firmly, incisively, nimbly, promptly, quickly, rapidly, readily, smartly, vigorously

bristle 1 *n.* barb, hair, prickle, spine, stubble, thorn, whisker 2. *v.* be angry, bridle, flare up, rage, see red, seethe

brittle breakable, crisp, crumbly, delicate, fragile, frail, shivery

broach bring up, hint at, introduce, mention, open up, propose, speak of, suggest, talk of, touch on

broad 1. ample, extensive, large, roomy, spa-

cious, vast, voluminous, wide, widespread 2. comprehensive, far-reaching, general, inclusive, sweeping, universal, unlimited, wide, wide-ranging

broadcast *v.* 1. air, beam, radio, relay, show, televise, transmit 2. advertise, announce, circulate, disseminate, make public, proclaim, promulgate, publish, report, spread ~*n.* 3. programme, show, transmission

broaden develop, enlarge, expand, extend, increase, open up, spread, stretch, swell, widen

broad-minded catholic, flexible, indulgent, liberal, open-minded, permissive, responsive, tolerant, unbiased, unprejudiced

broadside abuse, assault, attack, censure, criticism, diatribe

brochure booklet, circular, folder, handbill, leaflet, pamphlet

broken 1. burst, demolished, destroyed, fractured, fragmented, ruptured, separated, severed, shattered 2. disconnected, discontinuous, disturbed, erratic, fragmentary, incomplete, intermittent, interrupted, spasmodic

brokenhearted crestfallen, desolate, despairing, devastated, disappointed, disconsolate, grief-stricken, inconsolable, miserable, mournful, prostrated, sorrowful, wretched

broker agent, dealer, factor, go-between, intermediary, middleman

DICTIONARY

bronchus [bronk-uss] *n., pl.* **bronchi** [bronk-eye]. either of the two branches of the windpipe. —**bronchial** *adj.* —**bronchitis** *n.* inflammation of the bronchi.

bronco *n., pl.* **-cos.** (in the US) wild or partially tamed pony.

brontosaurus *n.* very large plant-eating four-footed dinosaur.

bronze *n.* alloy of copper and tin; statue, medal, etc. made of bronze. —*adj.* made of, or coloured like, bronze. —*v.* (esp. of the skin) make or become brown.

brooch *n.* ornament with a pin for attaching to clothes.

brood *n.* number of birds produced at one hatching; all the children of a family. —*v.* think long and morbidly. —**broody** *adj.* moody and sullen; (of a hen) wishing to hatch eggs.

brook[1] *n.* small stream.

brook[2] *v.* bear or tolerate.

broom *n.* long-handled sweeping brush; yellow-flowered shrub. —**broomstick** *n.* handle of a broom.

broth *n.* soup, usu. containing vegetables.

brothel *n.* house where men pay to have sex with prostitutes.

brother *n.* boy or man with the same parents as another person; member of a male religious order. —**brotherly** *adj.* —**brotherhood** *n.* fellowship; association, such as a trade union. —**brother-in-law** *n.* brother of one's husband or wife; husband of one's sister.

brought *v.* past of BRING.

brow *n.* forehead; eyebrow; top of a hill.

browbeat *v.* frighten (someone) with threats.

brown *n.* colour of earth or wood. —*adj.* of the colour brown. —*v.* make or become brown. —**brownish** *adj.* —**browned-off** *adj. Informal* bored and depressed.

Brownie (Guide) *n.* junior Girl Guide.

browse *v.* look through (a book or articles for sale) in a casual manner; nibble on young shoots or leaves. —*n.* instance of browsing.

bruise *n.* discoloured area on the skin caused by an injury. —*v.* cause a bruise on. —**bruiser** *n.* strong tough person.

brunch *n. Informal* breakfast and lunch combined.

brunette *n.* girl or woman with brown hair.

brunt *n.* main force or shock of a blow, attack, etc.

brush[1] *n.* device made of bristles, wires, etc. used for cleaning, painting, etc.; brief unpleasant encounter; fox's tail. —*v.* apply, remove, clean, etc. with a brush; touch lightly and briefly. —**brush off** *v. Slang* dismiss or ignore (someone). —**brush up** *v.* refresh one's knowledge of (a subject).

brush[2] *n.* thick growth of shrubs.

brusque *adj.* blunt or curt in manner or speech. —**brusquely** *adv.* —**brusqueness** *n.*

Brussels sprout *n.* vegetable like a tiny cabbage.

THESAURUS

bronze brownish, chestnut, copper, reddish-brown, rust, tan

brood 1. *v.* agonize, dwell upon, fret, meditate, mope, muse, repine, ruminate, think upon 2. *n.* breed, chicks, children, clutch, family, hatch, infants, issue, litter, offspring, progeny, young

brook beck, burn, rill, rivulet, stream, streamlet, watercourse

brother 1. kin, kinsman, relation, relative, sibling 2. cleric, friar, monk, regular, religious

brotherhood 1. camaraderie, companionship, comradeship, fellowship, friendliness, kinship 2. alliance, association, clan, clique, community, coterie, fraternity, guild, league, society, union

brotherly affectionate, amicable, benevolent, cordial, fraternal, friendly, kind, neighbourly, sympathetic

browbeat bulldoze (*Inf.*), bully, coerce, cow, domineer, dragoon, hector, intimidate, oppress, overawe, overbear, threaten, tyrannize

brown auburn, bronze, brunette, chestnut, chocolate, coffee, dark, dun, dusky, hazel, rust, sunburnt, tan, tanned, tawny, toasted, umber

browse 1. dip into, leaf through, look through, peruse, scan, skim, survey 2. crop, eat, feed, graze, nibble, pasture

bruise 1. *v.* blacken, blemish, contuse, crush, damage, deface, discolour, injure, mar, mark 2. *n.* blemish, contusion, discoloration, injury, mark, swelling

brunt burden, force, full force, impact, pressure, shock, strain, stress, thrust, violence

brush[1] *n.* 1. besom, broom, sweeper 2. clash, conflict, fight, fracas, scrap, set-to (*Inf.*), skirmish, tussle ~*v.* 3. buff, clean, paint, polish, sweep, wash 4. contact, flick, glance, graze, kiss, scrape, stroke, sweep, touch

brush[2] *n.* bushes, copse, scrub, shrubs, thicket, undergrowth

brush up go over, polish up, read up, relearn, revise, study

DICTIONARY

brute *n.* brutal person; animal other than man. —*adj.* wholly instinctive or physical, like that of an animal; without reason. —**brutish** *adj.* of or like an animal. —**brutal** *adj.* cruel and vicious. —**brutally** *adv.* —**brutality** *n.* —**brutalize** *v.*

BS British Standard.

BSc Bachelor of Science.

BSE bovine spongiform encephalopathy.

BST British Summer Time.

bubble *n.* ball of air in a liquid. —*v.* form bubbles; move or flow with a gurgling sound. —**bubbly** *adj.* excited and lively; full of bubbles. —**bubble over** *v.* express an emotion freely.

bubonic plague [bew-**bonn**-ik] *n.* acute infectious disease characterized by swellings.

buccaneer *n.* pirate.

buck[1] *n.* male of certain animals, such as the deer and hare. —*v.* (of a horse etc.) jump with legs stiff and back arched. —**buck up** *v.* make or become more cheerful.

buck[2] *n.* US & Aust. slang dollar.

buck[3] *n.* —**pass the buck** *Informal* shift blame or responsibility onto someone else.

bucket *n.* open-topped round container with a handle. —**bucketful** *n.* —**bucket down** *v.* **-eting, -eted.** rain heavily.

buckle *n.* metal clasp for fastening a belt or strap. —*v.* fasten or be fastened with a buckle; (cause to) bend out of shape through pressure and heat. —**buckle down** *v.* apply oneself with determination.

buckram *n.* coarse stiffened cloth.

buckshee *adj. Slang* free.

buckteeth *pl. n.* projecting upper front teeth. —**buck-toothed** *adj.*

buckwheat *n.* small black grain used for making flour.

bucolic [bew-**koll**-ik] *adj.* rustic.

bud *n.* swelling on a tree or plant that develops into a leaf or flower. —*v.* **budding, budded.** produce buds; develop or grow, e.g. *a budding actor.*

Buddhism *n.* eastern religion founded by Buddha. —**Buddhist** *n., adj.*

buddleia *n.* shrub with purple or yellow flowers.

buddy *n., pl.* **-dies.** *Informal, esp. US* friend.

budge *v.* move slightly.

budgerigar *n.* small brightly coloured Aust. bird.

budget *n.* financial plan for a period of time; money allocated for a specific purpose. —*v.* **-eting, -eted.** plan the expenditure of (money or time). —*adj.* cheap. —**budgetary** *adj.*

budgie *n. Informal* short for BUDGERIGAR.

buff[1] *adj.* dull yellowish-brown. —*v.* rub with soft material. —**in the buff** *Informal* naked.

buff[2] *n. Informal* expert on a given subject.

buffalo *n.* type of cattle; *US* bison.

buffer *n.* something that lessens shock or protects from damaging impact, circumstances, etc.

buffet[1] [**boof**-ay] *n.* refreshment bar; meal at which guests serve themselves.

buffet[2] [**buff**-it] *v.* **-feting, -feted.** knock against or about.

buffoon *n.* clown or fool. —**buffoonery** *n.*

bug *n.* small insect; *Informal* minor illness; small mistake in a computer programme; concealed microphone. —*v.* **bugging, bugged.** *Informal* irritate (someone); conceal a microphone in a room or phone).

THESAURUS

brutal bloodthirsty, cruel, ferocious, heartless, inhuman, merciless, pitiless, remorseless, ruthless, savage, uncivilized, vicious

brute 1. animal, beast, creature, wild animal 2. barbarian, beast, devil, fiend, monster, ogre, sadist, savage, swine

bubble *n.* 1. bead, blister, drop, droplet, globule, vesicle ~*v.* 2. boil, effervesce, fizz, foam, froth, seethe, sparkle 3. babble, burble, gurgle, murmur

buccaneer pirate, privateer, sea-rover

buckle *n.* 1. catch, clasp, clip, fastener ~*v.* 2. catch, clasp, close, fasten, hook, secure 3. bend, bulge, cave in, collapse, crumple, fold, twist, warp

bud 1. *n.* germ, shoot, sprout 2. *v.* burgeon, develop, grow, shoot, sprout

budding beginning, burgeoning, fledgling, flowering, growing, incipient, nascent, potential, promising

budge dislodge, give way, inch, move, propel, push, remove, roll, shift, slide, stir

budget 1. *n.* allowance, cost, finances, funds, means, resources 2. *v.* apportion, cost, cost out, estimate, plan, ration

buff addict, admirer, connoisseur, devotee, enthusiast, expert, fan

buffer bumper, cushion, fender, intermediary, safeguard, screen, shield

buffet[1] *n.* café, cafeteria, cold table, counter, cupboard, snack bar

buffet[2] *v.* bang, batter, beat, box, bump, knock, pound, push, rap, shove, slap, strike, thump

DICTIONARY

bugbear *n.* thing that causes obsessive anxiety.

bugger *n. Taboo slang* unpleasant or difficult person or thing; person who practises buggery. —*v. Slang* tire; practise buggery with. —**buggery** *n.* anal intercourse.

bugle *n.* instrument like a small trumpet. —**bugler** *n.*

build *v.* **building, built.** make, construct, or form by joining parts or materials. —*n.* shape of the body. —**builder** *n.* —**building** *n.* structure with walls and a roof. —**building society** organization where money can be borrowed or invested. —**build-up** *n.* gradual increase. —**built-up** *adj.* having many buildings.

bulb *n.* glass part of an electric lamp; onion-shaped root which grows into a flower or plant. —**bulbous** *adj.* round and fat.

bulge *n.* swelling on a normally flat surface; sudden increase in number. —*v.* swell outwards. —**bulging** *adj.*

bulk *n.* great size or volume; main part. —**in bulk** in large quantities. —**bulky** *adj.*

bulkhead *n.* partition in a ship or aeroplane.

bull[1] *n.* male of some animals, such as cattle, elephants, and whales. —**bullock** *n.* castrated bull. —**bulldog** *n.* sturdy thickset dog with a broad head and a muscular body. —**bulldozer** *n.* powerful tractor for moving earth. —**bulldoze** *v.* —**bullfight** *n.* public show in which a matador kills a bull. —**bull's-eye** *n.* central disc of a target.

bull[2] *n.* papal decree.

bull[3] *n. Informal* complete nonsense.

bullet *n.* small piece of metal fired from a gun.

bulletin *n.* short official report or announcement.

bullion *n.* gold or silver in the form of bars.

bully *n., pl.* **-lies.** person who hurts, persecutes, or intimidates a weaker person. —*v.* **-lying, -lied.** hurt, intimidate, or persecute (a weaker person).

bulrush *n.* tall stiff reed.

bulwark *n.* wall used as a fortification; person or thing acting as a defence.

bum[1] *n. Slang* buttocks or anus.

bum[2] *n. Informal, esp. US* person who avoids work, idler.

bumble *v.* speak, do, or move in a clumsy way. —**bumbling** *adj., n.*

bumblebee *n.* large hairy bee.

bump *v.* knock or strike with a jolt; travel in jerks and jolts. —*n.* (dull thud from an) impact or collision; raised uneven part. —**bumper** *n.* bar on the front and back of a vehicle to protect against damage. —*adj.* unusually large or abundant. —**bump off** *v. Informal* murder.

bumph, bumf *n. Informal* official documents or forms.

bumpkin *n.* awkward simple country person.

bumptious *adj.* offensively self-assertive.

bun *n.* small round cake; hair gathered into a bun shape.

bunch *n.* number of things growing, fastened, or

THESAURUS

buffoon clown, comedian, comic, droll, fool, harlequin, jester, joker, wag

bug *Inf. v.* 1. annoy, badger, bother, disturb, harass, irk, irritate, pester, plague, vex 2. eavesdrop, listen in, spy, tap, wiretap

build 1. *v.* assemble, construct, erect, fabricate, form, make, put up, raise 2. *n.* body, figure, form, frame, physique, shape

building 1. dwelling, edifice, fabric, house, pile, structure 2. construction, erection, raising

build-up development, enlargement, escalation, expansion, gain, growth, increase

bulge *n.* 1. bump, lump, protuberance, swelling 2. boost, increase, rise, surge ~*v.* 3. dilate, distend, enlarge, expand, project, protrude, puff out, sag, stand out, stick out, swell

bulk 1. immensity, largeness, magnitude, massiveness, size, substance, volume, weight 2. body, generality, lion's share, main part, majority, major part, mass, most, nearly all

bulldoze demolish, flatten, level, raze

bullet missile, pellet, projectile, shot, slug

bulletin announcement, communiqué, dispatch, message, news flash, notification, report, statement

bulwark bastion, buttress, defence, fortification, rampart, redoubt

bumbling awkward, blundering, botching, bungling, clumsy, incompetent, inefficient, inept, lumbering, maladroit, muddled, stumbling

bump *v.* 1. bang, crash, hit, knock, slam, smash into, strike 2. bounce, jar, jerk, jolt, rattle, shake ~*n.* 3. bang, blow, crash, hit, impact, jar, jolt, knock, rap, shock, smash, thud, thump 4. bulge, contusion, knob, knot, lump, protuberance, swelling

bumper *adj.* abundant, bountiful, excellent, exceptional, massive, prodigal

bunch 1. *n.* batch, bouquet, bundle, clump, cluster, collection, heap, lot, mass, parcel, pile, quantity, sheaf, spray, stack, tuft 2. *v.* assemble, bundle, cluster, collect, crowd, flock, group, herd, mass, pack

DICTIONARY

grouped together; group, e.g. *a bunch of boys.* —*v.* group or be grouped together in a bunch.

bundle *n.* number of things gathered loosely together. —*v.* cause to go roughly or unceremoniously. —**bundle up** *v.* make into a bundle.

bung *n.* stopper for a cask etc. —*v.* (foll. by *up*) *Informal* close with a bung; *Slang* throw (something) somewhere in a careless manner.

bungalow *n.* one-storey house.

bungle *v.* spoil through incompetence. —**bungler** *n.* —**bungling** *adj., n.*

bunion *n.* inflamed swelling on the big toe.

bunk¹ *n.* narrow shelflike bed. —**bunk bed** one of a pair of beds constructed one above the other.

bunk² *n.* same as BUNKUM.

bunk³ *n.* —**do a bunk** *Slang* leave a place without telling anyone.

bunker *n.* large storage container for coal etc.; sandy hollow on a golf course; underground shelter.

bunkum *n.* nonsense.

bunny *n., pl.* -**nies.** child's word for a rabbit.

Bunsen burner *n.* gas burner used in laboratories.

bunting *n.* decorative flags.

buoy *n.* floating marker anchored in the sea. —*v.* prevent from sinking; encourage or hearten. —**buoyant** *adj.* able to float; cheerful or resilient. —**buoyancy** *n.*

bur *n.* same as BURR¹.

burble *v.* make a bubbling sound; talk quickly and excitedly.

burden¹ *n.* heavy load; something difficult to cope with. —*v.* put a burden on; oppress. —**burdensome** *adj.*

burden² *n.* theme of a speech etc.

bureau *n., pl.* -**reaus,** -**reaux.** writing desk with shelves and drawers; office that provides a service.

bureaucracy *n., pl.* -**cies.** an administrative system based on complex rules and procedures; excessive adherence to complex procedures. —**bureaucrat** *n.* —**bureaucratic** *adj.*

burgeon *v.* develop or grow rapidly.

burgh *n.* Scottish borough.

burglar *n.* person who enters a building to commit a crime, esp. theft. —**burglary** *n.* —**burgle** *v.*

burgundy *n.* type of French wine.

burial *n.* burying of a dead body.

burlesque *n.* artistic work which satirizes a subject by caricature.

burly *adj.* -**lier,** -**liest.** (of a person) broad and strong.

burn¹ *v.* **burning, burnt** *or* **burned.** be or set on fire; destroy or be destroyed by fire; damage, injure, or mark by heat; feel strong emotion. —*n.* injury or mark caused by fire or exposure to heat. —**burning** *adj.* intense; urgent or crucial.

burn² *n. Scot.* small stream.

THESAURUS

bundle *n.* 1. assortment, batch, bunch, collection, group, heap, mass, pile, quantity 2. bag, bale, box, carton, crate, pack, package, packet, pallet, parcel, roll ~*v.* 3. **bundle up** bale, bind, fasten, pack, tie, tie up, truss, wrap

bungle blunder, butcher, make a mess of, mar, mess up, miscalculate, mismanage, muff, ruin, spoil

bungling awkward, blundering, incompetent, inept, maladroit

buoy beacon, float, guide, marker, signal

buoyant 1. afloat, floatable, floating, light 2. blithe, bouncy, breezy, bright, carefree, cheerful, happy, joyful, light-hearted, lively

burden 1. *n.* affliction, anxiety, care, clog, load, onus, sorrow, strain, stress, trial, trouble, weight, worry 2. *v.* bother, encumber, load, oppress, overload, saddle with, strain, tax, weigh down, worry

bureau 1. desk, writing desk 2. agency, branch, department, division, office, service

bureaucracy administration, civil service, government, ministry, officialdom

bureaucrat civil servant, mandarin, minister, officer, official, public servant

burglar housebreaker, pilferer, robber, sneak thief, thief

burial entombment, exequies, funeral, interment, obsequies

buried 1. entombed, interred, laid to rest 2. dead and buried, in the grave 3. covered, forgotten, hidden, suppressed 4. hidden, private, tucked away

burlesque *n.* caricature, mock, mockery, parody, satire

burly beefy, big, broad, bulky, hefty, muscular, powerful, stocky, stout, strapping, strong, sturdy, well-built

burn 1. be ablaze, be on fire, blaze, flame, flare, flash, flicker, glow, smoke 2. char, ignite, incinerate, kindle, light, parch, scorch, set on fire, shrivel, singe, toast, wither

burning ardent, eager, earnest, fervent, frantic, intense, passionate, vehement, zealous

burnish *v.* brighten, buff, furbish, glaze, polish, rub up, shine, smooth

DICTIONARY

burnish *v.* make smooth and shiny by rubbing.

burp *v., n. Informal* belch.

burr[1] *n.* head of a plant with prickles or hooks.

burr[2] *n.* soft trilling sound given to the letter (r) in some English dialects; whirring sound.

burrow *n.* hole dug in the ground by a rabbit etc. —*v.* dig holes in the ground.

bursar *n.* treasurer of a school, college, or university. —**bursary** *n.* scholarship.

burst *v.* **bursting, burst.** (cause to) break open or apart noisily and suddenly; come or go suddenly and forcibly; be full to the point of breaking open. —*n.* instance of breaking open suddenly; sudden and violent outbreak or occurrence. —**burst into** *v.* give vent to (an emotion) suddenly.

bury *v.* **burying, buried.** place in a grave; place in the earth and cover with soil; conceal or hide.

bus *n.* large motor vehicle for carrying passengers. —*v.* **bussing, bussed.** travel or transport by bus.

busby *n., pl.* **-bies.** tall fur hat worn by certain soldiers.

bush *n.* dense woody plant, smaller than a tree; wild uncultivated part of a country. —**bushy** *adj.* (of hair) thick and shaggy. —**bushbaby** *n.* small tree-living mammal with large eyes.

bushel *n.* unit of measure equal to eight gallons.

business *n.* trade or profession; purchase and sale of goods and services; commercial establishment; proper concern or responsibility; affair, e.g. *it's a dreadful business.* —**businesslike** *adj.* —**businessman, businesswoman** *n.*

busker *n.* street entertainer. —**busk** *v.* act as a busker.

bust[1] *n.* woman's bosom; sculpture of the head and shoulders.

bust[2] *Informal* —*v.* **busting, bust** or **busted.** break; (of the police) raid (a place) or arrest (someone). —*adj.* broken. —**go bust** become bankrupt.

bustle[1] *v.* hurry with a show of activity or energy. —*n.* energetic and noisy activity. —**bustling** *adj.*

bustle[2] *n. Hist.* cushion worn by women to hold out their dress below the waist at the back.

busy *adj.* **busier, busiest.** actively employed; full of activity. —*v.* **busying, busied.** keep (someone) busy. —**busily** *adv.* —**busybody** *n.* meddlesome or nosy person.

but *conj.* contrary to expectation; in contrast; other than; without it happening. —*prep.* except. —*adv.* only. —**but for** were it not for.

butane [**bew**-tane] *n.* gas used for fuel.

butch *adj. Slang* markedly or aggressively masculine.

butcher *n.* person who sells the meat of slaughtered animals; brutal murderer. —*v.* slaughter (animals) for meat; kill (people) brutally or indiscriminately. —**butchery** *n.*

THESAURUS

burrow 1. *n.* den, hole, lair, retreat, shelter, tunnel 2. *v.* delve, dig, excavate, hollow out, scoop out, tunnel

burst 1. *v.* blow up, break, crack, explode, fly open, fragment, puncture, rupture, shatter, shiver, split, tear apart 2. *n.* bang, blast, blowout, blow-up, breach, break, crack, discharge, explosion, rupture, split

bury 1. entomb, inearth, inhume, inter, lay to rest 2. conceal, cover, cover up, hide, secrete, stow away

bush 1. hedge, plant, shrub, shrubbery, thicket 2. brush, scrub, the wild

busily actively, briskly, carefully, diligently, earnestly, energetically, industriously, intently, speedily, strenuously

business 1. calling, career, craft, employment, function, job, line, métier, occupation, profession, pursuit, trade, vocation, work 2. company, concern, enterprise, firm, organization, venture 3. commerce, dealings, industry, manufacturing, selling, trade, trading, transaction

businesslike correct, efficient, methodical, orderly, organized, practical, professional, regular, systematic, thorough, well-ordered

businessman, businesswoman capitalist, employer, entrepreneur, executive, financier, industrialist, merchant, tradesman, tycoon

bust bosom, breast, chest, torso

bustle 1. *v.* bestir, dash, fuss, hasten, hurry, rush, scamper, scramble, scurry, stir 2. *n.* activity, ado, agitation, commotion, excitement, flurry, fuss, haste, hurry, stir, to-do, tumult

busy 1. active, assiduous, brisk, diligent, employed, engaged, engrossed, hard at work, industrious, occupied, on duty, slaving, working 2. active, energetic, full, hectic, hustling, lively, restless, tireless, tiring

but *conj.* 1. further, however, moreover, nevertheless, on the contrary, on the other hand, still, yet 2. bar, barring, except, excepting, excluding, notwithstanding, save, with the exception of ~*adv.* 3. just, merely, only, simply, singly solely

butcher *n.* 1. destroyer, killer, murderer, slaughterer, slayer ~*v.* 2. carve, clean, cut

DICTIONARY

butler *n.* chief male servant.

butt[1] *n.* thick end of something; unused end of a cigar or cigarette.

butt[2] *n.* person or thing that is the target of ridicule.

butt[3] *v.* strike with the head or horns. —**butt in** *v.* interrupt a conversation.

butt[4] *n.* large cask.

butter *n.* edible fatty solid made from cream by churning. —*v.* put butter on. —**buttery** *adj.* —**butter up** *v.* flatter.

buttercup *n.* small yellow flower.

butterfingers *n. Informal* person who drops things by mistake.

butterfly *n.* insect with brightly coloured wings; swimming stroke in which both arms move together in a forward circular action.

buttermilk *n.* sourish milk that remains after the butter has been separated from milk.

butterscotch *n.* kind of hard brittle toffee.

buttery *n., pl.* **-teries.** (in some universities) room where food and drink are sold.

buttock *n.* either of the two fleshy masses that form the human rump.

button *n.* small hard object sewn to clothing to fasten it; knob that operates a piece of equipment when pressed. —*v.* fasten with buttons. —**buttonhole** *n.* slit in a garment through which a button is passed; flower worn on a lapel. —*v.* detain (someone) in conversation.

buttress *n.* structure to support a wall. —*v.* support with a buttress.

buxom *adj.* (of a woman) healthily plump and full-bosomed.

buy *v.* **buying, bought.** acquire by paying money for; bribe; *Slang* accept as true. —*n.* thing acquired through payment. —**buyer** *n.* customer; person employed to buy merchandise.

buzz *n.* rapidly vibrating humming sound; *Informal* sense of excitement. —*v.* make a humming sound; be filled with an air of excitement. —**buzzer** *n.* —**buzz around** *v.* move around quickly and busily. —**buzz word** jargon word which becomes fashionably popular.

buzzard *n.* bird of prey of the hawk family.

by *adv.* near; past. —*prep.* used to indicate the person responsible for a creative work, e.g. *an opera by Verdi;* used to indicate a means used, e.g. *I go home by bus;* past; not later than; during; near; placed between measurements, e.g. *a plank fourteen inches by seven.* —**by and by** presently. —**by and large** in general.

by(e)law *n.* rule made by a local authority.

bye(-bye) *interj. Informal* goodbye.

by-election *n.* election held during parliament to fill a vacant seat.

bygone *adj.* past or former.

bypass *n.* main road built to avoid a city. —*v.* go round or avoid.

by-product *n.* secondary or incidental product of a process.

byre *n.* shelter for cows.

bystander *n.* person present but not involved.

byte *n. Computers* group of bits processed as one unit of data.

byway *n.* side road.

byword *n.* person or thing regarded as a perfect example of something.

THESAURUS

up, dress, joint, prepare, slaughter 3. assassinate, cut down, destroy, exterminate, kill, massacre, slaughter, slay

butt[1] handle, hilt, shaft, shank, stock

butt[2] dupe, mark, object, point, subject, target, victim

butt[3] *v./n. With or of the head or horns,* buck, buffet, bump, jab, knock, poke, prod, punch, push, ram, shove, thrust

buttonhole *v. Fig.* accost, bore, catch, grab, take aside, waylay

buttress 1. *n.* brace, mainstay, pier, prop, reinforcement, shore, stay, strut, support 2. *v.*

back up, bolster, brace, prop, prop up, reinforce, shore, shore up, strengthen, support, sustain, uphold

buy 1. *v.* get, invest in, obtain, pay for, procure, purchase, shop for 2. *n.* acquisition, bargain, deal, purchase

by *prep.* 1. along, beside, by way of, close to, near, next to, over, past, via 2. through, through the agency of, under the aegis of ~*adv.* 3. aside, at hand, away, beyond, close, handy, in reach, near, past, to one side

bystander eyewitness, looker-on, observer, onlooker, passer-by, spectator, viewer, watcher, witness

C

C *Chem.* carbon; Celsius; centigrade.

c. cent; century; circa; copyright.

Ca *Chem.* calcium.

cab *n.* taxi; enclosed driver's compartment on a train, lorry, etc. —**cabbie** *n. Informal* taxi driver.

cabal [kab-**bal**] *n.* small group of political plotters; secret plot.

cabaret [kab-a-ray] *n.* dancing and singing show in a nightclub.

cabbage *n.* vegetable with a large head of green leaves.

caber *n.* tree trunk tossed in competition at Highland games.

cabin *n.* compartment in a ship or aircraft; small hut. —**cabin cruiser** motorboat with a cabin.

cabinet *n.* piece of furniture with drawers or shelves; (**C-**) committee of senior government ministers. —**cabinet-maker** *n.* person who makes fine furniture.

cable *n.* strong thick rope; bundle of wires that carries electricity or telegraph messages; telegram sent abroad. —*v.* send (a message) to (someone) by cable. —**cable car** vehicle pulled up a steep slope by a moving cable. —**cable television** television service conveyed by cable to subscribers.

caboodle *n.* —**the whole caboodle** *Informal* the whole lot.

cabriolet [kab-ree-oh-**lay**] *n.* small horse-drawn carriage with a folding hood.

cacao [kak-**kah**-oh] *n.* tropical tree with seed pods from which chocolate and cocoa are made.

cache [kash] *n.* hiding place; hidden store of weapons or treasure.

cachet [**kash**-shay] *n.* prestige, distinction; distinctive mark.

cack-handed *adj. Informal* clumsy.

cackle *v.* laugh or chatter shrilly; (of a hen) squawk with shrill broken notes. —*n.* cackling noise.

cacophony [kak-**koff**-on-ee] *n.* harsh discordant sound. —**cacophonous** *adj.*

cactus *n., pl.* **-tuses, -ti.** fleshy desert plant with spines but no leaves.

cad *n. Old-fashioned* dishonourable man. —**caddish** *adj.*

cadaver [kad-**dav**-ver] *n.* corpse. —**cadaverous** *adj.* deathly pale; gaunt.

caddie, caddy *n., pl.* **-dies.** person who carries a golfer's clubs. —*v.* **-dying, -died.** act as a caddie.

caddis fly *n.* insect whose larva (**caddis worm**) lives underwater in a protective case of sand and stones.

caddy *n., pl.* **-dies.** small box for tea.

cadence [**kade**-enss] *n.* rise and fall in the pitch of a voice; close of a musical phrase.

cadenza *n.* complex passage for a soloist in a piece of music.

cadet *n.* young person training for the armed forces or police.

cadge *v.* get (food, money, etc.) by sponging or begging. —**cadger** *n.*

cadmium *n.* bluish-white metallic element used in alloys.

cadre [**kah**-der] *n.* (member of) a group of selected trained people forming the core of a military unit, Communist Party, etc.

caecum [**seek**-um] *n., pl.* **-ca.** pouch at the beginning of the large intestine.

Caesarean section [see-**zair**-ee-an] *n.* surgical incision into the womb to deliver a baby.

caesium *n.* silvery-white metallic element used in photocells.

café *n.* small or inexpensive restaurant serving light refreshments. —**cafeteria** *n.* self-service restaurant.

caffeine *n.* stimulant found in tea and coffee.

caftan *n.* same as KAFTAN.

cage *n.* enclosure of bars or wires, for keeping animals or birds; enclosed platform of a lift, esp. in a mine. —*v.* confine in a cage.

THESAURUS

cab minicab, taxi, taxicab

cabin 1. berth, chalet, cot, cottage, crib, hovel, hut, lodge, shack, shanty, shed 2. berth, compartment, deckhouse, quarters, room

cabinet 1. case, closet, commode, cupboard, dresser, locker 2. administration, assembly, council, counsellors, ministry

caddish despicable, dishonourable, ill-bred, low, ungentlemanly, unmannerly

café cafeteria, coffee bar, coffee shop, lunchroom, restaurant, snack bar, tearoom

cage *v.* confine, coop up, fence in, immure, impound, imprison, lock up, mew, restrain, shut up

DICTIONARY

cagey *adj.* **cagier, cagiest.** not frank; wary. —**caginess** *n.*

cagoule [kag-**gool**] *n.* lightweight hooded waterproof jacket.

cahoots *pl. n.* —**in cahoots** *Informal* conspiring together.

cairn *n.* mound of stones erected as a monument or landmark. —**cairn terrier** small rough-haired terrier.

cairngorm *n.* yellow or brownish quartz gemstone.

caisson [**kay**-son] *n.* watertight chamber used to carry out construction work under water.

cajole *v.* persuade by flattery. —**cajolery** *n.*

cake *n.* sweet food baked from a mixture of flour, eggs, etc.; flat compact mass. —*v.* form into a hardened mass or crust.

calabash *n.* type of large gourd.

calamine *n.* pink powder consisting chiefly of zinc oxide, used in skin lotions and ointments.

calamity *n., pl.* **-ties.** disaster. —**calamitous** *adj.*

calcify *v.* **-fying, -fied.** harden by the depositing of calcium salts. —**calcification** *n.*

calcium *n.* silvery-white metallic element found in bones, teeth, limestone, and chalk.

calculate *v.* solve (a problem) mathematically; estimate; plan deliberately. —**calculable** *adj.* —**calculating** *adj.* selfishly scheming. —**calculation** *n.* —**calculator** *n.* small electronic device for making calculations.

calculus *n., pl.* **-luses.** branch of mathematics dealing with infinitesimal changes to a variable number or quantity; *Pathol.* stone.

Caledonian *adj.* of Scotland.

calendar *n.* system for determining the beginning, length, and division of years; table showing such an arrangement; schedule of events or appointments.

calendula *n.* marigold.

calf[1] *n., pl.* **calves.** young cow, bull, elephant, whale, or seal; leather made from calf skin. —**calve** *v.* give birth to a calf. —**calf love** adolescent infatuation.

calf[2] *n., pl.* **calves.** back of the leg between the ankle and knee.

calibre [**kal**-lib-ber] *n.* ability, personal worth; diameter of the bore of a gun or of a shell or bullet. —**calibrate** *v.* mark the scale or check the accuracy of (a measuring instrument); measure the calibre of. —**calibration** *n.*

calico *n., pl.* **-coes, -co.** plain white cotton cloth.

caliph *n. Hist.* Muslim ruler.

call *v.* name; shout to attract attention; ask to come; (often foll. by *on*) visit; telephone; (of an animal or bird) utter its characteristic cry; read (a list) aloud for checking; awaken; arrange (a meeting, strike, etc.). —*n.* telephone communication; shout; animal's or bird's cry; summons or invitation; visit; need, demand. —**caller** *n.* —**calling** *n.* vocation or profession. —**call box** kiosk for a public telephone. —**call for** *v.* need, demand. —**call off** *v.* cancel. —**call up** *v.* summon to serve in the armed forces; evoke.

calligraphy *n.* (art of) beautiful handwriting. —**calligrapher** *n.*

calliper *n.* (*usu. pl.*) metal splint for the leg; instrument for measuring diameters.

callisthenics *pl. n.* light keep-fit exercises. —**callisthenic** *adj.*

callous *adj.* insensitive or heartless. —**calloused** *adj.* (of skin) thickened and hardened. —**callously** *adv.* —**callousness** *n.*

THESAURUS

cajole beguile, coax, decoy, entice, flatter, inveigle, lure, mislead, persuade, seduce, tempt, wheedle

cake bar, block, cube, loaf, lump, mass, slab

calamitous catastrophic, deadly, devastating, dire, disastrous, fatal, pernicious, ruinous, tragic, woeful

calamity affliction, cataclysm, catastrophe, disaster, distress, downfall, hardship, mischance, misfortune, mishap, reverse, ruin, scourge, tragedy, trial, woe

calculate adjust, compute, consider, count, determine, enumerate, estimate, figure, gauge, judge, rate, reckon, value, weigh, work out

calculation answer, computation, estimate, judgment, reckoning, result

calibre 1. bore, diameter, gauge, measure 2. *Fig.*

ability, capacity, endowment, faculty, force, gifts, merit, parts, quality, scope, stature, talent, worth

call *v.* 1. announce, arouse, awaken, cry, cry out, hail, proclaim, rouse, shout, waken, yell 2. assemble, bid, collect, contact, convene, convoke, gather, invite, muster, phone, rally, ring up, summon, telephone 3. christen, describe as, designate, dub, entitle, label, name, style, term ~*n.* 4. cry, hail, shout, signal, whoop, yell 5. announcement, appeal, command, demand, invitation, notice, order, plea, request, ring (*Brit. inf.*), summons, supplication, visit

call for demand, entail, need, occasion, require, suggest

calling employment, life's work, line, métier, mission, occupation, profession, province, pursuit, trade, vocation, work

DICTIONARY

callow *adj.* immature and inexperienced.

callus *n., pl.* **-luses.** area of thick hardened skin.

calm *adj.* serene, composed; still, peaceful; windless. —*n.* serenity, composure; stillness, peacefulness; absence of wind. —*v.* make or become calm. —**calmly** *adv.* —**calmness** *n.*

calorie *n.* unit of measurement for the energy value of food; unit of heat. —**calorific** *adj.* heat-producing.

calumny *n., pl.* **-nies.** slander. —**calumniate** *v.* slander.

calypso *n., pl.* **-sos.** West Indian song with improvised topical lyrics.

calyx *n., pl.* **calyxes, calyces.** ring of sepals protecting a flower bud.

cam *n.* device which converts rotary motion to to-and-fro motion. —**camshaft** *n.* part of an engine consisting of a rod to which cams are fixed.

camaraderie *n.* comradeship.

camber *n.* slight upward curve to the centre of a surface.

cambric *n.* fine white linen fabric.

camcorder *n.* combined portable video camera and recorder.

came *v.* past tense of COME.

camel *n.* humped mammal of Asia and Africa.

camellia [kam-**meal**-ya] *n.* evergreen ornamental shrub with roselike white, pink, or red flowers.

Camembert [kam-mem-bare] *n.* soft creamy French cheese.

cameo *n., pl.* **cameos.** brooch or ring with a profile head carved in relief; small part in a film or play performed by a well-known actor or actress.

camera *n.* apparatus used for taking photographs. —**in camera** in private. —**cameraman** *n.* photographer, esp. for television or cinema.

camiknickers *pl. n.* woman's undergarment consisting of knickers attached to a camisole.

camisole *n.* woman's bodice-like garment.

camomile *n.* aromatic plant, used to make herbal tea.

camouflage [kam-moo-flahzh] *n.* use of natural surroundings or artificial aids to conceal or disguise something. —*v.* conceal or disguise by camouflage.

camp[1] *n.* (place for) temporary lodgings consisting of tents, huts, or cabins; group supporting a particular doctrine. —*v.* stay in a camp. —**camper** *n.*

camp[2] *adj. Informal* homosexual; *Informal* consciously artificial or affected. —**camp it up** *Informal* behave in a camp way.

campaign *n.* series of coordinated activities designed to achieve a goal. —*v.* conduct or take part in a campaign.

campanology *n.* art of ringing bells. —**campanologist** *n.*

campanula *n.* plant with blue or white bell-shaped flowers.

camphor *n.* aromatic crystalline substance used medicinally and in mothballs. —**camphorated** *adj.*

campion *n.* white or pink wild flower.

campus *n., pl.* **-puses.** grounds of a college or university.

can[1] *v., past* **could.** be able; be allowed.

can[2] *n.* metal container for liquid or foods. —*v.* **canning, canned.** put (something) in a can. —**canned** *adj.* preserved in a can; (of music etc.) prerecorded. —**cannery** *n.* factory where food is canned.

Canadian *n., adj.* (person) from Canada.

canal *n.* artificial watercourse; duct in the body.

canapé [kan-nap-pay] *n.* small piece of bread or toast with a savoury topping.

canary *n., pl.* **-ries.** small yellow songbird often kept as a pet.

canasta *n.* card game like rummy, played with two packs.

cancan *n.* lively high-kicking dance performed by a female group.

THESAURUS

callous cold, hard-bitten, hardened, hard-hearted, heartless, indifferent, insensitive, obdurate, soulless, thick-skinned, uncaring, unfeeling, unresponsive, unsympathetic

calm *adj.* 1. balmy, mild, pacific, peaceful, placid, quiet, restful, serene, smooth, still, tranquil, windless 2. collected, composed, cool, equable, impassive, imperturbable, relaxed, sedate, self-possessed, unemotional, unexcited, unmoved, unruffled ~*v.* 3. hush, mollify, placate, quieten, relax, soothe

calmness 1. calm, composure, equability, hush, peace, peacefulness, placidity, quiet, repose, serenity, smoothness, stillness, tranquillity 2. composure, coolness, dispassion, equanimity, impassivity, imperturbability, self-possession

camouflage 1. *n.* blind, cloak, concealment, cover, deceptive markings, disguise, front, guise, mask, masquerade, mimicry, screen, subterfuge 2. *v.* cloak, conceal, cover, disguise, hide, mask, obscure, screen, veil

camp bivouac, camp site

campaign attack, crusade, drive, expedition, offensive, push

DICTIONARY

cancel v. **-celling, -celled.** postpone indefinitely; cross out; mark (a cheque or stamp) to prevent reuse. **—cancellation** n. **—cancel out** v. counterbalance or neutralize.

cancer n. malignant growth or tumour; disease resulting from this. **—cancerous** adj.

candela [kan-dee-la] n. unit of luminous intensity.

candelabrum n., pl. **-bra.** large branched candle holder.

candid adj. frank and outspoken. **—candidly** adv.

candidate n. person seeking a job or position; person taking an examination. **—candidacy, candidature** n.

candle n. stick of wax enclosing a wick, which is burned to produce light. **—candlestick** n. holder for a candle. **—candlewick** n. cotton fabric with a tufted surface.

candour n. frankness.

candy n., pl. **-dies.** US a sweet, or sweets in general. —v. **-dying, -died.** preserve with sugar. **—candyfloss** n. light fluffy mass of spun sugar on a stick. **—candy-striped** adj. having coloured stripes on a white background.

cane n. stem of the bamboo or similar plant; slender walking stick; flexible rod used to beat someone. —v. beat with a cane.

canine [kay-nine] adj. of or like a dog. **—canine tooth** sharp pointed tooth between the incisors and the molars.

canister n. metal container.

canker n. ulceration or ulcerous disease; something that spreads and corrupts. —v. infect or become infected with canker. **—cankerous** adj.

cannabis n. drug obtained from the hemp plant.

cannelloni pl. n. tubular pieces of pasta filled with meat etc.

cannibal n. person who eats human flesh; animal that eats others of its own kind. **—cannibalism** n. **—cannibalize** v. use parts from (one machine) to repair another.

cannon[1] n. large gun on wheels. **—cannonade** n. continuous heavy gunfire. **—cannonball** n. heavy metal ball fired from a cannon.

cannon[2] n. billiard stroke in which the cue ball hits two balls successively. —v. make this stroke; rebound, collide.

cannot can not.

canny adj. **-nier, -niest.** shrewd and cautious. **—cannily** adv.

canoe n. light narrow boat propelled by a paddle or paddles. —v. **-noeing, -noed.** go in a canoe. **—canoeist** n.

canon[1] n. Church law or decree; general rule or principle; set of writings accepted as genuine. **—canonical** adj. **—canonize** v. declare (a person) officially to be a saint. **—canonization** n.

canon[2] n. priest serving in a cathedral.

canoodle v. Slang kiss and cuddle.

canopy n., pl. **-pies.** covering above a throne, bed, etc.; any large or wide covering. —v. **-pying, -pied.** cover with a canopy.

can't can not.

cant[1] n. insincere talk; specialized vocabulary of a particular group.

cant[2] v., n. tilt or slope.

cantaloup(e) n. kind of melon with sweet orange flesh.

cantankerous adj. bad-tempered, quarrelsome.

cantata [kan-tah-ta] n. musical work consisting of arias, duets, and choruses.

canteen n. restaurant attached to a workplace; case of cutlery.

canter n. horse's gait between a trot and a gallop. —v. (cause to) move at a canter.

THESAURUS

cancel abolish, annul, blot out, call off, cross out, delete, efface, eliminate, erase, expunge, obliterate, quash, repeal, repudiate, rescind, revoke

cancellation abandonment, abolition, deletion, elimination, quashing, repeal, revocation

cancer blight, canker, carcinoma (*Pathol.*), corruption, evil, growth, malignancy, pestilence, rot, tumour

candid blunt, fair, frank, free, impartial, just, open, outspoken, plain, straightforward, truthful, unprejudiced

candidate applicant, aspirant, competitor, contender, contestant, entrant, nominee, runner

candour forthrightness, frankness, honesty, openness, outspokenness, truthfulness

canker bane, blight, cancer, corruption, infection, rot, ulcer

cannon big gun (*Inf.*), field gun, gun, mortar

canny acute, artful, astute, careful, cautious, circumspect, clever, judicious, knowing, prudent, sagacious, sharp, shrewd, subtle, wise

canopy awning, covering, shade, sunshade

cant[1] n. humbug, hypocrisy, insincerity, lip service, pretence, sanctimoniousness

cant[2] v./n. angle, incline, rise, slant, slope

cantankerous bad-tempered, captious, contra~

DICTIONARY

canticle *n.* short hymn with words from the Bible.

cantilever *n.* beam or girder fixed at one end only.

canto [**kan**-toe] *n., pl.* **-tos.** main division of a long poem.

canton *n.* political division of a country, esp. Switzerland.

cantonment [kan-**toon**-ment] *n.* military camp.

cantor *n.* man employed to lead services in a synagogue.

canvas *n.* heavy coarse cloth used for sails and tents, and for painting on; a painting on canvas.

canvass *v.* try to get votes or support (from); determine the opinions of (people) by conducting a survey. —*n.* canvassing.

canyon *n.* deep gorge.

cap *n.* soft close-fitting covering for the head; small lid; small explosive device used in a toy gun. —*v.* **capping, capped.** cover with or as if with a cap; outdo; select (a player) for a national team; impose an upper limit on (a tax).

capable *adj.* able, competent; (foll. by *of*) having the capacity (for). —**capably** *adv.* —**capability** *n.*

capacity *n., pl.* **-ties.** maximum amount that can be contained or produced; physical or mental ability; position or function. —**capacious** *adj.* roomy. —**capacitance** *n.* (measure of) the ability of a system to store electric charge. —**capacitor** *n.* device for storing electric charge.

caparisoned [kap-**par**-riss-sond] *adj.* dressed in rich clothing.

cape[1] *n.* short cloak.

cape[2] *n.* headland or promontory.

caper[1] *n.* high-spirited prank. —*v.* skip or dance about.

caper[2] *n.* pickled flower bud of a Mediterranean shrub used in sauces.

capercaillie, capercailzie [kap-per-**kale**-yee] *n.* large black European grouse.

capillary [kap-**pill**-a-ree] *n., pl.* **-laries.** very fine blood vessel.

capital *n.* chief town of a country; accumulated wealth; wealth used to produce more wealth; large letter, as used at the beginning of a name or sentence; top part of a pillar. —*adj.* involving or punishable by death; chief or principal; *Old-fashioned* excellent. —**capitalism** *n.* economic system based on the private ownership of industry. —**capitalist** *n.* supporter of capitalism; person who owns capital. —*adj.* of capitalists or capitalism. —**capitalize** *v.* convert into or provide with capital; write or print (text) in capital letters. —**capitalize on** *v.* take advantage of (a situation).

capitation *n.* charge or grant of a fixed amount per person.

capitulate *v.* surrender on agreed terms. —**capitulation** *n.*

capon [**kay**-pon] *n.* castrated cock fowl fattened for eating.

cappuccino [kap-poo-**cheen**-oh] *n., pl.* **-nos.** coffee with steamed milk.

THESAURUS

ry, crabby, crotchety (*Inf.*), crusty, difficult, disagreeable, grumpy, irascible, irritable, peevish, perverse, quarrelsome, testy

canter *n.* amble, jog, lope

canvass 1. *v.* analyse, campaign, electioneer, examine, inspect, investigate, poll, scan, sift, solicit, study, ventilate 2. *n.* examination, poll, scrutiny, survey

cap *v.* beat, better, cover, crown, exceed, excel, finish, outdo, outstrip, overtop, surpass, top, transcend

capability ability, capacity, facility, faculty, means, power, proficiency, wherewithal

capable able, accomplished, adapted, adept, apt, clever, competent, efficient, fitted, gifted, masterly, proficient, skilful, suited, talented

capacious ample, broad, commodious, expansive, extended, extensive, generous, liberal, roomy, sizable, spacious, substantial, vast, wide

capacity 1. amplitude, compass, extent, range, room, scope, size, space, volume 2. ability, brains, cleverness, competence, competency, facility, faculty, forte, genius, gift, intelligence, power, readiness, strength 3. function, office, position, post, province, role, service, sphere

cape head, headland, point, promontory

caper *v.* bounce, bound, cavort, dance, frisk, frolic, gambol, hop, jump, leap, romp, skip, spring

capital *adj.* 1. cardinal, central, chief, foremost, important, leading, main, major, paramount, pre-eminent, prime, principal, vital 2. excellent, fine, first, first-rate, prime, splendid, superb ~*n.* 3. assets, cash, finances, funds, investment(s), means, money, principal, property, resources, stock, wealth, wherewithal

capitalism free enterprise, *laissez faire*, private enterprise, private ownership

capitulate give in, give up, relent, submit, succumb, surrender, yield

DICTIONARY

caprice [kap-reess] *n.* whim. —**capricious** *adj.* changeable. —**capriciously** *adv.*

capsicum *n.* kind of pepper used as a vegetable or as a spice.

capsize *v.* overturn accidentally.

capstan *n.* rotating cylinder on which a rope etc. is wound.

capsule *n.* soluble case containing a dose of medicine; seed vessel of a plant; detachable crew compartment of a spacecraft.

captain *n.* leader of a team or group; commander of a ship or civil aircraft; middle-ranking naval officer; junior officer in the armed forces. —*v.* be captain of. —**captaincy** *n.*

caption *n.* title or explanation accompanying an illustration. —*v.* provide with a caption.

captious *adj.* tending to make trivial criticisms. —**captiously** *adv.* —**captiousness** *n.*

captivate *v.* fascinate or enchant. —**captivating** *adj.* —**captivation** *n.*

captive *n.* confined or restrained person or animal. —*adj.* held prisoner; obliged to stay. —**captivity** *n.*

captor *n.* person who holds someone captive.

capture *v.* take prisoner; gain control over. —*n.* capturing.

capybara *n.* very large S American rodent.

car *n.* motor vehicle designed to carry a small number of people; passenger compartment of a cable car, lift, etc.; *US* railway carriage. —**car park** area or building reserved for parking cars.

carafe [kar-**raff**] *n.* glass bottle for serving water or wine.

caramel *n.* chewy sweet made from sugar and milk; burnt sugar used for colouring and flavouring food. —**caramelize** *v.* turn into caramel.

carapace *n.* hard upper shell of tortoises and crustaceans.

carat *n.* unit of weight of precious stones; measure of the purity of gold in an alloy.

caravan *n.* large enclosed vehicle for living in,

able to be towed by a car or horse; group travelling together for safety in the East.

caraway *n.* plant whose seeds are used as a spice.

carbide *n.* compound of carbon with a metal.

carbine *n.* light automatic rifle.

carbohydrate *n.* any of a large group of energy-producing compounds in food, such as sugars and starches.

carbolic (**acid**) *n.* disinfectant derived from coal tar.

carbon *n.* nonmetallic element occurring as charcoal, graphite, and diamond, found in all organic matter. —**carbonate** *n.* salt or ester of carbonic acid. —*v.* impregnate with carbon dioxide. —**carbonize** *v.* turn into carbon as a result of heating; coat with carbon. —**carbon copy** copy made with carbon paper; very similar person or thing. —**carbon dioxide** colourless gas exhaled by people and animals. —**carbon paper** paper covered with a dark waxy pigment, used to make a duplicate of something as it is typed or written. —**carbonic acid** weak acid formed from carbon dioxide and water.

Carborundum *n.* ® compound of silicon and carbon, used for grinding and polishing.

carboy *n.* large bottle with a protective casing.

carbuncle *n.* inflamed boil; rounded garnet cut without facets.

carburettor *n.* device which mixes petrol and air in an internal-combustion engine.

carcass, carcase *n.* dead body or skeleton of an animal.

carcinogen *n.* substance producing cancer. —**carcinogenic** *adj.* —**carcinoma** *n.* malignant tumour, cancer.

card[1] *n.* piece of thick stiff paper or cardboard used for identification, reference, or sending greetings or messages; one of a set of cards with a printed pattern, used for playing games; small rectangle of stiff plastic for use as a credit card or banker's card; *Old-fashioned* witty or eccentric person. —*pl.* any card game, or card games

---

THESAURUS

capsize keel over, overturn, tip over, turn over, turn turtle, upset

capsule lozenge, pill, tablet

captain boss, chief, commander, head, leader, master, officer, skipper

captivate allure, attract, beguile, bewitch, charm, dazzle, enchant, enslave, enthral, entrance, fascinate, infatuate, lure, mesmerize, seduce, win

captive 1. *n.* convict, detainee, hostage, internee, prisoner, slave 2. *adj.* caged, confined,

ensnared, imprisoned, incarcerated, locked up, restricted, subjugated

captivity confinement, custody, detention, imprisonment, incarceration, internment, servitude, slavery

capture 1. *v.* arrest, catch, secure, seize, take, take prisoner 2. *n.* arrest, imprisonment, seizure

car automobile, machine, motor, motorcar, vehicle

carcass body, cadaver (*Medical*), corpse, dead body, hulk, remains, shell, skeleton

DICTIONARY

in general. —**cardboard** n. thin stiff board made from paper pulp. —**cardsharp(er)** n. professional card player who cheats.

card² n. machine or tool for combing wool before spinning. —**carder** n.

cardiac adj. of the heart. —**cardiograph** n. instrument which records heart movements. —**cardiogram** n. record of heart movements. —**cardiology** n. study of the heart and its diseases. —**cardiologist** n. —**cardiovascular** adj. of the heart and the blood vessels.

cardigan n. knitted jacket.

cardinal n. one of the high-ranking clergymen of the RC Church who elect the Pope and act as his counsellors. —adj. chief, principal; deep red. —**cardinal number** number indicating quantity but not order in a group, for example four as distinct from fourth. —**cardinal point** one of the four main points of the compass.

care v. be concerned; have regard or liking for; have a desire for; look after. —n. serious attention; protection or supervision; worry, anxiety; caution. —**careful** adj. —**carefully** adv. —**carefulness** n. —**careless** adj. —**carelessly** adv. —**carelessness** n. —**carefree** adj. without worry or responsibility. —**caretaker** n. person employed to look after a place. —**careworn** adj. showing signs of worry.

careen v. tilt over to one side.

career n. profession or occupation; course through life. —v. rush in an uncontrolled way.

—**careerist** n. person who seeks advancement by any possible means.

caress n. gentle affectionate touch or embrace. —v. touch gently and affectionately.

caret [**kar**-rett] n. symbol (ʌ) showing the place in written or printed matter where something is to be inserted.

cargo n., pl. **-goes.** goods carried by a ship, aircraft, etc.

caribou n. N American reindeer.

caricature n. likeness of a person which exaggerates features for comic effect. —v. portray by a caricature.

caries [**care**-reez] n. tooth decay.

carillon [kar-**rill**-yon] n. set of bells played by keyboard or mechanically; tune played on this.

carmine adj. vivid red.

carnage n. slaughter.

carnal adj. relating to the appetites and passions of the body. —**carnal knowledge** sexual intercourse.

carnation n. cultivated plant with fragrant white, pink, or red flowers.

carnival n. festive period with processions and entertainment.

carnivore n. flesh-eating animal. —**carnivorous** adj.

carob n. Mediterranean tree with edible pods used as a chocolate substitute.

THESAURUS

cardinal capital, central, chief, essential, first, foremost, greatest, highest, important, leading, main, pre-eminent, primary, prime, principal

care 1. anxiety, burden, concern, disquiet, interest, pressure, responsibility, solicitude, stress, trouble, vexation, woe, worry 2. attention, caution, consideration, direction, forethought, heed, management, pains, prudence, regard, vigilance, watchfulness 3. charge, control, custody, keeping, management, protection, supervision, ward

career n. calling, employment, life work, livelihood, occupation, profession, pursuit, vocation

careful 1. accurate, attentive, cautious, chary, circumspect, conscientious, discreet, fastidious, heedful, painstaking, precise, prudent, scrupulous, thoughtful, thrifty 2. alert, concerned, judicious, mindful, particular, protective, solicitous, vigilant, wary, watchful

careless 1. absent-minded, forgetful, hasty, heedless, incautious, indiscreet, negligent, perfunctory, remiss, thoughtless, uncon-

cerned, unguarded, unmindful, unthinking 2. inaccurate, irresponsible, lackadaisical, neglectful, offhand, slapdash, slipshod, sloppy (Inf.)

carelessness inaccuracy, indiscretion, irresponsibility, neglect, negligence, omission, remissness, slackness, thoughtlessness

caress 1. v. cuddle, embrace, fondle, hug, kiss, pet, stroke 2. n. cuddle, embrace, hug, kiss, pat, stroke

caretaker concierge, curator, custodian, janitor, keeper, porter, warden, watchman

cargo baggage, consignment, contents, freight, goods, lading, load, merchandise, shipment, tonnage, ware

caricature 1. n. burlesque, cartoon, farce, lampoon, parody, satire, takeoff (Inf.), travesty 2. v. burlesque, distort, lampoon, mimic, mock, parody, ridicule, satirize, send up (Brit. inf.), take off (Inf.)

carnival celebration, fair, festival, fête, fiesta, gala, holiday, revelry

carol chorus, hymn, lay, song, strain

DICTIONARY

carol *n.* joyful Christmas hymn. —*v.* **-olling, -olled.** sing carols; sing joyfully.

carotid [kar-**rot**-id] *adj., n.* (of) one of the two arteries supplying blood to the head.

carouse *v.* have a merry drinking party. —**carousal** *n.* merry drinking party.

carousel [kar-roo-**sell**] *n.* revolving conveyor; *US* merry-go-round.

carp¹ *n.* freshwater fish.

carp² *v.* complain or find fault.

carpel *n.* female reproductive organ of a flowering plant.

carpenter *n.* person who makes or repairs wooden structures. —**carpentry** *n.*

carpet *n.* heavy fabric for covering a floor. —*v.* **carpeting, carpeted.** cover with a carpet. —**on the carpet** *Informal* being reprimanded.

carpus *n., pl.* **-pi.** set of eight small bones forming the wrist.

carriage *n.* one of the sections of a train for passengers; four-wheeled horse-drawn vehicle; person's bearing; moving part of a machine that supports and shifts another part; act or cost of conveying goods. —**carriageway** *n.* part of a road along which traffic passes in one direction.

carrier *n.* person or thing that carries something; person or animal that does not show symptoms of a disease but can transmit it to others. —**carrier pigeon** homing pigeon used for carrying messages.

carrion *n.* dead and rotting flesh.

carrot *n.* long tapering orange root vegetable; incentive. —**carroty** *adj.* reddish.

carry *v.* **-rying, -ried.** take (something) from one place to another; transport; have on one's person; transmit; have as a penalty or result; bear (the head, body, etc.) in a specified manner; win acceptance for (a bill or motion); (of sound) travel over a distance. —**carry on** *v.* continue or persevere; *Informal* fuss unnecessarily. —**carry out** *v.* perform or complete.

cart *n.* open two-wheeled horse-drawn vehicle for carrying goods or passengers. —*v.* carry in a cart; carry with effort. —**carthorse** *n.* large heavily built horse. —**cartwheel** *n.* sideways somersault supported by the arms with the legs outstretched; large spoked wheel of a cart.

carte blanche *n. French* complete authority.

cartel *n.* association of competing firms formed to fix prices.

cartilage [kar-till-ij] *n.* firm elastic tissue forming part of the skeleton. —**cartilaginous** *adj.*

cartography *n.* map making. —**cartographer** *n.* —**cartographic** *adj.*

carton *n.* container made of cardboard or waxed paper.

cartoon *n.* humorous or satirical drawing; sequence of these telling a story; film made by photographing a series of drawings which give the illusion of movement when projected; preliminary sketch for a painting. —**cartoonist** *n.*

cartridge *n.* casing containing an explosive charge for a firearm; sealed container of film, tape, etc.; unit in the pick-up of a record player holding the stylus. —**cartridge paper** strong thick paper.

carve *v.* cut; form (an object or design) by cutting, esp. in stone or wood; slice (meat) into pieces. —**carving** *n.*

caryatid [kar-ree-**at**-id] *n.* supporting column in the shape of a female figure.

Casanova *n.* promiscuous man.

cascade *n.* waterfall; something that flows or falls like a waterfall. —*v.* fall in cascades.

case¹ *n.* instance or example; matter for discussion; condition or state of affairs; set of arguments for an action or cause; person attended to by a doctor, solicitor, or social worker; lawsuit; grounds for a lawsuit; *Grammar* form of a noun, pronoun, or adjective showing its relation to other words in the sentence. —**in case** so as to allow for eventualities.

THESAURUS

carp cavil, censure, complain, criticize, find fault, reproach

carpenter cabinet-maker, joiner, woodworker

carriage 1. conveyance, delivery, freight, transport 2. cab, coach, vehicle 3. *Fig.* air, bearing, behaviour, conduct, demeanour, gait, manner, mien, posture, presence

carry bear, bring, conduct, convey, fetch, haul, lift, lug, move, relay, take, transfer, transmit, transport

carry on continue, endure, keep going, last, maintain, persevere, persist

carry out accomplish, achieve, carry through,

complete, discharge, effect, execute, fulfil, perform, realize

carton box, case, pack, package

cartoon animated film, animation, comic strip, lampoon, parody, satire, sketch, takeoff

cartridge charge, round, shell

carve chip, chisel, cut, divide, engrave, etch, form, hack, hew, mould, sculpt, sculpture, slash, slice, whittle

cascade *n.* cataract, deluge, falls, flood, fountain, outpouring, shower, torrent, waterfall

DICTIONARY

case² *n.* container or protective covering; container and its contents. —*v. Slang* inspect (a building) with the intention of burgling it. —**case-harden** *v.* harden (an iron alloy) by carbonizing the surface; make callous.

casement *n.* window that is hinged on one side.

cash *n.* banknotes and coins. —*v.* obtain cash for. —**cash in on** *v. Informal* gain profit or advantage (from). —**cash register** till that displays and adds the prices of the goods sold.

cashew *n.* edible tropical American nut.

cashier¹ *n.* person responsible for handling cash in a bank or shop.

cashier² *v.* dismiss with dishonour from the armed forces.

cashmere *n.* fine soft wool; fabric made from this.

casing *n.* protective case or covering.

casino *n., pl.* **-nos.** building or room for gambling in.

cask *n.* barrel, usu. for holding alcoholic drink.

casket *n.* small box for valuables; *US* coffin.

cassava *n.* flour obtained from the roots of a tropical American plant, used to make tapioca.

casserole *n.* covered dish in which food is cooked and served; food so cooked. —*v.* cook (food) in a casserole.

cassette *n.* plastic case containing a reel of film or magnetic tape.

cassock *n.* long tunic worn by a clergyman.

cassowary *n., pl.* **-waries.** large flightless bird of Australia and New Guinea.

cast *v.* **casting, cast.** select (actors) to play parts in a play or film; direct (a glance); let fall, shed; throw with force; give (a vote); shape (molten material) in a mould. —*n.* actors in a play or film collectively; something shaped by a

mould while molten; mould used to shape something; quality or nature; slight squint in the eye; throw. —**castaway** *n.* shipwrecked person. —**casting vote** deciding vote used by the chairman when the votes on each side are equal. —**cast-iron** *adj.* made of a hard but brittle type of iron; rigid or unchallengeable. —**cast-off** *adj., n.* discarded (garment).

castanets *pl. n.* two small curved pieces of hollow wood clicked together in the hand, used esp. by Spanish dancers.

caste *n.* one of the hereditary classes into which Hindu society is divided; social rank.

castellated *adj.* having battlements.

caster *n.* small swivelled wheel on a chair leg etc.; bottle with a perforated top for sprinkling sugar or flour. —**caster sugar** finely ground white sugar.

castigate *v.* criticize or scold severely. —**castigation** *n.*

castle *n.* large fortified building; rook in chess.

castor *n.* same as CASTER.

castor oil *n.* oil obtained from an Indian plant, used as a lubricant and purgative.

castrate *v.* remove the testicles of; deprive of vigour or masculinity. —**castration** *n.*

casual *adj.* happening by chance; careless or offhand; appearing unconcerned; for informal wear; (of work or workers) occasional. —**casually** *adv.*

casualty *n., pl.* **-ties.** person killed or injured in an accident or war; anything lost or destroyed.

casuistry *n.* clever but false reasoning. —**casuist** *n.*

cat *n.* small domesticated furry mammal; related wild mammal, such as the lion or tiger; *Informal* spiteful woman. —**catty** *adj. Informal* spiteful. —**catkin** *n.* drooping flower spike of

---

THESAURUS

case¹ 1. circumstance(s), condition, context, dilemma, event, plight, position, predicament, situation, state 2. example, illustration, instance, occasion, occurrence, specimen 3. *Law* action, cause, dispute, lawsuit, proceedings, process, suit, trial

case² box, cabinet, capsule, carton, cartridge, casket, chest, compact, container, crate, holder, receptacle, shell, suitcase, tray, trunk

cash bullion, change, coin, coinage, currency, dough (*Sl.*), funds, money, notes, payment, ready money, resources, wherewithal

cashier¹ *n.* bank clerk, banker, bursar, clerk, teller

cashier² *v.* cast off, discard, discharge, dismiss, drum out, expel

cast *v.* 1. chuck, drive, drop, fling, hurl, impel, launch, lob, pitch, project, shed, shy, sling, throw, thrust, toss ~*n.* 2. fling, lob, throw, thrust, toss 3. actors, characters, company, players

castigate beat, cane, censure, chasten, chastise, correct, criticize, discipline, flay, flog, lash, rebuke, reprimand, scold, scourge, whip

castle chateau, citadel, fortress, keep, mansion, stronghold, tower

casual 1. accidental, chance, contingent, fortuitous, irregular, occasional, random, unexpected, unforeseen, unpremeditated 2. blasé, indifferent, informal, nonchalant, offhand, perfunctory, relaxed, unconcerned

casualty loss, sufferer, victim

DICTIONARY

certain trees. —**catcall** *n.* derisive whistle or cry. —**catgut** *n.* strong cord used to string musical instruments. —**catnap** *v., n.* doze. —**Catseye** *n.* ® glass reflector set in the road to indicate traffic lanes. —**cat's paw** person used as a tool by another. —**catwalk** *n.* narrow pathway or platform.

cataclysm [kat-a-kliz-zum] *n.* disaster, such as an earthquake; violent upheaval. —**cataclysmic** *adj.*

catacomb [kat-a-koom] *n.* underground burial place consisting of tunnels with recesses for tombs.

catafalque [kat-a-falk] *n.* raised platform on which a body lies in state before or during a funeral.

catalepsy *n.* trancelike state in which the body is rigid. —**cataleptic** *adj.*

catalogue *n.* systematic list of items. —*v.* make such a list; enter (an item) in a catalogue.

catalyst *n.* substance that speeds up a chemical reaction without itself changing. —**catalyse** *v.* speed up (a chemical reaction) by a catalyst. —**catalysis** *n.* —**catalytic** *adj.*

catamaran *n.* boat with twin parallel hulls.

catapult *n.* Y-shaped device with a loop of elastic used for firing stones; *Hist.* weapon used for hurling large rocks. —*v.* shoot from or as if from a catapult.

cataract *n.* waterfall; eye disease in which the lens becomes opaque; opaque area of an eye.

catarrh [kat-**tar**] *n.* inflammation of a mucous membrane causing a flow of mucus. —**catarrhal** *adj.*

catastrophe [kat-**ass**-trof-fee] *n.* great and sudden disaster. —**catastrophic** *adj.*

catch *v.* **catching, caught.** seize or capture; surprise, e.g. *catch someone red-handed;* hit unexpectedly; be in time for; see or hear by chance or with difficulty; contract (a disease); understand; entangle or become entangled; check (one's breath) suddenly; begin to burn. —*n.* catching; thing caught; device that fastens; *Informal* concealed or unforeseen difficulty. —**catch it** *Informal* be punished. —**catching** *adj.* infectious. —**catchy** *adj.* (of a tune) pleasant and easily remembered. —**catchment area** area served by a particular school or hospital. —**catch on** *v. Informal* become popular; understand. —**catch out** *v. Informal* trap (someone) in an error or lie. —**catch phrase, catchword** *n.* well-known and frequently used phrase or slogan. —**catch 22** inescapable dilemma.

catechism [**kat**-ti-kiz-zum] *n.* doctrine of a Christian Church in a series of questions and answers. —**catechize** *v.* instruct by using a catechism; question (someone) thoroughly. —**catechist** *n.*

category *n., pl.* **-ries.** class or group. —**categorical** *adj.* absolute or unconditional. —**categorically** *adv.* —**categorize** *v.* put in a category. —**categorization** *n.*

cater *v.* provide what is needed or wanted, esp. food or services. —**caterer** *n.*

caterpillar *n.* wormlike larva of a moth or butterfly; ® endless track, driven by cogged wheels, used to propel a heavy vehicle.

caterwaul *v.* wail, yowl.

catharsis [kath-**thar**-siss] *n., pl.* **-ses.** relief of strong suppressed emotions. —**cathartic** *adj.*

cathedral *n.* principal church of a diocese.

Catherine wheel *n.* rotating firework.

catheter [**kath**-it-er] *n.* tube inserted into a body cavity to drain fluid.

cathode *n.* negative electrode, by which electrons leave a circuit. —**cathode rays** stream of electrons from a cathode in a vacuum tube.

catholic *adj.* broad-minded; universal. —*n., adj.* (C-) (member) of the Roman Catholic Church. —**Catholicism** *n.*

cation [**kat**-eye-on] *n.* positively charged ion.

cattle *pl. n.* domesticated cows, bulls, or oxen.

THESAURUS

catalogue directory, index, inventory, list, record, register, roll, roster, schedule

catastrophe adversity, affliction, blow, calamity, cataclysm, devastation, disaster, failure, fiasco, ill, mischance, misfortune, mishap, reverse, tragedy, trial, trouble

catch *v.* 1. apprehend, arrest, capture, clutch, ensnare, entrap, grab, grasp, grip, lay hold of, seize, snare, snatch, take 2. detect, discover, expose, find out, surprise, unmask ~*n.* 3. bolt, clasp, clip, fastener, hasp, hook, hook and eye, latch 4. difficulty, disadvantage, drawback, fly in the ointment, hitch, snag, stumbling block, trap, trick

catching contagious, infectious, infective, transferable, transmittable

categorical absolute, direct, downright, emphatic, explicit, express, positive, unconditional, unequivocal, unqualified

category class, department, division, grade, group, head, heading, list, order, rank, section, sort, type

cater furnish, outfit, provide, provision, purvey, supply, victual

cattle beasts, cows, livestock, stock

catty ill-natured, malevolent, malicious, mean, rancorous, spiteful, venomous

DICTIONARY

Caucasoid *adj.* of the light-skinned racial group of mankind.

caucus *n., pl.* **-cuses.** local committee or faction of a political party; political meeting to decide future plans.

caught *v.* past of CATCH.

cauldron *n.* large pot used for boiling.

cauliflower *n.* type of cabbage with an edible white flower head.

caulk *v.* stop up (cracks, esp. in a ship) with filler.

causal *adj.* of or being a cause; of cause and effect. —**causally** *adv.* —**causality, causation** *n.* relationship of cause and effect.

cause *n.* aim or principle supported by a person or group; something that produces an effect; reason or motive. —*v.* be the cause of.

cause célèbre [kawz sill-**leb**-ra] *n., pl.* **causes célèbres** [kawz sill-**leb**-ra]. controversial legal case or issue.

causeway *n.* raised road or path across water or marshland.

caustic *adj.* capable of burning by chemical action; sarcastic or cutting. —*n.* caustic substance. —**caustically** *adv.*

cauterize *v.* burn (body tissue) with heat or a chemical to treat a wound. —**cauterization** *n.*

caution *n.* care, attention to safety; warning. —*v.* warn or advise. —**cautionary** *adj.* warning. —**cautious** *adj.* showing caution. —**cautiously** *adv.*

cavalcade *n.* procession of people on horseback or in cars.

cavalier *adj.* arrogant, offhand. —*n.* (**C-**) supporter of Charles I in the English Civil War.

cavalry *n., pl.* **-ries.** mounted troops.

cave *n.* large hole in a hill or cliff. —**caving** *n.*

sport of exploring caves. —**cave in** *v.* collapse inwards; give in. —**caveman** *n.* prehistoric cave dweller.

caveat [**kav**-vee-at] *n.* warning.

cavern *n.* large cave. —**cavernous** *adj.*

caviar(e) *n.* salted sturgeon roe.

cavil *v.* **-illing, -illed.** make petty objections. —*n.* petty objection.

cavity *n., pl.* **-ties.** hole; decayed area in a tooth.

cavort *v.* prance, caper.

caw *n.* cry of a crow, rook, or raven. —*v.* make this cry.

cayenne (pepper) *n.* hot red spice made from capsicum seeds.

cayman *n., pl.* **-mans.** S American reptile similar to an alligator.

CB Citizens' Band.

CBE Commander of the Order of the British Empire.

CBI Confederation of British Industry.

cc cubic centimetre(s).

CD compact disc.

Cd *Chem.* cadmium.

cease *v.* bring or come to an end. —**ceaseless** *adj.* —**ceaselessly** *adv.* —**cease-fire** *n.* order to stop firing; temporary truce.

cedar *n.* large evergreen tree; its wood.

cede *v.* surrender (territory or legal rights).

cedilla *n.* hooklike symbol placed under a letter *c* to show that it is pronounced *s*, not *k.*

ceilidh [**kay**-lee] *n.* informal social gathering for singing and dancing, esp. in Scotland.

ceiling *n.* inner upper surface of a room; upper limit set on something.

celandine *n.* wild plant with yellow flowers.

celebrate *v.* hold festivities to mark (a happy

THESAURUS

cause *n.* 1. agent, beginning, creator, genesis, maker, origin, prime mover, producer, root, source, spring 2. account, agency, aim, basis, consideration, end, grounds, incentive, inducement, motivation, motive, object, purpose, reason ~*v.* 3. begin, bring about, compel, create, effect, engender, generate, give rise to, incite, induce, lead to, motivate, occasion, precipitate, produce, provoke, result in

caustic acrid, astringent, biting, burning, corroding, corrosive, keen, mordant

caution *n.* 1. care, carefulness, circumspection, discretion, forethought, heed, prudence, vigilance, watchfulness 2. admonition, advice, counsel, injunction, warning ~*v.* 3. admonish, advise, tip off, urge, warn

cautious alert, cagey (*Inf.*), careful, chary, cir-

cumspect, discreet, guarded, heedful, judicious, prudent, tentative, vigilant, wary, watchful

cavalry horse, horsemen

cave cavern, den, grotto, hollow

cavern cave, hollow, pothole

cavity crater, hole, hollow, pit

cease come to an end, conclude, desist, die away, end, fail, finish, halt, leave off, refrain, stay, stop, terminate

ceaseless constant, continuous, endless, eternal, everlasting, incessant, never-ending, nonstop, perpetual, unending, untiring

cede allow, concede, grant, hand over, make over, renounce, resign, surrender, transfer, yield

DICTIONARY

event, anniversary, etc.); perform (a religious ceremony). **—celebrated** *adj.* famous. **—celebration** *n.* **—celebrant** *n.* person who performs a religious ceremony. **—celebrity** *n.* famous person; fame.

celeriac [sill-**ler**-ee-ak] *n.* kind of celery with a large turnip-like root.

celerity [sill-**ler**-rit-tee] *n.* swiftness.

celery *n.* vegetable with crisp juicy edible stalks.

celestial *adj.* heavenly, divine; of the sky.

celibate *adj.* unmarried or abstaining from sex, esp. because of a religious vow of chastity. **—***n.* celibate person. **—celibacy** *n.*

cell *n.* smallest unit of an organism that is able to function independently; small room for a prisoner, monk, or nun; small compartment; small group operating as the core of a larger organization; device which generates electrical energy from a chemical reaction. **—cellular** *adj.* of or consisting of cells; woven with an open texture.

cellar *n.* underground room for storage; stock of wine.

cello [**chell**-oh] *n., pl.* **-los.** low-pitched instrument of the violin family. **—cellist** *n.*

Cellophane *n.* ® thin transparent cellulose sheeting used as wrapping.

celluloid *n.* plastic formerly used to make photographic film.

cellulose *n.* main constituent of plant cell walls, used in making plastics, paper, etc.

Celsius *adj.* of the temperature scale in which water freezes at 0° and boils at 100°.

Celt [kelt] *n.* person who speaks a Celtic language. **—Celtic** [**kel**-tik *or* **sel**-tik] *n.* group of languages including Gaelic and Welsh. **—***adj.* of the Celts or the Celtic languages.

cement *n.* fine grey powder mixed with water and sand to make mortar or concrete; adhesive; material used to fill teeth. **—***v.* join with or as if with cement; cover with cement.

cemetery *n., pl.* **-teries.** burial ground not attached to a church.

cenotaph *n.* monument to people buried elsewhere.

censer *n.* container for burning incense.

censor *v.* ban or cut parts of (a film, book, etc.) considered obscene or otherwise unacceptable. **—***n.* official employed to examine and censor films, books, etc. **—censorship** *n.* **—censorial** *adj.* **—censorious** *adj.* harshly critical.

censure *n.* severe disapproval. **—***v.* criticize severely.

census *n., pl.* **-suses.** official count, esp. of population.

cent *n.* hundredth part of a monetary unit such as the dollar.

centaur *n.* mythical creature resembling a horse with the head, arms, and torso of a man.

centenary [sen-**teen**-a-ree] *n., pl.* **-naries.** 100th anniversary or its celebration. **—centenarian** *n.* person at least 100 years old. **—centennial** *n. US* centenary.

centigrade *adj.* same as CELSIUS.

centigram(me) *n.* hundredth part of a gram.

centilitre *n.* hundredth part of a litre.

centimetre *n.* hundredth part of a metre.

centipede *n.* small wormlike creature with many legs.

central *adj.* of, at, or forming the centre; main or principal. **—centrally** *adv.* **—centrality** *n.* **—centralism** *n.* principle of central control of a country or organization. **—centralize** *v.* bring under central control. **—centralization** *n.* **—central heating** system for heating a building from one central source of heat.

centre *n.* middle point or part; place for a specified activity; political party or group favouring moderation; *Sport* player who plays in the middle of the field. **—***v.* move towards, put, or be at the centre. **—centrist** *n., adj.* (person) favouring political moderation. **—centrifugal** *adj.* moving away from the centre. **—centrifuge**

THESAURUS

celebrate commend, drink to, eulogize, exalt, extol, glorify, honour, keep, laud, observe, praise, proclaim, rejoice, reverence, toast

celebrated distinguished, eminent, famed, famous, glorious, illustrious, notable, popular, prominent, renowned, well-known

celebration carousal, festival, festivity, gala, jubilee, revelry

celebrity big name, degnitary, luminary, name, personage, personality, star, superstar, V.I.P.

cell 1. cavity, chamber, compartment, cubicle, dungeon, stall 2. coterie, group, unit

cement *v.* attach, bind, bond, glue, gum, join, plaster, seal, solder, stick together, unite, weld

cemetery burial ground, churchyard, graveyard

censure 1. *v.* abuse, blame, castigate, condemn, criticize, denounce, rebuke, reprimand, reproach, reprove, scold, upbraid 2. *n.* blame, castigation, condemnation, criticism, disapproval, rebuke, remonstrance, reprimand, reproach, reproof, stricture

central chief, essential, fundamental, inner, interior, main, mean, median, mid, middle, principal

DICTIONARY

n. machine which separates substances by centrifugal force. —**centripetal** *adj.* moving towards the centre. —**centre on** *v.* have as a centre or main theme.

centurion *n.* Roman officer commanding 100 men.

century *n., pl.* **-ries.** period of 100 years; cricket score of 100.

cephalopod [seff-a-loh-pod] *n.* sea mollusc with a head and tentacles, such as the octopus.

ceramic *n.* hard brittle material made by firing clay; object made of this. —*pl.* art of producing ceramic objects. —*adj.* made of ceramic; of ceramics.

cereal *n.* grass plant with edible grain, such as wheat or rice; this grain; breakfast food made from this grain.

cerebral [ser-rib-ral] *adj.* of the brain; intellectual. —**cerebrum** *n.* main part of the human brain.

ceremony *n., pl.* **-nies.** formal act or ritual; formally polite behaviour. —**ceremonial** *adj., n.* —**ceremonially** *adv.* —**ceremonious** *adj.* —**ceremoniously** *adv.*

cerise [ser-reess] *adj.* cherry-red.

certain *adj.* sure, without doubt; reliable or unerring; some but not much. —**certainly** *adv.* —**certainty** *n.* state of being sure; thing sure to happen.

certificate *n.* official document stating the details of a birth, death, etc.

certify *v.* **-fying, -fied.** declare formally or officially; declare (someone) legally insane. —**certifiable** *adj.* —**certification** *n.*

certitude *n.* confidence, certainty.

cerulean [ser-rule-ee-an] *adj.* of a deep blue colour.

cervix *n., pl.* **cervixes, cervices.** narrow entrance of the womb; neck. —**cervical** [ser-vik-kl *or* ser-vie-kl] *adj.*

cessation *n.* ceasing.

cesspool, cesspit *n.* covered tank or pit for sewage.

cetacean [sit-tay-shun] *n., adj.* (member) of the whale family.

cf. compare.

CFC chlorofluorocarbon.

ch. chapter; church.

chafe *v.* make or become sore or worn by rubbing; make or be impatient or annoyed.

chafer *n.* large beetle.

chaff *n.* grain husks; chopped hay and straw used to feed cattle; light-hearted teasing. —*v.* tease good-naturedly.

chaffinch *n.* small European songbird.

chagrin [shag-grin] *n.* annoyance and embarrassment. —*v.* annoy and embarrass.

chain *n.* flexible length of connected metal links; connected series of things or events; group of shops, hotels, etc. owned by one firm; unit of length equal to 22 yards. —*v.* confine or fasten with or as if with a chain. —**chain reaction** series of events, each of which causes the next. —**chain-smoke** *v.* smoke (cigarettes) continuously. —**chain-smoker** *n.*

chair *n.* seat with a back, for one person; official position of authority; person holding this; professorship. —*v.* preside over (a meeting). —**chairlift** *n.* series of chairs on a cable for carrying people, esp. skiers, up a slope. —**chairman, chairperson, chairwoman** *n.* person who presides over a meeting.

chaise [shaze] *n.* light horse-drawn carriage.

chaise longue [long] *n.* sofa with a back and single armrest.

chalcedony [kal-sed-don-ee] *n., pl.* **-nies.** variety of quartz.

chalet *n.* kind of Swiss wooden house; house like this, used as a holiday home.

chalice [chal-liss] *n.* large goblet.

THESAURUS

centre core, crux, focus, heart, hub, mid, middle, pivot

ceremonial 1. *adj.* formal, ritual, solemn, stately 2. *n.* ceremony, formality, rite, ritual, solemnity

ceremony commemoration, function, observance, parade, rite, ritual, service, show

certain 1. assured, confident, convinced, positive, satisfied, sure 2. ascertained, conclusive, incontrovertible, indubitable, plain, true, undeniable, unmistakable, valid 3. decided, definite, established, fixed, settled

certainty assurance, confidence, conviction, faith, inevitability, positiveness, sureness, trust, validity

certificate credential(s), diploma, document, licence, testimonial

certify assure, attest, authenticate, aver, avow, confirm, declare, endorse, guarantee, show, testify, validate, verify, witness

chaff *n.* dregs, husks, refuse, remains, rubbish, waste

chain *v.* 1. bind, enslave, fasten, fetter, handcuff, manacle, restrain, shackle, tether ~*n.* 2. coupling, fetter, link, manacle, shackle 3. progression, sequence, series, set, string, succession, train

DICTIONARY

chalk *n.* soft white rock consisting of calcium carbonate; piece of this, often coloured, used for drawing and writing on blackboards. —*v.* draw or mark with chalk. —**chalky** *adj.*

challenge *v.* invite (someone) to take part in a contest or fight; call (something) into question; be difficult but stimulating to; order (someone) to stop and be identified. —*n.* act of challenging. —**challenger** *n.*

chamber *n.* hall used for formal meetings; legislative or judicial assembly; compartment or cavity; *Obs.* bedroom. —*pl.* set of rooms used as offices by a barrister. —**chamberlain** *n.* official who manages the household of a king or nobleman. —**chambermaid** *n.* woman employed to clean bedrooms in a hotel. —**chamber music** music for a small group of players. —**chamber pot** bowl for urine, formerly used in bedrooms.

chameleon [kam-**meal**-yon] *n.* small lizard that changes colour according to its surroundings.

chamfer [**cham**-fer] *v.* bevel the edge of.

chamois [**sham**-wah] *n., pl.* **-ois.** small mountain antelope; [**sham**-ee] soft leather; cloth of this.

chamomile [**kam**-mo-mile] *n.* same as CAMO-MILE.

champ[1] *v.* chew noisily; be impatient.

champ[2] *n.* short for CHAMPION.

champagne *n.* sparkling white French wine.

champion *n.* overall winner of a competition; someone who defends a person or cause. —*adj. Dialect* excellent. —*v.* support. —**championship** *n.*

chance *n.* likelihood, probability; opportunity; risk, gamble; unpredictable element that causes

things to happen one way rather than another; fortune, luck. —*v.* risk; happen by chance. —*adj.* accidental. —**chancy** *adj.* risky.

chancel *n.* part of a church containing the altar and choir.

chancellor *n.* state or legal officer of high rank; head of a university. —**chancellorship** *n.*

Chancery *n.* division of the British High Court of Justice.

chandelier [shan-dill-**eer**] *n.* hanging branched holder for lights.

chandler *n.* dealer, esp. in ships' supplies.

change *v.* make or become different; interchange or exchange; put different clothes or coverings on; exchange (money) for its equivalent in a smaller denomination or different currency; leave one vehicle and board another. —*n.* changing; variation or alteration; variety or novelty; coins of low value; balance received when the amount paid is more than the cost of a purchase. —**changeable** *adj.* changing often. —**changeling** *n.* child believed to have been exchanged by fairies for another.

channel *n.* band of broadcasting frequencies; means of access or communication; course along which a river, shipping, etc. moves; groove; broad strait connecting two areas of sea. —*v.* **-nelling, -nelled.** direct or convey through a channel.

chant *n.* short simple melody; psalm with such a melody; rhythmic or repetitious slogan. —*v.* sing or utter (a psalm or slogan).

chanter *n.* (on bagpipes) pipe on which the melody is played.

chaos *n.* complete disorder or confusion. —**chaotic** *adj.* —**chaotically** *adv.*

THESAURUS

challenge *v.* brave, claim, dare, defy, demand, dispute, investigate, object to, provoke, question, require, stimulate, summon, tax, try

chamber bedroom, compartment, cubicle, enclosure, hall, hollow, room

champion conqueror, defender, guardian, hero, patron, protector, title holder, upholder, victor, warrior, winner

chance *n.* 1. likelihood, occasion, odds, opening, opportunity, possibility, probability, prospect, scope, time 2. accident, casualty, coincidence, destiny, fate, fortune, luck, misfortune, peril, providence 3. gamble, hazard, risk, speculation, uncertainty ~*v.* 4. befall, betide, come about, come to pass, fall out, happen, occur 5. endanger, gamble, hazard, risk, stake, try, venture, wager

change *v.* 1. alter, convert, diversify, fluctuate, metamorphose, moderate, modify, mutate, re-

form, remodel, reorganize, restyle, shift, transform, vary, veer 2. barter, convert, displace, exchange, interchange, remove, replace, substitute, swap (*Inf.*), trade, transmit ~*n.* 3. alteration, difference, innovation, metamorphosis, modification, mutation, permutation, revolution, transformation, transition 4. conversion, exchange, interchange, substitution, trade

changeable capricious, erratic, fickle, fitful, fluid, inconstant, irregular, mercurial, mobile, protean, shifting, uncertain, unpredictable, unreliable, unsettled, unstable, unsteady, vacillating, variable, versatile, volatile, wavering

channel 1. *n.* canal, duct, furrow, groove, gutter, main, passage, route, strait 2. *v.* conduct, convey, direct, guide, transmit

DICTIONARY

chap[1] *n. Informal* fellow, man.

chap[2] *v.* **chapping, chapped.** (of the skin) make or become raw and cracked, by exposure to cold.

chapat(t)i *n.* (in Indian cookery) flat thin unleavened bread.

chapel *n.* place of worship with its own altar, within a church; similar place of worship in a large house or institution; Nonconformist place of worship; section of a trade union in the print industry.

chaperon(e) [**shap**-per-rone] *n.* older person who accompanies and supervises a young person. —*v.* act as a chaperone to.

chaplain *n.* clergyman attached to a chapel, military body, or institution. —**chaplaincy** *n.*

chaplet *n.* garland for the head.

chapter *n.* division of a book; period in a life or history; branch of a society or club; group of canons of a cathedral.

char[1] *Informal* —*n.* charwoman. —*v.* **charring, charred.** work as a charwoman.

char[2] *v.* **charring, charred.** blacken by partial burning.

char[3] *n. Slang* tea.

charabanc [**shar**-rab-bang] *n.* bus used for outings.

character *n.* combination of qualities distinguishing an individual; moral strength; reputation, esp. good reputation; person represented in a play, film, or story; notable or eccentric person; letter, numeral, or symbol used in writing or printing. —**characteristic** *n.* distinguishing feature or quality. —*adj.* distinguishing. —**characteristically** *adv.* —**characterize** *v.* be a characteristic of; describe the character of. —**characterization** *n.*

charade [shar-**rahd**] *n.* absurd pretence. —*pl.* game in which one team acts out a word, which the other team has to guess.

charcoal *n.* black substance formed by partially burning wood.

charge *v.* ask as a price; enter a debit against (a person or an account); accuse formally; assign a task to; make a rush or sudden attack (upon); fill (a battery) with electricity; fill or load. —*n.* price charged; formal accusation; attack or rush; command or exhortation; custody; person or thing entrusted to someone's care; amount of electricity stored in a battery. —**in charge** in command. —**chargeable** *adj.*

chargé d'affaires [**shar**-zhay daf-**fair**] *n., pl.* **chargés d'affaires.** head of a diplomatic mission in the absence of an ambassador or in a small mission.

chariot *n.* two-wheeled horse-drawn vehicle used in ancient times in wars and races. —**charioteer** *n.* chariot driver.

charisma [kar-**rizz**-ma] *n.* person's power to attract or influence people. —**charismatic** [kar-rizz-**mat**-ik] *adj.*

charity *n., pl.* **-ties.** giving of help, such as money or food, to those in need; organization that does this; help given; disposition to think kindly of others. —**charitable** *adj.* —**charitably** *adv.*

charlady *n.* same as CHARWOMAN.

charlatan [**shar**-lat-tan] *n.* person who claims expertise that he or she does not have.

charleston *n.* lively dance of the 1920s.

charm *n.* attractiveness; trinket worn on a bracelet; magic spell. —*v.* attract or delight; protect or influence as if by magic; influence by personal charm. —**charmer** *n.* —**charming** *adj.* attractive.

THESAURUS

chant 1. *n.* carol, chorus, melody, psalm, song 2. *v.* intone, recite, sing, warble

chaos anarchy, bedlam, confusion, disorder, pandemonium, tumult

chap character, customer, fellow, guy (*Inf.*), individual, man, person, sort, type

chapter clause, division, episode, part, period, phase, section, stage, topic

character 1. calibre, cast, complexion, constitution, disposition, make-up, nature, personality, quality, reputation, temper, temperament, type 2. honour, integrity, rectitude, strength, uprightness 3. card (*Inf.*), eccentric, oddball (*Inf.*), oddity, original, queer fish (*Inf.*) 4. part, persona, portrayal, role

characteristic 1. *adj.* distinctive, distinguish-

ing, individual, peculiar, representative, singular, special, specific, symbolic, typical 2. *n.* attribute, faculty, feature, mark, peculiarity, property, quality, trait

charge *v.* 1. accuse, arraign, blame, impeach, indict, involve 2. bid, command, enjoin, exhort, instruct, order, require ~*n.* 3. accusation, allegation, imputation, indictment 4. assault, attack, onset, rush, sortie 5. burden, care, concern, custody, duty, office, responsibility, safekeeping, trust, ward 6. amount, cost, expenditure, expense, outlay, payment, price, rate

charity alms-giving, assistance, benefaction, donations, fund, gift, hand-out, philanthropy, relief

charm 1. *v.* allure, attract, beguile, bewitch,

DICTIONARY

charnel house *n.* building or vault for the bones of the dead.

chart *n.* information shown in the form of a diagram, graph, or table; map to aid navigation. —*v.* make a chart of; plot the course of. —**the charts** *Informal* weekly list of best-selling pop records.

charter *n.* document granting or demanding certain rights; constitution of an organization; hire of transport for private use. —*v.* hire by charter; grant a charter to. —**chartered** *adj.* officially qualified to practise a profession, e.g. *chartered accountant.*

chartreuse [shar-**trerz**] *n.* sweet-smelling green or yellow liqueur.

charwoman *n.* woman employed as a cleaner.

chary [**chair**-ee] *adj.* -rier, -riest. cautious. —**charily** *adv.*

chase[1] *v.* run after quickly in order to catch or drive away; *Informal* hurry; *Informal* try energetically to obtain. —*n.* chasing or pursuit. —**chaser** *n.* drink drunk after another of a different kind.

chase[2] *v.* engrave or emboss (metal).

chasm [**kaz**-zum] *n.* deep crack or ravine in the earth.

chassis [**shass**-ee] *n., pl.* -**sis.** frame, wheels, and mechanical parts of a motor vehicle.

chaste *adj.* refraining from sex outside marriage or altogether; (of style) simple. —**chastely** *adv.* —**chastity** *n.*

chasten [**chase**-en] *v.* correct by punishment; subdue.

chastise *v.* punish severely, esp. by beating. —**chastisement** *n.*

chasuble [**chazz**-yew-bl] *n.* long sleeveless outer vestment worn by a priest while celebrating Mass.

chat *v.* chatting, chatted. talk in an easy familiar way. —*n.* easy familiar talk. —**chatty** *adj.* —**chattily** *adv.*

chateau [**shat**-toe] *n., pl.* -**teaux, -teaus.** French castle or country house.

chatelain [**shat**-tell-lane] *n.* (esp. formerly) mistress of a large house or castle.

chattels *pl. n.* movable possessions.

chatter *v.* talk about trivial matters rapidly and continuously; (of the teeth) rattle with cold or fear. —*n.* idle talk. —**chatterbox** *n.* person who chatters incessantly.

chauffeur *n.* person employed to drive a car. —**chauffeuse** *n. fem.*

chauvinism [**show**-vin-iz-zum] *n.* irrational belief that one's own race, group, or sex is superior; fanatical patriotism. —**chauvinist** *n., adj.* —**chauvinistic** *adj.*

cheap *adj.* low in price; of poor quality; of little value; mean, despicable. —**cheaply** *adv.* —**cheapen** *v.* make cheap or cheaper; degrade. —**cheapskate** *n. Informal* miserly person.

cheat *v.* act dishonestly to gain profit or advantage; deprive (someone) unfairly. —*n.* person who cheats; fraud or deception.

check *v.* examine or investigate; stop or hinder; *US* correspond. —*n.* examination or investigation; stoppage or restraint; *US* cheque; pattern of squares or crossing lines; *Chess* position of a king under attack. —**check in** *v.* register one's

THESAURUS

cajole, captivate, delight, enchant, entrance, fascinate, mesmerize, please 2. *n.* allure, appeal, attraction, desirability, enchantment, fascination, magic, magnetism, sorcery, spell

charming appealing, attractive, bewitching, captivating, delightful, engaging, lovely, pleasant, pleasing, seductive, winning, winsome

chart 1. *n.* blueprint, diagram, graph, map, plan, table 2. *v.* graph, map out, outline, plot, shape, sketch

charter *n.* contract, deed, document, franchise, indenture, privilege, right

chase course, drive, drive away, expel, follow, hound, hunt, pursue, put to flight, run after, track

chaste austere, decent, elegant, immaculate, incorrupt, innocent, modest, moral, neat, pure, quiet, refined, restrained, simple, unaffected, undefiled, virtuous, wholesome

chastise beat, castigate, censure, correct, flog, lash, punish, scold, scourge

chat 1. *n.* chatter, gossip, talk, tête-à-tête 2. *v.* chatter, gossip

chatter *n./v.* babble, blather, chat, gossip, natter, prattle

cheap 1. bargain, cut-price, economical, inexpensive, keen, low-priced, reduced, sale 2. common, inferior, paltry, poor, second-rate, shoddy, tatty, tawdry, worthless 3. base, contemptible, despicable, low, mean, scurvy, sordid, vulgar

cheat *v.* 1. beguile, deceive, defraud, double-cross (*Inf.*), dupe, fleece, fool, hoax, hoodwink, mislead, rip off (*Sl.*), swindle, thwart, trick, victimize 2. baffle, check, defeat, deprive, foil, frustrate, prevent, thwart ~*n.* 3. charlatan, cheater, con man (*Inf.*), deceiver, dodger, double-crosser (*Inf.*), impostor, rogue, shark, sharper, swindler, trickster

DICTIONARY

arrival. —**checkmate** n. Chess winning position in which an opponent's king is under attack and unable to escape; utter defeat. —v. Chess place (an opponent's king) in checkmate; defeat. —**check out** v. pay the bill and leave a hotel; examine or investigate; Informal have a look at. —**checkout** n. counter in a supermarket, where customers pay. —**checkup** n. general (medical) examination.

Cheddar n. smooth firm cheese.

cheek n. side of the face below the eye; Informal impudence. —v. Informal speak impudently to. —**cheeky** adj. impudent. —**cheekily** adv. —**cheekiness** n.

cheep n. young bird's high-pitched cry. —v. utter a cheep.

cheer v. applaud or encourage with shouts; (often foll. by up) comfort or gladden. —n. shout of applause or encouragement. —**cheerful, cheery** adj. —**cheerfully, cheerily** adv. —**cheerfulness** n. —**cheerless** adj. gloomy.

cheerio interj. Informal goodbye.

cheese n. food made from coagulated milk curd; shaped block of this. —**cheesy** adj. —**cheeseburger** n. hamburger with cheese on it. —**cheesecake** n. sweet tart with a cream cheese filling; Slang photographs of scantily clad women. —**cheesecloth** n. loosely woven cotton cloth. —**cheesed off** bored or annoyed. —**cheeseparing** adj. mean.

cheetah n. swift spotted African animal of the cat family.

chef n. cook in a restaurant.

chef-d'oeuvre [shay-**durv**] n., pl. **chefs-d'oeuvre.** masterpiece.

chemical n. substance used in or resulting from a reaction involving changes to atoms or molecules. —adj. of chemistry or chemicals. —**chemically** adv.

chemise [shem-**meez**] n. woman's loose-fitting slip or dress.

chemistry n. science of the composition, properties, and reactions of substances. —**chemist** n. qualified dispenser of prescribed medicines; shop that sells medicines; specialist in chemistry.

chemotherapy n. treatment of disease by chemical means.

chenille [shen-**neel**] n. (fabric of) thick tufty yarn.

cheque n. written order to one's bank to pay money from one's account. —**cheque card** card issued by a bank guaranteeing payment of a customer's cheques.

chequer n. piece used in Chinese chequers. —pl. game of draughts. —**chequered** adj. marked in squares; marked by varied fortunes, e.g. a chequered career.

cherish v. care for; hold dear; cling to (an idea or feeling).

cheroot [sher-**root**] n. cigar with both ends cut flat.

cherry n., pl. **-ries.** small red or black fruit with a stone; tree bearing this. —adj. deep red.

cherub n. angel, often represented as a winged child; sweet child. —**cherubic** [cher-**rew**-bik] adj.

chervil n. herb with an aniseed flavour.

chess n. game of skill for two players with 16 pieces each on a chequered board (**chessboard**)

THESAURUS

check v. 1. compare, confirm, enquire into, examine, inspect, investigate, look at, look over, make sure, monitor, note, probe, scrutinize, study, test, tick, verify 2. bar, bridle, control, curb, delay, halt, hinder, impede, inhibit, limit, obstruct, pause, repress, restrain, retard, stop, thwart ~n. 3. examination, inspection, investigation, research, scrutiny, test 4. constraint, control, curb, damper, hindrance, impediment, limitation, obstruction, restraint, stoppage

cheer v. 1. brighten, buoy up, cheer up, comfort, console, elate, elevate, encourage, enliven, exhilarate, gladden, hearten, incite, inspirit, solace, uplift, warm 2. acclaim, applaud, clap, hail, hurrah ~n. 3. cheerfulness, comfort, gaiety, gladness, glee, hopefulness, joy, liveliness, merriment, merry-making, mirth, optimism, solace

cheerful blithe, bright, buoyant, cheery, con-

tented, enthusiastic, gay, glad, gladsome, happy, hearty, jaunty, jolly, joyful, lighthearted, merry, optimistic, pleasant, sparkling, sprightly, sunny

cheerfulness exuberance, gaiety, geniality, gladness, good cheer, good humour, high spirits, joyousness, light-heartedness

cheerless austere, bleak, comfortless, dark, dejected, depressed, desolate, disconsolate, dismal, drab, dreary, dull, forlorn, gloomy, grim, joyless, melancholy, miserable, mournful, sad, sombre, sorrowful, sullen, unhappy, woeful

cheery breezy, cheerful, happy, jovial, lively, pleasant, sunny

cherish care for, cling to, comfort, encourage, entertain, foster, harbour, hold dear, nourish, nurse, prize, shelter, support, sustain, treasure

DICTIONARY

of 64 squares. —**chessman** n. piece used in chess.

chest n. front of the body, from the neck to the belly; large strong box. —**chest of drawers** piece of furniture consisting of drawers in a frame.

chesterfield n. sofa with high padded sides and back.

chestnut n. reddish-brown edible nut; tree bearing this; horse of a reddish-brown colour; *Informal* old joke. —*adj.* reddish-brown.

cheval glass [shev-**val**] n. full-length mirror mounted to swivel within a frame.

chevron [**shev**-ron] n. V-shaped pattern, esp. denoting rank.

chew v. grind (food etc.) between the teeth. —**chewy** adj. requiring chewing. —**chewing gum** flavoured gum used for chewing.

chianti [kee-**ant**-ee] n. dry red Italian wine.

chiaroscuro [kee-ah-roh-**skew**-roh] n., pl. **-ros.** distribution of light and shade in a picture.

chic [**sheek**] adj. stylish or elegant. —n. stylishness.

chicane [shik-**kane**] n. obstacle in a motor-racing circuit. —**chicanery** n. trickery.

chick n. young bird. —**chickpea** n. edible pea-like seed of an Asian plant. —**chickweed** n. weed with small white flowers.

chicken n. domestic fowl; flesh of this used as food; *Slang* coward. —*adj.* cowardly. —**chicken feed** *Slang* trifling amount of money. —**chicken out** v. *Informal* fail to do something through cowardice. —**chickenpox** n. infectious disease with an itchy rash.

chicory n., pl. **-ries.** plant whose leaves are used in salads; root of this plant, used as a coffee substitute.

chide v. chiding, chided or chid, chid or chidden. rebuke.

chief n. head of a group of people. —*adj.* principal, foremost. —**chiefly** adv. mainly; especially. —**chieftain** n. leader of a tribe.

chiffon [**shif**-fon] n. thin gauzy fabric.

chignon [**sheen**-yon] n. knot of hair worn at the back of the head.

chihuahua [chee-**wah**-wah] n. tiny short-haired dog.

chilblain n. inflammation on the fingers or toes, caused by exposure to cold.

child n., pl. **children.** young human being; son or daughter. —**childhood** n. —**childish** adj. of or like a child; immature or silly. —**childishly** adv. —**childless** adj. —**childlike** adj. simple or innocent. —**childbirth** n. giving birth to a child. —**child's play** very easy task.

chill n. unpleasant coldness; feverish cold. —*adj.* cold. —v. make or become cold. —**chilly** adj. cold; unfriendly. —**chilliness** n.

chilli n. small hot-tasting red or green pepper used in cooking.

chime n. bell or set of bells; sound of this. —v. ring or be rung; produce (sounds) or indicate (the time) by chiming; be in agreement.

chimera [kime-**meer**-a] n. illusory hope; fabled monster with a lion's head, goat's body, and serpent's tail.

chimney n. hollow vertical structure for carrying away smoke or steam. —**chimneypot** n. short pipe on the top of a chimney. —**chimney sweep** person who cleans soot from chimneys.

chimp n. *Informal* short for CHIMPANZEE.

chimpanzee n. intelligent ape of central W Africa.

THESAURUS

chest box, case, casket, crate, trunk

chew bite, champ, crunch, gnaw, grind, masticate, munch

chide admonish, blame, censure, check, criticize, lecture, rebuke, reproach, reprove, scold, tell off (*Inf.*), upbraid

chief 1. *adj.* capital, cardinal, central, especial, essential, foremost, grand, highest, key, leading, main, most important, outstanding, predominant, pre-eminent, premier, prevailing, principal, superior, supreme, uppermost, vital 2. *n.* boss (*Inf.*), captain, commander, director, governor, head, leader, lord, manager, master, principal, ruler, superintendent

chiefly especially, essentially, in general, in the main, mainly, mostly, on the whole, principally, usually

child baby, brat, descendant, infant, issue, juvenile, kid (*Inf.*), little one, minor, offspring, progeny, toddler, tot, youngster (*Inf.*)

childhood boyhood, girlhood, immaturity, infancy, minority, schooldays, youth

childlike artless, credulous, guileless, ingenuous, innocent, naive, simple, trustful, trusting, unfeigned

chill 1. *adj.* bleak, chilly, cold, freezing, raw, sharp, wintry 2. *v.* congeal, cool, freeze, refrigerate

chilly 1. breezy, brisk, cold, cool, crisp, draughty, fresh, nippy, sharp 2. hostile, unfriendly, unsympathetic, unwelcoming

china ceramics, crockery, porcelain, pottery, service, tableware, ware

DICTIONARY

chin *n.* part of the face below the mouth. —**chin-wag** *n. Brit. informal* chat.

china *n.* fine earthenware or porcelain; cups, saucers, etc.

chinchilla *n.* S American rodent with soft grey fur; its fur.

chine *n.* cut of meat including part of the backbone. —*v.* cut (meat) along the backbone.

Chinese *adj.* of China or its people. —*n., pl.* **-ese.** person from China; any of the languages of China.

chink¹ *n.* cleft or crack.

chink² *n.* light ringing sound. —*v.* make this sound.

chintz *n.* printed cotton fabric with a glazed finish.

chip *n.* strip of potato, fried; tiny wafer of a semiconductor forming an integrated circuit; small piece broken off; mark left where a small piece has broken off; counter used to represent money in gambling. —*v.* **chipping, chipped.** break small pieces from. —**have a chip on one's shoulder** *Informal* bear a grudge. —**chip in** *v. Informal* contribute (money); interrupt with a remark.

chipboard *n.* thin board made of compressed wood particles.

chipmunk *n.* small striped N American squirrel.

chipolata *n.* small sausage.

chiropodist [kir-**rop**-pod-ist] *n.* person who treats minor foot complaints. —**chiropody** *n.*

chiropractic [kire-oh-**prak**-tik] *n.* system of treating bodily disorders by manipulation of the spine. —**chiropractor** *n.*

chirp, chirrup *v.* (of a bird or insect) make a short high-pitched sound. —*n.* this sound. —**chirpy** *adj. Informal* cheerful and lively.

chisel *n.* metal tool with a sharp end for shaping wood or stone. —*v.* **-elling, -elled.** carve or form with a chisel.

chit¹ *n.* note or memorandum.

chit² *n.* pert young girl.

chitchat *n.* chat or gossip.

chitterlings *pl. n.* pig's intestines cooked as food.

chivalry *n.* courteous and considerate behaviour, esp. towards women; medieval system and principles of knighthood. —**chivalrous** *adj.*

chive *n.* herb with a mild onion flavour.

chivvy *v.* **-vying, -vied.** *Informal* urge to do something.

chlorine *n.* yellowish-green pungent gaseous element. —**chlorinate** *v.* disinfect or purify (esp. water) with chlorine. —**chlorination** *n.* —**chloride** *n.* compound of chlorine.

chlorofluorocarbon *n.* any of various gaseous compounds of chlorine, fluorine, and carbon, used in refrigerators and aerosol propellants, some of which cause a breakdown of ozone in the earth's atmosphere.

chloroform *n.* strong-smelling liquid formerly used as an anaesthetic. —*v.* make unconscious with chloroform.

chlorophyll *n.* green colouring matter in plants, which helps them convert sunlight into energy.

chock *n.* block or wedge used to prevent a heavy object from moving. —**chock-full, chock-a-block** *adj.* completely full.

chocolate *n.* food made from cacao seeds; sweet or drink made from this. —*adj.* dark brown.

choice *n.* choosing; opportunity or power of choosing; thing or person chosen; possibilities from which to choose. —*adj.* of superior quality.

choir *n.* organized group of singers, esp. in church; part of a church occupied by the choir.

choke *v.* hinder or stop the breathing of (a person) by squeezing or blocking the windpipe; have trouble in breathing; block or clog up. —*n.* device controlling the amount of air that is mixed with the fuel in a petrol engine. —**choker** *n.* tight-fitting necklace. —**choke back** *v.* suppress (anger, tears, etc.).

choler [**kol**-ler] *n.* anger or bad temper. —**choleric** *adj.*

cholera [**kol**-er-a] *n.* dangerous infectious disease characterized by vomiting and diarrhoea.

THESAURUS

chip *n.* dent, flake, flaw, fragment, nick, notch, paring, piece, scrap, scratch, shaving, wafer

chivalrous bold, brave, considerate, courteous, courtly, gallant, gentlemanly, heroic, high-minded, honourable, knightly, true, valiant

chivalry courage, courtesy, courtliness, gallantry, politeness

choice 1. *n.* alternative, election, option, pick, preference, say, selection, variety 2. *adj.* best, dainty, elect, elite, excellent, exclusive, exquisite, hand-picked, nice, precious, prize, rare, select, special, uncommon, valuable

choke bar, block, clog, close, congest, constrict, dam, obstruct, occlude, overpower, smother, stifle, stop, strangle, suffocate, suppress, throttle

DICTIONARY

cholesterol [kol-lest-er-oll] *n.* fatty substance found in animal tissue.

chomp *v.* chew noisily.

choose *v.* **choosing, chose, chosen.** select from a number of alternatives; decide (to do something). —**choosy** *adj. Informal* fussy, hard to please.

chop[1] *v.* **chopping, chopped.** cut with a blow from an axe or knife; cut into pieces; hit (an opponent) with a sharp blow. —*n.* sharp blow; slice of meat, usu. with a rib. —**chopper** *n.* small axe; *Informal* helicopter. —**choppy** *adj.* (of the sea) fairly rough.

chop[2] *v.* **chopping, chopped.** —**chop and change** change one's mind repeatedly.

chop suey *n.* Chinese dish of chopped meat and vegetables fried in soy sauce.

chops *pl. n. Informal* jaws or cheeks.

chopsticks *pl. n.* pair of thin sticks used to eat with by the Chinese and Japanese.

choral *adj.* of or for a choir.

chorale [kor-rahl] *n.* slow stately hymn tune.

chord *n.* simultaneous sounding of three or more musical notes; *Maths* straight line joining two points on a curve.

chore *n.* routine task.

choreography *n.* composition of steps and movements for ballet and other dancing. —**choreographer** *n.* —**choreographic** *adj.*

chorister *n.* singer in a choir.

chortle *v.* chuckle gleefully. —*n.* gleeful chuckle.

chorus *n., pl.* **-ruses.** large choir; group of singers or dancers who perform together; part of a song repeated after each verse; something expressed by many people at once. —*v.* **chorusing, chorused.** sing or say together. —**in chorus** in unison.

chose *v.* past tense of CHOOSE. —**chosen** *v.* past participle of CHOOSE.

choux pastry [shoo] *n.* very light pastry made with eggs.

chow[1] *n.* thick-coated dog with a curled tail, orig. from China.

chow[2] *n. Informal* food.

chow mein *n.* Chinese-American dish consist-

ing of chopped meat or vegetables fried with noodles.

chowder *n.* thick soup containing clams or fish.

Christ *n.* Jesus, regarded by Christians as the Messiah.

christen *v.* baptize; give a name to; use for the first time. —**christening** *n.*

Christendom *n.* all Christian people or countries.

Christian *n.* person who believes in and follows Christ. —*adj.* relating to Christ or Christianity; kind or good. —**Christianity** *n.* religion based on the life and teachings of Christ. —**Christian name** person's first name. —**Christian Science** religious system which emphasizes spiritual healing.

Christmas *n.* annual festival on Dec. 25 commemorating the birth of Christ; period around this time. —**Christmassy** *adj.* —**Christmas box** tip given at Christmas. —**Christmas Day** Dec. 25. —**Christmas Eve** Dec. 24. —**Christmas tree** evergreen tree or imitation of one, decorated as part of Christmas celebrations.

chromatic *adj.* of colour or colours; *Music* (of a scale) proceeding by semitones. —**chromatically** *adv.*

chromatography *n.* separation and analysis of the components of a substance by slowly passing it through an adsorbing material.

chrome, chromium *n.* metallic element used in steel alloys and for electroplating.

chromosome *n.* microscopic gene-carrying body in the nucleus of a cell.

chronic *adj.* lasting a long time; habitual, e.g. *a chronic smoker; Informal* very bad. —**chronically** *adv.*

chronicle *n.* record of events in chronological order. —*v.* record in or as if in a chronicle. —**chronicler** *n.*

chronology *n., pl.* **-gies.** list or arrangement of events in order of occurrence. —**chronological** *adj.* —**chronologically** *adv.*

chronometer *n.* timepiece designed to be accurate in all conditions.

chrysalis [kriss-a-liss] *n.* insect in the stage between larva and adult, when it is in a cocoon.

THESAURUS

choose adopt, designate, elect, fix on, opt for, pick, prefer, see fit, select, settle upon, single out, take, wish

chore burden, duty, job, task

chortle cackle, chuckle, crow, guffaw

chorus 1. choir, choristers, dancers, ensemble,

singers, vocalists 2. burden, refrain, response, strain

christen baptize, call, dub, name, style, title

chronicle 1. *n.* account, annals, diary, history, journal, narrative, record, story 2. *v.* enter, narrate, record, recount, register, relate, report, set down, tell

DICTIONARY

chrysanthemum *n.* garden plant with bright showy flowers.

chub *n.* freshwater fish of the carp family.

chubby *adj.* **-bier, -biest.** plump. —**chubbiness** *n.*

chuck[1] *v. Informal* throw; *Informal* give up, reject; touch (someone) affectionately under the chin.

chuck[2] *n.* cut of beef from the neck to the shoulder; device that holds a workpiece in a lathe or a tool in a drill.

chuckle *v.* laugh softly. —*n.* soft laugh.

chuffed *adj. Informal* pleased, delighted.

chug *n.* short dull sound, as of an engine. —*v.* **chugging, chugged.** operate or move with this sound.

chukker, chukka *n.* period of play in polo.

chum *n. Informal* close friend. —*v.* **chumming, chummed.** —**chum up with** form a close friendship with. —**chummy** *adj.*

chump *n. Informal* stupid person; thick piece of meat.

chunk *n.* thick solid piece; considerable amount. —**chunky** *adj.* thick and short; with thick pieces.

church *n.* building for public Christian worship; clergy; (**C-**) Christians collectively; particular Christian denomination. —**churchgoer** *n.* person who attends church regularly. —**churchwarden** *n.* lay assistant of a parish priest. —**churchyard** *n.* grounds round a church, used as a graveyard.

churlish *adj.* surly and rude.

churn *n.* machine in which cream is shaken to make butter; large container for milk. —*v.* stir (cream) vigorously or make butter in a churn; move about violently. —**churn out** *v. Informal* produce (things) rapidly in large numbers.

chute [**shoot**] *n.* steep channel down which things may be slid; *Informal* short for PARA-CHUTE.

chutney *n.* pickle made from fruit, vinegar, and spices.

CIA *US* Central Intelligence Agency.

cicada [sik-**kah**-da] *n.* large insect that makes a high-pitched drone.

cicatrix [**sik**-a-trix] *n., pl.* **-trices.** scar.

CID Criminal Investigation Department.

cider *n.* alcoholic drink made from fermented apple juice.

cigar *n.* roll of cured tobacco leaves for smoking. —**cigarette** *n.* shredded tobacco in a thin paper cylinder for smoking.

cinch [**sinch**] *n. Informal* easy task; certainty.

cinder *n.* piece of incombustible material left after burning coal.

cine camera *n.* camera for taking moving pictures.

cinema *n.* place for showing films; films collectively. —**cinematic** *adj.* —**cinematography** *n.* technique of making films. —**cinematographer** *n.*

cineraria *n.* garden plant with daisy-like flowers.

cinnamon *n.* spice obtained from the bark of an Asian tree.

cipher [**sife**-er] *n.* system of secret writing; unimportant person.

circa [**sir**-ka] *prep. Latin* about, approximately.

circle *n.* perfectly round geometric figure, line, or shape; group of people sharing an interest or activity; *Theatre* section of seats above the main level of the auditorium. —*v.* move in a circle; surround. —**circlet** *n.* circular ornament worn on the head. —**circular** *adj.* round; moving in a circle. —*n.* letter or notice for general distribution. —**circularity** *n.* —**circulate** *v.* send, go, or move around. —**circulation** *n.* flow of blood around the body; sending or moving around; number of copies of a newspaper or magazine sold. —**circulatory** *adj.*

circuit *n.* complete round or course; complete path through which an electric current can flow; periodical journey around a district, as made by judges; motor-racing track. —**circuitous** [sir-

---

THESAURUS

chuck cast, discard, fling, heave, hurl, pitch, shy, sling, throw, toss

churlish boorish, crabbed, harsh, ill-tempered, impolite, morose, oafish, rude, sullen, surly, uncivil, unmannerly, vulgar

cinema big screen (*Inf.*), films, flicks (*Sl.*), movies, pictures

cipher code, cryptograph

circle *n.* 1. band, circumference, coil, cordon, cycle, disc, globe, lap, loop, orb, perimeter, revolution, ring, round, sphere, turn 2. assembly, clique, club, company, coterie, crowd,

fellowship, fraternity, group, set, society ~*v.* 3. circumnavigate, coil, compass, curve, encircle, enclose, encompass, envelop, gird, hem in, revolve, ring, rotate, surround, tour

circuit area, compass, course, journey, orbit, revolution, round, route, tour, track

circulate broadcast, diffuse, distribute, issue, make known, promulgate, propagate, publicize, publish, spread

circulation 1. currency, distribution, spread, transmission, vogue 2. circling, flow, motion, rotation

DICTIONARY

kew-it-uss] *adj.* roundabout, indirect. —**circuitry** [sir-kit-tree] *n.* electrical circuit(s).

circumcise *v.* cut off the foreskin of. —**circumcision** *n.*

circumference *n.* boundary of a specified area or shape, esp. of a circle; distance round this.

circumflex *n.* accent (ˆ) over a vowel to show that it is pronounced in a particular way.

circumlocution *n.* indirect expression. —**circumlocutory** *adj.*

circumnavigate *v.* sail right round. —**circumnavigation** *n.*

circumscribe *v.* restrict; draw a line round. —**circumscription** *n.*

circumspect *adj.* cautious, prudent. —**circumspectly** *adv.* —**circumspection** *n.*

circumstance *n.* (*usu. pl.*) occurrence or condition that accompanies or influences a person or event. —**circumstantial** *adj.* (of evidence) strongly suggesting something but not proving it; detailed. —**circumstantiate** *v.* prove by giving details.

circumvent *v.* avoid or get round (a difficulty etc.). —**circumvention** *n.*

circus *n., pl.* **-cuses.** (performance given by) a travelling company of acrobats, clowns, performing animals, etc.

cirrhosis [sir-roh-siss] *n.* liver disease.

cirrus *n., pl.* **-ri.** high wispy cloud.

cistern *n.* water tank.

citadel *n.* fortress in a city.

cite *v.* quote; bring forward as proof. —**citation** *n.*

citizen *n.* native or naturalized member of a state or nation; inhabitant of a city or town. —**citizenship** *n.* —**Citizens' Band** range of radio

frequencies for private communication by the public.

citric acid *n.* weak acid found in citrus fruits.

citrus fruit *n.* juicy, sharp-tasting fruit such as an orange, lemon, or lime.

city *n., pl.* **-ties.** large or important town. —**the City** area of London as a financial centre.

civet [siv-vit] *n.* spotted catlike African mammal; musky fluid from its glands used in perfume.

civic *adj.* of a city or citizens. —**civics** *pl. n.* study of the rights and responsibilities of citizenship.

civil *adj.* relating to the citizens of a state as opposed to the armed forces or the Church; polite. —**civilly** *adv.* —**civility** *n.* politeness. —**civilian** *n., adj.* (person) not belonging to the armed forces. —**civil service** service responsible for the administration of the government. —**civil servant** member of the civil service. —**civil war** war between people of the same country.

civilize *v.* bring out of barbarism into a state of civilization; refine. —**civilization** *n.* high level of human cultural and social development; particular society which has reached this level.

civvies *pl. n. Slang* civilian clothes.

Cl *Chem.* chlorine.

clack *n.* sound made by two hard objects striking together. —*v.* (cause to) make this sound.

clad *v.* a past of CLOTHE.

cladding *n.* material used for the outside facing of a building etc.

claim *v.* demand as a right; assert; call for or need. —*n.* demand for something as due; assertion; right; thing claimed. —**claimant** *n.*

clairvoyance *n.* power of perceiving things

THESAURUS

circumference border, boundary, bounds, circuit, edge, extremity, fringe, limits, outline, perimeter, rim, verge

circumstance accident, condition, contingency, detail, element, event, fact, factor, happening, incident, item, occurrence, particular, position, respect, situation

cistern basin, reservoir, sink, tank, vat

citadel bastion, fastness, fortification, fortress, keep, stronghold, tower

cite adduce, advance, allude to, enumerate, evidence, extract, mention, name, quote, specify

citizen burgher, dweller, freeman, inhabitant, ratepayer, resident, townsman

city conurbation, megalopolis, metropolis, municipality

civil 1. civic, domestic, home, interior, municipal, political 2. affable, civilized, courteous, courtly, obliging, polished, polite, refined, urbane, well-bred, well-mannered

civilization 1. culture, development, education, enlightenment, progress, refinement, sophistication 2. community, nation, people, polity, society

civilize cultivate, educate, enlighten, improve, polish, refine, tame

claim 1. *v.* allege, ask, assert, call for, collect, demand, exact, hold, insist, maintain, need, pick up, profess, require, take, uphold 2. *n.* application, assertion, call, demand, petition, privilege, protestation, request, requirement, right, title

DICTIONARY

beyond the natural range of the senses. —**clair-voyant** n., adj.

clam n. edible shellfish with a hinged shell. —v. **clamming, clammed.** —**clam up** Informal refuse to talk.

clamber v. climb awkwardly or with difficulty.

clammy adj. -**mier**, -**miest.** unpleasantly moist and sticky. —**clamminess** n.

clamour n. loud protest; loud persistent outcry or noise. —v. make a loud outcry or noise. —**clamorous** adj. —**clamour for** v. demand noisily.

clamp n. tool with movable jaws for holding things together tightly. —v. fasten with a clamp. —**clamp down on** v. become stricter about; suppress.

clan n. group of families with a common ancestor; close group. —**clannish** adj. (of a group) tending to exclude outsiders.

clandestine adj. secret, furtive.

clang n. loud ringing sound. —v. (cause to) make this sound. —**clanger** n. Informal conspicuous mistake.

clangour n. loud continuous clanging sound. —**clangorous** adj.

clank n. harsh metallic sound. —v. (cause to) make this sound.

clap[1] v. **clapping, clapped.** applaud by striking the palms of one's hands sharply together; put quickly or forcibly. —n. act or sound of clapping; sharp abrupt sound, esp. of thunder. —**clapped out** Slang worn out. —**clapper** n. piece of metal inside a bell, which causes it to sound when struck against the side. —**clapperboard** n. pair of hinged boards clapped together during filming to aid synchronizing sound and picture. —**claptrap** n. empty words.

clap[2] n. Slang gonorrhoea.

claret [klar-rit] n. dry red wine from Bordeaux.

clarify v. -**fying**, -**fied.** make or become clear. —**clarification** n.

clarinet n. keyed woodwind instrument with a single reed. —**clarinettist** n.

clarion n. obsolete high-pitched trumpet; its sound. —**clarion call** rousing appeal.

clarity n. clearness.

clash v. come into conflict; (of events) coincide; (of colours) look unattractive together; (cause to) make a clashing sound. —n. conflict; loud harsh noise, esp. of things striking together.

clasp n. device for fastening things; firm grasp or embrace. —v. grasp or embrace firmly; fasten with a clasp. —**clasp knife** knife whose blade folds into the handle.

class n. group of people or things sharing a common characteristic; social group of a particular rank; system of dividing society into such groups; group of pupils or students taught together; standard of quality; Informal excellence or elegance. —v. place in a class. —**classy** adj. Informal stylish, elegant. —**classify** v. arrange in classes; designate (information) as officially secret. —**classifiable** adj. —**classification** n.

classic adj. of the highest class, esp. in art or literature; typical; characterized by simplicity and purity of form. —n. author, artist, or work of art of recognized excellence. —pl. study of ancient Greek and Roman literature and culture. —**classical** adj. traditional and standard; Music denoting serious art music; of or influenced by ancient Greek and Roman culture. —**classically** adv. —**classicism** n. artistic style showing regularity of form and emotional restraint. —**classicist** n.

clatter n. rattling noise. —v. (cause to) make a rattling noise.

THESAURUS

clan band, brotherhood, clique, faction, family, fraternity, group, race, sect, sept, set, society, tribe

clap acclaim, applaud, cheer

clarification elucidation, explanation, simplification

clarify clear up, elucidate, explain, make plain, resolve, simplify, shed light on

clarity clearness, definition, explicitness, intelligibility, lucidity, precision, simplicity, transparency

clash 1. v. conflict, cross swords, feud, grapple, quarrel, war, wrangle 2. n. brush, collision, conflict, confrontation, difference of opinion, disagreement, fight

clasp 1. v. clutch, connect, embrace, enfold,

fasten, grapple, grasp, grip, hold, hug, press, seize, squeeze 2. n. brooch, buckle, catch, clip, grip, hasp, hook, pin, snap

class caste, category, collection, department, division, genus, grade, group, grouping, kind, league, order, rank, set, sort, species, sphere, status, type, value

classic adj. 1. best, finest, first-rate, masterly 2. archetypal, definitive, exemplary, ideal, master, model, standard, typical ~n. 3. exemplar, masterpiece, model, standard

classical Attic, Augustan, Grecian, Greek, Hellenic, Latin, Roman

classification analysis, arrangement, codification, grading, sorting, taxonomy

classify arrange, catalogue, codify, dispose, distribute, file, grade, rank, sort

DICTIONARY

clause *n*. part of a sentence, containing a verb; section in a legal document.

claustrophobia *n*. abnormal fear of confined spaces. —**claustrophobic** *adj*.

clavichord *n*. early keyboard instrument.

clavicle *n*. collarbone.

claw *n*. sharp hooked nail of a bird or beast; similar part, such as a crab's pincer. —*v*. tear with claws or nails.

clay *n*. fine-grained earth, soft when moist and hardening when baked, used to make bricks and pottery. —**clayey** *adj*. —**clay pigeon** baked clay disc hurled into the air as a target for shooting.

claymore *n*. two-edged broadsword formerly used by Scottish Highlanders.

clean *adj*. free from dirt or impurities; not yet used; morally sound; smooth and regular; without obscenity; complete, e.g. *a clean break*. —*adv*. in a clean way. —*v*. free from dirt. —**come clean** *Informal* confess. —**cleaner** *n*. —**cleanly** *adv*. —**cleanliness** *n*. —**cleanse** *v*. make clean. —**cleanser** *n*.

clear *adj*. transparent; free from darkness or obscurity, bright; (of weather) free from clouds; plain, distinct; free from doubt or confusion; without blemish or defect; free from obstruction; (of money) net. —*adv*. clearly; completely; out of the way, e.g. *stand clear of the gates*. —*v*. make or become clear; acquit; pass by or over without touching; make as profit. —**clearly** *adv*. —**clearness** *n*. —**clearance** *n*. clearing; official permission. —**clearing** *n*. area cleared of trees. —**clear off** *v*. *Informal* go away. —**clear out** *v*. empty; *Informal* go away. —**clear-sighted** *adj*. percep-tive. —**clearway** *n*. stretch of road on which motorists may stop only in an emergency.

cleat *n*. wedge; piece of wood or iron with two projecting ends round which ropes are fastened.

cleave¹ *v*. **cleaving; cleft, cleaved,** *or* **clove; cleft, cleaved,** *or* **cloven.** split apart. —**cleavage** *n*. space between a woman's breasts, as revealed by a low-cut dress; division, split. —**cleaver** *n*. heavy butcher's knife.

cleave² *v*. cling or adhere.

clef *n*. *Music* symbol at the beginning of a stave to show the pitch.

cleft *n*. split or indentation. —*v*. a past of CLEAVE¹. —**in a cleft stick** in a very difficult position.

clematis *n*. climbing plant with showy flowers.

clement *adj*. (of weather) mild. —**clemency** *n*. mercy.

clementine *n*. small orange citrus fruit.

clench *v*. close or squeeze (one's teeth or fist) firmly together; grasp firmly.

clerestory [clear-store-ee] *n*., *pl*. **-ries.** row of windows at the top of a wall above an adjoining roof.

clergy *n*. priests and ministers as a group. —**clergyman** *n*.

cleric *n*. member of the clergy.

clerical *adj*. of clerks or office work; of the clergy.

clerk *n*. employee in an office, bank, or court who keeps records, files, and accounts.

clever *adj*. intelligent, quick at learning; showing skill. —**cleverly** *adv*. —**cleverness** *n*.

THESAURUS

clause article, chapter, condition, paragraph, part, passage, section

claw nail, nipper, pincer, talon, tentacle

clean *adj*. 1. faultless, fresh, hygienic, immaculate, pure, sanitary, spotless, unsoiled, unstained, unsullied, washed 2. chaste, decent, exemplary, good, honourable, innocent, moral, pure, respectable, undefiled, upright, virtuous ~*v*. 3. bath, cleanse, disinfect, do up, dust, launder, mop, purge, purify, rinse, scour, scrub, sponge, swab, sweep, wash, wipe

cleanser detergent, disinfectant, scourer, soap, soap powder, solvent

clear *adj*. 1. bright, cloudless, fair, fine, light, luminous, shining, sunny, unclouded, undimmed 2. apparent, audible, coherent, definite, distinct, evident, explicit, express, lucid, manifest, obvious, palpable, patent, plain, pronounced, recognizable, unambiguous, unequivocal 3. empty, free, open, smooth, unhampered, unhindered, unimpeded, unlimit-ed, unobstructed 4. certain, convinced, decided, definite, positive, resolved, satisfied, sure ~*v*. 5. clean, erase, purify, refine, sweep away, tidy (up), wipe 6. break up, brighten, clarify, lighten 7. absolve, acquit, excuse, exonerate, justify, vindicate 8. jump, leap, miss, pass over, vault

clearly beyond doubt, distinctly, evidently, obviously, openly, seemingly, undeniably, undoubtedly

clergy clerics, ecclesiastics, holy orders, ministry, priesthood, the cloth

clergyman chaplain, cleric, curate, divine, father, minister, padre, parson, pastor, priest, rabbi, rector, reverend (*Inf*.), vicar

clever able, adroit, apt, astute, brainy (*Inf*.), bright, canny, capable, cunning, deep, discerning, expert, gifted, ingenious, intelligent, inventive, keen, knowing, quick, rational, sagacious, sensible, shrewd, skilful, smart, talented, witty

DICTIONARY

cliché [klee-shay] n. hackneyed expression or idea. —**clichéd** adj.

click n. short slight sound. —v. (cause to) make this sound; Slang be a success; Informal become suddenly clear; Informal (of two people) get on well.

client n. person who uses the services of a professional; customer. —**clientele** [klee-on-tell] n. clients collectively.

cliff n. steep rock face, esp. along the sea shore. —**cliffhanger** n. film, game, etc. which is exciting and full of suspense because its outcome is uncertain.

climate n. prevalent weather conditions of an area. —**climatic** adj.

climax n. most intense point of an experience, series of events, or story; orgasm. —v. reach a climax. —**climactic** adj.

climb v. go up or ascend; rise. —n. place to be climbed. —**climber** n. —**climb down** v. retreat from an opinion or position.

clime n. Lit. region or its climate.

clinch v. settle (an argument or agreement) decisively. —n. clinching. —**clincher** n. Informal something decisive.

cling v. **clinging, clung.** hold fast or stick closely. —**clingfilm** n. thin polythene wrapping.

clinic n. place in which outpatients receive medical advice or treatment; private or specialized hospital. —**clinical** adj. of a clinic; scientifically detached. —**clinically** adv.

clink[1] n. light sharp metallic sound. —v. (cause to) make such a sound.

clink[2] n. Slang prison.

clinker n. fused coal residues from a fire or furnace.

clinker-built adj. (of a boat) made of overlapping planks.

clip[1] v. **clipping, clipped.** cut with shears or scissors; Informal hit sharply. —n. short extract of a film; Informal sharp blow. —**clippers** pl. n. tool for clipping. —**clipping** n. something cut out, esp. an article from a newspaper.

clip[2] n. device for attaching or holding things together. —v. **clipping, clipped.** attach or hold together with a clip.

clipper n. fast commercial sailing ship.

clique [kleek] n. small exclusive group. —**cliqueish** adj.

clitoris [klit-or-iss] n. small sexually sensitive part of the female genitals. —**clitoral** adj.

cloak n. loose sleeveless outer garment. —v. cover or conceal. —**cloakroom** n. room where coats may be left temporarily.

clobber Informal —v. batter; defeat utterly. —n. belongings.

cloche [klosh] n. cover to protect young plants; woman's close-fitting hat.

clock n. instrument for showing the time; device with a dial for recording or measuring. —**clockwise** adv., adj. in the direction in which the hands of a clock rotate. —**clock in** or **on**, **out** or **off** v. register arrival at or departure from work on an automatic time recorder. —**clock up** v. reach (a total). —**clockwork** n. mechanism similar to that of a clock, as in a wind-up toy.

clod n. lump of earth; stupid person. —**cloddish** adj.

clog v. **clogging, clogged.** block. —n. wooden-soled shoe.

cloisonné [klwah-zon-nay] n. design made by filling in a wire outline with coloured enamel.

cloister n. covered pillared arcade, usu. in a monastery. —**cloistered** adj. sheltered.

clone n. group of organisms or cells reproduced asexually from a single plant or animal; Informal person who closely resembles another. —v. produce as a clone.

close[1] adj. near; intimate; careful, thorough; oppressive or stifling; secretive; compact, dense.

THESAURUS

client applicant, buyer, consumer, customer, dependant, habitué, patient, protégé, shopper

clientele clients, customers, following, market, regulars, trade

cliff bluff, crag, escarpment, face, overhang, precipice, rock face, scar, scarp

climate region, temperature, weather

climax acme, apogee, culmination, head, height, highlight, high spot (Inf.), peak, summit, top, zenith

climb ascend, clamber, mount, rise, scale, shin up, soar, top

climb down 1. descend, dismount 2. back down, eat one's words, retract, retreat

cling adhere, be true to, clasp, cleave to, clutch, embrace, fasten, grasp, grip, hug, stick, twine round

clip[1] crop, curtail, cut, cut short, pare, prune, shear, shorten, snip, trim

clip[2] attach, fasten, fix, hold, pin, staple

cloak 1. v. camouflage, conceal, cover, disguise, hide, mask, obscure, screen, veil 2. n. cape, mantle, wrap

clog block, burden, congest, dam up, hamper, hinder, impede, jam, obstruct, occlude, shackle, stop up

DICTIONARY

—*adv.* closely or tightly. —*n.* street closed at one end; courtyard or quadrangle. —**closely** *adv.* —**closeness** *n.* —**close season** period when it is illegal to kill certain kinds of game and fish. —**close-up** *n.* photograph or film taken at very close range.

close² *v.* shut; prevent access to; finish; bring or come nearer together. —*n.* end. —**closed shop** place of work in which all workers must belong to a particular trade union.

closet *n.* US cupboard; small private room. —*adj.* private or secret. —*v.* **closeting, closeted.** shut away in private, esp. for conference.

closure *n.* closing or being closed.

clot *n.* soft thick lump formed from liquid; *Informal* fool. —*v.* **clotting, clotted.** form clots.

cloth *n.* woven fabric.

clothe *v.* **clothing, clothed** *or* **clad.** put clothes on; provide with clothes. —**clothes** *pl. n.* articles of dress; bed coverings. —**clothing** *n.* clothes collectively.

cloud *n.* mass of condensed water vapour floating in the sky; floating mass of smoke, dust, etc. —*v.* make or become cloudy; confuse; make gloomy or depressed. —**cloudless** *adj.* —**cloudy** *adj.* full of clouds; (of liquid) opaque. —**cloudburst** *n.* heavy fall of rain.

clout *Informal* —*n.* blow; influence, power. —*v.* hit.

clove¹ *n.* dried flower bud of a tropical tree, used as a spice; segment of a bulb of garlic.

clove² *v.* a past tense of CLEAVE¹. —**clove hitch** knot used to fasten a rope to a spar.

cloven *v.* a past participle of CLEAVE¹. —**cloven hoof** divided hoof of a sheep, goat, etc.

clover *n.* plant with three-lobed leaves. —**in clover** in luxury.

clown *n.* comic entertainer in a circus; amusing person; stupid person. —*v.* perform as a clown; behave foolishly. —**clownish** *adj.*

cloy *v.* sicken by an excess of something sweet or pleasurable.

club *n.* association of people with common interests; building used by such a group; thick stick used as a weapon; bat or stick used in some games; playing card of the suit marked with black three-leafed symbols. —*v.* **clubbing, clubbed.** strike with a club. —**club together** *v.* combine resources for a common purpose.

club foot *n.* congenitally deformed foot.

cluck *n.* low clicking noise made by a hen. —*v.* make this noise.

clue *n.* something that helps to solve a mystery or puzzle. —**not have a clue** be completely baffled. —**clueless** *adj.* stupid.

clump¹ *n.* cluster or mass. —*v.* form into a clump.

clump² *v.* walk or tread heavily. —*n.* dull heavy tread.

clumsy *adj.* **-sier, -siest.** lacking skill or physical coordination; badly made or done. —**clumsily** *adv.* —**clumsiness** *n.*

THESAURUS

close¹ 1. adjacent, adjoining, approaching, at hand, handy, hard by, imminent, impending, near, nearby, neighbouring, nigh 2. compact, congested, cramped, cropped, crowded, dense, impenetrable, jam-packed, packed, short, solid, thick, tight 3. attached, confidential, dear, devoted, familiar, inseparable, intimate, loving 4. airless, heavy, humid, muggy, oppressive, stale, stifling, stuffy, suffocating, sweltering, thick

close² *v.* 1. bar, block, choke, clog, confine, cork, fill, lock, obstruct, plug, seal, secure, shut, shut up, stop up 2. cease, complete, conclude, discontinue, end, finish, shut down, terminate, wind up

cloth dry goods, fabric, material, stuff, textiles

clothe apparel, array, attire, cover, deck, drape, dress, endow, enwrap, equip, fit out, garb, habit, invest, outfit, rig, robe, swathe

clothes, clothing attire, costume, dress, ensemble, garb, garments, gear (*Inf.*), get-up (*Inf.*), habits, outfit, raiment, togs (*Inf.*), vestments, vesture, wardrobe, wear

cloud 1. *n.* billow, darkness, fog, gloom, haze, mist, murk, obscurity, vapour 2. *v.* darken, dim, eclipse, obscure, overcast, overshadow, shade, shadow, veil

cloudy blurred, confused, dark, dim, dismal, dull, dusky, gloomy, hazy, indistinct, leaden, lowering, muddy, murky, nebulous, obscure, opaque, overcast, sombre, sullen, sunless

clown 1. *n.* buffoon, comedian, dolt, fool, harlequin, jester, joker, pierrot, prankster 2. *v.* act the fool, jest, mess about

club 1. bat, bludgeon, cosh, cudgel, stick, truncheon 2. association, circle, clique, company, fraternity, group, guild, lodge, order, set, society, union

clue evidence, hint, indication, inkling, intimation, lead, pointer, sign, suggestion, suspicion, tip, tip-off, trace

clumsy awkward, blundering, bumbling, bungling, gauche, gawky, heavy, ill-shaped, inept, lumbering, maladroit, ponderous, uncoordinated

DICTIONARY

clung *v.* past of CLING.

clunk *n.* dull metallic sound. —*v.* make such a sound.

cluster *n.* small close group. —*v.* (cause to) form a cluster.

clutch[1] *v.* grasp tightly; try to seize. —*n.* tight grasp; device enabling two revolving shafts to be connected and disconnected.

clutch[2] *n.* set of eggs laid at the same time; brood of chickens.

clutter *v.* strew objects about (a place) in disorder. —*n.* disordered heap or mass of objects.

cm centimetre(s).

CND Campaign for Nuclear Disarmament.

c/o care of; *Book-keeping* carried over.

CO Commanding Officer.

Co *Chem.* cobalt.

co- *prefix* together; joint or jointly, e.g. *coproduction.*

Co. Company; County.

coach *n.* long-distance bus; railway carriage; large four-wheeled horse-drawn carriage; tutor, trainer. —*v.* train or teach.

coagulate [koh-**ag**-yew-late] *v.* change from a liquid to a semisolid mass. —**coagulation** *n.* —**coagulant** *n.* substance causing coagulation.

coal *n.* black mineral consisting mainly of carbon, used as fuel. —**coalfield** *n.* area rich in coal.

coalesce [koh-a-**less**] *v.* come together, merge. —**coalescence** *n.*

coalition [koh-a-**lish**-un] *n.* temporary alliance, esp. between political parties.

coarse *adj.* rough in texture; unrefined or indecent. —**coarsely** *adv.* —**coarseness** *n.* —**coarsen** *v.* —**coarse fish** any freshwater fish not of the salmon family.

coast *n.* sea shore. —*v.* move by momentum, without the use of power. —**coastal** *adj.* —**coaster** *n.* small ship; small mat placed under a glass.

—coastguard *n.* organization which aids shipping and prevents smuggling; member of this. —**coastline** *n.* outline of a coast.

coat *n.* long outer garment with sleeves; animal's fur or hair; covering layer. —*v.* cover with a layer. —**coating** *n.* covering layer. —**coat of arms** heraldic emblem of a family or institution.

coax *v.* persuade gently; manipulate carefully and patiently.

coaxial [koh-**ax**-ee-al] *adj.* (of a cable) transmitting by means of two concentric conductors separated by an insulator.

cob *n.* thickset type of horse; male swan; stalk of an ear of maize; round loaf of bread.

cobalt *n.* metallic element; deep blue pigment made from it.

cobber *n. Aust. informal* friend, mate: used as a term of address between men.

cobble *v.* put together roughly. —*n.* (also **cobblestone**) round stone used for paving. —**cobbler** *n.* shoe mender.

cobra *n.* venomous hooded snake of Asia and Africa.

cobweb *n.* spider's web.

cocaine *n.* addictive drug used as a narcotic and local anaesthetic.

coccyx [**kok**-six] *n., pl.* **coccyges** [kok-**sije**-eez]. bone at the base of the spinal column.

cochineal *n.* scarlet dye obtained from a Mexican insect.

cock *n.* male bird, esp. of domestic fowl; stopcock; hammer of a gun. —*v.* draw back (the hammer of a gun) to firing position; lift and turn (part of the body). —**cockerel** *n.* young cock. —**cock-a-hoop** *adj.* in high spirits. —**cock-and-bull story** improbable story. —**cockeyed** *adj. Informal* askew; absurd.

cockade *n.* rosette or feather worn on a hat as a badge.

THESAURUS

cluster 1. *n.* batch, bunch, clump, collection, gathering, group, knot 2. *v.* assemble, bunch, collect, flock, gather

clutch catch, clasp, cling to, embrace, grab, grapple, grasp, grip, seize

coach *n.* 1. bus, car, carriage, vehicle 2. instructor, teacher, trainer, tutor ~*v.* 3. cram, drill, instruct, prepare, train, tutor

coalesce blend, combine, come together, consolidate, fuse, integrate, merge, mix, unite

coalition alliance, amalgamation, association, bloc, combination, compact, confederacy, confederation, integration, league, merger, union

coarse boorish, brutish, foul-mouthed, gruff, loutish, rough, rude, uncivil, unrefined

coarseness bawdiness, crudity, indelicacy, poor taste, ribaldry, roughness, smut, uncouthness, unevenness

coast 1. *n.* beach, border, coastline, seaside, shore, strand 2. *v.* cruise, drift, freewheel, get by, glide, sail, taxi

coat *n.* 1. fleece, fur, hair, hide, pelt, skin, wool 2. coating, covering, layer, overlay ~*v.* 3. apply, cover, plaster, smear, spread

coax allure, beguile, cajole, decoy, entice, flatter, persuade, prevail upon, soothe, talk into, wheedle

DICTIONARY

cockatoo *n.* crested parrot of Australia or the East Indies.

cockatrice [kok-a-triss] *n.* mythical animal like a small dragon.

cockchafer *n.* large flying beetle.

cocker spaniel *n.* small breed of spaniel.

cockle *n.* edible bivalve mollusc.

Cockney *n.* native of the East End of London; Cockney dialect.

cockpit *n.* pilot's compartment in an aircraft; driver's compartment in a racing car.

cockroach *n.* beetle-like insect which is a household pest.

cocksure *adj.* overconfident, arrogant.

cocktail *n.* mixed alcoholic drink; appetizer of seafood or mixed fruits.

cocky *adj.* **cockier, cockiest.** conceited and overconfident. **—cockily** *adv.* **—cockiness** *n.*

cocoa *n.* powder made from the seed of the cacao tree; drink made from this powder.

coconut *n.* large hard fruit of a type of palm tree; edible flesh of this fruit. **—coconut matting** coarse matting made from the fibrous husk of the coconut.

cocoon *n.* silky sheath of a chrysalis; protective covering. **—v.** wrap or protect as if in a cocoon.

COD cash on delivery.

cod *n.* large food fish of the North Atlantic.

coda [kode-a] *n.* final part of a musical composition.

coddle *v.* overprotect or pamper.

code *n.* system of letters, symbols, or prearranged signals by which messages can be communicated briefly or briefly; set of principles or rules. **—v.** put into code. **—codify** [kode-if-fie] *v.* organize (rules or procedures) systematically. **—codification** *n.*

codeine [kode-een] *n.* drug used as a painkiller.

codex *n., pl.* **codices.** volume of manuscripts of an ancient text.

codger *n. Informal* old man.

codicil [kode-iss-ill] *n.* addition to a will.

coeducation *n.* education of boys and girls together. **—coeducational** *adj.*

coefficient *n. Maths* number or constant placed before and multiplying a quantity.

coelacanth [seel-a-kanth] *n.* primitive marine fish.

coeliac disease [seel-ee-ak] *n.* disease which hampers digestion of food.

coerce [koh-urss] *v.* compel or force. **—coercion** *n.* **—coercive** *adj.*

coeval [koh-eev-al] *adj., n.* contemporary.

coexist *v.* exist together, esp. peacefully despite differences. **—coexistence** *n.*

C of E Church of England.

coffee *n.* drink made from the roasted and ground seeds of a tropical shrub; beanlike seeds of this shrub. **—adj.** light brown. **—coffee bar** café, snack bar. **—coffee table** small low table.

coffer *n.* chest for valuables. **—pl.** store of money.

cofferdam *n.* watertight enclosure pumped dry to enable construction work to be done.

coffin *n.* box in which a corpse is buried or cremated.

cog *n.* one of a series of teeth on the rim of a gearwheel; unimportant person in a big organization.

cogent [koh-jent] *adj.* forcefully convincing. **—cogency** *n.* **—cogently** *adv.*

cogitate [koj-it-tate] *v.* think deeply, ponder. **—cogitation** *n.*

cognac [kon-yak] *n.* French brandy.

cognate *adj.* related, akin.

cognition *n.* act or experience of knowing or acquiring knowledge. **—cognitive** *adj.*

cognizance *n.* knowledge, perception. **—cognizant** *adj.*

cognoscenti [kon-yo-shen-tee] *pl. n.* connoisseurs.

cohabit *v.* live together as husband and wife without being married. **—cohabitation** *n.*

cohere *v.* stick together; be logically connected and consistent. **—coherence** *n.* **—coherent** *adj.* capable of intelligible speech; logical and consistent. **—coherently** *adv.* **—cohesion** *n.* tendency to unite. **—cohesive** *adj.*

cohort *n.* band of associates; tenth part of a Roman legion.

coiffure *n.* hairstyle. **—coiffeur, coiffeuse** *n.* hairdresser.

coil *v.* wind or be wound in loops; move in a winding course. **—n.** something coiled; single loop of this; contraceptive device inserted in the womb.

THESAURUS

cocky arrogant, brash, cocksure, conceited, lordly, overconfident, swaggering, vain

code 1. cipher 2. canon, convention, custom, ethics, etiquette, manners, maxim, rules, system

cogitate consider, contemplate, deliberate, meditate, mull over, muse, ponder, reflect, ruminate, think

coil curl, entwine, loop, snake, spiral, twine, twist, wind, wreathe

DICTIONARY

coin *n.* piece of metal money; metal currency collectively. —*v.* invent (a word or phrase). —**coin it in** *Informal* make money rapidly. —**coinage** *n.* coining; coins collectively; word or phrase coined.

coincide *v.* happen at the same time; agree or correspond exactly. —**coincidence** *n.* occurrence of simultaneous or apparently connected events; coinciding. —**coincident** *adj.* —**coincidental** *adj.* —**coincidentally** *adv.*

coir *n.* coconut husk fibre.

coition [koh-**ish**-un], **coitus** [**koh**-it-uss] *n.* sexual intercourse. —**coital** *adj.*

coke[1] *n.* solid fuel left after gas has been distilled from coal.

coke[2] *n. Slang* cocaine.

col *n.* high mountain pass.

cola *n.* soft drink flavoured with an extract from the nuts of a tropical tree.

colander *n.* perforated bowl for straining or rinsing foods.

cold *adj.* lacking heat; lacking affection or enthusiasm; (of a colour) giving an impression of coldness; *Slang* unconscious, e.g. *out cold.* —*n.* lack of heat; illness characterized by catarrh and sneezing. —**coldly** *adv.* —**coldness** *n.* —**cold-blooded** *adj.* having a body temperature that varies with that of the surroundings; callous or cruel. —**cold cream** creamy preparation for softening and cleansing the skin. —**cold feet** *Slang* fear. —**cold-shoulder** *v.* treat (someone) with indifference. —**cold war** political hostility between countries without actual warfare.

coleslaw *n.* salad dish of shredded raw cabbage in a dressing.

coley *n.* codlike food fish of the N Atlantic.

colic *n.* severe pains in the stomach and bowels. —**colicky** *adj.*

colitis [koh-**lie**-tiss] *n.* inflammation of the colon.

collaborate *v.* work with another on a project; cooperate with an enemy invader. —**collaboration** *n.* —**collaborative** *adj.* —**collaborator** *n.*

collage [kol-**lahzh**] *n.* art form in which various materials or objects are glued onto a surface; picture made in this way.

collapse *v.* fall down or in suddenly; fail completely; fold compactly. —*n.* act of collapsing; sudden failure or breakdown. —**collapsible** *adj.*

collar *n.* part of a garment round the neck; band put round an animal's neck; cut of meat from an animal's neck; band round a pipe, rod, or shaft. —*v. Informal* seize, arrest; catch in order to speak to; take for oneself. —**collarbone** *n.* bone joining the shoulder blade to the breast bone.

collate *v.* compare carefully. —**collation** *n.* collating; light meal. —**collator** *n.*

collateral *n.* security pledged for the repayment of a loan.

colleague *n.* fellow worker, esp. in a profession.

collect[1] *v.* gather or be gathered together; accumulate (stamps etc.) as a hobby; fetch. —**collected** *adj.* calm and controlled. —**collection** *n.* collecting; things collected. —**collector** *n.* —**collective** *n.* group of people working together on an enterprise and sharing the benefits from it.

THESAURUS

coin 1. *v.* create, fabricate, forge, frame, invent, make up, mint, mould, originate, think up 2. *n.* cash, change, copper, money, silver

coincide 1. be concurrent, coexist, synchronize 2. accord, harmonize, match, square, tally

coincidence accident, chance, eventuality, fluke, luck, stroke of luck

cold *adj.* 1. arctic, biting, bitter, bleak, chill, chilly, cool, freezing, frigid, frosty, frozen, icy, raw, wintry 2. benumbed, chilled, chilly, freezing, numbed, shivery 3. aloof, apathetic, dead, distant, frigid, indifferent, reserved, spiritless, standoffish, stony, unfeeling, unmoved, unresponsive, unsympathetic ~*n.* 4. chill, chilliness, coldness, frigidity, frostiness, iciness, inclemency

collaborate cooperate, join forces, participate, team up, work together

collaborator associate, colleague, confederate, co-worker, partner, team-mate

collapse 1. *v.* break down, cave in, come to

nothing, crumple, fail, faint, fall, fold, founder, give way, subside 2. *n.* breakdown, cave-in, disintegration, downfall, exhaustion, failure, faint

collar *v.* apprehend, appropriate, capture, catch, grab, lay hands on, seize

colleague ally, assistant, associate, auxiliary, collaborator, companion, comrade, fellow worker, helper, partner, team-mate, workmate

collect 1. accumulate, amass, assemble, gather, heap, hoard, save, stockpile 2. assemble, congregate, convene, converge, flock together, rally

collected calm, composed, controlled, cool, placid, poised, self-possessed, serene, unruffled

collection 1. accumulation, anthology, compilation, heap, hoard, mass, pile, set, stockpile, store 2. assembly, assortment, cluster, company, crowd, gathering, group

DICTIONARY

—*adj.* of or done by a group, combined. —**collectively** *adv.*

collect² *n.* short prayer.

colleen *n. Irish* girl.

college *n.* place of higher education; group of people of the same profession or with special duties. —**collegiate** *adj.*

collide *v.* crash together violently; conflict. —**collision** *n.*

collie *n.* silky-coated sheepdog.

colliery *n., pl.* **-lieries.** coal mine. —**collier** *n.* coal miner; coal ship.

collocate *v.* (of words) occur together regularly. —**collocation** *n.*

colloid *n.* suspension of particles in a solution.

collop *n.* small slice of meat.

colloquial *adj.* suitable for informal speech or writing. —**colloquialism** *n.* colloquial expression.

colloquy *n., pl.* **-quies.** conversation or conference.

collusion *n.* secret agreement for a fraudulent purpose. —**collude** *v.* act in collusion.

collywobbles *pl. n. Slang* nervousness; upset stomach.

cologne *n.* perfumed toilet water.

colon¹ *n.* punctuation mark (:).

colon² *n.* part of the large intestine connected to the rectum.

colonel *n.* senior commissioned army or air-force officer.

colonnade *n.* row of columns.

colony *n., pl.* **-nies.** group of people who settle in a new country but remain subject to their parent state; territory occupied by a colony; group of people or animals of the same kind living together. —**colonial** *adj., n.* (inhabitant) of a colony. —**colonialism** *n.* policy of acquiring and maintaining colonies. —**colonist** *n.* settler in a colony.

—**colonize** *v.* make into a colony. —**colonization** *n.*

colophon *n.* publisher's emblem.

Colorado beetle *n.* black-and-yellow beetle that is a serious pest of potatoes.

coloration *n.* colouring.

colossal *adj.* huge.

colossus *n., pl.* **-si, -suses.** huge statue; huge or important person or thing.

colostomy *n., pl.* **-mies.** operation to form an opening from the colon onto the surface of the body, for emptying the bowel.

colour *n.* appearance of things as a result of reflecting light; paint or pigment; complexion. —*pl.* flag; *Sport* badge or symbol denoting membership of a team. —*v.* apply or give colour to; influence or distort; blush. —**Coloured** *adj.* non-White; (in S Africa) of mixed race. —**colourful** *adj.* with bright or varied colours; vivid or distinctive. —**colourfully** *adv.* —**colourless** *adj.* —**colour-blind** *adj.* unable to distinguish between certain colours.

colt *n.* young male horse.

columbine *n.* garden flower with five spurred petals.

column *n.* pillar; vertical arrangement of numbers; long narrow formation of troops; vertical division of a newspaper page; regular feature in a newspaper. —**columnist** *n.* journalist writing a regular feature for a newspaper.

coma *n.* state of deep unconsciousness. —**comatose** *adj.* in a coma; sound asleep.

comb *n.* toothed implement for arranging the hair; cock's crest; honeycomb. —*v.* use a comb on; search with great care.

combat *v.* **-bating, -bated.** *n.* fight, struggle. —**combatant** *n.* —**combative** *adj.*

THESAURUS

collide clash, conflict, crash, meet head-on

collision accident, bump, crash, impact, pile-up, smash

colony community, outpost, province, settlement, territory

colossal enormous, gigantic, huge, immense, massive, monstrous, monumental, mountainous, prodigious, titanic, vast

colour *n.* 1. dye, hue, paint, pigment, shade, tincture, tinge, tint 2. bloom, blush, brilliance, complexion, flush, glow, liveliness, rosiness, ruddiness, vividness ~*v.* 3. dye, paint, stain, tinge, tint 4. *Fig.* disguise, distort, embroider, falsify, garble, gloss over,

misrepresent, pervert, prejudice, slant, taint 5. blush, burn, crimson, flush, go crimson, redden

colourful 1. bright, brilliant, intense, motley, multicoloured, rich, variegated, vivid 2. characterful, distinctive, graphic, interesting, lively, picturesque, rich, stimulating, unusual, vivid

colourless characterless, dreary, insipid, lacklustre, tame, uninteresting, vapid

column 1. cavalcade, file, line, list, procession, queue, rank, row, string, train 2. pillar, post, shaft, support, upright

coma insensibility, oblivion, somnolence, stupor, trance, unconsciousness

DICTIONARY

combine *v.* join together. —*n.* association of people or firms for a common purpose. —**combination** *n.* combining; people or things combined; set of numbers that opens a special lock. —*pl.* one-piece undergarment with long sleeves and legs. —**combine harvester** machine which reaps and threshes grain in one operation.

combustion *n.* process of burning. —**combustible** *adj.* burning easily.

come *v.* **coming, came, come.** move towards a place, arrive; occur; be available; reach a specified point or condition; originate (from); become. —**come across** *v.* meet or find by accident; (foll. by *as*) give an impression (of being). —**comeback** *n. Informal* return to a former position; retort. —**comedown** *n.* decline in status; disappointment. —**come-uppance** *n. Informal* deserved punishment.

comedy *n., pl.* **-dies.** humorous play, film, or programme. —**comedian, comedienne** *n.* entertainer who tells jokes.

comely *adj.* **-lier, -liest.** *Old-fashioned* good-looking.

comestibles *pl. n.* food.

comet *n.* heavenly body with a long luminous tail.

comfit *n.* sugar-coated sweet.

comfort *n.* physical ease or wellbeing; consolation; means of consolation. —*v.* give comfort to. —**comfortable** *adj.* giving comfort; free from pain; *Informal* well-off financially. —**comfortably** *adv.* —**comforter** *n.*

comfrey *n.* tall plant with bell-shaped flowers.

comfy *adj.* **-fier, -fiest.** *Informal* comfortable.

comic *adj.* humorous, funny; relating to comedy. —*n.* comedian; *Brit.* magazine consisting of strip cartoons. —**comical** *adj.* amusing. —**comically** *adv.*

comma *n.* punctuation mark (,).

command *v.* order; have authority over; deserve and get; look down over. —*n.* authoritative instruction that something must be done; authority to command; knowledge, mastery; military or naval unit with a specific function. —**commandant** *n.* officer commanding a military group. —**commandeer** *v.* seize for military use. —**commander** *n.* military officer in command of a group or operation; middle-ranking naval officer. —**commander-in-chief** *n.* supreme commander. —**commandment** *n.* divine command.

THESAURUS

comb *v.* 1. dress, groom, untangle 2. *Fig.* go through with a fine-tooth comb, hunt, rake, ransack, rummage, scour, screen, search, sift, sweep

combat action, battle, conflict, contest, encounter, engagement, fight, skirmish, struggle, war, warfare

combatant belligerent, contender, enemy, fighter, fighting man, opponent, serviceman, soldier, warrior

combination 1. amalgam, blend, coalescence, composite, mix, mixture 2. alliance, association, cabal, cartel, coalition, compound, confederacy, consortium, federation, merger, syndicate, unification, union

combine amalgamate, bind, blend, bond, compound, connect, cooperate, fuse, incorporate, integrate, join (together), link, marry, merge, mix, pool, unify, unite

come 1. advance, appear, approach, arrive, become, draw near, enter, happen, materialize, move, move towards, near, occur, originate, turn out, turn up (*Inf.*) 2. appear, arrive, attain, enter, materialize, reach, show up (*Inf.*), turn up (*Inf.*) 3. fall, happen, occur, take place 4. arise, emanate, emerge, end up, flow, issue, originate, result, turn out 5. extend, reach

come across chance upon, discover, encounter,

find, happen upon, hit upon, meet, notice, unearth

comeback rally, rebound, recovery, resurgence, return, revival, triumph

comedown anticlimax, blow, decline, demotion, disappointment, humiliation, reverse

comedy chaffing, drollery, facetiousness, farce, fun, hilarity, humour, jesting, joking, slapstick, witticisms

comfort *v.* 1. cheer, commiserate with, console, ease, encourage, enliven, gladden, hearten, inspirit, invigorate, reassure, refresh, relieve, solace, soothe, strengthen ~*n.* 2. aid, alleviation, cheer, consolation, ease, encouragement, help, relief, succour, support 3. cosiness, creature comforts, ease, luxury, wellbeing

comfortable 1. agreeable, ample, commodious, convenient, cosy, delightful, easy, enjoyable, homely, loose, pleasant, relaxing, restful, roomy, snug 2. affluent, prosperous, well-off, well-to-do

comic *adj.* amusing, comical, droll, facetious, farcical, funny, humorous, joking, light, rich, waggish, witty

coming *adj.* approaching, at hand, due, en route, forthcoming, future, imminent, impending, in store, in the wind, near, next, nigh

command *v.* 1. bid, charge, compel, demand, direct, enjoin, order, require 2. control, domi-

DICTIONARY

commando *n., pl.* **-dos, -does.** (member of) a military unit trained for swift raids in enemy territory.

commemorate *v.* honour or keep alive the memory of. —**commemoration** *n.* —**commemorative** *adj.*

commence *v.* begin. —**commencement** *n.*

commend *v.* praise; recommend; entrust. —**commendable** *adj.* —**commendably** *adv.* —**commendation** *n.*

commensurable *adj.* measurable by the same standard. —**commensurability** *n.*

commensurate *adj.* corresponding in degree, size, or value.

comment *n.* remark; gossip; explanatory note. —*v.* make a comment or comments. —**commentary** *n.* spoken accompaniment to a broadcast or film; explanatory notes. —**commentate** *v.* provide a commentary. —**commentator** *n.*

commerce *n.* buying and selling, trade; dealings. —**commercial** *adj.* of commerce; (of television or radio) paid for by advertisers; having profit as the main aim. —*n.* television or radio advertisement. —**commercialize** *v.* make commercial. —**commercialization** *n.*

commiserate *v.* (foll. by *with*) express pity or sympathy (for). —**commiseration** *n.*

commissar *n.* official responsible for political education in Communist countries.

commissariat *n.* military department in charge of food supplies.

commission *n.* duty or task given to someone; delegated authority; group of people appointed to perform certain duties; percentage paid to a salesperson for each sale made; *Mil.* rank or authority officially given to an officer; committing. —*v.* grant authority to; *Mil.* give a commission to; place an order for. —**out of commission** not working. —**commissioner** *n.* appointed official in a government department; member of a commission.

commissionaire *n.* uniformed doorman at a hotel, theatre, etc.

commit *v.* **-mitting, -mitted.** perform (a crime or error); pledge to a cause or course of action; send (someone) to prison or hospital. —**committal** *n.* sending of someone for trial, etc. —**commitment** *n.* dedication to a cause; responsibility or promise that hinders freedom of action.

committee *n.* group of people appointed to perform a specified service or function.

commode *n.* seat with a compartment holding a chamber pot; chest of drawers.

commodious *adj.* roomy.

commodity *n., pl.* **-ities.** article of trade.

commodore *n.* senior naval or air-force officer; president of a yacht club.

common *adj.* occurring often; belonging to two or more people; public, general; low-class. —*n.*

THESAURUS

nate, govern, head, lead, manage, reign over, rule, supervise, sway ~*n.* 3. behest, bidding, decree, direction, directive, edict, fiat, injunction, instruction, mandate, order, precept, requirement

commander boss, captain, chief, C in C, C.O., commanding officer, director, head, leader, officer, ruler

commemorate celebrate, honour, immortalize, keep, observe, pay tribute to, remember, salute

commemoration ceremony, honouring, memorial service, observance, remembrance, tribute

commence begin, embark on, enter upon, initiate, open, originate, start

commend acclaim, applaud, approve, compliment, eulogize, extol, praise, recommend

commendation acclaim, acclamation, approbation, approval, credit, good opinion, panegyric, praise, recommendation

comment *v.* 1. mention, note, observe, opine, point out, remark, say 2. criticize, elucidate, explain, interpret ~*n.* 3. observation, remark, statement 4. commentary, criticism, elucidation, explanation, exposition, note

commentary analysis, critique, description, exegesis, explanation, narration, notes, review, treatise, voice-over

commentator reporter, sportscaster

commerce business, dealing, exchange, trade, traffic

commercial business, mercantile, sales, trade, trading

commission *n.* 1. appointment, authority, charge, duty, employment, errand, function, mandate, mission, task, trust, warrant 2. allowance, cut, fee, percentage, rake-off (*Sl.*) 3. board, committee, delegation, deputation, representative ~*v.* 4. appoint, authorize, contract, delegate, depute, empower, engage, nominate, order, select, send

commit carry out, do, enact, execute, perform, perpetrate

commitment 1. duty, engagement, liability, obligation, responsibility, tie 2. assurance, dedication, guarantee, pledge, promise, undertaking, vow, word

DICTIONARY

area of grassy land belonging to a community. —*pl.* ordinary people; (C-) House of Commons. —**commonly** *adv.* —**commoner** *n.* person who does not belong to the nobility. —**common-law** *adj.* (of a relationship) regarded as marriage through being longstanding. —**Common Market** European Community. —**commonplace** *adj.* ordinary, everyday. —*n.* trite remark. —**common sense** sound practical understanding. —**commonwealth** *n.* republic; (C-) federation of independent states that used to be ruled by Britain.

commotion *n.* noisy disturbance.

commune[1] *n.* group of people living together, sharing property and responsibilities. —**communal** *adj.* shared. —**communally** *adv.*

commune[2] *v.* (foll. by *with*) experience strong emotion (for). —**communion** *n.* sharing of thoughts or feelings; (C-) Christian ritual of sharing consecrated bread and wine; religious group with shared beliefs and practices.

communicate *v.* make known, reveal (information, thoughts, or feelings); (of rooms) have a connecting door. —**communicable** *adj.* (of a disease) able to be passed on. —**communicant** *n.* person who receives Communion. —**communication** *n.* communicating; thing communicated. —*pl.* means of travelling or sending messages. —**communicative** *adj.* willing to talk.

communiqué [kom-**mune**-ik-kay] *n.* official announcement.

communism *n.* doctrine that all property and means of production should be shared by the people; (C-) system of state control of the economy and society in some countries. —**communist** *n., adj.*

community *n., pl.* -ties. all the people living in one district; group having shared interests or origins; society, the public. —**community centre** building used by a community for activities. —**community charge** tax levied per head of adult population, to fund local government.

commute *v.* travel daily to and from work; reduce (a sentence) to a less severe one. —**commuter** *n.* person who commutes to and from work. —**commutator** *n.* device used to change alternating electric current into direct current.

compact[1] *adj.* closely packed; neatly arranged; concise, brief. —*n.* small flat case containing a mirror and face powder. —*v.* pack closely together. —**compactly** *adv.* —**compactness** *n.* —**compact disc** small digital audio disc on which the sound is read by an optical laser system.

compact[2] *n.* agreement, contract.

companion *n.* person who associates with or accompanies another. —**companionable** *adj.* friendly. —**companionship** *n.*

THESAURUS

common 1. average, conventional, customary, daily, everyday, familiar, frequent, general, humdrum, obscure, ordinary, plain, regular, routine, run-of-the-mill, simple, standard, stock, usual, workaday 2. accepted, general, popular, prevailing, universal, widespread 3. coarse, hackneyed, inferior, low, pedestrian, plebeian, stale, trite, undistinguished, vulgar

common sense good sense, level-headedness, mother wit, native intelligence, practicality, prudence, soundness, wit

commotion ado, agitation, bustle, disorder, disturbance, excitement, ferment, furore, fuss, hubbub, racket, riot, rumpus, to-do, tumult, turmoil, uproar

communal collective, community, general, joint, public, shared

commune *n.* collective, community, cooperative, kibbutz

communicate acquaint, announce, be in contact, be in touch, connect, convey, correspond, declare, disclose, divulge, impart, inform, make known, pass on, phone, proclaim, publish, report, reveal, ring up, signify, spread, transmit, unfold

communication 1. connection, contact, conver-

sation, correspondence, link, transmission 2. disclosure, dispatch, information, intelligence, message, news, report, statement, word

communiqué announcement, bulletin, dispatch, news flash, report

communism Bolshevism, collectivism, Marxism, socialism, state socialism

communist Bolshevik, collectivist, Marxist, socialist

community association, body politic, brotherhood, commonwealth, company, district, general public, locality, people, populace, population, public, residents, society, state

commuter daily traveller, straphanger, suburbanite

compact 1. close, compressed, condensed, dense, firm, impenetrable, impermeable, pressed together, solid, thick 2. brief, concise, epigrammatic, laconic, pithy, pointed, succinct, terse, to the point

companion accomplice, ally, associate, colleague, comrade, confederate, consort, crony, friend, partner

companionship amity, company, conviviality, fellowship, fraternity, friendship, rapport, togetherness

DICTIONARY

companionway n. ladder linking the decks of a ship.

company n., pl. **-nies.** business firm; small unit of troops; group of actors; crew of a ship; companionship; associates; guest or guests; gathering of people.

compare v. examine (things) to find the resemblances or differences; declare to be like; be worthy of comparison. —**comparable** adj. —**comparability** n. —**comparative** adj. relative; involving comparison; *Grammar* denoting the form of an adjective or adverb indicating *more*. —n. *Grammar* comparative form of a word. —**comparatively** adv. —**comparison** n.

compartment n. separate section; section of a railway carriage.

compass n. instrument for showing direction, with a needle that points north; range. —pl. hinged instrument for drawing circles.

compassion n. pity, sympathy. —**compassionate** adj.

compatible adj. able to exist, work, or be used together. —**compatibility** n.

compatriot n. fellow countryman or countrywoman.

compeer n. equal, companion.

compel v. **-pelling, -pelled.** force (to be or do).

compendium n., pl. **-diums, -dia.** selection of different table games in one container. —**compendious** adj. brief but inclusive.

compensate v. make amends to (someone), esp. for injury or loss; (foll. by *for*) cancel out a bad effect. —**compensation** n. —**compensatory** adj.

compère n. person who presents a stage, radio, or television show. —v. be the compère of.

compete v. take part in (a contest or competition). —**competition** n. competing; event in which people compete; people against whom one competes. —**competitive** adj. —**competitor** n.

competent adj. having sufficient skill or knowledge. —**competently** adv. —**competence** n.

compile v. collect and arrange (information), esp. to form a book. —**compilation** n. —**compiler** n.

complacent adj. self-satisfied. —**complacently** adv. —**complacency** n.

complain v. express resentment or displeasure; state that one is suffering from pain or illness. —**complaint** n. complaining; mild illness. —**complainant** n. plaintiff.

THESAURUS

company 1. assemblage, assembly, band, body, circle, collection, convention, coterie, crew, crowd, ensemble, gathering, group, league, party, set, throng, troop, troupe, turnout 2. association, business, concern, corporation, establishment, firm, house, partnership, syndicate

compare *With* with balance, collate, contrast, juxtapose, set against, weigh

comparison 1. contrast, distinction, juxtaposition 2. analogy, correlation, likeness, resemblance, similarity

compartment alcove, bay, berth, booth, carriage, cell, chamber, cubicle, locker, niche, pigeonhole, section

compass area, bound, boundary, circle, circuit, enclosure, extent, field, limit, range, reach, realm, round, scope, sphere, stretch, zone

compassion commiseration, condolence, fellow feeling, heart, humanity, kindness, mercy, pity, soft-heartedness, sorrow, sympathy, tenderness

compel coerce, constrain, dragoon, drive, enforce, exact, force, impel, make, oblige, restrain, squeeze, urge

compensate 1. atone, indemnify, make amends, make good, make restitution, recompense, refund, reimburse, remunerate, repay, requite, reward, satisfy 2. balance, cancel (out), counteract, make up for, offset, redress

compensation amends, atonement, damages, indemnity, payment, remuneration, reparation, restitution, reward, satisfaction

compete be in the running, challenge, contend, contest, emulate, fight, pit oneself against, rival, strive, struggle, vie

competent able, adapted, appropriate, capable, clever, equal, fit, proficient, qualified, sufficient, suitable

competition 1. contention, contest, emulation, opposition, rivalry, strife, struggle 2. championship, contest, event, puzzle, quiz, tournament

competitor adversary, antagonist, challenger, competition, contestant, opponent, opposition, rival

compile amass, collect, cull, garner, gather, organize, put together

complacent contented, gratified, pleased, satisfied, self-assured, self-righteous, self-satisfied, serene, smug, unconcerned

complain bemoan, bewail, carp, deplore, find fault, fuss, grieve, groan, grouse, growl, grumble, lament, moan, whine

DICTIONARY

complaisant [kom-**play**-zant] *adj.* obliging, willing to please. —**complaisance** *n.*

complement *n.* thing that completes something; complete amount or number; *Grammar* word or words added after a verb to complete the meaning. —*v.* make complete. —**complementary** *adj.*

complete *adj.* thorough; whole; finished; having all the necessary parts. —*v.* finish; make whole or perfect. —**completely** *adv.* —**completeness** *n.* wholeness. —**completion** *n.* finishing.

complex *adj.* made up of parts; complicated. —*n.* whole made up of parts; group of unconscious feelings that influences behaviour. —**complexity** *n.*

complexion *n.* natural appearance of the skin of the face; character or nature.

complicate *v.* make or become complex or difficult to deal with. —**complication** *n.*

complicity *n.* fact of being an accomplice, esp. in a crime.

compliment *n.* expression of praise. —*pl.* formal greetings. —*v.* praise. —**complimentary** *adj.* expressing praise; free of charge.

compline *n.* last service of the day in the Roman Catholic Church.

comply *v.* -**plying,** -**plied.** act in accordance (with a rule, order, or request). —**compliance** *n.* —**compliant** *adj.*

component *n.* part of a whole. —*adj.* being a component.

comport *v.* behave (oneself) in a specified way.

compos mentis *adj. Latin* sane.

compose *v.* put together; create (music or literature); arrange in order; calm (oneself). —**composer** *n.*

composite *adj.* made up of separate parts.

composition *n.* way that something is put together or arranged; musical work; essay; act of composing.

compositor *n.* person who arranges type for printing.

compost *n.* decayed plants used as a fertilizer.

composure *n.* calmness.

compote *n.* fruit stewed in syrup.

compound[1] *n., adj.* (thing, esp. chemical) made up of two or more combined parts or elements. —*v.* combine or make by combining; intensify, make worse.

compound[2] *n.* fenced enclosure containing buildings.

comprehend *v.* understand. —**comprehen-**

THESAURUS

complaint 1. accusation, annoyance, charge, criticism, dissatisfaction, fault-finding, grievance, grouse, grumble, lament, moan, plaint, remonstrance, trouble, wail 2. affliction, ailment, disease, disorder, illness, malady, sickness

complete *adj.* 1. all, entire, full, intact, integral, unabridged, unbroken, undivided, whole 2. accomplished, achieved, concluded, ended, finished 3. consummate, perfect, thorough, total, utter ~*v.* 4. accomplish, achieve, cap, close, conclude, crown, discharge, do, end, execute, fill in, finalize, finish, fulfil, perfect, perform, realize, round off, settle, terminate

completely absolutely, altogether, en masse, entirely, from beginning to end, fully, heart and soul, in full, *in toto*, perfectly, quite, solidly, thoroughly, totally, utterly, wholly

complex circuitous, complicated, intricate, involved, knotty, labyrinthine, mingled, mixed, tangled, tortuous

complicate confuse, entangle, interweave, involve, make intricate, muddle, snarl up

complication complexity, confusion, entanglement, intricacy, mixture, web

compliment 1. *n.* admiration, bouquet, commendation, congratulations, courtesy, eulogy, favour, flattery, honour, praise, tribute 2. *v.* commend, congratulate, extol, felicitate, flatter, laud, pay tribute to, praise, salute

comply accede, accord, acquiesce, adhere to, agree to, conform to, consent to, discharge, follow, fulfil, obey, observe, perform, respect, satisfy

component constituent, element, ingredient, item, part, piece, unit

compose build, compound, comprise, constitute, construct, fashion, form, make, make up, put together

composition 1. arrangement, configuration, constitution, design, form, formation, layout, make-up, structure 2. creation, essay, exercise, literary work, opus, piece, study, work, writing

composure aplomb, calm, calmness, collectedness, coolness, dignity, ease, equanimity, placidity, poise, sedateness, self-assurance, self-possession, serenity, tranquillity

compound 1. *v.* amalgamate, blend, coalesce, combine, concoct, fuse, intermingle, mingle, mix, synthesize, unite 2. *n.* alloy, amalgam, blend, combination, composite, composition, conglomerate, fusion, medley, mixture, synthesis 3. *adj.* complex, composite, conglomerate, intricate, multiple, not simple

DICTIONARY

sible *adj.* —**comprehension** *n.* —**comprehensive** *adj.* of broad scope, fully inclusive. —*n.* comprehensive school. —**comprehensive school** secondary school for children of all abilities.

compress *v.* squeeze together; condense. —*n.* pad applied to stop bleeding or cool inflammation. —**compressible** *adj.* —**compression** *n.* —**compressor** *n.* device that compresses a gas.

comprise *v.* be made up of, constitute.

compromise [**kom**-prom-mize] *n.* settlement reached by concessions on each side. —*v.* settle a dispute by making concessions; put in a dishonourable position.

comptroller *n.* (in titles) financial controller.

compulsion *n.* irresistible impulse; compelling or being compelled. —**compulsive** *adj.* —**compulsively** *adv.* —**compulsory** *adj.* required by rules or laws, obligatory.

compunction *n.* feeling of guilt or remorse.

compute *v.* calculate, esp. using a computer. —**computation** *n.* —**computer** *n.* electronic machine that stores and processes data. —**computerize** *v.* equip with a computer; perform or operate by computer. —**computerization** *n.*

comrade *n.* companion; fellow member of a union or socialist political party. —**comradeship** *n.*

con[1] *Informal* —*v.* **conning, conned.** deceive or swindle (someone) by gaining his or her trust. —*n.* such a deception or swindle.

con[2] *n.* —**pros and cons** see PRO[1].

concatenation *n.* linked series of events.

concave *adj.* curving inwards. —**concavity** *n.*

conceal *v.* cover and hide; keep secret. —**concealment** *n.*

concede *v.* admit to be true; grant as a right; acknowledge defeat in (a contest or argument).

conceit *n.* too high an opinion of oneself; *Lit.* far-fetched or clever comparison. —**conceited** *adj.*

conceive *v.* imagine or think; form in the mind; become pregnant. —**conceivable** *adj.* imaginable or possible. —**conceivably** *adv.*

concentrate *v.* fix one's attention or efforts (on); make (a substance) stronger; bring or come together in large numbers in one place. —*n.* concentrated substance. —**concentration** *n.* concentrating; concentrated substance. —**concentration camp** prison camp for civilian prisoners, esp. in Nazi Germany.

concentric *adj.* having the same centre.

concept *n.* abstract or general idea. —**conceptual** *adj.* of or based on concepts. —**conceptualize** *v.* form a concept of.

conception *n.* general idea; act of conceiving.

concern *v.* worry; involve or interest; be relevant or important to. —*n.* anxiety; something that concerns a person; business or firm. —**concerned** *adj.* interested or involved; anxious. —**concerning** *prep.* about, regarding.

THESAURUS

comprehend assimilate, conceive, discern, fathom, grasp, know, make out, perceive, see, take in, understand

comprehension discernment, grasp, intelligence, judgment, knowledge, perception, realization, sense, understanding

compress compact, concentrate, condense, constrict, cram, crowd, crush, press, shorten, summarize

comprise be composed of, consist of, constitute, contain, embrace, encompass, include, take in

compromise 1. *v.* adjust, agree, concede, give and take, go fifty-fifty (*Inf.*), meet halfway, settle, strike a balance 2. *n.* accommodation, accord, adjustment, agreement, concession, give-and-take, settlement, trade-off

compulsive compelling, driving, irresistible, obsessive, uncontrollable, urgent

compulsory binding, forced, imperative, mandatory, required, requisite

comrade ally, associate, colleague, companion, confederate, crony, fellow, friend, partner

conceal bury, cover, disguise, dissemble, hide, keep dark, keep secret, mask, obscure, screen, secrete, shelter

concede 1. acknowledge, admit, allow, confess, grant, own 2. cede, give up, hand over, surrender, yield

conceit arrogance, complacency, egotism, narcissism, pride, swagger, vainglory, vanity

conceited arrogant, cocky, egotistical, immodest, overweening, puffed up, self-important, swollen-headed, vain

conceivable believable, credible, imaginable, possible, thinkable

conceive 1. apprehend, believe, comprehend, envisage, fancy, grasp, imagine, realize, suppose, understand 2. create, design, devise, form, formulate, produce, project, purpose, think up

concentrate 1. consider closely, focus attention on, put one's mind to, rack one's brains 2. bring to bear, centre, cluster, converge, focus

concept hypothesis, idea, image, impression, notion, theory, view

DICTIONARY

concert *n.* musical entertainment. —**in concert** working together; (of musicians) performing live. —**concerted** *adj.* done together.

concertina *n.* small musical instrument similar to an accordion. —*v.* **-naing, -naed.** collapse or fold up like a concertina.

concerto [kon-**chair**-toe] *n., pl.* **-tos, -ti.** large-scale composition for a solo instrument and orchestra.

concession *n.* grant; reduction in price for a specified category of people; conceding; thing conceded. —**concessionary** *adj.*

conch *n.* marine mollusc with a large spiral shell; its shell.

concierge [kon-see-**airzh**] *n.* (in France) caretaker of a block of flats.

conciliate *v.* overcome the hostility of. —**conciliation** *n.* —**conciliator** *n.* —**conciliatory** *adj.*

concise *adj.* brief and to the point. —**concisely** *adv.* —**conciseness** *n.*

conclave *n.* secret meeting; private meeting of cardinals to elect a new pope.

conclude *v.* end, finish; decide by reasoning; arrange or settle finally. —**conclusion** *n.* ending; outcome; decision or opinion. —**conclusive** *adj.* ending doubt, convincing. —**conclusively** *adv.*

concoct *v.* make by combining ingredients; make up (a story or plan). —**concoction** *n.*

concomitant *adj.* accompanying.

concord *n.* state of peaceful agreement, harmony. —**concordance** *n.* similarity or consistency; index of words in a book. —**concordant** *adj.* agreeing.

concourse *n.* large open public place where people can gather; crowd.

concrete *n.* mixture of sand, gravel, and cement, used in building. —*adj.* made of concrete; particular, specific; real or solid, not abstract.

concubine [kon-**kew**-bine] *n.* woman living with a man as his wife, but not married to him; secondary wife in polygamous societies. —**concubinage** *n.*

concupiscence [kon-**kew**-piss-enss] *n.* lust. —**concupiscent** *adj.*

concur *v.* **-curring, -curred.** agree, be in accord. —**concurrence** *n.* —**concurrent** *adj.* —**concurrently** *adv.* at the same time.

concussion *n.* brain injury caused by a blow or fall. —**concuss** *v.* affect with concussion.

condemn *v.* express disapproval of; sentence; doom; declare unfit for use. —**condemnation** *n.* —**condemnatory** *adj.*

condense *v.* express in fewer words; concentrate, make more dense; turn from gas into liquid. —**condensation** *n.* —**condenser** *n. Electricity* capacitor.

THESAURUS

concern *v.* 1. affect, apply to, bear on, be relevant to, interest, involve, pertain to, regard, touch 2. bother, disquiet, distress, disturb, make anxious, make uneasy, perturb, trouble, worry ~*n.* 3. affair, business, charge, field, interest, involvement, job, matter, mission, responsibility, task 4. anxiety, attention, burden, care, consideration, disquiet, distress, heed, responsibility, solicitude, worry 5. business, company, enterprise, establishment, firm, house, organization

concerned 1. active, implicated, interested, involved, mixed up, privy to 2. anxious, bothered, distressed, disturbed, exercised, troubled, uneasy, upset, worried

concerning about, apropos of, as regards, as to, in the matter of, on the subject of, re, regarding, relating to, respecting, touching, with reference to

concise brief, compact, compressed, condensed, laconic, pithy, short, succinct, summary, terse, to the point

conclude 1. cease, close, come to an end, complete, end, finish, round off, terminate 2. assume, decide, deduce, gather, infer, judge, suppose, surmise

conclusion 1. close, completion, end, ending,

finale, finish, result 2. consequence, culmination, issue, outcome, result, upshot 3. agreement, conviction, decision, deduction, inference, judgment, opinion, resolution, settlement, verdict

conclusive clinching, convincing, decisive, definite, definitive, final, irrefutable, ultimate, unanswerable

concoction blend, brew, compound, creation, mixture, preparation

concrete *adj.* actual, definite, explicit, factual, material, real, sensible, specific, substantial, tangible

concur accord, acquiesce, agree, approve, assent, coincide, combine, consent, cooperate, harmonize, join

condemn 1. blame, censure, damn, denounce, disapprove, reproach, reprove, upbraid 2. convict, damn, doom, proscribe, sentence

condemnation 1. blame, censure, denouncement, denunciation, disapproval, reproach, reprobation, reproof, stricture 2. conviction, damnation, doom, judgment, proscription, sentence

condensation 1. abridgment, digest, précis,

DICTIONARY

condescend *v.* behave patronizingly towards; do something as if it were beneath one's dignity. **—condescension** *n.*

condiment *n.* relish or seasoning for food.

condition *n.* particular state of being; necessary prerequisite for something else to happen; restriction or qualification; state of health, physical fitness; ailment. **—***pl.* circumstances. **—***v.* accustom; make fit or healthy; subject to a condition. **—on condition that** only if. **—conditional** *adj.* dependent on circumstances. **—conditioner** *n.* thick liquid used when washing to make hair or clothes feel softer.

condole *v.* express sympathy (with someone). **—condolence** *n.*

condom *n.* rubber sheath worn on the penis during sexual intercourse to prevent conception or infection.

condominium *n.* *US* apartment building in which each apartment is individually owned.

condone *v.* overlook or forgive (an offence or wrongdoing).

condor *n.* large vulture of S America.

conducive *adj.* (foll. by *to*) likely to produce (a result).

conduct *n.* behaviour; management. **—***v.* behave (oneself); manage; transmit (heat or electricity); direct (musicians) by moving the hands or a baton; lead, guide. **—conduction** *n.* transmission of heat or electricity. **—conductive** *adj.* able to conduct heat or electricity. **—conductivity** *n.* **—conductor** *n.* person who conducts musicians; (*fem.* **conductress**) official on a bus who collects fares; *US* guard on a train; something that conducts electricity or heat.

conduit [kon-dew-it] *n.* channel or tube for fluid or cables.

cone *n.* hollow or solid object with a circular base, tapering to a point; scaly fruit of a conifer tree.

coney *n.* same as CONY.

confabulation, *Informal* **confab** *n.* conversation.

confection *n.* any sweet food; elaborate article of clothing. **—confectioner** *n.* maker or seller of confectionery. **—confectionery** *n.* sweets and cakes.

confederate *n.* member of a confederacy; accomplice. **—***v.* unite in a confederacy. **—***adj.* united, allied. **—confederacy** *n.* union of states or people for a common purpose. **—confederation** *n.* alliance of political units.

confer *v.* **-ferring, -ferred.** discuss together; give. **—conference** *n.* meeting for discussion. **—conferment** *n.* formal giving.

confess *v.* admit (a fault or crime); admit to be true; declare (one's sins) to God or a priest, in hope of forgiveness. **—confession** *n.* confessing; thing confessed. **—confessional** *n.* small stall in which a priest hears confessions. **—confessor** *n.* priest who hears confessions.

confetti *n.* small bits of coloured paper thrown at weddings.

confidant *n.* person confided in. **—confidante** *n. fem.*

THESAURUS

synopsis 2. concentration, crystallization, curtailment, reduction

condense abridge, compact, compress, concentrate, contract, curtail, epitomize, précis, shorten, summarize

condescend 1. bend, deign, lower oneself, see fit, stoop, submit, unbend (*Inf.*) 2. patronize, talk down to

condition *n.* 1. case, circumstances, plight, position, predicament, shape, situation, state, state of affairs, *status quo* 2. arrangement, article, demand, limitation, modification, prerequisite, provision, proviso, qualification, requirement, requisite, restriction, rule, stipulation, terms 3. fettle, fitness, health, kilter, order, shape, state of health, trim ~*v.* 4. accustom, adapt, educate, equip, habituate, inure, make ready, prepare, ready, tone up, train, work out

conditional contingent, dependent, limited, provisional, qualified, subject to, with reservations

conditions circumstances, environment, milieu, situation, surroundings

conduct *n.* 1. administration, control, direction, guidance, leadership, management, organization, running, supervision 2. attitude, bearing, behaviour, carriage, comportment, demeanour, deportment, manners, mien (*Literary*), ways ~*v.* 3. administer, carry on, control, direct, govern, handle, lead, manage, organize, preside over, regulate, run, supervise

confederacy alliance, bund, coalition, compact, confederation, league, union

confer consult, converse, deliberate, discourse, discuss, parley, talk

conference congress, consultation, convention, convocation, discussion, forum, meeting, seminar, symposium, teach-in

confess acknowledge, admit, allow, concede, confide, disclose, divulge, grant, own, own up, recognize

confession acknowledgment, admission, avowal, disclosure, revelation

DICTIONARY

confide *v.* (foll. by *in*) tell (something) in confidence (to); entrust. —**confidence** *n.* trust; self-assurance; something confided, secret. —**in confidence** as a secret. —**confidence trick** same as CON[1]. —**confident** *adj.* feeling or showing self-assurance. —**confidently** *adv.* —**confidential** *adj.* private or secret; entrusted with another's secret affairs. —**confidentially** *adv.* —**confidentiality** *n.*

configuration *n.* arrangement of parts; shape.

confine *v.* keep within bounds; restrict the free movement of. —**confines** *pl. n.* boundaries, limits. —**confinement** *n.* being confined; period of childbirth.

confirm *v.* prove to be true; reaffirm or strengthen; administer the rite of confirmation to. —**confirmation** *n.* confirming; something that confirms; *Christianity* rite which admits a baptized person to full church membership. —**confirmed** *adj.* long-established in a habit or condition.

confiscate *v.* seize (property) by authority. —**confiscation** *n.*

conflagration *n.* great destructive fire.

conflate *v.* combine or blend into a whole. —**conflation** *n.*

conflict *n.* struggle or fight; disagreement. —*v.* be incompatible.

confluence *n.* place where two rivers join. —**confluent** *adj.*

conform *v.* comply with accepted standards, rules, or customs; be like or in accordance with. —**conformist** *n.* person who conforms, esp. excessively. —**conformity** *n.*

confound *v.* astound, bewilder; confuse. —**confounded** *adj. Informal* damned.

confront *v.* come or bring face to face with. —**confrontation** *n.*

confuse *v.* mix up, mistake (one thing) for another; perplex or disconcert; make unclear. —**confusion** *n.*

confute *v.* prove wrong. —**confutation** *n.*

conga *n.* dance performed by a number of people in single file; large single-headed drum played with the hands.

congeal *v.* (of a liquid) coagulate, solidify.

congenial *adj.* pleasant, agreeable; of similar disposition or tastes. —**congenially** *adv.* —**congeniality** *n.*

congenital *adj.* (of a condition) existing from birth. —**congenitally** *adv.*

conger *n.* large sea eel.

THESAURUS

confide admit, breathe, confess, disclose, divulge, impart, reveal, whisper

confidence 1. belief, credence, dependence, faith, reliance, trust 2. aplomb, assurance, boldness, courage, firmness, nerve, self-possession, self-reliance 3. **in confidence** confidentially, in secrecy, privately

confident assured, bold, dauntless, fearless, self-assured, self-reliant

confidential classified, intimate, off the record, private, privy, secret

confidentially between ourselves, in camera, in confidence, in secret, personally, privately

confine bind, bound, cage, enclose, hem in, hold back, imprison, incarcerate, intern, keep, limit, repress, restrain, restrict, shut up

confines boundaries, bounds, edge, limits

confirm approve, authenticate, bear out, corroborate, endorse, ratify, sanction, substantiate, validate, verify

confirmation evidence, proof, substantiation, testimony, verification

confirmed chronic, habitual, hardened, ingrained, inured, inveterate, long-established, rooted, seasoned

conflict *n.* 1. battle, clash, combat, contention, contest, encounter, engagement, fight, strife, war, warfare 2. antagonism, bad blood, difference, disagreement, discord, dissension, divided loyalties, friction, hostility, interference, opposition, strife, variance ~*v.* 3. be at variance, clash, collide, combat, contend, contest, differ, disagree, fight, interfere, strive, struggle

confound amaze, astonish, astound, baffle, bewilder, confuse, dumbfound, mix up, mystify, nonplus, perplex, startle, surprise

confuse 1. baffle, bemuse, bewilder, mystify, obscure, perplex, puzzle 2. abash, addle, demoralize, discomfit, discompose, disconcert, discountenance, disorient, embarrass, fluster, mortify, nonplus, shame, upset

confusion 1. bemusement, bewilderment, mystification, perplexity, puzzlement 2. bustle, chaos, clutter, commotion, disarrangement, disorder, disorganization, jumble, mess, muddle, shambles, tangle, turmoil, untidiness, upheaval

congenial adapted, agreeable, compatible, favourable, fit, friendly, genial, kindly, kindred, like-minded, pleasant, pleasing, suitable, sympathetic, well-suited

congested clogged, crammed, crowded, jammed, overcrowded, overfilled, overflowing, packed, stuffed, stuffed-up, teeming

DICTIONARY

congested *adj.* too full; clogged or blocked. —**congestion** *n.*

conglomerate *n.* large corporation comprising many companies; mass composed of several different things. —*v.* form into a mass. —*adj.* made up of several different things. —**conglomeration** *n.*

congratulate *v.* express one's pleasure to (a person) at his or her good fortune or success. —**congratulations** *n., pl.* —**congratulatory** *adj.*

congregate *v.* gather together in or as a crowd. —**congregation** *n.* assembled group of worshippers. —**congregational** *adj.* —**Congregationalism** *n.* Protestant denomination in which each church is self-governing. —**Congregationalist** *n., adj.*

congress *n.* formal meeting for discussion; (C-) federal parliament of the U.S. —**congressional** *adj.* —**congressman** *n.* member of the U.S. Congress.

congruent *adj.* agreeing or corresponding; *Geom.* identical in shape and size. —**congruence** *n.*

conic *adj.* of a cone. —**conical** *adj.* cone-shaped.

conifer *n.* cone-bearing tree, such as the fir or pine. —**coniferous** *adj.*

conjecture *n., v.* guess. —**conjectural** *adj.*

conjugal [kon-jew-gal] *adj.* of marriage.

conjugate [kon-jew-gate] *v.* give the inflections of (a verb). —**conjugation** *n.* complete set of inflections of a verb.

conjunction *n.* combination; simultaneous oc-

currence of events; part of speech joining words, phrases, or clauses.

conjunctivitis *n.* inflammation of the membrane covering the eyeball and inner eyelid. —**conjunctiva** *n.* this membrane.

conjure *v.* perform tricks that appear to be magic. —**conjure up** *v.* produce as if by magic. —**conjurer, -or** *n.*

conk *n. Slang* head or nose. —**conk out** *v. Informal* (of a machine) break down.

conker *n. Informal* horse chestnut.

connect *v.* join together; associate in the mind. —**connection, connexion** *n.* association; opportunity to transfer from one public vehicle to another; influential acquaintance. —**connective** *adj.*

conning tower *n.* raised observation tower containing the periscope on a submarine.

connive *v.* (foll. by *at*) give assent to (wrongdoing) by ignoring it; conspire. —**connivance** *n.*

connoisseur [kon-noss-**sir**] *n.* person with special knowledge of the arts, food, or drink.

connote *v.* imply in addition to the literal meaning. —**connotation** *n.*

connubial [kon-**new**-bee-al] *adj.* of marriage.

conquer *v.* defeat; overcome; take (a place) by force. —**conqueror** *n.* —**conquest** *n.* conquering; person or thing conquered.

consanguineous *adj.* related by birth. —**consanguinity** *n.*

conscience *n.* sense of right or wrong as regards thoughts and actions. —**conscientious**

THESAURUS

congratulate compliment, felicitate

congratulations best wishes, compliments, felicitations, good wishes, greetings

congregate assemble, collect, come together, convene, converge, convoke, flock, forgather, gather, mass, meet, muster, rally, rendezvous, throng

congregation assembly, brethren, crowd, fellowship, flock, host, laity, multitude, parish, parishioners, throng

congress assembly, conclave, conference, convention, convocation, council, delegates, diet, legislature, meeting, parliament, representatives

conjecture 1. *v.* assume, fancy, guess, imagine, infer, suppose, surmise, suspect 2. *n.* assumption, conclusion, fancy, guess, guesswork, hypothesis, inference, notion, presumption, speculation, supposition, surmise, theorizing, theory

conjure juggle, play tricks

conjurer, conjuror magician, sorcerer, wizard

conjure up bring to mind, contrive, create, evoke, recall, recollect

connect affix, ally, cohere, combine, couple, fasten, join, link, relate, unite

connection 1. alliance, association, attachment, coupling, fastening, junction, link, tie, union 2. acquaintance, ally, associate, contact, friend, sponsor

connoisseur aficionado, arbiter, authority, buff (*Inf.*), devotee, expert, judge, savant, specialist

conquer beat, crush, defeat, get the better of, humble, master, overcome, overpower, overthrow, quell, rout, subdue, succeed, surmount, triumph, vanquish

conqueror champion, hero, lord, master, vanquisher, victor, winner

conquest 1. defeat, discomfiture, mastery, overthrow, rout, triumph, victory 2. annexation, appropriation, coup, invasion, occupation, subjection, takeover

DICTIONARY

adj. painstaking; governed by conscience. —**conscientious objector** person who refuses to serve in the armed forces on moral or religious grounds. —**conscientiously** *adv.*

conscious *adj.* alert and awake; aware; deliberate, intentional. —**consciously** *adv.* —**consciousness** *n.*

conscript *v.* enrol (someone) for compulsory military service. —*n.* conscripted person. —**conscription** *n.*

consecrate *v.* make sacred; dedicate to a specific purpose. —**consecration** *n.*

consecutive *adj.* in unbroken succession. —**consecutively** *adv.*

consensus *n.* general agreement.

consent *v.* permit, agree (to). —*n.* permission, agreement.

consequence *n.* result, effect; importance. —**consequent** *adj.* resulting. —**consequently** *adv.* therefore; as a result. —**consequential** *adj.* important.

conservative *adj.* opposing change; cautious; conventional in style; (**C-**) of or supporting the Conservative Party, the British right-wing political party which believes in private enterprise

and capitalism. —*n.* conservative person; (**C-**) supporter or member of the Conservative Party. —**conservatism** *n.*

conservatoire [kon-**serv**-a-twahr] *n.* school of music.

conservatory *n., pl.* **-ries.** greenhouse; conservatoire.

conserve *v.* protect from harm, decay, or loss; preserve (fruit) with sugar. —*n.* fruit preserved by cooking in sugar. —**conservancy** *n.* environmental conservation. —**conservation** *n.* conserving; protection of natural resources and the environment. —**conservationist** *n.*

consider *v.* be of the opinion that; think about; be considerate of; discuss; examine. —**considerable** *adj.* fairly large; much. —**considerably** *adv.* —**considerate** *adj.* thoughtful towards others. —**considerately** *adv.* —**consideration** *n.* careful thought; fact that must be considered; kindness; payment for a service. —**considering** *prep.* taking (a specified fact) into account.

consign *v.* deposit; entrust; address or deliver (goods). —**consignment** *n.* shipment of goods.

consist *v.* —**consist in** have as its main or only feature. —**consist of** be made up of.

THESAURUS

conscience moral sense, principles, scruples, still small voice

conscientious careful, diligent, exact, faithful, meticulous, painstaking, particular, punctilious, thorough

conscious 1. alert, alive to, awake, aware, cognizant, percipient, responsive, sensible, sentient, wise to (*Sl.*) 2. calculated, deliberate, intentional, knowing, premeditated, studied, wilful

consciousness apprehension, awareness, knowledge, realization, recognition, sensibility

consecrate dedicate, devote, exalt, hallow, ordain, sanctify, set apart

consecutive following, in sequence, in turn, running, sequential, successive, uninterrupted

consensus agreement, common consent, concord, harmony, unanimity

consent 1. *v.* accede, acquiesce, agree, allow, approve, assent, comply, concede, concur, permit, yield 2. *n.* agreement, approval, assent, compliance, go-ahead (*Inf.*), O.K. (*Inf.*), permission, sanction

consequence effect, end, event, issue, outcome, repercussion, result, upshot

consequently accordingly, ergo, hence, necessarily, therefore, thus

conservation custody, economy, maintenance, preservation, protection, safeguarding, safekeeping, saving, upkeep

conservative cautious, conventional, die-hard, guarded, hidebound, moderate, quiet, reactionary, right-wing, sober, tory, traditional

conserve hoard, husband, keep, nurse, preserve, protect, save, store up, take care of

consider 1. chew over, cogitate, consult, contemplate, deliberate, discuss, meditate, ponder, reflect, revolve, ruminate, study, weigh 2. bear in mind, care for, keep in view, make allowance for, regard, remember, respect

considerable abundant, ample, appreciable, goodly, great, large, lavish, marked, much, plentiful, reasonable, substantial, tidy, tolerable

considerably appreciably, greatly, markedly, noticeably, remarkably, significantly, substantially, very much

considerate concerned, discreet, kind, kindly, mindful, obliging, patient, tactful, thoughtful, unselfish

consideration 1. attention, contemplation, deliberation, discussion, examination, reflection, regard, review, scrutiny, study, thought 2. concern, friendliness, kindliness, kindness, respect, solicitude, tact, thoughtfulness

considering all in all, in the light of, in view of

DICTIONARY

consistency *n., pl.* **-cies.** degree of thickness or smoothness; being consistent. —**consistent** *adj.* unchanging, constant; in agreement. —**consistently** *adv.*

console[1] *v.* comfort in distress. —**consolation** *n.* consoling; person or thing that consoles.

console[2] *n.* panel of controls for electronic equipment; cabinet for a television or audio equipment; ornamental wall bracket; part of an organ containing the pedals, stops, and keys.

consolidate *v.* make or become stronger or more stable; combine into a whole. —**consolidation** *n.*

consommé [kon-**som**-may] *n.* thin clear meat soup.

consonant *n.* speech sound made by partially or completely blocking the breath stream; letter representing this. —*adj.* (foll. by *with*) agreeing (with). —**consonance** *n.*

consort *v.* (foll. by *with*) keep company (with). —*n.* husband or wife of a monarch.

consortium *n., pl.* **-tia.** association of business firms.

conspectus *n.* survey or summary.

conspicuous *adj.* clearly visible; striking. —**conspicuously** *adv.*

conspire *v.* plan a crime together in secret; act together as if by design. —**conspiracy** *n.* conspiring; plan made by conspiring. —**conspirator** *n.* —**conspiratorial** *adj.*

constable *n.* police officer of the lowest rank. —**constabulary** *n.* police force of an area.

constant *adj.* continuous; unchanging; faithful. —*n.* unvarying quantity; something unchanging. —**constantly** *adv.* —**constancy** *n.*

constellation *n.* group of stars.

consternation *n.* anxiety, dismay, or confusion.

constipation *n.* difficulty in defecating. —**constipated** *adj.* having constipation.

constituent *adj.* forming part of a whole. —*n.* member of a constituency; component part. —**constituency** *n.* area represented by a Member of Parliament; voters in such an area.

constitute *v.* form, compose. —**constitution** *n.* principles on which a state is governed; physical condition; structure. —**constitutional** *adj.* of a constitution; in accordance with a political constitution. —*n.* walk taken for exercise. —**constitutionally** *adv.*

constrain *v.* force, compel; restrain or confine. —**constraint** *n.* compulsion or restraint; forced unnatural manner.

THESAURUS

consignment batch, delivery, goods, shipment

consist *With of* be composed of, be made up of, amount to, comprise, contain, embody, include, incorporate, involve

consistent constant, dependable, regular, steady, true to type, unchanging, undeviating

consolation cheer, comfort, ease, encouragement, help, relief, solace, succour, support

console cheer, comfort, encourage, relieve, solace, soothe

consolidate fortify, reinforce, secure, stabilize, strengthen

consort 1. *n.* associate, companion, fellow, husband, partner, spouse (*of a reigning monarch*), wife 2. *v.* associate, fraternize, go around with, hang about *or* around with, keep company, mingle, mix

conspicuous clear, discernible, easily seen, evident, manifest, noticeable, obvious, patent, perceptible, striking, visible

conspiracy collusion, confederacy, frame-up (*Sl.*), intrigue, machination, plan, plot, scheme, treason

conspire contrive, devise, hatch treason, intrigue, machinate, manoeuvre, plan, plot, scheme

constant 1. even, firm, fixed, habitual, immutable, invariable, permanent, perpetual, regular, stable, steadfast, steady, unbroken, unchanging, unvarying 2. ceaseless, continuous, endless, eternal, everlasting, incessant, interminable, nonstop, perpetual, persistent, relentless, sustained, unrelenting, unremitting

constantly all the time, always, continually, endlessly, everlastingly, incessantly, interminably, invariably, nonstop, perpetually, relentlessly

consternation alarm, anxiety, awe, bewilderment, confusion, dismay, distress, dread, fear, fright, horror, panic, shock, terror

constituent 1. *adj.* basic, component, elemental, essential, integral 2. *n.* component, element, essential, factor, ingredient, part, principle, unit

constitute comprise, create, enact, establish, fix, form, found, make, make up, set up

constitution establishment, formation, organization

constitutional 1. *adj.* chartered, statutory, vested 2. *n.* airing, stroll, turn, walk

constrain bind, compel, drive, force, impel, oblige, pressure, urge

constraint 1. compulsion, force, necessity, pressure, restraint 2. check, curb, damper, deterrent, hindrance, limitation, restriction

DICTIONARY

constrict v. make narrower or tighter, esp. by squeezing. —**constriction** n. —**constrictive** adj. —**constrictor** n. large snake that squeezes its prey to death; muscle that constricts.

construct v. build or put together. —**construction** n. constructing; thing constructed; interpretation; *Grammar* way in which words are arranged in a sentence, clause, or phrase. —**constructive** adj. (of advice, criticism, etc.) useful and helpful. —**constructively** adv.

construe v. -**struing**, -**strued**. interpret; analyse grammatically.

consul n. official representing a state in a foreign country; one of the two chief magistrates in ancient Rome. —**consular** adj. —**consulate** n. position or offices of a consul. —**consulship** n.

consult v. go to for information or advice. —**consultant** n. specialist doctor with a senior position in a hospital; specialist who gives professional advice. —**consultancy** n. work or position of a consultant. —**consultation** n. (meeting for) consulting. —**consultative** adj. giving advice.

consume v. eat or drink; use up; destroy; obsess. —**consumer** n. person who buys goods or uses services. —**consumption** n. consuming; amount consumed; *Old-fashioned* tuberculosis. —**consumptive** adj., n. (person) having tuberculosis.

consummate [kon-sume-mate] v. make (a marriage) legal by sexual intercourse; complete or fulfil. —adj. [kon-sum-mit] supremely skilled; perfect. —**consummation** n.

cont. continued.

contact n. communicating; touching; useful acquaintance; connection between two electrical conductors in a circuit. —v. get in touch with. —**contact lens** lens fitting over the eyeball to correct defective vision.

contagion n. passing on of disease by contact; contagious disease; spreading of a harmful influence. —**contagious** adj. spreading by contact, catching.

contain v. hold or be capable of holding; consist of; control, restrain. —**container** n. receptacle used to hold something; large standard-sized box for transporting cargo by lorry or ship. —**containment** n. prevention of the spread of something harmful.

contaminate v. pollute, make impure; make radioactive. —**contaminant** n. contaminating substance. —**contamination** n.

contemplate v. think deeply (about); consider as a possibility; gaze at. —**contemplation** n. —**contemplative** adj. —**contemplatively** adv.

contemporary adj. present-day, modern; living or occurring at the same time. —n., pl. -**raries**. person or thing living or occurring at the same time as another. —**contemporaneous** adj.

contempt n. attitude of scornful disregard; open disrespect for the authority of a court. —**contemptible** adj. deserving contempt. —**contemptuous** adj. showing contempt. —**contemptuously** adv.

contend v. (foll. by with) deal with; assert; compete. —**contender** n. competitor. —**contention** n. disagreement or dispute; point asserted in argument. —**contentious** adj. causing dispute; quarrelsome.

THESAURUS

construct assemble, build, compose, create, design, erect, establish, fabricate, fashion, form, formulate, found, frame, make, manufacture, organize, put up, raise, set up, shape

construction assembly, building, composition, creation, edifice, erection, fabric, fabrication, figure, form, shape, structure

constructive helpful, positive, practical, productive, useful, valuable

consult ask, compare notes, confer, consider, debate, deliberate, interrogate, question, refer to, take counsel, turn to

consultant adviser, authority, specialist

consultation appointment, conference, council, deliberation, dialogue, discussion, examination, hearing, interview, meeting, session

consume absorb, deplete, drain, eat up, employ, exhaust, expend, finish up, lavish, lessen, spend, use, use up, utilize, vanish, waste, wear out

consumer buyer, customer, purchaser, shopper, user

contact n. 1. approximation, contiguity, junction, juxtaposition, touch, union 2. acquaintance, connection ~v. 3. approach, call, communicate with, get or be in touch with, get hold of, reach, ring (up), speak to, write to

contain accommodate, enclose, have capacity for, hold, incorporate, seat

container holder, receptacle, vessel

contemplate 1. brood over, consider, deliberate, meditate, observe, ponder, reflect upon, study 2. consider, design, envisage, expect, foresee, intend, mean, plan, propose, think of

contemporary adj. 1. coexistent, synchronous 2. à la mode, current, in fashion, latest, modern, newfangled, present, present-day, recent, up-to-date ~n. 3. compeer, fellow, peer

contempt contumely, derision, disdain, disre-

DICTIONARY

content[1] *n.* meaning or substance of a book etc.; amount of a substance in a mixture. —*pl.* what something contains; list of chapters at the front of a book.

content[2] *adj.* satisfied with things as they are. —*v.* make (someone) content. —*n.* peace of mind. —**contented** *adj.* —**contentment** *n.*

contest *n.* competition or struggle. —*v.* dispute; fight or compete for. —**contestant** *n.*

context *n.* words before and after a word or passage that contribute to its meaning; circumstances of an event or fact. —**contextual** *adj.*

contiguous *adj.* very near or touching. —**contiguity** *n.*

continent[1] *n.* one of the earth's large masses of land. —**the Continent** *Brit.* mainland of Europe. —**continental** *adj.* —**continental breakfast** light breakfast of rolls, coffee, etc.

continent[2] *adj.* able to control one's urination and defecation; sexually chaste. —**continence** *n.*

contingent *adj.* (foll. by *on*) dependent on (something uncertain). —*n.* group of people, esp. soldiers, that is part of a larger group. —**contingency** *n.* something that may happen.

continue *v.* **-tinuing, -tinued.** (cause to) remain in a condition or place; carry on (doing some-thing); resume. —**continual** *adj.* constant; frequently recurring. —**continually** *adv.* —**continuance** *n.* continuing. —**continuation** *n.* continuing; part added. —**continuity** *n.* smooth development or sequence. —**continuous** *adj.* continuing uninterrupted. —**continuously** *adv.*

continuo *n., pl.* **-tinuos.** *Music* continuous bass part, usually played on a keyboard instrument.

continuum *n., pl.* **-tinua, -tinuums.** continuous series.

contort *v.* twist out of normal shape. —**contortion** *n.* —**contortionist** *n.* performer who contorts his or her body to entertain.

contour *n.* outline; (also **contour line**) line on a map joining places of the same height.

contra- *prefix* against or contrasting, e.g. *contraflow.*

contraband *adj., n.* smuggled (goods).

contraception *n.* prevention of pregnancy by artificial means. —**contraceptive** *n.* device used or pill taken to prevent pregnancy. —*adj.* preventing pregnancy.

contract *v.* make or become smaller or shorter; make a formal agreement (to do something); catch (an illness). —*n.* formal agreement. —**contraction** *n.* —**contractor** *n.* firm that supplies

THESAURUS

gard, disrespect, mockery, neglect, scorn, slight

contend 1. clash, compete, contest, cope, emulate, grapple, jostle, litigate, skirmish, strive, struggle, vie 2. affirm, allege, argue, assert, aver, avow, debate, dispute, hold, maintain

content[1] burden, essence, gist, ideas, matter, meaning, significance, substance, text, thoughts

content[2] 1. *v.* appease, delight, gladden, gratify, humour, indulge, mollify, placate, please, reconcile, satisfy, suffice 2. *n.* comfort, ease, gratification, peace, peace of mind, pleasure, satisfaction 3. *adj.* agreeable, at ease, comfortable, contented, fulfilled, satisfied, willing to accept

contented at ease, at peace, cheerful, comfortable, glad, gratified, happy, pleased, satisfied, serene, thankful

contentment comfort, ease, equanimity, fulfilment, gladness, gratification, happiness, peace, pleasure, repletion, satisfaction, serenity

contents 1. elements, ingredients, load 2. chapters, divisions, subject matter, subjects, themes, topics

contest *n.* 1. competition, game, match, struggle, tournament, trial ~*v.* 2. compete, contend, fight, fight over, strive, vie 3. argue, challenge, debate, dispute, doubt, litigate, oppose, question

contestant aspirant, candidate, competitor, contender, entrant, player

context background, connection, frame of reference, framework, relation

continual constant, endless, eternal, everlasting, frequent, incessant, interminable, perpetual, recurrent, regular, repeated, unceasing, unremitting

continually all the time, always, constantly, endlessly, eternally, everlastingly, incessantly, interminably, repeatedly

continuation extension, furtherance, sequel, supplement

continue abide, carry on, endure, last, live on, persist, remain, rest, stay, stay on, survive

continuing enduring, in progress, lasting, ongoing, sustained

continuity cohesion, connection, flow, progression, sequence, succession

continuous connected, constant, extended, prolonged, unbroken, unceasing, undivided, uninterrupted

contraband 1. *n.* black-marketing, smuggling, trafficking 2. *adj.* banned, black-market, forbidden, illegal, illicit, prohibited, smuggled, unlawful

DICTIONARY

materials or labour, esp. for building. —**contractual** adj.

contradict v. declare the opposite of (a statement) to be true; be at variance with. —**contradiction** n. —**contradictory** adj.

contraflow n. flow of traffic going alongside but in an opposite direction to the usual flow.

contralto n., pl. -**tos.** (singer with) lowest female voice.

contraption n. strange-looking device.

contrapuntal adj. Music of or in counterpoint.

contrary adj. opposed, completely different; perverse, obstinate. —n. complete opposite. —adv. in opposition. —**contrarily** adv. —**contrariness** n. —**contrariwise** adv. conversely.

contrast v. compare or be compared in order to show differences. —n. striking difference; something showing this. —**contrastive** adj.

contravene v. break (a rule or law). —**contravention** n.

contretemps [kon-tra-tahn] n., pl. -**temps.** embarrassing minor disagreement.

contribute v. give to a common purpose or fund; (foll. by to) help (something) to occur. —**contribution** n. —**contributor** n. —**contributory** adj.

contrite adj. guilty and regretful. —**contritely** adv. —**contrition** n.

contrive v. make happen; invent and construct. —**contrivance** n. device; plan; contriving. —**contrived** adj. planned, artificial.

control v. -**trolling, -trolled.** have power over; curb or check; regulate. —n. power to direct something; curb or check; standard of comparison in an experiment. —pl. instruments used to operate a machine. —**controllable** adj. —**controller** n.

controversy n., pl. -**sies.** fierce argument or debate. —**controversial** adj. causing controversy.

contumacy [kon-tume-mass-ee] n. obstinate disobedience. —**contumacious** [kon-tume-may-shuss] adj.

contumely [kon-tume-mill-ee] n. scornful or insulting treatment.

THESAURUS

contract v. 1. abridge, compress, condense, confine, constrict, curtail, dwindle, lessen, narrow, purse, reduce, shrink, shrivel, tighten, wither, wrinkle 2. agree, arrange, bargain, clinch, close, come to terms, covenant, engage, enter into, negotiate, pledge, stipulate ~n. 3. agreement, arrangement, bargain, bond, commitment, compact, convention, covenant, deal (*Inf.*), engagement, pact, settlement, treaty, understanding

contradict be at variance with, belie, challenge, contravene, counter, counteract, deny, dispute, negate, oppose

contradiction conflict, contravention, denial, inconsistency, opposite

contradictory antagonistic, antithetical, conflicting, contrary, incompatible, inconsistent, opposite, paradoxical

contraption apparatus, contrivance, device, gadget, mechanism, rig

contrary adj. adverse, anti, clashing, contradictory, counter, discordant, hostile, inimical, opposed, opposite

contrast 1. n. comparison, difference, disparity, dissimilarity, distinction, divergence, foil, opposition 2. v. compare, differ, differentiate, distinguish, oppose, set in opposition, set off

contribute add, afford, bestow, chip in, donate, furnish, give, provide, subscribe, supply

contribution addition, bestowal, donation, gift, grant, subscription

contributor backer, bestower, donor, giver, patron, subscriber, supporter

contrite humble, penitent, regretful, remorseful, repentant, sorrowful, sorry

contrivance 1. artifice, design, dodge, expedient, formation, intrigue, measure, plan, plot, project, ruse, scheme, stratagem, trick 2. apparatus, appliance, contraption, device, equipment, gadget, gear, implement, invention, machine, mechanism

contrive concoct, construct, create, design, devise, engineer, fabricate, frame, improvise, invent

contrived artificial, elaborate, forced, laboured, overdone, planned, unnatural

control v. 1. command, conduct, direct, dominate, govern, have charge of, lead, manage, manipulate, oversee, pilot, reign over, rule, steer, superintend, supervise 2. bridle, check, constrain, contain, curb, hold back, limit, master, rein in, repress, restrain, subdue ~n. 3. authority, charge, command, direction, discipline, government, guidance, jurisdiction, management, mastery, oversight, rule, supervision, supremacy 4. brake, check, curb, limitation, regulation, restraint

controversial at issue, contentious, debatable, disputable, disputed, open to question, under discussion

controversy argument, contention, debate, discussion, dispute, dissension, polemic, quarrel, squabble, strife, wrangle

DICTIONARY

contusion *n.* bruise.

conundrum *n.* riddle.

conurbation *n.* large urban area formed by the growth and merging of towns.

convalesce *v.* recover health after an illness or operation. —**convalescence** *n.* —**convalescent** *adj., n.*

convection *n.* transmission of heat in liquids or gases by the circulation of currents. —**convector** *n.* heater which emits hot air.

convene *v.* gather or summon for a formal meeting. —**convener, -or** *n.* person who calls a meeting.

convenient *adj.* suitable or opportune; easy to use; nearby. —**conveniently** *adv.* —**convenience** *n.* quality of being convenient; convenient thing; public toilet.

convent *n.* building where nuns live; school run by nuns.

convention *n.* widely accepted view of proper behaviour; assembly or meeting; formal agreement. —**conventional** *adj.* (slavishly) following the accepted customs; customary; (of weapons or warfare) not nuclear. —**conventionally** *adv.* —**conventionality** *n.*

converge *v.* move towards the same point. —**convergence** *n.*

conversant *adj.* —**conversant with** having knowledge or experience of.

converse[1] *v.* have a conversation. —**conversation** *n.* informal talk. —**conversational** *adj.* —**conversationalist** *n.* person with a specified ability at conversation.

converse[2] *adj., n.* opposite or contrary. —**conversely** *adv.*

convert *v.* change in form, character, or function; cause to change in opinion or belief. —*n.* converted person. —**conversion** *n.* (thing resulting from) a converting or being converted. —**converter, -or** *n.* —**convertible** *adj.* capable of being converted. —*n.* car with a folding or removable roof.

convex *adj.* curving outwards. —**convexity** *n.*

convey *v.* communicate (information); carry, transport. —**conveyance** *n.* Old-fashioned vehicle; transfer of the legal title to property. —**conveyancing** *n.* branch of law dealing with the transfer of ownership of property. —**conveyor belt** continuous moving belt for transporting things, esp. in a factory.

convict *v.* declare guilty. —*n.* person serving a prison sentence. —**conviction** *n.* instance of being convicted; firm belief.

convince *v.* persuade by evidence or argument. —**convincing** *adj.* —**convincingly** *adv.*

convivial *adj.* sociable, lively. —**conviviality** *n.*

convoke *v.* call together. —**convocation** *n.* convoking; large formal meeting.

convoluted *adj.* coiled, twisted; (of an argument or sentence) complex and hard to understand. —**convolution** *n.*

convolvulus *n.* twining plant with funnel-shaped flowers.

convoy *n.* group of vehicles or ships travelling together.

convulse *v.* (of muscles) undergo violent

THESAURUS

convene assemble, bring together, call, come together, congregate, gather, meet, muster, rally, summon

convenience accessibility, appropriateness, availability, fitness, handiness, opportuneness, serviceability, suitability, usefulness, utility

convenient 1. appropriate, beneficial, commodious, fit, fitted, handy, helpful, labour-saving, opportune, seasonable, suitable, suited, timely, useful, well-timed 2. accessible, at hand, available, close at hand, handy

convention 1. assembly, conference, congress, convocation, council, delegates, meeting 2. code, custom, etiquette, formality, practice, propriety, protocol, tradition, usage

converge combine, come together, focus, gather, join, meet, merge, mingle

conversation chat, colloquy, communion, conference, converse, dialogue, discourse, discussion, exchange, gossip, talk, tête-à-tête

converse *n.* antithesis, contrary, obverse, opposite, reverse

conversion 1. change, transformation, transmutation 2. adaptation, alteration, modification, reconstruction, reorganization 3. change of heart, rebirth, reformation, regeneration

convert *v.* 1. alter, change, transform, transmute, transpose, turn 2. adapt, apply, modify, remodel, reorganize, restyle, revise

convey bear, bring, carry, conduct, fetch, forward, grant, guide, move, send, support, transmit, transport

convict 1. *v.* condemn, find guilty, imprison, sentence 2. *n.* criminal, culprit, felon, malefactor, prisoner

conviction assurance, certainty, confidence, firmness, reliance

convince assure, bring round, persuade, satisfy, sway, win over

DICTIONARY

spasms; *Informal* be overcome (with laughter or rage). —**convulsion** *n.* violent muscular spasm. —*pl.* uncontrollable laughter. —**convulsive** *adj.* —**convulsively** *adv.*

cony *n., pl.* **conies.** rabbit; rabbit fur.

coo *v.* **cooing, cooed.** (of a dove or pigeon) make a soft murmuring sound. —*n.* cooing sound.

cooee *interj.* call to attract attention.

cook *v.* prepare (food) by heating; (of food) be cooked; *Informal* falsify (accounts etc.). —*n.* person who cooks food. —**cooker** *n.* apparatus for cooking heated by gas or electricity; apple suitable for cooking. —**cookery** *n.* art of cooking. —**cookie** *n. US* biscuit. —**cook up** *v. Informal* devise (a story or scheme).

cool *adj.* moderately cold; calm and unemotional; indifferent or unfriendly; *Informal* sophisticated or excellent; *Informal* (of a large sum of money) without exaggeration, e.g. *a cool ten thousand.* —*v.* make or become cool. —*n.* coolness; *Slang* calmness, composure. —**coolly** *adv.* —**coolness** *n.* —**coolant** *n.* fluid used to cool machinery while it is working. —**cooler** *n.* container for making or keeping things cool; *Slang* prison.

coolie *n. Old-fashioned, Offens.* unskilled Oriental labourer.

coomb(e) *n.* valley.

co-op *n.* cooperative society; shop run by one.

coop *n.* cage or pen for poultry. —**coop up** *v.* confine in a restricted place.

cooper *n.* person who makes or repairs barrels or casks.

cooperate *v.* work or act together. —**cooperation** *n.* —**cooperative** *adj.* willing to cooperate; (of an enterprise) owned and managed collectively. —*n.* cooperative organization.

co-opt *v.* add (someone) to a group by the agreement of the existing members. —**co-option** *n.*

coordinate *v.* bring together and cause to work together efficiently. —*n. Maths* any of a set of numbers defining the location of a point. —*pl.* garments designed to be worn together. —**coordination** *n.* —**coordinator** *n.*

coot *n.* small black water bird.

cop *Slang* —*n.* policeman. —*v.* **copping, copped.** —**cop it** get into trouble or be punished. —**cop out** *v.* avoid taking responsibility or committing oneself.

cope[1] *v.* deal successfully (with).

cope[2] *n.* large ceremonial cloak worn by some Christian priests.

coping *n.* sloping top row of a wall. —**coping stone.**

copious [**kope**-ee-uss] *adj.* abundant, plentiful. —**copiously** *adv.*

copper[1] *n.* soft reddish-brown metal; copper or bronze coin; large metal container used to boil water. —**copper-bottomed** *adj.* financially reliable. —**copperplate** *n.* fine handwriting style.

copper[2] *n. Slang* policeman.

coppice, copse *n.* dense growth of small trees and undergrowth.

copra *n.* dried oil-yielding kernel of the coconut.

copulate *v.* have sexual intercourse. —**copulation** *n.*

copy *n., pl.* **copies.** thing made to look exactly like another; single specimen of a book etc.; material for printing. —*v.* **copying, copied.** make a copy of; act or try to be like another. —**copyright** *n.* exclusive legal right to reproduce and control a book, work of art, etc. —*v.* take out a copyright on. —*adj.* protected by copyright. —**copywriter** *n.* person who writes advertising copy.

THESAURUS

convulse agitate, derange, disorder, disturb, shake, shatter, twist, work

cool *adj.* 1. chilled, chilly, nippy, refreshing 2. calm, collected, composed, deliberate, imperturbable, level-headed, placid, quiet, relaxed, self-controlled, self-possessed, serene, unemotional, unexcited, unruffled 3. aloof, distant, frigid, indifferent, lukewarm, offhand, reserved, unfriendly, uninterested, unresponsive, unwelcoming~*v.* 4. chill, cool off, freeze, lose heat, refrigerate 5. abate, allay, assuage, calm (down), dampen, lessen, moderate, quiet, temper

cooperate aid, assist, collaborate, combine, concur, conspire, contribute, help, join forces, pitch in, pull together, work together

cooperation assistance, collaboration, give-and-take, helpfulness, participation, responsiveness, teamwork, unity

cooperative accommodating, helpful, obliging, responsive, supportive

coordinate correlate, harmonize, integrate, match, mesh, organize, relate

cope 1. carry on, manage, struggle through, survive 2. **cope with** deal, encounter, handle, struggle, tangle, tussle, weather, wrestle

copious abundant, ample, bountiful, extensive, exuberant, full, generous, lavish, liberal, luxuriant, overflowing, plenteous, plentiful, profuse, rich

copy *n.* 1. counterfeit, duplicate, facsimile, forgery, image, imitation, likeness, model, pattern, photocopy, print, replica, replication,

DICTIONARY

coquette *n.* woman who flirts. —**coquettish** *adj.* —**coquetry** *n.*

coracle *n.* small round boat of wicker covered with skins.

coral *n.* hard substance formed from the skeletons of very small sea animals. —*adj.* made of coral; orange-pink.

cor anglais *n., pl.* **cors anglais.** woodwind instrument similar to the oboe.

corbel *n.* stone or timber support projecting from a wall.

cord *n.* thin rope or thick string; cordlike structure in the body; corduroy. —*pl.* corduroy trousers. —*adj.* (of fabric) ribbed.

cordial *adj.* warm and friendly; strong, e.g. *cordial dislike.* —*n.* drink with a fruit base. —**cordially** *adv.* —**cordiality** *n.*

cordite *n.* explosive used in guns and bombs.

cordon *n.* chain of police, soldiers, etc. guarding an area; fruit tree grown as a single stem. —**cordon off** *v.* form a cordon round.

cordon bleu [**bluh**] *adj.* (of cookery or cooks) of the highest standard.

corduroy *n.* cotton fabric with a velvety ribbed surface.

core *n.* central part of certain fruits, containing the seeds; central or essential part. —*v.* remove the core from.

co-respondent *n.* person with whom someone being sued for divorce is claimed to have committed adultery.

corgi *n.* short-legged sturdy dog.

coriander *n.* plant with aromatic seeds and leaves used for flavouring.

cork *n.* thick light bark of a Mediterranean oak; piece of this used as a stopper. —*v.* stop up with a cork. —**corkage** *n.* restaurant's charge for serving wine bought elsewhere. —**corkscrew** *n.* tool for extracting corks from bottles.

corm *n.* bulblike underground stem of certain plants.

cormorant *n.* large dark-coloured long-necked sea bird.

corn[1] *n.* cereal plant; grain of such plants; *US* maize; *Slang* something unoriginal or oversentimental. —**corny** *adj. Slang* unoriginal or oversentimental. —**cornflakes** *pl. n.* breakfast cereal of toasted maize flakes. —**cornflour** *n.* finely ground maize. —**cornflower** *n.* plant with blue flowers.

corn[2] *n.* painful hard skin on the foot or toe.

cornea [**korn**-ee-a] *n., pl.* **-neas, -neae.** transparent membrane covering the eyeball. —**corneal** *adj.*

corned beef *n.* beef preserved in salt.

cornelian *n.* reddish semiprecious stone.

corner *n.* area or angle where two converging lines or surfaces meet; place where two streets meet; sharp bend in a road; remote or inaccessible place; *Sport* free kick or shot from the corner of the field. —*v.* (of a vehicle) turn a corner; force into a difficult or inescapable position; obtain a monopoly of. —**cornerstone** *n.* indispensable part or basis.

cornet *n.* brass instrument similar to the trumpet; cone-shaped ice-cream wafer.

cornice [**korn**-iss] *n.* decorative moulding round the top of a wall.

cornucopia [korn-yew-**kope**-ee-a] *n.* great abundance; symbol of plenty, consisting of a horn overflowing with fruit and flowers.

corolla *n.* petals of a flower collectively.

corollary [kor-**oll**-a-ree] *n., pl.* **-laries.** idea, fact, or proposition which is the natural result of something else.

corona [kor-**rone**-a] *n., pl.* **-nas, -nae.** ring of light round the moon or sun.

coronary [**kor**-ron-a-ree] *adj.* of the arteries surrounding the heart. —*n., pl.* **-naries.** coronary thrombosis. —**coronary thrombosis** condition in which the flow of blood to the heart is blocked by a blood clot.

coronation *n.* ceremony of crowning a monarch.

coroner *n.* official responsible for the investigation of violent, sudden, or suspicious deaths.

coronet *n.* small crown.

corpora *n.* plural of CORPUS.

THESAURUS

representation, reproduction ~*v.* 2. counterfeit, duplicate, photocopy, reproduce, transcribe 3. ape, echo, emulate, follow, follow the example of, imitate, mimic, mirror, parrot, repeat, simulate

cord line, rope, string, twine

cordial affable, affectionate, agreeable, cheerful, friendly, genial, hearty, sociable, warm, warmhearted, welcoming, wholehearted

cordon *n.* barrier, chain, line, ring

core centre, crux, essence, gist, heart, kernel, nub, nucleus, pith

corner *n.* 1. angle, bend, crook, joint 2. cavity, cranny, hideaway, hide-out, hole, niche, nook, recess, retreat ~*v.* 3. bring to bay, run to earth, trap

corny banal, commonplace, dull, feeble, hackneyed, maudlin, mawkish, old-fashioned, sentimental, stale, trite

DICTIONARY

corporal[1] *adj.* of the body. —**corporal punishment** physical punishment, such as caning.

corporal[2] *n.* noncommissioned officer below sergeant.

corporation *n.* large business or company; city or town council; *Informal* large paunch. —**corporate** *adj.* relating to business corporations; shared by a group.

corporeal [kore-**pore**-ee-al] *adj.* physical or tangible.

corps [**kore**] *n., pl.* **corps.** military unit with a specific function; organized body of people.

corpse *n.* dead body.

corpulent *adj.* fat or plump. —**corpulence** *n.*

corpus *n., pl.* **corpora.** collection of writings, esp. by a single author.

corpuscle *n.* red or white blood cell.

corral *US* —*n.* enclosure for cattle or horses. —*v.* -**ralling, -ralled.** put in a corral.

correct *adj.* free from error, true; in accordance with accepted standards. —*v.* put right; indicate the errors in; rebuke or punish. —**correctly** *adv.* —**correctness** *n.* —**correction** *n.* correcting; alteration correcting something. —**corrective** *n., adj.* (thing) intended or tending to correct.

correlate *v.* place or be placed in a mutual relationship. —*n.* either of two things mutually related. —**correlation** *n.* —**correlative** *adj., n.*

correspond *v.* be consistent or compatible

(with); be similar (to); communicate (with) by letter. —**corresponding** *adj.* —**correspondingly** *adv.* —**correspondence** *n.* communication by letters; letters so exchanged; relationship or similarity. —**correspondent** *n.* writer of letters; person employed by a newspaper etc. to report on a special subject or from a foreign country.

corridor *n.* passage in a building or train; strip of land or air space providing access through foreign territory.

corrigendum [kor-rij-**end**-um] *n., pl.* -**da.** thing to be corrected.

corroborate *v.* support (a fact or opinion) by giving proof. —**corroboration** *n.* —**corroborative** *adj.*

corrode *v.* eat or be eaten away by chemical action. —**corrosion** *n.* —**corrosive** *adj.*

corrugate *v.* fold into alternate grooves and ridges. —**corrugated** *adj.* —**corrugation** *n.*

corrupt *adj.* open to or involving bribery; morally wrong, depraved; (of a text, data, etc.) unreliable through errors or alterations. —*v.* make corrupt. —**corruptly** *adv.* —**corruption** *n.* —**corruptible** *adj.*

corsage [kor-**sahzh**] *n.* small bouquet worn on the bodice of a dress.

corsair *n.* pirate; pirate ship.

corset *n.* close-fitting undergarment worn to support or shape the torso.

THESAURUS

corps band, body, company, contingent, crew, detachment, division, regiment, squad, squadron, team, troop, unit

corpse body, cadaver, carcass

correct *v.* 1. adjust, amend, cure, improve, rectify, redress, reform, remedy, right 2. admonish, chastise, chide, discipline, punish, rebuke, reprimand, reprove ~*adj.* 3. accurate, exact, faultless, flawless, just, precise, regular, right, strict, true

correction 1. adjustment, alteration, amendment, improvement, modification 2. admonition, castigation, chastisement, discipline, punishment, reproof

correctly accurately, perfectly, precisely, properly, rightly

correctness accuracy, exactitude, fidelity, preciseness, precision, regularity, truth

correspond 1. accord, agree, be consistent, coincide, conform, dovetail, fit, harmonize, match, square, tally 2. communicate, exchange letters

correspondence 1. agreement, analogy, coincidence, comparison, conformity, congruity,

correlation, fitness, harmony, match, relation, similarity 2. communication, letters, mail, post, writing

correspondent *n.* 1. letter writer, pen friend *or* pal 2. contributor, journalist, reporter

corresponding analogous, answering, complementary, correlative, equivalent, interrelated, matching, reciprocal, similar

corridor aisle, hallway, passage, passageway

corrode canker, consume, corrupt, eat away, erode, gnaw, impair, rust, waste, wear away

corrosive acrid, caustic, erosive, virulent, wasting, wearing

corrupt *adj.* 1. dishonest, fraudulent, rotten, shady (*Inf.*), unethical, unprincipled, unscrupulous, venal 2. altered, contaminated, decayed, defiled, distorted, doctored, falsified, rotten, tainted ~*v* 3. bribe, debauch, demoralize, deprave, entice, fix (*Inf.*), lure, pervert, square (*Inf.*), suborn, subvert

corruption 1. breach of trust, bribery, bribing, demoralization, dishonesty, extortion, fraud, graft, jobbery, profiteering, shadiness, venality 2. decadence, degeneration, depravity, evil,

DICTIONARY

cortege [kor-tayzh] *n.* funeral procession.

cortex *n., pl.* **-tices.** *Anat.* outer layer of the brain or other internal organ. —**cortical** *adj.*

cortisone *n.* steroid hormone used to treat various diseases.

corundum *n.* hard mineral used as an abrasive.

coruscate *v.* sparkle. —**coruscation** *n.*

corvette *n.* lightly armed escort warship.

cos *Maths* cosine.

cosh *n.* heavy blunt weapon. —*v.* hit with a cosh.

cosine [**koh**-sine] *n.* (in trigonometry) ratio of the length of the adjacent side to that of the hypotenuse in a right-angled triangle.

cosmetic *n.* preparation used to improve the appearance of a person's skin. —*adj.* improving the appearance only.

cosmic *adj.* of the whole universe. —**cosmic rays** electromagnetic radiation from outer space.

cosmonaut *n.* Soviet astronaut.

cosmopolitan *adj.* composed of people or elements from many countries; having lived and travelled in many countries. —*n.* cosmopolitan person. —**cosmopolitanism** *n.*

cosmos *n.* the universe. —**cosmology** *n.* study of the origin and nature of the universe. —**cosmological** *adj.*

Cossack *n.* member of a S Russian people famous as horsemen.

cosset *v.* **cosseting, cosseted.** pamper or pet.

cost *n.* amount of money, time, labour, etc. required for something. —*pl.* expenses of a lawsuit. —*v.* **costing, cost.** have as its cost; involve the loss or sacrifice of; estimate the cost of. —**costly** *adj.* expensive; involving great loss or sacrifice. —**costliness** *n.*

costermonger *n.* person who sells fruit and vegetables from a barrow in the street.

costive *adj.* having or causing constipation.

costume *n.* style of dress of a particular place or time, or for a particular activity; clothes worn by an actor or performer. —**costumier** *n.* maker or seller of costumes. —**costume jewellery** inexpensive artificial jewellery.

cosy *adj.* **-sier, -siest.** snug and warm; intimate, friendly. —*n.* cover to keep a teapot etc. hot. —**cosily** *adv.* —**cosiness** *n.*

cot *n.* child's bed with high sides; small portable bed. —**cot death** unexplained death of a baby while asleep.

cote *n.* shelter for animals or birds.

coterie [**kote**-er-ee] *n.* exclusive group, clique.

cotoneaster [kot-tone-ee-**ass**-ter] *n.* garden shrub with red berries.

cottage *n.* small house in the country. —**cottage cheese** soft mild white cheese. —**cottage industry** craft industry in which employees work at home. —**cottage pie** dish of minced meat topped with mashed potato.

cotter *n.* pin or wedge used to secure machine parts.

cotton *n.* white downy fibre covering the seeds of a tropical plant; thread or cloth made of this. —**cottony** *adj.* —**cotton on (to)** *v. Informal* understand. —**cotton wool** fluffy cotton used for surgical dressings etc.

cotyledon [kot-ill-**ee**-don] *n.* first leaf of a plant embryo.

couch *n.* piece of upholstered furniture for seating more than one person. —*v.* express in a particular way.

couch grass *n.* quickly spreading grassy weed.

couchette [koo-**shett**] *n.* bed converted from seats in a train.

cougar [**koo**-gar] *n.* puma.

cough *v.* expel air from the lungs abruptly and noisily. —*n.* act or sound of coughing; illness which causes coughing.

could *v.* past tense of CAN[1].

couldn't could not.

coulomb [**koo**-lom] *n.* unit of electric charge.

coulter [**kole**-ter] *n.* blade at the front of a ploughshare.

THESAURUS

immorality, impurity, iniquity, perversion, sinfulness, vice, viciousness, wickedness

corset belt, bodice, girdle

cosmetic *adj.* beautifying, superficial, surface

cosmic huge, immense, infinite, limitless, measureless, universal, vast

cosmopolitan catholic, sophisticated, universal, urbane, well-travelled, worldly, worldly-wise

cost 1. *n.* amount, charge, expenditure, expense, figure, outlay payment, price, rate, worth 2. *v.* come to, sell at

costly dear, excessive, expensive, extortionate, highly-priced, steep (*Inf.*), valuable

costume attire, clothing, dress, ensemble, garb, get-up (*Inf.*), livery, outfit, robes, uniform

cosy comfortable, homely, intimate, secure, sheltered, snug, warm

cottage but-and-ben (*Scot.*), cabin, chalet, cot, hut, lodge, shack

cough 1. *n.* bark, hack 2. *v.* bark, clear one's throat, hack, hawk, hem

DICTIONARY

council *n.* group meeting for discussion or consultation; local governing body of a town or county. —**councillor** *n.* member of a council.

counsel *n.* advice or guidance; barrister or barristers. —*v.* **-selling, -selled.** give guidance to; urge or recommend. —**counsellor** *n.*

count[1] *v.* say numbers in order; find the total of; be important; regard as; take into account. —*n.* number reached by counting; counting; *Law* one of a number of charges. —**countless** *adj.* too many to be counted. —**count on** *v.* expect; rely on.

count[2] *n.* European nobleman. —**countess** *n. fem.*

countdown *n.* counting backwards to zero of the seconds before an event.

countenance *n.* (expression of) the face. —*v.* support or tolerate.

counter[1] *n.* long flat surface in a bank or shop, on which business is transacted; small flat disc used in board games.

counter[2] *adv.* in the opposite direction; in direct contrast. —*v.* oppose, retaliate against. —*n.* opposing or retaliatory action.

counter- *combining form* used with many main words to mean: against, opposite, e.g. *counterbalance;* retaliatory, rival, e.g. *counterrevolution, counterclaim.*

counteract *v.* neutralize or act against. —**counteraction** *n.*

counterattack *v., n.* attack in response to an attack.

counterbalance *n.* weight or force balancing or neutralizing another. —*v.* act as a counterbalance to.

counterblast *n.* aggressive response to a verbal attack.

counterfeit *adj.* fake, forged. —*n.* fake, forgery. —*v.* fake, forge.

counterfoil *n.* part of a cheque or receipt kept as a record.

countermand *v.* cancel (a previous order).

counterpane *n.* bed covering.

counterpart *n.* person or thing complementary to or corresponding to another.

counterpoint *n. Music* technique of combining melodies.

counterpoise *n., v.* counterbalance.

counterproductive *adj.* having an effect opposite to the one intended.

countersign *v.* sign (a document already signed by another) as confirmation.

countersink *v.* drive (a screw) into a shaped hole so that its head is below the surface.

countertenor *n.* male alto.

country *n., pl.* **-tries.** nation; nation's territory; nation's people; rural areas as opposed to town. —**countrified** *adj.* rustic in manner or appearance. —**countryman, countrywoman** *n.* compatriot; person who lives in the country. —**country music** popular music based on American White folk music. —**countryside** *n.* rural areas.

THESAURUS

council assembly, board, cabinet, chamber, committee, conference, congress, convention, convocation, diet, ministry, panel, parliament, synod

counsel *n.* 1. admonition, advice, caution, consideration, direction, forethought, guidance, information, recommendation, suggestion, warning 2. advocate, attorney, barrister, lawyer, legal adviser, solicitor ~*v.* 3. admonish, advise, advocate, caution, exhort, instruct, recommend, urge, warn

count 1. add (up), calculate, cast up, check, compute, enumerate, estimate, number, reckon, score, tally, tot up 2. be important, carry weight, matter, rate, signify, tell, weigh

counter 1. *adv.* against, contrarily, conversely, in defiance of, versus 2. *adj.* adverse, against, conflicting, contradictory, contrary, contrasting, obverse, opposing, opposite 3. *v.* answer, hit back, meet, offset, parry, resist, respond, retaliate, return, ward off

counterbalance balance, compensate, make up for, offset, set off

counterfeit 1. *v.* copy, fabricate, fake, feign, forge, imitate, impersonate, pretend, sham, simulate 2. *adj.* bogus, copied, faked, false, feigned, forged, fraudulent, imitation, phoney (*Sl.*), pseudo (*Inf.*), sham, simulated, spurious 3. *n.* copy, fake, forgery, fraud, imitation, reproduction, sham

countermand annul, cancel, override, repeal, rescind, retract, reverse, revoke

counterpart complement, copy, duplicate, equal, fellow, match, mate, supplement, tally, twin

countless endless, incalculable, infinite, legion, limitless, measureless, myriad, uncounted, untold

count on *or* **upon** bank on, believe (in), depend on, lean on, reckon on, rely on, take on trust, trust

country 1. commonwealth, kingdom, nation, people, realm, sovereign state, state 2. fatherland, homeland, motherland, nationality, native land 3. land, part, region, terrain, territory 4. citizens, community, electors, inhabitants,

DICTIONARY

county *n., pl.* **-ties.** division of a country.

coup [koo] *n.* successful action; coup d'état.

coup de grace [koo de grahss] *n.* final or decisive action.

coup d'état [koo day-**tah**] *n.* sudden violent overthrow of a government.

coupé [koo-pay] *n.* sports car with two doors and a sloping fixed roof.

couple *n.* two people who are married or romantically involved; two partners in a dance or game. —*v.* connect, associate; *Lit.* have sexual intercourse. —**a couple (of)** a pair (of); *Informal* a few. —**couplet** *n.* two consecutive lines of verse, usu. rhyming and of the same metre. —**coupling** *n.* device for connecting things, such as railway carriages.

coupon *n.* piece of paper entitling the holder to a discount or gift; detachable order form; football pools entry form.

courage *n.* ability to face danger or pain without fear. —**courageous** *adj.* —**courageously** *adv.*

courgette *n.* type of small vegetable marrow.

courier *n.* person who looks after and guides travellers; person paid to deliver urgent messages.

course *n.* onward movement in space or time; direction or route of movement; natural development of events; mode of conduct or action; series of lessons or medical treatment; any of the successive parts of a meal; area where golf is played or a race is run; continuous layer of masonry at one level in a building. —*v.* (of liquid) run swiftly; hunt with hounds that follow the quarry by sight and not scent. —**of course** naturally.

court *n.* body which decides legal cases; place where it meets; marked area for playing a racket game; courtyard; residence, household, or retinue of a sovereign. —*v. Old-fashioned* try to win (someone) as a spouse; try to win (someone's favour); invite, e.g. *court disaster.* —**courtier** *n.* attendant at a royal court. —**courtly** *adj.* ceremoniously polite. —**courtliness** *n.* —**courtship** *n.* courting of an intended spouse or mate. —**court martial** court for trying naval or military offences. —**court shoe** woman's low-cut shoe without straps or laces. —**courtyard** *n.* paved space enclosed by buildings or walls.

courtesan [kor-tiz-**zan**] *n. Hist.* mistress or high-class prostitute.

courtesy *n., pl.* **-sies.** politeness, good manners; courteous act. —**(by) courtesy of** by permission of. —**courteous** *adj.* polite. —**courteously** *adv.*

THESAURUS

nation, people, populace, public, society, voters 5. backwoods, farmland, green belt, outdoors, provinces, rural areas, wide open spaces (*Inf.*)

countryside country, farmland, green belt, outdoors, view, wide open spaces (*Inf.*)

county province, shire

coup action, deed, exploit, feat, manoeuvre, stratagem, stroke, stunt, *tour de force*

couple 1. *n.* brace, duo, pair, twosome 2. *v.* buckle, clasp, conjoin, connect, hitch, join, link, marry, pair, unite, wed, yoke

coupon card, certificate, slip, ticket, token, voucher

courage boldness, bravery, daring, fearlessness, firmness, fortitude, gallantry, grit, guts (*Inf.*), heroism, mettle, nerve, pluck, resolution, valour

courageous audacious, bold, brave, daring, fearless, gallant, hardy, heroic, indomitable, intrepid, plucky, resolute, valiant, valorous

course 1. advance, continuity, development, flow, march, movement, order, progress, sequence, succession 2. channel, direction, line, orbit, passage, path, road, route, tack, track, trail, trajectory, way 3. lapse, passage, passing, sweep, term, time 4. conduct, manner, method, mode, plan, policy, procedure, programme 5. circuit, lap, race, racecourse, round 6. classes, course of study, curriculum, lectures, programme, schedule, studies 7. **of course** certainly, definitely, naturally, obviously, undoubtedly

court *n.* 1. cloister, courtyard, piazza, plaza, quad (*Inf.*), quadrangle, square, yard 2. hall, manor, palace 3. attendants, retinue, royal household, suite, train 4. bar, bench, court of justice, lawcourt, tribunal ~*v.* 5. chase, date, go (out) with, keep company with, make love to, pay court to, pursue, run after, serenade, take out, walk out with, woo 6. cultivate, curry favour with, fawn upon, flatter, pander to, seek, solicit

courteous affable, attentive, civil, courtly, elegant, gallant, gracious, mannerly, polished, polite, refined, respectful, urbane, well-bred, well-mannered

courtesy affability, civility, elegance, gallantry, good breeding, good manners, graciousness, polish, politeness, urbanity

courtier attendant, follower, squire, trainbearer

courtly affable, ceremonious, chivalrous, civil, dignified, elegant, flattering, formal, gallant, lordly, polished, refined, stately, urbane

courtyard area, enclosure, playground, quad, quadrangle, yard

DICTIONARY

cousin n. child of one's uncle or aunt.

couturier n. person who designs women's fashion clothes.

cove n. small bay or inlet.

coven [kuv-ven] n. meeting of witches.

covenant [kuv-ven-ant] n. formal agreement, esp. to make an annual (charitable) payment. —v. agree (to pay) by a covenant.

Coventry n. —**send someone to Coventry** punish someone by refusing to speak to him or her.

cover v. place or spread or be placed or spread over; screen or conceal; protect from loss or risk by insurance; travel over; include; be enough to pay for; report (an event) for a newspaper; keep a gun aimed at. —n. anything which covers; outside of a book or magazine; shelter or protection; insurance. —**coverage** n. amount or extent covered. —**coverlet** n. bed cover.

covert adj. secret, concealed. —n. thicket giving shelter to game birds or animals. —**covertly** adv.

covet v. **coveting, coveted.** long to possess (what belongs to someone else). —**covetous** adj. —**covetousness** n.

covey [kuv-vee] n. small flock of grouse or partridge.

cow[1] n. mature female of cattle and of certain other animals, such as the elephant or whale. —**cowboy** n. ranch worker who herds and tends cattle, usu. on horseback; Informal irresponsible or unscrupulous worker.

cow[2] v. intimidate, subdue.

coward n. person who lacks courage. —**cowardly** adj. —**cowardice** n. lack of courage.

cower v. cringe or shrink in fear.

cowl n. loose hood; monk's hooded robe; cover on a chimney to increase ventilation.

cowling n. cover on an engine.

cowrie n. brightly-marked sea shell.

cowslip n. fragrant wild primrose.

cox n. coxswain. —v. act as cox of (a boat).

coxswain [kok-sn] n. person who steers a rowing boat.

coy adj. affectedly shy or modest. —**coyly** adv. —**coyness** n.

coyote [koy-ote-ee] n. prairie wolf of N America.

coypu n. beaver-like aquatic rodent, bred for its fur.

cozen v. cheat or trick.

Cr Chem. chromium.

crab n. edible shellfish with ten legs, the first pair modified into pincers.

crab apple n. small sour apple.

crabbed adj. (of handwriting) hard to read; (also **crabby**) bad-tempered.

crack v. break or split partially; break with a sharp noise; (cause to) make a sharp noise; break down or yield under strain; hit suddenly; tell (a joke); solve (a code or problem); (of the voice) become harsh or change pitch suddenly. —n. narrow gap; sudden sharp noise; sharp blow; Informal gibe or joke; Slang pure highly addictive form of cocaine. —adj. Informal excellent, first-rate, e.g. a crack shot. —**cracker** n. thin dry biscuit; decorated cardboard tube, pulled apart with a bang, containing a paper hat and a motto or toy; small explosive firework. —**crackers** adj. Slang crazy. —**cracking** adj. first-class. —**crackdown** n. severe disciplinary or repressive measure. —**crack down on** v. take severe measures against. —**crackpot** adj., n. Informal eccentric (person).

THESAURUS

cove bay, creek, inlet, sound

covenant 1. bargain, commitment, compact, concordat, contract, convention, pact, promise, stipulation, treaty, trust 2. bond, deed

cover n. 1. cloak, cover-up, disguise, façade, front, mask, pretence, screen, smoke screen, veil 2. concealment, defence, guard, hiding, place, protection, refuge, sanctuary, shelter, shield 3. compensation, indemnity, insurance, payment, protection ~v. 4. cloak, conceal, cover up, curtain, disguise, eclipse, hide, hood, house, mask, obscure, screen, secrete, shade, shroud, veil 5. defend, guard, protect, reinforce, shelter, shield 6. describe, detail, investigate, narrate, recount, relate, report, tell of, write up

covet begrudge, crave, desire, envy, fancy (Inf.),

hanker after, long for, lust after, thirst for, yearn for

covetous avaricious, envious, grasping, greedy, jealous, mercenary, yearning

coward craven, faint-heart, poltroon, renegade, sneak

cowardly base, craven, dastardly, faint-hearted, fearful, lily-livered, scared, shrinking, soft, spineless, timorous, weak, yellow (Inf.)

cower cringe, crouch, draw back, fawn, flinch, grovel, quail, shrink, skulk, sneak, tremble, truckle

coy arch, backward, bashful, demure, evasive, modest, prudish, reserved, retiring, self-effacing, shrinking, shy, skittish, timid

crack v. 1. break, burst, chip, chop, fracture, snap, splinter, split 2. break down, collapse,

DICTIONARY

crackle v. make small sharp popping noises. —n. crackling sound. —**crackling** n. crackle; crisp skin of roast pork.

cradle n. baby's bed on rockers; place where something originated; supporting structure. —v. hold gently as if in a cradle.

craft[1] n. skill or ability; skilled trade; cunning. —**crafty** adj. skilled in deception. —**craftily** adv. —**craftiness** n. —**craftsman, craftswoman** n. skilled worker. —**craftsmanship** n.

craft[2] n., pl. **craft**. boat, ship, aircraft, or spaceship.

crag n. steep rugged rock. —**craggy** adj.

cram v. **cramming, crammed**. force into too small a space; fill too full; study hard just before an examination.

cramp n. painful muscular contraction; clamp for holding masonry or timber together. —v. confine or restrict.

crampon n. spiked plate strapped to a boot for climbing on ice.

cranberry n. sour edible red berry.

crane n. machine for lifting and moving heavy weights; wading bird with long legs, neck, and bill. —v. stretch (one's neck) to see something.

crane fly n. long-legged insect with slender wings.

cranium n., pl. -**niums, -nia**. skull. —**cranial** adj.

crank n. arm projecting at right angles from a shaft, for transmitting or converting motion; Informal eccentric person. —v. start (an engine) with a crank. —**cranky** adj. eccentric; US bad-tempered. —**crankshaft** n. shaft driven by a crank.

cranny n., pl. -**nies**. small opening, chink.

crape n. same as CREPE.

craps n. gambling game played with two dice.

crash v. (cause to) collide violently with a vehicle, a stationary object, or the ground; (cause to) make a loud smashing noise; (cause to) fall with a crash; collapse or fail financially. —n. collision involving a vehicle or vehicles; sudden loud smashing noise; financial collapse. —adj. requiring or using great effort to achieve results quickly, e.g. a crash course. —**crash helmet** protective helmet worn by a motorcyclist. —**crash-land** v. land (an aircraft) in an emergency, causing it damage. —**crash-landing** n.

crass adj. grossly stupid. —**crassly** adv. —**crassness** n.

crate n. large wooden container for packing goods.

THESAURUS

give way, go to pieces, lose control, succumb, yield ~n. 3. breach, break, chink, chip, cleft, cranny, crevice, fissure, fracture, gap, rift 4. burst, clap, crash, explosion, pop, report, snap 5. Sl. dig, gag, insult, jibe, joke, quip, witticism ~adj. 6. Sl. ace, choice, elite, excellent, first-class, first-rate, hand-picked, superior

cradle n. 1. cot, crib, Moses basket 2. Fig. beginning, birthplace, fount, origin, source, spring ~v. 3. hold, lull, nestle, nurse, rock, support

craft[1] 1. ability, aptitude, art, artistry, cleverness, dexterity, expertise, ingenuity, skill, technique, workmanship 2. artfulness, contrivance, cunning, deceit, duplicity, guile, ruse, scheme, shrewdness, subtlety, trickery, wiles 3. business, calling, employment, handicraft, handiwork, line, occupation, pursuit, trade, vocation, work

craft[2] aircraft, barque, boat, plane, spacecraft, vessel

craftsman artificer, artisan, maker, master, skilled worker, smith, technician, wright

crafty artful, astute, calculating, canny, cunning, deceitful, designing, devious, foxy, fraudulent, guileful, knowing, scheming, sharp, shrewd, sly, subtle, tricky, wily

crag peak, pinnacle, rock, tor

cram compact, compress, crowd, crush, force, jam, overcrowd, overfill, pack, pack in, press, ram, shove, squeeze, stuff

cramp 1. v. check, clog, confine, encumber, hamper, handicap, hinder, impede, inhibit, obstruct, restrict, shackle 2. n. ache, crick, pain, pang, shooting pain, spasm, stiffness, twinge

cranny breach, chink, cleft, crack, crevice, fissure, gap, hole, interstice, nook, opening

crash n. 1. bang, boom, clang, clash, din, racket, smash, thunder 2. accident, bump, collision, jar, jolt, pile-up (Inf.), smash, thud, thump, wreck 3. bankruptcy, collapse, debacle, depression, downfall, failure, ruin, smash ~v. 4. come a cropper (Inf.), dash, fall, give way, hurtle, lurch, overbalance, pitch, plunge, precipitate oneself, sprawl, topple 5. bang, bump (into), collide, crash-land (an aircraft), drive into, have an accident, hit, hurtle into, plough into, run together, wreck

crass asinine, boorish, bovine, coarse, dense, doltish, gross, insensitive, obtuse, stupid, unrefined

crate n. box, case, container, packing case, tea chest

DICTIONARY

crater *n.* bowl-shaped cavity made by the impact of a meteorite or an explosion; mouth of a volcano.

cravat *n.* man's scarf worn like a tie.

crave *v.* desire intensely; beg or plead for. —**craving** *n.*

craven *adj.* cowardly.

craw *n.* bird's crop; animal's stomach.

crawfish *n.* same as CRAYFISH.

crawl *v.* move on one's hands and knees; move very slowly; act in a servile manner; be or feel as if covered with crawling creatures. —*n.* crawling motion or pace; overarm swimming stroke. —**crawler** *n.*

crayfish *n.* edible freshwater shellfish like a lobster.

crayon *n.* stick or pencil of coloured wax or clay. —*v.* draw or colour with a crayon.

craze *n.* short-lived fashion or enthusiasm. —**crazed** *adj.* demented; (of porcelain) having fine cracks. —**crazy** *adj.* ridiculous; (foll. by *about*) very fond (of); insane. —**craziness** *n.* —**crazy paving** paving made of irregularly shaped slabs of stone.

creak *v., n.* (make) a harsh squeaking sound. —**creaky** *adj.*

cream *n.* fatty part of milk; something, esp. a food or cosmetic, resembling cream in consistency; best part (of something). —*adj.* yellowish-white. —*v.* beat to a creamy consistency; (foll. by *off*) take the best part from. —**creamy** *adj.* —**cream cheese** rich soft white cheese.

crease *n.* line made by folding or pressing; *Cricket* line marking the bowler's and batsman's positions. —*v.* crush.

create *v.* bring into being; appoint to a new rank or position; *Slang* make an angry fuss. —**creation** *n.* —**creative** *adj.* imaginative or inventive. —**creativity** *n.* —**creator** *n.*

creature *n.* person, animal, or being.

crèche *n.* day nursery for very young children.

credence [**kreed**-enss] *n.* belief in the truth or accuracy of a statement.

credentials *pl. n.* document giving evidence of the bearer's identity or qualifications.

credible *adj.* believable; trustworthy. —**credibly** *adv.* —**credibility** *n.*

credit *n.* system of allowing customers to take goods and pay later; reputation for trustworthi-

THESAURUS

crater depression, dip, hollow, shell hole

crave 1. cry out for (*Inf.*), desire, fancy (*Inf.*), hanker after, hunger after, long for, lust after, need, pant for, pine for, require, sigh for, thirst for, want, yearn for 2. ask, beg, beseech, entreat, implore, petition, plead for, pray for, seek, solicit, supplicate

crawl 1. advance slowly, creep, drag, go on all fours, inch, pull *or* drag oneself along, slither, wriggle, writhe 2. cringe, fawn, grovel, humble oneself, toady

craze enthusiasm, fad, fashion, infatuation, mania, mode, novelty, passion, rage, thing, trend, vogue

crazy 1. berserk, cracked (*Sl.*), cuckoo (*Inf.*), delirious, demented, deranged, idiotic, insane, mad, maniacal, mental (*Sl.*), not all there (*Inf.*), nuts (*Sl.*), nutty (*Sl.*), off one's head (*Sl.*), of unsound mind, potty (*Inf.*), round the bend (*Sl.*), touched, unbalanced, unhinged 2. bizarre, eccentric, fantastic, odd, outrageous, peculiar, ridiculous, silly, strange, weird

creak *v.* grate, grind, groan, rasp, scrape, scratch, screech, squeak, squeal

cream 1. cosmetic, emulsion, liniment, lotion, oil, ointment, paste, salve, unguent 2. best, *crème de la crème*, elite, flower, pick, prime

crease 1. *v.* crinkle, crumple, crush, double up, fold, pucker, ridge, ruck up, rumple, screw up,

wrinkle 2. *n.* bulge, fold, groove, line, overlap, pucker, ridge, ruck, tuck, wrinkle

create beget, bring into being coin, compose, concoct, design, develop, devise, form, formulate, generate, hatch, initiate, invent, make, originate, produce, spawn

creation 1. formation, generation, genesis, making, procreation, siring 2. establishment, formation, foundation, inception, institution, laying down, origination, production, setting up

creative artistic, clever, fertile, gifted, imaginative, ingenious, inspired, inventive, original, productive, stimulating, visionary

creator architect, author, begetter, designer, father, framer, God, initiator, inventor, maker, originator, prime mover

creature animal, beast, being, brute, dumb animal, living thing, lower animal, quadruped

credentials authorization, card, certificate, deed, diploma, docket, licence, missive, passport, recommendation, reference(s), testimonial, title, voucher, warrant

credibility integrity, plausibility, reliability, tenability, trustworthiness

credible believable, conceivable, imaginable, likely, plausible, possible, probable, reasonable, tenable, thinkable

DICTIONARY

ness in paying debts; money at one's disposal in a bank account; side of an account book on which such sums are entered; (source or cause of) praise or approval; influence or reputation based on the good opinion of others; belief or trust. —*pl.* list of people responsible for the production of a film, programme, or record. —*v.* **crediting, credited.** enter as a credit in an account; (foll. by *with*) attribute (to); believe. —**creditable** *adj.* praiseworthy. —**creditably** *adv.* —**creditor** *n.* person to whom money is owed. —**credit card** card allowing a person to buy on credit.

credulous *adj.* too willing to believe. —**credulity** *n.*

creed *n.* statement or system of (Christian) beliefs or principles.

creek *n.* narrow inlet or bay; *US* small stream.

creel *n.* wicker basket used by anglers.

creep *v.* **creeping, crept.** crawl with the body near to the ground; move with stealthy slow movements; (of a plant) grow along the ground or over a surface. —*n. Slang* obnoxious or servile person. —*pl.* feeling of fear or disgust. —**creeper** *n.* creeping plant. —**creepy** *adj. Informal* causing a feeling of fear or disgust.

cremate *v.* burn (a corpse) to ash. —**cremation** *n.* —**crematorium** *n.* building where corpses are cremated.

crenellated *adj.* having battlements. —**crenellation** *n.*

creole *n.* language developed from a mixture of languages; (**C-**) native-born W Indian or Latin American of mixed European and African descent.

creosote *n.* dark oily liquid distilled from coal tar and used for preserving wood. —*v.* treat with creosote.

crepe [**krayp**] *n.* fabric or rubber with a crinkled texture; very thin pancake. —**crepe paper** paper with a crinkled texture.

crept *v.* past of CREEP.

crepuscular *adj.* of or like twilight.

crescendo [**krish-end-oh**] *n., pl.* **-dos.** gradual increase in loudness, esp. in music.

crescent *n.* (shape of) the moon as seen in its first or last quarter; crescent-shaped street.

cress *n.* plant with strong-tasting leaves, used in salads.

crest *n.* top of a mountain, hill, or wave; tuft or growth on a bird's or animal's head; heraldic device used on a coat of arms, notepaper, and elsewhere. —**crested** *adj.* —**crestfallen** *adj.* disheartened.

cretin *n.* person afflicted with physical and mental retardation caused by a thyroid deficiency; *Informal* stupid person. —**cretinous** *adj.*

cretonne *n.* heavy printed cotton fabric used in furnishings.

crevasse *n.* deep open chasm, esp. in a glacier.

crevice *n.* narrow fissure or crack.

crew *n.* people who man a ship or aircraft; group of people working together; *Informal* any group of people. —*v.* serve as a crew member on. —**crew cut** man's closely cropped haircut.

crewel *n.* fine worsted yarn used in embroidery.

crib *n.* piece of writing stolen from elsewhere; translation or list of answers used by students, often illicitly; baby's cradle; rack for fodder; short for CRIBBAGE. —*v.* **cribbing, cribbed.** copy (someone's work) dishonestly.

cribbage *n.* card game for two to four players.

crick *n.* muscle spasm or cramp, esp. in the back or neck. —*v.* cause a crick in.

THESAURUS

credit *n.* 1. acclaim, acknowledgment, approval, commendation, fame, glory, honour, kudos, merit, praise, recognition, thanks, tribute ~*v.* 2. *With* **with** accredit, ascribe to, assign to, attribute to, impute to, refer to 3. accept, bank on, believe, depend on, have faith in, rely on, trust

creditable admirable, commendable, deserving, estimable, exemplary, honourable, laudable, meritorious, praiseworthy, reputable, respectable, worthy

credulity blind faith, gullibility, naiveté, silliness, simplicity

creed articles of faith, belief, canon, catechism, confession, credo, doctrine, dogma, principles

creek bay, bight, cove, inlet

creep 1. crawl, glide, insinuate, slither, squirm,

worm, wriggle, writhe 2. skulk, slink, sneak, steal, tiptoe 3. crawl, dawdle, drag, edge, inch

creeper climber, rambler, runner, vine

crescent half-moon, new moon, old moon, sickle, sickle-shape

crest apex, crown, head, height, highest point, peak, pinnacle, ridge, summit, top

crestfallen dejected, depressed, despondent, disappointed, disconsolate, disheartened, downcast, downhearted

crevice chink, cleft, crack, cranny, fissure, fracture, gap, hole, rent, rift, slit, split

crew 1. hands, (ship's) company, (ship's) complement 2. company, corps, gang, party, posse, squad, team, working party

crib *v. Inf.* cheat, pilfer, pirate, plagiarize, purloin, steal

DICTIONARY

cricket¹ *n.* outdoor game played with bats, a ball, and wickets by two teams of eleven. —**cricketer** *n.*

cricket² *n.* chirping insect like a grasshopper.

crime *n.* unlawful act; unlawful acts collectively; *Informal* disgraceful act. —**criminal** *n.* person guilty of a crime. —*adj.* of crime. —**criminally** *adv.* —**criminality** *n.* —**criminology** *n.* study of crime. —**criminologist** *n.*

crimp *v.* fold or press into ridges.

crimson *adj.* deep red.

cringe *v.* flinch or shrink; behave in a servile or timid way.

crinkle *v., n.* wrinkle, twist, or fold.

crinoline *n.* hooped petticoat.

cripple *n.* person who is lame or disabled. —*v.* make a cripple of (someone); damage (something).

crisis *n., pl.* **-ses.** crucial stage, turning point; time of acute trouble or danger.

crisp *adj.* dry and brittle; fresh and firm; (of weather) cold but invigorating; brisk and lively; clean and neat. —*n.* thin slice of potato fried till crunchy. —**crisply** *adv.* —**crispness** *n.* —**crispy** *adj.* —**crispbread** *n.* thin dry biscuit.

crisscross *v.* move in, mark with, or consist of a crosswise pattern. —*adj.* (of lines) crossing in different directions.

criterion *n., pl.* **-ria.** standard of judgment.

critic *n.* professional judge of any of the arts;

person who finds fault. —**critical** *adj.* very important or dangerous; fault-finding; discerning; of a critic or criticism. —**critically** *adv.* —**criticism** *n.* fault-finding; evaluation of a work of art. —**criticize** *v.* find fault with. —**critique** *n.* critical essay.

croak *v.* (of a frog or crow) give a low hoarse cry; utter or speak with a croak. —*n.* low hoarse cry. —**croaky** *adj.* hoarse.

crochet [**kroh**-shay] *n.* handicraft like knitting, done with a single hooked needle. —*v.* do or make such work.

crock *n.* earthenware jar or pot; *Informal* old or decrepit person or thing. —**crockery** *n.* earthenware or china dishes.

crocodile *n.* large amphibious tropical reptile; line of children walking two by two. —**crocodile tears** insincere grief.

crocus *n., pl.* **-cuses.** small plant with yellow, white, or purple flowers in spring.

croft *n.* small farm worked by the occupier in Scotland. —**crofter** *n.*

croissant [**krwah**-son] *n.* rich flaky crescent-shaped roll.

cromlech *n.* circle of prehistoric standing stones.

crone *n.* witchlike old woman.

crony *n., pl.* **-nies.** close friend.

crook *n. Informal* criminal; bent or curved part; hooked pole. —**crooked** *adj.* bent or twisted; set at an angle; *Informal* dishonest.

THESAURUS

crime fault, felony, misdeed, misdemeanour, offence, outrage, transgression, trespass, unlawful act, violation, wrong

criminal 1. *n.* convict, crook (*Inf.*), culprit, delinquent, evildoer, felon, jailbird, lawbreaker, malefactor, offender, sinner, transgressor 2. *adj.* bent (*Sl.*), corrupt, crooked (*Inf.*), culpable, felonious, illegal, illicit, immoral, indictable, lawless, nefarious, unlawful, unrighteous, vicious, villainous, wicked, wrong

cripple *v.* disable, enfeeble, incapacitate, lame, maim, paralyse, weaken

crisis 1. climax, crunch (*Inf.*), crux, height, turning point 2. catastrophe, critical situation, dilemma, dire straits, disaster, emergency, exigency, extremity, mess, plight, predicament, quandary, strait, trouble

crisp 1. brittle, crispy, crumbly, crunchy, firm, fresh, unwilted 2. bracing, brisk, fresh, invigorating, refreshing

criterion canon, gauge, measure, norm, principle, rule, standard, test, yardstick

critic 1. analyst, arbiter, authority, commenta-

tor, connoisseur, expert, judge, pundit, reviewer 2. carper, caviller, censor, detractor, fault-finder

critical 1. captious, carping, cavilling, censorious, derogatory, disapproving, disparaging, fault-finding, nagging, niggling 2. accurate, analytical, diagnostic, discerning, discriminating, fastidious, judicious, penetrating, perceptive, precise 3. crucial, dangerous, deciding, decisive, grave, important, momentous, perilous, pivotal, precarious, pressing, risky, serious, urgent, vital

criticism 1. bad press, censure, disapproval, disparagement, fault-finding, stricture 2. analysis, appraisal, appreciation, assessment, comment, commentary, critique, elucidation, evaluation, judgment, notice, review

criticize carp, censure, condemn, disapprove of, disparage, nag at, pick to pieces, slate (*Inf.*)

croak *v.* caw, gasp, grunt, squawk, utter *or* speak harshly

crook cheat, criminal, racketeer, robber, rogue, shark, swindler, thief, villain

crooked 1. bent, bowed, crippled, curved, de-

DICTIONARY

croon v. hum, sing, or speak in a soft low tone. —**crooner** n.

crop n. cultivated plant; season's total yield of produce; group of things appearing at one time; short haircut; pouch in a bird's gullet; hunting whip. —v. **cropping, cropped.** cut short; produce or harvest as a crop; (of animals) feed on (grass etc.). —**cropper** n. —**come a cropper** Informal have a disastrous failure or heavy fall. —**crop up** v. Informal happen unexpectedly.

croquet [kroh-kay] n. game in which balls are hit through hoops.

croquette [kroh-kett] n. fried cake of potato, meat, or fish.

crosier n. same as CROZIER.

cross n. structure, symbol, or mark of two intersecting lines; such a structure of wood as a means of execution; representation of the Cross as an emblem of Christianity; affliction; mixture of two things. —v. move or go across (something); meet and pass; mark with lines across; draw a cross or lines through (something); place (one's arms or legs) crosswise; make the sign of the cross on (oneself); interbreed or cross-fertilize; thwart or oppose. —adj. angry, in a bad mood; lying or placed across; transverse. —**the Cross** Christianity the cross on which Christ was crucified. —**crossing** n. place where a street etc. may be crossed; place where things cross; journey across water. —**crossly** adv. —**crossness** n. —**crossbar** n. horizontal bar across goalposts or on a bicycle. —**crossbow** n. bow fixed across a wooden stock. —**crossbred** adj. bred from two different types of animal or plant. —**crossbreed** n. crossbred animal or plant. —**crosscheck** v. check using a different method. —**cross-country** adj., adv. by way of open country or fields.

—**cross-examine** v. question (a witness in court) to check his or her testimony. —**cross-examination** n. —**cross-eyed** adj. with eyes turning inwards. —**cross-fertilize** v. fertilize (an animal or plant) from one of a different kind. —**cross-fertilization** n. —**crossfire** n. gunfire crossing another line of fire. —**cross-ply** adj. (of a tyre) having the fabric cords in the outer casing running diagonally. —**cross-purposes** pl. n. —**at cross-purposes** misunderstanding each other. —**cross-reference** n. reference within a text to another part. —**crossroads** n. place where roads intersect. —**cross section** (diagram of) a surface made by cutting across something; representative sample. —**crosswise** adj., adv. transverse(ly); in the shape of a cross. —**crossword (puzzle)** n. puzzle in which words suggested by clues are written into a grid of squares.

crotch n. fork between the legs.

crotchet n. musical note half the length of a minim.

crotchety adj. Informal bad-tempered.

crouch v. bend low with the legs and body close. —n. this position.

croup[1] [kroop] n. throat disease of children, with a cough.

croup[2] [kroop] n. hind quarters of a horse.

croupier [kroop-ee-ay] n. person who collects bets and pays out winnings at a gambling table.

crouton n. small piece of fried or toasted bread served in soup.

crow[1] n. large black bird with a harsh call. —**as the crow flies** in a straight line. —**crow's feet** wrinkles at the corners of the eyes. —**crow's nest** lookout platform high on a ship's mast.

crow[2] v. (of a cock) utter a shrill squawking

THESAURUS

formed, deviating, disfigured, distorted, hooked, irregular, misshapen, tortuous, twisted, twisting, warped, winding, zigzag 2. askew, asymmetric, awry, lopsided, off-centre, slanted, slanting, squint 3. Inf. bent (Sl.), corrupt, crafty, criminal, deceitful, dishonest, dishonourable, dubious, fraudulent, illegal, knavish, nefarious, questionable, shady (Inf.), shifty, underhand, unlawful, unscrupulous

croon breathe, hum, purr, sing, warble

crop 1. n. fruits, gathering, harvest, produce, reaping, season's growth, vintage, yield 2. v. clip, curtail, cut, lop, mow, pare, prune, reduce, shear, shorten, snip, top, trim

crop up appear, arise, emerge, happen, occur, spring up, turn up

cross adj. 1. angry, annoyed, captious, churlish, crusty, disagreeable, fractious, fretful, ill-humoured, ill-tempered, impatient, in a bad

mood, irascible, irritable, out of humour, peevish, pettish, petulant, put out, querulous, short, snappish, snappy, sullen, surly, testy, vexed, waspish 2. crosswise, intersecting, oblique, transverse ~v. 3. bridge, cut across, extend over, ford, meet, pass over, ply, span, traverse, zigzag 4. crisscross, intersect, intertwine, lace 5. blend, crossbreed, hybridize, interbreed, mix ~n. 6. crucifix, rood 7. crossing, crossroads, intersection, junction 8. blend, combination, crossbreed, cur, hybrid, mixture, mongrel

cross-examine catechize, grill (Inf.), interrogate, pump, question, quiz

crouch bend down, bow, duck, hunch, kneel, squat, stoop

crow boast, brag, exult, gloat, glory in, strut, swagger, triumph, vaunt

DICTIONARY

sound; boast of one's superiority; (of a baby) utter cries of pleasure. —*n.* cock's cry.

crowbar *n.* iron bar used as a lever.

crowd *n.* large group of people or things; particular group of people. —*v.* flock together; fill or occupy fully.

crown *n.* monarch's headdress; wreath for the head; highest point of something arched or curved; former British coin worth twenty-five pence. —*v.* put a crown on (someone's head) to proclaim him or her monarch; form or put on the top of; put the finishing touch to (a series of events); *Informal* hit on the head. —**the Crown** power of the monarchy. —**Crown Court** local criminal court in England and Wales. —**crown prince,** *fem.* **crown princess** heir to the throne.

crozier *n.* bishop's hooked staff.

cruces *n.* a plural of CRUX.

crucial *adj.* very important, critical. —**crucially** *adv.*

crucible *n.* pot in which metals are melted.

crucify *v.* **-fying, -fied.** put to death by fastening to a cross; treat cruelly; *Informal* ridicule publicly. —**crucifix** *n.* model of Christ on the Cross. —**crucifixion** *n.* crucifying. —**the Crucifixion** *Christianity* crucifying of Christ; representation of this. —**cruciform** *adj.* cross-shaped.

crude *adj.* tasteless or vulgar; in a natural or raw state; rough, unfinished. —**crudely** *adv.* —**crudity** *n.*

cruel *adj.* delighting in others' pain; causing pain or suffering. —**cruelly** *adv.* —**cruelty** *n.*

cruet *n.* small container for salt, pepper, etc. at table.

cruise *v.* sail about for pleasure; (of a vehicle, aircraft, or ship) travel at a moderate and economical speed. —*n.* voyage for pleasure. —**cruiser** *n.* motorboat with a cabin; fast warship. —**cruise missile** low-flying guided missile.

crumb *n.* small fragment of bread or other dry food; small bit.

crumble *v.* break into fragments; fall apart or decay. —*n.* pudding of stewed fruit with a crumbly topping. —**crumbly** *adj.*

crummy *adj.* **-mier, -miest.** *Slang* inferior; squalid.

crumpet *n.* round soft yeast cake eaten buttered; *Slang* sexually attractive women collectively.

crumple *v.* crush and crease; collapse. —**crumpled** *adj.*

THESAURUS

crowd *n.* 1. army, assembly, company, flock, herd, horde, host, mass, mob, multitude, pack, press, rabble, swarm, throng, troupe 2. attendance, audience, gate, house, spectators ~*v.* 3. cluster, congregate, cram, flock, gather, huddle, mass, muster, press, push, stream, surge, swarm, throng

crown *n.* 1. chaplet, circlet, coronet, diadem, tiara 2. bays, distinction, garland, honour, kudos, laurels, prize, trophy ~*v.* 3. adorn, dignify, festoon, honour, invest, reward 4. be the climax *or* culmination of, cap, complete, consummate, finish, fulfil, perfect, put the finishing touch to, round off, surmount, terminate, top

crucial central, critical, decisive, pivotal, searching, testing, trying

crucify execute, harrow, persecute, rack, torment, torture

crude 1. boorish, coarse, crass, dirty, gross, indecent, lewd, obscene, smutty, tactless, tasteless, uncouth, vulgar 2. natural, raw, unpolished, unprepared, unprocessed, unrefined 3. clumsy, makeshift, outline, primitive, rough, rough-hewn, rude, rudimentary, sketchy, undeveloped, unfinished, unformed, unpolished

crudely bluntly, clumsily, coarsely, impolitely, indecently, roughly, rudely, tastelessly, vulgarly

crudity coarseness, crudeness, impropriety, indelicacy, lewdness, loudness, lowness, obscenity, vulgarity

cruel 1. barbarous, bitter, brutal, callous, cold-blooded, ferocious, fierce, grim, hard, hard-hearted, harsh, heartless, hellish, implacable, inclement, inhuman, inhumane, malevolent, painful, ravening, raw, remorseless, sadistic, savage, severe, spiteful, unfeeling, unkind, vengeful, vicious 2. merciless, pitiless, ruthless, unrelenting

cruelly brutally, callously, ferociously, fiercely, heartlessly, in cold blood, mercilessly, pitilessly, sadistically, savagely, spitefully, unmercifully, viciously

cruelty bestiality, bloodthirstiness, brutality, callousness, depravity, ferocity, hardheartedness, harshness, inhumanity, sadism, savagery, severity, spite, spitefulness, venom

cruise 1. *v.* coast, sail, voyage 2. *n.* boat trip, sail, sea trip, voyage

crumb atom, bit, grain, mite, morsel, particle, scrap, shred, sliver, snippet, *soupçon*, speck

crumble 1. bruise, crumb, crush, fragment, granulate, grind, pound, powder 2. break up, collapse, come to dust, decay, decompose,

DICTIONARY

crunch v. crush (food) noisily with the teeth; (cause to) make a crisp or brittle sound. —n. crunching sound; *Informal* critical moment. —**crunchy** adj.

crupper n. strap that passes from the back of a saddle under a horse's tail.

crusade n. medieval Christian war to recover the Holy Land from the Muslims; vigorous campaign in favour of a cause. —v. take part in a crusade. —**crusader** n.

crush v. compress so as to break, injure, or crumple; break into small pieces; defeat utterly. —n. dense crowd; *Informal* infatuation; drink made by crushing fruit.

crust n. hard outer part of something, esp. bread. —v. cover with or form a crust. —**crusty** adj. having a crust; irritable.

crustacean n. hard-shelled, usu. aquatic animal with several pairs of legs, such as the crab or lobster.

crutch n. staff with a rest for the armpit, used by a lame person; support; crotch.

crux n., pl. **cruxes, cruces.** crucial or decisive point.

cry v. **crying, cried.** shed tears; call or utter loudly; appeal urgently (for). —n., pl. **cries.** fit of weeping; loud utterance; urgent appeal. —**crybaby** n. person who cries too readily. —**cry off** v. *Informal* withdraw from an arrangement.

cryogenics n. branch of physics concerned with very low temperatures. —**cryogenic** adj.

crypt n. vault, esp. one under a church. —**cryptic** adj. obscure in meaning. —**cryptically** adv. —**cryptogram** n. message in code. —**cryptography** n. art of writing in and deciphering codes.

cryptogam n. plant that reproduces by spores, not seeds.

crystal n. glasslike mineral; very clear and brilliant glass; tumblers, vases, etc. made of such glass; (single grain of a) symmetrically shaped solid formed naturally by some substances. —adj. bright and clear. —**crystalline** adj. of or like crystal or crystals; clear. —**crystallize** v. make or become definite; form into crystals; preserve (fruit) in sugar. —**crystallization** n.

Cu *Chem.* copper.

cu. cubic.

cub n. young of certain mammals, such as the lion; (C-) Cub Scout. —v. **cubbing, cubbed.** give birth to (cubs). —**Cub Scout** member of the junior branch of the Scout Association.

cubbyhole n. small enclosed space or room.

cube n. solid with six equal square sides; product obtained by multiplying a number by itself twice. —v. find the cube of (a number); cut into cubes. —**cubic** adj. having three dimensions; cube-shaped. —**cubism** n. style of art in which objects are represented by geometrical shapes. —**cubist** n., adj. —**cube root** number whose cube is a given number.

cubicle n. enclosed part of a large room, screened for privacy.

cuckold n. man whose wife has committed adultery. —v. make a cuckold of.

cuckoo n. migratory bird with a characteristic two-note call, which lays its eggs in the nests of other birds. —adj. *Informal* crazy.

cucumber n. long green-skinned fleshy fruit used in salads.

cud n. partially digested food which a ruminant brings back into its mouth to chew again. —**chew the cud** reflect or ponder.

cuddle v. hug fondly; nestle. —n. fond hug. —**cuddly** adj.

THESAURUS

degenerate, deteriorate, disintegrate, fall apart, go to pieces (*Inf.*), moulder, perish, tumble down

crumple 1. crease, crush, pucker, rumple, screw up, wrinkle 2. break down, cave in, collapse, fall, give way, go to pieces

crusade campaign, cause, drive, holy war, movement

crush 1. break, bruise, compress, crease, crumble, crumple, crunch, mash, pound, pulverize, rumple, smash, squeeze, wrinkle 2. conquer, defeat, overcome, overpower, overwhelm, put down, quell, stamp out, subdue, vanquish

crust coat, coating, covering, layer, outside, shell, skin, surface

crusty 1. brittle, crisp, crispy, friable, hard, short, well-baked, well-done 2. brusque, cap-

tious, choleric, crabby, cross, curt, gruff, irritable, peevish, prickly, snarling, surly, testy, touchy

cry v. 1. bawl, bewail, blubber, lament, shed tears, snivel, sob, wail, weep, whimper, whine, whinge (*Inf.*) 2. bawl, bellow, call, call out, exclaim, hail, howl, roar, scream, screech, shout, shriek, sing out, whoop, yell ~n. 3. blubbering, howl, keening, lament, lamentation, snivel, snivelling, sob, sobbing, sorrowing, wailing, weep, weeping

cry off back out, beg off, excuse oneself, quit, withdraw, withdraw from

cub offspring, whelp, young

cudgel baton, bludgeon, club, cosh, stick, truncheon

DICTIONARY

cudgel *n.* short thick stick used as a weapon.

cue[1] *n.* signal to an actor or musician to begin speaking or playing; signal or reminder. —*v.* **cueing, cued.** give a cue to (someone).

cue[2] *n.* long tapering stick used in billiards, snooker, or pool. —*v.* **cueing, cued.** strike (a ball) with a cue.

cuff[1] *n.* end of a sleeve. —**off the cuff** *Informal* impromptu. —**cuff link** one of a pair of decorative fastenings for shirt cuffs.

cuff[2] *v.* strike with an open hand. —*n.* blow with an open hand.

cuisine [quiz-**zeen**] *n.* style of cooking.

cul-de-sac *n.* road with one end blocked off.

culinary *adj.* of the kitchen or cookery.

cull *v.* gather, select; remove or kill (inferior or surplus animals) from a herd. —*n.* culling.

culminate *v.* reach the highest point or climax. —**culmination** *n.*

culottes *pl. n.* women's flared trousers cut to look like a skirt.

culpable *adj.* deserving blame. —**culpability** *n.*

culprit *n.* person guilty of an offence or misdeed.

cult *n.* specific system of worship; devotion to a person, idea, or activity; popular fashion.

cultivate *v.* prepare (land) to grow crops; grow (plants); develop or improve (something); try to develop a friendship with (someone). —**cultivated** *adj.* cultured or well-educated. —**cultivation** *n.*

culture *n.* ideas, customs, and art of a particular society; particular society; developed understanding of the arts; cultivation of plants or rearing of animals; growth of bacteria for study. —**cultural** *adj.* —**cultured** *adj.* showing culture. —**cultured pearl** pearl artificially grown in an oyster shell.

culvert *n.* drain under a road or railway.

cumbersome *adj.* awkward or unwieldy.

cummerbund *n.* broad sash worn round the waist.

cum(m)in *n.* aromatic seeds of a Mediterranean plant, used in cooking.

cumulative [kew-myew-la-tiv] *adj.* increasing steadily.

cumulus [kew-myew-luss] *n., pl.* -li. cloud shaped in heaped-up rounded masses.

cuneiform [kew-nif-form] *n.* ancient system of writing using wedge-shaped characters. —*adj.* written in cuneiform.

cunning *adj.* clever at deceiving; ingenious. —*n.* cleverness at deceiving; ingenuity. —**cunningly** *adv.*

cup *n.* small bowl-shaped drinking container with a handle; contents of a cup; cup-shaped trophy given as a prize; hollow rounded shape; mixed drink with fruit juice or wine as a base. —*v.* **cupping, cupped.** form (one's hands) into the shape of a cup; hold in cupped hands. —**cupful** *n.*

cupboard *n.* piece of furniture or recess with a door, for storage.

THESAURUS

cue hint, key, nod, prompting, reminder, sign, signal, suggestion

culminate climax, close, conclude, end, end up, finish, terminate

culprit criminal, delinquent, felon, guilty party, miscreant, offender, rascal, sinner, wrongdoer

cult 1. body, church faction, clique, denomination, faith, following, party, religion, school, sect 2. admiration, craze, devotion, reverence, veneration, worship

cultivate 1. farm, harvest, plant, plough, prepare, tend, till, work 2. better, bring on, cherish, civilize, develop, discipline, elevate, enrich, foster, improve, polish, promote, refine, train

cultivation advancement, advocacy, development, encouragement, enhancement, fostering, furtherance, help, nurture, patronage, promotion, support

cultural artistic, broadening, civilizing, edifying, educational, educative, elevating, enriching, humane, humanizing, liberal

culture 1. civilization, customs, life style, mores, society, the arts, way of life 2. accomplishment, breeding, education, elevation, enlightenment, erudition, good taste, improvement, polish, politeness, refinement, urbanity

cultured accomplished, advanced, educated, enlightened, erudite, genteel, knowledgeable, polished, refined, scholarly, urbane, versed, well-bred, well-informed, well-read

culvert channel, conduit, drain, gutter, watercourse

cumbersome awkward, bulky, clumsy, heavy, incommodious, inconvenient, oppressive, unmanageable, unwieldy, weighty

cunning 1. *adj.* artful, astute, canny, crafty, devious, guileful, knowing, Machiavellian, sharp, shifty, shrewd, subtle, tricky, wily 2. *n.* artfulness, astuteness, craftiness, deceitfulness, deviousness, guile, shrewdness, slyness, trickery, wiliness

cup beaker, chalice, draught, drink, goblet, potion, teacup, trophy

DICTIONARY

cupidity [kew-**pid**-it-ee] *n.* greed for wealth or possessions.

cupola [kew-pol-la] *n.* domed roof or ceiling.

cur *n.* mongrel dog; contemptible person.

curaçao [kew-rah-so] *n.* orange-flavoured liqueur.

curare [kew-**rah**-ree] *n.* poisonous resin of a S American tree, used as a muscle relaxant in medicine.

curate *n.* clergyman who assists a parish priest. —**curacy** [kew-rah-see] *n.* work or position of a curate.

curative *adj.* able to cure. —*n.* something curative.

curator *n.* person in charge of a museum or art gallery. —**curatorship** *n.*

curb *n.* check or restraint. —*v.* restrain.

curd *n.* coagulated milk. —**curdle** *v.* turn into curd, coagulate.

cure *v.* heal (an ailment or problem); restore to health; preserve by salting, smoking, or drying. —*n.* restoration to health; medical treatment; remedy or solution. —**curable** *adj.*

curet(te) *n.* surgical instrument for scraping tissue from body cavities. —*v.* -**retting, -retted.** scrape with a curet. —**curettage** *n.*

curfew *n.* law ordering people to stay indoors after a specific time at night; time set as a deadline by such a law.

curie *n.* standard unit of radioactivity.

curio [kew-ree-oh] *n., pl.* -**rios.** strange or rare thing valued as a collector's item.

curious *adj.* eager to know; eager to find out private details; unusual or peculiar. —**curiously** *adv.* —**curiosity** *n.* eagerness to know; eagerness to find out private details; strange or rare thing.

curium [kew-ree-um] *n.* artificial radioactive element produced from plutonium.

curl *v.* twist (hair) or (of hair) be twisted into coils; twist into a spiral or curve. —*n.* coil of hair; spiral or curved shape. —**curly** *adj.* —**curling** *n.* game like bowls, played with heavy stones on ice.

curlew *n.* long-billed wading bird.

curmudgeon *n.* bad-tempered or mean person.

currant *n.* dried grape; small round berry, such as a redcurrant.

current *adj.* of the immediate present; most recent, up-to-date; commonly accepted. —*n.* flow of water or air in one direction; flow of electricity; general trend. —**currently** *adv.* —**currency** *n.* money in use in a particular country; state of being current.

curriculum *n., pl.* -**la, -lums.** specified course of study. —**curriculum vitae** [vee-tie] outline of someone's educational and professional history, prepared for job applications.

curry[1] *n., pl.* -**ries.** dish of meat or vegetables in a hot spicy sauce. —*v.* -**rying, -ried.** prepare (food) with curry powder. —**curry powder** mixture of spices for making curry.

curry[2] *v.* -**rying, -ried.** groom (a horse) with a currycomb. —**curry favour** ingratiate oneself, esp. with one's superiors. —**currycomb** *n.* ridged comb for grooming a horse.

curse *n.* profane or obscene expression, usu. of anger; call to a supernatural power for harm to come to a person; affliction, misfortune. —*v.* say profane or obscene things (to); utter a curse against. —**cursed** *adj.* hateful.

THESAURUS

curb 1. *v.* bite back, bridle, check, constrain, contain, control, hinder, impede, inhibit, moderate, muzzle, repress, restrain, restrict, retard, subdue, suppress 2. *n.* brake, bridle, check, control, deterrent, limitation, rein, restraint

cure *v.* 1. alleviate, correct, ease, heal, help, make better, mend, rehabilitate, relieve, remedy, restore, restore to health 2. dry, kipper, pickle, preserve, salt, smoke ~*n.* 3. antidote, healing, medicine, panacea, recovery, remedy, restorative, specific, treatment

curiosity 1. interest, prying 2. freak, marvel, novelty, oddity, phenomenon, rarity, sight, spectacle, wonder

curious 1. inquiring, inquisitive, interested, puzzled, questioning, searching 2. inquisitive, meddling, peeping, peering, prying 3. bizarre,

exotic, extraordinary, mysterious, novel, odd, peculiar, puzzling, quaint, queer, rare, singular, strange, unconventional, unique, unorthodox, unusual, wonderful

curl *v.* bend, coil, corkscrew, crimp, crinkle, crisp, curve, entwine, frizz, loop, meander, ripple, spiral, turn, twine, twirl, twist, wind, wreathe, writhe

currency bills, coinage, coins, money, notes

current *adj.* 1. accepted, circulating, common, customary, general, in circulation, in progress, in the air, in the news, ongoing, popular, present, prevailing, prevalent, rife, widespread 2. in, in fashion, in vogue, now (*Inf.*), present-day, up-to-date ~*n.* 3. course, draught, flow, jet, river, stream, tide

curse *n.* 1. blasphemy, expletive, oath, obscenity, swearing, swearword 2. ban, evil eye, ex-

DICTIONARY

cursive *n., adj.* (handwriting) done with joined letters.

cursor *n.* movable point of light that shows a specific position on a visual display unit.

cursory *adj.* hasty and superficial. —**cursorily** *adv.*

curt *adj.* (of speech) impolitely brief. —**curtly** *adv.* —**curtness** *n.*

curtail *v.* cut short; restrict. —**curtailment** *n.*

curtain *n.* piece of cloth hung at a window or opening as a screen; hanging cloth separating the audience and the stage in a theatre; end of a scene or act, marked by the fall or closing of the curtain; thing(s) forming a barrier or screen. —*v.* provide with curtains; conceal with a curtain.

curts(e)y *n., pl.* **-sies, -seys.** woman's gesture of respect made by bending the knees and bowing the head. —*v.* **-s(e)ying, -sied** *or* **-seyed.** make a curtsy.

curve *n.* continuously bending line with no straight parts. —*v.* bend into or move in a curve. —**curvy** *adj.* —**curvaceous** *adj. Informal* (of a woman) having a shapely body. —**curvature** *n.* state or degree of being curved. —**curvilinear** *adj.* consisting of or bounded by a curve.

cushion *n.* bag filled with soft material, to make a seat more comfortable; something that provides comfort or absorbs shock. —*v.* protect from injury or shock; lessen the effects of.

cushy *adj.* **cushier, cushiest.** *Informal* easy, e.g. *a cushy job.*

cusp *n.* pointed end, esp. on a tooth; *Astrol.* division between houses or signs of the zodiac.

cuss *Informal* —*n.* curse, oath; annoying person. —*v.* swear (at). —**cussed** [kuss-id] *adj. Informal* obstinate.

custard *n.* dish or sauce made of sweetened milk thickened with eggs or cornflour.

custody *n.* guardianship; imprisonment prior to being tried. —**custodial** *adj.* —**custodian** *n.* person in charge of a public building or museum collection.

custom *n.* usual habit; long-established activity or action; regular use of a shop or business. —*pl.* duty charged on imports or exports; government department which collects these; area at a port, airport, or border where baggage and freight are examined for dutiable goods. —**customary** *adj.* usual; established by custom. —**customarily** *adv.* —**customer** *n.* person who buys goods or services.

cut *v.* **cutting, cut.** open up, penetrate, wound, or divide with a sharp instrument; trim or shape by cutting; divide; intersect; reduce; abridge; *Informal* snub (a person); *Informal* absent oneself from (classes). —*n.* stroke or incision made by cutting; piece cut off; reduction; abridgement; style in which hair or a garment is cut; *Informal* share, esp. of profits. —**cutter** *n.* person or tool that cuts; any of various small fast boats. —**cutting** *n.* piece cut from a plant for rooting or grafting; article cut from a newspaper or magazine; passage cut through high ground for a road or railway. —*adj.* keen, piercing; (of a remark) hurtful. —**cut in** *v.* interrupt; obstruct another vehicle in overtaking it. —**cutthroat** *adj.* fierce or relentless. —*n.* murderer.

THESAURUS

communication, execration, imprecation, jinx, malediction 3. affliction, bane, burden, calamity, cross, disaster, evil, misfortune, ordeal, plague, scourge, torment, tribulation, trouble, vexation ~*v.* 4. blaspheme, swear, use bad language 5. damn, excommunicate, execrate, fulminate, imprecate

cursed abominable, damnable, detestable, devilish, fiendish, hateful, infamous, infernal, loathsome, odious, pernicious, pestilential, vile

curt abrupt, blunt, brief, brusque, gruff, offhand, pithy, rude, sharp, short, snappish, succinct, summary, tart, terse, unceremonious, uncivil, ungracious

curtail abbreviate, abridge, contract, cut, cut back, decrease, dock, lessen, lop, pare down, reduce, restrict, shorten, trim, truncate

curtain 1. *n.* drape (*Chiefly U.S.*), hanging 2. *v.* conceal, drape, hide, screen, shroud, shut off, shutter, veil

curve 1. *v.* arc, arch, bend, bow, coil, hook, inflect, turn, twist, wind 2. *n.* arc, bend, camber, half-moon, loop, turn

custody arrest, confinement, detention, imprisonment, incarceration

custom habit, manner, routine, way, wont

customary accepted, accustomed, acknowledged, common, confirmed, conventional, everyday, established, familiar, fashionable, general, normal, ordinary, popular, regular, routine, traditional, usual

customer buyer, client, consumer, habitué, patron, prospect, purchaser, regular (*Inf.*), shopper

customs duty, import charges, tariff, taxes, toll

cut *v.* 1. chop, cleave, divide, gash, incise, lacerate, nick, notch, penetrate, pierce, score, sever, slash, slice, slit, wound 2. carve, chip, chisel, chop, engrave, fashion, form, saw, sculpt, sculpture, shape, whittle 3. contract, cut back,

DICTIONARY

cutaneous [kew-**tane**-ee-uss] *adj.* of the skin.

cute *adj.* appealing or attractive; *Informal* clever or shrewd. —**cutely** *adv.* —**cuteness** *n.*

cuticle [kew-**tik**-kl] *n.* skin at the base of a fingernail or toenail.

cutlass *n.* short curved one-edged sword.

cutlery *n.* knives, forks, and spoons, used for eating. —**cutler** *n.* maker of cutlery.

cutlet *n.* small piece of meat from the neck; flat croquette of chopped meat or fish.

cuttlefish *n.* sea mollusc like a squid.

CV curriculum vitae.

cwt. hundredweight.

cyanide *n.* extremely poisonous chemical compound.

cyanosis *n.* blueness of the skin, caused by a deficiency of oxygen in the blood.

cybernetics *n.* branch of science in which electronic and mechanical systems are studied and compared to biological systems.

cyclamen [**sik**-la-men] *n.* plant with red, pink, or white flowers having turned-back petals.

cycle *n.* bicycle; motorcycle; recurrent series of events; time taken for one such series. —*v.* ride a cycle. —**cyclic(al)** *adj.* occurring in cycles. —**cyclist** *n.* person who rides a cycle.

cyclone *n.* violent wind moving clockwise round a central area. —**cyclonic** *adj.*

cyclotron *n.* apparatus which accelerates charged particles by means of a strong vertical magnetic field.

cygnet *n.* young swan.

cylinder *n.* solid or hollow body with straight sides and circular ends; chamber within which the piston moves in an internal-combustion engine. —**cylindrical** *adj.*

cymbal *n.* percussion instrument consisting of a brass plate which is struck against another or hit with a stick.

cynic [**sin**-ik] *n.* person who believes that people always act selfishly. —**cynical** *adj.* —**cynically** *adv.* —**cynicism** *n.*

cynosure [**sin**-oh-zyure] *n.* centre of attention.

cypher *n.* same as CIPHER.

cypress *n.* evergreen tree with very dark foliage.

cyst [**sist**] *n.* (abnormal) sac in the body containing fluid or soft matter. —**cystic** *adj.* —**cystitis** [siss-**tite**-iss] *n.* inflammation of the bladder.

cytology [site-**ol**-a-jee] *n.* study of plant and animal cells. —**cytological** *adj.* —**cytologist** *n.*

czar [**zahr**] *n.* same as TSAR.

THESAURUS

decrease, ease up on, lower, rationalize, reduce, slash, slim (down) 4. abbreviate, abridge, condense, curtail, delete, edit out, excise, precis, shorten ~*n.* 5. gash, graze, groove, incision, laceration, nick, rent, rip, slash, slit, stroke, wound 6. cutback, decrease, economy, fall, lowering, reduction, saving

cut in break in, butt in, interpose, interrupt, intervene, intrude, move in

cutting *adj.* biting, bitter, chill, keen, numbing, penetrating, piercing, raw, sharp, stinging

cycle age, circle, era, period, phase, revolution, rotation

cynic doubter, pessimist, sceptic, scoffer

cynical derisive, ironic, misanthropical, mocking, pessimistic, sarcastic, sardonic, sceptical, scornful, sneering, unbelieving

D

D *Chem.* deuterium.

d *Physics* density.

d. died; *Brit.* old penny.

dab[1] *v.* **dabbing, dabbed.** pat lightly; apply with short tapping strokes. —*n.* small amount of something soft or moist; light tap or stroke. —**dab hand** *Informal* person who is particularly good at something.

dab[2] *n.* small flatfish.

dabble *v.* deal in something superficially; splash about. —**dabbler** *n.*

dace *n.* small freshwater fish.

dachshund *n.* dog with a long body and short legs.

dactyl *n.* metrical foot of three syllables, one long followed by two short. —**dactylic** *adj.*

dad *n. Informal* father.

daddy *n., pl.* **-dies.** *Informal* father.

daddy-longlegs *n. Informal* crane fly.

dado [**day**-doe] *n., pl.* **-does, -dos.** lower part of an interior wall that is decorated differently from the upper part.

daffodil *n.* spring plant with yellow trumpet-shaped flowers.

daft *adj. Brit. informal* foolish or crazy.

dagger *n.* short stabbing weapon with a pointed blade.

dago [**day**-go] *n. Offens.* Spanish or other Latin person.

daguerreotype [dag-**gair**-oh-type] *n.* type of early photograph produced on chemically treated silver.

dahlia [**day**-lya] *n.* garden plant with showy flowers.

daily *adj.* occurring every day or every weekday. —*adv.* every day. —*n., pl.* **-lies.** daily newspaper; *Brit. informal* charwoman.

dainty *adj.* **-tier, -tiest.** delicate or elegant. —**daintily** *adv.*

daiquiri [**dak**-eer-ee] *n.* iced drink containing rum, lime juice, and sugar.

dairy *n., pl.* **dairies.** place for the processing or sale of milk and its products. —*adj.* of milk or its products.

dais [**day**-iss] *n.* raised platform in a hall.

daisy *n., pl.* **-sies.** flower with a yellow centre and white petals. —**daisywheel** *n.* flat disc in a word processor with radiating spokes for printing letters.

Dalai Lama *n.* chief lama and (until 1959) ruler of Tibet.

dale *n.* valley.

dally *v.* **-lying, -lied.** dawdle; (foll. by *with*) amuse oneself (with). —**dalliance** *n.* flirtation.

Dalmatian *n.* large dog with a white coat and black spots.

dam[1] *n.* barrier built across a river to create a lake; lake created by this. —*v.* **damming, dammed.** restrict by a dam.

dam[2] *n.* female parent of an animal.

damage *v.* harm. —*n.* injury or harm to a person or thing; *Informal* cost, e.g. *what's the damage?* —*pl.* money to be paid as compensation for injury or loss.

damask *n.* fabric with a pattern woven into it, used for tablecloths etc.

dame *n. Slang* woman; (**D-**) title of a woman who has been awarded the OBE or another order of chivalry.

damn *interj. Slang* exclamation of annoyance. —*adv., adj.* (also **damned**) *Slang* extreme or extremely. —*v.* declare to be bad or worthless; swear (at); (of God) condemn to hell; prove (someone) guilty, e.g. *damning evidence.* —**damnable** *adj.* annoying. —**damnably** *adv.* —**damnation** *n.*

THESAURUS

dagger bayonet, dirk, poniard, skean, stiletto

daily 1. *adj.* diurnal, everyday, quotidian 2. *adv.* day after day, every day, often, once a day, regularly

dainty charming, delicate, elegant, fine, graceful, neat, petite, pretty

dam 1. *n.* barrage, barrier, hindrance, obstruction, wall 2. *v.* barricade, block, check, choke, confine, hold back, hold in, obstruct, restrict

damage *n.* 1. destruction, devastation, harm, hurt, injury, loss, mischief, suffering 2. *Plural* fine, indemnity, reimbursement, reparation,

satisfaction ~*v.* 3. deface, harm, hurt, impair, injure, mar, mutilate, ruin, spoil, tamper with, weaken, wreck

dame baroness, dowager, lady, noblewoman, peeress

damn *v.* 1. blast, castigate, censure, condemn, criticize, denounce, denunciate, pan (*Inf.*), slam (*Sl.*), slate (*Inf.*) 2. abuse, curse, execrate, imprecate, revile, swear 3. condemn, doom, sentence

damned 1. accursed, condemned, doomed, infernal, lost, reprobate, unhappy 2. despicable,

DICTIONARY

damp *adj.* slightly wet. —*n.* slight wetness, moisture. —*v.* make damp; (foll. by *down*) reduce the force of (feelings or actions). —**damply** *adv.* —**dampness** *n.* —**dampen** *v.* damp. —**damper** *n.* depressing influence; movable plate to regulate the draught in a fire or furnace; pad in a piano that deadens the vibration of each string.

damsel *n. Obs.* young woman.

damson *n.* small blue-black plumlike fruit.

dance *v.* move the feet and body rhythmically in time to music; perform (a particular kind of dance); skip or leap; move rhythmically. —*n.* social meeting arranged for dancing; series of steps and movements in time to music. —**dancer** *n.*

D and C *Surgery* dilat(at)ion and curettage: an operation in which the neck of the womb is stretched and the lining of the womb is scraped, for example to remove diseased tissue.

dandelion *n.* yellow-flowered wild plant.

dander *n.* —**get one's dander up** *Slang* become angry.

dandle *v.* move (a child) up and down on one's knee.

dandruff *n.* loose scales of dry dead skin shed from the scalp.

dandy *n., pl.* **-dies.** man who is greatly concerned with the elegance of his appearance. —*adj.* **-dier, -diest.** *Informal* very good or fine. —**dandified** *adj.*

danger *n.* state of being vulnerable to injury or loss; person or thing that may cause injury; likelihood that something unpleasant will happen. —**dangerous** *adj.* —**dangerously** *adv.*

dangle *v.* hang freely; display as an enticement.

dank *adj.* unpleasantly damp and chilly.

daphne *n.* shrub with small bell-shaped flowers.

dapper *adj.* (of a man) neat in appearance and slight in build.

dappled *adj.* marked with spots of a different colour. —**dapple-grey** *n.* horse having a grey coat with spots of a different colour.

dare *v.* be courageous enough to try (to do something); challenge to do something risky. —*n.* challenge. —**daring** *adj.* willing to take risks. —*n.* courage to do dangerous things. —**daringly** *adv.* —**daredevil** *adj., n.* reckless (person).

daren't dare not.

dark *adj.* having little or no light; (of a colour) reflecting little light; (of hair or skin) brown or black; gloomy or sinister; secret, e.g. *keep it dark.* —*n.* absence of light; night. —**darkly** *adv.* —**darkness** *n.* —**darken** *v.* —**dark horse** person

THESAURUS

detestable, hateful, infamous, infernal, loathsome, revolting

damp *n.* 1. dampness, dankness, dew, drizzle, fog, humidity, mist, moisture, vapour ~*adj.* 2. clammy, dank, dewy, dripping, drizzly, humid, misty, moist, muggy, sodden, soggy, sopping, vaporous, wet ~*v.* 3. dampen, moisten, wet 4. *Fig.* allay, check, chill, cool, curb, dash, deaden, deject, depress, diminish, discourage, dispirit, dull, inhibit, moderate, restrain, stifle

dance 1. *v.* caper, frolic, gambol, hop, jig, prance, rock, skip, spin, sway, swing, whirl 2. *n.* ball, dancing party, social

danger hazard, insecurity, jeopardy, menace, peril, risk, threat, venture, vulnerability

dangerous alarming, breakneck, chancy (*Inf.*), exposed, hazardous, insecure, menacing, nasty, perilous, risky, threatening, treacherous, ugly, unsafe

dangerously alarmingly, carelessly, daringly, desperately, harmfully, hazardously, perilously, precariously, recklessly, riskily, unsafely, unsecurely

dangle 1. depend, flap, hang, hang down, sway, swing, trail 2. brandish, entice, flaunt, flourish, lure, tantalize, tempt, wave

dare *v.* 1. challenge, defy, goad, provoke, taunt

2. brave, gamble, hazard, make bold, presume, risk, stake, venture ~*n.* 3. challenge, defiance, provocation, taunt

daredevil 1. *n.* adventurer, desperado, madcap, show-off (*Inf.*), stunt man 2. *adj.* adventurous, audacious, bold, daring, death-defying, madcap, reckless

daring 1. *adj.* adventurous, bold, brave, fearless, game (*Inf.*), impulsive, intrepid, plucky, rash, reckless, valiant, venturesome 2. *n.* boldness, bravery, courage, fearlessness, grit, guts (*Inf.*), nerve (*Inf.*), pluck, rashness, spirit, temerity

dark *adj.* 1. black, dusky, ebony, sable, swarthy 2. cloudy, dim, dingy, indistinct, murky, overcast, pitch-black, pitchy, shadowy, shady, sunless, unlit 3. abstruse, arcane, concealed, cryptic, deep, enigmatic, hidden, mysterious, mystic, obscure, occult, recondite, secret 4. bleak, cheerless, dismal, doleful, drab, gloomy, grim, joyless, morbid, morose, mournful, sombre ~*n.* 5. darkness, dimness, dusk, gloom, murk, murkiness, obscurity, semi-darkness 6. evening, night, nightfall, nighttime, twilight

darkness dark, dimness, dusk, gloom, murk, nightfall, obscurity, shade, shadiness, shadows

DICTIONARY

who reveals unexpected talents. —**darkroom** *n.* darkened room for processing film.

darling *n.* much-loved person; favourite, e.g. *the darling of the gossip columns.* —*adj.* beloved.

darn[1] *v.* mend (a garment) with a series of interwoven stitches. —*n.* patch of darned work.

darn[2] *interj., adv., adj., v. Euphemistic* damn.

dart *n.* small narrow pointed missile that is thrown or shot, esp. in the game of darts; sudden quick movement; tuck made in dressmaking. —*pl.* indoor game in which darts are thrown at a circular numbered board (**dartboard**). —*v.* move or throw quickly and suddenly.

Darwinism *n.* theory of the origin of animal and plant species by evolution. —**Darwinian, Darwinist** *adj., n.*

dash *v.* move hastily; throw or strike violently; frustrate (someone's hopes). —*n.* sudden quick movement; small amount; mixture of style and courage; punctuation mark (-) showing a change of subject; longer symbol used in Morse code. —**dashing** *adj.* lively; stylish. —**dashboard** *n.* instrument panel in a car, boat, or aircraft.

dastardly *adj.* mean and cowardly.

data *n.* series of observations, measurements, or facts; numbers, digits, etc. operated on by a computer. —**data base** store of information that can be easily handled by a computer. —**data capture** process for converting information into a form that can be handled by a computer. —**data processing** series of operations performed on data, esp. by a computer, to extract or interpret information.

date[1] *n.* specified day of the month; particular day or year when an event happened; *Informal* appointment, esp. with a person of the opposite sex; *US informal* this person. —*v.* mark with the date; assign a date of occurrence to; (foll. by *from*) originate from (a date), e.g. *this house dates from the 16th century;* make or become old-fashioned. —**dated** *adj.*

date[2] *n.* dark-brown sweet-tasting fruit of the date palm. —**date palm** tall palm grown in tropical regions for its fruit.

dative *n.* (in certain languages) the form of the noun that expresses the indirect object.

daub *v.* smear or spread quickly or clumsily.

daughter *n.* female child; woman who comes from a certain place or is connected with a certain thing, e.g. *daughter of the church.* —**daughterly** *adj.* —**daughter-in-law** *n., pl.* **daughters-in-law.** son's wife.

daunt *v.* intimidate or dishearten. —**daunting** *adj.* —**dauntless** *adj.* fearless.

dauphin [daw-fin] *n.* (formerly) eldest son of the king of France.

davenport *n.* small writing table with drawers; *US* large couch.

davit [dav-vit] *n.* crane, usu. one of a pair, at a ship's side, for lowering and hoisting boats.

Davy lamp *n.* miner's lamp designed to prevent it from igniting gas.

dawdle *v.* be slow or lag behind; waste time. —**dawdler** *n.*

dawn *n.* daybreak; beginning (of something). —*v.* begin to grow light; begin to develop or appear; (foll. by *on* or *upon*) become apparent (to).

day *n.* period of 24 hours; period of light between sunrise and sunset; part of a day occupied with regular activity, esp. work; period or point in time; day of special observance; time of success. —**daybreak** *n.* time in the morning when light first appears. —**daydream** *n.* pleasant fantasy indulged in while awake. —*v.* indulge in idle

---

THESAURUS

darling *n.* 1. beloved, dear, dearest, love, sweet~heart 2. favourite, pet ~*adj.* 3. adored, beloved, cherished, dear, precious, treasured

darn mend, patch, repair, sew up, stitch

dart bound, dash, flash, flit, fly, race, run, rush, shoot, spring, sprint, start, tear, whiz

dash *v.* 1. cast, fling, hurl, slam, sling, throw 2. bolt, bound, dart, fly, haste, hasten, hurry, race, run, rush, speed, spring, sprint, tear 3. abash, chagrin, confound, dampen, disappoint, discomfort, discourage, frustrate ~*n* 4. brio, élan, flair, flourish, panache, spirit, style, verve, vigour, vivacity

dashing bold, daring, debonair, exuberant, gallant, lively, plucky, spirited, swashbuckling

data details, documents, facts, figures, information, input, materials, statistics

date 1. age, epoch, era, period, stage, time 2. appointment, assignation, engagement, meeting, rendezvous, tryst

dated antiquated, archaic, obsolete, old-fashioned, old hat, out, outdated, out of date, passé, unfashionable

daub *v.* coat, cover, paint, plaster, slap on (*Inf.*), smear

daunt alarm, appal, cow, dismay, frighten, intimidate, overawe, scare, subdue, terrify

dawdle dally, delay, hang about, idle, lag, loaf, loiter, potter, trail, waste time

dawn 1. *n.* daybreak, daylight, morning, sunrise 2. *v.* break, brighten, gleam, glimmer, grow light, lighten

DICTIONARY

fantasy. —**daydreamer** n. —**daylight** n. light from the sun. —**day release** system in which workers go to college one day a week. —**day-to-day** adj. routine.

daze v. stun, esp. by a blow or shock. —n. state of confusion or shock.

dazzle v. blind temporarily by sudden excessive light; impress greatly. —n. bright light that dazzles. —**dazzling** adj. —**dazzlingly** adv.

dB, db decibel(s).

DC direct current.

DCM Distinguished Conduct Medal.

DD Doctor of Divinity.

D-day n. day selected for the start of some operation, esp. the Allied invasion of Europe in 1944.

DDT kind of insecticide.

de facto adv. in fact. —adj. existing in fact, whether legally recognized or not.

de- prefix indicating: removal, e.g. deforest; reversal, e.g. decode; departure, e.g. decamp.

deacon n. Christianity ordained minister ranking immediately below a priest; (in some Protestant churches) lay official who assists the minister. —**deaconess** n. fem.

dead adj. no longer alive; no longer in use; numb, e.g. my leg has gone dead; complete, e.g. a dead stop; Informal very tired; (of a place) lacking activity. —n. period during which coldness or darkness is most intense, e.g. the dead of night. —adv. extremely; suddenly, e.g. stop dead. —**the dead** dead people. —**dead beat** Informal exhausted. —**dead set against** completely op-

posed to. —**deaden** v. make less sensitive or lively; make less resonant. —**deadly** adj. -**lier**, -**liest**. likely to cause death; Informal extremely boring. —adv. extremely. —**deadly nightshade** plant with poisonous black berries. —**deadbeat** n. Informal lazy useless person. —**dead end** road with one end blocked off; situation in which further progress is impossible. —**dead heat** tie for first place between two participants in a contest. —**dead letter** law or rule that is no longer enforced. —**deadline** n. time limit. —**deadlock** n. point in a dispute at which further progress is impossible. —v. bring to a deadlock. —**deadpan** adj., adv. showing no emotion or expression. —**dead reckoning** method of establishing one's position using the distance and direction travelled. —**dead weight** heavy weight.

deaf adj. unable to hear. —**deaf to** refusing to listen to or take notice of. —**deafen** v. make deaf, esp. temporarily. —**deafness** n.

deal[1] v. **dealing, dealt** [delt]. distribute; inflict (a blow) on; Cards give out (cards) to the players. —n. transaction or agreement; treatment, e.g. a fair deal; large amount. —**dealer** n. —**dealings** pl. n. transactions or business relations. —**deal in** v. engage in commercially. —**deal with** v. take action on; be concerned with.

deal[2] n. plank of fir or pine wood.

dean n. chief administrative official of a college or university faculty; chief administrator of a cathedral. —**deanery** n. office or residence of a dean; parishes of a dean.

dear adj. beloved; costly. —n. someone regarded with affection. —**dearly** adv. —**dearness** n.

THESAURUS

day 1. daylight, daytime, twenty-four hours, working day 2. date, particular day, point in time, set time, time

daydream n. 1. dream, musing, reverie, vision 2. dream, fancy, fantasy, fond hope, pipe dream, wish ~v. 3. dream, fancy, fantasize, imagine, muse

daylight sunlight, sunshine

daze 1. v. benumb, numb, paralyse, shock, stun, stupefy 2. n. bewilderment, confusion, shock, stupor, trance

dazzle 1. bedazzle, blind, blur, confuse, daze 2. amaze, astonish, awe, bowl over (Inf.), fascinate, impress, overawe, overpower, overwhelm, strike dumb, stupefy

dead 1. deceased, defunct, departed, extinct, gone, inanimate, late, lifeless, passed away, perished 2. inert, numb, paralysed 3. boring, dull, uninteresting

deadlock dead heat, draw, full stop, halt, impasse, stalemate, tie

deadly baleful, baneful, dangerous, deathly, destructive, fatal, lethal, malignant, mortal, noxious, pernicious, poisonous, venomous

deaf 1. hard of hearing, stone deaf 2. oblivious, unconcerned, unhearing, unmoved

deafen din, drown out, make deaf, split or burst the eardrums

deal 1. v. allot, apportion, assign, bestow, dispense, distribute, divide, dole out, give, reward, share 2. n. Inf. agreement, arrangement, bargain, contract, pact, transaction, understanding

dealer marketer, merchant, trader, tradesman, wholesaler

dear adj. 1. beloved, cherished, close, darling, esteemed, familiar, favourite, intimate, precious, prized, respected, treasured 2. costly,

DICTIONARY

dearth [dirth] *n.* inadequate amount, scarcity.

death *n.* permanent end of all functions of life in a person or animal; instance of this; ending, destruction. —**deathly** *adj., adv.* like death, e.g. *deathly quiet; deathly pale.* —**death duty** tax paid on property left at death. —**death's-head** *n.* human skull or a representation of one. —**death-trap** *n.* place or vehicle considered very unsafe. —**deathwatch beetle** beetle that bores into wood and makes a tapping sound.

deb *n. Informal* debutante.

debacle [day-**bah**-kl] *n.* disastrous collapse or defeat.

debar *v.* exclude or bar.

debase *v.* lower in value, quality, or character. —**debasement** *n.*

debate *n.* a discussion. —*v.* discuss, esp. in a formal assembly; consider (a course of action). —**in debate** in doubt, uncertain. —**debatable** *adj.* not absolutely certain.

debauched [dib-**bawcht**] *adj.* immoral, sexually corrupt. —**debauchery** *n.*

debenture *n.* long-term bond, bearing fixed interest, issued by a company or a government agency.

debilitate *v.* weaken. —**debilitation** *n.* —**debility** *n.* weakness, infirmity.

debit *n.* acknowledgment of a sum owing by entry on the left side of an account. —*v.* **debiting, debited.** record as a debit; charge with a debt.

debonair *adj.* suave or refined; carefree.

debouch *v.* move out from a narrow place to a wider one.

debrief *v.* receive a report from (a soldier, diplomat, etc.) after an event. —**debriefing** *n.*

debris [**deb**-ree] *n.* fragments of something destroyed.

debt *n.* something owed, esp. money; state of owing something. —**debtor** *n.*

debunk *v. Informal* expose the pretensions or falseness of.

debut [**day**-byoo] *n.* first public appearance of a performer. —**debutante** [**day**-byoo-tont] *n.* young upper-class woman making her first formal appearance in society.

Dec. December.

deca- *combining form* ten.

decade *n.* period of ten years.

decadence [**dek**-a-denss] *n.* state of deterioration of morality or culture. —**decadent** *adj.*

decaffeinated [dee-**kaf**-fin-ate-id] *adj.* (of coffee) with caffeine removed.

decagon *n.* geometric figure with ten sides. —**decagonal** *adj.*

decahedron [dek-a-**hee**-dron] *n.* solid figure with ten sides.

Decalogue *n.* the Ten Commandments.

decamp *v.* depart secretly or suddenly.

decant *v.* pour (a liquid) from one container to another; rehouse (people) while their homes are being refurbished. —**decanter** *n.* stoppered bottle for wine or spirits.

decapitate *v.* behead. —**decapitation** *n.*

decarbonize *v.* remove carbon from (an internal-combustion engine). —**decarbonization** *n.*

decathlon *n.* athletic contest with ten events.

decay *v.* rot; become weaker or more corrupt. —*n.* process of decaying; state brought about by this process.

THESAURUS

expensive, high-priced ~*n.* 3. angel, beloved, darling, loved one, precious, treasure

dearly extremely, greatly, profoundly, very much

death 1. bereavement, decease, demise, departure, dying, end, exit, expiration, loss, passing, quietus, release 2. destruction, downfall, extinction, finish, grave, ruin, undoing

deathly gaunt, ghastly, grim, haggard, pale, pallid, wan

debase cheapen, degrade, demean, devalue, disgrace, dishonour, drag down, humble, lower, reduce, shame

debatable arguable, borderline, controversial, disputable, doubtful, dubious, in dispute, moot, open to question, questionable, uncertain, unsettled

debate 1. *v.* argue, contend, contest, discuss,

dispute, question, wrangle 2. *n.* argument, contention, controversy, discussion, disputation, dispute

debris bits, dross, fragments, litter, pieces, remains, rubbish, rubble, ruins, waste, wreck, wreckage

debt arrears, bill, commitment, debit, due, duty, liability, obligation, score

debtor borrower, defaulter, insolvent

debunk cut down to size, deflate, disparage, expose, lampoon, mock, puncture, ridicule, show up

debut beginning, bow, coming out, entrance, inauguration, initiation, introduction, launching

decadent corrupt, debased, decaying, declining, degenerate, degraded, depraved, dissolute, immoral

DICTIONARY

decease n. Formal death. —**deceased** adj. Formal dead. —n. —**the deceased** person who has recently died.

deceive v. mislead by lying; be unfaithful to (one's sexual partner). —**deceiver** n. —**deceit** n. behaviour intended to deceive. —**deceitful** adj.

decelerate v. slow down. —**deceleration** n.

December n. twelfth month of the year.

decennial adj. lasting for ten years; happening every ten years.

decent adj. (of people) polite and morally acceptable; fitting or proper; conforming to conventions of sexual behaviour; Informal kind. —**decently** adv. —**decency** n.

decentralize v. reorganize into smaller local units. —**decentralization** n.

deception n. deceiving; something that deceives, trick. —**deceptive** adj. likely or designed to deceive. —**deceptively** adv. —**deceptiveness** n.

deci- combining form one tenth.

decibel n. unit for measuring the intensity of sound.

decide v. (cause to) reach a decision; settle (a contest or question). —**decided** adj. unmistakable; determined. —**decidedly** adv. —**decision** n. judgment, conclusion, or resolution; act of making up one's mind; firmness of purpose. —**deci-**

sive adj. indisputable, e.g. a decisive win; having the ability to make (quick) decisions. —**decisively** adv. —**decisiveness** n.

deciduous adj. (of a tree) shedding its leaves annually.

decimal n. fraction written in the form of a dot followed by one or more numbers. —adj. relating to or using powers of ten; expressed as a decimal. —**decimalize** v. change (a system or number) to the decimal system. —**decimalization** n. —**decimal currency** system of currency in which the units are parts or powers of ten. —**decimal point** dot between the unit and the fraction of a number in the decimal system. —**decimal system** number system with a base of ten, in which numbers are expressed by combinations of the digits 0 to 9.

decimate v. destroy or kill a large proportion of. —**decimation** n.

decipher v. decode; make out the meaning of (poor handwriting). —**decipherable** adj.

deck n. area of a ship that forms a floor; similar area in a bus; platform that supports the turntable and pick-up of a record player. —v. decorate. —**deck chair** folding chair made of canvas over a wooden frame. —**deck out** v. dress (oneself) or decorate (a room).

declaim v. speak loudly and dramatically; protest loudly. —**declamation** n. —**declamatory** adj.

THESAURUS

decay v. 1. crumble, decline, degenerate, deteriorate, disintegrate, dissolve, dwindle, moulder, shrivel, sink, spoil, wane, wither 2. decompose, mortify, perish, putrefy, rot

decease death, demise, departure, dissolution, dying, release

deceased adj. dead, defunct, departed, expired, finished, former, gone, late, lifeless, lost

deceit artifice, cheating, cunning, dissimulation, double-dealing, duplicity, fraud, guile, hypocrisy, imposition, pretence, slyness, treachery, trickery

deceitful crafty, designing, dishonest, disingenuous, double-dealing, duplicitous, fallacious, false, fraudulent, guileful, hypocritical, illusory, insincere, treacherous, tricky, two-faced, underhand, untrustworthy

deceive beguile, betray, cheat, con (Sl.), cozen, delude, double-cross (Inf.), dupe, ensnare, entrap, fool, hoax, hoodwink, mislead, outwit, swindle, take in (Inf.), trick

decency correctness, courtesy, decorum, etiquette, good form, good manners, modesty, propriety, seemliness

decent becoming, chaste, comely, decorous,

delicate, fit, modest, nice, polite, presentable, proper, pure, respectable, seemly, suitable

deception cunning, deceit, duplicity, fraud, fraudulence, guile, hypocrisy, imposition, insincerity, treachery, trickery

deceptive deceitful, delusive, dishonest, fake, false, fraudulent, illusory, misleading, mock, spurious, unreliable

decide adjudicate, choose, commit oneself, conclude, decree, determine, elect, end, purpose, resolve, settle

decipher construe, crack, decode, explain, interpret, make out, read, reveal, solve, understand, unfold, unravel

decision conclusion, finding, judgment, outcome, resolution, result, ruling, sentence, settlement, verdict

decisive 1. absolute, conclusive, critical, crucial, definite, definitive, fateful, final, influential, significant 2. determined, firm, forceful, incisive, resolute, strong-minded

deck v. adorn, array, attire, beautify, bedeck, bedight, clothe, decorate, dress, embellish, festoon, grace, ornament

declaim harangue, hold forth, lecture, proclaim, rant, recite, speak

DICTIONARY

declare v. state firmly and forcefully; announce officially; acknowledge for tax purposes. —**declaration** n. —**declaratory** adj.

decline v. say that one is unwilling to give, accept, or do (something); become smaller, weaker, or less important; *Grammar* list the inflections of (a noun, pronoun, or adjective). —n. gradual deterioration; movement downwards; diminution. —**declension** n. *Grammar* changes in the form of nouns, pronouns, or adjectives to show case, number, and gender.

declivity n., pl. **-ties.** downward slope. —**declivitous** adj.

declutch v. disengage the clutch of a motor vehicle.

decoct v. extract the essence from (a substance) by boiling. —**decoction** n.

decode v. convert from code into ordinary language. —**decoder** n.

décolleté [day-**kol**-tay] adj. (of a woman's garment) having a low neckline.

decompose v. be broken down through chemical or bacterial action. —**decomposition** n.

decompression n. gradual reduction in air pressure.

decongestant n. drug that relieves nasal congestion.

decontaminate v. render harmless by the removal of poisons, radioactivity, etc. —**decontamination** n.

décor [**day**-core] n. decorative scheme of a room or house.

decorate v. ornament; paint or wallpaper (a room); award a (military) medal to. —**decoration** n. —**decorative** adj. —**decorator** n.

decorous [**dek**-a-russ] adj. polite, calm, and sensible in behaviour. —**decorously** adv. —**decorousness** n. —**decorum** [dik-**core**-um] n. decorous behaviour.

decoy n. person or thing used to lure someone into danger; image of a bird or animal, used to lure game within shooting range. —v. lure into danger by means of a decoy.

decrease v. diminish. —n. lessening; amount by which something has been diminished.

decree n. law made by someone in authority; court judgment. —v. order by decree.

decrepit adj. weakened or worn out by age or long use. —**decrepitude** n.

decry v. **-crying, -cried.** express disapproval of.

dedicate v. commit (oneself or one's time) wholly to a special purpose or cause; inscribe or address (a book etc.) to someone as a tribute. —**dedicated** adj. devoted to a particular purpose or cause. —**dedication** n.

THESAURUS

declaration 1. affirmation, assertion, disclosure, revelation, statement, testimony 2. announcement, edict, manifesto, notification, promulgation, pronouncement

declare affirm, announce, assert, attest, aver, avow, claim, confirm, maintain, proclaim, profess, pronounce, state, swear, testify

decline v. 1. avoid, deny, forgo, refuse, reject, say 'no', turn down 2. decrease, diminish, dwindle, ebb, fade, fail, fall, fall off, flag, lessen, shrink, sink, wane ~n. 3. downturn, dwindling, falling off, lessening, recession, slump

décor colour scheme, decoration, ornamentation

decorate 1. adorn, beautify, deck, embellish, enrich, grace, ornament, trim 2. colour, furbish, paint, paper, renovate 3. cite, honour

decoration 1. adornment, embellishment, enrichment, ornamentation, trimming 2. flounce, flourish, frill, garnish, ornament, scroll, spangle, trimmings, trinket 3. award, badge, colours, emblem, garter, medal, order, ribbon, star

decorum behaviour, breeding, decency, dignity, etiquette, gentility, good grace, good manners, gravity, politeness, propriety, protocol, respectability, seemliness

decoy 1. n. attraction, bait, enticement, inducement, lure, pretence, trap 2. v. allure, bait, deceive, ensnare, entice, entrap, inveigle, lure, seduce, tempt

decrease 1. v. abate, contract, curtail, cut down, decline, diminish, drop, dwindle, ease, fall off, lessen, lower, reduce, shrink, slacken, subside, wane 2. n. cutback, decline, ebb, falling off, loss, reduction, shrinkage, subsidence

decree 1. n. act, command, edict, enactment, law, mandate, order, precept, proclamation, regulation, ruling, statute 2. v. command, decide, determine, dictate, enact, lay down, ordain, order, prescribe, proclaim, rule

decrepit aged, crippled, debilitated, effete, feeble, frail, incapacitated, infirm, wasted, weak

dedicate commit, devote, give over to, pledge, surrender

dedicated committed, devoted, enthusiastic, purposeful, single-minded, wholehearted, zealous

deduce conclude, derive, draw, gather, glean, infer, reason, understand

DICTIONARY

deduce v. reach (a conclusion) by reasoning from evidence. —**deducible** adj.

deduct v. subtract.

deduction n. deducting; something that is deducted; deducing; conclusion reached by deducing. —**deductive** adj.

deed n. something that is done; legal document.

deem v. have as an opinion.

deep adj. extending or situated far down, inwards, backwards, or sideways; of a specified dimension downwards, inwards, or backwards; coming from or penetrating to a great depth; difficult to understand; of great intensity; (foll. by in) immersed (in); (of a colour) strong or dark; low in pitch. —**the deep** Poetic the sea. —**deeply** adv. profoundly or intensely. —**deepen** v. —**deepfreeze** n. same as FREEZER.

deer n., pl. **deer.** hoofed mammal with antlers in the male. —**deerstalker** n. cloth hat with peaks back and front and earflaps.

deface v. spoil the surface or appearance of. —**defacement** n.

defame v. attack the good reputation of. —**defamation** n. —**defamatory** [dif-**fam**-a-tree] adj.

default n. failure to do something. —v. fail to fulfil an obligation. —**in default of** in the absence of. —**defaulter** n.

defeat v. overcome; thwart. —n. defeating or being defeated. —**defeatism** n. ready acceptance or expectation of defeat. —**defeatist** n., adj.

defecate v. discharge waste from the body through the anus. —**defecation** n.

defect n. imperfection. —v. desert one's cause or country to join the opposing forces. —**defective** adj. having a flaw. —**defection** n. —**defector** n.

defence n. resistance to attack; plea in support of something; a country's military resources; defendant's case in a court of law. —**defenceless** adj.

defend v. protect from harm or danger; support in the face of criticism, esp. by argument; represent (a defendant) in court; protect (a title) against a challenge. —**defendant** n. person accused of a crime. —**defender** n. —**defensible** adj. capable of being defended because believed to be right. —**defensibility** n. —**defensive** adj. intended for defence; overanxious to protect oneself against (threatened) criticism. —**defensively** adv.

defer[1] v. **-ferring, -ferred.** delay (something) until a future time. —**deferment, deferral** n.

defer[2] v. **-ferring, -ferred.** (foll. by to) comply with the wishes (of). —**deference** n. compliance with the wishes of another; respect. —**deferential** adj. —**deferentially** adv.

deficient adj. lacking some essential; inadequate in quality or quantity. —**deficiency** n. lack; state of being deficient. —**deficit** n. amount by which a sum of money is too small.

THESAURUS

deduct decrease by, reduce by, remove, subtract, take away, take from, withdraw

deduction 1. conclusion, consequence, finding, inference, reasoning, result 2. decrease, diminution, discount, reduction, subtraction

deed act, action, exploit, fact, feat, reality

deep adj. 1. bottomless, broad, far, profound, wide, yawning 2. extreme, grave, great, intense, profound 3. Of a sound bass, booming, full-toned, low, low-pitched, resonant, sonorous ~adv. 4. far down, far into, late

deeply completely, gravely, intensely, profoundly, seriously, thoroughly

default 1. n. absence, defect, failure, lack, lapse, neglect, nonpayment, omission, want 2. v. bilk, defraud, dodge, evade, fail, neglect, rat, swindle

defeat 1. v. beat, conquer, crush, overpower, overthrow, overwhelm, quell, repulse, rout, subdue, subjugate, vanquish 2. n. conquest, debacle, overthrow, repulse, rout

defect 1. n. blemish, blotch, error, failing, fault,

flaw, imperfection, mistake, spot, taint, want 2. v. change sides, desert, go over, rebel, revolt

defective broken, faulty, flawed, imperfect, inadequate, incomplete, insufficient, not working, out of order, scant, short

defence 1. armament, cover, deterrence, guard, immunity, protection, resistance, safeguard, security, shelter 2. apologia, argument, excuse, exoneration, explanation, justification, plea, vindication 3. Law alibi, case, declaration, denial, plea, pleading, rebuttal, testimony

defend 1. cover, fortify, guard, keep safe, preserve, protect, screen, secure, shelter, shield 2. assert, champion, endorse, espouse, justify, maintain, plead, speak up for, stand by, stand up for, support, sustain, uphold, vindicate

defender 1. bodyguard, escort, guard, protector 2. advocate, champion, patron, sponsor, supporter, vindicator

defer adjourn, delay, hold over, postpone, protract, put off, set aside, shelve, suspend, table

defiance challenge, contempt, disobedience,

DICTIONARY

defile[1] v. desecrate. —**defilement** n.

defile[2] n. narrow pass or valley.

define v. state precisely the meaning of; show clearly the outline of. —**definable** adj. —**definite** adj. clear in meaning; having precise limits; known for certain. —**definitely** adv. —**definition** n. statement of the meaning of a word or phrase; quality of being clear and distinct. —**definitive** adj. providing an unquestionable conclusion; being the best example of something.

deflate v. (cause to) collapse through the release of gas; take away the self-esteem or conceit from; *Economics* cause deflation of (an economy). —**deflation** n. *Economics* reduction in economic activity resulting in lower output and investment; feeling of sadness following excitement. —**deflationary** adj.

deflect v. (cause to) turn aside from a course. —**deflection** n. —**deflector** n.

deflower v. *Lit.* deprive (a woman) of her virginity.

defoliate v. deprive (a plant) of its leaves. —**defoliant** n. —**defoliation** n.

deforest v. clear of trees. —**deforestation** n.

deform v. cause to be misshapen; make ugly. —**deformity** n.

defraud v. take away or withhold money, rights, etc. from (a person) by fraud.

defray v. provide money for (costs or expenses).

defrock v. deprive (a priest) of priestly status.

defrost v. make or become free of frost or ice.

deft adj. quick and skilful in movement. —**deftly** adv. —**deftness** n.

defunct adj. no longer existing or operative.

defuse v. remove the triggering device from (an explosive device); remove the tension from (a situation).

defy v. -**fying**, -**fied**. resist openly and boldly; elude, esp. in a baffling way, e.g. *defy description*. —**defiance** n. open resistance or disobedience. —**defiant** adj.

degenerate adj. having deteriorated to a lower mental, moral, or physical level. —n. degenerate person. —v. become degenerate. —**degeneracy** n. degenerate behaviour. —**degeneration** n.

degrade v. reduce to dishonour or disgrace; reduce in status or quality; *Chem.* decompose into smaller molecules. —**degradation** n.

degree n. stage in a scale of relative amount or intensity; academic award given by a university or college on successful completion of a course; unit of measurement for temperature or angles.

dehumanize v. deprive of human qualities; make (an activity) mechanical or routine. —**dehumanization** n.

dehydrate v. cause to lose water; deprive the body of (someone) of water. —**dehydration** n.

de-ice v. free of ice. —**de-icer** n.

THESAURUS

disregard, insolence, insubordination, opposition, rebelliousness, spite

deficiency defect, demerit, failing, fault, flaw, frailty, shortcoming, weakness

deficit arrears, default, deficiency, loss, shortage, shortfall

define describe, designate, detail, determine, explain, expound, interpret, specify, spell out

definite clear, clear-cut, determined, exact, explicit, express, fixed, marked, obvious, particular, precise, specific

definitely absolutely, categorically, certainly, clearly, easily, finally, indubitably, obviously, plainly, positively, surely, undeniably, unequivocally, unmistakably, unquestionably, without doubt, without question

definition clarification, description, elucidation, explanation, exposition, statement of meaning

deflate 1. collapse, contract, exhaust, flatten, puncture, shrink, void 2. chasten, dash, disconcert, dispirit, squash

deflect bend, diverge, glance off, shy, sidetrack, swerve, turn, twist, veer, wind

defraud beguile, bilk, cheat, delude, dupe, embezzle, fleece, outwit, pilfer, rob, rook (*Sl.*), swindle, trick

deft able, adept, adroit, agile, clever, dexterous, expert, handy, neat, nimble, proficient, skilful

defunct dead, deceased, departed, extinct, gone

defy beard, brave, challenge, confront, dare, despise, disregard, face, flout, provoke, scorn, slight, spurn

degenerate 1. adj. base, corrupt, debased, debauched, decadent, degraded, depraved, dissolute, fallen, immoral, low, mean 2. v. decay, decline, deteriorate, fall off, lapse, regress, rot, sink, slip, worsen

degrade cheapen, corrupt, debase, demean, discredit, disgrace, humble, humiliate, impair, injure, pervert, shame

degree 1. class, grade, level, order, position, rank, standing, station, status 2. calibre, extent, intensity, level, measure, proportion, quality, quantity, range, rate, ratio, scale, scope, standard

DICTIONARY

deify [day-if-fie] *v.* -**fying**, -**fied**. treat or worship as a god. —**deification** *n.*

deign [dane] *v.* think it worthy of oneself (to do something), condescend.

deity [day-it-ee] *n., pl.* -**ties**. god or goddess; state of being divine.

déjà vu [day-zhah **voo**] *n.* feeling of having experienced before something that is actually happening now.

dejected *adj.* in low spirits. —**dejectedly** *adv.* —**dejection** *n.*

de jure *adv., adj.* according to law.

dekko *n. Brit. slang* —**have a dekko** have a look.

delay *v.* put off to a later time; slow up or cause to be late. —*n.* act of delaying; interval of time between events.

delectable *adj.* very attractive. —**delectation** *n. Formal* great pleasure.

delegate *n.* person chosen to act for others, esp. at a meeting. —*v.* entrust (duties or powers) to another person; appoint as a delegate. —**delegation** *n.* group of people appointed as delegates; delegating.

delete *v.* remove (something written or printed). —**deletion** *n.*

deleterious [del-lit-**eer**-ee-uss] *adj.* harmful, injurious.

deliberate *adj.* carefully thought out in advance; careful and unhurried. —*v.* consider (something) deeply. —**deliberately** *adv.* —**deliberation** *n.* —**deliberative** *adj.* for the purpose of deliberating, e.g. *a deliberative assembly.*

delicate *adj.* fine or subtle in quality or workmanship; having a fragile beauty; (of a taste etc.) pleasantly subtle; easily damaged; requiring tact. —**delicately** *adv.* —**delicacy** *n.* being delicate; something particularly good to eat.

delicatessen *n.* shop selling imported or unusual foods, already cooked or prepared.

delicious *adj.* very appealing, esp. to taste or smell. —**deliciously** *adv.*

delight *v.* please greatly; (foll. by *in*) take great pleasure (in). —*n.* great pleasure. —**delightful** *adj.* —**delightfully** *adv.*

delimit *v.* mark or prescribe the limits of. —**delimitation** *n.*

THESAURUS

deity divinity, god, goddess, godhead, idol, immortal

dejected cast down, crestfallen, depressed, despondent, disconsolate, disheartened, dismal, doleful, down, downcast, gloomy, glum, low, low-spirited, melancholy, miserable, morose, sad, wretched

de jure by right, legally, rightfully

delay *v.* 1. defer, hold over, postpone, procrastinate, prolong, protract, put off, shelve, stall, suspend, table, temporize ~*n.* 2. deferment, postponement, procrastination, stay, suspension 3. check, detention, hindrance, hold-up, impediment, interruption, interval, obstruction, setback, stoppage, wait

delegate *n.* agent, ambassador, commissioner, deputy, envoy, legate, representative, vicar

delegation commission, contingent, deputation, embassy, envoys, legation, mission

delete blot out, cancel, cross out, cut out, dele, edit, efface, erase, expunge, obliterate, remove, rub out

deliberate 1. *v.* cogitate, consider, consult, debate, discuss, meditate, mull over, ponder, reflect, think, weigh 2. *adj.* calculated, conscious, considered, designed, intentional, planned, premeditated, purposeful, studied, thoughtful, wilful

deliberately by design, calculatingly, consciously, determinedly, emphatically, in cold blood, intentionally, knowingly, on purpose, wilfully

deliberation care, carefulness, caution, circumspection, consideration, coolness, forethought, meditation, prudence, purpose, reflection, speculation, study, thought, wariness

delicacy 1. elegance, exquisiteness, fineness, lightness, nicety, precision, subtlety 2. discrimination, finesse, purity, refinement, sensibility, sensitivity, tact, taste 3. *bonne bouche*, dainty, luxury, relish, savoury, titbit, treat

delicate 1. flimsy, fragile, frail, slender, slight, weak 2. accurate, deft, detailed, minute, precise, skilled 3. critical, difficult, precarious, sensitive, ticklish, touchy

delicately carefully, deftly, elegantly, exquisitely, fastidiously, finely, gracefully, lightly, precisely, sensitively, skilfully, softly, subtly

delicious appetizing, choice, dainty, luscious, mouthwatering, savoury, tasty, toothsome

delight 1. *n.* ecstasy, enjoyment, gladness, gratification, happiness, joy, pleasure, rapture, transport 2. *v.* amuse, charm, cheer, divert, enchant, gratify, please, ravish, rejoice, satisfy, thrill

delightful agreeable, amusing, captivating, charming, congenial, delectable, engaging, enjoyable, entertaining, fascinating, heavenly, pleasant, pleasurable, ravishing, thrilling

DICTIONARY

delineate [dill-**lin**-ee-ate] *v.* show by drawing; describe in words. —**delineation** *n.*

delinquent *n.* someone, esp. a young person, who repeatedly breaks the law. —*adj.* repeatedly breaking the law. —**delinquency** *n.*

delirium *n.* state of excitement and mental confusion, often with hallucinations; violent excitement. —**delirious** *adj.* —**deliriously** *adv.*

deliver *v.* carry (goods etc.) to a destination; hand over; release or rescue; aid in the birth of; present (a speech etc.); strike (a blow) suddenly. —**deliverance** *n.* rescue from danger or captivity. —**delivery** *n.* act of delivering; something that is delivered; act of giving birth to a child; style, esp. in public speaking.

dell *n.* small wooded hollow.

Delphic *adj.* ambiguous, like the ancient Greek oracle at Delphi.

delphinium *n.* plant with spikes of blue flowers.

delta *n.* fourth letter of the Greek alphabet (Δ); flat area at the mouth of some rivers where the main stream splits up into several tributaries.

delude *v.* deceive. —**delusion** *n.* mistaken idea or belief; state of being deluded. —**delusive** *adj.*

deluge [**del**-lyooj] *n.* great flood of water; torrential rain; overwhelming number. —*v.* flood; overwhelm.

de luxe *adj.* rich or sumptuous; superior in quality.

delve *v.* research deeply (for information).

demagogue *n.* political agitator who appeals to the prejudice and passions of the mob. —**demagogic** *adj.* —**demagogy** *n.*

demand *v.* ask for forcefully; require as just, urgent, etc.; claim as a right. —*n.* forceful request; *Economics* willingness and ability to purchase goods and services. —*pl.* something that requires special effort or sacrifice. —**demanding** *adj.* requiring a lot of time or effort.

demarcation *n.* establishment of limits or boundaries, esp. between the work performed by different trade unions.

demean *v.* lower (someone) in dignity, character, or status.

demeanour *n.* way a person behaves.

demented *adj.* mad. —**dementedly** *adv.* —**dementia** [dim-**men**-sha] *n.* state of serious mental deterioration.

demerara sugar *n.* brown crystallized cane sugar.

demerit *n.* flaw, disadvantage.

demesne [dim-**mane**] *n.* land surrounding a house; *Law* possession of one's own property or land.

demi- *combining form* half.

demijohn *n.* large bottle with a short neck, often encased in wicker.

demilitarize *v.* remove the military forces from. —**demilitarization** *n.*

demimonde *n.* (esp. in the 19th century) class of women considered to be outside respectable society, because of promiscuity; group considered not wholly respectable.

demise *n. Formal* death; eventual failure (of something successful).

demo *n. Informal* demonstration, organized expression of public opinion.

demob *v. Informal* demobilize. —**demobilize** *v.* release from the armed forces. —**demobilization** *n.*

democracy *n., pl.* **-cies.** government by the people or their elected representatives; state governed in this way; social equality. —**democrat** *n.* advocate of democracy; (**D-**) member or supporter of the Democratic Party in the U.S. —**democratic** *adj.* connected with democracy; upholding democracy; (**D-**) of the Democratic Party, one of the two main political parties in the U.S. —**democratically** *adv.*

THESAURUS

deliver 1. bear, bring, carry, cart, convey, distribute, transport 2. cede, commit, give up, grant, hand over, make over, relinquish, resign, surrender, transfer, turn over, yield 3. acquit, discharge, emancipate, free, liberate, loose, ransom, redeem, release, rescue, save

delivery 1. consignment, conveyance, dispatch, distribution, handing over, surrender, transfer, transmission, transmittal 2. escape, liberation, release, rescue

delude beguile, cheat, cozen, deceive, dupe, fool, gull (*Archaic*), hoax, hoodwink, impose on, misguide, mislead, take in (*Inf.*), trick

deluge cataclysm, downpour, flood, inundation, overflowing, spate, torrent

de luxe choice, costly, elegant, exclusive, expensive, grand, opulent, palatial, rich, select, special, splendid, sumptuous, superior

demagogue agitator, firebrand, rabble-rouser, soapbox orator

demand *v.* 1. ask, challenge, inquire, interrogate, question, request 2. call for, cry out for, involve, necessitate, need, require, take, want ~*n.* 3. bidding, charge, inquiry, interrogation, order, question, request, requisition

DICTIONARY

demography *n.* study of human populations. —**demographic** *adj.*

demolish *v.* tear down or break up (buildings); put an end to (an argument etc.). —**demolisher** *n.* —**demolition** *n.*

demon *n.* evil spirit; person extremely skilful in or devoted to a given activity. —**demonic** *adj.* —**demoniac(al)** *adj.* appearing to be possessed by a devil; frenzied. —**demoniacally** *adv.* —**demonology** *n.* study of demons.

demonstrate *v.* show or prove by reasoning or evidence; reveal the existence of; display and explain the workings of; show support or protest by public parades or rallies. —**demonstrable** *adj.* able to be proved. —**demonstrably** *adv.* —**demonstration** *n.* organized expression of public opinion; proof; explanation or experiment showing how something works; show of emotion. —**demonstrative** *adj.* tending to express one's feelings unreservedly. —**demonstratively** *adv.* —**demonstrator** *n.* person who demonstrates machines, products, etc.; person who takes part in a public demonstration.

demoralize *v.* undermine the morale of. —**demoralization** *n.*

demote *v.* reduce in status or rank. —**demotion** *n.*

demur *v.* -murring, -murred. show reluctance. —**without demur** without objecting.

demure *adj.* quiet, reserved, and rather shy. —**demurely** *adv.* —**demureness** *n.*

den *n.* home of a wild animal; small secluded room in a home; place where people indulge in criminal or immoral activities, e.g *den of iniquity.*

denationalize *v.* transfer (an industry) from public to private ownership. —**denationalization** *n.*

denature *v.* change the nature of; make (alcohol) unfit to drink.

denier [den-yer] *n.* unit of weight used to measure the fineness of silk and man-made fibres.

denigrate *v.* criticize unfairly. —**denigration** *n.* —**denigrator** *n.*

denim *n.* hard-wearing cotton fabric. —*pl.* jeans made of denim.

denizen *n.* inhabitant.

denominate *v.* give a specific name to. —**denomination** *n.* group having a distinctive interpretation of a religious faith; grade or unit of value, measure, etc. —**denominational** *adj.* —**denominator** *n.* divisor of a fraction.

denote *v.* be a sign of; have as a literal meaning. —**denotation** *n.*

denouement [day-noo-mon] *n.* final outcome or solution, esp. in a play or book.

denounce *v.* speak violently against; give in-

THESAURUS

demanding challenging, difficult, exacting, exhausting, hard, taxing, tough, trying, wearing

demeanour air, bearing, behaviour, carriage, conduct, deportment, manner, mien

democracy commonwealth, government by the people, representative government, republic

democratic autonomous, egalitarian, popular, populist, representative, republican, self-governing

demolish bulldoze, destroy, dismantle, flatten, knock down, level, overthrow, pulverize, raze, ruin, tear down

demon devil, evil spirit, fiend, goblin, malignant spirit

demonstrable attestable, certain, evident, evincible, incontrovertible, indubitable, irrefutable, obvious, positive, self-evident, undeniable, unmistakable, verifiable

demonstrate 1. display, establish, evidence, exhibit, indicate, prove, show, testify to 2. describe, explain, illustrate, make clear, show how, teach 3. march, parade, picket, protest, rally

demonstration 1. confirmation, display, evidence, exhibition, expression, illustration,

manifestation, proof, testimony, validation 2. explanation, exposition, presentation, test, trial 3. march, mass lobby, parade, picket, protest, rally, sit-in

demur *v.* balk, cavil, disagree, dispute, doubt, hesitate, object, pause, protest, refuse, take exception, waver

demure decorous, diffident, grave, modest, reserved, reticent, retiring, sedate, shy, sober, staid, unassuming

den 1. cave, cavern, haunt, hide-out, hole, lair, shelter 2. cloister, cubbyhole, retreat, sanctum, snuggery, study

denial contradiction, disavowal, disclaimer, dismissal, dissent, negation, prohibition, rebuff, refusal, renunciation, repudiation, repulse, retraction, veto

denomination 1. belief, communion, creed, persuasion, religious group, school, sect 2. grade, size, unit, value

denote betoken, designate, express, imply, import, indicate, mark, mean, show, signify, typify

denounce accuse, attack, castigate, censure, condemn, decry, impugn, proscribe, revile, stigmatize, vilify

DICTIONARY

formation against. —**denunciation** n. open condemnation.

dense adj. closely packed; difficult to see through; stupid. —**densely** adv. —**density** n. degree to which something is filled or occupied; measure of the compactness of a substance, expressed as its mass per unit volume.

dent n. hollow in a surface, as made by a blow. —v. make a dent in.

dental adj. of or relating to the teeth or dentistry. —**dentifrice** [den-tif-riss] n. paste or powder for cleaning the teeth. —**dentine** [den-teen] n. calcified tissue comprising the bulk of a tooth. —**denture** n. artificial tooth. —pl. set of artificial teeth. —**dental floss** waxed thread used to remove food particles from between the teeth.

dentist n. person qualified to practise dentistry. —**dentistry** n. branch of medicine concerned with the teeth and gums.

denude v. (foll. by of) remove the covering or protection from. —**denudation** n.

deny v. -**nying**, -**nied**. declare to be untrue; refuse to give or allow; refuse to acknowledge. —**deniable** adj. —**denial** n. denying; statement that something is not true.

deodorize v. remove or disguise the smell of. —**deodorization** n. —**deodorant** n. substance applied to the body to mask the smell of perspiration.

dep. department; departure.

depart v. leave; differ. —**departed** adj. Euphemistic dead. —**the departed** dead people. —**departure** n.

department n. specialized division of a large

organization; major subdivision of the administration of a government. —**departmental** adj. —**department store** large shop selling many kinds of goods.

depend v. (foll. by on or upon) put trust (in); be influenced or determined (by); rely (on) for income or support. —**dependable** adj. —**dependably** adv. —**dependability** n. —**dependant** n. person who depends on another for financial support. —**dependence** n. state of being dependent. —**dependency** n. territory subject to a state on which it does not border; overreliance on another person or a drug. —**dependent** adj. depending on a person or thing for support.

depict v. give a picture of; describe in words. —**depiction** n.

depilatory [dip-**pill**-a-tree] n., pl. -**ries.** adj. (substance) designed to remove unwanted hair.

deplete v. use up; reduce in number. —**depletion** n.

deplore v. express or feel strong disapproval of. —**deplorable** adj. very bad.

deploy v. organize (troops or resources) into a position ready for immediate action. —**deployment** n.

depopulate v. cause to be reduced in population. —**depopulation** n.

deport v. remove forcibly from a country. —**deport oneself** behave oneself in a specified manner. —**deportation** n. —**deportee** n.

deportment n. manner in which a person behaves.

depose v. remove from an office or position of power; Law make a statement on oath.

THESAURUS

dense close, compact, compressed, condensed, heavy, impenetrable, opaque, solid, substantial, thick, thickset

dent 1. n. chip, crater, depression, dimple, dip, hollow, impression, indentation, pit 2. v. depress, dint, gouge, hollow, imprint, press in, push in

deny 1. contradict, disagree with, disprove, gainsay, oppose, rebuff, refute 2. abjure, disavow, discard, disclaim, disown, recant, renounce, repudiate, revoke

depart decamp, disappear, escape, exit, go, go away, leave, migrate, quit, remove, retire, retreat, set forth, start out, vanish, withdraw

department 1. district, division, province, region, sector 2. branch, bureau, division, office, section, station, subdivision, unit

departure 1. exit, exodus, going, leave-taking, leaving, removal, retirement, withdrawal 2. branching out, change, difference, innovation, novelty, shift

depend 1. bank on, build upon, calculate on, confide in, count on, lean on, reckon on, rely upon, trust in, turn to 2. be based on, be determined by, be subject to, hinge on, rest on

dependent counting on, defenceless, helpless, immature, reliant, relying on, vulnerable, weak

deplete consume, decrease, drain, empty, evacuate, exhaust, expend, impoverish, lessen, milk, reduce, use up

deplorable 1. calamitous, dire, disastrous, distressing, grievous, lamentable, melancholy, miserable, pitiable, regrettable, sad, unfortunate, wretched 2. disgraceful, disreputable, execrable, opprobrious, reprehensible, scandalous, shameful

deplore 1. bemoan, bewail, grieve for, lament, mourn, regret, rue, sorrow over 2. abhor, censure, condemn, denounce, deprecate, disapprove of, object to

depose break, cashier, degrade, demote, de-

DICTIONARY

deposit v. put down; entrust for safekeeping, esp. to a bank; lay down naturally. —n. entrusting of money to a bank; money entrusted; money given in part payment or as security; accumulation of sediments, minerals, etc. —**depositary** n. person to whom something is entrusted for safety. —**depositor** n. —**depository** n. store for furniture etc.

deposition n. Law sworn statement of a witness used in court in his or her absence; deposing; depositing; something deposited.

depot [**dep-oh**] n. building used for storage; Brit. building for the storage and servicing of buses or railway engines; US bus or railway station.

deprave v. make morally bad. —**depravity** n. moral corruption.

deprecate v. express disapproval of, protest against. —**deprecation** n. —**deprecatory** adj.

depreciate v. decline in value or price; criticize. —**depreciation** n. —**depreciatory** adj.

depredation n. plundering.

depress v. lower the spirits of (someone); lower (prices or wages); push down. —**depressing** adj. —**depressingly** adv. —**depressant** n. drug which reduces nervous activity. —**depression** n. mental state in which a person has feelings of gloom and inadequacy; economic condition in which there is a lot of unemployment and low output and investment; area of low air pressure; sunken place. —**depressive** adj. tending to cause depression.

deprive v. (foll. by of) prevent from (possessing or enjoying). —**deprivation** n. —**deprived** adj. lacking adequate living conditions, education, etc.

depth n. distance downwards, backwards, or inwards; intensity of emotion; profundity of character or thought; intensity of colour. —**depth charge** bomb used to attack submarines by exploding at a preset depth of water.

depute v. appoint (someone) to act on one's behalf. —**deputation** n. body of people appointed to represent others. —**deputize** v. act as a deputy. —**deputy** n. person appointed to act on behalf of another.

derail v. cause (a train) to go off the rails. —**derailment** n.

derange v. make insane; throw into disorder. —**derangement** n.

derby n., pl. **-bies.** sporting event between teams from the same area; US bowler hat. —**the Derby** annual horse race run at Epsom Downs.

deregulate v. remove regulations or controls from. —**deregulation** n.

derelict adj. deserted or abandoned; falling into ruins. —n. social outcast, vagrant. —**dereliction** n. wilful neglect (of duty); state of being abandoned.

deride v. speak of or treat with contempt or ridicule. —**derision** n. —**derisive** adj. mocking or scornful. —**derisory** adj. so small or inadequate that it is not worth serious consideration.

de rigueur [de rig-**gur**] adj. required by fashion.

THESAURUS

throne, dismiss, displace, downgrade, remove from office

deposit 1. v. drop, lay, locate, place, precipitate, put, put down, settle, sit down 2. n. down payment, instalment, money (in bank), part payment, pledge, retainer, security, stake, warranty

depot 1. repository, storehouse, warehouse 2. bus station, garage, terminus

deprave corrupt, debase, debauch, degrade, demoralize, pervert, seduce, vitiate

depreciate decrease, deflate, devalue, lessen, lose value, lower, reduce

depreciation 1. depression, devaluation, drop, fall, slump 2. belittlement, criticism, derogation, detraction, disparagement

depress cast down, chill, damp, deject, desolate, discourage, dishearten, dispirit, oppress, sadden, weigh down

depressing black, bleak, discouraging, disheartening, dismal, distressing, dreary, gloomy, heartbreaking, hopeless, melancholy, sad, sombre

depression 1. dejection, despair, despondency, dolefulness, downheartedness, gloominess, hopelessness, low spirits, melancholy, sadness 2. Commerce dullness, economic decline, hard or bad times, inactivity, lowness, recession, slump, stagnation

deprive bereave, despoil, dispossess, divest, expropriate, rob, strip, wrest

deprived bereft, destitute, disadvantaged, forlorn, in need, in want, lacking, needy, poor

depth abyss, deepness, drop, extent, measure, profundity

deputation commission, delegates, delegation, embassy, envoys, legation

deputize act for, stand in for, understudy

deputy n. agent, ambassador, commissioner, legate, lieutenant, proxy, representative, substitute, surrogate

derelict abandoned, deserted, discarded, forsaken, neglected, ruined

deride chaff, disdain, disparage, flout, gibe, in-

DICTIONARY

derive v. (foll. by *from*) draw or be drawn (from) in origin. —**derivation** n. —**derivative** adj., n.

dermatitis n. inflammation of the skin.

dermatology n. branch of medicine concerned with the skin. —**dermatologist** n.

derogatory [dir-**rog**-a-tree] adj. intentionally offensive.

derrick n. simple crane; framework erected over an oil well.

derv n. diesel oil, when used for road transport.

dervish n. member of a Muslim religious order noted for a frenzied whirling dance.

descant n. *Music* tune played or sung above a basic melody.

descend v. move down (a slope etc.); move to a lower level, pitch, etc.; (foll. by *to*) stoop to (unworthy behaviour); (foll. by *on*) visit unexpectedly. —**be descended from** be connected by a blood relationship to. —**descendant** n. person or animal descended from an individual, race, or species. —**descendent** adj. descending. —**descent** n. act of descending; downward slope; derivation from an ancestor.

describe v. give an account of (something or someone) in words; trace the outline of (a circle etc.). —**description** n. statement that describes something or someone; sort, e.g. *reptiles of every description*. —**descriptive** adj. —**descriptively** adv.

descry v. -**scrying**, -**scried**. catch sight of; discover by looking carefully.

desecrate v. violate the sacred character of (an object or place). —**desecration** n.

desegregate v. end racial segregation in. —**desegregation** n.

deselect v. *Brit. politics* refuse to select (an MP) for re-election. —**deselection** n.

desert[1] n. region that has little or no vegetation because of low rainfall.

desert[2] v. abandon (a person or place) without intending to return; *Mil.* abscond from (a post or duty) with no intention of returning. —**deserter** n. —**desertion** n.

deserts pl. n. —**get one's just deserts** get the punishment one deserves.

deserve v. be entitled to or worthy of. —**deserved** adj. rightfully earned. —**deservedly** adv. —**deserving** adj. worthy, esp. of praise or help.

deshabille [day-zab-**beel**] n. same as DISHA-BILLE.

desiccate v. remove most of the water from. —**desiccation** n.

design v. work out the structure or form of (something), as by making a sketch or plans; plan and make artistically; intend for a specific purpose. —n. preliminary drawing; arrangement or features of an artistic or decorative work; art of designing; intention, e.g. *by design*. —**designedly** adv. by intention. —**designer** n. person who draws up original sketches or plans from which things are made. —adj. designed by a well-known designer. —**designing** adj. crafty, cunning.

THESAURUS

sult, jeer, mock, pooh-pooh, ridicule, scoff, scorn, sneer, taunt

derivation ancestry, basis, beginning, descent, etymology, foundation, genealogy, origin, root, source

derive collect, deduce, draw, elicit, extract, follow, gain, gather, get, glean, infer, obtain, procure, receive, trace

descend 1. alight, dismount, drop, fall, go down, move down, plunge, sink, subside, tumble 2. dip, incline, slant, slope

descent 1. coming down, drop, fall, plunge, swoop 2. ancestry, extraction, family tree, genealogy, heredity, lineage, origin, parentage

describe characterize, define, depict, detail, explain, express, illustrate, narrate, portray, recount, relate, report, specify, tell

description account, characterization, detail, explanation, narrative, portrayal, report, representation, sketch

desert[1] solitude, waste, wasteland, wilderness, wilds

desert[2] v. abandon, abscond, betray, decamp, defect, forsake, give up, jilt, leave, leave stranded, maroon, quit, rat (on), relinquish, renounce, resign, throw over, vacate, walk out on (*Inf.*)

deserter absconder, defector, escapee, fugitive, runaway, traitor, truant

deserve be entitled to, be worthy of, earn, gain, justify, merit, procure, rate, warrant, win

deserved condign, due, earned, fair, fitting, just, justifiable, justified, merited, proper, right, rightful, suitable, well-earned

design v. 1. describe, draft, draw, outline, plan, sketch, trace ~n. 2. blueprint, draft, drawing, model, outline, plan, scheme, sketch ~v. 3. conceive, create, fabricate, fashion, invent, originate, think up 4. aim, contrive, destine, devise, intend, make, mean, plan, project, propose, purpose, scheme, tailor ~n. 5. aim, end, goal, intent, intention, meaning, object, objective, point, purport, purpose, target, view

DICTIONARY

designate [**dez**-zig-nate] *v.* give a name to; select (someone) for an office or duty. —*adj.* appointed but not yet in office. —**designation** *n.* name.

desire *v.* long for. —*n.* strong feeling of wanting something; sexual appetite; person or thing desired. —**desirable** *adj.* worth having; arousing sexual desire. —**desirability** *n.* —**desirous of** [diz-**zire**-uss] having a desire for.

desist *v.* (foll. by *from*) stop or abstain (from).

desk *n.* piece of furniture with a writing surface and usually drawers; service counter in a public building; section of a newspaper covering a specific subject, e.g. *the news desk.* —**desktop** *adj.* denoting a computer system small enough to use at a desk.

desolate *adj.* uninhabited and bleak; without hope. —*v.* lay waste; make (a person) very sad. —**desolation** *n.*

despair *v.* lose hope. —*n.* total loss of hope.

despatch *v., n.* same as DISPATCH.

desperado *n., pl.* **-does, -dos.** reckless person ready to commit any violent illegal act.

desperate *adj.* careless of danger, as from despair; (of an action) undertaken as a last resort; having a great need or desire. —**desperately** *adv.* —**desperation** *n.*

despise *v.* look down on with contempt. —**despicable** *adj.* worthy of being despised. —**despicably** *adv.*

despite *prep.* in spite of.

despoil *v. Formal* plunder. —**despoliation** *n.*

despondent *adj.* dejected or depressed. —**despondently** *adv.* —**despondency** *n.*

despot *n.* person in power who acts tyrannically. —**despotic** *adj.* —**despotically** *adv.* —**despotism** *n.* tyrannical government or behaviour.

dessert *n.* sweet course served at the end of a meal. —**dessertspoon** *n.* spoon between a tablespoon and a teaspoon in size.

destination *n.* place to which someone or something is going.

destine [**dess**-tin] *v.* set apart (for a certain purpose).

destiny *n., pl.* **-nies.** future destined for a person or thing; (**D-**) the power that predetermines the course of events.

destitute *adj.* totally impoverished. —**destitution** *n.*

THESAURUS

designation description, epithet, label, mark, name, title

designer artificer, creator, deviser, inventor, originator, stylist

desirable 1. advisable, agreeable, beneficial, eligible, enviable, good, pleasing, preferable, profitable, worthwhile 2. alluring, attractive, fascinating, fetching, seductive

desire *v.* 1. aspire to, covet, crave, fancy, hanker after, long for, want, wish for, yearn for ~*n.* 2. appetite, craving, hankering, longing, need, want, wish 3. appetite, concupiscence, lasciviousness, lechery, libido, lust, lustfulness, passion

desist abstain, break off, cease, discontinue, end, forbear, give up, leave off, pause, refrain from, stop, suspend

desolate 1. bare, barren, bleak, desert, dreary, ruined, solitary, uninhabited, waste, wild 2. abandoned, bereft, comfortless, dejected, depressing, despondent, dismal, downcast, forlorn, forsaken, gloomy, hopeless, lonely, melancholy, miserable, wretched

desolation destruction, devastation, havoc, ravages, ruin, ruination

despair 1. *v.* despond, give up, lose heart, lose hope 2. *n.* anguish, depression, desperation, gloom, hopelessness, melancholy, misery, wretchedness

desperado bandit, criminal, cutthroat, gangster, gunman, lawbreaker, outlaw, ruffian, thug

desperate dangerous, daring, determined, foolhardy, frantic, furious, hasty, headstrong, impetuous, madcap, rash, reckless, risky, violent, wild

desperately badly, dangerously, gravely, perilously, seriously, severely

despise abhor, deride, detest, disdain, disregard, flout, loathe, look down on, neglect, revile, scorn, slight

despite *prep.* against, even with, in spite of, in the face of, notwithstanding, regardless of

despondent blue, dejected, depressed, despairing, disconsolate, discouraged, disheartened, doleful, down, downcast, gloomy, glum, hopeless, in despair, low, melancholy, miserable, morose, sad, sorrowful, wretched

despot autocrat, dictator, tyrant

despotism autarchy, autocracy, dictatorship, oppression, tyranny

destination harbour, haven, journey's end, landing-place, resting-place, station, stop, terminus

destine allot, appoint, assign, consecrate, decree, design, devote, doom, earmark, fate, intend, mark out, ordain, predetermine, purpose, reserve, set apart

DICTIONARY

destroy v. ruin; put an end to; kill (an animal). —**destroyer** n. small heavily armed warship; person or thing that destroys. —**destructible** adj. —**destruction** n. destroying or being destroyed; cause of ruin. —**destructive** adj. causing destruction; intending to discredit someone, without positive suggestions, e.g. *destructive criticism.* —**destructively** adv.

desuetude [diss-**syoo**-it-tude] n. condition of not being in use.

desultory [**dez**-zl-tree] adj. changing fitfully from one thing to another; random. —**desultorily** adv.

detach v. disengage and separate. —**detachable** adj. —**detached** adj. standing apart; showing no emotional involvement. —**detachment** n. aloofness; small group of soldiers.

detail n. item that is considered separately; unimportant item; treatment of particulars; *Chiefly mil.* personnel assigned a specific duty. —v. list fully.

detain v. delay (someone); hold (someone) in custody. —**detainee** n. —**detainment** n.

detect v. notice; discover the existence or presence of. —**detectable** adj. —**detection** n. —**detective** n. policeman or private agent who investigates crime. —**detector** n. instrument used to find something, e.g. *smoke detector.*

detente [day-**tont**] n. easing of tension between nations.

detention n. imprisonment; form of punishment in which a pupil is detained after school.

deter v. **-terring, -terred.** discourage (someone) from doing something by instilling fear or doubt. —**deterrent** n. something that deters; weapon, esp. nuclear, to deter attack by another nation. —adj. tending to deter.

detergent n. chemical cleansing agent. —adj. having cleansing power.

deteriorate v. become worse. —**deterioration** n.

determine v. settle (an argument or a question) conclusively; find out the facts about (something); make a decision to do something. —**determinant** n. factor that determines. —**determinate** adj. definitely limited or fixed. —**determination** n. condition of being determined or resolute; act of determining. —**determined** adj. firmly decided, unable to be persuaded. —**determinedly** adv. —**determiner** n. *Grammar* word that determines the object to which a noun phrase refers, such as *all.* —**determinism** n. theory that human choice is not free, but decided by past events. —**determinist** n., adj.

THESAURUS

destiny doom, fate, fortune, lot, portion

destitute distressed, down and out, impecunious, impoverished, indigent, insolvent, moneyless, needy, penniless, penurious, poor

destroy annihilate, blow to bits, break down, crush, demolish, desolate, devastate, dismantle, dispatch, eradicate, extinguish, kill, ravage, raze, ruin, shatter, slay, smash, wipe out, wreck

destruction demolition, devastation, downfall, end, extermination, extinction, havoc, liquidation, massacre, overthrow, ruin, ruination, slaughter, wreckage, wrecking

destructive baleful, baneful, calamitous, cataclysmic, catastrophic, damaging, deadly, deleterious, detrimental, devastating, fatal, harmful, hurtful, injurious, lethal, pernicious, ruinous

detach cut off, disconnect, disengage, disentangle, disjoin, disunite, divide, free, isolate, loosen, remove, separate, sever, tear off, uncouple, unfasten

detachment aloofness, coolness, indifference, remoteness, unconcern

detail aspect, component, count, element, fact, factor, feature, item, particular, point, respect, specific, technicality

detain 1. check, delay, hinder, hold up, impede, keep, keep back, retard, slow up (*or* down), stay, stop 2. arrest, confine, hold, intern, restrain

detect 1. catch, descry, distinguish, identify, note, notice, observe, recognize, scent, spot 2. catch, disclose, discover, expose, find, reveal, track down, uncover, unmask

detective C.I.D. man, constable, investigator, private eye, sleuth (*Inf.*)

detention confinement, custody, delay, hindrance, holding back, imprisonment, keeping in, restraint

deter caution, check, damp, daunt, debar, discourage, dissuade, frighten, hinder, inhibit from, intimidate, prevent, prohibit, put off, restrain, stop, talk out of

deteriorate decline, degenerate, degrade, deprave, depreciate, go downhill (*Inf.*), lower, spoil, worsen

determination backbone, constancy, conviction, dedication, doggedness, drive, firmness, fortitude, perseverance, persistence, resolution, resolve, single-mindedness, steadfastness, tenacity, willpower

determine 1. arbitrate, conclude, decide, end, finish, fix upon, ordain, regulate, settle 2.

DICTIONARY

detest v. dislike intensely. —**detestable** adj. —**detestation** n.

dethrone v. remove from a throne or deprive of high position.

detonate v. cause (an explosive device) to explode or (of an explosive device) explode. —**detonation** n. —**detonator** n. small amount of explosive, or a device, used to set off an explosion.

detour n. deviation from a direct route or course of action.

detract v. (foll. by *from*) lessen the value of, diminish. —**detractor** n. —**detraction** n.

detriment n. disadvantage or damage. —**detrimental** adj. —**detrimentally** adv.

detritus [dit-**trite**-uss] n. loose mass of stones or silt worn away from rocks, debris. —**detrital** adj.

de trop [de **troh**] adj. not wanted; in the way.

deuce [**dyewss**] n. playing card or dice with two spots; *Tennis* score of forty all.

deuterium n. isotope of hydrogen twice as heavy as the normal atom.

Deutschmark [**doytch**-mark], **Deutsche Mark** [**doytch**-a] n. monetary unit of Germany.

devalue v. -**valuing**, -**valued**. reduce the exchange value of (a currency); reduce the value of (something or someone). —**devaluation** n.

devastate v. destroy; upset greatly. —**devastation** n.

develop v. grow or bring to a later, more

elaborate, or more advanced stage; come or bring into existence; improve the value or change the use of (land); treat (a photographic plate or film) to produce a visible image. —**developer** n. person who develops property; chemical used to develop photographs or films. —**development** n. —**developing country** poor or nonindustrial country that is seeking to develop its resources by industrialization.

deviate v. differ from others in belief or thought; turn aside from a course of action. —**deviation** n. —**deviant** n., adj. (person) deviating from what is considered acceptable behaviour. —**deviance** n.

device n. machine or tool used for a specific task; scheme or trick.

devil n. evil spirit; person regarded as wicked; person, e.g. *poor devil;* person regarded as daring; *Informal* something difficult or annoying. —v. -**illing**, -**illed**. prepare (food) with a highly flavoured spiced mixture; do routine literary work, esp. for a lawyer or author. —**the Devil** *Christianity* chief spirit of evil and enemy of God. —**devilish** adj. of or like the devil. —adv. (also **devilishly**) *Informal* extremely. —**devilment** n. mischievous conduct. —**devilry** n. reckless fun; wickedness. —**devil-may-care** adj. happy-go-lucky. —**devil's advocate** person who takes an opposing or unpopular point of view for the sake of argument.

THESAURUS

ascertain, certify, check, detect, discover, find out, learn, verify, work out

determined bent on, constant, dogged, firm, fixed, intent, persistent, purposeful, resolute, set on, single-minded, steadfast, tenacious, unflinching, unwavering

deterrent check, curb, discouragement, disincentive, hindrance, impediment, obstacle, restraint

detest abominate, despise, dislike intensely, execrate, hate, loathe

detour bypass, byway, diversion

detract diminish, lessen, lower, reduce, take away from

detriment damage, disservice, harm, hurt, injury, loss, mischief, prejudice

detrimental adverse, baleful, deleterious, destructive, harmful, inimical, injurious, pernicious, prejudicial, unfavourable

devastate demolish, desolate, despoil, destroy, lay waste, level, pillage, plunder, ravage, raze, ruin, sack, spoil, waste, wreck

develop 1. advance, cultivate, evolve, foster, grow, mature, progress, promote, prosper, rip-

en 2. amplify, augment, broaden, dilate upon, elaborate, enlarge, expand, unfold, work out 3. be a direct result of, break out, come about, ensue, follow, happen, result

development 1. advance, advancement, evolution, expansion, growth, improvement, increase, maturity, progress, progression, spread, unfolding 2. change, circumstance, event, happening, incident, issue, occurrence, outcome, result, situation, upshot

deviate avert, bend, deflect, depart, differ, digress, diverge, drift, err, part, stray, swerve, turn, turn aside, vary, veer, wander

deviation alteration, change, deflection, departure, digression, discrepancy, disparity, divergence, inconsistency, irregularity, shift, variance, variation

device 1. apparatus, appliance, contraption, contrivance, gadget, gimmick, implement, instrument, invention, tool, utensil 2. artifice, design, dodge, expedient, gambit, manoeuvre, plan, ploy, project, purpose, ruse, scheme, shift, stratagem, stunt, trick, wile

devil 1. demon, fiend, Satan 2. beast, brute,

DICTIONARY

devious *adj.* not sincere or straightforward; indirect. —**deviously** *adv.* —**deviousness** *n.*

devise *v.* work out (something) in one's mind.

devoid *adj.* (foll. by *of*) destitute (of) or free (from).

devolve *v.* (foll. by *on, upon,* or *to*) pass (power or duties) or (of power or duties) be passed to a successor or substitute. —**devolution** *n.* transfer of authority from a central government to regional governments.

devote *v.* apply or dedicate to some cause. —**devoted** *adj.* feeling loyalty or devotion. —**devotedly** *adv.* —**devotee** [dev-vote-**tee**] *n.* person ardently enthusiastic about something; zealous follower of a religion. —**devotion** *n.* strong affection for or loyalty to a cause or person; religious zeal or piety. —*pl.* prayers. —**devotional** *adj.*

devour *v.* eat up greedily; engulf and destroy; read or look at avidly. —**devouring** *adj.*

devout *adj.* deeply religious. —**devoutly** *adv.*

dew *n.* drops of water condensed on a cool surface at night from vapour in the air. —**dewy** *adj.*

dewclaw *n.* nonfunctional claw on a dog's leg.

dewlap *n.* loose fold of skin hanging under the throat in dogs, cattle, etc.

dexterity *n.* skill in using one's hands; mental quickness. —**dexterous** *adj.* —**dexterously** *adv.*

dextrose *n.* glucose occurring in fruit, honey, and the blood of animals.

dg decigram.

DH Department of Health.

diabetes [die-a-**beet**-eez] *n.* disorder in which an abnormal amount of urine containing an excess of sugar is excreted. —**diabetic** *n., adj.*

diabolic *adj.* of the devil; extremely cruel. —**diabolical** *adj. Informal* extremely bad. —**diabolically** *adv.* —**diabolism** *n.* witchcraft, devil worship.

diaconate *n.* position or period of office of a deacon. —**diaconal** *adj.*

diacritic *n.* sign above or below a letter or character to indicate phonetic value or stress.

diadem *n. Old-fashioned* crown.

diaeresis *n., pl.* -**ses.** same as DIERESIS.

diagnosis [die-ag-**no**-siss] *n., pl.* -**ses** [-seez]. discovery and identification of diseases from the examination of symptoms. —**diagnose** *v.* —**diagnostic** *adj.*

diagonal *adj.* from corner to corner; slanting. —*n.* diagonal line. —**diagonally** *adv.*

diagram *n.* sketch demonstrating the form or workings of something. —**diagrammatic** *adj.* —**diagrammatically** *adv.*

dial *n.* face of a clock or watch; graduated disc on a measuring instrument; control on a radio or television used to change the station; numbered disc on the front of some telephones. —*v.* **dialling, dialled.** try to establish a telephone connection with (someone) by operating the dial or buttons on a telephone.

dialect *n.* form of a language spoken in a particular area. —**dialectal** *adj.*

dialectic *n.* logical debate by question and

THESAURUS

demon, monster, ogre, rogue, savage, terror, villain

devilish accursed, damnable, detestable, diabolic, diabolical, fiendish, hellish, infernal, satanic, wicked

devious calculating, deceitful, dishonest, evasive, indirect, insidious, insincere, scheming, sly, surreptitious, treacherous, tricky, underhand, wily

devise arrange, conceive, concoct, construct, contrive, design, dream up, form, formulate, frame, imagine, invent, plan, plot, prepare, project, scheme, think up, work out

devoid barren, bereft, deficient, denuded, destitute, empty, free from, lacking, unprovided with, vacant, void, wanting, without

devote allot, apply, appropriate, assign, commit, concern oneself, dedicate, enshrine, give, pledge, reserve

devoted ardent, caring, committed, concerned, constant, dedicated, devout, faithful, fond, loving, loyal, staunch, steadfast, true

devour bolt, consume, cram, eat, gobble, gorge, gulp, guzzle, stuff, swallow, wolf

devout godly, holy, orthodox, pious, prayerful, pure, religious, reverent, saintly

dexterity adroitness, artistry, deftness, expertise, facility, finesse, handiness, knack, mastery, neatness, proficiency, skill, smoothness, touch

diagnose analyse, determine, distinguish, identify, interpret, pinpoint, pronounce, recognize

diagnosis 1. analysis, examination 2. conclusion, interpretation, opinion

diagonal *adj.* angled, cross, crossways, crosswise, oblique, slanting

diagonally aslant, at an angle, crosswise, obliquely

diagram chart, drawing, figure, layout, outline, plan, representation, sketch

dialect accent, idiom, jargon, language, patois, pronunciation, provincialism, speech, tongue, vernacular

DICTIONARY

answer to resolve differences between two views. **—dialectical** adj.

dialogue n. conversation between two people; discussion between representatives of two nations or groups.

dialysis [die-**al**-iss-iss] n. Med. filtering of blood through a membrane to remove waste products.

diamanté [die-a-**man**-tee] adj. decorated with artificial jewels or sequins.

diameter n. (length of) a straight line through the centre of a circle or sphere. **—diametrically** adv. completely, e.g. diametrically opposed.

diamond n. usually colourless, exceptionally hard precious stone; Geom. figure with four sides of equal length forming two acute and two obtuse angles; playing card marked with red diamond-shaped symbols. **—diamond wedding** sixtieth anniversary of a wedding.

diaper n. US nappy.

diaphanous [die-**af**-fan-ous] adj. fine and almost transparent.

diaphragm [die-a-fram] n. muscular partition that separates the abdominal cavity and chest cavity; contraceptive device placed over the neck of the womb.

diarrhoea [die-a-ree-a] n. frequent discharge of abnormally liquid faeces.

diary n., pl. **-ries.** (book for a) record of daily events, appointments, or observations. **—diarist** n.

diatribe n. bitter critical attack.

dibble n. small hand tool used to make holes in the ground for seeds or plants.

dice n., pl. **dice.** small cube each of whose sides has a different number of spots (1 to 6), used in games of chance. —v. cut (food) into small cubes. **—dice with death** take a risk. **—dicey** adj. Informal dangerous or risky.

dichotomy [die-**kot**-a-mee] n., pl. **-mies.** division into two opposed groups or parts.

dicky[1] n., pl. **dickies.** false shirt front. **—dicky-bird** n. child's word for a bird.

dicky[2] adj. **dickier, dickiest.** Informal shaky or weak, e.g. a dicky heart.

Dictaphone n. ® tape recorder for recording dictation for subsequent typing.

dictate v. say aloud for another person to transcribe; give (commands) authoritatively. —n. authoritative command; guiding principle. **—dictation** n. **—dictator** n. ruler who has complete power; tyrannical person. **—dictatorship** n. **—dictatorial** adj. like a dictator, tyrannical. **—dictatorially** adv.

diction n. manner of pronouncing words and sounds.

dictionary n., pl. **-aries.** book that consists of an alphabetical list of words with their meanings; reference book listing terms and giving information about a particular subject.

dictum n., pl. **-tums, -ta.** formal statement; popular saying.

did v. past tense of DO.

didactic adj. intended to instruct. **—didactically** adv.

diddle v. Brit. informal swindle.

didn't did not.

die[1] v. **dying, died.** (of a person, animal, or plant) cease all biological activity permanently; (of something inanimate) cease to exist or function. **—be dying for** Informal be eager for. **—die-hard** n. person who resists change.

die[2] n. shaped block used to cut or form metal; casting mould.

dieresis [die-**air**-iss-iss] n., pl. **-ses** [-seez]. mark (¨) placed over a vowel to show that it is pronounced separately from the preceding one, as in Noël.

diesel n. diesel engine; vehicle driven by a diesel engine; Informal diesel oil. **—diesel engine** internal-combustion engine in which oil is ignited by compression. **—diesel oil** fuel obtained from petroleum distillation.

diet[1] n. food that a person or animal regularly eats; specific allowance of food, to control

THESAURUS

dialogue communication, conference, conversation, converse, discourse, discussion, interlocution

diary appointment book, chronicle, daily record, day-to-day account, engagement book, journal

dicky adj. fluttery, queer, shaky, unreliable, unsound, unsteady, weak

dictate 1. read out, say, speak, transmit, utter 2. command, decree, direct, enjoin, impose, lay down, ordain, order, prescribe

dictator absolute ruler, autocrat, despot, oppressor, tyrant

diction articulation, delivery, elocution, enunciation, inflection, intonation, pronunciation, speech

dictionary concordance, encyclopedia, glossary, lexicon, vocabulary, wordbook

die 1. decease, depart, expire, finish, pass away, perish 2. decay, decline, disappear, dwindle, ebb, end, fade, lapse, pass, sink, vanish, wane, wilt, wither 3. break down, fail, fizzle out, halt, lose power, peter out, run down, stop

die-hard fanatic, old fogy, reactionary, zealot

DICTIONARY

weight or for health reasons. —*v.* follow a special diet so as to lose weight. —**dietary** *adj.* —**dietary fibre** fibrous substances in fruit and vegetables that aid digestion. —**dieter** *n.* —**dietetic** *adj.* prepared for special dietary requirements. —**dietetics** *pl. n.* study of food intake and preparation. —**dietician** *n.* person who specializes in dietetics.

diet[2] *n.* parliament of some countries.

differ *v.* be unlike; disagree. —**difference** *n.* state or quality of being unlike; disagreement; remainder left after subtraction. —**different** *adj.* unlike; unusual. —**differently** *adv.*

differential *adj.* of or using a difference; *Maths* involving differentials. —*n.* factor that differentiates between two comparable things; *Maths* slight difference between values in a scale; difference between rates of pay for different types of labour. —**differential calculus** branch of calculus concerned with derivatives and differentials. —**differential gear** mechanism in a road vehicle that allows one driving wheel to rotate faster than the other when cornering. —**differentiate** *v.* perceive or show the difference (between); make (one thing) distinct from other such things; *Maths* determine the derivative of (a function or variable). —**differentiation** *n.*

difficult *adj.* requiring effort or skill to do or understand; not easily pleased. —**difficulty** *n.*

diffident *adj.* lacking self-confidence. —**diffidence** *n.* —**diffidently** *adv.*

diffract *v.* cause to undergo diffraction. —**diffraction** *n.* *Physics* deviation in the direction of a wave at the edge of an obstacle in its path; formation of light and dark fringes by the passage of light through a small aperture.

diffuse *v.* spread in all directions. —*adj.* widely spread; lacking conciseness. —**diffusely** *adv.* —**diffusion** *n.*

dig *v.* **digging, dug.** (often foll. by *up*) cut into, break up, and turn over or remove (earth etc.), esp. with a spade; (foll. by *out* or *up*) find by effort or searching; (foll. by *in* or *into*) thrust or jab. —*n.* act of digging; thrust or poke; cutting remark; archaeological excavation. —*pl. Informal* lodgings. —**digger** *n.* machine used for digging.

digest *v.* subject to a process of digestion; absorb mentally. —*n.* methodical compilation of information, often a condensed one. —**digestible** *adj.* —**digestion** *n.* process of breaking down food into easily absorbed substances. —**digestive** *adj.* —**digestive biscuit** biscuit made from wholemeal flour.

digit [dij-it] *n.* finger or toe; numeral from 0 to 9. —**digital** *adj.* displaying information as numbers rather than with a dial, e.g. *digital clock.* —**digi-**

THESAURUS

diet[1] *n.* 1. abstinence, dietary, fast, regime, regimen 2. commons, fare, food, nourishment, provisions, rations, subsistence, sustenance, viands, victuals ~*v.* 3. fast, lose weight, reduce, slim

diet[2] chamber, congress, council, legislature, meeting, parliament, sitting

differ be dissimilar, be distinct, contradict, contrast, depart from, diverge, run counter to, stand apart, vary

difference 1. alteration, change, contrast, deviation, differentiation, discrepancy, disparity, dissimilarity, distinction, divergence, diversity, unlikeness, variation, variety 2. distinction, exception, idiosyncrasy, peculiarity, singularity 3. argument, clash, conflict, contention, contretemps, controversy, debate, disagreement, discordance, dispute, quarrel, strife, tiff, wrangle

different 1. altered, at variance, changed, clashing, contrasting, deviating, disparate, dissimilar, divergent, inconsistent, opposed, unlike 2. assorted, diverse, manifold, many, miscellaneous, multifarious, numerous, several, some, sundry, varied, various

differentiate contrast, discern, discriminate, distinguish, mark off, separate, tell apart

difficult 1. arduous, demanding, formidable, hard, laborious, onerous, painful, strenuous, toilsome, uphill, wearisome 2. fastidious, fractious, fussy, hard to please, obstreperous, perverse, refractory, rigid, tiresome, troublesome, trying, unmanageable

difficulty awkwardness, hardship, labour, pain, painfulness, strain, tribulation

diffident backward, bashful, constrained, doubtful, hesitant, insecure, meek, modest, reluctant, reserved, self-conscious, sheepish, shrinking, shy, suspicious, timid, timorous, unobtrusive, unsure, withdrawn

dig *v.* 1. break up, burrow, delve, excavate, grub, hoe, hollow out, mine, penetrate, pierce, quarry, scoop, till, tunnel, turn over 2. delve, dig down, go into, investigate, probe, research, search ~*n.* 3. jab, poke, prod, punch, thrust 4. cutting remark, gibe, insult, jeer, quip, taunt, wisecrack (*Inf.*)

digest 1. absorb, assimilate, concoct, dissolve, incorporate 2. absorb, assimilate, consider, contemplate, grasp, master, meditate, ponder, study, take in, understand

digestion assimilation, conversion, incorporation, transformation

DICTIONARY

tal **recording** sound-recording process that converts audio or analogue signals into a series of pulses. —**digitally** adv. —**digitate** adj. (of animals) having digits.

digitalis n. drug made from foxglove leaves, used as a heart stimulant.

dignity n., pl. **-ties.** serious, calm, and controlled behaviour or manner; quality of being worthy of honour; sense of self-importance. —**dignify** v. **-fying, -fied.** give dignity to. —**dignitary** n. person of high official position.

digress v. depart from the main subject in speech or writing. —**digression** n. —**digressive** adj.

dike n. same as DYKE.

dilapidated adj. (of a building) having fallen into ruin. —**dilapidation** n.

dilate v. make or become wider or larger. —**dilation, dilatation** n.

dilatory [dill-a-tree] adj. tending or intended to waste time.

dildo n., pl. **-dos.** object used as a substitute for an erect penis.

dilemma n. situation offering a choice between two equally undesirable alternatives.

dilettante [dill-it-**tan**-tee] n. person whose interest in a subject, esp. art, is superficial rather than serious. —**dilettantism** n.

diligent adj. careful and persevering in carrying out duties; carried out with care and perseverance. —**diligently** adv. —**diligence** n.

dill n. sweet-smelling herb used for flavouring.

dilly-dally v. **-lying, -lied.** Informal dawdle or waste time.

dilute v. make (a liquid) less concentrated, esp. by adding water; make (a quality etc.) weaker in force. —**dilution** n.

diluvial, diluvian adj. of a flood, esp. the great Flood described in the Old Testament.

dim adj. **dimmer, dimmest.** badly illuminated; not clearly seen; mentally dull. —v. **dimming, dimmed.** make or become dim. —**take a dim view of** disapprove of. —**dimly** adv. —**dimness** n. —**dimmer** n. device for dimming an electric light.

dime n. coin of the US and Canada, worth ten cents.

dimension n. measurement of the size of something in a particular direction; scope.

diminish v. make or become smaller, fewer, or less. —**diminution** n. —**diminutive** adj. very small. —n. word or affix which implies smallness or unimportance. —**diminutiveness** n.

diminuendo n. Music gradual decrease in loudness.

dimple n. small natural dent, esp. in the cheeks or chin. —v. produce dimples by smiling.

din n. loud discordant confused noise. —v. **dinning, dinned.** instil (something) into someone by constant repetition.

dinar [dee-nahr] n. monetary unit of Yugoslavia and various Middle Eastern and North African countries.

dine v. eat dinner. —**diner** n. person eating a meal; US small cheap restaurant. —**dining car**

THESAURUS

dignified august, distinguished, exalted, formal, grave, honourable, imposing, lofty, lordly, noble, solemn, stately

dignitary notability, notable, personage, public figure, V.I.P., worthy

dignity courtliness, decorum, grandeur, gravity, hauteur, loftiness, majesty, nobility, propriety, solemnity, stateliness

digress depart, deviate, diverge, drift, expatiate, ramble, stray, turn aside, wander

dilapidated battered, broken-down, crumbling, decayed, decaying, decrepit, fallen in, falling apart, in ruins, neglected, ramshackle, rickety, ruined, run-down, shabby, shaky, tumbledown, uncared for, worn-out

dilemma difficulty, embarrassment, mess, perplexity, plight, predicament, problem, puzzle, quandary, spot (Inf.), strait

diligence activity, application, assiduity, attention, attentiveness, care, constancy, industry, perseverance

diligent active, assiduous, attentive, busy, careful, conscientious, constant, earnest, hardworking, indefatigable, industrious, laborious, persevering, persistent, studious, tireless

dilute v. adulterate, cut, thin (out), water down, weaken

dim adj. 1. cloudy, dark, darkish, dusky, grey, overcast, poorly lit, shadowy 2. bleary, blurred, faint, fuzzy, ill-defined, indistinct, obscured, shadowy, unclear 3. dense, doltish, dull, obtuse, slow, stupid, thick ~v. 4. blur, cloud, darken, dull, fade, lower, obscure, tarnish, turn down

diminish abate, contract, curtail, cut, decrease, lessen, lower, reduce, retrench, shrink, weaken

diminutive bantam, little, midget, miniature, minute, petite, pygmy, small, tiny, wee

din babel, clamour, clangour, clash, clatter, commotion, crash, hullabaloo, noise, outcry, pandemonium, racket, row, shout, uproar

dine banquet, eat, feast, lunch, sup

DICTIONARY

railway coach in which meals are served. —**dining room** room where meals are eaten.

dinghy [**ding**-ee] *n., pl.* **-ghies.** small boat, powered by sails, oars, or an outboard motor.

dingle *n.* small wooded dell.

dingo *n., pl.* **-goes.** wild dog of Australia.

dingy [**din**-jee] *adj.* **-gier, -giest.** dirty-looking, dull. —**dinginess** *n.*

dinkum *adj. Aust. & NZ informal* genuine or right.

dinky *adj.* **-kier, -kiest.** *Brit. informal* small and neat.

dinner *n.* main meal of the day, taken either in the evening or at midday; official banquet. —**dinner jacket** man's semiformal evening jacket, usu. black.

dinosaur *n.* extinct prehistoric reptile, often of gigantic size.

dint *n.* —**by dint of** by means of.

diocese [**die**-a-siss] *n.* district under the jurisdiction of a bishop. —**diocesan** *adj.*

diode *n.* semiconductor device for converting alternating current to direct current.

dioptre [die-**op**-ter] *n.* unit for measuring the refractive power of a lens.

dioxide *n.* oxide containing two oxygen atoms per molecule.

dip *v.* **dipping, dipped.** plunge quickly or briefly into a liquid; slope downwards; switch (car headlights) from the main to the lower beam; lower briefly. —*n.* act of dipping; brief swim; liquid chemical in which farm animals are dipped to rid them of insects; depression, esp. in a landscape; creamy mixture into which pieces of food are dipped before being eaten. —**dip into** *v.* read passages at random from (a book or journal).

diphtheria [dif-**theer**-ya] *n.* contagious disease producing fever and difficulty in breathing and swallowing.

diphthong *n.* union of two vowel sounds in a single compound sound.

diploma *n.* document conferring a qualification or recording successful completion of a course of study.

diplomacy *n.* conduct of the relations between nations by peaceful means; tact or skill in dealing with people. —**diplomat** *n.* official engaged in diplomacy. —**diplomatic** *adj.* of or relating to diplomacy; tactful in dealing with people. —**diplomatically** *adv.*

dipper *n.* ladle used for dipping; kind of river bird.

dipsomania *n.* compulsive craving for alcohol. —**dipsomaniac** *n., adj.*

diptych [**dip**-tik] *n.* painting on two hinged panels.

dire *adj.* desperate or urgent; indicating disaster.

direct *v.* conduct or control the affairs of; give orders with authority to (a person or group); tell (someone) the way to a place; address (a letter, package, remarks, etc.); provide guidance to (actors, cameramen, etc.) in (a play or film). —*adj.* without evasion, straightforward; (of a route) shortest, straight; without anyone or anything intervening; honest, frank. —*adv.* in a direct manner. —**directly** *adv.* in a direct manner; at once. —*conj.* as soon as. —**directness** *n.* —**direction** *n.* course or line along which a person or thing moves, points, or lies; management or guidance. —*pl.* instructions for doing something or for reaching a place. —**directional** *adj.* —**directive** *n.* instruction, order. —**director** *n.* person or thing that directs or controls; member of the governing board of a business etc.; person responsible for the artistic and technical aspects of the making of a film etc. —**directorial** *adj.* —**directorship** *n.* —**directorate** *n.* board of directors; position of director. —**directory** *n.* book listing names, addresses, and telephone numbers of individuals and firms.

THESAURUS

dingy colourless, dark, dim, dirty, discoloured, drab, dreary, dull, dusky, faded, gloomy, grimy, murky, obscure, seedy, shabby, soiled, sombre

dinner banquet, collation, feast, meal, refection, repast, spread

dip *v.* 1. bathe, douse, duck, dunk, immerse, plunge, rinse, souse 2. *With* **in** *or* **into** draw upon, reach into ~*n.* 3. douche, drenching, ducking, immersion, plunge, soaking 4. bathe, dive, plunge, swim 5. concoction, dilution, infusion, mixture, preparation, solution, suspension 6. basin, concavity, depression, hole, hollow, incline, slope

diplomacy 1. statecraft, statesmanship 2. craft, delicacy, discretion, finesse, savoir faire, skill, subtlety, tact

diplomat go-between, mediator, moderator, negotiator, politician

diplomatic adept, discreet, polite, politic, prudent, sensitive, subtle, tactful

dire 1. alarming, awful, calamitous, cataclysmic, cruel, disastrous, horrible, ruinous, terrible, woeful 2. dismal, dreadful, fearful, gloomy, grim, ominous, portentous

direct *v.* 1. administer, advise, conduct, control, dispose, govern, guide, handle, lead, manage, oversee, preside over, regulate, rule, run,

DICTIONARY

dirge *n.* slow sad song of mourning.

dirigible [**dir**-rij-jib-bl] *adj.* able to be steered. —*n.* airship.

dirk *n.* dagger, formerly worn by Scottish Highlanders.

dirndl *n.* (dress with) full gathered skirt.

dirt *n.* unclean substance, filth; loose earth or soil; obscene speech or behaviour; *Informal* scandal, harmful gossip. —**dirt track** racetrack made of packed earth or cinders.

dirty *adj.* **dirtier, dirtiest.** covered or marked with dirt; obscene; unfair or dishonest. —*v.* **dirtying, dirtied.** make dirty. —**dirtiness** *n.*

dis- *prefix* indicating: reversal, e.g. *disconnect;* negation or lack, e.g. *dissimilar, disgrace;* removal or release, e.g. *disembowel.*

disable *v.* make ineffective, unfit, or incapable, as by crippling. —**disablement** *n.* —**disability** *n.* condition of being physically or mentally impaired; something that disables someone.

disabuse *v.* (foll. by *of*) rid (someone) of a mistaken idea.

disadvantage *n.* unfavourable circumstance, thing, or situation. —**disadvantageous** *adj.* —**disadvantaged** *adj.* socially or economically deprived.

disaffected *adj.* having lost loyalty to or affection for someone or something. —**disaffection** *n.*

disagree *v.* **-greeing, -greed.** have different opinions; fail to correspond; (foll. by *with*) cause physical discomfort (to), e.g. *curry disagrees with me.* —**disagreement** *n.* —**disagreeable** *adj.* (of a person) bad-tempered or disobliging; unpleasant. —**disagreeably** *adv.*

disallow *v.* reject as untrue or invalid.

disappear *v.* cease to be visible; cease to exist. —**disappearance** *n.*

disappoint *v.* fail to meet the expectations or hopes of. —**disappointment** *n.* feeling of being disappointed; person or thing that disappoints.

disapprobation *n.* disapproval.

THESAURUS

superintend, supervise 2. bid, charge, command, dictate, enjoin, instruct, order 3. guide, indicate, lead, show ~*adj.* 4. candid, frank, honest, open, outspoken, plain-spoken, sincere, straight 5. absolute, blunt, categorical, downright, explicit, express, plain, straightforward, unambiguous, unequivocal 6. nonstop, not crooked, shortest, straight, through, unbroken, uninterrupted

direction 1. administration, charge, command, control, government, guidance, leadership, management, order, oversight, supervision 2. aim, bearing, course, line, path, road, route, track, way

directive charge, command, decree, dictate, edict, injunction, instruction, notice, order, ordinance, ruling

directly 1. exactly, precisely, straight, unswervingly 2. candidly, face-to-face, honestly, in person, openly, personally, plainly, pointblank, straightforwardly, truthfully, unequivocally

director administrator, chairman, chief, controller, executive, governor, head, leader, manager, organizer, principal, producer

dirt 1. dust, filth, grime, impurity, mire, muck, mud, slime, smudge, stain, tarnish 2. clay, earth, loam, soil

dirty 1. filthy, foul, grimy, grubby, messy, mucky, muddy, nasty, polluted, soiled, sullied, unclean 2. corrupt, crooked, dishonest, fraudulent, illegal, treacherous, unfair, unscrupulous, unsporting

disability affliction, ailment, defect, disorder, handicap, impairment, infirmity, malady

disable cripple, damage, handicap, immobilize, impair, incapacitate, paralyse, prostrate, unfit, unman, weaken

disadvantage damage, detriment, disservice, harm, hurt, injury, loss, prejudice

disagree 1. be discordant, be dissimilar, conflict, contradict, counter, depart, deviate, differ, diverge, vary 2. argue, bicker, clash, contend, contest, debate, dispute, dissent, object, oppose, quarrel, take issue with, wrangle

disagreeable bad-tempered, brusque, churlish, contrary, cross, difficult, disobliging, ill-natured, irritable, nasty, peevish, rude, surly, unfriendly, ungracious, unlikable, unpleasant

disagreement 1. difference, discrepancy, disparity, dissimilarity, divergence, diversity, incompatibility, incongruity, variance 2. argument, clash, conflict, debate, difference, discord, dispute, dissent, division, falling out, quarrel, squabble, strife, wrangle

disappear 1. be lost to view, depart, drop out of sight, ebb, escape, fade away, flee, fly, go, pass, recede, retire, wane, withdraw 2. cease, die out, dissolve, end, evaporate, expire, fade, pass away, perish, vanish

disappearance departure, desertion, eclipse, evanescence, evaporation, fading, flight, loss, passing, vanishing

disappoint dash, deceive, disenchant, dishearten, disillusion, dismay, dissatisfy, fail, let down, sadden, vex

DICTIONARY

disapprove v. (foll. by *of*) consider wrong or bad. —**disapproval** n.

disarm v. deprive of weapons; win the confidence or affection of; (of a nation) decrease the size of one's armed forces. —**disarmament** n. —**disarming** adj. removing hostility or suspicion. —**disarmingly** adv.

disarrange v. throw into disorder. —**disarrangement** n.

disarray n. confusion and lack of discipline; extreme untidiness.

disaster n. occurrence that causes great distress or destruction; project etc. that fails. —**disastrous** adj. —**disastrously** adv.

disavow v. deny connection with or responsibility for (something). —**disavowal** n.

disband v. (cause to) cease to function as a group or unit.

disbelieve v. reject as false; (foll. by *in*) have no faith (in). —**disbelief** n.

disburse v. pay out. —**disbursement** n.

disc n. flat circular object; gramophone record; *Anat.* circular flat structure in the body, esp. between the vertebrae; *Computers* same as DISK. —**disc jockey** person who introduces and plays pop records on a radio programme or at a disco.

discard v. get rid of (something or someone) as useless or undesirable.

discern v. see or be aware of (something) clearly. —**discernible** adj. —**discerning** adj. having or showing good judgment. —**discernment** n.

discharge v. release, allow to go; dismiss (someone) from duty or employment; fire (a gun); pour forth, emit; meet the demands of (an obligation etc.); relieve oneself of (a responsibility or debt). —n. something that is discharged; dismissal from duty or employment; pouring forth of a fluid, emission.

disciple [diss-**sipe**-pl] n. follower of the doctrines of a teacher, esp. Jesus Christ.

discipline n. training imposed for the improvement of physical powers, self-control, etc.; state of improved behaviour resulting from such training; punishment; branch of learning. —v. (attempt to) improve the behaviour of (oneself or another) by training or rules; punish. —**disciplinarian** n. person who practises strict discipline. —**disciplinary** adj.

disclaim v. deny (responsibility for or knowledge of something). —**disclaimer** n. repudiation, denial.

THESAURUS

disappointment discontent, discouragement, disenchantment, disillusionment, displeasure, dissatisfaction, distress, failure, frustration, mortification, regret

disapproval censure, condemnation, criticism, deprecation, disapprobation, displeasure, dissatisfaction

disapprove *Often with* of blame, censure, condemn, deplore, deprecate, dislike, frown on, object to, reject

disarrange confuse, derange, discompose, disorder, disorganize, disturb, scatter, shake, shuffle, unsettle, untidy

disarray 1. confusion, dismay, disorder, disunity, indiscipline, unruliness, upset 2. chaos, clutter, jumble, mess, mix-up, muddle, shambles, tangle, untidiness

disaster accident, adversity, blow, calamity, catastrophe, misadventure, mischance, misfortune, mishap, reverse, ruin, stroke, tragedy, trouble

disastrous adverse, catastrophic, destructive, detrimental, devastating, dire, dreadful, fatal, hapless, harmful, ill-fated, ill-starred, ruinous, terrible, tragic, unfortunate, unlucky

disbelief distrust, doubt, dubiety, incredulity, mistrust, scepticism, unbelief

discard abandon, cast aside, dispense with, dispose of, ditch (*Sl.*), drop, get rid of, jettison, reject, relinquish, remove, repudiate, scrap, shed

discharge v. 1. absolve, acquit, allow to go, clear, free, liberate, pardon, release, set free ~n. 2. acquittal, clearance, liberation, pardon, release, remittance ~v. 3. discard, dismiss, expel, oust 4. detonate, explode, fire, let off, set off, shoot ~n. 5. blast, burst, discharging, explosion, firing, report, salvo, shot, volley ~v. 6. accomplish, carry out, do, execute, fulfil, observe, perform 7. clear, honour, meet, pay, relieve, satisfy, settle, square up

disciple apostle, believer, convert, devotee, follower, learner, partisan, proselyte, pupil, student, supporter

disciplinarian despot, martinet, stickler, taskmaster, tyrant

discipline n. 1. drill, exercise, method, practice, regulation 2. conduct, control, orderliness, regulation, restraint, strictness 3. chastisement, correction, punishment ~v. break in, bring up, check, control, drill, educate, exercise, form, govern, instruct, prepare, regulate, restrain, train

disclose broadcast, communicate, confess, divulge, impart, leak, let slip, make known, make public, publish, relate, reveal, tell, unveil, utter

DICTIONARY

disclose v. make known; allow to be seen.
—**disclosure** n.

disco n., pl. **-cos.** occasion at which people
dance to pop records; place where such dances
are held; mobile equipment for providing music
for a disco.

discolour v. change in colour, stain. —**discoloration** n.

discomfit v. make uneasy or confused. —**discomfiture** n.

discomfort n. inconvenience, distress, or mild
pain.

discommode v. cause inconvenience to.
—**discommodious** adj.

disconcert v. disturb the confidence or self-
possession of.

disconnect v. undo or break the connection
between (two things); stop the supply of (electricity or gas) of. —**disconnected** adj. (of speech
or ideas) not logically connected. —**disconnection** n.

disconsolate adj. sad beyond comfort. —**dis-
consolately** adv.

discontent n. lack of contentment, as with
one's lot in life. —**discontented** adj. —**discon-
tentedly** adv.

discontinue v. **-uing, -ued.** come or bring to an
end. —**discontinuous** adj. characterized by in-
terruptions. —**discontinuity** n. lack of smooth or
unbroken development.

discord n. lack of agreement or harmony between people; harsh confused sounds. —**discordant** adj. —**discordance** n.

discotheque n. full name for DISCO.

discount v. leave (something) out of account as
being unreliable, prejudiced, or irrelevant; deduct (an amount) from the price of something.
—n. deduction from the full price of something.

discourage v. deprive of the will to persist in
something; oppose by expressing disapproval.
—**discouragement** n.

discourse n. conversation; formal treatment of
a subject in speech or writing. —v. (foll. by *on*)
speak or write (about) at length.

discourteous adj. showing bad manners.
—**discourteously** adv. —**discourtesy** n.

discover v. be the first to find or to find out
about; learn about for the first time; find after
study or search. —**discoverer** n. —**discovery** n.
act of discovering; person, place, or thing that
has been discovered.

discredit v. damage the reputation of (someone); cause (an idea) to be disbelieved or dis-
trusted. —n. (something that causes) damage to

THESAURUS

discolour fade, mar, mark, rust, soil, stain,
streak, tarnish, tinge

discomfort ache, annoyance, disquiet, distress,
hardship, hurt, irritation, nuisance, pain,
soreness, trouble, uneasiness, vexation

disconcert abash, agitate, bewilder, discompose, disturb, flurry, fluster, nonplus, perplex,
perturb, rattle (*Inf.*), ruffle, take aback, trouble, unbalance, unsettle, upset, worry

disconnect cut off, detach, divide, part, separate, sever, take apart, uncouple

disconsolate dejected, desolate, despairing,
forlorn, gloomy, heartbroken, hopeless, inconsolable, melancholy, miserable, sad, unhappy,
wretched

discontinue abandon, break off, cease, drop,
end, finish, give up, halt, interrupt, leave off,
pause, put an end to, quit, refrain from, stop,
suspend, terminate

discord 1. clashing, conflict, contention, difference, dispute, dissension, disunity, division,
friction, opposition, rupture, strife, variance,
wrangling 2. cacophony, din, dissonance,
harshness, jangle, jarring

discount v. 1. disbelieve, disregard, ignore,
overlook, pass over 2. lower, mark down, rebate, reduce, take off ~n. 3. allowance, concession, cut, cut price, deduction, rebate, reduction

discourage abash, awe, cast down, damp,
dampen, dash, daunt, deject, demoralize, depress, dishearten, dismay, frighten, intimidate, overawe, scare, unnerve

discouragement dejection, depression, despair,
despondency, disappointment, dismay, hopelessness, low spirits, pessimism

discourse 1. n. chat, communication, conversation, converse, dialogue, discussion, speech,
talk 2. v. confer, converse, debate, declaim,
discuss, speak, talk

discourteous abrupt, bad-mannered, brusque,
curt, ill-mannered, impolite, insolent, offhand, rude, uncivil, ungentlemanly, ungracious, unmannerly

discover 1. come across, come upon, dig up,
find, light upon, locate, turn up, uncover,
unearth 2. ascertain, descry, detect, determine, discern, disclose, espy, find out, learn,
notice, perceive, realize, recognize, reveal, see,
spot, uncover

discovery 1. ascertainment, detection, disclosure, exploration, finding, introduction, location, origination, revelation 2. breakthrough,
coup, find, findings, innovation, invention,
secret

DICTIONARY

someone's reputation. **—discreditable** *adj.* bringing discredit.

discreet *adj.* careful to avoid embarrassment, esp. by keeping confidences secret; unobtrusive. **—discreetly** *adv.*

discrepancy *n., pl.* **-cies.** conflict or variation between facts, figures, or claims.

discrete *adj.* separate or distinct.

discretion [diss-**kresh**-on] *n.* quality of behaving in a discreet way; freedom or authority to make judgments and to act as one sees fit. **—discretionary** *adj.*

discriminate *v.* (foll. by *against* or *in favour of*) single out a particular person or group for special disfavour or favour; (foll. by *between* or *among*) recognize or understand the difference (between). **—discriminating** *adj.* showing good taste and judgment. **—discrimination** *n.* **—discriminatory** *adj.* based on prejudice.

discursive *adj.* passing from one topic to another.

discus *n.* disc-shaped object with a heavy middle, thrown in sports competitions.

discuss *v.* consider (something) by talking it over; treat (a subject) in speech or writing. **—discussion** *n.*

disdain *n.* feeling of superiority and dislike. *—v.*

refuse with disdain. **—disdainful** *adj.* **—disdainfully** *adv.*

disease *n.* illness, sickness. **—diseased** *adj.*

disembark *v.* (cause to) land from a ship, aircraft, or bus. **—disembarkation** *n.*

disembodied *adj.* lacking a body; seeming not to be attached to or coming from anyone.

disembowel *v.* **-elling, -elled.** remove the entrails of.

disenchanted *adj.* disappointed and disillusioned (with something). **—disenchantment** *n.*

disenfranchise *v.* deprive (a person) of the right to vote or of other rights of citizenship.

disengage *v.* release from a connection. **—disengagement** *n.*

disentangle *v.* release from entanglement or confusion. **—disentanglement** *n.*

disfavour *n.* disapproval or dislike.

disfigure *v.* spoil the appearance or shape of. **—disfigurement** *n.*

disfranchise *v.* same as DISENFRANCHISE.

disgorge *v.* vomit; discharge (contents).

disgrace *n.* condition of shame, loss of reputation, or dishonour; shameful person or thing. *—v.* bring shame upon (oneself or others). **—disgraceful** *adj.* **—disgracefully** *adv.*

THESAURUS

discreet careful, cautious, circumspect, considerate, diplomatic, discerning, guarded, judicious, politic, prudent, reserved, tactful, wary

discrepancy conflict, difference, disagreement, disparity, dissimilarity, dissonance, divergence, incongruity, inconsistency, variance, variation

discretion acumen, care, carefulness, caution, consideration, diplomacy, discernment, good sense, judgment, maturity, prudence, sagacity, tact, wariness

discriminate 1. favour, show bias, show prejudice, single out, treat differently, victimize 2. assess, differentiate, discern, distinguish, evaluate, separate, sift

discriminating acute, astute, critical, cultivated, discerning, fastidious, keen, particular, refined, selective, sensitive, tasteful

discrimination bias, bigotry, favouritism, inequity, intolerance, prejudice, unfairness

discuss argue, confer, consider, converse, debate, deliberate, examine, go into, review, sift, thrash out, ventilate

discussion analysis, argument, colloquy, conference, consideration, consultation, conversation, debate, deliberation, dialogue, discourse, examination, exchange, review, scrutiny, symposium

disdain *n.* arrogance, contempt, derision, dislike, hauteur, indifference, scorn, sneering

disease affliction, ailment, complaint, condition, disorder, ill health, illness, indisposition, infection, infirmity, malady, sickness, upset

diseased infected, rotten, sick, sickly, tainted, unhealthy, unsound, unwell

disembark alight, arrive, get off, go ashore, land

disengage disentangle, ease, extricate, free, liberate, loosen, release, set free, unloose, untie

disentangle detach, disengage, extricate, free, loose, separate, sever, unfold, unravel, unsnarl, untangle, untwist

disfavour disapprobation, disapproval, dislike, displeasure

disfigure blemish, damage, deface, deform, distort, injure, maim, mutilate, scar

disgorge belch, discharge, eject, empty, expel, regurgitate, spew, spit up, spout, throw up, vomit

disgrace *n.* 1. baseness, degradation, dishonour, disrepute, ignominy, infamy, odium, opprobrium, shame 2. aspersion, blemish, blot, defamation, reproach, scandal, slur, stain, stigma 3. contempt, discredit, disesteem, disfavour, obloquy ~*v.* 4. abase, bring shame

DICTIONARY

disgruntled *adj.* sulky or discontented. —**disgruntlement** *n.*

disguise *v.* change the appearance or manner in order to conceal the identity of (someone or something); misrepresent (something) in order to obscure its actual nature or meaning. —*n.* mask, costume, or manner that disguises; state of being disguised.

disgust *v.* sicken, fill with loathing. —*n.* great loathing or distaste.

dish *n.* shallow container used for holding or serving food; portion or variety of food; *Informal* attractive person. —**dishcloth** *n.* cloth for washing dishes. —**dish out** *v. Informal* distribute. —**dish up** *v. Informal* serve (food).

dishabille [diss-a-**beel**] *n.* state of being partly dressed.

dishearten *v.* weaken or destroy the hope, courage, or enthusiasm of.

dishevelled *adj.* (of a person's hair, clothes, or general appearance) disordered and untidy.

dishonest *adj.* not honest or fair. —**dishonestly** *adv.* —**dishonesty** *n.*

dishonour *v.* treat with disrespect. —*n.* lack of respect; state of shame or disgrace; something that causes a loss of honour. —**dishonourable** *adj.* —**dishonourably** *adv.*

disillusion *v.* destroy the illusions or false ideas of. —*n.* (also **disillusionment**) state of being disillusioned.

disincentive *n.* something that acts as a deterrent.

disinclined *adj.* unwilling. —**disinclination** *n.*

disinfect *v.* rid of harmful germs, esp. by chemical means. —**disinfectant** *n.* substance that destroys harmful germs. —**disinfection** *n.*

disinformation *n.* false information intended to mislead.

disingenuous *adj.* not sincere. —**disingenuously** *adv.*

disinherit *v. Law* deprive (an heir) of inheritance. —**disinheritance** *n.*

disintegrate *v.* break up into fragments. —**disintegration** *n.*

disinter *v.* **-terring, -terred.** dig up; reveal, make known.

disinterested *adj.* free from bias or involvement. —**disinterest** *n.*

THESAURUS

upon, defame, degrade, discredit, disfavour, dishonour, disparage, humiliate, reproach, shame, slur, stain, stigmatize, sully, taint

disgraceful contemptible, degrading, detestable, discreditable, dishonourable, disreputable, ignominious, infamous, low, mean, scandalous, shameful, shocking, unworthy

disgruntled annoyed, discontented, displeased, dissatisfied, grumpy, irritated, malcontent, peeved, peevish, petulant, put out, sulky, sullen, testy, vexed

disguise *v.* 1. cloak, conceal, cover, hide, mask, screen, secrete, shroud, veil 2. deceive, dissemble, dissimulate, fake, falsify, fudge, gloss over, misrepresent ~*n.* 3. cloak, costume, cover, mask, screen, veil

disgust 1. *v.* displease, nauseate, offend, outrage, put off, repel, revolt, sicken 2. *n.* abhorrence, abomination, antipathy, aversion, detestation, dislike, distaste, hatred, loathing, nausea, repugnance, repulsion, revulsion

dish 1. bowl, plate, platter, salver 2. fare, food, recipe

dishearten cast down, crush, damp, dampen, dash, daunt, deject, depress, deter, discourage, dismay, dispirit

dishonest corrupt, crafty, deceitful, deceiving, deceptive, designing, disreputable, double-dealing, false, fraudulent, guileful, lying, mendacious, perfidious, treacherous, unfair, unprincipled, unscrupulous, untrustworthy, untruthful

dishonesty corruption, craft, criminality, crookedness, deceit, duplicity, falsehood, falsity, fraud, fraudulence, graft, improbity, mendacity, perfidy, sharp practice, treachery, trickery, wiliness

dishonour 1. *v.* abase, blacken, corrupt, debase, debauch, defame, degrade, discredit, disgrace, shame, sully 2. *n.* discredit, disfavour, disgrace, disrepute, ignominy, infamy, obloquy, odium, opprobrium, reproach, scandal, shame

dishonourable base, despicable, discreditable, disgraceful, ignoble, infamous, scandalous, shameful

disinclination antipathy, aversion, demur, dislike, hesitance, objection, opposition, reluctance, repugnance, resistance, unwillingness

disinclined antipathetic, averse, indisposed, loath, opposed, reluctant, resistant, unwilling

disinfect clean, cleanse, decontaminate, fumigate, purify, sterilize

disinfectant antiseptic, germicide, sterilizer

disinherit cut off, disown, dispossess, oust, repudiate

disintegrate break up, crumble, disunite, fall apart, fall to pieces, separate, shatter, splinter

disinterest detachment, equity, fairness, impartiality, justice, neutrality

disinterested detached, equitable, even-

DICTIONARY

disjointed *adj.* having no coherence; disconnected.

disk *n. Computers* storage device, consisting of a stack of plates coated with a magnetic layer, which rotates rapidly as a single unit.

dislike *v.* consider unpleasant or disagreeable. —*n.* feeling of not liking something or someone.

dislocate *v.* displace (a bone or joint) from its normal position; disrupt or shift out of place. —**dislocation** *n.*

dislodge *v.* remove (something) from a previously fixed position.

disloyal *adj.* not loyal, deserting one's allegiance. —**disloyalty** *n.*

dismal *adj.* causing gloom or depression; *Informal* of poor quality. —**dismally** *adv.*

dismantle *v.* take apart piece by piece.

dismay *v.* fill with alarm or depression. —*n.* alarm mixed with sadness.

dismember *v.* remove the limbs of; cut to pieces. —**dismemberment** *n.*

dismiss *v.* remove (an employee) from a job; allow (someone) to leave; put out of one's mind; (of a judge) state that (a case) will not be brought to trial. —**dismissal** *n.* —**dismissive** *adj.* scornful, contemptuous.

dismount *v.* get off a horse or bicycle.

disobey *v.* neglect or refuse to obey. —**disobedient** *adj.* —**disobedience** *n.*

disobliging *adj.* unwilling to help.

disorder *n.* state of untidiness and disorganization; public violence or rioting; an illness. —**disordered** *adj.* untidy. —**disorderly** *adj.* very untidy, disorganized; uncontrolled, unruly.

disorganize *v.* disrupt the arrangement or system of. —**disorganization** *n.*

disorientate, disorient *v.* cause (someone) to lose his or her bearings. —**disorientation** *n.*

disown *v.* deny any connection with (someone).

disparage *v.* speak contemptuously of. —**disparagement** *n.*

disparate *adj.* utterly different in kind. —**disparity** *n.*

dispassionate *adj.* uninfluenced by emotion. —**dispassionately** *adv.*

dispatch *v.* send off to a destination or to perform a task; carry out (a duty or a task) with speed; *Old-fashioned* kill. —*n.* official communi-

---

THESAURUS

handed, impartial, impersonal, neutral, outside, unbiased, uninvolved, unprejudiced, unselfish

dislike 1. *n.* animosity, animus, antagonism, antipathy, aversion, detestation, disapproval, disgust, distaste, enmity, hatred, hostility, loathing, repugnance 2. *v.* abhor, abominate, be averse to, despise, detest, disapprove, disfavour, hate, loathe, object to, scorn, shun

disloyal disaffected, faithless, false, perfidious, seditious, subversive, traitorous, treacherous, two-faced, unfaithful, unpatriotic, untrustworthy

disloyalty deceitfulness, double-dealing, falseness, falsity, inconstancy, infidelity, perfidy, treachery, treason, unfaithfulness

dismal bleak, cheerless, dark, depressing, despondent, discouraging, dreary, forlorn, gloomy, gruesome, lowering, lugubrious, melancholy, sad, sombre, sorrowful

dismay 1. *v.* affright, alarm, appal, distress, frighten, horrify, paralyse, scare, terrify, unnerve 2. *n.* agitation, alarm, anxiety, apprehension, distress, dread, fear, fright, horror, panic, terror

dismember anatomize, disjoint, dislimb, dislocate, dissect, divide, rend, sever

dismiss 1. cashier, discharge, lay off, oust, remove 2. disband, disperse, dissolve, free, let go, release, send away

dismissal 1. adjournment, end, release 2. discharge, expulsion, notice, removal

disobedience insubordination, mutiny, noncompliance, recalcitrance, revolt, unruliness, waywardness

disobedient contrary, defiant, disorderly, insubordinate, intractable, mischievous, naughty, obstreperous, refractory, undisciplined, unruly, wilful

disobey defy, disregard, flout, ignore, infringe, overstep, rebel, resist, transgress, violate

disorderly 1. chaotic, confused, disorganized, indiscriminate, irregular, jumbled, messy, untidy 2. disruptive, lawless, obstreperous, rebellious, refractory, riotous, rowdy, tumultuous, turbulent, ungovernable, unlawful, unmanageable, unruly

disown cast off, deny, disallow, disavow, disclaim, reject, renounce, repudiate

dispassionate calm, collected, composed, cool, imperturbable, moderate, quiet, serene, sober, temperate, unemotional, unexcitable, unmoved

dispatch 1. *v.* conclude, discharge, dispose of, expedite, finish, perform, settle 2. *n.* account, bulletin, communication, communiqué, document, instruction, item, letter, message, missive, news, piece, report, story

DICTIONARY

cation or report, sent in haste; report sent to a newspaper by a correspondent. —**dispatch rider** motorcyclist who carries dispatches.

dispel v. **-pelling, -pelled.** disperse or drive away.

dispense v. distribute in portions; prepare and distribute (medicine); administer (the law etc.). —**dispensable** adj. not essential. —**dispensation** n. act of dispensing; exemption from an obligation; administrative system. —**dispenser** n. —**dispensary** n. place where medicine is dispensed. —**dispense with** v. do away with; manage without.

disperse v. scatter over a wide area; (cause to) leave a gathering. —**dispersal, dispersion** n.

dispirit v. make downhearted.

displace v. move from the usual location; remove from office. —**displacement** n. —**displaced person** person forced from his or her home or country, esp. by war or revolution.

display v. make visible or noticeable. —n. act of displaying; something displayed; exhibition.

displease v. annoy. —**displeasure** n.

disport v. —**disport oneself** indulge oneself in pleasure.

dispose v. make willing or receptive; place in a certain order. —**disposable** adj. designed to be thrown away after use; available for use if needed, e.g. *disposable assets.* —**disposal** n. getting rid of something. —**at one's disposal** available for use. —**disposition** n. person's usual temperament; tendency; arrangement. —**dispose of** v. deal with (a problem etc.); get rid of; kill.

dispossess v. (foll. by *of*) deprive (someone) of (a possession). —**dispossession** n.

disproportion n. lack of proportion or equality. —**disproportionate** adj. —**disproportionately** adv.

disprove v. show (an assertion or claim) to be incorrect.

dispute v. argue about (something); doubt the validity of; fight over possession of. —n. argument. —**disputation** n. *Formal* argument.

THESAURUS

dispense 1. allocate, allot, apportion, assign, deal out, disburse, distribute, dole out, mete out, share 2. administer, apply, carry out, direct, discharge, enforce, execute, implement, operate, undertake

disperse 1. broadcast, circulate, diffuse, disseminate, dissipate, distribute, scatter, spread, strew 2. disband, dismiss, dispel, dissolve, rout, scatter, send off, separate, vanish

displace 1. derange, disarrange, disturb, misplace, move, shift, transpose 2. crowd out, oust, replace, succeed, supersede, supplant, take the place of

display v. 1. betray, demonstrate, disclose, evidence, evince, exhibit, expose, manifest, open, present, reveal, show, unveil 2. expand, extend, model, open out, spread out, stretch out, unfold, unfurl ~n. 3. array, demonstration, exhibition, exposition, exposure, manifestation, presentation, revelation, show 4. flourish, ostentation, pageant, parade, pomp, show, spectacle

displease anger, annoy, disgust, dissatisfy, exasperate, incense, irk, irritate, nettle, offend, pique, provoke, put out, rile, upset, vex

displeasure anger, annoyance, disapproval, dislike, dissatisfaction, distaste, indignation, irritation, offence, pique, resentment, vexation, wrath

disposal clearance, discarding, ejection, relinquishment, removal, riddance, scrapping, throwing away

dispose adjust, arrange, array, determine, dis-

tribute, fix, group, marshal, order, place, put, range, rank, regulate, set, settle, stand

dispose of 1. deal with, decide, determine, end, finish with, settle 2. destroy, discard, dump (*Inf.*), get rid of, jettison, scrap, unload

disposition character, constitution, make-up, nature, spirit, temper, temperament

disproportion asymmetry, disparity, imbalance, inequality, insufficiency, lopsidedness, unevenness

disproportionate excessive, incommensurate, inordinate, out of proportion, too much, unbalanced, unequal, uneven, unreasonable

disprove confute, controvert, discredit, expose, invalidate, negate, prove false, rebut, refute

dispute v. 1. argue, brawl, clash, contend, debate, discuss, quarrel, squabble, wrangle 2. challenge, contest, contradict, controvert, deny, doubt, impugn, question ~n. 3. argument, brawl, conflict, disagreement, discord, disturbance, feud, friction, quarrel, strife, wrangle

disqualification 1. disablement, incapacitation, unfitness 2. disenablement, disentitlement, elimination, exclusion, incompetence, ineligibility, rejection

disqualified debarred, eliminated, ineligible, knocked out

disqualify 1. disable, incapacitate, invalidate 2. debar, declare ineligible, disentitle, preclude, prohibit, rule out

DICTIONARY

disqualify v. -**fying, -fied.** debar from a contest; make ineligible. —**disqualification** n.

disquiet n. feeling of anxiety. —v. make (someone) anxious. —**disquietude** n. anxiety, uneasiness.

disregard v. give little or no attention to. —n. lack of attention or respect.

disrepair n. condition of being worn out or in poor working order.

disrepute n. loss or lack of good reputation. —**disreputable** adj. having or causing a bad reputation.

disrespect n. lack of respect. —**disrespectful** adj. —**disrespectfully** adv.

disrobe v. undress.

disrupt v. interrupt the progress of. —**disruption** n. —**disruptive** adj.

dissatisfied adj. not pleased, disappointed. —**dissatisfaction** n.

dissect v. cut open (a dead body) to examine it; examine critically and minutely. —**dissection** n.

dissemble v. conceal one's real motives or emotions by pretence.

disseminate v. scatter about. —**dissemination** n.

dissent v. disagree; *Christianity* reject the doctrines of an established church. —n. disagreement; *Christianity* separation from an established church. —**dissension** n. —**dissenter** n.

dissertation n. written thesis, usu. required for a higher university degree; long formal speech.

disservice n. bad turn or wrong.

dissident adj. disagreeing. —n. person who disagrees, esp. with the government. —**dissidence** n.

dissimilar adj. not alike, different. —**dissimilarity** n.

dissimulate v. conceal one's real feelings by pretence. —**dissimulation** n.

dissipate v. waste or squander; scatter. —**dissipated** adj. showing signs of overindulging in alcohol and other pleasures. —**dissipation** n.

dissociate v. regard or treat as separate. —**dissociate oneself from** deny or break a connection with. —**dissociation** n.

dissolute adj. leading an immoral life.

THESAURUS

disquiet alarm, anxiety, concern, disquietude, distress, fear, foreboding, fretfulness, restlessness, trouble, uneasiness, unrest, worry

disregard 1. discount, disobey, ignore, laugh off, make light of, neglect, overlook, pass over 2. brush off (*Sl.*), cold-shoulder, contemn, despise, disdain, disparage, slight, snub

disreputable base, contemptible, derogatory, discreditable, disgraceful, dishonourable, disorderly, ignominious, infamous, low, mean, notorious, scandalous, shameful, shocking, unprincipled, vicious, vile

disrepute disesteem, disfavour, disgrace, dishonour, ignominy, ill favour, ill repute, infamy, obloquy, shame, unpopularity

disrespect contempt, discourtesy, dishonour, disregard, impertinence, impoliteness, impudence, insolence, irreverence, lack of respect, rudeness

disrespectful bad-mannered, cheeky, contemptuous, discourteous, ill-bred, impertinent, impolite, impudent, insolent, insulting, irreverent, misbehaved, rude, uncivil

disrupt agitate, confuse, disorder, disorganize, disturb, spoil, throw into disorder, upset

dissatisfaction annoyance, disappointment, discontent, dismay, displeasure, distress, exasperation, frustration, irritation, regret, unhappiness

dissatisfied disappointed, discontented, dis-

gruntled, displeased, fed up, frustrated, unfulfilled, ungratified, unhappy

dissect anatomize, cut up *or* apart, dismember, lay open

disseminate broadcast, circulate, diffuse, disperse, distribute, propagate, publish, scatter, sow, spread

dissension conflict, contention, difference, disagreement, discord, dispute, dissent, quarrel, strife

dissent 1. v. decline, differ, disagree, object, protest, refuse, withhold assent *or* approval 2. n. difference, disagreement, discord, nonconformity, objection, opposition, refusal, resistance

dissenter dissident, nonconformist, objector, protestant

dissertation discourse, essay, exposition, thesis, treatise

disservice bad turn, disfavour, harm, ill turn, injury, injustice, wrong

dissident 1. adj. differing, disagreeing, discordant, heterodox, nonconformist, schismatic 2. n. agitator, dissenter, rebel, recusant

dissimilar different, disparate, divergent, diverse

dissipate burn up, deplete, expend, fritter away, lavish, misspend, run through, spend, squander, waste

dissociate 1. break off, disband, disrupt, part

DICTIONARY

dissolve v. (cause to) become liquid; bring to an end; dismiss (a meeting, Parliament, etc.); collapse emotionally. —**dissolution** n. destruction by breaking up and dispersing; termination of a meeting, assembly, or legal relationship.

dissonance n. discordant combination of sounds; lack of agreement or consistency. —**dissonant** adj.

dissuade v. deter (someone) by persuasion from a course of action, policy, etc. —**dissuasion** n.

distaff n. rod on which wool, flax, etc. is wound for spinning. —**distaff side** female side of a family.

distance n. space between two points; state of being apart; distant place; remoteness in manner. —**distance oneself from** separate oneself mentally from. —**distant** adj. far apart; separated by a specified distance; remote in manner. —**distantly** adv.

distaste n. dislike, aversion. —**distasteful** adj. unpleasant or offensive.

distemper[1] n. highly contagious disease of animals, esp. dogs.

distemper[2] n. paint mixed with water, glue, etc., which is used for painting walls.

distend v. expand by pressure from within. —**distension** n.

distil v. **-tilling, -tilled.** subject to or obtain by distillation; give off (a substance) in drops; extract the essence of. —**distillation** n. process of evaporating a liquid and condensing its vapour; (also **distillate**) concentrated essence. —**distiller** n. person or company that makes spirits. —**distillery** n. place where alcoholic drinks are made by distillation.

distinct adj. easily sensed or understood; different; sharp or clear. —**distinctly** adv. —**distinction** n. act of distinguishing; distinguishing feature; state of being different; special honour, recognition, or fame. —**distinctive** adj. easily recognizable. —**distinctively** adv. —**distinctiveness** n.

distinguish v. (foll. by *between* or *among*) make, show, or recognize a difference (between *or* among); be a distinctive feature of; perceive. —**distinguishable** adj. —**distinguished** adj. noble or dignified in appearance; highly respected.

distort v. twist out of shape; alter or misrepresent (facts). —**distortion** n.

distract v. draw the attention of (a person) away from something; confuse, trouble; entertain. —**distraction** n.

THESAURUS

company, quit 2. detach, disconnect, distance, divorce, isolate, segregate, separate, set apart

dissolute abandoned, corrupt, debauched, degenerate, depraved, immoral, lax, lewd, libertine, licentious, loose, profligate, vicious, wanton, wild

dissolution breaking up, disintegration, division, divorce, parting, resolution, separation

dissolve flux, fuse, melt, soften, thaw

dissuade deter, discourage, disincline, divert, expostulate, put off, remonstrate, urge not to, warn

distance 1. n. absence, extent, gap, interval, lapse, length, range, reach, remoteness, remove, separation, space, span, stretch, width 2. v. dissociate oneself, separate oneself

distant 1. abroad, afar, far, faraway, far-flung, far-off, outlying, out-of-the-way, remote, removed 2. aloof, cold, cool, formal, haughty, reserved, restrained, standoffish, stiff, unapproachable, unfriendly, withdrawn

distaste abhorrence, antipathy, aversion, disfavour, disgust, disinclination, dislike, displeasure, horror, loathing, repugnance, revulsion

distasteful abhorrent, disagreeable, displeasing, obnoxious, offensive, repugnant, repulsive, undesirable, uninviting, unpalatable, unpleasant, unsavoury

distil condense, evaporate, express, purify, rectify, refine, vaporize

distinct 1. apparent, clear, clear-cut, decided, definite, evident, lucid, manifest, marked, noticeable, obvious, patent, plain, recognizable, sharp, well-defined 2. different, dissimilar, individual, separate, unconnected

distinction 1. discernment, discrimination, penetration, perception, separation 2. contrast, difference, differential, division, separation 3. celebrity, credit, eminence, excellence, fame, greatness, honour, importance, merit, name, note, prominence, quality, rank, renown, reputation, repute, superiority, worth

distinctly clearly, decidedly, definitely, evidently, manifestly, markedly, noticeably, obviously, plainly, precisely

distinguish 1. decide, determine, differentiate, discriminate, judge, tell apart 2. discern, know, make out, perceive, pick out, recognize, see, tell

distinguished celebrated, conspicuous, eminent, famed, famous, illustrious, notable, noted, well-known

distort 1. bend, buckle, contort, deform, disfigure, misshape, twist, warp, wrench, wrest 2.

DICTIONARY

distrait [diss-**tray**] *adj.* absent-minded or abstracted.

distraught [diss-**trawt**] *adj.* extremely anxious or agitated.

distress *v.* cause mental pain to, upset badly. —*n.* mental pain; physical or financial trouble. —**distressed** *adj.* much troubled; in financial difficulties. —**distressing** *adj.* —**distressingly** *adv.*

distribute *v.* give out in shares; hand out or deliver. —**distribution** *n.* act of distributing; arrangement or location. —**distributor** *n.* wholesaler who distributes goods to retailers in a specific area; device in a petrol engine that sends the electric current to the spark plugs.

district *n.* area of land regarded as an administrative or geographical unit.

distrust *v.* regard as untrustworthy. —*n.* suspicion or doubt. —**distrustful** *adj.*

disturb *v.* intrude on; disarrange; worry, make anxious. —**disturbance** *n.* —**disturbing** *adj.* —**disturbingly** *adv.* —**disturbed** *adj. Psychiatry* emotionally upset, troubled, or maladjusted.

disunite *v.* cause disagreement among. —**disunity** *n.*

disuse *n.* condition of being unused. —**disused** *adj.*

ditch *n.* narrow channel dug in the earth for drainage or irrigation. —*v. Slang* abandon.

dither *v. Brit.* be uncertain or indecisive. —*n.* state of indecision or agitation. —**ditherer** *n.* —**dithery** *adj.*

ditto *n., pl.* **-tos.** the same. —*adv.* in the same way.

ditty *n., pl.* **-ties.** short simple poem or song.

diuretic [die-yoor-**et**-ik] *n.* drug that increases the flow of urine.

diurnal [die-**urn**-al] *adj.* happening during the day or daily.

divan *n.* backless sofa or couch; low backless bed.

dive *v.* **diving, dived.** plunge headfirst into water; (of a submarine or diver) submerge under water; move quickly in a specified direction; (foll. by *in* or *into*) start (doing something) enthusiastically. —*n.* act of diving; steep nose-down descent; *Slang* disreputable bar or club. —**diver** *n.* person who works or explores underwater; person who dives for sport. —**dive bomber** military aircraft designed to release bombs during a dive.

diverge *v.* separate and go in different directions; deviate (from a prescribed course). —**divergence** *n.* —**divergent** *adj.*

THESAURUS

bias, colour, falsify, garble, misrepresent, pervert, slant, twist

distract 1. divert, draw away, sidetrack, turn aside 2. agitate, bewilder, confound, confuse, disturb, harass, madden, perplex, puzzle, torment, trouble

distraction 1. agitation, bewilderment, commotion, confusion, discord, disorder, disturbance 2. amusement, beguilement, diversion, entertainment, pastime, recreation

distress 1. *n.* affliction, agony, anguish, anxiety, desolation, discomfort, grief, heartache, misery, pain, sadness, sorrow, torment, torture, woe, worry, wretchedness 2. *v.* afflict, agonize, bother, disturb, grieve, harass, harrow, pain, perplex, sadden, torment, trouble, upset, worry, wound

distressed agitated, anxious, distracted, distraught, saddened, tormented, troubled, upset, worried, wretched

distressing affecting, afflicting, disturbing, grievous, heart-breaking, hurtful, lamentable, painful, sad

distribute administer, allocate, allot, assign, deal, dispense, dispose, divide, dole out, give, measure out, mete, share

distribution allocation, allotment, division, dole, partition, sharing

district area, community, locality, neighbourhood, parish, quarter, region, sector, vicinity, ward

distrust 1. *v.* be sceptical of, be suspicious of, disbelieve, discredit, doubt, misbelieve, question, suspect 2. *n.* disbelief, doubt, misgiving, mistrust, qualm, question, scepticism, suspicion, wariness

disturb 1. bother, disrupt, interfere with, interrupt, intrude on, pester, rouse, startle 2. agitate, alarm, annoy, distract, distress, excite, fluster, harass, perturb, ruffle, shake, trouble, unsettle, upset, worry

disturbance agitation, bother, confusion, disorder, distraction, hindrance, interruption, intrusion, perturbation, upset

disuse decay, discontinuance, idleness, neglect

ditch 1. *n.* channel, drain, dyke, furrow, gully, moat, trench, watercourse 2. *v.* discard, dispose of, drop, get rid of, jettison, scrap

dither falter, haver, hesitate, oscillate, waver

dive 1. *v.* dip, disappear, drop, duck, fall, jump, leap, pitch, plummet, plunge, submerge, swoop 2. *n.* dash, jump, leap, lunge, plunge, spring

diverge branch, divide, fork, part, radiate, separate, split, spread

DICTIONARY

divers *adj. Old-fashioned* various.

diverse *adj.* having variety; different in kind. **—diversity** *n.* quality of being different or varied; range of difference. **—diversify** *v.* **—diversification** *n.*

divert *v.* deflect; entertain, distract the attention of. **—diversion** *n.* act of diverting; *Brit.* official detour used by traffic when a main route is closed; something that distracts from business etc.; an entertainment. **—diversionary** *adj.*

divest *v.* strip (of clothes); dispossess or deprive.

divide *v.* separate into parts; share or be shared out in parts; (cause to) disagree; keep apart, be a boundary between; calculate how many times (one number) can be contained in (another). **—***n.* division, split. **—dividend** *n.* sum of money representing part of the profit made, paid by a company to its shareholders; bonus. **—dividers** *pl. n.* compasses with two pointed arms, used for measuring or dividing lines.

divine *adj.* of God or a god; godlike; *Informal* splendid. **—***v.* discover (something) by intuition or guessing. **—divinely** *adv.* **—divination** *n.* art of discovering future events, as though by supernatural powers. **—divinity** *n.* theology; state of being divine; god. **—divining rod** forked twig said to move when held over ground in which water or metal is to be found.

division *n.* act of dividing or sharing out; one of the parts into which something is divided; difference of opinion; mathematical operation of dividing. **—divisional** *adj.* of a division in an organization. **—divisible** *adj.* **—divisibility** *n.* **—divisive** [div-**vice**-iv] *adj.* tending to cause disagreement. **—divisor** *n.* number to be divided into another number.

divorce *n.* legal ending of a marriage; separation, esp. one that is total. **—***v.* separate or be separated by divorce; remove or separate. **—divorcé,** *(fem.)* **divorcée** *n.* person who is divorced.

divulge *v.* make known, disclose. **—divulgence** *n.*

Dixie *n.* southern states of the U.S.

dixie *n. Chiefly mil.* large metal cooking pot.

DIY *Brit.* do-it-yourself.

dizzy *adj.* **-zier, -ziest.** having or causing a whirling sensation; mentally confused. **—***v.* **-zying, -zied.** make dizzy. **—dizzily** *adv.* **—dizziness** *n.*

DJ disc jockey; dinner jacket.

dl decilitre.

dm decimetre.

DNA *n.* deoxyribonucleic acid, the main constituent of the chromosomes of all living things.

do *v.* **does, doing, did, done.** perform or complete (a deed or action); be suitable, suffice; provide, serve, e.g. *this place doesn't do lunch on Sundays;* make tidy, elegant, or ready, e.g *do one's hair;* improve, e.g. *that hat does nothing for you;* find the answer to (a problem or puzzle); cause or produce, e.g. *complaints do nothing to help;*

THESAURUS

diverse 1. assorted, miscellaneous, several, sundry, varied, various 2. different, dissimilar, distinct, separate, unlike, varying

diversion 1. change, deflection, detour, deviation, digression, variation 2. amusement, delight, distraction, enjoyment, entertainment, game, pastime, play, pleasure, recreation, relaxation, sport

diversity assortment, difference, heterogeneity, medley, multiplicity, range, variance, variegation, variety

divert deflect, redirect, switch, turn aside

divide 1. cut (up), detach, disconnect, part, partition, segregate, separate, sever, shear, split, subdivide 2. allocate, allot, apportion, deal out, dispense, distribute, dole out, measure out, portion, share

dividend bonus, extra, gain, plus, portion, share, surplus

divine *adj.* 1. celestial, godlike, heavenly, holy, spiritual, superhuman, supernatural 2. *Inf.* beautiful, excellent, glorious, marvellous, perfect, splendid, wonderful ~*v.* 3. conjecture,

deduce, discern, foretell, guess, infer, intuit, perceive, suppose, surmise, suspect, understand

divinity 1. deity, divine nature, godliness, holiness, sanctity 2. deity, genius, god, goddess, guardian spirit, spirit 3. religion, religious studies, theology

divisible fractional, separable, splittable

division 1. cutting up, detaching, dividing, partition, separation 2. allotment, apportionment, distribution, sharing 3. branch, category, class, compartment, department, group, head, part, portion, section, sector, segment

divorce 1. *n.* breach, break, decree nisi, dissolution, disunion, rupture, separation, severance, split-up 2. *v.* annul, disconnect, dissociate, disunite, divide, part, separate, sever, split up, sunder

divulge betray, confess, declare, disclose, exhibit, expose, impart, leak, let slip, make known, proclaim, publish, reveal, tell, uncover

dizzy faint, giddy, reeling, shaky, staggering, swimming, wobbly

DICTIONARY

give or render, e.g. *do me a favour;* work at, esp. as a course of study or a job; travel (a distance); *Informal* cheat or rob; used to form questions, e.g. *do you agree?;* used to intensify positive statements and commands, e.g. *I do like your new house; do hurry!;* used to form negative statements and commands, e.g. *do not leave me here alone!;* used to replace an earlier verb, e.g. *he likes you as much as I do.* —*n., pl.* **dos, do's.** *Informal* festive gathering or party. —**do away with** *v.* kill; get rid of. —**do-it-yourself** *n.* practice of constructing and repairing things oneself, esp. as a hobby. —**do up** *v.* fasten; renovate. —**do with** *v.* find useful or benefit from. —**do without** *v.* manage without.

Doberman (pinscher) *n.* large dog with a glossy black-and-tan coat.

docile *adj.* (of a person or animal) easily managed. —**docilely** *adv.* —**docility** *n.*

dock[1] *n.* enclosed area of water where ships are loaded, unloaded, or repaired. —*v.* moor or be moored at dock; link (two spacecraft) or (of two spacecraft) be linked together in space. —**docker** *n.* person employed in the loading or unloading of ships. —**dockyard** *n.* place with docks and equipment where ships are built or repaired.

dock[2] *v.* remove part of (an animal's tail) by cutting through the bone; deduct (an amount) from (a person's wages).

dock[3] *n.* enclosed space in a court of law where the accused person sits or stands.

dock[4] *n.* weed with broad leaves.

docket *n.* piece of paper accompanying a package or other delivery, stating contents, delivery instructions, etc. —*v.* fix a docket to (a package etc.).

doctor *n.* person licensed to practise medicine; person who has been awarded a doctorate. —*v.* make different in order to deceive; poison or drug (food or drink); *Informal* castrate or sterilize (a cat, dog, etc.). —**doctoral** *adj.* —**doctorate** *n.* highest academic degree in any field of knowledge.

doctrine [dock-trin] *n.* body of teachings of a religious, political, or philosophical group; principle or body of principles that is taught or advocated. —**doctrinal** *adj.* of or related to doctrine. —**doctrinaire** *adj.* stubbornly insistent on the application of a theory without regard to practicality.

document *n.* piece of paper, booklet, etc. providing information, esp. of an official nature. —*v.* record or report (something) in detail; support (a claim) with evidence. —**documentation** *n.*

documentary *n., pl.* **-ries.** film or television programme presenting the facts about a particular subject. —*adj.* of or based on documents.

dodder *v.* move unsteadily. —**dodderer** *n.* —**doddery** *adj.*

dodecagon [doe-**deck**-a-gon] *n.* geometric figure with twelve sides.

dodge *v.* avoid (a blow, being seen, etc.) by moving suddenly; evade by cleverness or trickery. —*n.* plan contrived to deceive; sudden evasive movement. —**dodger** *n.* —**dodgy** *adj. Informal* difficult or dangerous; untrustworthy.

Dodgem *n.* ® electrically propelled vehicle driven and bumped against similar cars in a rink at a funfair.

THESAURUS

do *v.* 1. accomplish, achieve, act, carry out, complete, conclude, discharge, end, execute, perform, produce, work 2. be adequate, be enough, be of use, be sufficient, pass muster, satisfy, serve, suffice, suit 3. behave, carry oneself, conduct oneself 4. fare, get along, get on, make out, manage, proceed 5. bring about, cause, create, effect, produce 6. *Sl.* cheat, deceive, defraud, dupe, fleece, hoax, swindle, trick ~*n.* 7. *Inf.* affair, event, function, gathering, occasion, party

do away with 1. destroy, exterminate, kill, liquidate, murder, slay 2. abolish, discard, discontinue, eliminate, get rid of, remove

docile biddable, compliant, manageable, obedient, pliant, submissive, tractable

docility compliance, manageability, meekness, obedience, pliancy, submissiveness, tractability

dock 1. *n.* harbour, pier, quay, waterfront, wharf

2. *v.* anchor, berth, drop anchor, land, moor, put in, tie up

doctor 1. *n.* general practitioner, G.P., medical practitioner, physician 2. *v.* alter, change, disguise, falsify, fudge, pervert, tamper with

doctrinaire *adj.* biased, dogmatic, fanatical, inflexible, insistent, opinionated, rigid

doctrine article, belief, canon, concept, conviction, creed, dogma, opinion, precept, principle, teaching, tenet

document 1. *n.* certificate, legal form, paper, record, report 2. *v.* authenticate, back up, certify, cite, corroborate, detail, instance, substantiate, support, validate, verify

dodge *v.* 1. dart, duck, shift, sidestep, swerve, turn aside 2. avoid, deceive, elude, evade, fend off, fudge, get out of, hedge, parry, shirk, shuffle, trick ~*n.* 3. device, feint, ploy, ruse, scheme, stratagem, subterfuge, trick, wile

DICTIONARY

dodo *n., pl.* **dodos, dodoes.** large flightless extinct bird.

doe *n.* female deer, hare, or rabbit.

does *v.* third person singular of the present tense of DO.

doesn't does not.

doff *v.* take off or lift (one's hat) as a mark of respect.

dog *n.* domesticated four-legged meat-eating mammal occurring in many different breeds; any other member of the dog family, such as the dingo or coyote; male of animals of the dog family; *Informal* fellow, chap, e.g. *you lucky dog!* —*v.* **dogging, dogged.** follow (someone) closely; trouble or plague. —**go to the dogs** go to ruin physically or morally. —**let sleeping dogs lie** leave things undisturbed. —**dogged** [dog-gid] *adj.* obstinately determined. —**doggedly** *adv.* —**doggedness** *n.* —**doggy, doggie** *n.* child's word for a dog. —**dogcart** *n.* light horse-drawn two-wheeled vehicle. —**dog collar** collar for a dog; *Informal* clerical collar. —**dog-eared** *adj.* (of a book) having pages folded down at the corner; shabby or worn. —**dogfight** *n.* close-quarters combat between fighter aircraft; any rough fight. —**dogfish** *n.* small shark. —**doghouse** *n. US* kennel. —**in the doghouse** *Informal* in disfavour. —**dogleg** *n.* sharp bend. —**dog rose** wild rose with pink or white flowers. —**dogsbody** *n. Informal* person who carries out menial tasks for others. —**dogtired** *adj. Informal* exhausted.

doge [doje] *n.* (formerly) chief magistrate of Venice or Genoa.

doggerel *n.* poorly written, usually comic verse.

doggo *adv.* —**lie doggo** *Informal* hide and keep quiet.

dogma *n.* doctrine or system of doctrines proclaimed by authority as true. —**dogmatic** *adj.* (of a statement or opinion) forcibly asserted as if unchallengeable; (of a person) prone to making such statements. —**dogmatically** *adv.* —**dogmatism** *n.*

doily *n., pl.* **-lies.** decorative mat of lace or lacelike paper, laid on plates.

doldrums *pl. n.* depressed state of mind; state of inactivity.

dole *n. Brit. informal* money received from the state while out of work. —*v.* (foll. by *out*) distribute (something), esp. in small portions.

doleful *adj.* dreary or mournful. —**dolefully** *adv.* —**dolefulness** *n.*

doll *n.* small model of a human being, used as a toy; *Slang* girl or young woman, esp. a pretty one.

dollar *n.* standard monetary unit of the U.S., Canada, and various other countries.

dollop *n. Informal* semisolid lump.

dolly *n., pl.* **-lies.** child's word for a doll; wheeled support on which a camera may be moved.

dolman sleeve *n.* sleeve that is very wide at the armhole and tapers to a tight wrist.

dolmen *n.* prehistoric monument consisting of a horizontal stone supported by vertical stones.

dolomite *n.* mineral consisting of calcium magnesium carbonate.

dolorous *adj.* causing or involving pain or sorrow.

dolphin *n.* sea mammal of the whale family, with a beaklike snout. —**dolphinarium** *n.* aquarium for dolphins, esp. one in which they give public displays.

dolt *n.* stupid person. —**doltish** *adj.*

domain *n.* field of knowledge or activity; land under one ruler or government.

dome *n.* rounded roof built on a circular base; something shaped like this. —**domed** *adj.*

domestic *adj.* of the home or family; home-loving; (of an animal) bred or kept as a pet or for the supply of food; of one's own country or a specific country, e.g. *domestic and foreign affairs.* —*n.* household servant. —**domestically** *adv.* —**domesticity** *n.* —**domesticate** *v.* bring or keep (wild animals or plants) under control or cultivation; accustom (someone) to home life. —**domestication** *n.* —**domestic science** study of household skills.

THESAURUS

dog 1. *n.* bitch, canine, cur, hound, man's best friend, mongrel, pup, puppy, tyke 2. *v.* haunt, hound, plague, pursue, shadow, track, trail, trouble

dogged determined, firm, persevering, persistent, resolute, staunch, steadfast, steady, tenacious, unflagging, unshakable

dogma article, belief, creed, doctrine, precept, principle, tenet

dogmatic arbitrary, arrogant, assertive, cat-egorical, dictatorial, downright, emphatic, imperious, obdurate, overbearing, peremptory

doldrums blues, boredom, depression, dullness, ennui, gloom, inertia, listlessness, malaise, stagnation, tedium

dole 1. *n.* allowance, alms, benefit, gift, grant, parcel, pittance, portion, quota, share 2. *v. Usually with* **out** administer, allocate, allot, assign, deal, dispense, distribute, divide, give, hand out, share

DICTIONARY

domicile [**dom**-miss-ile] *n.* person's regular dwelling place. —**domiciliary** *adj.*

dominant *adj.* having authority or influence; predominant. —**dominance** *n.*

dominate *v.* control or govern; tower above (surroundings); predominate in. —**domination** *n.*

domineering *adj.* acting arrogantly or tyrannically.

Dominican *n.* friar or nun of an order founded by Saint Dominic. —*adj.* of the Dominican order.

dominion *n.* rule or authority; land governed by one ruler or government; (formerly) self-governing division of the British Empire.

domino *n., pl.* -**noes.** small rectangular block marked with dots, used in dominoes. —*pl.* game in which dominoes with matching halves are laid together.

don[1] *v.* **donning, donned.** put on (clothing).

don[2] *n. Brit.* member of the teaching staff at a university or college; Spanish gentleman or nobleman. —**donnish** *adj.* resembling a university don.

donate *v.* give (something), esp. to a charity. —**donation** *n.* act of donating; a contribution. —**donor** *n.* person who makes a donation; *Med.* person who gives blood, organs, etc. for use in the treatment of another person.

done *v.* past participle of DO.

donkey *n.* long-eared member of the horse family. —**donkey jacket** man's thick hip-length jacket with a waterproof panel across the shoulders. —**donkey's years** *Informal* a long time. —**donkey-work** *n.* groundwork; drudgery.

don't do not.

doodle *v.* scribble or draw aimlessly. —*n.* shape or picture drawn aimlessly.

doom *n.* death or a terrible fate. —*v.* destine or condemn to death or a terrible fate. —**doomsday** *n. Christianity* day on which the Last Judgment will occur; any dreaded day.

door *n.* hinged or sliding panel for closing the entrance to a room, cupboard, etc.; entrance. —**doormat** *n.* mat, placed at an entrance, for wiping dirt from shoes; *Informal* person who offers little resistance to ill-treatment. —**doorway** *n.* opening into a building or room.

dope *n. Slang* illegal drug, usu. cannabis; drug, esp. one administered to a racehorse etc. to affect its performance; *Informal* slow-witted person; confidential information. —*v.* administer a drug to. —**dop(e)y** *adj.* half-asleep; *Slang* silly.

dormant *adj.* temporarily quiet, inactive, or not being used. —**dormancy** *n.*

dormer (window) *n.* window that projects from a sloping roof.

dormitory *n., pl.* -**ries.** large room, esp. at a school, containing several beds.

dormouse *n.* small rodent resembling a mouse with a furry tail.

dorsal *adj.* of or on the back.

dory *n., pl.* -**ries.** spiny-finned sea fish.

dose *n.* specific quantity of a medicine taken at one time; specific amount of something unpleasant to experience. —*v.* administer a dose to (someone). —**dosage** *n.* size of a dose.

doss *v.* —**doss down** *Brit. slang* sleep, esp. on a makeshift bed. —**dosshouse** *n. Brit. slang* cheap lodging house for homeless people.

THESAURUS

dolt ass, chump (*Inf.*), dullard, dunce, fool, idiot, ignoramus, nitwit, simpleton, thickhead

domestic 1. family, home, household, private 2. house, house-trained, pet, tame, trained 3. indigenous, internal, native, not foreign

dominant ascendant, assertive, commanding, controlling, governing, leading, predominant, presiding, ruling, superior, supreme

dominate 1. control, direct, govern, lead, master, monopolize, overbear, rule, tyrannize 2. bestride, loom over, overlook, stand over, survey, tower above

domination authority, command, control, influence, mastery, power, rule, superiority, supremacy, sway

dominion ascendancy, authority, command, control, government, mastery, power, rule, sovereignty, supremacy, sway

don dress in, get into, pull on, put on

donate bestow, gift, give, present, subscribe

donation alms, benefaction, boon, contribution, gift, grant, gratuity, largess, offering, present, subscription

donor almsgiver, benefactor, contributor, donator, giver

doom 1. *n.* catastrophe, death, destiny, destruction, downfall, fate, fortune, lot, portion, ruin 2. *v.* condemn, consign, damn, decree, destine, judge, sentence

door egress, entrance, entry, exit, ingress, opening

dope drugs, narcotic, opiate

dormant asleep, inactive, inert, latent, quiescent, sleeping, sluggish, slumbering, suspended

dose draught, drench, measure, portion, potion, prescription, quantity

DICTIONARY

dossier [**doss**-ee-ay] *n.* collection of papers with information about a subject or person.

dot *n.* small round mark; shorter symbol used in Morse code. —*v.* **dotting, dotted.** mark with a dot; scatter or intersperse. —**on the dot** at exactly the arranged time. —**dotty** *adj. Slang* slightly mad. —**dottiness** *n.*

dote *v.* —**dote on** love to an excessive or foolish degree. —**dotage** [**dote**-ij] *n.* feebleness of mind as a result of old age. —**dotard** [**dote**-ard] *n.* person who is feeble-minded through old age.

double *adj.* as much again in size, strength, number, value, etc.; composed of two equal or similar parts; designed for two users; folded in two. —*adv.* twice over, twofold. —*n.* twice the number, amount, size, etc.; duplicate or counterpart, esp. a person who closely resembles another. —*pl.* game between two pairs of players. —*v.* make or become twice as much; bend or fold (material etc.); play two parts; turn sharply. —**at the double** quickly or immediately. —**doubly** *adv.* —**double agent** spy employed simultaneously by two opposing sides. —**double bass** stringed instrument, largest and lowest member of the violin family. —**double chin** fold of fat under the chin. —**double cream** thick cream with a high fat content. —**double-cross** *v.* cheat or betray. —*n.* instance of double-crossing. —**double-dealing** *n.* treacherous or deceitful behaviour. —**double-decker** *n.* bus with two passenger decks one on top of the other; *Informal* sandwich made from three slices of bread with two fillings. —**double Dutch** *Informal* incomprehensible talk, gibberish. —**double glazing** two panes of glass in a window, fitted to reduce heat loss. —**double take** (esp. in comedy) delayed reaction by a person to a remark or situation. —**double talk** deceptive or ambiguous talk.

double entendre [**doob**-bl on-**tond**-ra] *n.* word or phrase that can be interpreted in two ways, esp. with one meaning that is rude.

doublet [**dub**-lit] *n.* (formerly) man's close-fitting jacket, with or without sleeves.

doubloon *n.* former Spanish gold coin.

doubt *n.* uncertainty about the truth, facts, or existence of something; unresolved difficulty or point. —*v.* be inclined to disbelieve (a fact or story); distrust or be suspicious of (a person). —**doubter** *n.* —**doubtful** *adj.* unlikely; feeling doubt. —**doubtfully** *adv.* —**doubtless** *adv.* certainly; probably.

douche [**doosh**] *n.* (instrument for applying a) stream of water directed onto or into the body for cleansing or medical purposes. —*v.* cleanse or treat by means of a douche.

dough *n.* thick mixture of flour and water or milk, used for making bread; *Slang* money. —**doughnut** *n.* small cake of sweetened dough cooked in hot fat.

doughty [**dowt**-ee] *adj.* **-tier, -tiest.** hardy or resolute.

dour [**doo**-er] *adj.* sullen and unfriendly. —**dourness** *n.*

douse [rhymes with **mouse**] *v.* drench with water or other liquid; put out (a light).

dove *n.* bird with a heavy body, small head, and short legs; *Politics* person opposed to war. —**dovecot(e)** *n.* structure for housing pigeons. —**dovetail** *n.* joint containing wedge-shaped tenons. —*v.* fit together neatly.

dowager *n.* widow possessing property or a title obtained from her husband.

dowdy *adj.* **-dier, -diest.** shabby or old-fashioned. —**dowdily** *adv.* —**dowdiness** *n.*

THESAURUS

dotage feebleness, imbecility, old age, second childhood, senility, weakness

dote on *or* **upon** admire, adore, hold dear, love, prize, treasure

double 1. *adj.* coupled, doubled, dual, duplicate, in pairs, paired, twice, twin, twofold 2. *v.* duplicate, enlarge, fold, grow, increase, magnify, multiply, plait, repeat

double-cross betray, cheat, defraud, hoodwink, mislead, swindle, trick

doubt *v.* 1. discredit, distrust, fear, misgive, mistrust, query, question, suspect 2. be dubious, be uncertain, demur, fluctuate, hesitate, scruple, vacillate, waver ~*n.* 3. apprehension, disquiet, distrust, fear, incredulity, lack of faith, misgiving, mistrust, qualm, scepticism, suspicion 4. ambiguity, confusion, difficulty, dilemma, perplexity, problem, quandary

doubtful 1. ambiguous, debatable, dubious, equivocal, hazardous, indefinite, obscure, problematic, questionable, unclear, unconfirmed, unsettled, vague 2. hesitating, irresolute, perplexed, sceptical, suspicious, tentative, uncertain, unconvinced, undecided, unresolved, unsettled, unsure, vacillating, wavering

doubtless 1. assuredly, certainly, clearly, of course, precisely, surely, truly, unquestionably 2. apparently, most likely, ostensibly, presumably, probably, seemingly

dour dismal, dreary, forbidding, gloomy, grim, morose, sour, sullen, unfriendly

dowdy dingy, drab, old-fashioned, shabby, unfashionable

DICTIONARY

dowel *n.* wooden or metal peg that fits into two corresponding holes to join two adjacent parts.

dower *n.* life interest in a part of her husband's estate allotted to a widow by law.

down[1] *prep.* from a higher to a lower position in or on; at a lower or further level or position on, in, or along. —*adv.* at or to a lower position or level; used to indicate lowering or destruction, e.g. *knock down;* used with several verbs to indicate intensity or completion, e.g. *calm down;* immediately, e.g. *cash down;* on paper, e.g. *write this down;* lower in price; from an earlier to a later time. —*adj.* depressed, sad. —*v. Informal* drink, esp. quickly. —**have a down on** *Informal* bear ill will towards. —**down under** *Informal* Australia or New Zealand. —**downward** *adj.* descending from a higher to a lower level, condition, or position. —*adv.* downwards. —**downwards** *adv.* from a higher to a lower place, level, etc. —**down-and-out** *adj.* without any means of livelihood. —*n.* person who is destitute and, often, homeless. —**downbeat** *adj. Informal* gloomy; relaxed. —**downcast** *adj.* dejected; (of the eyes) directed downwards. —**downfall** *n.* sudden loss of position or reputation; cause of this. —**downgrade** *v.* reduce in importance or value. —**downhearted** *adj.* sad and discouraged. —**downhill** *adj.* going or sloping down. —*adv.* towards the bottom of a hill. —**downpour** *n.* heavy fall of rain. —**downright** *adj., adv.* extreme(ly). —**downstairs** *adv.* to or on a lower floor. —*n.* lower or ground floor. —**down-to-earth** *adj.* sensible or practical. —**downtrodden** *adj.* oppressed and lacking the will to resist.

down[2] *n.* soft fine feathers or hair. —**downy** *adj.*

downs *pl. n.* rolling upland, esp. in the chalk areas of S England.

Down's syndrome *n.* genetic disorder characterized by a flat face, slanting eyes, and mental retardation.

dowry *n., pl.* **-ries.** property brought by a woman to her husband at marriage.

dowse [rhymes with **cows**] *v.* search for underground water or minerals using a divining rod.

doxology *n., pl.* **-gies.** short hymn of praise to God.

doyen [doy-en] *n.* senior member of a group, profession, or society. —**doyenne** [doy-en] *n. fem.*

doze *v.* sleep lightly or intermittently. —*n.* short sleep. —**dozy** *adj.* drowsy; *Informal* stupid. —**doze off** *v.* fall into a light sleep.

dozen *adj., n.* twelve. —**dozenth** *adj., n.*

DPP Director of Public Prosecutions.

Dr Doctor; Drive.

drab *adj.* **drabber, drabbest.** dull or dingy; cheerless or dreary. —**drabness** *n.*

drachm [dram] *n. Brit.* one eighth of a fluid ounce.

drachma *n., pl.* **-mas, -mae.** standard monetary unit of Greece.

draconian *adj.* harsh or severe.

draft *n.* plan, sketch, or drawing of something; preliminary outline of a book, speech, etc.; written order for payment of money by a bank; *US* selection for compulsory military service. —*v.* draw up an outline or plan of; detach (personnel) from one place to another; *US* select for compulsory military service.

drag *v.* **dragging, dragged.** pull with force, esp. along the ground; trail on the ground; (foll. by *along* or *to*) bring (oneself or someone else) with effort or difficulty; (foll. by *on* or *out*) last, prolong, or be prolonged tediously; search (a river) with a dragnet or hook. —*n.* person or thing that slows up progress; *Informal* tedious person or thing; *Slang* women's clothes worn by a man. —**dragnet** *n.* net used to scour the bottom of a pond or river, when searching for something. —**drag race** race in which specially built cars or motorcycles are timed over a measured course.

THESAURUS

down *adj.* blue, dejected, depressed, disheartened, downcast, low, miserable, sad, unhappy

down-and-out derelict, destitute, impoverished, penniless, ruined

downcast cheerless, dejected, depressed, despondent, disconsolate, discouraged, disheartened, dismayed, dispirited, miserable, sad, unhappy

downfall breakdown, collapse, debacle, descent, destruction, disgrace, fall, overthrow, ruin, undoing

downgrade degrade, demote, humble

downhearted crestfallen, dejected, depressed,

despondent, discouraged, disheartened, dismayed, downcast, low-spirited, sad, sorrowful, unhappy

downpour cloudburst, deluge, flood, inundation, rainstorm

down-to-earth common-sense, hard-headed, matter-of-fact, plain-spoken, practical, realistic, sane, sensible

doze *v.* catnap, drowse, nap, nod, sleep, slumber, zizz (*Inf.*)

drab cheerless, colourless, dingy, dismal, dreary, dull, flat, gloomy, grey, lacklustre, shabby, sombre, uninspired

DICTIONARY

dragon *n.* mythical fire-breathing monster with a scaly body, wings, claws, and a long tail; *Informal* fierce woman. —**dragonfly** *n., pl.* **-flies.** brightly coloured insect with a long slender body and two pairs of wings.

dragoon *n.* heavily armed cavalryman. —*v.* coerce or force.

drain *n.* pipe or channel that carries off water or sewage; cause of continuous diminution of resources or energy. —*v.* draw off or remove liquid from; flow away or filter off; drink the entire contents of (a glass or cup); make constant demands on (resources, energy, etc.); exhaust (someone) physically and emotionally. —**drainage** *n.* process or method of draining; system of drains.

drake *n.* male duck.

dram *n.* small amount of spirits, esp. whisky; one sixteenth of an ounce.

drama *n.* a work to be performed by actors; art of the writing or production of plays; situation that is highly emotional, turbulent, or tragic. —**dramatic** *adj.* of or like drama; striking or effective. —**dramatically** *adv.* —**dramatist** *n.* playwright. —**dramatize** *v.* put into dramatic form; express (something) in a dramatic or exaggerated way. —**dramatization** *n.*

drank *v.* past tense of DRINK.

drape *v.* cover with material, usu. in folds; place casually and loosely. —*n. US* curtain. —**draper** *n. Brit.* dealer in fabrics and sewing materials. —**drapery** *n.* fabric or clothing arranged and draped; fabrics and cloth collectively. —*pl.* curtains.

drastic *adj.* sudden and extreme.

draught *n.* current of air, esp. in an enclosed space; act of pulling a load by a vehicle or animal; portion of liquid to be drunk, esp. medicine; instance of drinking; one of the flat discs used in the game of draughts. —*pl.* game for two players using a chessboard and twelve draughts each. —**draughty** *adj.* exposed to draughts of air. —**draughtiness** *n.* —**draughtsman** *n.* person employed to prepare detailed scale drawings of machinery, buildings, etc. —**draughtsmanship** *n.* —**draught beer** beer stored in a cask.

draw *v.* **drawing, drew, drawn.** depict or sketch (a figure, picture, etc.) in lines, with a pencil or pen; cause (a person or thing) to move towards one or away from a place by pulling; bring, take, or pull (something) out, as from a drawer, holster, etc.; move in a specified direction; arouse the interest or attention of; formulate or derive, e.g. *draw conclusions;* take from a source, e.g. *draw money from the bank;* (of two teams or contestants) finish a game with an equal number of points. —*n.* raffle or lottery; contest or game ending in a tie; event, act, etc., that attracts a large audience. —**drawer** *n.* boxlike container in a chest, table, etc., made for sliding in and out. —*pl. Old-fashioned* undergarment worn below the waist. —**drawing** *n.* picture or plan made by means of lines on a surface; art of making drawings. —**drawing pin** short tack with a broad smooth head. —**drawing room** *Old-fashioned* room where visitors are received and entertained. —**drawback** *n.* disadvantage. —**drawbridge** *n.* bridge that may be raised to prevent access or to enable vessels to pass. —**draw out** *v.* extend; encourage (a person) to talk freely. —**drawstring** *n.* cord run through a hem around an opening, so that when it is pulled tighter, the opening closes. —**draw up** *v.* (of a vehicle) come to a halt; formulate and write out (a contract).

THESAURUS

draft 1. *v.* compose, design, draw, draw up, formulate, outline, plan, sketch 2. *n.* outline, plan, rough, sketch, version

drag draw, hale, haul, lug, pull, tow, trail, tug, yank

dragoon bully, coerce, compel, constrain, drive, force, impel, intimidate

drain *v.* 1. bleed, draw off, dry, empty, milk, remove, tap, withdraw 2. consume, deplete, dissipate, empty, exhaust, sap, strain, tax, use up, weary ~*n.* 3. channel, conduit, culvert, ditch, duct, outlet, pipe, sewer, sink, trench, watercourse 4. depletion, drag, exhaustion, reduction, sap, strain, withdrawal

drama 1. play, show 2. acting, dramaturgy, stagecraft, theatre 3. crisis, excitement, scene, spectacle, theatrics, turmoil

dramatic 1. theatrical 2. breathtaking, electrify-ing, emotional, exciting, melodramatic, sensational, startling, sudden, tense, thrilling

dramatist playwright, scriptwriter

dramatize act, overdo, overstate, play-act

drastic desperate, dire, extreme, forceful, harsh, radical, severe, strong

draught 1. *Of air* current, flow, movement 2. cup, dose, drench, drink, potion, quantity

draw *v.* 1. drag, haul, pull, tow, tug 2. depict, design, map out, mark out, outline, paint, portray, sketch, trace 3. allure, attract, bring forth, call forth, elicit, engage, entice, evoke, induce, influence, invite, persuade 4. elongate, extend, lengthen, stretch 5. breathe in, drain, inhale, inspire, pull, respire, suck 6. compose, draft, formulate, frame, prepare, write ~*n.* 7. *Inf.* attraction, enticement, lure *(Inf.)* 8. dead heat, stalemate, tie

DICTIONARY

drawl v. speak slowly, esp. prolonging the vowel sounds. —n. drawling manner of speech.

drawn v. past participle of DRAW. —adj. haggard, tired, or tense in appearance.

dray n. low cart used for carrying heavy loads.

dread v. anticipate with apprehension or terror. —n. great fear. —**dreadful** adj. extremely disagreeable, shocking, or bad; extreme. —**dreadfully** adv.

dream n. mental activity, usu. an imagined series of events, occurring during sleep; cherished hope; Informal something wonderful. —v. **dreaming, dreamt** or **dreamed.** experience (a dream); (foll. by of or about) have an image (of) or fantasy (about); (foll. by of) consider the possibility (of). —**dreamer** n. —**dreamy** adj. vague or impractical; Informal wonderful. —**dreamily** adv.

dreary adj. **drearier, dreariest.** dull or boring. —**drearily** adv. —**dreariness** n.

dredge[1] v. remove (silt or mud) from (a river bed etc.). —**dredger** n. boat fitted with machinery for dredging.

dredge[2] v. sprinkle (food) with flour etc.

dregs pl. n. solid particles that settle at the bottom of some liquids; most despised elements, e.g. the dregs of society.

drench v. make completely wet. —**drenching** n.

dress v. put clothes on; put on formal clothes; apply protective covering to (a wound); arrange or prepare. —n. one-piece garment for a woman or girl, consisting of a skirt and bodice and sometimes sleeves; complete style of clothing. —**dressing** n. sauce for salad; covering for a wound. —**dressing-down** n. Informal severe scolding. —**dressing gown** robe worn before dressing. —**dressing room** room used for changing clothes, esp. backstage in a theatre. —**dressy** adj. (of clothes) elegant. —**dressiness** n. —**dress circle** first gallery in a theatre. —**dressmaker** n. person who makes clothes for women. —**dressmaking** n. —**dress rehearsal** last rehearsal of a play, using costumes, lighting, etc., as for the first night.

dressage [dress-ahzh] n. training of a horse to perform manoeuvres in response to the rider's body signals.

dresser[1] n. set of shelves, usu. with cupboards, for storing or displaying dishes.

dresser[2] n. Theatre person employed to assist actors with their costumes.

drew v. past tense of DRAW.

drey n. squirrel's nest.

dribble v. (allow to) flow in drops; allow saliva to trickle from the mouth; propel (a ball) by repeatedly tapping it with the foot, hand, or a stick. —n. small quantity of liquid falling in drops. —**dribbler** n.

dried v. past of DRY.

drier adj. comparative of DRY. —n. same as DRYER.

driest adj. superlative of DRY.

THESAURUS

drawback defect, difficulty, disadvantage, fault, flaw, handicap, hindrance, hitch, impediment, nuisance, obstacle, snag, stumbling block, trouble

drawing cartoon, depiction, illustration, outline, picture, portrayal, representation, sketch, study

drawn fatigued, fraught, harassed, harrowed, pinched, sapped, strained, stressed, taut, tense, tired, worn

draw out drag out, extend, lengthen, prolong, protract, stretch

draw up compose, draft, formulate, frame, prepare, write out

dread 1. v. fear, quail, shrink from, shudder, tremble 2. n. alarm, apprehension, aversion, awe, dismay, fear, fright, horror, terror, trepidation

dreadful alarming, appalling, awful, distressing, fearful, formidable, frightful, ghastly, hideous, horrible, monstrous, shocking, terrible, tragic

dream n. 1. daydream, delusion, fantasy, illusion, imagination, reverie, speculation, trance, vision 2. ambition, aspiration, design, desire, goal, hope, notion, wish ~v. 3. daydream, envisage, fancy, imagine, stargaze, think, visualize

dreamy 1. chimerical, fantastic, misty, shadowy, unreal 2. absent, abstracted, daydreaming, faraway, impractical, musing, pensive, preoccupied, vague

dreary boring, drab, dull, lifeless, monotonous, routine, tedious, uneventful, wearisome

dregs deposit, dross, grounds, lees, residue, scum, sediment, trash, waste

drench drown, flood, inundate, saturate, soak, souse, steep, wet

dress n. 1. costume, ensemble, frock, garment, gown, outfit, robe, suit 2. attire, clothes, clothing, costume, garb, garments, guise ~v. 3. attire, change, clothe, don, garb, put on, robe 4. bandage, bind up, plaster, treat

dressmaker couturier, seamstress, tailor

dribble drip, drop, leak, ooze, run, seep, trickle

DICTIONARY

drift v. be carried along by currents of air or water; move aimlessly from one place or activity to another. —n. something piled up by the wind or current, such as a snowdrift; tendency or meaning; general movement or development. —**drifter** n. person who moves aimlessly from place to place or job to job. —**driftwood** n. wood floating on or washed ashore by the sea.

drill[1] n. tool or machine for boring holes; strict and often repetitive training; *Informal* correct procedure. —v. pierce, bore, or cut (a hole) in (material) (as if) with a drill; teach by rigorous exercises and training.

drill[2] n. hard-wearing cotton cloth.

drily adv. same as DRYLY.

drink v. **drinking, drank, drunk.** swallow (a liquid); consume alcohol, esp. to excess. —n. liquid suitable for drinking; portion of liquid for drinking; alcohol or its habitual or excessive consumption. —**drinkable** adj. —**drinker** n. —**drink in** v. pay close attention to. —**drink to** v. drink a toast to.

drip v. **dripping, dripped.** fall or let fall in drops. —n. falling of drops of liquid; sound made by falling drops; *Informal* inane insipid person; *Med.* apparatus for the administration of a solution drop by drop into a vein. —**drip-dry** adj. denoting clothing that will dry free of creases if hung up when wet.

dripping n. fat that comes from meat while it is being roasted or fried.

drive v. **driving, drove, driven.** guide the movement of (a vehicle); transport or be transported in a vehicle; goad into a specified state; push or propel; *Sport* hit (a ball) very hard and straight. —n. journey in a driven vehicle; road for vehicles, esp. a private road leading to a house; united effort towards a common goal, e.g. *an investment drive;* energy, ambition, or initiative;

Psychol. motive or interest, e.g. *sex drive;* means by which force, motion, etc. is transmitted in a mechanism. —**driver** n. person who drives a vehicle; *Golf* club used for tee shots. —**drive at** v. *Informal* intend or mean, e.g. *what are you driving at?* —**drive-in** n., adj. (denoting) a public facility used by patrons in their cars.

drivel n. foolish talk. —v. -**elling, -elled.** speak foolishly.

drizzle n. very light rain. —v. rain lightly. —**drizzly** adj.

droll adj. quaintly amusing. —**drolly** adv. —**drollery** n.

dromedary [drom-mid-er-ee] n., pl. -**daries.** camel with a single hump.

drone[1] n. male bee.

drone[2] v., n. (make) a monotonous low dull sound. —**drone on** v. talk for a long time in a monotonous tone.

drool v. (foll. by *over*) show excessive enthusiasm (for) or pleasure (in); allow saliva to flow from the mouth.

droop v. sag, as from weakness. —**droopy** adj.

drop n. small quantity of liquid forming a round shape; very small quantity of liquid; act of falling; decrease in amount or value; vertical distance that anything may fall. —pl. liquid medication applied drop by drop. —v. **dropping, dropped.** (allow to) fall in globules; (allow to) fall vertically; decrease in amount, strength, or value; mention casually; discontinue (an activity). —**droplet** n. —**droppings** pl. n. faeces of certain animals, such as rabbits or birds. —**drop in** or **by** v. pay someone a casual visit. —**drop off** v. grow smaller or less; *Informal* fall asleep. —**dropout** n. person who fails to complete a course of study; person who rejects conventional society. —**drop out (of)** v. abandon or withdraw (from a school, job, etc.).

THESAURUS

drift coast, float, meander, stray, waft, wander

drill v. 1. exercise, instruct, practise, rehearse, teach, train ~n. 2. discipline, exercise, practice, preparation, repetition, training ~v. 3. bore, pierce, puncture, sink in ~n. 4. bit, borer, gimlet

drink v. 1. drain, gulp, guzzle, imbibe, partake of, quaff, sip, suck, sup, swallow, swig, swill, wash down 2. revel, tipple, tope ~n. 3. beverage, liquid, potion, refreshment 4. alcohol, liquor, spirits

drip 1. v. drop, exude, filter, splash, sprinkle, trickle 2. n. dribble, drop, leak, trickle

drive v. 1. herd, hurl, impel, propel, push, send, urge 2. direct, go, guide, handle, manage, motor, operate, ride, steer, travel ~n. 3. excur-

sion, jaunt, journey, outing, ride, run, trip, turn 4. effort, energy, enterprise, initiative, vigour

drizzle 1. n. fine rain, Scotch mist 2. v. rain, shower, spray, sprinkle

droll amusing, comic, comical, diverting, eccentric, entertaining, farcical, funny, humorous, jocular, ludicrous, odd, quaint, ridiculous, risible, whimsical

droop bend, drop, fall down, hang (down), sag, sink

drop n. 1. bead, drip, globule, pearl, tear 2. dab, dash, mouthful, nip, pinch, sip, spot, taste, tot, trace, trickle 3. decline, decrease, downturn, fall-off, reduction ~v. 4. decline, depress, descend, diminish, dive, droop, fall,

DICTIONARY

dropsy *n.* illness in which watery fluid collects in the body.

dross *n.* scum formed on the surfaces of molten metals; worthless matter.

drought *n.* prolonged shortage of rainfall.

drove[1] *v.* past tense of DRIVE.

drove[2] *n.* moving herd of livestock; moving crowd of people. —**drover** *n.* person who drives sheep or cattle.

drown *v.* die or kill by immersion in liquid; forget (one's sorrows) temporarily by drinking alcohol; drench thoroughly; render (a sound) inaudible by making a loud noise.

drowse *v.* be sleepy, dull, or sluggish. —**drowsy** *adj.* —**drowsily** *adv.* —**drowsiness** *n.*

drubbing *n.* utter defeat, as in a contest.

drudge *n.* person who works hard at wearisome menial tasks. —*v.* toil at such tasks. —**drudgery** *n.*

drug *n.* substance used in the treatment or prevention of disease; chemical substance, esp. a narcotic, taken for the effect it produces. —*v.* **drugging, drugged.** mix a drug with (food or drink); administer a drug to (a person or animal) in order to induce sleepiness or unconsciousness. —**drugstore** *n. US* pharmacy where a wide variety of goods is available.

Druid *n.* member of an ancient order of Celtic priests. —**Druidic(al)** *adj.*

drum *n.* percussion instrument sounded by striking a skin stretched across the opening of a hollow cylinder; cylindrical object or container. —*v.* **drumming, drummed.** play (music) on a drum; tap rhythmically or regularly. —**drummer** *n.* —**drum into** *v.* instil into (someone) by constant repetition. —**drumstick** *n.* stick used

for playing a drum; lower joint of the leg of a cooked fowl. —**drum up** *v.* obtain (support) by solicitation or canvassing.

drunk *v.* past participle of DRINK. —*adj.* intoxicated with alcohol to the extent of losing control over normal functions; overwhelmed by a strong influence or emotion. —*n.* person who is drunk. —**drunkard** *n.* person who is frequently or habitually drunk. —**drunken** *adj.* drunk; caused by or relating to alcoholic intoxication. —**drunkenly** *adv.* —**drunkenness** *n.*

dry *adj.* **drier, driest** *or* **dryer, dryest.** lacking moisture; having little or no rainfall; *Informal* thirsty; (of wine) not sweet; uninteresting, e.g. *a dry book;* (of humour) subtle and sarcastic; prohibiting the sale of alcohol, e.g. *a dry area.* —*v.* **drying, dried.** make or become dry; preserve (food) by removing the moisture. —**dryly** *adv.* —**dryness** *n.* —**dryer** *n.* apparatus for removing moisture. —**dry-clean** *v.* clean (clothes etc.) with a solvent other than water. —**dry-cleaner** *n.* —**dry-cleaning** *n.* —**dry out** *v.* make or become dry; (cause to) undergo treatment for alcoholism or drug addiction. —**dry rot** crumbling and drying of timber, caused by certain fungi. —**dry run** *Informal* rehearsal.

dryad *n.* wood nymph.

DSc Doctor of Science.

DSS Department of Social Security.

dual *adj.* relating to or denoting two; twofold. —**duality** *n.* —**dual carriageway** *Brit.* road on which traffic travelling in opposite directions is separated by a central strip of turf or concrete.

dub[1] *v.* **dubbing, dubbed.** give (a person or place) a name or nickname.

dub[2] *v.* **dubbing, dubbed.** provide (a film) with a

THESAURUS

lower, plunge, sink, tumble 5. abandon, cease, desert, discontinue, forsake, give up, leave, relinquish, terminate

drop off decline, decrease, diminish, dwindle, fall off, lessen, slacken

drop out abandon, back out, forsake, give up, leave, quit, renege, stop, withdraw

drought dry spell, dry weather

drove collection, company, crowd, flock, gathering, herd, horde, mob, multitude, press, swarm, throng

drown deluge, drench, engulf, flood, go down, go under, immerse, inundate, sink, submerge, swamp

drudge factotum, hack, menial, plodder, servant, slave, toiler, worker

drudgery chore, hack work, hard work, labour, slavery, slog, toil

drug *n.* 1. medicine, physic, poison, remedy 2. narcotic, opiate ~*v.* 3. dose, medicate, treat

drum *v.* beat, pulsate, rap, reverberate, tap, tattoo, throb

drunk 1. *adj.* drunken, fuddled, inebriated, intoxicated, maudlin, merry (*Inf.*), tight (*Inf.*), tipsy, well-oiled (*Sl.*) 2. *n.* drunkard, inebriate, sot, toper

drunkenness alcoholism, dipsomania, insobriety, intemperance, intoxication, tipsiness

dry *adj.* 1. arid, barren, dehydrated, dried up, parched, sapless, thirsty, torrid, waterless 2. *Fig.* boring, dreary, dull, monotonous, plain, tedious, tiresome, uninteresting ~*v.* 3. dehydrate, desiccate, drain, make dry, parch, sear

dual coupled, double, duplicate, matched, paired, twin, twofold

DICTIONARY

new soundtrack, esp. in a different language; provide (a film or tape) with a soundtrack.

dubbin n. *Brit.* greasy preparation applied to leather to soften and waterproof it.

dubious [dew-bee-uss] *adj.* feeling or causing doubt. —**dubiously** *adv.* —**dubiety** [dew-by-it-ee] n.

ducal [duke-al] *adj.* of a duke.

ducat [duck-it] n. former European gold or silver coin.

duchess n. woman who holds the rank of duke in her own right; wife or widow of a duke.

duchy n., pl. **duchies.** territory of a duke or duchess.

duck[1] n. water bird with short legs, webbed feet, and a broad blunt bill; female of this bird; flesh of this bird, used as food; *Cricket* score of nothing. —**duckling** n. young duck.

duck[2] v. move (the head or body) quickly downwards, to escape observation or to dodge a blow; plunge suddenly into water; *Informal* dodge or escape (a duty etc.).

duct n. tube, pipe, or canal by means of which a fluid or gas is conveyed; bodily passage conveying secretions or excretions. —**ductile** *adj.* (of metal) able to be shaped into sheets or wires; easily influenced. —**ductility** n.

dud n. *Informal* person or thing that proves ineffectual. —*adj.* bad or useless.

dude n. *US old-fashioned informal* man, chap; dandy.

dudgeon n. —**in high dudgeon** angry or resentful.

due *adj.* expected or scheduled to be present or arrive; owed as a debt; fitting, proper. —n. something that is owed, required, or due. —*pl.* charges for membership of a club or organization. —*adv.* directly or exactly, e.g. *due north.* —**due to** attributable to or caused by.

duel n. formal prearranged combat with deadly weapons between two people, to settle a quarrel. —v. **duelling, duelled.** fight in a duel. —**duellist** n.

duenna n. (esp. in Spain) elderly woman acting as chaperone to a young woman.

duet n. piece of music for two performers.

duff *adj. Brit. informal* bad or useless. —**duff up** v. *Brit. informal* beat (a person) severely.

duffel, duffle n. coat made of heavy woollen cloth.

duffer n. *Informal* dull or incompetent person.

dug[1] v. past of DIG.

dug[2] n. teat or udder.

dugong n. whalelike mammal found in tropical waters.

dugout n. canoe made by hollowing out a log; *Mil.* covered excavation dug to provide shelter; (at a sports ground) covered bench where managers and substitutes sit.

duke n. nobleman of the highest rank; prince or ruler of a small principality or duchy. —**dukedom** n.

dulcet [dull-sit] *adj.* (of a sound) soothing or pleasant.

dulcimer n. tuned percussion instrument consisting of a set of strings stretched over a sounding board and struck with hammers.

dull *adj.* uninteresting; stupid; (of a blade) lacking sharpness; (of a pain) not acute or intense; (of weather) not bright or clear; lacking in spirit. —v. make or become dull. —**dullness** n. —**dully** *adv.* —**dullard** n. dull or stupid person.

duly *adv.* in a proper manner; at the proper time.

dumb *adj.* lacking the power to speak; silent; *Informal* stupid. —**dumbly** *adv.* —**dumbness** n. —**dumbbell** n. exercising weight consisting of a short bar with a heavy ball or disc at either end.

THESAURUS

dubious 1. doubtful, hesitant, uncertain, unconvinced, undecided, unsure, wavering 2. ambiguous, debatable, doubtful, equivocal, indefinite, obscure, problematical, unclear, unsettled 3. questionable, suspect, suspicious

duck 1. bend, bow, crouch, dodge, drop, lower, stoop 2. *Inf.* avoid, dodge, escape, evade, shirk, sidestep

dudgeon ire, resentment, umbrage, wrath

due *adj.* 1. outstanding, owed, owing, payable, unpaid 2. appropriate, becoming, bounden, deserved, fit, fitting, just, justified, merited, obligatory, proper, right, rightful, suitable 3. expected, expected to arrive, scheduled ~*adv.* 4. dead, direct, directly, exactly, straight

duel 1. affair of honour, single combat 2. clash, competition, contest, encounter, engagement, fight, rivalry

dues charge, charges, fee, levy

dull 1. dense, dim, slow, stolid, stupid, thick, unintelligent 2. apathetic, blank, callous, dead, empty, heavy, indifferent, lifeless, listless, slow, sluggish 3. boring, commonplace, dreary, dry, flat, plain, prosaic, tedious, tiresome, unimaginative, uninteresting 4. cloudy, dim, gloomy, overcast

duly 1. accordingly, befittingly, correctly, deservedly, fittingly, properly, rightfully, suitably 2. on time, punctually

DICTIONARY

—**dumbfound** v. strike dumb with astonishment. —**dumb show** meaningful gestures without speech.

dumdum n. soft-nosed bullet that expands on impact and inflicts extensive wounds.

dummy n., pl. **-mies.** figure representing the human form, used for displaying clothes etc.; copy of an object, often lacking some essential feature of the original; *Brit.* rubber teat for a baby to suck; *Slang* stupid person. —*adj.* sham or counterfeit. —**dummy run** practice, rehearsal.

dump v. drop or let fall heavily or in a mass; *Informal* dispose of (something or someone) carelessly; market (goods) in bulk and at low prices, esp. abroad. —*n.* place where waste materials are dumped; *Informal* dirty unattractive place; *Mil.* place where weapons or supplies are stored. —**down in the dumps** in a state of depression. —**dumpy** *adj.* short and plump.

dumpling n. small ball of dough cooked and served with stew; round pastry case filled with fruit.

dun *adj.* brownish-grey.

dunce n. person who is stupid or slow to learn.

dunderhead n. slow-witted person.

dune n. mound or ridge of drifted sand.

dung n. excrement of animals.

dungarees pl. n. trousers with a bib attached.

dungeon n. underground prison cell.

dunk v. dip (a biscuit etc.) into liquid before eating it; submerge (something) in liquid.

duo n., pl. **duos.** pair of performers; *Informal* pair of closely connected people.

duodecimal *adj.* reckoned in twelves or twelfths.

duodenum [dew-oh-**deen**-um] n., pl. **-nas, -nums.** first part of the small intestine, just below the stomach. —**duodenal** *adj.*

dupe v. deceive or cheat. —*n.* person who is easily deceived.

duple *adj. Music* having two beats in a bar.

duplex n. *US* apartment on two floors. —*adj.* having two parts.

duplicate *adj.* copied exactly from an original. —*n.* exact copy. —*v.* make a replica of; do again (something that has already been done). —**duplication** n. —**duplicator** n.

duplicity n. deception or double-dealing.

durable *adj.* long-lasting. —**durables, durable goods** pl. n. goods that require infrequent replacement. —**durability** n.

duration n. length of time that something lasts.

duress n. compulsion by use of force or threats.

during *prep.* throughout or within the limit of (a period of time).

dusk n. time just before nightfall, when it is almost dark. —**dusky** *adj.* dark in colour; shadowy. —**duskiness** n.

dust n. dry fine powdery material, such as particles of dirt. —*v.* remove dust from (furniture) by wiping; sprinkle (something) with dust or some other powdery substance. —**duster** n. cloth used for dusting. —**dusty** *adj.* covered with dust. —**dustbin** n. large usu. cylindrical container for household rubbish. —**dustbowl** n. dry area in which the surface soil is exposed to wind erosion. —**dust jacket, cover** removable paper cover used to protect a book. —**dustman** n. *Brit.* man whose job is to collect household rubbish. —**dustpan** n. short-handled hooded shovel into which dust is swept from floors.

Dutch *adj.* of the Netherlands, its inhabitants, or their language. —**go Dutch** *Informal* share the expenses on an outing. —**Dutch courage** false courage gained from drinking alcohol.

duty n., pl. **-ties.** task that a person is bound to

THESAURUS

dumb inarticulate, mute, silent, soundless, speechless, tongue-tied, voiceless, wordless

dummy n. 1. figure, form, model 2. copy, counterfeit, duplicate, imitation, sham, substitute ~*adj.* 3. artificial, bogus, counterfeit, fake, false, imitation, mock, sham, simulated

dump v. 1. deposit, drop, fling down, let fall, throw down ~*n.* 2. junkyard, refuse heap, rubbish heap, rubbish tip, tip 3. hovel, mess, pigsty, shack, shanty, slum

dungeon cage, cell, lockup, prison

duplicate 1. *adj.* corresponding, identical, matched, twin, twofold 2. *n.* carbon copy, copy, double, likeness, match, mate, replica, reproduction, twin 3. *v.* copy, double, echo, photocopy, repeat, reproduce

durability endurance, imperishability, permanence, persistence

durable abiding, constant, dependable, enduring, fast, firm, hard-wearing, persistent, reliable, resistant, sound, stable, strong, sturdy, substantial, tough

dusk dark, evening, nightfall, sundown, sunset, twilight

dusky dark, dark-hued, sable, swarthy

dust n. grime, grit, particles, powder

dusty dirty, grubby, sooty, unclean, undusted, unswept

dutiful compliant, conscientious devoted, docile, obedient, punctilious, respectful, submissive

DICTIONARY

perform for moral or legal reasons; government tax, esp. on imports. —**on duty** at work. —**dutiable** *adj.* (of goods) requiring payment of duty. —**dutiful** *adj.* showing or resulting from a sense of duty. —**dutifully** *adv.*

duvet [doo-vay] *n.* quilt filled with down or artificial fibre.

dwarf *n., pl.* **dwarfs, dwarves.** undersized person; (in folklore) small ugly manlike creature, often possessing magical powers. —*adj.* denoting an animal or plant much below the average size for a species. —*v.* cause (someone or something) to seem small by being much larger.

dwell *v.* **dwelling, dwelt** *or* **dwelled.** live as a permanent resident. —**dweller** *n.* —**dwelling** *n.* place of residence. —**dwell on, upon** *v.* think, speak, or write at length about.

dwindle *v.* grow less in size, intensity, or number.

dye *n.* staining or colouring substance; colour produced by dyeing. —*v.* **dyeing, dyed.** colour or stain (fabric, hair, etc.) by the application of dye. —**dyer** *n.* —**dyed-in-the-wool** *adj.* uncompromising or unchanging in attitude or opinion.

dying *v.* present participle of DIE[1].

dyke *n.* wall built to prevent flooding; ditch; *Slang* lesbian.

dynamic *adj.* characterized by force of personality, ambition, and energy; of or concerned with energy or forces that produce motion. —**dynamically** *adv.* —**dynamism** *n.* forcefulness of an energetic personality.

dynamics *n.* branch of mechanics concerned with the forces that change or produce the motions of bodies.

dynamite *n.* high-explosive mixture containing nitroglycerin; *Informal* spectacular or potentially dangerous person or thing. —*v.* mine or blow (something) up with dynamite.

dynamo *n., pl.* **-mos.** device for converting mechanical energy into electrical energy.

dynasty *n., pl.* **-ties.** sequence of hereditary rulers. —**dynastic** *adj.*

dysentery *n.* infection of the intestine causing severe diarrhoea.

dysfunction *n. Med.* disturbance or abnormality in the function of an organ or part.

dyslexia *n.* disorder causing impaired ability to read. —**dyslexic** *adj.*

dysmenorrhoea *n.* painful menstruation.

dyspepsia *n.* indigestion. —**dyspeptic** *adj.*

dystrophy [diss-trof-fee] *n.* wasting of the body tissues, esp. the muscles.

THESAURUS

duty 1. business, calling, charge, engagement, function, mission, obligation, office, onus, responsibility, role, service, task, work 2. customs, excise, impost, levy, tariff, tax, toll 3. **on duty** at work, busy, engaged

dwarf 1. *n.* bantam, midget, pygmy 2. *adj.* baby, diminutive, miniature, petite, pocket, small, tiny, undersized 3. *v.* dominate, overshadow, tower above *or* over

dwell abide, inhabit, live, lodge, remain, reside, rest, settle, sojourn, stay, stop

dwelling abode, domicile, establishment, habitation, home, house, quarters, residence

dye 1. *n.* colour, colouring, pigment, stain, tinge, tint 2. *v.* colour, pigment, stain, tincture, tinge, tint

dying ebbing, expiring, fading, failing, final, going, *in extremis,* moribund, mortal, passing, perishing, sinking

dynamic active, driving, energetic, forceful, go-ahead, high-powered, lively, magnetic, powerful, vigorous, vital

dynasty ascendancy, dominion, empire, government, house, regime, rule, sovereignty, sway

E

E East(ern).

each *adj., pron.* every (one) taken separately.

eager *adj.* showing or feeling great desire, keen. —**eagerly** *adv.* —**eagerness** *n.*

eagle *n.* large bird of prey with keen eyesight; *Golf* score of two strokes under par for a hole. —**eaglet** *n.* young eagle.

ear[1] *n.* organ of hearing, esp. the external part of it; sensitivity to musical or other sounds. —**earache** *n.* pain in the ear. —**eardrum** *n.* thin piece of skin inside the ear which enables one to hear sounds. —**earmark** *v.* set (something) aside for a specific purpose. —*n.* distinguishing mark. —**earphone** *n.* receiver for a radio etc., held to or put in the ear. —**earring** *n.* ornament for the lobe of the ear. —**earshot** *n.* hearing range.

ear[2] *n.* head of corn.

earl *n.* British nobleman ranking next below a marquess. —**earldom** *n.*

early *adj., adv.* **-lier, -liest.** before the expected or usual time; in the first part of a period; in a period far back in time.

earn *v.* obtain by work or merit; (of investments etc.) gain (interest). —**earnings** *pl. n.* money earned.

earnest[1] *adj.* serious and sincere. —**in earnest** seriously. —**earnestly** *adv.*

earnest[2] *n.* part payment given in advance, esp. to confirm a contract.

earth *n.* planet that we live on; land, the ground; soil; fox's hole; wire connecting an electrical apparatus with the earth. —*v.* connect (a circuit) to earth. —**earthen** *adj.* made of baked clay or earth. —**earthenware** *n.* pottery made of baked clay. —**earthly** *adj.* conceivable or possible, e.g. *no earthly reason.* —**earthy** *adj.* coarse or crude; of or like earth. —**earthquake** *n.* violent vibration of the earth's surface. —**earthwork** *n.* fortification made of earth. —**earthworm** *n.* worm which burrows in the soil.

earwig *n.* small insect with a pincer-like tail.

ease *n.* freedom from difficulty, discomfort, or worry; rest or leisure, e.g. *at one's ease.* —*v.* give bodily or mental ease to; lessen (severity, tension, pain, etc.); move carefully or gradually.

easel *n.* frame to support an artist's canvas or a blackboard.

east *n.* part of the horizon where the sun rises; eastern lands or the orient. —*adj.* on, in, or near the east; (of the wind) from the east. —*adv.* in, to, or towards the east. —**easterly** *adj., adv.* in the east; (of a wind) from the east. —**eastern** *adj.* of, in, or from the east. —**eastward** *adj., adv.* —**eastwards** *adv.*

Easter *n.* Christian spring festival commemorating the Resurrection of Jesus Christ. —**Easter egg** chocolate egg given at Easter.

easy *adj.* **easier, easiest.** not needing much work or effort; free from pain, care, or anxiety; easy-going. —**easily** *adv.* —**easiness** *n.* —**easy**

THESAURUS

each 1. *adj.* every 2. *pron.* every one, one and all

eager agog, anxious, ardent, athirst, earnest, enthusiastic, fervent, greedy, hungry, intent, keen, longing, raring, zealous

ear discrimination, sensitivity, taste

early 1. *adj.* forward, premature, untimely 2. *adv.* beforehand, in advance, in good time, prematurely, too soon

earn 1. collect, draw, gain, get, gross, make, net, obtain, procure, reap, receive 2. deserve, merit, rate, warrant, win

earnest close, constant, determined, firm, fixed, grave, intent, resolute, serious, sincere, solemn, stable, staid, steady

earnings gain, income, pay, proceeds, profits, receipts, remuneration, return, reward, salary, stipend, wages

earth 1. globe, orb, planet, sphere, world 2. clay, dirt, ground, land, loam, sod, soil, topsoil, turf

earthenware ceramics, crockery, crocks, pots, pottery, terra cotta

ease 1. *n.* affluence, calmness, comfort, contentment, enjoyment, happiness, leisure, peace, quiet, relaxation, repose, rest, serenity, tranquillity 2. *v.* abate, allay, alleviate, assuage, calm, comfort, disburden, lessen, lighten, moderate, pacify, palliate, quiet, relax, relent, relieve, slacken, soothe, still

easily comfortably, effortlessly, readily, simply, smoothly, with ease, without difficulty

easy child's play, clear, effortless, facile, light, no bother, not difficult, no trouble, painless, simple, smooth, straightforward, uncomplicated, undemanding

easy-going amenable, calm, carefree, casual, complacent, easy, even-tempered, flexible, indulgent, lenient, liberal, mild, moderate, nonchalant, permissive, placid, relaxed, serene, tolerant, uncritical, undemanding, unhurried chair comfortable armchair. —**easy-going** *adj.* relaxed in attitude, tolerant.

eat *v.* **eating, ate, eaten.** take (food) into the mouth and swallow it; (foll. by *away* or *up*) destroy; have a meal. —**eatable** *adj.* fit or suitable for eating.

eau de Cologne [**oh** de kol-**lone**] *n. French* light perfume.

eaves *pl. n.* overhanging edges of a roof.

eavesdrop *v.* **-dropping, -dropped.** listen secretly to a private conversation. —**eavesdropper** *n.* —**eavesdropping** *n.*

ebb *v.* (of tide water) flow back; become weaker. —*n.* flowing back of the tide. —**at a low ebb** in a state of weakness.

ebony *n., pl.* **-onies.** hard black wood. —*adj.* deep black.

ebullient *adj.* overflowing with enthusiasm and excitement. —**ebullience** *n.*

EC European Community.

eccentric *adj.* odd or unconventional; (of circles) not having the same centre. —*n.* eccentric person. —**eccentrically** *adv.* —**eccentricity** *n.*

ecclesiastic *adj.* (also **ecclesiastical**) of the Christian Church or clergy. —*n.* clergyman.

ECG electrocardiogram; electrocardiograph.

echelon [**esh**-a-lon] *n.* level of power or responsibility; *Mil.* formation in which units follow one another but are spaced out sideways to allow each a line of fire ahead.

echo *n., pl.* **-oes.** repetition of sounds by reflection of sound waves off a surface; close imitation. —*v.* **-oing, -oed.** repeat or be repeated as an echo; imitate closely. —**echo sounder** sonar. —**echo sounding** use of sonar to navigate.

éclair *n.* finger-shaped pastry filled with cream and covered with chocolate.

éclat [ake-**lah**] *n.* brilliant success; splendour.

eclectic *adj.* selecting from various ideas or sources. —**eclecticism** *n.*

eclipse *n.* temporary obscuring of one heavenly body by another. —*v.* surpass or outclass. —**ecliptic** *n.* apparent path of the sun.

eclogue *n.* short poem on a rural theme.

ecology *n.* study of the relationships between living things and their environment. —**ecological** *adj.* —**ecologically** *adv.* —**ecologist** *n.*

economy *n., pl.* **-mies.** system of interrelationship of money, industry, and employment in a country; careful management of resources to avoid waste. —**economic** *adj.* of economics; profitable. —**economics** *n.* social science concerned with the production and consumption of goods and services. —*pl.* financial aspects. —**economical** *adj.* not wasteful, thrifty. —**economically** *adv.* —**economist** *n.* specialist in economics. —**economize** *v.* limit or reduce waste.

ecru *adj.* greyish-yellow.

ecstasy *n.* state of intense delight. —**ecstatic** *adj.* —**ecstatically** *adv.*

ectoplasm *n. Spiritualism* substance that supposedly is emitted from the body of a medium during a trance.

ecumenical *adj.* of the Christian Church

THESAURUS

eat 1. chew, consume, devour, munch, swallow 2. dine, feed, have a meal, take food

eavesdrop listen in, monitor, overhear, spy

ebb *v.* 1. abate, fall away, flow back, go out, recede, retire, retreat, sink, subside, wane, withdraw 2. decay, decline, decrease, degenerate, deteriorate, diminish, drop, dwindle, fade away, fall away, flag, lessen, peter out, shrink, sink, slacken, weaken

eccentric abnormal, anomalous, bizarre, capricious, erratic, freakish, idiosyncratic, irregular, odd, outlandish, peculiar, singular, strange, uncommon, unconventional, weird

eccentricity abnormality, anomaly, caprice, foible, idiosyncrasy, irregularity, nonconformity, oddity, peculiarity, quirk, singularity, strangeness, unconventionality, waywardness, weirdness

ecclesiastic churchman, clergyman, cleric, divine, holy man, minister, parson, priest

echo *v.* 1. repeat, resound, reverberate ~*n.* 2. answer, repetition, reverberation 3. copy, imi-

tation, parallel, reflection, reproduction, ringing

economic 1. business, commercial, financial, industrial, mercantile, trade 2. productive, profitable, profit-making, remunerative, solvent, viable 3. budgetary, financial, fiscal, material, monetary, pecuniary

economical 1. cost-effective, efficient, money-saving, sparing, time-saving, unwasteful, work-saving 2. careful, frugal, prudent, saving, scrimping, sparing, thrifty

economize be economical, be frugal, be sparing, cut back, husband, retrench, save, scrimp, tighten one's belt

economy frugality, husbandry, parsimony, providence, prudence, restraint, saving, thrift

ecstasy bliss, delight, elation, enthusiasm, euphoria, exaltation, fervour, frenzy, joy, rapture, trance, transport

ecstatic blissful, delirious, elated, enthusiastic, euphoric, fervent, frenzied, joyful, joyous, overjoyed, rapturous, transported

DICTIONARY

throughout the world, esp. with regard to its unity.

eczema [ek-sim-a] *n*. skin disease causing intense itching.

Edam *n*. round Dutch cheese with a red rind.

eddy *n., pl.* **eddies.** small whirling movement in air, water, etc. —*v*. **eddied, eddying.** move in eddies.

edelweiss [ade-el-vice] *n*. alpine plant with white flowers.

Eden *n. Bible* garden in which Adam and Eve were placed at the Creation; place of delight or contentment.

edge *n*. border or line where something ends or begins; cutting side of a blade; sharpness of tone. —*v*. provide an edge or border for; push (one's way) gradually. —**have the edge on** have an advantage over. —**on edge** nervous or irritable. —**edgeways** *adv*. with the edge forwards or uppermost. —**edging** *n*. anything placed along an edge to finish it. —**edgy** *adj*. nervous or irritable.

edible *adj*. fit to be eaten. —**edibility** *n*.

edict [ee-dikt] *n*. order issued by an authority.

edifice [ed-if-iss] *n*. large building.

edify [ed-if-fie] *v*. **-fying, -fied.** improve morally by instruction. —**edification** *n*.

edit *v*. prepare (a book, film, etc.) for publication or broadcast. —**edition** *n*. form in which

something is published; number of copies of a new publication printed at one time. —**editor** *n*. person who edits; person in overall charge of a newspaper or periodical. —**editorial** *adj*. of editing or editors. —*n*. newspaper article stating the opinion of the editor.

educate *v*. teach; provide schooling for. —**education** *n*. —**educational** *adj*. —**educationally** *adv*. —**educationalist** *n*. expert in the theory of education. —**educative** *adj*. educating.

Edwardian *adj*. of the reign of King Edward VII of Great Britain and Ireland (1901–10).

EEG electroencephalogram.

eel *n*. snakelike fish.

eerie *adj*. uncannily frightening or disturbing. —**eerily** *adv*.

efface *v*. remove by rubbing; make (oneself) inconspicuous. —**effacement** *n*.

effect *n*. change or result caused by someone or something; overall impression; condition of being operative, e.g. *the law comes into effect next month*. —*pl*. property; lighting, sounds, etc. to accompany a film or a broadcast. —*v*. cause to happen, accomplish. —**effective** *adj*. producing a desired result; impressive; operative. —**effectively** *adv*. —**effectual** *adj*. successful in producing a desired result. —**effectually** *adv*.

effeminate *adj*. (of a man) displaying charac-

THESAURUS

eddy 1. *n*. swirl, vortex, whirlpool 2. *v*. swirl, whirl

edge 1. border, bound, boundary, brim, brink, fringe, limit, line, lip, margin, outline, perimeter, rim, side, threshold, verge 2. bite, force, incisiveness, interest, keenness, point, pungency, sharpness, sting, urgency, zest

edgy ill at ease, irascible, irritable, keyed up, nervous, on edge, restive, tense, touchy

edible eatable, fit to eat, good, harmless, palatable, wholesome

edict act, command, decree, dictate, dictum, fiat, injunction, law, mandate, manifesto, order, pronouncement, regulation, ruling, statute

edifice building, erection, habitation, house, pile, structure

edify educate, elevate, enlighten, guide, improve, inform, instruct, nurture, school, teach, uplift

edit adapt, annotate, censor, check, condense, correct, emend, polish, revise, rewrite

edition copy, impression, issue, number, printing, version, volume

educate civilize, coach, cultivate, develop, discipline, drill, edify, enlighten, exercise, foster, improve, inform, instruct, school, teach, train

education breeding, civilization, cultivation, culture, development, discipline, edification, enlightenment, erudition, improvement, indoctrination, instruction, knowledge, scholarship, training, tutoring

eerie awesome, fearful, frightening, ghostly, mysterious, spectral, strange, uncanny, unearthly, weird

efface blot out, cancel, cross out, delete, destroy, dim, erase, excise, expunge, obliterate, raze, rub out, wipe out

effect 1. *n*. conclusion, consequence, event, fruit, issue, outcome, result, upshot 2. *v*. accomplish, achieve, bring about, carry out, cause, complete, create, execute, fulfil, give rise to, initiate, make, perform, produce

effective 1. able, active, capable, competent, effectual, efficient, energetic, operative, productive, serviceable, useful 2. active, current, in force, in operation, operative, real

effects belongings, chattels, gear, goods, movables, paraphernalia, possessions, property, things

DICTIONARY

teristics thought to be typical of a woman. —**ef-feminacy** *n.*

effervescent *adj.* (of a liquid) giving off bubbles; (of a person) lively and enthusiastic. —**effervescence** *n.*

effete [if-**feet**] *adj.* powerless, feeble.

efficacious *adj.* producing the intended result, effective. —**efficacy** *n.*

efficient *adj.* functioning effectively with little waste of effort. —**efficiently** *adv.* —**efficiency** *n.*

effigy [**ef**-fij-ee] *n., pl.* **-gies.** image or likeness of a person.

efflorescence *n.* flowering.

effluent *n.* liquid discharged as waste. —**effluence** *n.* something that flows out. —**effluvium** *n., pl.* **-via.** unpleasant smell, as decaying matter or gaseous waste.

effort *n.* physical or mental exertion; attempt. —**effortless** *adj.*

effrontery *n.* brazen impudence.

effusion *n.* unrestrained outburst. —**effusive** *adj.* openly emotional, demonstrative. —**effusively** *adv.* —**effusiveness** *n.*

EFTA European Free Trade Association.

e.g. for example.

egalitarian *adj.* upholding the equality of all people. —*n.* person who holds egalitarian beliefs. —**egalitarianism** *n.*

egg[1] *n.* oval or round object laid by the females of birds and other creatures, containing a developing embryo; hen's egg used as food; (also **egg cell**) ovum. —**egghead** *n. Informal* intellectual person. —**eggplant** *n. US* aubergine.

egg[2] *v.* —**egg on** encourage or incite, esp. to do wrong.

eglantine *n.* sweetbrier.

ego *n., pl.* **egos.** self-esteem; the self of an individual person. —**egoism, egotism** *n.* excessive concern for one's own interests; excessively high opinion of oneself. —**egoist, egotist** *n.* —**egoistic, egotistic** *adj.* —**egocentric** *adj.* self-centred.

egregious [ig-**greej**-uss] *adj.* outstandingly bad.

egress [**ee**-gress] *n.* way out; departure.

egret [**ee**-grit] *n.* lesser white heron.

Egyptology *n.* study of the culture of ancient Egypt.

eider *n.* Arctic duck. —**eiderdown** *n.* quilt (orig. stuffed with eider feathers).

eight *adj., n.* one more than seven. —*n.* eight-oared boat; its crew. —**eighth** *adj., n.* (of) number eight in a series. —**eighteen** *adj., n.* eight and ten. —**eighteenth** *adj., n.* —**eighty** *adj., n.* eight times ten. —**eightieth** *adj., n.*

eisteddfod [ice-**sted**-fod] *n.* Welsh festival with competitions in music and other performing arts.

either *adj., pron.* one or the other (of two); each of two. —*conj.* used preceding two or more possibilities joined by *or.* —*adv.* likewise, e.g. *I don't eat meat and he doesn't either.*

ejaculate *v.* eject (semen); utter abruptly. —**ejaculation** *n.*

eject *v.* force out, expel. —**ejection** *n.* —**ejector** *n.*

eke *v.* —**eke out** make (a supply) last by frugal use; make (a living) with difficulty.

elaborate *adj.* with a lot of fine detail. —*v.* expand upon. —**elaboration** *n.*

THESAURUS

effervescent 1. bubbling, bubbly, foaming, foamy, frothing, sparkling 2. animated, buoyant, ebullient, enthusiastic, excited, exhilarated, exuberant, gay, in high spirits, irrepressible, lively, merry, vital, vivacious

effete corrupt, debased, decadent, decayed, decrepit, degenerate, dissipated, feeble, ineffectual, spoiled, weak

efficacious active, capable, competent, effective, effectual, efficient, energetic, operative, potent, powerful, successful, useful

efficiency adeptness, capability, competence, economy, effectiveness, power, skill

efficient able, adept, businesslike, capable, competent, economic, powerful, productive, proficient, ready, skilful, workmanlike

effluent effluvium, pollutant, sewage, waste

effort endeavour, energy, exertion, force, labour,

pains, power, strain, stress, stretch, striving, struggle, toil, trouble, work

effortless easy, facile, painless, simple, smooth, uncomplicated, undemanding

effusion discharge, emission, gush, outflow, outpouring, shedding, stream

effusive ebullient, enthusiastic, extravagant, exuberant, fulsome, gushing, lavish, profuse, talkative, unreserved, wordy

egocentric egotistic, self-centred, selfish

egoism egocentricity, narcissism, self-absorption, self-centredness, self-importance, self-love, self-regard

egotist boaster, braggart, egoist, egomaniac, self-admirer

egress escape, exit, exodus, issue, outlet, passage out, vent, way out, withdrawal

eject 1. cast out, discharge, disgorge, emit, ex-

DICTIONARY

élan [ale-**an**] *n.* style and vigour.

eland [eel-and] *n.* large antelope of southern Africa.

elapse *v.* (of time) pass by.

elastic *adj.* resuming normal shape after distortion; adapting easily to change. —*n.* tape or fabric containing interwoven strands of flexible rubber. —**elasticity** *n.*

elate *v.* fill with high spirits or pride. —**elation** *n.*

elbow *n.* joint between the upper arm and the forearm; part of a garment that covers this. —*v.* shove or strike with the elbow. —**elbow grease** vigorous physical labour. —**elbowroom** *n.* sufficient room to move freely.

elder[1] *adj.* older. —*n.* older person; (in certain Protestant Churches) lay officer. —**elderly** *adj.* (fairly) old. —**eldest** *adj.* oldest.

elder[2] *n.* small tree with white flowers and black berries.

El Dorado [el dor-**rah**-doe] *n.* fictitious country rich in gold.

eldritch *adj. Scot.* weird, uncanny.

elect *v.* choose by voting; decide (to do something). —*adj.* appointed but not yet in office, e.g. *president elect.* —**election** *n.* choosing of representatives by voting; act of choosing. —**electioneer** *v.* be active in a political election. —**elective** *adj.* chosen by election; optional. —**elector** *n.* someone who has the right to vote in an election. —**electoral** *adj.* —**electorate** *n.* people who have the right to vote.

electricity *n.* form of energy associated with stationary or moving electrons or other charged particles; electric current or charge. —**electric** *adj.* produced by, producing, transmitting, or powered by electricity; exciting or tense. —**electrics** *pl. n.* electric appliances. —**electric chair** *US* chair in which criminals who have been sentenced to death are electrocuted. —**electrical** *adj.* using or concerning electricity. —**electrician** *n.* person trained to install and repair electrical equipment. —**electrify** *v.* **-fying, -fied.** adapt for operation by electric power; charge with electricity; startle or excite intensely. —**electrification** *n.*

electro- *combining form* operated by or caused by electricity. —**electrocardiograph** *n.* instrument for recording the electrical activity of the heart. —**electrocardiogram** *n.* tracing produced by this. —**electrodynamics** *n.* branch of physics concerned with the interactions between electrical and mechanical forces. —**electroencephalograph** [ill-lek-tro-en-**sef**-a-loh-graf] *n.* instrument for recording the electrical activity of the brain. —**electroencephalogram** *n.* tracing produced by this. —**electromagnet** *n.* magnet containing a coil of wire through which an electric current is passed. —**electromagnetic** *adj.* —**electromagnetism** *n.* —**electroplate** *v.* coat with silver etc. by electrolysis.

electrocute *v.* kill or injure by electricity. —**electrocution** *n.*

electrode *n.* conductor through which an electric current enters or leaves a battery, vacuum tube, etc.

electrolysis [ill-lek-**troll**-iss-iss] *n.* conduction of electricity by an electrolyte, esp. to induce chemical change; destruction of living tissue such as hair roots by an electric current.

electrolyte *n.* solution or molten substance that conducts electricity. —**electrolytic** *adj.*

electron *n.* elementary particle in all atoms that has a negative electrical charge. —**electronic** *adj.* (of a device) dependent on the action of electrons; (of a process) using electronic devices. —**electronics** *n.* technology concerned with the development of electronic devices and circuits. —**electron microscope** microscope that uses electrons, rather than light, to produce a magnified image. —**electron volt** unit of energy used in nuclear physics.

THESAURUS

pel, throw out 2. discharge, dislodge, dismiss, get rid of, oust, throw out

elaborate *adj.* 1. careful, detailed, exact, intricate, laboured, minute, painstaking, precise, skilful, thorough 2. complex, complicated, detailed, fussy, involved, ornamented, showy ~*v.* 3. add detail, amplify, decorate, develop, devise, enhance, enlarge, garnish, improve, polish, produce, refine

elapse glide by, go, go by, lapse, pass, pass by, roll by, slip away

elastic flexible, plastic, pliable, resilient, rubbery, springy, supple, yielding

elbow bump, crowd, hustle, jostle, knock, nudge, push, shoulder, shove

elder 1. *adj.* ancient, first-born, older, senior 2. *n.* older person, senior

elect appoint, choose, decide upon, determine, opt for, pick, pick out, prefer, select, settle on, vote

election choice, choosing, decision, judgment, preference, selection, vote

elector constituent, voter

electric *Fig.* charged, dynamic, exciting, rousing, stimulating, stirring, tense, thrilling

DICTIONARY

elegant *adj.* tasteful in dress, style, or design; graceful. —**elegance** *n.*

elegy [el-lij-ee] *n., pl.* **-egies.** mournful poem, esp. a lament for the dead. —**elegiac** *adj.* mournful or plaintive.

element *n.* component part; small amount; section of people within a larger group, e.g. *the rowdy element;* substance which cannot be separated into other substances by ordinary chemical techniques; heating wire in an electric kettle, stove, etc. —*pl.* basic principles of something; weather conditions, esp. wind, rain, and cold. —**in one's element** in a situation where one is happiest. —**elemental** *adj.* fundamental; of primitive natural forces or passions. —**elementary** *adj.* simple and straightforward.

elephant *n.* huge four-footed thick-skinned animal with ivory tusks and a long trunk. —**elephantine** *adj.* unwieldy, clumsy. —**elephantiasis** [el-lee-fan-**tie**-a-siss] *n.* disease with hardening of the skin and enlargement of the legs etc.

elevate *v.* raise in rank or status; lift up. —**elevation** *n.* raising; scale drawing of one side of a building; height above sea level. —**elevator** *n. US* lift for carrying people.

eleven *adj., n.* one more than ten. —*n. Sport* team of eleven people. —**eleventh** *adj., n.* (of) number eleven in a series. —**elevenses** *n. Informal* light mid-morning snack.

elf *n., pl.* **elves.** (in folklore) small mischievous fairy. —**elfin** *adj.* small and delicate.

elicit *v.* draw out (information) from someone.

elide *v.* omit (a vowel or syllable) from a spoken word. —**elision** *n.*

eligible *adj.* qualified to be chosen; desirable as a spouse. —**eligibility** *n.*

eliminate *v.* get rid of. —**elimination** *n.*

elite [ill-**eet**] *n.* most powerful, rich, or gifted members of a group. —**elitism** *n.* belief that society should be governed by a small group of superior people. —**elitist** *n., adj.*

elixir [ill-**ix**-er] *n.* liquid medicine in syrup.

Elizabethan *adj.* of the reign of Elizabeth I of England (1558–1603).

elk *n.* large deer of N Europe and Asia.

ellipse *n.* oval shape. —**elliptical** *adj.* oval-shaped; (of speech or writing) obscure or ambiguous.

ellipsis [ill-**lip**-siss] *n., pl.* **-ses.** omission of letters or words in a sentence.

elm *n.* tree with serrated leaves.

elocution *n.* art of speaking clearly in public.

elongate [eel-long-gate] *v.* make or become longer. —**elongation** *n.*

elope *v.* run away secretly to get married. —**elopement** *n.*

eloquence *n.* fluent powerful use of language. —**eloquent** *adj.* —**eloquently** *adv.*

else *adv.* otherwise; besides; instead. —**elsewhere** *adv.* in or to another place.

elucidate *v.* make (something difficult) clear, explain. —**elucidation** *n.*

THESAURUS

electrify *Fig.* amaze, animate, astonish, astound, excite, fire, invigorate, jolt, rouse, shock, startle, stimulate, stir, thrill

elegance beauty, courtliness, dignity, gentility, grace, gracefulness, grandeur, luxury, polish, politeness, refinement, sumptuousness

elegant artistic, beautiful, chic, choice, comely, courtly, cultivated, delicate, exquisite, fashionable, fine, genteel, graceful, handsome, luxurious, nice, refined, stylish, sumptuous, tasteful

element basis, component, constituent, factor, feature, hint, ingredient, member, part, section, trace, unit

elementary clear, easy, facile, plain, rudimentary, simple, straightforward, uncomplicated

elements basics, essentials, foundations, fundamentals, principles, rudiments

elevate 1. heighten, hoist, lift, lift up, raise, uplift, upraise 2. advance, aggrandize, exalt, prefer, promote, upgrade

elevation 1. altitude, height 2. eminence, height, hill, hillock, mountain, rise

elicit bring out, call forth, cause, derive, draw out, educe, evoke, evolve, exact, extort, extract, obtain, wrest

eligible fit, preferable, proper, qualified, suitable, suited, worthy

eliminate cut out, dispose of, do away with, exterminate, get rid of, remove, stamp out, take out

elite aristocracy, best, cream, elect, flower, gentry, high society, nobility, pick, upper class

elocution articulation, delivery, diction, enunciation, oratory, public speaking, rhetoric, speech, utterance

elongate draw out, extend, lengthen, make longer, prolong, protract, stretch

elope abscond, bolt, decamp, disappear, escape, leave, run away, run off, slip away, steal away

eloquence expressiveness, fluency, oratory, persuasiveness, rhetoric

eloquent articulate, fluent, forceful, graceful, moving, persuasive, well-expressed

elsewhere abroad, absent, away, not here

DICTIONARY

elude v. baffle; escape from by cleverness or quickness. —**elusive** adj. difficult to catch or remember.

elver n. young eel.

elves n. plural of ELF.

emaciated [im-mace-ee-ate-id] adj. abnormally thin. —**emaciation** n.

emanate [em-a-nate] v. issue, proceed from a source. —**emanation** n.

emancipate v. free from social, political, or legal restraints. —**emancipation** n.

emasculate v. deprive of power. —**emasculation** n.

embalm v. preserve (a corpse) from decay by the use of chemicals etc. —**embalmment** n.

embankment n. man-made ridge that carries a road or railway or holds back water.

embargo n., pl. -**goes**. order stopping the movement of ships; legal stoppage of trade; ban. —v. -**going**, -**goed**. put an embargo on.

embark v. board a ship or aircraft; (foll. by on or upon) begin (a new project). —**embarkation** n.

embarrass v. cause to feel self-conscious or ashamed. —**embarrassment** n.

embassy n., pl. -**sies**. offices or official residence of an ambassador; ambassador and his staff.

embattled adj. having a lot of difficulties.

embed v. -**bedding**, -**bedded**. fix firmly in something solid.

embellish v. decorate; embroider (a story). —**embellishment** n.

ember n. glowing piece of wood or coal in a dying fire.

embezzle v. steal money that has been entrusted to one. —**embezzlement** n. —**embezzler** n.

embitter v. make bitter. —**embitterment** n.

emblazon [im-blaze-on] v. decorate with bright colours; proclaim or publicize.

emblem n. object or representation that symbolizes a quality, type, or group. —**emblematic** adj.

embody v. -**bodying**, -**bodied**. be an example or expression of; comprise, include. —**embodiment** n.

embolden v. encourage (someone).

embolism n. blocking of a blood vessel by a blood clot or air bubble.

emboss v. mould or carve a raised design on.

embrace v. clasp in the arms, hug; accept (an idea) eagerly; comprise. —n. act of embracing.

embrasure n. door or window having splayed sides so that the opening is larger on the inside; opening like this in a fortified wall, for shooting through.

embrocation n. lotion for rubbing into the skin to relieve pain.

embroider v. decorate with needlework; make (a story) more interesting with fictitious detail. —**embroidery** n.

embroil v. involve (a person) in problems. —**embroilment** n.

THESAURUS

elucidate clarify, clear up, explain, expound, gloss, illuminate, make plain, spell out, unfold

elude avoid, dodge, escape, evade, flee, get away from, shirk, shun

elusive shifty, slippery, tricky

emaciated attenuated, cadaverous, gaunt, haggard, lank, lean, meagre, pinched, thin, wasted

emanate arise, derive, emerge, flow, issue, originate, proceed, spring, stem

emancipate deliver, discharge, enfranchise, free, liberate, release, set free, unshackle

emancipation deliverance, enfranchisement, freedom, liberation, liberty

embargo ban, bar, barrier, blockage, check, hindrance, impediment, interdict, prohibition, restraint, restriction, stoppage

embark 1. board ship, go aboard, take ship 2. With on or upon begin, broach, commence, engage, enter, initiate, launch, plunge into, set about, set out, start, take up, undertake

embarrass chagrin, discompose, disconcert, distress, fluster, mortify

embarrassment awkwardness, bashfulness, chagrin, confusion, distress, humiliation, mortification, shame

embellish adorn, beautify, bedeck, deck, decorate, dress up, elaborate, embroider, enhance, enrich, garnish, gild, grace, ornament

embezzle abstract, appropriate, filch, misapply, misappropriate, misuse, peculate, pilfer, purloin, steal

embitter anger, disaffect, disillusion, envenom, poison, sour

emblem badge, crest, device, figure, image, insignia, mark, representation, sign, symbol, token, type

embolden cheer, encourage, fire, hearten, inflame, inspirit, invigorate, nerve, reassure, rouse, stimulate, vitalize

embrace v. 1. clasp, cuddle, encircle, enfold,

DICTIONARY

embryo [em-bree-oh] *n., pl.* **-bryos.** unborn creature in the early stages of development; something at an undeveloped stage. —**embryonic** *adj.* at an early stage. —**embryology** *n.*

emend *v.* remove errors from. —**emendation** *n.*

emerald *n.* bright green precious stone. —*adj.* bright green.

emerge *v.* come into view; (foll. by *from*) come out of; become known. —**emergence** *n.* —**emergent** *adj.*

emergency *n., pl.* **-cies.** sudden unforeseen occurrence needing immediate action.

emeritus [im-mer-rit-uss] *adj.* retired, but retaining an honorary title, e.g. *emeritus professor.*

emery *n.* hard mineral used for smoothing and polishing. —**emery board** cardboard strip coated with crushed emery, for filing the nails.

emetic [im-met-ik] *n.* substance that causes vomiting. —*adj.* causing vomiting.

emigrate *v.* go and settle in another country. —**emigrant** *n.* —**emigration** *n.*

émigré [em-mig-gray] *n.* someone who has left his native country for political reasons.

eminent *adj.* distinguished, well-known. —**emi**nently *adv.* —**eminence** *n.* position of superiority or fame; (E-) title of a cardinal.

emir [em-meer] *n.* Muslim ruler. —**emirate** *n.* his country.

emissary *n., pl.* **-saries.** agent sent on a mission by a government.

emit *v.* **emitting, emitted.** give out (heat, light, or a smell); utter. —**emission** *n.*

emollient *adj.* softening, soothing. —*n.* substance which softens or soothes something.

emolument *n. Formal* payment for work, salary.

emotion *n.* strong feeling. —**emotional** *adj.* readily affected by or appealing to the emotions. —**emotive** *adj.* tending to arouse emotion.

empathy *n.* power of imaginatively entering into and understanding another's feelings.

emperor *n.* ruler of an empire. —**empress** *n. fem.*

emphasis *n., pl.* **-ses.** special importance or significance; stress on a word or phrase in speech; intensity of expression. —**emphasize** *v.* —**emphatic** *adj.* showing emphasis. —**emphatically** *adv.*

emphysema [em-fiss-see-ma] *n.* condition in

THESAURUS

grasp, hold, hug, seize, squeeze 2. accept, adopt, espouse, grab, receive, seize, take up, welcome ~*n.* 3. clasp, cuddle, hug, squeeze

embroil complicate, confound, confuse, disorder, disturb, enmesh, entangle, implicate, incriminate, involve, mire, mix up, perplex, trouble

embryo germ, nucleus, root

emend amend, correct, edit, improve

emerge 1. appear, arise, come forth, come out, come up, emanate, issue, proceed, rise, spring up, surface 2. come out, crop up, develop, materialize, transpire, turn up

emergency crisis, danger, difficulty, extremity, necessity, pass, pinch, plight, predicament, quandary, strait

emigrate migrate, move, move abroad, remove

eminence celebrity, dignity, distinction, esteem, fame, greatness, importance, notability, note, prestige, rank, renown, reputation, repute, superiority

eminent celebrated, distinguished, esteemed, exalted, famous, grand, great, high, illustrious, important, notable, noted, noteworthy, outstanding, prestigious, renowned, signal, superior, well-known

emission diffusion, discharge, ejection, exhalation, issuance, issue, radiation

emit diffuse, discharge, eject, emanate, exhale, exude, give off, give out, issue, radiate, send out, shed, throw out, transmit, utter, vent

emolument benefit, earnings, fee, gain, hire, pay, payment, profits, recompense, remuneration, return, reward, salary, stipend, wages

emotion ardour, excitement, feeling, fervour, passion, sensation, sentiment, warmth

emotional 1. demonstrative, excitable, hotblooded, passionate, sensitive, susceptible, temperamental, tender, warm 2. ardent, enthusiastic, fervent, fervid, fiery, heated, passionate, roused, stirred, zealous

emphasis accent, attention, force, importance, insistence, intensity, moment, power, preeminence, priority, prominence, significance, strength, stress, weight

emphasize accent, dwell on, highlight, insist on, play up, press home, stress, underline, underscore, weight

emphatic absolute, certain, decided, definite, direct, distinct, earnest, forceful, forcible, important, impressive, insistent, marked, positive, powerful, resounding, significant, striking, strong, telling, vigorous

empire commonwealth, kingdom, realm

DICTIONARY

which the air sacs of the lungs are grossly enlarged, causing breathlessness.

empire *n.* group of territories under the rule of one state or person; large organization that is directed by one person or group.

empirical *adj.* relying on experiment or experience, not on theory. **—empirically** *adv.* **—empiricism** *n.* doctrine that all knowledge derives from experience. **—empiricist** *n.*

emplacement *n.* prepared position for a gun.

employ *v.* hire (a person); provide work or occupation for; use. **—***n.* state of being employed, e.g. *in someone's employ.* **—employee** *n.* **—employer** *n.* **—employment** *n.* state of being employed; work done by a person to earn money.

emporium *n. Old-fashioned* large general shop.

empower *v.* enable, authorize.

empress *n.* see EMPEROR.

empty *adj.* **-tier. -tiest.** containing nothing; unoccupied; without purpose or value; (of words) insincere. **—***v.* **-tying, -tied.** make or become empty. **—empties** *pl. n.* empty boxes, bottles, etc. **—emptiness** *n.*

emu *n.* large Aust. flightless bird with long legs.

emulate *v.* attempt to equal or surpass by imitating. **—emulation** *n.*

emulsion *n.* light-sensitive coating on photographic film; type of water-based paint. **—***v.* paint with emulsion paint. **—emulsify** *v.* **-fying, -fied.** make into an emulsion. **—emulsifier** *n.*

enable *v.* provide (a person) with the means, opportunity, or authority (to do something).

enact *v.* establish by law; represent as in a play. **—enactment** *n.*

enamel *n.* glasslike coating applied to metal etc. to preserve the surface; hard white coating on a tooth. **—***v.* **-elling, elled.** cover with enamel.

enamoured *adj.* inspired with love.

en bloc *adv. French* as a whole, all together.

encamp *v.* set up in a camp. **—encampment** *n.*

encapsulate *v.* abridge; enclose as in a capsule.

encephalitis [en-sef-a-**lite**-iss] *n.* inflammation of the brain.

encephalogram *n.* short for ELECTROENCEPHALOGRAM.

enchant *v.* bewitch or delight. **—enchantment** *n.* **—enchanter** *n.* **—enchantress** *n. fem.*

encircle *v.* form a circle around. **—encirclement** *n.*

enclave *n.* part of a country entirely surrounded by foreign territory.

enclose *v.* surround completely; include along with something else. **—enclosure** *n.*

encomium *n., pl.* **-miums, -mia.** formal expression of praise.

encompass *v.* surround; include comprehensively.

encore *interj.* again, once more. **—***n.* extra performance due to enthusiastic demand.

encounter *v.* meet unexpectedly; be faced with. **—***n.* unexpected meeting; contest.

THESAURUS

employ 1. engage, enlist, hire, retain, take on 2. engage, fill, occupy, spend, take up, use up

employee hand, staff member, wage-earner, worker, workman

employer business, company, establishment, firm, organization, owner, patron, proprietor

employment 1. engagement, enlistment, hire 2. application, exercise, exertion, use 3. business, calling, craft, employ, job, line, métier, occupation, profession, pursuit, service, trade, vocation, work

empower allow, authorize, commission, delegate, enable, entitle, license, permit, qualify, sanction, warrant

emptiness 1. bareness, blankness, desolation, vacancy, vacuum, void, waste 2. cheapness, hollowness, idleness, insincerity, triviality

empty *adj.* 1. bare, blank, clear, deserted, desolate, hollow, unfurnished, uninhabited, unoccupied, vacant, void, waste 2. aimless, banal, frivolous, fruitless, futile, hollow, inane, ineffective, meaningless, purposeless, silly, un~

real, vain, valueless, worthless ~*v.* 3. clear, consume, deplete, discharge, drain, evacuate, exhaust, pour out, unburden, unload, use up, vacate, void

enable allow, authorize, commission, empower, fit, license, permit, prepare, qualify, sanction, warrant

enact authorize, command, decree, legislate, ordain, order, pass, proclaim, ratify, sanction

enamoured bewitched, charmed, enchanted, enraptured, entranced, fascinated, fond, in love

enchant beguile, bewitch, captivate, charm, delight, enamour, enrapture, enthral, fascinate, hypnotize, spellbind

enchanter conjurer, magician, sorcerer, spell~binder, witch, wizard

enclose 1. bound, cover, encase, encircle, encompass, fence, hedge, hem in, pen, shut in, wall in, wrap 2. include, insert, put in, send with

DICTIONARY

encourage *v.* inspire with confidence; spur on. —**encouragement** *n.*

encroach *v.* intrude gradually on a person's rights or land. —**encroachment** *n.*

encrust *v.* cover with a layer of something.

encumber *v.* hamper or burden. —**encumbrance** *n.* impediment.

encyclical [en-**sik**-lik-kl] *n.* letter sent by the Pope to all bishops.

encyclop(a)edia *n.* book or set of books containing facts about many subjects, usually in alphabetical order. —**encyclop(a)edic** *adj.*

end *n.* furthest point or part; limit; last part of something; fragment; *Lit.* death; destruction; purpose; *Sport* either of the two defended areas of a playing field. —*v.* bring or come to a finish. —**make ends meet** have just enough money for one's needs. —**ending** *n.* —**endless** *adj.* —**endways** *adv.* having the end forwards or upwards.

endanger *v.* put in danger.

endear *v.* cause to be liked. —**endearing** *adj.* —**endearment** *n.* affectionate word or phrase.

endeavour *v.* try. —*n.* effort.

endemic *adj.* present within a localized area or peculiar to a particular group of people.

endive *n.* curly-leaved plant used in salads.

endocrine *adj.* relating to the glands which secrete hormones directly into the bloodstream.

endogenous [en-**dodge**-in-uss] *adj.* originating from within.

endorse *v.* give approval to; sign the back of (a cheque); record a conviction on (a driving licence). —**endorsement** *n.*

endow *v.* provide permanent income for. —**endowed with** provided with. —**endowment** *n.*

endure *v.* bear (hardship) patiently; last for a

THESAURUS

encompass circle, encircle, enclose, envelop, girdle, hem in, ring, surround

encounter 1. *v.* chance upon, come upon, confront, experience, face, meet, run across 2. *n.* brush, confrontation, meeting

encourage buoy up, cheer, comfort, console, embolden, hearten, incite, inspire, rally, reassure, rouse, stimulate

encouragement aid, boost, cheer, consolation, favour, help, inspiration, reassurance, stimulation, stimulus, succour, support, urging

encroach impinge, infringe, intrude, invade, make inroads, overstep, trench, trespass, usurp

encumber burden, clog, cramp, embarrass, hamper, handicap, hinder, impede, inconvenience, obstruct, oppress, overload, retard, saddle, slow down, trammel, weigh down

end *n.* 1. boundary, edge, extent, extremity, limit, point, terminus, tip 2. close, closure, completion, conclusion, consequence, culmination, denouement, ending, expiry, finale, finish, issue, outcome, resolution, result, stop, termination, wind-up 3. aim, aspiration, design, drift, goal, intention, object, objective, point, purpose, reason 4. death, demise, destruction, dissolution, doom, extinction, ruin, ruination ~*v.* 5. cease, close, complete, conclude, culminate, dissolve, expire, finish, resolve, stop, terminate, wind up

endanger compromise, hazard, imperil, jeopardize, put at risk, risk, threaten

endeavour 1. *n.* aim, attempt, effort, enterprise, essay, go, trial, try, venture 2. *v.* aim, aspire, attempt, essay, strive, struggle, try, undertake

ending close, completion, conclusion, denouement, finale, finish, resolution, termination, wind-up

endless 1. ceaseless, constant, continual, eternal, everlasting, immortal, incessant, infinite, interminable, perpetual, unbounded, unbroken, undying, unlimited 2. interminable, monotonous, overlong, whole 3. continuous, unbroken, undivided, whole

endorse advocate, affirm, approve, authorize, back, champion, confirm, favour, ratify, recommend, sanction, support, warrant

endorsement 1. countersignature, qualification, signature 2. advocacy, affirmation, approval, authorization, backing, confirmation, favour, fiat, ratification, recommendation, sanction, support, warrant

endow award, bequeath, bestow, confer, donate, endue, enrich, favour, finance, fund, furnish, give, grant, invest, leave, make over, provide, settle on, supply, will

endowment award, benefaction, bequest, bestowal, boon, donation, fund, gift, grant, income, largess, legacy, presentation, property, provision, revenue

endurable bearable, sufferable, supportable, sustainable, tolerable

endurance bearing, fortitude, patience, perseverance, resignation, resolution, stamina, staying power, strength, submission, sufferance, tenacity, toleration

endure 1. bear, brave, cope with, experience, go through, stand, suffer, support, sustain, undergo, weather, withstand 2. abide, allow, bear, brook, countenance, permit, stand, stomach, suffer, swallow, take patiently, tolerate

DICTIONARY

long time. —**endurable** *adj.* —**endurance** *n.* act or power of enduring.

enema [en-im-a] *n.* medicine injected into the rectum to empty the bowels.

enemy *n., pl.* -**mies.** hostile person or nation, opponent.

energy *n., pl.* -**gies.** capacity for intense activity; capacity to do work and overcome resistance; source of power, such as electricity. —**energetic** *adj.* —**energetically** *adv.* —**energize** *v.* give vigour to.

enervate *v.* weaken, deprive of vigour. —**enervation** *n.*

enfant terrible [on-fon ter-reeb-la] *n., pl.* **enfants terribles.** *French* clever but unconventional or indiscreet person.

enfeeble *v.* weaken. —**enfeeblement** *n.*

enfold *v.* cover by wrapping something around; embrace.

enforce *v.* impose obedience (to a law etc.); impose (a condition). —**enforceable** *adj.* —**enforcement** *n.*

enfranchise *v.* grant (a person) the right to vote. —**enfranchisement** *n.*

engage *v.* take part, participate; involve (a person or his or her attention) intensely; employ (a person); bring (a mechanism) into operation; begin a battle with. —**engaged** *adj.* pledged to be married; in use. —**engagement** *n.* —**engaging** *adj.* charming.

engender *v.* produce, cause to occur.

engine *n.* any machine which converts energy into mechanical work; railway locomotive. —**engineer** *n.* person trained in any branch of engineering. —*v.* plan in a clever manner; design or construct as an engineer. —**engineering** *n.* profession of applying scientific principles to the design and construction of engines, cars, buildings, or machines.

English *n.* language of Britain, the U.S., most parts of the Commonwealth, and certain other countries. —*adj.* relating to England. —**the English** the people of England.

engrave *v.* carve (a design) onto a hard surface; fix deeply in the mind. —**engraver** *n.* —**engraving** *n.* print made from an engraved plate.

engross [en-**groce**] *v.* occupy the attention of (a person) completely.

engulf *v.* cover or surround completely.

enhance *v.* increase in quality, value, or attractiveness. —**enhancement** *n.*

enigma *n.* puzzling thing or person. —**enigmatic** *adj.* —**enigmatically** *adv.*

enjoin *v.* order (someone) to do something.

enjoy *v.* take joy in; have the benefit of; experience. —**enjoyable** *adj.* —**enjoyment** *n.*

enlarge *v.* make or grow larger; (foll. by *on* or *upon*) speak or write about in greater detail. —**enlargement** *n.*

THESAURUS

enemy adversary, antagonist, competitor, foe, opponent, rival

energetic active, brisk, dynamic, forceful, forcible, indefatigable, lively, potent, powerful, spirited, strenuous, strong, tireless, vigorous

energy activity, ardour, drive, efficiency, élan, exertion, fire, force, intensity, life, liveliness, pluck, power, spirit, stamina, strength, verve, vigour, vitality, vivacity, zeal, zest

enforce apply, carry out, coerce, compel, constrain, exact, execute, impose, insist on, oblige, prosecute, reinforce, require, urge

enfranchise 1. give the vote to 2. emancipate, free, liberate, manumit, release, set free

engage 1. appoint, commission, employ, enlist, enrol, hire, retain, take on 2. absorb, busy, engross, grip, involve, occupy, preoccupy, tie up 3. assail, attack, combat, fall on, fight with, give battle to, meet, take on 4. activate, apply, bring into operation, energize, set going, switch on

engaged affianced, pledged, promised, spoken for

engagement 1. betrothal, bond, compact, contract, oath, obligation, pact, pledge, promise, vow, word 2. appointment, commitment, date, meeting 3. action, battle, combat, conflict, contest, fight

engine 1. machine, mechanism, motor 2. agency, agent, apparatus, appliance, contrivance, device, implement, instrument, means, tool, weapon

engineer *v.* bring about, cause, concoct, contrive, control, create, devise, effect, encompass, manage, mastermind, originate, plan, plot, scheme

engrave carve, chase, chisel, cut, etch, inscribe

enigma conundrum, mystery, problem, puzzle, riddle

enjoy 1. appreciate, delight in, like, rejoice in, relish, revel in, take joy in 2. experience, own, possess, use

enjoyable agreeable, amusing, delicious, delightful, entertaining, pleasant, pleasing, pleasurable, satisfying

enjoyment amusement, delight, entertainment,

DICTIONARY

enlighten v. give information to. —**enlightenment** n.

enlist v. enter the armed forces; obtain the support of. —**enlistment** n.

enliven v. make lively or cheerful.

en masse adv. French in a group, all together.

enmesh v. entangle.

enmity n., pl. -**ties.** ill will, hatred.

ennoble v. make noble, elevate. —**ennoblement** n.

ennui [on-**nwee**] n. boredom, dissatisfaction.

enormous adj. very big, vast. —**enormity** n., pl. -**ties.** great wickedness; gross offence; Informal great size.

enough adj. as much or as many as necessary. —n. sufficient quantity. —adv. sufficiently; just adequately.

en passant [on pass-on] adv. French in passing, by the way.

enquire v. same as INQUIRE. —**enquiry** n.

enrapture v. fill with delight.

enrich v. improve in quality; make rich.

enrol v. -**rolling, -rolled.** (cause to) become a member. —**enrolment** n.

en route adv. French on the way.

ensconce v. settle firmly or comfortably.

ensemble [on-**som**-bl] n. all the parts of something taken together; complete outfit of clothes; company of actors or dancers; Music group of musicians playing together.

enshrine v. cherish or treasure.

ensign n. naval flag; banner; US naval officer.

ensilage n. process of storing green fodder in a silo; silage.

enslave v. make a slave of (someone). —**enslavement** n.

ensnare v. catch in or as if in a snare.

ensue v. come next, result.

en suite adv. French as part of a set or single unit.

ensure v. make certain or sure; make safe or secure.

entail v. bring about or impose inevitably.

entangle v. catch or involve in or as if in a tangle. —**entanglement** n.

entente [on-**tont**] n. friendly understanding between nations.

enter v. come or go in; join; become involved in, take part in; record (an item) in a journal etc.; begin. —**entrance** n. way into a place; act of entering; right of entering. —**entrant** n. person who enters a university, contest, etc. —**entry** n., pl. -**tries.** entrance; entering; item entered in a journal etc.

THESAURUS

fun, gladness, gratification, gusto, happiness, indulgence, joy, pleasure, recreation, relish, satisfaction, zest

enlarge add to, augment, broaden, diffuse, dilate, distend, elongate, expand, extend, grow, heighten, increase, inflate, lengthen, magnify, multiply, stretch, swell, wax, widen

enlighten advise, apprise, civilize, counsel, edify, educate, inform, instruct, make aware, teach

enlist engage, enrol, gather, join, join up, muster, obtain, procure, recruit, register, secure, sign up

enliven brighten, buoy up, cheer up, excite, exhilarate, fire, gladden, hearten, inspire, inspirit, invigorate, quicken, rouse, spark, stimulate, vitalize, wake up

enmity animosity, animus, antagonism, antipathy, aversion, bad blood, bitterness, hate, hatred, hostility, ill will, malevolence, malice, rancour, spite, venom

enormity atrocity, depravity, disgrace, evilness, outrageousness, turpitude, viciousness, villainy, wickedness

enormous astronomic, colossal, gigantic, gross, huge, immense, mammoth, massive, monstrous, prodigious, tremendous, vast

enough 1. adj. abundant, adequate, ample, plenty, sufficient 2. adv. abundantly, adequately, amply, fairly, moderately, passably, reasonably, satisfactorily, sufficiently, tolerably

enquire 1. ask, query, question 2. Also **inquire** conduct an inquiry, examine, explore, inspect, investigate, look into, make inquiry, probe, scrutinize, search

enquiry examination, exploration, inquest, inspection, investigation, probe, research, scrutiny, search, study, survey

enrolment acceptance, admission, enlistment, recruitment, registration

en route in transit, on the way

ensign badge, banner, colours, flag, pennant, pennon, standard, streamer

ensue arise, attend, be consequent on, befall, come after, derive, flow, follow, issue, proceed, result, stem, succeed, supervene

entail bring about, call for, cause, demand, give rise to, impose, involve, lead to, necessitate, occasion, require, result in

entangle 1. catch, embroil, enmesh, ensnare,

DICTIONARY

enteric [en-ter-rik] *adj.* intestinal. **—enteritis** [en-ter-**rite**-iss] *n.* inflammation of the intestine, causing diarrhoea.

enterprise *n.* company or firm; bold or difficult undertaking; boldness and energy. **—enterprising** *adj.* full of boldness and initiative.

entertain *v.* amuse; receive as a guest; consider (an idea). **—entertainer** *n.* **—entertainment** *n.*

enthral [en-**thrawl**] *v.* **-thralling, -thralled.** hold the attention of. **—enthralment** *n.*

enthusiasm *n.* ardent interest, eagerness. **—enthuse** *v.* (cause to) show enthusiasm. **—enthusiast** *n.* ardent supporter of something. **—enthusiastic** *adj.* **—enthusiastically** *adv.*

entice *v.* attract by exciting hope or desire, tempt. **—enticement** *n.*

entire *adj.* complete; unbroken or undivided. **—entirely** *adv.* **—entirety** *n.*

entitle *v.* give a right to; give a title to. **—entitlement** *n.*

entity *n., pl.* **-ties.** separate distinct thing.

entomology *n.* study of insects. **—entomological** *adj.* **—entomologist** *n.*

entourage [**on**-toor-ahzh] *n.* group of people who assist an important person.

entrails *pl. n.* intestines; innermost parts of something.

entrance[1] *n.* see ENTER.

entrance[2] *v.* delight; put into a trance.

entreat *v.* ask earnestly. **—entreaty** *n., pl.* **-ties.** earnest request.

entrée [**on**-tray] *n.* main course of a meal; right of admission.

entrench *v.* establish firmly; establish in a fortified position with trenches. **—entrenchment** *n.*

entrepreneur *n.* business person who attempts to make a profit by risk and initiative.

entropy [en-trop-ee] *n. Formal* lack of organization.

entrust *v.* put into the care or protection of.

entwine *v.* twist together or around.

E number *n.* any of a series of numbers with

THESAURUS

implicate, involve, knot, mix up, snag, snare, tangle, trap 2. complicate, confuse, mix up, muddle, perplex, puzzle, snarl, twist

enter 1. arrive, come *or* go in *or* into, insert, introduce, penetrate, pierce 2. begin, commence, embark upon, enlist, enrol, join, sign up, start, take up 3. list, log, note, record, register, set down, take down

enterprise 1. adventure, effort, endeavour, essay, operation, plan, programme, project, undertaking, venture 2. activity, daring, dash, drive, energy, enthusiasm, initiative, readiness, resource, spirit, vigour, zeal 3. business, company, concern, establishment, firm, operation

enterprising active, adventurous, bold, daring, dashing, eager, go-ahead, intrepid, keen, ready, resourceful, spirited, stirring, vigorous, zealous

entertain 1. amuse, charm, cheer, delight, divert, occupy, please 2. be host to, harbour, have company, lodge, put up, treat

entertainment amusement, cheer, distraction, diversion, enjoyment, fun, good time, play, pleasure, recreation, satisfaction, sport, treat

enthusiasm ardour, eagerness, earnestness, excitement, fervour, frenzy, interest, keenness, passion, relish, vehemence, warmth, zeal, zest

enthusiast admirer, aficionado, devotee, fan, fanatic, follower, lover, zealot

enthusiastic ardent, avid, devoted, eager, earnest, ebullient, excited, fervent, fervid, hearty, keen, lively, spirited, unstinting, vigorous, warm, wholehearted, zealous

entice allure, attract, beguile, cajole, coax, decoy, draw, inveigle, lead on, lure, persuade, seduce, tempt, wheedle

entire complete, full, total, whole

entirely absolutely, altogether, completely, fully, perfectly, thoroughly, totally, unreservedly, utterly, wholly, without exception, without reservation

entitle 1. allow, authorize, empower, enable, fit for, license, permit, qualify for, warrant 2. call, christen, designate, dub, label, name, style, term, title

entrance[1] *n.* 1. access, door, doorway, entry, gate, inlet, opening, passage, way in 2. arrival, entry, ingress, introduction 3. access, admission, admittance, entrée, entry, ingress

entrance[2] *v.* bewitch, captivate, charm, delight, enchant, enthral, fascinate, ravish, transport

entrant 1. beginner, convert, initiate, newcomer, novice, probationer, tyro 2. candidate, competitor, contestant, entry, participant, player

entrust assign, charge, commend, commit, confide, consign, delegate, deliver, hand over, invest, trust

entry 1. appearance, initiation, introduction 2. access, door, doorway, entrance, gate, inlet, opening, passageway, portal, way in 3. access, admission, entrance, entrée

DICTIONARY

the prefix E indicating a specific food additive recognized by the EC.

enumerate *v.* name one by one. —**enumeration** *n.*

enunciate *v.* pronounce clearly; proclaim. —**enunciation** *n.*

envelop *v.* **enveloping, enveloped.** wrap up, enclose. —**envelopment** *n.*

envelope *n.* folded gummed paper cover for a letter.

environment [en-**vire**-on-ment] *n.* external conditions and surroundings in which people, animals, or plants live. —**environmental** *adj.* —**environmentalist** *n.* person concerned with the protection of the natural environment.

environs *pl. n.* surrounding area, esp. of a town.

envisage *v.* visualize; conceive of as a possibility.

envoy *n.* messenger; diplomatic minister ranking below an ambassador.

envy *v.* **-vying, -vied.** grudge (another's good fortune, success, or qualities). —*n.* bitter contemplation of another's good fortune. —**enviable** *adj.* arousing envy, fortunate. —**envious** *adj.* full of envy.

enzyme *n.* any of a group of complex proteins that act as catalysts in specific biochemical reactions.

Eolithic *adj.* of the early part of the Stone Age.

epaulette *n.* shoulder ornament on a uniform.

ephemeral *adj.* short-lived.

epic *n.* long poem, book, or film about heroic events or actions. —*adj.* very impressive or ambitious.

epicentre *n.* point on the earth's surface immediately above the origin of an earthquake.

epicure *n.* person who enjoys good food and drink. —**epicurism** *n.* —**epicurean** *adj.* devoted to sensual pleasures, esp. food and drink. —*n.* epicure. —**epicureanism** *n.*

epidemic *n.* widespread occurrence of a disease; rapid spread of something.

epidermis *n.* outer layer of the skin.

epidural [ep-pid-**dure**-al] *adj., n.* (of) spinal anaesthetic injected to relieve pain during childbirth.

epiglottis *n.* thin flap that covers the opening of the larynx during swallowing.

epigram *n.* short witty remark or poem. —**epigrammatic** *adj.*

epigraph *n.* quotation at the start of a book; inscription.

epilepsy *n.* disorder of the nervous system causing loss of consciousness and sometimes convulsions. —**epileptic** *n.* person who has epilepsy. —*adj.* of or having epilepsy.

epilogue *n.* short speech or poem at the end of a literary work, esp. a play.

Epiphany *n.* Christian festival held on January 6 commemorating the manifestation of Christ to the Magi.

episcopal [ip-**piss**-kop-al] *adj.* of or governed by bishops. —**episcopalian** *n.* member of an episcopal Church. —*adj.* advocating Church government by bishops.

episode *n.* incident in a series of incidents; section of a serialized book, television programme, etc. —**episodic** *adj.* occurring at irregular intervals.

epistemology [ip-iss-stem-**ol**-a-jee] *n.* study of the source, nature, and limitations of knowledge. —**epistemological** *adj.* —**epistemologist** *n.*

THESAURUS

enumerate cite, detail, itemize, list, mention, name, quote, recite, recount, rehearse, relate, specify, spell out, tell

envelop blanket, cloak, conceal, cover, embrace, encase, enclose, enfold, engulf, hide, obscure, sheathe, shroud, surround, swathe, veil, wrap

envelope case, casing, coating, cover, covering, jacket, sheath, shell, skin, wrapping

enviable blessed, desirable, favoured, fortunate, lucky, privileged

envious covetous, grudging, jaundiced, jealous, malicious, resentful, spiteful

environment atmosphere, background, conditions, context, element, habitat, locale, medium, milieu, scene, setting, situation, surroundings

environs district, locality, neighbourhood, outskirts, precincts, vicinity

envisage 1. contemplate, fancy, imagine, picture, think up, visualize 2. anticipate, envision, foresee, predict, see

envoy agent, ambassador, courier, delegate, diplomat, emissary, intermediary, messenger, minister, representative

envy 1. *n.* covetousness, grudge, hatred, ill will, jealousy, malice, resentment, spite 2. *v.* begrudge, be jealous (of), covet, grudge, resent

epidemic *n.* outbreak, plague, rash, spread, wave

epigram bon mot, quip, witticism

epilogue coda, conclusion, postscript

episode 1. adventure, affair, event, experience, happening, incident, matter, occurrence 2. chapter, instalment, part, passage, scene, section

DICTIONARY

epistle *n.* letter, esp. of an apostle. —**epistolary** *adj.*

epitaph *n.* commemorative inscription on a tomb; commemorative speech or passage.

epithet *n.* descriptive word or name.

epitome [ip-**pit**-a-mee] *n.* typical example. —**epitomize** *v.* be the epitome of.

epoch [**ee**-pok] *n.* period of notable events. —**epoch-making** *adj.* extremely important.

eponymous [ip-**pon**-im-uss] *adj.* after whom a book, play, etc. is named.

equable [**ek**-wab-bl] *adj.* even-tempered. —**equably** *adv.*

equal *adj.* identical in size, quantity, degree, etc.; having identical rights or status; evenly balanced; (foll. by *to*) having the necessary ability (for). —*v.* **equalling, equalled.** be equal to. —**equally** *adv.* —**equality** *n.* state of being equal. —**equalize** *v.* make or become equal; reach the same score as one's opponent. —**equalization** *n.* —**equal opportunity** nondiscrimination as to sex, race, etc. in employment.

equanimity *n.* calmness of mind.

equate *v.* make or regard as equivalent. —**equation** *n.* mathematical statement that two expressions are equal; act of equating.

equator *n.* imaginary circle round the earth, equidistant from the poles. —**equatorial** *adj.*

equerry [**ek**-kwer-ee] *n., pl.* **-ries.** officer who

acts as an attendant to a member of a royal family.

equestrian *adj.* of horses and riding.

equidistant *adj.* equally distant.

equilateral *adj.* having equal sides.

equilibrium *n., pl.* **-ria.** steadiness or stability.

equine *adj.* of or like a horse.

equinox *n.* time of year when day and night are of equal length. —**equinoctial** *adj.*

equip *v.* **equipping, equipped.** provide with what is needed. —**equipment** *n.* set of tools or devices used for a particular purpose; equipping.

equipoise *n.* perfect balance.

equity *n., pl.* **-ties.** fairness; legal system, founded on the principles of natural justice, that supplements common law. —*pl.* interest of ordinary shareholders in a company. —**equitable** *adj.* fair, just. —**equitably** *adv.*

equivalent *adj.* equal in value; having the same meaning or result. —**equivalence** *n.*

equivocal *adj.* ambiguous; deliberately misleading; of doubtful character or sincerity. —**equivocally** *adv.* —**equivocate** *v.* use equivocal words to mislead people. —**equivocation** *n.*

ER Queen Elizabeth.

era *n.* period of time considered as distinctive.

eradicate *v.* destroy completely. —**eradication** *n.*

THESAURUS

epistle communication, letter, message, missive, note

epithet description, designation, name, nickname, tag, title

epitome embodiment, essence, exemplar, personification, type

epoch age, date, era, period, time

equable agreeable, calm, composed, easy-going, placid, serene, temperate, unexcitable

equal *adj.* 1. alike, commensurate, equivalent, identical, like, proportionate, tantamount, uniform 2. balanced, egalitarian, even, evenly matched, matched, regular, symmetrical, uniform 3. able, adequate, capable, competent, fit, ready, suitable, up to ~*n.* 4. brother, compeer, equivalent, fellow, match, mate, peer, rival, twin

equality balance, egalitarianism, equivalence, evenness, fairness, identity, likeness, parity, sameness, similarity, uniformity

equate agree, balance, compare, correspond with, liken, match, offset, pair, square, tally

equation agreement, balancing, comparison,

correspondence, equivalence, likeness, match, pairing, parallel

equilibrium 1. balance, counterpoise, equipoise, evenness, rest, stability, steadiness 2. calm, calmness, composure, coolness, equanimity, poise, self-possession, stability, steadiness

equip accoutre, arm, array, attire, endow, fit out, furnish, kit out, outfit, prepare, provide, rig, stock, supply

equipment accoutrements, apparatus, baggage, furnishings, gear, outfit, stuff, supplies, tackle, tools

equivalence agreement, conformity, correspondence, evenness, identity, likeness, match, parity, similarity, synonymy

equivalent alike, commensurate, comparable, corresponding, equal, even, interchangeable, of a kind, same, similar, synonymous, tantamount

equivocal ambiguous, ambivalent, doubtful, dubious, evasive, indefinite, indeterminate, misleading, obscure, questionable, suspicious, uncertain

DICTIONARY

erase *v.* rub out; remove. **—eraser** *n.* object for erasing something written. **—erasure** *n.* erasing; place or mark where something has been erased.

ere *prep., conj. Poetic* before.

erect *adj.* upright; (of the penis, clitoris, or nipples) rigid as a result of sexual excitement. **—v.** build; set up. **—erectile** *adj.* capable of becoming erect from sexual excitement. **—erection** *n.*

erg *n.* unit of work or energy.

ergonomics *n.* study of the relationship between workers and their environment. **—ergonomic** *adj.*

ergot *n.* fungal disease of cereal; dried fungus used in medicine.

ermine *n.* stoat in northern regions; its white winter fur.

erode *v.* wear away. **—erosion** *n.*

erogenous [ir-**roj**-in-uss] *adj.* sexually sensitive or arousing.

erotic *adj.* relating to sexual pleasure or desire. **—eroticism** *n.* **—erotica** *n.* sexual literature or art.

err *v. Formal* make a mistake. **—erratum** *n., pl.* **-ta.** error in writing or printing. **—erroneous** *adj.* incorrect, mistaken. **—error** *n.* something considered to be wrong or incorrect.

errand *n.* short trip to do something for someone.

errant *adj.* behaving in a manner considered to be unacceptable.

erratic *adj.* irregular or unpredictable. **—erratically** *adv.*

ersatz [**air**-zats] *adj.* made in imitation, e.g *ersatz coffee.*

erstwhile *adj.* former.

erudite [**air**-rude-ite] *adj.* having great academic knowledge. **—erudition** *n.*

erupt *v.* eject (steam, water, or volcanic material) violently; (of a blemish) to appear on the skin; burst forth suddenly and violently. **—eruption** *n.*

erysipelas *n.* acute skin infection causing purplish patches.

escalate *v.* increase in extent or intensity. **—escalation** *n.*

escalator *n.* moving staircase.

escalope [**ess**-kal-lop] *n.* thin slice of meat, esp. veal.

escape *v.* get free (of); avoid, e.g. *escape attention;* (of a gas, liquid, etc.) leak gradually; be forgotten by, e.g. *the figure escapes me.* **—n.** act of escaping; means of distraction. **—escapade** *n.* mischievous adventure. **—escapee** *n.* person who has escaped. **—escapism** *n.* taking refuge in

---

THESAURUS

era age, cycle, date, day *or* days, epoch, generation, period, stage, time

eradicate annihilate, destroy, efface, eliminate, erase, expunge, extinguish, obliterate, remove, root out, stamp out, uproot, weed out, wipe out

erect 1. *adj.* firm, raised, rigid, standing, stiff, straight, upright, vertical 2. *v.* build, construct, lift, mount, pitch, put up

erode consume, corrode, destroy, deteriorate, eat away, grind down, spoil

err be inaccurate, be incorrect, blunder, go wrong, make a mistake, miscalculate, misjudge, mistake

errand charge, commission, job, message, mission, task

erratic aberrant, abnormal, capricious, changeable, desultory, fitful, inconsistent, irregular, shifting, unreliable, unstable, variable, wayward

erroneous amiss, fallacious, false, inaccurate, incorrect, inexact, invalid, mistaken, spurious, untrue, wrong

error blunder, delusion, erratum, fallacy, fault, flaw, inaccuracy, miscalculation, mistake, oversight, slip, solecism

erstwhile bygone, former, late, old, one-time, past, previous, sometime

erudite cultivated, educated, knowledgeable, learned, lettered, literate, scholarly, well-educated, well-read

erupt belch forth, blow up, break out, burst forth, burst out, discharge, explode, flare up, gush, pour forth, out, spit out, spout, throw off, vent, vomit

eruption discharge, ejection, explosion, flareup, outbreak, outburst

escalate ascend, be increased, enlarge, expand, extend, grow, heighten, increase, intensify, mount, raise, rise

escapade adventure, antic, caper, fling, mischief, spree, stunt, trick

escape *v.* 1. bolt, break free, decamp, flee, fly, get away, run away *or* off, skip, slip away ~*n.* 2. break, break-out, flight, getaway ~*v.* 3. avoid, dodge, duck, elude, evade, pass, shun, slip ~*n.* 4. elusion, evasion ~*v.* 5. drain, emanate, flow, gush, issue, leak, seep, spurt ~*n.* 6. drain, efflux, emission, gush, leak, leakage, outflow, outpour, seepage, spurt

DICTIONARY

fantasy to avoid unpleasant reality. —**escapologist** *n.* entertainer who specializes in freeing himself from confinement. —**escapology** *n.*

escarpment *n.* steep face of a ridge or mountain.

eschew [iss-**chew**] *v.* abstain from, avoid.

escort *n.* people or vehicles accompanying another person for protection or as an honour; person who accompanies a person of the opposite sex to a social event. —*v.* act as an escort to.

escudo [ess-**kyoo**-doe] *n., pl.* **-dos.** monetary unit of Portugal.

escutcheon *n.* shield with a coat of arms. —**blot on one's escutcheon** stain on one's honour.

Eskimo *n.* member of the aboriginal race inhabiting N Canada, Greenland, Alaska, and E Siberia; their language.

esoteric [ee-so-**ter**-rik] *adj.* understood by only a small number of people with special knowledge.

ESP extrasensory perception.

esp. especially.

espadrille [ess-pad-drill] *n.* light canvas shoe with a braided cord sole.

espalier [ess-**pal**-yer] *n.* shrub or fruit tree trained to grow flat; trellis for this.

esparto *n., pl.* **-tos.** grass used for making rope etc.

especial *adj. Formal* special. —**especially** *adv.* particularly.

Esperanto *n.* universal artificial language.

espionage [ess-pyon-ahzh] *n.* spying.

esplanade *n.* wide open road used as a public promenade.

espouse *v.* adopt or give support to (a cause etc.). —**espousal** *n.*

espresso *n., pl.* **-sos.** strong coffee made by forcing steam or boiling water through ground coffee beans.

esprit [ess-**pree**] *n.* spirit, liveliness. —**esprit de corps** [de **core**] pride in and loyalty to a group.

espy *v.* **espying, espied.** catch sight of.

Esq. esquire.

esquire *n.* courtesy title placed after a man's name.

essay *n.* short literary composition. —*v.* attempt. —**essayist** *n.*

essence *n.* most important feature of a thing which determines its identity; concentrated extract obtained by distillation, e.g. *vanilla essence.* —**essential** *adj.* vitally important; fundamental. —*n.* something essential. —**essentially** *adv.*

establish *v.* set up on a permanent basis; make secure or permanent in a certain place, job, etc.; prove; cause to be accepted. —**establishment** *n.* act of establishing; commercial or other institution. —**the Establishment** group of people having authority within a society.

estate *n.* landed property; large area of property development, esp. of new houses or factories; property of a deceased person. —**estate agent** agent concerned with the valuation, lease, and sale of property. —**estate car** car with a rear door and luggage space behind the rear seats.

esteem *v.* think highly of; judge or consider. —*n.* high regard.

THESAURUS

escort 1 *n.* bodyguard, company, convoy, cortege, entourage, guard, protection, retinue, safeguard, train 2. *v.* accompany, conduct, convoy, guard, guide, lead, partner, protect, squire, usher

especial chief, exceptional, extraordinary, marked, notable, noteworthy, outstanding, principal, signal, special, uncommon, unusual

especially chiefly, conspicuously, exceptionally, extraordinarily, mainly, markedly, notably, principally, remarkably, specially, strikingly, supremely, uncommonly, unusually

espousal advocacy, backing, championship, defence, embracing, maintenance, support, taking up

espouse adopt, advocate, back, champion, defend, embrace, maintain, stand up for, support, take up

essay article, composition, discourse, disquisition, dissertation, paper, piece, tract

essence 1. being, core, entity, heart, kernel, life, lifeblood, nature, pith, principle, soul, spirit, substance 2. concentrate, distillate, extract, spirits, tincture

essential *adj.* 1. crucial, important, indispensable, necessary, needed, requisite, vital 2. basic, cardinal, fundamental, inherent, innate, intrinsic, key, main, principal ~*n.* 3. basic, fundamental, necessity, requisite, rudiment, *sine qua non*

establish base, constitute, create, decree, enact, entrench, fix, form, found, ground, implant, inaugurate, install, institute, plant, root, secure, settle, set up, start

establishment 1. business, company, concern, enterprise, firm, house, institution, organization, outfit (*Inf.*), setup (*Inf.*), structure, sys-

DICTIONARY

ester n. Chem. compound produced by the reaction between an acid and an alcohol.

estimate v. calculate roughly; form an opinion about. —n. approximate calculation; opinion; statement from a workman etc. of the likely charge for a job. —**estimable** adj. worthy of respect. —**estimation** n. judgment, opinion.

estranged adj. no longer living with one's spouse; having lost someone's affection and loyalty. —**estrangement** n.

estuary n., pl. **-aries.** mouth of a river.

et cetera [et set-ra] n. and v. substitute and the rest, and others; or the like. —**etceteras** pl. n. miscellaneous extra things or people.

ETA estimated time of arrival.

etc. et cetera.

etch v. wear away or cut the surface of (metal, glass, etc.) with acid; imprint vividly (on someone's mind). —**etching** n.

eternal adj. without beginning or end; unchanging. —**eternally** adv. —**eternity** n. infinite time; timeless existence after death. —**eternity ring** ring given as a token of lasting affection.

ether n. colourless sweet-smelling liquid used as an anaesthetic; region above the clouds. —**ethereal** [eth-eer-ee-al] adj. extremely delicate.

ethic n. moral principle. —pl. code of behaviour; study of morals. —**ethical** adj. —**ethically** adv.

ethnic adj. relating to a people or group that shares a culture, religion, or language; belonging or relating to such a group, esp. one that is a minority group in a particular place. —**ethnology** n. study of human races. —**ethnological** adj. —**ethnologist** n.

ethos [eeth-oss] n. distinctive spirit and attitudes of a people, culture, etc.

ethyl [eth-ill] adj. of, consisting of, or containing the monovalent group C_2H_5. —**ethylene** n. poisonous gas used as an anaesthetic and as fuel.

etiolate [ee-tee-oh-late] v. become pale and weak; Botany whiten through lack of sunlight.

etiology n. study of the causes of diseases.

etiquette n. conventional code of conduct.

étude [ay-tewd] n. short musical composition for a solo instrument, esp. intended as a technical exercise.

etymology n., pl. **-gies.** study of the sources and development of words. —**etymological** adj. —**etymologist** n.

eucalypt(us) n. tree, mainly grown in Australia, that provides timber and gum.

Eucharist [yew-kar-ist] n. Christian sacrament commemorating Christ's Last Supper; consecrated elements of bread and wine. —**Eucharistic** adj.

eugenics [yew-jen-iks] n. study of methods of improving the human race.

eulogy n., pl. **-gies.** speech or writing in praise of a person. —**eulogize** v. praise (a person or thing) highly in speech or writing. —**eulogist** n. —**eulogistic** adj.

eunuch n. castrated man, esp. (formerly) a guard in a harem.

euphemism n. inoffensive word or phrase substituted for one considered offensive or upsetting. —**euphemistic** adj. —**euphemistically** adv.

euphony n., pl. **-nies.** pleasing sound. —**euphonious** adj. pleasing to the ear. —**euphonium** n. brass musical instrument, tenor tuba.

euphoria n. sense of elation. —**euphoric** adj.

Eurasian adj. of Europe and Asia; of mixed European and Asian parentage. —n. person of Eurasian parentage.

THESAURUS

tem 2. **the Establishment** established order, ruling class

estate area, domain, holdings, lands, manor, property

esteem 1. v. admire, be fond of, cherish, honour, like, love, prize, respect, revere, reverence, treasure, value, 2. n. credit, good opinion, honour, regard, respect, reverence

estimate v. 1. assess, calculate roughly, evaluate, gauge, guess, judge, number, reckon, value 2. assess, believe, conjecture, consider, guess, judge, rank, rate, reckon, surmise, think ~n. 3. approximate calculation, assessment, evaluation, guess, judgment, reckoning, valuation

estuary creek, firth, fjord, inlet, mouth

et cetera and others, and so forth, and so on, and the like, and the rest

eternal abiding, ceaseless, constant, deathless, endless, everlasting, immortal, infinite, interminable, never-ending, perennial, perpetual, timeless, unceasing, undying, unending, without end

ethical correct, fitting, good, honest, honourable, just, moral, principled, proper, right, upright

ethics conscience, moral code, morality, moral philosophy, moral values, principles, standards

etiquette civility, code, convention, courtesy, customs, decorum, manners, politeness, propriety, protocol, rules, usage

DICTIONARY

eureka [yew-reek-a] *interj.* exclamation of triumph at finding something.

European *n., adj.* (person) from Europe. —**European Community** association of a number of European nations for trade.

Eustachian tube *n.* passage leading from the ear to the throat.

euthanasia *n.* act of killing someone painlessly, esp. to relieve his or her suffering.

evacuate *v.* send (someone) away from a place of danger; empty. —**evacuation** *n.* —**evacuee** *n.*

evade *v.* get away from or avoid; elude. —**evasion** *n.* —**evasive** *adj.* not straightforward, e.g. *an evasive answer.* —**evasively** *adv.*

evaluate *v.* find or judge the value of. —**evaluation** *n.*

evanescent *adj.* quickly fading away. —**evanescence** *n.*

evangelical *adj.* of or according to gospel teaching; of certain Protestant sects which maintain the doctrine of salvation by faith. —*n.* member of an evangelical sect. —**evangelicalism** *n.*

evangelist *n.* writer of one of the four gospels; travelling preacher. —**evangelism** *n.* teaching and spreading of the Christian gospel. —**evangelize** *v.* preach the gospel. —**evangelization** *n.*

evaporate *v.* change from a liquid or solid to a vapour; disappear. —**evaporation** *n.* —**evaporated milk** thick unsweetened tinned milk.

eve *n.* evening or day before some special event; period immediately before an event. —**evensong** *n.* evening prayer.

even *adj.* flat or smooth; (foll. by *with*) on the same level (as); constant; calm; equally balanced; divisible by two. —*adv.* equally; simply; nevertheless. —*v.* make even.

evening *n.* end of the day or early part of the night; concluding period.

event *n.* anything that takes place; actual outcome; contest in a sporting programme. —**eventful** *adj.* full of exciting incidents. —**eventing** *n.* riding competitions, usually involving cross-country, jumping, and dressage. —**eventual** *adj.* ultimate. —**eventually** *adv.* —**eventuality** *n.* possible event.

ever *adv.* at any time; always. —**evergreen** *n., adj.* (tree or shrub) having leaves throughout the year. —**everlasting** *adj.* —**evermore** *adv.* all time to come.

every *adj.* each without exception; all possible. —**everybody** *pron.* every person. —**everyday** *adj.* usual or ordinary. —**everyone** *pron.* every person. —**everything** *pron.* —**everywhere** *adv.* in all places.

evict *v.* legally expel (someone) from his or her home. —**eviction** *n.*

THESAURUS

evacuate abandon, clear, decamp, depart, desert, forsake, leave, move out, pull out, quit, relinquish, remove, vacate, withdraw

evade avoid, circumvent, decline, dodge, duck, elude, escape, shirk, shun, sidestep

evaluate appraise, assay, assess, estimate, gauge, judge, rank, rate, reckon, value, weigh

evaporate 1. dry, dry up, vaporize 2. dematerialize, disappear, disperse, dissipate, dissolve, fade away, melt, vanish

evasion avoidance, cunning, dodge, equivocation, escape, evasiveness, excuse, prevarication, ruse, shift, shuffling, sophistry, subterfuge, trickery

eve day before, night before, vigil

even *adj.* 1. flat, flush, level, plane, plumb, smooth, steady, straight, true, uniform 2. cool, equable, imperturbable, peaceful, placid, serene, stable, steady, tranquil, undisturbed, unexcitable, unruffled, well-balanced 3. balanced, disinterested, dispassionate, equitable, fair, impartial, just, unbiased, unprejudiced ~*adv.* 4. all the more, equally, much, nevertheless, still, yet

event affair, business, circumstance, episode,

experience, fact, happening, incident, matter, milestone, occasion, occurrence

eventful active, busy, critical, crucial, decisive, exciting, fateful, full, historic, important, lively, memorable, momentous, notable, significant

eventually after all, finally, in the end, in the long run, one day, some day, some time, sooner or later, ultimately

ever 1. at all, at any time (period, point), in any case, on any occasion 2. always, at all times, constantly, continually, endlessly, eternally, incessantly, perpetually, relentlessly, to the end of time, unceasingly, unendingly

everlasting abiding, deathless, endless, eternal, immortal, imperishable, infinite, interminable, never-ending, perpetual, timeless, undying

evermore always, eternally, ever, for ever, *in perpetuum,* to the end of time

everyday accustomed, common, commonplace, conventional, dull, familiar, frequent, habitual, informal, mundane, ordinary, routine, stock, usual, wonted

evict boot out (*Inf.*), chuck out (*Inf.*), dislodge, dispossess, eject, expel, kick out (*Inf.*), oust,

DICTIONARY

evidence *n.* ground for belief; sign, indication; matter produced before a lawcourt to prove or disprove a point. —*v.* demonstrate, prove. —**in evidence** conspicuous. —**evident** *adj.* easily noticed or understood. —**evidently** *adv.* —**evidential** *adj.* of, serving as, or based on evidence. —**evidentially** *adv.*

evil *adj.* morally bad; harmful; very unpleasant. —*n.* wickedness; wicked deed. —**evilly** *adv.* —**evildoer** *n.* wicked person.

evince *v.* make evident.

eviscerate *v.* disembowel. —**evisceration** *n.*

evoke *v.* call or summon up (a memory, feeling, etc.). —**evocation** *n.* —**evocative** *adj.*

evolve *v.* develop gradually; (of an animal or plant species) undergo evolution. —**evolution** *n.* gradual change in the characteristics of living things over successive generations, esp. to a more complex form. —**evolutionary** *adj.*

ewe *n.* female sheep.

ewer *n.* large jug with a wide mouth.

ex *n. Informal* former wife or husband.

ex- *prefix* out of, outside, from, e.g. *exodus;* former, e.g. *ex-wife.*

exacerbate [ig-**zass**-er-bate] *v.* make (pain, emotion, or a situation) worse. —**exacerbation** *n.*

exact *adj.* correct and complete in every detail; precise, as opposed to approximate. —*v.* demand (payment or obedience). —**exactly** *adv.* precisely, in every respect. —**exactness, exactitude** *n.* —**exacting** *adj.* making rigorous or excessive demands.

exaggerate *v.* regard or represent as greater than is true; make greater or more noticeable. —**exaggeratedly** *adv.* —**exaggeration** *n.*

exalt *v.* praise highly; elevate in rank. —**exaltation** *n.* feeling of great joy; act of praising highly.

exam *n.* short for EXAMINATION.

examine *v.* look at closely; test the knowledge of; ask questions of. —**examination** *n.* examining; test of a candidate's knowledge or skill. —**examinee** *n.* —**examiner** *n.*

example *n.* specimen typical of its group; per-

THESAURUS

put out, remove, show the door (to), throw on to the streets, throw out, turf out (*Inf.*), turn out

evidence affirmation, confirmation, data, declaration, demonstration, grounds, indication, mark, proof, sign, substantiation, testimony, token, witness

evident apparent, clear, incontestable, indisputable, manifest, noticeable, obvious, patent, perceptible, plain, visible

evidently apparently, it seems, ostensibly, outwardly, semmingly

evil *adj.* 1. bad, base, corrupt, depraved, malicious, malignant, sinful, vicious, vile, villainous, wicked, wrong 2. calamitous, catastrophic, destructive, dire, harmful, hurtful, injurious, mischievous, painful, pernicious, ruinous, sorrowful, unfortunate, unlucky, woeful ~*n.* 3. badness, baseness, corruption, immorality, vice, villainy, wickedness, wrong, wrongdoing

evoke 1. arouse, awaken, call, excite, induce, recall, stimulate, stir up, summon up 2. call forth, elicit, produce, provoke

evolution development, enlargement, expansion, growth, increase, progress, unrolling

evolve develop, disclose, educe, elaborate, enlarge, expand, grow, increase, mature, open, progress, unfold, unroll, work out

exact *adj.* 1. accurate, careful, correct, definite, explicit, faithful, faultless, identical, literal, methodical, orderly, particular, precise, right, specific, true, unequivocal, unerring, vera-

cious, very 2. careful, meticulous, painstaking, punctilious, rigorous, scrupulous, severe, strict ~*v.* 3. call for, claim, command, compel, demand, extort, extract, force, impose, insist upon, require

exactly 1. accurately, carefully, correctly, definitely, explicitly, faithfully, faultlessly, literally, precisely, severely, strictly, truly, truthfully, veraciously 2. absolutely, expressly, indeed, just, particularly, precisely, quite, specifically

exactness carefulness, correctness, exactitude, faultlessness, nicety, precision, promptitude, regularity, rigorousness, scrupulousness, strictness, truth, veracity

exaggerate amplify, embroider, emphasize, enlarge, exalt, inflate, magnify, overdo, overestimate, overstate

exaggeration embellishment, emphasis, enlargement, excess, hyperbole, inflation, magnification, overstatement, pretension, pretentiousness

exalt advance, dignify, elevate, ennoble, honour, promote, raise, upgrade

examination analysis, catechism, checkup, exploration, inquiry, inquisition, inspection, interrogation, investigation, perusal, probe, questioning, quiz, review, scrutiny, search, study, survey, test, trial

examine analyse, appraise, check out, consider, explore, inspect, investigate, look over, peruse, ponder, probe, review, scan, scrutinize, sift, study, survey, test, vet, weigh

DICTIONARY

son or thing worthy of imitation; punishment regarded as a warning to others.

exasperate v. cause great irritation to. —**exasperation** n.

excavate v. unearth buried objects from (a piece of land) methodically to learn about the past; make (a hole) in solid matter by digging. —**excavation** n. —**excavator** n. large machine used for digging.

exceed v. be greater than; go beyond (a limit). —**exceedingly** adv. very.

excel v. -celling, -celled. be superior to; be outstandingly good at something. —**excellent** adj. very good. —**excellence** n. —**Excellency** n. title used to address a high-ranking official, such as an ambassador.

except prep. (sometimes foll. by for) other than, not including. —v. not include. —**except that** with the exception that. —**excepting** prep. except. —**exception** n. excepting; thing that is excluded from or does not conform to the general rule. —**exceptionable** adj. causing offence. —**exceptional** adj. not ordinary; much above the average.

excerpt n. passage taken from a book, speech, etc.

excess n. state or act of exceeding the permitted limits; immoderate amount; amount by which a thing exceeds the permitted limits. —**excessive** adj. —**excessively** adv.

exchange v. give or receive (something) in return for something else. —n. act of exchanging; thing given or received in place of another; centre in which telephone lines are interconnected; Finance place where securities or commodities are traded; transfer of sums of money of equal value between different currencies. —**exchangeable** adj.

Exchequer n. Brit. government department in charge of state money.

excise[1] n. tax on goods produced for the home market.

excise[2] v. cut out or away. —**excision** n.

excite v. arouse to strong emotion; arouse or evoke (an emotion); arouse sexually. —**excitement** n. —**excitable** adj. easily excited. —**excitability** n.

exclaim v. speak suddenly, cry out. —**exclamation** n. —**exclamation mark** punctuation mark (!) used after exclamations. —**exclamatory** adj.

THESAURUS

example case, illustration, instance, sample, specimen

exasperate anger, annoy, embitter, enrage, exacerbate, excite, gall, incense, inflame, infuriate, irk, irritate, madden, nettle, pique, provoke, rankle, rouse, vex

exasperation anger, annoyance, fury, irritation, passion, pique, rage, vexation, wrath

excavate burrow, delve, dig, dig out, dig up, gouge, hollow, mine, quarry, scoop, trench, tunnel, uncover, unearth

exceed beat, better, eclipse, excel, outdistance, outdo, outreach, outrun, outshine, outstrip, overtake, pass, surmount, surpass, top, transcend

exceedingly enormously, especially, exceptionally, extremely, greatly, highly, hugely, inordinately, superlatively, unusually, vastly, very

excel beat, be superior, better, eclipse, exceed, go beyond, outdo, outrival, outshine, pass, surmount, surpass, top, transcend

excellence distinction, eminence, goodness, greatness, high quality, merit, perfection, superiority, supremacy, virtue, worth

excellent admirable, capital, champion, choice, distinguished, exemplary, exquisite, fine, first-class, first-rate, good, great, meritorious, notable, noted, outstanding, prime, select, superb, superior, superlative, worthy

except, except for apart from, bar, barring, besides, but, excepting, excluding, exclusive of, omitting, other than

exception anomaly, deviation, freak, irregularity, oddity, peculiarity, quirk, special case

exceptional excellent, extraordinary, marvellous, outstanding, phenomenal, prodigious, remarkable, special, superior

excess n. 1. glut, leftover, overdose, overflow, plethora, remainder, superfluity, surfeit, surplus, too much 2. debauchery, dissipation, dissoluteness, extravagance, intemperance, overindulgence, prodigality

excessive enormous, exaggerated, extravagant, extreme, inordinate, needless, overdone, overmuch, prodigal, profligate, superfluous, too much, undue, unreasonable

exchange 1. v. bandy, barter, change, commute, switch, trade, truck 2. n. barter, dealing, substitution, switch, trade, traffic, truck

excitable edgy, hasty, highly strung, hotheaded, nervous, passionate, sensitive, temperamental, testy, touchy, violent, volatile

excite agitate, arouse, awaken, disturb, evoke, fire, foment, galvanize, incite, inflame, inspire, move, provoke, quicken, rouse, stimulate, stir up, thrill, waken

excitement action, ado, adventure, agitation, animation, commotion, elation, ferment, fe-

DICTIONARY

exclude v. leave out of consideration; keep out, leave out. —**exclusion** n. —**exclusive** adj. catering for a privileged minority; not shared; excluding everything else. —n. story reported in only one newspaper. —**exclusively** adv. —**exclusiveness, exclusivity** n.

excommunicate v. exclude from membership and the sacraments of the Church. —**excommunication** n.

excoriate v. censure severely; strip skin from. —**excoriation** n.

excrement n. waste matter discharged from the body.

excrescence n. lump or growth on the surface of an animal or plant.

excrete v. discharge (waste matter) from the body. —**excretion** n. —**excreta** [ik-**skree**-ta] n. excrement. —**excretory** adj.

excruciating adj. agonizing; very intense. —**excruciatingly** adv.

exculpate v. free from blame or guilt.

excursion n. short journey, esp. for pleasure.

excuse v. put forward a reason or justification for (a fault etc.); forgive (a person) or overlook (a fault etc.); make allowances for; exempt; allow to leave. —n. explanation offered to excuse (a fault etc.). —**excusable** adj.

ex-directory adj. not listed in a telephone directory by request.

execrable [eks-sik-rab-bl] adj. of very poor quality.

execute v. put (a condemned person) to death; perform (a plan or action); produce (a work of art); render (a legal document) effective, as by signing. —**execution** n. —**executioner** n. person employed to execute criminals. —**executor, executrix** n. person appointed to perform the instructions of a will.

executive n. person or group in an administrative position; branch of government responsible for carrying out laws etc. —adj. having the function of carrying out plans, orders, laws, etc.

exegesis [eks-sij-**jee**-siss] n., pl. -**ses**. explanation of a text, esp. of the Bible.

exemplar n. example; person or thing to be copied, model. —**exemplary** adj. being a good example; serving as a warning.

exemplify v. -**fying**, -**fied**. be an example of; show an example of. —**exemplification** n.

exempt adj. not subject to an obligation etc. —v. release from an obligation etc. —**exemption** n.

exequies [**eks**-sik-wiz] pl. n. funeral rites.

exercise n. activity to train the body or mind;

THESAURUS

ver, flurry, furore, heat, passion, thrill, tumult, warmth

exclaim call, call out, cry, cry out, declare, proclaim, shout, utter, yell

exclamation call, cry, expletive, interjection, outcry, shout, utterance, yell

exclude 1. ban, bar, debar, disallow, forbid, interdict, keep out, ostracize, prohibit, proscribe, refuse, shut out, veto 2. eliminate, except, ignore, leave out, omit, pass over, preclude, reject, repudiate, rule out

exclusive 1. aristocratic, chic, choice, clannish, closed, elegant, fashionable, limited, narrow, private, restricted, select, selfish, snobbish 2. confined, limited, peculiar, restricted, unique

excommunicate anathematize, ban, banish, cast out, denounce, eject, exclude, expel, proscribe, remove, repudiate, unchurch

exculpate absolve, acquit, clear, discharge, dismiss, excuse, exonerate, free, justify, pardon, release, vindicate

excursion airing, day trip, expedition, jaunt, journey, outing, pleasure trip, tour, trip

excuse v. 1. absolve, acquit, bear with, exculpate, exonerate, forgive, indulge, overlook, pardon, pass over, tolerate, wink at 2. absolve, discharge, exempt, free, let off, liberate, release, relieve, spare ~n. 3. apology, defence, explanation, grounds, justification, mitigation, plea, pretext, reason, vindication

execute behead, electrocute, guillotine, hang, kill, put to death, shoot

execution 1. accomplishment, achievement, administration, carrying out, completion, discharge, effect, enactment, enforcement, implementation, performance, prosecution, realization, rendering 2. hanging, killing

executive n. 1. administrator, director, manager, official 2. administration, directorate, directors, government, leadership, management ~adj. 3. administrative, controlling, decision-making, directing, governing, managerial

exemplary admirable, commendable, correct, estimable, excellent, good, ideal, laudable, meritorious, model, praiseworthy, sterling

exemplify demonstrate, depict, display, embody, evidence, exhibit, illustrate, instance, represent, show

exempt 1. v. absolve, discharge, except, excuse, exonerate, free, let off, liberate, release, relieve, spare 2. adj. absolved, clear, discharged, excused, favoured, free, immune, liberated, not liable, not subject, privileged, released, spared

DICTIONARY

set of movements or tasks designed to improve or test a person's ability; performance of a function. —*v.* take exercise or perform exercises; make use of, e.g. *to exercise one's rights*.

exert *v.* use (influence, authority, etc.) forcefully or effectively. —**exert oneself** make a special effort. —**exertion** *n.*

exeunt [eks-see-unt] *Latin* they go out: used as a stage direction.

ex gratia [eks gray-sha] *adj.* given as a favour where no legal obligation exists.

exhale *v.* breathe out. —**exhalation** *n.*

exhaust *v.* tire out; use up; discuss (a subject) thoroughly. —*n.* gases ejected from an engine as waste products; pipe through which an engine's exhaust fumes pass. —**exhaustible** *adj.* —**exhaustion** *n.* extreme tiredness; exhausting. —**exhaustive** *adj.* comprehensive. —**exhaustively** *adv.*

exhibit *v.* show (a quality); display to the public. —*n.* object exhibited to the public; *Law* document or object produced in court as evidence. —**exhibitor** *n.* —**exhibition** *n.* public display of art, skills, etc.; exhibiting. —**exhibitionism** *n.* compulsive desire to draw attention to oneself; compulsive desire to display one's genitals in public. —**exhibitionist** *n.*

exhilarate *v.* make lively and cheerful. —**exhilaration** *n.*

exhort *v.* urge earnestly. —**exhortation** *n.*

exhume [ig-**zyume**] *v.* dig up (something buried, esp. a corpse). —**exhumation** *n.*

exigency *n., pl.* **-cies.** urgent demand or need. —**exigent** *adj.*

exiguous *adj.* scanty, meagre.

exile *n.* prolonged, usu. enforced, absence from one's country; person banished or living away from his or her country. —*v.* expel from one's country.

exist *v.* have being or reality; eke out a living; live. —**existence** *n.* —**existent** *adj.*

existential *adj.* of or relating to existence, esp. human existence. —**existentialism** *n.* philosophical movement stressing the personal experience and responsibility of the individual, who is seen as a free agent. —**existentialist** *adj., n.*

exit *n.* way out; going out; actor's going off stage. —*v.* go out; go offstage: used as a stage direction.

exocrine *adj.* relating to a gland, such as the sweat gland, that secretes externally through a duct.

exodus [eks-so-duss] *n.* departure of a large number of people. —**the Exodus** departure of the Israelites from Egypt.

ex officio [eks off-**fish**-ee-oh] *adv., adj. Latin* by right of position or office.

exonerate *v.* free from blame or a criminal charge. —**exoneration** *n.*

exorbitant *adj.* (of prices, demands, etc.) excessive, immoderate. —**exorbitantly** *adv.*

exorcise *v.* expel (evil spirits) by prayers and religious rites. —**exorcism** *n.* —**exorcist** *n.*

exotic *adj.* having a strange allure or beauty;

THESAURUS

exercise *v.* 1. apply, bring to bear, employ, enjoy, exert, practise, put to use, use, utilize, wield 2. drill, inure, practise, train, work out ~*n.* 3. action, activity, discipline, drill, drilling, effort, labour, toil, training, work, workout 4. drill, lesson, practice, problem, schooling, task, work

exert bring into play, bring to bear, employ, exercise, expend, use, utilize, wield

exertion action, application, attempt, effort, industry, strain, stretch, struggle, toil, trial, use

exhaust 1. bankrupt, cripple, debilitate, disable, drain, enervate, fatigue, impoverish, prostrate, sap, tire, weaken, wear out 2. consume, deplete, dissipate, expend, finish, run through, spend, squander, use up, waste

exhibit 1. *v.* display, expose, express, indicate, manifest, offer, parade, present, put on view, reveal, show 2. *n.* display, exhibition, model, show

exhort advise, beseech, bid, call upon, encour-

age, entreat, goad, incite, persuade, spur, urge, warn

exigency 1. constraint, demand, necessity, need, requirement 2. crisis, difficulty, emergency, extremity, hardship, pass, pinch, plight, predicament, quandary, strait

exile *n.* 1. banishment, expatriation, expulsion, ostracism, proscription, separation 2. émigré, expatriate, outcast, refugee ~*v.* 3. banish, deport, drive out, eject, expel, oust, proscribe

exist abide, be, be living, be present, breathe, endure, happen, last, live, occur, prevail, remain, stand, survive

existence actuality, animation, being, breath, continuance, continuation, duration, endurance, life, subsistence, survival

exit door, egress, gate, outlet, passage out, vent, way out

exodus departure, evacuation, migration, retirement, retreat, withdrawal

exonerate absolve, acquit, clear, discharge, dismiss, excuse, justify, pardon, vindicate

DICTIONARY

originating in a foreign country. —*n.* exotic plant. —**exotically** *adv.* —**exotica** *pl. n.* (collection of) exotic objects.

expand *v.* make or become larger; spread out; (foll. by *on*) enlarge (on); become more relaxed, friendly, and talkative. —**expansion** *n.* —**expanse** *n.* uninterrupted wide area. —**expansive** *adj.* friendly and talkative; wide or extensive.

expatiate [iks-**pay**-shee-ate] *v.* (foll. by *on*) speak or write at great length (on). —**expatiation** *n.*

expatriate [eks-**pat**-ree-it] *n.* person living outside his or her native country. —*adj.* living outside one's native country. —**expatriation** *n.*

expect *v.* regard as probable; look forward to, await; require as an obligation. —**expectation** *n.* act or state of expecting; something looked forward to; attitude of anticipation or hope. —**expectancy** *n.* something expected on the basis of an average, e.g. *life expectancy;* feeling of anticipation. —**expectant** *adj.* expecting or hopeful; pregnant. —**expectantly** *adv.*

expectorate *v.* spit out (phlegm etc.). —**expectoration** *n.* —**expectorant** *n.* medicine that helps to bring up phlegm from the respiratory passages.

expedient [iks-**pee**-dee-ent] *n.* something that achieves a particular purpose. —*adj.* suitable to the circumstances, appropriate. —**expediency** *n.*

expedite *v.* hasten the progress of. —**expedition** *n.* organized journey, esp. for exploration; people and equipment comprising an expedition. —**expeditionary** *adj.* relating to an expedition, esp. a military one. —**expeditious** *adj.* prompt, speedy.

expel *v.* **-pelling, -pelled.** dismiss from a school etc. permanently; drive out with force. —**expulsion** *n.*

expend *v.* spend, use up. —**expendable** *adj.* able to be sacrificed to achieve an objective. —**expenditure** *n.* something expended, esp. money; amount expended. —**expense** *n.* cost; (cause of) spending. —*pl.* charges, outlay incurred. —**expensive** *adj.* high-priced.

experience *n.* direct personal participation; particular incident, feeling, etc. that a person has undergone; accumulated knowledge. —*v.* participate in; be affected by (an emotion). —**experienced** *adj.* skilful from extensive participation.

THESAURUS

expand amplify, augment, bloat, blow up, broaden, develop, dilate, distend, enlarge, extend, fatten, fill out, grow, heighten, increase, inflate, lengthen, magnify, multiply, prolong, protract, swell, thicken, wax, widen

expanse area, breadth, extent, field, plain, range, space, stretch, sweep, tract

expansive affable, communicative, effusive, free, friendly, garrulous, genial, loquacious, open, outgoing, sociable, talkative, warm

expect 1. assume, believe, calculate, conjecture, forecast, foresee, imagine, presume, reckon, suppose, surmise, think, trust 2. anticipate, await, contemplate, envisage, hope for, look ahead to, look for, look forward to, predict, watch for

expectation assumption, assurance, belief, calculation, confidence, conjecture, forecast, likelihood, presumption, probability, supposition, surmise, trust

expediency, expedience advisability, appropriateness, aptness, benefit, convenience, effectiveness, fitness, helpfulness, meetness, pragmatism, profitability, propriety, prudence, suitability, usefulness, utility

expedient advantageous, advisable, appropriate, beneficial, convenient, desirable, effective, fit, helpful, meet, opportune, politic, practical, pragmatic, profitable, proper, prudent, suitable, useful, worthwhile

expedition enterprise, excursion, exploration, journey, mission, quest, safari, tour, trek, trip, undertaking, voyage

expel 1. cast out, discharge, dislodge, drive out, eject, remove, throw out 2. ban, banish, bar, blackball, discharge, dismiss, evict, exclude, exile, oust, proscribe, throw out

expend consume, disburse, dissipate, employ, exhaust, go through, pay out, spend, use (up)

expendable inessential, replaceable, unimportant

expenditure charge, cost, disbursement, expense, outgoings, outlay, output, payment, spending, use

expense charge, cost, disbursement, loss, outlay, output, payment, sacrifice, spending, toll, use

expensive costly, dear, excessive, exorbitant, high-priced, inordinate, lavish, overpriced, rich, stiff

experience *n.* 1. contact, doing, evidence, exposure, familiarity, knowledge, observation, participation, practice, proof, training, trial, understanding 2. affair, encounter, episode, event, happening, incident, ordeal, test, trial ~*v.* 3. behold, encounter, endure, face, feel, go through, have, know, live through, meet, ob-

DICTIONARY

experiment *n.* test to provide evidence to prove or disprove a theory; attempt at something new. —*v.* make an experiment. —**experimental** *adj.* —**experimentally** *adv.* —**experimentation** *n.*

expert *n.* person with extensive skill or knowledge in a particular field. —*adj.* skilful or knowledgeable. —**expertise** [eks-per-**teez**] *n.* special skill or knowledge.

expiate *v.* make amends for. —**expiation** *n.*

expire *v.* finish or run out; *Lit.* die; breathe out. —**expiration** *n.* —**expiry** *n.* end, esp. of a contract period.

explain *v.* make clear and intelligible; account for. —**explanation** *n.* —**explanatory** *adj.*

expletive [iks-**plee**-tiv] *n.* swearword.

explicable *adj.* able to be explained. —**explicate** *v. Formal* explain. —**explication** *n.*

explicit *adj.* precisely and clearly expressed; shown in realistic detail. —**explicitly** *adv.*

explode *v.* burst with great violence, blow up; react suddenly with emotion; increase rapidly; show (a theory etc.) to be baseless. —**explosion** *n.* —**explosive** *adj., n.*

exploit *n.* notable feat or deed. —*v.* take advantage of for one's own purposes; make the best use of. —**exploitation** *n.* —**exploiter** *n.*

explore *v.* travel into (unfamiliar regions), esp. for scientific purposes; investigate. —**exploration** *n.* —**exploratory** *adj.* —**explorer** *n.*

expo *n. Informal* exposition, large public exhibition.

exponent *n.* person who advocates an idea, cause, etc.; skilful performer, esp. a musician. —**exponential** *adj.* very rapid. —**exponentially** *adv.*

export *n.* selling or shipping of goods to a foreign country; product shipped or sold to a foreign country. —*v.* sell or ship (goods) to a foreign country. —**exporter** *n.*

exposé [iks-**pose**-ay] *n.* bringing of a crime, scandal, etc. to public notice.

expose *v.* uncover or reveal; make vulnerable, leave unprotected; subject (a photographic film) to light. —**expose oneself** display one's sexual organs in public. —**exposure** *n.* exposing; lack of

---

THESAURUS

serve, perceive, sample, sense, suffer, sustain, taste, try, undergo

experienced accomplished, adept, capable, competent, expert, familiar, knowledgeable, practised, professional, qualified, seasoned, skilful, tested, trained, tried, veteran, well-versed

experiment 1. *n.* assay, attempt, investigation, procedure, proof, research, test, trial, trial run, venture 2. *v.* examine, investigate, research, sample, test, try, verify

experimental empirical, exploratory, pilot, preliminary, provisional, speculative, tentative, test, trial

expert 1. *n.* adept, authority, master, past master, professional, specialist, virtuoso, wizard 2. *adj.* able, adept, adroit, apt, clever, deft, experienced, handy, knowledgeable, masterly, practised, proficient, qualified, skilful, trained

expertise aptness, cleverness, command, deftness, dexterity, facility, judgment, knack, knowledge, mastery, proficiency, skilfulness, skill

expire 1. cease, close, come to an end, conclude, end, finish, lapse, run out, stop, terminate 2. depart, die, perish

explain clarify, clear up, define, demonstrate, describe, disclose, elucidate, expound, interpret, resolve, solve, teach, unfold

explanation 1. elucidation, exposition, interpretation, resolution 2. account, answer, cause, excuse, meaning, motive, reason, sense, vindication

explicit categorical, certain, clear, definite, direct, distinct, exact, express, frank, open, patent, plain, positive, precise, specific, stated, unqualified, unreserved

explode 1. blow up, burst, detonate, discharge, go off, set off, shatter, shiver 2. debunk, discredit, disprove, invalidate, refute, repudiate

exploit 1. *n.* achievement, adventure, attainment, deed, feat, stunt 2. *v.* abuse, manipulate, misuse, play on *or* upon, take advantage of

exploration examination, inquiry, inspection, investigation, probe, research, scrutiny, search, study

explore analyse, examine, inquire into, inspect, investigate, look into, probe, prospect, research, scrutinize, search

explosion bang, blast, burst, clap, crack, detonation, discharge, outburst, report

explosive 1. unstable, volatile 2. fiery, stormy, touchy, vehement, violent

exponent advocate, backer, champion, defender, promoter, spokesman, supporter, upholder

expose 1. display, exhibit, manifest, present, put on view, reveal, show, uncover, unveil 2. air, betray, bring to light, denounce, detect, disclose, divulge, lay bare, let out, make known, reveal, show up, uncover, unmask

DICTIONARY

shelter from the weather, esp. the cold; appearance before the public, as on television.

exposition *n.* see EXPOUND.

expostulate *v.* (foll. by *with*) reason (with), esp. to dissuade. —**expostulation** *n.*

expound *v.* explain in detail. —**exposition** *n.* explanation; large public exhibition.

express *v.* put into words; show (an emotion); indicate by a symbol or formula; squeeze out (juice etc.). —*adj.* explicitly stated; (of a purpose) particular; of or for rapid transportation of people, mail, etc. —*n.* fast train or bus stopping at only a few stations. —*adv.* by express delivery. —**expression** *n.* expressing; word or phrase; showing or communication of emotion; look on the face that indicates mood; *Maths* variable, function, or some combination of these. —**expressionless** *adj.* —**expressive** *adj.*

expressionism *n.* early 20th-century artistic movement which sought to express emotions rather than represent the physical world. —**expressionist** *n., adj.*

expropriate *v.* deprive an owner of (property). —**expropriation** *n.*

expunge [iks-**sponge**] *v.* delete, erase, blot out.

expurgate [**eks**-per-gate] *v.* remove objectionable parts from (a book etc.).

exquisite *adj.* of extreme beauty or delicacy; intense in feeling. —**exquisitely** *adv.*

extant *adj.* still existing.

extemporize *v.* speak, perform, or compose without preparation.

extend *v.* draw out or be drawn out, stretch; last for a certain time; (foll. by *to*) include; increase in size or scope; offer, e.g. *extend one's sympathy.* —**extendable** *adj.* —**extension** *n.* continuation or additional part of a building etc.; additional telephone connected to the same line as another; extending. —**extensive** *adj.* having a large extent, widespread. —**extensor** *n.* muscle that extends a part of the body. —**extent** *n.* range over which something extends, area.

extenuate *v.* make (an offence or fault) less blameworthy. —**extenuation** *n.*

exterior *n.* part or surface on the outside; outward appearance. —*adj.* of, on, or coming from the outside.

exterminate *v.* destroy (animals or people) completely. —**extermination** *n.* —**exterminator** *n.*

external *adj.* of, situated on, or coming from the outside. —**externally** *adv.*

extinct *adj.* having died out; (of a volcano) no longer liable to erupt. —**extinction** *n.*

THESAURUS

exposure 1. baring, display, manifestation, publicity, revelation, showing, uncovering, unveiling 2. airing, denunciation, detection, disclosure, divulgence, revelation, unmasking

expound describe, elucidate, explain, illustrate, interpret, spell out

express *v.* 1. articulate, assert, asseverate, communicate, couch, declare, phrase, pronounce, put, say, speak, state, tell, utter, voice, word ~*adj.* 2. clearcut, especial, particular, singular, special 3. direct, fast, high-speed, nonstop, quick, rapid, speedy, swift

expression 1. assertion, communication, declaration, mention, pronouncement, speaking, statement, utterance 2. demonstration, exhibition, indication, representation, show, sign, symbol, token 3. choice of words, delivery, diction, execution, language, phrasing, speech, style, wording 4. idiom, locution, phrase, remark, term, turn of phrase, word

expulsion banishment, discharge, dismissal, ejection, eviction, exclusion, exile, proscription, removal

exquisite 1. beautiful, dainty, delicate, elegant, fine, lovely, precious 2. attractive, beautiful, charming, comely, lovely, pleasing, striking

extend 1. carry on, continue, drag out, draw out, lengthen, prolong, protract, spin out, spread

out, stretch, unfurl, unroll 2. add to, augment, broaden, develop, dilate, enhance, enlarge, expand, increase, spread, widen

extension addendum, addition, adjunct, annexe, branch, supplement, wing

extensive broad, capacious, commodious, comprehensive, far-flung, far-reaching, general, great, huge, large, lengthy, long, prevalent, protracted, spacious, sweeping, thorough, universal, vast, wholesale, wide, widespread

extent 1. bounds, compass, play, range, reach, scope, sphere, sweep 2. amount, amplitude, area, breadth, bulk, degree, duration, expanse, expansion, length, magnitude, measure, quantity, size, stretch, term, time, volume, width

exterior 1. *n.* appearance, aspect, coating, covering, façade, face, finish, outside, shell, skin, surface 2. *adj.* external, outer, outermost, outside, outward, superficial, surface

exterminate abolish, annihilate, destroy, eliminate, eradicate, extirpate

external apparent, exterior, outer, outermost, outside, outward, superficial, surface, visible

extinct dead, defunct, gone, lost, vanished

extinction abolition, annihilation, death, dying out, excision, extermination, obliteration, oblivion

DICTIONARY

extinguish v. put out (a fire or light); remove or destroy entirely. —**extinguisher** n.

extirpate [**eks**-ter-pate] v. destroy utterly.

extol v. **-tolling, -tolled.** praise highly.

extort v. get (something) by force or threats. —**extortion** n. —**extortionate** adj. (of prices) excessive.

extra adj. additional; more than usual. —n. additional person or thing; something for which an additional charge is made; Films actor hired for crowd scenes. —adv. unusually or exceptionally.

extra- prefix outside or beyond an area or scope, e.g. extrasensory; extraterritorial.

extract v. pull out by force; remove; derive; copy out (an article, passage, etc.) from a publication. —n. something extracted, such as a passage from a book etc.; preparation containing the concentrated essence of a substance, e.g. beef extract. —**extraction** n. —**extractor** n.

extradite v. send (an accused person) back to his or her own country for trial. —**extradition** n.

extramural adj. connected with but outside the normal courses of a university or college.

extraneous [iks-**train**-ee-uss] adj. irrelevant.

extraordinary adj. very unusual; (of a meeting) unscheduled, arranged to deal with a particular subject. —**extraordinarily** adv.

extrapolate [iks-**trap**-a-late] v. infer (something not known) from the known facts; Maths estimate (a value of a function or measurement) beyond the known values by the extension of a curve. —**extrapolation** n.

extrasensory adj. —**extrasensory perception** supposed ability to obtain information other than through the normal senses.

extravagant adj. spending money excessively; going beyond reasonable limits. —**extravagance** n. —**extravaganza** n. elaborate and lavish entertainment, display, etc.

extreme adj. of a high or the highest degree or intensity; immoderate; severe; farthest or outermost. —n. either of the two limits of a scale or range. —**extremely** adv. —**extremist** n. person who favours immoderate methods. —adj. holding extreme opinions. —**extremity** n., pl. **-ties.** farthest point; extreme condition, as of misfortune. —pl. hands and feet.

extricate v. free from complication or difficulty. —**extrication** n.

extrovert adj. lively and outgoing; concerned more with external reality than inner feelings. —n. extrovert person.

extrude v. squeeze or force out. —**extrusion** n.

THESAURUS

extinguish 1. blow out, douse, put out, quench, smother, snuff out, stifle 2. abolish, destroy, eliminate, end, expunge, exterminate, kill, obscure, remove, suppress, wipe out

extol acclaim, applaud, celebrate, commend, eulogize, exalt, glorify, laud, praise

extort blackmail, bully, exact, extract, force, squeeze, wrest, wring

extra 1. adj. accessory, added, additional, auxiliary, fresh, further, more, new, other, supplemental, supplementary 2. n. addendum, addition, appurtenance, attachment, bonus, complement, extension, supernumerary, supplement 3. adv. especially, exceptionally, extraordinarily, extremely, particularly, remarkably, uncommonly, unusually

extract v. 1. draw, pluck out, pull, pull out, remove, take out, uproot, withdraw 2. derive, draw, elicit, evoke, exact, gather, get, glean, obtain, reap, wrest, wring ~n. 3. concentrate, decoction, distillate, distillation, essence, juice 4. abstract, citation, clipping, cutting, excerpt, passage, quotation, selection

extraordinary amazing, bizarre, curious, exceptional, fantastic, odd, outstanding, particular, peculiar, phenomenal, rare, remarkable, singular, special, strange, surprising, uncommon,

unfamiliar, unheard-of, unique, unprecedented, unusual, unwonted, weird, wonderful

extravagance improvidence, lavishness, overspending, prodigality, profligacy, profusion, squandering, waste

extravagant excessive, improvident, imprudent, lavish, prodigal, profligate, spendthrift, wasteful

extreme adj. 1. acute, great, greatest, high, highest, intense, maximum, severe, supreme, ultimate, utmost, uttermost, worst 2. faraway, far-off, farthest, final, last, most distant, outermost, remotest, terminal, ultimate, utmost, uttermost ~n. 3. acme, apex, boundary, climax, depth, edge, end, excess, extremity, height, limit, maximum, minimum, nadir, pinnacle, pole, termination, top, ultimate, zenith

extremely acutely, exceedingly, exceptionally, excessively, extraordinarily, greatly, highly, inordinately, intensely, markedly, quite, severely, uncommonly, unusually, utterly, very

extremity acme, apex, apogee, border, bound, boundary, brim, brink, edge, end, frontier, limit, margin, maximum, minimum, nadir, pinnacle, pole, rim, terminal, tip, top, ultimate, verge, zenith

extricate clear, deliver, disengage, disentangle,

DICTIONARY

exuberant *adj.* high-spirited; growing luxuriantly. —**exuberance** *n.*

exude *v.* make apparent by mood or behaviour, e.g. *exude confidence;* ooze out as sweat or sap.

exult *v.* be joyful or jubilant. —**exultation** *n.* —**exultant** *adj.*

eye *n.* organ of sight; (*often pl.*) ability to see; external part of an eye; attention, e.g. *his new shirt caught my eye;* ability to judge or appreciate, e.g *a good eye for detail;* one end of a sewing needle; dark spot on a potato from which a stem grows; small area of calm at the centre of a hurricane. —*v.* **ey(e)ing eyed.** look at carefully or warily. —**eyeless** *adj.* —**eyelet** *n.* small hole for a lace or cord to be passed through; ring that strengthens this. —**eyeball** *n.* ball-shaped part of the eye. —**eyebrow** *n.* line of hair on the bony ridge above the eye. —**eyeglass** *n.* lens for aiding defective vision. —**eyelash** *n.* short hair that grows out from the eyelid. —**eyelid** *n.* fold of skin that covers the eye when it is closed. —**eyeliner** *n.* cosmetic used to outline the eyes. —**eye-opener** *n. Informal* something startling or revealing. —**eye shadow** coloured cosmetic worn on the upper eyelids. —**eyesight** *n.* ability to see. —**eyesore** *n.* ugly object. —**eyetooth** *n.* canine tooth. —**eyewash** *n. Informal* nonsense. —**eyewitness** *n.* person who was present at an event and can describe what happened.

eyrie *n.* nest of an eagle; high isolated place.

THESAURUS

free, get out, liberate, release, relieve, remove, rescue, withdraw

exuberance 1. cheerfulness, eagerness, ebullience, effervescence, energy, enthusiasm, excitement, exhilaration, high spirits, life, liveliness, spirit, sprightliness, vigour, vitality, vivacity, zest 2. abundance, lavishness, lushness, luxuriance, profusion, rankness, richness, superabundance

exuberant 1. animated, buoyant, cheerful, eager, ebullient, effervescent, elated, energetic, enthusiastic, excited, exhilarated, high-spirited, lively, sparkling, spirited, sprightly, vigorous, vivacious, zestful 2. abundant, copious, lavish, lush, overflowing, plenteous, plentiful, profuse, rank, rich, teeming

exult be delighted, be elated, be joyful, be jubilant, be overjoyed, celebrate, jubilate, make merry, rejoice

eye *n.* 1. eyeball 2. appreciation, discernment, discrimination, judgment, perception, recognition, taste ~*v.* 3. contemplate, gaze at, glance at, inspect, look at, peruse, regard, scan, scrutinize, stare at, study, survey, view, watch

eyesight perception, sight, vision

eyesore atrocity, blemish, blight, blot, disfigurement, disgrace, horror, mess, monstrosity, ugliness

eyewitness looker-on, observer, onlooker, spectator, viewer, witness

F

F Fahrenheit; farad; *Chem.* fluorine.

f *Music* forte.

FA Football Association.

fable *n.* story with a moral; legend; lie. —**fabled** *adj.* made famous in legend.

fabric *n.* knitted or woven cloth; framework or structure. —**fabricate** *v.* make or build; make up (a story or lie). —**fabrication** *n.* —**fabricator** *n.*

fabulous *adj. Informal* excellent; astounding; told of in fables. —**fabulously** *adv.*

façade [fas-**sahd**] *n.* front of a building; (false) outward appearance.

face *n.* front of the head; facial expression; distorted expression; outward appearance; front or main side; dial of a clock; exposed area of coal or ore in a mine; dignity, self-respect. —*v.* look or turn towards; be opposite; be confronted by; provide with a surface. —**faceless** *adj.* impersonal, anonymous. —**facing** *n.* lining or covering for decoration or reinforcement. —*pl.* contrasting collar and cuffs on a jacket. —**face-lift** *n.* operation to tighten facial skin, to remove wrinkles. —**face-saving** *adj.* maintaining dignity or self-respect. —**face up to** *v.* accept (an unpleasant fact or reality). —**face value** apparent worth or meaning.

facet *n.* surface of a cut gem; aspect.

facetious [fas-**see**-shuss] *adj.* funny or trying to be funny, esp. at inappropriate times. —**facetiousness** *n.*

facia *n., pl.* -**ciae.** same as FASCIA.

facial *adj.* of the face. —*n.* beauty treatment for the face.

facile [**fas**-sile] *adj.* superficial and showing lack of real thought. —**facilitation** *n.*

facilitate *v.* make easy. —**facilitation** *n.*

facility *n., pl.* -**ties.** skill; easiness. —*pl.* means or equipment for an activity.

facsimile [fak-**sim**-ill-ee] *n.* exact copy.

fact *n.* event or thing known to have happened or existed; provable truth. —**facts of life** details of sex and reproduction. —**factual** *adj.*

faction *n.* (dissenting) minority group within a larger body; dissension. —**factious** *adj.* of or producing factions.

factitious *adj.* artificial.

factor *n.* element contributing to a result; *Maths* one of the integers multiplied together to give a given number; *Scot.* property manager. —**factorial** *n.* product of all the integers from one to a given number. —**factorize** *v.* calculate the factors of (a number).

factory *n., pl.* -**ries.** building where goods are manufactured.

THESAURUS

fabric 1. cloth, material, stuff, textile, web 2. constitution, framework, make-up, organization, structure

fabulous 1. amazing, astounding, breathtaking, fictitious, inconceivable, incredible, legendary, phenomenal, unbelievable 2. fictitious, imaginary, invented, legendary, made-up, mythical, unreal

façade appearance, exterior, face, front, frontage, guise, mask, pretence, semblance, show, veneer

face *n.* 1. countenance, features, physiognomy, visage 2. appearance, aspect, expression, frown, grimace, look, pout, scowl, smirk ~*v.* 3. brave, confront, cope with, deal with, defy, encounter, experience, meet, oppose 4. be opposite, front onto, give towards *or* onto, look onto, overlook

facet angle, aspect, face, part, phase, plane, side, slant, surface

facetious amusing, comical, droll, flippant, frivolous, funny, humorous, jesting, jocular, merry, playful, pleasant, waggish, witty

face up to accept, acknowledge, come to terms with, confront, cope with, deal with, meet head-on

facile adept, adroit, easy, effortless, fluent, light, quick, ready, simple, skilful, smooth, uncomplicated

facilitate ease, expedite, forward, further, help, make easy, promote, speed up

facility ability, adroitness, dexterity, ease, efficiency, effortlessness, fluency, knack, proficiency, quickness, readiness, skilfulness, skill, smoothness

facsimile copy, duplicate, photocopy, print, replica, reproduction, transcript

fact 1. act, deed, event, *fait accompli*, happening, incident, occurrence, performance 2. actuality, certainty, reality, truth

faction bloc, cabal, camp, caucus, clique, coalition, confederacy, division, gang, group, junta, lobby, minority, party, pressure group, section, sector, set, splinter group

factor aspect, cause, circumstance, component, consideration, element, influence, item, part, point, thing

factory mill, plant, works

DICTIONARY

factotum *n.* person employed to do all sorts of work.

faculty *n., pl.* **-ties.** physical or mental ability; department in a university or college.

fad *n.* short-lived fashion; whim. —**faddy, faddish** *adj.*

fade *v.* (cause to) lose brightness, colour, or strength; vanish slowly. —**fade-in, -out** *n.* gradual increase or decrease, as of vision or sound in a film or broadcast.

faeces [**fee**-seez] *pl. n.* waste matter discharged from the anus. —**faecal** [**fee**-kl] *adj.*

fag[1] *n. Slang* cigarette. —**fag end** cigarette stub; last and worst part.

fag[2] *n. Informal* boring task; young public schoolboy who does menial chores for a senior boy. —*v.* (often foll. by *out*) *Informal* tire; do menial chores in a public school.

fag[3] *n. US offens.* male homosexual.

faggot[1] *n.* ball of chopped liver, herbs, and bread; bundle of sticks for fuel.

faggot[2] *n. US offens.* male homosexual.

Fahrenheit [**far**-ren-hite] *adj.* of a temperature scale with the freezing point of water at 32° and the boiling point at 212°.

faïence [**fie**-ence] *n.* tin-glazed earthenware.

fail *v.* be unsuccessful; stop operating; be or judge to be below the required standard in a test; disappoint or be useless to (someone); omit or be unable to do (something); go bankrupt. —*n.* instance of not passing an exam or test. —**without fail** definitely; regularly. —**failing** *n.* weak point. —*prep.* in the absence of. —**failure** *n.* act or instance of failing; unsuccessful person or thing.

fain *adv. Obs.* gladly.

faint *adj.* lacking clarity, brightness, or volume; lacking conviction or force; feeling dizzy or weak. —*v.* lose consciousness temporarily. —*n.* temporary loss of consciousness.

fair[1] *adj.* unbiased and reasonable; light in colour; beautiful; quite good; unblemished; (of weather) fine. —*adv.* fairly; absolutely. —**fairly** *adv.* as deserved, reasonably; moderately; to a great degree or extent. —**fairness** *n.* —**fairway** *n. Golf* smooth area between the tee and the green.

fair[2] *n.* travelling entertainment with stalls and machines to ride on, etc.; exhibition of commercial or industrial products. —**fairground** *n.* open space used for a fair.

THESAURUS

factual accurate, authentic, close, correct, credible, exact, faithful, genuine, literal, objective, precise, real, sure, true, true-to-life, unadorned, unbiased, veritable

faculties intelligence, powers, reason, senses, wits

faculty branch of learning, department, discipline, profession, school, teaching staff

fad affectation, craze, fancy, fashion, mania, mode, rage, trend, vogue, whim

fade 1. blanch, bleach, blench, dim, discolour, dull, grow dim, lose colour, lose lustre, pale, wash out 2. decline, die out, dim, disperse, dissolve, droop, dwindle, ebb, fail, fall, flag, languish, melt away, perish, shrivel, vanish, waste away, wilt, wither

fail 1. be defeated, be unsuccessful, break down, come to grief, come to naught, come to nothing, fall short, founder, go astray, go down, miscarry, misfire, miss, run aground, turn out badly 2. abandon, desert, disappoint, forget, forsake, let down, neglect, omit

failing *n.* blemish, blind spot, defect, deficiency, drawback, error, failure, fault, flaw, imperfection, lapse, misfortune, shortcoming, weakness

failure 1. breakdown, collapse, defeat, downfall, fiasco, miscarriage, overthrow, wreck 2. disappointment, incompetent, loser, no-good, non-

starter 3. default, neglect, negligence, nonsuccess, omission, remissness, shortcoming 4. breakdown, decay, decline, failing, loss 5. bankruptcy, crash, downfall, insolvency, ruin

faint *adj.* 1. delicate, dim, distant, dull, faltering, feeble, hazy, hushed, ill-defined, indistinct, light, low, muted, soft, subdued, thin, vague, whispered 2. feeble, remote, slight, weak 3. dizzy, drooping, exhausted, fatigued, giddy, lethargic, light-headed, muzzy, vertiginous, weak ~*v.* 4. black out, collapse, fade, fail, languish, pass out, weaken

fair[1] *adj.* 1. above board, clean, disinterested, dispassionate, equal, even-handed, honest, honourable, impartial, just, lawful, legitimate, objective, proper, square, unbiased, upright 2. blonde, light 3. adequate, all right, average, decent, mediocre, middling, moderate, not bad, passable, reasonable, respectable, satisfactory, tolerable 4. beautiful, comely, handsome, lovely, pretty, well-favoured

fair[2] *n.* bazaar, carnival, festival, fête, gala, market, show

fairly 1. adequately, moderately, pretty well, quite, rather, reasonably, somewhat, tolerably 2. deservedly, equitably, honestly, justly, objectively, properly

fairness decency, equity, impartiality, justice, legitimacy, rightfulness, uprightness

DICTIONARY

Fair Isle *n.* intricate multicoloured knitted pattern.

fairy *n., pl.* **fairies.** imaginary small creature with magic powers; *Offens.* male homosexual. —**fairy godmother** person who helps in time of trouble. —**fairyland** *n.* —**fairy light** small coloured light used as decoration. —**fairy tale, story** story about fairies or magic; unbelievable story or explanation.

fait accompli [fate ak-kom-plee] *n. French* something already done that cannot be altered.

faith *n.* strong belief, esp. without proof; religion; complete confidence or trust; allegiance to a person or cause. —**faithful** *adj.* loyal; firm in support; accurate. —**faithfully** *adv.* —**faithless** *adj.* disloyal or dishonest.

fake *v.* cause (something) to appear real or more valuable by fraud; pretend to have (an illness, emotion, etc.). —*n.* person, thing, or act that is not genuine. —*adj.* not genuine. —**faker** *n.*

fakir [**fay**-keer] *n.* member of any Islamic religious order; Hindu holy man.

falcon *n.* small bird of prey. —**falconry** *n.* art of training falcons; sport of hunting with falcons. —**falconer** *n.*

fall *v.* **falling, fell, fallen.** drop from a higher to a lower place through the force of gravity; collapse to the ground; decrease in number or quality; slope downwards; die in battle; be captured; pass into a specified condition; (of the face) take on a sad expression; yield to temptation; occur. —*n.* falling; thing or amount that falls; decrease in value or number; decline in power or influence; *US* autumn; capture or overthrow. —*pl.* waterfall. —**fall for** *v. Informal* fall in love with; be taken in by. —**fall guy** *Informal* victim of a confidence trick; scapegoat. —**fallout** *n.* radioactive particles spread as a result of a nuclear explosion.

fallacy *n., pl.* **-cies.** false belief; unsound reasoning. —**fallacious** *adj.*

fallible *adj.* liable to error. —**fallibility** *n.*

Fallopian tube *n.* either of a pair of tubes through which egg cells pass from the ovary to the womb.

fallow[1] *adj.* (of land) ploughed but left unseeded to regain fertility.

fallow[2] *adj.* —**fallow deer** reddish-brown deer with white spots in summer.

false *adj.* not true or correct; artificial, fake; deceptive; treacherous. —**falsely** *adv.* —**falseness, falsity** *n.* —**falsehood** *n.* quality of being untrue; lie. —**falsify** *v.* **-fying, -fied.** alter fraudulently. —**falsification** *n.*

falsetto *n., pl.* **-tos.** voice pitched higher than one's natural range.

THESAURUS

fairy brownie, elf, hob, sprite

fairy tale *or* **fairy story** 1. folk tale, romance 2. fantasy, fiction, invention, lie, tall story, untruth

faith 1. assurance, confidence, conviction, credence, credit, reliance, trust 2. allegiance, constancy, faithfulness, fealty, fidelity, loyalty, truth, truthfulness

faithful 1. constant, dependable, devoted, loyal, reliable, staunch, steadfast, true, trusty, truthful, unwavering 2. accurate, close, exact, just, precise, strict, true

faithless disloyal, doubting, false, fickle, inconstant, perfidious, traitorous, treacherous, unbelieving, unfaithful, unreliable, untrue, untrustworthy, untruthful

fake 1. *v.* copy, counterfeit, fabricate, feign, forge, pretend, put on, sham, simulate 2. *n.* charlatan, copy, forgery, fraud, hoax, imitation, impostor, mountebank, reproduction, sham

fall *v.* 1. cascade, collapse, crash, descend, dive, drop, drop down, keel over, nose-dive, pitch, plummet, plunge, settle, sink, stumble, subside, topple, trip, trip over, tumble 2. abate, decline, decrease, depreciate, diminish, dwindle, ebb, fall off, flag, go down, lessen, slump,

subside 3. be taken, capitulate, give in *or* up, give way, go out of office, resign, succumb, surrender, yield ~*n.* 4. descent, dive, drop, plummet, plunge, slip, spill, tumble 5. cut, decline, decrease, dip, drop, dwindling, falling off, lessening, lowering, reduction, slump 6. capitulation, collapse, death, defeat, downfall, failure, overthrow, resignation, ruin, surrender 7. declivity, descent, incline, slant, slope

fallacy deceit, deception, delusion, error, falsehood, flaw, illusion, misconception, mistake, sophism, untruth

fallen *adj.* 1. collapsed, decayed, flat, ruinous, sunken 2. dead, killed, lost, perished, slain

fallible erring, frail, ignorant, imperfect, mortal, uncertain, weak

fallow dormant, idle, inert, resting, uncultivated, undeveloped, unplanted

false 1. concocted, erroneous, faulty, fictitious, improper, inaccurate, incorrect, inexact, invalid, mistaken, unfounded, unreal, wrong 2. lying, mendacious, unreliable, unsound, untrue, untrustworthy, untruthful 3. artificial, bogus, feigned, forged, imitation, mock, pretended, sham

falsehood 1. deceit, deception, dishonesty,

DICTIONARY

falter *v.* lose power momentarily; be unsure; utter hesitantly; move unsteadily.

fame *n.* state of being widely known or recognized. **—famed** *adj.* famous.

familiar *adj.* well-known; acquainted; too friendly; intimate, friendly. *—n.* friend; demon supposed to attend a witch. **—familiarly** *adv.* **—familiarity** *n.* **—familiarize** *v.* acquaint fully with a particular subject. **—familiarization** *n.*

family *n., pl.* **-lies.** group of parents and their children; one's spouse and children; one's children; group descended from a common ancestor; group of related objects or beings. *—adj.* suitable for parents and children together. **—familial** *adj.* **—family planning** control of the number of children in a family, esp. through contraception.

famine *n.* severe shortage of food.

famished *adj.* very hungry.

famous *adj.* very well-known. **—famously** *adv. Informal* excellently.

fan[1] *n.* hand-held or mechanical object used to create a current of air for ventilation or cooling. *—v.* **fanning, fanned.** blow or cool with a fan; spread out like a fan. **—fan belt** belt that drives a cooling fan in a car engine.

fan[2] *n. Informal* devotee of a pop star, sport, or hobby.

fanatic *n.* person who is excessively enthusiastic about something. **—fanatical** *adj.* **—fanatically** *adv.* **—fanaticism** *n.*

fancy *adj.* **-cier, -ciest.** elaborate, not plain; (of prices) higher than usual. *—n., pl.* **-cies.** sudden irrational liking or desire; uncontrolled imagination. *—v.* **-cying, -cied.** *Informal* have a wish for; *Informal* be sexually attracted to; picture in the imagination; suppose. **—fancy oneself** *Informal* have a high opinion of oneself. **—fanciful** *adj.* not based on fact; excessively elaborate. **—fancifully** *adv.* **—fancy dress** party costume representing a historical figure, animal, etc. **—fancy-free** *adj.* not in love.

fandango *n., pl.* **-gos.** lively Spanish dance.

fanfare *n.* short loud tune played on brass instruments.

fang *n.* snake's tooth which injects poison; long pointed tooth.

fantasy *n., pl.* **-sies.** imagination unrestricted by reality; far-fetched notion; daydream; fiction with a large fantasy content. **—fantasize** *v.* indulge in daydreams. **—fantasia** *n.* musical composition of an improvised nature. **—fantastic** *adj. Informal* very good; strange or difficult to believe; unrealistic or absurd. **—fantastically** *adv.*

far farther *or* **further, farthest** *or* **furthest.** *—adv.* at, to, or from a great distance; at or to a remote time; very much. *—adj.* remote in space or time. **—Far East** East Asia. **—far-fetched** *adj.* hard to believe.

farad *n.* unit of electrical capacitance.

farce *n.* boisterous comedy; ludicrous situation. **—farcical** *adj.* ludicrous. **—farcically** *adv.*

THESAURUS

mendacity, perjury, prevarication, untruthfulness 2. fib, fiction, lie, story, untruth

falsify alter, belie, counterfeit, distort, doctor, fake, forge, misrepresent, pervert

falter hesitate, shake, stammer, stutter, tremble, waver

fame celebrity, credit, eminence, glory, honour, name, prominence, renown, reputation, repute, stardom

familiar 1. common, conventional, customary, domestic, everyday, frequent, household, mundane, ordinary, recognizable, repeated, routine, stock, well-known 2. amicable, close, confidential, cordial, easy, free, friendly, informal, intimate, near, open, relaxed, unreserved

familiarity 1. acquaintance, awareness, experience, grasp 2. closeness, ease, fellowship, freedom, friendliness, informality, intimacy, naturalness, openness, sociability

family brood, children, household, issue, kin, offspring, people, progeny, relations, relatives

famine dearth, hunger, scarcity, starvation

famous celebrated, conspicuous, eminent, glorious, honoured, illustrious, legendary, notable, noted, prominent, remarkable, renowned, well-known

fanatic *n.* addict, bigot, devotee, enthusiast, extremist, visionary, zealot

fancy *v.* 1. believe, conceive, guess, imagine, infer, reckon, suppose, surmise, think, think likely 2. crave, desire, dream of, long for, relish, wish for, would like, yearn for *~adj.* 3. decorated, elaborate, elegant, intricate, ornamented, ornate

fantastic eccentric, exotic, fanciful, freakish, grotesque, imaginative, odd, peculiar, quaint, queer, rococo, strange, unreal, weird, whimsical

fantasy apparition, daydream, delusion, dream, fancy, hallucination, illusion, mirage, nightmare, pipe dream, reverie, vision

far *adv.* 1. afar, a good way, a great distance, a long way, deep 2. considerably, decidedly, ex-

DICTIONARY

fare *n.* charge for a passenger's journey; passenger; food provided. —*v.* get on (as specified), e.g. *we fared badly.* —**farewell** *interj.* goodbye. —*n.* act of saying goodbye and leaving.

farinaceous *adj.* mealy, starchy.

farm *n.* area of land for growing crops or rearing livestock. —*v.* cultivate (land); rear (stock). —**farmer** *n.* —**farmhouse** *n.* —**farm out** *v.* send (work) to be done by others. —**farmstead** *n.* farm and its buildings. —**farmyard** *n.*

farrago [far-**rah**-go] *n., pl.* **-gos, -goes.** jumbled mixture of things.

farrier *n.* person who shoes horses.

farrow *n.* litter of pigs. —*v.* (of a sow) give birth.

fart *Taboo* —*n.* emission of gas from the anus. —*v.* break wind.

farther, farthest *adv., adj.* see FAR.

farthing *n.* former British coin equivalent to a quarter of a penny.

farthingale *n. Obs.* hoop worn under skirts.

fascia [**fay**-shya] *n., pl.* **-ciae.** flat surface above a shop window; outer surface of a dashboard.

fascinate *v.* attract and interest strongly; make motionless from fear or awe. —**fascinating** *adj.* —**fascination** *n.*

fascism [**fash**-iz-zum] *n.* right-wing political system characterized by state control and extreme nationalism. —**fascist** *adj., n.*

fashion *n.* style in clothes, esp. the latest style; manner of doing something. —*v.* form or make into a particular shape. —**fashionable** *adj.* currently popular. —**fashionably** *adv.*

fast[1] *adj.* (capable of) acting or moving quickly; done in or lasting a short time; allowing rapid movement; (of a clock) showing a time later than the correct time; dissipated; firmly fixed; steadfast. —*adv.* quickly; tightly, firmly; soundly, deeply. —**fast food** food, such as hamburgers, prepared and served very quickly.

fast[2] *v.* go without food, esp. for religious reasons. —*n.* period of fasting.

fasten *v.* make or become firmly fixed or joined; close by fixing in place or locking; (foll. by *on*) direct (one's attention) towards. —**fastener, fastening** *n.* device that fastens.

fastidious *adj.* very fussy about details; easily disgusted. —**fastidiously** *adv.* —**fastidiousness** *n.*

fastness *n.* fortress, safe place.

fat *n.* extra flesh on the body; oily substance obtained from animals or plants. —*adj.* **fatter, fattest.** having excess flesh on the body; containing much fat; thick; profitable. —**fatness** *n.* —**fatten** *v.* (cause to) become fat. —**fatted** *adj.* fattened for slaughter. —**fatty** *adj.* containing fat. —**fathead** *n. Informal* fool. —**fat-headed** *adj.*

fatal *adj.* causing death or ruin. —**fatally** *adv.*

THESAURUS

tremely, greatly, incomparably, much ~*adj.* 3. distant, long, outlying, remote, removed

farce 1. buffoonery, comedy, satire, slapstick 2. absurdity, joke, mockery, nonsense, parody, ridiculousness, sham, travesty

fare *n.* 1. charge, price, ticket money, transport cost 2. diet, eatables, food, meals, menu, provisions, rations ~*v.* 3. do, get along, get on, make out, manage, prosper

farewell adieu, departure, goodbye, parting, valediction

far-fetched doubtful, dubious, improbable, incredible, preposterous, strained, unbelievable, unconvincing, unlikely, unnatural, unrealistic

farm 1. *n.* grange, holding, homestead, land, plantation, smallholding 2. *v.* cultivate, operate, plant, work

fascinate absorb, allure, beguile, bewitch, captivate, charm, delight, enchant, engross, enravish, enthral, entrance, hypnotize, infatuate, intrigue, rivet, transfix

fascination allure, attraction, charm, enchantment, glamour, lure, magic, magnetism, pull, sorcery, spell

fashion *n.* 1. convention, craze, custom, fad, latest, latest style, look, mode, prevailing

taste, rage, style, trend, usage, vogue 2. attitude, demeanour, manner, method, mode, style, way ~*v.* 3. construct, contrive, create, design, forge, form, make, manufacture, mould, shape, work

fashionable à la mode, chic, current, customary, genteel, in vogue, latest, modern, modish, popular, prevailing, smart, stylish, up-to-date, usual

fast[1] *adj.* 1. brisk, fleet, flying, hasty, hurried, nippy, quick, rapid, speedy, swiftly, winged 2. dissipated, dissolute, giddy, intemperate, licentious, loose, profligate, promiscuous, wild ~*adv.* 3. quickly, rapidly, speedily, swiftly, with all haste

fast[2] 1. *v.* abstain, deny oneself, go hungry, go without food, practise abstention, refrain from food *or* eating 2. *n.* abstinence, fasting

fasten affix, anchor, attach, bind, bolt, chain, connect, fix, grip, join, lace, link, lock, make fast, make firm, seal, secure, tie, unite

fat *adj.* 1. corpulent, fleshy, gross, heavy, obese, overweight, plump, podgy, portly, rotund, solid, stout, tubby 2. adipose, fatty, greasy, oily, suety ~*n.* 3. blubber, bulk, corpulence, flesh, obesity, overweight, paunch

DICTIONARY

—**fatality** *n.* death caused by an accident or disaster.

fatalism *n.* belief that all events are predetermined and man is powerless to change his destiny. —**fatalist** *n.* —**fatalistic** *adj.*

fate *n.* power supposed to predetermine events; inevitable fortune that befalls a person or thing. —**fated** *adj.* destined; doomed to death or destruction. —**fateful** *adj.* having important, usu. disastrous, consequences.

father *n.* male parent; man who originates or founds something; title of some priests; (**F-**) God. —*pl.* ancestors. —*v.* be the father of (offspring). —**fatherhood** *n.* —**fatherless** *adj.* —**fatherly** *adj.* —**father-in-law** *n.* father of one's husband or wife. —**fatherland** *n.* one's native country.

fathom *n.* unit of measurement of the depth of water, equal to six feet. —*v.* understand. —**fathomable** *adj.* —**fathomless** *adj.* too difficult to fathom.

fatigue [fat-**eeg**] *n.* physical or mental exhaustion caused by exertion; weakening of a material due to stress; soldier's nonmilitary duty. —*v.* tire out.

fatuous *adj.* foolish. —**fatuously** *adv.* —**fatuity** *n.*

faucet [**faw**-set] *n.* US tap.

fault *n.* responsibility for something wrong; mistake; defect or flaw; *Geology* break in layers of rock; *Tennis, squash, etc.* invalid serve. —*v.* criticize or find mistakes in. —**at fault** guilty of error. —**find fault with** seek out minor imperfections in. —**to a fault** excessively. —**faulty** *adj.* —**faultily** *adv.* —**faultless** *adj.* —**faultlessly** *adv.*

faun *n.* (in Roman legend) rural god with goat's horns and legs.

fauna *n., pl.* **-nas, -nae.** animals of a given place or time.

faux pas [foe pah] *n., pl.* **faux pas.** social blunder.

favour *n.* goodwill, approval; act of goodwill or generosity; partiality. —*v.* prefer; support or advocate; regard or treat with especial kindness; *Informal* resemble. —**favourable** *adj.* giving consent; encouraging; useful or beneficial. —**favourably** *adv.* —**favourite** *n.* preferred person or thing; *Sport* competitor expected to win. —*adj.* most liked. —**favouritism** *n.* practice of unfairly favouring one person or group.

fawn[1] *n.* young deer. —*adj.* light yellowish-brown.

fawn[2] *v.* (foll. by *on*) seek attention from (someone) by being obsequious; (of a dog) try to please by a show of extreme affection.

THESAURUS

fatal 1. deadly, final, incurable, killing, lethal, malignant, mortal, pernicious 2. baleful, baneful, calamitous, catastrophic, disastrous, lethal, ruinous

fate 1. chance, destiny, divine will, fortune, predestination, providence 2. end, future, issue, outcome, upshot

fated destined, doomed, foreordained, marked down, predestined, preordained, sure, written

fateful critical, crucial, decisive, important, significant

father *n.* 1. begetter, pater, patriarch, sire 2. ancestor, forebear, forefather, predecessor, progenitor 3. abbé, confessor, curé, pastor, priest ~*v.* 4. beget, get, procreate, sire

fatherly benevolent, benign, indulgent, kind, kindly, paternal, protective, supportive, tender

fathom comprehend, get to the bottom of, grasp, interpret, understand

fatigue 1. *v.* drain, exhaust, jade, overtire, tire, weaken, wear out, weary 2. *n.* debility, heaviness, languor, lethargy, overtiredness, tiredness

fatuous absurd, brainless, dense, dull, foolish, idiotic, inane, ludicrous, mindless, silly, stupid, witless

fault *n.* 1. blemish, defect, drawback, failing, flaw, imperfection, lack, shortcoming, snag, weakness, weak point 2. lapse, misconduct, misdeed, misdemeanour, mistake, offence, sin, trespass, wrong

faultless 1. accurate, classic, correct, exemplary, faithful, foolproof, impeccable, model, perfect 2. above reproach, blameless, guiltless, immaculate, innocent, pure, sinless, spotless, stainless

faulty bad, broken, damaged, defective, erroneous, impaired, imperfect, inaccurate, incorrect, invalid, malfunctioning, unsound, weak, wrong

favour *n.* 1. approval, backing, bias, esteem, good opinion, good will, grace, kindness, partiality, patronage, support 2. benefit, boon, courtesy, good turn, indulgence, kindness, service ~*v.* 3. be partial to, esteem, indulge, pamper, reward, smile upon, spoil, value

favourable advantageous, appropriate, auspicious, beneficial, convenient, fair, fit, good, helpful, hopeful, opportune, promising, propitious, suitable, timely

favourably advantageously, auspiciously, conveniently, fortunately, opportunely, profitably, well

favourite 1. *adj.* best-loved, choice, dearest, es-

DICTIONARY

fax n. electronic system for sending facsimiles of documents by telephone; document sent by this system. —v. send by this system.

FBI US Federal Bureau of Investigation.

FC Football Club.

Fe Chem. iron.

fealty n. Obs. subordinate's loyalty to his ruler or lord.

fear n. distress or alarm caused by impending danger or pain; cause of this. —v. feel anxiety about (something); be afraid of (something or someone). —**fearful** adj. feeling fear; causing fear; Informal very unpleasant. —**fearfully** adv. —**fearless** adj. —**fearlessly** adv. —**fearsome** adj. terrifying.

feasible adj. able to be done, possible. —**feasibly** adv. —**feasibility** n.

feast n. lavish meal; periodic religious celebration; something extremely pleasing. —v. eat a feast; (foll. by on) enjoy eating (something); give a feast to; delight.

feat n. remarkable, skilful, or daring action.

feather n. one of the barbed shafts forming the plumage of birds. —v. fit or cover with feathers; turn (an oar) edgeways. —**feather in one's cap** achievement one can be pleased with. —**feather one's nest** make one's life comfortable. —**feathered** adj. —**feathery** adj. —**featherbedding** n. overprotection. —**featherweight** n. boxer weigh-

ing up to 126lb (professional) or 57kg (amateur); insignificant person or thing.

feature n. prominent or distinctive part; part of the face, such as the eyes; special article in a newspaper or magazine; main film in a cinema programme. —v. have as a feature or be a feature in; give prominence to. —**featureless** adj.

Feb. February.

febrile [fee-brile] adj. feverish.

February n. second month.

feckless adj. ineffectual or irresponsible.

fecund adj. fertile. —**fecundity** n.

fed v. past of FEED. —**fed up** Informal bored, dissatisfied.

federal adj. of a system in which power is divided between one central government and several regional governments; of the central government of a federation. —**federalism** n. —**federalist** n. —**federate** v. unite in a federation. —**federation** n. union of several states, provinces, etc.; association.

fedora [fid-or-a] n. man's soft hat with a brim.

fee n. payment for professional services; charge paid to be allowed to do something.

feeble adj. lacking physical or mental power; unconvincing. —**feebleness** n. —**feebly** adv. —**feeble-minded** adj. mentally deficient.

THESAURUS

teemed, preferred 2. n. choice, darling, dear, idol, pet, pick, preference

fawn[1] adj. beige, buff, neutral

fawn[2] v. Often with on or upon be obsequious, be servile, court, crawl, creep, cringe, flatter, grovel, kneel, kowtow, toady

fear n. 1. alarm, awe, consternation, dismay, dread, fright, horror, panic, qualms, terror, timidity, tremors, trepidation 2. bogey, bugbear, horror, nightmare, phobia, spectre ~v. 3. dare not, dread, shudder at, take fright, tremble at

fearful 1. afraid, alarmed, anxious, apprehensive, diffident, frightened, hesitant, intimidated, nervous, panicky, scared, shrinking, tense, timid, timorous, uneasy 2. appalling, awful, dire, dreadful, frightful, ghastly, grievous, grim, hideous, horrible, monstrous, shocking, terrible

fearfully apprehensively, diffidently, nervously, timidly, timorously, uneasily

fearless bold, brave, confident, courageous, daring, gallant, heroic, indomitable, intrepid, plucky, unafraid, valiant, valorous

feasible attainable, likely, possible, practicable, reasonable, viable, workable

feast n. banquet, carousal, dinner, entertainment, junket, repast, revels, treat

feat achievement, act, attainment, deed, exploit, performance

feature n. 1. aspect, attribute, characteristic, facet, factor, hallmark, mark, peculiarity, point, property, quality, trait 2. article, column, comment, item, piece, report, story ~v. 3. accentuate, emphasize, headline, play up, present, promote, set off, spotlight, star

feckless aimless, feeble, futile, hopeless, incompetent, ineffectual, irresponsible, shiftless, useless, weak, worthless

fed up (with) annoyed, bored, depressed, discontented, dismal, dissatisfied, down, gloomy, glum, weary of

federation alliance, amalgamation, association, coalition, combination, confederacy, entente, federacy, league, syndicate, union

fee account, bill, charge, compensation, emolument, hire, pay, payment, remuneration, reward, toll

feeble delicate, doddering, effete, enervated, enfeebled, exhausted, failing, faint, frail, infirm,

DICTIONARY

feed v. **feeding, fed.** give food to; give (something) as food; eat; supply or prepare food for; supply (what is needed). —n. act of feeding; food, esp. for babies or animals; *Informal* meal. —**feeder** n. baby's bib; road or railway line linking outlying areas to the main traffic network. —**feedback** n. information received in response to something done; return of part of the output of an electrical circuit or loudspeaker to its source.

feel v. **feeling, felt.** have a physical or emotional sensation of; become aware of or examine by touch; believe. —n. act of feeling; way something feels; impression; sense of touch; instinctive aptitude. —**feeler** n. organ of touch in some animals; remark made to test others' opinion. —**feeling** n. emotional reaction; intuitive understanding; opinion; sympathy, understanding; ability to experience physical sensations; sensation experienced. —pl. emotional sensitivities. —**feel like** v. wish for, want.

feet n. plural of FOOT.

feign [fane] v. pretend.

feint[1] [faint] n. sham attack or blow meant to distract an opponent. —v. make a feint.

feint[2] [faint] n. narrow lines on ruled paper.

feldspar n. hard mineral that is the main constituent of igneous rocks.

felicity n., pl. **-ties.** happiness; appropriate expression or style. —**felicitate** v. congratulate. —**felicitation** n. —**felicitous** adj.

feline adj. of cats; catlike. —n. animal of the cat family.

fell[1] v. past tense of FALL.

fell[2] v. knock down; cut down (a tree).

fell[3] adj. *Old-fashioned* fierce, terrible. —**one fell swoop** single action or occurrence.

fell[4] n. (in N England) a mountain, hill, or moor.

felloe n. (segment of) the rim of a wheel.

fellow n. *Informal* man or boy; comrade or associate; person in the same group or condition; member of a learned society or the governing body of a college. —adj. in the same group or condition. —**fellowship** n. sharing of aims or interests; group with shared aims or interests; feeling of friendliness; college research post.

felon n. person guilty of a felony. —**felony** n., pl. **-nies.** serious crime. —**felonious** adj.

felspar n. same as FELDSPAR.

felt[1] v. past of FEEL.

felt[2] n. matted fabric made by bonding fibres by pressure. —**felt-tip pen** pen with a writing point made from pressed fibres.

fem. feminine.

female adj. of the sex which bears offspring; (of plants) producing fruits. —n. female person or animal.

feminine adj. of women; having qualities traditionally regarded as suitable for, or typical of, women; belonging to a particular class of grammatical inflection in some languages. —**femininity** n. —**feminism** n. advocacy of equal rights for women. —**feminist** n., adj.

femme fatale [fam fat-tahl] n., pl. **femmes fatales.** alluring woman who causes men distress.

femur [fee-mer] n. thighbone. —**femoral** adj. of the thigh.

fen n. low-lying flat marshy land.

fence n. barrier of posts linked by wire or wood,

THESAURUS

languid, powerless, puny, shilpit (*Scot.*), sickly, weak, weakened

feebleness debility, delicacy, exhaustion, frailty, incapacity, infirmity, languor, lassitude, sickliness, weakness

feed v. 1. cater for, nourish, provide for, supply, sustain, victual 2. *Sometimes with* **on** devour, eat, fare, graze, live on, nurture, pasture, subsist

feel v. 1. caress, finger, fondle, handle, manipulate, maul, paw, stroke, touch 2. be aware of, endure, enjoy, experience, go through, have, know, notice, observe, perceive, suffer, undergo 3. explore, fumble, grope, sound, test, try 4. be convinced, intuit, sense 5. believe, be of the opinion that, consider, deem, hold, judge, think 6. **feel like** desire, fancy, want

feeler antenna, tentacle, whisker

feeling 1. feel, perception, sensation, sense,

sense of touch, touch 2. consciousness, hunch, idea, impression, inkling, notion, presentiment, sense, suspicion 3. inclination, instinct, opinion, view

feelings ego, emotions, self-esteem, sensitivities, susceptibilities

fell v. cut, cut down, demolish, flatten, floor, hew, knock down, level, raze

fellow n. 1. boy, character, individual, man, person 2. associate, colleague, companion, compeer, comrade, co-worker, equal, friend, member, partner, peer

fellowship brotherhood, camaraderie, communion, familiarity, intercourse, intimacy, kindliness, sociability

feminine delicate, gentle, girlish, graceful, ladylike, modest, soft, tender, womanly

fen bog, marsh, morass, quagmire, slough, swamp

DICTIONARY

enclosing an area; *Slang* dealer in stolen property. —*v.* enclose with or as if with a fence; fight with swords as a sport; avoid a question. —**fencing** *n.* sport of fighting with swords; material for making fences. —**fencer** *n.*

fend *v.* —**fend for oneself** provide for oneself. —**fend off** *v.* ward off.

fender *n.* low metal frame in front of a fireplace; soft but solid object hung over a ship's side to prevent damage when docking; *US* wing of a car.

fennel *n.* fragrant plant whose seeds, leaves, and root are used in cookery.

fenugreek *n.* Mediterranean plant grown for its pungent seeds.

feral *adj.* wild.

ferment *n.* commotion, unrest. —*v.* undergo or cause to undergo fermentation. —**fermentation** *n.* reaction in which an organic molecule splits into simpler substances, esp. conversion of sugar to alcohol.

fern *n.* flowerless plant with fine fronds.

ferocious *adj.* fierce, violent. —**ferocity** *n.*

ferret *n.* tamed polecat used to catch rabbits or rats. —*v.* **ferreting, ferreted.** hunt with ferrets; search around. —**ferret out** *v.* find by searching.

ferric, ferrous *adj.* of or containing iron.

ferris wheel *n.* large vertical fairground wheel with hanging seats for riding in.

ferrule *n.* metal cap to strengthen the end of a stick.

ferry *n., pl.* **-ries.** boat for transporting people and vehicles. —*v.* **-rying, -ried.** carry by ferry; convey (goods or people). —**ferryman** *n.*

fertile *adj.* capable of producing young, crops, or vegetation; highly productive. —**fertility** *n.* —**fertilize** *v.* provide (an animal or plant) with sperm or pollen to bring about fertilization; supply (soil) with nutrients. —**fertilization** *n.* —**fertilizer** *n.*

fervent, fervid *adj.* intensely passionate and sincere. —**fervently** *adv.* —**fervour** *n.* intensity of feeling.

fescue *n.* pasture and lawn grass with stiff narrow leaves.

festal *adj.* festive.

fester *v.* form or cause to form pus; rot, decay; become worse.

festival *n.* organized series of special events or performances; day or period of celebration. —**festive** *adj.* of or like a celebration. —**festivity** *n., pl.* **-ties.** joyful celebration, merriment. —*pl.* celebrations.

festoon *v.* hang decorations in loops.

feta *n.* white salty Greek cheese.

fetch *v.* go after and bring back; be sold for; *Informal* deal (a blow). —**fetching** *adj.* attractive. —**fetch up** *v. Informal* arrive or end up.

fete, fête [fate] *n.* gala, bazaar, etc., usu. held outdoors. —*v.* honour or entertain regally.

fetid *adj.* stinking.

fetish *n.* form of behaviour in which sexual

THESAURUS

fence 1. *n.* barricade, barrier, defence, guard, hedge, paling, palisade, railings, rampart, shield, stockade, wall 2. *v.* bound, confine, coop, defend, enclose, guard, hedge, pen, protect, restrict, secure, separate, surround

ferment 1. *v.* boil, brew, bubble, concoct, foam, froth, heat, leaven, rise, seethe, work 2. *n. Fig.* agitation, commotion, excitement, fever, frenzy, glow, heat, stew, stir, tumult, turmoil, unrest, uproar

ferocious fierce, predatory, rapacious, ravening, savage, violent, wild

ferocity bloodthirstiness, brutality, cruelty, inhumanity, rapacity, ruthlessness, savagery, wildness

ferret out dig up, disclose, discover, drive out, elicit, get at, nose out, root out, search out, smell out, trace, track down, unearth

ferry 1. *n.* ferryboat, packet 2. *v.* carry, convey, ship, shuttle, transport

fertile abundant, fat, fecund, flowering, fruitful, luxuriant, plenteous, plentiful, productive, prolific, rich, teeming, yielding

fertility abundance, fecundity, fruitfulness, luxuriance, productiveness, richness

fertilizer compost, dressing, dung, guano, manure, marl

fervent, fervid ardent, devout, eager, earnest, emotional, enthusiastic, excited, fiery, heartfelt, impassioned, intense, vehement, warm

fervour ardour, eagerness, earnestness, enthusiasm, excitement, intensity, passion, vehemence, warmth, zeal

festival 1. commemoration, feast, fête, fiesta, holiday, saint's day 2. carnival, celebration, festivities, fête, field day, gala, jubilee, treat

festive back-slapping, carnival, celebratory, cheery, convivial, festal, gala, gay, happy, hearty, holiday, jolly, jovial, joyful, jubilant, light-hearted, merry, mirthful, sportive

festoon array, bedeck, deck, decorate, drape, garland, hang, swathe, wreathe

fetch 1. bring, carry, conduct, convey, deliver, escort, get, go for, lead, obtain, retrieve, transport 2. bring in, earn, go for, make, realize, sell for, yield

DICTIONARY

pleasure is derived from looking at or handling an inanimate object; thing with which one is excessively concerned; object believed to have magical powers. **—fetishism** *n.* **—fetishist** *n.*

fetlock *n.* projection behind and above a horse's hoof.

fetter *n.* chain or shackle for the foot. **—***pl.* restrictions. **—***v.* restrict; bind in fetters.

fettle *n.* state of health or spirits.

fetus [**fee**-tuss] *n., pl.* **-tuses.** embryo of a mammal in the later stages of development. **—fetal** *adj.*

feu *n.* (in Scotland) right of use of land in return for a fixed annual payment.

feud *n.* long bitter hostility between two people or groups. **—***v.* carry on a feud.

feudalism *n.* medieval system in which vassals held land from a lord, and in return worked and fought for him. **—feudal** *adj.* of or like feudalism.

fever *n.* (illness causing) high body temperature; nervous excitement. **—fevered** *adj.* **—feverish** *adj.* suffering from fever; in a state of nervous excitement. **—feverishly** *adv.*

few *adj.* not many. **—a few** a small number. **—good few, quite a few** several.

fey *adj.* whimsically strange; clairvoyant.

fez *n., pl.* **fezzes.** brimless tasselled cap, orig. from Turkey.

ff *Music* fortissimo.

fiancé [fee-**on**-say] *n.* man engaged to be married. **—fiancée** *n. fem.*

fiasco *n., pl.* **-cos, -coes.** ridiculous or humiliating failure.

fiat [**fee**-at] *n.* arbitrary order; official permission.

fib *n.* trivial lie. **—***v.* **fibbing, fibbed.** tell a fib. **—fibber** *n.*

fibre *n.* thread that can be spun into yarn; threadlike animal or plant tissue; essential substance or nature; strength of character; fibrous material in food. **—fibrous** *adj.* **—fibreboard** *n.* board made of compressed plant fibres. **—fibreglass** *n.* material made of fine glass fibres. **—fibre optics** transmission of information by light along very thin flexible fibres of glass.

fibroid [**fibe**-royd] *n.* benign tumour derived from fibrous connective tissue. **—fibrositis** [fibe-roh-**site**-iss] *n.* inflammation of the tissues of muscle sheaths.

fibula [**fib**-yew-la] *n., pl.* **-lae, -las.** slender outer bone of the lower leg. **—fibular** *adj.*

fiche [**feesh**] *n.* sheet of film for storing publications in miniaturized form.

fickle *adj.* changeable, inconstant. **—fickleness** *n.*

fiction *n.* literary works of the imagination, such as novels; invented story. **—fictional** *adj.* **—fictionalize** *v.* turn into fiction. **—fictitious** *adj.* not genuine; of or in fiction.

fiddle *n.* violin; *Informal* dishonest action or scheme. **—***v.* play the violin; move or touch something restlessly; falsify (accounts). **—fiddling** *adj.* trivial. **—fiddly** *adj.* awkward to do or use. **—fiddlesticks** *interj.* nonsense.

fidelity *n.* faithfulness; accuracy in detail; quality of sound reproduction.

fidget *v.* move about restlessly. **—***n.* person who fidgets. **—***pl.* restlessness. **—fidgety** *adj.*

THESAURUS

feud 1. *n.* argument, bad blood, broil, conflict, disagreement, discord, dissension, enmity, faction, grudge, hostility, quarrel, rivalry, strife, vendetta 2. *v.* bicker, brawl, clash, contend, dispute, duel, fall out, quarrel, row, squabble, war

fever *Fig.* agitation, delirium, ecstasy, excitement, ferment, fervour, flush, frenzy, heat, passion, turmoil, unrest

few 1. *adj.* inconsiderable, infrequent, insufficient, meagre, negligible, rare, scant, scanty, scarce, scattered, sparse, sporadic, thin 2. *pron.* handful, scarcely any, scattering, small number, some

fiancé, fiancée betrothed, intended, wife- or husband-to-be

fiasco catastrophe, debacle, disaster, failure, mess, rout, ruin

fib *n.* fiction, lie, prevarication, story, untruth, white lie

fibre 1. pile, staple, strand, texture, thread 2. *Fig.* essence, nature, quality

fickle capricious, changeable, faithless, fitful, flighty, inconstant, irresolute, mercurial, unfaithful, unstable, unsteady, vacillating, volatile

fiction 1. fable, fantasy, legend, myth, novel, romance, story, tale 2. fabrication, falsehood, fancy, fantasy, imagination, improvisation, invention, lie, tall story, untruth

fictitious apocryphal, artificial, assumed, bogus, false, fanciful, feigned, imaginary, imagined, improvised, invented, made-up, mythical, spurious, unreal, untrue

fiddling futile, petty, trifling, trivial

fidelity 1. constancy, devotion, faithfulness, integrity, loyalty, staunchness, trustworthiness

DICTIONARY

fiduciary [fid-yew-sheer-ee] *adj.* relating to a trust or trustee. —*n., pl.* **-aries.** trustee.

fief [feef] *n. Hist.* land granted by a lord in return for war service.

field *n.* enclosed piece of agricultural land; marked off area for sports; area rich in a specified natural resource; sphere of knowledge or activity; place away from the laboratory or classroom where practical work is done; all the competitors in a competition; all the competitors except the favourite; battlefield; area over which electric, gravitational, or magnetic force is exerted; background, as of a flag. —*v. Sport* catch and return (a ball); send a (player or team) on to the field; play as a fielder; deal with (a question) successfully. —**fielder** *n. Sport* player whose task is to field the ball. —**field day** day or time of exciting activity. —**field events** throwing and jumping events in athletics. —**fieldfare** *n.* type of large thrush. —**field glasses** binoculars. —**field marshal** army officer of the highest rank. —**field sports** hunting, shooting, and fishing. —**fieldwork** *n.* investigation made in the field as opposed to the classroom or the laboratory.

fiend [feend] *n.* evil spirit; cruel or wicked person; *Informal* person devoted to something, e.g. *fresh-air fiend.* —**fiendish** *adj.* cruel; *Informal* cunning; *Informal* very difficult. —**fiendishly** *adv.*

fierce *adj.* wild or aggressive; turbulent; intense. —**fiercely** *adv.* —**fierceness** *n.*

fiery [fire-ee] *adj.* **fierier, fieriest.** consisting of or like fire; easily angered; (of food) very spicy.

fiesta *n.* religious festival, carnival.

fife *n.* small high-pitched flute.

fifth, fifteen, fifteenth, fifty, fiftieth *n., adj.* see FIVE.

fig *n.* soft pear-shaped fruit; tree bearing it.

fight *v.* **fighting, fought.** struggle (against) in battle or physical combat; struggle to overcome someone or obtain something; carry on (a battle or struggle); make (a way) by fighting. —*n.* aggressive conflict between two (groups of) people; quarrel or contest; resistance; boxing match. —**fighter** *n.* boxer; determined person; aircraft designed to destroy other aircraft. —**fight off** *v.* repulse; struggle to avoid.

figment *n.* —**figment of one's imagination** imaginary thing.

figure *n.* numerical symbol; amount expressed in numbers; bodily shape; well-known person; representation in painting or sculpture of a human form; diagram or illustration; set of movements in dancing or skating; *Maths* any combination of lines, planes, points, or curves. —*v. US* consider, conclude; (usu. foll. by *in*) included (in); calculate. —**figure of speech** expression in which words do not have their literal meaning. —**figurative** *adj.* (of language) abstract, imaginative, or symbolic. —**figuratively** *adv.* —**figurine** *n.* statuette. —**figurehead** *n.* nominal leader; carved bust at the bow of a ship. —**figure out** *v.* solve or understand.

THESAURUS

2. accuracy, adherence, closeness, correspondence, exactness, precision

fidget bustle, chafe, fret, squirm, twitch, worry

fidgety impatient, jerky, nervous, on edge, restive, restless, uneasy

field 1. *n.* grassland, green, meadow, pasture 2. *v.* catch, pick up, retrieve, return, stop

fiend 1. demon, devil, evil spirit 2. addict, enthusiast, fanatic

fierce brutal, cruel, dangerous, feral, ferocious, menacing, murderous, passionate, savage, threatening, truculent, uncontrollable, untamed, vicious, wild

fiercely frenziedly, furiously, menacingly, passionately, savagely, tempestuously, tigerishly, viciously

fight *v.* 1. assault, battle, box, brawl, clash, close, combat, conflict, contend, engage, feud, grapple, joust, spar, struggle, take the field, tilt, tussle, war, wrestle 2. contest, defy, dispute, oppose, resist, strive, struggle, withstand 3. argue, bicker, dispute, squabble, wrangle 4. carry on, conduct, engage in, prosecute, wage ~*n.* 5. altercation, battle, bout, brawl, brush, clash, combat, conflict, contest, dispute, duel, encounter, engagement, fracas, fray, hostilities, joust, melee, riot, row, scuffle, skirmish, struggle, tussle, war

fighter 1. fighting man, soldier, warrior 2. boxer, pugilist

fighting *adj.* aggressive, belligerent, combative, contentious, disputatious, hawkish, martial, militant, pugnacious, truculent, warlike

fight off beat off, repel, repress, repulse, resist, stave off, ward off

figure *n.* 1. character, cipher, digit, number, numeral, symbol 2. amount, cost, price, sum, total, value 3. form, outline, shadow, shape, silhouette 4. body, build, frame, physique, proportions, shape, torso 5. celebrity, character, dignitary, force, leader, notability, notable, personage, personality, presence, worthy

figurehead cipher, dummy, mouthpiece, name, nonentity, puppet

figure out 1. calculate, compute, reckon, work

DICTIONARY

filament *n.* fine wire in a light bulb that gives out light; fine thread.

filbert *n.* hazelnut.

filch *v.* steal (small amounts).

file[1] *n.* box or folder used to keep documents in order; documents in a file; information about a person or subject; line of people one behind the other; *Computers* organized collection of related material. —*v.* place (a document) in a file; place (a legal document) on official record; bring a lawsuit, esp. for divorce; walk or march in a line.

file[2] *n.* tool with a roughened blade for smoothing or shaping. —*v.* shape or smooth with a file. —**filings** *pl. n.* shavings removed by a file.

filial *adj.* of or befitting a son or daughter.

filibuster *v.* obstruct legislation by making long speeches. —*n.* act of filibustering; person who filibusters.

filigree *n.* delicate ornamental work of gold or silver wire. —*adj.* made of filigree.

fill *v.* make or become full; occupy completely; plug (a gap); satisfy (a need); hold and perform the duties of (a position); appoint to (a job or position). —**one's fill** sufficient for one's needs or wants. —**filler** *n.* substance that fills a gap or increases bulk. —**filling** *n.* substance that fills a gap or cavity, esp. in a tooth. —*adj.* (of food) substantial and satisfying. —**filling station** garage selling petrol, oil, etc.

fillet *n.* boneless piece of meat or fish. —*v.* **filleting, filleted.** remove the bones from.

fillip *n.* something that adds stimulation or enjoyment.

filly *n., pl.* **-lies.** young female horse.

film *n.* sequence of images projected on a screen, creating the illusion of movement; story told in such a sequence of images; thin strip of light-sensitive cellulose used to make photographic negatives and transparencies; thin sheet or layer. —*v.* photograph with a movie or video camera; make a film of (a scene, story, etc.); cover or become covered with a thin layer. —*adj.* connected with cinema. —**filmy** *adj.* very thin, delicate. —**film strip** set of pictures on a strip of film, projected separately as slides.

filter *n.* material or device permitting fluid to pass but retaining solid particles; device that blocks certain frequencies of sound or light; traffic signal that allows vehicles to turn either left or right while the main signals are at red. —*v.* pass slowly or faintly; remove impurities from (a substance) with a filter. —**filtrate** *n.* filtered gas or liquid. —*v.* remove impurities with a filter. —**filtration** *n.*

filth *n.* disgusting dirt; offensive material or language. —**filthy** *adj.* —**filthily** *adv.* —**filthiness** *n.*

fin *n.* projection from a fish's body enabling it to balance and swim; vertical tailplane of an aircraft.

finagle [fin-**nay**-gl] *v.* get or achieve by craftiness or trickery.

final *adj.* at the end; having no possibility of further change, action, or discussion. —*n.* deciding contest in a competition. —*pl.* last examinations in an educational course. —**finally** *adv.* —**finality** *n.* —**finalist** *n.* competitor in a final. —**finalize** *v.* put into final form. —**finale** [fin-**nah**-lee] *n.* concluding part of a dramatic performance or musical work.

THESAURUS

out 2. comprehend, decipher, fathom, resolve, see, understand

filch abstract, embezzle, misappropriate, pilfer, purloin, steal, take, thieve

file[1] 1. *n.* case, data, documents, dossier, folder, information, portfolio 2. *v.* enter, record, register, slot in

file[2] *v.* abrade, burnish, furbish, polish, rasp, refine, rub, rub down, scrape, shape, smooth

fill brim over, cram, crowd, furnish, glut, gorge, pack, pervade, replenish, sate, satiate, satisfy, stock, store, stuff, supply, swell

filling 1. *n.* contents, insides, padding, stuffing, wadding 2. *adj.* ample, heavy, satisfying, square, substantial

film *n.* 1. coating, covering, gauze, layer, membrane, scum, skin, tissue 2. motion picture, movie (*U.S. inf.*) ~*v.* 3. photograph, shoot, take

filter 1. *v.* clarify, filtrate, purify, refine, screen, sieve, sift, strain, winnow 2. *n.* gauze, mesh, riddle, sieve, strainer

filth 1. contamination, defilement, dirt, dung, excrement, excreta, faeces, filthiness, foulness, garbage, grime, muck, nastiness, ordure, pollution, refuse, sewage, slime, sludge, squalor, uncleanness 2. corruption, dirtymindedness, impurity, indecency, obscenity, pornography, smut, vileness, vulgarity

filthy 1. dirty, faecal, feculent, foul, nasty, polluted, putrid, slimy, squalid, unclean, vile 2. begrimed, black, blackened, grimy, grubby, miry, mucky, muddy, smoky, sooty, unwashed 3. bawdy, coarse, corrupt, depraved, foul, impure, indecent, lewd, licentious, obscene, pornographic, smutty, suggestive

final 1. closing, end, eventual, last, latest, terminating, ultimate 2. absolute, conclusive, decided, decisive, definite, definitive, deter-

DICTIONARY

finance *n.* management of money; (provision of) funds. —*pl.* money resources. —*v.* provide funds for. —**financial** *adj.* —**financially** *adv.* —**financier** *n.* person involved in large-scale financial business. —**financial year** twelve-month period used for financial calculations.

finch *n.* small songbird with a stout bill.

find *v.* **finding, found.** discover by chance; discover by search or effort; become aware of; consider to have a particular quality; experience (a particular feeling); *Law* pronounce (the defendant) guilty or not guilty; provide, esp. with difficulty. —*n.* person or thing found, esp. when valuable. —**finder** *n.* —**finding** *n.* conclusion from an investigation. —**find out** *v.* gain knowledge of; detect (a crime, deception, etc.).

fine¹ *adj.* very good; in good health; acceptable; thin or slender; in small particles; subtle or abstruse, e.g. *a fine distinction;* of delicate workmanship; (of weather) clear and dry. —**finely** *adv.* —**fineness** *n.* —**finery** *n.* showy clothing. —**fine art** art produced to appeal to the sense of beauty. —**fine-tune** *v.* make small adjustments to (something) so that it works really well.

fine² *n.* payment imposed as a penalty. —*v.* impose a fine on.

finesse [fin-**ness**] *n.* delicate skill; subtlety and tact.

finger *n.* one of the four long jointed parts of the hand; part of a glove that covers a finger; quantity of liquid in a glass as deep as a finger is wide. —*v.* touch or handle with the fingers. —**fingering** *n.* technique of using the fingers in playing a musical instrument. —**fingerboard** *n.* part of a stringed instrument on which the fingers are placed. —**fingerprint** *n.* impression of the ridges on the tip of the finger. —*v.* take the fingerprints of (someone). —**fingerstall** *n.* cover to protect an injured finger.

finial *n. Archit.* ornament at the apex of a gable or spire.

finicky *adj.* excessively particular, fussy; over-elaborate.

finis *n. Latin* end: used at the end of a book.

finish *v.* bring to an end, stop; use up; bring to a desired or completed condition; put a surface texture on (wood, cloth, or metal); defeat or destroy. —*n.* end, last part; death or defeat; surface texture.

finite [**fine**-ite] *adj.* having limits in space, time, or size.

fiord *n.* same as FJORD.

THESAURUS

minate, finished, incontrovertible, irrevocable, settled

finalize agree, complete, conclude, decide, settle, tie up, work out

finally at last, at length, at long last, at the last, eventually, in the end, lastly, ultimately

finance 1. *n.* accounts, banking, business, commerce, economics, investment, money 2. *v.* back, float, fund, guarantee, pay for, subsidize, support, underwrite

finances affairs, assets, capital, cash, funds, money, resources, wherewithal

financial budgeting, economic, fiscal, monetary, money, pecuniary

find 1. *v.* chance upon, come across, descry, discover, encounter espy, expose, ferret out, hit upon, locate, meet, recognize, spot, turn up, uncover, unearth 2. *n.* acquisition, asset, bargain, catch, discovery, good buy

find out detect, discover, learn, note, observe, perceive, realize

fine¹ *adj.* 1. admirable, beautiful, choice, excellent, exceptional, exquisite, first-class, first-rate, great, magnificent, masterly, ornate, outstanding, rare, select, skilful, splendid, superior, supreme 2. balmy, bright, clear, cloudless, dry, fair, pleasant, sunny 3. dainty, delicate, elegant, exquisite, fragile 4. abstruse, acute, critical, discriminating, fastidious,

hairsplitting, intelligent, keen, minute, nice, precise, quick, refined, sensitive, sharp, subtle, tasteful, tenuous 5. acceptable, agreeable, all right, convenient, good, satisfactory, suitable

fine² 1. *v.* mulct, penalize, punish 2. *n.* damages, forfeit, penalty, punishment

finesse adroitness, artfulness, cleverness, craft, delicacy, diplomacy, discretion, polish, quickness, savoir-faire, skill, subtlety, tact

finger *v.* feel, handle, manipulate, maul, meddle with, touch, toy with

finish *v.* 1. accomplish, achieve, cease, close, complete, conclude, deal with, discharge, do, end, execute, finalize, fulfil, get done, round off, settle, stop, terminate 2. *Often with* **off** annihilate, best, bring down, defeat, destroy, dispose of, exterminate, get rid of, kill, overcome, overpower, rout, ruin, worst ~*n.* 3. cessation, close, closing, completion, conclusion, culmination, dénouement, end, ending, finale 4. annihilation, bankruptcy, death, defeat, end, liquidation, ruin ~*v.* 5. elaborate, perfect, polish, refine 6. coat, face, gild, lacquer, polish, smooth off, stain, texture, veneer, wax ~*n.* 7. appearance, grain, lustre, patina, polish, shine, smoothness, surface, texture

finite bounded, conditioned, limited, restricted, terminable

DICTIONARY

fir *n.* pyramid-shaped tree with needle-like leaves and erect cones.

fire *n.* state of combustion producing heat, flames, and smoke; uncontrolled destructive burning; burning coal or wood, or a gas or electric device, used to heat a room; shooting of guns; intense passion, ardour. —*v.* operate (a weapon) so that a bullet or missile is released; *Informal* dismiss from employment; excite; bake (ceramics etc.) in a kiln. —**firearm** *n.* rifle, pistol, or shotgun. —**firebrand** *n.* person who causes unrest. —**firebreak** *n.* strip of cleared land to stop the advance of a fire. —**fire brigade** organized body of people whose job is to put out fires. —**firedamp** *n.* explosive gas, composed mainly of methane, formed in mines. —**fire drill** rehearsal of procedures for escape from a fire. —**fire engine** vehicle with apparatus for extinguishing fires. —**fire escape** metal staircase or ladder down the outside of a building for escape in the event of fire. —**firefly** *n.* beetle that glows in the dark. —**fireguard** *n.* protective grating in front of a fire. —**fire irons** tongs, poker, and shovel for tending a domestic fire. —**fireman** *n.* member of a fire brigade. —**fireplace** *n.* recess in a room for a fire. —**firepower** *n. Mil.* amount a weapon or unit can fire. —**fireraiser** *n.* person who deliberately starts fires. —**fire station** headquarters of a fire brigade. —**firework** *n.* device containing chemicals that is ignited to produce spectacular explosions and coloured sparks. —*pl. n.* show of fireworks; *Informal* outburst of temper. —**firing squad** group of soldiers ordered to execute an offender by shooting.

firkin *n.* small cask.

firm¹ *adj.* not soft or yielding; securely in posi-

tion; definite; determined, resolute. —*adv.* in an unyielding manner, e.g. *hold firm.* —*v.* make or become firm. —**firmly** *adv.* —**firmness** *n.*

firm² *n.* business company.

firmament *n. Lit.* sky, heavens.

first *adj.* earliest in time or order; graded or ranked above all others. —*n.* person or thing coming before all others; outset, beginning; first-class honours degree at university; lowest forward gear in a motor vehicle. —*adv.* before anything else; for the first time. —**firstly** *adv.* —**first aid** immediate medical assistance given in an emergency. —**first-class** *adj.* of the highest quality; excellent. —**first-hand** *adj., adv.* (obtained) directly from the original source. —**first mate, officer** officer of a merchant ship second in command to the captain. —**first person** *Grammar* category of verbs and pronouns used by a speaker to refer to himself or herself. —**first-rate** *adj.* excellent. —**first-strike** *adj.* (of a nuclear missile) for use in an opening attack to destroy enemy weapons.

firth *n.* narrow inlet of the sea.

fiscal *adj.* of government finances, esp. taxes.

fish *n., pl.* **fish, fishes.** cold-blooded vertebrate with gills, that lives in water; its flesh as food. —*v.* try to catch fish; try to catch fish in (a specified place); (foll. by *for*) grope for and find with difficulty; (foll. by *for*) seek indirectly. —**fisherman** *n.* person who catches fish for a living or for pleasure. —**fishery** *n., pl.* **-eries.** area of the sea used for fishing. —**fishy** *adj.* of or like fish; *Informal* suspicious or questionable. —**fish finger** oblong piece of fish covered in breadcrumbs. —**fish meal** dried ground fish used as animal feed or fertilizer. —**fishmonger** *n.*

THESAURUS

fire *n.* 1. blaze, combustion, conflagration, flames, inferno 2. barrage, hail, salvo, shelling, sniping, volley ~*v.* 3. detonate, discharge, eject, explode, hurl, launch, let off, loose, set off, shell, shoot

firm¹ *adj.* 1. close-grained, compact, compressed, concentrated, dense, hard, inelastic, inflexible, rigid, set, solid, solidified, stiff, unyielding 2. braced, embedded, fast, fastened, fixed, immovable, motionless, riveted, robust, rooted, secure, secured, stable, stationary, steady, strong, sturdy, taut, tight, unshakable 3. adamant, constant, definite, determined, fixed, inflexible, obdurate, resolute, resolved, set on, settled, staunch, steadfast, strict, true, unflinching, unshakable, unswerving, unwavering, unyielding

firm² *n.* association, business, company, concern, corporation, enterprise, house, organization, partnership

firmly 1. immovably, motionlessly, securely, steadily, tightly, unshakably 2. determinedly, resolutely, staunchly, steadfastly, strictly, unchangeably, unwaveringly

firmness 1. density, fixedness, hardness, inelasticity, inflexibility, resistance, rigidity, solidity, stiffness 2. immovability, soundness, stability, steadiness, strength, tautness, tension, tightness 3. constancy, inflexibility, obduracy, resolution, resolve, staunchness, steadfastness, strictness

first *adj.* 1. chief, foremost, head, highest, leading, pre-eminent, prime, principal, ruling 2. earliest, initial, maiden, opening, original, premier, primitive, primordial, pristine 3. basic, cardinal, elementary, fundamental, key, primary ~*adv.* 4. beforehand, firstly, initially

first-rate admirable, elite, excellent, exceptional, first class, outstanding, prime, superb, superlative, tiptop, top

DICTIONARY

seller of fish. —**fishnet** *n.* open mesh fabric resembling netting. —**fishwife** *n.* coarse scolding woman.

fishplate *n.* metal plate holding rails together.

fission *n.* splitting; *Biol.* asexual reproduction involving a division into two or more equal parts; splitting of an atomic nucleus with the release of a large amount of energy. —**fissionable** *adj.* —**fissile** *adj.* capable of undergoing nuclear fission; tending to split.

fissure [fish-er] *n.* long narrow cleft or crack.

fist *n.* clenched hand. —**fisticuffs** *pl. n.* fighting with the fists.

fistula [fist-yew-la] *n.* long narrow ulcer.

fit[1] *v.* **fitting, fitted.** be appropriate or suitable for; be of the correct size or shape (for); adjust so as to make appropriate; try (clothes) on and note any adjustments needed; make competent or ready; correspond with the facts or circumstances. —*adj.* appropriate; in good health; worthy or deserving. —*n.* way in which something fits. —**fitness** *n.* —**fitter** *n.* person skilled in the installation and adjustment of machinery; person who fits garments. —**fitting** *adj.* appropriate, suitable. —*n.* accessory or part; trying on of clothes for size. —*pl.* furnishings and accessories in a building. —**fitment** *n.* detachable part of the furnishings of a room. —**fit in** *v.* give a place or time to; belong or conform. —**fit out** *v.* provide with the necessary equipment.

fit[2] *n.* sudden attack or convulsion, such as an epileptic seizure; sudden short burst or spell.

fitful *adj.* occurring in irregular spells. —**fitfully** *adv.*

five *adj., n.* one more than four. —**fiver** *n. Informal* five-pound note. —**fives** *n.* ball game resembling squash but played with bats or the hands. —**fifth** *adj., n.* (of) number five in a series. —**fifth column** group secretly helping the enemy. —**fifteen** *adj., n.* five and ten. —**fifteenth** *adj., n.* —**fifty** *adj., n.* five times ten. —**fiftieth** *adj., n.*

fix *v.* make or become firm, stable, or secure; place permanently; settle definitely; direct (the eyes etc.) steadily; repair; *Informal* unfairly influence the outcome of. —*n. Informal* difficult situation; ascertaining of the position of a ship by radar etc.; *Slang* injection of a narcotic drug. —**fixed** *adj.* —**fixedly** [fix-id-lee] *adv.* steadily. —**fixation** *n.* preoccupation, obsession. —**fixated** *adj.* obsessed. —**fixative** *n.* liquid used to preserve or hold things in place. —**fixer** *n.* solution used to make a photographic image permanent; *Slang* person who arranges things. —**fixture** *n.* permanently fitted piece of household equipment; person whose presence seems permanent; sports match or the date fixed for it. —**fix up** *v.* arrange; provide (with).

fizz *v.* give off small bubbles; make a hissing or bubbling noise. —*n.* hissing or bubbling noise; releasing of small bubbles of gas by a liquid; effervescent drink. —**fizzy** *adj.* —**fizziness** *n.*

fizzle *v.* make a weak hissing or bubbling sound. —**fizzle out** *v. Informal* come to nothing, fail.

fjord [fee-ord] *n.* long narrow inlet of the sea between cliffs, esp. in Norway.

flab *n. Informal* unsightly body fat.

flabbergast *v.* amaze utterly.

THESAURUS

fissure breach, break, chink, crack, cranny, crevice, fault, fracture, gap, hole, opening, rent, rift, rupture, slit, split

fit *adj.* 1. able, adequate, appropriate, apt, becoming, capable, competent, convenient, correct, deserving, equipped, expedient, good enough, prepared, proper, qualified, ready, right, seemly, suitable, trained, worthy 2. hale, healthy, robust, strapping, toned up, trim, well ∼*v.* 3. accord, agree, belong, concur, conform, correspond, dovetail, go, interlock, join, match, meet, suit, tally 4. adapt, adjust, alter, arrange, dispose, fashion, modify, place, position, shape

fitful broken, desultory, erratic, fluctuating, haphazard, impulsive, intermittent, irregular, spasmodic, sporadic, variable

fitness 1. adaptation, applicability, appropriateness, aptness, competence, eligibility, pertinence, preparedness, propriety, qualifications, readiness, seemliness, suitability 2.

good condition, good health, health, robustness, strength, vigour

fitting 1. *adj.* appropriate, becoming, correct, decent, decorous, desirable, proper, right, seemly, suitable 2. *n.* accessory, attachment, component, connection, part, piece, unit

fix *v.* 1. anchor, embed, establish, implant, install, locate, place, plant, position, root, set, settle 2. attach, bind, cement, connect, couple, fasten, glue, link, pin, secure, stick, tie 3. agree on, appoint, arrange, arrive at, conclude, decide, define, determine, establish, limit, name, resolve, set, settle, specify ∼*n.* 4. *Inf.* difficulty, dilemma, embarrassment, mess, plight, predicament, quandary

fixed 1. attached, established, immovable, made fast, permanent, rigid, rooted, secure, set 2. agreed, arranged, decided, definite, established, planned, resolved, settled

fix up agree on, arrange, fix, organize, plan, settle, sort out

DICTIONARY

flabby *adj.* **-bier, -biest.** loose or limp; having flabby flesh. —**flabbiness** *n.*

flaccid [**flas**-sid] *adj.* soft and limp. —**flaccidity** *n.*

flag[1] *n.* piece of cloth attached to a pole as an emblem or signal. —*v.* **flagging, flagged.** mark with a flag or sticker; (often foll. by *down*) signal (a vehicle) to stop by waving the arm. —**flag day** day on which small stickers are sold in the streets for charity. —**flagpole, flagstaff** *n.* pole for a flag. —**flagship** *n.* admiral's ship; most important product of an organization.

flag[2] *v.* **flagging, flagged.** lose enthusiasm or vigour.

flag[3]**, flagstone** *n.* flat paving-stone. —**flagged** *adj.* paved with flagstones.

flagellate [**flaj**-a-late] *v.* whip. —**flagellation** *n.* —**flagellant** *n.* person who whips himself, esp. in religious penance.

flageolet [flaj-a-**let**] *n.* small instrument like a recorder.

flagon *n.* wide bottle for wine or cider; narrow-necked jug for liquid.

flagrant [**flayg**-rant] *adj.* openly outrageous. —**flagrantly** *adv.* —**flagrancy** *n.*

flail *v.* wave about wildly; beat or thrash. —*n.* tool formerly used for threshing grain by hand.

flair *n.* natural ability; stylishness.

flak *n.* anti-aircraft fire; *Informal* adverse criticism.

flake *n.* small thin piece, esp. chipped off something. —*v.* peel off in flakes. —**flaky** *adj.* —**flake out** *v. Informal* collapse or fall asleep from exhaustion.

flambé [**flahm**-bay] *v.* **flambéing, flambéed.** cook or serve (food) in flaming brandy.

flamboyant *adj.* very bright and showy; behaving in a very noticeable, extravagant way. —**flamboyance** *n.*

flame *n.* luminous burning gas coming from burning material. —*v.* burn brightly; become bright red. —**old flame** *Informal* former sweetheart.

flamenco *n., pl.* **-cos.** rhythmical Spanish dance accompanied by a guitar and vocalist; music for this dance.

flamingo *n., pl.* **-gos, -goes.** large pink wading bird with a long neck and legs.

flammable *adj.* easily set on fire. —**flammability** *n.*

flan *n.* open sweet or savoury tart.

flange *n.* projecting rim or collar. —**flanged** *adj.*

flank *n.* part of the side between the hips and ribs; side of a body of troops. —*v.* be at or move along the side of.

flannel *n.* soft woollen fabric for clothing; small piece of cloth for washing the face and hands; *Informal* evasive talk. —*pl.* trousers made of flannel. —*v.* **-nelling, -nelled.** *Informal* talk evasively. —**flannelette** *n.* cotton imitation of flannel.

flap *v.* **flapping, flapped.** move back and forwards or up and down. —*n.* action or sound of flapping; piece of something attached by one edge only; *Informal* state of excitement or panic.

flapjack *n.* chewy biscuit made with oats.

flare *v.* blaze with a sudden unsteady flame; *Informal* (of temper, violence, or trouble) break out suddenly; (of a skirt or trousers) become wider towards the hem. —*n.* sudden unsteady flame; signal light. —*pl.* flared trousers. —**flared** *adj.* (of a skirt or trousers) becoming wider towards the hem.

flash *n.* sudden burst of light or flame; sudden occurrence (of intuition or emotion); very short time; brief unscheduled news announcement; *Photog.* small bulb that produces an intense

---

THESAURUS

flag[1] banner, colours, ensign, jack, pennant, pennon, standard, streamer

flag[2] *v.* abate, decline, die, droop, ebb, fade, fail, faint, fall, fall off, languish, pine, sag, sink, slump, succumb, wane, weaken, weary, wilt

flagging declining, decreasing, ebbing, fading, failing, sinking, tiring, waning, weakening, wilting

flagrant awful, barefaced, blatant, bold, brazen, crying, dreadful, egregious, enormous, flaunting, glaring, immodest, infamous, notorious, open, ostentatious, outrageous, scandalous, shameless

flagstone block, flag, slab

flail *v.* beat, thrash, thresh, windmill

flair 1. ability, aptitude, faculty, feel, genius, gift, knack, mastery, talent 2. chic, dash, discernment, elegance, panache, style, stylishness, taste

flamboyant 1. elaborate, florid, ornate, rich, rococo, showy, theatrical 2. brilliant, colourful, dashing, glamorous, swashbuckling

flame 1. *v.* blaze, burn, flare, flash, glare, glow, shine 2. *n.* blaze, fire, light

flap 1. *v.* agitate, beat, flail, flutter, shake, swing, swish, thrash, thresh, vibrate, wag, wave 2. *n.* apron, cover, fly, fold, lapel, skirt, tab, tail

flare blaze, burn up, dazzle, flicker, flutter, glare, waver

DICTIONARY

flash of light. —*v.* (cause to) burst into flame; (cause to) emit light suddenly or intermittently; move very fast; come rapidly (to mind or view); *Informal* display ostentatiously; *Slang* expose oneself indecently. —*adj.* (also **flashy**) vulgarly showy. —**flasher** *n. Slang* man who exposes himself indecently. —**flashing** *n.* watertight material used to cover joins in a roof. —**flashback** *n.* scene in a book, play, or film, that shows earlier events. —**flash flood** sudden short-lived flood. —**flashlight** *n. US* torch. —**flash point** critical point beyond which a situation will inevitably erupt into violence; lowest temperature at which vapour given off by a liquid can ignite.

flask *n.* vacuum flask; flat bottle for carrying alcoholic drink in the pocket; narrow-necked bottle.

flat¹ *adj.* **flatter, flattest.** level and horizontal; even, smooth; (of a tyre) deflated; outright; fixed; without variation or emotion; (of a battery) with no electrical charge; (of a drink) no longer fizzy; *Music* below the true pitch. —*adv.* in or into a flat position; exactly; completely, absolutely; *Music* too low in pitch. —*n.* flat surface; *Music* symbol lowering the pitch of a note by a semitone; punctured car tyre; level ground; mudbank exposed at low tide. —**flat out** with maximum speed or effort. —**flatly** *adv.* —**flatness** *n.* —**flatten** *v.* —**flatfish** *n.* sea fish, such as the sole, which has a flat body. —**flat racing** horse racing over level ground with no jumps.

flat² *n.* set of rooms for living in which are part of a larger building. —**flatlet** *n.* small flat. —**flatmate** *n.* person one shares a flat with.

flatter *v.* praise insincerely; show to advantage;

make (a person) appear more attractive in a picture than in reality. —**flatterer** *n.* —**flattery** *n.*

flatulent *adj.* suffering from, or caused by, excess gas in the intestines. —**flatulence** *n.*

flaunt *v.* display (oneself or one's possessions) arrogantly.

flautist [flaw-tist] *n.* flute player.

flavour *n.* distinctive taste; distinctive characteristic or quality. —*v.* give flavour to. —**flavouring** *n.* substance used to flavour food. —**flavourless** *adj.*

flaw *n.* imperfection or blemish; mistake that makes a plan or argument invalid. —**flawed** *adj.* —**flawless** *adj.*

flax *n.* plant grown for its stem fibres and seeds; its fibres, spun into linen thread. —**flaxen** *adj.* (of hair) pale yellow.

flay *v.* strip the skin off; criticize severely.

flea *n.* small wingless jumping bloodsucking insect. —**flea market** market for cheap goods. —**fleapit** *n. Informal* shabby cinema or theatre.

fleck *n.* small mark, streak, or speck. —*v.* speckle.

fled *v.* past of FLEE.

fledged *adj.* (of young birds) able to fly; (of people) fully trained. —**fledgling, fledgeling** *n.* young bird. —*adj.* new, inexperienced.

flee *v.* **fleeing, fled.** run away (from).

fleece *n.* sheep's coat of wool; sheepskin used as a lining for coats etc. —*v.* defraud or overcharge. —**fleecy** *adj.* made of or like fleece.

THESAURUS

flash *v.* 1. blaze, flare, flicker, glare, gleam, glint, glisten, glitter, light, shimmer, sparkle, twinkle 2. bolt, dart, fly, race, shoot, speed, sprint, streak, sweep, zoom ~*n.* 3. blaze, burst, dazzle, flare, flicker, gleam, ray, shaft, shimmer, spark, sparkle, streak, twinkle 4. instant, moment, second, shake, split second, trice, twinkling

flashy cheap, flaunting, garish, gaudy, glittery, loud, meretricious, ostentatious, showy, tasteless, tawdry, tinselly

flat¹ 1. even, horizontal, level, levelled, low, plane, smooth, unbroken 2. laid low, outstretched, prostrate, reclining, recumbent, supine 3. boring, dead, dull, insipid, lacklustre, lifeless, monotonous, prosaic, spiritless, stale, tedious, uninteresting, vapid, watery, weak

flat² apartment, rooms

flatly absolutely, categorically, completely, positively, unhesitatingly

flatness 1. evenness, smoothness, uniformity 2.

dullness, emptiness, insipidity, monotony, staleness, tedium, vapidity

flatten compress, even out, iron out, level, plaster, raze, roll, squash, trample

flatter blandish, butter up, cajole, compliment, court, fawn, humour, inveigle, praise, puff, wheedle

flattery blandishment, cajolery, fawning, obsequiousness, servility

flavour 1. *n.* aroma, essence, extract, odour, piquancy, relish, savour, seasoning, smack, tang, taste, zest 2. *v.* imbue, infuse, lace, leaven, season, spice

flaw blemish, defect, failing, fault, imperfection, speck, spot, weakness, weak spot

flawed broken, chipped, cracked, damaged, defective, faulty, unsound

flee avoid, bolt, decamp, depart, escape, fly, get away, leave, shun, take flight, vanish

DICTIONARY

fleet¹ *n.* number of warships organized as a unit; number of vehicles under the same ownership.

fleet² *adj.* swift in movement. **—fleeting** *adj.* rapid and soon passing. **—fleetingly** *adv.*

flesh *n.* soft part of a human or animal body; *Informal* excess fat; meat of animals as opposed to fish or fowl; thick soft part of a fruit or vegetable; human body as opposed to the soul. **—***adj.* yellowish-pink. **—in the flesh** in person, actually present. **—one's own flesh and blood** one's family. **—fleshly** *adj.* carnal; worldly. **—fleshy** *adj.* plump; like flesh. **—flesh wound** wound affecting only superficial tissue.

fleur-de-lis, fleur-de-lys [flur-de-lee] *n., pl.* **fleurs-de-lis, fleurs-de-lys.** heraldic lily with three petals.

flew *v.* past tense of FLY¹.

flex *n.* flexible insulated electric cable. **—***v.* bend. **—flexible** *adj.* easily bent; adaptable. **—flexibly** *adv.* **—flexibility** *n.* **—fleximtime** *n.* system permitting variation in starting and finishing times of work.

flibbertigibbet *n.* flighty gossiping person.

flick *v.* touch or strike lightly. **—***n.* tap or quick stroke. **—***pl. Slang* the cinema. **—flick knife** knife with a spring-loaded blade which shoots out when a button is pressed. **—flick through** *v.* look at (a book or magazine) quickly or idly.

flicker *v.* shine unsteadily or intermittently; move quickly to and fro. **—***n.* unsteady brief light; brief faint indication.

flier *n.* see FLY¹.

flight¹ *n.* act or manner of flying through the air; journey by air; group of birds or aircraft flying together; aircraft flying on a scheduled journey; set of stairs between two landings; stabilizing feathers or plastic fins on an arrow or dart. **—flightless** *adj.* (of certain birds or insects) unable to fly. **—flight deck** crew compartment in an airliner; runway deck on an aircraft carrier. **—flight recorder** electronic device in an aircraft storing information about its flight.

flight² *n.* act of running away.

flighty *adj.* **flightier, flightiest.** frivolous and fickle.

flimsy *adj.* **-sier, -siest.** not strong or substantial; thin; unconvincing, weak. **—flimsily** *adv.* **—flimsiness** *n.*

flinch *v.* draw back or wince, as from pain. **—flinch from** *v.* shrink from, avoid.

fling *v.* **flinging, flung.** throw, send, or move forcefully or hurriedly. **—***n.* spell of self-indulgent enjoyment; brief romantic or sexual relationship. **—fling oneself into** (start to) do with great vigour.

flint *n.* hard grey stone; piece of this; small piece of an iron alloy producing a spark when struck, as in a cigarette lighter. **—flinty** *adj.* cruel; of or like flint.

flip *v.* **flipping, flipped.** flick; turn (something) over; (also **flip one's lid**) *Slang* fly into an emotional state. **—***n.* snap or tap; alcoholic drink containing beaten egg. **—***adj. Informal* flippant. **—flipper** *n.* limb of a sea animal adapted for swimming; one of a pair of paddle-like rubber devices worn on the feet to help in swimming. **—flip-flop** *n.* rubber-soled sandal held on by a thong between the big toe and the next toe. **—flip side** less important side of a record. **—flip through** *v.* look at (a book or magazine) quickly or idly.

THESAURUS

fleet *n.* flotilla, naval force, navy, sea power, squadron, task force, vessels, warships

fleeting brief, ephemeral, flying, fugitive, momentary, passing, short, short-lived, temporary, transient, transitory

flesh 1. body, brawn, fatness, food, meat, tissue, weight 2. body, human nature, sensuality

flexibility adaptability, complaisance, elasticity, resilience, springiness

flexible 1. ductile, elastic, limber, lithe, plastic, pliable, springy, stretchy, supple 2. adaptable, adjustable, open, variable 3. amenable, biddable, docile, gentle, manageable, responsive, tractable

flicker *v.* 1. flutter, quiver, vibrate, waver ~*n.* 2. flare, flash, gleam, glimmer, spark 3. breath, drop, glimmer, spark, trace, vestige

flight¹ 1. mounting, soaring, winging 2. journey,

trip, voyage 3. cloud, flock, formation, squadron, swarm, unit, wing

flight² escape, exit, exodus, fleeing, getaway, retreat

flimsy 1. delicate, fragile, frail, insubstantial, makeshift, rickety, shaky, shallow, slight, superficial, unsubstantial 2. feeble, frivolous, implausible, inadequate, poor, thin, transparent, trivial, unconvincing, unsatisfactory, weak

flinch baulk, blench, cower, cringe, duck, flee, quail, recoil, retreat, shirk, shrink, start, swerve, wince, withdraw

fling *v.* cast, heave, hurl, jerk, pitch, precipitate, propel, send, shy, sling, throw, toss

flippancy cheekiness, frivolity, impertinence, irreverence, levity, pertness

flippant disrespectful, frivolous, glib, impertinent, impudent, irreverent, pert, rude

DICTIONARY

flippant *adj.* treating serious things lightly. —**flippantly** *adv.* —**flippancy** *n.*

flirt *v.* behave amorously without emotional commitment; consider lightly, toy (with). —*n.* person who flirts. —**flirtation** *n.* —**flirtatious** *adj.*

flit *v.* **flitting, flitted.** move lightly and rapidly; *Scot.* move house; *Informal* depart hurriedly and secretly. —*n.* act of flitting.

flitch *n.* side of bacon.

flitter *v., n.* same as FLUTTER.

float *v.* rest on the surface of liquid; move lightly and freely; move about aimlessly; launch (a company); offer for sale on the stock market; allow (a currency) to fluctuate against other currencies. —*n.* indicator on a fishing line that moves when a fish bites; small delivery vehicle; motor vehicle carrying a tableau in a parade; sum of money used for minor expenses or to provide change. —**floating** *adj.* moving about, changing, e.g. *floating population;* (of a voter) not committed to one party. —**flotation** *n.* launching or financing of a business enterprise.

flocculent *adj.* like tufts of wool.

flock[1] *n.* number of animals of one kind together; large group of people; *Christianity* congregation. —*v.* gather in a crowd.

flock[2] *n.* very small tufts of wool giving a raised pattern on wallpaper; wool or cotton waste used as stuffing.

floe *n.* sheet of floating ice.

flog *v.* **flogging, flogged.** beat with a whip, stick, etc.; *Slang* sell. —**flogging** *n.*

flood *n.* overflow of water onto a normally dry area; large amount of water; rising of the tide. —*v.* cover or become covered with water; fill to overflowing; come in large numbers or quantities. —**floodgate** *n.* gate used to control the flow of water. —**floodlight** *n.* lamp that casts a broad intense beam of light. —*v.* **-lighting, -lit.** illuminate by floodlight.

floor *n.* lower surface of a room; level of a building; flat bottom surface; (right to speak in) a legislative hall. —*v. Informal* disconcert or defeat; knock down; cover with a floor. —**flooring** *n.* material for floors. —**floor show** entertainment in a nightclub.

floozy *n., pl.* **-zies.** *Slang* disreputable woman.

flop *v.* **flopping, flopped.** bend, fall, or collapse loosely or carelessly; *Informal* fail. —*n.* flopping movement; *Informal* failure. —**floppy** *adj.* hanging downwards, loose. —**floppiness** *n.* —**floppy disk** *Computers* flexible magnetic disk that stores information.

flora *n.* plants of a given time or place. —**floral** *adj.* consisting of or decorated with flowers.

floret [**flaw**-ret] *n.* small flower forming part of a composite flower head.

floribunda *n.* type of rose whose flowers grow in large clusters.

florid *adj.* with a red or flushed complexion; ornate.

florin *n.* former British coin equivalent to ten pence.

florist *n.* seller of flowers.

floss *n.* fine silky fibres.

flotilla *n.* fleet of small ships; small fleet.

flotsam *n.* floating wreckage. —**flotsam and jetsam** odds and ends; homeless or vagrant people.

flounce[1] *v.* go with emphatic movements. —*n.* flouncing movement.

flounce[2] *n.* ornamental ruffle on a garment.

flounder[1] *v.* move with difficulty, as in mud;

THESAURUS

flirt 1. *v.* coquet, dally, make advances, philander 2. *n.* coquette, heart-breaker, philanderer, tease

float *v.* 1. be buoyant, hang, hover, poise 2. bob, drift, glide, move gently, sail, slide, slip along 3. launch, promote, set up

floating fluctuating, free, migratory, movable, unattached, uncommitted, variable, wandering

flock *v.* 1. collect, congregate, converge, crowd, gather, group, herd, huddle, mass, throng, troop ~*n.* 2. drove, flight, gaggle, herd, skein 3. collection, company, congregation, convoy, crowd, gathering, group, herd, host, mass, multitude, throng

flog beat, chastise, flay, lash, scourge, thrash, trounce, whack, whip

flood *v.* 1. deluge, drown, immerse, inundate, overflow, submerge, swamp 2. engulf, flow, gush, overwhelm, rush, surge, swarm, sweep 3. choke, fill, glut, oversupply, saturate ~*n.* 4. deluge, downpour, flash flood, inundation, overflow, spate, tide, torrent

floor 1. *n.* level, stage, storey, tier 2. *v. Fig.* baffle, beat, bewilder, confound, conquer, defeat, discomfit, disconcert, dumbfound, nonplus, overthrow, perplex, prostrate, puzzle, stump

floral flower-patterned, flowery

florid 1. flushed, high-coloured, rubicund, ruddy 2. baroque, busy, embellished, flamboyant, flowery, fussy, high-flown, ornate

flotsam debris, jetsam, junk, sweepings, wreckage

DICTIONARY

behave or speak in a bungling or hesitating manner.

flounder[2] *n.* edible flatfish.

flour *n.* powder made by grinding grain, esp. wheat. —*v.* sprinkle with flour. —**floury** *adj.* —**flouriness** *n.*

flourish *v.* be active, successful, or widespread; be at the peak of development; wave (something) dramatically. —*n.* dramatic waving motion; ornamental curly line in writing; fanfare. —**flourishing** *adj.*

flout [rhymes with **out**] *v.* deliberately disobey (a rule, law, etc.).

flow *v.* (of liquid) move in a stream; (of blood or electricity) circulate; proceed smoothly; hang loosely; be abundant. —*n.* act, rate, or manner of flowing; continuous stream or discharge. —**flow chart** diagram showing a sequence of operations in a process.

flower *n.* part of a plant that produces seeds; plant grown for its colourful flowers; best or finest part. —*v.* produce flowers, bloom; come to prime condition. —**in flower** with flowers open. —**flowered** *adj.* decorated with a floral design. —**flowery** *adj.* decorated with a floral design; (of language or style) elaborate. —**flowerbed** *n.* piece of ground for growing flowers on.

flown *v.* past participle of FLY[1].

fl. oz. fluid ounce(s).

flu *n.* short for INFLUENZA.

fluctuate *v.* change frequently and erratically. —**fluctuation** *n.*

flue *n.* passage or pipe for smoke or hot air.

fluent *adj.* able to speak or write with ease; spoken or written with ease. —**fluently** *adv.* —**fluency** *n.*

fluff *n.* soft fibres; down; *Informal* mistake. —*v.*

make or become soft and light; *Informal* make a mistake. —**fluffy** *adj.*

fluid *n.* liquid. —*adj.* able to flow or change shape easily. —**fluidity** *n.* —**fluid ounce** one twentieth of a pint.

fluke[1] *n.* accidental stroke of luck. —**fluky** *adj.*

fluke[2] *n.* flat triangular point of an anchor; lobe of a whale's tail.

fluke[3] *n.* parasitic worm.

flume *n.* narrow sloping channel for water.

flummox *v.* perplex or bewilder.

flung *v.* past of FLING.

flunk *v.* US & NZ *informal* fail.

flunky, flunkey *n., pl.* **flunkies, flunkeys.** manservant who wears a livery; servile person.

fluorescence *n.* emission of light from a substance bombarded by particles, such as electrons, or by radiation. —**fluorescent** *adj.* —**fluoresce** *v.* exhibit fluorescence.

fluoride *n.* compound containing fluorine. —**fluoridate** *v.* add fluoride to (water) as protection against tooth decay. —**fluoridation** *n.*

fluorine *n.* toxic yellow gas, most reactive of all the elements.

fluorspar *n.* mineral consisting of calcium fluoride.

flurry *n., pl.* **-ries.** sudden commotion; squall or gust of rain, wind, or snow. —*v.* **-rying, -ried.** fluster.

flush[1] *v.* blush; send water through (a toilet or pipe) so as to clean it; elate. —*n.* blush; rush of water; excitement or elation.

flush[2] *adj.* level with the surrounding surface; *Informal* having plenty of money.

flush[3] *n.* (in card games) hand all of one suit.

flush[4] *v.* drive out of a hiding place.

THESAURUS

flounder *v.* blunder, fumble, grope, muddle, plunge, struggle, stumble, toss, tumble, wallow

flourish 1. *v.* bear fruit, be successful, bloom, blossom, boom, burgeon, develop, flower, increase, prosper, succeed, thrive 2. *n.* dash, display, fanfare, parade, shaking, show, showy twirling, wave

flourishing blooming, lush, luxuriant, prospering, rampant, successful, thriving

flow circulate, course, glide, gush, move, pour, purl, ripple, roll, run, rush, slide, surge, sweep, swirl, whirl

flower *n.* 1. bloom, blossom, efflorescence 2. *Fig.* best, cream, elite, freshness, height, pick, vigour ∼*v.* 3. bloom, blossom, burgeon, effloresce, flourish, mature, open, unfold

flowery embellished, fancy, figurative, florid, ornate, rhetorical

fluctuate alternate, change, hesitate, oscillate, seesaw, shift, swing, undulate, vacillate, vary, veer, waver

fluency assurance, command, control, ease, facility, glibness, slickness, smoothness

fluent articulate, easy, effortless, facile, flowing, natural, ready, smooth, voluble

fluid *adj.* 1. flowing, liquefied, liquid, melted, molten, runny, watery 2. adaptable, adjustable, changeable, flexible, floating, indefinite, mercurial, mobile, mutable, shifting ∼*n.* 3. liquid, liquor, solution

flurry agitation, bustle, commotion, disturbance, excitement, ferment, flap, fluster, flut-

DICTIONARY

flute *n.* wind instrument consisting of a tube with sound holes and a mouth hole in the side; decorative groove. —**fluted** *adj.* having decorative grooves. —**fluting** *n.*

flutter *v.* wave rapidly; flap the wings; move quickly and irregularly; (of the heart) beat abnormally quickly. —*n.* flapping movement; nervous agitation; *Informal* small bet; abnormally fast heartbeat.

fluvial [flew-vee-al] *adj.* of rivers.

flux *n.* constant change or instability; flow or discharge; substance mixed with metal to assist in fusion.

fly¹ *v.* **flying, flew, flown.** move through the air on wings or in an aircraft; control the flight of; float, flutter, display, or be displayed in the air; transport or be transported by air; move quickly or suddenly; (of time) pass rapidly; flee. —*n., pl.* **flies.** (*often pl.*) fastening at the front of trousers; flap forming the entrance to a tent. —*pl.* space above a stage, used for storage. —**flyer, flier** *n.* aviator. —**flyleaf** *n.* blank leaf at the beginning or end of a book. —**flyover** *n.* road passing over another by a bridge. —**flywheel** *n.* heavy wheel regulating the speed of a machine.

fly² *n., pl.* **flies.** two-winged insect, esp. the housefly. —**flyblown** *adj.* covered with bluebottle eggs. —**flycatcher** *n.* small insect-eating songbird. —**fly-fishing** *n.* fishing with an artificial fly as a lure. —**flypaper** *n.* paper with a sticky poisonous coating, used to kill flies. —**flyweight** *n.* boxer weighing up to 112lb (professional) or 51kg (amateur).

fly³ *adj. Slang* sharp and cunning.

flying *adj.* hurried, brief. —**flying boat** aircraft fitted with floats instead of landing wheels. —**flying buttress** *Archit.* buttress supporting a wall

by an arch. —**flying colours** conspicuous success, e.g. *pass with flying colours.* —**flying fish** fish with winglike fins used for gliding above the water. —**flying fox** large fruit-eating bat. —**flying saucer** unidentified disc-shaped flying object, supposedly from outer space. —**flying squad** small group of police, soldiers, etc., ready to act quickly. —**flying start** very good start.

FM frequency modulation.

foal *n.* young of a horse or related animal. —*v.* give birth to a foal.

foam *n.* mass of small bubbles on a liquid; frothy saliva; light spongelike solid used for insulation, packing, etc. —*v.* produce foam. —**foamy** *adj.*

fob¹ *n.* short watch chain; small pocket in a waistcoat.

fob² *v.* **fobbing, fobbed.** (foll. by *off*) pretend to satisfy (a person) with lies or excuses; sell or pass off (something inferior) as valuable.

fo'c's'le *n.* same as FORECASTLE.

focus *n., pl.* **-cuses, -ci** [-sye]. point at which light or sound waves converge; state of an optical image when it is clearly defined; state of an instrument producing such an image; centre of interest or activity. —*v.* **-cus(s)ing, -cus(s)ed.** bring or come into focus; concentrate (on). —**focal** *adj.* of or at a focus.

fodder *n.* feed for livestock.

foe *n.* enemy, opponent.

foetid *adj.* same as FETID.

foetus *n., pl.* **-tuses.** same as FETUS.

fog *n.* mass of condensed water vapour in the lower air, often greatly reducing visibility. —*v.* **fogging, fogged.** cover with steam. —**foggy** *adj.* —**foghorn** *n.* large horn sounded to warn ships in fog.

THESAURUS

ter, furore, fuss, hurry, stir, to-do, tumult, whirl

flush¹ 1. *v.* blush, burn, colour, colour up, crimson, flame glow, go red, redden, suffuse 2. *n.* bloom, blush, colour, freshness, glow, redness, rosiness

flush² *adj.* 1. even, flat, level, plane, square, true 2. abundant, affluent, full, generous, lavish, liberal, overflowing, prodigal

fluster 1. *v.* agitate, bother, bustle, confound, confuse, disturb, excite, flurry, heat, hurry, perturb, ruffle, upset 2. *n.* bustle, commotion, disturbance, dither, flurry, flutter, furore, ruffle, turmoil

flutter 1. *v.* agitate, beat, flap, flicker, fluctuate, hover, palpitate, quiver, ripple, ruffle, shiver, tremble, vibrate, waver 2. *n.* palpitation, quiv-

er, shiver, shudder, tremble, tremor, twitching, vibration

fly *v.* 1. flit, flutter, hover, mount, sail, soar, take wing, wing 2. aviate, control, manoeuvre, operate, pilot 3. display, float, show, wave 4. elapse, flit, glide, pass, pass swiftly, roll on, run its course, slip away 5. bolt, career, dart, dash, hare, hasten, hurry, race, rush, scamper, scoot, shoot, speed, sprint, tear

flying *adj.* 1. brief, fleeting, hasty, hurried, rushed 2. express, fast, fleet, mercurial, mobile, rapid, speedy, winged

foam 1. *n.* bubbles, froth, head, lather, spray, spume, suds 2. *v.* boil, bubble, effervesce, fizz, froth, lather

focus *n.* centre, core, cynosure, headquarters, heart, hub, meeting place, target

DICTIONARY

fogy, fogey *n., pl.* -gies, -geys. old-fashioned person.

foible *n.* minor weakness, idiosyncrasy.

foil[1] *v.* ruin (someone's plan).

foil[2] *n.* metal in a thin sheet; anything which sets off another thing to advantage.

foil[3] *n.* light slender flexible sword tipped with a button.

foist *v.* (usu. foll. by *on*) force or impose on.

fold[1] *v.* bend so that one part covers another; interlace (the arms); clasp (in the arms); *Cooking* mix gently; *Informal* fail. —*n.* folded piece or part; mark, crease, or hollow made by folding. —**folder** *n.* piece of folded cardboard for loose papers.

fold[2] *n.* enclosure for sheep; church or its members.

foliage *n.* leaves. —**foliaceous** *adj.* of or like leaves. —**foliate** *adj.* having leaves; leaflike. —**foliation** *n.* process of producing leaves.

folio *n., pl.* -lios. sheet of paper folded in half to make two leaves of a book; book made up of such sheets; page number.

folk *n.* people in general; race of people; *Informal* folk music. —*pl.* relatives. —**folksy** *adj.* simple and unpretentious. —**folk dance** traditional country dance. —**folklore** *n.* traditional beliefs and stories of a people. —**folk song** song handed down among the common people; modern song like this. —**folk singer.**

follicle *n.* small cavity in the body, esp. one from which a hair grows.

follow *v.* go or come after; be a logical or natural consequence of; keep to the course or track of; act in accordance with; accept the ideas or beliefs of; understand; have a keen interest in. —**follower** *n.* disciple or supporter. —**following** *adj.* about to be mentioned; next in time. —*n.* group of supporters. —*prep.* as a result of. —**follow up** *v.* investigate; do a second, often similar, thing after (a first). —**follow-up** *n.* something done to reinforce an initial action.

folly *n., pl.* -lies. foolishness; foolish action or idea; useless extravagant building.

foment [foam-ent] *v.* encourage or stir up (trouble). —**fomentation** *n.*

fond *adj.* tender, loving; unlikely to be realized, e.g. *a fond hope;* indulgent. —**fond of** having a liking for. —**fondly** *adv.* —**fondness** *n.*

fondant *n.* (sweet made from) flavoured paste of sugar and water.

fondle *v.* caress.

fondue *n.* Swiss dish typically of a hot melted cheese sauce into which pieces of bread are dipped.

font *n.* bowl in a church for baptismal water.

fontanelle *n.* soft membranous gap between the bones of a baby's skull.

food *n.* what one eats, solid nourishment. —**foodie** *n. Informal* gourmet. —**foodstuff** *n.* substance used as food.

THESAURUS

foe adversary, antagonist, enemy, opponent, rival

fog *n.* gloom, miasma, mist, murk, murkiness, smog

foggy blurred, cloudy, dim, grey, hazy, indistinct, misty, murky, nebulous, obscure, vaporous

foil[1] *v.* baffle, balk, check, counter, defeat, elude, frustrate, nullify, outwit, stop, thwart

foil[2] antithesis, background, complement, contrast, setting

fold *v.* 1. bend, crease, crumple, double, gather, intertwine, overlap, pleat, tuck, turn under 2. do up, enclose, enfold, entwine, envelop, wrap, wrap up ~*n.* 3. bend, crease, furrow, layer, overlap, pleat, turn, wrinkle

folder binder, envelope, file, portfolio

folk clan, family, kin, people, race, tribe

follow 1. succeed, supersede, supplant 2. chase, dog, hound, hunt, pursue, shadow, stalk, tail, track, trail 3. comply, conform, heed, mind, note, obey, observe, regard, watch

follower adherent, admirer, apostle, backer, believer, convert, devotee, disciple, fan, fancier, habitué, partisan, pupil, supporter, votary, worshipper

following *adj.* consequent, ensuing, later, next, specified, subsequent, succeeding, successive

folly absurdity, foolishness, idiocy, imbecility, imprudence, indiscretion, irrationality, lunacy, madness, nonsense, recklessness, silliness, stupidity

fond adoring, affectionate, amorous, caring, devoted, doting, indulgent, loving, tender, warm

fondle caress, cuddle, dandle, pat, pet, stroke

fondly affectionately, dearly, indulgently, lovingly, possessively, tenderly

fondness attachment, fancy, liking, love, partiality, penchant, predilection, preference, soft spot, susceptibility, taste, weakness

food board, bread, commons, cooking, cuisine, diet, edibles, fare, foodstuffs, larder, meat, menu, nourishment, nutrition, provender, provisions, rations, refreshment, stores, sustenance, table, victuals

DICTIONARY

fool[1] *n.* person lacking sense or judgment; person made to appear ridiculous; *Hist.* jester, clown. —*v.* deceive (someone). —**foolish** *adj.* unwise, silly, or absurd. —**foolishly** *adv.* —**foolishness** *n.* —**foolery** *n.* foolish behaviour. —**fool around** *v.* act or play irresponsibly or aimlessly. —**foolproof** *adj.* unable to fail.

fool[2] *n.* dessert of puréed fruit mixed with cream.

foolhardy *adj.* recklessly adventurous. —**foolhardiness** *n.*

foolscap *n.* size of paper, 13.5 by 17 inches.

foot *n., pl.* **feet.** part of the leg below the ankle; unit of length of twelve inches (0.3048 metre); lowest part of anything; unit of poetic rhythm; *Obs.* infantry. —**foot it** *Informal* walk. —**foot the bill** pay the entire cost. —**footage** *n.* amount of film used. —**foot-and-mouth disease** infectious viral disease of sheep, cattle, etc. —**footbridge** *n.* bridge for pedestrians. —**footfall** *n.* sound of a footstep. —**foothills** *pl. n.* hills at the foot of a mountain. —**foothold** *n.* small place giving a secure grip for the foot; secure position from which progress may be made. —**footlights** *pl. n.* lights across the front of a stage. —**footloose** *adj.* free from ties. —**footman** *n.* male servant in livery. —**footnote** *n.* note printed at the foot of a page. —**footplate** *n.* platform in the cab of a locomotive for the driver. —**footprint** *n.* mark left by a foot. —**footsore** *adj.* having sore or tired feet. —**footstep** *n.* step in walking; sound made by walking. —**footstool** *n.* low stool used to rest the feet on while sitting. —**footwear** *n.* anything worn to cover the feet. —**footwork** *n.* skilful use of the feet, as in sport or dancing.

football *n.* game played by two teams of eleven players kicking a ball in an attempt to score goals, soccer; any of various similar games, such as rugby; ball used for this. —**footballer** *n.* —**football pools** form of gambling on the results of football matches.

footing *n.* secure grip by or for the feet; basis, foundation; relationship between people.

footle *v.* (often foll. by *around* or *about*) *Informal* loiter aimlessly. —**footling** *adj.* trivial.

footsie *n.* *Informal* flirtation involving the touching together of feet.

fop *n.* man excessively concerned with fashion. —**foppery** *n.* —**foppish** *adj.*

for *prep.* intended to be received or used by; in order to help or benefit; representing, e.g. *speaking for the opposition;* because of, e.g. *I could not see for the fog;* over a span of (time or distance); in the direction of, e.g. *heading for the border;* at a cost of; in favour of, e.g. *vote for me.* —*conj.* because. —**for it** *Informal* liable for punishment or blame.

forage [**for**-ridge] *v.* search about (for). —*n.* food for cattle or horses.

foray *n.* brief raid or attack; first attempt or new undertaking.

forbear *v.* cease or refrain (from doing something). —**forbearance** *n.* tolerance, patience. —**forbearing** *adj.*

forbid *v.* prohibit, refuse to allow. —**forbidden** *adj.* —**forbidding** *adj.* severe, threatening.

THESAURUS

fool *n.* 1. ass, dolt, dunce, dunderhead, halfwit, idiot, ignoramus, illiterate, jackass, loon, moron, nitwit, numskull, silly, simpleton 2. buffoon, clown, comic, harlequin, jester, motley, pierrot ~*v.* 3. beguile, bluff, cheat, deceive, delude, dupe, hoax, hoodwink, mislead, take in, trick

foolhardy bold, hot-headed, impetuous, imprudent, incautious, irresponsible, madcap, precipitate, rash, reckless, venturesome, venturous

foolish 1. absurd, ill-advised, ill-judged, imprudent, incautious, indiscreet, injudicious, senseless, short-sighted, silly, unintelligent, unreasonable, unwise 2. brainless, crazy, doltish, fatuous, half-witted, harebrained, idiotic, imbecilic, ludicrous, mad, ridiculous, senseless, silly, simple, stupid, weak, witless

foolishly absurdly, idiotically, ill-advisedly, imprudently, incautiously, indiscreetly, injudiciously, mistakenly, short-sightedly, stupidly, unwisely

foolishness absurdity, folly, imprudence, inanity, indiscretion, irresponsibility, silliness, stupidity, weakness

foolproof certain, guaranteed, infallible, safe, unassailable

footing basis, establishment, foot-hold, foundation, ground, groundwork, installation, settlement

footling fiddling, fussy, immaterial, insignificant, irrelevant, minor, niggly, petty, pointless, silly, time-wasting, trifling, trivial, unimportant

footstep footfall, step, tread

forage *n.* feed, fodder, food, foodstuffs, provender

forbear abstain, avoid, cease, decline, desist, eschew, omit, pause, refrain, stop, withhold

forbearance indulgence, leniency, lenity, mildness, moderation, patience, resignation, restraint, self-control, temperance, tolerance

forbearing easy, forgiving, indulgent, lenient,

DICTIONARY

force *n.* strength or power; compulsion; *Physics* influence tending to produce a change in a physical system; mental or moral strength; person or thing with strength or influence; vehemence or intensity; group of people organized for a particular task or duty; body of troops, police, etc. —*v.* compel, make (someone) do something; acquire or produce through effort, strength, etc.; propel or drive; break open; impose or inflict; cause to grow at an increased rate; strain to the utmost. —**in force** having legal validity; in great numbers. —**forced** *adj.* compulsory; false or unnatural; due to an emergency. —**forceful** *adj.* emphatic; effective. —**forcefully** *adv.* —**forcefulness** *n.* —**forcible** *adj.* involving physical force or violence; strong and emphatic. —**forcibly** *adv.*

forceps *pl. n.* surgical pincers.

ford *n.* shallow place where a river may be crossed. —*v.* cross (a river) at a ford. —**fordable** *adj.*

fore *adj.* in, at, or towards the front. —*n.* front part. —**to the fore** in a conspicuous position.

fore- *prefix* before in time or rank, e.g. *forefather;* at the front, e.g. *forecourt.*

fore-and-aft *adj.* located at both ends of a ship.

forearm[1] *n.* arm from the wrist to the elbow.

forearm[2] *v.* prepare beforehand.

forebear *n.* ancestor.

foreboding *n.* feeling that something bad is about to happen.

forecast *v.* **-casting, -cast** *or* **-casted.** predict (weather, events, etc.). —*n.* prediction.

forecastle [foke-sl] *n.* raised front part of a ship.

foreclose *v.* take possession of (property bought with borrowed money which has not been repaid). —**foreclosure** *n.*

forecourt *n.* courtyard or open space in front of a building.

forefather *n.* ancestor.

forefinger *n.* finger next to the thumb.

forefront *n.* most active or conspicuous position; very front.

forego *v.* same as FORGO.

foregoing *adj.* going before, preceding. —**foregone conclusion** inevitable result.

foreground *n* part of a view, esp. in a picture, nearest the observer.

forehand *adj.* (of a stroke in tennis, squash, etc.) made with the palm of the hand forward. —*n.* such a stroke.

forehead *n.* part of the face above the eyebrows.

foreign *adj.* not of, or in, one's own country; relating to or connected with other countries;

THESAURUS

long-suffering, merciful, mild, moderate, patient, tolerant

forbid ban, debar, disallow, exclude, hinder, inhibit, outlaw, preclude, prohibit, proscribe, rule out, veto

forbidden banned, outlawed, prohibited, proscribed, taboo, vetoed

force *n.* 1. energy, impact, impulse, life, might, muscle, potency, power, pressure, stimulus, strength, stress, vigour 2. coercion, compulsion, constraint, duress, enforcement, pressure, violence 3. bite, cogency, effect, effectiveness, efficacy, influence, power, strength, validity, weight 4. drive, emphasis, fierceness, intensity, persistence, vehemence, vigour ~*v.* 5. coerce, compel, constrain, drive, impel, impose, make, necessitate, obligate, oblige, overcome, press, press-gang, pressure, pressurize, urge 6. blast, break open, prise, propel, push, thrust, use violence on, wrench, wrest 7. drag, exact, extort, wring

forced 1. compulsory, involuntary, mandatory, obligatory, slave, unwilling 2. affected, artificial, contrived, false, insincere, laboured, stiff, strained, unnatural, wooden

forceful cogent, compelling, convincing, dy-

namic, effective, pithy, potent, powerful, telling, vigorous, weighty

forcible active, cogent, compelling, effective, efficient, energetic, forceful, impressive, mighty, potent, powerful, strong, telling, valid, weighty

forebear ancestor, father, forefather, forerunner, predecessor, progenitor

foreboding anxiety, apprehension, apprehensiveness, chill, dread, fear, misgiving, premonition, presentiment

forecast 1. *v.* augur, calculate, divine, estimate, foresee, foretell, plan, predict, prophesy 2. *n.* anticipation, conjecture, foresight, forethought, guess, outlook, planning, prediction, prognosis, projection, prophecy

forefather ancestor, father, forebear, forerunner, predecessor

foregoing above, antecedent, former, preceding, previous, prior

foreign alien, borrowed, distant, exotic, external, imported, outlandish, outside, overseas, remote, strange, unfamiliar, unknown

foreigner alien, immigrant, incomer, newcomer, outlander, stranger

DICTIONARY

unfamiliar, strange; in an abnormal place or position, e.g. *foreign matter*. —**foreigner** *n*.

foreland *n*. headland.

forelock *n*. lock of hair over the forehead.

foreman *n*. person in charge of a group of workers; leader of a jury.

foremast *n*. mast nearest the bow of a ship.

foremost *adj., adv.* first in time, place, or importance.

forename *n*. first name.

forenoon *n*. morning.

forensic [for-ren-sik] *adj.* used in or connected with courts of law. —**forensic medicine** use of medical knowledge for the purposes of the law.

foreplay *n*. sexual stimulation before intercourse.

forerunner *n*. person or thing that goes before, precursor.

foresee *v*. see or know beforehand. —**foreseeable** *adj.*

foreshadow *v*. show or indicate beforehand.

foreshore *n*. part of the shore between high- and low-tide marks.

foreshorten *v*. represent (an object) in a picture as shorter than it really is in accordance with perspective.

foresight *n*. ability to anticipate and provide for future needs.

foreskin *n*. fold of skin covering the tip of the penis.

forest *n*. large area with a thick growth of trees. —**forested** *adj.* —**forestry** *n*. science of planting and caring for trees; management of forests. —**forester** *n*. person skilled in forestry.

forestall *v*. prevent or guard against in advance.

foretaste *n*. early limited experience of something to come.

foretell *v*. tell or indicate beforehand.

forethought *n*. thoughtful planning for future events.

forever *adv.* without end; at all times; *Informal* for a long time.

forewarn *v*. warn beforehand.

foreword *n*. preface.

forfeit [for-fit] *n*. thing lost or given up as a penalty for a fault or mistake. —*v*. lose as a forfeit. —*adj.* lost as a forfeit. —**forfeiture** *n*.

forgather *v*. meet together, assemble.

forge[1] *n*. place where metal is worked, smithy; furnace for melting metal. —*v*. make a fraudulent imitation of (something); shape (metal) by heating and hammering it; create (an alliance etc.).

forge[2] *v*. advance steadily. —**forge ahead** *v*. increase speed or take the lead.

forgery *n., pl.* **-ries.** something forged; act of making a fraudulent imitation.

forget *v*. **-getting, -got, -gotten.** fail to remember; neglect; leave behind by mistake. —**forgetful** *adj.* tending to forget. —**forgetfulness** *n*. —**forget-me-not** *n*. plant with clusters of small blue flowers.

forgive *v*. cease to blame or hold resentment against, pardon. —**forgiveness** *n*.

forgo *v*. do without, give up.

forgot *v*. past tense of FORGET. —**forgotten** *v*. past participle of FORGET.

fork *n*. tool for eating food, with prongs and a

THESAURUS

foremost chief, first, front, highest, initial, leading, pre-eminent, principal, supreme

forerunner ancestor, envoy, forebear, foregoer, harbinger, herald, precursor, predecessor, progenitor, prototype

foresee anticipate, divine, envisage, forebode, forecast, foretell, predict, prophesy

foreshadow augur, betoken, bode, forebode, imply, indicate, portend, predict, presage, promise, signal

foresight anticipation, care, caution, forethought, precaution, preparedness, prescience, provision

foretell adumbrate, augur, forecast, foreshadow, forewarn, portend, predict, presage, prophesy, signify

forethought anticipation, precaution, providence, provision, prudence

forewarn admonish, advise, alert, caution, tip off

forfeit 1. *n*. damages, fine, loss, penalty 2. *v*. be deprived of, be stripped of, give up, lose, relinquish, surrender

forge *v*. 1. copy, counterfeit, fake, falsify, feign, imitate 2. coin

forget lose sight of, omit, overlook

forgive absolve, acquit, condone, excuse, exonerate, (*Inf.*), pardon, remit

forgo abandon, cede, do without, give up, relinquish, renounce, resign, sacrifice, surrender, waive, yield

forgotten buried, bygone, lost, obliterated, omitted, past, unremembered

DICTIONARY

handle; large similarly-shaped tool for digging or lifting; point where a road, river, etc. divides into branches; one of the branches. —v. branch; take one or other branch at a fork in the road; pick up, dig, etc. with a fork. —**forked** adj. —**fork-lift truck** vehicle with a forklike device at the front which can be raised or lowered to move loads. —**fork out** v. Informal pay.

forlorn adj. forsaken and unhappy. —**forlorn hope** hopeless enterprise. —**forlornly** adv.

form n. shape or appearance; mode in which something appears; type or kind; printed document with spaces for details; physical or mental condition; previous record of an athlete, racehorse, etc.; class in school; procedure or etiquette; bench; hare's nest. —v. give a (particular) shape to or take a (particular) shape; come or bring into existence; make or be made; train; acquire or develop; be an element of. —**formless** adj. —**formation** n. forming; thing formed; structure or shape; arrangement of people or things acting as a unit. —**formative** adj. shaping; of or relating to development.

formal adj. of or characterized by established conventions of ceremony and behaviour; of or for formal occasions; stiff in manner; organized; symmetrical. —**formally** adv. —**formality** n. requirement of custom or etiquette; necessary procedure without real importance. —**formalize** v. make official or formal.

formaldehyde [for-**mal**-de-hide] n. colourless pungent gas used to make formalin. —**formalin** n. solution of formaldehyde in water, used as a disinfectant or a preservative for biological specimens.

format n. size and shape of a publication; style in which something is arranged. —v. -**matting, -matted.** arrange in a format.

former adj. of an earlier time, previous. —**the former** first mentioned of two. —**formerly** adv.

formic acid n. acid derived from ants.

Formica n. ® kind of laminated sheet used to make heat-resistant surfaces.

formidable adj. arousing fear or dread; difficult to overcome or manage. —**formidably** adv.

formula n., pl. **-las, -lae.** group of numbers, letters, or symbols expressing a scientific or mathematical rule; set form of words used in religion, law, etc.; method or rule for doing or producing something; specific category of car in motor racing. —**formulaic** adj. —**formulate** v. plan or describe precisely and clearly. —**formulation** n.

fornicate v. have sexual intercourse without being married. —**fornication** n. —**fornicator** n.

forsake v. **-saking, -sook, -saken.** withdraw support or friendship from; give up, renounce.

forsooth adv. Obs. indeed.

forswear v. renounce or reject.

THESAURUS

forlorn abandoned, cheerless, comfortless, deserted, desolate, destitute, disconsolate, helpless, homeless, hopeless, lonely, lost, miserable, pathetic, pitiable, pitiful, unhappy, wretched

form v. 1. assemble, bring about, build, concoct, construct, contrive, create, devise, establish, fabricate, fashion, forge, found, invent, make, model, mould, produce, set up, shape 2. arrange, combine, design, dispose, draw up, frame, organize, pattern, plan ~n. 3. appearance, cast, cut, fashion, formation, model, mould, pattern, shape, structure 4. format, framework, harmony, order, orderliness, organization, plan, proportion, structure, symmetry 5. application, document, paper, sheet

formal approved, ceremonial, explicit, express, fixed, lawful, legal, methodical, official, prescribed, regular, rigid, ritualistic, set, solemn, strict

formality 1. ceremony, convention, custom, gesture, procedure, red tape, rite, ritual 2. correctness, decorum, etiquette, protocol, punctilio

formation 1. accumulation, composition, development, establishment, evolution, generation, genesis, manufacture, organization, production 2. arrangement, configuration, design, disposition, figure, grouping, pattern, rank, structure

former 1. ancient, bygone, departed, of yore, old, old-time, past 2. above, aforesaid, foregoing, preceding

formerly already, before, lately, once, previously

formidable 1. daunting, dreadful, fearful, frightful, horrible, intimidating, menacing, shocking, terrifying, threatening 2. arduous, challenging, colossal, difficult, onerous, overwhelming, toilsome

formula 1. rite, ritual, rubric 2. blueprint, method, precept, prescription, principle, procedure, recipe, rule, way

formulate codify, define, detail, express, frame, specify, systematize

forsake abandon, cast off, desert, disown, jilt, leave, quit, repudiate, throw over

forsaken abandoned, cast off, deserted, destitute, disowned, forlorn, friendless, ignored, isolated, jilted, left behind, left in the lurch, lonely, marooned, outcast, solitary

DICTIONARY

forsythia [for-**syth**-ee-a] *n.* shrub with yellow flowers in spring.

fort *n.* fortified building or place. —**hold the fort** *Informal* keep things going during someone's absence.

forte[1] [**for**-tay] *n.* thing at which a person excels.

forte[2] *Music* loudly.

forth *adv.* forwards, out, or away.

forthcoming *adj.* about to appear or happen; available; (of a person) communicative.

forthright *adj.* direct and outspoken.

forthwith *adv.* at once.

fortieth *adj., n.* see FOUR.

fortify *v.* -**fying**, -**fied.** make (a place) defensible, as by building walls; strengthen; add alcohol to (wine) to make sherry or port; add vitamins etc. to (food). —**fortification** *n.*

fortissimo *Music* very loudly.

fortitude *n.* courage in adversity or pain.

fortnight *n.* two weeks. —**fortnightly** *adv., adj.*

FORTRAN *n. Computers* programming language for mathematical and scientific purposes.

fortress *n.* large fort or fortified town.

fortuitous [for-**tyew**-it-uss] *adj.* happening by (lucky) chance. —**fortuitously** *adv.* —**fortuity** *n.*

fortunate *adj.* having good luck; occurring by good luck. —**fortunately** *adv.*

fortune *n.* luck, esp. when favourable; power regarded as influencing human destiny; wealth, large sum of money. —*pl.* person's destiny. —**fortune-teller** *n.* person who claims to predict the future of others.

forty *adj., n.* see FOUR.

forum *n.* meeting or medium for open discussion or debate.

forward *adj.* directed or moving ahead; in, at, or near the front; presumptuous; well developed or advanced; relating to the future. —*n.* attacking player in various team games, such as football or hockey. —*v.* send (a letter etc.) on to an ultimate destination; advance or promote. —*adv.* forwards. —**forwardly** *adv.* —**forwardness** *n.* —**forwards** *adv.* towards or at a place further ahead in space or time; towards the front.

fosse *n.* ditch or moat.

fossil *n.* hardened remains of a prehistoric animal or plant preserved in rock. —**fossilize** *v.* turn into a fossil; become out-of-date or inflexible. —**fossilization** *n.*

foster *v.* promote the growth or development of; bring up (a child not one's own). —*adj.* of or involved in fostering a child.

fought *v.* past of FIGHT.

foul *adj.* loathsome or offensive; stinking or dirty; (of language) obscene or vulgar; unfair. —*n. Sport* violation of the rules. —*v.* make dirty or polluted; make or become entangled or clogged; *Sport* commit a foul against (an opponent). —**fall foul of** come into conflict with.

THESAURUS

fort blockhouse, camp, castle, citadel, fortress, garrison, redoubt, station, stronghold

forte gift, métier, speciality, strength, strong point, talent

forth ahead, away, forward, onward, out, outward

forthcoming 1. approaching, coming, expected, future, imminent, impending, prospective 2. chatty, communicative, expansive, free, informative, open, sociable, talkative, unreserved

forthright above-board, blunt, candid, direct, frank, open, outspoken, straightforward

forthwith at once, directly, immediately, instantly, quickly, right away, straightaway

fortification bulwark, castle, citadel, defence, fastness, fort, fortress, keep, protection, stronghold

fortify brace, cheer, confirm, embolden, encourage, hearten, invigorate, reassure, stiffen, strengthen, sustain

fortress castle, citadel, fort, redoubt

fortunate bright, favoured, golden, happy, lucky, prosperous, rosy, successful, well-off

fortunately by good luck, happily, luckily, providentially

fortune 1. affluence, gold mine, possessions, property, prosperity, riches, treasure, wealth 2. accident, chance, destiny, fate, hazard, kismet, luck, providence

forward 1. *adj.* advanced, early, onward, precocious, premature, progressive, well-developed 2. *adv. Also* **forwards** ahead, forth, on, onward 3. *v.* advance, aid, assist, back, encourage, expedite, favour, foster, further, hasten, help, hurry, promote, speed, support

foster 1. cultivate, encourage, feed, nurture, promote, stimulate, support, uphold 2. bring up, mother, nurse, raise, rear, take care of 3. cherish, entertain, harbour, nourish, sustain

foul 1. *adj.* contaminated, dirty, disgusting, fetid, filthy, impure, loathsome, nasty, nauseating, noisome, offensive, polluted, putrid, rank, repulsive, revolting, rotten, squalid, stinking, sullied, tainted, unclean 2. *v.* besmear, besmirch, contaminate, defile, dirty, pollute, smear, soil, stain, sully, taint

DICTIONARY

—**foully** *adv.* —**foulness** *n.* —**foul-mouthed** *adj.* (habitually) using foul language. —**foul play** unfair conduct, esp. involving violence.

found[1] *v.* past of FIND.

found[2] *v.* establish or bring into being; lay the foundation of; (foll. by *on* or *upon*) have a basis (in). —**founder** *n.* —**foundation** *n.* basis or base; act of founding; institution supported by an endowment; cosmetic used as a base for make-up. —*pl.* part of a building or wall below the ground.

found[3] *v.* cast (metal or glass) by melting and setting in a mould; make (articles) by this method. —**founder** *n.* —**foundry** *n.* place where metal is melted and cast.

founder *v.* break down or fail; (of a ship) sink; stumble or fall.

foundling *n.* abandoned infant.

fount *n. Lit.* fountain; source; set of printing type of one style and size.

fountain *n.* jet of water; structure from which such a jet spurts; source. —**fountainhead** *n.* source. —**fountain pen** pen supplied with ink from a container inside it.

four *adj., n.* one more than three. —*n.* (crew of) four-oared rowing boat. —**on all fours** on hands and knees. —**fourth** *adj., n.* (of) number four in a series. —*n.* quarter. —**fourthly** *adv.* —**foursome** *n.* group of four people. —**fourteen** *adj., n.* four and ten. —**fourteenth** *adj., n.* —**forty** *adj., n.* four times ten. —**fortieth** *adj., n.* —**fourth dimension** time. —**fourth estate** the press. —**four-letter word** short obscene word referring to sex or excrement. —**four-poster** *n.* bed with four posts supporting a canopy.

fowl *n.* domestic cock or hen; any bird used for food or hunted as game. —*v.* hunt or snare wild birds. —**fowler** *n.*

fox *n.* reddish-brown bushy-tailed animal of the dog family; its fur; cunning person. —*v. Informal* perplex or deceive. —**foxy** *adj.* —**foxglove** *n.* tall plant with purple or white flowers. —**foxhole** *n. Mil.* small pit dug for protection. —**foxhound** *n.* dog bred for hunting foxes. —**fox terrier** small short-haired terrier. —**foxtrot** *n.* ballroom dance with slow and quick steps; music for this.

foyer [foy-ay] *n.* entrance hall in a theatre, cinema, or hotel.

fracas [frak-ah] *n., pl.* -**cas.** noisy quarrel.

fraction *n.* numerical quantity that is not a whole number; fragment, piece; *Chem.* substance separated by distillation. —**fractional** *adj.* —**fractionally** *adv.*

fractious *adj.* peevishly irritable.

fracture *n.* breaking, esp. of a bone. —*v.* break.

fragile *adj.* easily broken or damaged; in a weakened physical state. —**fragility** *n.*

fragment *n.* piece broken off; incomplete piece. —*v.* break into pieces. —**fragmentary** *adj.* —**fragmentation** *n.*

fragrant *adj.* sweet-smelling. —**fragrantly** *adv.* —**fragrance** *n.* pleasant smell; perfume, scent.

frail *adj.* physically weak; easily damaged. —**frailty** *n.*

frame *n.* structure giving shape or support;

THESAURUS

found constitute, construct, create, endow, erect, establish, fix, inaugurate, institute, organize, originate, plant, raise, settle, set up, start

foundation 1. base, basis, bedrock, bottom, footing, substructure, underpinning 2. endowment, establishment, inauguration, institution, settlement

founder[1] *n.* author, beginner, benefactor, builder, designer, establisher, father, framer, generator, initiator, inventor, maker, organizer, originator

founder[2] *v.* be lost, go down, go to the bottom, sink, submerge

foundling orphan, outcast, stray, waif

fountain fount, jet, reservoir, spout, spray, spring, well

foyer anteroom, entrance hall, lobby, vestibule

fracas brawl, disturbance, fight, melee, quarrel, riot, row, rumpus, scrimmage, scuffle, trouble, uproar

fractious awkward, captious, crabby, cross, fretful, irritable, peevish, recalcitrant, testy, touchy, unruly

fracture 1. *n.* breach, break, cleft, crack, fissure, gap, opening, rent, rift, rupture, schism, split 2. *v.* break, crack, rupture, splinter, split

fragile breakable, brittle, dainty, delicate, feeble, fine, flimsy, frail, infirm, slight, weak

fragment bit, chip, fraction, morsel, part, piece, portion, remnant, scrap, shiver, sliver

fragmentary bitty, broken, disconnected, discrete, disjointed, incoherent, incomplete, partial, piecemeal

fragrance aroma, balm, bouquet, perfume, scent, smell

fragrant aromatic, balmy, odorous, perfumed, sweet-scented, sweet-smelling

frail breakable, brittle, decrepit, delicate, feeble, flimsy, fragile, infirm, insubstantial, puny, slight, tender, unsound, vulnerable, weak

frailty feebleness, puniness, susceptibility, weakness

DICTIONARY

enclosing case or border, as round a picture; person's build; individual exposure on a strip of film; individual game of snooker in a match. —*v.* put into a frame; put together, construct; put into words; *Slang* incriminate (a person) on a false charge. —**frame of mind** mood, attitude. —**frame-up** *n. Slang* false incrimination. —**framework** *n.* supporting structure.

franc *n.* monetary unit of France, Switzerland, and Belgium.

franchise *n.* right to vote; authorization to sell a company's goods.

Franciscan *n., adj.* (friar or nun) of the order founded by St. Francis of Assisi.

Franco- *combining form* of France or the French.

frangipani [fran-jee-**pah**-nee] *n.* fragrant tropical American shrub.

frank *adj.* honest and straightforward; outspoken or blunt. —*v.* put such a mark on (a letter). —**frankly** *adv.* —**frankness** *n.*

frankfurter *n.* smoked sausage.

frankincense *n.* aromatic gum resin burned as incense.

frantic *adj.* distracted with rage, grief, joy, etc.; hurried and disorganized. —**frantically** *adv.*

fraternal *adj.* of a brother, brotherly. —**fraternally** *adv.* —**fraternity** *n.* group of people with shared interests, aims, etc.; brotherhood; *US* male social club at college. —**fraternize** *v.* associate on friendly terms. —**fraternization** *n.*

—**fratricide** *n.* crime of killing one's brother; person who does this.

Frau [rhymes with **how**] *n.* German title, equivalent to *Mrs.* —**Fräulein** [**froy**-line] *n.* German title, equivalent to *Miss.*

fraud *n.* (criminal) deception, swindle; person who acts in a deceitful way. —**fraudulent** *adj.* —**fraudulence** *n.*

fraught [frawt] *adj.* tense or anxious. —**fraught with** involving, filled with.

fray[1] *v.* make or become ragged at the edge; become strained.

fray[2] *n.* noisy quarrel or conflict.

frazzle *n. Informal* exhausted state.

freak *n.* abnormal person or thing; person who is excessively enthusiastic about something. —*adj.* abnormal. —**freakish** *adj.* —**freak out** *v. Slang* (cause to) be in a heightened emotional state.

freckle *n.* small brown spot on the skin. —**freckled** *adj.* marked with freckles.

-free *adj. combining form* without, e.g. *a trouble-free journey.*

free *adj.* **freer, freest.** able to act at will, not compelled or restrained; not subject (to); independent; provided without charge; generous, lavish; not in use; (of a person) not busy; not fixed or joined. —*v.* **freeing, freed.** release, liberate; remove (obstacles, pain, etc.) from; make available or usable. —**freely** *adv.* —**freedom** *n.* being free. —**freebooter** *n.* pirate. —**free fall** part of a parachute descent before the parachute opens.

THESAURUS

frame *v.* 1. assemble, build, constitute, construct, fabricate, fashion, forge, form, institute, invent, make, model, mould, set up 2. compose, contrive, devise, draft, draw up, form, formulate, hatch, plan, shape, sketch 3. case, enclose, mount, surround ~*n.* 4. casing, fabric, form, scheme, shell, structure, system 5. anatomy, body, build, physique, skeleton 6. mount, mounting, setting

framework core, fabric, foundation, groundwork, plan, schema, shell, skeleton, structure

franchise charter, exemption, freedom, immunity, right, suffrage, vote

frank artless, blunt, candid, direct, downright, forthright, free, honest, open, outright, outspoken, plain, sincere, straightforward, transparent, truthful, unconcealed, undisguised, unreserved, unrestricted

frankness bluntness, candour, forthrightness, openness, outspokenness, plain speaking

frantic berserk, distracted, distraught, frenetic, frenzied, furious, hectic, mad, overwrought, raging, raving, wild

fraternity association, brotherhood, circle, clan, club, companionship, company, comradeship, fellowship, guild, kinship, league, set, sodality, union

fraud 1. artifice, cheat, chicanery, craft, deceit, deception, double-dealing, duplicity, guile, hoax, humbug, imposture, spuriousness, stratagems, swindling, treachery, trickery 2. bluffer, charlatan, cheat, counterfeit, double-dealer, fake, forgery, hoax, hoaxer, impostor, mountebank, pretender, quack, sham, swindler

fraudulent crafty, criminal, deceitful, deceptive, dishonest, false, knavish, sham, spurious, swindling, treacherous

fray *v.* chafe, fret, rub, wear, wear away, wear thin

freak 1. *n.* aberration, abnormality, anomaly, malformation, monster, oddity 2. *adj.* aberrant, abnormal, atypical, bizarre, erratic, exceptional, fortuitous, odd, queer, unexpected, unforeseen, unpredictable, unusual

DICTIONARY

—**free-for-all** n. *Informal* brawl. —**freehand** adj. drawn without guiding instruments. —**free hand** unrestricted freedom to act. —**freehold** n. tenure of land for life without restrictions. —**freeholder** n. —**free house** public house not bound to sell only one brewer's products. —**freelance** adj., n. (of) self-employed person doing specific pieces of work for various employers. —**freeloader** n. *Slang* habitual scrounger. —**Freemason** n. member of a secret fraternity pledged to help each other. —**free-range** adj. kept or produced in natural conditions. —**free space** region with no gravitational or electromagnetic fields. —**freeway** n. *US* motorway. —**freewheel** v. travel downhill on a bicycle without pedalling.

freesia n. plant with fragrant tubular flowers.

freeze v. **freezing, froze, frozen.** change from a liquid to a solid by the reduction of temperature, as water to ice; preserve (food etc.) by extreme cold; (cause to) be very cold; become motionless with fear, shock, etc.; fix (prices or wages) at a particular level; ban the exchange or collection of (loans, assets, etc.). —n. period of very cold weather; freezing of prices or wages. —**freezer** n. insulated cabinet for cold-storage of perish-

able foods. —**freeze-dry** v. preserve (food) by rapid freezing and drying in a vacuum.

freight [frate] n. commercial transport of goods; cargo transported; cost of this. —v. send by freight. —**freighter** n. ship or aircraft for transporting goods.

French n. language of France. —adj. of France, its people, or their language. —**French bread** white bread in a long thin crusty loaf. —**French dressing** salad dressing of oil and vinegar. —**French fries** potato chips. —**French horn** brass wind instrument with a coiled tube. —**French leave** unauthorized absence or departure. —**French letter** *Slang* condom. —**French polish** shellac varnish for wood. —**French window** window extending to floor level, used as a door.

frenetic [frin-net-ik] adj. uncontrolled, excited. —**frenetically** adv.

frenzy n., pl. -zies. violent mental derangement; wild excitement. —**frenzied** adj. —**frenziedly** adv.

frequent adj. happening often; habitual. —v. visit habitually. —**frequently** adv. —**frequency**

THESAURUS

free adj. 1. complimentary, for nothing, gratis, gratuitous, unpaid 2. at large, at liberty, footloose, independent, liberated, loose, uncommitted, unconstrained, unfettered, unrestrained 3. able, allowed, clear, disengaged, loose, open, permitted, unattached, unhampered, unimpeded, unobstructed, unregulated, unrestricted, untrammelled 4. *With of* above, beyond, deficient in, devoid of, exempt from, immune to, lacking (in), not liable to, safe from, unaffected by, untouched by, without 5. autarchic, autonomous, democratic, emancipated, independent, self-governing, self-ruling, sovereign 6. available, empty, extra, idle, not tied down, spare, unemployed, uninhabited, unoccupied, unused, vacant 7. big (*Inf.*), bounteous, bountiful, charitable, eager, generous, hospitable, lavish, liberal, munificent, open-handed, prodigal, unsparing, unstinting, willing ~v. 8. deliver, discharge, emancipate, let go, let out, liberate, loose, manumit, release, turn loose, uncage, unchain, unfetter, unleash, untie 9. clear, cut loose, deliver, disengage, disentangle, exempt, extricate, ransom, redeem, relieve, rescue, rid, unburden, undo

freedom 1. autonomy, deliverance, emancipation, home rule, independence, liberty, release, self-government 2. exemption, immunity, impunity, privilege 3. ability, carte blanche, discretion, elbowroom, facility, flexi-

bility, free rein, latitude, leeway, licence, opportunity, play, power, range, scope

freely 1. of one's own accord, spontaneously, voluntarily, willingly 2. candidly, frankly, openly, plainly, unreservedly 3. unchallenged 4. abundantly, amply, bountifully, copiously, extravagantly, lavishly, liberally, openhandedly, unstintingly

freeze 1. benumb, chill, congeal, glaciate, harden, ice over *or* up, stiffen 2. fix, hold up, inhibit, peg, stop, suspend

freezing arctic, biting, bitter, chill, chilled, cutting, frosty, glacial, icy, numbing, penetrating, raw, wintry

freight n. bales, bulk, burden, cargo, consignment, contents, goods, haul, lading, load, merchandise, payload, tonnage

French adj. Gallic

frenzied agitated, convulsive, distracted, distraught, excited, frantic, frenetic, furious, hysterical, mad, maniacal, rabid, uncontrolled, wild

frequent 1. adj. common, constant, continual, customary, everyday, familiar, habitual, numerous, persistent, recurrent, repeated, usual 2. v. attend, be found at, haunt, patronize, resort, visit

frequently commonly, habitually, much, often, repeatedly, very often

DICTIONARY

n. rate of occurrence; *Physics* number of times a wave repeats itself in a given time.

fresco *n., pl.* **-coes, -cos.** watercolour painting done on wet plaster on a wall.

fresh *adj.* newly made, acquired, etc.; novel, original; most recent; further, additional; (of food) not preserved; (of water) not salty; (of weather) brisk or invigorating; not tired; *Informal* impudent. —**freshly** *adv.* —**freshness** *n.* —**freshen** *v.* —**freshman, fresher** *n.* first-year student.

fret[1] *v.* **fretting, fretted.** be worried. —**fretful** *adj.* irritable.

fret[2] *n.* small bar on the fingerboard of a guitar etc. —**fret saw** fine saw with a narrow blade, used for fretwork. —**fretwork** *n.* decorative carving in wood.

Freudian [froy-dee-an] *adj.* of or relating to the psychoanalyst Sigmund Freud or his theories.

friable [fry-a-bl] *adj.* easily crumbled. —**friability** *n.*

friar *n.* member of a male Roman Catholic religious order. —**friary** *n.* house of friars.

fricassee *n.* stewed meat served in a thick white sauce.

friction *n.* rubbing; resistance met with by a body moving over another; clash of wills or personalities. —**frictional** *adj.*

Friday *n.* sixth day of the week. —**Good Friday** Friday before Easter.

fridge *n.* short for REFRIGERATOR.

fried *v.* past of FRY[1].

friend *n.* person whom one knows well and likes; supporter; (F-) Quaker. —**friendly** *adj.* showing or expressing liking; not hostile, on the same side. —*n., pl.* **-lies.** *Sport* match played for its own sake and not as part of a competition. —**friendly** *combining form* good or easy for the person or thing specified, e.g. *user-friendly.* —**friendly society** association of people who pay regular dues in return for pensions, sickness benefits, etc. —**friendliness** *n.* —**friendless** *adj.* —**friendship** *n.*

Friesian [free-zhan] *n.* breed of black-and-white dairy cattle.

frieze [freeze] *n.* ornamental band on a wall.

frigate [frig-it] *n.* medium-sized fast warship.

fright *n.* sudden fear or alarm; sudden alarming shock; *Informal* grotesque person. —**frighten** *v.* scare or terrify; force (someone) to do something from fear. —**frightening** *adj.* —**frightful** *adj.* horrifying; *Informal* very great. —**frightfully** *adv.*

frigid [frij-id] *adj.* (of a woman) sexually unresponsive; very cold; excessively formal. —**frigidly** *adv.* —**frigidity** *n.*

frill *n.* gathered strip of fabric attached at one edge. —*pl.* superfluous decorations or details. —**frilled** *adj.* —**frilly** *adj.*

THESAURUS

fresh 1. different, latest, modern, new, novel, original, recent, unusual, up-to-date 2. added, additional, extra, further, more, other, renewed 3. bracing, bright, brisk, clean, clear, cool, crisp, invigorating, pure, refreshing, sparkling, stiff, sweet

freshen enliven, liven up, refresh, restore, revitalize, rouse, spruce up, titivate

freshness inventiveness, newness, novelty, originality

fret agonize, brood, grieve, worry

friction abrasion, erosion, fretting, grating, irritation, resistance, rubbing, scraping

friend chum, companion, comrade, confidant, crony, familiar, intimate, pal, partner, playmate, soul mate

friendliness amiability, congeniality, conviviality, geniality, kindliness, sociability, warmth

friendly affectionate, amiable, amicable, attentive, beneficial, benevolent, benign, close, companionable, comradely, convivial, cordial, familiar, favourable, fond, genial, good, helpful, intimate, kind, kindly, neighbourly, out-

going, peaceable, propitious, receptive, sociable, sympathetic, welcoming, well-disposed

friendship affection, affinity, alliance, amity, attachment, benevolence, closeness, concord, familiarity, fondness, good-fellowship, good will, harmony, intimacy, love, rapport, regard

fright alarm, apprehension, dismay, dread, fear, horror, panic, quaking, scare, shock, terror, trepidation

frighten alarm, appal, cow, daunt, dismay, intimidate, petrify, scare, shock, startle, terrify, terrorize, unman, unnerve

frightening alarming, appalling, dismaying, dreadful, fearful, fearsome, hair-raising, horrifying, intimidating, menacing, shocking, terrifying, unnerving

frightful appalling, awful, dire, dreadful, fearful, ghastly, grim, grisly, gruesome, harrowing, hideous, horrible, lurid, macabre, petrifying, shocking, terrible, terrifying, traumatic, unnerving, unspeakable

frigid 1. arctic, chill, cold, cool, frost-bound, frosty, frozen, gelid, glacial, hyperboreal, icy, Siberian, wintry 2. aloof, austere, forbidding, formal, icy, lifeless, passionless, passive, re-

DICTIONARY

fringe *n.* hair cut short over the forehead; ornamental edge of hanging threads, tassels, etc.; outer edge. —*v.* decorate with a fringe; be a fringe for, border. —*adj.* (of theatre etc.) unofficial or unconventional. —**fringe benefit** benefit given in addition to a regular salary.

frippery *n., pl.* **-peries.** useless ornamentation; trivia.

frisk *v.* move or leap playfully; *Informal* search (a person) for concealed weapons etc. —**frisky** *adj.* lively or high-spirited. —**friskily** *adv.*

frisson [frees-sonn] *n.* shiver of fear or excitement.

fritter *n.* piece of food fried in batter.

fritter away *v.* waste.

frivolous *adj.* not serious or sensible; enjoyable but trivial. —**frivolously** *adv.* —**frivolity** *n.*

frizz *v.* form (hair) into stiff wiry curls. —**frizzy** *adj.*

frizzle *v.* cook or heat until crisp and shrivelled.

frock *n.* dress. —**frock coat** man's skirted coat as worn in the 19th century.

frog *n.* smooth-skinned tailless amphibian with long back legs used for jumping. —**frog in one's throat** phlegm on the vocal cords, hindering speech. —**frogman** *n.* swimmer with a rubber suit and breathing equipment for working underwater. —**frogmarch** *v.* force (a resisting person) to move by holding his arms. —**frogspawn** *n.* jelly-like substance containing frog's eggs.

frolic *v.* **-icking, -icked.** run and play in a lively way. —*n.* lively and merry behaviour. —**frolicsome** *adj.* playful.

from *prep.* indicating the point of departure, source, distance, cause, change of state, etc.

frond *n.* long leaf or leaflike part of a fern, palm, or seaweed.

front *n.* fore part; position directly before or ahead; seaside promenade; battle line or area; *Meteorol.* dividing line between two different air masses; outward aspect; *Informal* cover for another, usu. criminal, activity; group with a common goal. —*v.* face (onto); be the presenter of (a television show). —*adj.* of or at the front. —**frontal** *adj.* —**frontage** *n.* façade of a building. —**frontispiece** *n.* illustration facing the title page of a book. —**front bench** parliamentary leaders of the government or opposition. —**front-bencher** *n.* —**frontrunner** *n. Informal* person regarded as most likely to win a race, election, etc.

frontier *n.* area of a country bordering on another.

frost *n.* white frozen dew or mist; atmospheric temperature below freezing point. —*v.* become covered with frost. —**frosted** *adj.* (of glass) having a rough surface to make it opaque; covered with frosting. —**frosting** *n. US* sugar icing. —**frosty** *adj.* characterized or covered by frost; unfriendly. —**frostily** *adv.* —**frostiness** *n.* —**frostbite** *n.* destruction of tissue, esp. of the fingers or ears, by cold. —**frostbitten** *adj.*

froth *n.* mass of small bubbles. —*v.* foam. —**frothy** *adj.*

frown *v.* wrinkle one's brows in worry, anger, or thought; look disapprovingly (on). —*n.* frowning expression.

THESAURUS

pellent, rigid, stiff, unapproachable, unbending, unfeeling, unloving, unresponsive

frills additions, affectation(s), decoration(s), embellishment(s), extras, finery, frippery, fuss, mannerisms, ornamentation, ostentation, superfluities, tomfoolery, trimmings

fringe 1. binding, border, edging, hem, tassel, trimming 2. borderline, edge, limits, march, marches, margin, outskirts, perimeter, periphery

frisk bounce, caper, cavort, dance, frolic, gambol, hop, jump, play, prance, rollick, romp, skip, sport, trip

fritter (away) dissipate, idle (away), misspend, run through, squander, waste

frivolity childishness, flippancy, folly, fun, gaiety, giddiness, jest, levity, lightness, nonsense, puerility, shallowness, silliness, superficiality, trifling, triviality

frivolous childish, dizzy, empty-headed, flighty,

flippant, foolish, giddy, idle, juvenile, light-minded, puerile, silly, superficial

frolic *v.* 1. caper, cavort, cut capers, frisk, gambol, lark, make merry, play, rollick, romp, sport ~*n.* 2. antic, escapade, gambol, game, lark, prank, revel, romp, spree 3. amusement, fun, gaiety, high jinks, merriment, sport

frolicsome coltish, frisky, gay, kittenish, lively, merry, playful, sportive, sprightly

front *n.* 1. exterior, façade, face, facing, foreground, forepart, frontage, obverse 2. beginning, fore, forefront, head, lead, top, van, vanguard 3. blind, cover, cover-up, disguise, façade, mask, pretext, show ~*adj.* 4. first, foremost, head, headmost, lead, leading, topmost ~*v.* 5. face (onto), look over *or* onto, overlook

frontier borderland, borderline, bound, boundary, confines, edge, limit, marches, perimeter, verge

frost freeze, hoarfrost, rime

frosty 1. chilly, cold, frozen, icy, rimy, wintry 2.

DICTIONARY

frowsty *adj.* stale or musty.

frowsy *adj.* **-sier, -siest.** dirty or unkempt.

froze *v.* past tense of FREEZE. **—frozen** *v.* past participle of FREEZE.

fructify *v.* **-fying, -fied.** (cause to) bear fruit. **—fructification** *n.*

frugal [froo-gl] *adj.* thrifty, sparing; meagre and inexpensive. **—frugally** *adv.* **—frugality** *n.*

fruit *n.* part of a plant containing seeds, esp. if edible; any plant product useful to man; (*often pl.*) result of an action or effort. **—***v.* bear fruit. **—fruiterer** *n.* person who sells fruit. **—fruitful** *adj.* useful or productive. **—fruitfully** *adv.* **—fruition** [froo-**ish**-on] *n.* fulfilment of something worked for or desired. **—fruitless** *adj.* useless or unproductive. **—fruitlessly** *adv.* **—fruity** *adj.* of or like fruit; (of a voice) mellow; *Informal* mildly bawdy. **—fruit machine** coin-operated gambling machine.

frump *n.* dowdy woman. **—frumpy** *adj.*

frustrate *v.* hinder or prevent; upset or anger. **—frustrated** *adj.* **—frustrating** *adj.* **—frustration** *n.*

fry[1] *v.* **frying, fried.** cook or be cooked in fat or oil. **—***n.* (also **fry-up**) dish of fried food.

fry[2] *pl. n.* young fishes. **—small fry** young or insignificant people.

ft. foot; feet.

fuchsia [**fyew**-sha] *n.* ornamental shrub with hanging flowers.

fuddle *v.* cause to be intoxicated or confused. **—fuddled** *adj.*

fuddy-duddy *n., pl.* **-dies.** *adj. Informal* old-fashioned (person).

fudge[1] *n.* soft caramel-like sweet.

fudge[2] *v.* avoid making a firm statement or decision.

fuel *n.* substance burned for heat or power; something that intensifies (a feeling etc.). **—***v.* **fuelling, fuelled.** provide with fuel.

fug *n.* hot stale atmosphere. **—fuggy** *adj.*

fugitive [**fyew**-jit-iv] *n.* person who flees, esp. from arrest or pursuit. **—***adj.* fleeing; transient.

fugue [fyewg] *n.* musical composition in which a theme is repeated in different parts.

fulcrum *n., pl.* **-crums, -cra.** pivot about which a lever turns.

fulfil *v.* **-filling, -filled.** bring about the achievement of (a desire or promise); carry out (a request or order); do what is required. **—fulfilment** *n.* **—fulfil oneself** *v.* achieve one's potential.

full *adj.* containing as much or as many as possible; abundant in supply; having had enough to eat; plump; complete, whole; (of a garment) of ample cut; (of a sound or flavour) rich and strong. **—***adv.* completely; directly; very. **—fully** *adv.* **—fullness** *n.* **—full-blooded** *adj.* vigorous or enthusiastic. **—full-blown** *adj* fully developed. **—full moon** phase of the moon when it is visible as a fully illuminated disc. **—full-scale** *adj.* (of a plan) of actual size; using all resources. **—full stop** punctuation mark (.) at the end of a sentence and after abbreviations.

THESAURUS

discouraging, frigid, off-putting, standoffish, unenthusiastic, unfriendly, unwelcoming

frown 1. glare, glower, lower, scowl 2. *With* **on** *or* **upon** disapprove of, discourage, dislike

frugal abstemious, careful, economical, meagre, niggardly, parsimonious, prudent, saving, sparing, thrifty

fruit 1. crop, harvest, produce, product, yield 2. advantage, benefit, consequence, effect, outcome, profit, result, return, reward

fruitful 1. fecund, fertile 2. abundant, copious, flush, plenteous, plentiful, productive, profuse, prolific, rich, spawning

fruition attainment, completion, consummation, enjoyment, fulfilment, materialization, maturity, perfection, realization, ripeness

fruitless abortive, barren, futile, idle, ineffectual, in vain, pointless, profitless, unavailing, unproductive, unprofitable, unsuccessful, useless, vain

frustrate baffle, balk, block, check, confront,

counter, defeat, disappoint, foil, forestall, inhibit, neutralize, nullify, stymie, thwart

frustrated disappointed, discontented, discouraged, disheartened, embittered, foiled, irked, resentful

fudge *v.* avoid, dodge, equivocate, evade, fake, falsify, hedge, misrepresent, patch up, shuffle, slant, stall

fuel ammunition, encouragement, fodder, food, incitement, material, means, nourishment, provocation

fugitive *n., adj.* runaway

fulfil accomplish, achieve, answer, carry out, complete, conclude, conform to, discharge, effect, execute, fill, finish, keep, meet, obey, observe, perfect, perform, realise, satisfy

fulfilment accomplishment, achievement, attainment, completion, consummation, crowning, discharge, end, implementation, observance, perfection, realization

full 1. brimful, complete, entire, filled, gorged, intact, loaded, replete, sated, satiated, satis-

DICTIONARY

fulmar *n.* Arctic sea bird.

fulminate *v.* (foll. by *against*) criticize angrily. —**fulmination** *n.*

fulsome *adj.* insincerely excessive.

fumble *v.* handle awkwardly; say awkwardly.

fume *v.* be very angry; give out smoke or vapour; treat with fumes. —*n.* (*usu. pl.*) pungent smoke or vapour.

fumigate [**fyew**-mig-gate] *v.* disinfect with fumes. —**fumigation** *n.*

fun *n.* enjoyment or amusement. —**make fun of** mock or tease. —**funny** *adj.* comical, humorous; odd. —**funny bone** part of the elbow where the nerve is near the surface. —**funnily** *adv.*

function *n.* purpose something exists for; way something works; large or formal social event; *Maths* quantity whose value depends on the varying value of another. —*v.* operate or work; (foll. by *as*) fill the role of. —**functional** *adj.* of or as a function; practical rather than decorative; in working order. —**functionally** *adv.* —**functionary** *n.* official.

fund *n.* stock of money for a special purpose; supply or store. —*pl.* money resources. —*v.* provide money to. —**funding** *n.*

fundamental *adj.* essential or primary; basic. —*n.* basic rule or fact. —**fundamentally** *adv.* —**fundamentalism** *n.* literal or strict interpretation of a religion. —**fundamentalist** *n., adj.*

funeral *n.* ceremony of burying or cremating a dead person. —**funerary** *adj.* of or for a funeral. —**funereal** [fyew-**neer**-ee-al] *adj.* gloomy or sombre.

funfair *n.* entertainment with machines to ride on and stalls.

fungus *n., pl.* **-gi, -guses.** plant without leaves, flowers, or roots, such as a mushroom or mould. —**fungal, fungous** *adj.* —**fungicide** *n.* substance that destroys fungi.

funicular [fyew-**nik**-yew-lar] *n.* cable railway on a mountainside or cliff.

funk[1] *n.* style of dance music with a strong beat. —**funky** *adj.* (of music) passionate or soulful.

funk[2] *Informal* —*n.* nervous or fearful state. —*v.* avoid (doing something) through fear.

funnel *n.* cone-shaped tube for pouring liquids into a narrow opening; chimney of a ship or locomotive. —*v.* **-nelling, -nelled.** (cause to) move through or as if through a funnel.

THESAURUS

fied, saturated, stocked, sufficient 2. abundant, ample, broad, comprehensive, copious, detailed, exhaustive, extensive, generous, maximum, plenary, plenteous, plentiful, thorough, unabridged 3. chock-full, crammed, crowded, in use, jammed, occupied, packed, taken

fullness broadness, completeness, comprehensiveness, entirety, extensiveness, plenitude, totality, vastness, wealth, wholeness

full-scale all-out, comprehensive, exhaustive, extensive, full-dress, in-depth, major, proper, sweeping, thorough, thoroughgoing, wide-ranging

fully 1. absolutely, altogether, completely, entirely, intimately, perfectly, positively, thoroughly, totally, utterly, wholly 2. abundantly, adequately, amply, enough, plentifully, satisfactorily, sufficiently

fulsome adulatory, excessive, extravagant, fawning, gross, ingratiating, inordinate, insincere, nauseating, saccharine, sickening, sycophantic, unctuous

fumble botch, bungle, make a hash of (*Inf.*), mess up, misfield, mishandle, mismanage, muff, spoil

fume boil, chafe, rage, rant, rave, seethe, smoulder, storm

fumes exhaust, gas, haze, pollution, reek, smog, smoke, stench, vapour

fumigate cleanse, disinfect, purify, sterilize

fun amusement, cheer, distraction, diversion, enjoyment, entertainment, frolic, gaiety, good time, jollity, joy, junketing, merriment, mirth, pleasure, recreation, romp, sport, treat

function *n.* 1. activity, business, capacity, charge, concern, duty, employment, exercise, job, mission, occupation, office, operation, part, post, province, purpose, responsibility, role, situation, task ~*v.* 2. act, behave, do duty, go, officiate, operate, perform, run, serve, work ~*n.* 3. affair, do (*Inf.*), gathering, reception, social occasion

functional practical, serviceable, useful, utilitarian, utility, working

fund *n.* 1. capital, endowment, foundation, kitty, pool, reserve, stock, store, supply 2. hoard, mine, repository, reserve, reservoir, source, storehouse, treasury, vein ~*v.* 3. capitalize, endow, finance, float, pay for, promote, stake, subsidize, support

fundamental *adj.* basic, cardinal, central, crucial, elementary, essential, first, important, indispensable, integral, intrinsic, key, necessary, prime, principal, underlying, vital

fundamentally at heart, basically, essentially, intrinsically, primarily

funds capital, cash, finance, hard cash, money, ready money, resources, savings

DICTIONARY

fur *n.* soft hair of a mammal; animal skin with the fur left on; garment made of this; whitish coating on the tongue or inside a kettle. —*v.* cover or become covered with fur. —**furry** *adj.* —**furrier** *n.* dealer in furs.

furbish *v.* smarten up.

furious *adj.* very angry; violent or unrestrained. —**furiously** *adv.*

furl *v.* roll up and fasten (a sail, umbrella, or flag).

furlong *n.* eighth of a mile.

furlough [fur-loh] *n.* leave of absence from military duty.

furnace *n.* enclosed chamber containing a very hot fire.

furnish *v.* fit up (a house or room) with furniture; (foll. by *with*) supply, provide. —**furnishings** *pl. n.* furniture, carpets, and fittings. —**furniture** *n.* large movable articles such as chairs and wardrobes.

furore [fyew-**ror**-ee] *n.* very excited or angry reaction.

furrow *n.* trench made by a plough; groove. —*v.* make or become wrinkled; make furrows in.

further *adv.* in addition; to a greater distance or extent. —*adj.* additional; more distant. —*v.* assist the progress of. —**further education** education beyond school other than at a university or polytechnic. —**furthest** *adv.* to the greatest distance or extent. —*adj.* most distant. —**furtherance** *n.* —**furthermore** *adv.* besides. —**furthermost** *adj.* most distant.

furtive *adj.* sly and secretive. —**furtively** *adv.*

fury *n., pl.* **-ries.** wild anger; uncontrolled violence.

furze *n.* gorse.

fuse[1] *n.* cord containing an explosive for detonating a bomb.

fuse[2] *v.* join or combine; melt with heat; unite by melting; (cause to) fail as a result of a blown fuse. —*n.* safety device for electric circuits, containing a wire that melts and breaks the connection when the circuit is overloaded. —**fusible** *adj.* —**fusion** *n.* melting; product of fusing; combination of two atoms with release of energy; popular music blending styles, esp. jazz and funk.

fuselage [fyew-zill-lahzh] *n.* body of an aircraft.

fusilier [fyew-zill-**leer**] *n.* soldier of certain regiments. —**fusillade** [fyew-zill-**lade**] *n.* continuous discharge of firearms; outburst of criticism, questions, etc.

fuss *n.* needless activity or worry; complaint or objection; great display of attention. —*v.* make a fuss. —**fussy** *adj.* inclined to fuss; overparticular; overelaborate. —**fussily** *adv.* —**fussiness** *n.*

THESAURUS

funeral burial, interment, obsequies

funnel *v.* channel, conduct, convey, direct, filter, move, pass, pour

funny 1. absurd, amusing, comic, comical, diverting, droll, entertaining, facetious, farcical, hilarious, humorous, jocular, jolly, laughable, ludicrous, rich, ridiculous, riotous, risible, silly, slapstick, waggish, witty 2. curious, dubious, mysterious, odd, peculiar, perplexing, puzzling, queer, remarkable, strange, suspicious, unusual, weird

furious angry, beside oneself, boiling, enraged, frantic, frenzied, fuming, incensed, infuriated, mad, maddened, raging, wrathful

furnish 1. appoint, decorate, equip, fit (out, up), outfit, provide, rig, stock, store, supply 2. afford, bestow, endow, give, grant, offer, present, provide, reveal, supply

furniture appointments, chattels, effects, equipment, fittings, furnishings, goods, household goods, movable property, possessions

furore commotion, disturbance, excitement, frenzy, fury, outburst, outcry, stir, uproar

furrow channel, crease, fluting, groove, hollow, line, rut, seam, trench, wrinkle

further 1. *adj.* additional, extra, fresh, more, new, other, supplementary 2. *adv.* additionally, also, as well as, besides, furthermore, in addition, moreover, on top of, what's more, yet 3. *v.* advance, aid, assist, champion, encourage, expedite, facilitate, forward, foster, hasten, help, patronize, promote, push, speed, succour, work for

furthermore additionally, as well, besides, in addition, moreover, to boot, too

furthest extreme, farthest, most distant, outermost, outmost, remotest, ultimate, uttermost

furtive clandestine, cloaked, covert, hidden, secret, secretive, skulking, slinking, sly, sneaking, sneaky, stealthy, surreptitious, underhand

fury 1. anger, frenzy, ire, madness, passion, rage, wrath 2. ferocity, force, intensity, power, savagery, severity, turbulence, vehemence, violence

fuss *n.* 1. ado, agitation, bother, bustle, commotion, confusion, excitement, fidget, flurry, fluster, flutter, hurry, stir, to-do, upset, worry 2. argument, bother, complaint, difficulty, display, furore, objection, row, squabble, trouble, unrest, upset ~*v.* 3. bustle, fidget, fret, fume

DICTIONARY

fusty *adj.* **-tier, -tiest.** stale-smelling; behind the times. **—fustiness** *n.*

futile [fyew-tile] *adj.* unsuccessful or useless. **—futility** *n.*

futon [foo-tonn] *n.* Japanese padded quilt, laid on the floor as a bed.

future *n.* time to come; what will happen; prospects. **—adj.** yet to come or be; of or relating to time to come; (of a verb tense) indicating that the action specified has not yet taken place. **—futuristic** *adj.* of a design appearing to belong to some future time.

fuzz[1] *n.* mass of fine or curly hairs or fibres. **—fuzzy** *adj.* of, like, or covered with fuzz; blurred or indistinct; (of hair) tightly curled. **—fuzzily** *adv.* **—fuzziness** *n.*

fuzz[2] *n. Slang* police(man).

THESAURUS

fussy choosy, difficult, exacting, faddy, fastidious, finicky, old-maidish, old womanish, overparticular, particular, pernickety, squeamish

futile abortive, barren, bootless, empty, forlorn, fruitless, hollow, ineffectual, nugatory, profitless, sterile, unavailing, unproductive, unprofitable, unsuccessful, useless, vain, valueless, worthless

future 1. *n.* expectation, hereafter, outlook, prospect, time to come 2. *adj.* approaching, coming, destined, eventual, expected, fated, forthcoming, impending, later, prospective, subsequent, to come, ultimate, unborn

G

g gram(s); (acceleration due to) gravity.

gab *n., v.* **gabbing, gabbed.** *Informal* talk or chatter. **—gift of the gab** eloquence. **—gabby** *adj. Informal* talkative.

gabardine, gaberdine *n.* strong twill cloth used esp. for raincoats.

gabble *v.* speak rapidly and indistinctly. *—n.* rapid indistinct speech.

gable *n.* triangular upper part of a wall between sloping roofs. **—gabled** *adj.*

gad *v.* **gadding, gadded. —gad about, around** go around in search of pleasure. **—gadabout** *n.* pleasure-seeker.

gadfly *n.* fly that bites cattle; constantly annoying person.

gadget *n.* small mechanical device or appliance. **—gadgetry** *n.* gadgets.

Gael [gayl] *n.* Gaelic-speaker. **—Gaelic** [gah-lik] *n.* Celtic language of Ireland and the Scottish Highlands. *—adj.* of the Gaels or their language.

gaff[1] *n.* stick with an iron hook for landing large fish. *—v.* hook or land (a fish) with a gaff.

gaff[2] *n.* **—blow the gaff** *Slang* divulge a secret.

gaffe *n.* social blunder.

gaffer *n.* old man; *Informal* foreman or boss.

gag[1] *v.* **gagging, gagged.** stop up the mouth of (a person) with cloth etc.; deprive of free speech; retch; choke. *—n.* cloth etc. put into or tied across the mouth.

gag[2] *n. Informal* joke.

gaga [gah-gah] *adj. Slang* senile; *Slang* crazy.

gage *n.* thing given as security; formerly, something thrown down as a challenge to combat.

gaggle *n.* flock of geese; *Informal* disorderly crowd.

gaiety *n.* cheerfulness; merrymaking. **—gaily** *adv.* merrily; colourfully.

gain *v.* acquire or obtain; win in competition; increase or improve; reach; (of a watch or clock) be or become too fast. *—n.* profit; increase or improvement. **—gainful** *adj.* useful or profitable. **—gainfully** *adv.* **—gain on, upon** *v.* get nearer to or catch up with.

gainsay *v.* **-saying, -said.** deny or contradict.

gait *n.* manner of walking.

gaiter *n.* cloth or leather covering for the lower leg.

gala [gah-la] *n.* festival; competitive sporting event.

galaxy *n., pl.* **-axies.** system of stars; gathering of famous people. **—galactic** *adj.*

gale *n.* strong wind; *Informal* loud outburst.

gall[1] [gawl] *n. Informal* impudence; bitter feeling. **—gall bladder** sac attached to the liver, storing bile. **—gallstone** *n.* hard growth in the gall bladder or its ducts.

gall[2] [gawl] *n.* sore caused by chafing. *—v.* make sore by rubbing; annoy.

gall[3] [gawl] *n.* abnormal outgrowth on a tree or plant.

gallant *adj.* brave and noble; (of a man) attentive to women. **—gallantly** *adv.* **—gallantry** *n.*

THESAURUS

gadget appliance, contrivance, device, gimmick, invention, novelty, tool

gaffe blunder, faux pas, gaucherie, howler, indiscretion, mistake, slip, solecism

gag curb, muffle, muzzle, quiet, silence, stifle, still, stop up, suppress, throttle

gaiety blitheness, cheerfulness, elation, glee, good humour, high spirits, hilarity, *joie de vivre*, jollity, joviality, joyousness, liveliness, merriment, mirth, vivacity

gaily blithely, cheerfully, gleefully, happily, joyfully, light-heartedly, merrily

gain *v.* 1. achieve, acquire, advance, attain, build up, capture, collect, enlist, gather, get, glean, harvest, improve, increase, net, obtain, pick up, procure, profit, realize, reap, secure, win, win over 2. acquire, bring in, clear, earn, get, make, net, obtain, produce, realize, win, yield ~*n.* 3. acquisition, advance, advantage, attainment, benefit, dividend, earnings, emolument, growth, headway, improvement, income, increase, increment, lucre, proceeds, produce, profit, return, rise, winnings, yield

gainsay contradict, controvert, deny, disaffirm, dispute

gait bearing, carriage, pace, step, stride, tread, walk

gala carnival, celebration, festival, festivity, fête, jamboree, pageant, party

gale blast, hurricane, squall, storm, tempest, tornado, typhoon

gallant *adj.* 1. bold, brave, courageous, daring, dashing, dauntless, doughty, fearless, heroic, honourable, intrepid, lion-hearted, manful, manly, noble, plucky, valiant, valorous 2. attentive, chivalrous, courteous, courtly, gentlemanly, gracious, magnanimous, noble, polite

gallantry audacity, boldness, bravery, courage, daring, fearlessness, heroism, intrepidity,

DICTIONARY

galleon n. large three-masted sailing ship of the 15th–17th centuries.

gallery n., pl. **-ries.** room or building for displaying works of art; balcony in a church, theatre, etc.; long narrow room for a specific purpose, e.g. *shooting gallery;* passage in a mine.

galley n. kitchen of a ship or aircraft; *Hist.* ship propelled by oars, usu. rowed by slaves. **—galley proof** printer's proof in long slip form. **—galley slave** slave forced to row in a galley; *Informal* drudge.

Gallic adj. French; of ancient Gaul. **—Gallicism** n. French word or idiom.

gallium n. soft grey metallic element used in semiconductors.

gallivant v. go about in search of pleasure.

gallon n. liquid measure of eight pints, equal to 4.55 litres.

gallop n. horse's fastest pace; galloping. **—v. galloping, galloped.** go or ride at a gallop; move or progress rapidly.

gallows n. wooden structure used for hanging criminals.

Gallup poll n. public opinion poll carried out by questioning a cross section of the population.

galore det. in plenty, e.g. *presents galore.*

galoshes pl. n. waterproof overshoes.

galumph v. *Informal* leap or move about clumsily.

galvanic adj. of or producing an electric current generated by chemical means; *Informal* stimulating or startling. **—galvanize** v. stimulate into action; coat (metal) with zinc.

gambit n. opening line or move intended to secure an advantage; *Chess* opening move involving the sacrifice of a pawn.

gamble v. play games of chance to win money; act on the expectation of something. **—n.** risky undertaking; bet or wager. **—gambler** n. **—gambling** n.

gamboge [gam-**boje**] n. gum resin used as a yellow pigment and purgative.

gambol v. **-bolling, -bolled.** jump about playfully, frolic. **—n.** frolic.

game[1] n. amusement or pastime; contest for amusement; single period of play in a contest; scheme or trick; animals or birds hunted for sport or food; their flesh. **—v.** gamble. **—adj.** brave; willing. **—gamely** adv. **—gaming** n. gambling. **—gamekeeper** n. person employed to breed game and prevent poaching. **—gamesmanship** n. art of winning by cunning practices without actually cheating.

game[2] adj. lame, crippled.

gamete [gam-eet] n. *Biol.* reproductive cell.

gamine [gam-een] n. slim boyish young woman.

gamma n. third letter of the Greek alphabet. **—gamma rays** electromagnetic rays of shorter wavelength and higher energy than x-rays.

gammon n. cured or smoked ham.

gammy adj. **-mier, -miest.** same as GAME[2].

gamut n. whole range or scale (of music etc.).

gander n. male goose; *Informal* quick look.

gang n. (criminal) group; organized group of workmen. **—gangland** n. criminal underworld. **—gang up** v. form an alliance (against).

gangling adj. lanky and awkward.

ganglion n. group of nerve cells; small harmless tumour.

gangplank n. portable bridge for boarding or leaving a ship.

gangrene n. decay of body tissue as a result of disease or injury. **—gangrenous** adj.

gangster n. member of a criminal gang.

gangway n. passage between rows of seats; gangplank.

THESAURUS

manliness, mettle, nerve, pluck, prowess, spirit, valiance, valour

gallop bolt, career, dart, dash, fly, hasten, hurry, race, run, rush, shoot, speed, sprint

galvanize arouse, awaken, electrify, excite, fire, inspire, invigorate, jolt, move, provoke, quicken, shock, spur, startle, stimulate, stir, thrill

gamble v. 1. back, bet, game, play, punt, stake, wager 2. back, chance, hazard, risk, speculate, stake, venture ~n. 3. chance, lottery, risk, speculation, uncertainty, venture 4. bet, punt, wager

gambol caper, cavort, frisk, frolic, hop, jump, prance, rollick, skip

game n. 1. amusement, distraction, diversion, entertainment, frolic, fun, jest, joke, lark, merriment, pastime, play, recreation, romp, sport 2. contest, event, match, meeting, round 3. chase, prey, quarry, wild animals ~adj. 4. bold, brave, courageous, dogged, fearless, gallant, heroic, intrepid, persistent, plucky, resolute, spirited, valiant, valorous

gamut compass, field, range, scale, scope, series, sweep

gang band, circle, clique, club, company, coterie, crowd, group, herd, horde, lot, mob, pack, party, ring, set, shift, squad, team, troupe

gangster bandit, brigand, desperado, hoodlum, racketeer, robber, ruffian, thug, tough

DICTIONARY

gannet n. large sea bird; *Slang* greedy person.

gantry n., pl. **-tries.** structure supporting something such as a crane or rocket.

gaol [jayl] n. same as JAIL.

gap n. break or opening; interruption or interval; divergence or difference. —**gappy** adj.

gape v. stare in wonder; open the mouth wide; be or become wide open. —**gaping** adj.

garage n. building used to house cars; place for the refuelling and repair of cars. —v. put or keep a car in a garage.

garb n. clothes. —v. clothe.

garbage n. rubbish.

garble v. jumble or distort (a story etc.).

garden n. piece of land for growing flowers, fruit, or vegetables. —pl. ornamental park. —v. cultivate a garden. —**gardener** n. —**gardening** n. —**garden centre** place selling plants and gardening equipment.

gardenia [gar-**deen**-ya] n. large fragrant white waxy flower; shrub bearing this.

gargantuan adj. huge.

gargle v. wash the throat with (a liquid) by breathing out slowly through the liquid. —n. act or sound of gargling; liquid used for gargling.

gargoyle n. waterspout carved in the form of a grotesque face, esp. on a church.

garish adj. crudely bright or colourful. —**garishly** adv. —**garishness** n.

garland n. wreath of flowers worn or hung as a decoration. —v. decorate with garlands.

garlic n. pungent bulb of a plant of the onion family, used in cooking.

garment n. article of clothing. —pl. clothes.

garner v. collect or store.

garnet n. red semiprecious stone.

garnish v. decorate (food). —n. decoration for food.

garret n. attic in a house.

garrison n. troops stationed in a town or fort; fortified place. —v. station troops in.

garrotte n. Spanish method of execution by strangling; cord or wire used for this. —v. kill by this method.

garrulous adj. talkative. —**garrulously** adv. —**garrulity** n.

garter n. band worn round the leg to hold up a sock or stocking.

gas n., pl. **gas(s)es.** airlike substance that is not liquid or solid; fossil fuel in the form of a gas, used for heating; gaseous anaesthetic; *US* petrol; *Informal* idle talk, boasting. —v. **gassing, gassed.** poison or render unconscious with gas; *Informal* talk idly or boastfully. —**gassy** adj. filled with gas. —**gaseous** adj. of or like gas. —**gasbag** n. *Informal* person who talks too much. —**gas chamber** airtight room which is filled with poison gas to kill people or animals. —**gasholder, gasometer** [gas-**som**-it-er] n. large tank for storing gas. —**gas mask** mask with a chemical filter to protect the wearer against poison gas.

gash v. make a long deep cut in. —n. long deep cut.

gasket n. piece of rubber etc. placed between two metal surfaces to act as a seal.

gasoline n. *US* petrol.

THESAURUS

gap blank, breach, break, chink, cleft, crack, cranny, crevice, divide, hiatus, hole, intermission, interruption, interstice, interval, lacuna, lull, opening, pause, recess, rent, rift, space, void

gape 1. gawk, goggle, stare, wonder 2. crack, open, split, yawn

gaping broad, cavernous, great, open, vast, wide, wide open, yawning

garbage debris, detritus, junk, litter, rubbish, scraps

garble 1. confuse, jumble, mix up 2. distort, doctor, falsify, misquote, misreport, misrepresent, mistranslate, mutilate, pervert, slant, tamper with, twist

garish brassy, cheap, flashy, gaudy, glaring, glittering, loud, raffish, showy, tasteless, vulgar

garland bays, chaplet, crown, festoon, honours, laurels, wreath

garments apparel, array, attire, clothes, clothing, costume, dress, garb, habit, outfit, robes, togs, uniform, vestments, wear

garner accumulate, amass, assemble, collect, deposit, gather, hoard, up, put by, reserve, save, stockpile, store, treasure

garnish adorn, beautify, bedeck, deck, decorate, embellish, enhance, grace, ornament, set off, trim

garrison 1. armed force, command, detachment, troops, unit 2. base, camp, encampment, fort, fortification, fortress, post, station, stronghold

garrulous babbling, chattering, chatty, effusive, glib, gossiping, gushing, loquacious, prattling, talkative, verbose, voluble

gash 1. v. cleave, cut, incise, lacerate, rend, slash, slit, split, tear, wound 2. n. cleft, cut, incision, laceration, rent, slash, slit, split, tear, wound

DICTIONARY

gasp *v.* draw in breath sharply or with difficulty; utter breathlessly. —*n.* convulsive intake of breath.

gastric *adj.* of the stomach. —**gastritis** *n.* inflammation of the stomach.

gastroenteritis *n.* inflammation of the stomach and intestines.

gastronomy *n.* art of good eating. —**gastronomic** *adj.*

gastropod *n.* mollusc, such as a snail, with a single flattened muscular foot.

gate *n.* movable barrier, usu. hinged, in a wall or fence; opening with a gate; any entrance or way in; (entrance money paid by) those attending a sporting event. —**gate-crash** *v.* enter (a party) uninvited. —**gatehouse** *n.* building at or above a gateway. —**gateway** *n.* entrance with a gate; means of access, e.g. *Bombay, gateway to India.*

gâteau [gat-toe] *n., pl.* **-teaux** [-toes]. rich elaborate cake.

gather *v.* assemble; collect gradually; increase gradually; learn from information given; pick or harvest; draw (material) into small tucks or folds. —**gathers** *pl. n.* gathered folds in material. —**gathering** *n.* assembly.

gauche [gohsh] *adj.* socially awkward. —**gaucheness** *n.* —**gaucherie** *n.* awkwardness; gauche act.

gaucho [gow-choh] *n., pl.* **-chos.** S American cowboy.

gaudy *adj.* **gaudier, gaudiest.** vulgarly bright or colourful. —**gaudily** *adv.* —**gaudiness** *n.*

gauge [gayj] *v.* measure the amount or condition of; estimate or judge. —*n.* scale or standard of measurement; measuring instrument; distance between the rails of a railway track.

gaunt *adj.* lean and haggard; (of a place) desolate or bleak. —**gauntness** *n.*

gauntlet[1] *n.* heavy glove with a long cuff. —**throw down the gauntlet** offer a challenge.

gauntlet[2] *n.* —**run the gauntlet** be forced to run between, and be struck by, two rows of men, as a former military punishment; be exposed to criticism or unpleasant treatment.

gauze *n.* transparent loosely-woven fabric; fine wire mesh. —**gauzy** *adj.*

gave *v.* past tense of GIVE.

gavel [gahv-el] *n.* small hammer banged on a table by a judge, auctioneer, or chairman to call for attention.

gavotte *n.* old formal dance; music for this.

gawk *v. Slang* stare stupidly. —**gawky** *adj.* clumsy or awkward. —**gawkiness** *n.*

gawp *v. Slang* stare stupidly.

gay *adj.* homosexual; carefree and merry; colourful. —*n.* homosexual. —**gayness** *n.* homosexuality.

gaze *v.* look fixedly. —*n.* fixed look.

gazebo [gaz-zee-boh] *n., pl.* **-bos, -boes.** summerhouse with a good view.

THESAURUS

gasp 1. *v.* blow, choke, gulp, pant, puff 2. *n.* blow, ejaculation, exclamation, gulp, pant, puff

gate access, barrier, door, doorway, egress, entrance, exit, passage, portal

gather 1. accumulate, amass, assemble, collect, congregate, convene, flock, garner, group, heap, hoard, marshal, mass, muster, pile up, round up, stack up, stockpile 2. assume, conclude, deduce, draw, hear, infer, learn, make, surmise, understand 3. crop, cull, garner, glean, harvest, pick, pluck, reap, select

gathering assemblage, company, conclave, concourse, congregation, congress, convention, convocation, crowd, flock, group, knot, meeting, muster, party, rally, throng, turnout

gauche awkward, clumsy, graceless, ignorant, ill-bred, ill-mannered, inelegant, inept, insensitive, maladroit, tactless, uncultured, unpolished, unsophisticated

gaudy bright, brilliant, flashy, florid, garish, gay, glaring, loud, ostentatious, raffish, showy, tasteless, tawdry, vulgar

gauge *v.* 1. ascertain, calculate, check, compute, count, determine, measure, weigh 2. adjudge, appraise, assess, estimate, evaluate, guess, judge, rate, reckon, value ~*n.* 3. basis, example, guide, indicator, measure, meter, model, pattern, rule, sample, standard, test, yardstick 4. bore, capacity, degree, depth, extent, height, magnitude, measure, scope, size, span, thickness, width

gaunt angular, attenuated, bony, cadaverous, emaciated, haggard, lank, lean, meagre, pinched, rawboned, scraggy, scrawny, skinny, spare, thin, wasted

gawky awkward, clownish, clumsy, gauche, loutish, lumbering, lumpish, maladroit, oafish, uncouth, ungainly

gay 1. animated, blithe, carefree, cheerful, debonair, glad, gleeful, happy, hilarious, jolly, jovial, joyful, joyous, lively, merry, sparkling, sunny, vivacious 2. bright, brilliant, colourful, flamboyant, flashy, fresh, garish, gaudy, rich, showy, vivid

gaze 1. *v.* contemplate, gape, look, regard, stare, view, watch, wonder 2. *n.* fixed look, look, stare

DICTIONARY

gazelle *n.* small graceful antelope.

gazette *n.* official publication containing announcements. —**gazetteer** *n.* (part of) a book that lists and describes places.

gazump *v.* raise the price of a house after verbally agreeing it with (a prospective buyer).

GB Great Britain.

GBH grievous bodily harm.

GCE General Certificate of Education.

GCSE General Certificate of Secondary Education.

gear *n.* set of toothed wheels connecting with another or with a rack to change the direction or speed of transmitted motion; mechanism for transmitting motion by gears; setting of a gear to suit engine speed, e.g. *first gear;* clothing or belongings; equipment. —*v.* adapt (one thing) to fit in with another. —**in** *or* **out of gear** with the gear mechanism engaged or disengaged. —**gearbox** *n.* case enclosing a set of gears in a motor vehicle. —**gear up** *v.* prepare for an activity.

gecko *n., pl.* **geckos, geckoes.** small tropical lizard.

geese *n.* plural of GOOSE.

geezer *n. Informal* (old or eccentric) man.

Geiger counter [**guy**-ger] *n.* instrument for detecting and measuring radiation.

geisha [**gay**-sha] *n., pl.* **-sha, -shas.** in Japan, professional female companion for men.

gel [**jell**] *n.* jelly-like substance. —*v.* **gelling, gelled.** form a gel; *Informal* take on a definite form.

gelatine [**jel**-at-een], **gelatin** *n.* substance made by boiling animal bones; edible jelly made of this. —**gelatinous** [jel-**at**-in-uss] *adj.* of or like jelly.

geld *v.* castrate. —**gelding** *n.* castrated horse.

gelid [**jel**-lid] *adj.* very cold.

gelignite *n.* type of dynamite used for blasting.

gem *n.* precious stone or jewel; highly valued person or thing.

gen *n. Informal* information. —**gen up on** *v.* **genning, genned.** *Informal* make or become fully informed about.

gendarme [**zhahn**-darm] *n.* member of the French police force.

gender *n.* state of being male or female, sex; *Grammar* classification of nouns in certain languages as masculine, feminine, or neuter.

gene [**jean**] *n.* part of a cell which determines inherited characteristics.

genealogy [jean-ee-**al**-a-gee] *n., pl.* **-gies.** (study of) the history and descent of a family or families. —**genealogical** *adj.* —**genealogist** *n.*

genera [**jen**-er-a] plural of GENUS.

general *adj.* common or widespread; of or affecting all or most; not specific; including or dealing with various or miscellaneous items; highest in authority or rank, e.g. *general manager;* true in most cases. —*n.* very senior army officer. —**generally** *adv.* —**generality** *n.* general principle; state of being general. —**generalize** *v.* draw general conclusions; speak in generalities; make widely known or used. —**generalization** *n.* —**general election** election in which representatives are chosen for every constituency. —**general practitioner** nonspecialist doctor serving a local area.

generate *v.* produce or bring into being. —**generative** *adj.* capable of producing. —**generator** *n.* machine for converting mechanical energy into electrical energy.

generation *n.* generating; all the people born about the same time; average time between two generations (about 30 years).

generic [jin-**ner**-ik] *adj.* of a class, group, or genus. —**generically** *adv.*

THESAURUS

gazette journal, newspaper, news-sheet, organ, paper, periodical

gear 1. cog, cogwheel, toothed wheel 2. accessories, accoutrements, apparatus, equipment, harness, instruments, outfit, rigging, supplies, tackle, tools, trappings 3. baggage, belongings, effects, kit, luggage, stuff, things

gelatinous gluey, glutinous, gummy, jelly-like, mucilaginous, sticky, viscid, viscous

gelid arctic, chilly, cold, freezing, frigid, frosty, frozen, glacial, ice-cold, icy, polar

gem 1. jewel, precious stone, stone 2. flower, jewel, masterpiece, pearl, pick, prize, treasure

general 1. accepted, broad, common, extensive, popular, prevailing, prevalent, public, univer-

sal, widespread 2. accustomed, conventional, customary, everyday, habitual, normal, ordinary, regular, typical, usual 3. approximate, ill-defined, imprecise, inaccurate, indefinite, inexact, loose, undetailed, unspecific, vague

generally 1. almost always, as a rule, by and large, conventionally, customarily, habitually, mainly, normally, ordinarily, regularly, typically, usually 2. commonly, extensively, popularly, publicly, universally, widely

generate beget, breed, cause, create, engender, form, initiate, make, originate, procreate, produce, propagate, spawn, whip up

generation begetting, breeding, creation, for-

DICTIONARY

generous *adj.* free in giving; free from pettiness; plentiful. —**generously** *adv.* —**generosity** *n.*

genesis [jen-iss-iss] *n., pl.* -**eses** [-iss-eez]. beginning or origin.

genetic [jin-**net**-tik] *adj.* of genes or genetics. —**genetics** *n.* study of heredity and variation in organisms. —**geneticist** *n.* —**genetic engineering** alteration of the genetic structure of an organism for a particular purpose. —**genetic fingerprinting** use of a person's unique DNA pattern for identification.

genial [**jean**-ee-al] *adj.* cheerful and friendly. —**genially** *adv.* —**geniality** *n.*

genie [**jean**-ee] *n.* in fairy tales, a servant who appears by magic and grants wishes.

genital *adj.* of the sexual organs or reproduction. —**genitals, genitalia** [jen-it-**ail**-ya] *pl. n.* external sexual organs.

genitive *adj., n.* (of) the grammatical case indicating possession or association.

genius [**jean**-yuss] *n.* (person with) exceptional ability in a particular field.

genocide [**jen**-no-side] *n.* murder of a race of people.

genre [**zhahn**-ra] *n.* style of literary, musical, or artistic work.

gent *Informal* —*n.* gentleman. —*pl.* men's public toilet.

genteel *adj.* affectedly proper and polite. —**genteelly** *adv.*

gentian [**jen**-shun] *n.* mountain plant with deep blue flowers.

gentile *adj., n.* non-Jewish (person).

gentle *adj.* mild or kindly; not rough or severe; gradual; easily controlled, tame; noble or well-born. —**gentleness** *n.* —**gently** *adv.* —**gentleman** *n.* polite well-bred man; man of high social position; polite name for a man. —**gentlemanly** *adj.* —**gentlewoman** *n.*

gentry *n.* people just below the nobility in social rank. —**gentrification** *n.* taking-over of a traditionally working-class area by middle-class incomers. —**gentrify** *v.*

genuflect *v.* bend the knee as a sign of reverence or deference. —**genuflection, genuflexion** *n.*

genuine *adj.* not fake, authentic; sincere. —**genuinely** *adv.* —**genuineness** *n.*

genus [**jean**-uss] *n., pl.* **genera.** group into which a family of animals or plants is divided; kind, type.

geocentric *adj.* having the earth as a centre; measured as from the earth's centre.

geode *n.* cavity lined with crystals within a rock.

geography *n.* study of the earth's physical features, climate, population, etc. —**geographer** *n.* —**geographic(al)** *adj.* —**geographically** *adv.*

geology *n.* study of the earth's origin, structure, and composition. —**geological** *adj.* —**geologically** *adv.* —**geologist** *n.*

geometry *n.* branch of mathematics dealing with points, lines, curves, and surfaces. —**geometric(al)** *adj.* —**geometrically** *adv.* —**geometrician** *n.*

geopolitics *n.* study of the effect of the geographical position of a country on its politics; global politics. —**geopolitical** *adj.*

THESAURUS

mation, genesis, procreation, production, propagation, reproduction

generosity benevolence, bounty, charity, kindness, liberality, munificence, open-handedness

generous 1. benevolent, bounteous, bountiful, charitable, free, hospitable, kind, lavish, liberal, munificent, open-handed, princely, ungrudging, unstinting 2. big-hearted, disinterested, good, high-minded, lofty, magnanimous, noble, unselfish

genial affable, agreeable, amiable, cheerful, cheery, convivial, cordial, easygoing, enlivening, friendly, happy, hearty, jolly, jovial, joyous, kind, kindly, merry, pleasant, sunny, warm

genius 1. adept, expert, maestro, master, virtuoso 2. ability, aptitude, bent, brilliance, capacity, endowment, faculty, flair, gift, inclination, knack, talent, turn

genteel aristocratic, civil, courteous, courtly, cultured, elegant, fashionable, formal, gentlemanly, ladylike, mannerly, polished, polite, refined, respectable, stylish, urbane, well-mannered

gentle 1. amiable, benign, bland, humane, kind, kindly, lenient, meek, merciful, mild, peaceful, placid, quiet, soft, tender 2. balmy, calm, clement, easy, light, low, mild, moderate, muted, placid, quiet, serene, slight, smooth, soft, soothing, temperate, tranquil, untroubled

gentlemanly civil, courteous, cultivated, gallant, genteel, honourable, mannerly, noble, obliging, polished, polite, refined, well-bred, well-mannered

genuine actual, authentic, honest, legitimate, natural, original, pure, real, sound, sterling, true, veritable

DICTIONARY

Geordie *n.* person from, or dialect of, Tyneside.

georgette [jor-**jet**] *n.* fine silky fabric.

Georgian *adj.* of the time of any of the kings of England called George, esp. 1714–1830; of or from Georgia.

geostationary *adj.* (of a satellite) orbiting so as to remain over the same point of the earth's surface.

geothermal *adj.* of or using the heat in the earth's interior.

geranium *n.* cultivated plant with red, pink, or white flowers.

gerbil [**jer**-bill] *n.* burrowing desert rodent of Asia and Africa.

geriatrics *n.* branch of medicine dealing with old age and its diseases. —**geriatric** *adj., n.* old (person).

germ *n.* microbe, esp. one causing disease; beginning from which something may develop; simple structure that can develop into a complete organism. —**germicide** *n.* substance that kills germs. —**germicidal** *adj.*

german *adj.* having the same parents, e.g. *brother-german;* being a first cousin, e.g. *cousin-german.*

German *n.* language of Germany, Austria, and part of Switzerland; person from Germany. —*adj.* of Germany or its language. —**German measles** contagious disease accompanied by a cough, sore throat, and red spots. —**German shepherd** (**dog**) Alsatian.

germane *adj.* —**germane to** relevant to.

germinate *v.* (cause to) sprout or begin to grow. —**germination** *n.* —**germinal** *adj.* of or in the earliest stage of development.

gerrymander *v.* manipulate political boundaries so as to favour one party.

gerund [**jer**-rund] *n.* noun formed from a verb, such as *living.*

Gestapo *n.* secret state police of Nazi Germany.

gestation *n.* (period of) carrying of young in the womb between conception and birth; developing of a plan or idea in the mind.

gesticulate *v.* make expressive movements of the hands and arms. —**gesticulation** *n.*

gesture *n.* movement to convey meaning; thing said or done to show one's feelings. —*v.* gesticulate.

get *v.* **getting, got.** obtain or receive; bring or fetch; contract (an illness); capture or seize; (cause to) become as specified, e.g. *get wet;* prepare (a meal); understand; go on board (a plane, bus, etc.); persuade; receive a broadcast signal; *Informal* annoy; *Informal* have the better of; be revenged on. —**get across** *v.* (cause to) be understood. —**get at** *v.* gain access to; criticize; influence. —**getaway** *adj., n.* (used in) escape. —**get by** *v.* manage in spite of difficulties. —**get off** *v.* (cause to) avoid the consequences of, or punishment for, an action. —**get off with** *v. Informal* start a romantic or sexual relationship with. —**get over** *v.* recover from. —**get through** *v.* (cause to) succeed; contact by telephone; use up (money or supplies). —**get through to** *v.* make (a person) understand. —**get to** *v.* come to or arrive at; —**get-up** *n. Informal* costume. —**get up to** *v.* be involved in.

geyser [**geez**-er] *n.* spring that discharges steam and hot water; domestic gas water heater.

ghastly *adj.* **-lier, -liest.** *Informal* unpleasant; deathly pale; *Informal* unwell; *Informal* horrible. —**ghastliness** *n.*

ghat *n.* (in India) steps leading down to a river; mountain pass.

ghee [**gee**] *n.* (in Indian cookery) clarified butter.

gherkin *n.* small pickled cucumber.

ghetto *n., pl.* **-tos, -toes.** slum area inhabited by

THESAURUS

germ 1. microbe, microorganism, virus 2. beginning, bud, cause, embryo, origin, root, rudiment, seed, source, spark

germinate bud, develop, grow, originate, shoot, sprout, swell

gesticulate gesture, indicate, motion, sign, signal, wave

gesture 1. *n.* action, indication, motion, sign, signal 2. *v.* indicate, motion, sign, signal, wave

get 1. achieve, acquire, attain, bring, come by, earn, fetch, gain, glean, inherit, make, net, obtain, pick up, procure, realize, reap, receive, secure, succeed to, win 2. arrest, capture, grab, lay hold of, seize, take, trap 3. become, come

to be, grow, turn, wax 4. coax, convince, induce, influence, persuade, sway, wheedle, win over

get across communicate, convey, impart, put over, transmit

get at 1. acquire, attain, reach 2. annoy, attack, blame, carp, criticize, nag, pick on, taunt

get over come round, mend, recover, revive, survive

ghastly ashen, deathlike, dreadful, frightful, grim, grisly, gruesome, hideous, horrible, livid, loathsome, pale, pallid, repellent, shocking, spectral, terrible, terrifying, wan

DICTIONARY

a deprived minority. —**ghetto-blaster** *n. Informal* large portable cassette-recorder.

ghillie *n.* same as GILLIE.

ghost *n.* disembodied spirit of a dead person; faint trace. —*v.* ghostwrite. —**ghostly** *adj.* —**ghost town** deserted town. —**ghostwrite** *v.* write (a book or article) on behalf of another person who is credited as the author. —**ghostwriter** *n.*

ghoul [**gool**] *n.* person with morbid interests; demon that eats corpses. —**ghoulish** *adj.*

GI *n. Informal* US soldier.

giant *n.* mythical being of superhuman size; very large person or thing. —*adj.* huge. —**giantess** *n. fem.*

gibber [**jib**-ber] *v.* speak or utter rapidly and unintelligibly. —**gibberish** *n.* rapid unintelligible talk.

gibbet [**jib**-bit] *n.* gallows.

gibbon [**gib**-bon] *n.* agile tree-dwelling ape of S Asia.

gibbous *adj.* (of the moon) more than half but less than fully illuminated.

gibe [**jibe**] *v.*, *n.* taunt or jeer.

giblets [**jib**-lets] *pl. n.* gizzard, liver, heart, and neck of a fowl.

giddy *adj.* **-dier, -diest.** having or causing a feeling of dizziness; scatter-brained. —**giddily** *adv.* —**giddiness** *n.*

gift *n.* present; natural talent. —*v.* present with. —**gifted** *adj.* talented.

gig[1] *n.* single performance by pop or jazz musicians. —*v.* **gigging, gigged.** play a gig or gigs.

gig[2] *n.* light two-wheeled horse-drawn carriage.

gigantic *adj.* enormous.

giggle *v.* laugh nervously or foolishly. —*n.* such a laugh. —**giggly** *adj.*

gigolo [**jig**-a-lo] *n., pl.* **-los.** man paid by an older woman to be her escort or lover.

gigot *n.* leg of lamb or mutton.

gild *v.* **gilding, gilded** *or* **gilt.** put a thin layer of gold on; make falsely attractive. —**gilt** *adj.* gilded. —*n.* thin layer of gold used as decoration. —**gilt-edged** *adj.* denoting government stocks on which interest payments and final repayment are guaranteed.

gill[1] [**gill**] *n.* (*usu. pl.*) breathing organ in most aquatic animals; radiating structure beneath the cap of a mushroom.

gill[2] [**jill**] *n.* liquid measure of quarter of a pint, equal to 0.142 litres.

gillie *n.* (in Scotland) attendant for hunting or fishing.

gimbals *pl. n.* set of pivoted rings which allow nautical instruments to remain horizontal at sea.

gimcrack [**jim**-krak] *adj.* showy but cheap; shoddy.

gimlet [**gim**-let] *n.* small tool with a screwlike tip for boring holes in wood. —**gimlet-eyed** *adj.* having a piercing glance.

gimmick *n.* something designed to attract attention or publicity. —**gimmickry** *n.* —**gimmicky** *adj.*

gin[1] *n.* alcoholic drink flavoured with juniper berries.

gin[2] *n.* machine for separating seeds from raw cotton; wire noose used to trap small animals.

ginger *n.* root of a tropical plant, used as a spice; light orange-brown colour. —**gingery** *adj.* —**ginger ale, beer** fizzy ginger-flavoured soft

---

THESAURUS

ghost apparition, phantom, revenant, soul, spectre, spirit, wraith

ghostly eerie, illusory, insubstantial, phantom, spectral, supernatural, uncanny, unearthly, weird

giant 1. *n.* colossus, leviathan, monster, titan 2. *adj.* colossal, elephantine, enormous, gargantuan, gigantic, huge, immense, jumbo (*Inf.*), large, mammoth, monstrous, prodigious, vast

gibberish babble, balderdash, blather, double talk, drivel, gabble, jabber, jargon, nonsense, prattle, twaddle

gibe 1. *v.* deride, flout, jeer, mock, ridicule, scoff, scorn, sneer, taunt, twit 2. *n.* derision, dig, jeer, mockery, ridicule, sarcasm, scoffing, sneer, taunt

giddiness dizziness, faintness, vertigo

giddy dizzy, faint, light-headed, reeling, unsteady, vertiginous

gift 1. benefaction, bequest, bounty, contribution, donation, grant, gratuity, largess, legacy, offering, present 2. ability, aptitude, attribute, bent, capability, capacity, faculty, flair, genius, knack, power, talent

gifted able, accomplished, adroit, brilliant, capable, clever, expert, ingenious, intelligent, masterly, skilled, talented

gigantic colossal, elephantine, enormous, giant, huge, immense, mammoth, monstrous, prodigious, stupendous, tremendous, vast

giggle *v./n.* chortle, chuckle, laugh, snigger, titter

gild adorn, beautify, bedeck, brighten, coat, deck, dress up, embellish, embroider, enhance, enrich, garnish, grace

gimmick contrivance, device, dodge, gadget, gambit, ploy, scheme, stratagem, stunt, trick

DICTIONARY

drink. —**gingerbread** *n.* moist cake flavoured with ginger. —**ginger group** group within a larger group that agitates for a more active policy. —**ginger nut, snap** crisp ginger-flavoured biscuit.

gingerly *adv.* cautiously. —*adj.* cautious.

gingham *n.* cotton cloth, usu. checked or striped.

gingivitis [jin-jiv-**vite**-iss] *n.* inflammation of the gums.

ginkgo [**gink**-go] *n., pl.* **-goes.** ornamental Chinese tree.

ginseng [**jin**-seng] *n.* (root of) a plant believed to have tonic and energy-giving properties.

Gipsy *n., pl.* **-sies.** same as GYPSY.

giraffe *n.* African ruminant mammal with a spotted yellow skin and long neck and legs.

gird *v.* **girding, girded** *or* **girt.** put a belt round; secure with or as if with a belt; surround. —**gird (up) one's loins** prepare for action.

girder *n.* large metal beam.

girdle¹ *n.* woman's elastic corset; belt; *Anat.* encircling structure or part. —*v.* surround or encircle.

girdle² *n. Scot.* griddle.

girl *n.* female child; young woman; girlfriend; *Informal* any woman. —**girlhood** *n.* —**girlish** *adj.* —**girlie** *adj. Informal* featuring photographs of naked or scantily clad women. —**girlfriend** *n.* girl or woman with whom a person is romantically or sexually involved; female friend.

giro [**jire**-oh] *n., pl.* **-ros.** system of transferring money within a post office or bank directly from one account to another; *Informal* social security payment by giro cheque.

girt *v.* past of GIRD.

girth *n.* measurement round something; band round a horse to hold the saddle in position.

gist [jist] *n.* substance or main point of a matter.

give *v.* **giving, gave, given.** present (something) to another person; transfer in exchange or payment; hand over temporarily; impart; attribute; administer; be a source of; utter or emit; concede; sacrifice or devote; organize or host; yield or break under pressure. —*n.* resilience or elasticity. —**give away** *v.* donate as a gift; reveal; hand over (a bride) formally to her husband in a marriage ceremony. —**giveaway** *n.* usu. unintentional disclosure. —*adj.* very cheap or free. —**give in** *v.* admit defeat. —**give off** *v.* emit. —**give out** *v.* distribute; emit; come to an end or fail. —**give over** *v.* set aside for a specific purpose; *Informal* cease. —**give up** *v.* acknowledge defeat; abandon.

gizzard *n.* part of a bird's stomach.

glacé [**glass**-say] *adj.* crystallized or candied.

glacier *n.* slow-moving mass of ice formed by accumulated snow. —**glacial** *adj.* of ice or glaciers; very cold; unfriendly. —**glaciated** *adj.* covered with or affected by glaciers. —**glaciation** *n.*

glad *adj.* **gladder, gladdest.** pleased and happy; causing happiness. —**glad to** very willing to (do something). —**the glad eye** *Informal* an inviting or seductive glance. —**gladly** *adv.* —**gladness** *n.* —**gladden** *v.* make glad. —**glad rags** *Informal* best clothes.

glade *n.* open space in a forest.

gladiator *n.* (in ancient Rome) man trained to fight in arenas to provide entertainment.

gladiolus *n., pl.* **-lus, -li, -luses.** garden plant with sword-shaped leaves.

THESAURUS

gingerly carefully, cautiously, charily, circumspectly, delicately, hesitantly, reluctantly, squeamishly, suspiciously, timidly, warily

gird 1. belt, bind, girdle 2. encircle, enclose, enfold, environ, hem in, pen, ring, surround

girdle 1. *n.* band, belt, cummerbund, fillet, sash, waistband 2. *v.* bind, bound, encircle, enclose, encompass, environ, hem, ring, surround

girl damsel, daughter, female child, lass, maid, maiden, miss, wench

girth bulk, measure, size

gist core, drift, essence, force, idea, import, marrow, meaning, nub, pith, point, sense, substance

give 1. accord, administer, allow, award, bestow, commit, confer, consign, contribute, deliver, donate, entrust, furnish, grant, permit, present, provide, supply 2. allow, cede, concede,

devote, grant, hand over, lend, relinquish, surrender, yield

give away betray, disclose, divulge, expose, leak, let out, reveal, uncover

give in capitulate, collapse, comply, concede, quit, submit, surrender, yield

give off discharge, emit, exhale, exude, produce, release, vent

give out discharge, emit, exhale, exude, produce, release, send out, smell of, throw out, vent

give up abandon, capitulate, cease, cede, cut out, desist, despair, forswear, hand over, leave off, quit, relinquish, renounce, resign, stop, surrender, waive

glad cheerful, contented, delighted, gay, gleeful, gratified, happy, jocund, jovial, joyful, overjoyed, pleased, willing

DICTIONARY

glair *n.* white of an egg; any similar sticky substance.

glamour *n.* alluring charm or fascination. —**glamorous** *adj.* alluring. —**glamorize** *v.*

glance *v.* look rapidly or briefly; glint or gleam. —*n.* brief look. —**glancing** *adj.* hitting at an oblique angle. —**glance off** *v.* strike and be deflected off (an object) at an oblique angle.

gland *n.* organ that produces and secretes substances in the body. —**glandular** *adj.*

glanders *n.* contagious disease of horses.

glare *v.* stare angrily; be unpleasantly bright. —*n.* angry stare; unpleasant brightness. —**glaring** *adj.* conspicuous; unpleasantly bright. —**glaringly** *adv.*

glasnost *n.* policy of openness and accountability, esp. in the USSR.

glass *n.* hard brittle, usu. transparent substance made by melting sand; objects made of glass; tumbler; its contents; mirror; barometer. —*pl.* spectacles. —**glassy** *adj.* like glass; expressionless. —**glassiness** *n.* —**glasshouse** *n.* greenhouse; *Informal* army prison. —**glass wool** fine glass fibres used for insulating.

glaucoma *n.* eye disease.

glaze *v.* fit or cover with glass; cover with a glassy substance; become glassy. —*n.* transparent coating; substance used for this. —**glazier** *n.* person who fits windows with glass.

gleam *n.* small beam or glow of light; brief or faint indication. —*v.* emit a gleam. —**gleaming** *adj.*

glean *v.* gather (facts etc.) bit by bit; gather (the useful remnants of a crop) after harvesting. —**gleaner** *n.*

glebe *n.* land belonging to a parish church.

glee *n.* triumph and delight; musical composition for three or more unaccompanied voices. —**gleeful** *adj.* —**gleefully** *adv.*

glen *n.* deep narrow valley.

glengarry *n., pl.* **-ries.** brimless Scottish cap with a crease down the crown.

glib *adj.* **glibber, glibbest.** fluent but insincere or superficial. —**glibly** *adv.* —**glibness** *n.*

glide *v.* move easily and smoothly; (of an aircraft) move without the use of engines. —*n.* smooth easy movement. —**glider** *n.* aircraft without an engine which floats on air currents. —**gliding** *n.* sport of flying gliders.

glimmer *v.* shine faintly, flicker. —*n.* faint gleam; faint indication.

THESAURUS

gladden cheer, delight, enliven, exhilarate, hearten, please, rejoice

gladly cheerfully, freely, gaily, gleefully, happily, joyfully, merrily, readily, willingly

gladness blitheness, cheerfulness, delight, felicity, gaiety, glee, happiness, high spirits, hilarity, jollity, joy, joyousness, mirth, pleasure

glamorous alluring, attractive, beautiful, captivating, charming, dazzling, elegant, enchanting, entrancing, exciting, fascinating, glittering, glossy, lovely, prestigious, smart

glamour allure, appeal, attraction, beauty, charm, enchantment, fascination, prestige

glance 1. *v.* gaze, glimpse, look, peep, scan, view 2. *n.* glimpse, look, peek, peep, quick look, squint, view

glare *v.* 1. frown, glower, lower, scowl, stare angrily ~*n.* 2. black look, dirty look, frown, glower, lower, scowl 3. blaze, brilliance, dazzle, flame, glow

glaring audacious, blatant, conspicuous, flagrant, gross, manifest, obvious, open, outstanding, overt, patent, rank, visible

glassy clear, glossy, icy, shiny, slick, slippery, smooth, transparent

glaze 1. *v.* burnish, coat, enamel, gloss, lacquer, polish, varnish 2. *n.* coat, enamel, finish, gloss, lacquer, lustre, patina, polish, shine, varnish

gleam 1. *n.* beam, flash, glow, ray, sparkle 2. *v.* flare, flash, glance, glimmer, glint, glisten, glitter, glow, shimmer, shine, sparkle

glee cheerfulness, delight, elation, exultation, fun, gaiety, gladness, hilarity, jollity, joy, joyfulness, liveliness, merriment, mirth, triumph, verve

gleeful cheerful, delighted, elated, exuberant, gay, happy, jocund, jovial, joyful, jubilant, merry, mirthful, overjoyed, pleased, triumphant

glib artful, easy, fluent, plausible, quick, ready, slick, smooth, suave, voluble

glide coast, drift, float, flow, fly, roll, run, sail, skate, skim, slide, slip, soar

glimmer 1. *v.* blink, flicker, gleam, glisten, glitter, glow, shimmer, shine, sparkle, twinkle 2. *n.* blink, flicker, gleam, glow, shimmer, sparkle, twinkle

glimpse 1. *n.* brief view, glance, look, peek, peep, quick look, sight, sighting 2. *v.* espy, sight, spot, spy, view

glint 1. *v.* flash, gleam, glimmer, glitter, shine, sparkle, twinkle 2. *n.* flash, gleam, glimmer, glitter, shine, sparkle

DICTIONARY

glimpse n. brief or incomplete view. —v. catch a glimpse of.

glint v. gleam brightly. —n. bright gleam.

glissando n. *Music* slide between two notes in which all intermediate notes are played.

glisten v. gleam by reflecting light.

glitch n. sudden malfunction in an electronic system.

glitter v. shine with bright flashes; be showy. —n. sparkle or brilliance; shiny powder used as decoration.

gloaming n. twilight.

gloat v. (often foll. by *over*) look (at) or think (of) with smug or malicious pleasure.

glob n. rounded mass of thick fluid.

globe n. sphere with a map of the earth on it; spherical object. —**the globe** the earth. —**global** adj. worldwide; total or comprehensive. —**globally** adv. —**globetrotter** n. habitual worldwide traveller. —**globetrotting** n., adj.

globule n. small round drop. —**globular** adj.

globulin n. simple protein found in living tissue.

glockenspiel n. percussion instrument consisting of small metal bars played with hammers.

gloom n. darkness; melancholy or depression. —**gloomy** adj. —**gloomily** adv.

glory n., pl. **-ries.** praise or honour; praiseworthy thing; splendour; heavenly bliss. —v. **-rying, -ried.** —**glorify** v. make glorious; praise; make (something) seem more worthy than it is. —**glorification** n. —**glorious** adj. full of or conferring glory; brilliantly beautiful; delightful. —**gloriously** adv. —**glory hole** *Informal* untidy cupboard or storeroom. —**glory in** v. triumph or exalt.

gloss[1] n. surface shine or lustre; paint or cosmetic giving a shiny finish. —**glossy** adj. smooth and shiny; (of a magazine) printed on shiny paper. —**glossily** adv. —**glossiness** n. —**gloss over** v. (try to) cover up or pass over (a fault or error).

gloss[2] n. explanatory comment added to the text of a book. —v. add glosses to.

glossary n., pl. **-ries.** list of special or technical words with definitions.

glottis n., pl. **-tises, -tides.** vocal cords and the space between them. —**glottal** adj.

glove n. covering for the hand with individual sheaths for each finger and the thumb. —v. cover with or as if with a glove. —**glove com-**

THESAURUS

glisten flash, gleam, glimmer, glint, glitter, shimmer, shine, sparkle, twinkle

glitter 1. v. coruscate, flare, flash, gleam, glimmer, glint, glisten, scintillate, shimmer, shine, sparkle, twinkle 2. n. beam, brightness, flash, glare, gleam, lustre, radiance, sheen, shimmer, shine, sparkle

gloat crow, exult, glory, relish, revel in, triumph, vaunt

global 1. international, planetary, universal, worldwide 2. all-inclusive, all-out, comprehensive, encyclopedic, exhaustive, general, thorough, total, unbounded, unlimited

globe ball, earth, orb, planet, round, sphere, world

globule bead, bubble, drop, droplet, particle

gloom 1. blackness, cloud, cloudiness, dark, darkness, dimness, dullness, dusk, murk, murkiness, obscurity, shade, shadow, twilight 2. blues, dejection, depression, despair, despondency, low spirits, melancholy, misery, sadness, sorrow, unhappiness, woe

gloomy 1. black, dark, dim, dismal, dreary, dull, dusky, murky, obscure, overcast, shadowy, sombre 2. bad, black, cheerless, comfortless, depressing, disheartening, dispiriting, dreary, joyless, sad, saddening, sombre 3. blue, cheerless, dejected, despondent, dismal, dispirited,

downcast, downhearted, glum, melancholy, miserable, moody, morose, pessimistic, sad

glorify 1. adorn, augment, dignify, elevate, enhance, ennoble, illuminate, immortalize, lift up, magnify, raise 2. celebrate, eulogize, extol, hymn, laud, lionize, magnify, praise

glorious 1. celebrated, distinguished, elevated, eminent, excellent, famed, famous, grand, honoured, illustrious, magnificent, majestic, noble, noted, renowned, sublime, triumphant 2. delightful, enjoyable, excellent, fine, great, marvellous, pleasurable, splendid, wonderful

glory n. 1. celebrity, dignity, distinction, eminence, exaltation, fame, honour, immortality, kudos, praise, prestige, renown 2. adoration, blessing, gratitude, homage, praise, veneration, worship 3. grandeur, greatness, magnificence, majesty, nobility, pageantry, pomp, splendour, sublimity, triumph ~v. 4. boast, crow, exult, gloat, relish, revel, triumph

gloss[1] 1. n. brightness, brilliance, burnish, gleam, lustre, polish, sheen, shine, varnish, veneer 2. v. (foll. by *over*) camouflage, conceal, cover up, disguise, hide, mask, veil

gloss[2] annotation, commentary, explanation, footnote, note, scholium, translation

glossy bright, brilliant, burnished, glassy, glazed, lustrous, polished, shining, shiny, sleek, smooth

DICTIONARY

partment small storage area in the dashboard of a car.

glow v. emit light and heat without flames; shine; have a feeling of wellbeing or satisfaction; (of a colour) look warm; be hot. —n. glowing light; warmth of colour; feeling of wellbeing. —**glow-worm** n. insect giving out a green light.

glower [rhymes with **power**] v., n. scowl.

gloxinia n. tropical plant with large bell-shaped flowers.

glucose n. kind of sugar found in fruit.

glue n. natural or synthetic sticky substance used as an adhesive. —v. **glu(e)ing, glued.** fasten with glue; (foll. by to) pay full attention to, e.g. *her eyes were glued to the TV.* —**gluey** adj. —**glue-sniffing** n. inhaling of glue fumes for intoxicating or hallucinatory effects.

glum adj. **glummer, glummest.** sullen or gloomy. —**glumly** adv.

glut n. excessive supply. —v. **glutting, glutted.** feed or fill to excess; oversupply.

gluten [**gloo**-ten] n. protein found in cereal grain.

glutinous [**gloo**-tin-uss] adj. sticky or gluey.

glutton[1] n. greedy person; person with a great capacity for something. —**gluttonous** adj. —**gluttony** n.

glutton[2] n. wolverine.

glycerin(e) n. colourless sweet liquid used widely in chemistry and industry.

glycerol n. technical name for GLYCERINE.

gm gram.

GMT Greenwich Mean Time.

gnarled adj. rough, twisted, and knobbly.

gnash v. grind (the teeth) together in anger or pain.

gnat n. small biting two-winged fly.

gnaw v. **gnawing, gnawed, gnawed** or **gnawn.** bite or chew steadily; (foll. by at) cause constant distress (to).

gneiss n. coarse-grained metamorphic rock.

gnome n. imaginary creature like a little old man.

gnomic [**no**-mik] adj. of pithy sayings.

Gnosticism n. religious movement believing in intuitive spiritual knowledge. —**Gnostic** n., adj.

gnu [**noo**] n. oxlike S African antelope.

go v. **going, went, gone.** move to or from a place; depart; make regular journeys; function; be, do, or become as specified; contribute to a result, e.g. *it just goes to show;* be allotted to a specific purpose or recipient; be sold; blend or harmonize; fail or break down; elapse; be got rid of; attend; reach or exceed certain limits, e.g. *she's gone too far this time;* be acceptable; carry authority. —n. attempt; verbal attack; turn; *Informal* energy or vigour. —**make a go of** be successful at. —**go back on** v. break (a promise etc.). —**go-between** n. intermediary. —**go for** v. *Informal* choose; attack; apply to equally. —**go-getter** n. energetically ambitious person. —**go-go dancer** scantily-dressed erotic dancer. —**go off** v. explode; ring or sound; *Informal* stop liking; *Informal* become stale or rotten. —**go out** v. be romantically involved (with); be extinguished; cease to be fashionable or popular. —**go over** v. examine or check. —**go-slow** n. deliberate slowing of work-rate as an industrial protest. —**go through** v. examine or search; suffer or undergo.

goad n. spiked stick for driving cattle; spur or incentive. —v. urge on with or as if with a goad.

goal n. aim or purpose; objective; *Sport* posts through which the ball or puck has to be propelled to score; score so made. —**goalie** n. *Infor-*

THESAURUS

glow n. 1. burning, gleam, glimmer, light 2. brightness, brilliance, effulgence, radiance, splendour, vividness ~v. 3. brighten, burn, gleam, glimmer, redden, shine, smoulder

glower frown, glare, lower, scowl

glue 1. n. adhesive, gum, paste 2. v. affix, fix, gum, paste, seal, stick

glum crestfallen, crusty, dejected, doleful, down, gloomy, gruff, grumpy, ill-humoured, low, moody, morose, saturnine, sour, sulky, sullen

glut excess, oversupply, saturation, superfluity, surfeit, surplus

glutton gobbler, gorger, gormandizer, gourmand

gluttony greed, rapacity, voraciousness, voracity

gnaw 1. bite, chew, munch, nibble, worry 2. consume, devour, erode, fret

go v. 1. advance, decamp, depart journey, leave, move, pass, proceed, repair, set off, travel, withdraw 2. function, move, operate, perform, run, work 3. develop, eventuate, fall out, fare, happen, proceed, result, turn out, work out 4. elapse, expire, flow, lapse, pass, slip away ~n. 5. attempt, bid, effort, essay, try, turn

goad 1. n. impetus, incentive, incitement, irritation, motivation, pressure, spur, stimulation, stimulus, urge 2. v. annoy, arouse, drive, egg on, exhort, harass, hound, impel, incite, instigate, irritate, lash, prick, prod, prompt, propel, spur, stimulate, sting, urge, worry

DICTIONARY

mal goalkeeper. —**goalkeeper** *n.* player whose task is to stop shots entering the goal. —**goalpost** *n.* one of the two posts supporting the crossbar of a goal. —**move the goalposts** change the aims of an activity to ensure the desired result.

goat *n.* sure-footed ruminant animal. —**get someone's goat** *Slang* annoy someone. —**goatee** *n.* pointed tuftlike beard.

gob *n.* lump of a soft substance; *Slang* mouth.

gobbet *n.* lump, esp. of food.

gobble¹ *v.* eat hastily and greedily.

gobble² *n.* rapid gurgling cry of the male turkey. —*v.* make this noise.

gobbledegook, gobbledygook *n.* unintelligible (official) language or jargon.

goblet *n.* drinking cup.

goblin *n.* (in folklore) small malevolent creature.

goby *n., pl.* **-by, -bies.** small spiny-finned fish.

god *n.* spirit or being worshipped as having supernatural power; object of worship, idol; (G-) in monotheistic religions, the Supreme Being, creator and ruler of the universe. —**goddess** *n. fem.* —**the gods** top balcony in a theatre. —**godlike** *adj.* —**godly** *adj.* devout or pious. —**godliness** *n.* —**god-fearing** *adj.* pious and devout. —**godforsaken** *adj.* desolate or dismal. —**godsend** *n.* something unexpected but welcome.

godetia *n.* garden plant with showy flowers.

godparent *n.* person who promises at a child's baptism to bring the child up as a Christian. —**godchild** *n.* child for whom a person stands as godparent. —**goddaughter** *n.* —**godfather** *n.* male godparent; head of a criminal, esp. Mafia, organization. —**godmother** *n.* —**godson** *n.*

goggle *v.* (of the eyes) bulge; stare. —**goggles** *pl. n.* protective spectacles.

going *n.* departure; condition of the ground for walking or riding over; rate of travel. —*adj.* thriving; current or accepted; available. —**going-over** *n., pl.* **goings-over.** *Informal* investigation or examination; scolding or thrashing. —**goings-on** *pl. n.* mysterious or unacceptable events.

goitre [goy-ter] *n.* swelling of the thyroid gland in the neck.

go-kart *n.* small low-powered racing car.

gold *n.* yellow precious metal; coins or articles made of this; colour of gold. —*adj.* made of gold; gold-coloured. —**goldcrest** *n.* small bird with a yellow crown. —**goldfinch** *n.* kind of finch, the male of which has yellow-and-black wings. —**goldfish** *n.* orange fish kept in ponds or aquariums. —**gold leaf** thin gold sheet used for gilding. —**gold medal** medal given to the winner of a competition or race.

golden *adj.* made of gold; gold-coloured; very successful or promising. —**golden eagle** large mountain eagle of the N hemisphere. —**golden handshake** *Informal* payment to a departing employee. —**golden mean** middle course between extremes. —**golden rule** important principle. —**golden wedding** fiftieth wedding anniversary.

golf *n.* outdoor game in which a ball is struck with clubs into a series of holes. —*v.* play golf. —**golfer** *n.*

golliwog *n.* soft black-faced male doll.

gonad *n.* organ producing reproductive cells, such as a testicle or ovary.

gondola *n.* long narrow boat used in Venice; suspended cabin of a cable car, airship, etc. —**gondolier** *n.* person who rows a gondola.

gone *v.* past participle of GO. —**goner** *n. Informal* person or thing beyond help or recovery.

gong *n.* rimmed metal disc that produces a note when struck; *Slang* medal.

gonorrhoea [gon-or-ree-a] *n.* venereal disease with a discharge from the genitals.

good *adj.* **better, best.** giving pleasure; kindly; commendable; morally excellent; talented; well-behaved; beneficial; valid; reliable; financially sound; complete or full. —*n.* benefit; positive moral qualities. —*pl.* property; merchandise. —**as good as** virtually. —**for good** permanently.

THESAURUS

goal aim, ambition, design, destination, end, intention, limit, mark, object, objective, purpose, target

gobble bolt, cram, devour, gorge, gulp, guzzle, stuff, swallow, wolf

go-between agent, broker, dealer, factor, intermediary, liaison, mediator

godforsaken abandoned, backward, bleak, deserted, desolate, dismal, dreary, forlorn, gloomy, lonely, remote

godly devout, good, holy, pious, religious, righteous, saintly

godsend blessing, windfall

go for assail, assault, attack

golden 1. bright, brilliant, flaxen, shining, yellow 2. best, blissful, flourishing, glorious, happy, joyful, joyous, precious, prosperous, rich, successful 3. auspicious, excellent, favourable, opportune, promising, propitious, rosy, valuable

gone 1. elapsed, ended, finished, over, past 2. absent, astray, away, lacking, lost, missing, vanished

DICTIONARY

—**goodness** n. —**goodly** adj. considerable. —**goody** n., pl. **-ies.** enjoyable thing; Informal hero in a book or film. —**goody-goody** adj., n. smugly virtuous (person). —**good-for-nothing** adj., n. irresponsible or worthless (person). —**Good Samaritan** person who helps another in distress. —**goodwill** n. kindly feeling; value of a business in reputation etc. over and above its tangible assets.

goodbye interj., n. expression used on parting.

gooey adj. **gooier, gooiest.** Informal sticky and soft.

goof Informal —n. mistake. —v. make a mistake.

googly n., pl. **-lies.** Cricket ball which changes direction unexpectedly on the bounce.

goon n. Informal stupid person; US hired thug.

goose n., pl. **geese.** web-footed bird like a large duck; female of this bird. —**goose flesh, pimples** bristling of the skin due to cold or fright. —**goose step** march step in which the leg is swung rigidly.

gooseberry n. edible yellowy-green berry; Informal unwanted single person accompanying a couple.

gopher [go-fer] n. American burrowing rodent.

gore[1] n. blood from a wound.

gore[2] v. pierce with horns.

gorge n. deep narrow valley. —v. eat greedily. —**make one's gorge rise** cause feelings of disgust.

gorgeous adj. strikingly beautiful or attractive; Informal very pleasant. —**gorgeously** adv.

gorgon n. terrifying or repulsive woman.

Gorgonzola n. sharp-flavoured blue-veined Italian cheese.

gorilla n. largest of the apes, found in Africa.

gormless adj. Informal stupid.

gorse n. prickly yellow-flowered shrub.

gory adj. **gorier, goriest.** horrific or bloodthirsty; involving bloodshed.

goshawk n. large hawk.

gosling n. young goose.

gospel n. unquestionable truth; (G-) any of the first four books of the New Testament.

gossamer n. filmy cobweb; very fine fabric.

gossip n. idle talk, esp. about other people; person who engages in gossip. —v. **gossiping, gossiped.** engage in gossip. —**gossipy** adj.

THESAURUS

good adj. 1. acceptable, admirable, agreeable, capital, choice, excellent, fine, first-class, first-rate, great, pleasant, pleasing, positive, precious, satisfactory, splendid, superior, tiptop, valuable, worthy 2. admirable, estimable, ethical, exemplary, honest, honourable, moral, praiseworthy, right, righteous, upright, virtuous, worthy 3. able, accomplished, adept, adroit, capable, clever, competent, dexterous, efficient, expert, first-rate, proficient, reliable, satisfactory, serviceable, skilled, sound, suitable, talented, thorough, trustworthy, useful 4. authentic, bona fide, dependable, genuine, honest, legitimate, proper, real, reliable, sound, true, trustworthy, valid 5. decorous, dutiful, mannerly, obedient, orderly, polite, proper, seemly, well-behaved 6. adequate, ample, complete, considerable, entire, extensive, full, large, long, sizable, solid, substantial, sufficient, whole ~n. 7. advantage, avail, behalf, benefit, gain, interest, profit, service, use, usefulness, welfare, wellbeing, worth 8. excellence, goodness, merit, morality, probity, rectitude, right, righteousness, uprightness, virtue, worth

goodbye adieu, farewell, parting

good-for-nothing 1. n. idler, layabout, profligate, scapegrace, waster, wastrel 2. adj. feckless, idle, irresponsible, useless, worthless

goodness 1. excellence, merit, quality, superiority, value, worth 2. benevolence, friendliness, generosity, good will, graciousness, kindness, mercy 3. honesty, honour, integrity, merit, morality, probity, rectitude, righteousness, uprightness, virtue

goods 1. belongings, chattels, effects, furniture, gear, movables, possessions, property, things, trappings 2. merchandise, stock, stuff, wares

goodwill favour, friendship, heartiness, kindliness, zeal

go off 1. blow up, detonate, explode 2. Inf. go bad, go stale, rot

go out die out, expire, fade out

go over 1. examine, inspect, review, revise, study 2. peruse, read, scan, skim

gorge 1. n. canyon, cleft, defile, fissure, pass, ravine 2. v. bolt, cram, devour, feed, fill, glut, gobble, gulp, guzzle, overeat, surfeit, swallow, wolf

gorgeous beautiful, brilliant, dazzling, elegant, glittering, grand, luxuriant, magnificent, opulent, ravishing, showy, splendid, sumptuous, superb

gossip n. 1. chitchat, hearsay, idle talk, prattle, scandal, small talk, tittle-tattle 2. babbler, blether, busybody, chatterer, scandalmonger, tattler, telltale ~v. 3. blether, chat, gabble, prate, prattle, tattle

DICTIONARY

got v. past of GET. —**have got** possess. —**have got to** need or be required to.

Gothic adj. (of architecture) of or in the style common in Europe from the 12th–16th centuries, with pointed arches; of or in an 18th-century literary style characterized by gloom and the supernatural; barbarous; (of print) using a heavy ornate typeface.

gouache n. (painting using) watercolours mixed with glue.

Gouda n. mild-flavoured Dutch cheese.

gouge [gowj] v. scoop or force out; cut (a hole or groove) in (something). —n. chisel with a curved cutting edge; hole or groove.

goulash [goo-lash] n. rich stew seasoned with paprika.

gourd [goord] n. fleshy fruit of a climbing plant; its dried shell, used as a container.

gourmand [goor-mand] n. person who is very keen on food and drink.

gourmet [goorm-may] n. connoisseur of food and drink.

gout [gowt] n. disease causing inflammation of the joints. —**gouty** adj.

govern v. rule, direct, or control; exercise restraint over (temper etc.). —**governable** adj. —**governance** n. governing. —**governess** n. woman teacher in a private household. —**government** n. executive policy-making body of a state; exercise of political authority over a coun-try or state; system by which a country or state is ruled. —**governmental** adj. —**governor** n. official governing a province or state; senior administrator of a society, institution, or prison. —**governor general** representative of the Crown in a Commonwealth dominion.

gown n. woman's long formal dress; surgeon's overall; official robe worn by judges, clergymen, etc.

goy n. Slang Jewish word for a non-Jew.

GP general practitioner.

grab v. **grabbing, grabbed.** grasp suddenly, snatch. —n. sudden snatch; mechanical device for gripping.

grace n. beauty and elegance; polite, kind behaviour; goodwill or favour; delay granted; courtesy or decency; short prayer of thanks for a meal; (**G-**) title of a duke, duchess, or archbishop. —v. add grace to; honour. —**graceful** adj. —**gracefully** adv. —**graceless** adj. —**gracious** adj. kind and courteous; condescendingly polite; elegant. —**graciously** adv. —**grace note** Music note ornamenting a melody.

grade n. place on a scale of quality, rank, or size; mark or rating; US class in school. —v. arrange in grades; assign a grade to; level (a road etc.) to a suitable gradient. —**make the grade** succeed. —**gradation** n. (stage in) a series of degrees or steps; arrangement in stages.

gradient n. (degree of) slope.

THESAURUS

govern administer, command, conduct, control, direct, guide, hold sway, lead, manage, order, oversee, pilot, reign, rule, steer, supervise

government 1. administration, authority, dominion, law, rule, sovereignty, state, statecraft 2. administration, executive, ministry, regime

governor administrator, chief, commander, controller, director, executive, head, leader, manager, overseer, ruler, supervisor

gown costume, dress, frock, garb, garment, habit, robe

grab bag, capture, catch, clutch, grasp, grip, pluck, seize, snap up, snatch

grace n. 1. beauty, charm, ease, elegance, finesse, loveliness, pleasantness, poise, polish, refinement 2. benefaction, beneficence, benevolence, favour, generosity, goodness, good will, kindliness, kindness 3. courtesy, cultivation, decency, decorum, etiquette, manners, propriety, tact 4. benediction, blessing, prayer, thanks, thanksgiving ~v. 5. adorn, beautify, bedeck, deck, decorate, dignify, distinguish, elevate, embellish, enhance, enrich, favour, garnish, glorify, honour, ornament, set off

graceful agile, beautiful, becoming, charming, comely, easy, elegant, fine, flowing, natural, pleasing, smooth, tasteful

gracious affable, amiable, beneficent, benevolent, benign, charitable, chivalrous, civil, compassionate, considerate, cordial, courteous, friendly, hospitable, indulgent, kind, lenient, loving, merciful, mild, obliging, pleasing, polite, well-mannered

grade 1. n. brand, category, class, condition, degree, echelon, group, level, mark, notch, order, place, position, quality, rank, rung, size, stage, station, step 2. v. arrange, brand, class, classify, evaluate, group, order, range, rank, rate, sort, value

gradient bank, grade, hill, incline, rise, slope

gradual even, gentle, graduated, moderate, piecemeal, progressive, regular, slow, steady, unhurried

gradually bit by bit, by degrees, evenly, gently, moderately, piecemeal, progressively, slowly, steadily

DICTIONARY

gradual *adj.* occurring, developing, or moving in small stages. —**gradually** *adv.*

graduate *v.* receive a degree or diploma; group by type or quality; mark (a container etc.) with units of measurement. —*n.* holder of a degree. —**graduation** *n.*

graffiti [graf-**fee**-tee] *pl. n.* words or drawings scribbled or sprayed on walls etc.

graft[1] *n.* shoot of a plant set in the stalk of another; surgical transplant of skin or tissue. —*v.* insert (a plant shoot) in another stalk; transplant (living tissue) surgically.

graft[2] *Informal* —*n.* hard work; obtaining of money by misusing one's position. —*v.* work hard. —**grafter** *n.*

grail *n.* same as HOLY GRAIL.

grain *n.* seedlike fruit of a cereal plant; cereal plants in general; small hard particle; arrangement of fibres, as in wood; texture or pattern resulting from this; very small amount. —**go against the grain** be contrary to one's natural inclination. —**grainy** *adj.*

grammar *n.* branch of linguistics dealing with the form, function, and order of words; book on the rules of grammar; use of words. —**grammarian** *n.* —**grammatical** *adj.* according to the rules of grammar. —**grammatically** *adv.* —**grammar school** esp. formerly, a secondary school providing an education with a strong academic bias.

gram(me) *n.* metric unit of mass equal to one thousandth of a kilogram.

gramophone *n.* record player.

grampus *n., pl.* **-puses.** sea mammal.

gran *n. Informal* grandmother.

granary *n., pl.* **-ries.** storehouse for grain.

grand *adj.* large or impressive, imposing; dignified or haughty; *Informal* excellent; (of a total) final; chief. —*n.* grand piano; *Slang* thousand pounds or dollars. —**grandchild** *n.* child of one's child. —**granddaughter** *n.* female grandchild. —**grandfather** *n.* male grandparent. —**grand-**

father clock tall standing clock with a pendulum and wooden case. —**grandmother** *n.* female grandparent. —**grandparent** *n.* parent of one's parent. —**grand piano** large harp-shaped piano with the strings horizontally. —**grand slam** winning of all the games or major tournaments in a sport in one season. —**grandson** *n.* male grandchild. —**grandstand** *n.* terraced block of seats giving the best view at a sports ground.

grandeur *n.* magnificence; nobility or dignity.

grandiloquent *adj.* using pompous language. —**grandiloquently** *adv.* —**grandiloquence** *n.*

grandiose *adj.* imposing; pretentiously grand. —**grandiosity** *n.*

grange *n.* country house with farm buildings.

granite [**gran**-nit] *n.* very hard igneous rock often used in building.

granivorous *adj.* feeding on grain or seeds.

granny, grannie *n. Informal* grandmother. —**granny flat** flat in or added to a house, suitable for an elderly parent.

grant *v.* consent to fulfil (a request); admit. —*n.* sum of money provided by a government for a specific purpose, such as education. —**take for granted** accept as true without proof; take advantage of without due appreciation.

granule *n.* small grain. —**granular** *adj.* of or like grains. —**granulate** *v.* make into grains; give a rough surface to. —**granulation** *n.*

grape *n.* small juicy green or purple berry, eaten raw or used to produce wine, raisins, currants, or sultanas. —**grapevine** *n.* grape-bearing vine; *Informal* unofficial way of spreading news.

grapefruit *n.* large round yellow citrus fruit.

graph *n.* drawing showing the relation of different numbers or quantities plotted against a set of axes.

graphic *adj.* vividly descriptive; of or using drawing, painting, etc. —**graphics** *pl. n.* diagrams, graphs, etc., esp. as used on a television

THESAURUS

graduate calibrate, grade, mark off, measure out, proportion, regulate

grain 1. cereals, corn 2. grist, kernel, seed

grand 1. ambitious, august, dignified, elevated, eminent, exalted, fine, glorious, great, haughty, illustrious, imposing, impressive, large, lofty, lordly, luxurious, magnificent, majestic, noble, opulent, palatial, pompous, pretentious, princely, regal, splendid, stately, striking, sumptuous 2. admirable, excellent, fine, first-class, first-rate, outstanding, splendid, superb, wonderful

grandeur dignity, greatness, importance, lofti-

ness, magnificence, majesty, nobility, pomp, splendour, state

grandiose affected, ambitious, bombastic, extravagant, flamboyant, pompous, pretentious, showy

grant 1. *v.* accede to, accord, acknowledge, admit, agree to, allocate, allot, allow, assign, award, bestow, cede, concede, confer, consent to, donate, give, impart, permit, present, yield 2. *n.* admission, allocation, allotment, allowance, award, bequest, bounty, concession, donation, endowment, gift, present, subsidy

DICTIONARY

programme or computer screen. —**graphically** *adv.*

graphite *n.* soft black form of carbon, used in pencil leads.

graphology *n.* study of handwriting. —**graphologist** *n.*

grapnel *n.* tool with several hooks, used to grasp or secure things.

grapple *v.* come to grips with (a person); try to cope with (something difficult). —**grappling iron** grapnel.

grasp *v.* grip something firmly; try to seize; understand. —*n.* grip or clasp; total rule or possession; understanding. —**grasping** *adj.* greedy or avaricious.

grass *n.* common type of plant with jointed stems and long narrow leaves, including cereals and bamboo; lawn; pasture land; *Slang* marijuana; *Slang* person who informs, esp. on criminals. —*v.* cover with grass; *Slang* inform on. —**grassy** *adj.* —**grasshopper** *n.* jumping insect with long hind legs. —**grass roots** ordinary members of a group, as distinct from its leaders; essentials. —**grassroots** *adj.* —**grass widow** wife whose husband is absent for a time.

grate[1] *n.* framework of metal bars for holding fuel in a fireplace. —**grating** *n.* framework of metal bars covering an opening.

grate[2] *v.* rub into small bits on a rough surface; scrape with a harsh rasping noise; annoy. —**grater** *n.* —**grating** *adj.* harsh or rasping; annoying.

grateful *adj.* feeling or showing gratitude. —**gratefully** *adv.* —**gratefulness** *n.*

gratify *v.* **-fying, -fied.** satisfy or please; indulge (a desire or whim). —**gratification** *n.*

gratis *adv., adj.* free, for nothing.

gratitude *n.* feeling of being thankful for a favour or gift.

gratuitous [grat-**tyoo**-it-uss] *adj.* given free; uncalled for. —**gratuitously** *adv.*

gratuity [grat-**tyoo**-it-ee] *n., pl.* **-ties.** money given for services rendered, tip.

grave[1] *n.* hole for burying a corpse. —**gravestone** *n.* stone marking a grave. —**graveyard** *n.* cemetery.

grave[2] *adj.* serious and solemn; causing concern. —**gravely** *adv.*

grave[3] [rhymes with **halve**] *n.* accent (`) over a vowel to indicate a special pronunciation.

gravel *n.* mixture of small stones and coarse sand. —**gravelled** *adj.* covered with gravel. —**gravelly** *adj.* covered with gravel; rough-sounding.

graven [grave-en] *adj.* carved or engraved.

gravid [grav-id] *adj. Med.* pregnant.

gravitate *v.* be influenced or drawn towards; *Physics* move by gravity. —**gravitation** *n.* —**gravitational** *adj.*

gravity *n., pl.* **-ties.** force of attraction of one object for another, esp. of objects to the earth; seriousness or importance; solemnity.

gravy *n., pl.* **-vies.** juices from meat in cooking; sauce made from these.

gray *adj. US* same as GREY.

grayling *n.* fish of the salmon family.

graze[1] *v.* feed on grass. —**grazier** *n.* person who feeds cattle for market.

THESAURUS

grasp *v.* 1. catch, clasp, clinch, clutch, grab, grapple, grip, hold, lay *or* take hold of, seize, snatch 2. comprehend, follow, realize, see, take in, understand ~*n.* 3. clasp, clutches, embrace, grip, hold, possession, tenure 4. comprehension, knowledge, mastery, perception, realization, understanding

grasping acquisitive, avaricious, close-fisted, covetous, greedy, mean, miserly, rapacious, selfish, stingy, tightfisted, venal

grate 1. creak, grind, rasp, rub, scrape, scratch 2. annoy, chafe, exasperate, fret, gall, irk, irritate, jar, nettle, peeve, rankle, vex

grateful appreciative, indebted, obliged, thankful

gratify delight, favour, fulfil, give pleasure, gladden, humour, indulge, please, recompense, thrill

gratitude appreciation, indebtedness, obligation, recognition, thanks

gratuitous free, unasked-for, unpaid, unrewarded, voluntary

gratuity benefaction, bonus, bounty, donation, gift, largess, perquisite, present, reward, tip

grave[1] *n.* crypt, mausoleum, pit, sepulchre, tomb, vault

grave[2] 1. dignified, dour, dull, earnest, gloomy, heavy, leaden, long-faced, muted, quiet, serious, sober, solemn, sombre, staid, subdued, thoughtful, unsmiling 2. acute, critical, crucial, dangerous, hazardous, important, momentous, perilous, pressing, serious, severe, threatening, vital, weighty

graveyard burial ground, cemetery, churchyard, necropolis

gravity acuteness, exigency, importance, moment, seriousness, severity, significance, urgency, weightiness

DICTIONARY

graze[2] *v.* touch lightly in passing; scratch or scrape the skin. —*n.* slight scratch or scrape.

grease *n.* soft melted animal fat; any thick oily substance. —*v.* apply grease to. —**greasy** *adj.* —**greasiness** *n.* —**grease gun** appliance for injecting oil or grease into machinery. —**greasepaint** *n.* theatrical make-up.

great *adj.* large in size or number; important; pre-eminent; *Informal* excellent. —**great-** *prefix* two generations older or younger than, e.g. *great-grandfather.* —**greatly** *adv.* —**greatness** *n.* —**greatcoat** *n.* heavy overcoat. —**Great Dane** very large graceful dog.

greave *n.* piece of armour for the shin.

grebe *n.* diving water bird.

Grecian [gree-shan] *adj.* of ancient Greece.

greed *n.* excessive desire for food, wealth, etc. —**greedy** *adj.* —**greedily** *adv.* —**greediness** *n.*

Greek *n.* language of Greece; person from Greece. —*adj.* of Greece, the Greeks, or the Greek language.

green *adj.* of a colour between blue and yellow; unripe; characterized by green plants or foliage; (*sometimes* **G-**) of or concerned with environmental issues; envious or jealous; immature or gullible; (of bacon) unsmoked. —*n.* colour between blue and yellow; area of grass kept for a special purpose; (*sometimes* **G-**) person concerned with environmental issues. —*pl.* green vegetables. —*v.* make or become green. —**greenness** *n.* —**greenish, greeny** *adj.* —**greenery** *n.* vegetation. —**green belt** protected area of open country around a town. —**greenfinch** *n.*

European finch with dull green plumage in the male. —**green fingers** skill in gardening. —**greenfly** *n.* green aphid, a common garden pest. —**greengage** *n.* sweet green plum. —**greengrocer** *n.* shopkeeper selling vegetables and fruit. —**greenhorn** *n.* novice. —**greenhouse** *n.* glass building for rearing plants. —**greenhouse effect** rise in the temperature of the earth caused by heat absorbed from the sun being unable to leave the atmosphere. —**green light** signal to go; permission to proceed with something. —**greenroom** *n.* room for actors when offstage. —**greenshank** *n.* large European sandpiper.

greet *v.* meet with expressions of welcome; receive in a specified manner; be immediately noticeable to. —**greeting** *n.*

gregarious *adj.* fond of company; (of animals) living in flocks or herds.

gremlin *n.* imaginary being blamed for mechanical malfunctions.

grenade *n.* small bomb thrown by hand or fired from a rifle. —**grenadier** *n.* soldier of a regiment formerly trained to throw grenades.

grenadine [gren-a-**deen**] *n.* syrup made from pomegranates.

grew *v.* past tense of GROW.

grey *adj.* of a colour between black and white; (of hair) partly turned white. —*n.* grey colour; grey or white horse. —*v.* make or become grey. —**greyness** *n.* —**grey matter** *Informal* brains. —**greyish** *adj.*

greyhound *n.* swift slender dog used in racing.

THESAURUS

greasy fatty, oily, slick, slimy, slippery

great 1. big, bulky, colossal, enormous, extensive, gigantic, huge, immense, large, mammoth, stupendous, tremendous, vast, voluminous 2. capital, chief, grand, leading, main, major, paramount, primary, principal, prominent, superior 3. consequential, critical, crucial, grave, heavy, important, momentous, serious, significant, weighty 4. celebrated, distinguished, eminent, exalted, excellent, famed, famous, glorious, illustrious, notable, outstanding, pre-eminent, prominent, remarkable, renowned 5. able, adept, adroit, excellent, expert, good, masterly, proficient, skilful, skilled 6. admirable, excellent, fine, first-rate, good, wonderful

greatly abundantly, by much, considerably, enormously, exceedingly, extremely, highly, hugely, immensely, mightily, much, notably, powerfully, remarkably, vastly, very much

greatness 1. bulk, enormity, hugeness, immensity, largeness, length, magnitude, mass, size

2. gravity, heaviness, import, importance, moment, seriousness, significance, urgency, weight 3. celebrity, distinction, eminence, fame, glory, grandeur, note, renown

greed, greediness 1. gluttony, hunger, ravenousness, voracity 2. avidity, covetousness, cupidity, desire, eagerness, longing, rapacity, selfishness

greedy 1. gluttonous, hungry, insatiable, ravenous, voracious 2. acquisitive, avaricious, avid, covetous, craving, desirous, eager, grasping, hungry, impatient, rapacious, selfish

green *adj.* 1. blooming, budding, fresh, grassy, leafy, new, undecayed, verdant 2. fresh, immature, new, raw, recent, unripe ~*n.* 3. common, grassplot, lawn, sward, turf

greet accost, address, hail, meet, receive, salute, welcome

greeting address, hail, reception, salute, welcome

gregarious affable, convivial, cordial, friendly, outgoing, sociable, social

DICTIONARY

grid *n.* network of horizontal and vertical lines, bars, etc.; national network of electricity supply cables.

griddle *n.* flat iron plate for cooking.

gridiron *n.* frame of metal bars for grilling food; American football pitch.

grief *n.* deep sadness. —**grieve** *v.* (cause to) feel grief. —**grievance** *n.* real or imaginary cause for complaint. —**grievous** *adj.* very severe or painful; very serious.

griffin *n.* mythical monster with an eagle's head and wings and a lion's body.

grill *n.* device on a cooker that radiates heat downwards; grilled food; gridiron. —*v.* cook under a grill; question relentlessly. —**grilling** *n.* relentless questioning.

grill(e) *n.* grating over an opening.

grilse [grills] *n.* salmon on its first return from the sea to fresh water.

grim *adj.* **grimmer, grimmest.** stern; harsh or forbidding; very unpleasant. —**grimly** *adv.* —**grimness** *n.*

grimace *n.* ugly or distorted facial expression of pain, disgust, etc. —*v.* make a grimace.

grime *n.* ingrained dirt. —*v.* make very dirty. —**grimy** *adj.* —**griminess** *n.*

grin *v.* **grinning, grinned.** smile broadly, showing the teeth. —*n.* broad smile.

grind *v.* **grinding, ground.** crush or rub to a powder; smooth or sharpen by friction; scrape together with a harsh noise; oppress; *Informal* work or study hard. —*n.* *Informal* hard work; act or sound of grinding. —**grind out** *v.* produce in a routine or uninspired manner. —**grindstone** *n.* stone used for grinding.

grip *n.* firm hold or grasp; way in which something is grasped; mastery or understanding; handle; *US* travelling bag. —*v.* **gripping, gripped.** grasp or hold tightly; hold the interest or attention of. —**gripping** *adj.*

gripe *v.* *Informal* complain persistently. —*n.* sudden intense bowel pain; *Informal* complaint.

grisly *adj.* **-lier, -liest.** horrifying or ghastly.

grist *n.* grain for grinding. —**grist to one's mill** something which can be turned to advantage.

gristle *n.* cartilage in meat. —**gristly** *adj.*

grit *n.* rough particles of sand; courage. —*pl.* coarsely ground grain. —*v.* **gritting, gritted.** clench or grind (the teeth); spread grit on (an icy road etc.). —**gritty** *adj.* —**grittiness** *n.*

grizzle *v.* *Informal* whine or complain.

grizzled *adj.* grey-haired.

grizzly *n.,* *pl.* **-zlies.** (also **grizzly bear**) large American bear.

groan *n.* deep sound of grief or pain; *Informal* complaint. —*v.* utter a groan; *Informal* complain.

THESAURUS

grief agony, anguish, bereavement, dejection, distress, grievance, heartache, heartbreak, misery, mourning, pain, regret, remorse, sadness, sorrow, suffering, trial, tribulation, trouble, woe

grievance complaint, damage, distress, hardship, injury, injustice, resentment, sorrow, trial, tribulation, trouble, wrong

grieve 1. ache, bemoan, bewail, complain, deplore, lament, mourn, regret, rue, sorrow, suffer, wail, weep 2. afflict, agonize, crush, distress, hurt, injure, pain, sadden, wound

grievous 1. calamitous, damaging, distressing, dreadful, grave, harmful, heavy, hurtful, injurious, lamentable, oppressive, painful, severe 2. deplorable, dreadful, flagrant, glaring, heinous, intolerable, lamentable, monstrous, offensive, outrageous, serious, shameful, shocking, unbearable

grim cruel, ferocious, fierce, forbidding, formidable, frightful, ghastly, grisly, gruesome, harsh, hideous, horrible, horrid, merciless, morose, relentless, resolute, ruthless, severe, shocking, sinister, stern, sullen, surly, terrible

grimace face, frown, mouth, scowl, sneer, wry face

grime dirt, filth, smut, soot

grimy begrimed, besmeared, besmirched, dirty, filthy, foul, grubby, smutty, soiled, sooty, unclean

grind *v.* 1. crush, granulate, grate, mill, pound, powder, pulverize 2. gnash, grate, grit, scrape ~*n.* 3. chore, drudgery, hard work, labour, task, toil

grip *n.* 1. clasp, purchase 2. control, domination, grasp, hold, influence, mastery, perception, possession, power, tenure, understanding ~*v.* 3. clasp, clutch, grasp, hold, seize 4. catch up, compel, engross, enthral, entrance, fascinate, hold, involve, mesmerize, rivet, spellbind

gripping compulsive, enthralling, exciting, fascinating, riveting, thrilling

grisly abominable, appalling, awful, dreadful, frightful, ghastly, grim, gruesome, hideous, horrid, macabre, terrible

grit 1. dust, gravel, sand 2. backbone, courage, fortitude, gameness, mettle, nerve, perseverance, pluck, resolution, spirit, tenacity, toughness

groan 1. *n.* cry, moan, sigh, whine 2. *v.* cry, grumble, moan, sigh, whine

DICTIONARY

groat *n. Hist.* fourpenny piece.

grocer *n.* shopkeeper selling foodstuffs. —**grocery** *n.*, *pl.* **-ceries.** business or premises of a grocer. —*pl.* goods sold by a grocer.

grog *n.* spirit, usu. rum, and water.

groggy *adj.* **-gier, -giest.** *Informal* faint, shaky, or dizzy.

groin *n.* place where the legs join the abdomen; edge made by the intersection of two vaults.

grommet *n.* ring or eyelet.

groom *n.* person who looks after horses; bridegroom; officer in a royal household. —*v.* make or keep one's clothes and appearance neat and tidy; brush or clean a horse; train (someone) for a future role.

groove *n.* long narrow channel in a surface. —*v.* cut groove(s) in.

grope *v.* feel about or search uncertainly. —**groping** *n.*

gross *adj.* repulsively fat; total, without deductions; vulgar; flagrant. —*n.* twelve dozen. —*v.* make as total revenue before deductions. —**grossly** *adv.* —**grossness** *n.*

grotesque [grow-**tesk**] *adj.* strangely distorted; absurd. —*n.* artistic style mixing distorted human, animal, and plant forms; grotesque person or thing. —**grotesquely** *adv.*

grotto *n.*, *pl.* **-toes, -tos.** small picturesque cave.

grotty *adj.* **-tier, -tiest.** *Informal* nasty or in bad condition.

grouch *Informal* —*v.* grumble. —*n.* grumble; persistent grumbler. —**grouchy** *adj.*

ground[1] *n.* surface of the earth; soil; area used for a specific purpose, e.g. *rugby ground;* position in an argument or controversy. —*pl.* enclosed land round a house; reason or motive; coffee dregs. —*v.* base; instruct in the basics; ban an aircraft or pilot from flying; run (a ship) aground. —**grounding** *adj.* without reason. —**grounding** *n.* basic knowledge of a subject. —**groundnut** *n.* peanut. —**groundsheet** *n.* waterproof sheet put on the ground under a tent. —**groundsman** *n.* person employed to maintain a sports ground or park. —**groundswell** *n.* smooth heavy waves. —**groundwork** *n.* preliminary work.

ground[2] *v.* past of GRIND.

group *n.* number of people or things regarded as a unit; small band of musicians or singers. —*v.* place or form into a group.

grouper *n.* large edible sea fish.

grouse[1] *n.* stocky game bird; its flesh.

grouse[2] *v.* grumble or complain. —*n.* complaint.

grout *n.* thin mortar. —*v.* fill up with grout.

grove *n.* small group of trees.

grovel [**grov**-el] *v.* **-elling, -elled.** humble oneself; lie or crawl face down.

grow *v.* **growing, grew, grown.** develop physically; (of a plant) exist; originate; increase in size or degree; become gradually, e.g. *it was growing dark;* cultivate (plants). —**growth** *n.* growing; increase; something grown or growing; tumour. —**grown-up** *adj.*, *n.* adult. —**grow up** *v.* mature.

THESAURUS

groggy confused, dazed, dizzy, faint, reeling, shaky, stunned, unsteady, weak

groom *n.* 1. stableboy, stableman ~*v.* 2. clean, dress, smarten up, tidy, turn out 3. coach, drill, educate, make ready, nurture, prepare, prime, ready, train

groove channel, cutting, flute, furrow, gutter, hollow, rut, score, trench

grope feel, finger, fish, flounder, fumble, grabble, search

gross *adj.* 1. big, bulky, corpulent, dense, fat, great, heavy, hulking, large, massive, obese, overweight, thick 2. aggregate, entire, total, whole 3. coarse, crude, improper, impure, indecent, indelicate, lewd, low, obscene, offensive, rude, sensual, unseemly, vulgar

grotesque deformed, distorted, fantastic, freakish, incongruous, malformed, misshapen, odd, outlandish, ridiculous, strange, unnatural, weird

ground *n.* 1. clod, dirt, dry land, dust, earth, field, land, mould, sod, soil, terrain, turf 2.

Often plural area, country, district, domain, estate, fields, gardens, land, property, realm, terrain, tract 3. arena, field, pitch, stadium ~*v.* 4. base, establish, fix, found, set, settle 5. coach, inform, initiate, instruct, prepare, teach, train, tutor

groundless baseless, empty, false, idle, imaginary, unfounded, unjustified, unwarranted

groundwork base, basis, footing, foundation, fundamentals, preliminaries, preparation, spadework

group 1. *n.* association, band, batch, bunch, category, circle, class, clique, clump, cluster, collection, company, coterie, crowd, faction, formation, gang, gathering, organization, pack, party, set, troop 2. *v.* arrange, assemble, associate, assort, bracket, class, classify, dispose, gather, marshal, order, organize, put together, range, sort

grouse 1. *v.* carp, complain, grumble, moan,

DICTIONARY

growl v. make a low rumbling sound; utter with a growl. —n. growling sound.

groyne n. wall built out from the shore to control erosion.

grub n. legless insect larva; *Slang* food. —v. **grubbing, grubbed.** dig out or uproot; dig up the surface of (soil); search.

grubby adj. **-bier, -biest.** dirty. —**grubbiness** n.

grudge v. be unwilling to give or allow. —n. resentment.

gruel n. thin porridge.

gruelling adj. exhausting or severe.

gruesome adj. causing horror and disgust.

gruff adj. rough or surly in manner or voice. —**gruffly** adv. —**gruffness** n.

grumble v. complain; rumble. —n. complaint; rumble. —**grumbler** n. —**grumbling** adj., n.

grumpy adj. **grumpier, grumpiest.** bad-tempered. —**grumpily** adv. —**grumpiness** n.

grunt v. (esp. of pigs) make a low short gruff sound. —n. pig's sound; gruff noise.

Gruyère [grew-yair] n. hard yellow Swiss cheese with holes.

gryphon n. same as GRIFFIN.

G-string n. small strip of cloth covering the genitals and attached to a waistband.

GT gran turismo, used of a sports car.

guano [gwa-no] n. dried sea-bird manure.

guarantee n. formal assurance, esp. in writing, that a product will meet certain standards; something that makes a specified condition or outcome certain. —v. **-teeing, -teed.** give a guarantee; secure against risk etc.; ensure. —**guarantor** n. person who gives or is bound by a guarantee.

guard v. watch over to protect or to prevent escape. —n. person or group that guards; official in charge of a train; protection; screen for enclosing anything dangerous; posture of defence in sports such as boxing or fencing. —**guard against** v. take precautions against. —**guarded** adj. cautious or noncommittal. —**guardedly** adv. —**Guards** pl n. regiment with ceremonial duties. —**guardsman** n. member of the Guards.

guardian n. keeper or protector; person legally

THESAURUS

whine 2. *n.* complaint, grievance, grumble, moan, objection

grow 1. develop, enlarge, expand, extend, fill out, heighten, increase, multiply, spread, stretch, swell, thicken, widen 2. develop, flourish, shoot, spring up, sprout, vegetate 3. advance, expand, improve, progress, prosper, succeed, thrive 4. breed, cultivate, farm, produce, raise

grown-up adult, fully-grown, mature

growth 1. development, enlargement, evolution, expansion, extension, growing, increase, multiplication 2. crop, cultivation, development, produce, shooting, sprouting, vegetation 3. advance, expansion, improvement, progress, prosperity, rise, success

grub v. 1. burrow, dig up, probe, pull up, search for, uproot 2. ferret, forage, hunt, rummage, scour, search, uncover, unearth ~n. 3. caterpillar, larva, maggot 4. food, rations, sustenance, victuals

grubby dirty, filthy, grimy, mean, messy, mucky, scruffy, seedy, shabby, slovenly, smutty, soiled, sordid, squalid, unkempt, untidy, unwashed

grudge 1. *n.* animus, antipathy, aversion, bitterness, dislike, enmity, grievance, hate, ill will, malevolence, malice, pique, rancour, resentment, spite, venom 2. v. begrudge, complain, covet, envy, mind, resent, stint

gruelling arduous, brutal, crushing, demanding, difficult, fierce, grinding, hard, harsh, laborious, punishing, severe, stiff, strenuous, taxing, tiring, trying

gruesome abominable, awful, fearful, ghastly, grim, grisly, horrendous, macabre, repugnant, repulsive, shocking, terrible

gruff bearish, blunt, brusque, churlish, crabbed, crusty, curt, discourteous, grumpy, illhumoured, ill-natured, impolite, rough, rude, sour, sullen, surly, uncivil, ungracious, unmannerly

grumble 1. *v.* carp, complain, find fault, grouse, moan, whine 2. *n.* complaint, grievance, grouse, moan, objection

guarantee 1. *n.* assurance, bond, certainty, covenant, earnest, pledge, promise, security, surety, undertaking, warranty, word 2. *v.* answer for, assure, certify, insure, maintain, pledge, promise, protect, secure, swear, vouch for, warrant

guard v. 1. cover, defend, escort, keep, mind, oversee, patrol, police, protect, safeguard, save, screen, secure, shelter, shield, tend, watch, watch over ~n. 2. custodian, defender, lookout, picket, sentinel, sentry, warder, watch, watchman 3. buffer, bulwark, bumper, defence, pad, protection, rampart, safeguard, screen, security, shield

guardian champion, curator, custodian, defender, escort, guard, keeper, preserver, protector, trustee, warden, warder

DICTIONARY

responsible for a child, mentally ill person, etc. **—guardianship** n.

guava [**gwah**-va] n. yellow-skinned tropical American fruit.

gudgeon[1] n. small freshwater fish.

gudgeon[2] n. socket for a hinge or rudder.

Guernsey [**gurn**-zee] n. breed of dairy cattle; (g-) seaman's knitted sweater.

guer(r)illa n. member of an unofficial armed force fighting regular forces.

guess v. estimate or draw a conclusion without proper knowledge; estimate correctly by guessing; *US* suppose. —n. estimate or conclusion reached by guessing. **—guesswork** n. process or results of guessing.

guest n. person entertained at another's house or at another's expense; invited performer or speaker; customer at a hotel or restaurant. **—guesthouse** n. boarding house.

guff n. *Slang* nonsense.

guffaw n. crude noisy laugh. —v. laugh in this way.

guide n. person who shows the way; adviser; book of instruction or information; device for directing motion; (G-) member of an organization for girls equivalent to the Scouts. —v. act as a guide for; control, supervise, or influence. **—guidance** n. leadership, instruction, or advice. **—guided missile** missile whose flight is controlled electronically. **—guide dog** dog trained to lead a blind person. **—guideline** n. set principle for doing something.

guild n. organization or club; *Hist.* society of men in the same trade or craft.

guilder n. monetary unit of the Netherlands.

guile [gile] n. cunning or deceit. **—guileful** adj. **—guileless** adj.

guillemot [**gil**-lee-mot] n. black-and-white diving sea bird.

guillotine n. machine for beheading people; device for cutting paper or sheet metal; method of preventing lengthy debate in parliament by fixing a time for taking the vote. —v. behead by guillotine; limit debate by the guillotine.

guilt n. fact or state of having done wrong; remorse for wrongdoing. **—guiltless** adj. innocent. **—guilty** adj. responsible for an offence or misdeed; feeling or showing guilt. **—guiltily** adv.

guinea n. former British monetary unit worth 21 shillings (1.05 pounds); former gold coin of this value. **—guinea fowl** bird related to the pheasant. **—guinea pig** tailless S American rodent; *Informal* person used for experimentation.

guise [rhymes with **size**] n. false appearance.

guitar n. six-stringed instrument played by plucking or strumming. **—guitarist** n.

gulch n. *US* deep narrow valley.

gulf n. large deep bay; chasm; large difference in opinion or understanding.

gull n. long-winged sea bird.

gullet n. muscular tube through which food passes from the mouth to the stomach.

gullible adj. easily tricked. **—gullibility** n.

THESAURUS

guerrilla freedom fighter, irregular, partisan, underground fighter

guess 1. v. conjecture, estimate, fathom, predict, solve, speculate, work out 2. n. conjecture, feeling, hypothesis, judgment, notion, prediction, reckoning, speculation, supposition, surmise, suspicion, theory

guest boarder, company, lodger, visitor

guidance advice, conduct, control, counsel, direction, government, help, instruction, intelligence, leadership, management, teaching

guide v. 1. accompany, attend, conduct, convoy, direct, escort, lead, pilot, shepherd, steer, usher 2. command, control, direct, handle, manage, manoeuvre, steer 3. advise, counsel, educate, govern, influence, instruct, regulate, rule, superintend, supervise, sway, teach, train ~n. 4. adviser, attendant, conductor, counsellor, director, escort, leader, mentor, monitor, pilot, steersman, teacher, usher 5. catalogue, directory, handbook, instructions, key, manual, vade mecum

guild brotherhood, club, company, corporation,

fellowship, fraternity, league, lodge, order, society, union

guile art, artifice, cleverness, craft, craftiness, cunning, deceit, deception, duplicity, knavery, ruse, slyness, treachery, trickery

guilt 1. blame, delinquency, iniquity, misconduct, responsibility, sinfulness, wickedness, wrong, wrongdoing 2. bad conscience, contrition, disgrace, dishonour, infamy, regret, remorse, self-reproach, shame, stigma

guiltless blameless, clear, impeccable, innocent, pure, sinless, spotless, unimpeachable, untainted, untarnished

guilty at fault, convicted, criminal, culpable, delinquent, erring, evil, felonious, offending, responsible, sinful, to blame, wicked, wrong

gulf 1. bay, bight, sea inlet 2. breach, chasm, cleft, gap, rent, rift, split, void

gullible credulous, foolish, green, innocent, naive, silly, simple, trusting, unsophisticated, unsuspecting

gully channel, ditch, gutter

DICTIONARY

gully *n., pl.* **-lies.** channel cut by running water.

gulp *v.* swallow hastily; gasp. —*n.* gulping; thing gulped.

gum[1] *n.* firm flesh in which the teeth are set. —**gummy** *adj.* toothless.

gum[2] *n.* sticky substance obtained from certain trees; adhesive; gumdrop; chewing gum; gumtree. —*v.* **gumming, gummed.** stick with gum. —**gummy** *adj.* —**gumboots** *pl. n.* Wellington boots. —**gumdrop** *n.* hard jelly-like sweet. —**gumtree** *n.* eucalypt tree.

gumption *n. Informal* resourcefulness; *Informal* courage.

gun *n.* weapon with a metal tube from which missiles are fired by explosion; device from which a substance is ejected under pressure. —*v.* **gunning, gunned.** cause (an engine) to run at high speed. —**jump the gun** act prematurely. —**gunner** *n.* artillery soldier. —**gunnery** *n.* use or science of large guns. —**gunboat** *n.* small warship. —**gun dog** dog used to retrieve game. —**gun down** *v.* shoot (a person). —**gun for** *v.* seek or pursue vigorously. —**gunman** *n.* armed criminal. —**gunmetal** *n.* alloy of copper, tin, and zinc. —*adj.* dark grey. —**gunpowder** *n.* explosive mixture of potassium nitrate, sulphur, and charcoal. —**gunrunning** *n.* smuggling of guns and ammunition. —**gunrunner** *n.* —**gunshot** *n.* shot or range of a gun.

gunge *n. Informal* sticky unpleasant substance. —**gungy** *adj.*

gunny *n.* strong coarse fabric used for sacks.

gunwale, gunnel [gun-nel] *n.* top of a ship's side.

guppy *n., pl.* **-pies.** small colourful aquarium fish.

gurgle *v., n.* (make) a bubbling noise.

Gurkha *n.* person, esp. a soldier, belonging to a Hindu people of Nepal.

guru *n.* Indian spiritual teacher; leader or adviser.

gush *v.* flow out suddenly and profusely; express admiration effusively. —*n.* sudden copious flow; effusiveness. —**gusher** *n.* spurting oil well.

gusset *n.* piece of material sewn into a garment to strengthen it.

gust *n.* sudden blast of wind. —*v.* blow in gusts. —**gusty** *adj.*

gusto *n.* enjoyment or zest.

gut *n.* intestine; short for CATGUT; *Informal* fat stomach. —*pl. Informal* courage; *Informal* essential part. —*v.* **gutting, gutted.** remove the guts from; (of a fire) destroy the inside of (a building). —*adj.* basic or instinctive, e.g. *a gut reaction.* —**gutsy** *adj. Informal* greedy; *Informal* courageous.

gutta-percha *n.* whitish rubbery substance obtained from an Asian tree.

gutter *n.* shallow trough for carrying off water from a roof or roadside. —*v.* (of a candle) burn unsteadily, with wax running down the sides. —**the gutter** degraded or criminal environment. —**guttering** *n.* material for gutters. —**gutter press** newspapers that rely on sensationalism. —**guttersnipe** *n.* neglected slum child.

guttural [gut-ter-al] *adj.* (of a sound) produced at the back of the throat; (of a voice) harshsounding.

guy[1] *n.* effigy of Guy Fawkes burnt on Nov. 5th (**Guy Fawkes Day**); *Informal* man or boy. —*v.* make fun of.

guy[2] *n.* rope or chain to steady or secure something. —**guyrope** *n.*

guzzle *v.* eat or drink greedily.

gybe [jibe] *v.* (of a fore-and-aft sail) swing suddenly from one side to the other; (of a boat) change course by gybing.

gym *n.* short for GYMNASIUM or GYMNASTICS.

THESAURUS

gulp 1. *v.* bolt, devour, gobble, quaff, swallow, swill, toss off, wolf 2. *n.* draught, mouthful, swallow

gum adhesive, exudate, glue, mucilage, paste, resin

gumption ability, acumen, common sense, enterprise, initiative, resourcefulness, sagacity, shrewdness, spirit

gurgle 1. *v.* babble, bubble, burble, crow, lap, murmur, plash, purl, ripple, splash 2. *n.* murmur, ripple

gush 1. *v.* burst, cascade, flood, flow, jet, pour, run, rush, spout, spurt, stream 2. *n.* burst, cascade, flood, flow, jet, outburst, outflow, rush, spout, spurt, stream, torrent

gust blast, blow, breeze, flurry, gale, puff, rush, squall

gusto appetite, brio, delight, enjoyment, enthusiasm, fervour, liking, pleasure, relish, verve, zeal, zest

guts backbone, boldness, courage, daring, grit, mettle, nerve, pluck, spirit

gutter channel, conduit, ditch, drain, duct, pipe, sluice, trench, trough, tube

guttural deep, gruff, hoarse, husky, low, rasping, rough, thick, throaty

guy 1. *n.* chap, fellow, lad, man, person, youth 2. *v.* caricature, mock, ridicule

DICTIONARY

gymkhana [jim-**kah**-na] *n.* horse-riding competition.

gymnasium *n.* large room with equipment for physical training. —**gymnast** *n.* expert in gymnastics. —**gymnastic** *adj.* —**gymnastics** *pl. n.* exercises to develop strength and agility.

gynaecology [guy-nee-**kol**-la-jee] *n.* branch of medicine dealing with diseases and conditions specific to women. —**gynaecological** *adj.* —**gynaecologist** *n.*

gypsophila *n.* garden plant with small white flowers.

gypsum *n.* chalklike mineral used to make plaster of Paris.

Gypsy *n., pl.* **-sies.** member of a travelling people found throughout Europe.

gyrate [jire-**rate**] *v.* rotate or spiral about a point or axis. —**gyration** *n.* —**gyratory** *adj.* gyrating.

gyrocompass *n.* compass using a gyroscope.

gyroscope [**jire**-oh-skohp] *n.* disc rotating on an axis that can turn in any direction, used to keep navigation instruments steady. —**gyroscopic** *adj.*

H

H *Chem.* hydrogen.

habeas corpus [hay-bee-ass kor-puss] *n.* writ ordering a prisoner to be brought before a court.

haberdasher *n. Brit.* dealer in small articles used for sewing. —**haberdashery** *n.*

habit *n.* established way of behaving; costume of a monk or nun; woman's riding costume. —**habitual** *adj.* done regularly and repeatedly. —**habitually** *adv.* —**habituate** *v.* accustom. —**habituation** *n.* —**habitué** [hab-it-yew-ay] *n.* frequent visitor to a place.

habitable *adj.* fit to be lived in. —**habitat** *n.* natural home of an animal or plant. —**habitation** *n.* dwelling place; occupation of a dwelling place.

hacienda [hass-ee-end-a] *n.* ranch or large estate in Latin America.

hack[1] *v.* cut or chop (at) violently; utter a harsh dry cough. —**hacker** *n. Slang* computer enthusiast, esp. one who breaks into the computer system of a company or government.

hack[2] *n.* horse kept for riding; *Informal* (inferior) writer or journalist. —**hackwork** *n.* dull repetitive work.

hackles *pl. n.* hairs or feathers on the back of the neck of some animals and birds, which are raised in anger.

hackney carriage *n.* taxi; coach or carriage for hire.

hackneyed [hak-need] *adj.* (of language) stale or trite because of overuse.

hacksaw *n.* small saw for cutting metal.

had *v.* past of HAVE.

haddock *n.* large edible sea fish.

Hades [hay-deez] *n. Greek myth* underworld home of the dead.

hadj *n.* same as HAJJ.

haematic *adj.* relating to or containing blood. —**haematology** *n.* study of blood.

haemoglobin [hee-moh-globe-in] *n.* protein found in red blood cells which carries oxygen.

haemophilia *n.* hereditary illness in which the blood does not clot. —**haemophiliac** *n.*

haemorrhage [hem-or-ij] *n.* heavy bleeding. —*v.* bleed heavily.

haemorrhoids [hem-or-oydz] *pl. n.* swollen veins in the anus (also called **piles**).

haft *n.* handle of an axe, knife, or dagger.

hag *n.* ugly old woman; witch. —**hag-ridden** *adj.* distressed or worried.

haggard *adj.* looking tired and ill.

haggis *n.* Scottish dish made from sheep's offal, oatmeal, suet, and onion.

haggle *v.* bargain or wrangle over a price.

hagiology *n., pl.* -**gies.** literature about the lives of the saints. —**hagiography** *n.* writing of this. —**hagiographer** *n.*

hail[1] *n.* (shower of) small pellets of ice; large amount of words, missiles, blows, etc. —*v.* fall as or like hail. —**hailstone** *n.*

hail[2] *v.* greet; call (out to); acclaim, acknowledge. —**hail from** *v.* come originally from.

hair *n.* threadlike growth on the skin; such growths collectively, esp. on the head. —**hairy** *adj.* covered with hair; *Slang* dangerous or exciting. —**hairiness** *n.* —**hairdo** *n.* style in which a person's hair is cut and arranged. —**hairdresser** *n.* person who cuts and styles hair. —**hairgrip** *n.*

THESAURUS

habit 1. bent, custom, disposition, manner, practice, propensity, quirk, tendency, way 2. custom, mode, practice, routine, rule, second nature, usage, wont 3. dress, garb, garment, riding dress

habitation abode, domicile, dwelling, home, house, living quarters, lodging, quarters, residence

habitual accustomed, common, customary, familiar, fixed, natural, normal, ordinary, regular, routine, standard, traditional, usual, wonted

hack[1] chop, cut, gash, hew, kick, lacerate, mangle, mutilate, notch, slash

hack[2] penny-a-liner, scribbler

hackneyed banal, common, commonplace, overworked, pedestrian, stale, stereotyped, stock, threadbare, timeworn, tired, trite, unoriginal, worn-out

hag crone, fury, harridan, shrew, termagant, virago, vixen, witch

haggard careworn, drawn, emaciated, gaunt, ghastly, pinched, shrunken, thin, wan, wasted, wrinkled

haggle bargain, barter, wrangle

hail[1] *Fig.* 1. *n.* barrage, pelting, rain, shower, storm, volley 2. *v.* barrage, batter, beat down upon, pelt, rain, shower, storm, volley

hail[2] acclaim, acknowledge, applaud, cheer, exalt, glorify, greet, honour, salute, welcome

DICTIONARY

small, tightly bent metal hairpin. —**hairline** *n.* margin of hair at the top of the forehead. —*adj.* very fine or narrow. —**hairpin** *n.* U-shaped wire used to hold the hair in place. —**hairpin bend** U-shaped bend in the road. —**hair-raising** *adj.* terrifying. —**hairsplitting** *n.* making of petty distinctions. —**hairspring** *n.* very fine spring in a watch or clock.

hajj *n.* pilgrimage a Muslim makes to Mecca. —**hajji** *n.* Muslim who has made a pilgrimage to Mecca.

hake *n.* edible fish of the cod family.

halal *n.* meat from animals slaughtered according to Muslim law.

halberd *n.* spear with an axe blade.

halcyon [hal-see-on] *adj.* peaceful and happy. —**halcyon days** time of peace and happiness.

hale *adj.* robust, healthy, e.g. *hale and hearty.*

half *n., pl.* **halves.** either of two equal parts; *Informal* half-pint; half-price ticket. —*adj.* incomplete. —*adv.* to the extent of half; partially. —**half-baked** *adj. Informal* poorly planned. —**half-breed** *n.* half-caste. —**half-brother, -sister** *n.* brother or sister related through one parent only. —**half-caste** *n.* person with parents of different races. —**half-cocked** *adj.* —**go off half-cocked** fail because of inadequate preparation. —**half-hearted** *adj.* unenthusiastic. —**half-life** *n.* time taken for half the atoms in radioactive material to decay. —**half-nelson** *n.* hold in wrestling in which one wrestler's arm is pinned behind his back by his opponent. —**halfpenny** [hayp-nee] *n.* former British coin worth half an old penny. —**half-timbered** *adj.* having an exposed wooden frame filled in with plaster. —**half-time** *n. Sport* interval between two halves of a game. —**halftone** *n.* illustration showing lights and shadows by means of very small dots.

—**halfway** *adv., adj.* at or to half the distance. —**halfwit** *n.* foolish or feeble-minded person.

halibut *n.* large edible flatfish.

halitosis *n.* bad-smelling breath.

hall *n.* (entrance) passage; large room or building belonging to a particular group or used for a particular purpose; large country house.

hallelujah [hal-ee-loo-ya] *interj.* exclamation of praise to God.

hallmark *n.* mark indicating the standard of tested gold and silver; distinguishing feature. —*v.* stamp with a hallmark.

hallo *interj.* same as HELLO.

hallowed *adj.* regarded as holy.

Hallowe'en *n.* October 31, the eve of All Saints' Day.

hallucinate *v.* seem to see something that is not really there. —**hallucination** *n.* experience of seeming to see something that is not really there. —**hallucinatory** *adj.* —**hallucinogen** *n.* drug that causes hallucinations.

halo [hay-loh] *n., pl.* **-loes, -los.** disc of light round the head of a sacred figure; ring of light round the sun or moon.

halogen [hal-oh-jen] *n. Chem.* any of a group of nonmetallic elements including chlorine and iodine.

halt *n.* temporary stop; minor railway station without a building. —*v.* stop. —**halting** *adj.* hesitant, e.g. *halting speech.*

halter *n.* strap around a horse's head with a rope to lead it with. —**halterneck** *n.* top or dress with a strap fastened at the back of the neck.

halve *v.* cut in half; reduce to half; share.

halves *n.* plural of HALF.

halyard *n.* rope for raising a ship's sail or flag.

ham *n.* smoked or salted meat from a pig's thigh; *Informal* actor who overacts; *Informal*

THESAURUS

hair locks, mane, mop, shock, tresses

hair-raising alarming, exciting, frightening, horrifying, shocking, startling, terrifying, thrilling

hale blooming, fit, flourishing, healthy, hearty, robust, sound, strong, vigorous

half 1. *n.* division, equal part, fifty per cent, fraction, portion, section 2. *adj.* divided, fractional, halved, incomplete, limited, moderate, partial 3. *adv.* all but, barely, inadequately, incompletely, in part, partially, partly, slightly

half-hearted cool, indifferent, listless, lukewarm, neutral, passive, perfunctory, spiritless, tame, uninterested

halfway 1. *adv.* midway 2. *adj.* central, equidistant, intermediate, mid, middle, midway

hall 1. corridor, entry, foyer, lobby, passage, vestibule 2. auditorium, chamber, meeting place

halo aura, corona, nimbus, radiance

halt *v.* 1. break off, cease, close down, desist, draw up, pull up, rest, stand still, stop, wait 2. arrest, block, check, curb, cut short, end, hold back, impede, obstruct, stem, step, terminate ~*n.* 3. arrest, break, close, end, pause, stand, standstill, stop, stoppage, termination

halting awkward, faltering, hesitant, laboured, stumbling, stuttering

halve bisect, cut in half, divide equally, split in two

DICTIONARY

amateur radio operator. —*v.* **hamming, hammed.** —**ham it up** *Informal* overact. —**ham-fisted, -handed** *adj.* clumsy.

hamburger *n.* flat round piece of minced beef, often served in a bread roll.

hamlet *n.* small village.

hammer *n.* tool with a heavy head, used to drive in nails, beat metal, etc.; metal ball on a wire, thrown as a sport; part of a gun which causes the bullet to be fired; auctioneer's mallet; striking mechanism in a piano. —*v.* strike (as if) with a hammer; *Informal* defeat. —**hammer and tongs** with great effort or energy. —**hammerhead** *n.* shark with a wide flattened head. —**hammertoe** *n.* condition in which the toe is permanently bent at the joint.

hammock *n.* hanging bed made of canvas or net.

hamper¹ *v.* make it difficult for (someone or something) to move or progress.

hamper² *n.* large basket with a lid; selection of food and drink packed as a gift.

hamster *n.* small rodent with a short tail and cheek pouches.

hamstring *n.* tendon at the back of the knee. —*v.* make it difficult for someone to take any action.

hand *n.* end of the arm beyond the wrist; style of writing; applause; manual worker; pointer on a dial; cards dealt to a player in a card game; unit of four inches used to measure horses. —*v.* pass or give. —**hands down** easily. —**have a hand in** be involved in. —**lend a hand** help. —**(near) at hand, on hand, to hand** nearby. —**out of hand** beyond

control. —**handful** *n.* the amount that can be held in the hand; small quantity or number; *Informal* person or thing that is difficult to control. —**handbag** *n.* small bag carried to contain personal articles. —**handbill** *n.* small printed notice. —**handbook** *n.* small reference or instruction book. —**handcuff** *n.* one of a linked pair of metal rings used for securing a prisoner. —*v.* put handcuffs on. —**handicraft** *n.* objects made by hand. —**handiwork** *n.* work of a particular person. —**hand-out** *n.* thing given free; written information given out at a talk etc. —**hands-on** *adj.* involving practical experience of equipment. —**handstand** *n.* act of supporting the body on the hands in an upside-down position. —**handwriting** *n.* (style of) writing by hand.

handicap *n.* any physical or mental disability; something that makes progress difficult; contest in which the competitors are given advantages or disadvantages in an attempt to equalize their chances; disadvantage or advantage given. —*v.* make it difficult for (someone) to do something.

handkerchief *n.* small square of fabric used to wipe the nose.

handle *n.* part of an object that is held so that it can be used. —*v.* hold, feel, or move with the hands; control or deal with. —**handler** *n.* person who controls an animal. —**handlebars** *pl. n.* curved metal bar used to steer a cycle.

handsome *adj.* attractive in appearance; large or generous, e.g. *a handsome reward.*

handy *adj.* **handier, handiest.** convenient, useful; good at manual work. —**handily** *adv.* —**handiness** *n.* —**handyman** *n.* man skilled at odd jobs.

THESAURUS

hammer *v.* 1. bang, beat, drive, hit, knock, strike, tap 2. beat out, fashion, forge, form, make, shape

hamper *v.* bind, cramp, curb, embarrass, encumber, entangle, fetter, frustrate, handicap, hinder, hold up, impede, interfere with, obstruct, prevent, restrict, slow down, thwart

hand *n.* 1. fist, palm 2. artisan, craftsman, employee, hired man, labourer, operative, worker, workman ~*v.* 3. deliver, pass

handbook guide, instruction book, manual

handcuff fetter, manacle, shackle

handful few, small number, small quantity, smattering, sprinkling

handicap 1. barrier, block, disadvantage, drawback, encumbrance, hindrance, impediment, limitation, obstacle, restriction, shortcoming 2. advantage, edge, head start, odds, penalty, upper hand 3. defect, disability, impairment

handicraft art, craft, handiwork, skill, workmanship

handiwork achievement, artefact, craft, creation, design, invention, product, production, result

handle *n.* 1. grip, haft, helve, hilt, knob, stock ~*v.* 2. feel, finger, fondle, grasp, hold, maul, poke, touch 3. control, direct, guide, manage, manipulate, manoeuvre, operate, steer, use, wield 4. administer, conduct, cope with, deal with, manage, supervise, treat

hand-out 1. alms, charity, dole 2. bulletin, circular, leaflet

handsome admirable, attractive, becoming, comely, elegant, fine, good-looking, graceful, majestic, personable, stately, well-proportioned

handwriting calligraphy, fist, hand, longhand, scrawl, script

handy 1. accessible, available, close, conveni-

DICTIONARY

hang v. **hanging, hung.** attach or be attached at the top with the lower part free; (past **hanged**) suspend or be suspended by the neck until dead; fasten to a wall; droop. —**get the hang of** Informal understand. —**hanger** n. curved piece of wood or hook for hanging clothes on. —**hang back** v. hesitate. —**hangdog** adj. sullen, dejected. —**hang-glider** n. glider with a light framework from which the pilot hangs in a harness. —**hang-gliding** n. —**hangman** n. person who executes people by hanging. —**hangover** n. aftereffects of drinking too much alcohol. —**hang-up** n. Informal emotional or psychological problem.

hangar n. large shed for storing aircraft.

hank n. coil or skein, esp. of yarn.

hanker v. (foll. by after) crave, long for.

hanky, hankie n., pl. **hankies.** Informal handkerchief.

hanky-panky n. Informal illicit sexual relations.

hansom n. formerly, a two-wheeled horse-drawn cab for hire.

haphazard adj. not organized or planned. —**haphazardly** adv.

hapless adj. unlucky.

happen v. occur, take place; do by chance. —**happening** n. occurrence, event.

happy adj. **-pier, -piest.** glad or content; lucky or fortunate; suitable. —**happily** adv. —**happiness** n. —**happy-go-lucky** adj. carefree and cheerful.

hara-kiri n. Japanese ritual suicide by disembowelment.

harangue v. address angrily or forcefully. —n. angry or forceful speech.

harass v. annoy or trouble constantly. —**harassed** adj. —**harassment** n.

harbinger [har-binge-er] n. person or thing that announces the approach of something.

harbour n. sheltered port. —v. give shelter or protection to; maintain secretly in the mind.

hard adj. firm, solid, or rigid; difficult; requiring a lot of effort; unkind or unfeeling; difficult to bear; (of water) containing calcium salts which stop soap lathering freely; (of a drug) strong and addictive. —adv. with great energy or effort; carefully; intensely. —**hard of hearing** slightly deaf. —**hard up** Informal short of money. —**harden** v. —**hardness** n. —**hardship** n. suffering; difficult circumstances. —**hard-bitten** adj. tough. —**hardboard** n. thin stiff board made of compressed sawdust and woodchips. —**hard-boiled** adj. (of eggs) boiled until solid; Informal tough, unemotional. —**hard copy** computer out-

THESAURUS

ent, near, nearby, within reach **2.** convenient, helpful, manageable, neat, practical, serviceable, useful **3.** adept, adroit, clever, deft, expert, nimble, ready, skilful, skilled

hang 1. dangle, depend, droop, incline, suspend **2.** execute **3.** attach, cover, deck, decorate, drape, fasten, fix, furnish

hang back demur, hesitate, recoil

hangdog adj. abject, browbeaten, cowed, cringing, dejected, downcast, furtive, guilty, shamefaced, wretched

hanging adj. dangling, drooping, flapping, floppy, loose, pendent, suspended, swinging, unattached, unsupported

hank coil, length, loop, piece, roll, skein

haphazard 1. accidental, arbitrary, chance, random **2.** aimless, careless, casual, disorderly, indiscriminate, slipshod, unsystematic

happen 1. appear, arise, come about, come to pass, develop, ensue, follow, materialize, occur, result, transpire **2.** befall, betide **3.** chance, fall out, supervene, turn out

happening accident, adventure, affair, case, chance, episode, event, experience, incident, occurrence, phenomenon

happily 1. agreeably, contentedly, delightedly, enthusiastically, freely, gladly, heartily, will-

ingly, with pleasure **2.** blithely, cheerfully, gaily, gleefully, joyfully, joyously, merrily **3.** auspiciously, favourably, felicitously, fortunately, luckily, propitiously **4.** appropriately, aptly, suitably

happiness beatitude, blessedness, bliss, cheer, cheerfulness, cheeriness, contentment, delight, ecstasy, elation, enjoyment, felicity, gaiety, gladness, high spirits, joy, jubilation, merriment, pleasure, prosperity, satisfaction

happy blessed, blithe, cheerful, content, contented, delighted, ecstatic, elated, glad, gratified, jolly, joyful, jubilant, merry, overjoyed, pleased, thrilled

happy-go-lucky blithe, carefree, casual, easygoing, heedless, improvident, insouciant, nonchalant, untroubled

harangue 1. n. address, diatribe, exhortation, lecture, oration, screed, speech, tirade **2.** v. address, declaim, exhort, hold forth, lecture, rant

harass annoy, badger, bait, beleaguer, bother, disturb, exasperate, exhaust, fatigue, harry, hound, perplex, persecute, pester, plague, tease, tire, torment, trouble, vex, weary, worry

harbour 1. n. destination, haven, port **2.** v. conceal, hide, lodge, protect, provide refuge, relieve, secrete, shelter, shield

DICTIONARY

put printed on paper. —**hard-headed** adj. shrewd, practical. —**hardhearted** adj. unfeeling, unkind. —**hard sell** aggressive sales technique. —**hard shoulder** surfaced verge at the motorway edge for emergency stops. —**hardware** n. metal tools or implements; machinery used in a computer system; military weapons. —**hardwood** n. wood of a deciduous tree such as oak or ash.

hardly adv. scarcely or not at all; with difficulty.

hardy adj. -**dier**, -**diest**. able to stand difficult conditions. —**hardiness** n.

hare n. animal like a large rabbit, with longer legs and ears. —v. run fast. —**harebell** n. blue bell-shaped flower. —**harebrained** adj. foolish or impractical. —**harelip** n. split in the upper lip.

harem n. (apartments of) a Muslim man's wives and concubines.

haricot [har-rik-oh] n. white bean which can be dried.

hark v. Old-fashioned listen. —**hark back** v. return (to an earlier subject).

harlequin n. stock comic character, with a diamond-patterned costume and mask. —adj. in varied colours.

harlot n. Obs. prostitute.

harm n. physical, mental, or moral injury. —v. injure physically, mentally, or morally. —**harmful** adj. —**harmless** adj.

harmony n., pl. -**nies**. peaceful agreement and cooperation; combination of notes to make a pleasing sound. —**harmonious** adj. —**harmoniously** adv. —**harmonic** adj. of harmony; harmonious. —**harmonics** n. science of musical sounds. —**harmonize** v. fit in or go well with each other. —**harmonization** n. —**harmonica** n. mouth organ. —**harmonium** n. small organ.

harness n. equipment for attaching a horse to a cart or plough; combination of straps fastened round someone's body to attach something, e.g. a parachute harness. —v. put a harness on; control (something) in order to use its energy.

harp n. large triangular stringed instrument

THESAURUS

hard adj. 1. compact, dense, firm, inflexible, rigid, rocklike, solid, stiff, stony, strong, tough, unyielding 2. arduous, backbreaking, exacting, exhausting, fatiguing, formidable, laborious, rigorous, strenuous, tough, uphill, wearying 3. baffling, complex, complicated, difficult, intricate, involved, knotty, perplexing, puzzling, tangled, thorny 4. callous, cold, cruel, exacting, grim, harsh, implacable, obdurate, pitiless, ruthless, severe, stern, strict, stubborn, unjust, unkind, unsympathetic ~adv. 5. energetically, fiercely, forcefully, forcibly, heavily, intensely, powerfully, severely, sharply, strongly, vigorously, violently 6. assiduously, determinedly, diligently, doggedly, earnestly, industriously, intently, persistently, steadily, strenuously, untiringly

harden 1. bake, cake, freeze, set, solidify, stiffen 2. brace, buttress, fortify, gird, indurate, nerve, reinforce, steel, strengthen, toughen

hard-headed astute, cool, practical, pragmatic, realistic, sensible, shrewd, tough

hardhearted callous, cold, cruel, hard, heartless, indifferent, insensitive, intolerant, merciless, pitiless, stony, uncaring, unfeeling, unkind, unsympathetic

hardiness boldness, courage, fortitude, resilience, resolution, robustness, ruggedness, toughness

hardly almost not, barely, by no means, faintly, infrequently, just, not at all, not quite, no way, only, only just, scarcely, with difficulty

hardship adversity, affliction, austerity, burden, calamity, destitution, difficulty, fatigue, grievance, labour, misery, misfortune, need, suffering, toil, torment, tribulation, trouble, want

hard up bankrupt, impecunious, impoverished, penniless, poor

hardy firm, fit, hale, healthy, hearty, in fine fettle, lusty, robust, rugged, sound, stalwart, stout, strong, sturdy, tough, vigorous

harm 1. n. abuse, damage, detriment, hurt, ill, impairment, injury, loss, mischief, misfortune 2. v. abuse, blemish, damage, hurt, ill-treat, ill-use, impair, injure, maltreat, mar, molest, ruin, spoil, wound

harmful baleful, baneful, destructive, detrimental, evil, hurtful, injurious, noxious, pernicious

harmless gentle, innocent, innocuous, inoffensive, safe

harmonious agreeable, compatible, concordant, congruous, coordinated, dulcet, euphonious, harmonizing, matching, melodious, musical, tuneful

harmony 1. accord, agreement, amicability, amity, compatibility, concord, conformity, cooperation, friendship, like-mindedness, peace, rapport, sympathy, unity 2. euphony, melody, tune, tunefulness

harness n. 1. equipment, gear, tack, tackle, trappings ~v. 2. couple, hitch up, saddle, yoke 3. apply, channel, control, employ, exploit, utilize

DICTIONARY

played with the fingers. —**harpist** *n.* —**harp on** (**about**) *v.* talk about continuously.

harpoon *n.* barbed spear attached to a rope used for hunting whales. —*v.* spear with a harpoon.

harpsichord *n.* stringed keyboard instrument.

harpy *n., pl.* -**pies.** cruel or grasping woman.

harridan *n.* shrewish (old) woman.

harrier *n.* cross-country runner.

harrow *n.* implement used to break up clods of soil. —*v.* draw a harrow over.

harrowing *adj.* very distressing.

harry *v.* -**rying, -ried.** keep asking (someone) to do something, pester.

harsh *adj.* unpleasant to the senses; severe or cruel. —**harshly** *adv.* —**harshness** *n.*

hart *n.* adult male deer.

hart(e)beest *n.* large African antelope.

harum-scarum *adj.* reckless.

harvest *n.* (season for) the gathering of crops; crops gathered. —*v.* gather (a ripened crop). —**harvester** *n.*

has *v.* third person singular of the present tense of HAVE. —**has-been** *n. Informal* person who is no longer popular or successful.

hash *n.* dish of diced meat and vegetables; *Informal* hashish. —**make a hash of** *Informal* mess up or destroy.

hashish [hash-**eesh**] *n.* drug made from the hemp plant, taken for its intoxicating effects.

hasp *n.* clasp which fits over a staple and is secured by a bolt or padlock, used as a fastening.

hassle *Informal* —*n.* trouble or difficulty; nuisance. —*v.* cause annoyance or trouble to.

hassock *n.* cushion for kneeling on in church.

haste *n.* speed or hurry. —**hasten** *v.* (cause to) hurry, increase speed. —**make haste** hurry or rush. —**hasty** *adj.* (too) quick. —**hastily** *adv.*

hat *n.* covering for the head, often with a brim, usually worn to give protection from the weather. —**keep something under one's hat** keep something secret. —**hat trick** any three successive achievements, esp. in sport.

hatch[1] *v.* (cause to) emerge from an egg; devise (a plot or plan). —**hatchery** *n.* place for hatching eggs.

hatch[2] *n.* (hinged door covering) an opening in a floor or wall; opening in the wall between a kitchen and a dining area; door in an aircraft or spacecraft. —**hatchback** *n.* car with a single lifting door in the rear. —**hatchway** *n.* opening in the deck of a ship.

hatchet *n.* small axe. —**bury the hatchet** make peace. —**hatchet job** malicious verbal or written attack. —**hatchet man** *Informal* person carrying out unpleasant tasks for an employer.

hate *v.* dislike intensely; be unwilling (to do something). —*n.* intense dislike; object of hatred.

THESAURUS

harry annoy, badger, chivvy, disturb, fret, harass, molest, pester, plague, tease, torment, trouble, vex, worry

harsh 1. coarse, croaking, crude, discordant, dissonant, glaring, grating, guttural, jarring, rasping, raucous, rough, strident 2. abusive, austere, bitter, bleak, brutal, cruel, dour, grim, hard, relentless, ruthless, severe, sharp, stern, unfeeling, unkind, unpleasant

harshly brutally, cruelly, grimly, roughly, severely, sharply, sternly, strictly

harshness acerbity, acrimony, asperity, austerity, bitterness, brutality, hardness, ill-temper, rigour, severity

harvest 1. ingathering, reaping 2. crop, produce, yield

hash hotchpotch, jumble, mess, mix-up, muddle, shambles

haste 1. briskness, celerity, dispatch, expedition, fleetness, quickness, rapidity, speed, swiftness, urgency 2. bustle, hurry, hustle, impetuosity, rashness, recklessness, rush

hasten bolt, dash, fly, haste, race, run, rush, scurry, scuttle, speed, sprint

hastily 1. apace, fast, promptly, quickly, rapidly, speedily 2. hurriedly, impetuously, impulsively, precipitately, rashly, recklessly, too quickly

hasty 1. brisk, eager, fast, fleet, hurried, prompt, rapid, speedy, swift, urgent 2. foolhardy, headlong, heedless, impetuous, impulsive, precipitate, rash, reckless

hatch 1. breed, brood, incubate 2. *Fig.* conceive, concoct, contrive, design, devise, plan, plot, project, scheme

hate 1. *v.* abhor, abominate, despise, detest, dislike, execrate 2. *n.* abhorrence, abomination, antagonism, antipathy, aversion, detestation, dislike, enmity, execration, hatred, hostility, loathing, odium

hateful abominable, despicable, detestable, disgusting, execrable, foul, horrible, loathsome, obnoxious, odious, offensive, repellent, repugnant, repulsive, revolting, vile

hatred animosity, animus, antagonism, antipathy, aversion, detestation, dislike, enmity, execration, hate, ill will, odium, repugnance, revulsion

DICTIONARY

—**hateful** *adj.* causing or deserving hate. —**hatred** *n.* intense dislike.

haughty *adj.* **-tier, -tiest.** proud, arrogant. —**haughtily** *adv.* —**haughtiness** *n.*

haul *v.* pull or drag with effort. —*n.* amount gained by effort or theft. —**long haul** something that takes a lot of time and effort to achieve. —**haulage** *n.* (charge for) transporting goods. —**haulier** *n.* firm or person that transports goods by road.

haunch *n.* human hip or fleshy hindquarter of an animal.

haunt *v.* visit in the form of a ghost; remain in the thoughts or memory of. —*n.* place visited frequently. —**haunted** *adj.* visited by ghosts; worried. —**haunting** *adj.* extremely beautiful or sad.

haute couture [oat koo-**ture**] *n. French* high fashion.

hauteur [oat-**ur**] *n.* haughtiness.

have *v.* **has, having, had.** hold, possess; experience or be affected with; be obliged (to do); *Slang* cheat or outwit; receive, take, or obtain; cause to be done; give birth to; used to form past tenses (with a past participle), e.g. *I have gone, I had gone.* —**have it out** *Informal* settle by argument. —**have on** *v. Informal* trick or tease. —**have up** *v.* bring to trial.

haven *n.* place of safety.

haversack *n.* canvas bag carried on the back or shoulder.

havoc *n.* disorder and confusion.

haw *n.* hawthorn berry.

hawk[1] *n.* bird of prey with short rounded wings and a long tail; supporter or advocate of warlike policies. —**hawkish, hawklike** *adj.* —**hawk-eyed** *adj.* having extremely good eyesight.

hawk[2] *v.* offer (goods) for sale in the street or door-to-door. —**hawker** *n.*

hawk[3] *v.* cough noisily.

hawser *n.* large rope used on a ship.

hawthorn *n.* thorny shrub or tree.

hay *n.* grass cut and dried as fodder. —**hay fever** allergic reaction to pollen or dust. —**haystack** *n.* large pile of stored hay. —**haywire** *adj.* —**go haywire** *Informal* not function properly.

hazard *n.* risk, danger. —*v.* put at danger; venture (a guess). —**hazardous** *adj.*

haze *n.* mist, often caused by heat. —**hazy** *adj.* misty; vague.

hazel *n.* bush producing nuts. —*adj.* (of eyes) greenish-brown. —**hazelnut** *n.*

H-bomb *n.* hydrogen bomb.

He *Chem.* helium.

he *pron.* refers to: a male person or animal; a person or animal of unspecified sex.

head *n.* upper or front part of the body, containing the sense organs and the brain; upper or most forward part of anything; chief of a group, organization, or school; aptitude; intellect; headline or title; person or animal considered as a unit; white froth on beer; *Informal* headache. —*adj.* chief, principal. —*v.* lead, direct; move (in a particular direction); be at the top or front of; provide with a heading; hit (a ball) with the head. —**go to someone's head** make someone drunk or conceited. —**head over heels (in love)** very much in love. —**not make head nor tail of** not understand. —**off one's head** *Slang* insane. —**header** *n.* action of striking a ball with the head; headlong dive. —**heading** *n.* title written or printed at the top of a page. —**heads** *adv. Informal* with the side of a coin which has a portrait of a head on it uppermost. —**heady** *adj.* intoxicating or exciting. —**headache** *n.* continuous pain in the head; cause of worry or annoy-

THESAURUS

haughty arrogant, conceited, disdainful, high, imperious, lofty, overweening, proud, scornful, snobbish, supercilious

haul 1. *v.* drag, draw, hale, heave, lug, pull, tow, trail, tug 2. *n.* booty, catch, find, gain, harvest, loot, spoils, takings, yield

haunt *v.* 1. visit, walk 2. beset, come back, obsess, plague, possess, prey on, recur, torment, trouble ~*n.* 3. rendezvous, resort

haunting eerie, evocative, nostalgic, poignant, recurrent, unforgettable

have 1. hold, keep, obtain, occupy, own, possess, retain 2. endure, enjoy, experience, feel, meet with, suffer, sustain, undergo 3. **have to** be bound, be compelled, be forced, be obliged, have got to, must, ought, should

haven *Fig.* asylum, refuge, retreat, sanctuary, shelter

havoc chaos, confusion, disorder, disruption, mayhem, shambles

hazardous dangerous, difficult, insecure, perilous, precarious, risky, unsafe

haze cloud, film, fog, mist, obscurity, smokiness, steam, vapour

hazy 1. blurry, cloudy, dim, dull, faint, foggy, misty, nebulous, obscure, overcast, smoky, veiled 2. *Fig.* fuzzy, indefinite, indistinct, loose, muddled, nebulous, uncertain, unclear, vague

DICTIONARY

ance. **—headboard** n. vertical board at the head of a bed. **—head-hunter** n. person who sets out to recruit someone from another company for a particular job. **—headland** n. area of land jutting out into the sea. **—headlight** n. powerful light on the front of a vehicle. **—headline** n. news summary in large type in a newspaper. **—pl.** main points of a news broadcast. **—headlong** adv. head foremost; with haste. **—headphones** pl. n. two small loudspeakers held against the ears by a strap. **—headquarters** pl. n. centre from which operations are directed. **—head start** advantage in a competition. **—headstone** n. gravestone. **—headstrong** adj. self-willed; obstinate. **—headway** n. progress. **—headwind** n. wind blowing against the course of an aircraft or ship.

heal v. make or become well. **—health** n. normal good condition of someone's body; toast drunk in a person's honour. **—healthy** adj. having good health; of or producing good health; functioning well, sound. **—healthily** adv. **—health food** natural food, organically grown and free from additives.

heap n. pile of things lying one on top of another; large quantity. **—v.** gather into a pile; (foll. by on) give abundantly (to).

hear v. **hearing, heard.** perceive (a sound) by ear; listen to; learn or be informed; Law try (a case). **—hear! hear!** exclamation of approval or

agreement. **—hearer** n. **—hearing** n. ability to hear; trial of a case. **—within hearing** close enough to be heard.

hearken v. Obs. listen.

hearsay n. gossip; rumour.

hearse n. funeral car used to carry a coffin.

heart n. organ which pumps blood round the body; centre of emotions and affections; tenderness; enthusiasm or courage; central or most important part; figure representing a heart; playing card of the suit marked with the figure of a heart. **—break someone's heart** cause someone great grief. **—by heart** from memory. **—set one's heart on something** greatly desire something. **—take to heart** get upset about. **—hearten** v. make cheerful, encourage. **—heartless** adj. cruel. **—hearty** adj. friendly, enthusiastic; substantial, nourishing. **—heartily** adv. **—heart attack** sudden severe malfunction of the heart. **—heartbeat** n. one complete pulsation of the heart. **—heartbreak** n. intense grief. **—heartburn** n. pain in the chest caused by indigestion. **—heart failure** sudden stopping of the heartbeat. **—heartfelt** adj. felt sincerely or strongly. **—heart-rending** adj. causing great sorrow. **—heart-throb** n. Slang very attractive person.

hearth n. floor of a fireplace; home.

THESAURUS

head n. 1. pate, skull 2. captain, chief, chieftain, commander, director, leader, manager, master, principal, supervisor 3. apex, crest, crown, height, peak, pitch, summit, tip, top, vertex 4. ability, aptitude, brain, capacity, faculty, flair, intellect, mind, talent, thought ~adj. 5. arch, chief, first, foremost, front, highest, leading, main, premier, prime, principal, supreme, topmost ~v. 6. be or go first, cap, crown, lead, precede, top 7. command, control, direct, govern, guide, lead, manage, rule, run, supervise

headache bane, bother, inconvenience, nuisance, problem, trouble, vexation, worry

heading caption, headline, name, rubric, title

headlong adv. hastily, heedlessly, helter-skelter, hurriedly, pell-mell, precipitately, rashly, wildly

headstrong contrary, heedless, impulsive, intractable, obstinate, perverse, rash, reckless, self-willed, stubborn, ungovernable, unruly, wilful

headway advance, improvement, progress, way

heal cure, make well, mend, remedy, restore, treat

health fitness, robustness, soundness, strength, vigour, wellbeing

healthy active, blooming, fit, flourishing, hale, hardy, robust, sound, strong, sturdy, vigorous, well

heap 1. n. accumulation, collection, hoard, lot, mass, mound, mountain, pile, stack, store 2. v. accumulate, amass, augment, bank, collect, gather, hoard, increase, mound, pile, stack, stockpile, store

hear 1. attend, catch, eavesdrop, hark, heed, listen to, overhear 2. ascertain, be informed, discover, find out, gather, learn, pick up, understand 3. Law examine, investigate, judge, try

hearing 1. audition, ear, perception 2. earshot, range, reach, sound 3. inquiry, investigation, review, trial

hearsay buzz, gossip, report, rumour, talk

heart n. 1. affection, benevolence, compassion, concern, humanity, love, pity, tenderness, understanding 2. boldness, bravery, courage, mettle, mind, nerve, pluck, purpose, resolution, spirit, will 3. centre, core, crux, essence, hub, kernel, marrow, middle, nucleus, pith, quintessence, root 4. **by heart** by memory, by rote, off pat, parrot-fashion (Inf.), pat, word for word

heartfelt ardent, cordial, deep, devout, earnest,

DICTIONARY

heat *n.* state of being hot; energy transferred as a result of a difference in temperature; hot weather; intensity of feeling; preliminary eliminating contest in a competition; readiness to mate in some female animals. —*v.* make hot. —**heated** *adj.* angry. —**heatedly** *adv.* —**heater** *n.*

heath *n.* area of open uncultivated land; low-growing evergreen shrub.

heathen *n.* person not believing in an established religion, pagan. —*adj.* of or relating to heathen peoples.

heather *n.* shrub with small bell-shaped flowers growing on heaths and mountains.

heave *v.* lift with effort; throw (something heavy); utter (a sigh); rise and fall; vomit. —*n.* act of heaving.

heaven *n.* home of God; place or state of bliss. —**the heavens** sky. —**heavenly** *adj.* wonderful or divine; of or like heaven; of or occurring in space.

heavy *adj.* **-vier, -viest.** of great weight; great in degree or amount; dense; difficult or severe; sorrowful; (of a situation) serious. —**heavily** *adv.* —**heaviness** *n.* —**heavy industry** large-scale production of raw material or machinery. —**heavy metal** very loud rock music featuring

guitar riffs. —**heavyweight** *n.* boxer weighing over 175lb (professional) or 81kg (amateur).

Hebrew *n.* ancient language of the Hebrews; its modern form, used in Israel; member of an ancient Semitic people. —*adj.* of this language or people.

heckle *v.* interrupt (a public speaker) with questions, taunts, and comments. —**heckler** *n.*

hectare *n.* one hundred ares or 10 000 square metres (2.471 acres).

hectic *adj.* rushed or busy.

hector *v.* bully.

hedge *n.* row of bushes forming a barrier or boundary. —*v.* be evasive or noncommittal; (foll. by *against*) protect oneself from (loss). —**hedgerow** *n.* bushes forming a hedge. —**hedge sparrow** small brownish songbird.

hedgehog *n.* small mammal with a protective covering of spines.

hedonism *n.* doctrine that pleasure is the most important thing in life. —**hedonist** *n.* —**hedonistic** *adj.*

heed *v.* pay close attention to. —**heedless** *adj.* —**heedless of** taking no notice of.

heel¹ *n.* back part of the foot; part of a shoe

THESAURUS

fervent, genuine, honest, profound, sincere, unfeigned, warm

heartily cordially, deeply, feelingly, genuinely, profoundly, sincerely, unfeignedly, warmly

heartless brutal, callous, cold, cruel, hard, harsh, inhuman, merciless, pitiless, uncaring, unfeeling, unkind

hearty affable, ardent, cordial, eager, effusive, friendly, generous, genial, jovial, unreserved, warm

heat *n.* 1. fever, sultriness, swelter, torridity, warmness, warmth 2. *Fig.* agitation, ardour, excitement, fervour, fever, fury, intensity, passion, vehemence, violence, warmth, zeal ~*v.* 3. flush, glow, grow hot, make hot, reheat, warm up

heated angry, bitter, excited, fierce, fiery, frenzied, furious, intense, passionate, raging, stormy, vehement, violent

heathen 1. *n.* idolater, infidel, pagan, unbeliever 2. *adj.* godless, heathenish, idolatrous, infidel, irreligious, pagan

heave 1. drag, elevate, haul, hoist, lever, lift, pull, raise, tug 2. cast, fling, hurl, pitch, send, sling, throw, toss

heaven *Fig.* bliss, dreamland, ecstasy, enchantment, happiness, paradise, rapture, transport, utopia

heavenly beautiful, blissful, delightful, en-

trancing, exquisite, glorious, lovely, rapturous, ravishing, sublime, wonderful

heavily 1. awkwardly, clumsily, ponderously 2. laboriously, painfully 3. completely, decisively, roundly, thoroughly, utterly

heaviness 1. gravity, weight 2. grievousness, oppressiveness, severity, weightiness

heavy 1. bulky, massive, ponderous, portly, weighty 2. burdensome, difficult, grievous, hard, harsh, intolerable, laborious, onerous, oppressive, severe, tedious, vexatious, wearisome

heckle disrupt, interrupt, jeer, pester, shout down, taunt

hectic boisterous, busy, chaotic, excited, fevered, feverish, flurrying, frantic, frenetic, frenzied, heated, riotous, rushed, turbulent, wild

hedge *n.* 1. hedgerow, quickset 2. barrier, boundary, screen, windbreak ~*v.* 3. dodge, duck, equivocate, evade, prevaricate, quibble, sidestep, temporize

heed *v.* attend, consider, follow, listen to, mark, mind, note, obey, observe, regard

heedless careless, imprudent, inattentive, incautious, negligent, oblivious, rash, reckless, thoughtless, unmindful

DICTIONARY

supporting the heel; *Slang* contemptible person.
—*v.* make or replace the heel of.

heel² *v.* lean to one side.

hefty *adj.* **heftier, heftiest.** large, heavy, or strong.

hegemony [hig-em-on-ee] *n.* political domination.

Hegira *n.* Mohammed's flight from Mecca to Medina in 622 AD.

heifer [hef-fer] *n.* young cow.

height *n.* distance from base to top; distance above sea level; highest degree or topmost point. —**heighten** *v.* make or become higher or more intense.

heinous *adj.* evil and shocking.

heir *n.* person entitled to inherit property or rank. —**heiress** *n. fem.* —**heirloom** *n.* object that has belonged to a family for generations.

held *v.* past of HOLD¹.

helicopter *n.* aircraft lifted and propelled by rotating overhead blades. —**heliport** *n.* airport for helicopters.

heliotrope *n.* plant with purple flowers. —*adj.* light purple.

helium [heel-ee-um] *n.* very light colourless odourless gas.

helix [heel-iks] *n., pl.* **helices, helixes.** spiral. —**helical** *adj.*

hell *n.* home of the wicked after death; place or state of wickedness, suffering, or punishment. —**hell for leather** at great speed. —**hellish** *adj.* —**hell-bent** *adj.* intent.

Hellenic *adj.* of the (ancient) Greeks or their language.

hello *interj.* expression of greeting or surprise.

helm *n.* tiller or wheel for steering a ship.

helmet *n.* hard hat worn for protection.

help *v.* make something easier, better, or quicker for (someone); improve (a situation); refrain from, e.g. *I can't help laughing.* —**help oneself** serve oneself; *Informal* steal something. —**helper** *n.* —**helpful** *adj.* —**helping** *n.* single portion of food. —**helpless** *adj.* weak or incapable. —**helplessly** *adv.* —**helpmate, -meet** *n.* companion and helper; husband or wife.

helter-skelter *adj.* haphazard and careless. —*adv.* in a haphazard and careless manner. —*n.* high spiral slide at a fairground.

hem *n.* border of cloth, folded under and stitched down. —*v.* **hemming, hemmed.** provide with a hem. —**hem in** *v.* surround and prevent from moving. —**hemline** *n.* level to which the hem of a skirt hangs.

hemisphere *n.* half of a sphere, esp. the earth. —**hemispherical** *adj.*

hemlock *n.* poison derived from a plant with spotted stems and small white flowers.

hemp *n.* Asian plant; its fibre, used to make canvas and rope; narcotic drug obtained from hemp.

hen *n.* female domestic fowl; female of any bird. —**hen party** party for women only. —**henpecked** *adj.* (of a man) dominated by his wife.

hence *adv.* for this reason; from this time. —**henceforward, henceforth** *adv.* from now on.

THESAURUS

height 1. altitude, elevation, highness, loftiness, stature 2. apex, apogee, crest, crown, hill, mountain, peak, pinnacle, summit, top, vertex, zenith 3. acme, dignity, eminence, exaltation, grandeur, loftiness, prominence

heighten add to, aggravate, amplify, augment, enhance, improve, increase, intensify, magnify, sharpen, strengthen

hell 1. abyss, bottomless pit, infernal regions, inferno, lower world, nether world, underworld 2. agony, anguish, martyrdom, misery, nightmare, ordeal, suffering, torment, trial, wretchedness

hellish damnable, damned, devilish, diabolical, fiendish, infernal

help *v.* 1. abet, aid, assist, back, befriend, cooperate, promote, relieve, save, second, serve, stand by, succour, support 2. alleviate, ameliorate, cure, ease, facilitate, heal, improve, mitigate, relieve, remedy, restore ~*n.* 3. advice, aid, assistance, avail, benefit, cooperation, guidance, service, support, use, utility

helper aide, ally, assistant, attendant, auxiliary, collaborator, colleague, deputy, helpmate, mate, partner, right-hand man, second, supporter

helpful 1. beneficial, constructive, favourable, fortunate, practical, productive, profitable, serviceable, timely, useful 2. beneficent, benevolent, caring, friendly, kind, supportive, sympathetic

helping *n.* piece, plateful, portion, ration, serving

helpless 1. abandoned, defenceless, dependent, destitute, exposed, forlorn, vulnerable, weak 2. disabled, feeble, impotent, incapable, incompetent, infirm, paralysed, powerless, unfit, weak

hem border, edge, fringe, margin, trimming

hence ergo, therefore, thus

henceforth from now on, hence, hereafter, hereinafter, in the future

DICTIONARY

henchman *n.* attendant or follower.

henna *n.* reddish dye made from a shrub or tree. —*v.* dye the hair with henna.

henry *n., pl.* **-ry, -ries, -rys.** unit of electrical inductance.

hepatic *adj.* of the liver. —**hepatitis** *n.* inflammation of the liver.

heptagon *n.* figure with seven sides. —**heptagonal** *adj.*

heptathlon *n.* athletic contest involving seven events.

her *pron.* refers to a female person or animal or anything personified as feminine (when the object of a sentence or clause). —*det.* of, belonging to, or associated with her.

herald *n.* person who announces important news; forerunner. —*v.* announce or signal the approach of. —**heraldry** *n.* study of coats of arms and the histories of families. —**heraldic** *adj.*

herb *n.* plant that is used for flavouring in cookery, and in medicine. —**herbal** *adj.* —**herbalist** *n.* person who grows or specializes in the use of medicinal herbs. —**herbaceous** *adj.* (of a plant) soft-stemmed. —**herbaceous border** flower bed that contains perennials rather than annuals. —**herbicide** *n.* chemical which destroys plants. —**herbivore** *n.* animal that feeds on plants. —**herbivorous** [her-biv-or-uss] *adj.*

herculean [her-kew-lee-an] *adj.* requiring great strength or effort.

herd *n.* group of animals feeding and living together; large crowd of people. —*v.* collect into a herd. —**herdsman** *n.* man who looks after a herd of animals.

here *adv.* in, at, or to this place or point. —**hereabouts** *adv.* near here. —**hereafter** *n.* life after death. —*adv.* in the future. —**hereby** *adv.* by means of or as a result of this. —**herein** *adv.* in this place, matter, or document. —**herewith** *adv.* with this.

heredity [hir-red-it-ee] *n.* passing on of characteristics from one generation to another. —**hereditary** *adj.* passed on genetically from one generation to another; passed on by inheritance.

heresy [herr-iss-ee] *n., pl.* **-sies.** opinion contrary to accepted opinion or belief. —**heretic** [herr-it-ik] *n.* person who holds unorthodox opinions. —**heretical** [hir-ret-ik-al] *adj.*

heritage *n.* thing that may be or is inherited; anything from the past, considered as the inheritance of present-day society.

hermaphrodite [her-maf-roe-dite] *n.* person, animal, or plant that has both male and female reproductive organs.

hermetic *adj.* sealed so as to be airtight. —**hermetically** *adv.*

hermit *n.* person living in solitude, esp. for religious reasons. —**hermitage** *n.* dwelling of a hermit.

hernia *n.* protrusion of (part of) an organ through the lining of the surrounding body cavity.

hero *n., pl.* **heroes.** principal character in a film, book, play, etc.; man greatly admired for exceptional qualities or achievements. —**heroine** *n. fem.* —**heroic** *adj.* of, like, or befitting a hero; courageous. —**heroics** *pl. n.* extravagant behaviour. —**heroically** *adv.* —**heroism** [herr-oh-izz-um] *n.*

heroin *n.* highly addictive drug derived from morphine.

heron *n.* long-legged wading bird. —**heronry** *n.* place where herons breed.

herpes [her-peez] *n.* any of several inflamma-

THESAURUS

herald *n.* 1. crier, messenger 2. forerunner, harbinger, indication, omen, precursor, sign, signal, token

herd 1. *n.* collection, crowd, crush, drove, flock, horde, mass, mob, multitude, press, swarm, throng 2. *v.* assemble, associate, collect, congregate, flock, gather, huddle, muster, rally

hereafter after this, from now on, henceforth, in future

hereditary family, genetic, inborn, inbred, inheritable

heredity constitution, genetics, inheritance

heresy apostasy, error, impiety, schism, unorthodoxy

heretic apostate, dissenter, renegade, sectarian, separatist

heritage bequest, birthright, endowment, estate, inheritance, legacy, lot, patrimony, portion, share, tradition

hermit anchorite, eremite, monk, recluse, solitary

hero 1. celebrity, champion, exemplar, great man, idol, star, superstar, victor 2. leading man, male lead, protagonist

heroic bold, brave, courageous, daring, doughty, fearless, gallant, intrepid, undaunted, valiant

heroine 1. celebrity, goddess, ideal 2. diva, female lead, leading lady, prima donna

heroism boldness, bravery, courage, daring, fearlessness, fortitude, gallantry, prowess, spirit, valour

DICTIONARY

tory skin diseases, including shingles and cold sores.

Herr [hair] *n., pl.* **Herren.** German title of address equivalent to Mr.

herring *n.* important food fish of northern seas. —**herringbone** *n.* pattern of zigzag lines.

hertz *n., pl.* **hertz.** *Physics* unit of frequency.

hesitate *v.* be slow or uncertain in acting; be reluctant (to do something). —**hesitation** *n.* —**hesitant** *adj.* undecided or wavering. —**hesitantly** *adv.* —**hesitancy** *n.*

hessian *n.* coarse jute cloth.

heterodox *adj.* not orthodox. —**heterodoxy** *n.*

heterogeneous [het-er-oh-**jean**-ee-uss] *adj.* composed of diverse elements. —**heterogeneity** *n.*

heterosexual *n., adj.* (person) sexually attracted to members of the opposite sex. —**heterosexuality** *n.*

heuristic [hew-**rist**-ik] *adj.* involving learning by investigation.

hew *v.* **hewing, hewed, hewed** *or* **hewn.** chop or cut with an axe; carve from a substance.

hexagon *n.* figure with six sides. —**hexagonal** *adj.*

hey *interj.* expression of surprise or for catching attention.

heyday *n.* time of greatest success, prime.

Hg *Chem.* mercury.

HGV heavy goods vehicle.

hiatus [hie-**ay**-tuss] *n., pl.* **-tuses, -tus.** break or interruption in continuity.

hibernate *v.* (of an animal) pass the winter as if in a deep sleep. —**hibernation** *n.*

Hibernia *n. Poetic* Ireland. —**Hibernian** *adj.*

hibiscus *n., pl.* **-cuses.** tropical plant with large brightly coloured flowers.

hiccup, hiccough *n.* spasm of the breathing organs with a sharp coughlike sound. —*v.* make a hiccup or hiccups.

hick *n. US informal* unsophisticated country person.

hickory *n., pl.* **-ries.** N American nut-bearing tree; its tough wood.

hide[1] *v.* **hiding, hid, hidden.** conceal or obscure (oneself or an object); keep secret. —*n.* place of concealment, esp. for a bird-watcher. —**hide-out** *n.* hiding place.

hide[2] *v.* skin of an animal. —**hiding** *n. Slang* thrashing. —**hidebound** *adj.* restricted by petty rules.

hideous [**hid**-ee-uss] *adj.* ugly, revolting. —**hideously** *adv.*

hierarchy [**hire**-ark-ee] *n., pl.* **-chies.** system of people or things arranged in a graded order. —**hierarchical** *adj.*

hieroglyphic [hire-oh-**gliff**-ik] *adj.* of a form of writing using picture symbols, as used in ancient Egypt. —*n.* (also **hieroglyph**) symbol representing an object, idea, or sound; symbol that is difficult to decipher.

hi-fi *n.* set of high-quality sound-reproducing equipment. —*adj.* short for HIGH-FIDELITY.

higgledy-piggledy *adv., adj.* in confusion.

high *adj.* tall, of greater than average height; far above ground or sea level; being at its peak; greater than usual in intensity or amount; of great importance, quality, or rank; (of a sound) acute in pitch; *Informal* under the influence of alcohol or drugs; (of food) slightly decomposed. —*adv.* at or to a high level. —**highly** *adv.* —**highly strung** nervous and easily upset. —**Highness** *n.* title used to address or refer to a royal person. —**highbrow** *n.* intellectual or scholar. —*adj.* appealing to highbrows. —**High Church** belonging to a section within the Church of England stressing the importance of ceremony and ritual. —**higher education** education at colleges, universities, and polytechnics. —**high-fidelity** *adj.* able to reproduce sound with little or no distortion. —**high-flown** *adj.* (of ideas or speech) grand and elaborate. —**high-handed** *adj.* over-

THESAURUS

hesitant diffident, doubtful, half-hearted, halting, irresolute, reluctant, sceptical, shy, timid, uncertain, unsure, vacillating, wavering

hesitate be uncertain, delay, dither, doubt, pause, vacillate, wait, waver

hesitation delay, doubt, indecision, irresolution, uncertainty, vacillation

hew 1. axe, chop, cut, hack, lop, split 2. carve, fashion, form, make, model, sculpt, sculpture, shape, smooth

heyday bloom, flowering, pink, prime

hidden abstruse, close, concealed, covert, cryptic, dark, masked, mysterious, mystic, mysti-

cal, obscure, occult, recondite, secret, shrouded, unseen, veiled

hide *v.* 1. cache, conceal, hole up, lie low, secrete, take cover 2. bury, cloak, conceal, cover, disguise, eclipse, mask, obscure, screen, shelter, shroud, veil

hidebound conventional, narrow-minded, rigid, set

hideous ghastly, grim, grisly, grotesque, gruesome, monstrous, repulsive, revolting, ugly, unsightly

hiding *n.* beating, caning, drubbing, flogging, spanking, thrashing, whipping

DICTIONARY

bearing and dogmatic. —**highlands** *pl. n.* area of relatively high ground. —**highlight** *n.* outstanding part or feature; light-toned area in a painting or photograph; lightened streak in the hair. —*v.* give emphasis to. —**high-rise** *adj.* (of a building) having many storeys. —**high tea** early evening meal consisting of a cooked dish, bread, cakes, and tea. —**high-tech** *adj.* same as HI-TECH. —**high time** latest possible time. —**highway** *n. US* main road. —**Highway Code** regulations and recommendations applying to all road users. —**highwayman** *n.* (formerly) robber, usually on horseback, who robbed travellers at gunpoint.

hijack *v.* seize control of (a vehicle or aircraft) while travelling. —**hijacker** *n.*

hike *v.* walk a long way (for pleasure) in the country; (foll. by *up*) pull (up) or raise. —**hiker** *n.*

hilarious *adj.* very funny. —**hilariously** *adv.* —**hilarity** *n.*

hill *n.* raised part of the earth's surface, less high than a mountain; incline or slope. —**hilly** *adj.* —**hillock** *n.* small hill. —**hillbilly** *n. US* unsophisticated country person.

hilt *n.* handle of a sword or knife.

him *pron.* refers to a male person or animal (when the object of a sentence or clause).

hind[1] *adj.* **hinder, hindmost.** situated at the back.

hind[2] *n.* female deer.

hinder *v.* obstruct the progress of. —**hindrance** *n.*

Hinduism *n.* dominant religion of India which involves the worship of many gods and a belief in reincarnation. —**Hindu** *n.* person who practises Hinduism. —*adj.* of Hinduism. —**Hindi** *n.* language of N central India.

hinge *n.* device for holding together two parts so that one can swing freely. —*v.* fit a hinge to; (foll. by *on*) depend (on).

hint *n.* indirect suggestion; piece of advice; small amount. —*v.* suggest indirectly.

hinterland *n.* land lying behind a coast or near a city, esp. a port.

hip[1] *n.* either side of the body below the waist and above the thigh.

hip[2] *n.* fruit of the rose bush.

hippie *n.* (esp. in the late 1960s) person whose behaviour and dress imply a rejection of conventional values.

hippo *n., pl.* **-pos.** *Informal* hippopotamus.

hippodrome *n.* music hall, variety theatre, or circus.

hippopotamus *n., pl.* **-muses, -mi.** large Afri-

THESAURUS

high *adj.* 1. elevated, lofty, soaring, steep, tall, towering 2. excessive, extreme, great, sharp, strong 3. arch, chief, eminent, exalted, important, influential, leading, powerful, prominent, ruling, significant, superior 4. acute, penetrating, piercing, piping, sharp, shrill, soprano, strident, treble ~*adv.* 5. aloft, at great height, far up, way up

highbrow 1. *n.* aesthete, intellectual, mastermind, savant, scholar 2. *adj.* bookish, cultivated, cultured, deep

high-flown elaborate, extravagant, florid, grandiose, lofty, overblown, pretentious

high-handed arbitrary, autocratic, despotic, domineering, imperious, oppressive, overbearing

highlight 1. *n.* climax, feature, focus, peak 2. *v.* accent, emphasize, feature, set off, show up, spotlight, stress, underline

highly decidedly, eminently, extraordinarily, extremely, greatly, immensely, supremely, tremendously, vastly, very, very much

hijack commandeer, expropriate, seize, skyjack, take over

hike *v.* back-pack, ramble, tramp, walk

hilarious amusing, comical, convivial, entertaining, funny, gay, happy, humorous, jolly, jovial, joyful, merry, noisy

hilarity amusement, boisterousness, cheerfulness, conviviality, exhilaration, exuberance, gaiety, glee, high spirits, jollification, jollity, joviality, joyousness, laughter, levity, merriment, mirth

hill elevation, eminence, fell, height, knoll, mound, mount, prominence, tor

hilt grip, haft, handgrip, handle, helve

hinder arrest, check, debar, delay, deter, encumber, hamper, handicap, impede, interrupt, obstruct, oppose, prevent, retard, stop, thwart

hindmost concluding, final, furthest, last, trailing, ultimate

hindrance bar, barrier, check, deterrent, difficulty, drag, drawback, encumbrance, handicap, hitch, impediment, limitation, obstacle, snag, stoppage

hinge *v.* depend, hang, pivot, rest, turn

hint *n.* 1. clue, implication, indication, inkling, innuendo, intimation, mention, reminder, suggestion, tip-off 2. advice, help, pointer, suggestion, tip 3. breath, dash, *soupçon*, speck, suggestion, suspicion, taste, tinge, touch, trace, whiff, whisper ~*v.* 4. allude, cue, imply, indicate, intimate, mention, prompt, suggest, tip off

DICTIONARY

can mammal with thick wrinkled skin, living in rivers.

hippy *n., pl.* **-pies.** same as HIPPIE.

hire *v.* obtain temporary use of by payment; employ for wages. —*n.* act of hiring; payment for the use of something. —**hireling** *n.* person who works only for wages. —**hire-purchase** *n.* system of purchase by which the buyer pays for goods by instalments.

hirsute [**her**-suit] *adj.* hairy.

his *pron., det.* (something) belonging to him.

Hispanic *adj.* of Spain or a Spanish-speaking country.

hiss *n.* sound like that of a long *s* (as an exclamation of contempt). —*v.* utter a hiss; show derision or anger towards.

histamine [**hiss**-ta-meen] *n.* substance released by the body tissues, causing allergic reactions.

histogram *n.* statistical graph in which the frequency of values is represented by vertical bars of varying heights and widths.

histology *n.* study of the tissues of an animal or plant.

history *n., pl.* **-ries.** (record or account of) past events and developments; study of these; record of someone's past; play that depicts historical events. —**historian** *n.* writer of history. —**historic** *adj.* famous or significant in history. —**historical** *adj.* based on history; occurring in the past. —**historically** *adv.*

histrionic *adj.* excessively dramatic. —**histrionics** *pl. n.* melodramatic behaviour.

hit *v.* **hitting, hit.** strike, touch forcefully; come into violent contact with; affect adversely; reach (a point or place). —*n.* impact or blow; success.

—**hit it off** *Informal* get on well together. —**hit the trail, road** *Informal* set out on a journey. —**hit man** hired assassin. —**hit on** *v.* think of (an idea). —**hit-or-miss** *adj.* haphazard.

hitch *v.* fasten with a loop or hook; pull up with a jerk. —*n.* slight difficulty.

hitch(hike) *v.* travel by obtaining free lifts. —**hitchhiker** *n.*

hi-tech *adj.* using sophisticated technology.

hither *adv.* to or towards this place. —**hitherto** *adv.* until this time.

HIV human immunodeficiency virus.

hive *n.* structure in which bees live. —**hive of activity** place where people are very busy. —**hive off** *v.* separate from a larger group.

hives *n.* disease causing itchy red or whitish patches on the skin.

HM Her (*or* His) Majesty.

HMS Her (*or* His) Majesty's Service *or* Ship.

HNC Higher National Certificate.

HND Higher National Diploma.

hoard *n.* store hidden away for future use. —*v.* gather or accumulate. —**hoarder** *n.*

hoarding *n.* large board for displaying advertisements.

hoarfrost *n.* white ground frost.

hoarse *adj.* (of a voice) rough and unclear; having a rough and unclear voice. —**hoarsely** *adv.* —**hoarseness** *n.*

hoary *adj.* **hoarier, hoariest.** grey or white (with age); very old.

hoax *n.* deception or trick. —*v.* deceive or play a trick upon. —**hoaxer** *n.*

THESAURUS

hire *v.* 1. appoint, employ, engage, sign up, take on 2. charter, engage, lease, let, rent ~*n.* 3. charge, cost, fee, price, rent, rental

hiss *n.* 1. buzz, hissing, sibilance 2. boo, catcall, contempt, derision, jeer ~*v.* 3. rasp, shrill, sibilate, wheeze, whirr, whistle, whiz 4. boo, catcall, condemn, damn, decry, deride, hoot, jeer, mock, revile, ridicule

historic celebrated, extraordinary, famous, momentous, notable, outstanding, remarkable, significant

history account, annals, chronicle, memoirs, narration, narrative, recital, record, relation, saga, story

hit *v.* 1. bang, batter, beat, cuff, flog, knock, lob, punch, slap, smack, sock (*Sl.*), strike, swat, thump, whack 2. bang into, bump, collide with, crash against, run into, smash into ~*n.* 3. blow, bump, clash, cuff, impact, knock, rap,

shot, slap, smack, stroke 4. *Inf.* sellout, sensation, success, triumph, winner

hitch 1. *v.* attach, connect, couple, fasten, harness, join, make fast, tether, tie, unite, yoke 2. *n.* catch, check, delay, difficulty, drawback, hindrance, hold-up, impediment, mishap, problem, snag, stoppage, trouble

hitherto heretofore, previously, so far, thus far, till now, until now, up to now

hit on *or* **upon** arrive at, chance upon, discover, guess, invent, realize, stumble on

hit-or-miss aimless, casual, cursory, haphazard, indiscriminate, random, uneven

hoard 1. *n.* cache, fund, heap, mass, pile, reserve, stockpile, store, supply 2. *v.* accumulate, amass, buy up, cache, collect, deposit, garner, gather, hive, lay up, put by, save, stockpile, store, treasure

hoarse croaky, grating, gravelly, growling, gruff,

DICTIONARY

hob *n.* flat top part of a cooker.

hobble *v.* walk lamely; tie the legs of (a horse) together.

hobby *n., pl.* **-bies.** activity pursued in one's spare time. —**hobbyhorse** *n.* favourite topic; toy horse.

hobgoblin *n.* mischievous goblin.

hobnail *n.* large-headed nail for boot soles.

hobnob *v.* **-nobbing, -nobbed.** (foll. by *with*) socialize (with).

hobo *n., pl.* **-bos.** *US* tramp or vagrant.

hock[1] *n.* joint in the leg of a horse or similar animal corresponding to the human ankle.

hock[2] *n.* white German wine.

hock[3] *Informal* —*v.* pawn. —**in hock** pawned; in debt.

hockey *n.* team game played on a field with a ball and curved sticks; *US* ice hockey.

hocus-pocus *n.* trickery.

hod *n.* open wooden box attached to a pole, for carrying bricks or mortar; type of coal scuttle.

hoe *n.* long-handled tool used to loosen soil or to weed. —*v.* scrape or weed using a hoe.

hog *n.* castrated male pig; *Informal* greedy person. —*v.* **hogging, hogged.** *Informal* take more than one's share of. —**hogshead** *n.* large cask. —**hogwash** *n.* *Informal* nonsense.

Hogmanay *n.* (in Scotland) New Year's Eve.

hoi polloi *n.* the ordinary people.

hoick *v.* raise abruptly and sharply.

hoist *v.* raise or lift up. —*n.* device for lifting things.

hoity-toity *adj. Informal* arrogant or haughty.

hold[1] *v.* **holding, held.** keep or support in or using the hands or arms; maintain in a specified position or state; have the capacity for; own, possess; keep possession of; reserve (a room etc.); restrain or keep back; not use; cause to take place, e.g. *hold a meeting;* (cause to) remain committed to (a promise etc.); believe. —*n.* act or method of holding; influence; something held onto for support. —**holder** *n.* —**holding** *n.* property, such as land or stocks and shares. —**holdall** *n.* large strong travelling bag. —**hold-up** *n.* armed robbery; delay.

hold[2] *n.* cargo compartment in a ship or aircraft.

hole *n.* area hollowed out in a solid; opening or hollow; animal's burrow; *Informal* unattractive place; *Informal* difficult situation. —*v.* make holes in; hit (a golf ball) into a hole. —**holey** *adj.*

holiday *n.* day or other period of rest from work or studies; time spent away from home for rest or recreation.

holism *n.* consideration of the complete person in the treatment of disease. —**holistic** *adj.*

hollow *adj.* having a hole or space inside; without any real value or worth; (of sounds) as if echoing in a hollow place. —*n.* cavity or space; dip in the land. —*v.* form a hollow in.

holly *n.* evergreen tree with prickly leaves and red berries.

hollyhock *n.* tall garden plant with spikes of colourful flowers.

holocaust *n.* destruction or loss of life on a massive scale.

THESAURUS

guttural, harsh, husky, rasping, raucous, rough, throaty

hoax cheat, deception, fraud, imposture, joke, practical joke, prank, ruse, swindle, trick

hobby activity, diversion, pastime, relaxation, sideline

hoist 1. *v.* elevate, erect, heave, lift, raise, rear 2. *n.* crane, elevator, lift, tackle, winch

hold *v.* 1. have, keep, maintain, occupy, own, possess, retain 2. adhere, clasp, cleave, clinch, cling, clutch, cradle, embrace, enfold, grasp, grip, stick 3. arrest, bind, check, confine, curb, detain, imprison, restrain, stay, stop, suspend 4. assume, believe, consider, deem, entertain, esteem, judge, maintain, presume, reckon, regard, think, view 5. assemble, call, carry on, celebrate, conduct, convene, have, run 6. bear, brace, carry, prop, shoulder, support, sustain, take 7. accommodate, comprise, contain, seat, take ~*n.* 8. clasp, clutch, grasp, grip 9. footing, leverage, prop, purchase, stay, support, vantage

holder bearer, custodian, incumbent, keeper, occupant, owner, possessor, proprietor, purchaser

hold-up bottleneck, delay, difficulty, hitch, obstruction, setback, snag, stoppage, trouble, wait

hole breach, break, crack, fissure, gap, opening, outlet, puncture, rent, split, tear, vent

holiday break, leave, recess, time off, vacation

holiness devoutness, divinity, godliness, piety, purity, sanctity, spirituality

hollow *adj.* 1. empty, unfilled, vacant, void 2. concave, depressed, indented, sunken 3. deep, dull, flat, low, muffled, muted, rumbling, toneless 4. empty, fruitless, futile, pointless, useless, vain, worthless ~*n.* 5. basin, bowl, cave, cavern, cavity, crater, cup, dent, depression, hole, indentation, pit, trough 6. bottom, dale, dell, dingle, glen, valley

DICTIONARY

hologram *n.* three-dimensional photographic image.

holograph *n.* document handwritten by the author.

holography *n.* science of using lasers to produce holograms.

holster *n.* leather case for a pistol, hung from a belt.

holy *adj.* **-lier, -liest.** of or associated with God or a deity; devout or virtuous. —**holiness** *n.* —**holier-than-thou** *adj.* self-righteous. —**Holy Communion** *Christianity* service in remembrance of the death and resurrection of Jesus Christ. —**Holy Grail** (in medieval legend) the bowl used by Jesus Christ at the Last Supper. —**Holy Spirit, Ghost** *Christianity* one of the three aspects of God. —**Holy Week** *Christianity* week before Easter.

homage *n.* show of respect or honour towards something or someone.

home *n.* place where one lives; institution to care for the elderly, infirm, etc. —*adj.* of one's home, birthplace, or native country. —*adv.* to or at home. —*v.* (foll. by *in on*) direct or be directed onto (a point or target). —**at home** at ease. —**bring home** to make clear to. —**home and dry** *Informal* safe or successful. —**homeless** *adj.* —**homelessness** *n.* —**homely** *adj.* simple, ordinary, and comfortable; *US* unattractive. —**homeward** *adj., adv.* —**homewards** *adv.* —**home-brew** *n.* beer made at home. —**home-made** *adj.* made at home or on the premises. —**homesick** *adj.* depressed by absence from home. —**homesickness** *n.* —**home truths** unpleasant facts told to a person about himself or herself. —**homework** *n.* school work done at home.

homeopathy [home-ee-**op**-ath-ee] *n.* treatment of disease by small doses of a drug that produces symptoms of the disease in healthy people.

—**homeopath** *n.* person who practises homeopathy. —**homeopathic** [home-ee-oh-**path**-ik] *adj.* —**homeopathically** *adv.*

homicide *n.* killing of a human being; person who kills another. —**homicidal** *adj.*

homily *n., pl.* **-lies.** speech telling people how they should behave.

hominid *n.* man or any extinct forerunner of man.

homo- *combining form* same, e.g. *homosexual.*

Homo sapiens [**hoe**-moh **sap**-ee-enz] *n.* human beings as a species.

homogeneous [home-oh-**jean**-ee-uss] *adj.* formed of similar parts. —**homogeneity** *n.* —**homogenize** *v.* make homogeneous; break up fat globules in (milk or cream) to distribute them evenly.

homograph *n.* word spelt the same as another.

homologous [hom-**ol**-log-uss] *adj.* having a related or similar position or structure.

homonym *n.* word with the same spelling or pronunciation as another, but with a different meaning.

homophobia *n.* hatred or fear of homosexuals. —**homophobic** *adj.*

homophone *n.* word with the same pronunciation as another.

homosexual *n., adj.* (person) sexually attracted to members of the same sex. —**homosexuality** *n.*

hone *v.* sharpen.

honest *adj.* not cheating, lying, or stealing; genuine or sincere; just or fair. —**honestly** *adv.* —**honesty** *n.* quality of being honest; plant with silvery seed pods.

honey *n.* sweet edible fluid made by bees from nectar; term of endearment. —**honeycomb** *n.* waxy structure of hexagonal cells in which hon-

---

THESAURUS

holy devout, divine, faithful, godly, hallowed, pious, pure, religious, righteous, saintly, sublime, virtuous

home 1. abode, dwelling, habitation, house, residence 2. birthplace, family, fireside, hearth, homestead, home town, household 3. element, habitat, haunt, range, territory 4. **at home** at ease, comfortable, familiar, relaxed

homicidal deadly, lethal, mortal, murderous

homicide bloodshed, killing, manslaughter, murder, slaying

homogeneity comparability, consistency, oneness, sameness, similarity, uniformity

homogeneous akin, alike, cognate, comparable, consistent, identical, kindred, similar, uniform, unvarying

honest 1. decent, ethical, high-minded, honourable, law-abiding, reliable, reputable, scrupulous, trustworthy, trusty, truthful, upright, veracious, virtuous 2. equitable, fair, impartial, just 3. candid, direct, forthright, frank, open, outright, plain, sincere

honestly 1. by fair means, cleanly, ethically, honourably, in good faith, lawfully, legally, legitimately, on the level (*Inf.*), with clean hands 2. candidly, frankly, in all sincerity, in plain English, plainly, straight (out), to one's face, truthfully

honesty fidelity, honour, integrity, morality, probity, rectitude, reputability, straightness, trustworthiness, truthfulness, uprightness, veracity, virtue

DICTIONARY

ey is stored. —**honeydew melon** melon with yellow skin and sweet pale flesh. —**honeymoon** *n.* holiday taken by a newly married couple. —**honeysuckle** *n.* climbing shrub with sweet-smelling flowers.

honk *n.* sound made by a car horn; sound made by a goose. —*v.* (cause to) make this sound.

honour *n.* personal integrity; (award given out of) respect; pleasure or privilege. —*pl.* rank or mark of the highest academic standard in a university degree course. —*v.* give praise and attention to; give an award to (someone) out of respect; keep (a promise); accept or pay (a cheque or bill). —**do the honours** act as host or hostess by pouring drinks or giving out food. —**honourable** *adj.* —**honourably** *adv.* —**honorary** *adj.* held or given only as an honour; holding a position or giving one's services without pay. —**honorific** *adj.* showing respect.

hood[1] *n.* head covering, often part of a coat etc.; folding roof of a convertible car or a pram; *US* car bonnet. —*v.* cover (as if) with a hood. —**hooded** *adj.* (of a garment) having a hood; (of eyes) having heavy eyelids that appear to be half closed.

hood[2] *n. Slang* hoodlum.

hoodlum *n. Slang* gangster, lawless youth.

hoodoo *n., pl.* **-doos.** (cause of) bad luck.

hoodwink *v.* trick or deceive.

hoof *n., pl.* **hooves, hoofs.** horny casing of the foot of a horse, deer, etc. —**hoof it** *Informal* walk.

hoo-ha *n.* fuss or commotion.

hook *n.* curved piece of metal used to hang, hold, or pull something; short swinging punch. —*v.* fasten or catch (as if) with a hook. —**hooked** *adj.* shaped like a hook; caught; (foll. by *on*) *Slang* addicted (to). —**hooker** *n. Slang* prostitute; *Rugby* player who uses his feet to get the ball in

a scrum. —**hook-up** *n.* linking of radio or television stations. —**hookworm** *n.* parasitic worm with hooked mouth parts.

hookah *n.* oriental pipe in which smoke is drawn through water and a long tube.

hooligan *n.* rowdy young person. —**hooliganism** *n.*

hoop *n.* rigid circular band, used esp. as a child's toy or for animals to jump through in the circus. —**be put through the hoops** go through an ordeal or test. —**hooped** *adj.*

hoopla *n.* fairground game in which hoops are thrown over objects in an attempt to win them.

hooray *interj.* same as HURRAH.

hoot *n.* owl's cry or similar sound; cry of derision; *Informal* amusing person or thing. —*v.* jeer or yell contemptuously at (someone); sound (a car horn); *Informal* laugh. —**hooter** *n.* device that hoots; *Slang* nose.

Hoover *n.* ® vacuum cleaner. —*v.* (**h-**) vacuum.

hooves *n.* a plural of HOOF.

hop[1] *v.* **hopping, hopped.** jump on one foot; move in short jumps; *Informal* move quickly. —*n.* instance of hopping; short journey, esp. by air; *Informal* dance. —**on the hop** *Informal* unawares, e.g. *caught on the hop;* active or busy.

hop[2] *n.* climbing plant with green conelike flowers used to give beer a bitter flavour. —*pl.* the dried flowers.

hope *n.* expectation of something desired; thing that gives cause for hope or is desired. —*v.* want (something) to happen or be true. —**hopeful** *adj.* having, expressing, or inspiring hope. —*n.* person considered to be on the brink of success. —**hopefully** *adv.* in a hopeful manner; it is hoped. —**hopeless** *adj.*

THESAURUS

honour *n.* 1. credit, dignity, distinction, esteem, fame, glory, prestige, rank, renown, reputation, repute 2. acclaim, accolade, commendation, deference, homage, kudos, praise, recognition, regard, respect, reverence, tribute 3. decency, fairness, goodness, integrity, morality, probity, rectitude, uprightness 4. compliment, credit, favour, pleasure, privilege ~*v.* 5. admire, adore, appreciate, esteem, exalt, glorify, hallow, prize, respect, revere, reverence, value, venerate, worship

honourable 1. ethical, fair, honest, just, moral, principled, true, trustworthy, trusty, upright, upstanding, virtuous 2. eminent, great, illustrious, noble, notable, noted, prestigious, renowned, venerable

honours awards, decorations, dignities, distinctions, laurels, titles

hoodwink befool, cheat, cozen, delude, dupe, fool, hoax, impose, mislead, swindle, trick

hook *n.* 1. catch, clasp, fastener, hasp, holder, link, lock, peg 2. noose, snare, springe, trap ~*v.* 3. catch, clasp, fasten, fix, hasp, secure 4. catch, enmesh, ensnare, entrap, snare, trap

hooligan delinquent, rowdy, ruffian, tough, vandal

hoop band, circlet, girdle, loop, ring, wheel

hoot *n.* 1. call, cry, toot 2. boo, catcall, hiss, jeer, yell ~*v.* 3. boo, catcall, condemn, decry, denounce, hiss, howl down, jeer, yell at

hop 1. *v.* bound, caper, dance, jump, leap, skip,

DICTIONARY

hopper *n.* container for storing things such as grain or sand.

hopscotch *n.* children's game of hopping in a pattern drawn on the ground.

horde *n.* large crowd.

horizon *n.* apparent line that divides the earth and the sky. —*pl.* limits of scope, interest, or knowledge.

horizontal *adj.* parallel to the horizon; level, flat. —**horizontally** *adv.*

hormone *n.* substance secreted by certain glands which stimulates certain organs of the body; synthetic substance with the same effect. —**hormonal** *adj.*

horn *n.* one of a pair of bony growths on the heads of animals such as cows and antelopes; substance of which this is made; wind instrument with a tube or pipe of brass fitted with a mouthpiece; device on a vehicle sounded as a warning. —**horned** *adj.* —**horny** *adj.* of or like horn; *Slang* sexually aroused. —**hornbeam** *n.* tree with smooth grey bark. —**hornbill** *n.* bird with a bony growth on its large beak. —**hornpipe** *n.* (music for) a lively solo dance, traditionally associated with sailors.

hornblende *n.* mineral containing aluminium, calcium, sodium, magnesium, and iron.

hornet *n.* large wasp with a severe sting.

horology *n.* art or science of clock-making and measuring time.

horoscope *n.* prediction of a person's future based on the positions of the planets, sun, and moon at his or her birth; diagram of the positions of these at a particular time and place.

horrendous *adj.* horrific.

horror *n.* (thing or person causing) terror or hatred. —**horrible** *adj.* disagreeable; causing horror. —**horribly** *adv.* —**horrid** *adj.* unpleasant or disagreeable; *Informal* unkind. —**horrify** *v.* cause feelings of horror in; shock. —**horrific** *adj.* particularly horrible.

hors d'oeuvre [or **durv**] *n.* appetizer served before a main meal.

horse *n.* four-footed animal with hooves, a mane, and a tail, used for riding and pulling carts, etc.; piece of gymnastic equipment for vaulting over. —**straight from the horse's mouth** from the most reliable source. —**horsy** *adj.* devoted to horses; like a horse. —**horse about, around** *v. Informal* play roughly or boisterously. —**horse chestnut** tree with broad leaves, white or pink flowers, and large brown shiny nuts. —**horsefly** *n.* large bloodsucking fly. —**horsehair** *n.* hair from the tail or mane of a horse. —**horse laugh** harsh boisterous laugh. —**horseman, horsewoman** *n.* rider on a horse. —**horseplay** *n.* rough or rowdy behaviour. —**horsepower** *n.* unit of power (equivalent to 745.7 watts), used to measure the power of an engine. —**horseradish** *n.* plant with a strong-tasting root, used to make a sauce. —**horseshoe** *n.* protective U-shaped piece of iron nailed to a horse's hoof, often regarded as a symbol of good luck.

horticulture *n.* art or science of cultivating gardens. —**horticultural** *adj.* —**horticulturist** *n.*

THESAURUS

spring, vault 2. *n.* bounce, bound, jump, leap, skip, spring, step, vault

hope 1. *n.* ambition, anticipation, assumption, belief, confidence, desire, dream, expectancy, faith, longing 2. *v.* anticipate, aspire, await, believe, desire, expect, foresee, long, rely, trust

hopeful 1. assured, buoyant, confident, expectant, optimistic, sanguine 2. auspicious, bright, cheerful, encouraging, heartening, promising, propitious, reassuring, rosy

hopefully 1. confidently, expectantly, optimistically, sanguinely 2. conceivably, expectedly, feasibly, probably

hopeless 1. defeatist, dejected, desperate, despondent, disconsolate, downhearted, forlorn, pessimistic 2. helpless, incurable, irremediable, irreparable, irreversible, lost 3. forlorn, futile, impossible, impracticable, pointless, unattainable, useless, vain

horde band, crew, crowd, drove, gang, host, mob, multitude, pack, press, swarm, throng, troop

horizon 1. skyline, vista 2. *Plural* compass, perspective, prospect, purview, range, realm, scope, sphere, stretch

horrible 1. abominable, appalling, awful, dreadful, fearful, frightful, ghastly, grim, grisly, gruesome, heinous, hideous, horrid, repulsive, revolting, shameful, shocking, terrible 2. awful, cruel, disagreeable, dreadful, mean, nasty, terrible, unkind, unpleasant

horrid awful, disagreeable, disgusting, dreadful, horrible, nasty, offensive, terrible, unpleasant

horrify 1. alarm, frighten, intimidate, petrify, scare, terrify 2. appal, disgust, dismay, outrage, shock, sicken

horror 1. alarm, apprehension, awe, consternation, dismay, dread, fear, fright, panic, terror 2. aversion, detestation, disgust, hatred, loathing, repugnance, revulsion

horseman cavalier, dragoon, equestrian, rider

horseplay buffoonery, clowning, pranks, romping

DICTIONARY

hosanna *interj.* exclamation of praise to God.

hose[1] *n.* flexible tube for conveying liquid or gas. —*v.* water with a hose.

hose[2] *n.* stockings, socks, and tights. —**hosiery** *n.* stockings, socks, etc. collectively.

hospice [**hoss**-piss] *n.* nursing home for the terminally ill.

hospital *n.* institution for the care and treatment of sick or injured people. —**hospitalize** *v.* send or admit for care in a hospital. —**hospitalization** *n.*

hospitality *n.* friendliness in welcoming strangers or guests. —**hospitable** *adj.* welcoming. —**hospitably** *adv.*

Host *n. Christianity* bread used in Holy Communion.

host[1] *n.* person who entertains another as a guest; compère of a show; animal or plant on which a parasite lives. —*v.* be the host of. —**hostess** *n.* woman who welcomes guests or visitors.

host[2] *n.* large number.

hostage *n.* person who is illegally held prisoner until certain demands are met by other people.

hostel *n.* building providing accommodation at a low cost for particular categories of people, such as homeless people.

hostelry *n., pl.* -**ries.** *Obs.* inn.

hostile *adj.* unfriendly; of an enemy; (foll. by *to*) opposed (to). —**hostility** *n.* unfriendly and aggressive feelings or behaviour. —*pl.* acts of warfare.

hot *adj.* **hotter, hottest.** having a high temperature; giving or feeling heat; (of a temper) quick to flare up; (of a competition) intense; recent or new; liked very much, e.g. *a hot favourite;* spicy; *Slang* stolen. —**in hot water** *Informal* in trouble.

—**hotly** *adv.* —**hotness** *n.* —**hot air** *Informal* empty talk. —**hotbed** *n.* any place encouraging a particular activity, e.g. *a hotbed of vice.* —**hotblooded** *adj.* passionate or excitable. —**hot dog** hot sausage (esp. a frankfurter) in a bread roll. —**hotfoot** *v., adv. Informal* (go) as fast as possible. —**hotheaded** *adj.* hasty, having a hot temper. —**hothouse** *n.* heated greenhouse. —**hot line** direct telephone link for emergency use. —**hotplate** *n.* heated metal surface on an electric cooker; portable device for keeping food warm.

hotchpotch *n.* jumbled mixture.

hotel *n.* commercial establishment providing lodging and meals. —**hotelier** *n.* owner or manager of a hotel.

Hottentot *n.* member of a race of people of southern Africa, now nearly extinct.

hound *n.* hunting dog. —*v.* pursue relentlessly.

hour *n.* twenty-fourth part of a day; sixty minutes; time of day; appointed time. —*pl.* period regularly appointed for work or business. —**hourly** *adj., adv.* (happening) every hour; frequent(ly). —**hourglass** *n.* device with two glass compartments, containing a quantity of sand that takes an hour to trickle from the top section to the bottom one.

houri *n. Islam* any of the beautiful nymphs of paradise.

house *n.* building used as a dwelling; building for some specific purpose, e.g. *schoolhouse;* lawmaking body or the hall where it meets; family or dynasty; business firm; theatre audience or performance. —*v.* give accommodation to; cover or contain. —**get on like a house on fire** *Informal* get on very well together. —**on the house** *Informal* provided free by the management. —**housing** *n.* (providing of) houses; protective case or covering of a machine. —**house**

THESAURUS

hospitable amicable, bountiful, cordial, friendly, generous, genial, gracious, kind, liberal, sociable, welcoming

hospitality cheer, conviviality, cordiality, friendliness, sociability, warmth, welcome

host[1] entertainer, innkeeper, landlord, proprietor

host[2] army, array, drove, horde, legion, multitude, myriad, swarm, throng

hostage captive, gage, pawn, pledge, prisoner, security, surety

hostile 1. antagonistic, contrary, inimical, malevolent, opposed, unkind, warlike 2. adverse, alien, unfriendly, unsympathetic, unwelcoming

hostilities conflict, fighting, state of war, war, warfare

hostility animosity, animus, antagonism, antipathy, aversion, detestation, enmity, hatred, ill will, malevolence, malice, opposition, unfriendliness

hot 1. boiling, burning, fiery, flaming, heated, roasting, scalding, scorching, searing, steaming, sultry, sweltering, torrid, warm 2. acrid, biting, peppery, piquant, pungent, sharp, spicy

hot air bombast, bunkum, rant, verbiage, wind

hotchpotch farrago, hash, jumble, medley, *mélange,* mess, mishmash, mixture, olio, potpourri

hotheaded fiery, foolhardy, hasty, impetuous, precipitate, rash, reckless, unruly, volatile

hound *v.* chase, drive, give chase, hunt, hunt down, pursue

DICTIONARY

arrest confinement to one's home rather than to prison. —**houseboat** n. stationary boat used as a home. —**housebreaker** n. burglar. —**housecoat** n. woman's long loose robelike garment for casual wear. —**household** n. all the people living in a house. —**householder** n. person who owns or rents a house. —**housekeeper** n. person employed to run someone else's household. —**housekeeping** n. (money for) running a household. —**housemaid** n. female servant who does housework. —**house-train** v. train (a domestic animal) to urinate and defecate outside. —**house-warming** n. party to celebrate moving into a new home. —**housewife** n. woman who runs her own household. —**housework** n. work of running a house, such as cleaning, cooking, and shopping.

House music, House n. kind of disco music based on funk, with fragments of other recordings edited in electronically.

hovel n. small dirty dwelling.

hover v. (of a bird etc.) remain suspended in one place in the air; loiter; be in a state of indecision. —**hovercraft** n. vehicle which can travel over both land and sea on a cushion of air.

how adv. in what way; by what means; in what condition; to what degree. —**however** adv. nevertheless; by whatever means; no matter how.

howdah n. canopied seat on an elephant's back.

howitzer n. cannon firing shells at a steep angle.

howl v. utter a long loud cry. —n. such a cry; loud burst of laughter. —**howler** n. Informal stupid mistake.

hoyden n. wild or boisterous girl, tomboy.

HP, hp hire-purchase; horsepower.

HQ headquarters.

HRH Her (or His) Royal Highness.

HRT hormone replacement therapy.

hub n. centre of a wheel, through which the axle passes; central point of activity.

hubbub n. confused noise of many voices, uproar.

hubby n., pl. -bies. Informal husband.

hubris [hew-briss] n. pride, arrogance.

huckster n. person using aggressive methods of selling.

huddle n. small group; Informal impromptu conference. —v. heap or crowd closely together; hunch (oneself) as through cold.

hue n. colour.

hue and cry n. public outcry.

huff n. passing mood of anger or resentment. —v. blow or puff heavily. —**huffy** adj. —**huffily** adv.

hug v. hugging, hugged. clasp tightly in the arms, usually with affection; keep close to. —n. tight or fond embrace.

huge adj. very big. —**hugely** adv. very much.

hula n. native dance of Hawaii.

Hula-Hoop n. ® plastic hoop swung round the body by wriggling the hips.

hulk n. body of an abandoned ship; Offens. large or unwieldy person or thing. —**hulking** adj. bulky or unwieldy.

hull n. main body of a boat; leaves round the stem of a strawberry, raspberry, or similar fruit;

THESAURUS

house n. 1. abode, building, dwelling, edifice, home, residence 2. family, household, ménage 3. ancestry, clan, dynasty, kindred, line, lineage, race, tribe 4. business, company, concern, establishment, firm, organization ~v. 5. accommodate, billet, board, domicile, harbour, lodge, put up, quarter, take in

household n. family, home, house, ménage

housing dwellings, homes, houses

hovel cabin, den, hole, hut, shack, shanty, shed

hover 1. drift, float, flutter, fly, hang, poise 2. linger, loiter

however after all, anyhow, but, nevertheless, nonetheless, notwithstanding, still, though, yet

howl 1. n. bay, bellow, clamour, cry, groan, hoot, outcry, roar, scream, shriek, wail, yelp, yowl 2. v. bellow, cry, cry out, lament, roar, scream, shout, shriek, wail, weep, yell, yelp

howler blunder, error, malapropism, mistake

huddle n. 1. crowd, disorder, heap, jumble, mass, mess, muddle 2. conference, discussion, meeting ~v. 3. cluster, converge, crowd, flock, gather, press, throng 4. crouch, cuddle, curl up, nestle, snuggle

hue colour, dye, shade, tincture, tinge, tint, tone

hug 1. v. clasp, cuddle, embrace, enfold, hold close, squeeze 2. n. bear hug, clasp, clinch (Sl.), embrace, squeeze

huge colossal, enormous, gargantuan, giant, gigantic, great, immense, large, massive, mountainous, prodigious, stupendous, tremendous, vast

hulk derelict, frame, hull, shell, shipwreck, wreck

hull n. 1. body, casing, covering, frame, framework, skeleton 2. husk, peel, pod, rind, shell, shuck, skin

DICTIONARY

shell or husk of a fruit or seed. —*v.* remove the hulls from (fruit or seeds).

hullabaloo *n., pl.* **-loos.** loud confused noise or clamour.

hum *v.* **humming, hummed.** make a low continuous vibrating sound; sing with closed lips; *Slang* be very active. —*n.* humming sound. —**hummingbird** *n.* very small American bird whose powerful wings make a humming noise as they vibrate.

human *adj.* of, concerning, or typical of people. —**humanity** *n.* human nature; mankind; kindness or mercy. —*pl.* study of literature, philosophy, and the arts. —**humanly** *adv.* by human powers or means. —**humanize** *v.* make human or humane. —**humankind** *n.* mankind.

humane *adj.* kind or merciful. —**humanely** *adv.*

humanism *n.* belief in human effort rather than religion. —**humanist** *n.* —**humanitarian** *n., adj.* (person) with the interest of mankind at heart.

humble *adj.* conscious of one's failings; modest, unpretentious; unimportant. —*v.* cause to become humble; humiliate. —**humbly** *adv.*

humbug *n.* boiled sweet flavoured with peppermint; nonsense; person or thing that deceives people.

humdinger *n. Slang* excellent person or thing.

humdrum *adj.* commonplace and dull.

humerus [hew-mer-uss] *n., pl.* **-eri.** bone from the shoulder to the elbow.

humid *adj.* (of the weather) damp and warm. —**humidity** *n.* —**humidify** *v.* —**humidifier** *n.* device for increasing the amount of water vapour in the air in a room.

humiliate *v.* lower the dignity or hurt the pride of. —**humiliating** *adj.* —**humiliation** *n.*

humility *n.* quality of being humble.

hummock *n.* hillock.

humour *n.* ability to say or perceive things that are amusing; situations, speech, or writings that are humorous; state of mind, mood; *Obs.* fluid in the body. —*v.* be kind and indulgent to. —**humorous** *adj.* —**humorously** *adv.* —**humorist** *n.* person who acts, speaks, or writes in a humorous way.

hump *n.* normal or deforming lump, esp. on the back; hillock; *Informal* fit of sulking. —*v. Slang* carry or heave. —**humpback** *n.* person with an abnormal curvature of the spine. —**humpbacked** *adj.* —**hump-back bridge** road bridge with a sharp slope on either side.

humus [hew-muss] *n.* decomposing vegetable and animal mould in the soil.

hunch *n. Informal* feeling or suspicion not based on facts. —*v.* draw (one's shoulders) up or together. —**hunchback** *n.* humpback.

hundred *adj., n.* ten times ten. —**hundredth** *adj., n.* (of) number one hundred in a series.

THESAURUS

hum 1. buzz, drone, mumble, murmur, purr, sing, throb, thrum, vibrate, whir 2. *Sl.* be active, be busy, bustle, buzz, move, pulsate, pulse, stir, vibrate

human fleshly, manlike, mortal

humane benign, charitable, clement, compassionate, forbearing, forgiving, gentle, good, kind, lenient, merciful, mild, sympathetic, tender, understanding

humanity flesh, man, mankind, men, mortality, people

humanize civilize, cultivate, educate, mellow, polish, refine, soften, tame

humble 1. meek, modest, submissive, unostentatious 2. common, commonplace, insignificant, low, low-born, lowly, mean, modest, obscure, ordinary, poor, simple, unimportant

humbug 1. bluff, cheat, deceit, dodge, feint, fraud, hoax, ruse, sham, swindle, trick, trickery, wile 2. charlatan, cheat, fraud, impostor, quack, swindler, trickster

humdrum boring, dreary, dull, mundane, ordinary, repetitious, routine, tedious, tiresome, unvaried

humid clammy, damp, dank, moist, muggy, steamy, sticky, sultry, wet

humiliate abase, bring low, chagrin, chasten, crush, debase, degrade, discomfit, disgrace, embarrass, humble, shame, subdue

humility diffidence, lowliness, meekness, modesty, servility, submissiveness

humorist comedian, comic, droll, jester, joker, wag, wit

humorous amusing, comic, comical, entertaining, facetious, farcical, funny, hilarious, laughable, ludicrous, merry, playful, pleasant, witty

humour *n.* 1. amusement, comedy, drollery, facetiousness, fun, funniness, wit 2. comedy, farce, jesting, jests, jokes, joking, pleasantry, wit, wittiness 3. mood, spirits, temper —*v.* 4. accommodate, cosset, favour, flatter, gratify, indulge, mollify, pamper, spoil

hump bulge, bump, knob, mound, projection, swelling

hunch feeling, idea, impression, inkling, intuition, premonition, presentiment, suspicion

DICTIONARY

—hundredfold adj., adv. **—hundredweight** n. unit of weight of 112 lbs. (50.8 kg).

hung v. past of HANG. **—adj.** (of a jury) unable to decide; (of a parliament) with no clear majority. **—hung over** Informal suffering the effects of a hangover.

hunger n. discomfort or weakness from lack of food; desire or craving. **—v.** (foll. by for) want very much. **—hungry** adj. desiring food. **—hungrily** adv. **—hunger strike** refusal of all food, as a means of protest.

hunk n. large piece; Slang sexually attractive man.

hunt v. seek out (animals) to kill or capture for sport or food; search (for). **—n.** act or instance of hunting; (party organized for) hunting wild animals for sport. **—hunter** n. man or animal that seeks out and kills or captures game; horse or dog bred for hunting. **—huntress** n. Obs. woman who seeks out and kills or captures game. **—huntsman** n. man in charge of a pack of hounds; man who hunts.

hurdle n. light barrier for jumping over; problem or difficulty. **—pl.** race involving hurdles. **—v.** jump over (something). **—hurdler** n. person who races over hurdles.

hurdy-gurdy n., pl. **-dies.** mechanical musical instrument, such as a barrel organ.

hurl v. throw or utter violently.

hurling, hurley n. Irish game resembling hockey.

hurly-burly n. loud confusion.

hurrah, hurray interj. exclamation of joy or applause.

hurricane n. very strong, often destructive wind or storm. **—hurricane lamp** paraffin lamp with a glass covering.

hurry v. **-rying, -ried.** (cause to) move or act in great haste. **—n.** haste; eagerness. **—hurriedly** adv.

hurt v. **hurting, hurt.** cause physical or mental pain to; wound the feelings of; Informal feel pain. **—n.** physical or mental pain or suffering. **—hurtful** adj.

hurtle v. move rapidly or violently.

husband n. woman's partner in marriage. **—v.** use economically. **—husbandry** n. farming; management of resources.

hush v. make or be silent. **—n.** stillness or quietness. **—hush-hush** adj. Informal secret. **—hush up** v. suppress information about.

husk n. outer covering of certain seeds and fruits. **—v.** remove the husk from.

husky[1] adj. **huskier, huskiest.** hoarse or dry in the throat; Informal big and strong. **—huskily** adv.

husky[2] n., pl. **huskies.** Arctic sledge dog with a thick coat and a curled tail.

hussar [hoo-zar] n. lightly armed cavalry soldier.

hussy n., pl. **-sies.** brazen or promiscuous woman.

hustings pl. n. proceedings at a parliamentary election.

hustle v. push about, jostle; US slang (of a prostitute) solicit. **—n.** lively activity or bustle.

THESAURUS

hunger n. 1. appetite, emptiness, famine, rav~enousness, starvation, voracity 2. appetite, craving, desire, itch, lust, yearning ~v. 3. crave, desire, hanker, itch, long, pine, starve, thirst, want, wish, yearn

hungry empty, famishing, hollow, ravenous, starved, starving, voracious

hunk block, chunk, lump, mass, piece, slab, wedge

hunt v. 1. chase, hound, pursue, stalk, track, trail 2. ferret about, forage, look, scour, search, seek, try to find ~n. 3. chase, hunting, inves~tigation, pursuit, quest, search

hurdle n. 1. barricade, barrier, fence, hedge, wall 2. barrier, difficulty, hindrance, impediment, obstacle, snag

hurl cast, fire, fling, heave, launch, pitch, proj~ect, propel, send, shy, sling, throw, toss

hurricane cyclone, gale, storm, tempest, torna~do, typhoon, windstorm

hurried brief, cursory, hasty, hectic, perfunc~tory, precipitate, quick, rushed, short, slap~dash, speedy, superficial, swift

hurry v. 1. dash, fly, rush, scurry 2. accelerate, expedite, goad, hasten, hustle, push on, quicken, urge ~n. 3. bustle, celerity, commo~tion, dispatch, expedition, flurry, haste, quickness, rush, speed, urgency

hurt v. 1. bruise, damage, disable, harm, impair, injure, mar, spoil, wound 2. ache, be sore, burn, pain, smart, sting, throb 3. afflict, ag~grieve, annoy, distress, grieve, pain, sadden, sting, upset, wound ~n. 4. discomfort, dis~tress, pain, pang, soreness, suffering

husband v. budget, conserve, economize, hoard, save, store

husbandry agriculture, cultivation, farming, tillage

hush 1. v. mute, quieten, silence, still, suppress 2. n. calm, peace, quiet, silence, stillness, tranquillity

DICTIONARY

hut *n.* small house or shelter.

hutch *n.* cage for small pet animals.

hyacinth *n.* sweet-smelling spring flower which grows from a bulb.

hyaena *n.* same as HYENA.

hybrid *n.* offspring of two plants or animals of different species; anything of mixed ancestry. —*adj.* of mixed ancestry.

hydatid disease *n.* condition caused by the presence of bladder-like cysts (**hydatids**) in the liver, lungs, or brain.

hydra *n.* mythical many-headed water serpent; any persistent problem; freshwater polyp.

hydrangea *n.* ornamental shrub with clusters of pink, blue, or white flowers.

hydrant *n.* outlet from a water main with a nozzle for a hose.

hydrate *n.* chemical compound of water with another substance.

hydraulic *adj.* operated by pressure forced through a pipe by a liquid such as water or oil. —**hydraulics** *n.* study of the mechanical properties of fluids as they apply to practical engineering. —**hydraulically** *adv.*

hydro[1] *n.* hotel offering hydropathy.

hydro[2] *adj.* short for **hydroelectric.**

hydro- *combining form* water; hydrogen.

hydrocarbon *n.* compound of hydrogen and carbon.

hydrochloric acid *n.* strong colourless acid used in many industrial and laboratory processes.

hydrodynamics *n.* science concerned with the mechanical properties of fluids.

hydroelectric *adj.* of the generation of electricity by the use of water.

hydrofoil *n.* fast light vessel with its hull raised out of the water on one or more pairs of fins.

hydrogen *n.* light flammable colourless gaseous element which combines with oxygen to form water. —**hydrogen bomb** atom bomb of enormous power in which energy is released by the fusion of hydrogen nucleii to give helium nucleii. —**hydrogen peroxide** colourless liquid used as a hair bleach and as an antiseptic.

hydrolysis [hie-**drol**-iss-iss] *n.* decomposition of a chemical compound reacting with water.

hydrometer [hie-**drom**-it-er] *n.* device for measuring the relative density of a liquid.

hydropathy *n.* method of treating disease by the use of large quantities of water both internally and externally.

hydrophobia *n.* fear of water; rabies.

hydroplane *n.* light motorboat which skims the water.

hydroponics *n.* science of cultivating plants in water without using soil.

hydrotherapy *n. Med.* treatment of certain diseases by exercise in water.

hydrous *adj.* containing water.

hyena *n.* scavenging doglike mammal of Africa and S Asia.

hygiene *n.* principles and practice of health and cleanliness; study of these principles. —**hygienic** *adj.* —**hygienically** *adv.*

hymen *n.* membrane covering the opening of a girl's vagina, which breaks before puberty or at the first occurrence of sexual intercourse.

hymn *n.* Christian song of praise sung to God or a saint. —**hymnal** *adj.* of hymns. —*n.* (also **hymn book**) book of hymns.

hype *n.* intensive or exaggerated publicity or sales promotion. —*v.* promote (a product) using intensive or exaggerated publicity.

hyper *adj. Informal* overactive or overexcited.

hyper- *prefix* over, above, excessively, e.g. *hyperactive, hypercritical.*

hyperbola [hie-per-**bol**-a] *n.* curve produced when a cone is cut by a plane at a steeper angle to its base than its side.

hyperbole [hie-per-**bol**-ee] *n.* deliberate exaggeration for effect. —**hyperbolic** *adj.*

hypermarket *n.* huge self-service store.

hypersensitive *adj.* unduly vulnerable emotionally or physically.

hypersonic *adj.* having a speed of at least five times the speed of sound.

hypertension *n.* abnormally high blood pressure.

hyphen *n.* punctuation mark (-) indicating that two words or syllables are connected. —**hyphenate** *v.* join with a hyphen. —**hyphenated** *adj.* having two words or syllables joined by a hyphen. —**hyphenation** *n.*

hypnosis *n.* artificially induced state of relaxa-

THESAURUS

husky croaking, croaky, gruff, guttural, harsh, hoarse, rasping, raucous, rough, throaty

hustle bustle, crowd, elbow, force, haste, hasten, hurry, impel, jog, jostle, push, rush, shove, thrust

hut cabin, den, hovel, lean-to, refuge, shanty, shed, shelter

hygiene cleanliness, sanitation

hygienic aseptic, clean, germ-free, healthy, pure, sanitary, sterile

DICTIONARY

tion in which the mind is more than usually receptive to suggestion. —**hypnotic** *adj.* of or (as if) producing hypnosis. —**hypnotism** *n.* —**hypnotist** *n.* —**hypnotize** *v.* induce hypnosis in (someone).

hypo- *prefix* below, less than, e.g. *hypocrite, hypodermic.*

hypoallergenic *adj.* (of cosmetics) not likely to cause an allergic reaction.

hypochondria *n.* undue preoccupation with one's health. —**hypochondriac** *n.*

hypocrisy [hip-**ok**-rass-ee] *n., pl.* -**sies.** (instance of) pretence of having standards or beliefs that are contrary to one's real character or actual behaviour. —**hypocrite** [**hip**-oh-krit] *n.* person who pretends to be what he or she is not. —**hypocritical** *adj.* —**hypocritically** *adv.*

hypodermic *adj., n.* (denoting) a syringe or needle used to inject a drug beneath the skin.

hypotension *n.* abnormally low blood pressure.

hypotenuse [hie-**pot**-a-news] *n.* side of a right-angled triangle opposite the right angle.

hypothermia *n.* condition in which a person's body temperature is reduced to a dangerously low level.

hypothesis [hie-**poth**-iss-iss] *n., pl.* -**ses** [-seez]. suggested but unproved explanation of something. —**hypothetical** *adj.* based on assumption rather than fact or reality. —**hypothetically** *adv.*

hysterectomy *n., pl.* -**mies.** surgical removal of the womb.

hysteria *n.* state of uncontrolled excitement, anger, or panic. —**hysterical** *adj.* —**hysterically** *adv.* —**hysterics** *pl. n.* attack of hysteria.

Hz hertz.

THESAURUS

hypnotize mesmerize

hypocrisy cant, deceit, deception, dissembling, duplicity, falsity, insincerity, pharisaism, pretence, two-facedness

hypocrite charlatan, deceiver, dissembler, fraud, impostor, pharisee, pretender

hypocritical canting, deceitful, deceptive, dissembling, duplicitous, false, fraudulent, hollow, insincere, sanctimonious, specious, spurious, two-faced

hypothesis assumption, postulate, premise, proposition, theory, thesis

hypothetical academic, assumed, conjectural, imaginary, putative

hysteria agitation, delirium, frenzy, hysterics, madness, panic, unreason

hysterical berserk, convulsive, crazed, distracted, distraught, frantic, frenzied, mad, overwrought, raving, uncontrollable

I

I *pron.* used by a speaker or writer to refer to himself or herself as the subject of a verb.

iambic *adj.* (of poetry) written in metrical units formed of one long and one short syllable.

IBA Independent Broadcasting Authority.

Iberian *adj.* of Iberia, the peninsula of Spain and Portugal.

ibex [ibe-eks] *n.* wild goat with large backward-curving horns.

ibid. (referring to a book, passage, etc. previously cited) in the same place.

ibis [ibe-iss] *n.* wading bird with long legs.

ice *n.* frozen water; portion of ice cream. —*v.* become covered with ice; cool with ice; cover with icing. —**break the ice** create a relaxed atmosphere, esp. between people meeting for the first time. —**iced** *adj.* served very cold; covered with icing. —**icy** *adj.* covered with ice; cold; aloof and unfriendly. —**icily** *adv.* —**iciness** *n.* —**ice age** period when much of the earth's surface was covered in glaciers. —**iceberg** *n.* large floating mass of ice. —**icebox** *n.* US refrigerator. —**ice cap** mass of ice permanently covering an area. —**ice cream** sweet creamy frozen food. —**ice cube** small square block of ice added to a drink to cool it. —**ice floe** sheet of floating ice. —**ice hockey** team game like hockey played on ice with a puck. —**ice lolly** flavoured ice on a stick. —**ice pick** axe-like tool for breaking ice. —**ice skate** boot with a steel blade fixed to the sole, to enable the wearer to glide over ice. —**ice-skate** *v.* —**ice-skater** *n.*

ichthyology [ik-thi-ol-a-jee] *n.* scientific study of fish.

icicle *n.* tapering spike of ice hanging where water has dripped.

icing *n.* mixture of sugar and water etc. used to cover and decorate cakes. —**icing sugar** finely ground sugar for making icing.

icon *n.* picture of Christ or another religious figure, venerated in the Orthodox Church; picture on a computer screen representing a computer function that can be activated by moving the cursor over it.

iconoclast *n.* person who attacks established principles or ideas. —**iconoclastic** *adj.*

id *n. Psychoanalysis* the mind's instinctive unconscious energies.

idea *n.* plan or thought formed in the mind; thought of something, e.g. *the idea horrified her;* belief or opinion.

ideal *n.* conception of something that is perfect; perfect person or thing. —*adj.* most suitable; perfect. —**ideally** *adv.* —**idealism** *n.* tendency to seek perfection in everything. —**idealist** *n.* —**idealistic** *adj.* —**idealize** *v.* regard or portray as perfect. —**idealization** *n.*

idem *pron., adj. Latin* the same: used to refer to a book, article, etc. already quoted.

identical *adj.* exactly the same. —**identically** *adv.*

identify *v.* **-fying, -fied.** prove or recognize as being a certain person or thing; treat as being the same; understand and sympathize with a person or group because one regards oneself as being similar or similarly situated. —**identifiable** *adj.* —**identification** *n.*

Identikit *n.* ® set of pictures of parts of faces that can be built up to form a likeness of a person wanted by the police.

identity *n., pl.* **-ties.** state of being a specified person or thing; individuality or personality; state of being the same.

ideogram, ideograph *n.* picture, symbol,

THESAURUS

icy 1. arctic, biting, bitter, chilly, cold, freezing, frosty, frozen over, ice-cold, raw 2. *Fig.* aloof, cold, distant, forbidding, frigid, frosty, glacial, hostile, indifferent, steely, stony, unfriendly

idea 1. concept, conclusion, fancy, impression, judgment, perception, thought, understanding 2. belief, conviction, doctrine, interpretation, notion, opinion, teaching, view, viewpoint

ideal 1. *n.* archetype, criterion, epitome, example, exemplar, last word, model, paradigm, paragon, pattern, perfection, prototype, standard, standard of perfection 2. *adj.* classic, complete, model, perfect, quintessential, supreme

idealist *n.* romantic, visionary

identical alike, duplicate, equal, equivalent, indistinguishable, interchangeable, like, selfsame, the same, twin

identification 1. cataloguing, labelling, naming, pinpointing, recognition 2. credentials, papers

identify catalogue, classify, diagnose, label, make out, name, pick out, pinpoint, place, recognize, spot, tag

identity distinctiveness, existence, individuality, oneness, particularity, personality, self, selfhood, singularity, uniqueness

DICTIONARY

etc. representing an object rather than the sounds of its name.

ideology *n., pl.* **-gies.** body of ideas and beliefs of a group, nation, etc. —**ideological** *adj.* —**ideologist** *n.*

idiocy *n., pl.* **-cies.** utter stupidity.

idiom *n.* group of words which when used together have a different meaning from the component words, e.g. *raining cats and dogs;* way of expression natural or peculiar to a language or group. —**idiomatic** *adj.* —**idiomatically** *adv.*

idiosyncrasy *n., pl.* **-sies.** personal peculiarity of mind, habit, or behaviour.

idiot *n.* foolish person; mentally retarded person. —**idiotic** *adj.* utterly stupid. —**idiotically** *adv.*

idle *adj.* not doing anything; not being used; lazy; useless, e.g. *idle thoughts.* —*v.* be idle; (of an engine) run slowly with the gears disengaged; (esp. foll. by *away*) waste (time). —**idleness** *n.* —**idler** *n.* —**idly** *adv.*

idol [**ide**-ol] *n.* image of a god as an object of worship; object of excessive devotion. —**idolatry** [ide-**ol**-a-tree] *n.* worship of idols; excessive devotion or reverence. —**idolater** *n.* —**idolatrous** *adj.* —**idolize** *v.* love or admire excessively.

idyll [**id**-ill] *n.* scene or time of peace and happiness; description in literature of a picturesque or charming scene or episode, esp. of country life. —**idyllic** *adj.* —**idyllically** *adv.*

i.e. that is to say.

if *conj.* on the condition or supposition that; whether; even though. —*n.* uncertainty or doubt, e.g. *I won't have any ifs or buts.* —**iffy** *adj. Informal* doubtful, uncertain.

igloo *n., pl.* **-loos.** dome-shaped Eskimo house of snow and ice.

igneous [ig-nee-uss] *adj.* (of rocks) formed as molten rock cools and hardens.

ignite *v.* catch fire or set fire to. —**ignition** *n.* system that ignites the fuel-air mixture to start an engine; igniting.

ignoble *adj.* dishonourable. —**ignobly** *adv.*

ignominy [ig-nom-in-ee] *n.* humiliating disgrace. —**ignominious** *adj.* —**ignominiously** *adv.*

ignoramus *n., pl.* **-muses.** ignorant person.

ignore *v.* refuse to notice, disregard deliberately. —**ignorance** *n.* lack of knowledge. —**ignorant** *adj.* lacking knowledge; rude through lack of knowledge of good manners. —**ignorantly** *adv.*

iguana *n.* large tropical American lizard.

iguanodon *n.* large plant-eating dinosaur.

ileum *n.* lower part of the small intestine. —**ileac** *adj.*

ilk *n.* —**of that ilk** of the same type.

ill *adj.* not in good health; bad, evil; unfavourable, e.g. *an ill omen.* —*n.* evil, harm. —*adv.* badly; hardly, with difficulty, e.g. *I can ill afford the*

THESAURUS

idiocy fatuity, fatuousness, foolishness, imbecility, insanity, lunacy

idiom 1. expression, locution, phrase 2. jargon, language, parlance, style, talk, usage, vernacular

idiosyncrasy characteristic, eccentricity, habit, mannerism, peculiarity, quirk, trick

idiot ass, cretin, dunderhead, fool, halfwit, imbecile, moron, nitwit, simpleton

idiotic asinine, crazy, fatuous, foolish, halfwitted, imbecile, insane, lunatic, moronic, senseless, stupid

idle *adj.* 1. dead, empty, inactive, jobless, out of work, redundant, stationary, unemployed, unoccupied, unused, vacant 2. indolent, lazy, shiftless, slothful, sluggish 3. frivolous, insignificant, irrelevant, superficial, trivial, unhelpful, useless ~*v.* 4. coast, drift, mark time, shirk, slack, slow down, vegetate

idleness 1. inaction, inactivity, leisure, unemployment 2. hibernation, inertia, laziness, shiftlessness, sloth, sluggishness, torpor 3. lazing, loafing, pottering, time-wasting, trifling

idol deity, god, graven image, image, pagan symbol

idolater 1. heathen, pagan 2. admirer, adorer, devotee, idolizer, votary, worshipper

idolatry adoration, adulation, apotheosis, exaltation, glorification

idolize admire, adore, deify, dote upon, exalt, glorify, hero-worship, look up to, love, revere, reverence, venerate, worship

ignite burn, catch fire, fire, inflame, kindle, light, set fire to

ignominious abject, disgraceful, dishonourable, disreputable, humiliating, indecorous, inglorious, scandalous, shameful, sorry, undignified

ignominy contempt, disgrace, dishonour, disrepute, infamy, obloquy, odium, reproach, shame, stigma

ignorance benightedness, blindness, illiteracy, unenlightenment, unintelligence

ignorant 1. benighted, blind to, inexperienced, innocent, oblivious, unaware, unconscious, unenlightened, uninformed, unknowing, unwitting 2. green, illiterate, naive, unaware, uneducated, unlettered, unread, untaught, untrained, untutored

ignore cold-shoulder, disregard, neglect, overlook, pass over, reject

DICTIONARY

expense. —**ill at ease** uncomfortable, unable to relax. —**illness** *n.* —**ill-advised** *adj.* badly thought out; unwise. —**ill-disposed** *adj.* (often foll. by *towards*) unfriendly or unsympathetic. —**ill-fated** *adj.* doomed or unlucky. —**ill-gotten** *adj.* obtained dishonestly. —**ill-health** *n.* condition of being unwell. —**ill-mannered** *adj.* rude. —**ill-treat** *v.* treat cruelly. —**ill will** unkind feeling, hostility.

illegal *adj.* against the law. —**illegally** *adv.* —**illegality** *n.*

illegible *adj.* unable to be read or deciphered.

illegitimate *adj.* born to parents not married to each other; unlawful. —**illegitimacy** *n.*

illicit *adj.* illegal; forbidden or disapproved of by society.

illiterate *adj.* unable to read or write; uneducated, ignorant. —**illiteracy** *n.*

illogical *adj.* unreasonable; not logical. —**illogicality** *n.*

illuminate *v.* light up; make clear, explain; decorate with lights; *Hist.* decorate (a manuscript) with designs of gold and bright colours. —**illumination** *n.* —**illuminating** *adj.* helping to explain.

illusion *n.* deceptive appearance or belief. —**illusionist** *n.* conjurer. —**illusory** *adj.* false.

illustrate *v.* explain by use of examples; provide (a book or text) with pictures; be an example of. —**illustration** *n.* picture or diagram; example. —**illustrative** *adj.* —**illustrator** *n.*

illustrious *adj.* famous and distinguished.

THESAURUS

ill *adj.* 1. ailing, diseased, indisposed, infirm, off-colour, queasy, queer, sick, unwell 2. bad, damaging, evil, foul, harmful, injurious, ruinous, unfortunate, unlucky, vile, wicked, wrong 3. disturbing, ominous, sinister, threatening, unfavourable, unlucky, unpropitious, unwholesome ~*n.* 4. affliction, harm, hurt, injury, misery, misfortune, pain, trial, tribulation, trouble, unpleasantness, woe 5. abuse, badness, cruelty, damage, destruction, evil, malice, mischief, suffering, wickedness ~*adv.* 6. badly, hard, poorly, unfavourably, unfortunately, unluckily

ill-advised foolish, impolitic, imprudent, inappropriate, incautious, indiscreet, injudicious, misguided, overhasty, rash, reckless, unseemly, unwise

illegal banned, black-market, bootleg, criminal, felonious, forbidden, illicit, lawless, outlawed, prohibited, proscribed, unauthorized, unconstitutional, unlawful, unlicensed, unofficial, wrongful

illegality crime, felony, illicitness, lawlessness, unlawfulness, wrong, wrongness

illegible faint, indecipherable, obscure, scrawled, unreadable

illegitimate 1. illegal, illicit, improper, unconstitutional, unlawful 2. bastard, fatherless, natural

ill-fated blighted, doomed, hapless, ill-omened, luckless, unfortunate, unhappy, unlucky

illicit 1. bootleg, contraband, criminal, felonious, illegal, prohibited, unlawful, unlicensed 2. forbidden, furtive, guilty, immoral, improper, wrong

illiterate benighted, ignorant, uncultured, uneducated

ill-mannered boorish, churlish, coarse, discourteous, impolite, insolent, loutish, rude, uncivil, uncouth, unmannerly

illness affliction, ailment, attack, complaint, disability, disease, disorder, indisposition, infirmity, malady, malaise, poor health, sickness

illogical absurd, fallacious, faulty, inconsistent, incorrect, invalid, irrational, meaningless, senseless, specious, spurious, unreasonable, unsound

ill-treat abuse, damage, harass, harm, harry, injure, maltreat, mishandle, misuse, oppress, wrong

illuminate 1. brighten, light, light up 2. clarify, clear up, elucidate, enlighten, explain, instruct, make clear

illuminating explanatory, helpful, informative, instructive, revealing

illumination awareness, clarification, enlightenment, perception, revelation, understanding

illusion 1. chimera, daydream, fantasy, hallucination, mirage, mockery, phantasm, semblance 2. delusion, error, fallacy, fancy

illusory apparent, beguiling, deceitful, delusive, fallacious, false, misleading, mistaken, sham, unreal, untrue

illustrate 1. bring home, clarify, demonstrate, elucidate, emphasize, exhibit, explain, interpret, show 2. adorn, decorate, depict, draw, picture, sketch

illustration 1. analogy, case, clarification, demonstration, elucidation, example, explanation, instance, specimen 2. adornment, decoration, figure, picture, plate, sketch

illustrious brilliant, celebrated, distinguished, eminent, famous, glorious, great, noble, notable, noted, prominent, remarkable, renowned, signal, splendid

DICTIONARY

image *n.* representation or likeness of a person or thing; optical counterpart, as in a mirror; double, copy; impression people have of a politician, organization, etc.; simile or metaphor. —*v.* make an image of; reflect. —**imagery** *n.* images collectively, esp. in literature.

imagine *v.* form a mental image of; think, believe, or guess. —**imaginable** *adj.* —**imaginary** *adj.* existing only in the imagination. —**imagination** *n.* ability to make mental images of things not present; creative mental ability. —**imaginative** *adj.* —**imaginatively** *adv.*

imago [im-**may**-go] *n., pl.* **imagoes, imagines** [im-**maj**-in-ees]. sexually mature adult insect.

imam *n.* leader of prayers in a mosque; title of some Islamic leaders.

imbalance *n.* lack of proportion.

imbecile [**imb**-ess-eel] *n.* idiot. —*adj.* idiotic. —**imbecility** *n.*

imbibe *v.* drink (esp. alcohol); *Lit.* absorb (ideas etc.).

imbroglio [imb-**role**-ee-oh] *n., pl.* **-ios.** confusing and complicated situation.

imbue *v.* **-buing, -bued.** (usu. foll. by *with*) fill or inspire with (ideals or principles).

IMF International Monetary Fund.

imitate *v.* take as a model; mimic or copy. —**imitation** *n.* imitating; copy of an original. —**imitative** *adj.* —**imitator** *n.*

immaculate *adj.* completely clean or tidy; completely flawless. —**immaculately** *adv.*

immanent *adj.* present within and throughout something. —**immanence** *n.*

immaterial *adj.* not important, not relevant.

immature *adj.* not fully developed; lacking wisdom or stability because of youth. —**immaturity** *n.*

immediate *adj.* occurring at once; next or nearest in time, space, or relationship. —**immediately** *adv.* —**immediacy** *n.*

immemorial *adj.* having existed or happened for longer than anyone can remember. —**immemorially** *adv.*

immense *adj.* huge or vast. —**immensely** *adv.* —**immensity** *n.*

THESAURUS

ill will acrimony, animosity, antagonism, antipathy, aversion, dislike, enmity, envy, grudge, hatred, hostility, malice, rancour, resentment, spite, unfriendliness, venom

image 1. appearance, effigy, figure, icon, idol, likeness, picture, portrait, reflection, statue 2. conceit, concept, figure, idea, impression, perception

imaginable conceivable, credible, likely, plausible, possible, thinkable

imaginary assumed, dreamlike, fanciful, fictional, ideal, illusive, illusory, imagined, invented, legendary, made-up, mythological, nonexistent, shadowy, supposed, unreal, unsubstantial, visionary

imagination creativity, enterprise, fancy, ingenuity, insight, inspiration, inventiveness, originality, vision, wit

imaginative clever, creative, dreamy, enterprising, fanciful, ingenious, inspired, inventive, original, poetical, visionary, vivid

imagine conceive, conjure up, create, devise, envisage, frame, invent, picture, plan, project, scheme, think up, think of, visualize

imbecile 1. *n.* bungler, dolt, dotard, fool, half-wit, idiot, moron 2. *adj.* asinine, fatuous, foolish, idiotic, inane, moronic, simple, stupid, thick

imbibe consume, drink, quaff, suck, swallow

imitate affect, ape, burlesque, copy, counterfeit, duplicate, echo, emulate, follow, impersonate, mimic, mirror, mock, parody, personate, repeat, simulate

imitation *n.* 1. aping, copy, counterfeit, echoing, imitating, likeness, mimicry, resemblance, simulation 2. fake, forgery, impersonation, impression, mockery, parody, reflection, reproduction, sham, substitution, travesty

imitative copied, derivative, mock, onomatopoeic, parrotlike, plagiarized, put-on, second-hand, simulated, unoriginal

imitator echo, follower, impersonator, impressionist, mimic, parrot, shadow

immaculate 1. clean, impeccable, neat, spruce, trim, unexceptionable 2. faultless, flawless, guiltless, incorrupt, innocent, perfect, pure, sinless, spotless, stainless, unpolluted, unsullied, untarnished, virtuous

immaterial extraneous, impertinent, inapposite, inconsequential, inessential, insignificant, irrelevant, trifling, trivial, unimportant

immature 1. adolescent, crude, green, premature, raw, undeveloped, unformed, unripe, unseasonable, untimely, young 2. callow, childish, inexperienced, infantile, jejune, juvenile, puerile

immaturity crudeness, crudity, greenness, imperfection, rawness, unpreparedness, unripeness

immediate 1. instant, instantaneous 2. adjacent, close, direct, near, nearest, next, recent

immediately at once, directly, forthwith, in-

DICTIONARY

immerse v. plunge (something) into liquid; involve deeply, e.g. *I immersed myself in my work.* —**immersion** n. immersing. —**immersion heater, immerser** n. electric heater contained in a domestic hot-water tank.

immigrant n. person who comes into a country to live there. —**immigration** n.

imminent adj. about to happen. —**imminently** adv. —**imminence** n.

immobile adj. unable to move; not moving. —**immobility** n. —**immobilize** v. make unable to move or work.

immoderate adj. excessive or unreasonable.

immolate v. kill as a sacrifice. —**immolation** n.

immoral adj. morally wrong, corrupt; sexually depraved or promiscuous. —**immorality** n.

immortal adj. living forever; famed for all time. —n. immortal being; person whose fame will last for all time. —**immortality** n. —**immortalize** v.

immune adj. protected against a specific disease; secure (against); exempt (from). —**immunity** n. ability to resist disease; freedom from prosecution, tax, etc. —**immunize** v. make immune to a disease. —**immunization** n.

immunodeficiency n. deficiency in or breakdown of a person's immune system.

immunology n. study of immunity. —**immunological** adj. —**immunologist** n.

immure v. Lit. imprison.

immutable [im-mute-a-bl] adj. unchangeable. —**immutability** n.

imp n. demon; mischievous child.

impact n. collision; strong effect. —v. press firmly against or into. —**impaction** n.

impair v. weaken or damage. —**impairment** n.

impala [imp-ah-la] n. southern African antelope.

impale v. pierce with a sharp object. —**impalement** n.

impalpable adj. imperceptible to the touch; difficult to understand.

impart v. communicate (information); give, e.g. *impart flavour.*

impartial adj. not favouring one side or the other. —**impartially** adv. —**impartiality** n.

impassable adj. (of a road etc.) impossible to travel over or through.

impasse [am-pass] n. situation in which progress is impossible.

impassioned adj. full of emotion.

THESAURUS

stantly, now, promptly, right away, this instant, unhesitatingly, without delay

immense colossal, elephantine, enormous, extensive, giant, gigantic, great, huge, infinite, large, mammoth, massive, monumental, prodigious, stupendous, titanic, tremendous, vast

immigrant incomer, newcomer, settler

imminent at hand, close, coming, forthcoming, gathering, impending, looming, menacing, near, threatening

immobile fixed, frozen, immovable, motionless, rigid, riveted, rooted, stable, static, stationary, stiff, still, stolid, unmoving

immobilize cripple, disable, freeze, halt, paralyse, stop, transfix

immoderate enormous, excessive, exorbitant, extreme, inordinate, intemperate, profligate, uncontrolled, undue, unjustified, unreasonable, unrestrained, unwarranted

immoral abandoned, bad, corrupt, debauched, degenerate, depraved, evil, impure, indecent, lewd, licentious, nefarious, obscene, profligate, reprobate, sinful, unchaste, unethical, unprincipled, vicious, vile, wicked, wrong

immorality corruption, debauchery, depravity, dissoluteness, evil, licentiousness, profligacy, sin, vice, wickedness

immortal adj. 1. abiding, constant, deathless,

endless, enduring, eternal, everlasting, imperishable, incorruptible, indestructible, lasting, perennial, perpetual, timeless, undying, unfading ~n. 2. god, goddess 3. hero

immortality 1. deathlessness, endlessness, eternity, indestructibility, perpetuity 2. celebrity, fame, glorification, greatness, renown

immune clear, exempt, free, invulnerable, proof (against), protected, resistant, safe, unaffected

immunity amnesty, charter, exemption, franchise, freedom, indemnity, liberty, prerogative, privilege, release, right

impact bang, blow, bump, collision, contact, crash, force, jolt, knock, shock, smash, stroke, thump

impair blunt, damage, deteriorate, diminish, enfeeble, harm, hinder, injure, lessen, mar, reduce, spoil, undermine, weaken, worsen

impart communicate, convey, disclose, discover, divulge, make known, pass on, relate, reveal, tell

impartial detached, disinterested, equal, equitable, even-handed, fair, just, neutral, objective, open-minded, unbiased, unprejudiced

impartiality detachment, disinterest, dispassion, equality, equity, fairness, neutrality, objectivity

DICTIONARY

impassive *adj.* showing no emotion, calm. —**impassivity** *n.*

impatient *adj.* irritable at any delay or difficulty; restless to have or do something. —**impatiently** *adv.* —**impatience** *n.*

impeach *v.* charge with a serious crime against the state. —**impeachment** *n.*

impeccable *adj.* without fault, excellent. —**impeccably** *adv.*

impecunious *adj.* penniless.

impedance [imp-eed-anss] *n. Electricity* measure of the opposition to the flow of an alternating current.

impede *v.* hinder in action or progress. —**impediment** *n.* something that makes action, speech, or progress difficult. —**impedimenta** *pl. n.* objects impeding progress, esp. baggage or equipment.

impel *v.* -**pelling, -pelled.** drive (a person) to do something.

impending *adj.* (esp. of something bad) about to happen.

impenetrable *adj.* impossible to get through; impossible to understand.

imperative *adj.* extremely urgent, vital; *Gram-*

mar denoting a mood of verbs used in commands. —*n. Grammar* imperative mood.

imperceptible *adj.* too slight or gradual to be noticed. —**imperceptibly** *adv.*

imperfect *adj.* having faults or mistakes; not complete; *Grammar* denoting a tense of verbs describing continuous, incomplete, or repeated past actions. —*n. Grammar* imperfect tense. —**imperfection** *n.*

imperial *adj.* of an empire or emperor; majestic; denoting weights and measures formerly official in Britain. —**imperialism** *n.* rule by one country over many others. —**imperialist** *n., adj.*

imperil *v.* -**illing, -illed.** endanger.

imperious *adj.* used to being obeyed, domineering.

impersonal *adj.* not influenced by emotion; lacking human warmth or personality; *Grammar* (of a verb) without a personal subject, as in *it is snowing.* —**impersonality** *n.*

impersonate *v.* pretend to be (another person); imitate the mannerisms of (someone). —**impersonation** *n.* —**impersonator** *n.*

impertinent *adj.* disrespectful or rude. —**impertinently** *adv.* —**impertinence** *n.*

THESAURUS

impasse deadlock, stalemate

impassioned ardent, blazing, excited, fervid, fiery, furious, glowing, heated, inflamed, inspired, intense, passionate, rousing, stirring, violent, vivid, warm

impatience haste, heat, impetuosity, intolerance, shortness, vehemence

impatient 1. abrupt, brusque, curt, demanding, edgy, hasty, intolerant, irritable, sudden, testy 2. agog, chafing, eager, fretful, headlong, impetuous, restless

impeach accuse, arraign, blame, censure, charge, denounce, indict, tax

impeccable exact, exquisite, faultless, flawless, incorrupt, innocent, perfect, precise, pure, sinless, stainless

impecunious destitute, indigent, insolvent, penniless

impede bar, block, brake, check, clog, curb, delay, hamper, hinder, obstruct, restrain, retard, stop

impediment bar, barrier, block, check, clog, curb, defect, difficulty, hindrance, obstacle, snag

impel drive, force, incite, induce, influence, instigate, motivate, move, oblige, power, prod, prompt, propel, push, require, spur, stimulate, urge

impending approaching, coming, gathering, im-

minent, looming, menacing, near, nearing, threatening

imperative compulsory, crucial, essential, insistent, obligatory, pressing, urgent, vital

imperceptible faint, fine, gradual, inaudible, infinitesimal, insensible, invisible, microscopic, minute, shadowy, slight, small, subtle, tiny

imperfect broken, damaged, defective, faulty, flawed, immature, impaired, incomplete, inexact, limited, partial, patchy, sketchy, unfinished

imperfection blemish, defect, deficiency, failing, fault, flaw, frailty, infirmity, shortcoming, stain, taint, weakness

imperial 1. kingly, majestic, princely, queenly, regal, royal, sovereign 2. august, exalted, grand, great, high, lofty, magnificent, majestic, noble, superior, supreme

imperil endanger, expose, hazard, jeopardize, risk

impersonal cold, detached, dispassionate, formal, inhuman, neutral, remote

impersonate act, ape, enact, imitate, mimic, personate

impertinence audacity, boldness, brazenness, disrespect, effrontery, impudence, incivility, insolence rudeness

impertinent bold, brazen, disrespectful, impo-

DICTIONARY

imperturbable *adj.* calm, not excitable. —**imperturbability** *n.*

impervious *adj.* not letting (water etc.) through; not influenced by (a feeling, argument, etc.).

impetigo [imp-it-**tie**-go] *n.* contagious skin disease.

impetuous *adj.* done or acting without thought, rash. —**impetuously** *adv.* —**impetuosity** *n.*

impetus [**imp**-it-uss] *n., pl.* **-tuses.** force with which a body moves; impulse.

impinge *v.* encroach (upon), affect or restrict.

impious [**imp**-ee-uss] *adj.* showing a lack of respect or reverence.

impish *adj.* mischievous.

implacable *adj.* not to be appeased; unyielding. —**implacably** *adv.* —**implacability** *n.*

implant *v.* fix firmly in the mind; insert or embed. —*n. Med.* anything implanted in the body, such as a tissue graft. —**implantation** *n.*

implement *n.* tool or instrument. —*v.* carry out (instructions etc.). —**implementation** *n.*

implicate *v.* show to be involved, esp. in a crime. —**implication** *n.* something implied.

implicit *adj.* expressed indirectly; absolute, e.g. *implicit belief.* —**implicitly** *adv.*

implore *v.* beg desperately.

imply *v.* **-plying, -plied.** indicate by hinting, suggest; mean.

impolitic *adj.* unwise, ill-advised.

imponderable *n., adj.* (something) impossible to assess.

import *v.* bring in (goods) from another country. —*n.* something imported; meaning; importance. —**importation** *n.* —**importer** *n.*

important *adj.* of great significance or value; famous, powerful. —**importance** *n.*

importunate *adj.* persistent in making demands. —**importune** *v.* persist in demands. —**importunity** *n.*

impose *v.* force the acceptance of; take unfair

THESAURUS

lite, impudent, insolent, rude, uncivil, unmannerly

imperturbable calm, collected, complacent, composed, cool, sedate, self-possessed, tranquil, unmoved, unruffled

impetuous ardent, eager, fierce, furious, hasty, headlong, impulsive, precipitate, rash, spontaneous, unplanned, unthinking, vehement, violent

impetus 1. goad, impulse, incentive, push, spur, stimulus 2. energy, force, momentum, power

impious godless, irreligious, irreverent, profane, sacrilegious, sinful, ungodly, unholy, wicked

impish elfin, mischievous, puckish, rascally, roguish, sportive, waggish

implant inculcate, infix, infuse, instil, sow

implement 1. *n.* apparatus, appliance, device, gadget, instrument, tool 2. *v.* bring about, carry out, complete, effect, enforce, execute, fulfil, perform, realize

implicate associate, compromise, concern, embroil, entangle, imply, include, incriminate, involve, mire

implication inference, innuendo, meaning, overtone, presumption, significance, signification, suggestion

implicit contained, implied, inferred, inherent, latent, tacit, understood, unspoken

implied implicit, indirect, inherent, insinuated, suggested, tacit, undeclared, unspoken

implore beg, beseech, crave, entreat, importune, plead with, pray, solicit, supplicate

imply 1. connote, hint, insinuate, intimate, signify, suggest 2. betoken, denote, entail, evidence, import, include, indicate, involve, mean, point to, presuppose

import 1. *n.* bearing, drift, gist, implication, intention, meaning, message, purport, sense, significance, thrust 2. *v.* bring in, introduce, land

importance 1. concern, consequence, import, interest, moment, significance, substance, value, weight 2. distinction, eminence, esteem, influence, mark, pre-eminence, prestige, prominence, standing, status, usefulness, worth

important 1. far-reaching, grave, large, material, momentous, primary, salient, serious, signal, significant, substantial, urgent, weighty 2. eminent, foremost, high-level, high-ranking, influential, leading, notable, noteworthy, outstanding, powerful, pre-eminent, prominent, seminal

importunate clamorous, demanding, dogged, earnest, exigent, insistent, persistent, pressing, urgent

impose decree, establish, exact, fix, institute, introduce, lay, levy, ordain, place, promulgate, put, set

imposing august, commanding, dignified, effective, grand, impressive, majestic, stately, striking

imposition demand, encroachment, intrusion, liberty, presumption

DICTIONARY

advantage of. —**imposing** adj. impressive. —**imposition** n. unreasonable demand, burden.

impossible adj. incapable of being done or experienced; absurd or unreasonable. —**impossibly** adv. —**impossibility** n.

impostor n. person who cheats or swindles by pretending to be someone else.

impotent [**imp**-a-tent] adj. powerless; (of a man) incapable of sexual intercourse. —**impotence** n. —**impotently** adv.

impound v. take legal possession of, confiscate.

impoverish v. make poor or weak. —**impoverishment** n.

impracticable adj. incapable of being put into practice.

impractical adj. not sensible.

imprecation n. curse.

impregnable adj. impossible to break into. —**impregnability** n.

impregnate v. saturate, spread all through; make pregnant. —**impregnation** n.

impresario n., pl. **-ios.** person who runs theatre performances, concerts, etc.

impress v. affect strongly, usu. favourably; imprint or stamp; stress or emphasize. —**impres-**

sion n. strong or favourable effect; vague idea; mark made by pressing; impersonation for entertainment. —**impressionable** adj. easily influenced.

impressionism n. art style that gives a general effect or mood rather than form or structure. —**impressionist** n. —**impressionistic** adj.

impressive adj. making a strong impression, esp. through size, importance, or quality.

imprimatur [imp-rim-**ah**-ter] n. official approval to print a book.

imprint n. mark made by printing or stamping; publisher's name and address on a book. —v. produce (a mark) by printing or stamping.

imprison v. put in prison. —**imprisonment** n.

improbable adj. unlikely. —**improbability** n.

impromptu adv., adj. without preparation, improvised.

improper adj. indecent; incorrect or irregular; (of a fraction) with a numerator larger than the denominator, as in ⅝.

impropriety [imp-roe-**pry**-a-tee] n., pl. **-ties.** improper behaviour.

improve v. make or become better. —**improvement** n.

THESAURUS

impossible hopeless, impracticable, inconceivable, unattainable, unobtainable, unthinkable

impostor charlatan, cheat, deceiver, fake, fraud, hypocrite, pretender, quack, rogue, sham, trickster

impotence disability, feebleness, frailty, inability, inadequacy, incapacity, incompetence, ineffectiveness, infirmity, paralysis, powerlessness, uselessness, weakness

impotent disabled, feeble, frail, helpless, incapable, ineffective, infirm, nerveless, paralysed, powerless, unable, weak

impoverish 1. bankrupt, beggar, break, ruin 2. deplete, diminish, drain, exhaust, reduce, sap

impracticable 1. impossible, unattainable, unfeasible, unworkable 2. awkward, inapplicable, inconvenient, unsuitable, useless

impractical 1. impossible, unrealistic, unserviceable, unworkable, visionary, wild 2. idealistic, romantic, unrealistic, visionary

impress affect, excite, influence, inspire, move, stir, strike, sway, touch

impression 1. effect, feeling, impact, influence, reaction, sway 2. belief, concept, conviction, fancy, feeling, hunch, idea, memory, notion, opinion, sense, suspicion 3. imitation, impersonation, parody

impressive exciting, forcible, moving, powerful, stirring, touching

imprint 1. n. impression, mark, print, sign, stamp 2. v. engrave, establish, etch, fix, impress, print, stamp

imprison confine, constrain, detain, immure, jail, lock up, put away

imprisonment confinement, custody, detention, duress, incarceration

improbability doubt, dubiety, uncertainty, unlikelihood

improbable doubtful, dubious, fanciful, farfetched, implausible, questionable, unbelievable, uncertain, unconvincing, unlikely, weak

impromptu ad-lib, extempore, improvised, offhand, spontaneous, unpremeditated, unprepared, unrehearsed, unscripted

improper 1. impolite, indecent, indecorous, indelicate, risqué, smutty, suggestive, unfitting, unseemly, untoward, vulgar 2. abnormal, false, inaccurate, incorrect, irregular, wrong

impropriety 1. bad taste, indecency, indecorum, unsuitability, vulgarity 2. blunder, faux pas, gaffe, gaucherie, mistake, slip, solecism

improve 1. advance, amend, augment, better, correct, help, mend, polish, rectify, touch up, upgrade 2. develop, enhance, gain strength, increase, pick up, progress, rally, reform, rise

improvement 1. amelioration, amendment,

DICTIONARY

improvident *adj.* not planning for future needs. —**improvidence** *n.*

improvise *v.* make use of materials at hand; make up (a piece of music, speech, etc.) as one goes along. —**improvisation** *n.*

impudent *adj.* cheeky. —**impudently** *adv.* —**impudence** *n.*

impugn [imp-**yoon**] *v.* call in question, cast doubt on.

impulse *n.* sudden urge to do something; short electrical signal passing along a wire or nerve or through the air. —**on impulse** suddenly and without planning. —**impulsive** *adj.* tending to act without thinking first. —**impulsively** *adv.*

impunity [imp-**yoon**-it-ee] *n.* —**with impunity** without punishment or unpleasant consequences.

impure *adj.* having unwanted substances mixed in; immoral or obscene. —**impurity** *n.*

impute *v.* attribute responsibility to. —**imputation** *n.*

in *prep.* inside, within; during; at the end of (a period of time); indicating a state, situation, or manner; into. —*adv.* in or into a particular place; at one's home or place of work; in office or power; in fashion. —*adj.* fashionable.

inability *n.* lack of means or skill to do something.

inaccurate *adj.* not correct. —**inaccuracy** *n.*

inadequate *adj.* not enough; not good enough. —**inadequacy** *n.*

inadvertent *adj.* done unintentionally.

inalienable *adj.* not able to be taken away, e.g. *an inalienable right.*

inane *adj.* senseless or silly. —**inanity** *n.*

inanimate *adj.* not living.

inanition *n.* exhaustion or weakness, as from lack of food.

inappropriate *adj.* not suitable.

inarticulate *adj.* unable to express oneself clearly or well.

inasmuch as *conj.* seeing that, because.

inaugurate *v.* open or begin the use of, esp.

THESAURUS

betterment, correction, gain, rectification 2. advance, development, enhancement, increase, progress, rally, recovery, rise

improvisation ad-lib, expedient, impromptu, invention, makeshift

improvise 1. ad-lib, extemporize, invent 2. concoct, contrive, devise, make do

impudence audacity, boldness, effrontery, impertinence, insolence, presumption, rudeness, sauciness, shamelessness

impudent audacious, bold, bold-faced, brazen, forward, impertinent, insolent, presumptuous, rude

impulse force, impetus, momentum, movement, pressure, push, stimulus, surge, thrust

impulsive emotional, hasty, headlong, impetuous, instinctive, intuitive, passionate, precipitate, quick, rash

impure 1. adulterated, alloyed, debased, mixed, unrefined 2. contaminated, defiled, dirty, filthy, foul, infected, polluted, sullied, tainted, unclean

impurity 1. adulteration, mixture 2. contamination, defilement, dirtiness, filth, foulness, infection, pollution, taint, uncleanness

imputation accusation, attribution, blame, censure, charge, insinuation, reproach, slander, slur

inability impotence, inadequacy, incapability, incapacity, incompetence, ineptitude, powerlessness

inaccuracy 1. imprecision, inexactness, unfaithfulness, unreliability 2. blunder, defect, erratum, error, fault, miscalculation, mistake, slip

inaccurate careless, defective, faulty, imprecise, incorrect, in error, inexact, mistaken, out, unfaithful, unreliable, unsound, wild, wrong

inadequacy 1. dearth, deficiency, insufficiency, meagreness, paucity, poverty, scantiness, shortage, skimpiness 2. faultiness, inability, inaptness, incompetence, incompetency, inefficacy, unfitness, unsuitableness

inadequate 1. defective, deficient, faulty, imperfect, incomplete, insubstantial, insufficient, meagre, niggardly, scanty, short, sketchy, skimpy, sparse 2. inapt, incapable, incompetent, unequal, unfitted, unqualified

inane empty, fatuous, frivolous, futile, idiotic, mindless, puerile, senseless, silly, stupid, trifling, unintelligent, vacuous, vain, vapid, worthless

inanimate cold, dead, defunct, extinct, inactive, inert, lifeless, quiescent, soulless, spiritless

inappropriate ill-suited, ill-timed, improper, incongruous, malapropos, tasteless, unbecoming, unbefitting, unfit, unfitting, unseemly, unsuitable, untimely

inarticulate 1. blurred, indistinct, muffled, mumbled, unclear, unintelligible 2. dumb, mute, silent, unspoken, unvoiced, voiceless, wordless 3. faltering, halting, hesitant, poorly spoken

inaugural dedicatory, first, initial, introductory, maiden, opening

DICTIONARY

with ceremony; formally establish (a new leader) in office. —**inaugural** *adj.* —**inauguration** *n.*

inauspicious *adj.* unlucky, suggesting an unfavourable outcome.

inboard *adj.* (of a boat's engine) inside the hull.

inborn *adj.* existing from birth, natural.

inbred *adj.* produced as a result of inbreeding; inborn or ingrained.

inbreeding *n.* breeding from closely related individuals.

inbuilt *adj.* present from the start.

Inc. *US* (of a company) incorporated.

incalculable *adj.* impossible to estimate, very great.

in camera *adv.* in private session.

incandescent *adj.* glowing with heat; (of artificial light) produced by a glowing filament. —**incandescence** *n.*

incantation *n.* ritual chanting of magic words or sounds. —**incantatory** *adj.*

incapable *adj.* (foll. by *of*) lacking the ability to; helpless.

incapacitate *v.* deprive of strength or ability, disable. —**incapacity** *n.*

incarcerate *v.* imprison. —**incarceration** *n.*

incarnate *adj.* possessing human form; typified, e.g. *stupidity incarnate.* —**incarnation** *n.* —**Incarnation** *n. Christianity* God's coming to earth in human form as Jesus Christ.

incendiary [in-**send**-ya-ree] *adj.* (of bombs etc.) designed to cause fires. —*n.* bomb designed to cause fires; fire raiser or arsonist.

incense[1] *v.* make very angry.

incense[2] *n.* substance that gives off a sweet perfume when burned; its smoke.

incentive *n.* something that encourages effort or action.

inception *n.* beginning.

incessant *adj.* never stopping. —**incessantly** *adv.*

incest *n.* sexual intercourse between two people too closely related to marry. —**incestuous** *adj.*

inch *n.* unit of length equal to one twelfth of a foot or 2.54 centimetres. —*v.* move very slowly.

inchoate [in-**koe**-ate] *adj.* just begun and not yet properly developed.

incidence *n.* extent or frequency of occurrence.

incident *n.* (memorable) event; event involving violence.

incidental *adj.* occurring as a minor part of or accompaniment to something else; happening by chance. —**incidentally** *adv.* —**incidental music** background music for a film or play.

incinerate *v.* burn to ashes. —**incineration** *n.* —**incinerator** *n.* furnace for burning rubbish.

incipient *adj.* just starting to appear or happen.

THESAURUS

inaugurate 1. begin, commence, initiate, institute, introduce, launch, originate, set in motion, set up 2. induct, install, instate, invest

inauguration initiation, institution, launch, launching, opening

inauspicious bad, black, discouraging, ill-omened, ominous, unfortunate, unlucky, unpropitious

incalculable boundless, countless, enormous, immense, inestimable, infinite, limitless, measureless, numberless, untold, vast

incapable feeble, incompetent, ineffective, inept, insufficient, unfit, unfitted, unqualified, weak

incapacitate cripple, disable, disqualify, immobilize, paralyse, prostrate

incapacity disqualification, feebleness, impotence, inability, inadequacy, incapability, incompetency, ineffectiveness, powerlessness, unfitness, weakness

incarcerate commit, confine, detain, gaol, immure, impound, imprison, intern, jail, lock up, restrain, restrict

incense *v.* anger, enrage, exasperate, excite, inflame, infuriate, irritate, madden, provoke

incentive bait, encouragement, goad, impetus, impulse, inducement, lure, motivation, motive, spur, stimulus

inception beginning, birth, dawn, initiation, origin, outset, rise, start

incessant ceaseless, constant, continuous, endless, eternal, everlasting, interminable, perpetual, persistent, relentless, unending, unrelenting, unremitting

incident 1. adventure, circumstance, episode, event, fact, happening, matter, occurrence 2. brush, clash, commotion, mishap, scene, skirmish

incidental accidental, casual, chance, fortuitous, odd, random

incipient beginning, developing, embryonic, inceptive, inchoate, starting

incision cut, gash, slash, slit

incisive 1. acute, keen, piercing, trenchant 2. acid, biting, caustic, cutting, direct, forceful, mordant, sarcastic, sardonic, satirical, severe, sharp

DICTIONARY

incise v. cut into with a sharp tool. —**incision** n. —**incisive** adj. direct and forceful. —**incisor** n. cutting tooth.

incite v. stir up or provoke. —**incitement** n.

incivility n., pl. -**ties**. rudeness.

inclement adj. (of weather) bad. —**inclemency** n.

incline v. lean, slope; (cause to) have a certain disposition or tendency. —n. slope. —**inclination** n. liking, tendency, or preference; slope; degree of deviation from the horizontal or vertical.

include v. have as (part of) the contents; put in as part of a set or group. —**inclusion** n. —**inclusive** adj. including everything. —**inclusively** adv.

incognito [in-kog-**nee**-toe] adv., adj. under an assumed identity. —n., pl. -**tos**. false identity.

incoherent adj. (of speech) unclear and impossible to understand. —**incoherence** n. —**incoherently** adv.

income n. amount of money earned from work, investments, etc. —**income support** (in Britain) allowance paid by the government to the very poor. —**income tax** personal tax levied on annual income.

incoming adj. about to arrive; about to come into office.

incommode v. inconvenience.

incommodious adj. cramped.

incommunicado adj., adv. deprived of communication with other people.

incomparable adj. beyond comparison, unequalled. —**incomparably** adv.

incompatible adj. inconsistent or conflicting. —**incompatibility** n.

inconceivable adj. impossible to imagine.

inconclusive adj. not giving a final decision or result.

incongruous adj. inappropriate or out of place. —**incongruously** adv. —**incongruity** n.

inconsequential adj. unimportant or irrelevant.

inconsiderable adj. relatively small; insignificant.

inconstant adj. liable to change one's loyalties or opinions.

incontinent adj. not able to control one's bladder or bowels. —**incontinence** n.

THESAURUS

incite animate, drive, egg on, encourage, excite, goad, impel, inflame, instigate, prompt, provoke, rouse, spur, stimulate, urge

incitement encouragement, goad, impetus, impulse, instigation, motivation, motive, provocation, spur, stimulus

incivility bad manners, discourteousness, disrespect, impoliteness, rudeness

inclement bitter, boisterous, foul, harsh, intemperate, rigorous, rough, severe, stormy, tempestuous

inclination affection, aptitude, bent, bias, desire, disposition, fancy, fondness, leaning, liking, partiality, penchant, predilection, predisposition, proclivity, propensity, stomach, taste, tendency, turn, wish

incline v. 1. be disposed, bias, influence, persuade, prejudice, sway, tend, turn 2. bend, bevel, cant, deviate, diverge, lean, slant, slope, tend, tilt, tip, veer ~n. 3. ascent, descent, dip, grade, gradient, ramp, rise, slope

include comprehend, comprise, contain, cover, embody, embrace, encompass, incorporate, involve, take in

inclusion incorporation, insertion

inclusive all in, all together, blanket, comprehensive, full, general, overall, sweeping, umbrella

incoherent confused, disjointed, inarticulate, inconsistent, loose, muddled, rambling, uncoordinated, unintelligible, wandering, wild

income earnings, gains, interest, means, pay, proceeds, profits, receipts, revenue, salary, takings, wages

incoming approaching, arriving, entering, homeward, landing, new

incomparable inimitable, matchless, paramount, peerless, superlative, supreme, unequalled, unmatched, unrivalled

incompatible antipathetic, conflicting, contradictory, discordant, disparate, incongruous, inconsistent, mismatched, uncongenial, unsuitable

inconceivable impossible, incredible, unbelievable, unheard-of, unimaginable, unknowable, unthinkable

inconclusive ambiguous, indecisive, indeterminate, open, uncertain, undecided, unsettled, vague

incongruous absurd, conflicting, contradictory, contrary, discordant, extraneous, improper, inapt, incoherent, inconsistent, unbecoming, unsuitable, unsuited

incontrovertible certain, established, incontestable, indisputable, indubitable, irrefutable, positive, sure, undeniable, unquestionable

DICTIONARY

incontrovertible *adj.* impossible to deny or disprove.

inconvenience *n.* trouble or difficulty. —*v.* cause trouble or difficulty to. —**inconvenient** *adj.*

incorporate *v.* include or be included as part of a larger unit. —**incorporation** *n.*

incorporeal *adj.* without bodily existence.

incorrigible *adj.* beyond correction or reform. —**incorrigibility** *n.*

incorruptible *adj.* impossible to bribe or corrupt, honest; not subject to decay.

increase *v.* make or become greater in size, number, etc. —*n.* rise in number, size, etc.; amount by which something increases. —**on the increase** becoming more common. —**increasingly** *adv.* more and more.

incredible *adj.* unbelievable; *Informal* marvellous, amazing. —**incredibly** *adv.*

incredulous *adj.* not willing or able to believe something. —**incredulity** *n.*

increment *n.* increase in money or value, esp. a regular salary increase. —**incremental** *adj.*

incriminate *v.* make (someone) seem guilty of a crime. —**incriminating** *adj.* —**incrimination** *n.*

incubate [in-cube-ate] *v.* (of birds) hatch eggs by sitting on them; grow (bacteria); (of bacteria) remain inactive in an animal or person before causing disease. —**incubation** *n.* —**incubator** *n.*

heated enclosed apparatus for rearing premature babies; apparatus for artificially hatching eggs.

incubus [in-cube-uss] *n., pl.* **-bi, -buses.** demon believed to have sex with sleeping women; nightmare.

inculcate *v.* fix in someone's mind by constant repetition. —**inculcation** *n.*

incumbent *adj.* —**it is incumbent on** it is the duty of. —*n.* person holding a particular office or position. —**incumbency** *n.*

incur *v.* **-curring, -curred.** bring (something unpleasant) upon oneself.

incurable *adj.* not able to be cured. —**incurably** *adv.*

incurious *adj.* showing no curiosity or interest.

incursion *n.* sudden brief invasion; inroad.

indaba *n. S Afr.* meeting or discussion; problem.

indebted *adj.* owing gratitude for help or favours; owing money. —**indebtedness** *n.*

indecent *adj.* morally or sexually offensive; unsuitable or unseemly, e.g. *indecent haste.* —**indecently** *adv.* —**indecency** *n.* —**indecent assault** sexual attack which does not include rape. —**indecent exposure** showing of one's genitals in public.

indecipherable *adj.* impossible to read.

indeed *adv.* really, certainly. —*interj.* showing surprise, doubt, etc.

THESAURUS

inconvenience *n.* annoyance, awkwardness, bother, difficulty, disadvantage, disruption, disturbance, drawback, fuss, hindrance, nuisance, trouble, uneasiness, upset, vexation

inconvenient annoying, awkward, bothersome, disturbing, embarrassing, inopportune, tiresome, troublesome, unseasonable, unsuitable, untimely, vexatious

incorporate absorb, amalgamate, assimilate, blend, coalesce, combine, consolidate, embody, fuse, include, integrate, merge, mix, unite

incorrigible hardened, hopeless, incurable, intractable, inveterate

incorruptible honest, honourable, just, straight, trustworthy, unbribable, upright

increase 1. *v.* add to, advance, amplify, augment, boost, build up, develop, dilate, enhance, enlarge, escalate, expand, extend, grow, heighten, inflate, intensify, magnify, mount, multiply, proliferate, prolong, raise, snowball, spread, strengthen, swell, wax 2. *n.* addition, boost, development, enlargement, escalation, expansion, extension, gain, growth, increment, intensification, rise, upsurge, upturn

incredible absurd, beyond belief, far-fetched, implausible, impossible, improbable, inconceivable, preposterous, unbelievable, unimaginable, unthinkable

incredulous disbelieving, doubtful, doubting, dubious, sceptical, suspicious, unbelieving

increment accretion, addition, advancement, augmentation, enlargement, gain, increase

incriminate accuse, arraign, blame, charge, impeach, implicate, indict, involve

incumbent binding, compulsory, mandatory, necessary, obligatory

incur arouse, contract, draw, earn, gain, induce, meet with, provoke

incurable *adj.* fatal, irrecoverable, irremediable, terminal

indebted beholden, grateful, obligated, obliged

indecency coarseness, crudity, foulness, grossness, immodesty, impurity, indecorum, indelicacy, lewdness, obscenity, pornography, smut, smuttiness, vileness, vulgarity

indecent blue, coarse, crude, dirty, filthy, foul, gross, improper, impure, indelicate, lewd, licentious, pornographic, salacious, scatological, smutty, vile

DICTIONARY

indefatigable *adj.* never getting tired. —**indefatigably** *adv.*

indefensible *adj.* not justifiable; unable to be defended. —**indefensibly** *adv.*

indefinite *adj.* without exact limits, e.g. *an indefinite period;* vague. —**indefinite article** *Grammar* the word *a or an.* —**indefinitely** *adv.*

indelible *adj.* impossible to erase or remove; producing indelible marks. —**indelibly** *adv.*

indelicate *adj.* embarrassing, tasteless. —**indelicacy** *n.*

indemnify *v.* -**ifying, -ified.** give indemnity to; compensate. —**indemnification** *n.*

indemnity *n., pl.* -**ties.** insurance against loss or damage; compensation for loss or damage suffered.

indent *v.* start (a line of writing) further from the margin than the other lines; order (goods) using a special order form. —**indentation** *n.* dent in a surface or edge.

indenture *n.* contract, esp. one binding an apprentice to his employer.

independent *adj.* free from the control or influence of others; separate; financially self-reliant; capable of acting for oneself or on one's own. —*n.* politician who does not belong to any party. —**independently** *adv.* —**independence** *n.*

indescribable *adj.* too intense or extreme for words. —**indescribably** *adv.*

indeterminate *adj.* uncertain in extent, amount, or nature. —**indeterminacy** *n.*

index *n., pl.* **indexes,** *Maths* **indices [in-diss-eez].** alphabetical list of names or subjects dealt with in a book; file or catalogue used to find things; pointer or indicator; *Maths* exponent. —*v.* provide (a book) with an index; enter in an index; make index-linked. —**index finger** finger next to the thumb. —**index-linked** *adj.* (of pensions, wages, etc.) rising or falling in line with the cost of living.

Indian *n., adj.* (person) from India; (person) descended from the original inhabitants of the American continent. —**Indian summer** period of warm sunny weather in autumn.

India rubber *n.* eraser.

indicate *v.* be a sign or symptom of; point out; state briefly; (of a measuring instrument) show a reading of. —**indication** *n.* —**indicative [in-dik-a-tiv]** *adj.* suggesting, e.g. *clouds indicative of rain; Grammar* denoting a mood of verbs used to make a statement. —**indicator** *n.* something acting as a sign or indication; flashing light on a vehicle showing the driver's intention to turn; dial or gauge.

indict [in-dite] *v.* formally accuse of a crime. —**indictable** *adj.* —**indictment** *n.*

indifferent *adj.* showing no interest or concern; of poor quality or low standard. —**indifference** *n.* —**indifferently** *adv.*

THESAURUS

indeed actually, certainly, doubtlessly, positively, really, strictly, truly, undeniably, undoubtedly, veritably

indefensible faulty, inexcusable, unforgivable, unpardonable, unwarrantable, wrong

indefinite confused, doubtful, equivocal, evasive, general, imprecise, indeterminate, indistinct, inexact, loose, obscure, uncertain, unclear, undetermined, unfixed, unknown, unlimited, unsettled, vague

indelible enduring, indestructible, ineffaceable, ineradicable, permanent

indelicacy bad taste, coarseness, crudity, grossness, immodesty, impropriety, indecency, obscenity, offensiveness, vulgarity

indelicate blue, coarse, crude, embarrassing, gross, immodest, improper, indecent, low, obscene, off-colour, offensive, risqué, rude, suggestive, tasteless, vulgar

indemnify 1. endorse, insure, protect, secure, underwrite 2. compensate, pay, repair, repay, requite, satisfy

independence autarchy, autonomy, freedom, home rule, liberty, self-government, self-rule, sovereignty

independent absolute, free, liberated, separate, unconnected, uncontrolled, unrelated

independently alone, autonomously, individually, solo, unaided

indescribable ineffable, inexpressible, unutterable

indeterminate imprecise, inconclusive, indefinite, inexact, uncertain, undefined, unfixed, unspecified, vague

index 1. clue, guide, indication, mark, sign, symptom, token 2. director, forefinger, hand, indicator, needle, pointer

indicate betoken, denote, evince, imply, manifest, point to, reveal, show, signify, suggest

indication clue, evidence, explanation, hint, index, manifestation, mark, note, omen, portent, sign, signal, symptom, warning

indicator display, gauge, guide, index, mark, marker, meter, pointer, sign, signal, signpost, symbol

indictment accusation, allegation, charge, impeachment, prosecution, summons

indifference aloofness, apathy, callousness, carelessness, coldness, coolness, detachment, disregard, unconcern

DICTIONARY

indigenous [in-**dij**-in-uss] *adj.* born in or natural to a country.

indigent *adj.* so poor as to lack necessities. —**indigence** *n.*

indigestion *n.* (discomfort or pain caused by) difficulty in digesting food. —**indigestible** *adj.*

indignation *n.* anger caused by something unfair or wrong. —**indignant** *adj.* feeling or showing indignation. —**indignantly** *adv.*

indignity *n., pl.* -**ties.** embarrassing or humiliating treatment.

indigo *n.* deep violet-blue; dye of this colour.

indirect *adj.* done or caused by someone or something else; not by a straight route. —**indirect object** *Grammar* person or thing indirectly affected by an action, such as *Sue* in *I bought Sue a book.* —**indirect speech** report that gives the content of what someone said but not the actual words. —**indirect tax** tax, such as VAT, added to the price of something.

indiscreet *adj.* incautious or tactless in revealing secrets. —**indiscreetly** *adv.* —**indiscretion** *n.*

indiscriminate *adj.* chosen or choosing without thought or care.

indispensable *adj.* impossible to do without.

indisposed *adj.* unwell or ill; unwilling. —**indisposition** *n.*

indisputable *adj.* without doubt. —**indisputably** *adv.*

indissoluble *adj.* permanent.

indium *n.* soft silver-white metallic element.

individual *adj.* characteristic of or meant for a single person or thing; separate or distinct; distinctive, unusual. —*n.* single person or thing. —**individually** *adv.* singly. —**individualism** *n.* principle of living one's life in one's own way. —**individualist** *n.* —**individualistic** *adj.* —**individuality** *n.* distinctive character or personality.

indoctrinate *v.* teach (someone) to accept a doctrine or belief uncritically. —**indoctrination** *n.*

Indo-European *adj., n.* (of) a family of languages spoken in most of Europe and much of Asia, including English, Russian, and Hindi.

indolent *adj.* lazy. —**indolence** *n.*

indomitable *adj.* too strong to be defeated or discouraged. —**indomitably** *adv.*

indoor *adj.* inside a building. —**indoors** *adv.*

indubitable [in-**dew**-bit-a-bl] *adj.* beyond doubt, certain. —**indubitably** *adv.*

induce *v.* persuade; cause; *Med.* bring on (labour) by the use of drugs etc. —**inducement** *n.* something that encourages someone to do something.

THESAURUS

indifferent 1. aloof, apathetic, callous, careless, cold, cool, detached, distant, heedless, inattentive, regardless, unconcerned, unimpressed, unresponsive 2. average, fair, mediocre, middling, moderate, ordinary, passable, perfunctory, undistinguished, uninspired

indignant angry, annoyed, disgruntled, exasperated, furious, heated, incensed, irate, resentful, riled, scornful, wrathful

indignation anger, fury, rage, resentment, scorn, umbrage, wrath

indirect circuitous, crooked, devious, meandering, oblique, rambling, roundabout, tortuous, wandering, winding, zigzag

indiscreet foolish, hasty, ill-advised, ill-considered, ill-judged, impolitic, imprudent, incautious, injudicious, naive, rash, reckless, tactless, unwise

indiscriminate aimless, careless, desultory, general, random, sweeping, uncritical, unselective, unsystematic, wholesale

indispensable crucial, essential, imperative, key, necessary, needed, needful, requisite, vital

indisposed ailing, ill, sick, unwell

indisposition ailment, ill health, illness, sickness

indisputable absolute, beyond doubt, certain, evident, incontestable, incontrovertible, positive, sure, undeniable

individual 1. *adj.* characteristic, discrete, distinct, exclusive, identical, own, particular, peculiar, personal, proper, respective, separate, several, single, singular, special, specific, unique 2. *n.* being, character, creature, mortal, party, person, soul, type, unit

individuality character, distinction, originality, personality, uniqueness

indolent idle, inactive, inert, lackadaisical, languid, lazy, lethargic, listless, slack, slothful, slow, sluggish, torpid

indomitable invincible, resolute, staunch, steadfast

indubitable certain, evident, incontrovertible, obvious, sure, unarguable, undeniable, undoubted

induce actuate, convince, draw, encourage, get, impel, incite, influence, move, persuade, press, prompt

inducement attraction, bait, cause, consideration, encouragement, impulse, incentive, incitement, influence, lure, motive, reward, spur, stimulus, urge

DICTIONARY

induct *v.* formally install someone, esp. a clergyman, in office.

induction *n.* reasoning process by which general conclusions are drawn from particular instances; process by which electrical or magnetic properties are produced by the proximity of an electrified or magnetic object; formal installing of a person into office. —**inductance** *n.* —**inductive** *adj.* —**induction coil** transformer for producing high voltage from a low voltage. —**induction course** training course to help familiarize someone with a new job.

indulge *v.* allow (someone) to have or do everything he or she wants; allow oneself pleasure, e.g. *indulge in daydreaming.* —**indulgence** *n.* something allowed because it gives pleasure; act of indulging oneself or someone else; favourable or tolerant treatment. —**indulgent** *adj.* —**indulgently** *adv.*

industrial *adj.* of, used in, or employed in industry. —**industrial action** action such as a strike or work-to-rule, by which workers can protest about their conditions. —**industrialize** *v.* develop large-scale industry in (a country or region). —**industrial estate** area of land set aside for factories and warehouses. —**industrial relations** relations between management and workers.

industry *n., pl.* **-tries.** manufacture of goods; branch of this, e.g. *the publishing industry;* quality of working hard. —**industrious** *adj.* hardworking.

inebriate *v.* make drunk. —*adj.* habitually drunk. —**inebriated** *adj.* drunk. —**inebriation** *n.* drunkenness.

inedible *adj.* not fit to be eaten.

ineffable *adj.* too great for words. —**ineffably** *adv.*

ineffectual *adj.* having no effect or an inadequate effect.

ineligible *adj.* not qualified for or entitled to something.

ineluctable *adj.* impossible to avoid.

inept *adj.* clumsy, lacking skill. —**ineptitude** *n.*

inequitable *adj.* unfair.

ineradicable *adj.* impossible to remove.

inert *adj.* without the power of motion or resistance; chemically unreactive. —**inertly** *adv.* —**inertness** *n.*

inertia *n.* feeling of unwillingness to do anything; *Physics* property by which a body remains still or continues to move unless a force is applied to it. —**inertial** *adj.*

inescapable *adj.* unavoidable.

inestimable *adj.* too great to be estimated. —**inestimably** *adv.*

inevitable *adj.* unavoidable, sure to happen.

THESAURUS

indulge 1. cater to, give way to, gratify, pander to, regale, satiate, satisfy, yield to 2. *With* **in** bask in, luxuriate in, revel in, wallow in

indulgence 1. excess, fondness, intemperance, kindness, leniency, partiality, profligacy, spoiling 2. courtesy, forbearance, good will, patience, tolerance, understanding

indulgent compliant, easy-going, favourable, fond, forbearing, gentle, kind, lenient, liberal, mild, permissive, tender, tolerant

industrious active, busy, diligent, energetic, hard-working, laborious, persistent, productive, purposeful, steady, tireless, zealous

industry 1. business, commerce, manufacturing, production, trade 2. activity, application, assiduity, determination, diligence, effort, labour, perseverance, persistence, toil, vigour, zeal

ineffectual bootless, emasculate, feeble, fruitless, futile, idle, impotent, inadequate, incompetent, inept, lame, powerless, unavailing, useless, vain, weak

inefficient disorganized, feeble, inept, inexpert, slipshod, wasteful, weak

ineligible disqualified, ruled out, unacceptable, undesirable, unfit, unqualified, unsuitable

inept awkward, bungling, clumsy, gauche, maladroit, unskilful

ineptitude clumsiness, gaucheness, incapacity, unfitness, unhandiness

inequitable biased, one-sided, partial, prejudiced, unfair, unjust

inert dead, dormant, dull, idle, immobile, inactive, inanimate, leaden, lifeless, motionless, passive, quiescent, slack, sluggish, static, still, torpid, unresponsive

inertia apathy, deadness, drowsiness, dullness, idleness, immobility, laziness, lethargy, listlessness, passivity, sloth, stillness, stupor, torpor

inescapable certain, destined, fated, inevitable, inexorable, sure

inestimable incalculable, invaluable, precious, priceless, prodigious

inevitable assured, certain, decreed, destined, fixed, necessary, ordained, settled, sure, unavoidable

inevitably automatically, certainly, necessarily, perforce, surely, unavoidably

DICTIONARY

—*n.* something inevitable. —**inevitably** *adv.* —**inevitability** *n.*

inexorable *adj.* relentless; unavoidable. —**inexorably** *adv.*

inexpert *adj.* lacking skill.

inexplicable *adj.* impossible to explain. —**inexplicably** *adv.*

in extremis *adv. Latin* in great difficulty; at the point of death.

inextricable *adj.* impossible to escape from; impossible to disentangle or separate.

infallible *adj.* never wrong; always successful. —**infallibly** *adv.* —**infallibility** *n.*

infamous [**in**-fam-uss] *adj.* well-known for something bad. —**infamously** *adv.* —**infamy** *n.*

infant *n.* very young child. —**infancy** *n.* early childhood; early stage of development. —**infantile** *adj.* childish.

infanticide *n.* murder of an infant; person guilty of this.

infantry *n.* foot soldiers.

infatuate *v.* inspire with intense unreasonable passion. —**infatuated** *adj.* —**infatuation** *n.*

infect *v.* affect with a disease. —**infection** *n.* —**infectious** *adj.* (of a disease) spreading without actual contact; spreading from person to person, e.g. *infectious laughter*.

infer *v.* -**ferring,** -**ferred.** work out from evidence. —**inference** *n.*

inferior *adj.* lower in position, status, or quality. —*n.* person of lower position or status. —**inferiority** *n.*

infernal *adj.* of hell; *Informal* irritating. —**infernally** *adv.*

inferno *n., pl.* -**nos.** intense raging fire.

infertile *adj.* unable to produce offspring; (of soil) barren, not productive. —**infertility** *n.*

infest *v.* inhabit or overrun in unpleasantly large numbers. —**infestation** *n.*

infidel *n.* person with no religion; person who rejects a particular religion, esp. Christianity or Islam.

infidelity *n., pl.* -**ties.** sexual unfaithfulness to one's husband, wife, or lover.

infighting *n.* quarrelling within a group.

infiltrate *v.* enter gradually and secretly. —**infiltration** *n.* —**infiltrator** *n.*

infinite [**in**-fin-it] *adj.* without any limit or end. —**infinitely** *adv.*

infinitesimal *adj.* extremely small.

infinitive [in-**fin**-it-iv] *n. Grammar* form of a verb not showing tense, person, or number, such as *to sleep.*

infinity *n.* endless space, time, or number.

THESAURUS

inexpert awkward, bungling, clumsy, inept, maladroit, unpractised, unprofessional, unskilful

inexplicable baffling, enigmatic, inscrutable, insoluble, mysterious, strange, unaccountable

infallible 1. faultless, impeccable, perfect, unerring, unimpeachable 2. certain, dependable, foolproof, reliable, sure, trustworthy, unfailing

infamous base, disgraceful, dishonourable, disreputable, hateful, heinous, ignominious, ill-famed, iniquitous, loathsome, monstrous, nefarious, notorious, odious, outrageous, scandalous, scurvy, shameful, shocking, vile, villainous, wicked

infancy 1. babyhood, early childhood 2. beginnings, cradle, dawn, early stages, emergence, inception, origins, outset, start

infant *n.* baby, child, suckling, toddler, tot

infantile babyish, childish, immature, puerile, tender, weak, young

infatuate befool, beguile, besot, bewitch, captivate, delude, enchant, fascinate, mislead, obsess, stupefy

infatuated beguiled, besotted, bewitched, captivated, enraptured, fascinated, inflamed, intoxicated, obsessed, possessed, spellbound

infect blight, contaminate, corrupt, defile, influence, poison, pollute, taint, touch

infection contagion, contamination, corruption, poison, pollution

infectious catching, communicable, contagious, contaminating, corrupting, infective, pestilential, poisoning

infer conclude, conjecture, deduce, derive, gather, presume, understand

inference assumption, conclusion, conjecture, consequence, corollary, deduction, presumption, surmise

inferior junior, lesser, lower, menial, minor, secondary, subordinate, subsidiary, underneath

inferiority imperfection, inadequacy, meanness, mediocrity, shoddiness

infertile barren, sterile, unfruitful

infest beset, flood, invade, overrun, ravage, swarm, throng

infiltrate creep in, penetrate, percolate, permeate, pervade

infinite absolute, all-embracing, boundless, enormous, eternal, immense, inestimable, inexhaustible, interminable, limitless, measureless, numberless, perpetual, stupendous,

DICTIONARY

infirm *adj.* physically or mentally weak. —**infirmity** *n.*

infirmary *n., pl.* **-ries.** hospital.

inflame *v.* make angry or excited. —**inflamed** *adj.* (of part of the body) red and swollen because of infection. —**inflammation** *n.* inflamed part of the body. —**inflammatory** *adj.* likely to provoke anger or excitement.

inflammable *adj.* easily set on fire. —**inflammability** *n.*

inflate *v.* expand by filling with air or gas; cause economic inflation in. —**inflatable** *adj.* able to be inflated. —*n.* plastic or rubber object which can be inflated.

inflation *n.* inflating; increase in prices and fall in the value of money. —**inflationary** *adj.*

inflection, inflexion *n.* change in the pitch of the voice; *Grammar* change in the form of a word to show grammatical use.

inflexible *adj.* obstinate or unyielding; fixed and unalterable. —**inflexibly** *adv.* —**inflexibility** *n.*

inflict *v.* impose (something unpleasant) on. —**infliction** *n.*

inflorescence *n. Botany* arrangement of flowers on a stem.

influence *n.* effect of one person or thing on another; (person with) the power to have such an effect. —*v.* have an effect on. —**influential** *adj.* —**influentially** *adv.*

influenza *n.* viral disease causing muscle pains, fever, and catarrh.

influx *n.* arrival or entry of many people or things; a flowing in.

info *n. Informal* information.

inform *v.* tell; give incriminating information to the police. —**informant** *n.* person who gives information. —**information** *n.* what is told, knowledge. —**informative** *adj.* giving useful information. —**information technology** use of computers and electronic technology to store and communicate information. —**informer** *n.* person who informs to the police.

informal *adj.* relaxed and friendly; appropriate for everyday life or use. —**informally** *adv.* —**informality** *n.*

infra dig *adj. Informal* beneath one's dignity.

infrared *adj.* of or using rays below the red end of the visible spectrum.

infrastructure *n.* basic facilities, services, and equipment needed for a country or organization to function properly.

infringe *v.* break (a law or agreement). —**infringement** *n.*

infuriate *v.* make very angry.

THESAURUS

total, unbounded, uncounted, untold, vast, wide, without end, without number

infinity boundlessness, endlessness, eternity, immensity, vastness

infirm decrepit, doddering, doddery, failing, feeble, frail, lame, weak

inflame anger, arouse, embitter, enrage, excite, fire, heat, ignite, impassion, incense, infuriate, kindle, madden, provoke, rile, rouse, stimulate

inflamed angry, festering, fevered, heated, hot, red, septic, sore, swollen

inflammable combustible, flammable, incendiary

inflate amplify, balloon, blow up, boost, dilate, distend, enlarge, escalate, exaggerate, expand, increase, swell

inflation blowing up, distension, enlargement, escalation, expansion, increase, rise, spread, swelling

inflection 1. bend, bow, crook, curvature, intonation, modulation 2. *Gram.* conjugation, declension

inflexibility 1. hardness, inelasticity, rigidity, stiffness, stringency 2. fixity, intransigence, obstinacy

inflexible adamant, firm, fixed, immovable, im~

placable, inexorable, intractable, iron, obdurate, relentless, resolute, rigorous, set, steadfast, steely, strict, stringent, stubborn, unbending, unyielding

inflict apply, deliver, exact, impose, levy, visit, wreak

influence *n.* 1. agency, authority, control, credit, direction, domination, effect, guidance, mastery, power, pressure, rule, spell, sway, weight 2. hold, importance, leverage, power, prestige, weight ~*v.* 3. affect, arouse, bias, control, count, direct, dispose, guide, impel, impress, incite, incline, induce, instigate, manipulate, modify, move, persuade, predispose, prompt, rouse, sway

influx arrival, flow, incursion, inflow, inrush, invasion, rush

inform acquaint, advise, apprise, communicate, enlighten, instruct, notify, teach, tell, tip off

informal casual, easy, familiar, natural, relaxed, simple

information advice, counsel, data, facts, instruction, intelligence, knowledge, material, message, news, notice, report, tidings, word

informer accuser, betrayer, sneak, stool pigeon

infringe break, contravene, disobey, transgress, violate

DICTIONARY

infuse *v.* fill with (an emotion or quality); soak to extract flavour. —**infusion** *n.* infusing; liquid obtained by infusing.

ingenious [in-**jean**-ee-uss] *adj.* clever at contriving; cleverly contrived. —**ingeniously** *adv.* —**ingenuity** [in-jen-**new**-it-ee] *n.*

ingénue [an-jay-new] *n.* naive young woman, esp. as a role played by an actress.

ingenuous [in-**jen**-new-uss] *adj.* unsophisticated and trusting. —**ingenuously** *adv.*

ingest *v.* take (food or drink) into the body. —**ingestion** *n.*

inglorious *adj.* dishonourable or shameful.

ingot *n.* oblong block of cast metal.

ingrained *adj.* (of a habit etc.) deep-rooted; (of dirt) deeply fixed.

ingratiate *v.* bring (oneself) into favour (with). —**ingratiating** *adj.* —**ingratiatingly** *adv.*

ingredient *n.* component of a mixture or compound.

ingress *n.* act or right of entering.

ingrowing *adj.* (of a toenail) growing abnormally into the flesh.

inhabit *v.* -**habiting**, -**habited**. live in. —**inhabitable** *adj.* —**inhabitant** *n.*

inhale *v.* breathe in (air, smoke, etc.). —**inhalation** *n.* —**inhalant** [in-**hale**-ant] *n.* medical preparation inhaled to help breathing problems. —**inhaler** *n.* container for an inhalant.

inherent *adj.* existing as an inseparable part. —**inherently** *adv.*

inherit *v.* -**heriting**, -**herited**. receive (money etc.) from someone who has died; receive (a characteristic) from parents etc.; receive from predecessors. —**inheritance** *n.* —**inheritor** *n.*

inhibit *v.* -**hibiting**, -**hibited**. restrain (an impulse or desire); hinder or prevent (action). —**inhibition** *n.* feeling of fear or embarrassment that stops one from behaving naturally. —**inhibited** *adj.*

inhospitable *adj.* not hospitable, unfriendly; difficult to live in, harsh.

inhuman *adj.* cruel or brutal; not human.

inhumane *adj.* cruel or brutal. —**inhumanity** *n.*

inimical *adj.* unfavourable or hostile. —**inimically** *adv.*

inimitable *adj.* impossible to imitate, unique. —**inimitably** *adv.*

iniquity *n., pl.* -**ties**. great injustice; wickedness; sin. —**iniquitous** *adj.*

initial *adj.* first, at the beginning. —*n.* first letter, esp. of someone's name. —*v.* -**tialling**, -**tialled**. sign with one's initials. —**initially** *adv.* first, originally.

initiate *v.* begin or set going; admit (someone)

THESAURUS

infuriate anger, enrage, exasperate, incense, irritate, madden, provoke, rile

ingenious adroit, bright, brilliant, clever, crafty, creative, dexterous, fertile, inventive, masterly, original, ready, resourceful, shrewd, skilful, subtle

ingenuous artless, candid, childlike, frank, guileless, honest, innocent, naive, open, plain, simple, sincere, trustful, unreserved, unsophisticated

ingratiate blandish, crawl, fawn, flatter, grovel

ingredient component, constituent, element, part

inhabit abide, dwell, live, lodge, occupy, people, populate, possess, reside, in, tenant

inhabitant aborigine, citizen, denizen, dweller, indweller, inmate, native, occupant, occupier, resident, tenant

inhabited colonized, developed, held, occupied, peopled, populated, settled, tenanted

inherit accede to, be left, fall heir to, succeed to

inheritance bequest, birthright, heritage, legacy, patrimony

inhibit arrest, bar, bridle, check, constrain, curb, debar, discourage, forbid, frustrate, hinder, impede, obstruct, prevent, restrain, stop

inhibition bar, check, embargo, hindrance, interdict, obstacle, prohibition, reserve, restraint, restriction, reticence, shyness

inhospitable 1. unfriendly, ungenerous, unkind, unsociable, unwelcoming 2. bare, barren, bleak, desolate, empty, hostile, lonely, sterile

inhuman animal, barbaric, bestial, brutal, cruel, diabolical, fiendish, heartless, merciless, pitiless, remorseless, ruthless, savage, unfeeling, vicious

inhumane brutal, cruel, heartless, pitiless, unfeeling, unkind

iniquitous atrocious, base, criminal, evil, heinous, immoral, infamous, nefarious, reprehensible, sinful, unjust, unrighteous, vicious, wicked

initial *adj.* beginning, early, first, inaugural, introductory, opening, primary

initially at *or* in the beginning, at first, first, firstly, originally, primarily

initiate 1. begin, break the ice, inaugurate, institute, launch, open, originate, pioneer, start 2. indoctrinate, induct, instate, instruct, introduce, invest, teach, train

DICTIONARY

into a closed group; instruct in the basics of something. —*n.* initiated person. —**initiation** *n.* —**initiator** *n.* —**initiatory** *adj.*

initiative *n.* first step, commencing move; ability to act independently.

inject *v.* put (a fluid) into the body with a syringe; introduce (a new element), e.g. *he injected some humour into the scene.* —**injection** *n.*

injudicious *adj.* showing poor judgment, unwise.

injunction *n.* court order not to do something.

injure *v.* hurt physically or mentally; damage. —**injury** *n.* physical hurt; damage. —**injury time** *Sport* time added at the end of a match to compensate for time spent treating injured players. —**injurious** *adj.*

injustice *n.* unfairness; unfair treatment or action.

ink *n.* coloured liquid used for writing or printing. —*v.* mark or cover with ink. —**inky** *adj.* dark or black; stained with ink.

inkling *n.* slight idea or suspicion.

inlaid *adj.* set in another material so that the surface is smooth; made like this, e.g. *an inlaid table.*

inland *adj., adv.* in or towards the interior of a country, away from the sea. —**Inland Revenue** government department that collects taxes.

in-laws *pl. n.* relatives by marriage.

inlay *n.* inlaid substance or pattern.

inlet *n.* narrow piece of water extending from the sea into the land; valve etc. through which liquid or gas enters.

in loco parentis [par-**rent**-iss] *Latin* in place of a parent.

inmate *n.* person living in an institution such as a prison.

inmost *adj.* furthest inside, most secret.

inn *n.* pub or small hotel, esp. in the country. —**innkeeper** *n.*

innards *pl. n. Informal* internal organs; working parts.

innate *adj.* being part of someone's nature, inborn.

inner *adj.* happening or located within; of the mind or spirit, e.g. *inner peace.* —**innermost** *adj.* —**inner city** parts of a city near the centre, esp. when seen as poor or violent.

innings *n. Sport* player's or side's turn of batting; spell or turn.

innocent *adj.* not guilty of a crime; without experience of evil; trustful or naive. —*n.* innocent person, esp. a child. —**innocently** *adv.* —**innocence** *n.*

innocuous *adj.* harmless. —**innocuously** *adv.*

THESAURUS

initiative advantage, beginning, first move, first step, lead

inject 1. inoculate, vaccinate 2. infuse, insert, instil, interject, introduce

injudicious foolish, hasty, ill-advised, ill-judged, ill-timed, imprudent, indiscreet, inexpedient, rash, unthinking, unwise

injunction command, dictate, mandate, order, precept, ruling

injure abuse, blemish, blight, break, damage, deface, disable, harm, hurt, impair, maltreat, mar, ruin, spoil, tarnish, undermine, vitiate, weaken, wound, wrong

injury abuse, damage, evil, grievance, harm, hurt, ill, injustice, mischief, ruin, wound, wrong

injustice bias, favouritism, inequality, oppression, partiality, prejudice, unfairness, unlawfulness, wrong

inkling clue, glimmering, hint, idea, indication, intimation, notion, suggestion, suspicion, whisper

inland *adj.* domestic, interior, internal

inlet arm (of the sea), bay, bight, cove, creek, entrance, ingress, passage

inmost basic, buried, central, deep, deepest, essential, intimate, personal, private, secret

innate congenital, essential, inborn, inbred, inherent, inherited, instinctive, intrinsic, intuitive, native, natural

inner central, essential, inside, interior, internal, intestinal, inward, middle

innkeeper host, hostess, hotelier, landlady, landlord, publican

innocence 1. blamelessness, chastity, probity, purity, righteousness, uprightness, virginity, virtue 2. artlessness, freshness, gullibility, naiveté, simplicity

innocent 1. blameless, clear, faultless, guiltless, honest, uninvolved, unoffending 2. chaste, immaculate, impeccable, incorrupt, pristine, pure, righteous, sinless, spotless, stainless, upright, virginal 3. artless, childlike, credulous, frank, guileless, gullible, ingenuous, naive, open, simple, unworldly

innovation change, departure, introduction, novelty, variation

innuendo aspersion, hint, implication, insinuation, suggestion, whisper

DICTIONARY

innovate v. introduce new ideas or methods. —**innovation** n. —**innovative** adj. —**innovator** n.

innuendo n., pl. -**does**. indirect accusation.

innumerable adj. too many to be counted. —**innumerably** adv.

innumerate adj. having no understanding of mathematics or science. —**innumeracy** n.

inoculate v. protect against disease by injecting with a vaccine. —**inoculation** n.

inoperable adj. Med. that cannot safely be operated on.

inopportune adj. badly timed.

inordinate adj. excessive.

inorganic adj. not having the characteristics of living organisms; of or denoting chemical substances that do not contain carbon. —**inorganically** adv.

inpatient n. patient who stays in a hospital for treatment.

input n. resources put into a project etc.; data fed into a computer. —v. -**putting**, -**put**. enter (data) in a computer.

inquest n. official inquiry, esp. into a sudden death.

inquire v. seek information or ask about. —**inquirer** n. —**inquiry** n. question; investigation.

inquisition n. thorough investigation; Hist. (**I**-) organization within the Catholic Church for suppressing heresy. —**inquisitor** n. —**inquisitorial** adj.

inquisitive adj. too curious about other people's business. —**inquisitively** adv.

inquorate adj. without enough people present to make a quorum.

inroads pl. n. —**make inroads into** start affecting or reducing, e.g. my gambling has made inroads into my savings.

insalubrious adj. likely to cause ill-health.

insane adj. mentally ill; stupidly irresponsible. —**insanely** adv. —**insanity** n.

insanitary adj. dirty or unhealthy.

insatiable [in-**saysh**-a-bl] adj. impossible to satisfy.

inscribe v. write or carve words on. —**inscription** n. words inscribed.

inscrutable adj. mysterious or enigmatic; incomprehensible. —**inscrutably** adv. —**inscrutability** n.

insect n. small invertebrate animal with six legs, a segmented body, and usu. two or four wings. —**insecticide** n. substance for killing insects. —**insectivorous** adj. insect-eating.

insecure adj. not safe or firm; anxious, not confident.

inseminate v. implant semen into. —**insemination** n.

insensate adj. without sensation, unconscious; unfeeling.

insensible adj. unconscious; without feeling; not aware; imperceptible. —**insensibility** n.

insensitive adj. unaware of or ignoring other people's feelings. —**insensitivity** n.

insert v. put inside or between. —n. something inserted. —**insertion** n.

THESAURUS

innumerable countless, incalculable, infinite, many, myriad, untold

inopportune ill-timed, inauspicious, malapropos, mistimed, unpropitious, untimely

inordinate disproportionate, excessive, exorbitant, extravagant, immoderate, intemperate, undue, unreasonable

inquest inquiry, inquisition, investigation, probe

inquire examine, explore, inspect, investigate, make inquiries, probe, scrutinize, search

inquiry examination, exploration, inquest, investigation, probe, research, scrutiny, search, study, survey

inquisition cross-examination, examination, inquest, inquiry, investigation, question

inquisitive curious, inquiring, intrusive, peering, probing, prying, questioning, scrutinizing

insane crazed, crazy, demented, deranged, mad, unhinged

insanitary dirty, disease-ridden, filthy, impure,

infected, infested, noxious, polluted, unclean, unhealthy, unhygienic

insanity dementia, frenzy, madness

insatiable greedy, intemperate, rapacious, ravenous, voracious

inscribe carve, cut, engrave, etch, impress, imprint

inscription dedication, engraving, label, legend, lettering, saying, words

inscrutable 1. blank, deadpan, enigmatic 2. hidden, mysterious, unexplainable, unfathomable, unintelligible

insecure 1. afraid, anxious, uncertain, unconfident, unsure 2. flimsy, frail, insubstantial, loose, precarious, rickety, rocky, shaky, unreliable, unsound, unstable, unsteady, weak

insensible benumbed, dull, inert, numbed, stupid, torpid

insensitive callous, crass, hardened, imperceptive, indifferent, obtuse, tactless, thick-skinned, tough, unfeeling

DICTIONARY

inset *adj.* decorated with something inserted. —*n.* small map or diagram within a larger one.

inshore *adj.* close to the shore. —*adj., adv.* towards the shore.

inside *n.* inner side, surface, or part. —*prep.* in or to the inside of. —*adj.* of or on the inside; by or from someone within an organization, e.g. *inside information.* —*adv.* in or into the inside; *Slang* in prison. —**inside out** with the interior facing outwards; thoroughly. —**insider** *n.* member of a group who has exclusive knowledge about it.

insidious *adj.* subtle or unseen but dangerous. —**insidiously** *adv.*

insight *n.* clear understanding.

insignia [in-**sig**-nee-a] *n., pl.* **-nias, -nia.** badge or emblem of honour or office.

insignificant *adj.* not important. —**insignificance** *n.*

insincere *adj.* pretending what one does not feel. —**insincerely** *adv.* —**insincerity** *n.*

insinuate *v.* suggest indirectly; work oneself into a position by gradual manoeuvres. —**insinuation** *n.*

insipid *adj.* lacking interest, spirit, or flavour. —**insipidity** *n.*

insist *v.* demand or state firmly. —**insistent** *adj.* making persistent demands; demanding attention. —**insistently** *adv.* —**insistence** *n.*

in situ *adv., adj. Latin* in its original position.

insofar as *adv.* to the extent that.

insole *n.* inner sole of a shoe or boot.

insolent *adj.* arrogantly rude. —**insolence** *n.* —**insolently** *adv.*

insoluble *adj.* incapable of being solved; incapable of being dissolved.

insolvent *adj.* unable to pay one's debts. —**insolvency** *n.*

insomnia *n.* sleeplessness. —**insomniac** *n.*

insouciant *adj.* carefree and unconcerned. —**insouciance** *n.*

inspect *v.* check closely or officially. —**inspection** *n.* —**inspector** *n.* person who inspects; high-ranking police officer.

THESAURUS

insert enter, interpolate, interpose, introduce, place, put, set, stick in, tuck in

insertion addition, implant, inclusion, inset, interpolation, introduction

inside 1. *n.* contents, inner part, interior 2. *adv.* indoors, under cover, within 3. *adj.* inner, innermost, interior, internal, inward

insidious artful, crafty, cunning, deceptive, designing, duplicitous, guileful, slick, sly, smooth, sneaking, stealthy, subtle, tricky, wily

insight awareness, discernment, intuition, judgment, observation, perception, understanding, vision

insignia badge, crest, emblem, ensign, symbol

insignificance inconsequence, irrelevance, paltriness, pettiness, triviality, unimportance, worthlessness

insignificant flimsy, inconsiderable, irrelevant, meaningless, minor, negligible, nugatory, paltry, petty, scanty, trifling, trivial, unimportant, unsubstantial

insincere devious, dishonest, dissembling, double-dealing, duplicitous, evasive, faithless, false, hollow, hypocritical, lying, perfidious, two-faced, unfaithful, untrue, untruthful

insincerity deviousness, dishonesty, dissimulation, duplicity, hypocrisy, mendacity, perfidy, pretence, untruthfulness

insinuate 1. allude, hint, imply, indicate, intimate, suggest 2. infiltrate, infuse, inject, instil, introduce

insinuation allusion, aspersion, hint, implication, innuendo, slur, suggestion

insipid 1. banal, bland, colourless, drab, dry, dull, flat, lifeless, limp, pointless, prosaic, stale, stupid, tame, tedious, trite, vapid, weak, wearisome 2. bland, flavourless, tasteless, unappetizing, watery

insist 1. be firm, demand, persist, require 2. aver, claim, contend, hold, maintain, reiterate, repeat, state, swear, urge, vow

insistence assertion, contention, emphasis, reiteration, stress, urging

insistent demanding, dogged, emphatic, exigent, forceful, incessant unrelenting, urgent

insolence abuse, audacity, boldness, disrespect, effrontery, gall (*Inf.*), impertinence, impudence, insubordination, rudeness

insolent abusive, bold, contemptuous, impertinent, impudent, insubordinate, insulting, pert, rude, saucy, uncivil

insoluble baffling, inexplicable, mysterious, mystifying, obscure, unfathomable

insolvency bankruptcy, failure, liquidation, ruin

insolvent bankrupt, failed, ruined

insomnia sleeplessness, wakefulness

inspect check, examine, investigate, look over, oversee, scan, scrutinize, search, supervise, survey, vet

inspection check, examination, investigation,

DICTIONARY

inspire v. fill with enthusiasm, stimulate; arouse (an emotion). —**inspiration** n. good idea; creative influence or stimulus. —**inspirational** adj.

instability n. lack of steadiness or reliability.

install v. put in and prepare (equipment) for use; formally place (a person) in a position or rank. —**installation** n. installing; equipment installed; place containing equipment for a particular purpose, e.g. radar installation.

instalment n. any of the portions of a thing presented or a debt paid in successive parts.

instance n. particular example. —v. mention as an example. —**for instance** for example.

instant n. very brief time; particular moment. —adj. immediate; (of foods) requiring little preparation. —**instantly** adv. at once.

instantaneous adj. happening at once. —**instantaneously** adv.

instead adv. as a replacement or substitute.

instep n. part of the foot forming the arch between the ankle and toes; part of a shoe etc. covering this.

instigate v. cause to happen, bring about. —**instigation** n. —**instigator** n.

instil v. -stilling, -stilled. introduce (an idea etc.) gradually in someone's mind. —**instilment** n.

instinct n. inborn tendency to behave in a certain way. —**instinctive** adj. —**instinctively** adv.

institute n. organization set up for a specific purpose, esp. teaching or research. —v. start or establish. —**institution** n. long-established custom; large important organization such as a university or bank; hospital etc. for people with special needs. —**institutional** adj. —**institutionalize** v. make unable to cope with life outside an institution.

instruct v. order to do something; teach (someone) how to do something; brief (a solicitor or barrister). —**instruction** n. teaching; order. —pl. information on how to do or use something. —**instructive** adj. informative or helpful. —**instructor** n.

THESAURUS

look-over, review, scan, scrutiny, search, supervision, surveillance, survey

inspector censor, checker, critic, examiner, investigator, overseer, scrutineer, supervisor

inspiration arousal, awakening, encouragement, influence, muse, spur, stimulus

inspire animate, encourage, enliven, galvanize, hearten, imbue, influence, infuse, inspirit, instil, spark off, spur, stimulate

instability fickleness, fluctuation, fluidity, frailty, imbalance, insecurity, restlessness, unsteadiness, vacillation, variability, volatility, weakness

install 1. fix, lay, lodge, place, position, put in, set up, station 2. establish, induct, institute, introduce, invest, set up

installation 1. inauguration, induction, investiture 2. equipment, machinery, plant, system

instalment chapter, division, episode, part, portion, repayment, section

instance 1. n. case, example, illustration, occasion, occurrence, precedent, situation, time 2. v. adduce, cite, mention, name, quote, specify

instant 1. n. flash, moment, second, split second, trice, twinkling 2. adj. direct, immediate, instantaneous, prompt, quick, urgent

instantaneous direct, immediate, instant, on-the-spot

instantaneously at once, forthwith, immediately, instantly, promptly, straight away

instantly at once, directly, forthwith, immediately, instantaneously, now, without delay

instead alternatively, preferably, rather

instigate actuate, encourage, impel, incite, influence, initiate, kindle, move, prompt, provoke, rouse, set on, spur, start, stimulate, stir up, urge, whip up

instil engender, implant, impress, infix, infuse, insinuate

instinct aptitude, faculty, feeling, gift, impulse, intuition, knack, proclivity, talent, tendency, urge

instinctive inborn, inherent, innate, intuitional, intuitive, natural, reflex

institute 1. v. appoint, begin, enact, establish, fix, found, induct, initiate, install, introduce, invest, ordain, organize, pioneer, settle, set up, start 2. n. academy, college, conservatory, foundation, guild, school, seminary, society

institution 1. academy, college, foundation, hospital, institute, school, seminary, society, university 2. custom, fixture, law, practice, ritual, rule, tradition

instruct 1. bid, charge, direct, enjoin, order, tell 2. coach, discipline, drill, educate, ground, guide, inform, school, teach, train, tutor

instruction coaching, discipline, drilling, education, grounding, guidance, information, lesson(s), schooling, teaching, training, tuition

instructions advice, directions, guidance, information, orders, rules

instructor adviser, coach, guide, master, mentor, mistress, pedagogue, teacher, trainer, tutor

DICTIONARY

instrument *n.* tool used for particular work; object played to produce a musical sound; measuring device to show height, speed, etc.; *Informal* person used by another. —**instrumental** *adj.* helping to cause; played by or composed for musical instruments. —**instrumentalist** *n.* player of a musical instrument. —**instrumentation** *n.* set of instruments in a car etc.; arrangement of music for instruments.

insubordinate *adj.* not submissive to authority. —**insubordination** *n.*

insufferable *adj.* unbearable.

insular *adj.* not open to new ideas, narrow-minded; of or like an island. —**insularity** *n.*

insulate *v.* prevent or reduce the transfer of electricity, heat, sound, etc. by surrounding or lining with nonconductive material; isolate or set apart. —**insulation** *n.* —**insulator** *n.*

insulin [**in-**syoo-lin] *n.* hormone produced by the pancreas which controls the amount of sugar in the blood.

insult *v.* behave rudely to, offend. —*n.* insulting remark or action. —**insulting** *adj.*

insuperable *adj.* impossible to overcome. —**insuperability** *n.* —**insuperably** *adv.*

insupportable *adj.* incapable of being tolerated; indefensible.

insurance *n.* agreement by which one makes regular payments to a company who pay an agreed sum if damage, loss, or death occurs; money paid by or for insurance; means of protection. —**insure** *v.* protect by insurance. —**insurance policy** contract of insurance.

insurgent *adj.* in revolt. —*n.* rebel. —**insurgence** *n.* revolt.

insurrection *n.* rebellion.

intact *adj.* untouched; left complete or unharmed.

intaglio [in-**tah**-lee-oh] *n., pl.* **-lios, -li.** (gem carved with) an engraved design.

intake *n.* thing or quantity taken in; opening through which fluid or gas enters an engine, pipe, etc.

integer *n.* positive or negative whole number or zero.

integral *adj.* being an essential part of a whole. —*n. Maths* sum of a large number of very small quantities.

integrate *v.* combine into a whole; amalgamate (a religious or racial group) into a community. —**integration** *n.* —**integrated circuit** tiny electronic circuit on a silicon chip.

integrity *n.* honesty; quality of being sound or whole.

integument *n.* natural covering such as skin or rind.

intellect *n.* power of thinking and reasoning. —**intellectual** *adj.* of or appealing to the intellect; clever or intelligent. —*n.* intellectual person. —**intellectually** *adv.*

THESAURUS

instrument appliance, contrivance, device, gadget, implement, mechanism, tool, utensil

instrumental active, assisting, auxiliary, conducive, helpful, involved, of help *or* service, subsidiary, useful

insubordinate defiant, disobedient, disorderly, rebellious, recalcitrant, riotous, seditious, turbulent, undisciplined, unruly

insubordination defiance, disobedience, indiscipline, insurrection, mutiny, rebellion, revolt, riotousness, sedition

insufferable detestable, impossible, intolerable, outrageous, unbearable, unendurable, unspeakable

insular *Fig.* blinkered, closed, illiberal, isolated, limited, narrow, parochial, petty, provincial

insulate *Fig.* close off, cut off, isolate, protect

insult 1. *n.* abuse, indignity, insolence, outrage, rudeness, slight, snub 2. *v.* abuse, injure, offend, outrage, revile, slander, slight

insupportable insufferable, intolerable, past bearing, unbearable, unendurable

insurance cover, guarantee, indemnity, protection, provision, safeguard, security, warranty

insurgent *n.* insurrectionist, rebel, revolutionary, rioter

intact complete, entire, perfect, sound, together, unbroken, undamaged, unharmed, unhurt, untouched, unviolated, virgin, whole

integral basic, component, constituent, essential

integrate accommodate, assimilate, blend, coalesce, combine, fuse, harmonize, join, knit, merge, mesh, unite

integrity goodness, honesty, honour, principle, probity, purity, rectitude, righteousness, uprightness, virtue

intellect brains (*Inf.*), intelligence, judgment, mind, reason, sense, understanding

intellectual 1. *adj.* bookish, highbrow, intelligent, mental, rational, scholarly, studious, thoughtful 2. *n.* academic, highbrow

intelligence 1. acumen, alertness, brightness, capacity, cleverness, discernment, intellect, mind, perception, quickness, reason, understanding 2. advice, data, disclosure, facts, findings, information, knowledge, news, notice, report, rumour, tidings, tip-off, word

DICTIONARY

intelligent *adj.* able to understand, learn, and think things out quickly; (of a computerized device) able to initiate or modify action in the light of ongoing events. —**intelligence** *n.* quality of being intelligent; information or news, esp. military information; people or department collecting military information. —**intelligently** *adv.*

intelligentsia *n.* intellectual or cultured classes.

intelligible *adj.* understandable. —**intelligibility** *n.*

intemperate *adj.* extreme; uncontrolled; drinking alcohol to excess. —**intemperance** *n.*

intend *v.* propose or plan (something or to do something); have as one's purpose.

intense *adj.* of great strength or degree; deeply emotional. —**intensity** *n.*

intensify *v.* **-fying, -fied.** make or become more intense. —**intensification** *n.*

intensive *adj.* using or needing concentrated effort or resources. —**intensively** *adv.*

intent *n.* intention. —*adj.* paying close attention. —**intently** *adv.* —**intentness** *n.* —**intent on** determined to.

intention *n.* something intended. —**intentional** *adj.* deliberate. —**intentionally** *adv.*

inter [in-**ter**] *v.* **-terring, -terred.** bury (a corpse). —**interment** *n.* burial (of a corpse).

inter- *prefix* between or among, e.g. *intercontinental.*

inter-city *adj.* (of a passenger service) travelling fast between cities.

interact *v.* act on or in close relation with each other. —**interaction** *n.* —**interactive** *adj.*

interbreed *v.* breed within a related group.

intercede *v.* plead in favour of; mediate. —**intercession** *n.* —**intercessor** *n.*

intercept *v.* seize or stop in transit. —**interception** *n.*

interchange *v.* (cause to) exchange places. —*n.* motorway junction. —**interchangeable** *adj.*

intercom *n.* internal communication system with loudspeakers.

intercontinental *adj.* travelling between or linking continents.

intercourse *n.* act of having sex; communication or dealings between people or groups.

interdict, interdiction *n.* formal order forbidding something.

interdisciplinary *adj.* involving more than one academic discipline.

interest *n.* desire to know or hear more about something; hobby or subject that one enjoys; (often *pl.*) advantage, e.g. *in one's own interests;* sum paid for use of borrowed money; right or share. —*v.* arouse the interest of. —**interested** *adj.* feeling or showing interest; involved in or affected by. —**interesting** *adj.* —**interestingly** *adv.*

THESAURUS

intelligent acute, alert, apt, bright, clever, discerning, knowing, perspicacious, quick, rational, sharp, smart

intelligentsia highbrows, illuminati, intellectuals, literati

intelligible clear, distinct, lucid, open, plain, understandable

intemperate excessive, extreme, immoderate, incontinent, inordinate, prodigal, profligate, self-indulgent, severe, unrestrained, violent, wild

intend aim, contemplate, determine, mean, meditate, plan, propose, purpose, scheme

intense 1. acute, close, concentrated, deep, extreme, fierce, forceful, great, harsh, powerful, profound, protracted, severe, strained 2. ardent, burning, eager, earnest, fanatical, fervent, fierce, heightened, impassioned, keen, passionate, vehement

intensify add to, aggravate, boost, concentrate, deepen, emphasize, enhance, heighten, increase, magnify, quicken, reinforce, set off, sharpen, strengthen

intensity ardour, concentration, depth, emotion, energy, excess, fervour, fierceness, fire, force, keenness, passion, potency, power, severity, strain, strength, tension, vehemence, vigour

intensive all-out, concentrated, demanding, exhaustive, thorough

intent absorbed, alert, attentive, committed, concentrated, determined, eager, earnest, fixed, occupied, preoccupied, rapt, resolute, resolved, steadfast, steady, watchful, wrapped up

intention aim, design, end, goal, idea, object, objective, point, purpose, scope, target, view

intentional deliberate, designed, meant, planned, premeditated, purposed, studied

inter bury, lay to rest, sepulchre

intercede interpose, intervene, mediate, plead, speak

intercept arrest, block, catch, check, cut off, deflect, head off, stop, take

interchangeable equivalent, identical, reciprocal, synonymous, the same

intercourse 1. association, commerce, communion, connection, contact, converse, deal-

DICTIONARY

interface *n.* area where two things interact or link; circuit linking a computer and another device.

interfere *v.* try to influence other people's affairs where one is not involved or wanted; clash (with); *Euphemistic* abuse sexually. —**interfering** *adj.* —**interference** *n.* interfering; *Radio* interruption of reception by atmospherics or unwanted signals.

interferon *n.* protein that stops the development of an invading virus.

interim *adj.* temporary or provisional.

interior *adj.* inside, inner; mental or spiritual. —*n.* inside; inland region.

interject *v.* make (a remark) suddenly or as an interruption. —**interjection** *n.*

interlace *v.* join by lacing or weaving together.

interlay *v.* insert (layers) between.

interlink *v.* connect together.

interlock *v.* join firmly together. —*adj.* closely knitted.

interlocutor [in-ter-**lok**-yew-ter] *n.* person who takes part in a conversation.

interloper [**in**-ter-lope-er] *n.* person in a place or situation where he or she has no right to be.

interlude *n.* short rest or break in an activity or event.

intermarry *v.* (of families, races, or religions) become linked by marriage. —**intermarriage** *n.*

intermediate *adj.* coming between two points or extremes. —**intermediary** *n.* person trying to create agreement between others; messenger.

intermezzo [in-ter-**met**-so] *n., pl.* **-zos, -zi.** short piece of music, esp. one performed between the acts of an opera.

interminable *adj.* seemingly endless because boring. —**interminably** *adv.*

intermingle *v.* mix together.

intermission *n.* interval between parts of a play, film, etc.

intermittent *adj.* occurring at intervals. —**intermittently** *adv.*

intern *v.* imprison, esp. during a war. —*n. US* trainee doctor in a hospital. —**internment** *n.* —**internee** *n.* person who has been interned.

internal *adj.* of or on the inside; within a country or organization; spiritual or mental. —**internally** *adv.* —**internal-combustion engine** engine powered by the explosion of a fuel-and-air mixture within the cylinders.

international *adj.* of or involving two or more countries. —*n.* game or match between teams of different countries; player in such a match. —**internationally** *adv.*

internecine *adj.* mutually destructive.

interplanetary *adj.* of or linking planets.

interplay *n.* action and reaction of two things upon each other.

interpolate [in-**ter**-pole-ate] *v.* insert (a comment or passage) in (a conversation or text). —**interpolation** *n.*

interpose *v.* insert between or among things; say as an interruption. —**interposition** *n.*

THESAURUS

ings, trade, traffic, truck 2. carnal knowledge, coition, coitus, congress, copulation, intimacy

interest *n.* 1. affection, attention, attraction, concern, curiosity, notice, regard, suspicion, sympathy 2. activity, diversion, hobby, pastime, pursuit, relaxation 3. advantage, benefit, gain, good, profit ~*v.* 4. amuse, attract, divert, engross, fascinate 5. affect, concern, engage, involve

interested 1. affected, attentive, attracted, curious, drawn, excited, fascinated, intent, keen, moved, stimulated 2. concerned, implicated, involved, partial, partisan

interesting absorbing, amusing, appealing, attractive, compelling, curious, engaging, engrossing, entertaining, gripping, intriguing, pleasing, stimulating, suspicious, unusual

interfere butt in, intervene, intrude, meddle, tamper

interference 1. intervention, intrusion, meddling 2. collision, conflict, obstruction, opposition

interim *adj.* acting, caretaker, improvised, makeshift, provisional, stopgap, temporary

interior *adj.* 1. inner, inside, internal, inward 2. *Geog.* central, inland, inner, remote 3. hidden, inner, personal, private, secret, spiritual ~*n.* 4. *Geog.* centre, heartland, upcountry

interloper intruder, trespasser

interlude break, delay, episode, halt, hiatus, intermission, interval, pause, respite, rest, spell, stop, stoppage, wait

intermediate halfway, intervening, mean, mid, middle, midway

interment burial, burying, funeral

interminable ceaseless, dragging, endless, everlasting, infinite, limitless, long, protracted, unbounded, unlimited, wearisome

intermittent broken, discontinuous, fitful, irregular, occasional, periodic, punctuated, recurrent, spasmodic, sporadic

intern confine, detain, hold

internal inner, inside, interior, intimate, private

DICTIONARY

interpret v. explain the meaning of; translate orally from one language into another; convey the meaning of (a poem, song, etc.) in performance. —**interpretation** n. —**interpreter** n.

interregnum n., pl. **-nums, -na.** interval between reigns.

interrogate v. question closely. —**interrogation** n. —**interrogative** adj. questioning. —n. word used in asking a question, such as how or why. —**interrogator** n.

interrupt v. break into (a conversation etc.); temporarily stop (a process or activity). —**interruption** n.

intersect v. divide by passing across or through; (of roads) meet and cross. —**intersection** n.

interspersed adj. scattered among, between, or on.

interstate adj. US between or involving two or more states.

interstellar adj. between or among stars.

interstice [in-ter-stiss] n. small crack or gap between things.

intertwine v. twist together or entwine.

interval n. time between two particular moments or events; break between parts of a play, concert, etc.; difference in pitch between notes. —**at intervals** repeatedly; with spaces left between.

intervene v. involve oneself in a situation, esp. to prevent conflict; happen so as to stop something. —**intervention** n.

interview n. formal discussion, esp. between a job-seeker and employer; questioning of a well-known person about his or her career, views, etc., by a reporter. —v. have an interview with. —**interviewee** n. —**interviewer** n.

interwar adj. of or during the period 1919–39.

interweave v. weave together.

intestate adj. not having made a will. —**intestacy** n.

intestine n. (usu. pl.) lower part of the alimentary canal between the stomach and the anus. —**intestinal** adj.

intimate[1] adj. having a close personal relationship; private; (of knowledge) extensive and detailed; Euphemistic having sexual relations; having a friendly quiet atmosphere. —n. intimate friend. —**intimately** adv. —**intimacy** n.

intimate[2] v. hint or suggest; announce. —**intimation** n.

THESAURUS

international cosmopolitan, global, intercontinental, universal, worldwide

interpose 1. interfere, intervene, intrude, step in 2. insert, interject, introduce

interpret adapt, clarify, construe, decipher, decode, define, elucidate, explain, expound, paraphrase, read, render, solve, take, translate

interpretation analysis, clarification, construction, diagnosis, elucidation, exegesis, explanation, explication, meaning, performance, reading, rendering, sense, translation, version

interpreter annotator, exponent, scholiast, translator

interrogate ask, cross-examine, enquire, examine, inquire, investigate, pump, question, quiz

interrogation cross-examination, cross-questioning, enquiry, examination, inquisition, probing, questioning

interrupt break in, butt in, check, cut off, delay, disconnect, discontinue, disturb, divide, heckle, hinder, hold up, intrude, obstruct, separate, sever, stay, stop, suspend

interruption break, disconnection, disruption, disturbance, division, halt, hiatus, hitch, impediment, intrusion, obstacle, obstruction, pause, stop, stoppage

intersection crossing, crossroads, interchange, junction

interval break, delay, gap, interlude, intermission, meantime, meanwhile, opening, pause, period, playtime, rest, season, space, spell, term, time, wait

intervene arbitrate, intercede, interfere, intrude, mediate

interview 1. n. audience, conference, consultation, dialogue, meeting, talk 2. v. examine, interrogate, question, talk to

interviewer examiner questioner, reporter

intimacy closeness, confidence, familiarity, understanding

intimate[1] adj. 1. bosom, cherished, close, confidential, dear, friendly, near, warm 2. personal, private, privy, secret 3. cosy, friendly, informal, snug, warm ~n. 4. bosom friend, comrade, confidant, companion, crony, familiar, friend, pal

intimate[2] v. allude, communicate, declare, hint, impart, imply, indicate, insinuate, remind, state, suggest, warn

intimately 1. closely, confidentially, warmly 2. fully, thoroughly, very well

intimidate alarm, appal, bully, coerce, dishearten, dismay, frighten, overawe, scare, subdue, terrify, terrorize, threaten

intimidation browbeating, bullying, fear, menaces, pressure, terror, threat

DICTIONARY

intimidate v. subdue or influence by frightening. —**intimidation** n. —**intimidating** adj.

into prep. to the inner part of; to the middle of; (up) against; used to indicate the result of a change, e.g. *he turned into a monster; Maths* used to indicate division, e.g. *three into six is two; Informal* interested in.

intolerable adj. more than can be endured. —**intolerably** adv.

intolerant adj. narrow-minded or bigoted. —**intolerance** n.

intonation n. sound pattern produced by variations in the voice.

intone v. speak or recite in an unvarying tone of voice.

intoxicate v. make drunk; excite to excess. —**intoxicant** n., adj. (drink) capable of intoxicating. —**intoxication** n.

intractable adj. (of a person) difficult to influence; (of a problem or illness) hard to solve or cure.

intransigent adj. refusing to change one's attitude. —**intransigence** n.

intransitive adj. (of a verb) not taking a direct object.

intrauterine adj. within the womb.

intravenous [in-tra-vee-nuss] adj. into a vein. —**intravenously** adv.

intrepid adj. fearless or bold. —**intrepidity** n.

intricate adj. involved or complicated; full of fine detail. —**intricately** adv. —**intricacy** n.

intrigue v. make interested or curious; plot secretly. —n. secret plotting; secret love affair. —**intriguing** adj.

intrinsic adj. part of the basic nature of. —**intrinsically** adv.

introduce v. present (someone) by name (to another person); present (a radio or television programme); bring forward for discussion; bring into use; insert. —**introduction** n. presentation of one person to another; preliminary part or treatment. —**introductory** adj. preliminary.

introspection n. examination of one's own thoughts and feelings. —**introspective** adj.

introvert n. person concerned more with his or her thoughts and feelings than with external reality. —**introverted** adj. —**introversion** n.

intrude v. come in or join in without being invited. —**intruder** n. —**intrusion** n. —**intrusive** adj.

intuition n. instinctive knowledge or insight without conscious reasoning. —**intuitive** adj. —**intuitively** adv.

THESAURUS

intolerable excruciating, impossible, insufferable, insupportable, painful, unbearable, unendurable

intolerance chauvinism, fanaticism, narrow-mindedness, prejudice, racialism, racism

intolerant chauvinistic, fanatical, narrow, narrow-minded, one-sided, prejudiced, racist, small-minded, uncharitable

intoxication drunkenness, inebriation, tipsiness

intrepid bold, brave, courageous, daring, doughty, fearless, gallant, heroic, plucky, resolute, stalwart, unafraid, unflinching, valiant, valorous

intricacy complexity, involvement, knottiness

intricate baroque, complex, complicated, difficult, elaborate, fancy, involved, knotty, obscure, perplexing, tangled, tortuous

intrigue v. 1. attract, charm, fascinate, interest, rivet, titillate 2. connive, conspire, machinate, plot, scheme ~n. 3. collusion, conspiracy, double-dealing, knavery, manipulation, manoeuvre, plot, ruse, scheme, stratagem, trickery, wile 4. affair, amour, liaison, romance

intriguing diverting, exciting, fascinating, interesting, tantalizing, titillating

intrinsic basic, built-in, central, congenital, essential, genuine, inborn, inbred, inherent, native, natural, real, true

introduce 1. acquaint, familiarize, make known, present 2. begin, bring in, commence, establish, found, inaugurate, initiate, institute, launch, organize, pioneer, set up, start, usher in 3. announce, open, preface

introduction 1. baptism, debut, inauguration, induction, initiation, institution, launch, presentation 2. foreword, lead-in, opening, overture, preamble, preface, prelude, proem, prologue

introductory early, elementary, first, inaugural, initial, opening, prefatory, preliminary, preparatory, starting

intrude encroach, infringe, interfere, interrupt, obtrude, trespass, violate

intruder burglar, interloper, invader, prowler, raider, thief, trespasser

intrusion infringement, interruption, invasion, trespass, violation

intuition hunch, insight, instinct, perception, presentiment

inundate deluge, drown, engulf, flood, glut, overflow, overrun, overwhelm, submerge, swamp

DICTIONARY

Inuit *n.* Eskimo of North America or Greenland.

inundate *v.* flood; overwhelm. **—inundation** *n.*

inure *v.* accustom, esp. to hardship or danger.

invade *v.* enter (a country) by military force; enter in large numbers; disturb (privacy etc.). **—invader** *n.*

invalid[1] *n.* disabled or chronically ill person. **—v.** dismiss from active service because of illness etc. **—invalidity** *n.*

invalid[2] *adj.* having no legal force; (of an argument etc.) not valid because based on a mistake. **—invalidate** *v.* make or show to be invalid.

invaluable *adj.* priceless.

invasion *n.* act of invading; intrusion.

invective *n.* abusive speech or writing.

inveigh [in-**vay**] *v.* (foll. by *against*) criticize (something) harshly.

inveigle *v.* coax or entice. **—inveiglement** *n.*

invent *v.* think up or create (something new); make up (an excuse, lie, etc.). **—invention** *n.* something invented; ability to invent. **—inventive** *adj.* resourceful; creative. **—inventiveness** *n.* **—inventor** *n.*

inventory [**in**-ven-tree] *n., pl.* **-tories.** detailed list of goods or furnishings.

inverse *adj.* opposite, inverted; *Maths* linking two variables in such a way that one increases as the other decreases. **—inversely** *adv.*

invert *v.* turn upside down or inside out. **—inversion** *n.* **—inverted commas** raised commas in writing to show where speech begins and ends.

invertebrate *n.* animal with no backbone.

invest *v.* spend (money, time, etc.) on something with the expectation of profit. **—investment** *n.* money invested; something invested in. **—investor** *n.* **—invest in** *v.* buy. **—invest with** *v.* give (power or rights) to.

investigate *v.* inquire into; examine. **—investigation** *n.* **—investigative** *adj.* **—investigator** *n.*

investiture *n.* formal installation of a person in an office or rank.

inveterate *adj.* deep-rooted; confirmed in a habit or practice. **—inveteracy** *n.*

invidious *adj.* likely to cause resentment. **—invidiously** *adv.*

invigilate [in-**vij**-il-late] *v.* supervise examination candidates. **—invigilator** *n.*

invigorate *v.* give energy to or refresh.

invincible *adj.* unconquerable. **—invincibly** *adv.* **—invincibility** *n.*

THESAURUS

invade assail, assault, attack, burst in, encroach, infringe, occupy, raid, violate

invader aggressor, attacker, plunderer, raider, trespasser

invalid *adj.* baseless, false, ill-founded, illogical, irrational, null and void, unfounded, unsound, untrue, void, worthless

invaluable costly, inestimable, precious, priceless, valuable

invasion assault, attack, foray, incursion, inroad, irruption, offensive, onslaught, raid

invective abuse, censure, contumely, diatribe, obloquy, reproach, sarcasm, tirade, vituperation

invent coin, conceive, contrive, create, design, devise, discover, formulate, imagine, improvise, originate, think up

invention 1. contraption, contrivance, creation, design, development, device, discovery, gadget 2. deceit, fabrication, fake, falsehood, fantasy, fiction, forgery, lie, prevarication, sham, story, untruth

inventive creative, fertile, gifted, imaginative, ingenious, resourceful

inventor author, coiner, creator, designer, father, maker, originator

inventory *n.* account, catalogue, list, record, register, roll, roster, schedule

inverse *adj.* contrary, inverted, opposite, reverse, transposed

invert capsize, overturn, reverse, transpose, upset, upturn

invest advance, devote, lay out, put in, sink, spend

investigate consider, enquire into, examine, explore, inspect, probe, scrutinize, search, sift, study

investigation analysis, enquiry, examination, exploration, hearing, inquest, inquiry, inspection, probe, research, review, scrutiny, search, study, survey

investigator examiner, inquirer, (private) detective, researcher, reviewer, sleuth

investiture admission, enthronement, inauguration, induction, installation

investment asset, speculation, transaction, venture

inveterate chronic, confirmed, deep-dyed, entrenched, established, hardened, incorrigible, ineradicable, long-standing

invigorate brace, energize, enliven, exhilarate, fortify, galvanize, harden, quicken, refresh, rejuvenate, stimulate, strengthen

invincible indestructible, insuperable, unassailable, unbeatable, unconquerable

DICTIONARY

inviolable *adj.* that must not be broken or violated.

inviolate *adj.* unharmed, unaffected.

invisible *adj.* not able to be seen. —**invisibly** *adv.* —**invisibility** *n.*

invite *v.* request the company of; ask politely for; attract, e.g. *the plan invited criticism.* —*n. Informal* invitation. —**inviting** *adj.* —**invitation** *n.*

in vitro *adj.* (of a biological process) happening outside the body in an artificial environment.

invoice *v., n.* (send) a bill for goods or services supplied.

invoke *v.* call on (a god) for help, inspiration, etc.; put (a law or penalty) into operation; summon (a spirit). —**invocation** *n.*

involuntary *adj.* not done consciously; unintentional. —**involuntarily** *adv.*

involve *v.* include as a necessary part; affect; implicate (a person); make complicated. —**involved** *adj.* complicated; concerned in. —**involvement** *n.*

invulnerable *adj.* not able to be wounded or harmed.

inward *adj.* internal; situated within; spiritual or mental. —*adv.* (also **inwards**) towards the inside or middle. —**inwardly** *adv.*

iodine *n.* bluish-black element used in medicine, photography, and dyeing. —**iodize** *v.* treat with iodine.

ion *n.* electrically charged atom. —**ionic** *adj.* —**ionize** *v.* change into ions. —**ionization** *n.* —**ionosphere** *n.* region of ionized air in the upper atmosphere which reflects radio waves.

iota [eye-**oh**-ta] *n.* Greek letter *i*; very small amount.

IOU *n.* signed paper acknowledging debt.

IPA International Phonetic Alphabet.

ipso facto *adv. Latin* by that very fact.

IQ intelligence quotient.

IRA Irish Republican Army.

irascible *adj.* easily angered. —**irascibly** *adv.* —**irascibility** *n.*

irate *adj.* very angry.

ire *n. Lit.* anger.

iridescent *adj.* having shimmering changing colours like a rainbow. —**iridescence** *n.*

iris *n.* circular membrane of the eye containing the pupil; plant with sword-shaped leaves and showy flowers.

Irish *adj.* of Ireland. —**Irish coffee** hot coffee mixed with whiskey and topped with cream.

irk *v.* irritate or annoy. —**irksome** *adj.* tiresome.

iron *n.* metallic element widely used for structural and engineering purposes; tool made of iron; appliance used, when heated, to press clothes or fabric; metal-headed golf club. —*pl.* fetters or chains. —*adj.* made of iron; inflexible, e.g. *an iron will.* —*v.* smooth (clothes or fabric) with an iron. —**iron out** *v.* settle (a problem) through discussion. —**Iron Age** era when iron tools were used. —**ironing** *n.* clothes to be ironed. —**ironing board** long cloth-covered board, usu. with folding legs, on which to iron clothes.

ironic, ironical *adj.* using irony. —**ironically** *adv.*

THESAURUS

invisible 1. indiscernible, out of sight, unseen 2. concealed, disguised, hidden, inconspicuous

invitation 1. asking, begging, bidding, call, request, solicitation, summons 2. coquetry, enticement, incitement, inducement, overture, provocation, temptation

invite 1. ask, beg, bid, call, request, solicit, summon 2. allure, attract, bring on, court, draw, encourage, entice, lead, provoke, solicit, tempt, welcome

inviting alluring, appealing, attractive, captivating, delightful, engaging, fascinating, pleasing, seductive, tempting, warm, welcoming

invocation appeal, entreaty, petition, prayer, supplication

invoke adjure, beg, beseech, call upon, conjure, entreat, implore, petition, pray, solicit, supplicate

involuntary compulsory, forced, obligatory, reluctant, unwilling

involve 1. entail, imply, mean, necessitate, presuppose, require 2. affect, associate, concern, connect, draw in, implicate, incriminate, inculpate, touch

involvement association, commitment, concern, connection, interest, responsibility

inward *adj.* 1. entering, incoming, ingoing, penetrating 2. confidential, hidden, inmost, innermost, inside, interior, internal, mental, personal, private, secret, spiritual

inwardly at heart, inside, privately, secretly, within

irksome annoying, boring, burdensome, disagreeable, exasperating, tedious, tiresome, troublesome, unwelcome, vexatious, vexing, wearisome

iron *adj. Fig.* adamant, cruel, hard, heavy, im-

DICTIONARY

ironmonger *n.* shopkeeper or shop dealing in hardware. —**ironmongery** *n.*

ironstone *n.* rock consisting mainly of iron ore; tough durable earthenware.

irony *n., pl.* **-nies.** mildly sarcastic use of words to imply the opposite of what is said; event or situation the opposite of that expected.

irradiate *v.* subject to or treat with radiation. —**irradiation** *n.*

irrational *adj.* not based on logical reasoning.

irredeemable *adj.* not able to be reformed, improved, or corrected; not able to be recovered, bought back, or converted into coin.

irreducible *adj.* impossible to put in a reduced or simpler form.

irrefutable *adj.* impossible to deny or disprove.

irregular *adj.* not regular or even; unconventional; (of a word) not following the typical pattern of formation in a language. —**irregularly** *adv.* —**irregularity** *n.*

irrelevant *adj.* not connected with the matter in hand. —**irrelevantly** *adv.* —**irrelevance** *n.*

irreparable *adj.* not able to be repaired or put right. —**irreparably** *adv.*

irreproachable *adj.* blameless, faultless. —**irreproachably** *adv.*

irresistible *adj.* too attractive or strong to resist. —**irresistibly** *adv.*

irrespective of *prep.* without taking account of.

irreverence *n.* lack of due respect; disrespectful remark or act. —**irreverent** *adj.*

irrevocable *adj.* not possible to change or undo. —**irrevocably** *adv.*

irrigate *v.* water by artificial channels or pipes. —**irrigation** *n.*

irritate *v.* annoy or anger; cause (a body part) to itch or become inflamed. —**irritable** *adj.* easily annoyed. —**irritably** *adv.* —**irritant** *n., adj.* (person or thing) causing irritation. —**irritation** *n.*

irrupt *v.* enter forcibly or suddenly. —**irruption** *n.*

is *v.* third person singular present tense of BE.

ISBN International Standard Book Number.

isinglass [**ize-ing-glass**] *n.* kind of gelatine obtained from some freshwater fish.

Islam *n.* Muslim religion teaching that there is

THESAURUS

movable, implacable, inflexible, obdurate, rigid, steel, strong, tough, unbending, unyielding

ironic, ironical 1. mocking, sarcastic, sardonic, satirical, sneering, wry 2. incongruous, paradoxical

iron out clear up, eliminate, erase, expedite, harmonize, put right, reconcile, resolve, settle, simplify, sort out, unravel

irony 1. mockery, sarcasm, satire 2. contrariness, incongruity, paradox

irrational absurd, crazy, foolish, illogical, silly, unreasonable, unsound, unthinking, unwise

irrefutable certain, incontestable, incontrovertible, indisputable, indubitable, invincible, sure, unanswerable, undeniable

irregular *adj.* 1. eccentric, erratic, fitful, fluctuating, fragmentary, haphazard, intermittent, occasional, patchy, random, shifting, spasmodic, sporadic, uncertain, unpunctual, unsteady, unsystematic, variable, wavering 2. asymmetrical, broken, bumpy, craggy, crooked, elliptic, jagged, lopsided, pitted, ragged, rough, unequal, uneven

irregularity 1. asymmetry, bumpiness, crookedness, lopsidedness, patchiness, raggedness, roughness, unevenness 2. aberration, anomaly, breach, deviation, eccentricity, freak, malfunction, malpractice, oddity, peculiarity, singularity, unconventionality, unorthodoxy

irrelevance inappositeness, inappropriateness

irrelevant extraneous, immaterial, impertinent, inapplicable, inappropriate, unrelated

irreparable beyond repair, irremediable, irretrievable, irreversible

irreproachable blameless, faultless, guiltless, impeccable, innocent, perfect, pure, unimpeachable

irresistible 1. compelling, imperative, overpowering, overwhelming, potent, urgent 2. alluring, enchanting, fascinating, ravishing, seductive, tempting

irreverent derisive, disrespectful, flippant, impertinent, impious, mocking, saucy

irrevocable changeless, fated, fixed, irreversible, predestined, settled, unalterable, unreversible

irrigate flood, inundate, moisten, water, wet

irritable bad-tempered, cantankerous, choleric, crabbed, cross, dyspeptic, exasperated, fiery, fretful, hasty, hot, ill-humoured, ill-tempered, irascible, peevish, petulant, prickly, snappish, snarling, tense, testy, touchy

irritate 1. anger, annoy, bother, enrage, exasperate, fret, harass, incense, inflame, infuriate, nettle, offend, pester, provoke, ruffle, vex 2. aggravate, chafe, fret, inflame, intensify, pain, rub

irritation anger, annoyance, displeasure, exasperation, impatience, indignation, irritability, resentment, testiness, vexation, wrath

DICTIONARY

one God and that Mohammed is his prophet; Muslim countries and civilization. —**Islamic** *adj.*

island *n.* piece of land surrounded by water. —**islander** *n.* person who lives on an island.

isle *n.* island. —**islet** *n.* little island.

isobar [ice-oh-bar] *n.* line on a map connecting places of equal barometric pressure. —**isobaric** *adj.*

isolate *v.* place apart or alone; obtain (a substance) in uncombined form. —**isolation** *n.* —**isolationism** *n.* policy of not participating in international affairs. —**isolationist** *n., adj.*

isomer [ice-oh-mer] *n.* substance whose molecules contain the same atoms as another but in a different arrangement. —**isomeric** *adj.* —**isomerism** *n.*

isometric *adj.* having equal dimensions; relating to muscular contraction without movement; (of a three-dimensional drawing) having three equally inclined axes and drawn to scale in every direction. —**isometrics** *pl. n.* system of isometric exercises.

isosceles triangle [ice-soss-ill-eez] *n.* triangle with two sides of equal length.

isotherm [ice-oh-therm] *n.* line on a map connecting points of equal mean temperature.

isotope [ice-oh-tope] *n.* one of two or more atoms with the same number of protons in the nucleus but a different number of neutrons.

issue *n.* topic of interest or discussion; particular edition of a magazine or newspaper; question requiring a decision; outcome or result; *Law* children. —*v.* make (a statement etc.) publicly;

officially supply (with); send out or distribute; publish. —**take issue** disagree.

isthmus [iss-muss] *n., pl.* -**muses.** narrow strip of land connecting two areas of land.

IT information technology.

it *pron.* refers to a nonhuman, animal, plant, or inanimate object; thing mentioned or being discussed; used as the subject of impersonal verbs, e.g. *it is snowing; Informal* crucial or ultimate point. —**its** *adj.* belonging to it. —**it's** it is. —**itself** *pron.* emphatic form of IT.

italic *adj.* (of printing type) sloping to the right. —**italics** *pl. n.* this type, now used for emphasis etc. —**italicize** *v.* put in italics.

itch *n.* skin irritation causing a desire to scratch; restless desire. —*v.* have an itch. —**itchy** *adj.*

item *n.* single thing in a list or collection; piece of information. —**itemize** *v.* put on a list; make a list of.

iterate *v.* repeat. —**iteration** *n.*

itinerant *adj.* travelling from place to place.

itinerary *n., pl.* -**aries.** detailed plan of a journey; route.

ITV Independent Television.

IUD intrauterine device: coil-shaped contraceptive fitted into the womb.

IVF in vitro fertilization.

ivory *n., pl.* -**ries.** hard white bony substance forming the tusks of elephants. —*adj.* yellowish-white. —**ivory tower** remoteness from the realities of everyday life.

ivy *n., pl.* **ivies.** climbing evergreen plant.

THESAURUS

isolate cut off, detach, disconnect, divorce, insulate, quarantine, segregate, separate, sequester, set apart

isolation aloofness, detachment, disconnection, exile, loneliness, quarantine, retirement, seclusion, separation, solitude, withdrawal

issue *n.* 1. affair, argument, concern, matter, point, problem, question, subject, topic 2. copy, edition, instalment, number 3. children, descendants, heirs, offspring, progeny, scions ~*n.* 4. announce, broadcast, circulate, deliver, distribute, emit, give out, promulgate, publish, release

itch *v.* 1. crawl, irritate, prickle, tickle, tingle 2.

ache, burn, crave, hanker, hunger, long, lust, pant, pine, yearn ~*n.* 3. irritation, prickling, tingling 4. craving, desire, hunger, longing, lust, passion, yearning

item 1. article, aspect, component, consideration, detail, entry, matter, particular, point, thing 2. account, article, bulletin, dispatch, feature, note, paragraph, piece, report

itinerant *adj.* ambulatory, migratory, nomadic, peripatetic, roaming, roving, travelling, unsettled, vagabond, vagrant

itinerary circuit, journey, line, programme, route, schedule, tour

J

jab *v.* **jabbing, jabbed.** poke roughly. —*n.* poke; *Informal* injection.

jabber *v.* talk rapidly or incoherently.

jacaranda *n.* tropical tree with sweet-smelling wood.

jacinth *n.* reddish-orange precious stone.

jack *n.* device for raising a motor-car or other heavy object; playing card with a picture of a pageboy; *Bowls* small white ball aimed at by the players; socket in electrical equipment into which a plug fits; flag flown at the bow of a ship, showing nationality. —**jack up** *v.* lift with a jack.

jackal *n.* doglike wild animal of Asia and Africa.

jackass *n.* male of the ass; fool. —**laughing jackass** kookaburra.

jackboot *n.* high military boot.

jackdaw *n.* black-and-grey bird of the crow family.

jacket *n.* short coat; outer paper cover on a hardback book; skin of a baked potato.

jackknife *n.* large clasp knife; dive with a sharp bend at the waist in mid-air. —*v.* (of an articulated lorry) go out of control so that the trailer swings round at a sharp angle to the cab.

jackpot *n.* large prize or accumulated stake that may be won in a game. —**hit the jackpot** be very successful through luck.

Jacobean [jak-a-**bee**-an] *adj.* of the reign of James I of England.

Jacobite *n.* supporter of the exiled Stuarts after the overthrow of James II of England.

Jacquard [**jak**-ard] *n.* fabric in which the design is incorporated into the weave.

Jacuzzi [jak-**oo**-zee] *n.* ® device in a bath that swirls the water.

jade *n.* ornamental semiprecious stone, usu. dark green. —*adj.* bluish-green.

jaded *adj.* tired and unenthusiastic.

jag[1] *n.* sharp or ragged projection; *Informal* injection. —**jagged** [**jag**-gid] *adj.*

jag[2] *n.* spree or drinking bout.

jaguar *n.* large S American spotted cat.

jail *n.* building for confinement of criminals or suspects. —*v.* send to jail. —**jailer** *n.* —**jailbird** *n.* *Informal* hardened criminal.

jalopy [jal-**lop**-ee] *n., pl.* **-lopies.** *Informal* old car.

jam[1] *n.* spread made from fruit boiled with sugar.

jam[2] *v.* **jamming, jammed.** pack tightly into a place; crowd or congest; make or become stuck; *Radio* block (another station) with impulses of equal wavelength. —*n.* hold-up of traffic; *Informal* awkward situation. —**jam on** *v.* apply (brakes) fiercely. —**jam-packed** *adj.* filled to capacity. —**jam session** informal rock or jazz performance.

jamb *n.* side post of a door or window frame.

jamboree *n.* large rally of Scouts; large celebration.

Jan. January.

jangle *v.* (cause to) make a harsh ringing noise; (of nerves) be upset or irritated.

janitor *n.* caretaker of a school or other building.

January *n.* first month of the year.

japan *n.* very hard varnish, usu. black. —*v.* **-panning, -panned.** cover with this varnish.

jape *n.* joke or prank.

japonica *n.* shrub with red flowers.

jar[1] *n.* wide-mouthed container, usu. cylindrical and made of glass.

jar[2] *v.* **jarring, jarred.** have a disturbing or unpleasant effect on; (cause to) vibrate suddenly or violently. —*n.* jolt or shock.

THESAURUS

jab *v./n.* dig, lunge, nudge, poke, prod, punch, stab, tap, thrust

jack up elevate, heave, hoist, lift, lift up, raise, rear

jacket case, casing, coat, covering, envelope, folder, sheath, skin, wrapper

jackpot award, bonanza, kitty, pool, pot, prize, reward, winnings

jaded exhausted, fatigued, spent, tired, weary

jagged barbed, broken, cleft, craggy, notched, pointed, ragged, ridged, rough, serrated, spiked, toothed, uneven

jail 1. *n.* borstal, prison, reformatory 2. *v.* con-

fine, detain, immure, impound, imprison, incarcerate, lock up

jailer captor, guard, keeper, warder

jam *v.* 1. cram, crowd, crush, force, pack, press, squeeze, stuff, throng, wedge 2. block, clog, congest, halt, obstruct, stall, stick ~*n.* 3. bind, dilemma, plight, predicament, quandary, strait, trouble

jangle chime, clank, clash, rattle, vibrate

janitor caretaker, concierge, custodian, doorkeeper, porter

jar[1] *n.* crock, flagon, jug, pitcher, pot, urn,

DICTIONARY

jardinière *n.* ornamental plant pot.

jargon *n.* specialized technical language of a particular subject.

jasmine *n.* shrub with sweet-smelling yellow or white flowers.

jasper *n.* red, yellow, dark green, or brown variety of quartz.

jaundice *n.* disease marked by yellowness of the skin. —**jaundiced** *adj.* (of an attitude or opinion) bitter or cynical; having jaundice.

jaunt *n.* short journey for pleasure. —*v.* make such a journey.

jaunty *adj.* **-tier, -tiest.** sprightly and cheerful; smart. —**jauntily** *adv.*

javelin *n.* light spear thrown in sports competitions.

jaw *n.* one of the bones in which the teeth are set; gripping part of a vice etc. —*pl.* mouth. —*v. Slang* talk lengthily.

jay *n.* bird with a pinkish body and blue-and-black wings.

jaywalking *n.* crossing the road in a careless or dangerous manner. —**jaywalker** *n.*

jazz *n.* rhythmic music of Black American origin. —**jazzy** *adj.* flashy or showy. —**jazz up** *v.* make more lively.

JCB *n.* ® construction machine with a shovel at the front and an excavator at the rear.

jealous *adj.* fearful of losing a partner or possession to a rival; envious; suspiciously watchful. —**jealously** *adv.* —**jealousy** *n.*

jeans *pl. n.* casual denim trousers.

Jeep *n.* ® four-wheel-drive motor vehicle.

jeer *v.* scoff or deride. —*n.* cry of derision.

Jehovah *n.* God.

jejune *adj.* simple or naive; dull or boring.

jell *v.* congeal; *Informal* assume a definite form.

jelly *n., pl.* **-lies.** soft food made of liquid set with gelatine; jam made from fruit juice and sugar.

jellyfish *n.* small jelly-like sea animal.

jemmy *n., pl.* **-mies.** short steel crowbar used by burglars.

jenny *n., pl.* **-nies.** female ass; female wren.

jeopardy *n.* danger. —**jeopardize** *v.* place in danger.

jerboa *n.* small mouselike African rodent with long hind legs.

jeremiad *n.* long lamenting complaint.

jerk *n.* sharp or abruptly stopped movement; sharp pull; *Slang* contemptible person. —*v.* move or throw with a jerk. —**jerky** *adj.* sudden or abrupt. —**jerkily** *adv.* —**jerkiness** *n.*

jerkin *n.* sleeveless jacket.

jerry can *n.* flat-sided can for carrying petrol etc.

jerry-built *adj.* built badly using flimsy materials.

jersey *n.* knitted jumper; machine-knitted fabric; (**J-**) breed of cow.

Jerusalem artichoke *n.* small yellowish-white root vegetable.

jest *n., v.* joke. —**jester** *n.* joker; *Hist.* professional clown at court.

Jesuit [**jezz**-yoo-it] *n.* member of the Society of Jesus, a Roman Catholic order. —**jesuitical** *adj.* crafty through using oversubtle reasoning.

jet¹ *n.* stream of liquid or gas, esp. one forced from a small hole; nozzle from which gas or liquid is forced; burner on a gas fire; aircraft driven by jet propulsion. —*v.* **jetting, jetted.** shoot forth as a jet; fly by jet aircraft. —**jet lag** fatigue caused by crossing time zones in an

---

THESAURUS

vase, vessel

jar² *v.* 1. agitate, disturb, grate, irritate, jolt, offend, rasp, rock, shake, vibrate 2. annoy, clash, grate, grind, irk, irritate, nettle

jargon argot, cant, dialect, idiom, parlance, patois, slang, tongue, usage

jaundiced bigoted, bitter, distorted, envious, hostile, jealous, partial, prejudiced, resentful, spiteful, suspicious

jaunt airing, excursion, expedition, outing, ramble, stroll, tour, trip

jaunty airy, breezy, buoyant, carefree, dapper, gay, high-spirited, lively, perky, showy, smart, sprightly, spruce, trim

jaw *v.* babble, chat, chatter, gossip, lecture, talk

jealous covetous, desirous, envious, green, grudging, intolerant, resentful, rival

jealousy covetousness, distrust, envy, ill-will, mistrust, resentment, spite

jeer *v.* banter, barrack, deride, flout, gibe, heckle, hector, mock, ridicule, scoff, sneer, taunt

jeopardize chance, endanger, gamble, hazard, imperil, risk, stake, venture

jeopardy danger, exposure, hazard, peril, risk, venture

jerk *v./n.* jolt, lurch, pull, throw, thrust, tug, tweak, twitch, wrench, yank

jest 1. *n.* banter, bon mot, fun, hoax, jape, joke, play, prank, quip, sally, sport, witticism 2. *v.* banter, chaff, deride, gibe, jeer, joke, mock, quip, scoff, sneer, tease

jester 1. comedian, comic, humorist, joker, wag, wit 2. buffoon, clown, fool, madcap, mummer, pantaloon

DICTIONARY

aircraft. —**jet propulsion** propulsion by thrust provided by a jet of gas or liquid. —**jet-propelled** *adj.* —**jet set** rich and fashionable people who travel the world for pleasure.

jet² *n.* hard black mineral. —**jet-black** *adj.* glossy black.

jetsam *n.* goods thrown overboard to lighten a ship.

jettison *v.* **-soning, -soned.** abandon; throw overboard.

jetty *n., pl.* **-ties.** small pier.

Jew *n.* person whose religion is Judaism; descendant of the ancient Hebrews. —**Jewish** *adj.* —**Jewry** *n.* Jews collectively. —**jew's-harp** *n.* musical instrument held between the teeth and played by plucking a metal strip.

jewel *n.* precious stone; ornament containing one. —**jeweller** *n.* dealer in jewels. —**jewellery** *n.*

jib¹ *v.* **jibbing, jibbed.** (of a horse, person, etc.) stop and refuse to go on. —**jib at** *v.* object to (a proposal etc.).

jib² *n.* projecting arm of a crane or derrick; triangular sail set in front of a mast.

jibe *v., n.* same as GIBE. —*v.* same as GYBE.

jiffy *n., pl.* **-fies.** *Informal* very short period of time.

jig *n.* type of lively dance; music for it; device that holds a component in place for cutting etc. —*v.* **jigging, jigged.** make jerky up-and-down movements.

jiggery-pokery *n.* *Informal* trickery or mischief.

jiggle *v.* move up and down with short jerky movements.

jigsaw *n.* machine fret saw. —**jigsaw (puzzle)** picture cut into interlocking pieces, which the user tries to fit together again.

jihad *n.* Islamic holy war against unbelievers.

jilt *v.* leave or reject (one's lover).

jingle *n.* gentle ringing noise, as of a shaken chain; catchy rhythmic verse or song, as on a television advert. —*v.* (cause to) make a jingling sound.

jingoism *n.* aggressive nationalism. —**jingoist** *n.* —**jingoistic** *adj.*

jinks *pl. n.* —**high jinks** boisterous merrymaking.

jinni *n., pl.* **jinn.** spirit in Muslim mythology.

jinx *n.* person or thing bringing bad luck.

jitters *pl. n.* worried nervousness. —**jittery** *adj.* nervous.

jiujitsu *n.* same as JUJITSU.

jive *n.* lively dance of the 1940s and 50s. —*v.* dance the jive.

job *n.* task to be done; occupation or paid employment; *Informal* difficult task; *Informal* crime, esp. robbery. —**jobbing** *adj.* doing individual jobs for payment. —**jobless** *adj., pl. n.* unemployed (people). —**job lot** assortment sold together. —**job sharing** splitting of one post between two people working part-time.

jockey *n.* (professional) rider of racehorses. —*v.* —**jockey for position** manoeuvre to obtain an advantage.

jockstrap *n.* belt with a pouch to support the genitals, worn by male athletes.

jocose [joke-**kohss**] *adj.* playful or humorous. —**jocosely** *adv.*

jocular *adj.* joking; fond of joking. —**jocularly** *adv.* —**jocularity** *n.*

jocund [**jok**-kund] *adj. Lit.* merry or cheerful.

jodhpurs *pl. n.* riding breeches, stretchy or loose-fitting above the knee but tight below.

jog *v.* **jogging, jogged.** run at a gentle pace, esp. for exercise; nudge slightly. —*n.* jogging. —**jogger** *n.* —**jogging** *n.*

THESAURUS

jet¹ *n.* 1. flow, fountain, gush, spout, spray, spring, stream 2. nozzle, rose, spout, sprinkler ~*v.* 3. flow, gush, issue, rush, shoot, spout, squirt, stream, surge

jet² black, ebony, inky, raven, sable

jettison abandon, discard, dump, eject, expel, heave, scrap, unload

jetty breakwater, dock, mole, pier, quay, wharf

jewel 1. brilliant, ornament, precious stone, trinket 2. charm, gem, paragon, pearl, prize, rarity, wonder

jib balk, recoil, refuse, retreat, shrink

jig *v.* bounce, caper, prance, shake, skip, twitch, wobble

jingle *v.* 1. chime, clatter, clink, rattle, ring,

tinkle ~*n.* 2. clang, clink, rattle, ringing, tinkle 3. chorus, ditty, doggerel, melody, song, tune

jinx curse, evil eye, plague, voodoo

job 1. affair, charge, chore, concern, duty, errand, function, pursuit, responsibility, role, stint, task, undertaking, venture, work 2. business, calling, capacity, career, craft, employment, function, livelihood, métier, occupation, office, position, post, profession, situation, trade, vocation

jobless idle, inactive, out of work, unemployed, unoccupied

jocular amusing, comical, droll, facetious, fun-

DICTIONARY

joggle v. move to and fro in jerks; shake.

joie de vivre [jwah de **veev**-ra] n. French enjoyment of life.

join v. come or bring together; become a member (of); come into someone's company; take part (in). —n. place of joining. —**join up** v. enlist in the armed services.

joiner n. maker of finished woodwork. —**joinery** n. joiner's work.

joint n. junction of two or more parts or objects; place where bones meet but can move; piece of meat for roasting; Slang house or place, esp. a disreputable bar or nightclub; Slang marijuana cigarette. —adj. shared by two or more. —v. divide meat into joints. —**out of joint** dislocated; disorganized. —**jointed** adj. —**jointly** adv. —**joint-stock company** firm whose capital is jointly owned by shareholders.

jointure n. property settled on a wife for her use after her husband's death.

joist n. horizontal beam that helps support a floor or ceiling.

jojoba [hoe-**hoe**-ba] n. shrub whose seeds yield oil used in cosmetics.

joke n. thing said or done to cause laughter; amusing or ridiculous person or thing. —v. make jokes. —**jokey** adj. —**jokingly** adv. —**joker** n. person who jokes; Slang fellow; extra card in a pack, of variable value.

jolly adj. -**lier,** -**liest.** happy and cheerful; merry and festive. —v. -**lying,** -**lied.** —**jolly along** try to keep (someone) cheerful by flattery or coaxing. —**jolliness** n. —**jollity** n. —**jollification** n. merrymaking.

jolt n. sudden jerk or bump; unpleasant surprise or shock. —v. move or shake with jolts; surprise or shock.

jonquil n. fragrant narcissus.

joss stick n. stick of incense giving off a sweet smell when burnt.

jostle v. knock or push against.

jot n. very small amount. —v. **jotting, jotted.** write briefly; make a note of. —**jotter** n. notebook.

joule [jool] n. Physics unit of work or energy.

journal n. daily newspaper or other periodical; daily record of events. —**journalese** n. superficial and clichéd writing. —**journalism** n. writing in or editing of periodicals. —**journalist** n. —**journalistic** adj.

journey n. act or process of travelling from one place to another. —v. travel.

journeyman n. qualified craftsman employed by another.

joust Hist. —n. combat with lances between two mounted knights. —v. fight on horseback using lances.

jovial adj. happy and cheerful. —**jovially** adv. —**joviality** n.

jowl n. lower jaw; fatty flesh hanging from the lower jaw. —pl. cheeks.

joy n. feeling of great delight or pleasure; cause of this feeling. —**joyful** adj. —**joyless** adj. —**joyous** adj. extremely happy and enthusiastic. —**joy ride** pleasure trip, esp. in a stolen car. —**joystick** n. Informal control device for an aircraft or computer.

THESAURUS

ny, humorous, jolly, jovial, playful, roguish, sportive, teasing, waggish, witty

jog 1. arouse, nudge, prod, prompt, push, remind, shake, stimulate, stir, suggest 2. canter, lope, run, trot

join 1. accompany, add, adhere, annex, append, attach, cement, combine, connect, couple, fasten, knit, link, marry, splice, tie, unite, yoke 2. enlist, enrol, enter, sign up

joint 1. n. connection, hinge, junction, knot, nexus, node, seam, union 2. adj. collective, combined, communal, concerted, cooperative, joined, mutual, shared, united

jointly as one, collectively, mutually, together, unitedly

joke 1. n. frolic, fun, jape, jest, lark, play, pun, quip, quirk, sally, sport, witticism, yarn 2. v. banter, chaff, deride, frolic, gambol, jest, mock, quip, ridicule, taunt, tease

jolly carefree, cheerful, convivial, festive, funny,

gay, gladsome, hilarious, jocund, jovial, joyful, joyous, jubilant, merry, mirthful, playful

jolt v. 1. jar, jerk, knock, push, shake, shove 2. astonish, disturb, perturb, stagger, startle, stun, surprise, upset ~n. 3. bump, jar, jerk, jump, quiver, shake, start 4. blow, bombshell, reversal, setback, shock, surprise

jostle bump, butt, crowd, elbow, jog, jolt, press, push, shove, squeeze, throng, thrust

journal 1. daily, gazette, magazine, monthly, newspaper, paper, periodical, record, register, review, tabloid, weekly 2. diary, log, record

journalist broadcaster, columnist, commentator, contributor, correspondent, hack, newspaperman, pressman, reporter, stringer

journey excursion, expedition, jaunt, odyssey, outing, passage, pilgrimage, progress, ramble, tour, travel, trek, trip, voyage

jovial airy, blithe, buoyant, cheery, convivial, cordial, gay, glad, happy, jolly, jubilant, merry, mirthful

DICTIONARY

JP Justice of the Peace.

Jr Junior.

jubilant *adj.* feeling or expressing great joy. —**jubilantly** *adv.* —**jubilation** *n.*

jubilee *n.* special anniversary, esp. 25th (**silver jubilee**) or 50th (**golden jubilee**).

Judaism *n.* religion of the Jews, having only one God and based on the teachings of the Old Testament and the Talmud. —**Judaic** *adj.*

judder *v.* vibrate violently. —*n.* violent vibration.

judge *n.* public official who tries cases and passes sentence in a court of law; person who decides the outcome of a contest. —*v.* act as a judge; appraise critically; consider something to be the case. —**judg(e)ment** *n.* faculty of judging; sentence of a court; opinion reached after careful thought. —**judg(e)mental** *adj.*

judicature *n.* administration of justice; body of judges.

judicial *adj.* of or by a court or judge; showing or using judgment. —**judicially** *adv.*

judiciary *n.* system of courts and judges.

judicious *adj.* well-judged, sensible. —**judiciously** *adv.*

judo *n.* modern sport derived from jujitsu, where the opponent must be defeated using the minimum physical effort.

jug *n.* container for liquids, with a handle and small spout; its contents; *Slang* prison. —**jugged hare** hare stewed in an earthenware pot.

juggernaut *n.* large heavy lorry; any irresistible destructive force.

juggle *v.* throw and catch (several objects) so that most are in the air at the same time; manipulate (figures, situations, etc.) to suit one's purposes. —**juggler** *n.*

jugular vein *n.* one of three large veins of the neck returning blood from the head.

juice *n.* liquid part of vegetables, fruit, or meat; fluid secreted by an organ of the body; *Informal* petrol. —**juicy** *adj.* succulent; interesting.

jujitsu *n.* Japanese art of wrestling and self-defence.

juju *n.* W African magic charm or fetish.

jujube *n.* chewy sweet of flavoured gelatine.

jukebox *n.* automatic coin-operated record player.

julep *n.* sweet alcoholic drink.

julienne *n.* clear soup containing thinly shredded vegetables.

July *n.* seventh month of the year.

jumble *v.* mix in a disordered way. —*n.* confused heap or state; articles for a jumble sale. —**jumble sale** sale of miscellaneous second-hand items.

jumbo *adj. Informal* very large. —**jumbo jet** large jet airliner.

THESAURUS

joy bliss, delight, ecstasy, elation, exultation, felicity, festivity, gaiety, gladness, glee, pleasure, rapture, ravishment, satisfaction, transport

joyful blithesome, delighted, glad, gratified, happy, jubilant, light-hearted, merry, pleased, satisfied

joyless cheerless, dejected, depressed, dismal, dispirited, downcast, dreary, gloomy, miserable, sad, unhappy

jubilant elated, enraptured, excited, exuberant, exultant, glad, joyous, overjoyed, rejoicing, thrilled, triumphant

judge *n.* 1. adjudicator, arbiter, moderator, referee, umpire 2. arbiter, assessor, authority, connoisseur, critic, evaluator, expert 3. justice, magistrate ~*v.* 4. adjudge, adjudicate, arbitrate, ascertain, conclude, decide, determine, discern, mediate, referee, umpire 5. appreciate, assess, consider, criticize, esteem, estimate, evaluate, examine, review, value

judgment 1. acumen, common sense, discernment, discrimination, intelligence, perspicacity, prudence, sagacity, sense, shrewdness, taste, understanding, wisdom 2. arbitration, award, conclusion, decision, decree, finding, order, result, ruling, sentence, verdict 3. appraisal, assessment, conviction, deduction, diagnosis, estimate, finding, opinion, valuation, view

judicial judiciary, legal, official

judicious acute, astute, careful, cautious, circumspect, considered, diplomatic, discerning, discreet, expedient, informed, politic, prudent, rational, sage, sane, sensible, shrewd, skilful, sober, sound, thoughtful, well-judged, wise

jug carafe, crock, ewer, jar, pitcher, urn, vessel

juggle alter, change, disguise, falsify, manipulate, manoeuvre, misrepresent, modify

juice fluid, liquid, liquor, nectar, sap

juicy 1. lush, moist, succulent, watery 2. colourful, interesting, racy, risqué, sensational, spicy, suggestive

jumble 1. *v.* confound, confuse, disarrange, dishevel, disorder, disorganize, entangle, mix, muddle, shuffle, tangle 2. *n.* chaos, clutter, confusion, disarray, disorder, litter, medley, mélange, mess, miscellany, mixture, muddle

jumbo giant, huge, immense, large

DICTIONARY

jump *v.* leap or spring into the air using the leg muscles; leap over (an obstacle); move quickly and suddenly; jerk with surprise; increase suddenly; pass over or miss out (intervening material); change the subject abruptly; come off (tracks, rails, etc.); *Informal* attack without warning; *Informal* pass through (a red traffic light). —*n.* jumping; obstacle to be jumped; sudden nervous jerk; sudden rise in prices; break in continuity. —**jump the gun** act prematurely. —**jump the queue** not wait one's turn. —**jumpy** *adj.* nervous. —**jump at** *v.* accept (a chance etc.) gladly. —**jumped-up** *adj.* arrogant because of recent promotion. —**jump jet** fixed-wing jet that can take off and land vertically. —**jump leads** electric cables to connect a discharged car battery to an external battery to aid starting an engine. —**jump on** *v.* criticize suddenly and forcefully. —**jump suit** one-piece garment of trousers and top.

jumper *n.* sweater or pullover.

junction *n.* place where routes, railway lines, or roads meet; point where traffic can leave or enter a motorway; join.

juncture *n.* point in time, esp. a critical one.

June *n.* sixth month of the year.

jungle *n.* tropical forest of dense tangled vegetation; tangled mass; place of intense struggle for survival.

junior *adj.* younger; of lower standing. —*n.* junior person.

juniper *n.* evergreen shrub with berries yielding oil.

junk[1] *n.* discarded or useless objects; *Informal* rubbish; *Slang* narcotic drug, esp. heroin.

—**junkie, junky** *n. Slang* drug addict. —**junk food** snack food of low nutritional value.

junk[2] *n.* flat-bottomed Chinese sailing vessel.

junket *n.* sweetened milk set with rennet; excursion by public officials paid for from public funds. —**junketing** *n.*

junta *n.* group of military officers holding power in a country, esp. after a coup.

Jupiter *n.* Roman chief of the gods; largest of the planets.

juridical *adj.* of law or the administration of justice.

jurisdiction *n.* right or power to administer justice and apply laws; extent of this right or power.

jurisprudence *n.* science or philosophy of law.

jurist *n.* expert in law.

jury *n., pl.* **-ries.** group of people sworn to deliver a verdict in a court of law. —**juror, juryman, jurywoman** *n.*

just *adv.* very recently; exactly; barely; at this instant; merely, only; really. —*adj.* fair or impartial in action or judgment; proper or right; well-founded. —**justly** *adv.* —**justness** *n.*

justice *n.* quality of being just; fairness; judicial proceedings; judge or magistrate. —**justice of the peace** person who is authorized to act as a judge in a local court of law.

justify *v.* **-fying, -fied.** prove right or reasonable; show to be free from blame or guilt; align (text) so the margins are straight. —**justifiable** *adj.* —**justifiably** *adv.* —**justification** *n.*

jut *v.* **jutting, jutted.** project or stick out.

jute *n.* fibre of certain plants, used for rope, canvas, etc.

THESAURUS

jump *v.* 1. bounce, bound, caper, clear, gambol, hop, hurdle, leap, skip, spring, vault 2. avoid, digress, evade, miss, omit, overshoot, skip, switch ~*n.* 3. bound, caper, hop, leap, skip, spring, vault

jumper pullover, sweater, woolly

jumpy agitated, anxious, fidgety, jittery, nervous, restless, tense

junction alliance, combination, connection, coupling, joint, juncture, linking, seam, union

junior inferior, lesser, lower, minor, secondary, subordinate, younger

junk clutter, debris, leavings, litter, oddments, refuse, rubbish, rummage, scrap, trash, waste

jurisdiction authority, command, control, dominion, influence, power, prerogative, rule, say, sway

just *adj.* 1. blameless, decent, equitable, fair,

good, honest, honourable, impartial, lawful, pure, right, righteous, unbiased, upright, virtuous 2. appropriate, apt, deserved, due, fitting, justified, merited, proper, reasonable, suitable ~*adv.* 3. absolutely, completely, entirely, exactly, perfectly, precisely 4. hardly, lately, only now, recently, scarcely

justice equity, fairness, honesty, impartiality, integrity, justness, law, legality, legitimacy, rectitude, right

justifiable acceptable, defensible, excusable, fit, lawful, legitimate, proper, right, sound, tenable, valid, warrantable, well-founded

justification apology, approval, defence, excuse, explanation, extenuation, plea, vindication

justify absolve, acquit, approve, confirm, defend, establish, excuse, exonerate, explain, legalize, maintain, substantiate, support, sustain, uphold, validate, vindicate, warrant

DICTIONARY

juvenile *adj.* young; suitable for young people; immature and rather silly. —*n.* young person or child. —**juvenilia** *pl. n.* works produced in an author's youth. —**juvenile delinquent** young person guilty of a crime.

juxtapose *v.* put side by side. —**juxtaposition** *n.*

THESAURUS

juvenile adolescent, boy, child, girl, infant, minor, youth

juxtaposition adjacency, closeness, contact, nearness, vicinity

K

K Kelvin; *Chem.* potassium; *Informal* thousand(s).

Kaffir [kaf-fer] *n. S Afr. offens. & obs.* a Black African.

kaftan *n.* long loose Eastern garment; woman's dress resembling this.

kai *n. NZ* food.

kail *n.* same as KALE.

kaiser [kize-er] *n. Hist.* German or Austro-Hungarian emperor.

Kalashnikov *n.* Russian-made automatic rifle.

kale *n.* cabbage with crinkled leaves.

kaleidoscope *n.* tube-shaped toy containing loose pieces of coloured glass reflected by mirrors so that various symmetrical patterns form when the tube is twisted. —**kaleidoscopic** *adj.*

kamikaze [kam-mee-kah-zee] *n.* (in World War II) Japanese pilot who performed a suicide mission. —*adj.* (of an action) undertaken in the knowledge that it will kill or injure the person performing it.

kangaroo *n., pl.* **-roos.** *Aust.* marsupial which moves by jumping with its powerful hind legs. —**kangaroo court** unofficial court set up by a group to discipline its members.

kaolin *n.* fine white clay used to make porcelain and in some medicines.

kapok *n.* fluffy fibre from a tropical tree, used to stuff cushions etc.

kaput [kap-poot] *adj. Informal* ruined or broken.

karate *n.* Japanese system of unarmed combat using blows with feet, hands, elbows, and legs.

karma *n. Buddhism & Hinduism* person's actions affecting his or her fate for his or her next reincarnation.

karoo *n. S Afr.* high arid plateau.

kasbah *n.* citadel of N African town.

kauri *n., pl.* **kauris.** large NZ conifer grown for its valuable timber and resin.

kayak *n.* Inuit canoe made of sealskins stretched over a frame; fibreglass or canvas-covered canoe of this design.

kbyte *Computers* kilobyte.

kebab *n.* dish of small pieces of meat grilled on skewers.

kedge *n.* small anchor. —*v.* move (a ship) by hauling on a cable attached to a kedge.

kedgeree *n.* dish of fish with rice and eggs.

keel *n.* main lengthways timber or steel support along the base of a ship. —**keel over** *v.* turn upside down; *Informal* collapse suddenly.

keen[1] *adj.* eager or enthusiastic; intense or strong; (of the senses) capable of recognizing small distinctions; intellectually acute; competitive; cold and penetrating; sharp. —**keenly** *adv.* —**keenness** *n.*

keen[2] *v.* wail over the dead. —*n.* funeral lament.

keep *v.* **keeping, kept.** stay (in, on, or at a place or position); have or retain possession of; take temporary charge of; look after or maintain; detain (someone); store; continue or persist; support financially; remain good. —*n.* cost of food and everyday expenses; central tower of a castle. —**keeper** *n.* person who looks after animals in a zoo; person in charge of a museum or collection; short for GOALKEEPER. —**keeping** *n.* care or charge. —**in** *or* **out of keeping** appropriate or inappropriate. —**keep fit** exercises designed to promote physical fitness. —**keepsake** *n.* gift treasured for the sake of the giver. —**keep up** *v.* maintain at the current level. —**keep up with** maintain a pace set by (someone).

THESAURUS

keen 1. ardent, avid, eager, earnest, enthusiastic, fervid, fierce, intense, zealous 2. acid, acute, biting, caustic, cutting, edged, incisive, piercing, pointed, sardonic, satirical, sharp, tart, trenchant

keenness ardour, avidity, diligence, eagerness, enthusiasm, fervour, impatience, intensity, passion, zeal, zest

keep *v.* 1. conserve, control, hold, maintain, possess, preserve, retain 2. amass, carry, deal in, deposit, furnish, garner, heap, hold, pile, place, stack, stock, store, trade in 3. care for, defend, guard, look after, maintain, manage, mind, operate, protect, safeguard, shelter, shield, tend, watch over 4. board, feed, main-

tain, nourish, subsidize, support, sustain, victual ~*n.* 5. board, food, livelihood, living, maintenance, means, nourishment, subsistence, support 6. castle, citadel, dungeon, fastness, stronghold, tower

keeper attendant, caretaker, curator, custodian, defender, gaoler, governor, guard, jailer, overseer, preserver, steward, warden, warder

keeping care, charge, custody, patronage, possession, protection, safekeeping, trust

keepsake emblem, favour, memento, relic, remembrance, reminder, souvenir, symbol, token

keep up balance, compete, contend, continue, maintain, match, persevere, preserve, rival,

DICTIONARY

keg *n.* small metal beer barrel.

kelp *n.* large brown seaweed.

Kelvin *n.* SI unit of temperature. —**Kelvin scale** temperature scale starting at absolute zero (-273.15° Celsius).

ken *n.* range of knowledge. —*v.* **kenning, kenned** or **kent**. *Scot.* know.

kendo *n.* Japanese sport of fencing using wooden staves.

kennel *n.* hutlike shelter for a dog. —*pl.* place for breeding, boarding, or training dogs.

kepi *n.* French military cap with a flat top and horizontal peak.

kept *v.* past of KEEP.

keratin *n.* fibrous protein found in the hair and nails.

kerb *n.* stone edging to a footpath. —**kerb crawling** act of driving slowly beside a pavement to pick up a prostitute.

kerchief *n.* piece of cloth worn over the head or round the neck.

kerfuffle *n. Informal* commotion or disorder.

kermes [**kur**-meez] *n.* red dyestuff obtained from dried insects.

kernel *n.* inner seed of a nut or fruit stone; central and essential part of something.

kerosene *n. US* paraffin.

kestrel *n.* small falcon.

ketch *n.* two-masted sailing ship.

ketchup *n.* thick cold sauce, usu. of tomatoes.

kettle *n.* container with a spout and handle used for boiling water. —**a fine kettle of fish** an awkward situation.

kettledrum *n.* large metal drum with a brass bottom.

key *n.* device for operating a lock by moving a bolt; device turned to wind a clock, operate a machine, etc.; any of a set of levers or buttons pressed to operate a piano, typewriter, etc.; *Music* set of related notes; list of explanations of codes, symbols, etc.; something crucial in providing an explanation or interpretation; means of achieving a desired end. —*v.* (foll. by *to*) adjust to. —*adj.* of great importance. —**keyed up** very excited or nervous. —**key in** *v.* keyboard.

keyboard *n.* set of keys on a piano, typewriter, etc.; musical instrument played using a keyboard. —*v.* enter (text) using a keyboard.

keyhole *n.* opening for inserting a key into a lock.

keynote *n.* dominant idea of a speech etc.; basic note of a musical key.

keystone *n.* central stone of an arch which locks others in position.

kg kilogram(s).

KGB *n.* Soviet secret police.

khaki *adj.* dull yellowish-brown. —*n.* hard-wearing fabric of this colour used for military uniforms.

kHz kilohertz.

kibbutz *n., pl.* **kibbutzim.** communal farm or factory in Israel.

kibosh *n.* —**put the kibosh on** *Slang* put a stop to.

kick *v.* drive, push, or strike with the foot; score with a kick; (of a gun) recoil when fired; *Informal* object or resist; *Informal* free oneself of (an addiction). —*n.* thrust or blow with the foot; recoil; *Informal* excitement or thrill. —**kickback** *n.* money paid illegally for favours done. —**kick off** *v.* start a game of football; *Informal* begin. —**kick out** *v.* dismiss or expel forcibly. —**kick-start** *v.* start a motorcycle engine by kicking a pedal. —**kick up** *v. Informal* create (a fuss).

kid[1] *n.* young goat; leather made from the skin of a kid; *Informal* child.

kid[2] *v.* **kidding, kidded.** *Informal* tease or deceive (someone).

kidnap *v.* **-napping, -napped.** seize and hold (a person) to ransom. —**kidnapper** *n.*

kidney *n.* either of the pair of organs which filter waste products from the blood to produce urine; animal kidney used as food. —**kidney bean** usu. reddish-brown kidney-shaped bean, edible when cooked.

THESAURUS

sustain, vie

key *n.* 1. latchkey, opener 2. *Fig.* answer, clue, cue, explanation, guide, interpretation, lead, means, pointer, sign, solution, translation ~*adj.* 3. basic, chief, crucial, decisive, essential, fundamental, important, leading, main, major, pivotal, principal

keynote centre, core, essence, gist, kernel, marrow, pith, substance

kick boot, punt

kick off begin, commence, initiate, open, start

kick out discharge, dismiss, eject, evict, expel, oust, reject, remove, sack, toss out

kid 1. *n.* baby, bairn, boy, child, girl, infant, lad, little one, stripling, teenager, tot, youngster, youth 2. *v.* bamboozle, beguile, cozen, delude, fool, hoax, hoodwink, jest, joke, mock, plague, pretend, ridicule, tease, trick

kidnap abduct, capture, hijack, remove, seize, skyjack, steal

DICTIONARY

kill v. cause the death of; put an end to; pass (time); *Informal* cause (someone) pain or discomfort. —n. act of killing; animals or birds killed in a hunt. —**killer** n. —**killing** *Informal* —adj. very tiring; very funny. —n. sudden financial success. —**killjoy** n. person who spoils others' pleasure.

kiln n. oven for baking, drying, or processing pottery, bricks, etc.

kilo n. short for KILOGRAM.

kilo- *combining form* one thousand, e.g. *kilolitre.*

kilobyte n. *Computers* 1000 or 1024 units of information.

kilogram(me) n. unit of mass, equal to 1000 grams.

kilohertz n. one thousand hertz.

kilometre n. one thousand metres.

kilowatt n. *Electricity* one thousand watts.

kilt n. knee-length pleated tartan skirt worn orig. by Scottish Highlanders. —**kilted** adj.

kimono [kim-**moan**-no] n., pl. **-nos.** loose wide-sleeved Japanese robe, fastened with a sash; European dressing gown like this.

kin n. (also **kinsfolk**) person's relatives collectively. —**kinship** n.

kind[1] adj. considerate, friendly, and helpful. —**kindly** adj. **-lier, -liest.** having a warm-hearted nature; pleasant or agreeable. —adv. in a considerate way; please, e.g. *will you kindly be quiet!* —**kindliness** n. —**kindness** n. —**kind-hearted** adj.

kind[2] n. class or group having common characteristics; essential nature or character. —**in kind** (of payment) in goods rather than money; with something similar. —**kind of** to a certain extent.

kindergarten n. class or school for children of about four to six years old.

kindle v. set (a fire) alight; (of a fire) start to burn; arouse or be aroused. —**kindling** n. dry wood or straw for starting fires.

kindred adj. having similar qualities; related. —n. person's relatives collectively.

kine pl. n. *Obs.* cows or cattle.

kinetic [kin-**net**-ik] adj. relating to or caused by motion.

king n. male ruler of a monarchy; ruler or chief; best or most important of its kind; most important piece in chess; playing card with a picture of a king on it. —**kingly** adj. —**kingship** n. —**kingdom** n. state ruled by a king or queen; division of the natural world. —**king-size(d)** adj. *Informal* larger than standard size.

kingfisher n. small bird with a bright plumage that dives for fish.

kingpin n. most important person in an organization.

kink n. twist or bend in rope, wire, hair, etc.; *Informal* quirk in personality. —**kinky** adj. full of kinks; *Slang* given to deviant or unusual sexual practices.

kiosk n. small booth selling drinks, cigarettes, newspapers, etc.; public telephone box.

THESAURUS

kill 1. annihilate, assassinate, butcher, destroy, dispatch, execute, exterminate, extirpate, massacre, murder, neutralize, obliterate, slaughter, slay 2. *Fig.* cancel, cease, deaden, defeat, halt, quash, quell, ruin, scotch, smother, stifle, stop, suppress, veto

killer assassin, butcher, executioner, exterminator, gunman, murderer, slaughterer, slayer

killing bloodshed, carnage, extermination, fatality, homicide, manslaughter, massacre, murder, slaughter, slaying

kind[1] adj. affectionate, amiable, beneficent, benevolent, benign, bounteous, charitable, compassionate, congenial, considerate, cordial, courteous, friendly, generous, gentle, good, gracious, humane, indulgent, lenient, loving, mild, neighbourly, obliging, propitious, tender-hearted, thoughtful

kind[2] n. brand, breed, class, family, genus, race, set, sort, species, variety

kindle fire, ignite, inflame, light, set fire to

kindliness amiability, benevolence, charity, compassion, friendliness, gentleness, humanity, sympathy

kindly 1. adj. benevolent, compassionate, cordial, favourable, genial, gentle, good-natured, hearty, helpful, kind, mild, pleasant, polite, sympathetic, warm 2. adv. agreeably, graciously, politely, tenderly, thoughtfully

kindness 1. affection, benevolence, charity, compassion, fellow-feeling, generosity, goodness, grace, humanity, indulgence, tenderness, tolerance, understanding 2. aid, assistance, benefaction, bounty, favour, generosity, good deed, help, service

king emperor, majesty, monarch, overlord, prince, ruler, sovereign

kingdom 1. dominion, dynasty, empire, monarchy, realm, reign, sovereignty 2. county, division, nation, province, state, territory, tract

kink 1. bend, coil, entanglement, knot, tangle, twist, wrinkle 2. crotchet, eccentricity, fetish, foible, quirk, singularity, vagary, whim

kiosk bookstall, booth, counter, newsstand, stall, stand

DICTIONARY

kip *n., v.* **kipping, kipped.** *Informal* sleep.

kipper *n.* cleaned, salted, and smoked herring.

kirk *n. Scot.* church.

Kirsch *n.* brandy made from cherries.

kismet *n.* fate or destiny.

kiss *v.* touch with the lips in affection or greeting; join lips with a person in love or desire. —*n.* touch with the lips. —**kisser** *n. Slang* mouth or face. —**kissagram** *n.* greetings service in which a messenger kisses the person celebrating. —**kiss of life** mouth-to-mouth resuscitation.

kit *n.* outfit or equipment for a specific purpose; set of pieces of equipment sold ready to be assembled. —**kitbag** *n.* bag for a soldier's or traveller's belongings. —**kit out** *v.* **kitting, kitted.** provide with clothes or equipment needed for a particular activity.

kitchen *n.* room used for cooking. —**kitchenette** *n.* small kitchen. —**kitchen garden** garden for growing vegetables, herbs, etc.

kite *n.* light frame covered with a thin material flown on a string in the wind; large hawk with a forked tail. —**Kite mark** official mark on articles approved by the British Standards Institution.

kith *n.* —**kith and kin** friends and relatives.

kitsch *n.* vulgarized or pretentious art or literature with popular sentimental appeal.

kitten *n.* young cat. —**kittenish** *adj.* lively and flirtatious.

kittiwake *n.* type of seagull.

kitty *n., pl.* **-ties.** pool in certain gambling games; communal fund for buying drinks etc.

kiwi *n.* NZ flightless bird with a stout beak and no tail; *Informal* a New Zealander. —**kiwi fruit** edible fruit with a fuzzy brown skin and green flesh.

klaxon *n.* loud horn used on emergency vehicles as a warning signal.

kleptomania *n.* compulsive tendency to steal. —**kleptomaniac** *n.*

km kilometre(s).

knack *n.* skilful way of doing something; innate ability.

knacker *n.* buyer of old horses for killing. —*v. Slang* exhaust. —**knackered** *adj.*

knapsack *n.* soldier's or traveller's bag worn strapped on the back.

knave *n.* jack at cards; *Obs.* rogue. —**knavish** *adj.* —**knavery** *n.* dishonest behaviour.

knead *v.* work (flour) into dough using the hands; squeeze or press with the hands.

knee *n.* joint between thigh and lower leg; part of a garment covering the knee; lap. —*v.* **kneeing, kneed.** strike or push with the knee. —**kneecap** *n.* bone in front of the knee. —*v.* shoot in the kneecap. —**kneejerk** *adj.* (esp. of a reply or reaction) automatic and predictable. —**knees-up** *n. Informal* party.

kneel *v.* **kneeling, kneeled** or **knelt.** fall or rest on one's knees.

knell *n.* sound of a bell, esp. at a funeral or death; portent of doom.

knew *v.* past tense of KNOW.

knickerbockers *pl. n.* loose-fitting short trousers gathered in at the knee.

knickers *pl. n.* woman's or girl's undergarment covering the lower trunk and having legs or legholes.

knick-knack *n.* trifle or trinket.

knife *n., pl.* **knives.** cutting tool or weapon consisting of a sharp-edged blade with a handle. —*v.* cut or stab with a knife.

knight *n.* honorary title given to a man by the British sovereign; *Hist.* man who served his lord as a mounted armoured soldier; chess piece shaped like a horse's head. —*v.* award a knighthood to. —**knighthood** *n.* —**knightly** *adj.*

knit *v.* **knitting, knitted** or **knit.** make (a garment) by interlocking a series of loops in wool or other yarn; draw (one's eyebrows) together; join closely together. —**knitter** *n.* —**knitting** *n.* —**knitwear** *n.* knitted clothes, such as sweaters.

knob *n.* rounded projection, such as a switch on a radio; rounded handle on a door or drawer; small amount of butter. —**knobbly** *adj.* covered with small bumps.

THESAURUS

kiss *v.* greet, osculate, salute

kit apparatus, effects, equipment, gear, outfit, rig, supplies, tackle, tools

knack ability, aptitude, bent, capacity, dexterity, expertise, flair, forte, genius, gift, handiness, ingenuity, skill, talent, trick

knave blackguard, cheat, rascal, reprobate, rogue, scamp, scoundrel, swindler, villain

knavery chicanery, corruption, deceit, dishonesty, fraud, roguery, trickery, villainy

kneel bow, curtsey, genuflect, kowtow, stoop

knell chime, peal, toll

knickers bloomers, briefs, drawers, panties, smalls, underwear

knick-knack bauble, bric-a-brac, plaything, trifle, trinket

knife blade, cutter, cutting tool

knit affix, ally, bind, connect, contract, fasten, heal, intertwine, join, link, loop, mend, secure, tie, unite, weave

DICTIONARY

knock v. give a blow or push to; rap audibly with the knuckles; make or drive by striking; *Informal* criticize adversely; (of an engine) make a regular banging noise as a result of a fault. —n. blow or rap; knocking sound. —**knocker** n. metal fitting for knocking on a door. —**knock about, around** v. travel or wander; hit or kick brutally. —**knockabout** adj. (of comedy) boisterous. —**knock back** v. *Informal* drink quickly; cost; reject or refuse. —**knock down** v. reduce the price of. —**knockdown** adj. (of a price) very low. —**knock-kneed** adj. having legs which curve in at the knees. —**knock off** v. take (a specified amount) off a price; *Informal* make or do (something) hurriedly or easily; *Informal* cease work; *Informal* steal. —**knock out** v. render (someone) unconscious; *Informal* overwhelm or amaze; defeat in a knockout competition. —**knockout** n. blow that renders an opponent unconscious; competition from which competitors are progressively eliminated; *Informal* overwhelmingly attractive person or thing. —**knock up** v. assemble (something) quickly; *Informal* waken. —**knock-up** n. practice session at tennis, squash, or badminton.

knoll n. small rounded hill.

knot n. fastening made by looping and pulling tight strands of string, cord, or rope; tangle, as of hair; small cluster or huddled group; round lump or spot in timber; unit of speed used by ships, equal to one nautical mile per hour. —v. **knotting, knotted.** tie with or into a knot. —**knotty** adj. full of knots; puzzling or difficult.

know v. **knowing, knew, known.** be aware of; be or feel certain of the truth of (information etc.); be acquainted with; have a grasp of or understand (a skill or language). —**in the know** *Informal* informed or aware. —**knowable** adj. —**knowing** adj. cunning or shrewd. —**knowingly**

adv. shrewdly; deliberately. —**know-all** n. *Offens.* person who acts as if knowing more than other people. —**know-how** n. *Informal* ingenuity, aptitude, or skill.

knowledge n. facts or experiences known by a person; state of knowing; specific information on a subject. —**knowledg(e)able** adj. intelligent or well-informed.

knuckle n. bone at the finger joint; knee joint of a calf or pig. —**near the knuckle** *Informal* approaching indecency. —**knuckle-duster** n. metal appliance worn on the knuckles to add force to a blow. —**knuckle under** v. yield or submit.

KO knockout.

koala n. tree-dwelling Aust. marsupial with dense grey fur.

kohl n. cosmetic powder used to darken the edges of the eyelids.

kohlrabi [kole-**rah**-bee] n., pl. **-bies.** type of cabbage with an edible stem.

kookaburra n. large Aust. kingfisher with a cackling cry.

kopeck n. Soviet monetary unit, one hundredth of a rouble.

kopje, koppie n. *S Afr.* small hill.

Koran n. sacred book of Islam.

kosher [**koh**-sher] adj. conforming to Jewish religious law, esp. (of food) to Jewish dietary law; *Informal* legitimate or authentic. —n. kosher food.

kowtow v. touch one's forehead to the ground in deference; be servile (towards).

kph kilometres per hour.

kraal n. S African village surrounded by a strong fence.

kraken n. mythical Norwegian sea monster.

THESAURUS

knob boss, bulk, bump, bunch, knot, lump, nub, projection, protrusion, snag, stud, swelling, tumour

knock 1. v. buffet, clap, cuff, hit, punch, rap, slap, smack, strike, thump, thwack 2. n. blow, box, clip, clout, cuff, hammering, rap, slap, smack, thump

knockout hit, sensation, smash, success, triumph, winner

knot 1. v. bind, entangle, knit, loop, secure, tether, tie, weave 2. n. bond, bow, braid, connection, joint, ligature, loop, rosette, tie

know 1. apprehend, experience, fathom, feel certain, learn, notice, perceive, realize, recognize, see, undergo, understand 2. be acquainted with, be familiar with, fraternize with, have dealings with, have knowledge of, recognize 3.

discern, distinguish, identify, make out, perceive, recognize, see, tell

knowing astute, clever, competent, discerning, experienced, expert, intelligent, qualified, skilful, well-informed

knowledge 1. enlightenment, erudition, instruction, intelligence, learning, scholarship, science, tuition, wisdom 2. ability, cognition, consciousness, discernment, grasp, judgment, recognition, understanding

knowledgeable acquainted, au fait, aware, cognizant, conscious, experienced, familiar, understanding, well-informed

known admitted, avowed, celebrated, common, confessed, familiar, famous, manifest, noted, obvious, patent, plain, popular, published, recognized, well-known

DICTIONARY

Kremlin *n.* central government of the Soviet Union.

krill *n., pl.* **krill.** small shrimplike sea creature.

krypton *n.* colourless gas present in the atmosphere and used in fluorescent lights.

kudos [kyoo-doss] *n.* fame or credit.

kulak *n. Hist.* independent well-to-do Russian peasant.

kümmel *n.* German liqueur flavoured with caraway seeds.

kumquat *n.* citrus fruit resembling a tiny orange.

kung fu *n.* Chinese martial art combining techniques of judo and karate.

kW kilowatt.

kWh kilowatt-hour.

L

L large; Latin; learner (driver).

l litre.

laager *n. S Afr.* camp defended by a circle of wagons.

lab *n. Informal* short for LABORATORY.

label *n.* piece of card or other material fixed to an object to show its ownership, destination, etc. —*v.* **labelling, labelled.** give a label to.

labia *pl. n., sing.* **labium.** four liplike folds of skin forming part of the female genitals. —**labial** [lay-bee-al] *adj.* of the lips; pronounced with the lips.

laboratory *n., pl.* **-ries.** building or room designed for scientific research or for the teaching of practical science.

laborious *adj.* involving great prolonged effort. —**laboriously** *adv.*

labour *n.* physical work or exertion; final stage of pregnancy, leading to childbirth; workers in industry. —*v.* work hard; be at a disadvantage because of a mistake or false belief; stress to excess or too persistently. —**laboured** *adj.* uttered or done with difficulty. —**labourer** *n.* person who labours, esp. someone doing manual work for wages. —**Labour Party** major British left-wing political party advocating democratic socialism and social equality.

labrador *n.* large retriever dog with a yellow or black coat.

laburnum *n.* ornamental tree with yellow hanging flowers.

labyrinth [lab-er-inth] *n.* network of tortuous passages, maze; interconnecting cavities in the internal ear. —**labyrinthine** *adj.*

lace *n.* delicate decorative fabric made from threads woven into an open weblike pattern; cord drawn through eyelets and tied. —*v.* fasten with laces; thread a cord or string through holes in something; add a small amount of alcohol, a drug, etc. to (food or drink). —**lacy** *adj.* fine, like lace. —**lace-ups** *pl. n.* shoes which fasten with laces.

lacerate [lass-er-rate] *v.* tear (flesh) jaggedly; wound (feelings). —**laceration** *n.*

lachrymose *adj.* tearful; sad.

lack *n.* shortage or absence of something needed or wanted. —*v.* need or be short of (something).

lackadaisical *adj.* lacking vitality and purpose; lazy and careless in a dreamy way.

lackey *n.* servile follower; uniformed male servant.

lacklustre *adj.* lacking brilliance or vitality.

laconic *adj.* using only a few words, terse. —**laconically** *adv.*

lacquer *n.* hard varnish for wood or metal; clear sticky substance sprayed onto the hair to hold it in place. —*v.* apply lacquer to.

lacrimal, lachrymal *adj.* of tears or the glands which produce them.

lacrosse *n.* sport in which teams catch and throw a ball using long sticks with a pouched net at the end, in an attempt to score goals.

lactation *n.* secretion of milk by female mammals to feed young. —**lactic** *adj.* of or derived from milk. —**lactose** *n.* white crystalline sugar found in milk.

lacuna [lak-kew-na] *n., pl.* **-nae, -nas.** gap or missing part, esp. in a document or series.

THESAURUS

label *n.* 1. marker, sticker, tag, tally, ticket ~*v.* 2. mark, stamp, sticker, tag, tally 3. brand, call, class, classify, define, describe, designate, identify, name

labour *n.* 1. industry, toil, work 2. employees, hands, labourers, workers, work force, workmen 3. drudgery, effort, exertion, industry, pains, toil 4. childbirth, contractions, delivery, labour pains, pains, parturition, throes, travail ~*v.* 5. dwell on, elaborate, overdo, overemphasize, strain

laboured awkward, difficult, forced, heavy, stiff, strained

labourer blue-collar worker, drudge, hand, labouring man, manual worker, worker, workman

lacerate claw, cut, gash, jag, maim, mangle, rend, rip, slash, tear, wound

lack 1. *n.* absence, dearth, deficiency, deprivation, destitution, need, scantiness, scarcity, shortage, want 2. *v.* miss, need, require, want

lackadaisical apathetic, dull, half-hearted, indifferent, limp, listless, spiritless

lacklustre boring, dim, drab, dry, dull, flat, leaden, lifeless, muted, prosaic, sombre, vapid

laconic brief, compact, concise, crisp, curt, pithy, short, succinct, terse

lad boy, fellow, juvenile, kid, schoolboy, stripling, youngster, youth

DICTIONARY

lad *n.* boy or young fellow.

ladder *n.* frame of two poles connected by horizontal steps used for climbing; line of stitches that have come undone in a stocking or tights. —*v.* have or cause to have such a line of undone stitches.

laden *adj.* loaded; burdened.

la-di-da, lah-di-dah *adj. Informal* affected or pretentious.

ladle *n.* spoon with a long handle and a large bowl, used for serving soup etc. —*v.* serve out liquid with a ladle.

lady *n., pl.* **-dies.** woman regarded as having characteristics of good breeding or high rank; polite term of address for a woman; (**L-**) title of some women of rank. —**Our Lady** the Virgin Mary. —**lady-in-waiting** *n., pl.* **ladies-in-waiting.** female servant of a queen or princess. —**lady-killer** *n. Informal* man who is or thinks he is irresistible to women. —**ladylike** *adj.* polite, well-mannered.

ladybird *n.* small red beetle with black spots.

lag[1] *v.* **lagging, lagged.** go too slowly, fall behind. —*n.* delay between events. —**laggard** *n.* person who lags behind.

lag[2] *v.* **lagging, lagged.** wrap (a boiler, pipes, etc.) with insulating material. —**lagging** *n.* insulating material.

lag[3] *n.* —**old lag** *Slang* convict.

lager *n.* light-bodied type of beer.

lagoon *n.* saltwater lake enclosed by an atoll or separated by a sandbank from the sea.

laid *v.* past of LAY[1]. —**laid-back** *adj. Informal* relaxed.

lain *v.* past participle of LIE[2].

lair *n.* resting place of an animal.

laird *n.* Scottish landowner.

laissez-faire [less-ay-**fair**] *n.* principle of non-intervention, esp. by a government in commercial affairs.

laity [**lay**-it-ee] *n.* people who are not members of the clergy.

lake[1] *n.* expanse of water entirely surrounded by land. —**lakeside** *n.*

lake[2] *n.* red pigment.

lam *v.* **lamming, lammed.** *Slang* beat or hit.

lama *n.* Buddhist priest in Tibet or Mongolia. —**lamasery** *n.* monastery of lamas.

lamb *n.* young of sheep; its meat; innocent or helpless creature. —*v.* (of sheep) give birth to a lamb or lambs. —**lambskin** *n.* —**lambswool** *n.*

lambast(e) *v.* beat or thrash; reprimand severely.

lambent *adj. Lit.* (of a flame) flickering softly.

lamé [**lah**-may] *n., adj.* (fabric) interwoven with gold or silver thread.

lame *adj.* having an injured or disabled leg or foot; (of an excuse) unconvincing. —*v.* make lame. —**lamely** *adv.* —**lameness** *n.* —**lame duck** person or thing unable to cope without help.

lament *v.* feel or express sorrow (for). —*n.* passionate expression of grief; song of grief. —**lamentable** *adj.* deplorable. —**lamentation** *n.* —**lamented** *adj.* grieved for.

laminate *v.* make (a sheet of material) by bonding together two or more thin sheets; cover with a thin sheet of material. —*n.* laminated sheet. —**laminated** *adj.* —**lamination** *n.*

Lammas *n.* August 1st, formerly a harvest festival.

lamp *n.* device which produces light from electricity, oil, or gas. —**lampblack** *n.* pigment made from soot. —**lamppost** *n.* post supporting a lamp in the street. —**lampshade** *n.*

lampoon *n.* humorous satire ridiculing someone. —*v.* satirize or ridicule.

lamprey *n.* eel-like fish with a round sucking mouth.

lance *n.* long spear used by a mounted soldier. —*v.* pierce (a boil or abscess) with a lancet. —**lancer** *n.* formerly, cavalry soldier armed with

---

THESAURUS

laden burdened, charged, full, hampered, loaded, oppressed, taxed

ladylike courtly, cultured, decorous, elegant, genteel, modest, polite, proper, refined, respectable, well-bred

lag dawdle, delay, idle, linger, loiter, saunter, straggle, tarry, trail

laggard dawdler, idler, loiterer, lounger, straggler

laid-back at ease, casual, easy-going, relaxed, unhurried

lame 1. crippled, disabled, game, hobbling,

limping 2. *Fig.* feeble, flimsy, inadequate, poor, thin, unconvincing, weak

lament 1. *v.* bemoan, bewail, complain, deplore, grieve, mourn, regret, sorrow, wail, weep 2. *n.* complaint, moan, moaning, plaint, wail, wailing

lamentable distressing, grievous, mournful, regrettable, sorrowful, tragic, unfortunate, woeful

lampoon 1. *n.* burlesque, parody, satire, skit, squib 2. *v.* burlesque, caricature, mock, parody, ridicule, satirize

DICTIONARY

a lance. —**lance corporal** lowest noncommissioned rank in the army.

lanceolate *adj.* narrow and tapering to a point at each end.

lancet *n.* pointed two-edged surgical knife; narrow window in the shape of a pointed arch.

land *n.* solid part of the earth's surface; ground, esp. with reference to its type or use; rural or agricultural area; property consisting of land; country or region. —*v.* come or bring to earth after a flight, jump, or fall; go or take from a ship at the end of a voyage; come to or touch shore; come or bring to some point or condition; *Informal* obtain; take (a hooked fish) from the water; *Informal* deliver (a punch). —**landed** *adj.* possessing or consisting of lands. —**landless** *adj.* —**landward** *adj.* nearest to or facing the land. —**land up** *v.* arrive at a final point or condition.

landau [**lan**-daw] *n.* four-wheeled carriage with a folding hood.

landfall *n.* ship's first landing after a voyage.

landing *n.* floor area at the top of a flight of stairs; bringing or coming to land; (also **landing stage**) place where people or goods go onto or come off a boat.

landlocked *adj.* completely surrounded by land.

landlord, landlady *n.* person who rents out land, houses, etc.; owner or manager of a pub or boarding house.

landlubber *n.* person who is not experienced at sea.

landmark *n.* prominent object in or feature of a landscape; event, decision, etc. considered as an important development.

landscape *n.* extensive piece of inland scenery seen from one place; picture of it. —*v.* improve natural features of (a piece of land).

landslide *n.* (also **landslip**) falling of soil, rock,

etc. down the side of a mountain; overwhelming electoral victory.

lane *n.* narrow road; area of road for one stream of traffic; specified route followed by ships or aircraft; strip of a running track or swimming pool for use by one competitor.

language *n.* system of sounds, symbols, etc. for communicating thought; particular system used by a nation or people.

languid *adj.* lacking energy or enthusiasm. —**languidly** *adv.*

languish *v.* suffer neglect or hardship; lose or diminish in strength or vigour; pine (for). —**languishing** *adj.*

languor [**lang**-ger] *n.* laziness or weariness; dreamy relaxation; oppressive stillness. —**languorous** *adj.*

lank *adj.* (of hair) greasy and limp; lean and tall. —**lanky** *adj.* ungracefully tall and thin. —**lankiness** *n.*

lanolin *n.* grease from sheep's wool used in ointments etc.

lantern *n.* light in a transparent protective case. —**lantern jaw** long thin jaw. —**lantern-jawed** *adj.*

lanthanum *n.* silvery-white metallic element. —**lanthanide series** class of 15 elements chemically related to lanthanum.

lanyard *n.* short cord worn round the neck to hold a knife or whistle; *Naut.* short rope.

lap[1] *n.* part between the waist and knees of a person when sitting. —**lapdog** *n.* small pet dog. —**laptop** *adj.* (of a computer) small enough to fit on a user's lap.

lap[2] *n.* single circuit of a racecourse or track; stage of a journey; overlap. —*v.* **lapping, lapped.** overtake an opponent so as to be one or more circuits ahead; enfold or wrap around.

lap[3] *v.* **lapping, lapped.** (of waves) beat softly

THESAURUS

land *n.* 1. earth, ground, terra firma 2. dirt, ground, loam, soil 3. acres, estate, grounds, property, realty 4. country, district, nation, province, region, territory, tract ~*v.* 5. alight, arrive, berth, debark, disembark, dock, touch down

landlord host, hotelier, hotel-keeper, innkeeper

landmark 1. feature, monument 2. crisis, mile~stone, turning point, watershed

landscape countryside, outlook, panorama, prospect, scene, scenery, view, vista

language 1. conversation, discourse, expres~sion, parlance, speech, talk, vocalization 2. argot, cant, dialect, idiom, jargon, patois, speech, tongue, vernacular, vocabulary

languid 1. drooping, faint, feeble, limp, pining, sickly, weak, weary 2. lazy, listless, spiritless, unenthusiastic, uninterested 3. dull, heavy, inactive, inert, lethargic, sluggish, torpid

languish decline, droop, fade, fail, faint, flag, sicken, waste, weaken, wilt, wither

lank 1. dull, lifeless, limp, long, straggling 2. emaciated, gaunt, lanky, lean, scrawny, skin~ny, slender, slim, spare, thin

lanky angular, bony, gaunt, rangy, spare, tall, thin

lap 1. *n.* circle, circuit, course, loop, orbit, round, tour 2. *v.* cover, enfold, fold, swathe, turn, twist, wrap

DICTIONARY

against (a shore etc.). —**lap up** v. drink by scooping up with the tongue; accept (information or attention) eagerly.

lapel [lap-**pel**] n. part of the front of a coat or jacket folded back towards the shoulders.

lapidary adj. of stones, esp. gemstones.

lapis lazuli [lap-iss **lazz**-yoo-lie] n. bright blue gemstone.

lapse n. temporary drop in a standard, esp. through forgetfulness or carelessness; instance of bad behaviour by someone usually well-behaved; break in occurrence or usage. —v. drop in standard; end or become invalid, esp. through disuse; (of time) slip away; abandon religious faith. —**lapsed** adj.

lapwing n. plover with a tuft of feathers on the head.

larboard n., adj. Old-fashioned port (side of a ship).

larceny n., pl. -**nies.** theft.

larch n. deciduous coniferous tree.

lard n. soft white fat obtained from a pig. —v. insert strips of bacon in (meat) before cooking; decorate (speech or writing) with strange words unnecessarily.

larder n. storeroom for food.

large adj. great in size, number, or extent. —**at large** free, not confined; in general; fully. —**largely** adv. —**largish** adj. —**large-scale** adj. wide-ranging or extensive.

largesse, largess [lar-**jess**] n. generous giving, esp. of money.

largo Music in a slow and dignified manner.

lariat n. lasso.

lark[1] n. small brown songbird, skylark.

lark[2] Informal —n. harmless piece of mischief; unnecessary activity or job. —**lark about** v. play pranks.

larkspur n. plant with spikes of blue, pink, or white flowers with spurs.

larva n., pl. -**vae.** insect in an immature stage, often resembling a worm. —**larval** adj.

larynx n., pl. **larynges.** part of the throat containing the vocal cords. —**laryngeal** adj. —**laryngitis** n. inflammation of the larynx.

lasagne, lasagna [laz-**zan**-ya] n. pasta in wide flat sheets; dish made from layers of lasagne, meat, vegetables, etc.

lascivious [lass-iv-ee-uss] adj. lustful. —**lasciviously** adv.

laser [**lay**-zer] n. device for concentrating light of mixed frequencies into an intense narrow beam.

lash[1] n. sharp blow with a whip; eyelash. —v. hit with a whip; (of rain or waves) beat forcefully against; attack verbally; scold; flick or wave sharply to and fro. —**lash out** v. make a sudden physical or verbal attack; Informal spend (money) extravagantly.

lash[2] v. fasten or bind tightly with cord etc.

lashings pl. n. Informal large amount.

lass, lassie n. girl.

lassitude n. physical or mental weariness.

lasso [lass-**oo**] n., pl. -**sos, -soes.** rope with a noose for catching cattle and horses. —v. -**soing, -soed.** catch with a lasso.

last[1] adj., adv. coming at the end or after all others; most recent(ly). —adj. only remaining. —n. last person or thing. —**lastly** adv. finally. —**last-ditch** adj. done as a final resort. —**last post** army bugle-call played at sunset or funerals. —**last straw** small irritation or setback that, coming after others, is too much to bear. —**last thing** at the end of the day. —**last word** final comment in an argument; most recent or best example of something.

last[2] v. continue; be sufficient for (a specified amount of time); remain fresh, uninjured, or unaltered. —**lasting** adj.

last[3] n. model of a foot on which shoes and boots are made or repaired.

THESAURUS

lapse n. 1. error, failing, fault, indiscretion, mistake, omission, oversight, slip ~v. 2. decline, drop, fail, fall, sink, slide, slip 3. end, expire, run out, stop, terminate

lapsed discontinued, ended, expired, finished, invalid

large 1. big, bulky, enormous, giant, goodly, great, huge, immense, king-size, massive, monumental, sizable, substantial, vast 2. ample, broad, capacious, copious, extensive, full, generous, grand, liberal, plentiful, roomy, spacious, sweeping, wide

largely chiefly, generally, mainly, mostly, predominantly, primarily, principally, widely

largess 1. benefaction, bounty, charity, generosity, liberality, philanthropy 2. bequest, bounty, donation, gift, grant, present

lark antic, caper, fling, frolic, fun, gambol, game, jape, mischief, prank, revel, rollick, romp, spree

lash[1] n. 1. blow, hit, stripe, stroke ~v. 2. beat, birch, flog, horsewhip, lam (Sl.), scourge, thrash, whip 3. beat, buffet, dash, drum, hammer, hit, knock, pound, smack, strike

DICTIONARY

latch *n.* fastening for a door with a bar and lever; lock which can only be opened from the outside with a key. —*v.* fasten with a latch. —**latchkey** *n.* key for a latch. —**latch onto** *v.* become attached to (a person or idea).

late *adj.* arriving or occurring after the normal or expected time; towards the end of (a period of time); recently dead; recent; former. —*adv.* after the normal or expected time; recently; at a relatively advanced age. —**lately** *adv.* not long since. —**lateness** *n.* —**latish** *adj., adv.* —**late-comer** *n.*

lateen sail *n.* triangular sail on a long yard hoisted to the head of a mast.

latent *adj.* hidden and not yet developed. —**latency** *n.*

lateral [lat-ter-al] *adj.* of, at, to, or from the side. —**laterally** *adv.*

latex *n.* milky sap found in some plants, esp. the rubber tree, used in making rubber and glues.

lath *n.* thin strip of wood used to support plaster, tiles, etc.

lathe *n.* machine for turning wood or metal while it is being shaped.

lather *n.* froth of soap and water; frothy sweat; *Informal* state of agitation. —*v.* make frothy; rub with soap until lather appears.

Latin *n.* language of the ancient Romans. —*adj.* of or in Latin; of a people whose language derives from Latin. —**Latin America** parts of South and Central America whose official language is Spanish or Portuguese. —**Latin American** *n., adj.*

latitude *n.* angular distance measured in degrees N or S of the equator; scope for freedom of action or thought. —*pl.* regions considered in relation to their distance from the equator. —**latitudinal** *adj.*

latitudinarian *adj.* liberal, esp. in religious matters.

latrine *n.* toilet in a barracks or camp.

latter *adj.* second of two; later; more recent. —**latterly** *adv.* —**latter-day** modern.

lattice [lat-iss] *n.* framework of intersecting strips of wood, metal, etc.; gate, screen, etc. formed of such a framework. —**latticed** *adj.*

laud *v.* praise or glorify. —**laudable** *adj.* praiseworthy. —**laudably** *adv.* —**laudatory** *adj.* praising or glorifying.

laudanum [lawd-a-num] *n.* opium-based sedative.

laugh *v.* make inarticulate sounds with the voice expressing amusement, merriment, or scorn; utter or express with laughter. —*n.* laughing; manner of laughing; *Informal* person or thing causing amusement. —**laughable** *adj.* ludicrous. —**laughter** *n.* sound or action of laughing. —**laughing gas** nitrous oxide as an anaesthetic. —**laughing stock** object of general derision. —**laugh off** *v.* treat (something serious or difficult) lightly.

launch[1] *v.* put (a ship or boat) into the water, esp. for the first time; send (a missile or space-

THESAURUS

lash[2] bind, fasten, join, make fast, rope, secure, strap, tie

lass damsel, girl, maid, maiden, miss, young woman

last[1] *adj.* 1. aftermost, hindmost, rearmost 2. latest, most recent 3. closing, concluding, extreme, final, furthest, remotest, ultimate, utmost ~*adv.* 4. after, behind

last[2] *v.* abide, continue, endure, keep, persist, remain, survive, wear

lasting abiding, continuing, durable, enduring, long-term, permanent, perpetual, unceasing, undying, unending

latch bar, bolt, catch, clamp, fastening, hasp, hook, lock

late 1. behind, belated, delayed, overdue, slow, tardy, unpunctual 2. advanced, fresh, modern, new, recent 3. dead, deceased, defunct, departed, ex-, former, old, past

lately just now, latterly, of, late, recently

lateness belatedness, delay, retardation, unpunctuality

lateral edgeways, flanking, sideways

lather bubbles, foam, froth, soap, soapsuds, suds

latitude 1. breadth, compass, extent, range, room, scope, space, span, spread, sweep, width 2. freedom, indulgence, leeway, liberty, unrestrictedness

latter closing, concluding, last, later, latest, modern, recent, second

latterly hitherto, lately, recently

lattice fretwork, grating, grid, grille, mesh, network, trellis, web

laudable admirable, creditable, excellent, meritorious, praiseworthy, worthy

laugh 1. *v.* chortle, chuckle, giggle, guffaw, snigger, titter 2. *n.* belly laugh (*Inf.*), chortle, chuckle, giggle, guffaw, snigger, titter

laughable absurd, derisory, ludicrous, nonsensical, preposterous, ridiculous

laughter amusement, glee, hilarity, merriment, mirth

DICTIONARY

craft) into space or the air; begin (a campaign, project, etc.); put a new product on the market. —*n.* launching. —**launcher** *n.* —**launch into** *v.* start doing something enthusiastically. —**launch out** *v.* start doing something new.

launch[2] *n.* large open motorboat.

launder *v.* wash and iron (clothes and linen); make (illegally obtained money) seem legal by passing it through foreign banks or legitimate businesses. —**laundry** *n., pl.* **-dries.** place for washing clothes and linen, esp. as a business; clothes etc. for washing or which have recently been washed. —**Launderette** *n.* ® shop with coin-operated washing and drying machines.

laureate [lor-ee-at] *adj.* —**poet laureate** poet appointed to write poems for special occasions.

laurel *n.* glossy-leaved shrub, bay tree. —*pl.* wreath of laurel, an emblem of victory or merit.

lava *n.* molten rock thrown out by volcanoes, which hardens as it cools.

lavatory *n., pl.* **-ries.** toilet.

lavender *n.* shrub with fragrant flowers. —*adj.* bluish-purple. —**lavender water** light perfume made from lavender.

lavish *adj.* great in quantity or richness; giving or spending generously; extravagant. —*v.* give or spend generously. —**lavishly** *adv.*

law *n.* rule binding on a community; system of such rules; *Informal* police; general principle deduced from facts; invariable sequence of events in nature. —**lawful** *adj.* allowed by law.

—**lawfully** *adv.* —**lawless** *adj.* breaking the law, esp. in a violent way. —**lawlessly** *adv.* —**lawabiding** *adj.* adhering to the laws. —**law-breaker** *n.* —**lawsuit** *n.* court case brought by one person or group against another.

lawn[1] *n.* area of tended and mown grass. —**lawn mower** machine for cutting grass. —**lawn tennis** tennis, esp. when played on a grass court.

lawn[2] *n.* fine linen or cotton fabric.

lawyer *n.* professionally qualified legal expert.

lax *adj.* not strict. —**laxity** *n.* —**laxly** *adv.*

laxative *n., adj.* (medicine) having a loosening effect on the bowels.

lay[1] *v.* **laying, laid.** cause to lie; set in a particular place or position; arrange a table for a meal; put forward (a plan, argument, etc.); attribute (blame); (of a bird or reptile) produce eggs; devise or prepare; place (a bet). —**lay waste** devastate. —**lay-by** *n.* stopping place for traffic beside a road. —**lay off** *v.* dismiss staff during a slack period. —**lay-off** *n.* —**lay on** *v.* provide or supply. —**lay out** *v.* arrange or spread out; prepare (a corpse) for burial; *Informal* spend money, esp. lavishly; *Slang* knock unconscious. —**layout** *n.* arrangement, esp. of matter for printing or of a building.

lay[2] *v.* past tense of LIE[2]. —**layabout** *n.* lazy person, loafer.

lay[3] *adj.* of or involving people who are not clergymen; nonspecialist. —**layman** *n.* ordinary person.

THESAURUS

launch 1. cast, discharge, dispatch, fire, project, propel, throw 2. begin, commence, embark upon, inaugurate, initiate, instigate, introduce, open, start

laurels acclaim, awards, bays, commendation, credit, distinction, fame, glory, honour, praise, renown, reward

lavatory bathroom, convenience, loo, powder room, (public) convenience, toilet, washroom, water closet

lavish 1. copious, exuberant, lush, opulent, plentiful, profuse, prolific, sumptuous 2. bountiful, free, generous, liberal, munificent, open-handed

law 1. charter, code, jurisprudence 2. act, code, commandment, covenant, decree, edict, enactment, order, ordinance, rule, statute

law-abiding compliant, dutiful, good, honest, lawful, obedient, orderly, peaceful

lawbreaker convict, criminal, culprit, delinquent, miscreant, offender, sinner, trespasser, wrongdoer

lawful allowable, authorized, constitutional,

just, legal, legalized, legitimate, licit, permissible, proper, rightful, valid

lawless anarchic, chaotic, disorderly, insubordinate, insurgent, mutinous, rebellious, reckless, riotous, seditious, unruly, wild

lawsuit action, argument, case, cause, contest, dispute, litigation, proceedings, prosecution, suit, trial

lawyer advocate, attorney, barrister, legal adviser, solicitor

lax careless, casual, easy-going, lenient, negligent, remiss, slack, slipshod

lay[1] 1. deposit, establish, leave, place, plant, posit, put, set, set down, settle, spread 2. arrange, dispose, locate, organize, position, set out 3. bear, deposit, produce 4. allot, ascribe, assign, attribute, charge, impute 5. concoct, contrive, design, devise, hatch, plan, plot, prepare, work out 6. bet, gamble, hazard, risk, stake, wager

lay[2] 1. laic, nonclerical, secular 2. amateur, inexpert

layabout good-for-nothing, idler, laggard, loafer, lounger, shirker, vagrant, wastrel

DICTIONARY

lay⁴ n. short narrative poem designed to be sung.

layer n. single thickness of some substance, as a stratum or coating on a surface; laying hen; shoot of a plant pegged down or partly covered with earth to encourage root growth. —v. form a layer; propagate plants by layers. —**layered** adj.

layette n. clothes for a newborn baby.

lay figure n. jointed figure of the body used by artists; nonentity.

laze v. be idle or lazy. —n. lazing.

lazy adj. **lazier, laziest.** not inclined to work or exert oneself; done in a relaxed manner without much effort; (of movement) slow and gentle. —**lazily** adv. —**laziness** n. —**lazybones** n. Informal lazy person.

lb pound (weight).

lbw Cricket leg before wicket.

lea n. Poetic meadow.

leach v. remove or be removed from a substance by a liquid passing through it.

lead¹ v. **leading, led.** guide or conduct; cause to feel, think, or behave in a certain way; (of a road, path, etc.) go towards; control or direct; be, go, or play first; be the most important person or thing in; result in; pass or spend (one's life). —n. first or most prominent place; example or leadership; clue; amount by which a person or group is ahead of another; length of leather or chain attached to a dog's collar to control it; principal role or actor in a film, play, etc.; cable bringing current to an electrical device. —adj. acting as a leader or lead. —**leading** adj. —**leading question**

question worded to prompt the answer desired. —**lead-in** n. introduction to a subject.

lead² n. soft heavy grey metal; (in a pencil) graphite; lead weight on a line, used for sounding depths of water. —**leaded** adj. (of windows) made from many small panes of glass held together by lead strips. —**leaden** adj. heavy or sluggish; made from lead; dull grey.

leader n. person who leads; (also **leading article**) article in a newspaper expressing editorial views. —**leadership** n.

leaf n., pl. **leaves.** flat usu. green blade attached to the stem of a plant; single sheet of paper in a book; very thin sheet of metal; extending flap on a table. —**leafy** adj. —**leafless** adj. —**leaf mould** rich soil composed of decayed leaves. —**leaf through** v. turn pages without reading them.

leaflet n. sheet of printed matter for distribution; small leaf.

league¹ n. association promoting the interests of its members; association of sports clubs organizing competitions between its members; Informal class or level.

league² n. Obs. measure of distance, about three miles.

leak n. hole or defect that allows the escape or entrance of liquid, gas, radiation etc.; liquid etc. that escapes or enters; disclosure of secrets. —v. let fluid etc. in or out; (of fluid etc.) find its way through a leak; disclose secret information. —**leakage** n. leaking; gradual escape or loss. —**leaky** adj.

THESAURUS

layer bed, ply, row, seam, stratum, thickness, tier

layman amateur, lay person, nonprofessional, outsider

lay-off discharge, dismissal, unemployment

lay off discharge, dismiss, drop, let go, oust, pay off

lay on cater (for), furnish, give, provide, supply

layout arrangement, design, draft, outline, plan

lay out arrange, design, display, exhibit, plan, spread out

laziness idleness, inactivity, indolence, slackness, sloth, slowness, tardiness

lazy idle, inactive, indolent, inert, slack, slothful, slow

leach drain, extract, filter, filtrate, lixiviate (Chem.), percolate, seep, strain

lead v. 1. conduct, escort, guide, pilot, precede, steer, usher 2. cause, dispose, draw, incline, induce, influence, persuade, prevail, prompt 3. command, direct, govern, head, manage, supervise 4. be ahead (of), exceed, excel, out-

do, outstrip, surpass, transcend 5. have, live, pass, spend, undergo ~n. 6. advantage, edge, first place, margin, precedence, priority, start, supremacy, van 7. direction, example, guidance, leadership, model 8. clue, guide, hint, indication, suggestion, tip 9. leading role, principal, protagonist, star part

leader captain, chief, chieftain, commander, conductor, director, guide, head, principal, ruler, superior

leadership 1. direction, domination, guidance, management, running 2. authority, command, control, influence, initiative, pre-eminence, supremacy, sway

leading chief, first, foremost, greatest, highest, main, outstanding, principal, ruling, superior

leaf n. 1. blade, flag, needle, pad 2. folio, page, sheet

leaflet bill, booklet, circular, handbill, pamphlet

league alliance, association, band, coalition, combination, compact, confederacy, fellow-

DICTIONARY

lean[1] *v.* **leaning, leant** or **leaned.** rest against; bend or slope from an upright position; tend (towards). —**leaning** *n.* tendency. —**lean on** *v. Informal* threaten or intimidate; depend on for help or advice. —**lean-to** *n.* shed built against an existing wall.

lean[2] *adj.* thin but healthy-looking; (of meat) lacking fat; unproductive. —*n.* lean part of meat. —**leanness** *n.*

leap *v.* **leaping, leapt** or **leaped.** make a sudden powerful jump. —*n.* sudden powerful jump; abrupt increase, as in costs or prices. —**leapfrog** *n.* game in which a player vaults over another bending down. —**leap year** year with February 29th as an extra day.

learn *v.* **learning, learnt** or **learned.** gain skill or knowledge by study, practice, or teaching; memorize (something); find out or discover. —**learned** *adj.* erudite, deeply read; showing much learning. —**learner** *n.* —**learning** *n.* knowledge got by study.

lease *n.* contract by which land or property is rented for a stated time by the owner to a tenant. —*v.* let or rent on lease. —**leasehold** *adj.* held on lease. —**leaseholder** *n.*

leash *n.* lead for a dog.

least *adj.* smallest; superlative of LITTLE. —*n.* smallest one. —*adv.* in the smallest degree.

leather *n.* material made from specially treated animal skins. —*v.* beat or thrash. —**leathery** *adj.* like leather, tough.

leave[1] *v.* **leaving, left.** go away from; allow to remain, accidentally or deliberately; cause to be or remain in a specified state; discontinue membership of; permit; deposit; entrust; bequeath. —**leave out** *v.* exclude or omit.

leave[2] *n.* permission to be absent from work or duty; period of such absence; permission to do something; formal parting.

leaven [lev-ven] *n.* yeast; influence that produces a gradual change. —*v.* raise with leaven; spread through and influence (something).

lecher *n.* lecherous man. —**lechery** *n.*

lecherous [letch-er-uss] *adj.* (of a man) having or showing excessive sexual desire. —**lecherously** *adv.* —**lecherousness** *n.*

lectern *n.* sloping reading desk, esp. in a church.

lecture *n.* informative talk to an audience on a subject; lengthy rebuke or scolding. —*v.* give a talk; reprove. —**lecturer** *n.* —**lectureship** *n.* appointment as a lecturer.

THESAURUS

ship, fraternity, group, guild, partnership, union

leak *n.* 1. chink, crack, crevice, fissure, hole, opening, puncture 2. drip, leakage, percolation, seepage 3. disclosure, divulgence ~*v.* 4. discharge, drip, escape, exude, pass, percolate, seep, spill, trickle 5. disclose, divulge

lean[1] *v.* 1. be supported, prop, recline, repose, rest 2. bend, incline, slant, slope, tilt, tip

lean[2] *adj.* 1. bony, emaciated, gaunt, lank, rangy, skinny, slender, slim, spare, thin, wiry 2. bare, barren, meagre, pitiful, poor, scanty, sparse

leaning aptitude, bent, bias, inclination, liking, partiality, penchant, proneness, taste, tendency

leap 1. *v.* bounce, bound, caper, cavort, frisk, gambol, hop, jump, skip, spring 2. *n.* bound, caper, frisk, hop, jump, skip, spring, vault

learn 1. acquire, attain, grasp, imbibe, master, pick up 2. get off, pat, learn by heart, memorize 3. detect, discern, discover, find out, gain, gather, hear, understand

learned academic, cultured, erudite, expert, highbrow, lettered, literate, scholarly, skilled, versed, well-read

learner beginner, disciple, novice, pupil, scholar, student, trainee, tyro

learning culture, education, erudition, information, knowledge, letters, lore, research, schooling, study, tuition, wisdom

lease *v.* charter, hire, let, loan, rent

least fewest, last, lowest, meanest, minimum, poorest, smallest, tiniest

leave[1] *v.* 1. abandon, decamp, depart, desert, disappear, exit, forsake, go, move, quit, relinquish, retire, withdraw 2. abandon, cease, desert, desist, drop, forbear, give up, refrain, relinquish, renounce, stop 3. allot, assign, cede, commit, consign, entrust, refer 4. bequeath, transmit, will

leave[2] *n.* 1. allowance, concession, consent, freedom, liberty, permission, sanction 2. furlough, holiday, sabbatical, time off, vacation

leave out bar, cast aside, count out, disregard, except, exclude, ignore, neglect, omit, overlook, reject

lecture *n.* 1. address, discourse, harangue, instruction, lesson, speech, talk ~*v.* 2. address, discourse, expound, harangue, speak, talk, teach ~*n.* 3. censure, chiding, rebuke, reprimand, reproof, scolding ~*v.* 4. admonish, castigate, censure, chide, rate, reprimand, reprove, scold

DICTIONARY

ledge *n.* narrow shelf sticking out from a wall; shelflike projection from a cliff etc.

ledger *n.* book of debit and credit accounts of a firm.

lee *n.* sheltered part or side; side away from the wind. **—leeward** *adj., n.* (on) the lee side. **—adv.** towards this side. **—leeway** *n.* room for free movement within limits.

leech *n.* species of bloodsucking worm; person who lives off others.

leek *n.* vegetable of the onion family with a long bulb and thick stem.

leer *v.* look or grin at in a sneering or suggestive manner. **—n.** sneering or suggestive look or grin.

leery *adj. Informal* suspicious or wary (of).

lees *pl. n.* sediment of wine.

leet *n. Scot.* list of candidates for a job.

left[1] *adj.* denotes the side that faces west when the front faces north; opposite to right. **—n.** left hand or part; *Politics* people supporting socialism rather than capitalism. **—adv.** on or towards the left. **—leftist** *n., adj.* (person) of the political left. **—left-handed** *adj.* more adept with the left hand than with the right. **—left-wing** *adj.* socialist; belonging to the more radical part of a political party.

left[2] *v.* past of LEAVE[1].

leftover *n.* unused portion of food or material.

leg *n.* one of the limbs on which a person or animal walks, runs, or stands; part of a garment covering the leg; structure that supports, such as one of the legs of a table; stage of a journey; *Sport* (part of) one game or race in a series. **—pull someone's leg** tease someone. **—leggy** *adj.* long-legged. **—legless** *adj.* without legs; *Slang* very drunk. **—leggings** *pl. n.* covering of leather or other material for the legs.

legacy *n., pl.* **-cies.** thing left in a will; thing handed down to a successor.

legal *adj.* established or permitted by law; relating to law or lawyers. **—legally** *adv.* **—legalize** *v.* make legal. **—legalization** *n.* **—legality** *n.*

legate *n.* messenger or representative, esp. from the Pope. **—legation** *n.* diplomatic minister and his staff; official residence of a diplomatic minister.

legatee *n.* recipient of a legacy.

legato [leg-**ah**-toe] *Music* smoothly.

legend *n.* traditional story or myth; traditional literature; famous person or event; stories about such a person or event; inscription. **—legendary** *adj.* of or in legend; famous.

legerdemain [lej-er-de-**main**] *n.* sleight of hand; cunning deception.

legible *adj.* easily read. **—legibility** *n.* **—legibly** *adv.*

legion *n.* large military force; large number; association of veterans; infantry unit in the Roman army. **—legionary** *adj., n.* **—legionnaire** *n.* member of a legion. **—legionnaire's disease** serious bacterial disease similar to pneumonia.

legislate *v.* make laws. **—legislation** *n.* legislating; laws made. **—legislative** *adj.* **—legislator** *n.* maker of laws. **—legislature** *n.* body of persons that makes, amends, or repeals the laws of a state.

legitimate *adj.* authorized by or in accordance with law; fairly deduced; born to parents married to each other. **—v.** make legitimate. **—legitimacy** *adv.* **—legitimacy** *n.* **—legitimize** *v.* make legitimate, legalize. **—legitimization** *n.*

Lego *n.* ® construction toy of plastic bricks fitted together by studs.

leguaan *n.* large S African lizard.

THESAURUS

lees deposit, dregs, grounds, sediment

leeway latitude, margin, play, room, scope, space

leg 1. limb, member 2. brace, prop, support, upright 3. lap, part, portion, section, segment, stage, stretch

legacy 1. bequest, estate, gift, heirloom, inheritance 2. heritage, patrimony, tradition

legal allowed, authorized, lawful, legalized, legitimate, licit, permissible, proper, rightful, sanctioned, valid

legalize allow, approve, license, permit, sanction, validate

legend 1. fable, fiction, folk tale, myth, narrative, saga, story, tale 2. caption, device, motto

legendary fabled, fabulous, fanciful, fictitious, mythical, romantic, storied, traditional

legibility clarity, neatness, plainness, readability

legible clear, distinct, neat, plain, readable

legion 1. army, brigade, company, division, force, troop 2. drove, horde, host, mass, multitude, myriad, number, throng

legislate enact, establish, ordain, prescribe

legislation 1. enactment, prescription, regulation 2. act, bill, charter, law, measure

legislative *adj.* congressional, judicial, ordaining, parliamentary

legislator lawgiver, parliamentarian

legislature assembly, chamber, congress, diet, parliament, senate

legitimate authentic, genuine, lawful, legal, licit, proper, real, rightful, sanctioned, statutory, true

DICTIONARY

legume *n.* pod of a plant of the pea or bean family. —*pl.* peas or beans. —**leguminous** *adj.* (of plants) pod-bearing.

lei *n.* in Hawaii, garland of flowers.

leisure *n.* time for relaxation or hobbies. —**at one's leisure** when one has time. —**leisurely** *adj.* deliberate, unhurried. —*adv.* slowly. —**leisured** *adj.* with plenty of spare time. —**leisure centre** building with facilities such as a swimming pool, gymnasium, and café.

leitmotif [**lite**-mote-eef] *n.* Music recurring theme associated with a person, situation, or thought.

lemming *n.* rodent of arctic regions, reputed to run into the sea and drown during mass migrations.

lemon *n.* yellow acid fruit that grows on trees; *Slang* useless or defective person or thing. —*adj.* pale-yellow. —**lemonade** *n.* lemon-flavoured soft drink, often fizzy. —**lemon curd** creamy spread made of lemons, butter, etc. —**lemon sole** edible flatfish.

lemur *n.* nocturnal animal like a small monkey, found on Madagascar.

lend *v.* **lending, lent.** give the temporary use of; provide (money) temporarily, often for interest; add (a quality or effect), e.g. *her presence lent beauty to the scene.* —**lend itself to** be suitable for. —**lender** *n.*

length *n.* quality of being long; extent or measurement from end to end; duration; piece of something narrow and long. —**at length** in full detail; at last. —**lengthy** *adj.* very long or tiresome. —**lengthily** *adv.* —**lengthen** *v.* make or become longer. —**lengthways, -wise** *adj., adv.*

lenient [**lee**-nee-ent] *adj.* tolerant, not strict or severe. —**leniency** *n.* —**leniently** *adv.*

lenity *n., pl.* **-ties.** mercy or clemency.

lens *n., pl.* **lenses.** piece of glass or similar material with one or both sides curved, used to converge or diverge light rays in cameras, spectacles, telescopes, etc.; transparent structure in the eye that focuses light.

Lent *n.* period from Ash Wednesday to Easter Eve. —**Lenten** *adj.* of, in, or suitable to Lent.

lent *v.* past of LEND.

lentil *n.* edible seed of a leguminous Asian plant.

lento *Music* slowly.

leonine *adj.* like a lion.

leopard *n.* large spotted carnivorous animal of the cat family. —**leopardess** *n. fem.*

leotard *n.* tight-fitting garment covering most of the body, worn by acrobats, dancers, etc.

leper *n.* person suffering from leprosy; ignored or despised person.

lepidoptera *pl. n.* order of insects with four wings covered with fine gossamer scales, as moths and butterflies. —**lepidopterous** *adj.* —**lepidopterist** *n.* person who studies or collects butterflies or moths.

leprechaun *n.* mischievous elf of Irish folklore.

leprosy *n.* disease attacking the nerves and skin, resulting in loss of feeling in the affected parts. —**leprous** *adj.*

lesbian *n.* homosexual woman. —*adj.* of homosexual women. —**lesbianism** *n.*

lèse-majesté [lezz-**maj**-est-ay] *n.* treason; taking of liberties against people in authority.

lesion *n.* structural change in an organ of the body caused by illness or injury.

less *adj.* smaller in extent, degree, or duration; not so much; comparative of LITTLE. —*n.* smaller part or quantity; lesser amount. —*adv.* to a smaller extent or degree. —*prep.* after deducting, minus. —**lessen** *v.* make or become smaller or not as much. —**lesser** *adj.* not as great in quantity, size, or worth.

lessee *n.* person to whom a lease is granted.

lesson *n.* single period of instruction in a subject; content of this; experience that teaches; portion of Scripture read in church.

THESAURUS

leisure ease, freedom, holiday, liberty, opportunity, pause, quiet, recreation, relaxation, respite, rest, retirement, spare time, vacation

leisurely comfortable, easy, gentle, lazy, relaxed, restful, slow, unhurried

lend 1. advance, loan 2. add, afford, bestow, confer, contribute, furnish, give, grant, impart, present, provide, supply

length 1. *Of linear extent* distance, extent, measure, reach, span 2. *Of time* duration, period, space, span, stretch, term

lengthen continue, draw out, elongate, expand, extend, increase, prolong, protract, stretch

lengthy diffuse, extended, interminable, long, prolix, tedious, verbose

leniency clemency, forbearance, gentleness, indulgence, mercy, mildness, tolerance

lenient forbearing, forgiving, gentle, indulgent, kind, merciful, mild, tender, tolerant

less 1. *adj.* shorter, slighter, smaller 2. *adv.* barely, little, meagrely

lessen abate, abridge, contract, curtail, decrease, die down, diminish, ease, impair, lighten, lower, moderate, narrow, reduce, shrink, slacken, weaken

DICTIONARY

lessor *n.* person who grants a lease.

lest *conj.* so as to prevent any possibility that; for fear that.

let¹ *v.* **letting, let.** allow, enable, or cause; allow to escape; grant use of for rent, lease; used as an auxiliary to express a proposal, command, threat, or assumption. —**let alone** not to mention. —**let down** *v.* disappoint; lower; deflate. —**letdown** *n.* disappointment. —**let off** *v.* excuse from (a duty or punishment); fire or explode (a weapon); emit (gas, steam, etc.). —**let on** *v. Informal* reveal (a secret). —**let out** *v.* emit; release. —**let up** *v.* diminish or stop. —**let-up** *n.* lessening.

let² *n.* hindrance; *Tennis* minor infringement or obstruction of the ball requiring a replay of the point.

lethal *adj.* deadly.

lethargy *n.* sluggishness or dullness; abnormal lack of energy. —**lethargic** *adj.* —**lethargically** *adv.*

letter *n.* alphabetical symbol; written message, usu. sent by post; strict meaning (of a law etc.). —*pl. n.* literary knowledge or ability. —**lettered** *adj.* learned. —**lettering** *n.* —**letter box** slot in a door through which letters are delivered; box in a street or post office where letters are posted. —**letterhead** *n.* printed heading on stationery giving the sender's name and address.

lettuce *n.* plant with large green leaves used in salads.

leucocyte [**loo**-koh-site] *n.* white blood corpuscle.

leukaemia [loo-**kee**-mee-a] *n.* disease caused by uncontrolled overproduction of white blood corpuscles.

levee¹ *n. US* natural or artificial river embankment; landing-place.

levee² *n. Hist.* reception held by the sovereign on rising.

level *adj.* horizontal; having an even surface; of the same height as something else; equal to or even with (someone or something else); not going above the top edge of (a spoon etc.). —*v.* **-elling, -elled.** make even or horizontal; make equal in position or status; direct (a gun, accusation, etc.) at; raze to the ground. —*n.* horizontal line or surface; device for showing or testing if something is horizontal; position on a scale; standard or grade; flat area of land. —**on the level** *Informal* honest or trustworthy. —**level crossing** point where a railway line and road cross. —**level-headed** *adj.* not apt to be carried away by emotion.

lever *n.* rigid bar pivoted about a fulcrum to transfer a force with mechanical advantage; bar used to move a heavy object or to open something; handle pressed, pulled, etc. to operate machinery; means of exerting pressure to achieve an aim. —*v.* prise or move with a lever. —**leverage** *n.* action or power of a lever; influence or strategic advantage.

leveret [**lev**-ver-it] *n.* young hare.

THESAURUS

lesser inferior, lower, minor, secondary, slighter, subordinate

lesson 1. class, coaching, instruction, period, schooling, teaching, tutoring 2. deterrent, example, exemplar, message, model, moral, precept

let *v.* 1. allow, authorize, give leave, grant, permit, sanction, tolerate, warrant 2. hire, lease, rent

let down disappoint, fail, leave stranded

lethal baleful, deadly, destructive, devastating, fatal, mortal, murderous, pernicious, virulent

lethargic apathetic, comatose, drowsy, dull, heavy, inactive, inert, languid, lazy, listless, sleepy, slothful, slow, sluggish, somnolent, torpid

lethargy apathy, inaction, inertia, languor, lassitude, listlessness, sloth, stupor, torpidity, torpor

let off 1. discharge, emit, explode, fire, give off, leak, release 2. absolve, discharge, excuse, exempt, exonerate, forgive, pardon, release, spare

let out 1. emit, produce 2. discharge, free, liberate, release

letter 1. character, sign, symbol 2. acknowledgment, answer, communication, dispatch, epistle, line, message, missive, note, reply

let-up abatement, break, cessation, interval, lull, pause, recess, respite

let up abate, decrease, diminish, moderate, slacken, stop, subside

level *adj.* 1. even, flat, horizontal, plain, plane, smooth, uniform 2. balanced, comparable, equivalent, even, flush, in line, on a line, on a par, proportionate ~*v.* 3. flatten, plane, smooth 4. bulldoze, demolish, destroy, flatten, raze, smooth, wreck ~*n.* 5. altitude, elevation, height 6. bed, floor, layer, storey, stratum

level-headed balanced, calm, collected, composed, cool, dependable, reasonable, sane, sensible, steady

lever 1. *n.* bar, crowbar, handle 2. *v.* force, move, prise, purchase, raise

DICTIONARY

leviathan [lev-**vie**-ath-an] *n.* sea monster; anything huge or formidable.

Levis *pl. n.* ® denim jeans.

levitation *n.* raising of a solid body into the air supernaturally. —**levitate** *v.* rise or cause to rise into the air.

levity *n., pl.* **-ties.** inclination to make a joke of serious matters.

levy [lev-vee] *v.* **levying, levied.** impose and collect (a tax); raise (troops). —*n., pl.* **levies.** imposition or collection of taxes; enrolling of troops; amount or number levied.

lewd *adj.* lustful or indecent. —**lewdly** *adv.* —**lewdness** *n.*

lexicon *n.* dictionary; vocabulary of a language. —**lexical** *adj.* relating to the vocabulary of a language. —**lexicographer** *n.* writer of dictionaries. —**lexicography** *n.*

liable *adj.* legally obliged or responsible; given to or at risk from a condition. —**liability** *n.* state of being liable; financial obligation; hindrance or disadvantage.

liaise *v.* establish and maintain communication (with). —**liaison** *n.* communication and contact between groups; secret or adulterous relationship.

liana *n.* climbing plant in tropical forests.

liar *n.* person who tells lies.

lib *n. Informal* short for LIBERATION.

libation [lie-**bay**-shun] *n.* drink poured as an offering to the gods.

libel *n.* published statement falsely damaging a person's reputation. —*v.* **-belling, -belled.** defame falsely. —**libellous** *adj.* defamatory.

liberal *adj.* (also L-) of a political party favouring progress and reform; generous in behaviour or temperament; tolerant; abundant; (of education) designed to develop general cultural interests. —*n.* person who has liberal ideas or opinions. —**liberally** *adv.* —**liberalism** *n.* belief in democratic reforms and individual freedom. —**liberality** *n.* generosity. —**liberalize** *v.* make (laws, a country, etc.) less restrictive. —**liberalization** *n.*

liberate *v.* set free. —**liberation** *n.* —**liberator** *n.*

libertarian *n.* believer in freedom of thought and action. —*adj.* having such a belief.

libertine [lib-er-teen] *n.* morally dissolute person.

liberty *n., pl.* **-ties.** freedom; act or comment regarded as forward or socially unacceptable.

THESAURUS

levity facetiousness, flightiness, frivolity, giddiness, silliness, skittishness, triviality

levy 1. *v.* charge, collect, demand, exact, gather, impose, tax 2. *n.* assessment, collection, exaction, gathering, imposition

lewd bawdy, blue, dirty, impure, indecent, libidinous, licentious, loose, obscene, pornographic, salacious, smutty, unchaste, vile, vulgar, wanton

lewdness crudity, depravity, impurity, indecency, lechery, licentiousness, obscenity, profligacy, smut, unchastity, vulgarity

liability 1. accountability, duty, obligation, onus, responsibility 2. arrear, debit, debt, obligation 3. burden, disadvantage, drag, drawback, encumbrance, handicap, hindrance, impediment, millstone, nuisance

liable 1. accountable, answerable, bound, responsible 2. exposed, open, subject, susceptible, vulnerable

liaison 1. communication, connection, contact, go-between, hook-up, interchange 2. affair, amour, intrigue, romance

liar fibber, perjurer, prevaricator

libel 1. *n.* aspersion, calumny, defamation, slander, smear 2. *v.* blacken, calumniate, defame, malign, revile, slander, slur, smear, traduce, vilify

libellous aspersive, defamatory, derogatory, false, injurious, malicious, scurrilous, slanderous, traducing, untrue, vituperative

liberal 1. advanced, libertarian, progressive, radical, reformist 2. altruistic, bountiful, charitable, free-handed, generous, kind, open handed, unstinting 3. abundant, ample, bountiful, copious, handsome, lavish, munificent, plentiful, profuse, rich

liberality altruism, bounty, charity, generosity, kindness, largess, munificence, open-handedness, philanthropy

liberalize broaden, ease, expand, extend, loosen, moderate, relax, slacken, soften, stretch

liberate deliver, discharge, emancipate, free, redeem, release, rescue, set free

liberation deliverance, emancipation, freedom, release

liberator deliverer, rescuer, saviour

libertine debauchee, lecher, rake, reprobate, roué, seducer, womanizer

liberty 1. *n.* autonomy, emancipation, freedom, immunity, independence, release, self-determination, sovereignty 2. carte blanche, dispensation, franchise, freedom, leave, licence, permission, privilege, right, sanction

DICTIONARY

—**at liberty** free; having the right. —**take liberties** be presumptuous.

libido [lib-ee-doe] *n., pl.* **-dos.** life force; emotional drive, esp. of sexual origin. —**libidinous** *adj.* lustful.

library *n., pl.* **-braries.** room or building where books are kept; collection of books, records, etc. for consultation or borrowing. —**librarian** *n.* keeper of or worker in a library. —**librarianship** *n.*

libretto *n., pl.* **-tos, -ti.** words of an opera. —**librettist** *n.*

Librium *n.* ® drug used as a tranquillizer.

lice *n.* a plural of LOUSE.

licence *n.* document giving official permission to do something; formal permission; excessive liberty; disregard of conventions for effect, e.g. *poetic licence.* —**license** *v.* grant a licence to. —**licensed** *adj.* —**licensee** *n.* holder of a licence, esp. to sell alcohol.

licentiate *n.* person licensed as competent to practise a profession.

licentious *adj.* sexually immoral, dissolute. —**licentiously** *adv.*

lichen *n.* small flowerless plant forming a crust on rocks, trees, etc.

lichgate, lychgate *n.* roofed gate to a churchyard.

licit *n.* lawful, permitted.

lick *v.* pass the tongue over; touch lightly or flicker round; *Slang* defeat. —*n.* licking; small amount (of paint etc.); *Informal* fast pace.

licorice *n.* same as LIQUORICE.

lid *n.* movable cover; short for EYELID.

lido [lee-doe] *n., pl.* **-dos.** pleasure centre with swimming and water sports.

lie¹ *v.* **lying, lied.** make a deliberately false statement. —*n.* deliberate falsehood. —**white lie** untruth said without evil intent.

lie² *v.* **lying, lay, lain.** place oneself or be in a horizontal position; be situated; be or remain in a certain state or position; exist or be found. —*n.* way something lies. —**lie-down** *n.* rest. —**lie in** *v.* remain in bed late into the morning. —**lie-in** *n.* long stay in bed in the morning.

lied [leed] *n., pl.* **lieder.** *Music* setting for voice and piano of a romantic poem.

lief *adv. Obs.* gladly, willingly.

liege [leej] *n.* lord; vassal or subject. —*adj.* bound to give or receive feudal service; faithful.

lien *n.* right to hold another's property until a debt is paid.

lieu [lyew] *n.* —**in lieu of** instead of.

lieutenant [lef-ten-ant] *n.* junior officer in the army or navy; main assistant.

life *n., pl.* **lives.** state of living beings, characterized by growth, reproduction, and response to stimuli; period between birth and death or between birth and the present time; amount of time something is active or functions; biography; way of living; liveliness or high spirits; living beings collectively. —**lifeless** *adj.* dead; inert; dull. —**lifelike** *adj.* —**lifelong** *adj.* lasting all of a person's life. —**life belt, jacket** buoyant device to keep afloat a person in danger of drowning. —**life cycle** series of changes undergone by each generation of an animal or plant. —**lifeline** *n.* means of contact or support; rope used in rescuing a person in danger. —**life science** any science concerned with living organisms, such as biology, botany, or zoology. —**lifestyle** *n.* particular attitudes, habits, etc. —**life-support** *adj.* (of equipment or treatment) necessary to keep a person alive. —**lifetime** *n.* length of time a person is alive.

THESAURUS

licence *n.* 1. authority, carte blanche, certificate, charter, dispensation, entitlement, exemption, immunity, leave, liberty, permission, permit, privilege, right, warrant 2. abandon, anarchy, disorder, excess, indulgence, lawlessness, laxity, unruliness

license *v.* accredit, allow, authorize, certify, commission, empower, permit, sanction, warrant

licentious abandoned, debauched, disorderly, dissolute, immoral, impure, lascivious, lax, lewd, profligate, sensual, uncontrolled, unruly, wanton

lick brush, lap, taste, tongue, touch, wash

lie¹ 1. *v.* equivocate, fabricate, falsify, fib, invent, misrepresent, perjure, prevaricate 2. *n.* deceit, fabrication, falsehood, fib, fiction, invention, mendacity, prevarication, untruth

lie² *v.* 1. be prone, be recumbent, be supine, couch, loll, lounge, recline, repose, rest, sprawl, stretch out 2. be interred, be located, belong, be placed, be situated, exist, extend, remain

life 1. being, breath, entity, growth, vitality 2. being, career, course, duration, existence, span, time 3. human, individual, mortal, person, soul 4. autobiography, biography, career, confessions, history, memoirs, story 5. behaviour, conduct 6. activity, brio, energy, go (*Inf.*), high spirits, liveliness, sparkle, spirit, verve, vigour, vitality, vivacity, zest

lifeless 1. cold, dead, deceased, defunct, extinct,

DICTIONARY

lift v. move upwards in position, status, volume, etc.; revoke or cancel; take (plants) out of the ground for harvesting; disappear; make or become more cheerful. —n. lifting; cage raised and lowered in a vertical shaft to transport people or goods; ride in a car etc. as a passenger; *Informal* feeling of cheerfulness. —**liftoff** n. moment a rocket leaves the ground.

ligament n. band of tissue joining bones.

ligature n. thread for tying, esp. as used in surgery.

light[1] n. electromagnetic radiation by which things are visible; source of this, lamp; anything that lets in light, such as a window; mental vision; light part of a photograph etc.; means of setting fire to; understanding. —pl. traffic lights. —adj. bright; (of a colour) pale. —v. **lighting, lighted** or **lit**. ignite; illuminate or cause to illuminate. —**lighten** v. make less dark. —**lighting** n. apparatus for supplying artificial light; use of artificial light in theatres, films, etc. —**lighthouse** n. tower with a light to guide ships. —**light year** *Astronomy* distance light travels in one year, about six million million miles.

light[2] adj. not heavy, weighing relatively little; relatively low in strength, amount, density, etc.; not serious or profound; not clumsy; easily digested; carrying light arms or equipment; (of industry) producing small goods, using light machinery. —adv. with little equipment or luggage. —v. **lighting, lighted** or **lit**. (esp. of birds) settle after flight; come (upon) by chance. —**lightly** adv. —**lightness** n. —**lighten** v. make less heavy or burdensome; make more cheerful or lively. —**light-fingered** adj. liable to steal. —**light-headed** adj. feeling faint, dizzy; frivolous. —**light-hearted** adj. carefree. —**lightweight** n., adj. (person) of little importance. —n. boxer weighing up to 135lb (professional) or 60kg (amateur).

lighter[1] n. device for lighting cigarettes etc.

lighter[2] n. flat-bottomed boat for unloading ships.

lightning n. visible discharge of electricity in the atmosphere. —adj. fast and sudden.

lights pl. n. lungs of animals as animal food.

ligneous adj. of or like wood.

lignite [lig-nite] n. woody textured rock used as fuel.

like[1] adj. resembling; similar; characteristic of. —prep. in the manner of; such as. —adv. in the manner of. —pron. similar thing. —**liken** v. compare. —**likeness** n. resemblance; portrait. —**likewise** adv. in a similar manner.

like[2] v. find enjoyable; be fond of; prefer, choose, or wish. —**lik- (e)able** adj. —**liking** n. fondness; preference.

THESAURUS

inanimate, inert 2. comatose, inert, insensate, insensible

lifelike authentic, exact, faithful, natural, real, realistic, vivid

lifelong constant, enduring, lasting, long-lasting, long-standing, perennial, permanent, persistent

lift v. 1. elevate, hoist, pick up, raise, rear, upheave, uplift, upraise 2. annul, cancel, end, relax, remove, rescind, revoke, stop, terminate 3. ascend, be dispelled, climb, disappear, disperse, dissipate, mount, rise, vanish ~n. 4. car ride, drive, ride, run, transport 5. boost, encouragement, fillip, pick-me-up, reassurance, uplift

light[1] n. 1. blaze, brilliance, flash, glare, gleam, glint, glow, illumination, radiance, ray, shine, sparkle 2. beacon, bulb, candle, flare, lamp, lantern, star, taper, torch 3. flame, lighter, match ~adj. 4. aglow, bright, glowing, shining, sunny 5. blond, faded, fair, pale, pastel ~v. 6. fire, ignite, inflame, kindle 7. brighten, clarify, illuminate, irradiate, put on, switch on, turn on

light[2] adj. 1. airy, delicate, easy, flimsy, portable, slight 2. faint, gentle, indistinct, mild, moderate, slight, soft, weak 3. inconsiderable, minute, scanty, slight, small, thin, tiny, trifling, trivial 4. easy, effortless, manageable, moderate, simple, untaxing 5. agile, airy, graceful, lithe, nimble 6. entertaining, frivolous, funny, gay, humorous, pleasing, superficial, trifling, trivial, witty ~v. 7. alight, land, perch, settle

lighten[1] brighten, flash, gleam, illuminate, irradiate, make bright, shine

lighten[2] 1. ease, unload 2. alleviate, assuage, ease, lessen, mitigate, reduce, relieve

light-headed fickle, flighty, flippant, foolish, frivolous, giddy, inane, shallow, silly, superficial, trifling

light-hearted blithe, bright, carefree, cheerful, gay, glad, gleeful, insouciant, jolly, merry, playful, sunny, untroubled

lightly airily, delicately, faintly, gently, gingerly, slightly, softly, timidly

lightweight adj. insignificant, paltry, petty, slight, trifling, trivial, unimportant, worthless

likable, likeable agreeable, amiable, attractive, charming, engaging, friendly, genial, nice, pleasant, pleasing, sympathetic, winning, winsome

like[1] adj. akin, alike, allied, analogous, corre-

DICTIONARY

likely *adj.* probable; tending or inclined; hopeful; promising. —*adv.* probably. —**not likely** *Informal* definitely not. —**likelihood** *n.* probability.

lilac *n.* shrub bearing pale mauve or white flowers. —*adj.* light-purple.

Lilliputian [lil-lip-**pew**-shun] *adj.* tiny.

Lilo *n., pl.* -**los.** ® inflatable rubber mattress.

lilt *n.* pleasing musical quality in speaking; jaunty rhythm; graceful rhythmic motion. —**lilting** *adj.*

lily *n., pl.* **lilies.** plant which grows from a bulb and has large, often white, flowers.

limb *n.* arm or leg; wing; main branch of a tree.

limber *adj.* pliant or supple. —**limber up** *v.* loosen stiff muscles by exercising.

limbo[1] *n., pl.* -**bos.** supposed region intermediate between Heaven and Hell for the unbaptized; unknown intermediate place or state.

limbo[2] *n., pl.* -**bos.** West Indian dance in which dancers lean backwards to pass under a bar.

lime[1] *n.* calcium compound used as a fertilizer or in making cement. —*v.* treat (land) with lime. —**limelight** *n.* glare of publicity. —**limestone** *n.* sedimentary rock used in building.

lime[2] *n.* small green citrus fruit. —**lime-green** *adj.* greenish-yellow.

lime[3] *n.* linden tree.

limerick [**lim**-mer-ik] *n.* nonsensical humorous verse of five lines.

limey *n. US slang* British person.

limit *n.* ultimate extent, degree, or amount of something; boundary or edge. —*v.* -**iting,** -**ited.** restrict or confine. —**limitation** *n.* —**limitless**

adj. —**limited company** company whose shareholders' liability is restricted.

limousine *n.* large luxurious car.

limp[1] *adj.* without firmness or stiffness. —**limply** *adv.*

limp[2] *v.* walk lamely. —*n.* limping gait.

limpet *n.* shellfish which sticks tightly to rocks.

limpid *adj.* clear or transparent; easy to understand. —**limpidity** *n.*

linchpin *n.* pin to hold a wheel on its axle; essential person or thing.

linctus *n., pl.* -**tuses.** syrupy cough medicine.

linden *n.* deciduous tree with heart-shaped leaves and fragrant flowers, the lime.

line *n.* long narrow mark; continuous length without breadth; row of words; queue of people; boundary or limit; mark on a sports ground showing divisions of a pitch or track; string or wire for a particular use; telephone connection; wire or cable for transmitting electricity; shipping company; railway track; class of goods; prescribed way of thinking; field of interest or activity; ancestors collectively. —*pl.* words of a theatrical part; school punishment of writing out a sentence a specified number of times; protected boundary of an area occupied by an army. —*v.* mark with lines; bring into line; be or form a border or edge; give a lining to; cover the inside of. —**in line for** candidate for. —**in line with** in accordance with. —**line-up** *n.* people or things assembled for a particular purpose.

THESAURUS

sponding, identical, relating, resembling, same, similar

like[2] *v.* 1. delight in, enjoy, love, relish, revel in 2. admire, appreciate, approve, cherish, esteem, prize

likelihood chance, liability, likeliness, possibility, probability, prospect

likely 1. *adj.* anticipated, apt, disposed, expected, inclined, liable, possible, probable, prone, tending 2. *adv.* doubtlessly, no doubt, presumably, probably

liken compare, match, parallel, relate

likeness 1. affinity, resemblance, similarity 2. copy, depiction, effigy, facsimile, image, model, picture, portrait, replica, study

liking affection, appreciation, attraction, bent, bias, desire, fondness, love, penchant, preference, stomach, taste, tendency, weakness

limb appendage, arm, extension, extremity, leg, member, part, wing

limelight attention, fame, prominence, publicity, recognition, stardom

limit *n.* 1. bound, deadline, end, termination, ultimate, utmost 2. *Often plural* border, boundary, edge, end, extent, frontier, perimeter, periphery ~*v.* 3. bound, check, confine, curb, fix, hinder, ration, restrain, restrict, specify

limitation block, check, condition, constraint, control, curb, drawback, impediment, qualification, restraint, restriction, snag

limited bounded, checked, confined, curbed, defined, finite, fixed, hampered, restricted

limitless boundless, countless, endless, immense, infinite, numberless, unbounded, undefined, unending, untold, vast

limp[1] *adj.* drooping, flabby, flaccid, floppy, lax, loose, relaxed, slack, soft

limp[2] *v.* falter, hobble, hop, shamble, shuffle

line *n.* 1. band, bar, channel, dash, groove, mark, rule, score, scratch, streak, stripe, stroke 2.

DICTIONARY

lineage [**lin**-ee-ij] *n.* descent from or descendants of an ancestor. —**lineal** *adj.* in direct line of descent.

lineament *n.* facial feature.

linear [**lin**-ee-er] *adj.* of or in lines.

linen *n.* cloth or thread made from flax; sheets, tablecloths, etc.

liner *n.* large passenger ship; something used as a lining.

linesman *n.* in some sports, an official who helps the referee or umpire; person who maintains railway, electricity, or telephone lines.

ling[1] *n.* slender food fish.

ling[2] *n.* heather.

linger *v.* delay or prolong departure; continue in a weakened state for a long time before dying or disappearing; spend a long time doing something. —**lingering** *adj.*

lingerie [**lan**-zher-ee] *n.* women's underwear or nightwear.

lingo *n., pl.* **-goes.** *Informal* foreign or unfamiliar language or jargon.

lingua franca *n., pl.* **lingua francas, linguae francae.** language used for communication between people of different mother tongues.

lingual *adj.* of the tongue; made by the tongue.

linguist *n.* person skilled in foreign languages; person who studies linguistics. —**linguistic** *adj.* of languages. —**linguistics** *pl. n.* scientific study of language.

liniment *n.* medicated liquid rubbed on the skin to relieve pain or stiffness.

lining *n.* layer of cloth attached to the inside of a garment etc.; inner covering of anything.

link *n.* any of the rings forming a chain; person or thing forming a connection. —*v.* connect with or as if with links; connect by association. —**link-age** *n.* —**link-up** *n.* joining together of two systems or groups.

links *pl. n.* golf course, esp. one by the sea.

linnet *n.* songbird of the finch family.

lino *n.* short for LINOLEUM.

linocut *n.* design cut in relief on a block of linoleum; print from such a block.

linoleum *n.* floor covering of hessian or jute with a smooth decorative coating of powdered cork.

Linotype *n.* ® typesetting machine which casts lines of words in one piece.

linseed *n.* seed of the flax plant.

lint *n.* soft material for dressing a wound.

lintel *n.* horizontal beam at the top of a door or window.

lion *n.* large animal of the cat family, the male of which has a shaggy mane. —**lioness** *n. fem.* —**the lion's share** the biggest part. —**lionize** *v.* treat as a celebrity. —**lion-hearted** *adj.* brave.

lip *n.* either of the fleshy edges of the mouth; rim of a jug etc.; *Slang* impudence. —**lip-reading** *n.* method of understanding speech by interpreting lip movements. —**lip service** insincere tribute or respect. —**lipstick** *n.* cosmetic in stick form, for colouring the lips.

liquefy *v.* **-fying, -fied.** make or become liquid. —**liquefaction** *n.*

liqueur [lik-**cure**] *n.* flavoured and sweetened alcoholic spirit.

liquid *n.* substance in a physical state which can change shape but not size. —*adj.* of or being a liquid; flowing smoothly; (of assets) in the form of money or easily converted into money. —**liquidize** *v.* make or become liquid. —**liquidizer** *n.* kitchen appliance that liquidizes food. —**liquidity** *n.* state of being able to meet financial obligations.

THESAURUS

crease, furrow, mark, wrinkle 3. border, boundary, demarcation, edge, frontier, limit, mark 4. contour, figure, profile, silhouette 5. cable, cord, filament, rope, strand, string, thread, wire 6. approach, avenue, belief, course, ideology, method, policy, position, practice, procedure, scheme, system 7. activity, area, business, calling, department, employment, field, forte, interest, job, occupation, profession, pursuit, trade, vocation 8. ancestry, breed, family, race, stock, strain, succession ~*v.* 9. crease, cut, draw, furrow, inscribe, mark, rule, score, trace 10. border, bound, edge, fringe, rank, rim, skirt, verge

lines part, script, words

line-up arrangement, array, row, selection, team

linger 1. loiter, remain, stay, stop, tarry, wait 2. abide, continue, endure, persist, remain, stay

lingering dragging, persistent, remaining, slow

link *n.* 1. component, element, member, part, piece 2. association, attachment, bond, connection, joint, knot, tie, tie-up, vinculum ~*v.* 3. attach, bind, connect, couple, fasten, join, tie, unite, yoke 4. associate, bracket, connect, identify

lip 1. brim, brink, edge, margin, rim 2. *Sl.* effrontery, insolence, rudeness

liquid *n.* 1. fluid, juice, liquor ~*adj.* 2. fluid, melted, molten, running, runny, thawed, wet 3. dulcet, fluent, mellifluent, mellifluous, melting, smooth, soft, sweet 4. *Of assets* convertible, negotiable

DICTIONARY

liquidate *v.* pay (a debt); dissolve a company and share its assets between creditors; wipe out or kill. —**liquidation** *n.* —**liquidator** *n.* official appointed to liquidate a business.

liquor *n.* alcoholic drink, esp. spirits; liquid in which food has been cooked.

liquorice [lik-ker-iss] *n.* black substance used in medicine and as a sweet.

lira *n., pl.* **-re, -ras.** monetary unit of Italy and Turkey.

lisle [rhymes with **mile**] *n.* strong fine cotton thread or fabric.

lisp *n.* speech defect in which 's' and 'z' are pronounced 'th'. —*v.* speak or utter with a lisp.

lissom(e) *adj.* supple, agile.

list[1] *n.* item-by-item record of names or things, usu. written one below another. —*v.* make a list of; include in a list.

list[2] *v.* (of a ship) lean to one side. —*n.* leaning to one side.

listen *v.* concentrate on hearing something; heed or pay attention to. —**listener** *n.* —**listen in** *v.* listen secretly, eavesdrop.

listeriosis *n.* dangerous form of food poisoning.

listless *adj.* lacking interest or energy. —**listlessly** *adv.*

lit *v.* past of LIGHT[1], LIGHT[2].

litany *n., pl.* **-nies.** prayer with responses from the congregation; any tedious recital.

literacy *n.* ability to read and write.

literal *adj.* according to the explicit meaning of a word or text, not figurative; (of a translation) word for word; actual, true. —**literally** *adv.*

literary *adj.* of or learned in literature; (of a word) formal, not colloquial. —**literariness** *n.*

literate *adj.* able to read and write; educated. —**literati** *pl. n.* literary people.

literature *n.* written works such as novels, plays, and poetry; books and writings of a country, period, or subject.

lithe *adj.* flexible or supple, pliant.

lithium *n.* chemical element, the lightest known metal.

litho *n., pl.* **-thos.** short for LITHOGRAPH. —*adj.* short for LITHOGRAPHIC.

lithography [lith-og-ra-fee] *n.* method of printing from a metal or stone surface in which the printing areas are made receptive to ink. —**lithograph** *n.* print made by lithography. —*v.* reproduce by lithography. —**lithographer** *n.* —**lithographic** *adj.*

litigate *v.* bring or contest a law suit; engage in legal action. —**litigant** *n.* person involved in a lawsuit. —**litigation** *n.* lawsuit. —**litigious** [lit-ij-uss] *adj.* frequently going to law.

litmus *n.* blue dye turned red by acids and restored to blue by alkali. —**litmus paper** paper impregnated with litmus.

litotes *n.* ironical understatement for rhetorical effect.

litre *n.* unit of liquid measure equal to 1.76 pints.

litter *n.* untidy rubbish dropped in public places; group of young animals produced at one birth; straw etc. as bedding for an animal; dry material

THESAURUS

liquidate 1. clear, discharge, pay, settle, square 2. abolish, annul, cancel, dissolve, terminate 3. annihilate, destroy, dispatch, eliminate, exterminate, kill, murder, remove, silence

liquor alcohol, drink, grog, intoxicant, spirits, strong drink

list[1] 1. *n.* catalogue, directory, file, index, inventory, invoice, register, roll, schedule, tally 2. *v.* bill, book, catalogue, enrol, enter, enumerate, file, index, itemize, note, record, register, schedule

list[2] 1. *v.* cant, heel over, incline, lean, tilt, tip 2. *n.* cant, tilt

listen 1. attend, hark, hear 2. concentrate, heed, mind, obey, observe

listless apathetic, heavy, indolent, inert, languid, lethargic, limp, sluggish, supine, torpid

literacy articulacy, education, learning, proficiency, scholarship

literal 1. close, exact, faithful, strict, verbatim 2. actual, genuine, plain, real, simple, true

literally actually, exactly, faithfully, plainly, precisely, really, simply, strictly, truly, verbatim

literary bookish, erudite, formal, learned, literate, well-read

literate cultivated, educated, erudite, informed, learned, lettered, scholarly

literature letters, lore, writings

lithe flexible, lissom, pliable, pliant, supple

litigant claimant, contestant, disputant, party, plaintiff

litigate go to law, prosecute, sue

litigation action, case, contending, disputing, lawsuit, process

litter *n.* 1. debris, fragments, muck, refuse, rubbish, shreds 2. brood, family, offspring, progeny, young 3. bedding, couch ~*v.* 4. clutter, derange, disorder, scatter, strew

DICTIONARY

to absorb a cat's excrement. —v. strew with litter; scatter or be scattered about untidily; give birth to young.

little *adj.* small or smaller than average; young. —*det.* small amount, extent, or duration of. —*adv.* not a lot; hardly; not much or often.

littoral *adj.* of or by the seashore. —*n.* coastal district.

liturgy *n., pl.* **-gies.** prescribed form of public worship. —**liturgical** *adj.*

live[1] *v.* be alive; remain in life or existence; exist in a specified way, e.g. *we live well;* reside; continue or last; subsist; enjoy life to the full. —**live down** *v.* wait till people forget a past mistake or misdeed. —**live-in** *adj.* sharing a house with one's sexual partner. —**live together** *v.* (of an unmarried couple) share a house and have a sexual relationship. —**live up to** *v.* meet (expectations). —**live with** *v.* tolerate.

live[2] *adj.* living, alive; current; glowing or burning; capable of exploding; (of a wire, circuit, etc.) carrying an electric current; (of a broadcast) transmitted during the actual performance. —**lively** *adj.* full of life or vigour; animated; vivid. —**liveliness** *n.* —**liven up** *v.* make (more) lively.

livelong [liv-long] *adj. Lit.* long.

liver *n.* organ secreting bile; animal liver as food. —**liverish** *adj.* unwell; touchy or irritable.

livery *n., pl.* **-eries.** distinctive dress, esp. of a servant or servants. —**liveried** *adj.* —**livery sta-**ble stable where horses are kept at a charge or hired out.

livestock *n.* farm animals.

livid *adj. Informal* angry or furious; bluish-grey.

living *adj.* possessing life, not dead or inanimate; currently in use or existing; of everyday life, e.g. *living conditions.* —*n.* condition of being alive; manner of life; financial means; church benefice. —**living-room** *n.* room in a house used for relaxation and entertainment.

lizard *n.* four-footed reptile with a long body and tail.

llama *n.* woolly animal of the camel family used as a beast of burden in S America.

LLB Bachelor of Laws.

loach *n.* carplike freshwater fish.

load *n.* burden or weight; amount carried; amount of electrical energy drawn from a source; source of worry. —*pl. Informal* lots. —*v.* put a load on or into; burden or oppress; cause to be biased; put ammunition into a weapon; put film into a camera. —**loaded** *adj.* (of a question) containing a hidden trap or implication; *Slang* wealthy; (of dice) dishonestly weighted.

loadstar, -stone *n.* same as LODESTAR, -STONE.

loaf[1] *n., pl.* **loaves.** shaped mass of baked bread; shaped mass of food; *Slang* common sense, e.g. *use your loaf.*

loaf[2] *v.* idle, loiter. —**loafer** *n.*

loam *n.* fertile soil.

THESAURUS

little *adj.* 1. diminutive, dwarf, elfin, infinitesimal, mini, miniature, minute, petite, pygmy, short, slender, small, tiny, wee 2. infant, junior, undeveloped, young ~*adv.* 3. barely, hardly 4. rarely, scarcely, seldom

live[1] *v.* 1. be, breathe, exist, have life 2. last, persist, prevail 3. abide, dwell, inhabit, lodge, occupy, reside, settle 4. endure, fare, feed, lead, pass, remain, subsist, survive

live[2] *adj.* 1. alive, animate, breathing, existent, living, vital 2. active, burning, current, hot, pressing, prevalent, topical, unsettled, vital

livelihood job, living, maintenance, means, occupation, subsistence, work

liveliness activity, boisterousness, briskness, dynamism, energy, gaiety, smartness, spirit, vitality, vivacity

lively 1. active, agile, alert, brisk, chirpy, energetic, keen, nimble, perky, quick, sprightly, spry, vigorous 2. blithe, cheerful, frisky, gay, merry, spirited, vivacious 3. bright, colourful, exciting, forceful, invigorating, racy, refreshing, stimulating, vivid

liverish 1. bilious, queasy 2. crusty, disagreeable, grumpy, ill-humoured, irritable, peevish, snappy

livery attire, clothing, costume, dress, garb, regalia, suit, uniform

livid 1. ashen, bloodless, greyish, leaden, pale, pallid, pasty, wan, waxen 2. enraged, fuming, furious, incensed, indignant

living *adj.* 1. active, alive, breathing, existing, strong, vigorous, vital ~*n.* 2. being, existence, life, subsistence 3. job, livelihood, maintenance, occupation, subsistence, sustenance, work

load *n.* 1. bale, cargo, freight, lading, shipment 2. burden, incubus, millstone, onus, oppression, pressure, trouble, weight, worry ~*v.* 3. cram, fill, freight, heap, lade, pack, pile, stack, stuff 4. burden, hamper, oppress, trouble, worry 5. charge, prime

loaded 1. biased, distorted, weighted 2. charged, primed 3. *Sl.* affluent, moneyed, rich, wealthy, well off, well-to-do

loaf block, cake, cube, lump, slab

loan *n.* advance, credit, mortgage

DICTIONARY

loan *n.* money borrowed at interest; lending; thing lent. —*v.* lend, grant a loan of.

lo(a)th [rhymes with **both**] *adj.* unwilling or reluctant (to).

loathe *v.* hate, be disgusted by. —**loathing** *n.* —**loathsome** *adj.*

lob *Sport* —*n.* ball struck or thrown high in the air. —*v.* **lobbing, lobbed.** strike or throw (a ball) high in the air.

lobby *n., pl.* **-bies.** corridor into which rooms open; hall in a legislative building to which the public has access; group which tries to influence legislators. —*v.* **-bying, -bied.** try to influence (legislators) in the formulation of policy. —**lobbyist** *n.*

lobe *n.* rounded projection; soft hanging part of the ear; subdivision of a body organ. —**lobed** *adj.* —**lobar** [loh-ber] *adj.* of or affecting a lobe.

lobelia *n.* garden plant with blue, red, or white lobed flowers.

lobotomy *n., pl.* **-mies.** surgical incision into a lobe of the brain.

lobster *n.* shellfish with a long tail and claws, which turns red when boiled. —**lobster pot** basket-like trap for catching lobsters.

local *adj.* of or existing in a particular place; confined to a particular place. —*n.* person belonging to a particular district; *Informal* (nearby) pub. —**locally** *adv.* —**locality** *n.* neighbourhood or area. —**localize** *v.* restrict to a definite place. —**locale** [loh-**kahl**] *n.* scene of an event. —**local anaesthetic** anaesthetic which produces insensibility in one part of the body. —**local authority** governing body of a county or district. —**local government** government of towns, counties, and districts by locally elected political bodies.

locate *v.* discover the whereabouts of; situate or place. —**location** *n.* site or position; site of a film production away from the studio; *S Afr.* Black African or coloured township.

loch *n. Scot.* lake; long narrow bay.

lock[1] *n.* appliance for fastening a door, case, etc.; section of a canal shut off by gates between which the water level can be altered to aid boats moving from one level to another; extent to which a vehicle's front wheels will turn; interlocking of parts; mechanism for firing a gun; wrestling hold. —*v.* fasten or become fastened securely; become or cause to become immovable; become or cause to become fixed or united; embrace closely. —**lockout** *n.* exclusion of workers by an employer as a means of coercion. —**locksmith** *n.* person who makes and mends locks. —**lockup** *n.* prison; garage or storage place away from the main premises.

lock[2] *n.* tress of hair.

locker *n.* small cupboard with a lock.

locket *n.* small hinged pendant for a portrait etc.

lockjaw *n.* tetanus.

locomotive *n.* self-propelled engine for pulling trains. —*adj.* of locomotion. —**locomotion** *n.* action or power of moving.

locum *n.* temporary stand-in for a doctor or clergyman.

locus *n., pl.* **loci.** area or place where something happens; *Maths* set of points or lines satisfying one or more specified conditions.

locust *n.* destructive African insect that flies in swarms and eats crops.

locution *n.* word or phrase.

lode *n.* vein of ore. —**lodestar** *n.* Pole Star. —**lodestone** *n.* magnetic iron ore.

lodge *n.* house or cabin used occasionally by hunters, skiers, etc.; gatekeeper's house; porters' room in a university or college; local branch of some societies. —*v.* live in another's house at a fixed charge; stick or become stuck (in a place); make (a complaint etc.) formally; deposit for safety or storage. —**lodger** *n.* —**lodgings** *pl. n.* rented room or rooms in another person's house.

THESAURUS

loathing abhorrence, antipathy, aversion, disgust, hatred, horror, odium, repugnance, repulsion, revulsion

loathsome abhorrent, disgusting, execrable, hateful, horrible, nasty, odious, offensive, repugnant, revolting, vile

lobby *n.* 1. corridor, foyer, hall, hallway, passage, porch, vestibule 2. pressure group ~*v.* 3. campaign for, influence, persuade, pressure, promote

local *adj.* 1. community, district, parish, region~al 2. confined, limited, narrow, parish, paro~

chial, provincial, restricted ~*n.* 3. inhabitant, native, resident

locality area, district, region, vicinity

locate detect, discover, find, pinpoint, unearth

location bearings, locale, place, point, site, situation, spot, venue

lock 1. *n.* bolt, clasp, padlock 2. *v.* bolt, close, fasten, latch, seal, secure, shut

lockup cell, gaol, jail

lodge *n.* 1. cabin, chalet, cottage, gatehouse, house, hut, shelter 2. association, branch, club, group, society ~*v.* 3. accommodate, bil~

DICTIONARY

loft *n.* space between the top storey and roof of a building; gallery in a church etc. —*v. Sport* strike, throw, or kick (a ball) high into the air.

lofty *adj.* **loftier, loftiest.** of great height; exalted or noble; haughty. —**loftily** *adv.* haughtily. —**loftiness** *n.*

log[1] *n.* portion of a felled tree stripped of branches; detailed record of a journey of a ship, aircraft, etc. —*v.* **logging, logged.** record in a log; saw logs from a tree. —**logging** *n.* work of cutting and transporting logs. —**logbook** *n.* —**log in** *or* **out** *v.* gain entrance to *or* leave a computer system by keying in a special command.

log[2] *n.* short for LOGARITHM.

loganberry *n.* purplish-red fruit, a cross between a raspberry and a blackberry.

logarithm *n.* one of a series of arithmetical functions used to make certain calculations easier. —**logarithmic** *adj.*

loggerheads *pl. n.* —**at loggerheads** quarrelling, disputing.

loggia [**loj**-ya] *n.* covered gallery at the side of a building.

logic *n.* philosophy of reasoning; reasoned thought or argument. —**logical** *adj.* of logic; reasonable; capable of or using clear valid reasoning. —**logically** *adv.* —**logician** *n.*

logistics *pl. n.* detailed planning and organization of a large, esp. military, operation. —**logistical** *adj.*

logo [**loh**-go] *n., pl.* **-os.** company emblem or similar device.

loin *n.* part of the body between the ribs and the hips; cut of meat from this part of an animal. —*pl.* hips and inner thighs. —**loincloth** *n.* piece of cloth covering the loins only.

loiter *v.* stand or wait aimlessly or idly. —**loiterer** *n.*

loll *v.* lounge lazily; (esp. of the tongue) hang out.

lollipop *n.* boiled sweet on a small wooden stick. —**lollipop man, lady** *Informal* person holding a circular sign on a pole, who controls traffic so that children may cross the road safely.

lolly *n., pl.* **-ies.** *Informal* lollipop or ice lolly; *Slang* money.

lone *adj.* solitary. —**lonely** *adj.* sad because alone; unfrequented; resulting from being alone. —**loneliness** *n.* —**loner** *n. Informal* person who prefers to be alone. —**lonesome** *adj.* lonely.

long[1] *adj.* having length, esp. great length, in space or time. —*adv.* for a long time. —**longdistance** *adj.* going between places far apart. —**long-drawn-out** *adj.* lasting too long. —**long face** glum expression. —**longhand** *n.* ordinary writing, not shorthand or typing. —**long johns** *Informal* long underpants. —**long-life** *adj.* (of milk, batteries, etc.) lasting longer than the regular kind. —**long-lived** living or lasting for a long time. —**long-range** *adj.* (of weapons) designed to hit a distant target; into the future. —**long shot** competitor, undertaking, or bet with little chance of success. —**long-sighted** *adj.* able to see distant objects in focus but not nearby ones. —**long-standing** *adj.* existing for a long time. —**long-suffering** *adj.* enduring trouble or unhappiness without complaint. —**long-term** *adj.* lasting or effective for a long time. —**long wave** radio wave with a wavelength of over 1000 metres. —**long-winded** *adj.* speaking or writing at tedious length.

long[2] *v.* (foll. by *for*) have a strong desire for. —**longing** *n.* yearning. —**longingly** *adv.*

longevity [lon-**jev**-it-ee] *n.* long existence or life.

THESAURUS

let, board, entertain, harbour, put up, shelter, stay, stop 4. catch, imbed, implant, stick

lodger boarder, guest, paying guest, resident, tenant

lodging abode, accommodation, boarding, dwelling, habitation, residence, rooms, shelter

lofty 1. high, raised, soaring, tall, towering 2. distinguished, elevated, grand, illustrious, imposing, majestic, noble, stately, superior 3. condescending, haughty, lordly, patronizing, proud, supercilious

log *n.* 1. block, chunk, stump, trunk 2. account, chart, journal, listing, record, tally ~*v.* 3. book, chart, note, record, register, tally

loggerhead at loggerheads estranged, feuding, opposed, quarrelling

logic reason, sense, sound judgment

logical clear, cogent, coherent, consistent, rational, relevant, sound, valid

loiter dally, dawdle, delay, idle, lag, linger, loaf, stroll

lone isolated, one, only, separate, single, sole, unaccompanied

loneliness desolation, isolation, seclusion, solitude

lonely 1. abandoned, estranged, forlorn, forsaken, friendless, outcast 2. alone, apart, single, solitary, withdrawn 3. deserted, remote, secluded, solitary, uninhabited

long[1] *adj.* expanded, extended, lengthy, stretched

long[2] *v.* covet, crave, desire, hanker, hunger, itch, lust, pine, want, yearn

longing ambition, aspiration, coveting, craving, desire, hungering, itch, thirst, urge, wish

DICTIONARY

longitude *n.* distance east or west from a standard meridian. —**longitudinal** *adj.* of length or longitude; lengthwise.

longshoreman *n. US* docker.

loo *n. Informal* lavatory.

loofah *n.* dried pod of a gourd, used as a sponge.

look *v.* direct the eyes or attention (towards); seem; face in a particular direction; search (for); hope (for). —*n.* looking; search; (often *pl.*) appearance. —**look after** *v.* take care of. —**look-alike** *n.* person who is the double of another. —**look down on** *v.* treat as inferior or unimportant. —**look forward to** *v.* anticipate with pleasure. —**look on** *v.* be an onlooker; consider or regard. —**lookout** *n.* guard; place for watching; chances or prospect; *Informal* worry or concern. —**look up** *v.* discover or confirm by checking in a book; visit; improve. —**look up to** *v.* respect.

loom[1] *n.* machine for weaving cloth.

loom[2] *v.* appear dimly; seem ominously close; assume great importance.

loony *n., pl.* **loonies.** *Slang* foolish or insane person. —*adj.* **loonier, looniest.** foolish or insane. —**loony bin** *Slang* mental hospital.

loop *n.* rounded shape made by a curved line or rope crossing itself. —*v.* form a loop. —**loop the loop** fly or be flown in a complete vertical circle. —**loophole** *n.* means of evading a rule without breaking it.

loose *adj.* not tight, fastened, fixed, or tense; slack; vague; dissolute or promiscuous. —*v.* free; unfasten; slacken; let fly (an arrow, bullet, etc.). —**at a loose end** bored, with nothing to do. —**loosely** *adv.* —**looseness** *n.* —**loosen** *v.* make loose. —**loosen up** *v.* relax, stop worrying. —**loose-leaf** *adj.* allowing the addition or removal of pages.

loot *n., v.* plunder. —**looter** *n.* —**looting** *n.*

lop *v.* **lopping, lopped.** cut away twigs and branches; chop off.

lope *v.* run with long easy strides.

lopeared *adj.* having drooping ears.

lopsided *adj.* greater in height, weight, or size on one side.

loquacious *adj.* talkative. —**loquacity** *n.*

lord *n.* person with power over others, such as a monarch or master; male member of the nobility; *Hist.* feudal superior; (**L-**) God; title given to certain male officials and peers. —**House of Lords** unelected upper chamber of the British parliament. —**lord it over** act in a superior manner towards. —**the Lord's Prayer** prayer

---

THESAURUS

long-standing enduring, established, fixed, time-honoured

long-suffering easygoing, patient, resigned, stoical, tolerant

long-winded garrulous, lengthy, prolix, rambling, repetitious, tedious, verbose, wordy

look *v.* 1. consider, contemplate, examine, eye, gaze, glance, inspect, observe, peep, regard, scan, scrutinize, see, study, survey, view, watch 2. appear, display, evidence, exhibit, present, seem, show 3. forage, hunt, search, seek ~*n.* 4. gaze, glance, glimpse, inspection, observation, review, sight, survey, view 5. air, appearance, aspect, bearing, cast, complexion, demeanour, effect, expression, face, fashion, guise, manner

look after guard, mind, nurse, protect, tend, watch

look down on *or* **upon** despise, disdain, scorn, sneer, spurn

look forward to anticipate, await, expect

lookout 1. guard, vigil, watch 2. guard, sentinel, sentry 3. beacon, citadel, post, watchtower

look up 1. find, research 2. ameliorate, improve, progress

loom appear, bulk, emerge, hover, impend, menace, take shape, threaten

loop 1. *n.* bend, circle, coil, curl, curve, eyelet, kink, noose, ring, spiral, twirl, twist 2. *v.* bend, circle, coil, connect, curl, encircle, fold, join, knot, roll, turn, twist

loophole *Fig.* avoidance, escape, evasion, excuse, plea, pretext

loose *adj.* 1. floating, free, insecure, movable, released, unattached, unfastened, unsecured, untied, wobbly 2. baggy, easy, relaxed, slack, sloppy 3. diffuse, ill-defined, imprecise, inaccurate, indefinite, inexact, rambling, random, vague 4. abandoned, disreputable, dissipated, dissolute, fast, immoral, lewd, licentious, promiscuous, unchaste, wanton ~*v.* 5. detach, disengage, ease, free, release, slacken, unbind, undo, unfasten, unloose, untie

loosen 1. detach, separate, slacken, undo, unstick, untie 2. deliver, free, liberate, release

loot booty, goods, haul, plunder, prize, spoils

lopsided askew, awry, crooked, off balance, squint, tilting, unbalanced, uneven

lord 1. commander, governor, leader, master, potentate, prince, ruler, seigneur, sovereign, superior 2. earl, noble, nobleman, peer, viscount

lordly arrogant, despotic, dictatorial, disdainful, haughty, imperious, lofty, patronizing, proud, supercilious

DICTIONARY

taught by Christ to his disciples. —**lordly** *adj.* imperious, proud. —**Lordship** *n.* title of some male officials and peers.

lore *n.* body of traditions on a subject.

lorgnette [lor-**nyet**] *n.* pair of spectacles mounted on a long handle.

lorry *n., pl.* **-ries.** large vehicle for transporting loads by road.

lose *v.* **losing, lost.** come to be without, as by accident or carelessness; fail to keep or maintain; be deprived of; fail to get or make use of; have an income less than one's expenditure; fail to perceive or understand; be defeated in a competition etc.; be or become engrossed, e.g. *lost in thought;* go astray or allow to go astray; die or be destroyed; (of a clock etc.) run slow (by a specified amount). —**loser** *n.*

loss *n.* losing; that which is lost; damage resulting from losing. —**at a loss** confused or bewildered; not earning enough to cover costs. —**loss leader** item sold at a loss to attract customers.

lot *pron.* great number. —*n.* collection of people or things; large quantity; fate or destiny; item at auction; one of a set of objects drawn at random to make a selection or choice. —*pl. Informal* great numbers or quantities. —**a lot** *adv. Informal* a great deal.

loth *adj.* same as LOATH.

lotion *n.* medical or cosmetic liquid for use on the skin.

lottery *n., pl.* **-teries.** method of raising funds by selling tickets that win prizes by chance; gamble.

lotto *n.* game of chance like bingo.

lotus *n.* legendary plant whose fruit induces forgetfulness; Egyptian water lily.

loud *adj.* relatively great in volume; capable of making much noise; insistent and emphatic; unpleasantly patterned or colourful. —**loudly** *adv.* —**loudness** *n.* —**loudspeaker** *n.* instrument for converting electrical signals into sound.

lough *n. Irish* loch.

lounge *v.* sit, lie, or stand in a relaxed manner. —*n.* living room in a private house; area for waiting in an airport; more expensive bar in a pub. —**lounge suit** man's suit for daytime wear.

lour *v.* same as LOWER[2].

louse *n.* (*pl.* **lice**) wingless parasitic insect; (*pl.* **louses**) unpleasant person. —**lousy** *adj. Slang* mean or unpleasant; bad, inferior; unwell.

lout *n.* crude, oafish, or aggressive person. —**loutish** *adj.*

louvre [**loo**-ver] *n.* one of a set of parallel slats slanted to admit air but not rain. —**louvred** *adj.*

love *n.* warm affection; sexual passion; wholehearted liking for something; beloved person; *Tennis, squash, etc.* score of nothing. —*v.* have a great affection for; feel sexual passion for; enjoy (something) very much. —**fall in love** become in love. —**in love (with)** feeling a strong emotional (and sexual) attraction (for). —**make love (to)** have sexual intercourse (with). —**lov(e)able** *adj.* —**loveless** *adj.* —**lover** *n.* —**loving** *adj.* affection-

THESAURUS

lore beliefs, doctrine, folk-wisdom, teaching, wisdom

lose 1. displace, drop, forget, mislay, misplace, miss 2. capitulate, default, fail, forfeit, miss, yield 3. be defeated

loser also-ran, failure, underdog

loss 1. deprivation, failure, losing, misfortune, privation, waste 2. cost, damage, defeat, destruction, detriment, harm, hurt, injury, ruin

lost 1. disappeared, forfeited, mislaid, misplaced, missing, strayed, vanished, wayward 2. adrift, astray, at sea, disoriented, off-course 3. baffled, bewildered, confused, helpless, ignorant, mystified, perplexed, puzzled 4. absent, absorbed, distracted, dreamy, entranced, preoccupied, rapt, spellbound 5. bygone, dead, extinct, forgotten, gone, lapsed, obsolete, past 6. abandoned, corrupt, damned, depraved, fallen

lot 1. batch, collection, crowd, group, quantity, set 2. accident, chance, destiny, doom, fate, fortune, hazard, plight, portion 3. allowance, parcel, part, piece, portion, quota, ration,

share 4. **a lot** *or* **lots** abundance, a great deal, heap(s), numbers, piles, plenty, quantities, scores

lotion balm, cream, liniment, solution

lottery 1. draw, raffle, sweepstake 2. chance, gamble, hazard, risk

loud 1. blaring, blatant, deafening, ear-piercing, noisy, piercing, resounding, rowdy, sonorous, stentorian, strident, strong, thundering, tumultuous, turbulent, vehement 2. *Fig.* brassy, flamboyant, flashy, garish, gaudy, glaring, lurid, ostentatious, showy, tasteless, vulgar

loudly deafeningly, noisily, shrilly, vigorously

lounge *v.* laze, loaf, loiter, recline, relax, saunter, sprawl

lout bear, boor, churl, clod, dolt, gawk, lubber, oaf, yahoo

lovable amiable, attractive, charming, cuddly, delightful, enchanting, endearing, lovely, pleasing, sweet, winning

DICTIONARY

ate, tender. —**lovingly** *adv.* —**love affair** romantic or sexual relationship between two people who are not married to each other. —**lovebird** *n.* small parrot. —**love child** *Euphemistic* child of an unmarried couple. —**love life** person's romantic or sexual relationships. —**lovelorn** *adj.* forsaken by or pining for a lover. —**lovemaking** *n.*

low[1] *adj.* not tall, high, or elevated; of little or less than the usual amount, degree, quality, or cost; coarse or vulgar; dejected; ill; not loud; deep in pitch; (of a gear) providing a relatively low speed. —*n.* low position, level, or degree; area of low atmospheric pressure, depression. —*adv.* in or to a low position, level, or degree. —**lowly** *adj.* modest, humble. —**lowliness** *n.* —**lowbrow** *n., adj.* (person) with nonintellectual tastes and interests. —**Low Church** section of the Anglican Church stressing evangelical beliefs and practices. —**lowdown** *n. Informal* inside information. —**low-down** *adj. Informal* mean, shabby, or dishonest. —**low-key** *adj.* subdued, restrained, not intense. —**lowland** *n.* low-lying country. —*pl.* (**L-**) less mountainous parts of Scotland. —**low profile** position or attitude avoiding prominence or publicity. —**low-spirited** *adj.* depressed.

low[2] *n.* cry of cattle, moo. —*v.* moo.

lower[1] *v.* cause or allow to move down; diminish or degrade; lessen. —*adj.* below one or more other things; smaller or reduced in amount or value. —**lower case** small, as distinct from capital, letters.

lower[2], **lour** *v.* (of the sky or weather) look gloomy or threatening. —**lowering** *adj.*

loyal *adj.* faithful to one's friends, country, or government. —**loyally** *adv.* —**loyalty** *n.* —**loyalist** *n.*

lozenge *n.* medicated tablet held in the mouth until it dissolves; four-sided diamond-shaped figure.

LP *n.* record playing approximately 20-25 minutes each side.

L-plate *n.* sign on a car being driven by a learner driver.

LSD lysergic acid diethylamide, a hallucinogenic drug.

Lt Lieutenant.

Ltd Limited (Liability).

lubricate [loo-brik-ate] *v.* oil or grease to lessen friction. —**lubricant** *n.* lubricating substance such as oil. —**lubrication** *n.*

lubricious [loo-**brish**-uss] *adj. Lit.* lewd.

lucerne *n.* fodder plant like clover, alfalfa.

lucid *adj.* clear and easily understood; able to think clearly; bright and clear. —**lucidly** *adv.* —**lucidity** *n.*

Lucifer *n.* Satan.

luck *n.* fortune, good or bad; good fortune; chance. —**lucky** *adj.* having good luck. —**lucky dip** game in which prizes are picked from a tub at random. —**luckily** *adv.* fortunately. —**luckless** *adj.* having bad luck.

THESAURUS

love *v.* 1. cherish, hold dear, idolize, prize, treasure, worship 2. appreciate, desire, enjoy, fancy, like, relish, savour 3. caress, cuddle, embrace, fondle, kiss, pet ~*n.* 4. adulation, affection, ardour, devotion, fondness, friendship, infatuation, liking, passion, rapture, regard, tenderness, warmth

lover admirer, beau, beloved, boyfriend, girlfriend, mistress, paramour, suitor, sweetheart

loving affectionate, ardent, cordial, dear, devoted, doting, fond, friendly, kind, tender, warm

low 1. little, short, small, squat, stunted 2. deep, shallow, subsided, sunken 3. depleted, little, meagre, paltry, reduced, scant, small, sparse, trifling 4. deficient, inadequate, inferior, mediocre, poor, puny, second-rate, shoddy, worthless 5. coarse, common, crude, disgraceful, dishonourable, disreputable, gross, obscene, rough, rude, unrefined, vulgar 6. blue, dejected, depressed, despondent, disheartened, down, forlorn, gloomy, glum, miserable, morose, sad, unhappy 7. gentle, hushed, muffled, muted, quiet, soft, subdued, whispered 8.

cheap, economical, inexpensive, moderate, modest, reasonable

lower *adj.* 1. inferior, junior, lesser, minor, secondary, smaller subordinate ~*v.* 2. depress, drop, fall, sink, submerge 3. abase, belittle, debase, degrade, deign, demean, devalue, disgrace, humiliate

lowly docile, dutiful, gentle, meek, modest, unassuming

low-spirited apathetic, blue, dejected, depressed, despondent, down, gloomy, low, miserable, moody, sad, unhappy

loyal attached, constant, dependable, devoted, dutiful, faithful, staunch, steadfast, true, trustworthy, unswerving, unwavering

loyalty allegiance, faithfulness, fidelity, patriotism, staunchness, steadfastness, trustiness

lubricate grease, oil, smear

lucid 1. clear, distinct, evident, explicit, intelligible, limpid, obvious, plain, transparent 2. beaming, bright, brilliant, effulgent, gleaming, radiant, shining 3. clear, diaphanous, limpid, pure, transparent

DICTIONARY

lucrative *adj.* very profitable.

lucre [**loo**-ker] *n.* —**filthy lucre** *Informal, usu. facetious.* money.

Luddite *n. Offens.* person opposed to change in industrial methods.

ludicrous *adj.* absurd or ridiculous. —**ludicrously** *adv.*

ludo *n.* game played with dice and counters on a board.

lug[1] *v.* **lugging, lugged.** carry or drag with great effort.

lug[2] *n.* projection serving as a handle; *Informal* ear.

luggage *n.* traveller's cases, bags, etc.

lugger *n.* working boat rigged with an oblong sail.

lugubrious [loo-**goo**-bree-uss] *adj.* mournful, gloomy. —**lugubriously** *adv.*

lugworm *n.* large worm used as bait.

lukewarm *adj.* moderately warm, tepid; indifferent or half-hearted.

lull *n.* brief time of quiet in a storm etc. —*v.* soothe (someone) by soft sounds or motions; calm (fears or suspicions) by deception.

lullaby *n., pl.* **-bies.** quiet song to send a child to sleep.

lumbago [lum-**bay**-go] *n.* pain in the lower back. —**lumbar** *adj.* relating to the lower back.

lumber[1] *n.* useless disused articles, such as old furniture; *US* sawn timber. —*v. Informal* burden with something unpleasant. —**lumberjack** *n. US* man who fells trees and prepares logs for transport.

lumber[2] *v.* move heavily and awkwardly. —**lumbering** *adj.*

luminous *adj.* reflecting or giving off light. —**luminosity** *n.* —**luminary** *n.* famous person; *Lit.* heavenly body giving off light. —**luminescence** *n.* emission of light at low temperatures by any process other than burning. —**luminescent** *adj.*

lump[1] *n.* shapeless piece or mass; swelling; *Informal* awkward or stupid person. —*v.* consider as a single group. —**lump in one's throat** tight dry feeling in one's throat, usu. caused by great emotion. —**lumpy** *adj.* —**lump sum** relatively large sum of money paid at one time.

lump[2] *v.* —**lump it** *Informal* tolerate or put up with it.

lunar *adj.* relating to the moon. —**lunar month, lunation** *n.* time taken for the moon to go once round the earth, approx. 29 days.

lunatic *adj.* foolish and irresponsible. —*n.* foolish or annoying person; *Old-fashioned* insane person. —**lunacy** *n.*

lunch *n.* meal taken in the middle of the day. —*v.* eat lunch. —**luncheon** *n.* formal lunch. —**luncheon meat** tinned ground mixture of meat and cereal. —**luncheon voucher** voucher for a certain amount, given to an employee and ac-

THESAURUS

luck 1. accident, chance, destiny, fate, fortune 2. advantage, blessing, fluke, prosperity, stroke, success, windfall

luckily favourably, fortunately, happily, opportunely

luckless cursed, disastrous, doomed, hapless, hopeless, jinxed, unfortunate, unhappy, unpropitious, unsuccessful

lucky blessed, charmed, favoured, fortunate, prosperous, successful

lucrative fat, fruitful, gainful, paying, productive, profitable, remunerative, well-paid

lucre gain, mammon, money, profit, riches, spoils, wealth

ludicrous absurd, burlesque, comic, crazy, droll, funny, laughable, odd, preposterous, ridiculous, silly

luggage baggage, bags, cases, gear, suitcases, trunks

lugubrious dismal, doleful, dreary, funereal, gloomy, melancholy, mournful, sad, serious, sombre, woebegone, woeful

lukewarm apathetic, cold, cool, half-hearted, indifferent, unenthusiastic, uninterested

lull 1. *v.* allay, calm, compose, hush, pacify, quell, quiet, soothe, still, subdue 2. *n.* calm, calmness, hush, pause, quiet, respite, silence

lullaby berceuse, cradlesong

lumber[1] *n.* clutter, discards, junk, refuse, rubbish, trash

lumber[2] *v.* clump, plod, shamble, shuffle, stump, trudge, trundle

lumbering awkward, blundering, bovine, clumsy, heavy, hulking, overgrown, ponderous, ungainly, unwieldy

luminous bright, brilliant, glowing, lighted, lit, lustrous, radiant, resplendent, shining, vivid

lump *n.* 1. ball, bunch, cake, chunk, gob, group, hunk, mass, piece, spot, wedge 2. bulge, bump, growth, protrusion, protererance, swelling, tumour ~*v.* 3. bunch, collect, combine, group, mass, pool, unite

lunacy 1. derangement, idiocy, insanity, madness 2. absurdity, craziness, folly, foolishness, idiocy, madness, stupidity

lunatic 1. *adj.* crazy, daft, demented, deranged, insane, irrational, mad, unhinged 2. *n.* madman, maniac, psychopath

DICTIONARY

cepted by some restaurants as payment for a meal.

lung *n.* organ that allows an animal or bird to breathe air: humans have two lungs in the chest.

lunge *n.* sudden forward motion; thrust with a sword. —*v.* move with or make a lunge.

lupin *n.* garden plant with tall spikes of flowers.

lupine *adj.* like a wolf.

lupus *n.* ulcerous skin disease.

lurch¹ *v.* tilt or lean suddenly to one side; stagger. —*n.* lurching movement.

lurch² *n.* —**leave someone in the lurch** abandon someone in difficulties.

lurcher *n.* crossbred dog trained to hunt silently.

lure *v.* tempt or attract by the promise of reward. —*n.* person or thing that lures; brightly-coloured artificial angling bait.

lurid *adj.* vivid in shocking detail, sensational; glaring in colour. —**luridly** *adv.*

lurk *v.* lie hidden or move stealthily, esp. for sinister purposes; be latent.

luscious [lush-uss] *adj.* extremely pleasurable to taste or smell; very attractive.

lush¹ *adj.* (of grass etc.) growing thickly and healthily; opulent. —**lushly** *adv.* —**lushness** *n.*

lush² *n. US slang* alcoholic.

lust *n.* strong sexual desire; any strong desire. —*v.* have passionate desire (for). —**lustful** *adj.* —**lusty** *adj.* vigorous, healthy. —**lustily** *adv.*

lustre *n.* gloss, sheen; splendour or glory; metallic pottery glaze. —**lustrous** *adj.* shining, luminous.

lute *n.* ancient guitar-like musical instrument with a body shaped like a half pear. —**lutenist** *n.* person who plays a lute.

Lutheran *adj.* of Martin Luther (1483–1546), German Reformation leader, his doctrines, or a Church following these doctrines.

lux *n., pl.* **lux.** unit of illumination.

luxuriant *adj.* rich and abundant; very elaborate. —**luxuriantly** *adv.* —**luxuriance** *n.*

luxuriate *v.* take self-indulgent pleasure (in); flourish.

luxury *n., pl.* **-ries.** enjoyment of rich, very comfortable living; enjoyable but not essential thing. —*adj.* of or providing luxury. —**luxurious** *adj.* full of luxury, sumptuous. —**luxuriously** *adv.*

lychee *n.* Chinese fruit with a whitish juicy pulp.

lychgate *n.* same as LICHGATE.

Lycra *n.* ® elastic fabric used for tight-fitting garments, such as swimming costumes.

lye *n.* water made alkaline with wood ashes etc., esp. as formerly used for washing.

lying *v.* present participle of LIE¹, LIE². —**lying-in** *n. Old-fashioned* period of confinement during childbirth.

lymph *n.* colourless bodily fluid consisting mainly of white blood cells. —**lymphatic** *adj.*

lymphocyte *n.* type of white blood cell.

lynch *v.* put to death without a trial.

lynx *n.* animal of the cat family with tufted ears and a short tail.

lyre *n.* ancient musical instrument like a U-shaped harp.

lyric *n.* short poem expressing personal emotion in a songlike style. —*pl.* words of a popular song. —*adj.* of such poems; in the style of a song. —**lyrical** *adj.* lyric; enthusiastic. —**lyricist** *n.* person who writes the words of songs or musicals.

THESAURUS

lunge 1. *n.* charge, cut, jab, pass, spring, stab, swing, swipe, thrust 2. *v.* bound, charge, cut, dash, dive, jab, leap, poke, stab, thrust

lure 1. *v.* attract, beckon, decoy, draw, ensnare, entice, inveigle, invite, lead on, seduce, tempt 2. *n.* attraction, bait, decoy, magnet, temptation

lurid graphic, melodramatic, sensational, shocking, startling, unrestrained, vivid

lurk crouch, hide, prowl, skulk, slink, sneak, snoop

luscious appetizing, delectable, delicious, honeyed, juicy, mouth-watering, palatable, rich, savoury, succulent, sweet

lush abundant, dense, green, lavish, prolific, rank, teeming, verdant

lust *n.* 1. carnaliy, lechery, lewdness, libido, salaciousness, sensuality, wantonness 2. appetite, avidity, craving, cupidity, desire, greed, longing, passion, thirst ~*v.* 3. covet, crave, desire, need, want, yearn

lustre 1. burnish, gleam, glint, glitter, gloss, glow, sheen, shimmer, shine, sparkle 2. distinction, fame, glory, honour, prestige, renown

lusty hale, healthy, hearty, powerful, robust, stalwart, stout, strapping, strong, sturdy, vigorous, virile

luxurious comfortable, costly, expensive, lavish, opulent, rich, splendid, sumptuous

luxury 1. affluence, opulence, richness, splendour 2. comfort, delight, enjoyment, gratification, indulgence, pleasure, satisfaction, well-being 3. extra, extravagance, treat

M

m metre(s); mile(s); minute(s).

M Monsieur; Motorway.

m. male; married; masculine; meridian; month.

MA Master of Arts.

ma n. *Informal* mother.

ma'am n. madam.

mac n. *Informal* mackintosh.

macabre [mak-**kahb**-ra] *adj.* strange and horrible, gruesome.

macadam n. road surface of pressed layers of small broken stones. —**macadamize** v. pave a road with macadam.

macaroni n. pasta in short tubes.

macaroon n. small biscuit or cake made with ground almonds.

macaw n. large tropical American parrot.

mace[1] n. ceremonial staff of office; medieval weapon with a spiked metal head.

mace[2] n. spice made from the dried husk of the nutmeg.

macerate [**mass**-a-rate] v. soften by soaking. —**maceration** n.

Mach (number) [mak] n. ratio of the speed of a body in a particular medium to the speed of sound in that medium.

machete [mash-**ett**-ee] n. broad heavy knife used for cutting or as a weapon.

Machiavellian [mak-ee-a-**vel**-yan] *adj.* unprincipled, crafty, and opportunist.

machinations [mak-in-**nay**-shunz] *pl. n.* cunning plots and ploys.

machine n. apparatus, usu. powered by electricity, designed to perform a particular task; vehicle, such as a car or aircraft; controlling system of an organization. —v. make or produce by machine. —**machinery** n. machines or machine parts collectively. —**machinist** n. person who operates a machine. —**machine gun** automatic gun that fires rapidly and continuously.

—**machine-gun** v. fire at with such a gun.

—**machine-readable** *adj.* (of data) in a form suitable for processing by a computer.

machismo [mak-**izz**-mow] n. strong or exaggerated masculinity.

macho [**match**-oh] *adj.* strongly or exaggeratedly masculine.

mackerel n. edible sea fish with blue and silver stripes.

mackintosh n. waterproof raincoat of rubberized cloth; any raincoat.

macramé [mak-**rah**-mee] n. ornamental work of knotted cord.

macrobiotics n. dietary system advocating whole grains and vegetables grown without chemical additives. —**macrobiotic** *adj.*

macrocosm n. the universe; any large complete system.

mad *adj.* **madder, maddest.** mentally deranged, insane; very foolish; (foll. by *about* or *on*) very enthusiastic (about); frantic; *Informal* angry. —**like mad** *Informal* with great energy, enthusiasm, or haste. —**madly** *adv.* —**madness** n. —**madman, madwoman** n.

madam n. polite form of address to a woman; *Informal* precocious or conceited girl.

madame [mad-**dam**] *n., pl.* **mesdames** [may-**dam**]. French title equivalent to *Mrs.*

madcap *adj., n.* reckless (person).

madden v. make mad. —**maddening** *adj.* irritating.

madder n. climbing plant; red dye made from its root.

made v. past of MAKE.

Madeira [mad-**deer**-a] n. fortified white wine. —**Madeira cake** rich sponge cake.

mademoiselle [mad-mwah-**zel**] *n., pl.* **mesdemoiselles** [maid-mwah-**zel**]. French title equivalent to *Miss.*

THESAURUS

macabre deathly, dreadful, frightening, frightful, ghastly, ghostly, grim, grisly, gruesome, hideous, horrid, unearthly, weird

machine 1. apparatus, appliance, contraption, contrivance, device, engine, instrument, tool 2. agency, organization, party, structure, system

machinery 1. apparatus, equipment, gear, tackle, tools, works 2. agency, channels, organization, procedure, structure, system

mad 1. crazed, delirious, demented, deranged,

distracted, frantic, frenzied, insane, lunatic, psychotic, raving, unbalanced, unhinged 2. absurd, foolhardy, foolish, imprudent, irrational, ludicrous, preposterous, senseless, unreasonable, unsafe, unsound, wild

madden annoy, craze, enrage, exasperate, inflame, infuriate, provoke, upset, vex

madly 1. crazily, dementedly, distractedly, frantically, frenziedly, hysterically, insanely 2. absurdly, foolishly, irrationally, unreasonably, wildly 3. energetically, excitedly, furiously, hastily, hurriedly, quickly, rapidly, recklessly,

DICTIONARY

Madonna *n.* the Virgin Mary; picture or statue of her.

madrigal *n.* 16th–17th century part song for unaccompanied voices.

maelstrom [**male**-strom] *n.* great whirlpool; turmoil.

maestro [**my**-stroh] *n., pl.* **-tri, -tros.** outstanding musician or conductor; any master of an art.

Mafia *n.* international secret criminal organization founded in Sicily. —**mafioso** *n.* member of the Mafia.

magazine *n.* periodical publication with articles by different writers; appliance for automatically supplying cartridges to a gun or slides to a projector; storehouse for explosives or arms.

magenta [maj-**jen**-ta] *adj.* deep purplish-red.

maggot *n.* larva of an insect, esp. the blowfly. —**maggoty** *adj.*

Magi [**maje**-eye] *pl. n.* wise men from the East at the Nativity.

magic *n.* supposed art of invoking supernatural powers to influence events; mysterious quality or power. —*adj.* (also **magical**) of, using, or like magic. —**magically** *adv.* —**magician** *n.* conjurer; person with magic powers.

magistrate *n.* public officer administering the law; justice of the peace. —**magisterial** *adj.* commanding or authoritative; of a magistrate.

magma *n.* molten rock inside the earth's crust.

magnanimous *adj.* noble and generous. —**magnanimously** *adv.* —**magnanimity** *n.*

magnate *n.* influential or wealthy person, esp. in industry.

magnesium *n.* silvery-white metallic element. —**magnesia** *n.* compound of magnesium used in medicine.

magnet *n.* piece of iron or steel capable of attracting iron and pointing north when suspended. —**magnetic** *adj.* having the properties of a magnet; powerfully attractive. —**magnetically** *adv.* —**magnetism** *n.* magnetic property; science of this; powerful personal charm. —**magnetize** *v.* make into a magnet; attract strongly. —**magnetization** *n.* —**magnetic tape** plastic strip coated with a magnetic substance for recording sound or video signals.

magneto [mag-**nee**-toe] *n., pl.* **-tos.** apparatus for ignition in an internal-combustion engine.

magnificent *adj.* splendid or impressive; excellent. —**magnificently** *adv.* —**magnificence** *n.*

magnify *v.* **-fying, -fied.** increase in apparent size, as with a lens; exaggerate. —**magnification** *n.*

magniloquent *adj.* speaking pompously. —**magniloquence** *n.*

magnitude *n.* relative importance or size.

THESAURUS

speedily, violently, wildly

madness 1. aberration, craziness, delusion, dementia, derangement, distraction, insanity, lunacy, mania, mental illness, psychopathy, psychosis 2. absurdity, daftness (*Inf.*), folly, foolhardiness, foolishness, nonsense, preposterousness, wildness 3. anger, exasperation, frenzy, fury, ire, rage, raving, wildness, wrath 4. ardour, craze, enthusiasm, fanaticism, fondness, infatuation, keenness, passion, rage, zeal 5. abandon, agitation, excitement, frenzy, furore, intoxication, riot, unrestraint, uproar

magazine 1. journal, pamphlet, paper, periodical 2. arsenal, depot, store, warehouse

magic *n.* 1. enchantment, occultism, sorcery, spell, witchcraft 2. allurement, charm, enchantment, fascination, glamour, magnetism, power ~*adj.* 3. *Also* **magical** charming, enchanting, entrancing, fascinating, magnetic, marvellous, miraculous

magistrate judge, justice

magnanimity charitableness, generosity, munificence, nobility, selflessness, unselfishness

magnanimous big, charitable, free, generous, handsome, kind, munificent, noble, selfless, ungrudging, unselfish

magnate 1. baron, chief, leader, mogul, plutocrat, tycoon 2. baron, grandee, magnifico, merchant, notable, personage, prince

magnetic alluring, attractive, captivating, charming, enchanting, entrancing, hypnotic, irresistible, seductive

magnetism allure, appeal, attraction, charisma, charm, draw, enchantment, fascination, magic, power, pull, spell

magnificence brilliance, glory, grandeur, luxury, majesty, nobility, opulence, pomp, splendour, sublimity

magnificent brilliant, elegant, elevated, exalted, excellent, fine, glorious, gorgeous, grand, imposing, impressive, lavish, noble, opulent, princely, regal, rich, splendid, stately, sumptuous, superb, superior

magnify 1. amplify, augment, boost, deepen, dilate, enlarge, expand, heighten, increase, intensify 2. blow up, dramatize, enhance, exaggerate, inflate, overdo

magnitude 1. consequence, eminence, grandeur, greatness, importance, mark, moment, note, significance, weight 2. amount, amplitude, bulk, capacity, dimensions, expanse, extent, hugeness, immensity, largeness, mass,

DICTIONARY

magnolia *n.* shrub or tree with showy white or pink flowers.

magnum *n.* large wine bottle holding about 1.5 litres.

magpie *n.* black-and-white bird.

Magyar *n.* member of the prevailing race in Hungary; Hungarian language. —*adj.* of the Magyars or their language.

maharajah *n.* former title of some Indian princes. —**maharanee** *n. fem.*

maharishi *n.* Hindu religious teacher or mystic.

mahatma *n. Hinduism* person revered for holiness and wisdom.

mahjong(g) *n.* Chinese table game for four, played with tiles bearing different designs.

mahogany *n., pl.* **-nies.** hard reddish-brown wood of several tropical trees.

mahout [ma-**howt**] *n.* elephant driver or keeper.

maid *n.* (also **maidservant**) female servant; *Lit.* young unmarried woman.

maiden *n. Lit.* young unmarried woman. —*adj.* unmarried; first, e.g. *maiden voyage.* —**maidenly** *adj.* modest. —**maidenhood** *n.* —**maidenhair** *n.* fern with delicate fronds. —**maidenhead** *n.* virginity. —**maiden name** woman's surname before marriage. —**maiden over** *Cricket* over in which no runs are scored.

mail[1] *n.* letters and packages transported and delivered by the post office; postal system; letters and packages conveyed at one time; train, ship, or aircraft carrying mail. —*v.* send by post.

—**mail order** system of buying goods by post. —**mailshot** *n.* posting of advertising material to many selected people at once.

mail[2] *n.* flexible armour of interlaced rings or links. —**mailed** *adj.*

maim *v.* cripple or mutilate.

main *adj.* chief or principal. —*n.* principal pipe or line carrying water, gas, or electricity. —**in the main** on the whole. —**mainly** *adv.* for the most part, chiefly. —**mainland** *n.* stretch of land which forms the main part of a country. —**mainmast** *n.* chief mast in a ship. —**mainsail** *n.* largest sail on a mainmast. —**mainspring** *n.* chief spring of a watch or clock; chief cause or motive. —**mainstay** *n.* rope securing a mainmast; chief support. —**mainstream** *n.* prevailing cultural trend.

mainframe *n. Computers* high-speed general-purpose computer.

maintain *v.* continue or keep in existence; keep up or preserve; support financially; assert. —**maintenance** *n.* maintaining; upkeep of a building, car, etc.; provision of money for a separated or divorced spouse.

maisonette *n.* flat with more than one floor.

maître d'hôtel [**met**-ra dote-**tell**] *n. French* head waiter.

maize *n.* type of corn with spikes of yellow grains.

majesty *n., pl.* **-ties.** stateliness or grandeur; supreme power. —**majestic** *adj.* —**majestically** *adv.*

major *adj.* greater in number, quality, or extent; significant or serious. —*n.* middle-ranking army

THESAURUS

measure, quantity, size, space, strength, volume

maid 1. damsel, girl, maiden, miss, wench 2. housemaid, servant

maiden *n.* 1. damsel, girl, maid, miss, nymph, virgin, wench ~*adj.* 2. chaste, intact, pure, virgin 3. first, initial, introductory

mail *n.* 1. letters, packages, parcels, post 2. post, postal service ~*v.* 3. dispatch, forward, post, send

maim cripple, disable, hurt, impair, incapacitate, injure, lame, mangle, mar, mutilate, wound

main 1. *adj.* capital, cardinal, central, chief, critical, crucial, essential, foremost, head, leading, necessary, paramount, particular, pre-eminent, primary, prime, principal, special, supreme, vital 2. *n.* cable, channel, conduit, duct, line, pipe

mainly chiefly, generally, largely, mostly, overall, predominantly, primarily

mainstay anchor, backbone, bulwark, linchpin, pillar, prop

maintain 1. conserve, continue, finance, keep, prolong, look after, nurture, perpetuate, preserve, provide, retain, supply, support, sustain, uphold 2. affirm, allege, assert, asseverate, aver, avow, claim, contend, declare, hold, insist, profess, state 3. back, champion, defend, justify, plead for, uphold, vindicate

maintenance 1. care, conservation, continuation, nurture, perpetuation, preservation, provision, repairs, supply, support, upkeep 2. aliment, alimony, allowance, food, keep, living, subsistence, support, upkeep

majestic awesome, elevated, exalted, grand, imperial, imposing, impressive, kingly, lofty, magnificent, monumental, noble, princely, regal, royal, splendid, stately, sublime, superb

majesty dignity, glory, grandeur, kingliness, magnificence, nobility, pomp, royalty, splendour, state, sublimity

DICTIONARY

officer; scale in music; *US* principal field of study at a university etc. —*v.* (foll. by *in*) *US* do one's principal study in (a particular subject). —**major-domo** *n.* chief steward of a great household.

majority *n., pl.* **-ties.** greater number; largest party voting together; number by which the votes on one side exceed those on the other; full legal age.

make *v.* **making, made.** create, construct, or establish; cause to do or be; bring about or produce; perform (an action); amount to; earn; serve as or become. —*n.* brand, type, or style. —**on the make** *Informal* intent on gain. —**maker** *n.* —**making** *n.* creation or production. —*pl.* necessary requirements or qualities. —**make-believe** *n.* fantasy or pretence. —**make do** manage with an inferior alternative.—**make for** *v.* head towards. —**make it** *Informal* be successful. —**make off with** *v.* steal or abduct. —**makeshift** *n.* temporary expedient. —**make up** *v.* form or constitute; prepare; invent; supply what is lacking, complete; (foll. by *for*) compensate (for); settle a quarrel; apply cosmetics. —**make-up** *n.* cosmetics; mental or physical constitution; way something is made. —**makeweight** *n.* something unimportant added to make up a lack.

mal- *combining form* bad or badly, e.g. *malformation, malfunction.*

malachite [**mal**-a-kite] *n.* green mineral.

maladjusted *adj. Psychol.* unable to meet the demands of society. —**maladjustment** *n.*

maladministration *n.* inefficient or dishonest administration.

maladroit [mal-a-**droyt**] *adj.* clumsy or awkward.

malady [**mal**-a-dee] *n., pl.* **-dies.** disease or illness.

malaise [mal-**laze**] *n.* vague feeling of illness or unease.

malapropism *n.* comical misuse of a word by confusion with one which sounds similar.

malaria *n.* infectious disease caused by the bite of some mosquitoes. —**malarial** *adj.*

Malay *n.* member of a people of Malaysia or Indonesia; language of this people. —**Malayan** *adj., n.*

malcontent *n.* discontented person.

male *adj.* of the sex which can fertilize female reproductive cells. —*n.* male person or animal.

malediction [mal-lid-**dik**-shun] *n.* curse.

malefactor [**mal**-if-act-or] *n.* criminal or wrongdoer.

malevolent [mal-**lev**-a-lent] *adj.* wishing evil to others. —**malevolently** *adv.* —**malevolence** *n.*

malfeasance [mal-**fee**-zanss] *n.* misconduct, esp. by a public official.

malformed *adj.* misshapen or deformed. —**malformation** *n.*

THESAURUS

major better, bigger, chief, elder, greater, higher, larger, leading, main, most, senior, superior, supreme, uppermost

majority 1. best part, bulk, mass, more, most, plurality, preponderance, superiority 2. manhood, maturity, seniority

make *v.* 1. assemble, build, compose, constitute, construct, create, fabricate, fashion, forge, form, frame, manufacture, originate, produce, shape, synthesize 2. accomplish, beget, cause, create, effect, generate, occasion, produce 3. cause, coerce, compel, constrain, dragoon, drive, force, impel, induce, oblige, press, require 4. acquire, clear, earn, gain, get, net, obtain, realize, secure, take in, win ~*n.* 5. brand, build, character, composition, construction, cut, designation, form, kind, mark, model, shape, sort, structure, style, type, variety

make-believe *n.* charade, dream, fantasy, imagination, pretence, unreality

make do cope, improvise, manage

maker author, builder, director, framer, manufacturer, producer

makeshift expedient, shift, stopgap, substitute

make-up 1. cosmetics, powder 2. arrangement, assembly, composition, configuration, constitution, construction, format, formation, organization, structure

make up 1. compose, comprise, constitute, form 2. coin, compose, concoct, construct, create, devise, fabricate, formulate, frame, hatch, invent, originate 3. complete, fill, meet, supply

maladjusted disturbed, neurotic, unstable

malady ailment, complaint, disease, illness, indisposition, infirmity, sickness

malcontent agitator, complainer, grouser, grumbler, rebel, troublemaker

male manlike, manly, masculine, virile

malefactor convict, criminal, culprit, delinquent, felon, lawbreaker, offender, outlaw, villain, wrongdoer

malevolence hate, ill will, malice, malignity, rancour, spite, vindictiveness

malevolent baleful, evil-minded, hostile, malicious, malignant, pernicious, spiteful, vengeful, vicious, vindictive

malformation deformity, distortion, misshape

DICTIONARY

malfunction *v.* function imperfectly or fail to function. —*n.* defective functioning or failure to function.

malice [mal-iss] *n.* desire to cause harm to others. —**malicious** *adj.* —**maliciously** *adv.*

malign [mal-line] *v.* slander or defame. —*adj.* evil in influence or effect. —**malignity** *n.* evil disposition.

malignant [mal-lig-nant] *adj.* seeking to harm others; (of a tumour) harmful and uncontrollable. —**malignancy** *n.*

malinger [mal-ling-ger] *v.* feign illness to avoid work. —**malingerer** *n.*

mall *n.* street or shopping area closed to vehicles.

mallard *n.* wild duck.

malleable [mal-lee-a-bl] *adj.* capable of being hammered or pressed into shape; easily influenced. —**malleability** *n.*

mallet *n.* (wooden) hammer; stick with a head like a hammer, used in croquet or polo.

mallow *n.* plant with pink or purple flowers.

malmsey *n.* kind of strong sweet wine.

malnutrition *n.* inadequate nutrition.

malodorous [mal-lode-or-uss] *adj.* bad-smelling.

malpractice *n.* immoral, illegal, or unethical professional conduct.

malt *n.* grain, such as barley, prepared for use in making beer or whisky.

maltreat *v.* treat badly. —**maltreatment** *n.*

mamba *n.* deadly S African snake.

ma(m)ma *n. Old-fashioned* mother.

mammal *n.* animal of the type that suckles its young. —**mammalian** *adj.*

mammary *adj.* of the breasts or milk-producing glands.

mammon *n.* wealth regarded as a source of evil; (**M-**) wealth personified in the New Testament as a false god.

mammoth *n.* extinct animal like an elephant. —*adj.* colossal.

man *n., pl.* **men.** adult male; human being or person; mankind; manservant; piece used in chess etc. —*v.* **manning, manned.** supply with sufficient people for operation or defence. —**manful** *adj.* determined and brave. —**manfully** *adv.* —**manhood** *n.* —**mankind** *n.* human beings collectively. —**manly** *adj.* (possessing qualities) appropriate to a man. —**manliness** *n.* —**mannish** *adj.* like a man. —**manhandle** *v.* treat roughly. —**manhole** *n.* hole with a cover, through which a person can enter a drain or sewer. —**man-hour** *n.* work done by one person in one hour. —**man-made** *adj.* synthetic. —**manpower** *n.* available number of workers. —**manservant** *n.* male servant, esp. a valet. —**manslaughter** *n.* unlawful but unintentional killing of a person.

manacle [man-a-kl] *n., v.* handcuff or fetter.

manage *v.* succeed in doing; be in charge of, administer; handle or control; cope with (financial) difficulties. —**manageable** *adj.* —**management** *n.* managers collectively; administration or organization. —**manager, manageress** *n.* person in charge of a business, institution, actor, sports team, etc. —**managerial** *adj.*

THESAURUS

malfunction 1. *v.* break down, fail 2. *n.* breakdown, defect, failure, fault, flaw

malice animosity, bitterness, enmity, hate, hatred, rancour, spite, venom, vindictiveness

malicious baleful, bitter, hateful, injurious, malevolent, pernicious, rancorous, resentful, spiteful, vengeful, vicious

malign 1. *adj.* bad, baleful, baneful, evil, harmful, hostile, hurtful, pernicious, vicious, wicked 2. *v.* abuse, defame, denigrate, disparage, harm, injure, libel, revile, slander, smear, traduce

malignant baleful, bitter, harmful, hostile, hurtful, malevolent, malicious, pernicious, spiteful, vicious

malpractice misbehaviour, misconduct, misdeed, offence

maltreat abuse, damage, harm, hurt, injure, mistreat

mammoth colossal, enormous, giant, huge, immense, massive, mighty, prodigious, titanic, vast

man *n.* 1. gentleman, male 2. adult, being, body, human being, individual, one, person, personage, somebody, soul 3. humanity, human race, mankind, mortals, people 4. attendant, employee, hand, retainer, servant, soldier, subject, valet, vassal, worker, workman ~*v.* 5. crew, fill, garrison, occupy, people, staff

manacle bond, chain, fetter, handcuff, iron, shackle, tie

manage 1. administer, command, concert, conduct, direct, govern, oversee, rule, run, supervise 2. accomplish, arrange, contrive, deal with, effect, engineer, succeed 3. control, guide, handle, influence, manipulate, operate, pilot, ply, steer, train, use, wield

manageable compliant, controllable, docile, easy, handy, submissive, tractable, wieldy

management administration, board, directorate, employers

DICTIONARY

manatee *n.* large tropical plant-eating aquatic mammal.

mandarin *n.* high-ranking government official; kind of small orange.

mandate *n.* official or authoritative command; authorization or instruction from an electorate to its representative or government. —*v.* give authority to. —**mandatory** *adj.* compulsory.

mandible *n.* lower jawbone or jawlike part.

mandolin *n.* musical instrument with four pairs of strings.

mandrake *n.* plant with a forked root, formerly used as a narcotic.

mandrel *n.* shaft on which work is held in a lathe.

mandrill *n.* large blue-faced baboon.

mane *n.* long hair on the neck of a horse, lion, etc.

manganese *n.* brittle greyish-white metallic element.

mange *n.* skin disease of domestic animals. —**mangy** *adj.* having mange; scruffy or shabby.

mangelwurzel *n.* variety of beet used as cattle food.

manger *n.* eating trough in a stable or barn.

mangetout [mawnzh-too] *n.* variety of pea with an edible pod.

mangle[1] *v.* destroy by crushing and twisting; spoil.

mangle[2] *n.* machine with rollers for squeezing water from washed clothes. —*v.* put through a mangle.

mango *n., pl.* **-goes, -gos.** tropical fruit with sweet juicy yellow flesh.

mangrove *n.* tropical tree with exposed roots, which grows beside water.

mania *n.* madness; extreme enthusiasm. —**maniac** *n.* mad person; *Informal* person who has an extreme enthusiasm for something. —**maniacal** [man-**eye**-a-kl], **manic** *adj.* affected by mania.

manicure *n.* cosmetic care of the fingernails and hands. —*v.* care for (the hands and fingernails) in this way. —**manicurist** *n.*

manifest *adj.* easily noticed, obvious. —*v.* show plainly; be evidence of. —*n.* list of cargo or passengers for customs. —**manifestation** *n.*

manifesto *n., pl.* **-toes, -tos.** declaration of policy as issued by a political party.

manifold *adj.* numerous and varied. —*n.* pipe with several outlets, esp. in an internal-combustion engine.

manikin *n.* little man or dwarf; model of the human body.

manil(l)a *n.* strong brown paper used for envelopes.

manipulate *v.* handle skilfully; control cleverly or deviously. —**manipulation** *n.* —**manipulative** *adj.* —**manipulator** *n.*

manna *n. Bible* miraculous food which sustained the Israelites in the wilderness; windfall.

mannequin *n.* woman who models clothes at a fashion show; life-size dummy of the human body used to fit or display clothes.

manner *n.* way a thing happens or is done; person's bearing or behaviour; type or kind; custom or style. —*pl.* (polite) social behaviour. —**mannered** *adj.* affected. —**mannerism** *n.* person's distinctive habit or trait.

THESAURUS

manager conductor, controller, director, executive, governor, head, organizer, proprietor, supervisor

mandate authority, bidding, charge, command, decree, directive, edict, fiat, instruction, order, sanction, warrant

mandatory binding, compulsory, obligatory, required, requisite

mangle butcher, crush, cut, deform, destroy, distort, hack, maim, mar, mutilate, spoil, tear, wreck

mangy dirty, mean, scruffy, seedy, shabby, shoddy, squalid

manhandle maul, pull, push

manhood bravery, courage, firmness, masculinity, maturity, mettle, resolution, spirit, strength, valour, virility

mania craziness, delirium, derangement, disorder, frenzy, insanity, lunacy, madness

maniac lunatic, madman, psychopath

manifest *adj.* apparent, clear, distinct, evident, glaring, noticeable, obvious, open, patent, plain, visible

manifestation disclosure, display, exhibition, exposure, instance, mark, materialization, revelation, show, sign, symptom, token

manifold abundant, assorted, diverse, many, multiple, numerous, varied, various

manipulate 1. employ, handle, operate, ply, use, wield, work 2. direct, guide, influence, negotiate, steer

mankind humanity, human race, man, people

manliness boldness, bravery, courage, heroism, masculinity, valour, vigour, virility

manly bold, brave, courageous, daring, fearless, gallant, hardy, heroic, male, masculine, noble, powerful, resolute, robust, strong, valiant, valorous, vigorous, virile

DICTIONARY

mannikin *n.* same as MANIKIN.

manoeuvre [man-**noo**-ver] *n.* contrived, complicated, and possibly deceptive plan or action; skilful movement. —*pl.* military or naval exercises. —*v.* manipulate or contrive skilfully or cunningly; perform manoeuvres. —**manoeuvrable** *adj.*

manor *n.* large country house (**manor house**) and its lands. —**manorial** *adj.*

manqué [**mong**-kay] *adj.* would-be, e.g. *an actor manqué.*

mansard roof *n.* roof with a break in its slope, the lower part being steeper than the upper.

manse *n.* minister's house in some religious denominations.

mansion *n.* large house.

mantel *n.* structure round a fireplace. —**mantel shelf, mantelpiece** *n.* shelf above a fireplace.

mantilla *n.* in Spain, a lace scarf covering a woman's head and shoulders.

mantis *n., pl.* -**tises, -tes.** carnivorous insect like a grasshopper.

mantle *n.* loose cloak; covering; incandescent gauze round a gas jet.

mantra *n. Hinduism & Buddhism* any sacred word or syllable used as an object of concentration.

manual *adj.* of or done with the hands; by human labour rather than automatic means. —*n.* handbook; organ keyboard. —**manually** *adv.*

manufacture *v.* process or make (goods) on a large scale using machinery; invent or concoct (an excuse etc.). —*n.* process of manufacturing goods. —**manufacturer** *n.*

manure *n.* animal excrement used as a fertilizer. —*v.* fertilize (land) with this.

manuscript *n.* book or document, orig. one written by hand; copy for printing.

Manx *adj.* of the Isle of Man or its inhabitants. —*n.* Manx language. —**Manx cat** tailless breed of cat.

many *adj.* **more, most.** numerous. —*n.* large number.

Maoism *n.* form of Marxism advanced by Mao Tse-tung in China. —**Maoist** *n., adj.*

Maori *n.* member of the indigenous race of New Zealand; Maori language. —*adj.* of the Maoris or their language.

map *n.* representation of the earth's surface or some part of it, showing geographical features. —*v.* **mapping, mapped.** make a map of. —**map out** *v.* plan.

maple *n.* tree with broad leaves, a variety of which yields sugar.

mar *v.* **marring, marred.** spoil or impair.

Mar. March.

marabou *n.* kind of African stork; its soft white down, used to trim hats etc.

maraca [mar-**rak**-a] *n.* shaken percussion instrument made from a gourd containing dried seeds etc.

maraschino [mar-rass-**kee**-no] *n.* liqueur made from cherries.

marathon *n.* long-distance race of just over 26 miles; long or arduous task.

marauding *adj.* hunting for plunder; pillaging. —**marauder** *n.*

marble *n.* kind of limestone with a mottled appearance, which can be highly polished; slab of or sculpture in this; small glass ball used in playing marbles. —*pl.* game of rolling these.

THESAURUS

man-made artificial, manufactured, synthetic

manner 1. air, appearance, aspect, bearing, behaviour, conduct, demeanour, deportment, look, presence, tone 2. approach, custom, genre, habit, line, method, mode, practice, process, routine, style, tenor, usage, way, wont

mannerism foible, habit, peculiarity, quirk, trait, trick

manners 1. bearing, behaviour, breeding, carriage, conduct, demeanour, deportment 2. courtesy, decorum, etiquette, polish, politeness, protocol, refinement

manoeuvre *n.* 1. action, artifice, dodge, intrigue, machination, move, plan, plot, ploy, ruse, scheme, subterfuge, tactic, trick ~*v.* 2. contrive, devise, engineer, intrigue, manage, plan, plot, scheme 3. direct, drive, guide, handle, navigate, pilot, steer

mansion abode, dwelling, habitation, hall, manor, residence, seat, villa

manual 1. *adj.* hand-operated, human, physical 2. *n.* bible, guide, handbook, instructions

manufacture 1. *v.* assemble, build, compose, construct, create, forge, form, make, mould, process, produce, shape, think up, trump up 2. *n.* assembly, construction, fabrication, production

manure compost, droppings, dung, muck, ordure

many *adj.* abundant, copious, countless, frequent, manifold, myriad, numerous, profuse, sundry, varied, various

mar blemish, blight, blot, damage, deface, harm, hurt, injure, ruin, scar, spoil, stain, taint, tarnish, vitiate

DICTIONARY

—**marbled** *adj.* having a mottled appearance like marble.

marcasite *n.* crystals of iron pyrites, used in jewellery.

March *n.* third month of the year.

march[1] *v.* walk with a military step; make (a person or group) proceed; progress steadily. —*n.* action of marching; distance covered by marching; steady progress; piece of music, as for a march.

march[2] *n.* border or frontier.

marchioness [marsh-on-**ness**] *n.* woman holding the rank of marquis; wife or widow of a marquis.

mare *n.* female horse. —**mare's nest** discovery which proves worthless.

margarine *n.* butter substitute made from animal or vegetable fats.

marge *n. Informal* margarine.

margin *n.* edge or border; blank space round a printed page; additional amount or one greater than necessary; limit. —**marginal** *adj.* insignificant, unimportant; near a limit; (of a constituency) won by only a small margin. —*n.* marginal constituency. —**marginally** *adv.*

marguerite *n.* large daisy.

marigold *n.* plant with yellow flowers.

marijuana, marihuana [mar-ri-**wah**-na] *n.* dried flowers and leaves of the hemp plant, used as a drug, esp. in cigarettes.

marina *n.* harbour for yachts and other pleasure boats.

marinade *n.* seasoned liquid in which fish or meat is soaked before cooking. —*v.* (also **marinate**) soak in marinade.

marine *adj.* of the sea or shipping; used at or found in the sea. —*n.* country's shipping or fleet; soldier trained for land or sea combat. —**mariner** *n.* sailor.

marionette *n.* puppet worked with strings.

marital *adj.* relating to marriage.

maritime *adj.* relating to shipping; of, near, or living in the sea.

marjoram *n.* aromatic herb.

mark[1] *n.* line, dot, scar, etc. visible on a surface; distinguishing sign or symbol; written or printed symbol; letter or number used to grade academic work; indication of position; indication of some quality; target or goal. —*v.* make a mark on; be a distinguishing mark of; indicate; pay attention to; notice or watch; grade (academic work); stay close to (a sporting opponent) to hamper his play. —**marked** *adj.* noticeable. —**markedly** [mark-id-lee] *adv.* —**marker** *n.*

mark[2] *n.* same as DEUTSCHMARK.

market *n.* assembly or place for buying and selling; demand for goods. —*v.* -**keting, -keted.** offer or produce for sale. —**on the market** for sale. —**marketable** *adj.* —**market garden** place where fruit and vegetables are grown for sale. —**market maker** *Stock Exchange* person who uses a firm's money to create a market for a stock. —**marketplace** *n.* market; commercial world. —**market research** research into consumers' needs and purchases.

marksman *n.* person skilled at shooting. —**marksmanship** *n.*

marl *n.* soil formed of clay and lime, used as fertilizer.

THESAURUS

march 1. *v.* file, pace, parade, stalk, stride, strut, tramp, tread, walk 2. *n.* tramp, trek, walk

margin 1. border, bound, brim, brink, confine, edge, limit, rim, side, verge 2. allowance, extra, latitude, leeway, play, room, scope, space

marginal borderline, peripheral

marine maritime, nautical, naval, oceanic, seafaring

mariner bluejacket, hand, sailor, salt, seafarer, seaman, tar

marital conjugal, married, matrimonial, nuptial, wedded

maritime marine, nautical, naval, oceanic, sea, seafaring

mark *n.* 1. blot, bruise, dent, impression, line, nick, scar, scratch, smudge, spot, stain, streak 2. badge, blaze, brand, emblem, evidence, feature, hallmark, indication, label, note, print, proof, seal, sign, stamp, symbol, symptom, token 3. aim, end, goal, object, objective, purpose, target 4. footprint, sign, trace, track, trail, vestige ~*v.* 5. blemish, blot, blotch, brand, bruise, dent, impress, imprint, nick, scar, scratch, smudge, stain, streak 6. brand, identify, label, stamp 7. attend, mind, note, notice, observe, regard, remark, watch

marked apparent, clear, conspicuous, decided, distinct, evident, manifest, notable, noted, obvious, patent, remarkable, signal, striking

markedly clearly, conspicuously, decidedly, distinctly, evidently, greatly, manifestly, notably, obviously, patently, remarkably, signally, strikingly

market 1. *n.* bazaar, fair, mart 2. *v.* retail, sell, vend

DICTIONARY

marlin(e)spike *n.* pointed hook used to separate strands of rope.

marmalade *n.* jam made from citrus fruits.

marmoreal [mar-**more**-ee-al] *adj.* of or like marble.

marmoset *n.* small bushy-tailed monkey.

marmot *n.* burrowing rodent.

maroon[1] *adj.* reddish-purple.

maroon[2] *v.* abandon ashore, esp. on an island; isolate without resources.

marquee *n.* large tent used for a party or exhibition.

marquess [mar-kwiss] *n.* nobleman of the rank below a duke.

marquetry *n., pl.* **-quetries.** ornamental inlaid work of wood.

marquis *n., pl.* **-quises, -quis.** (in various countries) nobleman of the rank above a count.

marram grass *n.* grass that grows on sandy shores.

marrow *n.* fatty substance inside bones; oblong green striped vegetable.

marry *v.* **-rying, -ried.** take as a husband or wife; join or give in marriage; unite closely. —**marriage** *n.* state of being married; wedding. —**marriageable** *adj.*

Mars *n.* Roman god of war; fourth planet from the sun. —**Martian** *adj.* of Mars. —*n.* supposed inhabitant of Mars.

Marsala [mar-**sah**-la] *n.* dark sweet wine.

marsh *n.* low-lying wet land. —**marshy** *adj.*

marshal *n.* officer of the highest rank; official who organizes ceremonies or events; *US* law officer. —*v.* **-shalling, -shalled.** arrange in order; assemble; conduct with ceremony. —**marshalling yard** railway depot for goods trains.

marshmallow *n.* spongy pink or white sweet.

marsupial [mar-**soop**-yal] *n.* animal that carries its young in a pouch, such as a kangaroo.

mart *n.* market.

Martello tower *n.* round tower for coastal defence.

marten *n.* weasel-like animal; its fur.

martial *adj.* of war, warlike. —**martial art** any of various philosophies and techniques of self-defence, orig. Eastern, such as karate. —**martial law** law enforced by military authorities in times of danger or emergency.

martin *n.* bird with a slightly forked tail.

martinet *n.* strict disciplinarian.

martini *n.* cocktail of vermouth and gin.

martyr *n.* person who dies or suffers for his beliefs. —*v.* make a martyr of. —**be a martyr to** be constantly suffering from. —**martyrdom** *n.*

marvel *v.* **-velling, -velled.** be filled with wonder. —*n.* wonderful thing. —**marvellous** *adj.* amazing; wonderful.

Marxism *n.* state socialism as conceived by Karl Marx. —**Marxist** *n., adj.*

marzipan *n.* paste of ground almonds, sugar, and egg whites.

masc. masculine.

mascara *n.* cosmetic for darkening the eyelashes.

mascot *n.* thing supposed to bring good luck.

masculine *adj.* relating to males; manly; *Grammar* of the gender of nouns that includes some male animate things. —**masculinity** *n.*

mash *n.* bran or meal mixed with warm water as food for horses etc.; *Informal* mashed potatoes. —*v.* crush into a soft mass.

mask *n.* covering for the face, as a disguise or protection; behaviour that hides one's true feelings. —*v.* cover with a mask; hide or disguise.

masochism [**mass**-oh-kiz-zum] *n.* form of (sexual) perversion marked by love of pain or of being humiliated. —**masochist** *n.* —**masochistic** *adj.*

THESAURUS

maroon abandon, cast away, desert, leave, strand

marriage 1. match, matrimony, wedding, wedlock 2. alliance, association, coupling, link, merger, union

married 1. joined, one, united, wed, wedded 2. conjugal, connubial, marital, matrimonial, nuptial, wifely

marry 1. espouse, wed 2. ally, bond, join, knit, link, match, merge, tie, unite, yoke

marsh bog, fen, quagmire, slough, swamp

marshal align, arrange, array, assemble, collect, deploy, dispose, gather, group, muster, order, rank

marshy boggy, miry, spongy, swampy, wet

martial bellicose, heroic, military

martinet disciplinarian, stickler

martyrdom agony, anguish, ordeal, persecution, suffering, torment, torture

marvel 1. *v.* gape, gaze, goggle, wonder 2. *n.* genius, miracle, phenomenon, portent, prodigy, wonder

marvellous amazing, astounding, breathtaking, extraordinary, miraculous, prodigious, remarkable, stupendous, wondrous

masculine male, manful, manlike, manly, virile

DICTIONARY

mason n. person who works with stone; (**M-**) Freemason. —**Masonic** adj. of Freemasonry. —**masonry** n. stonework; (**M-**) Freemasonry.

masque [mask] n. Hist. 16th–17th-century form of dramatic entertainment.

masquerade [mask-a-**raid**] n. deceptive show or pretence; party at which masks and costumes are worn. —v. pretend to be someone or something else.

mass n. coherent body of matter; large quantity or number; Physics amount of matter in a body. —adj. large-scale; involving many people. —v. form into a mass. —**the masses** ordinary people. —**massive** adj. large and heavy. —**mass-market** adj. for or appealing to a large number of people. —**mass media** means of communication to many people, such as television and newspapers. —**mass-produce** v. manufacture standardized goods in large quantities.

Mass n. service of the Eucharist, esp. in the RC Church.

massacre [mass-a-ker] n. indiscriminate killing of large numbers of people. —v. kill in large numbers.

massage [mass-ahzh] n. rubbing and kneading of parts of the body to reduce pain or stiffness. —v. give a massage to. —**masseur** [mass-ur], **masseuse** [mass-uhz] n. person who gives massages.

massif [mass-seef] n. connected group of mountains.

mast¹ n. tall pole for supporting something, esp. a ship's sails.

mast² n. fruit of the beech, oak, etc., used as pig fodder.

mastectomy [mass-**tek**-tom-ee] n., pl. -**mies.** surgical removal of a breast.

master n. person in control, such as an employer or an owner of slaves or animals; expert; great artist; male teacher; original thing from which copies are made. —adj. overall or controlling; main or principal. —v. overcome; acquire knowledge of or skill in. —**masterful** adj. domineering; showing great skill. —**masterly** adj. showing great skill. —**mastery** n. expertise; control or command. —**master key** key that opens all the locks of a set. —**mastermind** v. plan and direct (a complex task). —n. person who plans and directs a complex task. —**masterpiece** n. outstanding work of art.

mastic n. gum obtained from certain trees; putty-like substance used as a filler, adhesive, or seal.

masticate v. chew. —**mastication** n.

mastiff n. large dog.

mastitis n. inflammation of a breast or udder.

mastodon n. extinct elephant-like mammal.

mastoid n. projection of the bone behind the ear. —**mastoiditis** n. inflammation of this area.

masturbate v. stimulate the genitals (of). —**masturbation** n.

mat n. piece of fabric used as a floor covering or to protect a surface; thick tangled mass. —v. **matting, matted.** form into a mat. —**on the mat** Informal summoned for a reprimand.

matador n. man who kills the bull in bullfights.

match¹ n. contest in a game or sport; person or thing exactly like, equal to, or in harmony with another; marriage. —v. be exactly like, equal to, or in harmony with; put in competition (with); find a match for; join (in marriage). —**match-**

THESAURUS

mass n. 1. block, chunk, hunk, lump, piece 2. body, collection, entirety, sum, totality, whole 3. batch, bunch, collection, combination, heap, load, lot, pile, quantity, stack 4. assemblage, band, body, crowd, group, horde, host, lot, mob, number, throng, troop ~adj. 5. extensive, indiscriminate, large-scale, pandemic, popular, wholesale, widespread ~v. 6. accumulate, assemble, collect, forgather, gather, mob, muster, rally, swarm, throng

massacre 1. n. butchery, carnage, killing, murder, slaughter 2. v. butcher, exterminate, kill, mow down, murder, slaughter, slay

massage 1. n. manipulation, rub-down 2. v. manipulate, rub down

massive big, bulky, enormous, extensive, gigantic, great, heavy, huge, hulking, immense, imposing, impressive, ponderous, solid, substantial, vast, weighty

master n. 1. captain, chief, commander, controller, director, employer, governor, head, lord, manager, overlord, overseer, owner, principal, ruler 2. adept, expert, genius, maestro, virtuoso, wizard ~v. 3. acquire, grasp, learn 4. bridle, check, conquer, curb, defeat, overcome, quash, quell, subdue, subjugate, suppress, tame, vanquish

masterful 1. adept, adroit, clever, deft, expert, first-rate, skilful, skilled, superior, supreme 2. arrogant, dictatorial, domineering, highhanded

masterly adept, adroit, clever, fine, first-rate, skilful, superior

masterpiece classic, jewel, tour de force

mastery 1. command, familiarity, grasp, knowledge, understanding 2. ability, attainment, expertise, prowess, skill

DICTIONARY

less *adj.* unequalled. —**matchmaker** *n.* person who schemes to bring about a marriage. —**matchmaking** *n.*

match² *n.* small stick with a tip which ignites when scraped on a rough surface. —**matchbox** *n.* —**matchstick** *n.* wooden part of a match. —*adj.* (of drawn figures) thin and straight. —**matchwood** *n.* small splinters.

mate¹ *n. Informal* common Brit. and Aust. term of address between males; sexual partner of an animal; officer in a merchant ship; tradesman's assistant. —*v.* pair (animals) or (of animals) be paired for reproduction. —**matey** *adj. Informal* friendly or intimate.

mate² *n., v. Chess* checkmate.

material *n.* substance of which a thing is made; cloth; information on which a piece of work may be based. —*pl.* things needed for an activity. —*adj.* of matter or substance; affecting physical wellbeing; unspiritual; relevant. —**materially** *adv.* considerably. —**materialism** *n.* excessive interest in or desire for money and possessions; belief that only the material world exists. —**materialist** *adj., n.* —**materialistic** *adj.* —**materialize** *v.* come into existence or view; actually happen. —**materialization** *n.*

maternal *adj.* of a mother; related through one's mother. —**maternity** *n.* motherhood. —*adj.* of or for pregnant women.

mathematics *n.* science of number, quantity, shape, and space. —**mathematical** *adj.* —**mathematically** *adv.* —**mathematician** *n.*

maths *n. Informal* mathematics.

matinée [mat-in-nay] *n.* afternoon performance in a theatre.

matins *pl. n.* early morning service in various Christian Churches.

matriarch [mate-ree-ark] *n.* female head of a tribe or family. —**matriarchal** *adj.* —**matriarchy** *n.* society with matriarchal government and descent traced through the female line.

matricide *n.* crime of killing one's mother; person who does this.

matriculate *v.* enrol or be enrolled in a college or university. —**matriculation** *n.*

matrimony *n.* marriage. —**matrimonial** *adj.*

matrix [may-trix] *n., pl.* **matrices** [may-trisseez]. substance or situation in which something originates, takes form, or is enclosed; mould for casting; *Maths* rectangular array of numbers or elements.

matron *n.* staid or dignified married woman; *former name for* NURSING OFFICER; woman who supervises the domestic or medical arrangements of an institution. —**matronly** *adj.*

matt *adj.* dull, not shiny.

matter *n.* substance of which something is made; physical substance; event, situation, or subject; written material in general; pus. —*v.* be of importance. —**what's the matter?** what's wrong? what's the trouble?

mattock *n.* large pick with one of its blade ends flattened for loosening soil.

mattress *n.* large stuffed flat case, often with springs, used on or as a bed.

mature *adj.* fully developed or grown-up; ripe. —*v.* make or become mature; (of a bill or bond)

THESAURUS

match *n.* 1. bout, contest, game, test, trial 2. counterpart, equal, equivalent, peer, rival 3. copy, double, duplicate, equal, replica, twin 4. affiliation, alliance, combination, couple, duet, marriage, pair, pairing, partnership, union ~*v.* 5. ally, combine, couple, join, link, marry, mate, pair, unite, yoke 6. adapt, agree, blend, correspond, fit, go with, harmonize, suit, tally 7. compare, contend, equal, oppose, pit against, rival, vie

matchless consummate, incomparable, inimitable, peerless, perfect, superlative, supreme, unequalled, unique, unrivalled

mate *n.* 1. colleague, companion, fellow-worker 2. assistant, helper, subordinate ~*v.* 3. breed, copulate, couple, pair

material *n.* 1. body, element, matter, stuff, substance 2. data, evidence, facts, information, notes, work 3. cloth, fabric, stuff ~*adj.* 4. bodily, concrete, fleshly, physical, substantial, tangible, worldly 5. essential, grave, im-

portant, key, meaningful, momentous, serious, significant, vital, weighty

materialize appear, happen, occur, turn up

materially considerably, essentially, gravely, greatly, much, seriously, significantly, substantially

matrimonial conjugal, marital, married, nuptial, wedding

matrimony marriage, nuptials, wedlock

matrix forge, mould, origin, source

matter *n.* 1. body, stuff, substance 2. affair, business, concern, episode, event, incident, occurrence, question, situation, subject, topic ~*v.* 3. signify

mature 1. *adj.* adult, fit, grown, matured, mellow, of age, perfect, prepared, ready, ripe, seasoned 2. *v.* age, bloom, develop, mellow, perfect, ripen, season

maturity adulthood, experience, fullness, majority, manhood, perfection, ripeness, wisdom

DICTIONARY

become due for payment. —**maturity** n. —**maturation** n.

maudlin adj. foolishly or tearfully sentimental.

maul v. handle roughly; beat or tear.

maunder v. talk or act aimlessly or idly.

Maundy money n. special silver coins given to the poor in a symbolic ceremony on the Thursday before Easter (**Maundy Thursday**).

mausoleum [maw-so-lee-um] n. stately tomb.

mauve adj. pale purple.

maverick n. independent unorthodox person.

maw n. animal's mouth, throat, or stomach.

mawkish adj. foolishly sentimental.

maxim n. general truth or principle.

maximum n., pl. -**mums**, -**ma**. greatest possible amount or number. —adj. greatest. —**maximal** adj. —**maximize** v. increase to a maximum.

May n. fifth month of the year; (**m-**) same as HAWTHORN. —**mayfly** n. short-lived aquatic insect. —**maypole** n. pole set up for dancing round on the first day of May (**May Day**).

may v., past tense **might**. used as an auxiliary to express possibility, permission, opportunity, etc.

maybe adv. perhaps; possibly.

Mayday n. international radiotelephone distress signal.

mayhem n. violent destruction or confusion.

mayonnaise n. creamy sauce of egg yolks, oil, and vinegar.

mayor n. head of a municipality. —**mayoress** n. mayor's wife; lady mayor. —**mayoral** adj. —**mayoralty** n. (term of) office of a mayor.

maze n. complex network of paths or lines designed to puzzle; state of confusion.

mazurka n. lively Polish dance; music for this.

MB Bachelor of Medicine.

MBE Member of the Order of the British Empire.

MC Master of Ceremonies.

MD Doctor of Medicine.

ME myalgic encephalomyelitis, postviral syndrome.

me pron. objective form of I.

mead n. alcoholic drink made from honey.

meadow n. piece of grassland. —**meadowsweet** n. plant with dense heads of small fragrant flowers.

meagre adj. scanty or insufficient.

meal[1] n. occasion when food is served and eaten; the food itself.

meal[2] n. grain ground to powder. —**mealy** adj. —**mealy-mouthed** adj. not outspoken enough.

mealie n. S Afr. maize.

mean[1] v. **meaning**, **meant**. intend to convey or express; intend; signify, denote, or portend; have importance as specified. —**meaning** n. sense, significance. —adj. expressive. —**meaningful** adj. —**meaningless** adj.

mean[2] adj. miserly, ungenerous, or petty; despicable or callous; US informal bad-tempered. —**meanly** adv. —**meanness** n. —**meanie, meany** n. miserly person.

mean[3] n. middle point between two extremes; average. —pl. that by which something is done; money. —adj. intermediate in size or quantity; average. —**by all means** certainly. —**by no means** not at all. —**means test** enquiry into a person's means to decide eligibility for financial

THESAURUS

maudlin lachrymose, sentimental, tearful

maul 1. abuse, ill-treat, manhandle, molest, paw 2. batter, beat, claw, lacerate, mangle, pummel, thrash

maxim adage, aphorism, axiom, byword, motto, proverb, rule, saw, saying

maximum 1. n. ceiling, crest, extremity, height, most, peak, pinnacle, summit, top, utmost, uttermost, zenith 2. adj. greatest, highest, most, topmost, utmost

maybe perchance, perhaps, possibly

mayhem chaos, commotion, confusion, destruction, disorder, fracas, havoc, trouble, violence

maze 1. intricacy, labyrinth, meander 2. Fig. imbroglio, perplexity, puzzle, snarl, tangle, web

meadow field, grassland, pasture

meagre deficient, inadequate, little, paltry, poor, puny, scanty, short, slender, slight, small, spare, sparse

mean[1] v. 1. betoken, convey, denote, express, imply, indicate, purport, represent, say, signify, spell, suggest, symbolize 2. aim, aspire, design, desire, intend, plan, propose, purpose, set out, want, wish

mean[2] adj. 1. beggarly, close, mercenary, miserly, parsimonious, stingy, tight, ungenerous 2. abject, base, callous, contemptible, degraded, despicable, ignoble, low-minded, petty, scurvy, shabby, shameful, sordid, vile, wretched 3. beggarly, insignificant, miserable, paltry, petty, poor, scruffy, seedy, shabby, sordid, squalid, tawdry, wretched

mean[3] 1. n. average, balance, median, middle, mid-point, norm 2. adj. average, intermediate, medial, median, medium, middle, standard

DICTIONARY

aid. —**meantime** *n.* intervening period. —*adv.* meanwhile. —**meanwhile** *adv.* during the intervening period; at the same time.

meander [mee-**and**-er] *v.* follow a winding course; wander aimlessly. —*n.* winding course.

measles *n.* infectious disease producing red spots. —**measly** *adj. Informal* meagre.

measure *n.* size or quantity; graduated scale etc. for measuring size or quantity; unit of size or quantity; extent; action taken; law; poetical rhythm. —*v.* determine the size or quantity of; be (a specified amount) in size or quantity. —**measurable** *adj.* —**measured** *adj.* slow and steady; carefully considered. —**measurement** *n.* measuring; size. —**measure up to** *v.* fulfil (expectations or requirements).

meat *n.* animal flesh as food. —**meaty** *adj.* (tasting) of or like meat; brawny; full of significance or interest.

Mecca *n.* holy city of Islam; place that attracts visitors.

mechanic *n.* person skilled in repairing or operating machinery. —**mechanical** *adj.* of or done by machines; (of an action) without thought or feeling. —**mechanically** *adv.*

mechanism *n.* way a machine works; piece of machinery; process or technique, e.g. *defence mechanism*. —**mechanize** *v.* equip with machinery; make mechanical or automatic; *Mil.* equip (an army) with armoured vehicles. —**mechanization** *n.*

med. medical; medicine; medieval; medium.

medal *n.* piece of metal with an inscription etc., given as a reward or memento. —**medallion** *n.* large medal; circular decorative device in architecture. —**medallist** *n.* winner of a medal.

meddle *v.* interfere annoyingly. —**meddler** *n.* —**meddlesome** *adj.*

media *n.* a plural of MEDIUM; the mass media collectively.

mediaeval [med-ee-**eve**-al] *adj.* same as MEDIEVAL.

medial [**mee**-dee-al] *adj.* of or in the middle. —**median** *adj., n.* middle (point or line).

mediate [**mee**-dee-ate] *v.* intervene to bring about agreement; resolve (a dispute) by mediation. —**mediation** *n.* —**mediator** *n.*

medic *n. Informal* doctor or medical student.

medicine *n.* substance used to treat disease; science of preventing, diagnosing, or curing dis-

THESAURUS

meander 1. *v.* ramble, snake, stray, stroll, turn, wander, wind 2. *n.* bend, coil, curve, loop, turn, twist, zigzag

meaning drift, explanation, gist, implication, import, interpretation, message, purport, sense, significance, substance, upshot, value

meaningful 1. important, material, purposeful, relevant, serious, significant, valid 2. eloquent, expressive, meaning, pointed, speaking

meaningless aimless, empty, futile, hollow, in~ ane, insignificant, nonsensical, pointless, trifling, trivial, useless, vain, worthless

meanness 1. miserliness, parsimony, selfishness, tight-fistedness 2. bad temper, churlishness, hostility, ill temper, malice, nastiness, rudeness, unpleasantness 3. baseness, degradation, narrow-mindedness, pettiness, shabbiness, vileness

means 1. agency, avenue, course, instrument, medium, method, mode, process, way 2. affluence, estate, fortune, funds, income, money, property, resources, riches, substance, wealth

measurable determinable, material, perceptible, quantifiable, significant

measure *n.* 1. allowance, amount, amplitude, capacity, degree, extent, proportion, quantity, quota, range, ration, reach, scope, share, size 2. gauge, metre, rule, scale 3. act, action, course, deed, expedient, means, procedure,

step 4. act, bill, enactment, law, resolution, statute 5. beat, cadence, foot, metre, rhythm, verse ~*v.* 6. assess, calculate, calibrate, compute, determine, estimate, evaluate, gauge, judge, quantify, rate, size, sound, survey, value, weigh

measurement assessment, calculation, calibration, estimation, evaluation, mensuration, survey, valuation

measure up (**to**) be adequate, be fit, compare, equal, match, meet, rival

meat aliment, cheer, comestibles, fare, flesh, food, nourishment, provender, provisions, rations, subsistence, viands, victuals

mechanical 1. automatic 2. automatic, cold, cursory, dead, habitual, impersonal, instinctive, lacklustre, lifeless, perfunctory, routine, unconscious, unfeeling

mechanism 1. apparatus, appliance, contrivance, device, instrument, structure, system, tool 2. agency, execution, means, medium, method, operation, performance, procedure, system, technique

meddle interfere, intervene, intrude, pry

mediate arbitrate, conciliate, intercede, intervene, reconcile, referee, resolve, settle, umpire

mediator advocate, arbiter, go-between, intermediary, judge, negotiator, peacemaker, referee, umpire

DICTIONARY

ease. —**medical** *adj.* of the science of medicine. —*n. Informal* medical examination. —**medically** *adv.* —**medicament** *n.* a medicine. —**medicate** *v.* treat with a medicinal substance. —**medication** *n.* (treatment with) a medicinal substance. —**medicinal** [med-**diss**-in-al] *adj.* having therapeutic properties. —**medicine man** witch doctor.

medieval [med-ee-**eve**-al] *adj.* of the Middle Ages.

mediocre [mee-dee-**oak**-er] *adj.* average in quality; second-rate. —**mediocrity** [mee-dee-**ok**-rit-ee] *n.*

meditate *v.* reflect deeply, esp. on spiritual matters; think about or plan. —**meditation** *n.* meditating. —**meditative** *adj.* —**meditatively** *adv.* —**meditator** *n.*

medium *adj.* midway between extremes, average. —*n., pl.* **-dia** *or* **-diums.** middle state, degree, or condition; intervening substance producing an effect; means of communicating news or information to the public, such as radio or newspapers; person who can supposedly communicate with the dead; surroundings or environment; category of art according to the material used. —**medium wave** radio wave with a wavelength between 100 and 1000 metres.

medlar *n.* apple-like fruit of a small tree, eaten when it begins to decay.

medley *n.* miscellaneous mixture; musical sequence of different tunes.

medulla [mid-**dull**-la] *n., pl.* **-las, -lae.** marrow, pith, or inner tissue. —**medullary** *adj.*

meek *adj.* submissive or humble. —**meekly** *adv.* —**meekness** *n.*

meerkat *n.* S African mongoose.

meerschaum [**meer**-shum] *n.* white substance like clay; tobacco pipe with a bowl made of this.

meet[1] *v.* **meeting, met.** come together (with); come into contact (with); be at the place of arrival of; make the acquaintance of; satisfy (a need etc.); experience. —*n.* assembly of a hunt; sports meeting. —**meeting** *n.* coming together; assembly.

meet[2] *adj. Obs.* fit or suitable.

mega- *combining form* denoting one million, e.g. *mega*watt; very great, e.g. *megastar.*

megabyte *n. Computers* 2^{20} or 1 048 576 bytes.

megalith *n.* great stone, esp. as part of a prehistoric monument. —**megalithic** *adj.*

megalomania *n.* craving for or mental delusions of power. —**megalomaniac** *adj., n.*

megaphone *n.* cone-shaped instrument used to amplify the voice.

megaton *n.* explosive power equal to that of one million tons of TNT.

melancholy [mel-an-kol-lee] *n.* sadness or gloom. —*adj.* sad or gloomy. —**melancholia** [mel-an-**kole**-ya] *n.* old name for depression. —**melancholic** *adj., n.*

melange [may-lahnzh] *n.* mixture.

melanin *n.* dark pigment found in the hair, skin, and eyes of man and animals.

mêlée [**mel**-lay] *n.* noisy confused fight or crowd.

mellifluous [mel-**lif**-flew-uss] *adj.* (of sound) smooth and sweet.

mellow *adj.* (of fruit) ripe; kind-hearted, esp. through maturity; soft, not harsh. —*v.* make or become mellow.

THESAURUS

medicine cure, drug, physic, remedy

medieval antiquated, archaic, old-fashioned, primitive

mediocre average, indifferent, inferior, mean, middling, ordinary, passable, pedestrian, tolerable, undistinguished, uninspired

mediocrity 1. indifference, insignificance, poorness 2. nobody, nonentity

meditate cogitate, consider, contemplate, deliberate, muse, ponder, reflect, study, think

medium *adj.* 1. average, fair, intermediate, mean, mediocre, middle ~*n.* 2. average, centre, mean, middle 3. agency, avenue, channel, form, instrument, means, mode, organ, vehicle, way

medley jumble, miscellany, mishmash, mixture, pastiche, patchwork

meek deferential, docile, gentle, humble, mild, modest, patient, peaceful, soft, submissive, unpretentious, yielding

meekness deference, docility, gentleness, humbleness, humility, mildness, modesty, patience, softness, submission

meet 1. confront, contact, encounter, find 2. abut, adjoin, connect, converge, cross, intersect, join, touch, unite 3. answer, comply, discharge, equal, fulfil, gratify, handle, match, perform, satisfy 4. assemble, collect, come together, gather, muster, rally

meeting 1. assignation, encounter, engagement, introduction, rendezvous 2. assembly, audience, company, conference, congregation, convention, gathering, rally, reunion, session 3. concourse, confluence, convergence, crossing, intersection, junction, union

melancholy 1. *n.* dejection, depression, despondency, gloom, sadness, sorrow, unhappiness, woe 2. *adj.* gloomy, glum, joyless, low, lugubrious, miserable, mournful, pensive, sad, sombre, sorrowful, unhappy

DICTIONARY

melodrama *n.* play full of extravagant action and emotion; overdramatic behaviour or emotion. —**melodramatic** *adj.*

melody *n., pl.* **-dies.** series of musical notes which make a tune; sweet sound. —**melodic** [mel-**lod**-ik] *adj.* of melody; melodious. —**melodious** [mel-**lode**-ee-uss] *adj.* pleasing to the ear; tuneful.

melon *n.* large round juicy fruit with a hard rind.

melt *v.* (cause to) become liquid by heat; dissolve; soften through emotion; blend (into); disappear. —**meltdown** *n.* (in a nuclear reactor) melting of the fuel rods, with the possible release of radiation.

member *n.* individual making up a body or society; limb. —**membership** *n.* —**Member of Parliament** person elected to parliament.

membrane *n.* thin flexible tissue in a plant or animal body. —**membranous** *adj.*

memento *n., pl.* **-tos, -toes.** thing serving to remind, souvenir.

memo *n., pl.* **memos.** short for MEMORANDUM.

memoir [**mem**-wahr] *n.* biography or historical account based on personal knowledge. —*pl.* collection of these; autobiography.

memory *n., pl.* **-ries.** ability to remember; sum of things remembered; particular recollection; length of time one can remember; commemoration; part of a computer which stores information. —**memorial** *n.* something serving to commemorate a person or thing. —*adj.* serving as a memorial. —**memorable** *adj.* worth remembering, noteworthy. —**memorably** *adv.* —**memorandum** *n.* written record or communication within a business; note of things to be remembered. —**memorize** *v.* commit to memory.

men *n.* plural of MAN.

menace *n.* threat; *Informal* nuisance. —*v.* threaten, endanger. —**menacing** *adj.*

ménage [may-**nahzh**] *n.* household.

menagerie [min-**naj**-er-ee] *n.* collection of wild animals for exhibition.

mend *v.* repair or patch; make or become better; recover or heal. —*n.* mended area. —**on the mend** regaining health.

mendacity *n.* (tendency to) untruthfulness. —**mendacious** *adj.*

mendicant *adj.* begging. —*n.* beggar.

menhir [**men**-hear] *n.* single upright prehistoric stone.

menial [**mean**-yal] *adj.* involving boring work of low status. —*n.* domestic servant.

meningitis [men-in-**jite**-iss] *n.* inflammation of the membranes of the brain.

meniscus *n., pl.* **-nisci, -niscuses.** curved surface of a liquid; crescent-shaped lens.

menopause *n.* time when a woman's menstrual cycle ceases. —**menopausal** *adj.*

menstruation *n.* approximately monthly discharge of blood and cellular debris from the womb of a nonpregnant woman. —**menstruate** *v.* —**menstrual** *adj.*

mensuration *n.* measuring, esp. in geometry.

THESAURUS

mellow *adj.* 1. delicate, juicy, mature, perfect, rich, ripe, soft, sweet 2. cheerful, cordial, elevated, expansive, genial, happy, jolly, jovial, relaxed ~*v.* 3. develop, improve, mature, perfect, ripen, season, soften, sweeten

melodious dulcet, musical, silvery, sweet-sounding, tuneful

melodramatic extravagant, histrionic, over-dramatic, theatrical

melody air, descant, music, refrain, song, strain, theme, tune

melt 1. diffuse, dissolve, flux, fuse, liquefy, soften, thaw 2. disarm

member 1. fellow, representative 2. arm, component, constituent, element, leg, limb, organ, part, portion

memoir account, biography, essay, journal, life, narrative

memoirs autobiography, diary, experiences, journals, life, life story, memories, recollections

memorable celebrated, distinguished, famous, historic, illustrious, important, notable, remarkable, significant, striking, unforgettable

memorial 1. *adj.* commemorative, monumental 2. *n.* monument, plaque, record, souvenir

memorize learn, learn by heart, learn by rote, remember

memory 1. recall, recollection, reminiscence 2. honour, remembrance

menace 1. *v.* alarm, browbeat, bully, frighten, impend, intimidate, loom, lour, lower, terrorize, threaten 2. *n.* scare, threat, warning

menacing alarming, dangerous, frightening, intimidating, looming, louring, lowering, ominous, threatening

mend *v.* 1. cure, darn, fix, heal, patch, rectify, refit, reform, remedy, renew, repair, restore 2. amend, better, correct, emend, improve, rectify, reform, revise ~*n.* 3. darn, patch, repair, stitch

menial *adj.* boring, dull, humdrum, routine, unskilled

DICTIONARY

mental *adj.* of, in, or done by the mind; of or for mental illness; *Informal* insane. —**mentally** *adv.* —**mentality** *n.* way of thinking.

menthol *n.* organic compound found in peppermint, used medicinally.

mention *v.* refer to briefly; acknowledge. —*n.* acknowledgment; brief reference to a person or thing.

mentor *n.* adviser or guide.

menu *n.* list of dishes to be served, or from which to order; *Computers* list of options displayed on a screen.

MEP Member of the European Parliament.

mercantile *adj.* of trade or traders.

Mercator projection [mer-**kate**-er] *n.* method of map-making in which latitude and longitude form a rectangular grid.

mercenary *adj.* influenced by greed; working merely for reward. —*n., pl.* -**aries.** hired soldier.

mercerized *adj.* (of cotton) given lustre by treating with chemicals.

merchant *n.* person engaged in trade, wholesale trader. —**merchandise** *n.* commodities. —**merchant bank** bank dealing mainly with businesses and investment. —**merchantman** *n.* trading ship. —**merchant navy** ships or crew engaged in a nation's commercial shipping.

mercury *n.* silvery liquid metal; (**M-**) *Roman myth* messenger of the gods; (**M-**) planet nearest the sun. —**mercurial** [mer-**cure**-ee-al] *adj.* lively, changeable.

mercy *n., pl.* -**cies.** compassionate treatment of an offender or enemy who is in one's power; merciful act. —**merciful** *adj.* compassionate; giving relief. —**merciless** *adj.*

mere[1] *adj.* nothing more than, e.g. *mere chance.* —**merely** *adv.*

mere[2] *n. Obs.* lake.

meretricious *adj.* superficially or garishly attractive but of no real value.

merganser [mer-**gan**-ser] *n.* large crested diving duck.

merge *v.* (cause to) combine or blend. —**merger** *n.* combination of business firms into one.

meridian *n.* imaginary circle of the earth passing through both poles; peak or zenith.

meringue [mer-**rang**] *n.* baked mixture of egg whites and sugar; small cake of this.

merino *n., pl.* -**nos.** breed of sheep with fine soft wool; this wool.

merit *n.* excellence or worth. —*pl.* admirable qualities. —*v.* -**iting, -ited.** deserve. —**meritorious** *adj.* deserving praise. —**meritocracy** [mer-it-**tok**-rass-ee] *n.* rule by people of superior talent or intellect.

merlin *n.* small falcon.

mermaid *n.* imaginary sea creature with the upper part of a woman and the lower part of a fish. —**merman** *n. masc.*

merry *adj.* -**rier, -riest.** cheerful or jolly; *Informal* slightly drunk. —**merrily** *adv.* —**merriment** *n.* —**merry-go-round** *n.* roundabout. —**merrymaking** *n.* revelry.

mesdames *n.* plural of MADAME.

THESAURUS

mental cerebral, intellectual

mentality attitude, disposition, outlook, personality

mentally intellectually, inwardly, rationally, subjectively

mention *v.* 1. adduce, broach, cite, communicate, declare, disclose, divulge, impart, intimate, name, recount, refer to, report, reveal, state, tell, touch upon ~*n.* 2. citation, recognition, tribute 3. allusion, indication, remark

mentor adviser, coach, counsellor, guide, instructor, teacher, tutor

mercantile commercial, trading

mercenary 1. *adj.* avaricious, covetous, grasping, greedy, sordid, venal 2. *n.* hireling

merchandise goods, produce, stock, wares

merchant broker, dealer, retailer, salesman, seller, shopkeeper, trader, tradesman, trafficker, vendor, wholesaler

merciful compassionate, forbearing, forgiving, generous, gracious, humane, kind, lenient, liberal, soft, sparing, sympathetic

merciless callous, cruel, hard-hearted, heartless, inexorable, relentless, severe, unfeeling, unsympathetic

mercy charity, clemency, compassion, favour, forbearance, forgiveness, grace, kindness, pity, quarter

mere *adj.* absolute, bare, common, entire, plain, pure, sheer, simple, stark, unmixed, utter

merge amalgamate, blend, combine, fuse, intermix, join, meet, mingle, mix, unite

merger amalgamation, coalition, fusion, incorporation, union

merit 1. *n.* asset, excellence, good, goodness, integrity, quality, talent, value, virtue, worth, worthiness 2. *v.* deserve, earn, incur, warrant

merriment amusement, conviviality, festivity, frolic, fun, gaiety, laughter, mirth, revelry, sport

merry blithe, carefree, cheerful, convivial, festive, gay, glad, gleeful, happy, jolly, joyful, joyous, light-hearted, mirthful, rollicking, sportive, vivacious

DICTIONARY

mesdemoiselles *n.* plural of MADEMOISELLE.

mesembryanthemum *n.* low-growing plant with bright daisylike flowers.

mesh *n.* network or net; (open space between) strands forming a network. —*v.* (of gear teeth) engage.

mesmerize *v.* hold spellbound; *Obs.* hypnotize.

meson [mee-zon] *n.* elementary atomic particle.

mess *n.* untidy or dirty confusion; trouble or difficulty; group of servicemen who regularly eat together; place where they eat. —*v.* muddle or dirty; (foll. by *about*) potter about; (foll. by *with*) interfere with; (of servicemen) eat in a group.

message *n.* communication sent; meaning or moral. —**messenger** *n.* bearer of a message.

Messiah *n.* Jews' promised deliverer; Christ. —**Messianic** *adj.*

messieurs *n.* plural of MONSIEUR.

Messrs [mess-erz] *n.* plural of MR.

messy *adj.* **messier, messiest.** dirty, confused, or untidy. —**messily** *adv.* —**messiness** *n.*

met *v.* past of MEET[1].

metabolism [met-**tab**-oh-liz-zum] *n.* chemical processes of a living body. —**metabolic** *adj.* —**metabolize** *v.* produce or be produced by metabolism.

metal *n.* chemical element, such as iron or copper, that is malleable and capable of conducting heat and electricity; short for ROAD METAL. —**metallic** *adj.* —**metallurgy** *n.* scientific study of the structure, properties, extraction, and refining of metals. —**metallurgical** *adj.* —**metallurgist** *n.*

metamorphosis [met-a-**more**-foss-is] *n., pl.* **-phoses** [-foss-eez]. change of form or character. —**metamorphic** *adj.* (of rocks) changed in texture or structure by heat and pressure. —**metamorphose** *v.* transform.

metaphor *n.* figure of speech in which a term is applied to something it does not literally denote in order to imply a resemblance, such as *he is a lion in battle.* —**metaphorical** *adj.* —**metaphorically** *adv.*

metaphysics *n.* branch of philosophy concerned with being and knowing. —**metaphysical** *adj.*

mete *v.* (usu. with *out*) deal out as punishment.

meteor *n.* small fast-moving heavenly body, visible as a streak of incandescence if it enters the earth's atmosphere. —**meteoric** [meet-ee-or-rik] *adj.* of a meteor; brilliant but short-lived. —**meteorite** *n.* meteor that has fallen to earth.

meteorology *n.* study of the earth's atmosphere, esp. for weather forecasting. —**meteorological** *adj.* —**meteorologist** *n.*

meter *n.* instrument for measuring and recording something, such as the consumption of gas or electricity. —*v.* measure by meter.

methane *n.* colourless inflammable gas.

methanol *n.* colourless poisonous liquid used as a solvent and fuel (also called **methyl alcohol**).

methinks *v., past tense* **methought.** *Obs.* it seems to me.

method *n.* way or manner; technique; orderliness. —**methodical** *adj.* orderly. —**methodically** *adv.* —**methodology** *n.* particular method or procedure.

Methodist *n.* member of any of the Protestant churches originated by Wesley and his followers. —*adj.* of Methodists or their Church. —**Methodism** *n.*

meths *n. Informal* methylated spirits.

methyl *n.* (compound containing) a saturated hydrocarbon group of atoms. —**methylated spir-**

THESAURUS

mesh 1. *n.* net, network, web 2. *v.* combine, connect, dovetail, engage, harmonize, knit

mess *n.* 1. botch, chaos, clutter, confusion, dirtiness, disarray, disorder, jumble, litter, shambles, turmoil, untidiness 2. difficulty, muddle, perplexity, plight, predicament ~*v.* 3. *Often with* **up** botch, bungle, clutter, dirty, disarrange, dishevel, foul, litter, pollute, scramble

message 1. bulletin, communication, dispatch, letter, missive, note, notice, tidings, word 2. idea, import, moral, point, theme

messenger agent, bearer, carrier, courier, emis~ sary, envoy, go-between, herald, runner

messy chaotic, cluttered, confused, dirty, di~

shevelled, disordered, disorganized, grubby, littered, muddled

metaphor allegory, analogy, image, symbol

meteoric brief, brilliant, ephemeral, fast, flashing, fleeting, momentary, rapid, sudden, swift

method approach, course, fashion, form, manner, mode, plan, practice, procedure, programme, routine, rule, scheme, style, system, technique, way

methodical businesslike, deliberate, disciplined, efficient, meticulous, neat, organized, planned, precise, regular, structured, tidy

meticulous detailed, exact, fastidious, painstaking, precise, scrupulous, strict, thorough

DICTIONARY

its alcohol with methanol added, used as a solvent and for heating.

meticulous *adj.* very careful about details. —**meticulously** *adv.*

métier [met-ee-ay] *n.* profession or trade; one's strong point.

metonymy [mit-on-im-ee] *n.* figure of speech in which one thing is replaced by another associated with it, such as 'the Crown' for 'the king'.

metre *n.* basic unit of length equal to about 1.094 yards; rhythm of poetry. —**metric** *adj.* of the decimal system of weights and measures based on the metre. —**metrical** *adj.* of measurement; of poetic metre. —**metrication** *n.* conversion to the metric system.

metronome *n.* instrument which marks musical time by means of a ticking pendulum.

metropolis [mit-trop-oh-liss] *n.* chief city of a country or region. —**metropolitan** *adj.* of a metropolis.

mettle *n.* courage or spirit.

mew *n.* cry of a cat. — *v.* utter this cry.

mews *n.* yard or street orig. of stables, now often converted to houses.

mezzanine [mez-zan-een] *n.* intermediate storey, esp. between the ground and first floor.

mezzo-soprano [met-so-] *n.* voice or singer between a soprano and contralto.

mezzotint [met-so-tint] *n.* method of engraving by scraping the roughened surface of a metal plate; print so made.

mg milligram(s).

Mg *Chem.* magnesium.

MHz megahertz.

miaow [mee-ow] *n., v.* same as MEW.

miasma [mee-azz-ma] *n.* unwholesome or foreboding atmosphere.

mica [my-ka] *n.* glasslike mineral used as an electrical insulator.

mice *n.* plural of MOUSE.

Michaelmas [mik-kl-mass] *n.* Sept. 29th, feast of St Michael the archangel. —**Michaelmas daisy** garden plant with small daisy-shaped flowers.

mickey *n.* —**take the mickey (out of)** *Informal* tease.

micro *n., pl.* -**cros.** short for MICROCOMPUTER, MICROPROCESSOR.

microbe *n.* minute organism, esp. one causing disease. —**microbial** *adj.*

microchip *n.* small wafer of silicon containing electronic circuits.

microcomputer *n.* computer having a central

processing unit contained in one or more silicon chips.

microcosm *n.* miniature representation of something; man as an epitome of the universe.

microfiche [my-crow-feesh] *n.* microfilm in sheet form.

microfilm *n.* miniaturized recording of books or documents on a roll of film.

microlight *n.* very small light private aircraft with large wings.

micrometer [my-krom-it-er] *n.* instrument for measuring very small distances or angles.

micron [my-kron] *n.* one millionth of a metre.

microorganism *n.* organism of microscopic size.

microphone *n.* instrument for amplifying or transmitting sounds.

microprocessor *n.* integrated circuit acting as the central processing unit in a small computer.

microscope *n.* instrument with lens(es) which produces a magnified image of a very small body. —**microscopic** *adj.* too small to be seen except with a microscope; very small; of a microscope. —**microscopically** *adv.* —**microscopy** *n.* use of a microscope.

microsurgery *n.* intricate surgery using a special microscope and miniature precision instruments.

microwave *n.* electromagnetic wave with a wavelength of a few centimetres, used in radar and cooking; microwave oven. — *v.* cook in a microwave oven. —**microwave oven** oven using microwaves to cook food quickly.

mid *adj.* intermediate, middle. —**midday** *n.* noon. —**midland** *n.* middle part of a country. —*pl.* (**M-**) central England. —**midnight** *n.* twelve o'clock at night. —**midshipman** *n.* naval officer of the lowest commissioned rank. —**midsummer** *n.* summer solstice; middle of summer. —**Midsummer Day** June 24th. —**midway** *adj., adv.* halfway. —**midwinter** *n.*

midden *n.* dunghill or rubbish heap.

middle *adj.* equidistant from two extremes; medium, intermediate. —*n.* middle point or part. —**middle age** period of life between youth and old age. —**middle-aged** *adj.* —**Middle Ages** period from about 1000 AD to the 15th century. —**middle class** social class of businessmen and professional people. —**middle-class** *adj.* —**Middle East** area around the eastern Mediterranean up to and including Iran. —**middleman** *n.* trader who buys from the producer and sells to the

THESAURUS

microscopic imperceptible, infinitesimal, tiny

midday noon, noonday, twelve o'clock

DICTIONARY

consumer. —**middle-of-the-road** *adj.* politically moderate; (of music) generally popular. —**middleweight** *n.* boxer weighing up to 160lb (professional) or 75kg (amateur).

middling *adj.* mediocre; moderate. —*adv.* moderately.

midge *n.* small mosquito-like insect.

midget *n.* very small person or thing.

midriff *n.* middle part of the body.

midst *n.* —**in the midst of** surrounded by; at a point during.

midwife *n.* trained person who assists at childbirth. —**midwifery** *n.*

mien [**mean**] *n. Lit.* person's bearing, demeanour, or appearance.

miffed *adj. Informal* offended or upset.

might[1] *v.* past tense of MAY.

might[2] *n.* power or strength. —**with might and main** energetically or forcefully. —**mighty** *adj.* powerful; important. —*adv. US informal* very. —**mightily** *adv.*

mignonette [min-yon-**net**] *n.* grey-green plant with sweet-smelling flowers.

migraine [**mee**-grain] *n.* severe headache, often with nausea and other symptoms.

migrate *v.* move from one place to settle in another; (of animals) journey between different habitats at specific seasons. —**migration** *n.* —**migrant** *n., adj.* (person or animal) that migrates. —**migratory** *adj.*

mike *n. Informal* microphone.

milch [**miltch**] *adj.* (of a cow) giving milk.

mild *adj.* not strongly flavoured; gentle; calm or temperate. —**mildly** *adv.* —**mildness** *n.*

mildew *n.* destructive fungus on plants or things exposed to damp. —**mildewed** *adj.*

mile *n.* unit of length equal to 1760 yards or 1.609 km. —**mileage** *n.* distance travelled in miles; miles travelled by a motor vehicle per gallon of petrol; *Informal* usefulness of something. —**milestone** *n.* stone marker showing the distance to a certain place; significant event.

mileometer [mile-**om**-it-er] *n.* device that records the number of miles a vehicle has travelled.

milieu [**meal**-yuh] *n., pl.* **milieus, milieux** [**meal**-yuhz]. environment or surroundings.

militant *adj.* aggressive or vigorous in support of a cause. —**militancy** *n.*

military *adj.* of or for soldiers, armies, or war. —*n.* armed services. —**militarism** *n.* belief in the use of military force and methods. —**militarist** *n.* —**militia** [mill-**ish**-a] *n.* military force of trained citizens for use in emergency only.

militate *v.* (usu. with *against* or *for*) have a strong influence or effect.

milk *n.* white fluid produced by female mammals to feed their young; milk of cows, goats, etc. used by man as food; fluid in some plants. —*v.* draw milk from; exploit (a person or situation). —**milky** *adj.* —**Milky Way** luminous band of stars stretching across the night sky. —**milkmaid** *n.* (esp. in former times) woman who milks cows. —**milkman** *n.* man who delivers milk to people's houses. —**milkshake** *n.* frothy flavoured cold milk drink. —**milksop** *n.* feeble man. —**milk teeth** first set of teeth in young mammals.

mill *n.* factory; machine for grinding, processing, or rolling. —*v.* put through a mill; cut fine grooves across the edges of (coins); move in a confused manner. —**miller** *n.* person who works in a mill. —**millstone** *n.* flat circular stone for grinding corn. —**millwheel** *n.* waterwheel that drives a mill.

THESAURUS

middle 1. *adj.* central, halfway, inner, inside, mean, medial, median, medium, mid 2. *n.* centre, focus, heart, inside, mean, midpoint, midst, thick

middling adequate, all right, average, fair, indifferent, mediocre, medium, moderate, modest, ordinary, passable, tolerable, unremarkable

midget dwarf, gnome, pygmy

might ability, capability, efficacy, energy, force, potency, power, prowess, strength, sway, valour, vigour

mighty forceful, hardy, potent, powerful, robust, stalwart, stout, strong, sturdy, vigorous

migrant drifter, gypsy, itinerant, nomad, rover, tinker, transient, vagrant, wanderer

migrate journey, move, roam, rove, shift, travel, trek, wander

migration journey, movement, roving, shift, travel, trek, voyage

migratory gypsy, itinerant, nomadic, roving, shifting, transient, unsettled, vagrant

mild amiable, balmy, bland, calm, docile, easy, forbearing, forgiving, gentle, indulgent, kind, meek, mellow, merciful, moderate, peaceable, placid, pleasant, serene, smooth, soft, temperate, tender, tranquil, warm

mildness blandness, calmness, docility, gentleness, indulgence, kindness, leniency, meekness, placidity, smoothness, softness, tenderness, warmth

militant active, aggressive, assertive, combative

DICTIONARY

millennium [mill-**en**-yum] *n., pl.* **-niums, -nia.**
period of a thousand years; future period of
peace and happiness.

millepede, millipede [**mill**-lip-peed] *n.* small
animal with a jointed body and many pairs of
legs.

millet *n.* a cereal grass.

milli- *prefix* denoting a thousandth part, as in
milligram, millilitre.

millibar *n.* unit of atmospheric pressure.

milliner *n.* maker or seller of women's hats.
—**millinery** *n.*

million *n.* one thousand thousands. —**millionth**
adj., n. —**millionaire** *n.* person who owns at least
a million pounds, dollars, etc.

milometer [mile-**om**-it-er] *n.* same as MILEOM-
ETER.

milt *n.* sperm of fish.

mime *n.* acting without the use of words; performer who does this. —*v.* act in mime.

mimic *v.* **-icking, -icked.** imitate (a person or
manner), esp. for satirical effect. —*n.* person or
animal clever at mimicking. —**mimicry** *n.*

mimosa *n.* shrub with fluffy yellow flowers and
sensitive leaves.

min. minimum; minute(s).

minaret *n.* tall slender tower of a mosque.

mince *v.* cut or grind into very small pieces;
soften or moderate (one's words); walk or speak
in an affected manner. —*n.* minced meat.
—**mincer** *n.* machine for mincing meat. —**mincing** *adj.* affected in manner. —**mincemeat** *n.*
sweet mixture of dried fruit and spices. —**mince
pie** pie containing mincemeat.

mind *n.* thinking faculties; memory or attention;
intention; sanity. —*v.* take offence at; take care
of; pay attention to; be cautious or careful about

(something). —**minded** *adj.* having an inclination as specified, e.g. *politically minded.* —**mind-
er** *n. Slang* aide or bodyguard. —**mindful** *adj.*
keeping aware; heedful. —**mindless** *adj.* stupid;
requiring no thought; careless.

mine[1] *pron.* belonging to me.

mine[2] *n.* deep hole for digging out coal, ores,
etc.; bomb placed under the ground or in water;
profitable source. —*v.* dig for minerals; dig (minerals) from a mine; place explosive mines in or
on. —**miner** *n.* person who works in a mine.
—**minefield** *n.* area of land or water containing
mines. —**minesweeper** *n.* ship for clearing away
mines.

mineral *n.* naturally occurring inorganic substance, such as metal or coal. —*adj.* of, containing, or like minerals. —**mineralogy** [min-er-**al**-a-
jee] *n.* study of minerals. —**mineralogist** *n.*
—**mineral water** water containing dissolved
mineral salts or gases.

minestrone [min-ness-**strone**-ee] *n.* soup containing vegetables and pasta.

mingle *v.* mix or blend; come into association
(with).

mingy *adj.* **-gier, -giest.** *Informal* miserly.

mini *n., adj.* (something) small or miniature;
short (skirt).

miniature *n.* small portrait, model, or copy.
—*adj.* small-scale. —**miniaturist** *n.* —**miniatur-
ize** *v.* make to a very small scale.

minibus *n.* small bus.

minicab *n.* ordinary car used as a taxi.

minicomputer *n.* computer smaller than a
mainframe but more powerful than a microcomputer.

minim *n. Music* note half the length of a semibreve.

THESAURUS

military 1. *adj.* armed, martial, soldierly, warlike 2. *n.* armed forces, army, forces, services

milk *v.* drain, express, extract, press, tap

mill *n.* 1. factory, foundry, plant, shop, works 2.
crusher, grinder

mime 1. *n.* dumb show, gesture 2. *v.* gesture,
represent, simulate

mimic 1. *v.* ape, caricature, imitate, impersonate, parody 2. *n.* caricaturist, imitator, impersonator, parodist, parrot

mind *n.* 1. intellect, mentality, reason, sense,
spirit, understanding, wits 2. memory, recollection, remembrance 3. bent, desire, disposition, fancy, inclination, intention, leaning,
notion, purpose, tendency, urge, will, wish 4.
attention, concentration, thinking, thoughts
~*v.* 5. care, disapprove, dislike, object, resent

6. attend, follow, heed, mark, note, notice,
obey, observe, regard, respect, watch 7. guard,
look after, take care of, tend, watch

mindful alert, attentive, aware, careful, chary,
cognizant, conscious, heedful, wary, watchful

mine *n.* 1. colliery, deposit, lode, pit, shaft, vein
2. fund, hoard, reserve, source, stock, store,
supply ~*v.* 3. delve, excavate, extract, hew,
quarry, unearth

mingle 1. alloy, blend, combine, compound,
intermix, join, marry, merge, mix, unite 2.
associate, circulate, fraternize, hobnob, socialize

miniature *adj.* baby, diminutive, dwarf, little,
midget, pocket, reduced, small, tiny, toy, wee

minimal least, littlest, nominal, slightest,
smallest, token

DICTIONARY

minimum *adj., n.* least possible (amount or quantity). —**minimal** *adj.* minimum. —**minimize** *v.* reduce to a minimum; belittle. —**minimum lending rate** minimum rate of interest at which the Bank of England will lend money.

minion *n.* servile assistant.

miniseries *n.* TV programme in several parts, usu. shown on consecutive days.

minister *n.* head of a government department; diplomatic representative; clergyman. —*v.* (foll. by *to*) attend to the needs of. —**ministerial** *adj.* —**ministration** *n.* giving of help. —**ministry** *n.* profession or duties of a clergyman; ministers collectively; government department.

mink *n.* stoatlike animal; its highly valued fur.

minnow *n.* small freshwater fish.

minor *adj.* lesser; under age; *Music* (of a scale) having a semitone above the second note. —*n.* person below the age of legal majority; *Music* minor scale. —**minority** *n.* lesser number; smaller party voting together; group in a minority in any state; state of being a minor.

minster *n.* cathedral or large church.

minstrel *n.* medieval singer or musician.

mint[1] *n.* place where money is coined. —*v.* make (coins).

mint[2] *n.* aromatic herb; peppermint; sweet flavoured with this.

minuet [min-new-**wet**] *n.* stately dance; music for this.

minus *prep., adj.* reduced by the subtraction of; *Informal* without; less than zero. —*n.* sign (−) denoting subtraction or a number less than zero.

minuscule [min-niss-skyool] *adj.* very small.

minute[1] *adj.* very small; precise. —**minutely** *adv.* —**minutiae** [my-**new**-shee-eye] *pl. n.* trifling or precise details.

minute[2] *n.* 60th part of an hour or degree; moment. —*pl.* record of the proceedings of a meeting. —*v.* record in the minutes.

minx *n.* bold or flirtatious girl.

miracle *n.* wonderful supernatural event; marvel. —**miraculous** *adj.* —**miraculously** *adv.* —**miracle play** medieval play based on a sacred subject.

mirage [mir-**rahzh**] *n.* optical illusion, esp. one caused by hot air.

mire *n.* swampy ground; mud.

mirror *n.* coated glass surface for reflecting images. —*v.* reflect in or as if in a mirror.

mirth *n.* laughter, merriment, or gaiety. —**mirthful** *adj.* —**mirthless** *adj.*

mis- *prefix* wrong(ly), bad(ly), e.g. *misbehave.*

misadventure *n.* unlucky chance.

misanthrope [**miz**-zan-thrope], **misanthropist** [miz-**zan**-thrope-ist] *n.* person who dislikes people in general. —**misanthropic** [miz-zan-**throp**-ik] *adj.* —**misanthropy** [miz-**zan**-thropee] *n.*

misapprehend *v.* misunderstand. —**misapprehension** *n.*

misappropriate *v.* take and use (money) dishonestly. —**misappropriation** *n.*

THESAURUS

minimize 1. attenuate, curtail, decrease, diminish, prune, reduce, shrink 2. belittle, decry, deprecate, discount, underestimate, underrate

minimum 1. *n.* bottom, depth, least, lowest, nadir, slightest 2. *adj.* least, lowest, slightest, smallest

minion creature, flatterer, flunky, follower, hanger-on, henchman, hireling, lackey, pet, toady, yes man

minister *n.* 1. churchman, clergyman, cleric, divine, ecclesiastic, parson, pastor, preacher, priest, vicar 2. ambassador, delegate, diplomat, envoy, executive, office-holder, official, plenipotentiary ~*v.* 3. attend, tend

ministry administration, cabinet, council, government, holy orders

minor inconsiderable, inferior, junior, lesser, light, paltry, petty, secondary, slight, small, subordinate, trivial, younger

mint *v.* cast, coin, make, produce, stamp, strike

minute[1] *adj.* fine, little, slender, small, tiny

minute[2] *n.* flash, instant, moment, second

minutes notes, proceedings, record(s), transcript

minx coquette, flirt, hoyden, hussy, jade, tomboy, wanton

miracle marvel, prodigy, wonder

miraculous amazing, astonishing, astounding, extraordinary, incredible, magical, marvellous, phenomenal, supernatural, wonderful

mirage illusion, phantasm

mire bog, marsh, morass, quagmire, swamp

mirror 1. *n.* glass, reflector 2. *v.* copy, depict, echo, emulate, follow, reflect, represent, show

mirth amusement, cheerfulness, festivity, frolic, fun, gaiety, glee, laughter, levity, merriment, pleasure, rejoicing, revelry, sport

mirthful amusing, blithe, cheerful, cheery, festive, funny, gay, glad, happy, jolly, jovial, laughable, light-hearted, merry, playful, sportive

misadventure accident, calamity, catastrophe,

DICTIONARY

miscarriage *n.* spontaneous premature expulsion of a fetus from the womb; failure, e.g. *a miscarriage of justice*. —**miscarry** *v.* have a miscarriage; fail.

miscast *v.* **-casting, -cast.** cast (a role or actor) in (a play or film) inappropriately.

miscegenation [miss-ij-in-**nay**-shun] *n.* interbreeding of races.

miscellaneous [miss-sell-**lane**-ee-uss] *adj.* mixed or assorted. —**miscellany** [miss-**sell**-a-nee] *n.* mixed assortment.

mischance *n.* unlucky event.

mischief *n.* annoying but not malicious behaviour; inclination to tease; harm. —**mischievous** [**miss**-chiv-uss] *adj.* full of mischief; intended to cause harm. —**mischievously** *adv.*

miscible [**miss**-sib-bl] *adj.* able to be mixed.

misconception *n.* wrong idea or belief.

misconduct *n.* immoral or unethical behaviour.

miscreant [**miss**-kree-ant] *n.* wrongdoer.

misdeed *n.* wrongful act.

misdemeanour *n.* minor wrongdoing.

miser *n.* person who hoards money and hates spending it. —**miserly** *adj.*

miserable *adj.* very unhappy, wretched; causing misery; squalid; mean. —**misery** *n.* great unhappiness; *Informal* complaining person.

misfire *v.* (of a firearm or engine) fail to fire correctly; (of a plan) fail to turn out as intended.

misfit *n.* person not suited to his or her environment.

misfortune *n.* (piece of) bad luck.

misgiving *n.* feeling of fear or doubt.

misguided *adj.* mistaken or unwise.

mishap *n.* minor accident.

misinform *v.* give incorrect information to. —**misinformation** *n.*

misjudge *v.* judge wrongly or unfairly. —**misjudg(e)ment** *n.*

mislay *v.* lose (something) temporarily.

mislead *v.* give false or confusing information to.

mismanage *v.* organize or run (something) badly. —**mismanagement** *n.*

THESAURUS

debacle, disaster, failure, mischance, misfortune, mishap, reverse, setback

misappropriate embezzle, misapply, misuse, pocket, steal, swindle

miscellaneous assorted, diverse, indiscriminate, jumbled, many, mingled, mixed, motley, promiscuous, sundry, varied, various

miscellany anthology, assortment, collection, jumble, medley, mixture, variety

mischance accident, calamity, disaster, misadventure, misfortune, mishap

mischief 1. devilment, impishness, misbehaviour, naughtiness, roguery, trouble, waywardness 2. damage, detriment, disruption, evil, harm, hurt, injury, trouble

mischievous 1. arch, bad, badly behaved, impish, naughty, playful, puckish, roguish, sportive, teasing, vexatious, wayward 2. bad, damaging, destructive, evil, harmful, hurtful, injurious, malignant, pernicious, sinful, spiteful, wicked

misconception delusion, error, misunderstanding

misconduct delinquency, immorality, impropriety, malpractice, misbehaviour, transgression, wrongdoing

misdemeanour fault, misconduct, offence, peccadillo, transgression

miser niggard, skinflint

miserable 1. afflicted, crestfallen, dejected, depressed, despondent, distressed, downcast,

forlorn, gloomy, melancholy, mournful, sorrowful, unhappy, woebegone, wretched 2. abject, bad, contemptible, despicable, disgraceful, low, mean, pathetic, piteous, pitiable, shabby, shameful, sordid, sorry, squalid, vile, worthless, wretched

miserly avaricious, close, covetous, grasping, illiberal, mean, niggardly, parsimonious, sordid, stingy

misery agony, anguish, depression, desolation, despair, discomfort, distress, gloom, grief, hardship, melancholy, sadness, sorrow, suffering, torment, torture, unhappiness, woe

misfire fail, fall through, miscarry

misfit eccentric, nonconformist

misfortune bad luck, infelicity

misgiving anxiety, distrust, doubt, hesitation, reservation, suspicion, uncertainty, unease, worry

misguided deluded, foolish, ill-advised, imprudent, misled, misplaced, mistaken, unreasonable, unwise

mishap accident, adversity, bad luck, calamity, contretemps, disaster, hard luck, misadventure, mischance, misfortune

misinform deceive, misdirect, misguide, mislead

mislead beguile, bluff, deceive, delude, fool, hoodwink, misdirect, misguide, misinform

mismanage botch, bungle, maladminister, misdirect, misgovern, mishandle

DICTIONARY

misnomer [miss-**no**-mer] *n.* wrongly applied name; use of this.

misogyny [miss-**oj**-in-ee] *n.* hatred of women. —**misogynist** *n.*

misplace *v.* put in the wrong place; mislay; give (trust or affection) inappropriately.

misprint *n.* printing error.

misrepresent *v.* represent wrongly or inaccurately.

Miss *n.* title of a girl or unmarried woman.

miss *v.* fail to hit, reach, find, catch, or notice; not be in time for; notice or regret the absence of; avoid; (of an engine) misfire. —*n.* fact or instance of missing. —**missing** *adj.* lost or absent.

missal *n.* book containing the prayers and rites of the Mass.

misshapen *adj.* badly shaped, deformed.

missile *n.* object or weapon thrown, shot, or launched at a target.

mission *n.* specific task or duty; group of people sent on a mission; building in which missionaries work. —**missionary** *n., pl.* **-aries.** person sent abroad to spread religion.

missive *n.* letter.

misspent *adj.* wasted or misused.

mist *n.* thin fog; fine spray of liquid. —**misty** *adj.* full of mist; dim or obscure. —**mistiness** *n.*

mistake *n.* error or blunder. —*v.* **-taking, -took,**
-taken. misunderstand; confuse (a person or thing) with another.

Mister *n.* polite form of address to a man.

mistletoe *n.* evergreen plant with white berries growing as a parasite on trees.

mistral *n.* strong dry northerly wind of S France.

mistress *n.* woman who is the illicit lover of a married man; woman in control of people or things; female teacher.

mistrust *v.* not trust. —*n.* lack of trust. —**mistrustful** *adj.*

misunderstand *v.* fail to understand properly. —**misunderstanding** *n.*

misuse *n.* incorrect, improper, or careless use. —*v.* use wrongly; treat badly.

mite *n.* very small spiderlike animal; very small thing or amount.

mitigate *v.* make less severe. —**mitigation** *n.*

mitre [**my**-ter] *n.* bishop's pointed headdress; joint between two pieces of wood bevelled to meet at right angles. —*v.* join with a mitre joint.

mitt *n.* same as MITTEN; baseball catcher's glove.

mitten *n.* glove with one section for the thumb and a single section for the fingers.

mix *v.* combine or blend into one mass; form (something) by mixing; be sociable. —*n.* mixture. —**mixed** *adj.* —**mixer** *n.* —**mixture** *n.* something mixed; combination. —**mix-up** *n.* con-

THESAURUS

misrepresent disguise, distort, falsify, garble, pervert, twist

miss *v.* 1. avoid, blunder, err, escape, evade, fail, forego, lack, lose, miscarry, mistake, omit, overlook, skip, slip, trip 2. need, pine for, want, wish ~*n.* 3. blunder, error, failure, fault, loss, mistake, omission, oversight, want

misshapen contorted, crippled, crooked, deformed, distorted, grotesque, twisted, ugly, ungainly, warped

missile projectile, rocket, weapon

missing absent, astray, gone, lacking, lost, mislaid, misplaced

mission 1. aim, assignment, business, calling, charge, duty, errand, goal, job, office, operation, purpose, pursuit, quest, task, trust, undertaking, vocation, work 2. delegation, deputation, task force

missionary converter, evangelist, preacher

missive dispatch, epistle, letter, message, note, report

mist cloud, dew, drizzle, film, fog, haze, smog, spray, steam, vapour

mistake 1. *n.* blunder, error, fault, gaffe, over-
sight, slip, solecism 2. *v.* misconceive, misconstrue, misjudge, misread, misunderstand

mistaken fallacious, false, faulty, inaccurate, incorrect, misguided, misinformed, unfounded, wrong

mistress concubine, girlfriend, kept woman, lover, paramour

mistrust 1. *v.* beware, doubt, fear, suspect 2. *n.* doubt, fear, misgiving, scepticism, suspicion, uncertainty

misty bleary, cloudy, dark, dim, foggy, hazy, indistinct, obscure, vague

misunderstand misconceive, misconstrue, mishear, misinterpret, misjudge, mistake

misunderstanding error, misconstruction, misjudgment, misreading, mistake, mix-up

misuse 1. *n.* abuse, corruption, malapropism, perversion, profanation, solecism, waste 2. *v.* abuse, corrupt, desecrate, dissipate, misapply, pervert, profane, prostitute, squander, waste

mitigate abate, allay, appease, assuage, blunt, calm, check, dull, ease, extenuate, lessen, lighten, modify, mollify, pacify, palliate, placate, quiet, remit, soften, soothe, subdue, temper, weaken

DICTIONARY

fused situation. —**mixed-up** *adj. Informal* confused.

mizzenmast *n.* mast nearest the stern of a full-rigged ship.

mks units *pl. n.* metric system of units based on the metre, kilogram, and second.

ml millilitre(s).

mm millimetre(s).

Mn *Chem.* manganese.

mnemonic [nim-**on**-ik] *n., adj.* (rhyme etc.) intended to help the memory.

MO Medical Officer.

mo *n. Informal* short for MOMENT.

moan *n.* low cry of pain; *Informal* grumble. —*v.* make or utter with a moan; *Informal* grumble.

moat *n.* deep wide ditch, esp. round a castle.

mob *n.* disorderly crowd; *Slang* gang. —*v.* **mobbing, mobbed.** surround in a mob to acclaim or attack.

mobile *adj.* able to move. —*n.* hanging structure designed to move in air currents. —**mobility** *n.*

mobilize *v.* (of the armed services) prepare for active service; organize for a purpose. —**mobilization** *n.*

moccasin *n.* soft leather shoe.

mocha [**mock**-a] *n.* kind of strong dark coffee; flavouring made from coffee and chocolate.

mock *v.* make fun of; mimic. —*n.* imitation. —*pl. Informal* practice exams taken before public exams. —*adj.* sham or imitation. —**put the mockers on** *Informal* ruin the chances of success of. —**mockery** *n.* derision; inadequate attempt. —**mocking bird** N American bird which imitates other birds' songs. —**mock orange** shrub with white fragrant flowers. —**mock-up** *n.* full-scale model for test or study.

mod. moderate; modern.

mode *n.* method or manner; current fashion. —**modish** [**mow**-dish] *adj.* in fashion.

model *n.* (miniature) representation; pattern; person or thing worthy of imitation; person who poses for an artist or photographer; person who wears clothes to display them to prospective buyers. —*v.* **-elling, -elled.** make a model of; mould; display (clothing) as a model.

modem [**mow**-dem] *n.* device for connecting two computers by a telephone line.

moderate *adj.* not extreme; temperate; average. —*n.* person of moderate views. —*v.* make or become less violent or extreme; preside over a meeting etc. —**moderately** *adv.* —**moderation**

THESAURUS

mix 1. alloy, amalgamate, blend, coalesce, combine, compound, cross, fuse, incorporate, intermingle, join, merge, mingle, unite 2. associate, consort, fraternize, join, mingle, socialize

mixed 1. alloyed, amalgamated, blended, combined, composite, compound, fused, incorporated, joint, mingled, united 2. assorted, diverse, motley, varied

mixture alloy, amalgam, association, assortment, blend, brew, combine, compound, concoction, conglomeration, cross, fusion, medley, miscellany, mix, union, variety

mix-up confusion, disorder, jumble, mess, mistake, muddle

moan 1. *n.* groan, lament, sigh, sob, sough, wail, whine 2. *v.* bewail, deplore, grieve, groan, lament, mourn, sigh, sob, whine

mob 1. *n.* body, collection, crowd, drove, flock, gang, gathering, herd, horde, host, mass, pack, press, swarm, throng 2. *v.* jostle, overrun, surround

mobile itinerant, migrant, movable, peripatetic, portable, travelling, wandering

mobilize call up, marshal, muster, organize, prepare, rally, ready

mock *v.* 1. chaff, deride, flout, insult, jeer, ridicule, scoff, scorn, sneer, taunt, tease ~*n.* 2.

fake, forgery, fraud, imitation, sham ~*adj.* 3. artificial, bogus, counterfeit, dummy, fake, false, feigned, forged, fraudulent, imitation, pretended, sham, spurious

mockery contempt, contumely, derision, disdain, jeering, ridicule, scorn

model *n.* 1. copy, facsimile, image, imitation, mock-up, replica, representation 2. archetype, design, epitome, example, exemplar, gauge, ideal, mould, original, paradigm, paragon, pattern, prototype, standard, type 3. poser, sitter, subject 4. mannequin ~*v.* 5. base, carve, cast, design, fashion, form, mould, pattern, plan, sculpt, shape 6. display, show off, wear

moderate 1. *adj.* calm, cool, deliberate, equable, gentle, limited, mild, modest, peaceable, reasonable, restrained, sober, steady, temperate 2. *v.* abate, allay, appease, assuage, calm, control, curb, decrease, diminish, lessen, mitigate, modulate, pacify, quiet, regulate, repress, restrain, soften, subdue, tame, temper

moderately fairly, gently, passably, quite, rather, reasonably, slightly, somewhat, tolerably

moderation calmness, composure, coolness, equanimity, fairness, justice, mildness, reasonableness, restraint, sedateness, temperance

DICTIONARY

n. —**moderator** *n.* president of a Presbyterian body; arbitrator.

modern *adj.* of present or recent times; in current fashion. —**modernity** *n.* —**modernism** *n.* (support of) modern tendencies, thoughts, or styles. —**modernist** *n.* —**modernize** *v.* bring up to date. —**modernization** *n.*

modest *adj.* not vain or boastful; shy; not excessive; decorous or decent. —**modestly** *adv.* —**modesty** *n.*

modicum *n.* small quantity.

modify *v.* -**fying, -fied.** change slightly; tone down; (of a word) qualify (another word). —**modifier** *n.* word that qualifies another. —**modification** *n.*

modulate *v.* vary in tone; adjust; change the key of (music). —**modulation** *n.* modulating; *Electronics* superimposing of a wave or signal on to another wave or signal. —**modulator** *n.*

module *n.* self-contained unit, section, or component with a specific function.

modus operandi [mow-duss op-er-**an**-die] *n.* *Latin* method of operating.

mogul [**mow**-gl] *n.* important or powerful person.

MOH Medical Officer of Health.

mohair *n.* fine hair of the Angora goat; yarn or fabric made from this.

Mohammedan *adj., n.* another word (not in Muslim use) for MUSLIM.

mohican *n.* punk hairstyle with shaved sides and a stiff central strip of hair, often brightly coloured.

moiety [**moy**-it-ee] *n., pl.* -**ties.** half.

moist *adj.* slightly wet. —**moisten** *v.* make or become moist. —**moisture** *n.* liquid diffused as

vapour or condensed in drops. —**moisturize** *v.* add moisture to (the skin etc.).

moke *n.* *Slang* donkey.

molar *n.* large back tooth used for grinding.

molasses *n.* dark syrup, a by-product of sugar refining.

mole[1] *n.* small dark raised spot on the skin.

mole[2] *n.* small burrowing mammal; *Informal* spy who has infiltrated and become a trusted member of an organization.

mole[3] *n.* breakwater; harbour protected by this.

mole[4] *n.* unit of amount of substance.

molecule [**mol**-lik-kyool] *n.* simplest freely existing chemical unit, composed of two or more atoms; very small particle. —**molecular** [mol-**lek**-yew-lar] *adj.*

molest *v.* interfere with sexually; annoy or injure. —**molester** *n.* —**molestation** *n.*

moll *n.* *Slang* gangster's female accomplice; prostitute.

mollify *v.* -**fying, fied.** pacify or soothe. —**mollification** *n.*

mollusc *n.* soft-bodied, usu. hard-shelled animal such as a snail or oyster.

mollycoddle *v.* pamper.

Molotov cocktail *n.* petrol bomb.

molten *adj.* liquefied or melted.

molybdenum [mol-**lib**-din-um] *n.* silver-white metallic element.

moment *n.* short space of time; (present) point in time. —**momentary** *adj.* lasting only a moment. —**momentarily** *adv.*

momentous [mow-**men**-tuss] *adj.* of great significance.

momentum [mow-**men**-tum] *n., pl.* -**ta, -tums.**

THESAURUS

modern contemporary, current, fresh, late, latest, new, novel, present, recent

modernize bring up to date, rejuvenate, remake, remodel, renew, renovate, revamp, update

modest 1. bashful, coy, demure, discreet, humble, meek, quiet, reserved, reticent, retiring, shy, simple 2. fair, limited, ordinary, small

modesty demureness, diffidence, humility, meekness, propriety, reserve, reticence, shyness, timidity

modification adjustment, refinement, revision, variation

modify adapt, adjust, alter, change, convert, recast, reform, reorganize, reshape, revise, transform, vary

mogul baron, lord, magnate, notable, personage, tycoon

moist clammy, damp, dank, dewy, drizzly, humid, rainy, wet, wettish

moisten damp, soak, water, wet

moisture damp, dew, humidity, liquid, sweat, water

molecule atom, mite, particle

molest abuse, afflict, annoy, badger, bother, disturb, harass, harry, hector, irritate, persecute, pester, torment, upset, vex, worry

moment 1. flash, instant, minute, second, twinkling 2. hour, instant, juncture, point, stage, time

momentous critical, crucial, decisive, fateful, grave, historic, important, serious, significant, vital

momentum drive, energy, force, impetus, power, push, thrust

DICTIONARY

product of a body's mass and velocity; impetus of a moving body.

monarch *n.* sovereign ruler of a state. **—monarchic(al)** *adj.* **—monarchist** *n.* supporter of monarchy. **—monarchy** *n.* government by or a state ruled by a sovereign.

monastery *n., pl.* **-teries.** residence of a religious order. **—monastic** *adj.* of monks, nuns, or monasteries; ascetic. **—monasticism** *n.*

Monday *n.* second day of the week.

money *n.* medium of exchange, coins or banknotes. **—moneyed, monied** *adj.* rich. **—monetary** *adj.* of money or currency. **—monetarism** *n.* theory that inflation is caused by an increase in the money supply. **—monetarist** *n., adj.*

mongolism *n. Offens.* Down's syndrome. **—mongol** *n., adj. Offens.* (person) affected by this.

mongoose *n., pl.* **-gooses.** stoatlike mammal of Asia and Africa that kills snakes.

mongrel *n.* animal, esp. a dog, of mixed breed; hybrid. **—adj.** of mixed breed.

monitor *n.* person or device that checks, controls, warns, or keeps a record of something; pupil assisting a teacher with duties; television set used in a studio to check what is being transmitted; type of large lizard. **—v.** watch and check on.

monk *n.* member of an all-male religious community bound by vows. **—monkish** *adj.* **—monkshood** *n.* poisonous plant with hooded flowers.

monkey *n.* long-tailed primate; mischievous child. **—v.** (usu. foll. by *about* or *around*) meddle or fool. **—monkey nut** peanut. **—monkey puzzle** coniferous tree with sharp stiff leaves. **—monkey wrench** wrench with adjustable jaws.

mono- *prefix* single, e.g. *monosyllable.*

monochrome *adj.* in only one colour; black-and-white.

monocle [mon-a-kl] *n.* eyeglass for one eye only.

monocular *adj.* having or for one eye only.

monogamy *n.* custom of being married to one person at a time.

monogram *n.* design of combined letters, esp. a person's initials.

monograph *n.* book or paper on a single subject.

monolith *n.* large upright block of stone. **—monolithic** *adj.*

monologue *n.* dramatic piece for one performer; long speech by one person.

monomania *n.* obsession with one thing. **—monomaniac** *n., adj.*

monoplane *n.* aeroplane with one pair of wings.

monopoly *n., pl.* **-lies.** exclusive possession of or right to do something. **—monopolist** *n.* **—monopolize** *v.* have or take exclusive possession of.

monorail *n.* single-rail railway.

monotheism *n.* belief in only one God. **—monotheist** *n.* **—monotheistic** *adj.*

monotone *n.* unvaried pitch in speech or sound. **—monotonous** *adj.* tedious due to lack of variety. **—monotonously** *adv.* **—monotony** *n.*

Monseigneur [mon-sen-nyur] *n., pl.* **Messeigneurs** [may-sen-**nyur**]. title of French prelates.

monsieur [muss-**syur**] *n., pl.* **messieurs** [may-**syur**]. French title of address equivalent to *sir* or *Mr.*

Monsignor *n. RC Church* title attached to certain offices.

monsoon *n.* seasonal wind of SE Asia; rainy season accompanying this.

THESAURUS

monarch king, potentate, prince, princess, queen, ruler, sovereign

monastery abbey, cloister, convent, friary, house, nunnery, priory

monastic ascetic, austere, cloistered, recluse, secluded, withdrawn

monetary capital, cash, financial, fiscal

money banknotes, capital, cash, coin, currency, funds, hard cash, legal tender

mongrel 1. *n.* cross, crossbreed, hybrid 2. *adj.* crossbred, half-breed, hybrid

monitor 1. *n.* guide, overseer, supervisor, watchdog 2. *v.* check, follow, observe, record, scan, supervise, survey, watch

monk brother, monastic, religious

monkey *n.* 1. primate, simian 2. devil, imp,

rascal, rogue, scamp ~*v.* 3. fool, interfere, meddle, mess, play, tamper, tinker, trifle

monolithic colossal, giant, gigantic, huge, immovable, massive, monumental, solid, substantial

monologue harangue, lecture, sermon, speech

monopolize control, corner, dominate, engross, take up

monotonous boring, colourless, droning, dull, flat, humdrum, plodding, repetitious, repetitive, samey (*Inf.*), soporific, tedious, tiresome, toneless, unchanging, uniform, uninflected, unvaried, wearisome

monotony boredom, dullness, flatness, repetitiveness, routine, sameness, tedium, uniformity

DICTIONARY

monster *n.* imaginary, usu. frightening beast; very wicked person; huge person, animal, or thing. —*adj.* huge. —**monstrosity** *n.* large ugly thing. —**monstrous** *adj.* unnatural or ugly; outrageous or shocking; huge. —**monstrously** *adv.*

monstrance *n. RC Church* container in which the consecrated Host is exposed for adoration.

montage [mon-tahzh] *n.* (making of) a picture composed from pieces of others; method of film editing incorporating several shots to form a single image.

month *n.* one of the twelve divisions of the calendar year; period of four weeks. —**monthly** *adj.* happening or payable once a month. —*adv.* once a month. —*n.* monthly periodical.

monument *n.* something that commemorates, esp. a building or statue. —**monumental** *adj.* large, impressive, or lasting; of or being a monument; *Informal* extreme. —**monumentally** *adv.*

moo *n.* long deep cry of a cow. —*v.* make this noise.

mooch *v. Slang* loiter about aimlessly.

mood[1] *n.* temporary (gloomy) state of mind. —**moody** *adj.* gloomy or sullen; changeable in mood. —**moodily** *adv.*

mood[2] *n. Grammar* form of a verb indicating whether it expresses a fact, wish, supposition, or command.

moon *n.* natural satellite of the earth; natural satellite of any planet. —*v.* (foll. by *about* or *around*) be idle in a listless or dreamy way. —**moonlight** *n.* light from the moon. —*v. Informal* work at a secondary job, esp. illegally. —**moonshine** *n.* illicitly distilled whisky; non-

sense. —**moonstone** *n.* translucent semiprecious stone. —**moonstruck** *adj.* deranged.

Moor *n.* member of a Muslim people of NW Africa who ruled Spain between the 8th and 15th centuries. —**Moorish** *adj.*

moor[1] *n.* tract of open uncultivated ground covered with grass and heather.

moor[2] *v.* secure (a ship) with ropes etc. —**mooring** *n.* place for mooring a ship. —*pl.* ropes etc. used in mooring a ship.

moorhen *n.* small black water bird.

moose *n.* large N American deer.

moot *adj.* debatable, e.g. *a moot point.* —*v.* bring up for discussion.

mop *n.* long stick with twists of cotton or a sponge on the end, used for cleaning; thick mass of hair. —*v.* **mopping, mopped.** clean or soak up with or as if with a mop.

mope *v.* be gloomy and apathetic.

moped *n.* light motorized cycle.

moraine *n.* accumulated mass of debris deposited by a glacier.

moral *adj.* concerned with right and wrong conduct; based on a sense of right and wrong; (of support or a victory) psychological rather than practical. —*n.* lesson to be obtained from a story or event. —*pl.* behaviour with respect to right and wrong. —**morally** *adv.* —**moralist** *n.* person who lives by or expresses moral principles. —**morality** *n.* good moral conduct; moral goodness or badness. —**morality play** medieval play with a moral lesson. —**moralize** *v.* make moral pronouncements.

THESAURUS

monster 1. *n.* barbarian, beast, brute, demon, devil, fiend, ogre, savage, villain 2. *adj.* colossal, enormous, giant, huge, immense, massive, tremendous

monstrosity atrocity, evil, frightfulness, horror, obscenity

monstrous 1. abnormal, dreadful, fiendish, freakish, frightful, grotesque, gruesome, hellish, hideous, horrible, obscene, terrible, unnatural 2. atrocious, cruel, devilish, diabolical, disgraceful, evil, fiendish, foul, horrifying, infamous, inhuman, intolerable, loathsome, odious, outrageous, satanic, scandalous, shocking, vicious, villainous 3. colossal, enormous, giant, gigantic, great, huge, immense, massive, prodigious, stupendous, tremendous, vast

monument cairn, gravestone, marker, mausoleum, memorial, obelisk, pillar, shrine, statue, tombstone

monumental awesome, classic, enduring, enor-

mous, historic, immortal, important, lasting, majestic, memorable, outstanding, prodigious, significant, unforgettable

mood blues, depression, doldrums, melancholy, sulk

moody angry, broody, crabbed, crestfallen, cross, crusty, curt, dismal, doleful, dour, downcast, frowning, gloomy, glum, illtempered, irritable, lugubrious, melancholy, miserable, morose, offended, pensive, petulant, sad, saturnine, sulky, sullen, temperamental, testy, touchy

moon 1. *n.* satellite 2. *v.* daydream, idle, languish

moor[1] heath, moorland

moor[2] anchor, berth, dock, fasten, fix, lash, secure

moot *adj.* arguable, contestable, controversial, debatable, doubtful, unsettled

moral *adj.* 1. ethical 2. blameless, chaste, decent, good, honest, innocent, just, noble, prin-

DICTIONARY

morale [mor-**rahl**] *n.* degree of confidence or hope of a person or group.

morass *n.* marsh; mess.

moratorium *n., pl.* **-ria, -riums.** legally authorized ban or delay.

moray *n.* large voracious eel.

morbid *adj.* unduly interested in death or unpleasant events; gruesome.

mordant *adj.* sarcastic or scathing. —*n.* substance used to fix dyes.

more *adj.* greater in amount or degree; comparative of MUCH and MANY; additional or further. —*adv.* to a greater extent; in addition. —*pron.* greater or additional amount or number. —**moreover** *adv.* besides.

mores [**more**-rayz] *pl. n.* customs and conventions embodying the fundamental values of a community.

morganatic marriage *n.* marriage of a person of high rank to a lower-ranking person whose status remains unchanged.

morgue *n.* mortuary.

moribund *adj.* without force or vitality.

Mormon *n.* member of a religious sect founded in the U.S.A. —**Mormonism** *n.*

morn *n. Poetic* morning.

morning *n.* part of the day before noon. —**morning-glory** *n.* plant with trumpet-shaped flowers which close in the late afternoon.

morocco *n.* goatskin leather.

moron *n.* mentally deficient person; *Informal* fool. —**moronic** *adj.*

morose [mor-**rohss**] *adj.* sullen or moody.

morphine, morphia *n.* drug extracted from opium, used as an anaesthetic and sedative.

morphology *n.* science of forms and structures of organisms or words. —**morphological** *adj.*

morris dance *n.* traditional English folk dance perfomed by men.

morrow *n. Poetic* next day.

Morse *n.* system of signalling in which letters of the alphabet are represented by combinations of short and long signals.

morsel *n.* small piece, esp. of food.

mortal *adj.* subject to death; causing death. —*n.* mortal creature. —**mortally** *adv.* —**mortality** *n.* state of being mortal; great loss of life; death rate. —**mortal sin** *RC Church* sin meriting damnation.

mortar *n.* mixture of lime, sand, and water for holding bricks and stones together; small cannon with a short range; bowl in which substances are pounded. —**mortarboard** *n.* square academic cap.

mortgage *n.* conditional pledging of property, esp. a house, as security for the repayment of a loan; the loan itself. —*v.* pledge (property) as security thus. —**mortgagee** *n.* creditor in a mortgage. —**mortgagor, -ger** *n.* debtor in a mortgage.

mortify *v.* **-fying, -fied.** humiliate; subdue by self-denial; (of flesh) become gangrenous. —**mortification** *n.*

THESAURUS

cipled, proper, pure, right, righteous, upright, virtuous ~*n.* 3. lesson, meaning, message, point, significance

morale confidence, heart, mettle, spirit, temper

morality chastity, decency, goodness, honesty, integrity, justice, principle, righteousness, virtue

morals conduct, integrity, manners, principles, scruples, standards

moratorium freeze, halt, respite, standstill, stay, suspension

morbid 1. brooding, gloomy, grim, pessimistic, sick, sombre, unhealthy, unwholesome 2. dreadful, ghastly, grisly, gruesome, hideous, horrid, macabre

more 1. *adj.* added, extra, fresh, further, new, other, spare, supplementary 2. *adv.* better, further, longer

moreover additionally, also, besides, further

moribund declining, forceless, stagnant, waning, weak

morning dawn, daybreak, forenoon, sunrise

moron ass, blockhead, cretin, dolt, dunce, fool, halfwit, idiot, imbecile, numskull, simpleton, thickhead

morose churlish, crabbed, cross, depressed, dour, down, gloomy, glum, gruff, ill-tempered, low, melancholy, moody, mournful, perverse, pessimistic, saturnine, sour, sulky, sullen, surly, taciturn

morsel bit, bite, crumb, fraction, fragment, grain, mouthful, piece, scrap, segment, slice, soupçon, taste

mortal *adj.* 1. earthly, ephemeral, human, temporal, transient, worldly 2. deadly, destructive, fatal, killing, lethal, murderous ~*n.* 3. being, body, earthling, human, individual, man, person, woman

mortality 1. humanity, transience 2. bloodshed, carnage, death, destruction, fatality, killing

mortified abashed, affronted, annoyed, ashamed, confounded, crushed, deflated, dis-

DICTIONARY

mortise, mortice [**more-**tiss] *n.* hole in a piece of wood or stone shaped to receive a matching projection on another piece. —**mortise lock** lock set into a door.

mortuary *n., pl.* **-aries.** building where corpses are kept before burial or cremation.

mosaic [mow-**zay**-ik] *n.* design or decoration using small bits of coloured stone or glass.

Mosaic *adj.* of Moses.

Moselle *n.* light white wine.

Moslem *n., adj.* same as MUSLIM.

mosque *n.* Muslim temple.

mosquito *n., pl.* **-toes, -tos.** blood-sucking flying insect.

moss *n.* small flowerless plant growing in masses on moist surfaces. —**mossy** *adj.*

most *adj.* greatest in number or degree; superlative of MUCH and MANY. —*n.* greatest number or degree. —*adv.* in the greatest degree. —**mostly** *adv.* for the most part, generally.

MOT (test) *n.* compulsory annual test of the roadworthiness of vehicles over a certain age.

motel *n.* roadside hotel for motorists.

motet [mow-**tet**] *n.* short sacred choral song.

moth *n.* nocturnal insect like a butterfly. —**mothball** *n.* small ball of camphor or naphthalene used to repel moths from stored clothes. —*v.* store (something operational) for future use; postpone (a project etc.). —**motheaten** *adj.* eaten or damaged by moth larvae; decayed or scruffy.

mother *n.* female parent; head of a female religious community. —*adj.* native or inborn, e.g. *mother wit.* —*v.* look after as a mother. —**motherhood** *n.* —**motherly** *adj.* —**motherless** *adj.*

—**mother-in-law** *n.* mother of one's husband or wife. —**mother of pearl** iridescent lining of certain shells. —**mother tongue** one's native language.

motif [mow-**teef**] *n.* (recurring) theme or design.

motion *n.* process, action, or way of moving; proposal in a meeting; evacuation of the bowels. —*v.* direct (someone) by gesture. —**motionless** *adj.* not moving. —**motion picture** *US* film.

motive *n.* reason for a course of action. —*adj.* causing motion. —**motivate** *v.* give incentive to. —**motivation** *n.*

motley *adj.* miscellaneous; multicoloured. —*n. Hist.* jester's costume.

motocross *n.* motorcycle race over a rough course.

motor *n.* engine, esp. of a vehicle; machine that converts electrical energy into mechanical energy; car. —*v.* travel by car. —**motorist** *n.* driver of a car. —**motorize** *v.* equip with a motor or motor transport. —**motorbike** *n.* —**motorboat** *n.* —**motorcar** *n.* —**motorcycle** *n.* —**motorcyclist** *n.* —**motor scooter** —**motorway** *n.* main road for fast-moving traffic.

mottled *adj.* marked with blotches.

motto *n., pl.* **-toes, -tos.** saying expressing an ideal or rule of conduct; verse or maxim in a paper cracker.

mould[1] *n.* hollow container in which metal etc. is cast; shape, form, or pattern; nature or character. —*v.* shape; influence or direct. —**moulding** *n.* moulded ornamental edging.

mould[2] *n.* fungal growth caused by dampness. —**mouldy** *adj.* stale or musty; dull or boring.

mould[3] *n.* loose soil. —**moulder** *v.* decay into dust.

THESAURUS

pleased, embarrassed, humbled, shamed, vexed

mortify abase, abash, annoy, chasten, confound, crush, disappoint, displease, embarrass, humble, shame, vex

mostly chiefly, customarily, generally, largely, mainly, particularly, predominantly, principally, usually

moth-eaten antiquated, decrepit, outdated, outworn, ragged, seedy, shabby, stale, tattered, threadbare

mother 1. *n.* dam, mater 2. *adj.* inborn, innate, native, natural 3. *v.* cherish, nurse, nurture, protect, raise, rear, tend

motherly affectionate, caring, fond, gentle, kind, loving, maternal, tender

motion *n.* 1. action, change, flow, move, movement, passage, progress, travel 2. proposal,

proposition, submission, suggestion ∼*v.* 3. beckon, direct, gesture, nod, signal, wave

motionless calm, frozen, halted, immobile, lifeless, static, stationary, still, unmoving

motivate actuate, arouse, bring, cause, draw, drive, impel, induce, inspire, inspirit, instigate, lead, move, persuade, prompt, stimulate, stir

motivation ambition, desire, drive, hunger, inspiration, interest, wish

motive *n.* cause, design, ground(s), incentive, inducement, influence, inspiration, intention, occasion, purpose, reason, spur, stimulus

motley assorted, dissimilar, diversified, mingled, mixed, unlike, varied

mottled blotchy, chequered, dappled, flecked, marbled, piebald, pied, speckled, stippled, streaked, variegated

DICTIONARY

moult v. shed feathers, hair, or skin to make way for new growth. —n. process of moulting.

mound n. heap, esp. of earth or stones; small hill.

mount v. climb or ascend; get up on (a horse etc.); increase; fix on a support or backing; organize, e.g. *mount a campaign*. —n. backing or support on which something is fixed; horse for riding; hill.

mountain n. hill of great size; large heap. —**mountainous** adj. full of mountains; huge. —**mountaineer** n. person who climbs mountains. —**mountaineering** n. —**mountain bike** bicycle with straight handlebars and heavy-duty tyres.

mountebank n. charlatan or fake.

Mountie n. Informal member of the Royal Canadian Mounted Police.

mourn v. feel or express sorrow for (a dead person or lost thing). —**mourning** n. grieving; conventional symbols of grief for death, such as the wearing of black. —**mourner** n. —**mournful** adj. sad or dismal. —**mournfully** adv.

mouse n., pl. **mice**. small long-tailed rodent; timid person; Computers hand-held device for moving the cursor without keying. —v. catch or hunt mice. —**mouser** n. cat used to catch mice. —**mousy** adj. like a mouse, esp. in hair colour; meek and shy.

mousse n. dish of flavoured cream whipped and set.

moustache n. hair on the upper lip.

mouth n. opening in the head for eating and issuing sounds; opening; entrance; point where a river enters the sea. —v. speak or utter insincerely, esp. in public; form (words) with the lips without speaking. —**mouth organ** small musical instrument played by sucking and blowing. —**mouthpiece** n. part of a telephone into which a person speaks; part of a wind instrument into which the player blows; spokesman.

move v. change in place or position; change (one's house etc.); take action; stir the emotions of; incite; suggest (a proposal) formally. —n. moving; action towards some goal. —**mov(e)able** adj., n. —**movement** n. action or process of moving; moving parts of a machine; group with a common aim; division of a piece of music.

movie n. US informal film.

mow v. **mowing**, **mowed**, **mowed** or **mown**. cut (grass or crops). —**mower** n. —**mow down** v. kill in large numbers.

mozzarella [mot-sa-rel-la] n. moist white cheese originally made in Italy from buffalo milk.

MP Member of Parliament; Military Police.

mpg miles per gallon.

mph miles per hour.

Mr. n. short for MISTER.

Mrs. n. title of a married woman.

Ms [mizz] n. title used instead of Miss or Mrs.

THESAURUS

motto adage, cry, maxim, precept, proverb, rule, saw, saying, slogan

mould n. 1. cast, die, form, pattern, shape 2. brand, build, cut, design, fashion, form, format, frame, kind, line, make, pattern, shape, style ~v. 3. carve, cast, construct, create, fashion, forge, form, make, model, sculpt, shape, stamp, work

mouldy bad, decaying, rotten, spoiled, stale

mound 1. heap, pile, stack 2. bank, dune, hill, hillock, knoll, rise

mount v. 1. ascend, climb, escalade, scale 2. bestride, jump on 3. build, grow, increase, intensify, multiply, pile up, swell 4. display, frame, set 5. exhibit, prepare, produce, put on, stage ~n. 6. backing, base, fixture, foil, frame, mounting, setting, stand, support 7. horse

mountain alp, elevation, eminence, height, mount, peak

mountainous alpine, high, highland, rocky, soaring, steep, towering, upland

mourn bewail, deplore, grieve, lament, miss, rue, sorrow, wail, weep

mournful afflicting, distressing, grievous, lam~entable, melancholy, painful, piteous, plaintive, sad, sorrowful, tragic, unhappy, woeful

mourning grief, lamentation, weeping, woe

mouth n. 1. jaws, lips 2. door, entrance, gateway, inlet, opening, orifice, rim

mouthpiece agent, delegate, representative

move v. 1. advance, budge, drift, go, march, proceed, progress, shift, stir, walk 2. carry, change, shift, switch, transfer, transport, transpose 3. leave, migrate, quit, relocate, remove 4. activate, drive, impel, motivate, operate, propel, push, shift, shove, start, turn 5. affect, agitate, cause, excite, incite, induce, influence, inspire, lead 6. advocate, propose, recommend, suggest, urge ~n. 7. act, action, deed, measure, motion, ploy, shift, step, stratagem, stroke, turn

movement 1. act, action, activity, advance, agitation, change, exercise, flow, gesture, motion, operation, progress, shift, steps, stir, stirring, transfer 2. campaign, crusade, drive, faction, front, group, party 3. Music division, part, passage, section

mow crop, cut, scythe, shear, trim

DICTIONARY

MSc Master of Science.

MS(S) manuscript(s).

Mt. Mount.

much *adj.* **more, most.** existing in quantity. —*n.* large amount or degree. —*adv.* **more, most.** to a great degree; nearly.

mucilage [mew-sill-ij] *n.* gum or glue.

muck *n.* cattle dung; unclean refuse. —**mucky** *adj.*

mucus [mew-kuss] *n.* slimy secretion of the mucous membranes. —**mucous membrane** membrane lining body cavities or passages.

mud *n.* wet soft earth. —**muddy** *adj.* —**mudguard** *n.* cover over a wheel to prevent mud or water being thrown up by it. —**mudpack** *n.* cosmetic paste to improve the complexion.

muddle *v.* (often with *up*) confuse; mix up. —*n.* state of confusion.

muesli [mewz-lee] *n.* mixture of grain, nuts, and dried fruit eaten with milk.

muezzin [moo-ezz-in] *n.* official who summons Muslims to prayer.

muff[1] *n.* tube-shaped covering to keep the hands warm.

muff[2] *v.* bungle (an action).

muffin *n.* light round yeast cake.

muffle *v.* wrap up for warmth or to deaden sound. —**muffler** *n.* scarf.

mufti *n.* civilian clothes worn by a person who usually wears a uniform.

mug[1] *n.* large drinking cup.

mug[2] *n. Slang* face; *Slang* person who is easily swindled. —*v.* **mugging, mugged.** *Informal* rob violently. —**mugger** *n.*

mug[3] *v.* **mugging, mugged.** (esp. with *up*) *Informal* study hard.

muggins *n. Informal* simpleton.

muggy *adj.* **-gier, -giest.** (of weather) damp and stifling.

mulatto [mew-lat-toe] *n., pl.* **-tos, -toes.** child of one Black and one White parent.

mulberry *n.* tree whose leaves are used to feed silkworms; purple fruit of this tree.

mulch *n.* mixture of wet straw, leaves, etc., used to protect the roots of plants. —*v.* cover (land) with mulch.

mulct *v.* fine (a person).

mule[1] *n.* offspring of a horse and a donkey. —**mulish** *adj.* obstinate. —**muleteer** *n.* mule driver.

mule[2] *n.* backless shoe or slipper.

mull *v.* heat (wine) with sugar and spices; think (over) or ponder.

mullah *n.* Muslim theologian.

mullet *n.* edible sea fish.

mulligatawny *n.* soup made with curry powder.

mullion *n.* upright dividing bar in a window. —**mullioned** *adj.*

multi- *combining form* many, e.g. *multiracial.*

multifarious [mull-tiff-fare-ee-uss] *adj.* having many various parts.

multiple *adj.* having many parts. —*n.* quantity which contains another an exact number of times.

multiplex *adj.* having many elements, complex.

multiplicity *n., pl.* **-ties.** large number or great variety.

multiply *v.* **-plying, -plied.** (cause to) increase in number, quantity, or degree; add (a number or quantity) to itself a given number of times; increase in number by reproduction. —**multiplication** *n.* —**multiplicand** *n. Maths* number to be multiplied.

multitude *n.* great number; great crowd. —**multitudinous** *adj.* very numerous.

mum[1] *n. Informal* mother.

mum[2] *adj.* silent, e.g. *keep mum.*

THESAURUS

much 1. *adj.* abundant, ample, considerable, copious, great, plenteous, substantial 2. *adv.* a lot, considerably, decidedly, exceedingly, frequently, greatly, indeed, often, regularly

mud clay, dirt, mire, ooze, silt, sludge

muddle *v.* 1. confuse, disorder, mess, scramble, spoil, tangle 2. bewilder, confound, confuse, daze, perplex, stupefy ~*n.* 3. chaos, clutter, confusion, daze, disarray, disorder, mess, mix-up, tangle

muddy boggy, dirty, marshy, soiled

muffle cloak, conceal, cover, disguise, envelop, hood, mask, shroud

mug beaker, cup, flagon, jug, pot, tankard

muggy close, damp, humid, sticky, stuffy, sultry

multifarious different, diversified, legion, manifold, many, numerous, sundry, varied

multiple collective, many, several, sundry, various

multiply augment, breed, expand, extend, increase, reproduce, spread

multitude army, assembly, collection, congregation, crowd, horde, host, legion, lot, mass, mob, myriad, sea, swarm, throng

DICTIONARY

mumble *v.* speak indistinctly, mutter.

mumbo jumbo *n.* meaningless religious ritual; deliberately complicated language.

mummer *n.* actor in a folk play or mime.

mummy[1] *n., pl.* **-mies.** body embalmed and wrapped for burial in ancient Egypt. —**mummify** *v.* **-fying, -fied.** preserve (a body) as a mummy.

mummy[2] *n., pl.* **-mies.** child's word for MOTHER.

mumps *n.* infectious disease with swelling in the glands of the neck.

munch *v.* chew noisily and steadily.

mundane *adj.* everyday; earthly.

municipal *adj.* relating to a city or town. —**municipality** *n.* city or town with local self-government; governing body of this.

munificent [mew-**niff**-fiss-sent] *adj.* very generous. —**munificence** *n.*

muniments [mew-nim-ments] *pl. n.* title deeds or similar documents.

munitions [mew-**nish**-unz] *pl. n.* military stores.

mural [**myoor**-al] *n.* painting on a wall. —*adj.* of or on a wall.

murder *n.* unlawful intentional killing of a human being. —*v.* kill thus. —**murderer, murderess** *n.* —**murderous** *adj.*

murk *n.* thick darkness. —**murky** *adj.* dark or gloomy.

murmur *n.* continuous low indistinct sound. —*v.* **-muring, -mured.** make such a sound; complain; utter in a murmur.

murrain [**murr**-rin] *n.* cattle plague.

muscat *n.* sweet white grape. —**muscatel** [musk-a-**tell**] *n.* wine from muscat grapes; muscat grape or raisin.

muscle *n.* tissue in the body which produces movement by contracting; strength or power. —**muscular** *adj.* with well-developed muscles; of muscles. —**muscular dystrophy** disease with wasting of the muscles. —**muscle in** *v. Informal* force one's way in.

Muse *n. Greek myth* one of nine goddesses, each of whom inspired an art or science; (**m-**) force that inspires a creative artist.

muse *v.* ponder.

museum *n.* building where natural, artistic, historical, or scientific objects are exhibited and preserved.

mush *n.* soft pulpy mass; *Informal* cloying sentimentality. —**mushy** *adj.*

mushroom *n.* edible fungus with a stem and cap. —*v.* grow rapidly.

music *n.* art form using a melodious and harmonious combination of notes; written or printed form of this. —**musical** *adj.* of or like music; talented in or fond of music; pleasant-sounding. —*n.* play or film with songs and dancing. —**musically** *adv.* —**musician** *n.* —**musicology** *n.* scientific study of music. —**musicologist** *n.* —**music centre** combined record player, radio, and cassette player. —**music hall** variety theatre.

musk *n.* scent obtained from a gland of the **musk deer** or produced synthetically. —**musky** *adj.* —**muskrat** *n.* N American beaver-like rodent; its fur.

musket *n. Hist.* long-barrelled gun. —**musketeer** *n.* —**musketry** *n.* (use of) muskets.

Muslim *n.* follower of the religion of Islam. —*adj.* of or relating to Islam.

THESAURUS

mundane banal, everyday, humdrum, ordinary, prosaic, routine, workaday

municipal borough, city, civic, community, public, town, urban

municipality borough, city, district, town, township

munificence benevolence, big-heartedness, bounty, generosity, largess, liberality, philanthropy

munificent big-hearted, bountiful, generous, lavish, liberal, philanthropical, princely, rich

murder 1. *n.* assassination, bloodshed, butchery, carnage, homicide, killing, manslaughter, massacre, slaying 2. *v.* assassinate, butcher, destroy, dispatch, kill, massacre, slaughter

murderer assassin, butcher, cutthroat, killer, slayer

murderous barbarous, bloodthirsty, bloody, brutal, cruel, deadly, fatal, internecine, lethal, sanguinary, savage

murky cheerless, cloudy, dark, dim, dreary, dull, dusky, foggy, gloomy, grey, misty, obscure, overcast

murmur 1. *n.* babble, drone, humming, mumble, muttering, purr, rumble, undertone, whisper 2. *v.* babble, buzz, drone, hum, mumble, mutter, purr, rumble, whisper

muscle 1. sinew, tendon, thew 2. brawn, force, might, potency, power, stamina, strength, weight

muscular athletic, lusty, powerful, robust, sinewy, stalwart, strapping, strong, vigorous

muse brood, cogitate, deliberate, dream, meditate, ponder, reflect, ruminate, speculate, think, weigh

musical dulcet, lilting, lyrical, melodious, tuneful

DICTIONARY

muslin *n.* fine cotton fabric.

musquash *n.* muskrat.

mussel *n.* kind of bivalve mollusc.

must[1] *v.* used as an auxiliary to express obligation, certainty, or resolution. —*n.* something one must do.

must[2] *n.* newly pressed grape juice.

mustang *n.* wild horse of SW America.

mustard *n.* paste made from the powdered seeds of a plant, used as a condiment; the plant. —**mustard gas** poisonous gas causing blistering.

muster *v.* assemble. —*n.* assembly.

musty *adj.* **-tier, -tiest.** smelling mouldy and stale. —**mustiness** *n.*

mutable [mew-tab-bl] *adj.* liable to change. —**mutability** *n.*

mutation [mew-tay-shun] *n.* (genetic) change. —**mutate** [mew-tate] *v.* (cause to) undergo mutation. —**mutant** [mew-tant] *n.* mutated animal, plant, etc.

mute *adj.* unable to speak; silent. —*n.* person unable to speak; *Music* device to soften the tone of an instrument. —**muted** *adj.* (of sound or colour) softened; (of a reaction) subdued. —**mutely** *adv.*

mutilate [mew-till-ate] *v.* deprive of a limb or other part; damage (a book or text). —**mutilation** *n.*

mutiny [mew-tin-ee] *n., pl.* **-nies.** rebellion against authority, esp. by soldiers or sailors. —*v.* **-nying, -nied.** commit mutiny. —**mutineer** *n.* —**mutinous** *adj.*

mutt *n. Slang* stupid person; mongrel dog.

mutter *v.* utter or speak indistinctly; grumble. —*n.* muttered sound or grumble.

mutton *n.* flesh of sheep, used as food.

mutual [mew-chew-al] *adj.* felt or expressed by each of two people about the other; *Informal* common to both or all. —**mutually** *adv.*

Muzak *n.* ® recorded light music played in shops etc.

muzzle *n.* animal's mouth and nose; cover for these to prevent biting; open end of a gun. —*v.* put a muzzle on; force to keep silent.

muzzy *adj.* **-zier, -ziest.** confused or muddled; blurred or hazy. —**muzziness** *n.*

MW megawatt(s).

mW milliwatt(s).

my *det.* belonging to me.

mycology *n.* study of fungi.

myna(h) *n.* Indian bird which can mimic human speech.

myopia [my-oh-pee-a] *n.* short-sightedness. —**myopic** [my-op-ic] *adj.*

myriad [mir-ree-ad] *adj.* innumerable. —*n.* large indefinite number.

myrrh [mur] *n.* aromatic gum, formerly used in incense.

myrtle [mur-tl] *n.* flowering evergreen shrub.

myself *pron.* emphatic or reflexive form of I or ME.

mystery *n., pl.* **-teries.** strange or inexplicable event or phenomenon; obscure or secret thing; story or film that arouses suspense. —**mysterious** *adj.* —**mysteriously** *adv.*

THESAURUS

must *n.* duty, essential, imperative, necessity, obligation, requirement, requisite, *sine qua non*

muster 1. *v.* assemble, call up, collect, congregate, convene, convoke, enrol, gather, group, marshal, meet, mobilize, rally, summon 2. *n.* assembly, collection, concourse, congregation, convention, gathering, meeting, rally

musty airless, dank, decayed, frowsty, fusty, mildewed, mouldy, old, smelly, stale, stuffy

mutable adaptable, alterable, changeable, fickle, flexible, uncertain, unreliable, variable, volatile

mute *adj.* dumb, silent, speechless, unspoken, wordless

mutilate butcher, cripple, damage, disable, disfigure, dismember, hack, injure, lacerate, lame, maim, mangle

mutinous disobedient, insubordinate, rebellious, refractory, revolutionary, seditious, subversive, unruly

mutiny 1. *n.* disobedience, insubordination, insurrection, rebellion, resistance, revolt, revolution, riot, rising, strike, uprising 2. *v.* disobey, rebel, resist, revolt, strike

mutter complain, mumble, murmur, rumble

mutual common, interactive, joint, reciprocal, returned, shared

muzzle censor, choke, curb, restrain, silence, stifle, suppress

myopic near-sighted, short-sighted

myriad 1. *adj.* countless, incalculable, innumerable, untold 2. *n.* army, flood, horde, host, millions, scores, swarm, thousands

mysterious abstruse, arcane, baffling, concealed, cryptic, curious, dark, furtive, hidden, inexplicable, inscrutable, obscure, recondite, secret, strange, uncanny, unknown, weird

mystery conundrum, enigma, problem, puzzle, question, riddle, secrecy, secret

DICTIONARY

mystic *n.* person who seeks spiritual knowledge. —*adj.* having a spiritual or religious significance beyond human understanding. —**mystical** *adj.* mystic. —**mysticism** *n.*

mystify *v.* -**fying, -fied.** bewilder or puzzle. —**mystification** *n.*

mystique [miss-**steek**] *n.* aura of mystery or power.

myth *n.* tale with supernatural characters, usu. of how the world and mankind began; imaginary person or object. —**mythical** *adj.* —**mythology** *n.* myths collectively; study of myths. —**mythological** *adj.*

myxomatosis [mix-a-mat-**oh**-siss] *n.* contagious fatal viral disease of rabbits.

THESAURUS

mystify baffle, bewilder, confound, confuse, escape, perplex, puzzle, stump

myth allegory, fable, fiction, legend, parable, saga, story, tradition

mythical 1. fabled, fairy-tale, legendary 2. fabricated, fanciful, fictitious, invented, pretended, unreal, untrue

mythology folklore, legend, stories, tradition

N

N *Chess* knight; *Chem.* nitrogen; *Physics* newton(s); north(ern).

n. neuter; noun; number.

Na *Chem.* sodium.

Naafi Navy, Army, and Air Force Institutes.

naan *n.* same as NAN BREAD.

nab *v.* **nabbing, nabbed.** *Informal* arrest (someone); catch (someone) in wrongdoing.

nadir *n.* point in the sky opposite the zenith; lowest point.

naevus [nee-vuss] *n., pl.* **-vi.** birthmark or mole.

naff *adj. Slang* inferior or useless.

nag[1] *v.* **nagging, nagged.** scold or find fault (with) constantly; be a constant source of discomfort, pain, or worry (to). —*n.* person who nags. —**nagging** *adj., n.*

nag[2] *n. Informal* (old) horse.

naiad [nye-ad] *n. Greek myth* water nymph.

nail *n.* hard covering of the upper tips of the fingers and toes; pointed piece of metal with a head, hit with a hammer to join two objects together. —*v.* attach (something) with nails; *Informal* catch or arrest. —**hit the nail on the head** say something exactly correct. —**nailfile** *n.* small metal file used to smooth or shape the finger or toe nails. —**nail polish, varnish** cosmetic lacquer applied to the finger or toe nails.

naive [nye-eev] *adj.* innocent and credulous; lacking developed powers of reasoning and criticism. —**naively** *adv.* —**naivety, naiveté** [nye-eev-tee] *n.*

naked *adj.* without clothes or covering. —**the naked eye** the eye unassisted by any optical instrument. —**nakedness** *n.*

namby-pamby *adj.* sentimental or insipid.

name *n.* word by which a person or thing is known; reputation, esp. a good one; abusive word or description. —*v.* give a name to; refer to by name; specify. —**nameless** *adj.* without a name; unspecified; too horrible to be mentioned. —**namely** *adv.* that is to say. —**namesake** *n.* person with the same name as another.

nan bread *n.* slightly leavened Indian bread in a large flat leaf shape.

nanny *n., pl.* **-nies.** woman whose job is looking after young children. —**nanny goat** female goat.

nap[1] *n.* short sleep. —*v.* **napping, napped.** have a short sleep.

nap[2] *n.* raised fibres of velvet or similar cloth.

nap[3] *n.* card game similar to whist.

napalm *n.* highly inflammable petrol, used in bombs.

nape *n.* back of the neck.

naphtha *n.* liquid mixture distilled from coal tar or petroleum, used as a solvent and in petrol. —**naphthalene** *n.* white crystalline product distilled from coal tar or petroleum, used in disinfectants, mothballs, and explosives.

napkin *n.* piece of cloth or paper for wiping the mouth or protecting the clothes while eating.

nappy *n., pl.* **-pies.** piece of absorbent material fastened round a baby's lower torso to absorb urine and faeces.

narcissism *n.* abnormal love and admiration for oneself. —**narcissistic** *adj.*

narcissus *n., pl.* **-cissi.** yellow, orange, or white flower related to the daffodil.

narcotic *n., adj.* (of) a drug, such as morphine

THESAURUS

nadir bottom, depths, zero

nag[1] 1. *v.* annoy, badger, chivvy, goad, harass, harry, henpeck, pester, plague, provoke, scold, vex, worry 2. *n.* harpy, scold, shrew, termagant, virago

nag[2] hack, horse, jade

nail *v.* attach, beat, fasten, fix, hammer, join, pin, secure, tack

naive artless, candid, childlike, guileless, ingenuous, innocent, open, simple, trusting, unaffected, unpretentious, unsophisticated

naiveté artlessness, candour, frankness, inexperience, ingenuousness, innocence, naturalness, simplicity

naked bare, divested, exposed, nude, stripped, unclothed, unconcealed, uncovered, undraped, undressed

nakedness bareness, nudity, undress

name *n.* 1. denomination, designation, epithet, nickname, sobriquet, term, title 2. distinction, eminence, esteem, fame, honour, note, praise, renown, repute 3. credit, reputation ~*v.* 4. baptize, call, christen, dub, entitle, label, style, term 5. appoint, choose, commission, designate, identify, nominate, select, specify

nameless 1. anonymous, untitled 2. horrible, indescribable, unmentionable, unspeakable

namely specifically, to wit, viz.

nap 1. *v.* doze, drowse, nod, rest, sleep 2. *n.* rest, siesta, sleep

DICTIONARY

or opium, which produces numbness and drowsiness, used medicinally but addictive. —**narcosis** n. effect of a narcotic.

nark *Slang* —v. annoy. —n. someone who complains in an irritating manner; informer. —**narky** adj. *Slang* irritable or complaining.

narrate v. tell (a story). —**narration** n. —**narrator** n. —**narrative** n. account, story.

narrow adj. of little breadth in comparison to length; limited in range, extent, or outlook; with little margin, e.g. *a narrow escape.* —v. make or become narrow. —**narrows** pl. n. narrow part of a strait, river, or current. —**narrowly** adv. —**narrowness** n. —**narrow-minded** adj. intolerant or bigoted.

narwhal n. arctic porpoise with a long spiral tusk.

NASA *US* National Aeronautics and Space Administration.

nasal adj. of the nose; pronounced with air passing through the nose. —**nasally** adv.

nascent adj. starting to grow or develop.

nasturtium n. plant with yellow, red, or orange trumpet-shaped flowers.

nasty adj. **-tier, -tiest.** unpleasant; (of an injury) dangerous or painful; spiteful or unkind. —**nastily** adv. —**nastiness** n.

natal [nay-tal] adj. of or relating to birth.

nation n. people of one or more cultures or races organized as a single state. —**national** adj. of or characteristic of a nation. —n. citizen of a nation. —**nationally** adv. —**nationalism** n. policy of national independence; patriotism. —**nationalist** n., adj. —**nationality** n. fact of being a citizen of a particular nation; nation. —**national-**

ize v. put (an industry or a company) under state control. —**nationalization** n. —**National Health Service** system of national medical services financed mainly by taxation. —**national insurance** state insurance scheme providing payments to the unemployed, sick, and retired. —**national service** compulsory military service.

native adj. relating to a place where a person was born; born in a specified place; (foll. by *to*) originating (in); inborn. —n. person born in a specified place; member of the original race of a country; indigenous animal or plant.

Nativity n. *Christianity* birth of Jesus Christ.

NATO North Atlantic Treaty Organization.

natter *Informal* —v. talk idly or chatter. —n. long idle chat.

natty adj. **-tier, -tiest.** *Informal* smart and spruce.

natural adj. normal; of, according to, existing in, or produced by nature; genuine, not affected; not created by human beings; not synthetic; (of a parent) not adoptive; (of a child) illegitimate; *Music* not sharp or flat. —n. person with an inborn talent or skill. —**naturally** adv. of course; in a natural or normal way; instinctively. —**naturalist** n. student of natural history. —**naturalism** n. movement in art and literature advocating detailed realism. —**naturalistic** adj. —**naturalize** v. give citizenship to (a person born in another country). —**naturalization** n. —**natural gas** gas found below the ground, used mainly as a fuel. —**natural history** study of animals and plants.

THESAURUS

narcotic analgesic, anodyne, drug, opiate, painkiller, sedative, tranquillizer

narrate describe, detail, recite, recount, rehearse, relate, repeat, report, tell

narration description, explanation, reading, recital, relation, storytelling

narrative account, chronicle, detail, history, report, statement, story, tale

narrator author, bard, chronicler, commentator, reporter, storyteller

narrow adj. 1. close, confined, cramped, limited, meagre, near, pinched, restricted, scanty, straitened, tight 2. biased, bigoted, dogmatic, illiberal, intolerant, partial, prejudiced, small-minded ~v. 3. diminish, limit, reduce, simplify, straiten, tighten

narrowly barely, just, scarcely

narrow-minded biased, bigoted, hidebound, il-

liberal, insular, intolerant, parochial, petty, strait-laced

nastiness malice, meanness, spitefulness, unpleasantness

nasty abusive, annoying, despicable, disagreeable, distasteful, malicious, mean, spiteful, unpleasant, vicious, vile

nation community, country, people, race, realm, society, state

national civil, countrywide, governmental, public, state

nationalism allegiance, chauvinism, loyalty, patriotism

nationality birth, race

native adj. 1. congenital, endemic, hereditary, inborn, inbred, indigenous, inherited, innate, instinctive 2. domestic, home, home-made, indigenous, local, mother ~n. 3. aborigine, citizen, countryman, dweller, inhabitant

DICTIONARY

nature *n.* whole system of the existence, forces, and events of the physical world that are not controlled by human beings; fundamental or essential qualities of a person or thing; kind or sort.

naturism *n.* nudism. —**naturist** *n.*

naught *n. Obs.* nothing; figure 0.

naughty *adj.* -**tier**, -**tiest.** disobedient or mischievous; mildly indecent. —**naughtily** *adv.* —**naughtiness** *n.*

nausea [naw-zee-a] *n.* feeling of being about to vomit. —**nauseate** *v.* make (someone) feel sick; disgust. —**nauseous** *adj.* as if about to vomit; sickening.

nautical *adj.* of the sea or ships. —**nautical mile** 1852 metres.

nautilus *n., pl.* -**luses**, -**li.** shellfish with many tentacles.

naval *adj.* see NAVY.

nave *n.* main part of a church.

navel *n.* hollow in the middle of the abdomen where the umbilical cord was attached.

navigate *v.* direct or plot the path or position of a ship, aircraft, or car; travel over or through. —**navigation** *n.* —**navigator** *n.* —**navigable** *adj.* wide, deep, or safe enough to be sailed through; able to be steered.

navvy *n., pl.* -**vies.** labourer employed on a road or a building site.

navy *n., pl.* -**vies.** branch of a country's armed services comprising warships with their crews and organization; warships of a nation. —*adj.* navy-blue. —**naval** *adj.* of or relating to a navy or ships. —**navy-blue** *adj.* very dark blue.

nay *interj. Obs.* no.

Nazi *n.* member of the National Socialist Party, which seized political control in Germany in 1933 under Adolf Hitler. —*adj.* of or relating to the Nazis. —**Nazism** *n.*

NB note well.

NCO noncommissioned officer.

NE northeast(ern).

Ne *Chem.* neon.

Neanderthal [nee-**ann**-der-tahl] *adj.* of a type of primitive man that lived in Europe before 12 000 BC.

neap tide *n.* tide at the first and last quarters of the moon when there is the smallest rise and fall in tidal level.

near *prep.* close to, not far from. —*adv.* at or to a place or time not far away. —*adj.* (situated) at or in a place or time not far away; (of people) closely related; almost being the thing specified, e.g. *a near tragedy.* —*v.* approach and be about to reach. —**nearly** *adv.* almost. —**nearness** *n.* —**nearby** *adj.* not far away. —**nearside** *n.* side of a vehicle that is nearer the kerb.

neat *adj.* tidy and clean; smoothly or competently done; undiluted. —**neatly** *adv.* —**neatness** *n.*

THESAURUS

natty chic, dapper, elegant, neat, smart, spruce, stylish, trim

natural 1. common, everyday, logical, normal, ordinary, regular, typical, usual 2. characteristic, essential, inborn, inherent, innate, instinctive, intuitive 3. artless, candid, frank, genuine, ingenuous, open, real, simple, spontaneous, unaffected, unpretentious

naturalist biologist, botanist, ecologist, zoologist

naturally customarily, genuinely, informally, normally, simply, spontaneously, typically, unaffectedly, unpretentiously

nature 1. character, complexion, essence, features, make-up, quality, traits 2. category, description, kind, sort, species, style, type, variety 3. creation, earth, environment, universe, world

naughty annoying, bad, disobedient, exasperating, impish, misbehaved, mischievous, perverse, playful, roguish, sinful, teasing, wayward, wicked, worthless

nausea biliousness, qualm(s), sickness, vomiting

nauseate disgust, horrify, offend, repel, repulse, revolt, sicken

nautical maritime, naval, seafaring, yachting

naval marine, maritime, nautical

navigable clear, negotiable, passable, unobstructed

navigate cross, cruise, direct, drive, guide, handle, journey, manoeuvre, pilot, plan, plot, sail, steer, voyage

navigation cruising, pilotage, sailing, seamanship, steering, voyaging

navy fleet, flotilla, warships

near *adj.* 1. adjacent, adjoining, alongside, beside, bordering, close, contiguous, nearby, neighbouring, nigh, touching 2. forthcoming, imminent, impending, looming, next 3. akin, allied, attached, connected, dear, familiar, intimate, related

nearby adjacent, adjoining, convenient, handy, neighbouring

nearly about, all but, almost, approaching, approximately, closely, not quite, practically, roughly, virtually, well-nigh

DICTIONARY

nebula [neb-yew-la] *n. Astronomy* hazy cloud of particles and gases. **—nebulous** *adj.* vague, indistinct.

necessary *adj.* indispensable or required. **—necessarily** *adv.* **—necessitate** *v.* compel or require. **—necessitous** *adj.* very needy. **—necessity** *n.* something needed; compulsion.

neck *n.* part of the body joining the head to the shoulders; part of a garment round the neck; narrow part of something such as a bottle or violin. *—v. Slang* kiss and cuddle. **—neckerchief** *n.* piece of cloth worn tied round the neck. **—necklace** *n.* decorative piece of jewellery worn around the neck.

necromancy [neck-rome-man-see] *n.* communication with the dead; sorcery.

necropolis [neck-rop-pol-liss] *n.* cemetery.

nectar *n.* sweet liquid collected from flowers by bees; drink of the gods.

nectarine *n.* smooth-skinned peach.

née [nay] *prep.* indicating the maiden name of a married woman.

need *v.* want or require; be obliged (to do something). *—n.* condition of lacking something; requirement, necessity; poverty. **—needs** *adv.*

(preceded or foll. by *must*) necessarily. **—needy** *adj.* poor, in need of financial support. **—needful** *adj.* necessary or required. **—needless** *adj.* unnecessary.

needle *n.* thin pointed piece of metal with an eye through which thread is passed for sewing; long pointed rod used in knitting; pointed part of a hypodermic syringe; small pointed part in a record player that touches the record and picks up the sound signals; pointer on a measuring instrument or compass; long narrow stiff leaf. *—v. Informal* goad or provoke. **—needlework** *n.* sewing and embroidery.

ne'er *adv. Lit.* never. **—ne'er-do-well** *n.* useless or lazy person.

nefarious [nif-fair-ee-uss] *adj.* wicked.

negate *v.* invalidate; deny. **—negation** *n.*

negative *adj.* expressing a denial or refusal; lacking positive qualities; (of an electrical charge) having the same electrical charge as an electron. *—n.* negative word or statement; *Photog.* image with a reversal of tones or colours from which positive prints are made.

neglect *v.* take no care of; disregard; fail (to do something) through carelessness. *—n.* neglecting or being neglected. **—neglectful** *adj.*

THESAURUS

nearness 1. accessibility, availability, closeness, handiness, proximity, vicinity 2. immediacy, imminence

neat 1. accurate, dainty, fastidious, methodical, nice, orderly, shipshape, smart, spruce, straight, systematic, tidy, trim 2. adept, adroit, agile, apt, clever, deft, dexterous, efficient, effortless, elegant, expert, graceful, handy, nimble, precise, skilful, stylish 3. *Of alcoholic drinks* pure, straight, undiluted, unmixed

neatly accurately, daintily, fastidiously, methodically, nicely, smartly, sprucely, systematically, tidily

neatness 1. accuracy, daintiness, fastidiousness, orderliness, smartness, tidiness 2. agility, aptness, cleverness, dexterity, efficiency, elegance, grace, gracefulness, precision, skill, style

nebulous cloudy, confused, dim, hazy, imprecise, indefinite, indistinct, misty, murky, obscure, shadowy, uncertain, unclear, vague

necessarily automatically, by definition, certainly, compulsorily, consequently, inevitably, inexorably, naturally, of course, perforce, willy-nilly

necessary compulsory, essential, imperative, mandatory, needful, obligatory, required, vital

necessitate call for, coerce, compel, constrain, demand, force, oblige, require

necessity demand, exigency, need, requirement

need *v.* 1. call for, demand, lack, miss, necessitate, require, want ~*n.* 2. destitution, distress, extremity, inadequacy, insufficiency, lack, neediness, paucity, penury, poverty, privation, shortage 3. demand, desideratum, essential, requirement, requisite

needless dispensable, excessive, expendable, groundless, pointless, redundant, superfluous, unwanted, useless

needy deprived, destitute, impoverished, penniless, poor, underprivileged

nefarious atrocious, base, criminal, depraved, dreadful, evil, execrable, horrible, infamous, infernal, odious, shameful, sinful, vicious, vile, wicked

negate annul, cancel, invalidate, neutralize, nullify, repeal, rescind, retract, reverse, revoke, void, wipe out

negation antithesis, contrary, converse, denial, disavowal, disclaimer, inverse, opposite, rejection, reverse

negative *adj.* 1. contrary, denying, dissenting, opposing, refusing, resisting 2. antagonistic, colourless, contrary, cynical, gloomy, jaundiced, neutral, pessimistic, unenthusiastic,

DICTIONARY

negligee [**neg**-lee-zhay] *n.* woman's lightweight usu. lace-trimmed dressing gown.

negligence *n.* neglect or carelessness. —**negligent** *adj.*

negligible *adj.* so small or unimportant as to be not worth considering.

negotiate *v.* discuss in order to reach (an agreement); succeed in passing round or over (a place or problem). —**negotiation** *n.* —**negotiator** *n.* —**negotiable** *adj.*

Negro *n., pl.* **-groes.** member of any of the Black peoples originating in Africa. —**Negress** *n. fem.* —**Negroid** *adj.* of or relating to the Negro race.

neigh *n.* loud high-pitched sound made by a horse. —*v.* make this sound.

neighbour *n.* one who lives or is situated near another. —**neighbouring** *adj.* situated nearby. —**neighbourhood** *n.* district; people of a district; surroundings. —**neighbourly** *adj.* kind, friendly, and helpful.

neither *det.* not one nor the other. —*conj.* not.

nemesis [**nem**-miss-iss] *n., pl.* **-ses.** retribution or vengeance.

neo- *combining form* new, recent, or a modern form of, e.g. *neoclassicism.*

neolithic *adj.* of the later Stone Age.

neologism [nee-**ol**-a-jiz-zum] *n.* new-coined word or an established word used in a new sense.

neon *n.* colourless odourless gaseous element used in illuminated signs and lights.

neophyte *n.* beginner or novice; new convert.

nephew *n.* son of one's sister or brother.

nephritis [nif-**frite**-tiss] *n.* inflammation of a kidney.

nepotism [**nep**-a-tiz-zum] *n.* favouritism in business shown to relatives and friends.

Neptune *n.* Roman god of the sea; eighth planet from the sun.

neptunium *n.* synthetic metallic element.

nerve *n.* cordlike bundle of fibres that conducts impulses between the brain and other parts of the body; bravery and determination; impudence. —*pl.* anxiety or tension; ability or inability to remain calm in a difficult situation. —**get on someone's nerves** irritate someone. —**nerve oneself** prepare oneself (to do something difficult or unpleasant). —**nerveless** *adj.* fearless; numb, without feeling. —**nervy** *adj.* excitable or nervous. —**nerve centre** place from which a system or organization is controlled. —**nerve-racking** *adj.* very distressing or harrowing.

nervous *adj.* apprehensive or worried; of or relating to the nerves. —**nervously** *adv.* —**nervousness** *n.* —**nervous breakdown** mental illness in which the sufferer ceases to function properly.

nest *n.* place or structure in which birds or certain animals lay eggs or give birth to young;

THESAURUS

uninterested, unwilling, weak ~*n.* 3. denial, refusal

neglect *v.* 1. disdain, disregard, ignore, overlook, rebuff, scorn, slight, spurn 2. be remiss, evade, forget, omit, procrastinate, shirk, skimp ~*n.* 3. disdain, disregard, disrespect, indifference, slight, unconcern 4. carelessness, default, failure, forgetfulness, laxity, oversight, remissness, slackness

negligence carelessness, default, disregard, failure, inadvertence, inattention, indifference, laxity, omission, oversight, shortcoming, slackness, thoughtlessness

negligent careless, forgetful, heedless, inadvertent, inattentive, indifferent, offhand, regardless, remiss, slack, thoughtless, unthinking

negligible insignificant, minor, minute, petty, small, trifling, trivial, unimportant

negotiate arbitrate, arrange, bargain, confer, consult, contract, deal, debate, discuss, handle, manage, mediate, parley, settle, transact, work out

negotiation arbitration, bargaining, debate, diplomacy, discussion

neighbourhood community, district, environs, locality, precincts, proximity, quarter, region, vicinity

neighbouring adjacent, adjoining, bordering, near, nearby, nearest, next, surrounding

nerve 1. bravery, coolness, courage, daring, endurance, energy, fearlessness, firmness, force, fortitude, gameness, mettle, might, pluck, resolution, spirit, vigour, will 2. *Inf.* audacity, boldness, brazenness, effrontery, gall, impertinence, impudence, insolence

nerves anxiety, nervousness, strain, stress, tension

nervous agitated, anxious, apprehensive, edgy, fearful, fidgety, hysterical, jumpy, neurotic, ruffled, shaky, tense, timid, uneasy, weak, worried

nervousness agitation, anxiety, disquiet, excitability, fluster, tension, timidity, worry

nest 1. den, haunt, refuge, resort, retreat 2. breeding-ground, den

nestle cuddle, huddle, snuggle

DICTIONARY

snug retreat; set of things of graduated sizes designed to fit together. —*v.* make or inhabit a nest. —**nest egg** fund of money kept in reserve.

nestle *v.* snuggle; be in a sheltered position.

nestling *n.* bird too young to leave the nest.

net[1] *n.* openwork fabric of meshes of string, thread, or wire; piece of net used to protect or hold things or to trap animals. —*v.* **netting, netted.** cover with or catch in a net. —**netting** *n.* material made of net. —**netball** *n.* team game in which a ball has to be thrown through a net hanging from a ring at the top of a pole.

net[2], **nett** *adj.* left after all deductions; (of weight) excluding the wrapping or container. —*v.* **netting, netted.** yield or earn as a clear profit.

nether *adj.* lower.

nettle *n.* plant with stinging hairs on the leaves. —*v.* irritate.

network *n.* system of intersecting lines, roads, etc.; interconnecting group or system; in broadcasting, group of stations that all transmit the same programmes simultaneously.

neural *adj.* of a nerve or the nervous system.

neuralgia *n.* severe pain along a nerve.

neuritis [nyoor-**rite**-tiss] *n.* inflammation of a nerve or nerves.

neurology *n.* scientific study of the nervous system. —**neurologist** *n.*

neurosis *n., pl.* **-ses.** mental disorder producing hysteria, anxiety, depression, or obsessive behaviour. —**neurotic** *adj.* abnormally sensitive; suffering from neurosis. —*n.* neurotic person.

neuter *adj.* belonging to a particular class of grammatical inflections in some languages. —*v.* castrate (an animal).

neutral *adj.* taking neither side in a war or dispute; of or belonging to a neutral party or country; (of a colour) not definite or striking; of no distinctive quality or type. —*n.* neutral person or nation; neutral gear. —**neutrality** *n.* —**neutralize** *v.* make ineffective or neutral. —**neutral gear** position of the controls of a gearbox that leaves the gears unconnected to the engine.

neutrino [new-**tree**-no] *n., pl.* **-nos.** elementary particle with no mass or electrical charge.

neutron *n.* electrically neutral elementary particle of about the same mass as a proton. —**neutron bomb** nuclear bomb designed to kill people and animals while leaving buildings virtually undamaged.

never *adv.* at no time. —**nevertheless** *adv.* in spite of that.

never-never *n. Informal* hire-purchase.

new *adj.* not existing before; having lately come into some state; additional; (foll. by *to*) unfamiliar. —*adv.* recently. —**newness** *n.* —**newborn** *adj.* recently or just born. —**newcomer** *n.* recent arrival or participant. —**new-fangled** *adj.* objectionably or unnecessarily modern. —**new moon** moon when it appears as a narrow crescent at the beginning of its cycle.

newel *n.* post at the top or bottom of a flight of stairs that supports the handrail.

news *n.* important or interesting recent happenings; information about such events reported in the mass media. —**newsy** *adj.* full of news. —**newsagent** *n.* shopkeeper who sells newspapers and magazines. —**newscaster** *n.* person who reads the news on the television or radio. —**newsflash** *n.* brief important news item, which interrupts a radio or television programme. —**newsletter** *n.* bulletin issued periodi-

---

THESAURUS

nestling chick, fledgling

net[1] 1. *n.* lattice, mesh, tracery, web 2. *v.* bag, capture, catch, enmesh, ensnare, entangle, trap

net[2], **nett** 1. *adj.* clear, final, take-home 2. *v.* clear, earn, gain, make, realize, reap

nether below, beneath, bottom, inferior, lower, under

nettle annoy, goad, harass, irritate, pique, provoke, ruffle, sting, tease, vex

network arrangement, channels, complex, grid, grill, maze, mesh, organization, structure, system, web

neurosis abnormality, deviation, instability, obsession, phobia

neurotic abnormal, anxious, compulsive, disordered, disturbed, nervous, unstable

neuter *v.* castrate, geld, spay

neutral disinterested, dispassionate, impartial, noncombatant, unaligned, unbiased, uncommitted, undecided, unprejudiced

neutrality detachment, impartiality

neutralize cancel, counteract, frustrate, nullify, offset, undo

nevertheless but, however, notwithstanding, regardless, still, yet

new 1. advanced, contemporary, current, different, fresh, latest, modern, newfangled, novel, original, recent, topical, unfamiliar, unknown, unused, unusual, up-to-date, virgin 2. added, extra, more 3. altered, changed, improved, modernized, redesigned, renewed, restored

newcomer alien, arrival, beginner, foreigner, incomer, novice, outsider

newfangled contemporary, modern, new, newfashioned, novel, recent

DICTIONARY

cally to members of a group. —**newspaper** *n.* weekly or daily publication containing news. —**newsprint** *n.* inexpensive paper used for newspapers. —**newsreel** *n.* short film giving news. —**newsroom** *n.* room where news is received and prepared for publication or broadcasting. —**newsworthy** *adj.* sufficiently interesting to be reported as news.

newt *n.* small amphibious creature with a long slender body and tail.

newton *n.* unit of force.

next *adj., adv.* immediately following; nearest. —**next-of-kin** *n.* closest relative.

nexus *n., pl.* **nexus.** connection or link.

NHS National Health Service.

Ni *Chem.* nickel.

nib *n.* writing point of a pen.

nibble *v.* take little bites (of). —*n.* little bite; light meal.

nibs *n.* —**his** *or* **her nibs** *Slang* mock title of respect.

nice *adj.* pleasant; kind, e.g. *a nice gesture;* good or satisfactory, e.g. *they made a nice job of it;* subtle, e.g. *a nice distinction.* —**nicely** *adv.* —**niceness** *n.* —**nicety** *n.* subtle point; refinement or delicacy.

niche [neesh] *n.* hollow area in a wall; suitable position for a particular person.

nick *v.* make a small cut in; *Slang* steal; *Slang* arrest. —*n.* small cut; *Slang* prison or police station. —**in good nick** *Informal* in good condition. —**in the nick of time** just in time.

nickel *n.* silvery-white metal often used in alloys; US coin worth five cents.

nickelodeon *n. US* early type of jukebox.

nickname *n.* familiar name given to a person or place. —*v.* call by a nickname.

nicotine *n.* poisonous substance found in tobacco.

niece *n.* daughter of one's sister or brother.

nifty *adj.* **-tier, -tiest.** *Informal* neat or smart.

niggard *n.* stingy person. —**niggardly** *adj.*

nigger *n. Offens.* Black person.

niggle *v.* continually find fault (with); worry slightly. —*n.* small worry or doubt.

nigh *adv., prep. Lit.* near.

night *n.* time of darkness between sunset and sunrise. —**nightly** *adj., adv.* (happening) each night. —**nightcap** *n.* drink taken just before bedtime; soft cap formerly worn in bed. —**nightclub** *n.* establishment for dancing, music, etc., open late at night. —**nightdress** *n.* woman's loose dress worn in bed. —**nightfall** *n.* approach of darkness. —**nightie** *n. Informal* nightdress. —**nightingale** *n.* small bird with a musical song usually heard at night. —**nightjar** *n.* nocturnal bird with a harsh cry. —**nightlife** *n.* entertainment and social activities available at night in a town or city. —**nightmare** *n.* very bad dream; very unpleasant experience. —**nightshade** *n.* plant with bell-shaped flowers which are often poisonous. —**nightshirt** *n.* man's long loose shirt worn in bed. —**night-time** *n.* time from sunset to sunrise.

nihilism [nye-ill-liz-zum] *n.* rejection of all established authority and institutions. —**nihilist** *n.* —**nihilistic** *adj.*

nil *n.* nothing, zero.

nimble *adj.* agile and quick; mentally alert or acute. —**nimbly** *adv.*

THESAURUS

news account, advice, bulletin, dispatch, exposé, gossip, hearsay, information, intelligence, leak, release, report, revelation, rumour, scandal, statement, story, tidings, word

next *adj.* 1. consequent, ensuing, following, later, subsequent, succeeding 2. adjacent, adjoining, closest, nearest, neighbouring ~*adv.* 3. afterwards, closely, following, later, subsequently, thereafter

nice 1. agreeable, amiable, attractive, charming, courteous, friendly, good, kind, pleasant, polite, refined, well-mannered 2. accurate, careful, critical, delicate, exact, fastidious, fine, meticulous, precise, rigorous, scrupulous, strict, subtle

nicely 1. acceptably, agreeably, amiably, attractively, charmingly, courteously, kindly, pleasantly, politely, well 2. critically, delicately, exactly, fastidiously, finely, meticulously,

precisely, rigorously, scrupulously, strictly, subtly

nicety accuracy, exactness, meticulousness, minuteness, precision

niche alcove, corner, hollow, nook, opening, recess

nick chip, cut, damage, dent, mark, notch, scar, score, scratch

nickname diminutive, epithet, label, pet name, sobriquet

niggardly close, covetous, frugal, grudging, mean, mercenary, miserly, parsimonious, penurious, sparing, stingy, tightfisted

niggle 1. carp, cavil, criticize, find fault, fuss 2. annoy, irritate, rankle, worry

night dark, night-time

nightfall dusk, evening, sunset, twilight

nightmare 1. hallucination 2. horror, ordeal, torment, trial, tribulation

DICTIONARY

nimbus *n., pl.* **-bi, -buses.** dark grey rain cloud.

nincompoop *n. Informal* stupid person.

nine *adj., n.* one more than eight. —**ninth** *adj., n.* (of) number nine in a series. —**nineteen** *adj., n.* ten and nine. —**nineteenth** *adj., n.* —**ninety** *adj., n.* ten times nine. —**ninetieth** *adj., n.* —**ninepins** *n.* game of skittles.

nip *v.* **nipping, nipped.** pinch or squeeze; bite lightly; *Informal* hurry. —*n.* pinch; light bite; small alcoholic drink; sharp coldness, e.g. *a nip in the air.* —**nippy** *adj.* frosty or chilly; *Informal* quick or nimble. —**nipper** *n. Informal* small child.

nipple *n.* projection in the centre of a breast.

nirvana [near-**vah**-na] *n. Buddhism & Hinduism* absolute spiritual enlightenment and bliss.

nit *n.* egg or larva of a louse; *Informal* short for NITWIT. —**nit-picking** *adj. Informal* overconcerned with insignificant detail, esp. to find fault. —**nitwit** *n. Informal* stupid person.

nitrogen [**nite**-roj-jen] *n.* colourless odourless gas that forms four fifths of the air. —**nitric, nitrous, nitrogenous** *adj.* of or containing nitrogen. —**nitrate** *n.* compound of nitric acid, used as a fertilizer. —**nitroglycerin(e)** *n.* explosive liquid.

nitty-gritty *n. Informal* basic facts.

no *interj.* expresses denial, disagreement, or refusal. —*det.* not any, not a; not at all. —*n., pl.* **noes** or **nos.** answer or vote of 'no'; person who answers or votes 'no'. —**no-go area** district barricaded off so that the police or army can enter only by force. —**no-man's-land** *n.* land between boundaries, esp. contested land between two opposing forces. —**no-one, no one** *pron.* nobody.

no. number.

nob *n. Slang* person of wealth or social distinction.

nobble *v. Slang* attract the attention of (someone) in order to talk to him or her; *Slang* bribe or threaten.

Nobel Prize [no-**bell**] *n.* prize awarded annually for outstanding achievement in various fields.

noble *adj.* showing or having high moral qualities; of the nobility; impressive and magnificent. —*n.* member of the nobility. —**nobility** *n.* quality of being noble; class of people holding titles and high social rank. —**nobly** *adv.* —**nobleman, noblewoman** *n.*

nobody *pron.* no person. —*n., pl.* **-bodies.** person of no importance.

nocturnal *adj.* of the night; active at night.

nocturne *n.* short dreamy piece of music.

nod *v.* **nodding, nodded.** lower and raise (one's head) briefly in agreement or greeting; let one's head fall forward with sleep. —*n.* act of nodding. —**nod off** *v. Informal* fall asleep.

noddle *n. Informal* the head.

node *n.* point on a plant stem from which leaves grow; point at which a curve crosses itself.

nodule *n.* small knot or lump; rounded mineral growth on the root of a plant.

Noel *n.* Christmas.

noggin *n.* small quantity of an alcoholic drink; *Informal* head.

noise *n.* sound, usually a loud or disturbing one. —**be noised abroad** be rumoured. —**noisy** *adj.* making a lot of noise; full of noise. —**noisily** *adv.* —**noiseless** *adj.*

noisome *adj.* (of smells) offensive; harmful or poisonous.

THESAURUS

nil duck, love, none, nothing, zero

nimble active, agile, alert, brisk, deft, lively, prompt, quick, ready, smart, sprightly, spry, swift

nip[1] *v.* bite, catch, clip, grip, pinch, snag, snap, snip, tweak, twitch

nip[2] *n.* dram, draught, drop, finger, portion, sip, *soupçon*, taste

nipple breast, dug, pap, teat, tit, udder

nippy biting, chilly, sharp, stinging

nitty-gritty basics, core, crux, essence, facts, gist, reality, substance

nobble bribe, get at, influence, intimidate, outwit

nobility 1. aristocracy, elite, lords, nobles, peerage 2. dignity, eminence, excellence, grandeur, greatness, majesty, nobleness, superiority,

worthiness 3. honour, integrity, uprightness, virtue

noble *n.* 1. lord, nobleman, peer ~*adj.* 2. aristocratic, highborn, lordly 3. august, dignified, distinguished, elevated, eminent, grand, great, imposing, impressive, lofty, splendid, stately 4. generous, honourable, upright, virtuous, worthy

nobody 1. no-one 2. cipher, menial, nonentity

nocturnal night, nightly, night-time

nod *v.* 1. bow, dip, duck, gesture, indicate, salute, signal 2. agree, assent, concur 3. doze, droop, drowse, nap, sleep, slump ~*n.* 4. beck, gesture, greeting, salute, sign, signal

noise babble, blare, clamour, clatter, commotion, cry, din, fracas, hubbub, outcry, pandemonium, racket, row, sound, talk, tumult, uproar

DICTIONARY

nomad *n.* member of a tribe with no fixed dwelling place, wanderer. **—nomadic** *adj.*

nom de plume *n., pl.* **noms de plume.** pen name.

nomenclature [no-**men**-klatch-er] *n.* system of names used in a particular subject.

nominal *adj.* in name only; very small in comparison with real worth. **—nominally** *adv.*

nominate *v.* suggest as a candidate; appoint to an office or position. **—nomination** *n.* **—nominee** *n.* candidate. **—nominative** *n.* form of a noun indicating subject of a verb.

non- *prefix* indicating: negation, e.g. *nonexistent;* refusal or failure, e.g. *noncooperation;* exclusion from a specified class, e.g. *nonfiction;* lack or absence, e.g. *nonevent.*

nonagenarian *n.* person aged between ninety and ninety-nine.

nonaggression *n.* (of countries) not attacking.

nonagon *n.* geometric figure with nine sides. **—nonagonal** *adj.*

nonalcoholic *adj.* containing no alcohol.

nonaligned *adj.* (of a country) not part of a major alliance or power bloc.

nonce *n.* **—for the nonce** for the present.

nonchalant [**non**-shall-ant] *adj.* casually unconcerned or indifferent. **—nonchalantly** *adv.* **—nonchalance** *n.*

noncombatant *n.* member of the armed forces whose duties do not include fighting.

noncommissioned officer *n.* (in the armed forces) a subordinate officer, risen from the ranks.

noncommittal *adj.* not committing oneself to any particular opinion.

non compos mentis *adj.* of unsound mind.

nonconductor *n.* substance that is a poor conductor of heat, electricity, or sound.

nonconformist *n.* person who does not conform to generally accepted patterns of behaviour or thought; (N-) member of a Protestant group separated from the Church of England. **—adj.** (of behaviour or ideas) not conforming to accepted patterns. **—nonconformity** *n.*

noncontributory *adj.* denoting a pension scheme for employees, the premiums of which are paid entirely by the employer.

nondescript *adj.* lacking outstanding features.

none *pron.* not any; no-one. **—nonetheless** *adv.* despite that, however.

nonentity [non-**enn**-tit-tee] *n., pl.* **-ties.** insignificant person or thing.

nonevent *n.* disappointing or insignificant occurrence.

nonflammable *adj.* not easily set on fire.

nonintervention *n.* refusal to intervene in the affairs of others.

nonpareil [non-par-**rail**] *n.* person or thing that is unsurpassed.

nonpayment *n.* failure to pay money owed.

nonplussed *adj.* perplexed.

nonsense *n.* something that has or makes no sense; absurd language; foolish behaviour. **—nonsensical** *adj.*

THESAURUS

noiseless hushed, mute, quiet, silent, soundless, still

noisy boisterous, chattering, deafening, loud, piercing, riotous, strident, turbulent, uproarious, vociferous

nomad drifter, migrant, rambler, rover, vagabond, wanderer

nomadic itinerant, migrant, pastoral, peripatetic, roaming, roving, travelling, vagrant, wandering

nom de plume alias, pseudonym

nomenclature classification, codification, locution, vocabulary

nominal formal, ostensible, pretended, professed, puppet, self-styled, so-called, supposed, theoretical, titular

nominate appoint, assign, choose, designate, elect, elevate, name, present, propose, recommend, select, submit, suggest, term

nomination appointment, choice, election, proposal, selection, suggestion

nominee aspirant, candidate, contestant, entrant, runner

nonchalance calm, composure, equanimity, indifference, unconcern

nonchalant airy, apathetic, calm, careless, casual, collected, cool, detached, indifferent, offhand, unconcerned

noncommittal careful, cautious, discreet, evasive, guarded, indefinite, neutral, politic, reserved, tactful, vague, wary

non compos mentis crazy, deranged, insane, mentally ill, of unsound mind

nonconformist dissenter, eccentric, heretic, maverick, protester, radical, rebel

nondescript characterless, dull, indeterminate, mousy, ordinary, undistinguished, uninspiring, uninteresting, unremarkable, vague

none nil, nobody, no-one, nothing, not one, zero

DICTIONARY

non sequitur [sek-wit-tur] *n.* statement with little or no relation to what preceded it.

nonstandard *adj.* denoting language that is not regarded as correct by educated native speakers.

nonstarter *n.* person or idea that has little chance of success.

nonstick *adj.* coated with a substance that food will not stick to when cooked.

nonstop *adj., adv.* without a stop.

nontoxic *adj.* not poisonous.

noodle *n.* strip of pasta.

nook *n.* sheltered place.

noon *n.* twelve o'clock midday. **—noonday** *n. Lit.* noon.

noose *n.* loop in the end of a rope, tied with a slipknot.

nor *conj.* and not.

Nordic *adj.* of Scandinavia.

norm *n.* standard that is regarded as normal.

normal *adj.* usual, regular, or typical; free from mental or physical disorder. **—normally** *adv.* **—normality** *n.* **—normalize** *v.*

Norse *n., adj.* (language) of ancient and medieval Norway.

north *n.* direction towards the North Pole, opposite south; area lying in or towards the north. *—adv.* in, to, or towards the north. *—adj.* to or in the north; (of a wind) from the north. **—northerly** *adj.* **—northern** *adj.* **—northerner** *n.* person from the north of a country or area. **—north-**

wards *adv.* **—North Pole** northernmost point on the earth's axis.

nos. numbers.

nose *n.* organ of smell, used also in breathing; front part of a vehicle. *—v.* move forward slowly and carefully; pry or snoop. **—nos(e)y** *adj. Informal* prying or inquisitive. **—nosiness** *n.* **—nose dive** (of an aircraft) sudden drop. **—nosegay** *n.* small bunch of flowers.

nosh *Slang —n.* food. *—v.* eat.

nostalgia *n.* sentimental longing for the past. **—nostalgic** *adj.*

nostril *n.* one of the two openings at the end of the nose.

nostrum *n.* quack medicine; favourite remedy.

not *adv.* expressing negation, refusal, or denial.

notable [note-a-bl] *adj.* worthy of being noted, remarkable. *—n.* person of distinction. **—notably** *adv.* **—notability** [note-a-**bill**-lit-tee] *n.*

notary [note-a-ree] *n., pl.* **-ries.** person authorized to witness the signing of legal documents.

notation [no-tay-shun] *n.* representation of numbers or quantities in a system by a series of symbols; set of such symbols.

notch *n.* V-shaped cut; *Informal* step or level. *—v.* make a notch in.

note *n.* short letter; brief comment or record; banknote; (symbol for) a musical sound; hint or mood. *—v.* notice, pay attention to; record in writing; remark upon. **—noted** *adj.* well-known. **—notebook** *n.* book for writing in. **—noteworthy** *adj.* worth noting, remarkable.

THESAURUS

nonentity cipher, mediocrity, nobody

nonetheless despite that, even so, however, nevertheless, yet

nonsense absurdity, balderdash, blather, bombast, drivel, folly, gibberish, inanity, jest, rot, rubbish, silliness, stuff, stupidity, trash, twaddle

nonstop 1. *adj.* ceaseless, constant, continuous, direct, endless, steady, unbroken, unending, uninterrupted 2. *adv.* constantly, directly, endlessly, steadily

nook alcove, cavity, corner, cranny, crevice, niche, opening, recess, retreat

norm average, criterion, mean, model, pattern, rule, standard, type

normal accustomed, average, common, natural, ordinary, popular, regular, routine, standard, typical, usual

normality naturalness, popularity, regularity

normally commonly, ordinarily, regularly, typically, usually

nosegay bouquet, posy

nostalgia homesickness, longing, yearning

nostalgic homesick, longing, regretful

nostrum cure, drug, elixir, medicine, potion, remedy, specific

notability celebrity, distinction, eminence, esteem, fame, renown

notable 1. *adj.* celebrated, distinguished, eminent, famous, manifest, marked, memorable, noteworthy, noticeable, pre-eminent, pronounced, rare, remarkable, renowned, striking, uncommon, unusual, well-known 2. *n.* celebrity, dignitary, personage

notably distinctly, especially, markedly, outstandingly, particularly, remarkably

notation characters, code, script, signs, symbols, system

notch cleft, cut, incision, mark, nick, score

note 1. *n.* comment, epistle, gloss, letter, memo, message, minute, record, remark, reminder 2. *v.* designate, indicate, mark, mention, notice, observe, record, register, remark, see

noted acclaimed, celebrated, distinguished,

DICTIONARY

nothing *pron.* not anything; matter of no importance; figure 0. —*adv.* not at all. —**nothingness** *n.* nonexistence; insignificance.

notice *n.* observation or attention; sign giving warning or an announcement; advance notification of intention to end a contract of employment. —*v.* observe, become aware of; point out or remark upon. —**noticeable** *adj.* easily seen or detected, appreciable.

notify *v.* -fying, -fied. inform. —**notification** *n.* —**notifiable** *adj.* having to be reported to the authorities.

notion *n.* vague idea; whim. —**notional** *adj.* speculative, imaginary, or unreal.

notorious *adj.* well known for something bad. —**notoriously** *adv.* —**notoriety** *n.*

notwithstanding *prep.* in spite of.

nougat *n.* chewy sweet containing nuts and fruit.

nought *n.* nothing; figure 0.

noun *n.* word that refers to a person, place, or thing.

nourish *v.* feed; encourage or foster (an idea or feeling). —**nourishment** *n.* —**nourishing** *adj.* providing the food necessary for life and growth.

nouvelle cuisine [noo-vell kwee-zeen] *n.* style of preparing and presenting food with light sauces and unusual combinations of flavours.

Nov. November.

nova *n., pl.* -vae, -vas. star that suddenly becomes brighter and then gradually decreases to its original brightness.

novel[1] *n.* long fictitious story in book form. —**novelist** *n.* writer of novels. —**novelette** *n.* short novel.

novel[2] *adj.* fresh, new, or original. —**novelty** *n.* newness; something new or unusual; cheap toy or trinket.

November *n.* eleventh month of the year.

novena [no-vee-na] *n., pl.* -nae. *RC Church* set of prayers or services on nine consecutive days.

novice [nov-viss] *n.* beginner; person who has entered a religious order but has not yet taken vows.

now *adv.* at or for the present time; immediately. —*conj.* seeing that, since. —**just now** very recently. —**now and again, then** occasionally. —**nowadays** *adv.* in these times.

Nowel(l) *n.* same as NOEL.

nowhere *adv.* not anywhere.

noxious *adj.* poisonous or harmful; extremely unpleasant.

nozzle *n.* projecting spout through which fluid is discharged.

NSPCC National Society for the Prevention of Cruelty to Children.

NT National Trust; New Testament.

nuance [new-ahnss] *n.* subtle difference in colour, meaning, or tone.

nub *n.* point or gist (of a story etc.).

nubile [new-bile] *adj.* (of a young woman) sexually attractive; old enough to get married.

nuclear *adj.* of nuclear weapons or energy; of a

THESAURUS

eminent, famous, illustrious, prominent, recognized, well-known

noteworthy exceptional, important, remarkable, significant, unusual

nothing cipher, naught, nonentity, nonexistence, nought, nullity, trifle, void, zero

notice *v.* 1. detect, discern, distinguish, heed, mark, mind, note, observe, perceive, remark, see, spot ~*n.* 2. heed, note, observation, regard 3. advice, announcement, instruction, intelligence, intimation, news, order, warning

noticeable clear, conspicuous, distinct, evident, manifest, obvious, perceptible, plain, striking

notification advice, alert, declaration, information, intelligence, message, notice, publication, statement

notify acquaint, advise, alert, announce, declare, inform, tell, warn

notion 1. belief, concept, idea, impression, inkling, judgment, knowledge, opinion, view 2. caprice, desire, fancy, impulse, whim, wish

notoriety dishonour, disrepute, scandal

notorious disreputable, infamous, scandalous

notoriously disreputably, infamously

notwithstanding although, despite, however, nevertheless, nonetheless, though, yet

nought naught, nil, nothing, zero

nourish attend, feed, nurse, nurture, supply, sustain, tend

nourishing healthful, nutritious, wholesome

nourishment diet, food, nutrition, sustenance, victuals

novel 1. *adj.* different, fresh, new, original, rare, singular, strange, uncommon, unfamiliar, unusual 2. *n.* fiction, romance, story, tale

novelty 1. freshness, newness, oddity, strangeness, surprise 2. bauble, curiosity, gadget, gewgaw, gimcrack, gimmick, memento, souvenir, trifle, trinket

novice amateur, apprentice, beginner, learner, newcomer, probationer, proselyte, pupil, tyro

now at once, immediately, instantly, promptly, straightaway

DICTIONARY

nucleus, esp. the nucleus of an atom. —**nuclear bomb** bomb whose force is due to uncontrolled nuclear fusion or fission. —**nuclear energy** energy released as a result of nuclear fission or fusion. —**nuclear fission** splitting of an atomic nucleus. —**nuclear fusion** combination of two nuclei to form a heavier nucleus with the release of energy. —**nuclear power** power produced by a nuclear reactor. —**nuclear reaction** change in structure and energy content of an atomic nucleus by interaction with another nucleus or particle. —**nuclear reactor** device in which a nuclear reaction is maintained and controlled to produce nuclear energy. —**nuclear winter** theoretical period of low temperatures and little light after a nuclear war.

nucleic acid n. complex compound, such as DNA or RNA, found in all living cells.

nucleonics n. branch of physics dealing with the applications of nuclear energy.

nucleus n., pl. -**clei**. centre, esp. of an atom or cell; central thing around which others are grouped.

nude adj. naked. —n. naked figure in painting, sculpture, or photography. —**nudity** n. —**nudism** n. practice of not wearing clothes. —**nudist** n.

nudge v. push gently, esp. with the elbow. —n. gentle push or touch.

nugatory [new-gat-tree] adj. trifling; not valid.

nugget n. small lump of gold in its natural state; something small but valuable.

nuisance n. something or someone that causes annoyance or bother.

nuke Slang —v. attack with nuclear weapons. —n. nuclear bomb.

null adj. —**null and void** not legally valid. —**nullity** n. —**nullify** v. make ineffective; cancel.

numb adj. without feeling, as through cold, shock, or fear. —v. make numb. —**numbly** adv.

—**numbness** n. —**numbskull** n. same as NUMSKULL.

number n. sum or quantity; word or symbol used to express a sum or quantity, numeral; one of a series, such as a copy of a magazine; Grammar classification of words depending on how many persons or things are referred to; song or piece of music; group of people; numeral or string of numerals used to identify a person or thing. —v. count; give a number to; amount to; include in a group. —**numberless** adj. too many to be counted. —**number crunching** Computers large-scale processing of numerical data. —**number one** Informal oneself. —**numberplate** n. plate on a car showing the registration number.

numeral n. word or symbol used to express a sum or quantity.

numerate adj. able to do basic arithmetic. —**numeracy** n.

numeration n. act or process of numbering or counting.

numerator n. Maths number above the line in a fraction.

numerical adj. measured or expressed in numbers. —**numerically** adv.

numerous adj. existing or happening in large numbers.

numismatist n. coin collector.

numskull n. stupid person.

nun n. female member of a religious order. —**nunnery** n. convent.

nuncio n. RC Church pope's ambassador.

nuptial adj. relating to marriage. —**nuptials** pl. n. wedding.

nurse n. person employed to look after sick people, usu. in hospital; woman employed to look after children. —v. look after (a sick person); breast-feed (a baby); try to cure (an ailment);

THESAURUS

nucleus basis, centre, core, heart, kernel, pivot

nude bare, disrobed, exposed, naked, stripped, unclad, unclothed, undressed

nudge v. bump, dig, elbow, jog, poke, prod, push, shove, touch

nudity bareness, nakedness, undress

nuisance bore, bother, irritation, offence, pest, plague, problem, trouble, vexation

nullify abolish, annul, cancel, invalidate, negate, neutralize, quash, repeal, rescind, revoke, veto, void

numb 1. adj. dead, deadened, frozen, insensible, paralysed, stupefied, torpid 2. v. benumb, deaden, dull, freeze, paralyse, stun, stupefy

number n. 1. count, digit, figure, integer, nu-

meral, sum, total, unit 2. amount, collection, company, crowd, horde, many, multitude, quantity, throng 3. copy, edition ~v. 4. account, add, calculate, compute, count, reckon, tell, total

numberless countless, endless, infinite, untold

numbness deadness, dullness, insensibility, paralysis, torpor

numeral character, cipher, digit, figure, integer, number, symbol

numerous abundant, copious, many, plentiful, profuse, several

nunnery abbey, cloister, convent, house, monastery

DICTIONARY

harbour or foster (a feeling). —**nursery** *n.* room where children sleep or play; place where children are taken care of while their parents are at work; place where plants are grown for sale. —**nurseryman** *n.* person who raises plants for sale. —**nursery school** school for children from 3 to 5 years old. —**nursery slope** gentle ski slope for beginners. —**nursing home** private hospital or home for old people. —**nursing officer** administrative head of the nursing staff of a hospital.

nurture *n.* act or process of promoting the development of a child or young plant. —*v.* promote or encourage the development of.

nut *n.* fruit consisting of a hard shell and a kernel; small piece of metal that screws onto a bolt; *Slang* head; *Slang* eccentric person. —**nutty** *adj.* containing or resembling nuts; *Slang* insane or eccentric. —**nutter** *n. Slang* insane or violent person. —**nutcracker** *n.* device for cracking the shells of nuts. —**nuthatch** *n.* small songbird. —**nutmeg** *n.* spice made from the seed of a tropical tree.

nutria [new-tree-a] *n.* fur of the coypu.

nutrient [new-tree-ent] *n.* substance that provides nourishment.

nutriment [new-tree-ment] *n.* food or nourishment required by all living things to grow and stay healthy.

nutrition [new-trish-shun] *n.* process of taking in and absorbing nutrients; process of being nourished. —**nutritious, nutritive** *adj.* nourishing.

nuzzle *v.* push or rub gently with the nose or snout.

NW northwest(ern).

nylon *n.* synthetic material used for clothing etc. —*pl.* stockings made of nylon.

nymph *n.* mythical spirit of nature, represented as a beautiful young woman.

nymphet *n.* sexually precocious young girl.

nymphomaniac *n.* woman with an abnormally intense sexual desire.

NZ New Zealand.

THESAURUS

nurse *v.* 1. tend, treat 2. feed, nourish, nurture, suckle 3. *Fig.* cherish, encourage, foster, preserve, promote, succour, support

nurture *v.* 1. feed, nourish, nurse, support, sustain, tend 2. bring up, develop, educate, instruct, rear, school, train

nutrition food, nourishment, sustenance

nutritious beneficial, healthful, nourishing, wholesome

O

oaf *n.* stupid or clumsy person. —**oafish** *adj.*

oak *n.* deciduous forest tree; its wood, used for furniture. —**oaken** *adj.* —**oak apple** brownish lump found on oak trees.

oakum *n.* fibre obtained by unravelling old rope.

OAP old-age pensioner.

oar *n.* pole with a broad blade, used for rowing a boat.

oasis *n., pl.* **-ses.** fertile area in a desert.

oast *n.* kiln for drying hops.

oath *n.* solemn promise, esp. to be truthful in court; swearword.

oats *pl. n.* grain of a cereal plant, used for food. —**sow one's wild oats** have many sexual relationships when young. —**oaten** *adj.* —**oatmeal** *adj.* pale brownish-cream.

obbligato [ob-lig-**gah**-toe] *n. Music* essential part or accompaniment.

obdurate *adj.* hardhearted; stubborn. —**obduracy** *n.*

OBE Officer of the Order of the British Empire.

obedient *adj.* obeying or willing to obey. —**obediently** *adv.* —**obedience** *n.*

obeisance [oh-**bay**-sanss] *n.* attitude of respect; bow or curtsy.

obelisk [**ob**-bill-isk] *n.* four-sided stone column tapering to a pyramid at the top.

obese [oh-**beess**] *adj.* very fat. —**obesity** *n.*

obey *v.* carry out the instructions of (someone); comply with (instructions).

obfuscate *v.* darken; make (something) confusing.

obituary *n., pl.* **-aries.** announcement of someone's death, esp. in a newspaper. —**obituarist** *n.*

object[1] *n.* physical thing; focus of thoughts or action; aim or purpose; *Grammar* word that a verb or preposition affects. —**no object** not a hindrance.

object[2] *v.* (foll. by *to*) oppose. —**objection** *n.* —**objectionable** *adj.* unpleasant. —**objector** *n.*

objective *adj.* existing in the real world outside the human mind; not biased. —*n.* aim or purpose. —**objectively** *adv.* —**objectivity** *n.*

objet d'art [ob-zhay **dahr**] *n., pi.* **objets d'art.** small object of artistic value.

oblate *adj.* (of a sphere) flattened at the poles.

oblation *n.* religious offering.

THESAURUS

oasis *Fig.* haven, island, refuge, retreat, sanctuary, sanctum

oath 1. affirmation, avowal, bond, pledge, promise, vow, word 2. curse, expletive, imprecation, profanity

obdurate adamant, callous, dogged, firm, fixed, hard, implacable, inexorable, inflexible, iron, mulish, obstinate, pig-headed, relentless, stubborn, unbending, unshakable

obedience acquiescence, agreement, compliance, deference, docility, duty, observance, respect, submissiveness

obedient acquiescent, amenable, biddable, compliant, docile, duteous, dutiful, regardful, respectful, submissive, well-trained

obelisk column, monolith, monument, needle, pillar, shaft

obese corpulent, fat, fleshy, gross, heavy, outsize, plump, podgy, portly, rotund, stout, tubby

obesity bulk, corpulence, fatness, fleshiness, grossness, overweight, portliness, stoutness

obey 1. comply, conform, discharge, execute, follow, fulfil, heed, keep, mind, observe, perform, respond, serve 2. bow to, submit, yield

object[1] *n.* 1. article, body, fact, item, reality, thing 2. aim, butt, focus, target, victim 3. design, end, goal, idea, intent, motive, objective, point, purpose, reason

object[2] *v.* demur, expostulate, oppose, protest

objection cavil, censure, demur, doubt, exception, opposition, protest, remonstrance, scruple

objectionable deplorable, distasteful, indecorous, insufferable, intolerable, obnoxious, offensive, regrettable, repugnant, undesirable, unpleasant

objective 1. *adj.* detached, dispassionate, fair, impartial, impersonal, judicial, just, unemotional, unprejudiced 2. *n.* aim, ambition, aspiration, design, end, goal, mark, object, purpose, target

objectively dispassionately, even-handedly, impartially

obligation burden, charge, compulsion, duty, liability, must, onus, requirement, responsibility, trust

obligatory binding, compulsory, essential, imperative, mandatory, necessary, required

DICTIONARY

oblige *v.* compel (someone) morally or by law to do (something); do a favour for (someone). **—obliging** *adj.* ready to help other people. **—obligingly** *adv.* **—obligate** *v.* cause (someone) to be obliged to do (something). **—obligation** *n.* duty. **—obligatory** *adj.* required by a rule or law.

oblique [oh-**bleak**] *adj.* slanting; indirect. **—n.** the symbol (/). **—obliquely** *adv.* **—obliqueness** *n.* **—oblique angle** angle that is not a right angle.

obliterate *v.* wipe out, destroy. **—obliteration** *n.*

oblivious *adj.* (foll. by *to* or *of*) unaware (of). **—oblivion** *n.* state of being forgotten; state of being unaware or unconscious.

oblong *adj.* shape with two long sides, two short sides, and four right angles. **—n.** oblong figure.

obloquy [**ob**-lock-wee] *n., pl.* **-quies.** verbal abuse; discredit.

obnoxious *adj.* offensive. **—obnoxiousness** *n.*

oboe *n.* double-reeded woodwind instrument. **—oboist** *n.*

obscene *adj.* portraying sex offensively; disgusting. **—obscenity** *n.*

obscure *adj.* not well known; hard to understand; indistinct. **—v.** make (something) obscure. **—obscurity** *n.*

obsequies [**ob**-sick-weez] *pl. n.* funeral rites.

obsequious [ob-**seek**-wee-uss] *adj.* too eager to please in order to be liked. **—obsequiousness** *n.*

observe *v.* watch (someone or something) carefully; perceive visually; remark; act according to (a law or custom). **—observation** *n.* action or habit of observing; something observed; remark. **—observer** *n.* **—observable** *adj.* **—observably** *adv.* **—observance** *n.* observing of a custom. **—observant** *adj.* quick to notice things. **—observatory** *n.* building equipped for astronomical or meteorological observations.

THESAURUS

oblige 1. bind, compel, force, impel, make, require 2. accommodate, benefit, favour, gratify, indulge, please, serve

obliging agreeable, amiable, civil, considerate, cooperative, courteous, friendly, good-natured, helpful, kind, polite, willing

oblique angled, aslant, inclined, slanted, slanting, sloped, sloping

obliterate cancel, delete, destroy, efface, eradicate, erase, expunge, extirpate, wipe out

oblivion forgetfulness, insensibility, neglect, unawareness, unconsciousness, (waters of) Lethe

oblivious blind, careless, deaf, forgetful, heedless, ignorant, neglectful, regardless, unaware

obnoxious abominable, detestable, disgusting, foul, hateful, horrid, insufferable, nasty, odious, offensive, repellent, repugnant, repulsive, revolting, unpleasant

obscene bawdy, blue, coarse, dirty, disgusting, filthy, foul, gross, immoral, improper, impure, indecent, lewd, offensive, pornographic, prurient, ribald, salacious, shameless, suggestive

obscenity bawdiness, coarseness, dirtiness, filthiness, grossness, immodesty, impurity, lewdness, pornography, salacity, suggestiveness, vileness

obscure *adj.* 1. ambiguous, arcane, confusing, cryptic, deep, doubtful, esoteric, hazy, hidden, involved, mysterious, occult, opaque, recondite, unclear, vague 2. blurred, cloudy, dim, dusky, faint, gloomy, indistinct, murky, shadowy, shady, sombre, tenebrous, unlit, veiled ~*v.* 3. conceal, cover, disguise, hide, screen, veil 4. bedim, befog, block, blur, cloak, cloud,

darken, dim, dull, eclipse, mask, overshadow, shade, shroud

obscurity 1. ambiguity, complexity, intricacy, vagueness 2. darkness, dimness, dusk, gloom, haze, haziness, murkiness, shadows 3. insignificance, lowliness, unimportance

observable apparent, clear, discernible, evident, noticeable, obvious, open, patent, perceptible, recognizable, visible

observance ceremonial, custom, fashion, form, practice, rite, ritual, tradition

observant alert, attentive, heedful, mindful, perceptive, quick, vigilant, watchful

observation attention, consideration, examination, experience, information, inspection, knowledge, notice, review, scrutiny, study, surveillance

observe 1. detect, discern, discover, espy, note, notice, perceive, see, spot, witness 2. monitor, regard, scrutinize, study, survey, view, watch 3. comment, declare, mention, note, opine, remark, say, state 4. comply, follow, fulfil, heed, honour, keep, mind, obey, respect 5. keep, remember, solemnize

observer commentator, eyewitness, onlooker, spectator, viewer, witness

obsessive compulsive, consuming, fixed, unforgettable

obsolescent ageing, declining, waning

obsolete ancient, antiquated, archaic, bygone, dated, *démodé*, extinct, musty, old, outmoded, outworn, passé

DICTIONARY

obsess v. preoccupy (someone) compulsively. —**obsessive** adj. —**obsession** n.

obsidian n. dark glassy volcanic rock.

obsolete adj. no longer in use. —**obsolescent** adj. becoming obsolete. —**obsolescence** n.

obstacle n. something that makes progress difficult.

obstetrics n. branch of medicine concerned with pregnancy and childbirth. —**obstetric** adj. —**obstetrician** n.

obstinate adj. stubborn; (of a stain) difficult to remove. —**obstinately** adv. —**obstinacy** n.

obstreperous adj. unruly, noisy.

obstruct v. block with an obstacle. —**obstruction** n. —**obstructionist** n. person who deliberately obstructs formal proceedings. —**obstructive** adj.

obtain v. acquire intentionally; be customary. —**obtainable** adj.

obtrude v. push oneself or one's ideas on others. —**obtrusion** n. —**obtrusive** adj. —**obtrusively** adv.

obtuse adj. mentally slow; Maths (of an angle) between 90° and 180°; not pointed. —**obtusely** adv. —**obtuseness** n.

obverse n. opposite way of looking at an idea; main side of a coin or medal.

obviate v. make unnecessary.

obvious adj. easy to see or understand, evident. —**obviously** adv.

ocarina n. small oval wind instrument made of clay.

occasion n. time at which a particular thing happens; special event; reason, e.g. no occasion for complaint. —v. cause. —**occasional** adj. happening sometimes; for a special event. —**occasionally** adv.

Occident n. Lit. the West. —**Occidental** adj.

occiput [ox-sip-put] n. back of the head.

occlude v. obstruct; close off. —**occlusion** n. —**occlusive** adj. —**occluded front** Meteorol. front formed when a cold front overtakes a warm front and warm air rises.

occult n. —**the occult** knowledge or study of the supernatural. —adj. relating to the supernatural.

occupant n. person occupying a specified place. —**occupancy** n. (length of a) person's stay in a specified place.

occupation n. profession; activity that occupies one's time; being occupied. —**occupational** adj. —**occupational therapy** activities, esp. crafts, designed to aid recovery from illness.

occupy v. -**pying**, -**pied**. live or work in (a building); take up the attention of (someone); take up (space or time); take possession of (a place) by force. —**occupier** n.

THESAURUS

obstacle bar, barrier, check, hindrance, hitch, hurdle, interruption, obstruction, snag

obstinacy firmness, inflexibility, intransigence, persistence, pertinacity, resoluteness, stubbornness, tenacity, wilfulness

obstinate determined, dogged, firm, immovable, inflexible, intractable, opinionated, pertinacious, perverse, recalcitrant, refractory, self-willed, steadfast, stubborn, tenacious

obstreperous boisterous, disorderly, loud, noisy, rackety, restive, riotous, rough, rowdy, tumultuous, turbulent, uncontrolled, undisciplined, unruly, wild

obstruct arrest, bar, block, check, choke, clog, cumber, curb, cut off, frustrate, hamper, hamstring, hide, hinder, impede, inhibit, interrupt, mask, obscure, prevent, restrict, stop

obstruction bar, barrier, blockage, check, hindrance, impediment, snag, stop, stoppage

obstructive awkward, preventative, restrictive, unhelpful

obtain achieve, acquire, earn, gain, get, procure, secure

obtrusive forward, meddling, nosy, officious, prying

obvious apparent, clear, conspicuous, distinct,

evident, manifest, open, overt, palpable, patent, perceptible, plain, pronounced, recognizable, self-evident, straightforward, transparent, unmistakable, unsubtle, visible

obviously certainly, clearly, distinctly, palpably, patently, plainly

occasion 1. chance, incident, moment, occurrence, opening, time 2. affair, event, experience, occurrence 3. call, cause, excuse, ground(s), motive, prompting, provocation, reason

occasional casual, desultory, incidental, infrequent, irregular, odd, rare, sporadic

occasionally irregularly, periodically, sometimes

occupant holder, indweller, inhabitant, inmate, lessee, occupier, resident, tenant, user

occupation 1. activity, business, calling, craft, employment, job, post, profession, pursuit, trade, vocation, work 2. control, holding, occupancy, possession, residence, tenancy, tenure, use 3. conquest, invasion

occupied 1. busy, employed, engaged, working 2. engaged, full, taken, unavailable

occupy 1. Often passive absorb, amuse, busy, divert, employ, engage, engross, entertain, im-

DICTIONARY

occur v. **-curring, -curred.** take place; exist; (foll. by *to*) come to the mind (of). **—occurrence** n. something that occurs; occurring.

ocean n. vast area of sea between continents. **—oceanic** adj. **—oceanography** n. scientific study of the oceans. **—ocean-going** adj. able to sail on the open sea.

ocelot [oss-ill-lot] n. American wild cat with a spotted coat.

oche [ok-kee] n. Darts mark on the floor behind which a player must stand.

ochre [oak-er] adj. brownish-yellow.

o'clock adv. used after a number to specify an hour.

Oct. October.

octagon n. geometric figure with eight sides. **—octagonal** adj.

octahedron [ok-ta-heed-ron] n., pl. **-drons, -dra.** three-dimensional geometric figure with eight faces.

octane n. hydrocarbon found in petrol. **—octane rating** measure of petrol quality.

octave n. Music (interval between the first and) eighth note of a scale.

octet n. group of eight performers; music for such a group.

October n. tenth month of the year.

octogenarian n. person aged between eighty and eighty-nine.

octopus n., pl. **-puses.** sea creature with a soft body and eight tentacles.

ocular adj. relating to the eyes or sight.

OD n. Med. overdose. **—v. OD'ing, OD'd.** Informal take an overdose.

odd adj. unusual; occasional; not divisible by two; not part of a set. **—odds** pl. n. (ratio showing) the probability of something happening. **—odds and ends** small miscellaneous items. **—oddness** n. quality of being odd. **—oddity** n. odd person or thing. **—oddments** pl. n. things left over.

ode n. lyric poem, usu. addressed to a particular subject.

odium [oh-dee-um] n. widespread dislike. **—odious** adj. offensive.

odour n. particular smell. **—odorous** adj. **—odourless** adj. **—odoriferous** adj. giving off a pleasant smell. **—odorize** v. fill (something) with scent.

odyssey [odd-iss-ee] n. long eventful journey.

OECD Organization for Economic Cooperation and Development.

oedema [id-deem-a] n., pl. **-mata.** abnormal swelling.

oesophagus [ee-soff-a-guss] n., pl. **-gi.** passage between the mouth and stomach.

oestrogen [ee-stra-jen] n. female hormone that controls the reproductive cycle.

of prep. belonging to; consisting of; connected with; characteristic of.

off prep. away from. **—adv.** away. **—adj.** not operating; cancelled; (of food) gone bad. **—n.** Cricket side of the field on the bowler's left. **—off colour** slightly ill.

offal n. edible organs of an animal, such as liver or kidneys.

offcut n. piece remaining after the required parts have been cut out.

offend v. hurt the feelings of; insult; commit a crime. **—offender** n. **—offence** n. (cause of) hurt feelings or annoyance; illegal act. **—offensive** adj. insulting; aggressive; disagreeable. **—n.** position or action of attack.

THESAURUS

merse, interest, involve, monopolize, preoccupy 2. capture, hold, invade, keep, seize

occur arise, befall, betide, chance, eventuate, happen, materialize, result

occurrence affair, circumstance, episode, event, happening, incident, proceeding

odd 1. abnormal, bizarre, curious, deviant, different, eccentric, extraordinary, freak, funny, irregular, peculiar, quaint, queer, rare, remarkable, singular, strange, uncommon, unusual, weird, whimsical 2. lone, remaining, single, solitary, spare, unpaired

oddity abnormality, anomaly, freak, irregularity, peculiarity, phenomenon, quirk, rarity

odds balance, chances, likelihood, probability

odious abominable, detestable, disgusting, ex-ecrable, foul, hateful, horrible, loathsome, offensive, repellent, repugnant, repulsive, revolting, unpleasant

odour aroma, bouquet, essence, fragrance, perfume, scent, smell, stink

off adj. 1. absent, cancelled, finished, gone, inoperative, postponed, unavailable 2. bad, decomposed, high, mouldy, rancid, rotten, sour, turned

off colour ill, peaky, queasy, sick, unwell

offence 1. crime, fault, lapse, misdeed, misdemeanour, peccadillo, sin, transgression, trespass, wrong 2. anger, annoyance, displeasure, pique, resentment, umbrage, wrath

offend affront, annoy, displease, fret, gall, insult, irritate, outrage, pain, pique, provoke, rile, slight, snub, upset, vex, wound

DICTIONARY

offer v. present (something) for acceptance or rejection; provide; propose (a sum of money) as payment. —n. instance of offering something. —**offering** n. thing offered. —**offertory** n. *Christianity* offering of the bread and wine for Communion.

offhand adj. (also **offhanded**) casual, curt. —adv. without preparation.

office n. room or building where people work at desks; department of a commercial organization; formal position of responsibility; duty, function; (esp. pl.) something done for another. —**officer** n. person in authority in the armed services; a member of the police force; person with special responsibility in an organization.

official adj. approved or arranged by someone in authority; of a position of authority. —n. person who holds a position of authority. —**officialdom** n. *Offens.* officials collectively. —**Official Receiver** person who deals with the affairs of a bankrupt company.

officiate v. conduct a ceremony in an official role.

officious adj. giving unnecessary instructions; interfering.

offing n. area of the sea visible from the shore. —**in the offing** likely to happen soon.

off-licence n. shop licensed to sell alcohol.

offset v. cancel out, compensate for.

offside adj., adv. *Sport* (positioned) illegally ahead of the ball.

offspring n., pl. **offspring.** one's child.

often adv. frequently, much of the time. —**oft** adv. *Poetic* often.

ogle v. stare at (someone) lustfully.

ogre n. giant that eats human flesh.

oh interj. exclamation of surprise, pain, etc.

ohm n. unit of electrical resistance.

OHMS On Her *or* His Majesty's Service.

oil n. viscous liquid, insoluble in water and usu. flammable; same as PETROLEUM; petroleum derivative, used as a fuel or lubricant. —pl. oil-based paints used in art. —v. lubricate (a machine) with oil. —**oily** adj. —**oilfield** n. area containing oil reserves. —**oil rig** platform constructed for boring oil wells. —**oilskins** pl. n. waterproof clothing.

ointment n. greasy substance used for healing skin or as a cosmetic.

O.K., okay *Informal* —interj. all right. —n. approval. —v. approve (something).

okapi [ok-**kah**-pee] n. African animal related to the giraffe but with a shorter neck.

okra n. tropical plant with edible green pods.

old adj. having lived or existed for a long time; of a specified age, e.g. *two years old;* former. —**olden** adj. old, e.g. *in the olden days.* —**oldie** n. *Informal* old but popular song or film. —**old-fashioned** adj. no longer commonly used or valued. —**old guard** group of people in an organization who have traditional values. —**old hat** boring because so familiar. —**old maid** elderly unmarried woman. —**old master** European painter or painting from the period 1500–1800. —**Old Nick** *Informal* the Devil. —**old school tie** system of mutual help between former pupils of a public school. —**Old Testament** part of the Bible recording Hebrew history. —**Old World** world as it was known before the discovery of the Americas.

THESAURUS

offender criminal, culprit, lawbreaker, malefactor, miscreant, transgressor

offensive adj. 1. abusive, annoying, detestable, displeasing, insolent, insulting, irritating, rude, uncivil, unmannerly 2. disagreeable, disgusting, grisly, loathsome, nasty, noisome, obnoxious, odious, repellent, revolting, sickening, unpleasant, unsavoury, vile 3. aggressive, attacking, invading ~n. 4. attack, drive, onslaught

offer v. 1. bid, extend, give, proffer, tender 2. afford, furnish, present, provide, show 3. advance, extend, move, propose, submit, suggest ~n. 4. attempt, bid, essay, overture, proposal, suggestion, tender

offering contribution, gift, present, sacrifice

offhand abrupt, aloof, brusque, careless, casual, cavalier, curt, glib, offhanded, perfunctory, uninterested

office appointment, business, capacity, charge, commission, duty, employment, obligation, occupation, place, post, responsibility, role, service, situation, station, trust, work

officer agent, bureaucrat, executive, representative

official 1. adj. authentic, authoritative, bona fide, certified, ex officio, formal, legitimate, licensed, proper 2. n. agent, bureaucrat, executive, representative

officiate chair, conduct, manage, preside, serve

officious bustling, forward, impertinent, interfering, intrusive, meddlesome, mischievous, obtrusive, opinionated, overbusy, overzealous

offset counteract, counterbalance, counterpoise, countervail, neutralize

often frequently, generally, much, repeatedly

oil v. grease, lubricate

old 1. aged, ancient, decrepit, elderly, grey, ma~

DICTIONARY

oleaginous [ol-lee-aj-in-uss] *adj.* oily, producing oil.

oleander [ol-lee-ann-der] *n.* Mediterranean flowering evergreen shrub.

olfactory *adj.* relating to the sense of smell.

oligarchy [ol-lee-gark-ee] *n., pl.* **-chies.** government by a small group of people; state governed this way. —**oligarch** *n.* member of an oligarchy. —**oligarchic(al)** *adj.*

olive *n.* small green or black fruit used as food or pressed for its oil; tree on which this fruit grows. —*adj.* greyish-green. —**olive branch** conciliatory gesture.

Olympic Games *pl. n.* four-yearly international sports competition.

ombudsman *n.* official who investigates complaints against government organizations.

omelette *n.* dish of eggs beaten and fried.

omen *n.* happening or object thought to foretell success or misfortune. —**ominous** *adj.* worrying, seeming to foretell of misfortune.

omit *v.* **omitting, omitted.** leave out; neglect (to do something). —**omission** *n.*

omni- *combining form* all, everywhere, e.g. *omnidirectional.*

omnibus *n. Old-fashioned* bus; several books or TV or radio programmes made into one.

omnipotent [om-nip-a-tent] *adj.* having unlimited power. —**omnipotence** *n.*

omnipresent *adj.* present everywhere. —**omnipresence** *n.*

omniscient [om-niss-ee-ent] *adj.* knowing everything. —**omniscience** *n.*

omnivorous [om-niv-vor-uss] *adj.* eating food obtained from both animals and plants. —**omnivore** *n.* omnivorous animal.

on *prep.* above and touching; attached to; concerning; during, e.g. *on Monday;* through the medium of, e.g. *on television.* —*adv.* in operation; forwards; continuing. —*adj.* operating; taking place. —*n. Cricket* side of the field on the bowler's right.

on-line *adj. Computers* (of equipment) directly connected to and controlled by the computer.

once *adv.* on one occasion; formerly. —*conj.* as soon as. —**at once** immediately; simultaneously. —**once-over** *n. Informal* quick examination.

oncogene [on-koh-jean] *n.* gene that can cause cancer when abnormally activated.

oncoming *adj.* approaching from the front.

one *adj.* single, lone. —*n.* number or figure 1; single unit. —*pron.* any person. —**oneness** *n.* unity. —**oneself** *pron.* reflexive form of ONE. —**one-armed bandit** fruit machine operated by a lever on one side. —**one-liner** *n.* witty remark. —**one-night stand** sexual encounter lasting one night. —**one-sided** *adj.* considering only one point of view. —**one-way** *adj.* allowing movement in one direction only.

onerous [own-er-uss] *adj.* (of a task) difficult to carry out.

ongoing *adj.* in progress, continuing.

onion *n.* strongly flavoured edible bulb.

onlooker *n.* person who watches something happening without taking part.

only *adj.* alone of its kind. —*adv.* exclusively; merely; no more than. —*conj.* but.

onomatopoeia [on-a-mat-a-pee-a] *n.* formation of a word which imitates the sound it represents, such as *hiss.* —**onomatopoeic** *adj.*

onset *n.* beginning.

onslaught *n.* violent attack.

onto *prep.* to a position on; aware of, e.g. *she's onto us.*

ontology *n. Philosophy* study of existence. —**ontological** *adj.*

onus [own-uss] *n., pl.* **onuses.** responsibility or burden.

THESAURUS

ture, senile, venerable 2. antiquated, antique, cast-off, crumbling, dated, decayed, done, obsolete, old-fashioned, outdated, passé, stale, timeworn, unoriginal, worn-out

old-fashioned ancient, antiquated, archaic, dated, dead, démodé, obsolescent, past

omen augury, foreboding, indication, portent, presage, sign

ominous dark, fateful, menacing, portentous, sinister, threatening

omission default, failure, gap, lack, leaving out, neglect, oversight

omit disregard, drop, eliminate, exclude, fail, forget, miss (out), neglect, overlook, skip

omnipotent all-powerful, supreme

once 1. long ago, previously 2. **at once** directly, forthwith, immediately, instantly, now, right away

onerous burdensome, crushing, demanding, difficult, exacting, grave, hard, heavy, laborious, oppressive, taxing, weighty

one-sided biased, coloured, lopsided, partial, partisan, prejudiced, unfair, unjust

onlooker bystander, eyewitness, observer, spectator, witness

only 1. *adv.* exclusively, just, merely, purely 2. *adj.* exclusive, individual, lone, single, sole, solitary, unique

onslaught assault, attack, offensive

DICTIONARY

onward *adj.* directed or moving forward. —*adv.* (also **onwards**) ahead, forward.

onyx *n.* type of quartz with coloured layers.

oodles *pl. n. Informal* great quantities.

ooze *v.* flow slowly. —*n.* sluggish flow; soft mud at the bottom of a lake or river. —**oozy** *adj.*

opacity [oh-**pass**-it-tee] *n.* state of being opaque.

opal *n.* iridescent precious stone. —**opalescent** *adj.* iridescent like an opal.

opaque *adj.* not able to be seen through, not transparent.

op. cit. [**op** sit] in the work cited.

OPEC Organization of Petroleum Exporting Countries.

open *adj.* not closed; uncovered; unfolded; free from obstruction, accessible; unrestricted; not finalized; frank. —*v.* (cause to) become open; begin. —*n. Sport* competition open to everyone. —**in the open** outdoors. —**openly** *adv.* without concealment. —**opening** *n.* hole; opportunity. —*adj.* first. —**open-and-shut case** problem that is easily solved. —**opencast mining** mining at the surface and not underground. —**open day** day on which a school or college is open to the public. —**open-handed** *adj.* generous. —**open-hearted** *adj.* generous; frank. —**open-heart surgery** surgery on the heart during which the blood circulation is maintained by machine. —**open house** hospitality to visitors at any time. —**open letter** letter to an individual that the writer makes public in a newspaper or maga-

zine. —**open-minded** *adj.* receptive to new ideas. —**open-plan** *adj.* (of a house or office) having few interior walls. —**open prison** prison with minimal security. —**open verdict** coroner's verdict not stating the cause of death. —**openwork** *n.* patterns made by leaving spaces in a design.

opera[1] *n.* drama in which the text is sung to an orchestral accompaniment. —**operatic** *adj.* —**operetta** *n.* light-hearted comic opera.

opera[2] *n.* a plural of OPUS.

operate *v.* (cause to) function; direct; perform an operation. —**operator** *n.* —**operation** *n.* method or procedure of working; medical procedure in which the body is worked on to repair a damaged part. —**operational** *adj.* relating to an operation; in working order. —**operative** [**op**-rat-tiv] *adj.* working —*n.* worker with a special skill.

ophidian *adj., n.* (reptile) of the snake family.

ophthalmic *adj.* relating to the eyes. —**ophthalmology** *n.* study of the eye and its diseases. —**ophthalmologist** *n.* —**ophthalmic optician** see OPTICIAN.

opiate [oh-pee-ate] *n.* narcotic drug containing opium.

opinion *n.* personal belief or judgment. —**opinion poll** see POLL. —**opinionated** *adj.* having strong opinions. —**opine** *v. Old-fashioned* express an opinion.

opium [oh-pee-um] *n.* addictive narcotic drug made from poppy seeds.

opossum *n.* small marsupial of America or Australia.

THESAURUS

onus burden, liability, load, obligation, responsibility, task

ooze bleed, discharge, drain, drop, emit, escape, filter, leach, leak, seep, strain, sweat, weep

opaque clouded, cloudy, dim, dull, filmy, hazy, muddied, murky

open *adj.* 1. agape, ajar, extended, gaping, revealed, unclosed, uncovered, unfastened, unfurled, unlocked, unsealed, yawning 2. airy, bare, clear, exposed, extensive, free, navigable, passable, rolling, spacious, sweeping, unfenced, wide 3. available, free, general, public, unengaged, unoccupied, unqualified, unrestricted, vacant 4. arguable, debatable, moot, undecided, unresolved, unsettled 5. artless, candid, fair, frank, guileless, honest, innocent, natural, sincere, transparent ~*v.* 6. begin, commence, inaugurate, initiate, kick off (*Inf.*), launch, start 7. clear, crack, unbar, unblock, unclose, uncork, uncover, undo, unfasten, unlock, unseal, untie, unwrap

opening *n.* 1. aperture, breach, break, cleft, crack, gap, hole, rent, rupture, slot, space,

split, vent 2. chance, occasion, opportunity, place, vacancy ~*adj.* 3. beginning, early, first, inaugural, initial, introductory, primary

openly blatantly, brazenly, publicly, shamelessly, unashamedly, wantonly

open-minded broad, catholic, dispassionate, enlightened, free, impartial, liberal, reasonable, receptive, tolerant, unbiased, unprejudiced

operate act, function, go, perform, run, work

operation action, affair, course, exercise, motion, movement, procedure, process, use, working

operational functional, going, ready, usable, viable, working

operator conductor, driver, handler, mechanic, practitioner, technician, worker

opinion assessment, belief, conjecture, feeling, idea, judgment, mind, notion, persuasion, sentiment, theory, view

opinionated bigoted, cocksure, dictatorial, doctrinaire, dogmatic, inflexible, obstinate, prejudiced, stubborn

DICTIONARY

opponent *n.* person one is working against in a contest, battle, or argument.

opportunity *n., pl.* **-ties.** favourable time or condition; good chance. **—opportune** *adj.* happening at a suitable time. **—opportunist** *n.* person who does whatever is advantageous without regard for principles. **—opportunism** *n.*

oppose *v.* work against. **—be opposed to** disagree with or disapprove of. **—opposition** *n.* obstruction or hostility; largest political party not in power; group opposing another.

opposite *adj.* situated on the other side; facing; diametrically different. *—n.* person or thing that is opposite. *—prep., adv.* facing; on the other side (from).

oppress *v.* subjugate by cruelty or force; depress. **—oppression** *n.* **—oppressor** *n.* **—oppressive** *adj.* tyrannical; (of weather) hot and humid. **—oppressively** *adv.*

opprobrium [op-**probe**-ree-um] *n.* state of being criticized severely for wrong one has done. **—opprobrious** *adj.*

oppugn [op-**pewn**] *v.* dispute; question.

opt *v.* (foll. by *for*) show a preference (for), choose.

optic *adj.* relating to the eyes or sight. **—optics** *n.* science of sight and light. **—optical** *adj.* **—optical character reader** device that electronically reads and stores text. **—optical fibre** fine glass-fibre tube used to transmit information.

optician *n.* person who makes or sells glasses. **—dispensing optician** person who supplies and fits glasses. **—ophthalmic optician** person qualified to prescribe glasses.

optimism *n.* tendency to always take the most hopeful view. **—optimist** *n.* **—optimistic** *adj.* **—optimistically** *adv.*

optimum *n., pl.* **-ma, -mums.** best possible conditions. **—optimal** *adj.* **—optimize** *v.* make the most of.

option *n.* choice; thing chosen; right to buy or sell something at a specified price within a given time. **—optional** *adj.* possible but not compulsory.

optometrist [op-**tom**-met-trist] *n.* person qualified to prescribe glasses. **—optometry** *n.*

opulent [op-**pew**-lent] *adj.* having or indicating wealth. **—opulence** *n.*

opus [**oh**-puss] *n., pl.* **opuses** *or* **opera.** artistic creation, esp. a musical work.

or *conj.* used to join alternatives, e.g. *tea or coffee.*

oracle *n.* shrine of an ancient god; prophecy, often obscure, revealed at a shrine; person believed to make infallible predictions. **—oracular** *adj.*

oral *adj.* spoken; (of a drug) to be taken by mouth. *—n.* spoken examination. **—orally** *adv.*

orange *adj.* reddish-yellow. *—n.* reddish-yellow

THESAURUS

opponent adversary, antagonist, challenger, competitor, contestant, disputant, enemy, foe, rival

opportune appropriate, apt, auspicious, convenient, favourable, felicitous, fitting, happy, lucky, proper, propitious, seasonable, suitable, timely, well-timed

opportunity chance, hour, moment, occasion, opening, scope, time

oppose bar, check, combat, counter, defy, face, fight, hinder, obstruct, prevent, resist, take on, withstand

opposite *adj.* 1. corresponding, facing, fronting 2. adverse, conflicting, contradictory, contrary, contrasted, diverse, hostile, inimical, irreconcilable, opposed, reverse, unlike ~*n.* 3. antithesis, contradiction, contrary, converse, inverse, reverse

opposition 1. antagonism, competition, disapproval, hostility, prevention, resistance 2. antagonist, foe, other side, rival

oppress 1. afflict, burden, dispirit, harass, sadden, torment, vex 2. abuse, crush, harry, maltreat, overpower, persecute, subdue, subjugate, suppress, wrong

oppression abuse, brutality, cruelty, harshness, injury, injustice, misery, persecution, severity, tyranny

oppressive 1. brutal, cruel, despotic, grinding, harsh, heavy, onerous, repressive, severe, tyrannical, unjust 2. airless, close, heavy, stifling, stuffy, sultry, torrid

oppressor autocrat, despot, persecutor, scourge, tormentor, tyrant

opt (for) choose, elect, prefer

optimistic assured, bright, buoyant, cheerful, confident, expectant, hopeful, positive

option alternative, choice, election, preference, selection

optional extra, open, possible, voluntary

opulence affluence, fortune, luxury, plenty, prosperity, riches, richness

opulent affluent, luxurious, moneyed, prosperous, rich, sumptuous, wealthy

oracle 1. prophet, seer, sibyl, soothsayer 2. divination, prediction, prognostication, prophecy, revelation, vision

oral spoken, verbal, viva voce, vocal

DICTIONARY

citrus fruit. —**orangeade** n. orange-flavoured, usu. fizzy drink. —**orangery** n. greenhouse for growing orange trees.

orang-utang, orang-outan n. large reddish-brown ape with long arms.

orator [or-rat-tor] n. skilful public speaker. —**oration** n. formal speech. —**oratorical** adj. —**oratory** [or-rat-tree] n. art of making speeches; small private chapel.

oratorio [or-rat-**tor**-ee-oh] n., pl. **-rios**. musical composition for choir and orchestra, usu. with a religious theme.

orb n. ceremonial decorated sphere with a cross on top, carried by a monarch.

orbit n. curved path of a planet, satellite, or spacecraft around another heavenly body; sphere of influence. —v. **orbiting, orbited.** move in an orbit around; put (a satellite or spacecraft) into orbit.

orchard n. area where fruit trees are grown.

orchestra n. large group of musicians, esp. playing a variety of instruments. —**orchestral** adj. —**orchestrate** v. arrange (music) for orchestra; organize (something) to particular effect. —**orchestration** n. —**orchestra pit** area of a theatre in front of the stage, for the orchestra.

orchid n. plant with flowers that have unusual lip-shaped petals.

ordain v. make (someone) a member of the clergy; order or establish with authority.

ordeal n. painful or difficult experience.

order n. instruction to be carried out; request for goods to be supplied; methodical arrangement or sequence; established social system; condition of a law-abiding society; social class; group of similar plants or animals; kind, sort; religious society, usu. of monks or nuns. —v. give an instruction to; request (something) to be supplied; arrange methodically. —**in order** so that it is possible. —**orderly** adj. well organized; well behaved. —n., pl. **-lies.** male hospital attendant. —**orderliness** n.

ordinal number n. number showing a position in a series, e.g. first, second.

ordinance n. official rule or order.

ordinary adj. usual or normal. —**ordinarily** adv.

ordination n. ordaining.

ordnance n. weapons and military supplies. —**ordnance survey** official map-making survey of Britain.

ordure n. excrement.

ore n. (rock containing) a mineral which yields metal.

oregano [or-rig-**gah**-no] n. aromatic herb used in cooking.

organ n. part of an animal or plant that has a particular function, such as the heart or lungs;

THESAURUS

oration address, discourse, harangue, lecture, speech

orator declaimer, lecturer, rhetorician, speaker

oratorical declamatory, eloquent, high-flown, rhetorical, sonorous

oratory declamation, eloquence, rhetoric

orbit n. 1. circle, course, cycle, path, revolution, rotation, track, trajectory 2. Fig. ambit, compass, course, domain, influence, range, reach, scope, sphere, sweep ~v. 3. circle, encircle, revolve around

orchestrate 1. arrange, score 2. arrange, concert, coordinate, present

ordain 1. anoint, appoint, call, consecrate, destine, elect, frock, invest, nominate 2. decree, dictate, enact, enjoin, fix, lay down, order, prescribe, rule, set, will

ordeal affliction, agony, anguish, nightmare, suffering, test, torture, trial

order n. 1. arrangement, method, neatness, pattern, plan, regularity, symmetry, system, tidiness 2. array, disposal, disposition, grouping, layout, line, placement, progression, sequence, series, structure, succession 3. caste, class, degree, grade, hierarchy, position, rank, status 4. breed, cast, class, family, genre, genus, ilk, kind, sort, species, tribe, type 5. behest, command, decree, dictate, direction, directive, injunction, instruction, law, precept, regulation, rule, stipulation 6. application, booking, commission, request, reservation 7. brotherhood, community, company, fraternity, guild, league, lodge, sect, sisterhood, society, union ~v. 8. adjure, bid, charge, command, decree, direct, enact, enjoin, instruct, ordain, prescribe, require 9. book, call for, contract for, engage, prescribe, request, reserve 10. adjust, align, arrange, catalogue, class, classify, conduct, control, dispose, group, manage, marshal, neaten, organize, regulate, systematize, tabulate, tidy

orderly adj. 1. businesslike, in order, methodical, neat, regular, shipshape, systematic, tidy, trim 2. controlled, decorous, disciplined, lawabiding, quiet, restrained, well-behaved

ordinarily commonly, customarily, generally, habitually, normally, usually

ordinary accustomed, common, customary, established, everyday, normal, prevailing, regular, routine, settled, standard, stock, typical, usual, wonted

DICTIONARY

means of conveying information, esp. a newspaper; musical keyboard instrument in which notes are produced by forcing air through pipes. —**organic** *adj.* of or produced from animals or plants; *Chem.* relating to compounds of carbon; grown without artificial fertilizers or pesticides; organized systematically. —**organically** *adv.* —**organism** *n.* any living animal or plant. —**organist** *n.* organ player.

organdie *n.* fine cotton fabric.

organize *v.* make arrangements for; arrange systematically; unite (people) for a shared purpose. —**organization** *n.* group of people working together; act of organizing. —**organizer** *n.*

orgasm *n.* most intense point of sexual pleasure. —**orgasmic** *adj.*

orgy *n., pl.* -**gies.** party involving promiscuous sexual activity; unrestrained indulgence, e.g. *an orgy of destruction.*

oriel *n.* upper window built out from a wall.

Orient *n.* —**the Orient** *Lit.* East Asia. —**Oriental** *adj.* —**Orientalist** *n.* specialist in the languages and history of the Far East. —**orient(ate)** *v.* position (oneself) according to one's surroundings; position (a map) in relation to the points of the compass. —**orientation** *n.* —**orienteering** *n.* sport in which competitors hike over a course using a compass and map.

orifice [or-rif-fiss] *n.* opening or hole.

origami [or-rig-**gah**-mee] *n.* Japanese decorative art of paper folding.

origin *n.* point from which something develops.

—**original** *adj.* earliest; new, not copied or based on something else; able to think up new ideas. —*n.* first version, from which others are copied. —**original sin** human imperfection and mortality as a result of Adam's disobedience. —**originally** *adv.* —**originality** *n.* —**originate** *v.* come or bring into existence. —**origination** *n.* —**originator** *n.*

oriole *n.* tropical or American songbird.

ormolu *n.* gold-coloured alloy used for decoration.

ornament *n.* decorative object. —*v.* decorate. —**ornamental** *adj.* —**ornamentation** *n.*

ornate *adj.* highly decorated, elaborate.

ornithology *n.* study of birds. —**ornithological** *adj.* —**ornithologist** *n.*

orotund *adj.* (of a voice) resonant; (of language) pompous.

orphan *n.* child whose parents are dead. —**orphanage** *n.* children's home for orphans. —**orphaned** *adj.* having no living parents.

orrery *n., pl.* -**ries.** mechanical model of the solar system.

orris *n.* kind of iris; (also **orrisroot**) fragrant root used for perfume.

orthodontics *n.* branch of dentistry concerned with correcting irregular teeth. —**orthodontist** *n.*

orthodox *adj.* conforming to established views. —**orthodoxy** *n.* —**Orthodox Church** dominant Christian Church in Eastern Europe.

THESAURUS

organ agency, channel, forum, medium, mouthpiece, newspaper, publication, vehicle, voice

organism animal, being, body, creature, entity, structure

organization 1. assembly, construction, disposal, formation, management, regulation, running, standardization 2. association, body, combine, company, concern, consortium, group, institution, league, syndicate

organize arrange, catalogue, classify, codify, constitute, construct, coordinate, dispose, establish, form, frame, group, marshal, pigeonhole, set up, shape

orgy 1. debauch, revelry 2. bout, excess, indulgence, spree, surfeit

orientation bearings, direction, location, position

orifice aperture, cleft, hole, mouth, opening, perforation, pore, rent, vent

origin base, cause, derivation, fountain, occasion, roots, source, spring

original *adj.* 1. earliest, first, initial, introduc-

tory, opening, primary, pristine, rudimentary, starting 2. creative, fertile, fresh, ingenious, inventive, new, novel, resourceful, untried, unusual 3. archetypal, authentic, first, genuine, master, primary ~*n.* 4. archetype, master, model, pattern, precedent, prototype, standard, type

originality boldness, break with tradition, cleverness, creativeness, creative spirit, creativity, daring, freshness, imagination, imaginativeness, individuality, ingenuity, innovation, innovativeness, inventiveness, new ideas, newness, novelty, resourcefulness, unconventionality, unorthodoxy

originate 1. arise, begin, come, derive, emerge, flow, issue, result, rise, spring, start, stem 2. conceive, create, discover, evolve, formulate, generate, initiate, institute, introduce, invent, launch, pioneer, produce

ornament adornment, bauble, decoration, frill, garnish, trinket

ornamental attractive, decorative, showy

DICTIONARY

orthography *n.* correct spelling.

orthopaedics *n.* branch of medicine concerned with disorders of the muscles or joints. —**orthopaedic** *adj.* —**orthopaedist** *n.*

ortolan *n.* small European bird eaten as a delicacy.

oryx *n.* large African antelope.

Oscar *n.* award in the form of a statuette given for achievements in films.

oscillate [oss-ill-late] *v.* swing back and forth. —**oscillation** *n.* —**oscillator** *n.* —**oscillatory** *adj.* —**oscilloscope** [oss-**sill**-oh-scope] *n.* instrument that shows the shape of a wave on a cathode-ray tube.

osier [oh-zee-er] *n.* willow tree; willow branch used in basketwork.

osmium *n.* heaviest known metallic element.

osmosis *n.* movement of a liquid through a membrane from a higher to a lower concentration; process of subtle influence. —**osmotic** *adj.*

osprey *n.* large fish-eating bird of prey.

osseous *adj.* made of or like bone.

ossify *v.* -**fying,** -**fied.** (cause to) become bone, harden; become inflexible. —**ossification** *n.*

ostensible *adj.* apparent, seeming. —**ostensibly** *adv.*

ostentation *n.* pretentious display. —**ostentatious** *adj.* —**ostentatiously** *adv.*

osteopathy *n.* medical treatment involving manipulation of the joints. —**osteopath** *n.*

ostracize *v.* exclude (a person) from a group. —**ostracism** *n.*

ostrich *n.* large flightless African bird that runs fast but cannot fly.

OT Old Testament.

other *adj.* remaining in a group of which one or some have been specified; different from the ones specified or understood; additional. —*n.* other person or thing. —**otherwise** *adv.* differently, in another way. —*conj.* or else, if not. —**otherworldly** *adj.* concerned with spiritual rather than practical matters.

otiose [oh-tee-oze] *adj.* not useful, e.g. *otiose language.*

otter *n.* small brown freshwater mammal that eats fish.

ottoman *n.*, *pl.* -**mans.** storage chest with a padded lid for use as a seat. —**Ottoman** *n.*, *adj. Hist.* (member) of the former Turkish empire.

oubliette [oo-blee-ett] *n.* dungeon entered only by a trapdoor.

ouch *interj.* exclamation of sudden pain.

ought *v.* (foll. by *to*) used to express: obligation, e.g. *you ought to pay;* advisability, e.g. *you ought to diet;* probability, e.g. *you ought to know by then.*

Ouija *n.* ® lettered board on which supposed messages from the dead are spelt out.

ounce *n.* unit of weight equal to one sixteenth of a pound (28.4 grams).

our *det.* belonging to us. —**ours** *pron.* thing(s) belonging to us. —**ourselves** *pron.* emphatic and reflexive form of WE or US.

ousel *n.* same as DIPPER (the bird).

oust *v.* force (someone) out, expel.

out *adv.*, *adj.* away from inside; not at home; revealed or made public; used up; not correct, e.g. *the calculations were out;* not fashionable; on strike; openly homosexual; *Sport* dismissed. —**out of** at or to a point outside. —**outer** *adj.* on the outside. —**out(er)most** *adj.* furthest out. —**outing** *n.* leisure trip. —**outward** *adj.* apparent. —*adv.* (also **outwards**) away from somewhere. —**outwardly** *adv.*

out- *prefix* surpassing, e.g. *outlive, outdistance.*

outback *n.* remote bush country of Australia.

outbid *v.* offer a higher price than.

outboard motor *n.* engine externally attached to the stern of a boat.

outbreak *n.* sudden occurrence (of something unpleasant).

outburst *n.* sudden expression of emotion.

outcast *n.* person rejected by a particular group.

THESAURUS

ornate beautiful, bedecked, busy, decorated, elaborate, elegant, fancy, florid, rococo

orthodox accepted, approved, conformist, conventional, doctrinal, established, official, received, sound, traditional, true

orthodoxy authenticity, authority, conformity, inflexibility, soundness

ostensible alleged, apparent, manifest, outward, plausible, professed, seeming, specious

ostentation affectation, boasting, display, exhibitionism, flourish, parade, pomp, pretentiousness, show, window-dressing

ostentatious boastful, conspicuous, extravagant, flamboyant, gaudy, loud, pompous, pretentious, showy, vulgar

other *adj.* 1. added, alternative, extra, further, more, spare, supplementary 2. different, dissimilar, distinct, diverse, remaining, separate

otherwise if not, or else, or then

out *adj.* abroad, absent, away, elsewhere, gone, not at home, outside

DICTIONARY

outclass v. surpass in quality.

outcome n. result.

outcrop n. *Geology* area where bedrock is covered by little or no soil.

outcry n., pl. **-cries.** expression of vehement or widespread protest.

outdo v. surpass in performance.

outdoors adv. in(to) the open air. **—outdoor** adj.

outface v. subdue or disconcert (someone) by staring.

outfield n. *Cricket* area far from the pitch.

outfit n. matching set of clothes; *Informal* group of people working together. **—outfitter** n. *Old-fashioned* supplier of men's clothes.

outflank v. get round the side of (an enemy army); outdo (someone).

outgoing adj. leaving; sociable. **—outgoings** pl. n. expenses.

outgrow v. become too large or too old for. **—outgrowth** n. thing growing out from a main body; natural development.

outhouse n. building near a main building.

outlandish adj. extravagantly eccentric.

outlaw n. *Hist.* criminal deprived of legal protection, bandit **—v.** make illegal; *Hist.* make (someone) an outlaw.

outlay n. expenditure.

outlet n. means of expressing emotion; market

for a product; place where a product is sold; opening or way out.

outline n. line defining the shape of something; short general explanation. **—v.** draw the outline of; summarize.

outlook n. attitude; probable outcome.

outlying adj. distant from the main area.

outmanoeuvre v. get an advantage over.

outmoded adj. no longer fashionable or accepted.

outnumber v. exceed in number.

outpatient n. patient who does not stay in hospital overnight.

outpost n. outlying settlement.

output n. amount produced; *Computers* data produced. **—v.** *Computers* produce (data) at the end of a process.

outrage n. great moral indignation; gross violation of morality. **—v.** offend morally. **—outrageous** adj. shocking; offensive. **—outrageously** adv.

outré [oo-tray] adj. shockingly eccentric.

outrider n. motorcyclist acting as an escort.

outrigger n. stabilizing frame projecting from a boat.

outright adj., adv. absolute(ly); open(ly); direct(ly).

outrun v. run faster than; exceed.

outset n. beginning.

THESAURUS

outbreak burst, explosion, flare-up, flash, outburst, rash, spasm

outcast n. castaway, exile, leper, pariah, refugee, untouchable, wretch

outclass beat, eclipse, exceed, excel, outdistance, outdo, outrank, outstrip, surpass

outcome aftermath, consequence, end, issue, result, upshot

outcry clamour, complaint, cry, howl, noise, outburst, protest, scream, screech, uproar, yell

outdoor alfresco, open-air, outside

outer exposed, exterior, external, outward, remote, superficial, surface

outfit n. clothes, costume, ensemble, garb, gear, kit, suit, trappings

outgoing departing, former, last, leaving, past, retiring

outgoings costs, expenditure, expenses, outlay, overheads

outing excursion, jaunt, trip

outlandish alien, barbarous, eccentric, exotic, foreign, grotesque, queer, strange, weird

outlaw 1. n. bandit, brigand, highwayman, marauder, robber 2. v. ban, banish, bar, condemn, forbid, prohibit, proscribe

outlay n. cost, expenses, investment, outgoings

outlet avenue, channel, opening, release, vent

outline n. 1. résumé, rundown, summary, synopsis 2. contour, figure, form, profile, shape, silhouette ~v. 3. adumbrate, delineate, draft, plan, summarize, trace

outlook 1. angle, attitude, perspective, slant, viewpoint, views 2. forecast, future, prospect

output manufacture, production, yield

outrage n. 1. atrocity, enormity, evil, inhumanity 2. abuse, affront, indignity, injury, insult, offence, shock, violation, violence 3. anger, fury, hurt, indignation, resentment, shock, wrath ~v. 4. affront, incense, offend, scandalize, shock

outrageous 1. atrocious, beastly, flagrant, horrible, infamous, inhuman, scandalous, shocking, villainous, violent, wicked 2. disgraceful, offensive, scandalous, shocking, unreasonable

outright adj. 1. absolute, arrant, complete, perfect, pure, thorough, total, unconditional, utter, wholesale 2. definite, direct, flat ~adv. 3.

DICTIONARY

outshine *v.* surpass (someone) in excellence.

outside *prep.* to the exterior of; beyond the limits of. —*adv.* on or to the exterior; in(to) the open air. —*n.* external area or surface. —*adj.* exterior; unlikely, e.g. *an outside chance;* coming from outside. —**outsider** *n.* person outside a specific group; contestant thought unlikely to win.

outsize(d) *adj.* larger than normal.

outskirts *pl. n.* outer areas, esp. of a town.

outsmart *v. Informal* outwit.

outspoken *adj.* tending to say what one thinks; said openly.

outstanding *adj.* excellent; still to be dealt with or paid.

outstrip *v.* go faster than; surpass.

outtake *n.* unreleased take from a recording session, film, or TV programme.

outweigh *v.* be more important, significant or influential than.

outwit *v.* get the better of (someone) by cunning.

outworks *pl. n.* secondary external defences of a fort.

ouzel [ooze-el] *n.* same as DIPPER (the bird).

ova *n.* plural of OVUM.

oval *adj.* egg-shaped. —*n.* anything that is oval in shape.

ovary *n., pl.* **-ries.** female egg-producing organ. —**ovarian** *adj.*

ovation *n.* enthusiastic round of applause.

oven *n.* heated compartment or container for cooking or for drying or firing ceramics.

over *prep.* higher than; on or across the top of; on or to the other side of; during; more than; recovered from. —*adv.* above or across something; onto its side, e.g. *the jug toppled over;* in excess. —*adj.* finished. —*n.* Cricket series of six balls bowled from one end. —**overly** *adv.* excessively.

over- *prefix* too much, e.g. *overeat;* above, e.g. *overlord;* on top, e.g. *overshoe.*

overall *n.* coat-shaped protective garment. —*pl.* protective garment consisting of trousers with a jacket or bib and braces attached. —*adj., adv.* in total.

overarm *adv., adj.* (thrown) with the arm above the shoulder.

overawe *v.* affect (someone) with an overpowering sense of awe.

overbalance *v.* lose balance.

overbearing *adj.* domineering.

overboard *adv.* from a boat into the water. —**go overboard** go to extremes, esp. in enthusiasm.

overcast *adj.* (of the sky) covered by clouds.

overcoat *n.* heavy coat.

overcome *v.* gain control over after an effort; (of an emotion) affect strongly.

THESAURUS

absolutely, completely, explicitly, openly, overtly, straightforwardly, thoroughly

outset beginning, inception, opening, start

outshine eclipse, outclass, outstrip, surpass, top

outside *adj.* 1. exterior, external, extramural, extreme, outdoor, outer, outward, surface 2. distant, faint, marginal, negligible, remote, slight, slim, small, unlikely ~*n.* 3. exterior, façade, face, front, skin, surface, topside

outskirts borders, boundary, edge, environs, suburbs, vicinity

outspoken abrupt, blunt, candid, direct, explicit, frank, free, open, round

outstanding 1. celebrated, distinguished, eminent, excellent, exceptional, great, important, impressive, special, superior, well-known 2. due, ongoing, open, owing, payable, pending, unpaid, unsettled

outward *adj.* apparent, evident, exterior, external, obvious, ostensible, outer, outside, perceptible, superficial, surface, visible

outwardly apparently, externally, officially, ostensibly

outweigh compensate for, eclipse, override, predominate

outwit cheat, deceive, defraud, dupe, outjockey, outmanoeuvre, swindle

ovation acclaim, applause, cheers, plaudits, tribute

over *adj.* 1. accomplished, by, bygone, closed, completed, concluded, finished, gone, past ~*adv.* 2. beyond, extra, left over, remaining, superfluous, surplus, unused ~*prep.* 3. above, on, on top of, upon 4. above, exceeding, in excess of, more than ~*adv.* 5. above, aloft, on high, overhead

overall *adj.* blanket, complete, general, inclusive, umbrella

overbalance capsize, overturn, slip, tumble, upset

overbearing arrogant, despotic, dogmatic, domineering, lordly, officious, oppressive, overweening, peremptory, superior

overcast clouded, darkened, dismal, dreary,

DICTIONARY

overdo v. do to excess; exaggerate (something). **—overdo it** do something to a greater degree than is advisable.

overdose n. excessive dose of a drug. —v. take an overdose.

overdraft n. overdrawing; amount overdrawn.

overdraw v. withdraw more money than is in (one's bank account). **—overdrawn** adj. having overdrawn one's account; (of an account) in debit. **—overdraft** n. amount of money overdrawn.

overdrive n. very high gear in a motor vehicle.

overdue adj. still due after the time allowed.

overgrown adj. thickly covered with plants and weeds.

overhaul v. examine and repair. —n. examination and repair.

overhead adv. in the sky. —adj. over one's head. **—overheads** pl. n. general cost of maintaining a business.

overhear v. hear (a speaker or remark) unintentionally or without the speaker's knowledge.

overjoyed adj. extremely pleased.

overkill n. treatment that is greater than required.

overland adj., adv. by land.

overlap v. share part of the same space or period of time (as). —n. area overlapping.

overleaf adv. on the back of the current page.

overlook v. fail to notice; ignore; look at from above.

overnight adj., adv. (taking place) during one night; (happening) very quickly.

overpower v. subdue or overcome (someone).

overreach v. **—overreach oneself** fail by trying to be too clever.

override v. overrule; replace.

overrule v. reverse the decision of (a person with less power); reverse (someone else's decision).

overrun v. spread over (a place) rapidly; extend beyond a set limit.

overseas adj., adv. to, of, or from a distant country.

oversee v. watch over from a position of authority. **—overseer** n.

overshadow v. reduce the significance of (a person or thing) by comparison; sadden the atmosphere of.

oversight n. mistake caused by not noticing something.

overspill n. rehousing of people from crowded cities to smaller towns.

overstay v. **—overstay one's welcome** stay longer than one's host or hostess would like.

overt adj. open, not hidden. **—overtly** adv.

overtake v. move past (a vehicle or person) while travelling in the same direction.

THESAURUS

dull, grey, hazy, lowering, murky, sombre, threatening

overcome beat, best, conquer, crush, defeat, master, overpower, prevail, subdue, subjugate, surmount, survive, vanquish, worst

overdo belabour, exaggerate, overindulge, overplay

overdue behindhand, belated, late, owing, tardy, unpunctual

overhaul 1. v. check, do up (Inf.), examine, inspect, recondition, re-examine, repair, restore, service, survey 2. n. checkup, examination, inspection, service

overhead 1. adv. above, skyward, up above, upward 2. adj. overhanging, roof, upper

overheads burden, running cost(s)

overjoyed delighted, elated, joyful, jubilant, rapturous, thrilled

overlook 1. disregard, forget, ignore, miss, neglect, omit, pass, slight 2. condone, disregard, excuse, forgive

overpower beat, conquer, crush, defeat, master, overcome, overwhelm, quell, subdue, subjugate, vanquish

override annul, cancel, disregard, ignore, nullify, outweigh, quash, reverse, set aside, supersede, upset, vanquish

overrule alter, annul, cancel, invalidate, override, overturn, recall, repeal, rescind, reverse, revoke, veto

overrun 1. invade, occupy, rout, swamp 2. choke, infest, inundate, overgrow, permeate, ravage 3. exceed, overshoot

overseer chief, foreman, master, manager, supervisor

overshadow 1. dominate, dwarf, eclipse, excel, outshine, surpass 2. bedim, cloud, darken, dim, obfuscate, obscure, veil

oversight blunder, error, fault, lapse, laxity, mistake, neglect, omission, slip

overtake outdistance, outdo, outstrip, overhaul, pass

overthrow 1. v. abolish, beat, conquer, crush, defeat, depose, dethrone, master, oust, overwhelm, topple, unseat 2. n. defeat, discomfiture, displacement, dispossession, downfall, end, fall, ousting, rout, ruin, undoing

DICTIONARY

overthrow v. defeat and replace. —n. downfall, destruction.

overtime n., adv. (paid work done) in addition to one's normal working hours.

overtone n. additional meaning.

overture n. Music orchestral introduction; opening moves in a new relationship.

overturn v. turn upside down; overrule (a legal decision); overthrow (a government).

overweight adj. weighing more than is healthy.

overwhelm v. overpower, esp. emotionally; defeat by force. —**overwhelming** adj. —**overwhelmingly** adv.

overwrought adj. nervous and agitated.

oviparous [oh-**vip**-par-uss] adj. producing young by laying eggs.

ovoid [**oh**-void] adj. egg-shaped.

ovulate [**ov**-yew-late] v. release an egg cell from an ovary. —**ovulation** n.

ovum [**oh**-vum] n., pl. **ova**. unfertilized egg cell.

owe v. be obliged to pay (a sum of money) to (a person). —**owing to** as result of.

owl n. night bird of prey. —**owlish** adj. —**owlet** n. young owl.

own det. used to emphasize possession; e.g. my own idea. —v. possess. —**owner** n. —**ownership** n. —**own up** v. confess.

ox n., pl. **oxen**. castrated bull.

oxeye n. plant with daisy-like flowers.

Oxfam Oxford Committee for Famine Relief.

oxide n. compound of oxygen and one other element. —**oxidize** v. combine chemically with oxygen, as in burning or rusting.

oxygen n. gaseous element essential to life and combustion. —**oxygenate** v. add oxygen to. —**oxyacetylene** n. mixture of oxygen and acetylene used in high-temperature welding.

oxymoron [ox-see-**more**-on] n. figure of speech that combines two apparently contradictory ideas, such as cruel kindness.

oyez interj. Hist. (shouted three times by a public crier) listen.

oyster n. edible shellfish. —**oystercatcher** n. wading bird with black-and-white feathers.

oz. ounce.

ozone n. highly reactive strong-smelling form of oxygen. —**ozone layer** layer of ozone in the upper atmosphere that filters out ultraviolet radiation.

THESAURUS

overture Often plural advance, approach, invitation, offer, proposal, signal, tender

overturn 1. capsize, overbalance, reverse, spill, topple, tumble, upend, upset, upturn 2. abolish, annul, countermand, depose, destroy, invalidate, overthrow, repeal, rescind, reverse

overwhelm 1. bury, crush, deluge, engulf, flood, inundate, submerge, swamp 2. confuse, devastate, prostrate, stagger

overwhelming crushing, devastating, overpowering, shattering, stunning, vast

overwrought agitated, distracted, excited, frantic, keyed up, on edge, tense

own adj. 1. individual, particular, personal, private ~v. 2. enjoy, have, hold, keep, possess, retain 3. **own up** (**to**) admit, confess 4. acknowledge, admit, allow, avow, concede, confess, disclose, grant, recognize

owner holder, landlord, lord, master, mistress, possessor, proprietor

ownership dominion, possession, proprietorship, title

P

P (car) park; *Chess* pawn; *Chem.* phosphorus.

p page; penny or pence; *Music* piano.

p.a. each year.

PA personal assistant; public-address system.

pace *n.* single step in walking; length of a step; rate of progress. —*v.* walk with regular steps; set the speed for (competitors in a race); cross or measure with steps. —**put someone through his** *or* **her paces** test someone's ability. —**pacemaker** *n.* person who sets the speed of a race; electronic device surgically implanted in a person with heart disease to regulate the heartbeat.

pachyderm [**pak**-ee-durm] *n.* thick-skinned animal such as an elephant.

pacifist *n.* person who refuses on principle to take part in war. —**pacifism** *n.*

pacify *v.* **-fying, -fied.** soothe, calm; establish peace in. —**pacification** *n.*

pack *n.* load carried on the back; set of things sold together; container for things sold; set of playing cards; group of hunting animals. —*v.* put (clothes etc.) together in a suitcase or bag; press tightly together, cram; fill with things. —**packhorse** *n.* horse for carrying goods. —**pack ice** mass of floating ice in the sea. —**pack in** *v.* *Informal* stop doing. —**pack off** *v.* send away.

package *n.* parcel; set of things offered together. —*v.* put into packages. —**packaging** *n.* —**package holiday** holiday in which everything is arranged by one company for a fixed price.

packet *n.* small parcel; small container (and contents); *Slang* large sum of money. —**packet** (**boat**) *n.* *Hist.* boat that carried mail, goods, or passengers on a fixed short route.

pact *n.* formal agreement.

pad *n.* piece of soft material used for protection, support, absorption of liquid, etc.; block of sheets of paper fastened at the edge; fleshy underpart of an animal's paw; place for launching rockets; *Slang* home. —*v.* **padding, padded.** protect or fill in with soft material; walk with soft or muffled steps. —**padding** *n.* material used to pad; words put in simply to increase length.

paddle[1] *n.* short oar with a broad blade at one or each end. —*v.* move (a canoe etc.) with a paddle. —**paddle steamer** ship propelled by paddle wheels. —**paddle wheel** wheel with crosswise blades that strike the water successively to propel a ship.

paddle[2] *v.* walk with bare feet in shallow water.

paddock *n.* small field or enclosure for horses.

paddy *n.* *Informal* fit of temper.

paddy field *n.* field where rice is grown.

padlock *n.* detachable lock with a hinged hoop fastened over a ring on the object to be secured.

padre [**pah**-dray] *n.* chaplain in the armed forces.

paean [**pee**-an] *n.* song of triumph or thanksgiving.

paediatrics *n.* branch of medicine concerned with diseases of children. —**paediatrician** *n.*

paedophilia *n.* condition of being sexually attracted to children. —**paedophile** *n.* person who is sexually attracted to children.

paella [pie-**ell**-a] *n.* Spanish dish made of rice, chicken, shellfish, and vegetables.

pagan *adj.* not belonging to one of the world's main religions. —*n.* pagan person.

page[1] *n.* (one side of) a sheet of paper forming a book etc.

THESAURUS

pace *n.* 1. gait, measure, step, stride, tread, walk 2. momentum, motion, movement, progress, rate, speed, tempo, time, velocity ~*v.* 3. march, patrol, pound, stride 4. count, determine, mark out, measure, step

pacifist dove, peace lover, peacemonger

pack *n.* 1. bale, bundle, burden, kit, kitbag, knapsack, load, package, packet, parcel, rucksack, truss ~*v.* 2. bundle, burden, load, package, store, stow 3. charge, compact, compress, cram, crowd, fill, jam, mob, press, ram, stuff, tamp, throng, wedge

package *n.* 1. box, carton, container, parcel 2. combination, entity, unit, whole ~*v.* 3. batch, box, pack, wrap

packet bag, carton, container, package, parcel

pact agreement, alliance, bargain, bond, concord, contract, covenant, deal, league, protocol, treaty, understanding

pad *n.* 1. buffer, cushion, protection, stiffening, stuffing, wad 2. block, jotter, notepad, tablet, writing pad 3. foot, paw, sole ~*v.* 4. cushion, pack, protect, shape, stuff

padding filling, packing, stuffing, wadding

paddle[1] 1. *n.* oar, scull, sweep 2. *v.* oar, propel, pull, row, scull

paddle[2] dabble, plash, slop, wade

pagan 1. *n.* heathen, infidel, unbeliever 2. *adj.* heathen, infidel

DICTIONARY

page[2] *n. Hist.* boy in training for knighthood; attendant. —*v.* summon (a person whose whereabouts are unknown), for example by electronic bleeper or loudspeaker announcement.

pageant *n.* parade or display of people in costume, usu. illustrating a scene from history. —**pageantry** *n.*

paginate *v.* number the pages of (a book etc.). —**pagination** *n.*

pagoda *n.* pyramid-shaped Asian temple or tower.

paid *v.* past of PAY. —**put paid to** *Informal* end, destroy.

pail *n.* bucket. —**pailful** *n.*

pain *n.* bodily or mental suffering. —*pl.* trouble, effort. —**on pain of** subject to the penalty of. —**painful** *adj.* —**painfully** *adv.* —**painless** *adj.* —**painlessly** *adv.* —**painkiller** *n.* drug that reduces pain.

painstaking *adj.* thorough and careful.

paint *n.* colouring spread on a surface with a brush or roller. —*v.* colour or coat with paint; make a picture of. —**painter** *n.* —**painting** *n.*

painter *n.* rope at the bow of a boat for tying it up.

pair *n.* set of two things. —*v.* group or be grouped in twos.

paisley *n.* pattern of small curving shapes.

pal *n. Informal* friend.

palace *n.* residence of a king, bishop, etc.; large grand building.

palaeography [pal-ee-**og**-ra-fee] *n.* study of ancient writings.

palaeolithic [pal-ee-oh-**lith**-ik] *adj.* of the Old Stone Age.

palaeontology [pal-ee-on-**tol**-a-jee] *n.* study of past geological periods and fossils. —**palaeontological** *adj.*

palatable *adj.* pleasant to eat.

palate *n.* roof of the mouth; sense of taste.

palatial *adj.* like a palace; magnificent.

palaver [pal-**lah**-ver] *n.* time-wasting fuss.

pale[1] *adj.* light, whitish; having less colour than normal. —*v.* become pale.

pale[2] *n. Hist.* fence; boundary. —**beyond the pale** outside the limits of social convention.

palette *n.* artist's flat board for mixing colours on.

palindrome *n.* word, phrase, or sentence that reads the same backwards as forwards.

paling *n.* any of the upright planks in a fence.

palisade *n.* fence made of stakes.

pall[1] *n.* cloth spread over a coffin; depressing oppressive atmosphere; dark cloud (of smoke). —**pallbearer** *n.* person carrying a coffin at a funeral.

pall[2] *v.* become boring.

pallet[1] *n.* portable platform for storing and moving goods.

pallet[2] *n.* straw mattress; small bed.

palliasse *n.* straw mattress.

palliate *v.* lessen the severity of (something) without curing it. —**palliative** *adj.* giving temporary or partial relief. —*n.* something, for example a drug, that palliates.

THESAURUS

page[1] folio, leaf, sheet, side

page[2] 1. *n.* attendant, footboy, pageboy, servant, squire 2. *v.* call, seek, summon

pageant display, parade, procession, ritual, show, spectacle, tableau

pain *n.* 1. ache, cramp, hurt, irritation, pang, soreness, spasm, tenderness, throb, trouble, twinge 2. agony, anguish, bitterness, distress, grief, heartache, misery, suffering, torment, torture, woe

painful 1. agonizing, harrowing, inflamed, raw, smarting, sore, tender 2. arduous, difficult, hard, laborious, severe, tedious, troublesome, trying, vexatious

painkiller anaesthetic, analgesic, drug, remedy, sedative

painless easy, effortless, fast, pain-free, quick, simple

pains bother, care, diligence, effort, industry, labour, trouble

painstaking assiduous, careful, conscientious, diligent, earnest, meticulous, punctilious, scrupulous, sedulous, strenuous, thorough

paint *n.* 1. colour, colouring, dye, emulsion, pigment, stain, tint ~*v.* 2. delineate, depict, draw, figure, picture, portray, represent, sketch 3. apply, coat, colour, cover, daub, decorate

pair 1. *n.* brace, couple, doublet, duo, match, span, twins 2. *v.* bracket, couple, join, marry, match, mate, team, twin, wed, yoke

palatable appetizing, delicious, luscious, mouthwatering, savoury, tasty

palate appetite, heart, stomach, taste

palatial de luxe, grand, illustrious, imposing, magnificent, majestic, opulent, regal, spacious, splendid, stately, sumptuous

pale ashen, ashy, bleached, colourless, faded, light, pasty, sallow, wan, white

DICTIONARY

pallid *adj.* pale, esp. because ill or weak. —**pallor** *n.*

pally *adj.* -**lier**, -**liest.** *Informal* on friendly terms.

palm *n.* inner surface of the hand; tropical tree with a straight trunk crowned with long pointed leaves. —**palm off** *v.* get rid of (an unwanted thing or person), esp. by deceit. —**Palm Sunday** the Sunday before Easter.

palmistry *n.* fortune-telling from lines on the palm of the hand. —**palmist** *n.*

palomino *n., pl.* -**nos.** gold-coloured horse with a white mane and tail.

palpable *adj.* obvious; able to be touched or felt. —**palpably** *adv.*

palpate *v. Med.* examine (an area of the body) by touching.

palpitate *v.* (of the heart) beat rapidly; flutter or tremble. —**palpitation** *n.*

palsy [**pawl**-zee] *n.* paralysis. —**palsied** *adj.* affected with palsy.

paltry *adj.* -**trier**, -**triest.** worthless, insignificant.

pampas *pl. n.* vast grassy treeless plains in S America. —**pampas grass** tall grass with feathery ornamental flower branches.

pamper *v.* treat (someone) with great indulgence, spoil.

pamphlet *n.* thin paper-covered booklet. —**pamphleteer** *n.* writer of pamphlets.

pan[1] *n.* wide long-handled metal container used in cooking; bowl of a lavatory. —*v.* **panning, panned.** sift gravel from (a riverbed) in a pan to search for gold; *Informal* criticize harshly. —**pan out** *v.* result.

pan[2] *v.* **panning, panned.** move a film camera slowly so as to cover a whole scene or follow a moving object.

pan- *combining form* all, e.g. *pan-African.*

panacea [pan-a-**see**-a] *n.* remedy for all diseases or problems.

panache [pan-**ash**] *n.* confident elegant style.

panama *n.* straw hat.

panatella *n.* long slender cigar.

pancake *n.* thin flat circle of fried batter.

panchromatic *adj. Photog.* sensitive to light of all colours.

pancreas [**pang**-kree-ass] *n.* large gland behind the stomach that produces insulin and helps digestion. —**pancreatic** *adj.*

panda *n.* large black-and-white bearlike mammal from China. —**panda car** police patrol car.

pandemic *adj.* (of a disease) occurring over a wide area.

pandemonium *n.* wild confusion; uproar.

pander *n.* person who procures a sexual partner for someone. —**pander to** *v.* indulge (a person or his or her desires).

p & p postage and packing.

pane *n.* single piece of glass in a window or door.

panegyric [pan-ee-**jire**-ik] *n.* formal speech or piece of writing in praise of someone or something.

panel *n.* flat distinct section of a larger surface, such as that in a door; group of people as a team in a quiz etc.; list of jurors, doctors, etc. —*v.* -**elling, -elled.** decorate or cover with panels. —**panelling** *n.* panels collectively, such as those on a wall. —**panellist** *n.* member of a panel. —**panel beater** person who repairs damage to car bodies.

pang *n.* sudden sharp feeling of pain or sadness.

pangolin *n.* scaly anteater.

panic *n.* sudden overwhelming fear, often infectious. —*v.* -**icking, -icked.** feel or cause to feel panic. —**panicky** *adj.* —**panic-stricken, -struck** *adj.*

THESAURUS

palpable apparent, blatant, clear, conspicuous, evident, manifest, obvious, open, patent, plain, visible

palpitate beat, flutter, pound, pulsate, quiver, shiver, throb, tremble, vibrate

paltry base, beggarly, derisory, despicable, insignificant, low, meagre, mean, minor, miserable, petty, pitiful, poor, puny, slight, small, sorry, trifling, trivial, unimportant, worthless, wretched

pamper baby, coddle, cosset, fondle, gratify, humour, indulge, pet, spoil

pamphlet booklet, brochure, circular, folder, leaflet, tract

pan 1. *n.* container, pot, saucepan, vessel 2. *v. Inf.* censure, criticize, flay

panacea cure-all, elixir, nostrum

panache dash, élan, flamboyance, flourish, spirit, style, verve

pandemonium babel, bedlam, chaos, confusion, din, racket, rumpus, tumult, turmoil, uproar

pang ache, agony, distress, gripe, pain, prick, spasm, stab, sting, stitch, twinge

panic agitation, alarm, dismay, fear, fright, horror, scare, terror

panoply array, attire, dress, garb, regalia, show

DICTIONARY

pannier *n.* bag fixed on the back of a bike or motorbike; basket carried by a beast of burden.

panoply [**pan**-a-plee] *n.* magnificent array.

panorama *n.* wide or complete view. —**panoramic** *adj.*

pansy *n., pl.* **-sies.** garden flower with velvety petals; *Offens.* effeminate or homosexual man.

pant *v.* breathe quickly and noisily after exertion.

pantaloons *pl. n.* baggy trousers gathered at the ankles.

pantechnicon *n.* large van for furniture removals.

pantheism *n.* belief that God is present in everything. —**pantheist** *n.* —**pantheistic** *adj.*

pantheon *n.* (in ancient Greece and Rome) temple to all the gods.

panther *n.* leopard, esp. a black one.

panties *pl. n.* women's underpants.

pantile *n.* roofing tile with an S-shaped cross section.

pantograph *n.* instrument for copying maps etc. to any scale; device on the roof of an electric train for picking up the electric current.

pantomime *n.* play based on a fairy tale, performed at Christmas time.

pantry *n., pl.* **-tries.** room or cupboard for storing food or cooking utensils.

pants *pl. n.* undergarment for the lower part of the body; *US* trousers.

pap[1] *n.* soft food for babies or invalids; worthless or oversimplified ideas.

pap[2] *n. Obs.* nipple.

papacy [**pay**-pa-see] *n., pl.* **-cies.** the position or term of office of a pope. —**papal** *adj.* of the pope or papacy.

paparazzo [pap-a-**rat**-so] *n., pl.* **-razzi.** photographer specializing in unposed shots of famous people.

papaya [pa-**pie**-ya], **pa(w)paw** [pa-paw] *n.* large sweet West Indian fruit.

paper *n.* material made in sheets from wood pulp or other fibres; printed sheet of this; newspaper; article or essay; set of examination questions. —*pl.* personal documents. —*v.* cover (walls) with wallpaper. —**paperback** *n.* book with flexible paper covers. —**paperweight** *n.* heavy decorative object placed on top of loose papers. —**paperwork** *n.* the part of a job that consists of dealing with routine letters, forms, etc.

papier-mâché [pap-yay **mash**-ay] *n.* material made from paper mixed with paste, shaped by moulding and dried hard.

papist *n., adj. Offens.* Roman Catholic.

papoose *n.* N American Indian child.

paprika *n.* (powdered seasoning made from) a type of red pepper.

papyrus [pap-**ire**-uss] *n., pl.* **-ri, -ruses.** tall water plant; (manuscript written on) a kind of paper made from this plant.

par *n.* usual or average condition; face value of stocks and shares; *Golf* expected standard score. —**on a par with** equal to.

parable *n.* story that illustrates a religious teaching.

parabola [par-**ab**-bol-a] *n.* regular curve resembling the course of an object thrown forward and up. —**parabolic** *adj.*

paracetamol *n.* mild pain-relieving drug.

parachute *n.* large fabric canopy that slows the descent of a person or object from an aircraft. —*v.* land or drop by parachute. —**parachutist** *n.*

parade *n.* procession; public display by soldiers; street or promenade. —*v.* march in procession; display or flaunt.

paradigm [**par**-a-dime] *n.* example or model.

paradise *n.* heaven; state of bliss; Garden of Eden.

paradox *n.* statement that seems self-contradictory but may be true. —**paradoxical** *adj.* —**paradoxically** *adv.*

paraffin *n.* liquid mixture distilled from petroleum and used as a fuel, solvent, etc.

paragliding *n.* cross-country gliding using a parachute.

paragon *n.* model of perfection.

THESAURUS

panorama prospect, scenery, view, vista

pant blow, breathe, gasp, heave, huff, puff, throb, wheeze

paper *n.* 1. *Often plural* certificate, deed, documents, instrument, record 2. daily, gazette, journal, news, organ ~*v.* 3. hang, line, wallpaper

par *n.* average, level, mean, norm, standard, usual

parable allegory, exemplum, fable, lesson, moral tale, story

parade *n.* 1. array, ceremony, column, march, pageant, procession, review, spectacle, train 2. array, display, ostentation, pomp, show, spectacle, vaunting ~*v.* 3. march, process 4. air,

DICTIONARY

paragraph *n.* section of a piece of writing starting on a new line.

parakeet *n.* small long-tailed parrot.

parallax *n.* apparent difference in an object's position or direction as viewed from different points.

parallel *adj.* separated by equal distance at every point; precisely corresponding. —*n.* line equidistant from another at all points; thing with similar features to another; line of latitude. —*v.* be parallel to; correspond to. —**parallelism** *n.*

parallelogram *n.* four-sided geometric figure with opposite sides parallel.

paralysis *n.* inability to move or feel, because of damage to the nervous system. —**paralyse** *v.* affect with paralysis; make immobile. —**paralytic** *n., adj.* (person) affected with paralysis.

paramedic *n.* person working in support of the medical profession. —**paramedical** *adj.*

parameter [par-**am**-it-er] *n.* limiting factor, boundary.

paramilitary *adj.* organized on military lines.

paramount *adj.* of the greatest importance.

paramour *n. Obs.* illicit lover, mistress.

paranoia *n.* mental illness causing delusions of fame or persecution; *Informal* intense fear or suspicion. —**paranoiac, paranoid** *adj., n.*

paranormal *adj.* beyond scientific explanation.

parapet *n.* low wall or railing along the edge of a balcony, bridge, etc.

paraphernalia *n.* personal belongings or bits of equipment.

paraphrase *v.* express (meaning) in different words.

paraplegia [par-a-**plee**-ya] *n.* paralysis of the lower half of the body. —**paraplegic** *n., adj.*

parapsychology *n.* study of phenomena outside normal human ability, such as telepathy.

Paraquat *n.* ® very poisonous weedkiller.

parasite *n.* animal or plant living in or on another; person who lives at the expense of others, sponger. —**parasitic** *adj.*

parasol *n.* umbrella-like sunshade.

paratroops, -troopers *pl. n.* troops trained to attack by descending by parachute.

parboil *v.* boil until partly cooked.

parcel *n.* something wrapped up, package. —*v.* -**celling, -celled.** wrap up. —**parcel out** *v.* divide into parts.

parch *v.* make very hot and dry; make thirsty.

parchment *n.* thick smooth writing material made from animal skin.

pardon *v.* forgive or excuse. —*n.* forgiveness; official release from punishment. —**pardonable** *adj.* —**pardonably** *adv.*

pare *v.* trim or cut the edge of. —**paring** *n.* piece pared off.

parent *n.* father or mother. —**parental** *adj.* —**parenthood** *n.* —**parentage** *n.* ancestry or family. —**parenting** *n.* activity of bringing up children.

THESAURUS

brandish, display, exhibit, flaunt, show, strut, swagger, vaunt

paradise bliss, delight, felicity, heaven

paradox ambiguity, anomaly, contradiction, enigma, oddity, puzzle

paragon archetype, criterion, exemplar, ideal, jewel, model, pattern, prototype

paragraph clause, item, notice, part, passage, portion, section, subdivision

parallel *adj.* 1. alongside, equidistant 2. akin, analogous, complementary, like, matching, resembling, similar, uniform ~*n.* 3. analogue, corollary, counterpart, duplicate, equal, equivalent, match, twin

paralyse 1. cripple, disable, incapacitate, lame 2. arrest, benumb, freeze, halt, numb, petrify, stun, stupefy, transfix

paralysis immobility, palsy

paralytic *adj.* crippled, disabled, immobile, incapacitated, lame, numb, palsied, paralysed

paramount capital, cardinal, chief, dominant, eminent, first, foremost, main, outstanding,

pre-eminent, primary, principal, superior, supreme

paraphernalia apparatus, baggage, belongings, effects, gear, material, stuff, tackle, things, trappings

parasite hanger-on, leech

parcel 1. *n.* bundle, carton, package 2. *v.* Often *with up* do up, pack, package, tie up, wrap

parch blister, burn, dry up, evaporate, scorch, sear, shrivel, wither

pardon 1. *v.* absolve, acquit, amnesty, condone, exculpate, excuse, exonerate, forgive, free, overlook, release, remit, reprieve 2. *n.* absolution, acquittal, allowance, amnesty, discharge, excuse, grace, indulgence, release, remission, reprieve

pardonable excusable, forgivable, minor, understandable, venial

parent father, guardian, mother, sire

parentage ancestry, birth, descent, family, line, lineage, origin, pedigree, race, stock

DICTIONARY

parenthesis [par-en-thiss-iss] *n., pl.* **-ses.** word or sentence inserted in a passage, usu. marked off by brackets, dashes, or commas. —*pl.* round brackets, ( ). —**parenthetical** *adj.*

pargeting *n.* ornamental plasterwork on the outside of a house.

pariah [par-rye-a] *n.* social outcast.

parietal [par-rye-it-al] *adj.* of the walls of body cavities such as the skull.

parish *n.* area that has its own church and clergyman. —**parishioner** *n.* inhabitant of a parish.

parity *n.* equality or equivalence.

park *n.* area of open land for recreational use by the public; area containing a number of related businesses; large enclosed piece of ground attached to a country house. —*v.* stop and leave (a vehicle) temporarily.

parka *n.* warm waterproof hooded jacket.

parky *adj.* **parkier, parkiest.** *Informal* (of the weather) chilly.

parlance *n.* particular way of speaking, idiom.

parley *n.* meeting between leaders or representatives of opposing forces to discuss terms. —*v.* have a parley.

parliament *n.* law-making assembly of a country. —**parliamentary** *adj.*

parlour *n.* *Old-fashioned* living room for receiving visitors.

parlous *adj. Obs.* dangerous.

Parmesan *n.* hard strong-flavoured Italian cheese.

parochial *adj.* narrow in outlook, provincial; of a parish. —**parochialism** *n.*

parody *n., pl.* **-dies.** exaggerated and amusing imitation of someone else's style. —*v.* **-dying, -died.** make a parody of.

parole *n.* early freeing of a prisoner on condition that he or she behaves well. —*v.* place on parole. —**on parole** (of a prisoner) released on condition that he or she behaves well.

paroxysm *n.* uncontrollable outburst, as of laughter; spasm or convulsion, as of pain.

parquet [par-kay] *n.* wooden blocks arranged in a pattern and forming a floor. —**parquetry** *n.*

parricide *n.* person who kills one of his or her parents; act of killing either of one's parents.

parrot *n.* tropical bird with a short hooked beak, some varieties of which can imitate speaking. —*v.* **-roting, -roted.** repeat (words) without thinking.

parry *v.* **-rying, -ried.** ward off (an attack); cleverly avoid (an awkward question).

parse [parz] *v.* analyse (a sentence) in terms of grammar.

parsec *n.* unit of length used in expressing the distance of stars.

parsimony *n.* stinginess. —**parsimonious** *adj.*

parsley *n.* herb used for seasoning and decorating food.

parsnip *n.* long tapering cream-coloured root vegetable.

parson *n.* parish priest in the Church of England. —**parsonage** *n.* parson's house. —**parson's nose** rump of a cooked fowl.

part *n.* piece or portion; one of several equal divisions; actor's role; (often *pl.*) region, area; component of a vehicle or machine. —*v.* divide; (of people) leave each other. —**take someone's part** support someone in an argument etc. —**take something in good part** respond (to criticism etc.) with good humour. —**parting** *n.* division between sections of hair on the head; separation; leave-taking. —**partly** *adv.* not completely. —**part of speech** particular grammatical class of words, such as noun or verb. —**part song** song for several voices singing in harmony. —**part-time** *adj.* occupying or working less than the full working week. —**part with** *v.* give up ownership of.

THESAURUS

parish church, community, congregation, flock, fold

parity consistency, equality, par, uniformity, unity

park estate, garden, grounds, parkland, woodland

parliament assembly, congress, convocation, council, diet, legislature, senate

parliamentary deliberative, governmental, lawmaking, legislative

parlour front room, lounge, sitting room

parlous dangerous, desperate, difficult, dire, hazardous, risky

parody 1. *n.* burlesque, caricature, imitation, satire, skit 2. *v.* burlesque, caricature, mimic, satirize, travesty

parry 1. block, deflect, rebuff, repel, repulse 2. avoid, dodge, evade, fence, shun, sidestep

parsimonious close, frugal, grasping, mean, miserable, miserly, niggardly, penny-pinching (*Inf.*), penurious, saving, scrimpy, sparing, stingy, tightfisted

parson churchman, clergyman, cleric, divine,

DICTIONARY

partake v. **-taking, -took, -taken.** (foll. by of) take food or drink; (foll. by in) take part in.

parterre n. formally patterned flower garden.

partial adj. not general or complete; prejudiced. —**partial to** very fond of. —**partiality** n. favouritism; fondness for. —**partially** adv.

participate v. become actively involved in. —**participant** n. —**participation** n. —**participator** n.

participle n. form of a verb used in compound tenses or as an adjective, e.g. worried, worrying. —**participial** adj.

particle n. extremely small piece or amount; Physics minute piece of matter, such as a proton or electron.

parti-coloured adj. differently coloured in different parts.

particular adj. relating to one person or thing, not general; exceptional or special; very exact; not easily satisfied, fastidious. —n. detail; item of information. —**particularly** adv. —**particularize** v. give details about. —**particularity** n.

partisan n. strong supporter of a party or group; guerilla, member of a resistance movement. —adj. prejudiced or one-sided.

partition n. screen or thin wall that divides a room; division of a country into independent parts. —v. divide with a partition.

partner n. either member of a couple in a relationship or activity; member of a business partnership. —v. be the partner of (someone). —**partnership** n. joint business venture between two or more people.

partridge n. game bird of the grouse family.

parturition n. act of giving birth.

party n., pl. **-ties.** social gathering for pleasure; group of people travelling or working together; group of people with a common political aim; person or people forming one side in a lawsuit etc. —**party line** telephone line shared by two or more subscribers; official view of a political party. —**party wall** common wall separating adjoining buildings.

parvenu [par-ven-new] n. person newly risen to a position of power or wealth, upstart.

pascal n. unit of pressure.

THESAURUS

incumbent, minister, pastor, preacher, priest, rector, vicar

part n. 1. bit, fraction, fragment, lot, piece, portion, scrap, section, share, slice 2. branch, constituent, division, element, ingredient, limb, member, organ, piece, unit 3. Theat. character, lines, role 4. **in good part** cheerfully, cordially, well ~v. 5. break, cleave, come apart, detach, disunite, divide, rend, separate, sever, split, tear 6. depart, go, go away, leave, quit, separate, withdraw

partake With in engage, participate, share, take part

partial 1. imperfect, incomplete, limited, unfinished 2. biased, influenced, interested, one-sided, partisan, prejudiced, tendentious, unfair, unjust

partiality 1. bias, preference, prejudice 2. fondness, inclination, liking, love, penchant, predilection, proclivity, taste, weakness

partially fractionally, halfway, incompletely, in part, moderately, partly, piecemeal, somewhat

participant associate, contributor, member, party, shareholder

participate enter into, join in, perform, share, take part

particle atom, bit, crumb, grain, iota, jot, mite, mote, piece, scrap, shred, speck, tittle, whit

particular adj. 1. distinct, exact, express, peculiar, precise, special, specific 2. especial, marked, notable, remarkable, singular, un~ common, unusual 3. critical, dainty, demanding, discriminating, exacting, fastidious, finicky, fussy ~n. 4. Usually plural circumstance, detail, fact, feature, item, specification

particularly especially, exceptionally, markedly, singularly, surprisingly, uncommonly, unusually

parting 1. adieu, farewell, going, goodbye 2. breaking, division, partition, rift, rupture, separation, split

partisan n. 1. backer, devotee, stalwart, supporter, upholder, votary 2. guerrilla, irregular ~adj. 3. biased, factional, interested, one-sided, partial, prejudiced, sectarian

partition 1. n. barrier, screen, wall 2. v. apportion, cut up, divide, separate, share, split up, subdivide

partly partially, relatively, slightly, somewhat

partner 1. ally, associate, bedfellow, colleague, companion, comrade, helper, mate, teammate 2. consort, helpmate, husband, mate, spouse, wife

partnership alliance, combine, company, cooperative, firm, house, society, union

party 1. celebration, festivity, function, gathering, reception, social 2. band, body, company, crew, gang, group, squad, team, unit 3. alliance, cabal, clique, coalition, confederacy, coterie, faction, grouping, league, set, side 4. individual, person

DICTIONARY

paschal [pass-kal] *adj.* of the Passover or Easter.

pass *v.* go by, beyond, through, etc.; exceed; be accepted; be successful in a test etc.; examine and declare satisfactory; spend (time) or (of time) elapse; transfer; exchange; change or move from one state or person to another; bring (a law) into force; come to an end; choose not to take one's turn in a game or quiz. —*n.* successful result in a test; *Sport* transfer of a ball; permit or licence; narrow gap through mountains. —**make a pass at** *Informal* try to start a sexual relationship. —**passable** *adj.* (just) acceptable. —**passing** *adj.* brief or transitory; cursory or casual. —**pass away** *v.* die. —**pass out** *v. Informal* faint. —**pass up** *v. Informal* ignore or reject.

passage *n.* channel or opening providing a way through; hall or corridor; section of a book etc.; journey by sea; right or freedom to pass. —**passageway** *n.* passage or corridor.

passé [pas-say] *adj.* out-of-date.

passenger *n.* person travelling in a vehicle driven by someone else; one of a team who does not pull his or her weight.

passer-by *n., pl.* **passers-by.** person who is walking past something or someone.

passerine *adj.* belonging to the order of perching birds.

passim *adv. Latin* everywhere, throughout.

passion *n.* intense sexual love; any strong emotion; great enthusiasm; (**P-**) *Christianity* the suffering of Christ. —**passionate** *adj.* —**passionflower** *n.* tropical American plant. —**passion fruit** edible fruit of the passionflower. —**Passion play** play about Christ's suffering.

passive *adj.* not playing an active part; submissive and receptive to outside forces; denoting a form of verbs indicating that the subject receives the action, such as *was jeered* in *He was jeered by the crowd.* —**passive resistance** resistance to a government, law, etc. by nonviolent acts. —**passive smoking** inhalation of smoke from others' cigarettes by a nonsmoker.

Passover *n.* Jewish festival commemorating the sparing of the Jews in Egypt.

passport *n.* official document granting permission to travel abroad.

password *n.* secret word or phrase that ensures admission.

past *adj.* of the time before the present; ended, gone by; (of a verb tense) indicating that the action specified took place earlier. —*n.* bygone times; person's past life, esp. an earlier, disreputable period; past tense. —*adv.* by; along. —*prep.* beyond. —**past it** *Informal* unable to do the things one could do when younger. —**past master** person with great talent or experience in a particular subject.

pasta *n.* type of food, such as spaghetti, that is made in different shapes from flour and water.

THESAURUS

pass¹ *v.* 1. depart, elapse, flow, go, leave, move, proceed, roll, run 2. beat, exceed, excel, outdo, outstrip, surmount, surpass 3. answer, graduate, qualify, succeed, suffice, suit 4. convey, deliver, exchange, give, hand, kick, reach, send, throw, transfer 5. accept, adopt, approve, decree, enact, legislate, ordain, ratify

pass² *n.* 1. canyon, col, defile, gap, gorge, ravine 2. identification, licence, passport, permission, permit, safe-conduct, ticket, warrant

passable adequate, average, fair, mediocre, middling, moderate, ordinary, presentable, tolerable

passage 1. avenue, channel, course, lane, path, road, route, thoroughfare, way 2. corridor, doorway, entrance, hall, lobby, vestibule 3. extract, paragraph, piece, quotation, section, sentence, text, verse 4. crossing, journey, tour, trek, trip, voyage 5. allowance, freedom, permission, right, visa, warrant

passenger fare, rider, traveller

passing *adj.* 1. brief, fleeting, momentary, short, temporary, transient, transitory 2. casual, cursory, glancing, hasty, quick, shallow, short, slight, superficial

passion 1. ardour, eagerness, emotion, excitement, feeling, fire, heat, intensity, joy, rapture, spirit, transport, warmth, zeal 2. ardour, concupiscence, desire, fondness, infatuation, itch, keenness, love, lust 3. bug (*Inf.*), craving, craze, enthusiasm, fancy, fascination, idol, infatuation, mania, obsession 4. anger, fit, flare-up (*Inf.*), frenzy, fury, indignation, ire, outburst, paroxysm, rage, resentment, storm

passionate 1. amorous, ardent, aroused, desirous, erotic, hot, loving, lustful, sensual 2. animated, ardent, eager, emotional, excited, fierce, frenzied, heartfelt, impassioned, intense, strong, vehement, warm, wild

passive compliant, docile, enduring, inactive, inert, lifeless, nonviolent, patient, receptive, resigned, submissive

past *adj.* 1. completed, done, elapsed, ended, extinct, finished, forgotten, gone, over, spent 2. ancient, bygone, early, foregoing, former, late, olden, recent ~*n.* 3. background, experience, history, life, past life ~*adv.* 4. across, beyond, by, on, over

DICTIONARY

paste *n.* moist soft mixture, such as toothpaste; adhesive, esp. for paper; pastry dough; shiny glass used to make imitation jewellery. —*v.* fasten with paste. —**pasting** *n. Slang* defeat; strong criticism. —**pasteboard** *n.* stiff thick paper.

pastel *n.* coloured chalk crayon for drawing; picture drawn in pastels; pale delicate colour. —*adj.* pale and delicate in colour.

pasteurize *v.* sterilize by heat. —**pasteurization** *n.*

pastiche [pass-**teesh**] *n.* work of art that mixes styles or copies the style of another artist.

pastille *n.* small fruit-flavoured and sometimes medicated sweet.

pastime *n.* activity that makes time pass pleasantly.

pastor *n.* clergyman in charge of a congregation. —**pastoral** *adj.* of or depicting country life; of a clergyman or his duties.

pastrami *n.* highly seasoned smoked beef.

pastry *n., pl.* **-ries.** baking dough made of flour, fat, and water; cake or pie.

pasture *n.* grassy land for farm animals to graze on. —**pasturage** *n.* (right to) pasture.

pasty¹ [**pay**-stee] *adj.* **pastier, pastiest.** (of a complexion) pale and unhealthy.

pasty² [**pass**-tee] *n., pl.* **pasties.** round of pastry folded over a savoury filling.

pat *v.* **patting, patted.** tap lightly. —*n.* gentle tap or stroke; small shaped mass of butter etc. —*adj.* quick, ready, or glib. —**off pat** learned thoroughly.

patch *n.* piece of material sewn on a garment; small contrasting section; plot of ground; protecting pad for the eye. —*v.* mend with a patch; repair clumsily. —**patchy** *adj.* of uneven quality or intensity. —**patch up** *v.* make up (a quarrel). —**patchwork** *n.* needlework made of pieces of different materials sewn together.

pate *n. Old-fashioned* head.

pâté [pat-ay] *n.* spread of finely minced liver etc.

patella *n., pl.* **-lae.** kneecap.

paten [pat-in] *n.* plate for bread in Communion.

patent *n.* document giving the exclusive right to make or sell an invention. —*adj.* open to public inspection, e.g. *letters patent;* obvious; protected by a patent. —*v.* obtain a patent for. —**patently** *adv.* obviously. —**patent leather** leather processed to give a hard glossy surface.

paternal *adj.* fatherly; related through one's father. —**paternity** *n.* relation of a father to his offspring; fatherhood. —**paternalism** *n.* authority exercised in a way that limits individual responsibility. —**paternalistic** *adj.*

Paternoster *n. RC Church* the Lord's Prayer.

path *n.* surfaced walk or track; course of action.

pathetic *adj.* causing feelings of pity or sadness; distressingly inadequate. —**pathetically** *adv.*

pathogenic *adj.* producing disease.

pathology *n.* scientific study of diseases. —**pathological** *adj.* of pathology; *Informal* compulsively motivated. —**pathologist** *n.*

pathos *n.* power of arousing pity or sadness.

patient *adj.* enduring difficulties calmly. —*n.* person receiving medical treatment. —**patience** *n.* quality of being patient; card game for one.

patina *n.* fine layer on a surface; sheen of age on woodwork.

THESAURUS

pastel delicate, light, soft

pastime activity, amusement, diversion, entertainment, game, hobby, leisure, play, recreation, sport

pastor churchman, clergyman, divine, minister, parson, priest, rector, vicar

pastoral *adj.* 1. bucolic, idyllic, rural, rustic, simple 2. clerical, ministerial, priestly

pasture grass, grazing, meadow, pasturage

pat 1. *v.* caress, dab, fondle, pet, slap, stroke, tap, touch 2. *n.* clap, dab, light blow, slap, stroke, tap

patch *n.* 1. reinforcement 2. bit, scrap, shred, small piece, spot, stretch 3. area, ground, land, plot, tract ~*v.* 4. cover, fix, mend, repair, sew up

patchy bitty, erratic, fitful, irregular, random, sketchy, spotty, uneven

patent 1. *adj.* blatant, clear, downright, evident,

flagrant, glaring, manifest, obvious, open 2. *n.* copyright, invention, licence

paternal concerned, fatherly, protective, solicitous, vigilant

path 1. footway, track, trail 2. avenue, course, direction, passage, procedure, road, route, track, walk, way

pathetic affecting, distressing, melting, moving, pitiable, plaintive, poignant, sad, tender, touching

pathos pitifulness, plaintiveness, poignancy, sadness

patience calmness, forbearance, restraint, serenity, sufferance, tolerance, toleration

patient 1. *adj.* calm, composed, long-suffering, philosophical, quiet, resigned, serene, stoical, submissive, uncomplaining 2. *n.* case, invalid, sufferer

DICTIONARY

patio *n., pl.* **-tios.** paved area adjoining a house.

patois [pat-wah] *n., pl.* **patois** [pat-wahz]. regional dialect.

patriarch *n.* male head of a family or tribe; highest-ranking bishop in Orthodox Churches. —**patriarchal** *adj.* —**patriarchy** *n.* society in which men have most of the power.

patrician *n.* member of the nobility, esp. of ancient Rome. —*adj.* of noble birth.

patricide *n.* crime of killing one's father; person who does this.

patrimony *n., pl.* **-nies.** property inherited from ancestors.

patriot *n.* person who loves his or her country and supports its interests. —**patriotic** *adj.* —**patriotism** *n.*

patrol *n.* regular circuit by a guard; person or small group patrolling; unit of Scouts or Guides. —*v.* **-trolling, -trolled.** go round on guard, or reconnoitring.

patron *n.* person who gives (financial) support to charities, artists, etc.; regular customer of a shop, pub, etc. —**patronage** *n.* support given by a patron. —**patronize** *v.* treat in a condescending way; be a patron of. —**patron saint** saint regarded as the guardian of a country or group.

patronymic *n.* name derived from one's father or a male ancestor.

patten *n. Hist.* type of clog.

patter *v.* make repeated soft tapping sounds. —*n.* quick succession of taps; glib rapid speech.

pattern *n.* arrangement of repeated parts or decorative designs; diagram or shape used as a guide to make something. —*v.* (foll. by *on*) make or do on the model of. —**patterned** *adj.* decorated with a pattern.

patty *n., pl.* **-ties.** small pie; minced meat formed into a small disc.

paucity *n.* scarcity; smallness of amount or number.

paunch *n.* belly.

pauper *n.* very poor person.

pause *v.* stop for a time. —*n.* stop or rest.

pave *v.* form (a surface) with stone or brick. —**pavement** *n.* paved path for pedestrians.

pavilion *n.* clubhouse on a playing field etc.; building for housing an exhibition etc.

paw *n.* animal's foot with claws and pads. —*v.* scrape with the paw or hoof; handle roughly; stroke in an overfamiliar way.

pawn¹ *v.* deposit (an article) as security for money borrowed. —**in pawn** deposited as security with a pawnbroker. —**pawnbroker** *n.* lender of money on goods deposited.

pawn² *n.* chessman of the lowest value; person manipulated by someone else.

pay *v.* **paying, paid.** give money etc. in return for goods or services; settle a debt or obligation; compensate (for); give, bestow; be profitable to. —*n.* wages or salary. —**payment** *n.* act of paying; money paid. —**payable** *adj.* due to be paid. —**payee** *n.* person to whom money is paid or due. —**paying guest** lodger. —**pay off** *v.* pay (debt) in full; turn out successfully. —**pay out** *v.* spend; release (a rope) bit by bit.

THESAURUS

patriot chauvinist, loyalist, nationalist

patriotic chauvinistic, loyal, nationalistic

patrol *n.* 1. guarding, policing, protecting, vigilance, watching 2. garrison, guard, patrolman, sentinel, watchman ~*v.* 3. cruise, guard, inspect, police, pound, range, safeguard

patron 1. advocate, backer, benefactor, champion, defender, friend, guardian, helper, sponsor, supporter 2. buyer, client, customer, habitué, shopper

patronage 1. aid, assistance, backing, encouragement, help, promotion, sponsorship, support 2. business, clientele, commerce, custom, trade, trading, traffic

patronize 1. look down on 2. assist, back, befriend, foster, fund, help, sponsor, support 3. deal with, frequent

patter *n.* chatter, nattering, prattle

pattern *n.* 1. decoration, decorative design, design, device, figure 2. design, diagram, guide, instructions, original, plan, stencil, template

~*v.* 3. copy, emulate, follow, form, imitate, model, mould, order, shape, style

paucity dearth, lack, poverty, rarity, scarcity, shortage

pauper bankrupt, beggar, insolvent, mendicant

pause 1. *v.* break, cease, delay, desist, discontinue, halt, hesitate, interrupt, rest, wait, waver 2. *n.* break, cessation, delay, gap, halt, hesitation, interlude, interval, lull, respite, rest, stay, stoppage, wait

pawn deposit, hazard, mortgage, pledge, stake, wager

pay *v.* 1. clear, compensate, cough up (*Inf.*), discharge, foot, give, honour, liquidate, meet, offer, recompense, reimburse, remit, remunerate, render, requite, reward, settle 2. bestow, extend, give, grant, present, proffer, render 3. bring in, produce, profit, return, yield ~*n.* 4. allowance, earnings, emoluments, fee, hire, income, recompense, remuneration, reward, salary, stipend, takings, wages

payable due, mature, outstanding, owed, owing

DICTIONARY

PAYE pay as you earn: system by which income tax is paid by an employer straight to the government.

payload *n.* passengers or cargo of an aircraft; explosive power of a missile etc.

payola *n. Informal* bribe to get special treatment, esp. to promote a commercial product.

Pb *Chem.* lead.

pc per cent; postcard.

PC Police Constable; Privy Councillor.

PE physical education.

pea *n.* climbing plant with seeds growing in pods; its seed, eaten as a vegetable. —**pea-green** *adj.* yellowish-green. —**peasouper** *n. Informal* thick fog.

peace *n.* calm, quietness; absence of anxiety; freedom from war; harmony between people. —**peaceable** *adj.* inclined towards peace. —**peaceably** *adv.* —**peaceful** *adj.* —**peacefully** *adv.*

peach *n.* soft juicy fruit with a stone and a downy skin; *Informal* very pleasing person or thing. —*adj.* pinkish-orange.

peacock *n.* large male bird with a brilliantly coloured fanlike tail. —**peahen** *n. fem.* —**peafowl** *n.* peacock or peahen.

peak *n.* pointed top, esp. of a mountain; point of greatest development etc.; projecting piece on the front of a cap. —*adj.* of or at the point of greatest demand. —*v.* (cause to) form or reach peaks. —**peaked** *adj.* —**peaky** *adj. Informal* looking pale and sickly.

peal *n.* long loud echoing sound, esp. of bells or thunder. —*v.* sound with a peal or peals.

peanut *n.* pea-shaped nut that ripens underground. —*pl. Informal* trifling amount of money.

pear *n.* sweet juicy fruit with a narrow top and rounded base.

pearl *n.* hard round lustrous object found inside some oyster shells and used as a jewel. —**pearly** *adj.*

peasant *n.* (in some countries) farmer or farmworker of a low social class. —**peasantry** *n.* peasants collectively.

peat *n.* decayed vegetable material found in bogs, used as fertilizer or fuel.

pebble *n.* small roundish stone. —**pebbly** *adj.* —**pebble dash** coating for exterior walls consisting of small stones set in plaster.

pecan [**pee**-kan] *n.* edible nut of a N American tree.

peccadillo *n., pl.* **-los, -loes.** trivial misdeed.

peccary *n., pl.* **-ries.** wild pig of American forests.

peck *v.* strike or pick up with the beak; *Informal* kiss quickly. —*n.* pecking movement. —**peckish** *adj. Informal* hungry. —**peck at** *v.* nibble, eat reluctantly.

pectin *n.* substance in fruit that makes jam set.

pectoral *adj.* of the chest or thorax. —*n.* pectoral muscle or fin.

peculation *n.* embezzlement, theft.

peculiar *adj.* strange; distinct, special; belonging exclusively to. —**peculiarity** *n.* oddity, eccentricity; characteristic.

pecuniary *adj.* relating to, or consisting of, money.

pedagogue *n.* schoolteacher, esp. a pedantic one.

THESAURUS

payment 1. discharge, outlay, paying, remittance, settlement 2. fee, hire, remuneration, reward, wage

pay off 1. clear, discharge, settle, square 2. be effective, succeed, work

pay out disburse, expend, spend

peace 1. accord, agreement, concord, harmony 2. conciliation, treaty, truce 3. calm, composure, contentment, relaxation, repose, serenity 4. calm, calmness, hush, quiet, repose, rest, silence, tranquillity

peaceable 1. friendly, gentle, mild, pacific, placid, unwarlike 2. balmy, calm, peaceful, quiet, restful, serene, still, tranquil, undisturbed

peaceful 1. amicable, friendly, harmonious 2. calm, gentle, placid, quiet, restful, serene, still, tranquil 3. pacific, placatory

peak *n.* 1. apex, brow, crest, pinnacle, point, summit, tip, top 2. acme, apogee, climax, crown, zenith ~*v.* 3. climax, culminate

peal 1. *n.* blast, chime, clang, clap, crash, reverberation, ring, roar, rumble, sound 2. *v.* chime, crack, crash, resonate, resound, ring, roar, roll, rumble, sound, toll

peasant 1. countryman, rustic 2. boor, churl, lout, provincial, yokel

peccadillo error, indiscretion, lapse, misdeed

peculiar abnormal, bizarre, curious, eccentric, freakish, funny, odd, offbeat, outlandish, quaint, queer, singular, strange, uncommon, unusual, weird

peculiarity abnormality, eccentricity, foible, mannerism, oddity, quirk

pedagogue instructor, schoolmaster, schoolmistress, teacher

DICTIONARY

pedal *n.* foot-operated lever used to control a vehicle or machine, or to modify the tone of a musical instrument. —*v.* **-alling, -alled.** propel (a bicycle) by using its pedals.

pedant *n.* person who is overconcerned with details and rules, esp. in academic work. —**pedantic** *adj.* —**pedantry** *n.*

peddle *v.* sell (goods) from door to door. —**peddler** *n.* person who sells illegal drugs.

pederast *n.* man who has homosexual relations with boys. —**pederasty** *n.*

pedestal *n.* base supporting a column, statue, etc.

pedestrian *n.* person who is walking, esp. in a street. —*adj.* dull, uninspiring. —**pedestrian crossing** place marked where pedestrians may cross a road. —**pedestrian precinct** (shopping) area for pedestrians only.

pedicel *n.* small short stalk of a leaf, flower, or fruit.

pedicure *n.* medical or cosmetic treatment of the feet.

pedigree *n.* register of ancestors, esp. of a purebred animal.

pediment *n.* triangular part over a door etc.

pedlar *n.* person who sells goods from door to door.

pedometer [pid-**dom**-it-er] *n.* instrument which measures the distance walked.

peduncle *n.* flower stalk; *Anat.* stalklike structure.

pee *Informal* —*v.* **peeing, peed.** urinate. —*n.* urinating.

peek *v., n.* peep or glance.

peel *v.* remove the skin or rind of (a vegetable or fruit); (of skin or a surface) come off in flakes. —*n.* rind or skin. —**peelings** *pl. n.*

peep[1] *v.* look slyly or quickly. —*n.* peeping look. —**Peeping Tom** man who furtively watches women undressing.

peep[2] *v.* make a small shrill noise. —*n.* small shrill noise.

peer[1] *n.* nobleman (**peeress** *fem.*); person of the same status, age, etc. —**peerage** *n.* whole body of peers; rank of a peer. —**peerless** *adj.* unequalled, unsurpassed. —**peer group** group of people of similar age, status, etc.

peer[2] *v.* look closely and intently.

peeved *adj. Informal* annoyed.

peevish *adj.* fretful; irritable. —**peevishly** *adv.* —**peevishness** *n.*

peewit *n.* same as LAPWING.

peg *n.* pin or clip for joining, fastening, marking, etc.; hook or knob for hanging things on. —*v.* **pegging, pegged.** fasten with pegs; stabilize (prices). —**off the peg** (of clothes) ready-to-wear, not tailor-made.

peignoir [pay-**nwahr**] *n.* woman's light dressing gown.

pejorative [pij-**jor**-a-tiv] *adj.* (of words etc.) with an insulting or critical connotation.

Pekin(g)ese *n., pl.* **-ese.** small dog with a short wrinkled muzzle.

pelargonium *n.* plant with red, white, or pink flowers.

pelican *n.* large water bird with a pouch beneath its bill for storing fish. —**pelican crossing** pedestrian crossing with pedestrian-operated traffic lights.

pellagra *n.* disease caused by lack of vitamin B.

pellet *n.* small ball of something.

pell-mell *adv.* in utter confusion, headlong.

pellucid *adj.* very clear.

pelmet *n.* ornamental drapery or board, concealing a curtain rail.

pelt[1] *v.* throw missiles at; run fast, rush; rain heavily. —**at full pelt** at top speed.

pelt[2] *n.* skin of a fur-bearing animal.

THESAURUS

pedantic abstruse, academic, bookish, didactic, donnish, formal, fussy, overnice, particular, pedagogic, pompous, precise, priggish, stilted

peddle hawk, market, sell, trade, vend

pedestal base, foot, foundation, mounting, pier, plinth, stand, support

pedestrian 1. *n.* foot-traveller, walker 2. *adj.* banal, boring, commonplace, dull, flat, humdrum, mediocre, mundane, ordinary, plodding, prosaic

pedigree ancestry, blood, breed, derivation, descent, extraction, family, family tree, genealogy, heritage, line, lineage, race, stemma, stirps, stock

peek spy

peel flake off, pare, scale, skin

peer[1] *n.* 1. baron, count, duke, earl, lord, marquess, nobleman, viscount 2. equal, fellow, like, match

peer[2] *v.* gaze, inspect, peep, scan, snoop, spy

peerage aristocracy, lords and ladies, nobility, peers

peerless excellent, incomparable, matchless, outstanding, unmatched, unrivalled

peevish acrimonious, captious, childish, churlish, cross, crusty, fractious, fretful, grumpy,

DICTIONARY

pelvis *n.* framework of bones at the base of the spine, to which the hips are attached. —**pelvic** *adj.*

pen[1] *n.* instrument for writing in ink. —*v.* **penning, penned.** write or compose. —**pen friend** friend with whom a person corresponds without meeting. —**penknife** *n.* small knife with blade(s) that fold into the handle. —**pen name** name used by an author instead of his or her real name.

pen[2] *n.* small enclosure for domestic animals. —*v.* **penning, penned.** put or keep in a pen.

pen[3] *n.* female swan.

penal [pee-nal] *adj.* of or used in punishment. —**penalize** *v.* impose a penalty on; handicap, hinder. —**penalty** *n.* punishment for a crime or offence; *Sports* handicap or disadvantage imposed for an infringement of a rule.

penance *n.* voluntary self-punishment to make amends for wrongdoing.

pence *n.* a plural of PENNY.

penchant [pon-shon] *n.* inclination or liking.

pencil *n.* thin cylindrical instrument containing graphite, for writing or drawing. —*v.* **-cilling, -cilled.** draw, write, or mark with a pencil.

pendant *n.* ornament worn on a chain round the neck.

pendent *adj.* hanging.

pending *prep.* while waiting for. —*adj.* not yet decided or settled.

pendulous *adj.* hanging, swinging.

pendulum *n.* suspended weight swinging to and fro, esp. as a regulator for a clock.

penetrate *v.* find or force a way into or through; arrive at the meaning of. —**penetrable** *adj.* capable of being penetrated. —**penetrating** *adj.* quick to understand; (of a sound) loud and unpleasant. —**penetration** *n.*

penguin *n.* flightless black-and-white Antarctic sea bird.

penicillin *n.* antibiotic drug effective against a wide range of diseases and infections.

peninsula *n.* strip of land nearly surrounded by water. —**peninsular** *adj.*

penis *n.* organ of copulation and urination in male mammals.

penitent *adj.* feeling sorry for having done wrong. —*n.* someone who is penitent. —**penitence** *n.* —**penitentiary** *n.* *US* prison. —*adj.* (also **penitential**) relating to penance.

pennant *n.* long narrow flag.

pennon *n.* small triangular or swallow-tailed flag.

penny *n., pl.* **pence, pennies.** Brit. bronze coin worth one hundredth of a pound; former Brit. coin worth one twelfth of a shilling. —**penniless** *adj.* having no money; poor.

penology [pee-nol-a-jee] *n.* study of punishment and prison management.

pension[1] *n.* regular payment to people above a certain age, retired employees, widows, etc. —**pensionable** *adj.* —**pensioner** *n.* person receiving a pension. —**pension off** *v.* force (someone) to retire from a job and pay him or her a pension.

pension[2] [pon-syon] *n.* boarding house in Europe.

pensive *adj.* deeply thoughtful, often with a tinge of sadness.

pentacle, pentagram *n.* five-pointed star.

THESAURUS

irritable, petulant, sulky, sullen, surly, testy, touchy, waspish

peg *v.* attach, fasten, fix, join, secure

pelt assail, batter, cast, hurl, pepper, shower, sling, strike, thrash, throw

pen[1] *v.* compose, draft, jot down, write

pen[2] 1. *n.* cage, coop, fold, hutch, sty 2. *v.* cage, confine, enclose, hedge, hurdle

penal corrective, disciplinary, punitive, retributive

penalize discipline, handicap, punish

penalty fine, forfeit, handicap, price, punishment, retribution

penance atonement, penalty, reparation

penchant bent, bias, fondness, inclination, leaning, partiality, predilection, proclivity, propensity, taste, tendency, turn

pending awaiting, imminent, undecided, undetermined, unsettled

penetrate 1. bore, enter, pierce, prick, probe, stab 2. diffuse, enter, get in, infiltrate, permeate, pervade, seep, suffuse

penetration 1. entrance, incision, inroad, piercing, puncturing 2. astuteness, discernment, insight, keenness, perception, shrewdness, wit

penitence contrition, regret, remorse, repentance, shame, sorrow

penitent *adj.* abject, contrite, regretful, remorseful, sorrowful, sorry

pennant banner, ensign, flag, jack, streamer

penniless bankrupt, destitute, needy, poor, ruined

pension allowance, annuity, benefit, superannuation

pensive contemplative, dreamy, grave, melancholy, mournful, musing, preoccupied, reflective, ruminative, sad, serious, sober, solemn, sorrowful, thoughtful, wistful

DICTIONARY

pentagon *n.* geometric figure with five sides; (**P-**) headquarters of the US military. —**pentagonal** *adj.*

pentameter [pen-**tam**-it-er] *n.* line of poetry with five metrical feet.

Pentateuch [**pent**-a-tyuke] *n.* first five books of the Old Testament.

pentathlon *n.* athletic event consisting of five sports.

Pentecost *n.* Christian festival celebrating the descent of the Holy Spirit to the apostles, Whitsuntide; Jewish harvest festival fifty days after Passover.

penthouse *n.* flat built on the roof or top floor of a building.

pent-up *adj.* (of an emotion) not released, repressed.

penultimate *adj.* second last.

penumbra *n., pl.* **-brae, -bras.** partial shadow; in an eclipse, the partially shadowed region which surrounds the full shadow. —**penumbral** *adj.*

penury *n.* extreme poverty. —**penurious** *adj.*

peony *n., pl.* **-nies.** garden plant with showy red, pink, or white flowers.

people *pl. n.* persons generally; the community; one's family. —*sing.* race or nation. —*v.* stock with inhabitants; populate.

pep *n. Informal* high spirits, energy or enthusiasm. —**pep talk** *Informal* talk designed to increase confidence, enthusiasm, etc. —**pep up** *v.* stimulate, invigorate.

pepper *n.* sharp hot condiment made from the fruit of an East Indian climbing plant; colourful tropical fruit used as a vegetable, capsicum. —*v.* season with pepper; sprinkle, dot; pelt with missiles. —**peppery** *adj.* tasting of pepper; irritable. —**peppercorn** *n.* dried berry of the pepper plant. —**peppercorn rent** low or nominal rent.

peppermint *n.* plant that yields an oil with a strong sharp flavour; sweet flavoured with this.

peptic *adj.* relating to digestion or the digestive juices.

per *prep.* for each; in the manner of.

per annum *adv. Latin* in each year.

per capita *adj., adv. Latin* of or for each person.

per se [per say] *adv. Latin* in itself.

perambulate *v.* walk through or about (a place). —**perambulation** *n.* —**perambulator** *n.* pram.

percale *n.* woven cotton used esp. for sheets.

perceive *v.* become aware of (something) through the senses; understand.

percentage *n.* proportion or rate per hundred. —**per cent** in each hundred.

perceptible *adj.* discernible, recognizable.

perception *n.* act of perceiving; intuitive judgment. —**perceptive** *adj.*

perch[1] *n.* resting place for a bird. —*v.* alight, rest, or place on or as if on a perch.

perch[2] *n.* edible freshwater fish.

perchance *adv. Old-fashioned* perhaps.

percipient *adj.* quick to notice things, observant. —**percipience** *n.*

percolate *v.* pass or filter through small holes; permeate; make (coffee) or (of coffee) be made in a percolator. —**percolation** *n.* —**percolator** *n.* coffeepot in which boiling water is forced through a tube and filters down through coffee.

percussion *n.* striking of one thing against another. —**percussion instrument** musical instrument played by being struck, such as drums or cymbals.

perdition *n.* spiritual ruin.

peregrination *n.* travels, roaming.

peregrine *n.* falcon with dark upper parts and a light underside.

peremptory *adj.* authoritative, imperious.

perennial *adj.* lasting through the years; recurring perpetually. —*n.* plant lasting more than two years. —**perennially** *adv.*

THESAURUS

people *n.* 1. humanity, mankind, mortals, persons 2. citizens, clan, community, family, folk, nation, population, public, race, tribe ~*v.* 3. colonize, inhabit, occupy, populate, settle

perceive behold, descry, discern, discover, espy, note, notice, observe, recognize, remark, see, spot

perceptible appreciable, clear, detectable, discernible, distinct, evident, noticeable, obvious, recognizable, tangible, visible

perception awareness, conception, discernment, feeling, grasp, idea, insight, notion, recognition, sensation, sense, taste, understanding

perceptive acute, alert, astute, aware, discerning, observant, percipient, perspicacious, quick, responsive, sharp

perch 1. *n.* branch, pole, post, roost 2. *v.* alight, balance, land, rest, roost, settle, sit on

percussion blow, brunt, bump, clash, concussion, crash, impact, jolt, knock, shock, smash, thump

peremptory binding, compelling, decisive, final, imperative, obligatory, undeniable

DICTIONARY

perestroika *n.* policy of restructuring the Soviet economy and political system.

perfect *adj.* having all the essential elements, complete; unspoilt; faultless; correct, precise; excellent. —*n.* tense of verb describing an action that has been completed. —*v.* improve; make skilful. —**perfectly** *adv.* —**perfection** *n.* state of being perfect. —**perfectionist** *n.* person who demands the highest standards of excellence. —**perfectionism** *n.*

perfidy *n., pl.* -**dies.** treachery, disloyalty. —**perfidious** *adj.*

perforate *v.* make holes in. —**perforation** *n.*

perforce *adv.* of necessity.

perform *v.* carry out (an action); fulfil (a request etc.); act, sing, or present a play before an audience; work or function. —**performance** *n.* —**performer** *n.*

perfume *n.* liquid cosmetic worn for its pleasant smell; fragrance. —*v.* give a pleasant smell to. —**perfumery** *n.* perfumes in general.

perfunctory *adj.* done only as a matter of routine, superficial. —**perfunctorily** *adv.*

pergola *n.* arch or framework of trellis supporting climbing plants.

perhaps *adv.* it may be (so), possibly.

pericardium *n., pl.* -**dia.** membrane enclosing the heart.

perihelion *n., pl.* -**lia.** point in the orbit of a planet or comet nearest to the sun.

peril *n.* great danger. —**perilous** *adj.* —**perilously** *adv.*

perimeter [per-**rim**-it-er] *n.* (length of) the outer edge of an area.

perinatal *adj.* of or in the weeks shortly before or after birth.

period *n.* particular portion of time; series of years; single occurrence of menstruation; same as FULL STOP. —*adj.* (of furniture, dress, a play, etc.) dating from or in the style of an earlier time in history. —**periodic** *adj.* recurring at intervals. —**periodic table** chart of the elements, arranged to show their relationship to each other. —**periodical** *n.* magazine issued at regular intervals. —*adj.* periodic.

peripatetic [per-rip-a-**tet**-ik] *adj.* travelling about from place to place.

periphery [per-**if**-er-ee] *n., pl.* -**eries.** circumference; fringes of a field of activity. —**peripheral** [per-**if**-er-al] *adj.* unimportant, not central; of or on the periphery.

periphrasis [per-**if**-ra-siss] *n., pl.* -**rases** [-ra-seez]. roundabout speech or expression. —**periphrastic** *adj.*

periscope *n.* instrument used, esp. in submarines, for giving a view of objects on a different level.

perish *v.* be destroyed or die; decay, rot. —**per-**

THESAURUS

perennial abiding, constant, continual, enduring, incessant, inveterate, lifelong, persistent, recurrent, unchanging

perfect *adj.* 1. absolute, complete, consummate, entire, finished, full, sheer, unadulterated, unalloyed, unmitigated, utter, whole 2. blameless, excellent, faultless, flawless, ideal, impeccable, pure, splendid, sublime, superb, supreme, unblemished, unmarred, untarnished

perfection 1. achievement, completion, consummation, evolution, fulfilment, realization 2. completeness, exactness, excellence, faultlessness, integrity, maturity, precision, purity, sublimity, superiority, wholeness 3. acme, crown, ideal, paragon

perfectly 1. altogether, completely, entirely, fully, quite, thoroughly, totally, utterly, wholly 2. admirably, exquisitely, faultlessly, superbly, supremely, wonderfully

perform 1. accomplish, achieve, act, complete, discharge, do, effect, execute, fulfil, satisfy, transact, work 2. act, depict, enact, play, present, produce, render, represent, stage

performance 1. achievement, act, carrying out, completion, conduct, discharge, execution, exploit, feat, fulfilment, work 2. acting, appearance, exhibition, play, portrayal, presentation, production, show

performer actor, actress, artiste, player

perfume aroma, bouquet, fragrance, incense, odour, scent, smell

perfunctory careless, cursory, heedless, indifferent, mechanical, offhand, routine, sketchy, slipshod, slovenly, superficial

perhaps conceivably, feasibly, maybe, possibly

peril danger, hazard, insecurity, jeopardy, menace, pitfall, risk, uncertainty

perimeter ambit, border, bounds, circumference, confines, edge, limit

period interval, season, space, span, spell, stretch, term, time, while

periodical *n.* journal, magazine, monthly, organ, paper, publication, quarterly, review, serial, weekly

perish 1. die, expire, pass away 2. decay, decompose, disintegrate, moulder, rot, waste, wither

perishable decaying, short-lived, unstable

DICTIONARY

ishable *adj.* liable to rot quickly. —**perishing** *adj. Informal* very cold.

peritoneum [per-rit-toe-**nee**-um] *n., pl.* -**nea,** -**neums.** membrane lining the internal surface of the abdomen. —**peritonitis** [per-rit-tone-**ite**-iss] *n.* inflammation of the peritoneum.

periwig *n. Hist.* wig.

periwinkle[1] *n.* small edible shellfish, the winkle.

periwinkle[2] *n.* plant with trailing stems and blue flowers.

perjury [per-jer-ee] *n., pl.* -**juries.** act or crime of lying while under oath in a court. —**perjure** *v.* —**perjure oneself** commit perjury.

perk *n. Informal* incidental benefit gained from a job, such as a company car.

perk up *v.* cheer up. —**perky** *adj.* lively or cheerful.

perm *n.* long-lasting curly hairstyle produced by treating the hair with chemicals. —*v.* give (hair) a perm.

permafrost *n.* permanently frozen ground.

permanent *adj.* lasting forever. —**permanently** *adv.* —**permanence** *n.*

permanganate *n.* a salt of an acid of manganese.

permeate *v.* pervade or pass through the whole of (something). —**permeable** *adj.* able to be permeated, esp. by liquid.

permit *v.* -**mitting,** -**mitted.** give permission; allow, agree to. —*n.* document giving permission to do something. —**permission** *n.* authorization to do something. —**permissible** *adj.* —**permissive** *adj.* (excessively) tolerant, esp. in sexual matters.

permutation *n.* any of the ways a number of things can be arranged or combined.

pernicious *adj.* wicked; extremely harmful, deadly.

pernickety *adj. Informal* (excessively) fussy about details.

peroration *n.* concluding part of a speech, usu. summing up the main points.

peroxide *n.* oxide of a given base containing a high proportion of oxygen; short for HYDROGEN PEROXIDE.

perpendicular *adj.* at right angles to a line or surface; upright or vertical. —*n.* line at right angles to another line or plane.

perpetrate *v.* commit or be responsible for (a wrongdoing). —**perpetration** *n.* —**perpetrator** *n.*

perpetual *adj.* lasting forever; continually repeated. —**perpetually** *adv.* —**perpetuate** *v.* cause to continue or be remembered. —**perpetuation** *n.* —**perpetuity** *n.* eternity. —**in perpetuity** forever.

perplex *v.* puzzle, bewilder. —**perplexity** *n.*

perquisite *n.* same as PERK.

perry *n., pl.* -**ries.** alcoholic drink made from fermented pears.

persecute *v.* treat cruelly because of race, religion, etc.; subject to persistent harassment. —**persecution** *n.* —**persecutor** *n.*

THESAURUS

perjury false statement, forswearing, oath breaking

permanence constancy, continuance, duration, endurance, finality, fixedness, indestructibility, lastingness, perpetuity, stability, survival

permanent abiding, constant, durable, enduring, fixed, immutable, indestructible, invariable, lasting, perpetual, persistent, stable, steadfast

permeate charge, fill, impregnate, infiltrate, penetrate, percolate, pervade, saturate

permissible acceptable, allowable, authorized, lawful, legal, permitted, proper

permission allowance, approval, assent, authorization, consent, dispensation, freedom, go-ahead (*Inf.*), green light, leave, liberty, licence, permit, sanction, sufferance, tolerance

permissive easy-going, forbearing, free, indulgent, lax, lenient, liberal, tolerant

permit 1. *v.* agree, allow, authorize, consent, empower, enable, give leave *or* permission, grant, let, license, sanction, suffer, tolerate, warrant 2. *n.* liberty, licence, pass, passport, permission, sanction, warrant

pernicious bad, baleful, damaging, deadly, deleterious, destructive, detrimental, evil, fatal, harmful, hurtful, offensive, pestilent, poisonous, ruinous, wicked

pernickety carping, exacting, fastidious, finicky, fussy, nice, particular

peroration conclusion, recapitulation

perpendicular at right angles to, straight, upright, vertical

perpetrate commit, do, effect, enact, execute, inflict, perform, wreak

perpetual abiding, endless, enduring, eternal, everlasting, immortal, infinite, lasting, permanent, unchanging, unending

perpetuate maintain, preserve, sustain

perplex baffle, bewilder, confound, confuse, mystify, puzzle, stump

perquisite benefit, bonus, dividend, extra, plus

persecute 1. afflict, distress, harass, hound,

DICTIONARY

persevere v. keep making an effort despite difficulties. **—perseverance** n.

persiflage [per-sif-flahzh] n. light frivolous talk or writing.

persimmon n. sweet red tropical fruit.

persist v. continue in spite of obstacles or objections; continue to be or happen, last. **—persistent** adj. **—persistently** adv. **—persistence** n.

person n. human being; body of a human being; Grammar form of pronouns and verbs that shows if a person is speaking, spoken to, or spoken of. **—in person** actually present.

persona [per-**soh**-na] n., pl. **-nae.** someone's personality as presented to others.

personable adj. pleasant in appearance and personality.

personage n. important person.

personal adj. individual or private; of the body, e.g. personal hygiene; (of a remark etc.) offensive. **—personally** adv. in one's own opinion; directly, not by delegation to others. **—personal computer** small computer used for word processing or computer games. **—personal pronoun** pronoun like I or she that stands for a definite

person. **—personal stereo** very small portable cassette player with headphones.

personify v. **-fying, -fied.** give human characteristics to; be an example of, typify. **—personification** n.

personnel n. people employed in an organization.

perspective n. mental view; method of drawing that gives the effect of solidity and relative distances and sizes.

Perspex n. ® transparent acrylic substitute for glass.

perspicacious adj. having quick mental insight. **—perspicacity** n.

perspire v. sweat. **—perspiration** n. sweat.

persuade v. make (someone) do something by argument, charm, etc.; convince. **—persuasion** n. act of persuading; way of thinking or belief. **—persuasive** adj.

pert adj. bright and cheeky.

pertain v. belong or be relevant (to).

pertinacious adj. very persistent and determined. **—pertinacity** n.

pertinent adj. relevant. **—pertinence** n.

THESAURUS

hunt, ill-treat, injure, maltreat, martyr, molest, oppress, pursue, torment, torture, victimize 2. annoy, badger, bait, bother, pester, tease, vex, worry

perseverance dedication, diligence, endurance, persistence, pertinacity, resolution, stamina, tenacity

persevere carry on, continue, endure, go on, hang on, hold fast, maintain, persist, pursue, remain

persist 1. continue, insist, persevere 2. abide, continue, endure, keep up, last, linger, remain

persistence constancy, diligence, endurance, grit, perseverance, pertinacity, pluck, resolution, tenacity

persistent determined, dogged, immovable, indefatigable, obdurate, obstinate, persevering, pertinacious, resolute, steadfast, steady, stubborn, tenacious, tireless

person being, body, human, individual, soul

personage celebrity, dignitary, luminary, notable, somebody, V.I.P., worthy

personal exclusive, individual, intimate, own, particular, peculiar, private, special

personally 1. alone, independently, solely 2. individually, privately, specially, subjectively

personification embodiment, image, incarnation, likeness, portrayal, recreation, representation, semblance

personify embody, epitomize, exemplify, express, mirror, represent, symbolize, typify

personnel employees, helpers, liveware, members, people, staff, workers

perspective angle, attitude, context, outlook, proportion, relation, relativity

perspire drip, exude, glow, secrete, sweat, swelter

persuade actuate, advise, allure, coax, counsel, entice, impel, induce, influence, prompt, sway, urge

persuasion 1. cajolery, conversion, enticement, inducement, wheedling 2. cogency, force, potency, power 3. belief, conviction, credo, creed, faith, opinion, tenet, views

persuasive cogent, convincing, credible, effective, eloquent, forceful, impressive, influential, logical, moving, plausible, sound, telling, touching, valid, weighty, winning

pertain apply, befit, belong, concern, refer, regard, relate

pertinent admissible, applicable, apposite, appropriate, apt, fit, fitting, germane, material, proper, relevant, suitable

perturb agitate, alarm, bother, disconcert, disquiet, disturb, fluster, trouble, unsettle, upset, vex, worry

DICTIONARY

perturb v. disturb greatly; alarm. —**perturbation** n.

peruke n. Hist. wig.

peruse v. read in a careful or leisurely manner. —**perusal** n.

pervade v. spread right through (something). —**pervasive** adj.

perverse adj. deliberately doing something different from what is thought normal or proper. —**perversely** adv. —**perversity** n.

pervert v. use or alter for a wrong purpose; lead into abnormal (sexual) behaviour. —n. person who practises sexual perversion. —**perversion** n. sexual act or desire considered abnormal; act of perverting.

pervious adj. able to be penetrated, permeable.

peseta n. monetary unit of Spain.

pessary n., pl. **-ries.** appliance worn in the vagina, either to prevent conception or to support the womb; medicated suppository.

pessimism n. tendency to expect the worst in all things. —**pessimist** n. —**pessimistic** adj. —**pessimistically** adv.

pest n. annoying person; insect or animal that damages crops. —**pesticide** n. chemical for killing insect pests.

pester v. annoy or nag continually.

pestilence n. deadly epidemic disease. —**pestilential** adj. annoying, troublesome; deadly.

pestle n. club-shaped implement for grinding things to powder in a mortar.

pet n. animal kept for pleasure and companionship; person favoured or indulged. —v. **petting,**

petted. treat as a pet; pat or stroke affectionately; Informal kiss and caress erotically.

petal n. one of the white or coloured outer parts of a flower. —**petalled** adj.

petard n. Hist. explosive device. —**hoist with one's own petard** being the victim of one's own schemes.

peter out v. gradually come to an end.

petite adj. (of a woman) small and dainty.

petition n. formal request, esp. one signed by many people and presented to parliament. —v. present a petition to. —**petitioner** n.

petrel n. long-winged dark-coloured sea bird.

petrify v. **-fying, -fied.** frighten severely; turn to stone. —**petrification** n.

petrochemical n. a substance, such as acetone, obtained from petroleum.

petrol n. inflammable liquid obtained from petroleum, used as fuel in internal-combustion engines. —**petrol bomb** home-made incendiary device consisting of a bottle filled with petrol.

petroleum n. crude oil found underground.

petticoat n. woman's skirt-shaped undergarment.

pettifogging adj. overconcerned with unimportant detail.

pettish adj. fretful, irritable.

petty adj., **-tier, -tiest.** unimportant, trivial; small-minded; on a small scale, e.g. petty crime. —**pettiness** n. —**petty cash** cash kept by a firm to pay minor expenses. —**petty officer** noncommissioned officer in the navy.

THESAURUS

peruse browse, check, examine, inspect, read, scan, scrutinize, study

pervade affect, charge, diffuse, extend, fill, imbue, infuse, penetrate, percolate, permeate, suffuse

pervasive common, extensive, general, inescapable, prevalent, rife, universal, widespread

perverse abnormal, contradictory, deviant, improper, incorrect, miscreant, rebellious, refractory, troublesome, unhealthy, unreasonable

pervert v. 1. abuse, distort, falsify, garble, misuse, twist, warp 2. corrupt, debase, debauch, degrade, deprave, subvert ~n. 3. debauchee, degenerate, deviant

pessimism cynicism, depression, despair, despondency, distrust, gloom, hopelessness, melancholy

pessimist cynic, defeatist, worrier

pessimistic bleak, cynical, dark, dejected, depressed, distrustful, gloomy, glum, hopeless, morose, resigned, sad

pest 1. annoyance, bother, irritation, nuisance, thorn in one's flesh, trial, vexation 2. bane, blight, bug, curse, epidemic, infection, pestilence, plague, scourge

pester annoy, badger, bother, disturb, fret, get at, harass, harry, irk, nag, pick on, plague, torment, worry

pestilence 1. epidemic, plague, visitation 2. blight, cancer, curse, scourge

pestilential annoying, dangerous, destructive, evil, foul, harmful, injurious, pernicious, ruinous

pet n. 1. darling, favourite, idol, jewel, treasure ~v. 2. baby, coddle, cosset, pamper, spoil 3. caress, fondle, pat, stroke

peter out dwindle, ebb, evaporate, fade, fail, stop, wane

petition 1. n. address, appeal, entreaty, plea, prayer, request, suit, supplication 2. v. adjure,

DICTIONARY

petulant *adj.* childishly irritable or peevish. —**petulantly** *adv.* —**petulance** *n.*

petunia *n.* garden plant with funnel-shaped flowers.

pew *n.* fixed benchlike seat in a church; *Informal* chair, seat.

pewter *n.* greyish metal made of tin and lead.

phalanger *n.* long-tailed Aust. tree-dwelling marsupial.

phalanx *n., pl.* **phalanxes, phalanges.** closely grouped mass of people.

phalarope *n.* small wading bird.

phallus *n., pl.* **-li, -luses.** penis, esp. as a symbol of reproductive power in primitive rites. —**phallic** *adj.*

phantasm *n.* unreal vision, illusion. —**phantasmal** *adj.*

phantasmagoria *n.* shifting medley of dreamlike figures.

phantasy *n., pl.* **-sies.** same as FANTASY.

phantom *n.* ghost; unreal vision.

Pharaoh [**fare**-oh] *n.* title of the ancient Egyptian kings.

pharisee *n.* self-righteous hypocrite. —**pharisaic(al)** *adj.*

pharmaceutical *adj.* of pharmacy.

pharmacology *n.* study of drugs. —**pharmacological** *adj.* —**pharmacologist** *n.*

pharmacopoeia [far-ma-koh-**pee**-a] *n.* book with a list of and directions for the use of drugs.

pharmacy *n., pl.* **-cies.** preparation and dispensing of drugs and medicines; pharmacist's shop. —**pharmacist** *n.* person qualified to prepare and sell drugs and medicines.

pharynx [**far**-rinks] *n., pl.* **pharynges, phar-**ynxes. cavity forming the back part of the mouth. —**pharyngeal** *adj.* —**pharyngitis** [far-rin-**jite**-iss] *n.* inflammation of the pharynx.

phase *n.* any distinct or characteristic stage in a development or chain of events. —*v.* arrange or carry out in stages or to coincide with something else. —**phase in** *or* **out** *v.* introduce *or* discontinue gradually.

PhD Doctor of Philosophy.

pheasant *n.* game bird with bright plumage.

phenobarbitone *n.* drug inducing sleep or relaxation.

phenol *n.* chemical used in disinfectants and antiseptics.

phenomenon *n., pl.* **-ena.** anything appearing or observed; remarkable person or thing. —**phenomenal** *adj.* extraordinary, outstanding. —**phenomenally** *adv.*

phial *n.* small bottle for medicine etc.

philadelphus *n.* shrub with sweet-scented flowers.

philanderer *n.* man who flirts or has many casual love affairs. —**philandering** *n.*

philanthropy *n.* practice of helping people less well-off than oneself. —**philanthropic** *adj.* —**philanthropist** *n.*

philately [fill-**lat**-a-lee] *n.* stamp collecting. —**philatelic** *adj.* —**philatelist** *n.*

philharmonic *adj.* (in names of orchestras etc.) music-loving.

philistine *adj., n.* boorishly uncultivated (person). —**philistinism** *n.*

philology *n.* science of the structure and development of languages. —**philological** *adj.* —**philologist** *n.*

THESAURUS

appeal, ask, beg, beseech, crave, entreat, plead, pray, press, solicit, sue, urge

petty inferior, insignificant, little, negligible, paltry, slight, small, trifling

petulance ill humour, irritability, peevishness, pique, sulkiness, sullenness

petulant bad-tempered, captious, crabbed, cross, crusty, fretful, impatient, irritable, moody, peevish, querulous, sour, sulky, sullen

phantom apparition, ghost, spectre, spirit, wraith

phase aspect, chapter, juncture, period, point, position, stage, state, step, time

phase out close, ease off, eliminate, pull out, remove, replace, terminate, wind down, withdraw

phenomenal fantastic, marvellous, miraculous,

prodigious, remarkable, sensational, singular, unique, unusual, wondrous

phenomenon 1. circumstance, episode, event, fact, happening, incident, occurrence 2. marvel, miracle, prodigy, rarity, sensation, sight, spectacle

philanthropic altruistic, benevolent, benignant, charitable, gracious, humanitarian, kind, munificent

philanthropist alms-giver, altruist, benefactor, contributor, donor, patron

philanthropy altruism, benevolence, benignity, bounty, charitableness, charity, generosity, kind-heartedness, liberality, munificence, patronage

philistine 1. *n.* barbarian, bourgeois, lout, lowbrow, vulgarian, yahoo 2. *adj.* anti-

DICTIONARY

philosophy *n., pl.* **-phies.** study of the meaning of life, knowledge, thought, etc.; theory or set of ideas held by a particular philosopher; person's outlook on life. —**philosopher** *n.* person who studies philosophy. —**philosophical** *adj.* of philosophy; calm in the face of difficulties or disappointments. —**philosophically** *adv.* —**philosophize** *v.* talk in a boring and pretentious manner about basic things.

philtre *n.* magic drink supposed to arouse love in the person who drinks it.

phlebitis [fleb-**bite**-iss] *n.* inflammation of a vein.

phlegm [**flem**] *n.* thick yellowish substance formed in the nose and throat during a cold.

phlegmatic [fleg-**mat**-ik] *adj.* not easily excited, unemotional. —**phlegmatically** *adv.*

phlox *n., pl.* **phlox, phloxes.** flowering garden plant.

phobia *n.* intense and unreasoning fear or dislike.

phoenix *n.* legendary bird said to set fire to itself and rise anew from its ashes.

phone *n., v. Informal* telephone. —**phonecard** *n.* public telephone operated by a special card; the card itself. —**phone-in** *n.* broadcast in which telephone comments or questions from the public are transmitted live.

phonetic *adj.* of speech sounds; (of spelling) written as sounded. —**phonetics** *pl. n.* science of speech sounds. —**phonetically** *adv.*

phon(e)y *Informal* —*adj.* **phonier, phoniest.** not genuine; false; insincere. —*n., pl.* **phonies.** phoney person or thing.

phonograph *n. US or Old-fashioned* record player.

phonology *n., pl.* **-gies.** study of the speech sounds in a language. —**phonological** *adj.*

phosgene [**foz**-jean] *n.* poisonous gas used in warfare.

phosphorescence *n.* faint glow in the dark. —**phosphorescent** *adj.*

phosphorus *n.* toxic flammable nonmetallic element which appears luminous in the dark. —**phosphate** *n.* compound of phosphorus; fertilizer containing phosphorus.

photo *n., pl.* **photos.** short for PHOTOGRAPH. —**photo finish** finish of a race in which the contestants are so close that a photo is needed to decide the result.

photocopy *n., pl.* **-copies.** photographic reproduction. —*v.* make a photocopy of.

photoelectric *adj.* using or worked by electricity produced by the action of light.

photogenic *adj.* always looking attractive in photographs.

photograph *n.* picture made by the chemical action of light on sensitive film. —*v.* take a photograph of. —**photographer** *n.* —**photographic** *adj.* —**photography** *n.* art of taking photographs.

photogravure *n.* process in which an etched metal plate for printing is produced by photography.

photolithography *n.* lithographic printing process using photographically made plates.

photometer [foe-**tom**-it-er] *n.* instrument for measuring the intensity of light.

Photostat *n.* ® type of photocopying machine; copy made by it.

photosynthesis *n.* process by which a green plant uses sunlight to build up carbohydrate reserves.

phrase *n.* group of words forming a unit of meaning, esp. within a sentence; short effective expression. —*v.* express in words. —**phrasal verb** phrase consisting of a verb and an adverb or preposition, with a meaning different from the parts, such as *take in* meaning *deceive.*

THESAURUS

intellectual, crass, ignorant, lowbrow, tasteless, uneducated, unrefined

philosopher logician, metaphysician, sage, theorist, thinker

philosophical 1. abstract, erudite, learned, logical, rational, theoretical, thoughtful, wise 2. calm, collected, composed, cool, impassive, imperturbable, patient, resigned, serene, stoical, tranquil, unruffled

philosophy 1. knowledge, logic, metaphysics, rationalism, reason, reasoning, thinking, thought, wisdom 2. beliefs, doctrine, ideology, principle, tenets, thinking, values, viewpoint

phlegmatic apathetic, cold, dull, frigid, heavy,

impassive, listless, placid, sluggish, stoical, stolid, unemotional

phobia aversion, dislike, distaste, dread, fear, hatred, horror, obsession, repulsion, revulsion, terror

phone *n.* 1. telephone 2. call, ring ~*v.* 3. ring, ring up, telephone

phoney 1. *adj.* affected, assumed, bogus, fake, false, forged, imitation, sham, trick 2. *n.* fake, forgery, fraud, humbug, impostor, pretender, sham

photograph 1. *n.* image, likeness, picture, print, shot, slide, snapshot 2. *v.* film, record, shoot, take

DICTIONARY

phraseology *n., pl.* **-gies.** way in which words are used.

phut *n. Informal* **—go phut** *v.* (of a machine) break down.

phylactery *n., pl.* **-teries.** leather case containing religious texts, worn by Jewish men.

physical *adj.* of the body, as contrasted with the mind or spirit; of material things or nature; of physics. **—physically** *adv.* **—physical geography** branch of geography dealing with the features of the earth's surface.

physician *n.* doctor of medicine.

physics *n.* science of the properties of matter and energy. **—physicist** *n.* person skilled in, or studying, physics.

physiognomy [fiz-ee-**on**-om-ee] *n., pl.* **-mies.** face.

physiology *n.* science of the normal function of living things. **—physiological** *adj.* **—physiologist** *n.*

physiotherapy *n.* treatment of disease or injury by physical means such as massage, rather than by drugs. **—physiotherapist** *n.*

physique *n.* person's bodily build and muscular development.

pi *n., pl.* **pis.** *Maths* ratio of the circumference of a circle to its diameter.

pianissimo *Music* very quietly.

piano[1] *n., pl.* **pianos.** (*orig.* **pianoforte**) musical instrument with strings which are struck by hammers worked by a keyboard. **—pianist** *n.* **—Pianola** *n.* ® mechanically played piano.

piano[2] *Music* quietly.

piazza *n.* square or marketplace, esp. in Italy.

pibroch [**pee**-brok] *n.* form of bagpipe music.

pic *n., pl.* **pics, pix.** *Informal* photograph or illustration.

pica [**pie**-ka] *n.* printing type of 6 lines to the inch; typewriter typesize of 10 letters to the inch.

picador *n.* mounted bullfighter with a lance.

picaresque *adj.* denoting a type of fiction in which the hero, a rogue, has a series of adventures.

piccalilli *n.* pickle of vegetables in mustard sauce.

piccaninny *n., pl.* **-nies.** *Offens.* Black child.

piccolo *n., pl.* **-los.** small flute.

pick[1] *v.* choose; remove (flowers or fruit) from a plant; remove loose particles from; take hold of and move with the fingers; provoke (a fight etc.) deliberately; open (a lock) by means other than a key. **—***n.* choice, e.g. *take your pick;* best part. **—pick-me-up** *n. Informal* tonic; stimulating drink. **—pick on** *v.* find fault with. **—pick out** *v.* recognize, distinguish. **—pickpocket** *n.* thief who steals from someone's pocket. **—pick up** *v.* raise, lift; collect; improve, get better; become acquainted with for a sexual purpose; accelerate. **—pick-up** *n.* device for conversion of mechanical energy into electric signals, as in a record player; small truck; casual acquaintance made for a sexual purpose.

pick[2] *n.* tool with a curved iron crossbar and wooden shaft, for breaking up hard ground or masonry.

pickaback *n.* same as PIGGYBACK.

pickaxe *n.* large pick.

picket *n.* person or group standing outside a workplace to deter would-be workers during a strike; sentry or sentries posted to give warning of an attack; pointed stick used as part of a fence. **—***v.* form a picket outside (a workplace). **—picket line** line of people acting as pickets.

pickings *pl. n.* money easily acquired.

pickle *n.* food preserved in vinegar or salt water; *Informal* awkward situation. **—***v.* preserve in vinegar or salt water. **—pickled** *adj. Informal* drunk.

picnic *n.* informal meal out of doors. **—***v.* **-nicking, -nicked.** have a picnic.

Pict *n.* member of an ancient race of N Britain. **—Pictish** *adj.*

pictorial *adj.* of or in painting or pictures; illustrated. **—***n.* newspaper etc. with many pictures. **—pictorially** *adv.*

THESAURUS

phrase 1. *n.* expression, idiom, locution, motto, remark, saying, tag, utterance 2. *v.* couch, express, formulate, frame, present, put, say, term, utter, voice, word

physical 1. bodily, corporal, earthly, fleshly, incarnate, mortal 2. material, natural, real, sensible, solid, substantial, visible

physique body, build, constitution, figure, form, frame, make-up, shape

pick *v.* 1. choose, elect, hand-pick, mark out, opt

for, select, sort out 2. collect, cull, cut, gather, harvest, pluck, pull ~*n.* 3. choice, decision, option, preference, selection 4. elect, elite, flower, pride, prize

picket *n.* 1. pale, paling, post, stake, stanchion, upright 2. protester 3. guard, lookout, patrol, scout, sentinel, sentry, spotter, watch ~*v.* 4. blockade, boycott, demonstrate

pick-me-up drink, refreshment, restorative, stimulant, tonic

pick up 1. gather, grasp, hoist, lift, raise, take

DICTIONARY

picture *n.* drawing or painting; photograph; mental image; beautiful or picturesque object; image on a TV screen. —*pl.* cinema. —*v.* visualize, imagine; represent in a picture. —**picturesque** *adj.* (of a place or view) pleasant to look at; (of language) forceful, vivid. —**picture window** large window made of a single sheet of glass.

piddle *v. Informal* urinate.

pidgin *n.* language, not a mother tongue, made up of elements of two or more other languages.

pie *n.* dish of meat, fruit, etc. baked in pastry. —**pie chart** circular diagram with sectors representing quantities.

piebald *n., adj.* (horse) with irregular black-and-white markings.

piece *n.* separate bit or part; instance, e.g. *a piece of luck;* example, specimen; coin; literary or musical composition; small object used in draughts, chess, etc. —**piece together** *v.* make or assemble bit by bit.

pièce de résistance [pyess de ray-**ziss**-tonss] *n. French* most impressive item.

piecemeal *adv.* a bit at a time.

piecework *n.* work paid for according to the quantity produced.

pied *adj.* having markings of two or more colours.

pied-à-terre [pyay da **tair**] *n., pl.* **pieds-à-terre** [pyay da **tair**]. small flat or house for occasional use.

pie-eyed *adj. Slang* drunk.

pier *n.* platform on stilts sticking out into the sea; pillar, esp. one supporting a bridge.

pierce *v.* make a hole in or through with a sharp instrument; make a way through. —**piercing** *adj.*

(of a sound) shrill and high-pitched; (of wind or cold) fierce, penetrating.

pierrot [**pier**-roe] *n.* pantomime character, clown.

piety *n., pl.* **-ties.** deep devotion to God and religion.

piffle *n. Informal* nonsense.

pig *n.* animal kept and killed for pork, ham, and bacon; *Informal* greedy, dirty, or rude person. —**piggish, piggy** *adj. Informal* dirty; greedy; stubborn. —**piggery** *n.* place for keeping and breeding pigs. —**pig-headed** *adj.* obstinate. —**pig iron** crude iron produced in a blast furnace.

pigeon *n.* bird with a heavy body and short legs, sometimes trained to carry messages; *Informal* concern or responsibility. —**pigeonhole** *n.* compartment for papers in a desk etc. —*v.* classify; put aside and do nothing about. —**pigeon-toed** *adj.* with the feet or toes turned inwards.

piggyback *n.* ride on someone's shoulders. —*adv.* carried on someone's shoulders.

pigment *n.* colouring matter, paint or dye. —**pigmentation** *n.*

Pigmy *n., pl.* **-mies,** *adj.* same as PYGMY.

pigtail *n.* plait of hair hanging from the back or either side of the head.

pike[1] *n.* large predatory freshwater fish.

pike[2] *n. Hist.* long-handled spear.

pilaster *n.* square column, usu. set in a wall.

pilau, pilaf(f) *n.* Middle Eastern dish of meat or poultry boiled with rice, spices, etc.

pilchard *n.* small edible sea fish of the herring family.

pile[1] *n.* number of things lying on top of each other; *Informal* large amount; large building. —*v.* collect into a pile; (foll. by *in, out, off,* etc.).

THESAURUS

up, uplift 2. gain, improve, mend, rally, recover 3. call for, collect, get

pictorial graphic, picturesque, scenic, striking, vivid

picture *n.* 1. drawing, effigy, engraving, illustration, image, likeness, painting, photograph, portrait, portrayal, print, sketch 2. account, description, image, impression, report 3. film, movie ~*v.* 4. visualize

picturesque attractive, beautiful, charming, colourful, graphic, pretty, quaint, scenic, striking, vivid

piece 1. bit, chunk, division, fraction, fragment, length, morsel, part, portion, quantity, scrap, section, segment, share, shred, slice 2. article, composition, creation, item, production, study, work

pier 1. jetty, quay, wharf 2. buttress, column, pile, piling, pillar, support, upright

pierce bore, drill, enter, prick, probe, puncture, spike, stab, stick into, transfix

piety devotion, dutifulness, duty, faith, grace, holiness, religion, reverence, veneration

pig boar, hog, piglet, sow, swine

pigeonhole 1. *n.* compartment, locker, niche, place, section 2. *v.* defer, file, postpone, put off, shelve

pig-headed contrary, inflexible, mulish, obstinate, perverse, self-willed, stubborn, stupid, wilful

pigment colour, dye, dyestuff, paint, stain, tincture, tint

DICTIONARY

move in a group. —**pile-up** *n.* *Informal* traffic accident involving several vehicles.

pile² *n.* beam driven into the ground, esp. as a foundation for building in water or wet ground.

pile³ *n.* fibres of a carpet or a fabric, esp. velvet, that stand up from the weave.

piles *pl. n.* swollen veins in the rectum, haemorrhoids.

pilfer *v.* steal in small quantities.

pilgrim *n.* person who journeys to a holy place. —**pilgrimage** *n.*

pill *n.* small ball of medicine swallowed whole. —**the pill** pill taken by a woman to prevent pregnancy. —**pillbox** *n.* small box for pills; small concrete fort.

pillage *v.* steal property by violence in war. —*n.* violent seizure of goods, esp. in war.

pillar *n.* slender upright post, usu. supporting a roof; strong supporter. —**pillar box** red pillar-shaped letter box in the street.

pillion *n.* seat for a passenger behind the rider of a motorcycle.

pillory *n.*, *pl.* **-ries.** *Hist.* frame with holes for the head and hands in which an offender was locked and exposed to public abuse. —*v.* **-rying, -ried.** ridicule publicly.

pillow *n.* stuffed cloth bag for supporting the head in bed. —*v.* rest as if on a pillow. —**pillow case** removable cover for a pillow.

pilot *n.* person qualified to fly an aircraft or spacecraft; person employed to steer a ship entering or leaving a harbour. —*adj.* experimental and preliminary. —*v.* act as the pilot of; guide, steer. —**pilot light** small flame lighting the main one in a gas appliance.

pimento *n.*, *pl.* **-tos.** mild-tasting red pepper.

pimp *n.* man who gets customers for a prostitute in return for a share of his or her earnings. —*v.* act as a pimp.

pimpernel *n.* wild plant with small flowers that close in dull weather.

pimple *n.* small pus-filled spot on the skin. —**pimply** *adj.*

pin *n.* short thin piece of stiff wire with a point and head, for fastening things; wooden or metal peg or stake. —*v.* **pinning, pinned.** fasten with a pin; seize and hold fast. —**pin down** *v.* force (someone) to make a decision, take action, etc.; define clearly. —**pinball** *n.* electrically operated table game, in which a small ball is shot through various hazards. —**pin money** small amount earned to buy small luxuries. —**pinpoint** *v.* locate or identify exactly. —**pinstripe** *n.* very narrow stripe in fabric; the fabric itself. —**pin-up** *n.* picture of a sexually attractive person, esp. (partly) naked.

pinafore *n.* apron; dress with a bib top.

pince-nez [panss-**nay**] *n.*, *pl.* **pince-nez.** glasses kept in place only by a clip on the bridge of the nose.

pincers *pl. n.* tool consisting of two hinged arms, for gripping; claws of a lobster etc.

pinch *v.* squeeze between finger and thumb; cause pain by being too tight; *Informal* steal; *Informal* arrest. —*n.* act of pinching; as much as can be taken up between the finger and thumb. —**at a pinch** if absolutely necessary. —**feel the pinch** have to economize.

pinchbeck *n.* alloy of zinc and copper, used as imitation gold.

pine¹ *n.* evergreen coniferous tree; its wood. —**pine cone** woody cone-shaped fruit of the pine tree. —**pine marten** wild mammal of the coniferous forests of Europe and Asia.

THESAURUS

pile *n.* 1. collection, heap, hoard, mass, mound, mountain, stack, stockpile 2. building, edifice, erection, structure ~*v.* 3. amass, assemble, collect, gather, heap, hoard, load up, mass, stack, store

pile-up accident, collision, crash, smash

pilfer appropriate, embezzle, filch, purloin, rob, steal, take, thieve

pilgrim crusader, traveller, wanderer, wayfarer

pilgrimage crusade, excursion, expedition, journey, mission, tour, trip

pillage 1. *v.* despoil, loot, maraud, plunder, raid, ransack, ravage, rifle, rob, sack, strip 2. *n.* depredation, plunder, rapine, robbery, sack

pillar 1. column, pier, post, prop, shaft, support, upright 2. leader, mainstay, rock, supporter, upholder, worthy

pillory *v.* brand, denounce, lash, show up, stigmatize

pilot 1. *n.* airman, aviator, captain, coxswain, director, flier, guide, helmsman, leader, navigator, steersman 2. *v.* conduct, control, direct, drive, fly, guide, handle, lead, manage, navigate, operate, steer 3. *adj.* model, test, trial

pin *v.* 1. affix, attach, fasten, fix, join, secure 2. fix, hold down, hold fast, immobilize, pinion, press, restrain

pinch *v.* 1. grasp, nip, press, squeeze, tweak 2. chafe, confine, cramp, crush, hurt, pain ~*n.* 3. nip, squeeze, tweak 4. bit, dash, jot, mite, small quantity, *soupçon*, speck, taste

pin down constrain, force, make, press, pressurize

DICTIONARY

pine[2] v. (foll. by *for*) feel great longing (for); become thin and ill through grief etc.

pineal gland [pin-ee-al] n. small cone-shaped gland at the base of the brain.

pineapple n. large tropical fruit with juicy yellow flesh and a hard skin.

ping v., n. (make) a short high-pitched sound. —**pinger** n. device, esp. a timer, that makes a pinging sound.

Ping-Pong n. ® table tennis.

pinion[1] n. bird's wing. —v. immobilize (someone) by tying or holding his or her arms.

pinion[2] n. small cogwheel.

pink n. pale reddish colour; fragrant garden plant. —adj. of the colour pink. —v. (of an engine) make a metallic noise because not working properly, knock. —**in the pink** in good health.

pinking shears pl. n. scissors with a serrated edge that give a wavy edge to material to prevent fraying.

pinnacle n. highest point of success etc.; mountain peak; small slender spire.

pint n. liquid measure, half a quart, gallon (.568 litre).

Pinyin n. system for representing Chinese in Roman letters.

pioneer n. explorer or early settler of a new country; originator or developer of something new. —v. be the pioneer or leader of.

pious adj. deeply religious, devout.

pip[1] n. small seed in a fruit.

pip[2] n. high-pitched sound used as a time signal on radio; *Informal* star on a junior army officer's shoulder showing rank.

pip[3] n. —**give someone the pip** *Slang* annoy someone.

pipe n. tube for conveying liquid or gas; tube with a small bowl at the end for smoking tobacco; tubular musical instrument. —pl. bagpipes. —v. play on a pipe; utter in a shrill tone; convey by pipe; decorate with piping. —**piper** n. player on a pipe or bagpipes. —**piping** n. system of pipes; decoration of icing on a cake etc.; fancy edging on clothes. —**piped music** recorded music played as background music in public places. —**pipe down** v. *Informal* stop talking. —**pipe dream** fanciful impossible plan etc. —**pipeline** n. long pipe for transporting oil, water, etc.; means of communication. —**in the pipeline** in preparation. —**pipe up** v. speak suddenly or shrilly.

pipette n. slender glass tube used to transfer or measure fluids.

pipit n. small brownish bird.

pippin n. type of eating apple.

piquant [pee-kant] adj. having a pleasant spicy taste; mentally stimulating. —**piquancy** n.

piqué [pee-kay] n. stiff ribbed cotton fabric.

pique [peek] n. feeling of hurt pride, baffled curiosity, or resentment. —v. hurt the pride of; arouse (curiosity).

piquet [pik-ket] n. card game for two.

piranha n. small fierce freshwater fish of tropical America.

pirate n. sea robber; person who illegally publishes or sells work owned by someone else; person or company that broadcasts illegally. —v. sell or reproduce (artistic work etc.) illegally. —**piracy** n. —**piratical** adj.

pirouette v., n. (make) a spinning turn balanced on the toes of one foot.

piscatorial adj. of fishing or fishes.

piss *Taboo* —v. to urinate. —n. act of urinating; urine.

THESAURUS

pinion v. bind, chain, fasten, manacle, shackle, tie

pink adj. flesh, flushed, reddish, rose, roseate, rosy, salmon

pinnacle acme, apex, crest, crown, height, meridian, peak, summit, top, vertex, zenith

pinpoint define, distinguish, identify, locate, spot

pioneer n. 1. colonist, explorer, settler 2. developer, founder, innovator, leader, trailblazer ~v. 3. create, develop, discover, establish, initiate, instigate, institute, invent, launch, originate, prepare, start

pious dedicated, devoted, devout, godly, holy, religious, reverent, saintly, spiritual

pipe n. 1. conduit, duct, hose, line, main, passage, tube 2. briar, clay, meerschaum 3. fife, horn, tooter, whistle ~v. 4. cheep, peep, play, sing, sound, warble, whistle

pipe down hush, shush, silence

piquant biting, peppery, pungent, savoury, sharp, spicy, tart

pique 1. n. annoyance, displeasure, grudge, huff, irritation, offence, resentment, umbrage, vexation 2. v. affront, annoy, displease, incense, irk, mortify, nettle, offend, provoke, rile, sting, vex, wound

piracy freebooting, hijacking, plagiarism, rapine, stealing, theft

pirate n. 1. corsair, freebooter, marauder, raider, rover 2. infringer, plagiarist ~v. 3. borrow, copy, plagiarize, poach, reproduce, steal

DICTIONARY

pistachio *n., pl.* **-os.** edible nut of a Mediterranean tree.

piste [**peest**] *n.* ski slope.

pistil *n.* seed-bearing part of a flower.

pistol *n.* short-barrelled handgun.

piston *n.* cylindrical part in an engine that slides to and fro in a cylinder.

pit *n.* deep hole in the ground; coal mine; dent or depression; servicing and refuelling area on a motor-racing track; same as ORCHESTRA PIT. —*v.* **pitting, pitted.** mark with small dents or scars. —**pit one's wits against** compete against in a test or contest.

pitch[1] *v.* throw, hurl; set up (a tent); fall headlong; (of a ship or plane) move with the front and back going up and down alternately; set the level or tone of. —*n.* area marked out for playing sport; degree or angle of slope; degree of highness or lowness of a (musical) sound; place where a street or market trader regularly sells; *Informal* persuasive sales talk. —**pitcher** *n.* —**pitch in** *v.* join in enthusiastically. —**pitch into** *v. Informal* attack.

pitch[2] *n.* dark sticky substance obtained from tar. —**pitch-black, -dark** *adj.* very dark.

pitchblende *n.* mineral composed largely of uranium oxide, yielding radium.

pitcher *n.* large jug with a narrow neck.

pitchfork *n.* large long-handled fork for lifting hay. —*v.* thrust abruptly or violently.

pitfall *n.* hidden difficulty or danger.

pith *n.* soft white lining of the rind of oranges etc.; soft tissue in the stems of certain plants; essential part. —**pithy** *adj.* short and full of meaning.

piton [**peet**-on] *n.* metal spike used in climbing to secure a rope.

pittance *n.* very small allowance of money.

pituitary *n., pl.* **-taries.** (also **pituitary gland**) gland at the base of the brain, that helps to control growth.

pity *n., pl.* **-ties.** sympathy or sorrow for others' suffering; regrettable fact. —*v.* **pitying, pitied.** feel pity for. —**piteous, pitiable** *adj.* arousing pity. —**pitiful** *adj.* arousing pity; woeful, contemptible. —**pitifully** *adv.* —**pitiless** *adj.* feeling no pity, hard, merciless.

pivot *n.* central shaft on which something turns. —*v.* provide with or turn on a pivot. —**pivotal** *adj.* of crucial importance.

pix *n. Informal* a plural of PIC.

pixie *n.* (in folklore) fairy.

pizza *n.* flat disc of dough covered with a wide variety of savoury toppings and baked.

pizzazz *n. Informal* attractive combination of energy and style.

pizzicato [pit-see-**kah**-toe] *Music* played by plucking the string of a violin etc. with the finger.

placard *n.* large board with a slogan on it that is carried or displayed in public.

placate *v.* make (someone) stop feeling angry or upset. —**placatory** *adj.*

place *n.* particular part of an area or space; particular town, building, etc.; position or point reached; usual position; duty or right; position of employment; seat or space. —*v.* put in a particular place; identify, put in context; make (an order, bet, etc.). —**be placed** (of a competitor in a race) be among the first three. —**take place** happen, occur.

THESAURUS

pit abyss, cavity, chasm, coal mine, crater, dent, depression, dimple, gulf, hole, hollow, mine, pothole

pitch *v.* 1. cast, fling, hurl, launch, sling, throw, toss 2. erect, fix, locate, place, plant, put up, raise, settle, set up, station ~*n.* 3. angle, dip, gradient, incline, slope, tilt 4. degree, height, level, point, summit 5. harmonic, modulation, sound, timbre, tone 6. line, patter, sales talk 7. ground, sports field

pitch-black dark, ebony, inky, jet, jet-black, pitch-dark, raven, sable, unlit

piteous affecting, deplorable, distressing, grievous, lamentable, miserable, mournful, moving, plaintive, poignant, sad, sorrowful, woeful, wretched

pitfall catch, danger, difficulty, drawback, hazard, peril, snag, trap

pith core, crux, essence, gist, heart, kernel, marrow, meat, nub, point, salient point

pitiful distressing, grievous, lamentable, miserable, pathetic, sad, woeful, wretched

pitiless brutal, callous, cruel, harsh, heartless, implacable, inhuman, merciless, relentless, ruthless, unmerciful

pittance allowance, drop, mite, modicum, ration, slave wages, trifle

pity 1. *n.* charity, compassion, condolence, fellow feeling, forbearance, kindness, mercy, sympathy, tenderness, understanding 2. *v.* commiserate with, feel for, grieve for, weep for

pivot 1. *n.* axis, spindle, swivel 2. *v.* revolve, rotate, spin, swivel, turn, twirl

placard advertisement, bill, poster, sticker

placate appease, calm, conciliate, humour, mollify, pacify, satisfy, soothe

DICTIONARY

placebo [plas-see-bo] *n., pl.* **-bos, -boes.** sugar pill etc. given to an unsuspecting patient as an active drug.

placenta [plass-ent-a] *n., pl.* **-tas, -tae.** organ formed in the womb during pregnancy, providing nutrients for the fetus. —**placental** *adj.*

placid *adj.* calm, not easily excited or upset. —**placidity** *n.*

placket *n.* opening at the top of a skirt etc. fastened with buttons or a zip.

plagiarize [play-jer-ize] *v.* steal ideas, passages, etc. from (someone else's work) and present them as one's own. —**plagiarism** *n.*

plague *n.* fast-spreading fatal disease; *Hist.* bubonic plague; widespread infestation. —*v.* **plaguing, plagued.** trouble or annoy continually.

plaice *n.* edible European flatfish.

plaid *n.* long piece of tartan cloth worn as part of Highland dress; tartan cloth or pattern.

plain *adj.* obvious, unmistakable; easy to see or understand; simple, ordinary; without decoration or pattern; expressed honestly and clearly; not beautiful. —*n.* large stretch of level country. —**plainly** *adv.* —**plainness** *n.* —**plain clothes** ordinary clothes, as opposed to uniform. —**plain sailing** easy progress. —**plain speaking** saying exactly what one thinks.

plainsong *n.* unaccompanied singing, esp. in a medieval church.

plaintiff *n.* person who sues in a court of law.

plaintive *adj.* sad, mournful. —**plaintively** *adv.*

plait [platt] *v.* intertwine separate strands to form one ropelike length. —*n.* length of hair that has been plaited.

plan *n.* way thought out to do or achieve something; diagram showing the layout or design of something. —*v.* **planning, planned.** arrange beforehand; make a diagram of.

plane[1] *n.* an aircraft. —*v.* (of a boat) rise and partly skim over water.

plane[2] *n. Maths* flat surface; level of attainment etc.; tool for smoothing wood. —*v.* smooth (wood) with a plane. —*adj.* perfectly flat or level.

plane[3] *n.* tree with broad leaves.

planet *n.* large body in space that revolves round the sun or another star. —**planetary** *adj.*

planetarium *n., pl.* **-iums, -ia.** building where the movements of the stars, planets, etc. are shown by projecting lights on the inside of a dome.

plangent [plan-jent] *adj.* (of sounds) mournful and resounding.

plank *n.* long flat piece of sawn timber.

THESAURUS

place *n.* 1. area, location, locus, point, position, site, situation, spot, station, venue, whereabouts 2. city, district, hamlet, locale, locality, neighbourhood, quarter, region, town, vicinity, village 3. grade, position, rank, station, status 4. appointment, billet (*Inf.*), employment, job, position, post 5. affair, charge, concern, duty, function, prerogative, responsibility, right, role 6. **take place** befall, betide, go on, happen, occur, transpire (*Inf.*) ~*v.* 7. deposit, dispose, establish, fix, install, lay, locate, plant, position, put, rest, set, settle, situate, stand, station, stick 8. arrange, class, classify, grade, group, order, rank, sort

placid calm, collected, composed, cool, even, gentle, mild, peaceful, quiet, serene, still, tranquil

plague 1. *n.* disease, epidemic, infection, pestilence 2. *v.* afflict, annoy, badger, bedevil, bother, disturb, fret, harass, harry, haunt, molest, pain, persecute, pester, tease, torment, torture, trouble, vex

plain *adj.* 1. apparent, clear, comprehensible, distinct, evident, legible, lucid, manifest, obvious, patent, transparent, unmistakable, visible 2. artless, blunt, candid, direct, downright, forthright, frank, guileless, honest, ingenuous, open, outspoken, sincere 3. common, commonplace, everyday, frugal, homely, lowly, modest, ordinary, simple, workaday 4. austere, bare, basic, discreet, modest, muted, pure, restrained, severe, simple, stark, unembellished, unornamented, unvarnished 5. illfavoured, ordinary, ugly, unattractive, unprepossessing ~*n.* 6. flatland, grassland, lowland, plateau, prairie, tableland

plaintive disconsolate, doleful, grief-stricken, grievous, melancholy, mournful, pathetic, piteous, pitiful, rueful, sad, sorrowful, wistful, woeful

plan *n.* 1. design, device, idea, method, plot, procedure, programme, project, proposal, proposition, scenario, scheme, strategy, suggestion, system 2. blueprint, chart, delineation, diagram, drawing, layout, map, representation, scale drawing, sketch ~*v.* 3. arrange, concoct, contrive, design, devise, draft, invent, organize, outline, plot, prepare, represent, scheme, think out

plane *n.* 1. flat surface, level surface 2. condition, degree, footing, level, position, stratum ~*adj.* 3. even, flat, flush, horizontal, level, regular, smooth, uniform

DICTIONARY

plankton *n.* minute animals and plants floating in the surface water of a sea or lake.

plant *n.* living organism that grows in the ground and has no power to move; equipment or machinery used in industrial processes; factory or other industrial premises. —*v.* put in the ground to grow; place firmly in position; *Informal* hide (stolen goods etc.) on a person to make him or her seem guilty; *Informal* put (a person) secretly in an organization to spy. —**planter** *n.* ornamental pot for house plants; owner of a plantation.

plantain[1] *n.* low-growing wild plant with broad leaves.

plantain[2] *n.* tropical fruit like a green banana.

plantation *n.* estate for the cultivation of tea, tobacco, etc.; wood of cultivated trees.

plaque *n.* inscribed commemorative stone or metal plate fixed to a wall; filmy deposit on teeth that causes decay.

plasma *n.* clear liquid part of blood.

plaster *n.* mixture of lime, sand, etc. for coating walls; adhesive strip of material for dressing cuts etc. —*v.* cover with plaster; coat thickly. —**plaster of Paris** white powder which dries to form a hard solid when mixed with water, used for sculptures and casts for broken limbs. —**plastered** *adj. Slang* drunk.

plastic *n.* synthetic material that can be moulded when soft but sets in a hard long-lasting shape. —*adj.* made of plastic; easily moulded, pliant. —**plasticity** *n.* ability to be moulded. —**plastic bullet** solid PVC cylinder fired by police in riot control. —**plastic surgery** repair or reconstruction of missing or malformed parts of the body for medical or cosmetic reasons.

Plasticine *n.* ® soft coloured modelling material used esp. by children.

plate *n.* shallow round dish for holding food; flat thin sheet of metal, glass, etc.; thin coating of metal on another metal; dishes or cutlery made of gold or silver; illustration, usu. on fine quality paper, in a book; *Informal* set of false teeth. —*v.* cover with a thin coating of gold, silver, or other metal. —**plateful** *n.* —**plate glass** kind of thick glass used for mirrors and windows. —**plate tectonics** study of the structure of the earth's crust, esp. the movement of layers of rocks.

plateau *n., pl.* -**teaus,** -**teaux.** area of level high land; stage when there is no change or development.

platen *n.* roller of a typewriter, against which the paper is held; plate in a printing press by which the paper is pressed against the type.

platform *n.* raised floor for speakers; raised area in a station from which passengers board trains; programme of a political party; structure in the sea which holds machinery, stores, etc. for drilling an oil well.

platinum *n.* very valuable silvery-white metal. —**platinum blonde** woman with silvery-blonde hair.

platitude *n.* remark that is true but not interesting or original. —**platitudinous** *adj.*

platonic *adj.* friendly or affectionate but not sexual.

platoon *n.* subunit of a company of soldiers.

platteland *n. S Afr.* rural district.

platter *n.* large dish.

platypus *n.* (also **duck-billed platypus**) Aust. egg-laying amphibious mammal, with dense fur, webbed feet, and a ducklike bill.

plaudit *n.* expression of approval.

plausible *adj.* apparently true or reasonable; persuasive but insincere. —**plausibly** *adv.* —**plausibility** *n.*

play *v.* occupy oneself in (a game or recreation); compete against in a game or sport; behave carelessly; act (a part) on the stage; perform on (a musical instrument); cause (a radio, record player, etc.) to give out sound; move lightly or irregularly, flicker. —*n.* story performed on stage or broadcast; activities children take part in for amusement; playing of a game; conduct, e.g. *fair play*; (scope for) freedom of movement. —**player** *n.* —**playful** *adj.* lively. —**play back** *v.* listen to or watch (something recorded). —**playboy** *n.* rich man who lives only for pleasure.

THESAURUS

plant *n.* 1. bush, flower, herb, shrub, vegetable, weed 2. factory, foundry, mill, shop, works, yard 3. equipment, gear, machinery ~*v.* 4. scatter, seed, set out, sow, transplant

plaster *n.* 1. mortar, stucco 2. bandage, dressing ~*v.* 3. bedaub, besmear, coat, cover, daub, overlay, smear, spread

plastic *adj.* 1. docile, malleable, manageable, pliable, receptive, responsive, tractable 2. ductile, fictile, flexible, mouldable, pliable, pliant, soft, supple

plate 1. dish, platter 2. layer, panel, sheet, slab

plateau highland, table, upland

platform dais, podium, rostrum, stage, stand

platitude bromide, cliché, commonplace, stereotype, truism

plausible believable, credible, glib, possible, probable, reasonable, smooth, specious, tenable

DICTIONARY

—**play down** v. minimize the importance of.
—**playgroup** n. regular meeting of very young children for supervised play. —**playhouse** n. theatre. —**playing card** one of a set of 52 cards used in card games. —**playing fields** extensive piece of ground for open-air games. —**play off** v. set (two people) against each other for one's own ends. —**play on** v. exploit or encourage (someone's) sympathy or weakness. —**play-school** n. nursery group for young children. —**plaything** n. toy. —**play up** v. cause trouble; give prominence to. —**playwright** n. author of plays.

plaza n. modern shopping complex; open space or square.

PLC, plc Public Limited Company.

plea n. serious or urgent request, entreaty; statement of a prisoner or defendant; excuse.

plead v. ask urgently or with deep feeling; give as an excuse; Law declare oneself to be guilty or innocent of a charge made against one.

pleasant adj. pleasing, enjoyable. —**pleasantly** adv. —**pleasantry** n. polite or joking remark.

please v. give pleasure or satisfaction to. —adv. polite word of request. —**please oneself** do as one likes. —**pleased** adj. —**pleasing** adj. giving pleasure or satisfaction.

pleasure n. feeling of happiness and satisfac-

tion; something that causes this. —**pleasurable** adj. giving pleasure. —**pleasurably** adv.

pleat n. fold made by doubling material back on itself. —v. arrange (material) in pleats.

plebeian [pleb-ee-an] adj. of the lower social classes; vulgar or rough. —n. (also (Offens.) **pleb**) member of the lower social classes.

plebiscite [pleb-iss-ite] n. decision by direct voting of the people of a country.

plectrum n., pl. **-trums, -tra.** small implement for plucking the strings of a guitar etc.

pledge n. solemn promise; something valuable given as a guarantee that a promise will be kept or a debt paid. —v. promise solemnly; bind by or as if by a pledge, e.g. pledge to secrecy.

plenary adj. (of a meeting) attended by all members.

plenipotentiary n., pl. **-aries.** diplomat or representative having full powers. —adj. having full powers.

plenitude n. completeness, abundance.

plenteous adj. plentiful.

plentiful adj. existing in large amounts or numbers. —**plentifully** adv.

plenty n. large amount or number; quite enough.

THESAURUS

play v. 1. caper, frisk, frolic, gambol, revel, romp, sport, trifle 2. challenge, compete, participate, rival, take on, take part, vie with 3. act, execute, impersonate, perform, personate, portray, represent ~n. 4. comedy, drama, dramatic piece, entertainment, farce, masque, performance, piece, radio play, show, tragedy 5. diversion, entertainment, frolic, fun, gambol, game, recreation, romp, sport

playboy philanderer, rake, roué, socialite, womanizer

player 1. competitor, contestant, team member 2. actor, actress, entertainer, performer 3. artist, musician, performer, virtuoso

playful cheerful, frolicsome, gay, impish, lively, merry, mischievous, puckish, rollicking, spirited, sprightly, vivacious

plaything amusement, game, pastime, toy, trifle, trinket

play up emphasize, highlight, stress, underline

plea appeal, entreaty, overture, petition, prayer, request, suit, supplication

plead 1. ask, beg, beseech, crave, entreat, implore, petition, request, solicit 2. adduce, allege, argue, assert, maintain

pleasant agreeable, amusing, delectable, de-

lightful, enjoyable, fine, gratifying, lovely, nice, refreshing, satisfying, welcome

pleasantry badinage, banter, jest, joke, quip, sally, witticism

please amuse, charm, cheer, content, delight, gladden, gratify, humour, indulge, rejoice, satisfy, suit, tickle, tickle pink

pleased contented, delighted, euphoric, glad, gratified, happy, satisfied, thrilled

pleasing agreeable, amiable, amusing, attractive, charming, delightful, enjoyable, entertaining, gratifying, polite, satisfying

pleasure bliss, comfort, contentment, delight, ease, enjoyment, gladness, happiness, joy, recreation, satisfaction, solace

plebeian adj. base, coarse, common, ignoble, low, mean, proletarian, unrefined, vulgar, working-class

pledge n. 1. covenant, oath, promise, undertaking, vow, warrant, word 2. bail, bond, collateral, deposit, earnest, gage, guarantee, pawn, security, surety ~v. 3. contract, engage, promise, swear, undertake, vouch, vow

plentiful abundant, ample, bountiful, complete, copious, generous, infinite, lavish, liberal, profuse

plenty 1. enough, fund, mass, mine, moun-

DICTIONARY

pleonasm *n.* use of more words than necessary. **—pleonastic** *adj.*

plethora *n.* oversupply.

pleurisy *n.* inflammation of the membrane lining the chest and covering the lungs.

pliable *adj.* easily bent; easily influenced. **—pliability** *n.*

pliant *adj.* pliable. **—pliancy** *n.*

pliers *pl. n.* tool with hinged arms and jaws for gripping.

plight[1] *n.* difficult or dangerous situation.

plight[2] *v.* **—plight one's troth** *Old-fashioned* promise to marry.

Plimsoll line *n.* mark on a ship showing the level water should reach when the ship is fully loaded.

plimsolls *pl. n.* rubber-soled canvas shoes.

plinth *n.* slab forming the base of a column etc.

PLO Palestine Liberation Organization.

plod *v.* **plodding, plodded.** walk with slow heavy steps; work slowly but determinedly. **—plodder** *n.*

plonk[1] *v.* put (something) down heavily and carelessly.

plonk[2] *n. Informal* cheap inferior wine.

plop *n.* sound of an object falling into water without a splash. **—***v.* **plopping, plopped.** make this sound.

plot[1] *n.* secret plan to do something illegal or wrong; sequence of events on which a film, novel, etc. is based. **—***v.* **plotting, plotted.** plan secretly, conspire; mark the position or course of (a ship or aircraft) on a map; mark and join up (points on a graph).

plot[2] *n.* small piece of land.

plough *n.* agricultural tool for turning over soil.

—*v.* turn over (earth) with a plough; move or work through slowly and laboriously. **—ploughman** *n.* **—ploughshare** *n.* blade of a plough.

plover *n.* shore bird with a straight bill and long pointed wings.

ploy *n.* manoeuvre designed to gain an advantage.

pluck *v.* pull or pick off; pull out the feathers of (a bird for cooking); sound the strings of (a guitar etc.) with the fingers or a plectrum. **—***n.* courage. **—plucky** *adj.* brave. **—pluckily** *adv.* **—pluck up** *v.* summon up (courage).

plug *n.* thing fitting into and filling a hole; device connecting an appliance to an electricity supply; *Informal* favourable mention of a product etc., designed to encourage people to buy it. **—***v.* **plugging, plugged.** block or seal (a hole or gap) with a plug; *Informal* advertise (a product etc.) by constant repetition. **—plug away** *v. Informal* work steadily. **—plug in** *v.* connect (an electrical appliance) to a power source by pushing a plug into a socket.

plum *n.* oval usu. dark red fruit with a stone in the middle. **—***adj.* dark purplish-red; very desirable.

plumage *n.* bird's feathers.

plumb *v.* understand (something obscure); test with a plumb line. **—***adv.* exactly. **—plumb the depths of** experience the worst extremes of (an unpleasant quality or emotion). **—plumber** *n.* person who fits and repairs pipes and fixtures for water and drainage systems. **—plumbing** *n.* pipes and fixtures used in water and drainage systems. **—plumb in** *v.* connect (an appliance such as a washing machine) to a water supply. **—plumb line** string with a weight at the end, used to test the depth of water or to test whether something is vertical.

THESAURUS

tain(s), plethora, quantity, store, sufficiency 2. abundance, affluence, copiousness, fertility, luxury, opulence, profusion, prosperity, wealth

plethora excess, glut, profusion, superabundance, surfeit, surplus

pliable 1. ductile, flexible, limber, lithe, plastic, pliant, supple 2. adaptable, compliant, docile, pliant, receptive, responsive, susceptible, tractable, yielding

plight *n.* case, condition, difficulty, dilemma, extremity, predicament, situation, state, straits, trouble

plod clump, drag, lumber, slog, tramp, tread, trudge

plot[1] *n.* 1. conspiracy, intrigue, plan, scheme, stratagem 2. action, narrative, outline, sce-

nario, story, subject, theme, thread ~*v.* 3. collude, conspire, contrive, hatch, intrigue, manoeuvre, plan, scheme 4. chart, draft, draw, locate, map, mark, outline

plot[2] *n.* area, ground, lot, patch

plough *v.* cultivate, dig, furrow, ridge, till, turn over

pluck[1] *n.* boldness, bravery, courage, grit, heart, mettle, nerve, resolution, spirit

pluck[2] *v.* 1. catch, clutch, snatch, tug, tweak, yank 2. finger, pick

plucky bold, brave, daring, game, gritty, valiant

plug *n.* 1. bung, cork, spigot, stopper 2. mention, publicity, puff, push ~*v.* 3. block, bung, choke, close, cork, cover, fill, pack, seal, stop, stopper, stopple, stop up, stuff 4. mention, promote, publicize, puff, push

DICTIONARY

plume *n.* feather, esp. one worn as an ornament. —**plume oneself on** be proud of oneself because of.

plummet *v.* **-meting, -meted.** plunge downward.

plump[1] *adj.* moderately or attractively fat. —**plumpness** *n.* —**plump up** *v.* make (a pillow) fuller or rounded.

plump[2] *v.* sit or fall heavily and suddenly. —*adv.* suddenly and heavily; directly. —**plump for** *v.* choose, vote only for.

plunder *v.* take by force, esp. in time of war. —*n.* things plundered, spoils.

plunge *v.* put or throw forcibly or suddenly (into). —*n.* plunging, dive. —**take the plunge** *Informal* embark on a risky enterprise; get married. —**plunger** *n.* rubber suction cup used to clear blocked pipes. —**plunging** *adj.* (of the neckline of a dress) cut low so as to show the top of the breasts. —**plunge into** *v.* become deeply involved in.

plunk *v.* pluck the strings of (a banjo etc.) to produce a twanging sound.

pluperfect *adj., n. Grammar* (tense) expressing action completed before a past time, such as *had gone* in *his wife had gone already.*

plural *adj.* of or consisting of more than one. —*n.* a word in its plural form.

pluralism *n.* existence and toleration of a variety of peoples, opinions, etc. in a society. —**pluralist** *n.* —**pluralistic** *adj.*

plus *prep.* with the addition of: usu. indicated by the sign (+). —*adj.* more than zero or the number already mentioned; positive; advantageous. —*n.* plus sign; advantage.

plus fours *pl. n.* trousers gathered in at the knee.

plush *n.* fabric with long velvety pile. —*adj.* (also **plushy**) luxurious.

Pluto *n.* Greek god of the underworld; farthest planet from the sun.

plutocrat *n.* person who is powerful because of being very rich. —**plutocratic** *adj.*

plutonium *n.* radioactive metallic element used esp. in nuclear reactors and weapons.

pluvial *adj.* of or caused by the action of rain.

ply[1] *v.* **plying, plied.** work at (a job or trade); use (a tool); (of a ship) travel regularly along or between. —**ply with** *v.* supply with or subject to persistently.

ply[2] *n.* thickness of wool, fabric, etc.

plywood *n.* board made of thin layers of wood glued together.

PM prime minister.

pm, PM after noon; postmortem.

PMT premenstrual tension.

pneumatic *adj.* worked by or inflated with wind or air.

pneumonia *n.* inflammation of the lungs.

PO postal order; Post Office.

poach[1] *v.* catch (animals) illegally on someone else's land; encroach on or steal something belonging to someone else. —**poacher** *n.*

poach[2] *v.* simmer (food) gently in liquid.

pocket *n.* small bag sewn into clothing for carrying things; pouchlike container, esp. for catching balls at the edge of a snooker table; isolated or distinct group or area. —*v.* **pocketing, pocketed.** put into one's pocket; take secretly or dishonestly. —*adj.* small. —**in** *or* **out of pocket** having made a profit *or* loss. —**pocket money** small regular allowance given to children by parents; allowance for small personal expenses.

pockmarked *adj.* (of the skin) marked with hollow scars where diseased spots have been.

pod *n.* long narrow seed case of peas, beans, etc.

podgy *adj.* **podgier, podgiest.** short and fat.

podium *n., pl.* **-diums, -dia.** small raised platform for a conductor or speaker.

THESAURUS

plum *adj.* best, choice

plumb 1. *adv.* bang, exactly, precisely, slap 2. *v.* delve, explore, fathom, gauge, measure, probe, search, sound

plump burly, buxom, chubby, full, obese, podgy, portly, rotund, round, stout, tubby

plunder 1. *v.* despoil, loot, pillage, raid, ransack, ravage, rifle, rob, sack, spoil, steal, strip 2. *n.* booty, loot, pillage, prize, spoils

plunge 1. *v.* cast, descend, dip, dive, douse, drop, fall, immerse, jump, pitch, sink, submerge, swoop, throw, tumble 2. *n.* descent, dive, drop, fall, jump, swoop

plus 1. *prep.* added to, and, with 2. *adj.* added, additional, extra, positive

ply carry on, exercise, follow, practise, pursue, work at

poach infringe, intrude, plunder, rob, trespass

pocket 1. *n.* bag, hollow, pouch, receptacle, sack 2. *adj.* abridged, compact, concise, little, portable, small

podium dais, platform, rostrum, stage

poem lyric, ode, rhyme, song, sonnet, verse

DICTIONARY

poem *n.* imaginative piece of writing in rhythmic lines.

poesy *n. Obs.* poetry.

poet *n.* writer of poems. —**poet laureate** poet appointed by the British sovereign to write poems on important occasions. —**poetry** *n.* poems; art of writing poems; beautiful or pleasing quality. —**poetic** *adj.* (also **poetical**) of or like poetry. —**poetically** *adv.* —**poetic justice** suitable reward or punishment for someone's past actions. —**poetaster** *n.* would-be or inferior poet.

pogrom *n.* organized persecution and massacre.

poignant *adj.* sharply painful to the feelings. —**poignancy** *n.*

poinsettia *n.* Central American shrub widely cultivated for its clusters of scarlet leaves, which resemble petals.

point *n.* single idea in a discussion, argument, etc.; main or essential aspect; aim or purpose; detail or item; characteristic; particular position, stage, or time; unit for recording a value or score; dot indicating decimals; full stop; sharp end; headland; one of the direction marks of a compass; movable rail used to change a train to other rails; electrical socket. —*pl.* electrical contacts in the distributor of an engine. —*v.* show the direction or position of something or draw attention to it by extending a finger or other pointed object towards it; direct (a gun etc.) towards; finish or repair the joints in brickwork with mortar; (of a gun dog) show where game is by standing rigidly with the muzzle towards it. —**on the point of** very shortly going to. —**pointed** *adj.* having a sharp end; (of a remark) obviously directed at a particular person. —**pointedly** *adv.* —**pointer** *n.* indicator on a measuring instrument; breed of gun dog; helpful hint. —**pointless** *adj.* meaningless, irrelevant. —**point-blank** *adj., adv.* fired at a very close target; (of a remark or question) direct, blunt. —**point duty** policeman's position at a road junction to control traffic. —**point of view** way of considering something. —**point-to-point** *n.* horse race across open country.

poise *n.* calm dignified manner. —**poised** *adj.* absolutely ready; behaving with or showing poise.

poison *n.* substance that kills or injures when swallowed or absorbed. —*v.* give poison to; have a harmful or evil effect on, spoil. —**poisoner** *n.* —**poisonous** *adj.* —**poison-pen letter** malicious anonymous letter.

poke *v.* jab or prod with one's finger, a stick, etc.; thrust forward or out. —*n.* poking. —**poky** *adj. Informal* small and cramped.

poker[1] *n.* metal rod for stirring a fire to make it burn more brightly.

poker[2] *n.* card game involving bluff. —**poker-faced** *adj.* expressionless.

polar *adj.* of or near either of the earth's poles. —**polar bear** white bear that lives in the regions around the North Pole.

polarize *v.* form or cause to form into groups with directly opposite views; *Physics* restrict (light waves) to certain directions of vibration. —**polarization** *n.*

Polaroid *n.* ® plastic which polarizes light and so reduces glare; camera that develops a print very quickly inside itself.

polder *n.* land reclaimed from the sea.

THESAURUS

poet bard, lyricist, versifier

poetic elegiac, lyrical, metrical

poetry rhyme, rhyming, verse

poignancy emotion, feeling, pathos, sadness, sentiment, tenderness

poignant agonizing, bitter, distressing, intense, moving, painful, sad, touching, upsetting

point *n.* 1. dot, mark, period, stop 2. location, place, position, site, spot, stage, station 3. apex, end, nib, prong, spike, spur, summit, tip, top 4. bill, cape, headland, promontory 5. instant, juncture, moment, time 6. aim, design, end, goal, intent, intention, motive, object, purpose, reason, use 7. burden, core, drift, essence, gist, heart, import, matter, question, subject, text, theme 8. aspect, attribute, characteristic, peculiarity 9. score, unit ~*v.* 10. bespeak, denote, designate, direct, indicate, show

point-blank 1. *adj.* abrupt, blunt, direct, explicit, express, plain 2. *adv.* bluntly, brusquely, frankly, openly, plainly, straight

pointer 1. guide, hand, needle 2. advice, caution, hint, tip, warning

pointless aimless, futile, inane, senseless, silly, stupid, useless, vague, vain, worthless

poise *n.* aplomb, calmness, composure, dignity, elegance, grace, presence, serenity

poised 1. collected, composed, dignified, graceful, self-confident, serene, urbane 2. prepared, ready, waiting

poison 1. *n.* bane, toxin, venom 2. *v.* contaminate, envenom, infect, kill, murder, pollute

poisonous deadly, fatal, lethal, mortal, virulent

poke 1. *v.* butt, dig, elbow, hit, jab, nudge, prod, punch, push shove, stab, stick, thrust 2. *n.* butt, dig, hit, jab, nudge, prod, punch, thrust

DICTIONARY

pole[1] *n.* long rounded piece of wood etc.

pole[2] *n.* point furthest north (**North Pole**) or furthest south (**South Pole**) on the earth's axis of rotation; either of the opposite ends of a magnet or electric cell. —**Pole Star** star nearest to the North Pole in the northern hemisphere.

poleaxe *v.* hit or stun with a heavy blow.

polecat *n.* small animal of the weasel family.

polemic [pol-em-ik] *n.* fierce attack on or defence of a particular opinion, belief, etc. —**polemical** *adj.*

police *n.* organized force in a state which keeps law and order. —*v.* control or watch over with police or a similar body. —**policeman, policewoman** *n.* member of a police force.

policy[1] *n., pl.* **-cies.** plan of action adopted by a person, group, or state.

policy[2] *n., pl.* **-cies.** document containing an insurance contract.

polio *n.* (also called **poliomyelitis**) disease affecting the spinal cord, which often causes paralysis.

polish *v.* make smooth and shiny by rubbing; make more nearly perfect. —*n.* liquid, aerosol, etc. for polishing; pleasing elegant style. —**polished** *adj.* (of a person) socially sophisticated in manner; done or performed well or professionally. —**polish off** *v.* finish completely, dispose of.

Politburo *n.* decision-making committee in a Communist country.

polite *adj.* showing consideration for others in one's manners, speech, etc.; socially correct or refined. —**politely** *adv.* —**politeness** *n.*

politic *adj.* wise and likely to prove advantageous.

politics *n.* winning and using of power to govern society; person's beliefs about how a country should be governed; (study of) the art of government. —**political** *adj.* of the state, government, or public administration. —**politically** *adv.* —**political prisoner** person imprisoned because of his or her political beliefs. —**politician** *n.* person actively engaged in politics, esp. a member of parliament.

polka *n.* lively 19th-century dance; music for this. —**polka dots** pattern of bold spots on fabric.

poll *n.* (also **opinion poll**) questioning of a random sample of people to find out general opinion; voting; number of votes recorded. —*v.* receive (votes); question in an opinion poll. —**polling station** building where people vote in an election. —**pollster** *n.* person who conducts opinion polls. —**poll tax** (also called **community charge**) tax levied on every adult person.

pollarded *adj.* (of a tree) growing very bushy because its top branches have been cut short.

pollen *n.* fine dust produced by flowers that fertilizes other flowers. —**pollinate** *v.* fertilize with pollen. —**pollen count** measure of the amount of pollen in the air, esp. as a warning to people with hay fever.

pollute *v.* contaminate with something poisonous or harmful. —**pollution** *n.* —**pollutant** *n.* something that pollutes.

polo *n.* game like hockey played by teams of players on horseback. —**polo neck** sweater with tight turned-over collar.

polonaise *n.* old stately dance; music for this.

poltergeist *n.* spirit believed to move furniture and throw objects around.

poltroon *n. Obs.* utter coward.

poly *n., pl.* **polys.** *Informal* polytechnic.

poly- *combining form* many, much.

polyandry *n.* practice of having more than one husband at the same time.

polyanthus *n.* garden primrose.

polychromatic *adj.* many-coloured.

polyester *n.* synthetic material used to make plastics and textile fibres.

polygamy [pol-ig-a-mee] *n.* practice of having more than one husband or wife at the same time. —**polygamous** *adj.* —**polygamist** *n.*

THESAURUS

pole bar, mast, post, rod, shaft, spar, staff, standard, stick

police 1. *n.* constabulary 2. *v.* control, guard, patrol, protect, regulate, watch

policeman bobby, constable

policy action, approach, code, course, custom, plan, practice, programme, rule, scheme, theory

polish *v.* 1. brighten, buff, burnish, clean, rub, shine, smooth, wax 2. enhance, refine ~*n.* 3. varnish, wax 4. elegance, finesse, grace, refinement

polished 1. *Fig.* accomplished, civilized, cultivated, polite, refined, urbane, well-bred 2. adept, expert, fine, masterly, skilful

polite affable, civil, courteous, gracious, mannerly, obliging, respectful, well-mannered

politic discreet, expedient, judicious, prudent, sensible, wise

politician legislator, statesman

politics civics, government, statesmanship

poll *n.* 1. figures, vote, voting 2. ballot, canvass, census, count, sampling, survey

pollute befoul, contaminate, dirty, foul, infect, mar, poison, soil, spoil, stain, taint

DICTIONARY

polyglot *adj., n.* (person) able to speak or write several languages.

polygon *n.* geometrical figure with three or more angles and sides. —**polygonal** *adj.*

polygyny *n.* practice of having more than one wife at the same time.

polyhedron *n., pl.* **-drons, -dra.** solid figure with four or more sides.

polymer *n.* chemical compound with large molecules made of simple molecules of the same kind. —**polymerize** *v.* form into polymers. —**polymerization** *n.*

polyp *n.* small simple sea creature with a hollow cylindrical body; small growth on a mucous membrane.

polyphonic *adj. Music* consisting of several melodies played simultaneously.

polystyrene *n.* synthetic material used esp. as white rigid foam for packing and insulation.

polytechnic *n.* college offering courses in many subjects at and below degree level.

polytheism *n.* belief in many gods. —**polytheist** *n.* —**polytheistic** *adj.*

polythene *n.* light plastic used for many everyday articles.

polyunsaturated *adj.* of a group of fats that do not form cholesterol in the blood.

polyurethane *n.* synthetic material used esp. in paints.

polyvinyl chloride *n.* see PVC.

pomander *n.* (container for) a mixture of sweet-smelling petals, herbs, etc.

pomegranate *n.* round tropical fruit with a thick rind containing many seeds in a red pulp.

Pomeranian *n.* small dog with long straight hair.

pommel *n.* raised part on the front of a saddle; knob at the top of a sword hilt.

pommy *n., pl.* **-ies.** *Aust. & NZ slang* (also **pom**) person from Britain.

pomp *n.* stately display or ceremony.

pompom *n.* decorative ball of tufted wool, silk, etc.

pompous *adj.* foolishly serious and grand, self-important. —**pompously** *adv.* —**pomposity** *n.*

ponce *Offens.* —*n.* effeminate man; pimp. —**ponce around** *v.* act stupidly, waste time.

poncho *n., pl.* **-chos.** loose circular cloak with a hole for the head.

pond *n.* small area of still water. —**pondweed** *n.* plant that grows in ponds.

ponder *v.* think thoroughly or deeply (about).

ponderous *adj.* serious and dull; heavy and unwieldy; (of movement) slow and clumsy. —**ponderously** *adv.*

pong *n., v. Informal* (give off a) strong unpleasant smell.

pontiff *n.* the Pope. —**pontifical** *adj.* pompous and dogmatic. —**pontificate** *v.* state one's opinions as if they were the only possible correct ones. —*n.* period of office of a Pope.

pontoon[1] *n.* floating platform supporting a temporary bridge.

pontoon[2] *n.* gambling card game.

pony *n.* small horse. —**ponytail** *n.* long hair tied in one bunch at the back of the head.

poodle *n.* dog with curly hair often clipped fancifully.

poof *n. Offens.* homosexual man.

pool[1] *n.* small body of still water; puddle of spilt liquid; swimming pool.

pool[2] *n.* shared fund or group of workers or resources; game like snooker. —*pl.* see FOOTBALL POOLS. —*v.* put in a common fund.

poop *n.* raised part at the back of a sailing ship.

poor *adj.* having little money and few possessions; less, smaller, or weaker than is needed or expected; unproductive; unlucky; pitiable. —**poorly** *adv.* in a poor manner. —*adj.* not in good health. —**poorness** *n.*

THESAURUS

pomp 1. ceremony, flourish, grandeur, pageantry, splendour, state 2. display, ostentation, show

pompous 1. arrogant, grandiose, imperious, ostentatious, portentous, pretentious, showy 2. boastful, bombastic, inflated, turgid

ponder brood, cogitate, consider, deliberate, meditate, muse, reflect, ruminate, study, think, weigh

pool[1] 1. lake, mere, pond, splash, tarn 2. swimming bath

pool[2] *n.* 1. combine, consortium, group, syndicate, team, trust 2. bank, funds, jackpot, kitty, pot, stakes ~*v.* 3. combine, league, merge, share

poor 1. destitute, impoverished, indigent, needy, penniless, penurious 2. deficient, inadequate, incomplete, insufficient, meagre, miserable, niggardly, pitiable, reduced, scanty, slight, sparse 3. bad, bare, barren, depleted, exhausted, fruitless, infertile, sterile, unfruitful, unproductive 4. hapless, luckless, miserable, pathetic, pitiable, unfortunate, unlucky, wretched

poorly badly, crudely, inadequately, incompetently, insufficiently, meanly, unsatisfactorily

DICTIONARY

pop[1] v. **popping, popped.** make or cause to make a small explosive sound; *Informal* go, put, or come unexpectedly or suddenly. —n. small explosive sound; nonalcoholic fizzy drink. —**popcorn** n. maize kernels heated until they puff up and burst.

pop[2] n. music of general appeal, esp. to young people. —adj. short for POPULAR.

pop[3] n. *Informal* father.

Pope n. head of the Roman Catholic Church. —**popish** adj. *Offens.* Roman Catholic.

poplar n. tall slender tree.

poplin n. ribbed cotton material.

poppadom n. thin round crisp Indian bread.

poppy n., pl. **-ies.** plant with a large delicate red flower.

populace n. the ordinary people; the masses.

popular adj. widely liked and admired; of or for the public in general. —**popularly** adv. —**popularity** n. —**popularize** v. make popular; make (something technical or specialist) easily understood.

populate v. fill with inhabitants. —**population** n. all the people who live in a particular place; the number of people living in a particular place. —**populous** adj. thickly populated.

porbeagle n. kind of shark.

porcelain n. fine china; objects made of it.

porch n. covered approach to the entrance of a building.

porcine adj. of or like a pig.

porcupine n. animal covered with long pointed quills.

pore n. tiny opening in the skin or in the surface of a plant.

pork n. pig meat. —**porker** n. pig raised for food.

porn, porno n., adj. *Informal* short for PORNOGRAPHY or PORNOGRAPHIC.

pornography n. writing, films, or pictures designed to be sexually exciting. —**pornographer** n. producer of pornography. —**pornographic** adj.

porous adj. allowing liquid to pass through gradually. —**porosity** n.

porphyry [por-fir-ee] n. reddish rock with large crystals in it.

porpoise n. fish-like sea mammal.

porridge n. breakfast food made of oatmeal cooked in water or milk; *Slang* prison term.

port[1] n. harbour; town with a harbour.

port[2] n. left side of a ship or aircraft when facing the front of it.

port[3] n. strong sweet wine, usu. red.

port[4] n. opening in the side of a ship; porthole.

portable adj. easily carried. —**portability** n.

portal n. large imposing doorway or gate.

portcullis n. grating suspended above a castle gateway, that can be lowered to block the entrance.

portend v. be a sign of.

portent n. sign of a future event. —**portentous** adj. of great or ominous significance; pompous, self-important.

porter n. man on duty at the entrance to a hotel etc.; man who carries luggage; hospital worker who transfers patients between rooms etc.

portfolio n., pl. **-os.** (flat case for carrying) examples of an artist's work; area of responsibility of a minister of state; list of investments held by an investor.

porthole n. small round window in a ship or aircraft.

portico n., pl. **-cos, -coes.** porch or covered walkway with columns supporting the roof.

portion n. part or share; helping of food for one person; destiny or fate. —**portion out** v. divide into shares.

THESAURUS

pop v. 1. bang, burst, crack, explode, go off, report, snap 2. insert, push, put, shove, slip, stick, thrust, tuck ~n. 3. bang, burst, crack, explosion, noise, report

populace crowd, masses, mob, multitude, people, rabble, throng

popular 1. accepted, approved, famous, fashionable, favourite, in, in demand, in favour, liked 2. common, conventional, current, general, prevailing, public, standard, stock, universal

popularity acceptance, acclaim, approval, celebrity, esteem, fame, favour, recognition, regard, renown, repute, vogue

popularly commonly, customarily, generally, ordinarily, regularly, usually, widely

populate colonize, occupy, settle

population community, inhabitants, natives, people, residents, society

port anchorage, harbour, haven

portable compact, convenient, handy, light, manageable, movable

portend augur, betoken, bode, foreshadow, foretell, herald, indicate, omen, predict, presage, promise, threaten

portent augury, harbinger, omen, presage, presentiment, prognostication, sign, threat, warning

porter[1] bearer, carrier

DICTIONARY

portly *adj.* **-lier, -liest.** rather fat.

portmanteau *n., pl.* **-teaus, -teaux.** *Old-fashioned* large suitcase that opens into two compartments. *—adj.* combining aspects of different things.

portrait *n.* picture of a person; lifelike description.

portray *v.* describe or represent by artistic means, as in writing or film. **—portrayal** *n.*

Portuguese *adj.* of Portugal or its inhabitants. *—n.* person from Portugal; language of Portugal and Brazil. **—Portuguese man-of-war** sea creature resembling a jellyfish, with stinging tentacles.

pose *v.* place in or take up a particular position to be photographed or drawn; ask (a question); raise (a problem). *—n.* position while posing; behaviour adopted for effect. **—pose as** pretend to be. **—poser** *n.* puzzling question; poseur. **—poseur** *n.* person who behaves in an affected way to impress others.

posh *adj. Informal* smart, luxurious; affectedly upper-class.

posit [**pozz**-it] *v.* lay down as a basis for argument.

position *n.* place; usual or expected place; way in which something is placed or arranged; attitude, point of view; social standing; state of affairs; job. *—v.* place.

positive *adj.* feeling no doubts, certain; helpful, providing encouragement; confident, hopeful; absolute, downright; *Maths* greater than zero; *Electricity* having a deficiency of electrons. **—positively** *adv.* **—positive discrimination** provision of special opportunities for a disadvantaged group.

positron *n.* positive electron.

posse [**poss**-ee] *n. US* group of men organized to maintain law and order; *Informal* group or gang.

possess *v.* have as one's property; (of a feeling, belief, etc.) have complete control of, dominate. **—possessor** *n.* **—possession** *n.* state of possessing, ownership. *—pl.* things a person possesses. **—possessive** *adj.* wanting all the attention or love of another person; (of a word) indicating the person or thing that something belongs to. **—possessiveness** *n.*

possible *adj.* able to exist, happen, or be done; worthy of consideration. *—n.* person or thing that might be suitable or chosen. **—possibility** *n.* **—possibly** *adv.* perhaps, not necessarily.

possum *n.* same as OPOSSUM. **—play possum** pretend to be dead or asleep to deceive an opponent.

post[1] *n.* official system of carrying and delivering letters and parcels; (single collection or delivery of) letters and parcels sent by this system. *—v.* send by post. **—keep someone posted** supply someone regularly with the latest information. **—postage** *n.* charge for sending a

---

THESAURUS

porter[2] caretaker, doorman, gatekeeper

portion 1. bit, fragment, morsel, part, piece, scrap, section, segment 2. allocation, allotment, lot, measure, parcel, quantity, quota, ration, share 3. helping, piece 4. fate, fortune, lot, luck

portrait image, likeness, painting, photograph, picture

portray depict, draw, figure, illustrate, paint, picture, render, represent, sketch

pose *v.* 1. arrange, model, position, sit 2. *Often with* **as** feign, impersonate, sham 3. advance, put, set, state, submit *~n.* 4. attitude, bearing, position, posture, stance 5. act, air, façade, front, posturing, pretence, role

poser enigma, problem, puzzle, question, riddle

position *n.* 1. area, bearings, location, place, point, post, reference, site, situation, spot, station 2. arrangement, attitude, pose, posture, stance 3. angle, attitude, belief, opinion, outlook, slant, stance, standpoint, view 4. circumstances, condition, pass, plight, situation, state 5. caste, class, importance, place, prestige, rank, reputation, standing, station, stature, status 6. capacity, duty, function, job,

occupation, office, place, post, role, situation *~v.* 7. arrange, array, dispose, fix, locate, place, put, set, settle, stand

positive 1. absolute, actual, affirmative, categorical, certain, clear-cut, decisive, definite, direct, explicit, express, firm, real 2. assured, certain, confident, convinced, sure 3. assertive, cocksure, decided, emphatic, firm, forceful, resolute 4. beneficial, constructive, efficacious, forward-looking, helpful, practical, productive, progressive, useful

positively absolutely, certainly, definitely, emphatically, firmly, surely

possess 1. enjoy, have, hold, own 2. acquire, control, dominate, hold, occupy, seize

possession 1. control, custody, hold, occupation, ownership, title 2. *Plural* assets, belongings, chattels, estate, property

possibility likelihood, potentiality, workableness

possible 1. conceivable, credible, hypothetical, imaginable, likely, potential 2. feasible, viable, workable 3. hopeful, likely, potential, probable, promising

possibly perhaps

DICTIONARY

letter or parcel by post. —**postal** *adj.* —**postal order** written money order sent by post and cashed at a post office by the person who receives it. —**postbag** *n.* postman's bag; post received by a magazine, famous person, etc. —**postcard** *n.* card for sending a message by post without an envelope. —**postcode** *n.* system of letters and numbers used to aid the sorting of mail. —**postman** *n.* man who collects and delivers post. —**postmark** *n.* official mark stamped on letters showing place and date of posting. —**postmaster, postmistress** *n.* official in charge of a post office. —**post office** place where postal business is conducted.

post² *n.* length of wood, concrete, etc. fixed upright to support or mark something. —*v.* put up (a notice) in a public place.

post³ *n.* job; position to which someone, esp. a soldier, is assigned for duty; military establishment. —*v.* send (a person) to a new place to work; put (a guard etc.) on duty.

post- *prefix* after, later than, e.g. *postwar*.

postdate *v.* write a date on (a cheque) that is later than the actual date.

poster *n.* large picture or notice stuck on a wall.

poste restante *n. French* post-office department where a traveller's letters are kept until called for.

posterior *n.* buttocks. —*adj.* behind, at the back of.

posterity *n.* future generations, descendants.

postern *n.* small back door or gate.

postgraduate *n.* person with a degree who is studying for a more advanced qualification.

posthaste *adv.* with great speed.

posthumous [**poss**-tume-uss] *adj.* occurring after one's death; born after one's father's death; published after the author's death. —**posthumously** *adv.*

postil(l)ion *n. Hist.* person riding one of a pair of horses drawing a carriage.

postmortem *n.* medical examination of a body to establish the cause of death.

postnatal *adj.* occurring after childbirth.

postpone *v.* put off to a later time. —**postponement** *n.*

postprandial *adj.* after dinner.

postscript *n.* passage added at the end of a letter.

postulant *n.* candidate for admission to a religious order.

postulate *v.* assume to be true as the basis of an argument or theory. —**postulation** *n.*

posture *n.* position or way in which someone stands, walks, etc. —*v.* behave in an exaggerated way to get attention.

posy *n., pl.* **-sies.** small bunch of flowers.

pot *n.* round deep container; teapot; *Slang* cannabis. —*pl. Informal* a lot. —*v.* **potting, potted.** plant in a pot; *Snooker* hit (a ball) into a pocket. —**potted** *adj.* grown in a pot; (of meat or fish) preserved in a pot; *Informal* abridged. —**potluck** *n.* whatever is available. —**potsherd** *n.* broken fragment of pottery. —**pot shot** shot taken without aiming carefully. —**potting shed** shed where plants are potted.

potable [**pote**-a-bl] *adj.* drinkable.

potash *n.* white powdery substance obtained from ashes and used as fertilizer.

potassium *n.* white metallic element.

potato *n., pl.* **-toes.** roundish starchy vegetable that grows underground.

poteen *n.* (in Ireland) illicitly distilled alcoholic drink.

potent *adj.* having great power or influence; (of a male) capable of having sexual intercourse. —**potency** *n.*

potentate *n.* ruler or monarch.

potential *adj.* possible but not yet actual. —*n.* ability or talent not yet fully used; *Electricity*

THESAURUS

post¹ 1. *n.* collection, delivery, mail 2. *v.* dispatch, mail, send, transmit

post² 1. *n.* column, newel, pale, picket, pillar, pole, shaft, stake, stock, support, upright 2. *v.* advertise, affix, announce, display, proclaim, promulgate, publicize, publish

post³ 1. *n.* appointment, employment, job, office, place, position, situation 2. *v.* assign, establish, locate, place, put, situate, station

poster advertisement, bill, notice, placard, sticker

posterity children, descendants, family, heirs, issue, offspring

postpone adjourn, defer, delay, shelve, suspend, table

postscript addition, afterthought, supplement

postulate advance, assume, predicate, propose, suppose

posture 1. *n.* attitude, bearing, carriage, disposition, set, stance 2. *v.* affect

potent forceful, mighty, powerful, strong, vigorous

potential 1. *adj.* dormant, future, hidden, inherent, latent, likely, possible, promising 2. *n.* ability, aptitude, capacity, power, the makings, wherewithal

DICTIONARY

level of electric pressure. —**potentially** *adv.* —**potentiality** *n.*

pothole *n.* hole in the surface of a road; deep hole in a limestone area. —**potholing** *n.* sport of exploring underground caves. —**potholer** *n.*

potion *n.* dose of medicine or poison.

potpourri [po-**poor**-ee] *n.* fragrant mixture of dried flower petals; musical or literary medley.

pottage *n.* thick soup or stew.

potter[1] *n.* person who makes pottery.

potter[2] *v.* be busy in a pleasant but aimless way.

pottery *n., pl.* -**ries.** articles made from baked clay; place where they are made.

potty[1] *adj.* -**tier, -tiest.** *Informal* crazy or silly.

potty[2] *n., pl.* -**ties.** bowl used by a small child as a toilet.

pouch *n.* small bag; baglike pocket of skin on an animal.

pouf(fe) [poof] *n.* large solid cushion used as a seat.

poulterer *n.* person who sells poultry.

poultice [**pole**-tiss] *n.* moist dressing, often heated, applied to inflamed skin.

poultry *n.* domestic fowls.

pounce *v.* spring upon suddenly to attack or capture. —*n.* pouncing.

pound[1] *n.* monetary unit of Britain and some other countries; unit of weight equal to 0.454 kg.

pound[2] *v.* hit heavily and repeatedly; crush to pieces or powder; (of the heart) throb heavily; run heavily.

pound[3] *n.* enclosure for stray animals or officially removed vehicles.

pour *v.* flow or cause to flow out in a stream; rain heavily; come or go in large numbers.

pout *v.* thrust out one's lips, look sulky. —*n.* pouting look.

pouter *n.* pigeon that can puff out its crop.

poverty *n.* state of being without enough food or money; lack of, scarcity.

POW prisoner of war.

powder *n.* substance in the form of tiny loose particles; medicine or cosmetic in this form. —*v.* apply powder to. —**powdered** *adj.* in the form of a powder, e.g. *powdered milk.* —**powdery** *adj.* —**powder room** ladies' toilet.

power *n.* ability to do or act; strength; position of authority or control; person or thing having authority; particular form of energy, e.g. *nuclear power;* electricity supply; *Physics* rate at which work is done; *Maths* product from continuous multiplication of a number by itself. —**powered** *adj.* having or operated by mechanical or electrical power. —**powerful** *adj.* —**powerless** *adj.* —**power cut** temporary interruption in the supply of electricity. —**power point** socket on a wall for plugging in electrical appliances. —**power station** installation for generating and distributing electric power.

powwow *n.* talk, conference.

pox *n.* disease in which skin pustules form; *Informal* syphilis.

pp pages.

PR proportional representation; public relations.

practicable *adj.* capable of being carried out successfully. —**practicability** *n.*

practical *adj.* involving experience or actual use rather than theory; sensible; adapted for use;

THESAURUS

potter dabble, fritter, tinker

pouch bag, pocket, purse, sack

pounce 1. *v.* ambush, attack, drop, jump, snatch, spring, strike, swoop 2. *n.* assault, attack, bound, jump, leap, spring, swoop

pound 1. batter, beat, strike, thrash, thump 2. bruise, crush, powder, pulverize

pour 1. decant, spill, splash 2. course, emit, flow, gush, run, rush, spout, stream 3. teem

pout lower, mope, sulk

poverty 1. beggary, distress, hardship, insolvency, necessity, need, penury, privation, want 2. dearth, deficiency, lack, paucity, scarcity, shortage

powder 1. *n.* dust, pounce, talc 2. *v.* cover, dredge, dust, scatter, sprinkle, strew

power 1. ability, capacity, competence, faculty, potential 2. brawn, energy, force, intensity, might, muscle, strength, vigour, weight 3.

authority, command, control, dominance, dominion, influence, mastery, rule, sovereignty, sway 4. authorization, licence, prerogative, privilege, right, warrant

powerful 1. energetic, mighty, potent, robust, stalwart, strapping, strong, sturdy, vigorous 2. authoritative, commanding, dominant, influential, prevailing, supreme 3. cogent, compelling, convincing, effective, forceful, impressive, persuasive, telling, weighty

powerless 1. disabled, feeble, frail, helpless, impotent, incapable, infirm, paralysed, prostrate, weak 2. dependent, ineffective, subject, tied, unarmed, vulnerable

practicability feasibility, possibility, use

practicable attainable, doable, feasible, possible, workable

DICTIONARY

good at making or doing things; in effect though not in name. —*n.* examination in which something has to be done or made. —**practically** *adv.* —**practical joke** trick intended to make someone look foolish.

practice *n.* something done regularly or habitually; repetition of something so as to gain skill; doctor's or lawyer's place of work. —**in practice** what actually happens as distinct from what is supposed to happen. —**put into practice** carry out, do.

practise *v.* do repeatedly so as to gain skill; take part in, follow (a religion etc.); work at, e.g. *practise medicine;* do habitually.

practitioner *n.* person who practises a profession.

pragmatic *adj.* concerned with practical consequences rather than theory. —**pragmatism** *n.* —**pragmatist** *n.*

prairie *n.* large treeless area of grassland, esp. in N America. —**prairie dog** rodent that lives in burrows in the N American prairies.

praise *v.* express approval or admiration of (someone or something); express honour and thanks to (God). —*n.* something said or written to show approval or admiration. —**sing someone's praises** praise someone highly. —**praiseworthy** *adj.*

praline [prah-leen] *n.* sweet made of nuts and caramelized sugar.

pram *n.* four-wheeled carriage for a baby, pushed by hand.

prance *v.* walk with exaggerated bouncing steps.

prang *n. Old-fashioned slang* crash (a car or aircraft).

prank *n.* mischievous trick or escapade, frolic.

prat *n. Offens.* stupid person.

prattle *v.* chatter in a childish or foolish way. —*n.* childish or foolish talk. —**prattler** *n.*

prawn *n.* edible shellfish like a large shrimp.

praxis *n.* practice as opposed to theory.

pray *v.* say prayers; ask earnestly, entreat. —**prayer** *n.* thanks or appeal addressed to God; set form of words used in praying; earnest request.

pre- *prefix* before, beforehand, e.g. *prenatal, prerecord, preshrunk.*

preach *v.* give a talk on a religious theme as part of a church service; speak in support of (an idea, principle, etc.). —**preacher** *n.*

preamble *n.* introductory part to something said or written.

prearranged *adj.* arranged beforehand.

prebendary *n., pl.* **-daries.** clergyman who is a member of the chapter of a cathedral.

precarious *adj.* insecure, unsafe, likely to fall or collapse. —**precariously** *adv.*

precaution *n.* action taken in advance to pre-

THESAURUS

practical 1. applied, empirical, factual, pragmatic, realistic, utilitarian 2. businesslike, down-to-earth, hard-headed, mundane 3. proficient, qualified, seasoned, skilled, trained, veteran

practically 1. almost, basically, essentially, fundamentally, nearly, virtually, well-nigh 2. clearly, matter-of-factly, rationally, realistically, sensibly

practice 1. custom, habit, method, routine, rule, system, usage, way, wont 2. drill, exercise, rehearsal, repetition, study, training, work-out

practise 1. drill, exercise, polish, prepare, rehearse, repeat, study, train 2. apply, do, follow, observe, perform 3. carry on, engage in, ply, pursue, undertake

pragmatic efficient, practical, realistic, sensible, utilitarian

praise *n.* 1. acclaim, accolade, applause, approval, commendation, compliment, congratulation, eulogy, kudos, panegyric, plaudit, tribute 2. devotion, glory, homage, thanks, worship ~*v.* 3. acclaim, admire, applaud, ap-

prove, cheer, congratulate, eulogize, extol, honour, laud 4. bless, exalt, glorify, worship

pray ask, beg, beseech, crave, entreat, implore, importune, invoke, petition, plead, request, sue, supplicate, urge

prayer 1. devotion, litany, orison, supplication 2. appeal, entreaty, petition, plea, request, suit

preach 1. address, evangelize, exhort, orate 2. admonish, advocate, exhort, harangue, lecture, moralize, sermonize, urge

preacher evangelist, minister, missionary, parson

preamble foreword, introduction, preface, prelude

precarious dangerous, doubtful, hazardous, insecure, perilous, risky, tricky, uncertain, unsafe, unsure

precaution 1. insurance, protection, provision, safeguard 2. care, caution, forethought, providence, prudence, wariness

DICTIONARY

vent something bad happening. —**precautionary** *adj.*

precede *v.* go or be before. —**precedence** [**press**-ee-denss] *n.* formal order of rank or position. —**take precedence over** be more important than. —**precedent** *n.* previous case or occurrence regarded as an example to be followed.

precentor *n.* person who leads the singing in a church.

precept *n.* rule of behaviour.

precession *n.* —**precession of the equinoxes** slightly earlier occurrence of the equinoxes each year.

precinct *n.* area in a town closed to traffic; enclosed area round a building, e.g. *cathedral precinct; US* administrative area of a city. —*pl.* surrounding region.

precious *adj.* of great value and importance; loved and treasured; (of behaviour) affected, unnatural. —**precious metal** gold, silver or platinum. —**precious stone** rare mineral, such as a ruby, valued as a gem.

precipice *n.* very steep cliff or rockface. —**precipitous** *adj.* sheer.

precipitant *adj.* hasty or rash.

precipitate *v.* cause to happen suddenly; throw headlong; *Chem.* cause to be deposited in solid form from a solution. —*adj.* done rashly or hastily. —*n. Chem.* substance precipitated from a solution. —**precipitately** *adv.* —**precipitation** *n.* precipitating; rain, snow, etc.

précis [**pray**-see] *n., pl.* **précis.** short written summary of the main points of a longer piece. —*v.* make a précis of.

precise *adj.* exact, accurate in every detail; strict in observing rules or standards. —**precisely** *adv.* —**precision** *n.*

preclude *v.* make impossible to happen.

precocious *adj.* having developed or matured early or too soon. —**precocity, precociousness** *n.*

precognition *n.* alleged ability to foretell the future.

preconceived *adj.* (of an idea) formed without real experience or reliable information. —**preconception** *n.*

precondition *n.* something that must happen or exist before something else can.

precursor *n.* something that precedes and is a signal of something else, forerunner.

predate *v.* write a date on (a document) that is earlier than the actual date.

predatory [**pred**-a-tree] *adj.* habitually hunting and killing other animals for food. —**predator** *n.* predatory animal.

predecease *v.* die before (someone else).

predecessor *n.* person who precedes another in an office or position; ancestor.

predestination *n.* belief that future events have already been decided by God. —**predestined** *adj.*

predetermined *adj.* decided in advance.

predicament *n.* embarrassing or difficult situation.

predicate *n.* part of a sentence in which something is said about the subject, e.g. *went home* in *I went home.* —*v.* declare or assert. —**predicative** *adj.* of or in the predicate of a sentence.

predict *v.* tell about in advance, prophesy. —**predictable** *adj.* —**prediction** *n.*

THESAURUS

precede antedate, head, herald, introduce, lead, preface, usher

precedent *n.* authority, criterion, example, instance, model, pattern, standard

precept 1. canon, command, decree, direction, instruction, law, mandate, order, principle, rule, statute 2. guideline, maxim, motto, principle, rule, saying

precinct 1. confine, enclosure, limit 2. area, district, quarter, section

precious 1. beloved, cherished, darling, dear, favourite, idolized, loved, prized, treasured, valued 2. costly, dear, exquisite, fine, priceless, prized, rare, valuable

precipice bluff, brink, cliff, crag, height

precipitate 1. *v.* advance, dispatch, expedite, further, hasten, hurry, press, quicken 2. *adj.* breakneck, headlong, plunging, rapid, rushing, swift, violent

precise accurate, clear-cut, correct, definite, exact, express, fixed, literal, particular, specific, strict

precisely accurately, correctly, exactly, just so, strictly

precision accuracy, care, exactitude, nicety, particularity, rigour

preclude check, debar, exclude, inhibit, obviate, prevent, prohibit, restrain, stop

precocious advanced, ahead, bright, developed, forward, quick, smart

precursor forerunner, herald, messenger, usher, vanguard

predatory hunting, rapacious

predecessor antecedent, forerunner

predetermined agreed, fixed, prearranged

predicament corner, dilemma, emergency, mess, pinch, quandary, situation

DICTIONARY

predilection *n.* preference or liking.

predispose *v.* influence (someone) in favour of something; make (someone) susceptible to something. —**predisposition** *n.*

predominate *v.* be the main or controlling element. —**predominance** *n.* —**predominant** *adj.* —**predominantly** *adv.*

pre-eminent *adj.* excelling all others, outstanding. —**pre-eminently** *adv.* —**pre-eminence** *n.*

pre-empt *v.* get or do in advance of or to the exclusion of others. —**pre-emption** *n.* —**pre-emptive** *adj.*

preen *v.* (of a bird) clean or trim (its feathers) with its beak. —**preen oneself** smarten oneself; show self-satisfaction.

prefab *n.* prefabricated house.

prefabricated *adj.* (of a building) manufactured in shaped sections for rapid assembly on site.

preface [pref-iss] *n.* introduction to a book. —*v.* serve as an introduction to (a book, speech, etc.). —**prefatory** *adj.*

prefect *n.* senior pupil in a school, with limited power over others; senior administrative officer in some countries. —**prefecture** *n.* office or area of authority of a prefect.

prefer *v.* -**ferring**, -**ferred.** like better; *Law* bring (charges) before a court. —**preferable** *adj.* more desirable. —**preferably** *adv.* —**preference** *n.* —**preferential** *adj.* showing preference. —**preferment** *n.* promotion or advancement.

prefigure *v.* represent or suggest in advance.

prefix *n.* letter or group of letters put at the beginning of a word to make a new word, such as *un-* in *unhappy.* —*v.* put as an introduction or prefix (to).

pregnant *adj.* carrying a fetus in the womb; full of meaning or significance. —**pregnancy** *n.*

prehensile *adj.* capable of grasping. —**prehensility** *n.*

prehistoric *adj.* of the period before written history begins. —**prehistory** *n.*

prejudice *n.* unreasonable or unfair dislike or preference. —*v.* cause (someone) to have a prejudice; harm, cause disadvantage to. —**prejudicial** *adj.* harmful, disadvantageous.

prelate [prel-it] *n.* bishop or other churchman of high rank. —**prelacy** *n.*

preliminary *adj.* happening before and in preparation, introductory. —*n., pl.* -**naries.** preliminary remarks, contest, etc.

prelude [prel-yewd] *n.* introductory movement in music; event preceding and introducing something else.

premarital *adj.* occurring before marriage.

premature *adj.* happening or done before the normal or expected time; (of a baby) born before the end of the normal period of pregnancy. —**prematurely** *adv.*

premedication *n.* drugs given to prepare a patient for a general anaesthetic.

THESAURUS

predict augur, divine, forecast, foretell, portend, prophesy

predictable certain, expected, foreseeable, reliable

prediction augury, forecast, prophecy

predominant chief, leading, main, prevailing, principal, ruling, superior, supreme

pre-eminence distinction, prestige, renown, superiority, transcendence

pre-eminent chief, distinguished, excellent, matchless, peerless, renowned, superior, supreme, transcendent, unrivalled, unsurpassed

preface 1. *n.* foreword, introduction, preamble, preliminary, prelude, prologue 2. *v.* begin, introduce, launch, open, precede, prefix

prefer choose, desire, elect, fancy, favour, pick, select, wish

preferable best, better, choice, chosen, worthier

preferably rather, sooner

preference 1. choice, desire, favourite, option, partiality, pick, selection 2. advantage, favouritism, precedence, priority

preferment advancement, dignity, elevation, promotion, rise

prejudice *n.* 1. bias, partiality, prejudgment 2. chauvinism, intolerance, racism, sexism, unfairness ~*v.* 3. bias, colour, distort, influence, poison, prepossess, slant, sway, warp 4. damage, harm, hinder, hurt, impair, injure, mar, spoil, undermine

prejudicial damaging, harmful, hurtful, inimical, injurious

preliminary 1. *adj.* first, initial, introductory, opening, pilot, preparatory, prior, qualifying, test, trial 2. *n.* beginning, groundwork, initiation, introduction, opening, preamble, preface, prelims, prelude, start

prelude beginning, introduction, overture, preamble, preface, prologue, start

premature early, immature, incomplete, raw, unripe, unseasonable, untimely

premeditated calculated, considered, deliberate, intentional, planned

DICTIONARY

premeditated *adj.* planned in advance. —**premeditation** *n.*

premenstrual *adj.* occurring or experienced before a menstrual period, e.g. *premenstrual tension.*

premier *n.* prime minister. —*adj.* chief, leading. —**premiership** *n.*

première *n.* first performance of a play, film, etc.

premise, premiss *n.* statement assumed to be true and used as the basis of reasoning.

premises *pl. n.* house or other building and its land.

premium *n.* additional sum of money, as on a wage or charge; (regular) sum paid for insurance. —**at a premium** in great demand because scarce. —**Premium (Savings) Bond** savings certificate issued by the government, on which no interest is paid but cash prizes can be won.

premonition *n.* feeling that something unpleasant is going to happen. —**premonitory** *adj.*

prenatal *adj.* before birth; during pregnancy.

preoccupy *v.* **-pying, -pied.** fill the thoughts or attention of (someone) to the exclusion of other things. —**preoccupation** *n.*

preordained *adj.* decreed or determined in advance.

prep school *n.* short for PREPARATORY SCHOOL.

prep. preparatory; preposition.

prepacked *adj.* sold already wrapped.

prepaid *adj.* paid for in advance.

prepare *v.* make or get ready. —**prepared** *adj.* willing; ready. —**preparation** *n.* preparing; something done in readiness for something else;

mixture prepared for use as a cosmetic, medicine, etc. —**preparatory** [prip-**par**-a-tree] *adj.* preparing for. —**preparatory school** private school for children going on to public school.

preponderant *adj.* greater in amount, force, or influence. —**preponderantly** *adv.* —**preponderance** *n.*

preposition *n.* word used before a noun or pronoun to show its relationship with other words, such as *by* in *go by bus.* —**prepositional** *adj.*

prepossessing *adj.* making a favourable impression, attractive.

preposterous *adj.* utterly absurd.

prepuce [**pree**-pyewss] *n.* retractable fold of skin covering the tip of the penis, foreskin.

prerecorded *adj.* recorded in advance to be played or broadcast later.

prerequisite *n., adj.* (something) that must happen or exist before something else is possible.

prerogative *n.* special power or privilege.

presage [**press**-ij] *v.* be a sign or warning of.

presbyopia *n.* inability of the eye to focus on nearby objects.

Presbyterian *adj., n.* (member) of a Protestant church governed by lay elders. —**Presbyterianism** *n.*

presbytery *n., pl.* **-teries.** *Presbyterian Church* local church court; *RC Church* priest's house.

prescience [**press**-ee-enss] *n.* knowledge of events before they happen. —**prescient** *adj.*

prescribe *v.* recommend the use of (a medicine); lay down as a rule. —**prescription** *n.* written instructions from a doctor for the mak-

THESAURUS

premier 1. *n.* chancellor, prime minister 2. *adj.* arch, chief, first, foremost, head, highest, leading, main, primary, prime, principal, top

premiere debut, opening

premises building, place, property, site

premiss, premise argument, assertion, ground, hypothesis, postulate

premium bonus, boon, bounty, fee, perquisite, prize, recompense, reward

premonition feeling, foreboding, hunch, idea, intuition, omen, portent, presentiment, sign, suspicion

preoccupation absorption, daydreaming, musing, oblivion, reverie

preoccupied absorbed, distrait, engrossed, heedless, immersed, intent, oblivious, rapt, unaware

preparation 1. groundwork, preparing 2. anticipation, foresight, precaution, provision,

readiness, safeguard 3. compound, concoction, medicine, mixture

prepare 1. adapt, adjust, arrange, coach, dispose, form, groom, plan, practise, prime, train, warm up 2. brace, fortify, gird, ready, steel, strengthen 3. assemble, concoct, construct, contrive, fashion, make, produce

prepared 1. ready, set 2. able, disposed, inclined, minded, willing

preposterous absurd, bizarre, crazy, excessive, extreme, foolish, impossible, insane, monstrous, outrageous, ridiculous, senseless, shocking, unthinkable

prerequisite 1. *adj.* essential, indispensable, mandatory, necessary, required, vital 2. *n.* condition, necessity, qualification, requirement

prerogative authority, choice, claim, due, liberty, privilege, right

DICTIONARY

ing up and use of a medicine. —**prescriptive** *adj.* laying down rules.

presence *n.* fact of being in a specified place; impressive dignified appearance. —**presence of mind** ability to act sensibly in a crisis.

present[1] *adj.* being in a specified place; existing or happening now; (of a verb tense) indicating that the action specified is taking place now. —*n.* present time or tense. —**presently** *adv.* soon; *US & Scot.* now.

present[2] *n.* something given to bring pleasure to another person. —*v.* introduce formally or publicly; introduce and compère (a TV or radio show); cause, e.g. *present a difficulty;* give, award. —**presentation** *n.* —**presentable** *adj.* attractive, neat, fit for people to see. —**presenter** *n.* person introducing a TV or radio show.

presentiment [pree-**zen**-tim-ent] *n.* sense of something usu. unpleasant about to happen.

preserve *v.* keep from being damaged, changed, or ended; treat (food) to prevent it decaying. —*n.* area of interest restricted to a particular person or group; fruit preserved by cooking in sugar; area where game is kept for private fishing or shooting. —**preservation** *n.* —**preservative** *n.* chemical that prevents decay.

preside *v.* be in charge, esp. of a meeting.

president *n.* head of state in countries without a king or queen; head of a society, institution, etc. —**presidential** *adj.* —**presidency** *n.*

press[1] *v.* apply force or weight to; squeeze; smooth by applying pressure or heat; crowd, push; urge insistently. —*n.* newspapers collectively; reporters, journalists; printing machine.

—**pressed for** short of. —**pressing** *adj.* urgent. —**press box** room at a sports ground reserved for reporters. —**press conference** interview for reporters given by a celebrity.

press[2] *v.* —**press into service** force to be involved or used. —**press gang** *Hist.* group of men who captured men and boys and forced them to join the navy.

pressure *n.* force produced by pressing; urgent claims or demands, e.g. *working under pressure; Physics* force applied to a surface per unit of area. —**bring pressure to bear on** use influence or authority to persuade. —**pressure cooker** airtight pot which cooks food quickly by steam under pressure. —**pressure group** group that tries to influence policies, public opinion, etc.

prestidigitation *n.* skilful quickness with the hands, conjuring.

prestige *n.* high status or respect resulting from success or achievements. —**prestigious** *adj.*

presto *Music* very quickly.

prestressed *adj.* (of concrete) containing stretched steel wires to strengthen it.

presume *v.* suppose to be the case; (foll. by *to*) dare (to), take the liberty (of). —**presumably** *adv.* one supposes (that). —**presumption** *n.* bold insolent behaviour; strong probability. —**presumptuous** *adj.* doing things one has no right or authority to do. —**presumptuously** *adv.* —**presumptive** *adj.* assumed to be true or valid until the contrary is proved. —**heir presumptive** heir whose right may be defeated by the birth of a closer relative.

THESAURUS

prescribe appoint, assign, decree, define, dictate, direct, lay down, ordain, require, rule, set, specify, stipulate

prescription drug, medicine, mixture, remedy

presence 1. company, existence, occupancy, residence 2. air, appearance, aspect, aura, bearing, demeanour, ease, personality, poise, self-assurance

present[1] *adj.* 1. existing, immediate, instant 2. accounted for, available, here, nearby, ready, there ~*n.* 3. today

present[2] *v.* 1. introduce 2. demonstrate, display, exhibit, give, mount, put on, show, stage 3. advance, declare, expound, extend, offer, pose, proffer, relate, state, submit, suggest, tender ~*n.* 4. boon, bounty, donation, favour, gift, grant, gratuity, largess, offering

presentation 1. award, bestowal, conferral, donation, investiture, offering 2. arrangement, delivery, staging, submission 3. display, exhibition, performance, production, show

presently by and by, shortly, soon

preservation protection, safekeeping, safety, salvation, security, storage, support

preserve 1. *v.* care for, defend, guard, keep, protect, safeguard, save, secure, shelter 2. *n.* area, domain, field, realm, sphere

preside administer, chair, conduct, control, direct, govern, head, lead, manage, run

press *v.* 1. condense, crush, jam, mash, push, reduce, squeeze, stuff 2. finish, flatten, iron, mangle, smooth 3. compel, constrain, demand, enforce, enjoin, force 4. beg, entreat, exhort, implore, importune, petition, plead, sue, urge 5. cluster, crowd, flock, gather, hasten, herd, hurry, mill, push, rush, seethe, surge, swarm, throng

pressure 1. crushing, force, squeezing, weight 2. compulsion, constraint, force, influence, power, sway

prestige authority, credit, distinction, esteem,

DICTIONARY

presuppose v. need as a previous condition in order to be true. —**presupposition** n.

pretend v. claim or give the appearance of (something untrue) to deceive or in play. —**pretender** n. person who makes a false or disputed claim to a position of power. —**pretence** n. behaviour intended to deceive, pretending. —**pretentious** adj. making (unjustified) claims to special merit or importance. —**pretension** n.

preterite [pret-er-it] adj., n. Grammar (expressing) a past tense, such as jumped, swam.

preternatural adj. beyond what is natural, supernatural.

pretext n. false reason given to hide the real one.

pretty adj. **-tier, -tiest.** pleasing to look at. —adv. fairly, moderately. —**prettily** adv. —**prettiness** n.

pretzel n. brittle salted biscuit.

prevail v. gain mastery; be generally established. —**prevailing** adj. widespread; predominant. —**prevalence** n. —**prevalent** adj. widespread, common.

prevaricate v. be evasive, avoid giving a direct or truthful answer. —**prevarication** n.

prevent v. keep from happening or doing. —**preventable** adj. —**prevention** n. —**preventive** adj., n.

preview n. advance showing of a film or exhibition before it is shown to the public.

previous adj. coming or happening before. —**previously** adv.

prey n. animal hunted and killed for food by another animal; victim. —**bird of prey** bird that kills and eats other birds or animals. —**prey on** v. hunt and kill for food; worry, obsess.

price n. amount of money for which a thing is bought or sold; unpleasant thing that must be endured to get something desirable. —v. fix or ask the price of. —**priceless** adj. very valuable; Informal very funny. —**pric(e)y** adj. Informal expensive.

prick v. pierce slightly with a sharp point; cause to feel mental pain; (of an animal) make (the ears) stand erect. —n. sudden sharp pain caused by pricking; mark made by pricking; remorse. —**prick up one's ears** listen intently.

THESAURUS

fame, honour, importance, influence, renown, reputation, status

presume believe, conjecture, infer, suppose, surmise, think

presumption audacity, boldness, effrontery, insolence, temerity

presuppose accept, assume, consider, imply, postulate, presume

pretence 1. acting, charade, deceit, deception, falsehood, feigning, invention, sham, simulation, trickery 2. affectation, artifice, display, façade, show, veneer

pretend 1. affect, allege, assume, fake, falsify, feign, impersonate, profess, sham, simulate 2. act, imagine, play, suppose

pretender aspirant, claimant, claimer

pretension 1. aspiration, assumption, claim, demand, pretence, profession 2. affectation, airs, conceit, hypocrisy, show, snobbery, vanity

pretentious affected, conceited, exaggerated, extravagant, grandiose, high-flown, hollow, inflated, mannered, ostentatious, showy, snobbish

pretext cloak, cover, device, excuse, guise, mask, ploy, pretence, ruse, semblance, show, veil

pretty 1. adj. attractive, beautiful, charming, cute, fair, good-looking, graceful, lovely 2. adv. moderately, quite, rather, reasonably, somewhat

prevail overcome, overrule, succeed, triumph, win

prevailing common, current, customary, fashionable, general, ordinary, popular, prevalent, set, usual, widespread

prevaricate cavil, deceive, dodge, equivocate, evade, hedge, lie, palter, quibble, shift, shuffle

prevent avert, avoid, balk, bar, block, check, forestall, frustrate, hamper, hinder, impede, inhibit, obstruct, obviate, preclude, restrain, stop, thwart

prevention 1. avoidance, deterrence, elimination, precaution, safeguard, thwarting 2. bar, check, deterrence, hindrance, impediment, interruption, obstacle, obstruction, stoppage

preventive 1. adj. hampering, hindering, impeding, obstructive 2. n. block, hindrance, impediment, obstacle, obstruction

previous earlier, former, past, preceding, prior

previously before, earlier, formerly, once, then

prey 1. game, kill, quarry 2. dupe, target, victim

price n. 1. amount, assessment, bill, charge, cost, estimate, expense, fee, figure, outlay, payment, rate, valuation, worth 2. consequences, cost, penalty, sacrifice, toll ~v. 3. assess, cost, estimate, evaluate, rate, value

priceless cherished, costly, dear, expensive, precious, rare, rich, treasured

prick v. 1. bore, jab, lance, pierce, pink, punch, stab 2. bite, itch, prickle, smart, sting, tingle

DICTIONARY

prickle *n.* thorn or spike on a plant. —*v.* have a tingling or pricking sensation. —**prickly** *adj.* —**prickly heat** itchy rash occurring in hot moist weather.

pride *n.* feeling of pleasure and satisfaction when one has done well; too high an opinion of oneself; something that causes one to feel pride; group of lions. —**pride of place** most important position. —**pride oneself on** feel pride about.

priest *n.* (in the Christian church) a person who can administer the sacraments and preach; in some other religions, an official who performs religious ceremonies. —**priestess** *n.* woman priest. —**priesthood** *n.* —**priestly** *adj.*

prig *n.* self-righteous person who acts as if superior to others. —**priggish** *adj.* —**priggishness** *n.*

prim *adj.* **primmer, primmest.** formal, proper, and rather prudish. —**primly** *adv.* —**primness** *n.*

prima ballerina *n.* leading female ballet dancer.

primacy *n., pl.* **-cies.** state of being first in rank, grade, etc.; office of an archbishop.

prima donna *n.* leading female opera singer; *Informal* temperamental person.

primaeval *adj.* same as PRIMEVAL.

prima facie [**prime-**a **fay-**shee] *Latin* as it seems at first.

primal *adj.* of basic causes or origins.

primary *adj.* chief, most important. —**primarily** *adv.* —**primary colours** (in physics) red, green, and blue or (in art) red, yellow, and blue, from which all other colours can be produced by mixing. —**primary school** school for children from five to eleven years.

primate[1] *n.* archbishop.

primate[2] *n.* member of an order of mammals including monkeys and humans.

prime *adj.* main, most important; of the highest quality. —*n.* time when someone is at his or her best or most vigorous. —*v.* give (someone) information in advance to prepare them for something; prepare (a surface) for painting; prepare (a gun, pump, etc.) for use. —**Prime Minister** leader of a government. —**prime number** number that can be divided exactly only by itself and one.

primer *n.* special paint applied to bare wood etc. before the main paint; beginners' school book or manual.

primeval [prime-**ee**-val] *adj.* of the earliest age of the world.

primitive *adj.* of an early simple stage of development; basic, crude, e.g. *a primitive hut.*

primogeniture *n.* system under which the eldest son inherits all his parents' property.

primordial *adj.* existing at or from the beginning.

primrose *n.* pale yellow spring flower.

primula *n.* type of primrose with brightly coloured flowers.

Primus *n.* ® portable cooking stove used esp. by campers.

prince *n.* male member of a royal family, esp. the son of the king or queen; male ruler of a small country. —**princely** *adj.* of or like a prince; generous, lavish, or magnificent. —**prince consort** husband of a reigning queen. —**Prince of Wales** eldest son of the British sovereign. —**princess** *n.* female member of a royal family, esp. the daughter of the king or queen. —**Princess Royal** title sometimes given to the eldest daughter of the British sovereign.

principal *adj.* main, most important. —*n.* head of a school or college; person taking a leading part in something; sum of money lent on which interest is paid. —**principally** *adv.* —**principal boy** leading male role in pantomime, played by a woman.

THESAURUS

~*n.* 3. cut, gash, hole, pinhole, puncture, wound

prickly 1. barbed, bristly, spiny, thorny 2. scratchy, sharp, smarting, stinging, tingling

pride *n.* 1. arrogance, conceit, egotism, hauteur, loftiness, pretension, self-importance, snobbery, vanity 2. boast, gem, jewel, prize, treasure

priest clergyman, cleric, curate, divine, father, minister, vicar

prig pedant, prude, puritan

prim demure, fastidious, formal, fussy, particular, precise, proper, strait-laced

primarily basically, chiefly, essentially, fundamentally, generally, mainly, mostly

primary best, capital, cardinal, chief, first, greatest, highest, leading, main, prime, principal, top

prime *adj.* 1. best, choice, first-class, first-rate, highest, quality, select, selected, superior, top 2. chief, leading, main, pre-eminent, principal, ruling, senior ~*n.* 3. bloom, flower, height, peak, zenith ~*v.* 4. coach, fit, groom, prepare, train 5. brief, inform, notify, tell

primitive 1. earliest, original, primary, primeval, primordial, pristine 2. barbarian, crude, rough, rude, simple, uncivilized, unrefined

prince lord, monarch, ruler, sovereign

DICTIONARY

principality *n., pl.* **-ties.** territory ruled by a prince.

principle *n.* moral rule guiding behaviour; general or basic truth, e.g. *the principle of equality;* scientific law concerning the working of something. —**in principle** in theory but not always in practice. —**on principle** because of one's beliefs.

print *v.* reproduce (a newspaper, book, etc.) in large quantities by mechanical or electronic means; reproduce (text or pictures) by pressing ink onto paper etc.; write in letters that are not joined up; *Photog.* produce (pictures) from negatives; stamp (fabric) with a design. —*n.* printed words etc.; printed lettering; photograph; printed copy of a painting; mark left on a surface by something that has pressed against it; printed fabric. —**out of print** no longer available from a publisher. —**printer** *n.* person or company engaged in printing; machine that prints. —**printed circuit** electronic circuit with wiring printed on an insulating base. —**print-out** *n.* printed information from a computer.

prior¹ *adj.* earlier. —**prior to** before.

prior² *n.* head monk in a priory. —**prioress** *n.* deputy head nun in a convent. —**priory** *n.* place where certain orders of monks or nuns live.

priority *n., pl.* **-ties.** most important thing that must be dealt with first; right to be or go before others.

prise *v.* force open by levering.

prism *n.* transparent block usu. with triangular ends and rectangular sides, used to disperse light into a spectrum or refract it in optical instruments. —**prismatic** *adj.* of or shaped like a prism; (of colour) as if produced by refraction through a prism, rainbow-like.

prison *n.* building where criminals and accused people are held. —**prisoner** *n.* person held captive. —**prisoner of war** serviceman captured by an enemy in wartime.

prissy *adj.* **-sier, -siest.** prim, correct, and easily shocked. —**prissily** *adv.*

pristine *adj.* clean, new, and unused.

private *adj.* for the use of one person or group only; secret; owned or paid for by individuals rather than by the government; quiet, not likely to be disturbed; personal, unconnected with one's work. —*n.* soldier of the lowest rank. —**privately** *adv.* —**privacy** *n.*

privateer *n. Hist.* privately owned armed vessel authorized by the government to take part in a war; captain of such a ship.

privation *n.* loss or lack of the necessities of life.

privatize *n.* sell (a publicly owned company) to individuals or a private company. —**privatization** *n.*

privet *n.* bushy evergreen shrub used for hedges.

privilege *n.* advantage or favour that only some people have. —**privileged** *adj.* enjoying a special right or immunity.

privy *adj.* sharing knowledge of something secret. —*n., pl.* **privies.** *Obs.* toilet, esp. an outside one. —**privy council** council of state of a monarch.

prize¹ *n.* reward given for success in a competition etc. —*adj.* winning or likely to win a prize. —*v.* value highly. —**prizefighter** *n.* boxer who fights for money. —**prizefight** *n.*

prize² *v.* same as PRISE.

THESAURUS

princely bounteous, generous, gracious, lavish, liberal, rich

principal *adj.* 1. cardinal, chief, dominant, first, foremost, highest, key, leading, main, paramount, pre-eminent, prime, strongest ~*n.* 2. chief, director, head, leader, master, ruler 3. dean, director, headmaster, headmistress, master, rector 4. assets, capital, money

principally chiefly, especially, mainly, mostly, predominantly, primarily

principle 1. axiom, canon, criterion, doctrine, dogma, ethic, formula, law, maxim, precept, proposition, rule, standard, truth 2. belief, code, ethic, morality, opinion 3. integrity, morals, probity, rectitude, scruples

print *v.* 1. engrave, issue, mark, publish, stamp ~*n.* 2. book, magazine, newspaper, periodical, publication, typescript 3. copy, engraving, photograph, picture

priority precedence, preference, rank, seniority, superiority, supremacy

prison confinement, dungeon, gaol, jail

prisoner 1. convict, jailbird 2. captive, hostage, internee

privacy isolation, retirement, retreat, seclusion, solitude

private 1. confidential, inside, secret, unofficial 2. exclusive, intimate, own, personal, special 3. concealed, isolated, retired, secluded, secret, separate, solitary, withdrawn

privilege birthright, claim, concession, due, entitlement, freedom, immunity, liberty, right

prize¹ *n.* 1. award, honour, reward, trophy 2. purse, stakes, winnings ~*adj.* 3. best, champion, outstanding, top

prize² *v.* cherish, esteem, treasure, value

DICTIONARY

pro[1] *adj., adv.* in favour of. **—pros and cons** arguments for and against.

pro[2] *n.* professional; prostitute.

pro- *prefix* in favour of, e.g. *pro-Russian;* instead of, e.g. *pronoun.*

probable *adj.* likely to happen or be true. **—probably** *adv.* **—probability** *n.*

probate *n.* process of proving the authenticity of a will; certificate of this.

probation *n.* system of dealing with law-breakers, esp. juvenile ones, by placing them under supervision; period when someone is assessed for suitability for a job etc. **—probationer** *n.* person on probation.

probe *v.* search into or examine closely. *—n.* surgical instrument used to examine a wound, cavity, etc.

probity *n.* honesty, integrity.

problem *n.* something difficult to deal with or solve; question or puzzle set for solution. **—problematic(al)** *adj.*

proboscis [pro-**boss**-iss] *n.* elephant's trunk; long snout; elongated mouthpart of some insects.

procedure *n.* way of doing something, esp. the correct or usual one.

proceed *v.* start or continue doing; *Formal* walk, go; start a legal action; arise from. **—proceeds** *pl. n.* money obtained from an event or activity. **—proceedings** *pl. n.* organized or related series of events; minutes of a meeting; legal action.

process *n.* series of actions or changes; method of doing or producing something. *—v.* handle or prepare by a special method of manufacture; treat (food) to prevent it decaying. **—processsor** *n.*

procession *n.* line of people or vehicles moving forward together in order.

proclaim *v.* declare publicly. **—proclamation** *n.*

proclivity *n., pl.* **-ties.** inclination, tendency.

proconsul *n. Hist.* governor of a province, esp. of the Roman Empire.

procrastinate *v.* put off taking action, delay. **—procrastination** *n.* **—procrastinator** *n.*

procreate *v. Formal* produce offspring. **—procreation** *n.*

Procrustean *adj.* ruthlessly enforcing uniformity.

procurator fiscal *n.* (in Scotland) law officer who acts as public prosecutor and coroner.

procure *v.* get, provide; obtain (people) to act as prostitutes. **—procurement** *n.* **—procurer, procuress** *n.* person who obtains people to act as prostitutes.

prod *v.* **prodding, prodded.** poke with something pointed; goad (someone) to take action. *—n.* prodding.

prodigal *adj.* recklessly extravagant, wasteful. **—prodigality** *n.*

THESAURUS

probability expectation, likelihood, odds, prospect

probable apparent, credible, feasible, likely, ostensible, plausible, presumable, reasonable

probably doubtless, likely, maybe, perhaps, possibly

probe *v.* examine, explore, go into, investigate, query, scrutinize, search, sift, sound, test, verify

problem *n.* 1. difficulty, dispute, doubt, predicament, quandary, trouble 2. conundrum, enigma, poser, puzzle, question, riddle

procedure action, conduct, course, custom, form, method, performance, policy, practice, process, routine, scheme, step, strategy, system

proceed 1. advance, continue, go on, press on, progress 2. arise, come, derive, emanate, ensue, flow, follow, issue, result, spring, stem

proceeds earnings, gain, income, profit, receipts, returns, takings, yield

process *n.* 1. action, course, manner, means, measure, method, mode, operation, performance, practice, system, transaction 2. advance, course, development, evolution, formation, growth, movement, progress, stage, step ~*v.* 3. fulfil, handle 4. alter, convert, prepare, refine, transform, treat

procession column, cortege, file, march, parade, train

proclaim announce, circulate, declare, herald, indicate, profess, promulgate, publish

proclamation declaration, decree, edict, notice, pronouncement, publication

procrastinate adjourn, dally, defer, delay, postpone, prolong, protract, put off, retard, stall, temporize

procure acquire, buy, earn, effect, find, gain, get, obtain, pick up, purchase, secure, win

prod *v.* 1. dig, drive, elbow, jab, nudge, poke, prick, push, shove 2. goad, impel, move, prompt, rouse, spur, stimulate, urge ~*n.* 3. boost, dig, elbow, jab, nudge, poke, push, shove 4. goad, spur, stick

prodigal excessive, extravagant, improvident,

DICTIONARY

prodigy *n., pl.* **-gies.** person with some marvellous talent; wonderful thing. —**prodigious** *adj.* very large, immense; wonderful. —**prodigiously** *adv.*

produce *v.* bring into existence; present to view, show; make, manufacture; present on stage, film, or television. —*n.* food grown for sale. —**producer** *n.* person with financial and administrative control of a film etc.; person or company that produces something.

product *n.* something produced; number resulting from multiplication. —**production** *n.* producing; things produced. —**productive** *adj.* producing large quantities; useful, profitable. —**productivity** *n.*

profane *adj.* showing disrespect for religion or holy things; (of language) coarse, blasphemous. —*v.* treat (something sacred) irreverently, desecrate. —**profanation** *n.* act of profaning. —**profanity** *n.* profane talk or behaviour, blasphemy.

profess *v.* state or claim (something as true), sometimes falsely; have as one's belief or religion. —**professed** *adj.* supposed.

profession *n.* type of work, such as being a doctor, that needs special training; all the people employed in a profession, e.g. *the legal profession;* declaration of a belief or feeling. —**professional** *adj.* working in a profession; taking part in an activity, such as sport or music, for money; very competent. —*n.* person who works in a profession; person paid to take part in sport, music, etc. —**professionally** *adv.* —**professionalism** *n.*

professor *n.* teacher of the highest rank in a university. —**professorial** *adj.* —**professorship** *n.*

proffer *v.* offer.

proficient *adj.* skilled, expert. —**proficiency** *n.*

profile *n.* outline, esp. of the face, as seen from the side; brief biographical sketch.

profit *n.* money gained; benefit obtained. —*v.* gain or benefit. —**profitable** *adj.* making profit. —**profitably** *adv.* —**profitability** *n.* —**profiteer** *n.* person who makes excessive profits at the expense of the public. —**profiteering** *n.*

THESAURUS

profligate, reckless, spendthrift, wanton, wasteful

prodigious 1. enormous, huge, immense, massive, stupendous, tremendous, vast 2. abnormal, astounding, fabulous, impressive, marvellous, miraculous, remarkable, startling, striking, wonderful

prodigy 1. genius, mastermind, talent 2. marvel, miracle, phenomenon, wonder

produce *v.* 1. compose, construct, create, develop, invent, make, originate, turn out 2. bear, beget, breed, deliver, furnish, give, render, supply, yield 3. advance, demonstrate, exhibit, offer, present, show 4. direct, do, exhibit, mount, present, show, stage ~*n.* 5. crop, greengrocery, harvest, product, yield

producer 1. director, impresario 2. farmer, grower, maker

product 1. artefact, creation, goods, invention, merchandise, work 2. consequence, effect, fruit, issue, legacy, offshoot, outcome, result, returns, spin-off, upshot, yield

production 1. construction, creation, fabrication, manufacture, origination, preparation, producing 2. direction, management, presentation, staging

productive creative, dynamic, fecund, fertile, fruitful, generative, inventive, plentiful, prolific, rich, teeming, vigorous

productivity output, production, work rate, yield

profane *adj.* 1. godless, heathen, impious, irreverent, pagan, sinful, ungodly, wicked 2. abusive, coarse, crude, filthy, foul, obscene, vulgar ~*v.* 3. abuse, contaminate, debase, defile, desecrate, misuse, pervert, pollute, vitiate

profanity blasphemy, curse, execration, impiety, malediction, obscenity, sacrilege, swearword

profess admit, affirm, announce, assert, aver, avow, certify, confess, confirm, declare, maintain, own, proclaim, state, vouch

professed alleged, apparent

profession 1. business, calling, career, employment, line, occupation, office, position, sphere 2. assertion, avowal, claim, declaration, statement, testimony, vow

professional 1. *adj.* adept, competent, efficient, expert, masterly, polished, practised, proficient, qualified, skilled, trained 2. *n.* adept, expert, master, virtuoso

professor don, fellow

proficiency ability, aptitude, competence, expertise, facility, knack, skill, talent

proficient able, adept, apt, capable, clever, competent, expert, gifted, masterly, qualified, skilful, talented, trained

profile *n.* 1. drawing, figure, form, outline, portrait, shape, silhouette, sketch 2. biography, sketch

profit *n.* 1. earnings, emoluments, gain, proceeds, receipts, return, revenue, surplus, takings, winnings, yield 2. advantage, avail, benefit, gain, good, interest, use, value ~*v.* 3. aid,

DICTIONARY

profligate *adj.* recklessly extravagant; shamelessly immoral. —*n.* dissolute person. —**profligacy** *n.*

pro forma *Latin* prescribing a set form.

profound *adj.* showing or needing great knowledge; strongly felt, intense. —**profundity** *n.*

profuse *adj.* plentiful. —**profusion** *n.*

progeny [**proj**-in-ee] *n., pl.* **-nies.** children. —**progenitor** [pro-**jen**-it-er] *n.* ancestor.

progesterone *n.* hormone which prepares the womb for pregnancy and prevents further ovulation.

prognathous *adj.* having a projecting lower jaw.

prognosis *n., pl.* **-noses.** doctor's forecast about the progress of an illness; any forecast.

prognostication *n.* forecast or prediction.

program *n.* sequence of coded instructions for a computer. —*v.* **-gramming, -grammed.** arrange (data) so that it can be processed by a computer; feed a program into (a computer). —**programmer** *n.* —**programmable** *adj.*

programme *n.* planned series of events; broadcast on radio or television; list of items or performers in an entertainment.

progress *n.* improvement, development; movement forward. —*v.* become more advanced or skilful; move forward. —**in progress** taking place. —**progression** *n.* act of progressing, advance; sequence of numbers in which each differs from the next by a fixed ratio. —**progressive** *adj.* favouring political or social reform; happening gradually. —**progressively** *adv.*

prohibit *v.* forbid or prevent from happening. —**prohibition** *n.* act of forbidding; ban on the sale or drinking of alcohol. —**prohibitive** *adj.* (of prices) too high to be affordable. —**prohibitively** *adv.*

project *n.* planned scheme to do or examine something over a period. —*v.* make a forecast based on known data; make (a film or slide) appear on a screen; communicate (an impression); stick out beyond a surface or edge. —**projector** *n.* apparatus for projecting photographic images, films, or slides on a screen. —**projection** *n.* —**projectionist** *n.* person who operates a projector.

projectile *n.* object thrown as a weapon or fired from a gun.

prolapse *n.* slipping down of an internal organ of the body from its normal position.

prole *adj., n. Offens.* proletarian.

THESAURUS

avail, benefit, better, contribute, gain, help, improve, promote, serve 4. clear, earn, gain, make money

profitable 1. commercial, cost-effective, fruitful, paying, rewarding, worthwhile 2. beneficial, fruitful, productive, rewarding, serviceable, useful, valuable, worthwhile

profligate *adj.* 1. debauched, degenerate, depraved, dissipated, dissolute, immoral, licentious, loose, shameless, vicious, wicked, wild 2. extravagant, immoderate, reckless, spend~ thrift, wasteful ~*n.* 3. degenerate, libertine, rake, reprobate, roué

profound 1. abstruse, deep, discerning, erudite, learned, serious, skilled, subtle, thoughtful, weighty, wise 2. extreme, great, heartfelt, in~ tense, keen, sincere

profuse ample, copious, overflowing, plentiful, prolific, teeming

profusion bounty, excess, extravagance, glut, multitude, plethora, quantity, riot, surplus, wealth

progeny children, descendants, family, issue, offspring, race, seed, stock, young

programme *n.* 1. curriculum, line-up, list, list~ ing, plan, schedule, syllabus 2. broadcast, performance, production, show

progress *n.* 1. advance, course, movement, pas~ sage, way 2. advance, breakthrough, develop~ ment, gain, growth, headway, improvement, increase ~*v.* 3. advance, continue, move on, proceed, travel 4. advance, blossom, develop, gain, grow, improve, increase

progressive 1. advancing, continuing, growing, increasing, intensifying, ongoing 2. avant-garde, dynamic, enlightened, liberal, modern, radical, reformist

prohibit 1. ban, debar, forbid, outlaw, veto 2. constrain, hamper, hinder, impede, obstruct, preclude, prevent, stop

prohibition 1. constraint, exclusion, obstruc~ tion, prevention, restriction 2. ban, bar, em~ bargo, injunction, interdict, proscription, veto

prohibitive *Esp. of prices* excessive, exorbitant, extortionate

project *n.* 1. activity, design, enterprise, job, plan, programme, proposal, scheme, task, venture, work ~*v.* 2. contemplate, contrive, design, devise, draft, frame, outline, plan, propose, purpose, scheme 3. cast, discharge, fling, hurl, launch, propel, shoot, throw, transmit 4. extend, jut, overhang, protrude

projectile bullet, missile, rocket, shell

proletariat commoners, labouring classes, plebs, the common people, the masses, wage-earners, working class

DICTIONARY

proletariat [pro-lit-**air**-ee-at] *n.* working class. —**proletarian** *adj., n.*

proliferate *v.* grow or reproduce rapidly. —**proliferation** *n.*

prolific *adj.* very productive. —**prolifically** *adv.*

prolix *adj.* (of speech or a piece of writing) overlong and boring. —**prolixity** *n.*

prologue *n.* introduction to a play or book.

prolong *v.* make (something) last longer. —**prolongation** *n.*

prom *n.* short for PROMENADE or PROMENADE CONCERT.

promenade *n.* paved walkway along the seafront at a holiday resort. —*v., n. Old-fashioned* (take) a leisurely walk. —**promenade concert** concert at which part of the audience stands rather than sits.

prominent *adj.* very noticeable; famous, widely known. —**prominently** *adv.* —**prominence** *n.*

promiscuous *adj.* having many casual sexual relationships. —**promiscuity** *n.*

promise *v.* say that one will definitely do or not do something; show signs of, seem likely. —*n.* undertaking to do or not to do something; indication of future success. —**show promise** seem likely to succeed. —**promising** *adj.* likely to succeed or turn out well.

promo *n. Informal* short video film made to promote a pop record.

promontory *n., pl.* **-ries.** point of high land jutting out into the sea.

promote *v.* help to make (something) happen or increase; raise to a higher rank or position; encourage the sale of by advertising. —**promoter** *n.* person who organizes or finances an event etc. —**promotion** *n.* —**promotional** *adj.*

prompt *v.* cause (an action); remind (an actor or speaker) of words that he or she has forgotten. —*adj.* done without delay. —*adv.* exactly, e.g. *six o'clock prompt.* —**promptly** *adv.* immediately, without delay. —**promptness** *n.* —**prompter** *n.* person offstage who prompts actors.

promulgate *v.* put (a law etc.) into effect by announcing it officially; make widely known. —**promulgation** *n.* —**promulgator** *n.*

THESAURUS

prolific bountiful, copious, fertile, fruitful, luxuriant, productive, profuse, rank, rich, teeming

prologue foreword, introduction, preamble, preface, prelude

prolong continue, delay, extend, lengthen, perpetuate, protract, spin out, stretch

promenade *n.* 1. esplanade, parade, walkway 2. airing, saunter, stroll, turn, walk ~*v.* 3. saunter, stroll, walk

prominence 1. conspicuousness, precedence, salience, weight 2. celebrity, distinction, eminence, fame, greatness, importance, name, prestige, rank, reputation

prominent 1. conspicuous, eye-catching, noticeable, obtrusive, obvious, remarkable, striking 2. celebrated, chief, distinguished, eminent, famous, foremost, important, leading, main, renowned, respected, top, well-known

promiscuous debauched, dissipated, dissolute, fast, immoral, lax, loose, wanton, wild

promise *v.* 1. assure, contract, engage, guarantee, pledge, plight, stipulate, swear, undertake, vouch, vow, warrant 2. augur, bespeak, betoken, bid fair, denote, indicate, suggest ~*n.* 3. assurance, bond, commitment, compact, covenant, engagement, guarantee, oath, pledge, undertaking, vow, word 4. ability, capacity, flair, potential, talent

promising 1. bright, encouraging, favourable, hopeful, likely, propitious, reassuring, rosy 2. able, gifted, likely, rising, talented

promote 1. aid, assist, back, boost, develop, encourage, forward, foster, help, stimulate, support 2. dignify, elevate, exalt, honour, prefer, raise, upgrade 3. advertise, publicize, push, sell

promotion 1. advancement, elevation, exaltation, honour, preferment, rise 2. advancement, backing, cultivation, encouragement, furtherance, progress, support 3. advertising, propaganda, publicity

prompt *adj.* 1. early, instant, punctual, quick, rapid, speedy, swift, timely, unhesitating ~*adv.* 2. *Inf.* exactly, punctually, sharp ~*v.* 3. cause, impel, incite, induce, inspire, instigate, motivate, move, provoke, spur, stimulate, urge 4. assist, cue, prod, remind

promptly directly, immediately, punctually, quickly, speedily, swiftly, unhesitatingly

promptness alertness, briskness, eagerness, haste, punctuality, quickness, readiness, speed, willingness

promulgate advertise, broadcast, circulate, declare, decree, issue, notify, proclaim, promote, publish, spread

prone 1. flat, horizontal, prostrate, recumbent, supine 2. apt, bent, disposed, given, inclined, liable, likely, predisposed, subject, susceptible, tending

DICTIONARY

prone *adj.* (foll. by *to*) likely to do or be affected by (something); lying face downwards.

prong *n.* one spike of a fork or similar instrument. —**pronged** *adj.*

pronoun *n.* word, such as *she, it,* used to replace a noun. —**pronominal** *adj.*

pronounce *v.* form the sounds of (words or letters), esp. clearly or in a particular way; declare formally or officially. —**pronounceable** *adj.* —**pronounced** *adj.* very noticeable. —**pronouncement** *n.* formal announcement. —**pronunciation** *n.* way in which a word or language is pronounced.

pronto *adv. Informal* at once.

proof *n.* evidence that shows that something is true or has happened; copy of something printed, such as the pages of a book, for checking before final production. —*adj.* able to withstand, e.g. *proof against criticism;* denoting the strength of an alcoholic drink, e.g. *seventy proof.* —**proofread** *v.* read and correct (printer's proofs). —**proofreader** *n.*

prop¹ *v.* **propping, propped.** support (something) so that it stays upright or in place. —*n.* pole, beam, etc. used as a support.

prop² *n.* movable object used on the set of a film or play.

prop³ *n. Informal* propeller.

propaganda *n.* (organized promotion of) infor-

mation to assist or damage the cause of a government or movement. —**propagandist** *n.*

propagate *v.* reproduce, breed, or grow; spread (information and ideas). —**propagation** *n.*

propane *n.* flammable gas found in petroleum and used as a fuel.

propel *v.* **-pelling, -pelled.** cause to move forward. —**propellant** *n.* something that provides or causes propulsion; gas used in an aerosol spray. —**propeller** *n.* revolving shaft with blades for driving a ship or aircraft. —**propulsion** *n.* propelling or being propelled; method by which something is propelled.

propensity *n., pl.* **-ties.** natural tendency.

proper *adj.* real or genuine; appropriate; suited to a particular purpose; correct in behaviour; excessively moral; *Informal* complete. —**properly** *adv.*

property *n., pl.* **-ties.** something owned; possessions collectively; land or buildings owned by somebody; quality or attribute.

prophet *n.* person supposedly chosen by God to spread His word; person who predicts the future. —**prophetic** *adj.* —**prophetically** *adv.* —**prophecy** *n.* prediction; message revealing God's will. —**prophesy** *v.* foretell.

prophylactic *n., adj.* (drug) used to prevent disease.

propinquity *n.* nearness in time, place, or relationship.

THESAURUS

pronounce 1. accent, articulate, say, sound, speak, stress, utter, vocalize, voice 2. announce, declare, decree, deliver, proclaim

pronouncement declaration, decree, dictum, edict, judgment, proclamation, statement

pronunciation accent, articulation, diction, elocution, inflection, intonation, speech, stress

proof *n.* 1. attestation, confirmation, demonstration, evidence, substantiation, testimony, verification 2. *Printing* galley, pull, slip ~*adj.* 3. impenetrable, impervious, repellent, resistant, strong, tight, treated

prop 1. *v.* bolster, brace, buttress, maintain, shore, stay, support, sustain, truss, uphold 2. *n.* brace, buttress, stay, support

propaganda advertising, information, newspeak, promotion, publicity

propagate 1. beget, breed, engender, generate, increase, multiply, procreate, produce, reproduce 2. broadcast, circulate, disseminate, promote, promulgate, publicize, spread

propel drive, force, impel, launch, push, send, shoot, shove, start, thrust

propensity aptness, bent, bias, inclination, leaning, penchant, proclivity, tendency, weakness

proper 1. apt, becoming, befitting, fit, fitting, legitimate, right, suitable, suited 2. decent, decorous, genteel, mannerly, polite, refined, respectable, seemly 3. accepted, accurate, conventional, correct, established, exact, formal, orthodox, precise, right

property 1. assets, belongings, building(s), capital, chattels, effects, estate, goods, holdings, house(s), means, possessions, resources, riches, wealth 2. estate, freehold, holding, land, title 3. ability, attribute, feature, hallmark, idiosyncrasy, mark, peculiarity, quality, trait, virtue

prophecy forecast, prediction, prognosis, soothsaying

prophesy divine, forecast, foresee, foretell, forewarn, predict, presage

prophet clairvoyant, diviner, forecaster, oracle, seer, sibyl

prophetic oracular, predictive, prescient, prognostic

DICTIONARY

propitiate *v.* appease, win the favour of. **—propitiation** *n.* **—propitiatory** *adj.* intended to appease someone. **—propitious** *adj.* favourable or auspicious.

proponent *n.* person who argues in favour of something.

proportion *n.* relative size or extent; correct relation between connected parts; part considered with respect to the whole. **—***pl.* dimensions or size. **—***v.* adjust in relative amount or size. **—in proportion** comparable in size, rate of increase, etc.; without exaggerating. **—proportional, proportionate** *adj.* being in proportion. **—proportionally** *adv.*

propose *v.* put forward for consideration; nominate; intend or plan (to do); make an offer of marriage. **—proposal** *n.* **—proposition** *n.* offer; statement or assertion; theorem; *Informal* thing to be dealt with. **—***v. Informal* ask (someone) to have sexual intercourse with one.

propound *v.* put forward for consideration.

proprietor *n.* owner of a business establishment. **—proprietress** *n. fem.* **—proprietary** *adj.* made and distributed under a trade name; denoting or suggesting ownership.

propriety *n., pl.* **-ties.** correct conduct.

propulsion *n.* see PROPEL.

pro rata *Latin* in proportion.

prorogue *v.* suspend (parliament) without dissolving it. **—prorogation** *n.*

prosaic [pro-**zay**-ik] *adj.* lacking imagination, dull. **—prosaically** *adv.*

proscenium *n., pl.* **-niums, -nia.** arch in a theatre separating the stage from the auditorium.

proscribe *v.* prohibit, outlaw. **—proscription** *n.* **—proscriptive** *adj.*

prose *n.* ordinary speech or writing in contrast to poetry.

prosecute *v.* bring a criminal charge against; continue to do. **—prosecution** *n.* **—prosecutor** *n.*

proselyte [**pross**-ill-ite] *n.* recent convert. **—proselytize** [**pross**-ill-it-ize] *v.* attempt to convert.

prosody [**pross**-a-dee] *n.* study of poetic metre and techniques. **—prosodic** *adj.* **—prosodist** *n.*

prospect *n.* something anticipated, e.g. *the prospect of defeat; Old-fashioned* view from a place. **—***pl.* probability of future success. **—***v.* explore, esp. for gold. **—prospective** *adj.* expected; future. **—prospector** *n.* **—prospectus** *n.* booklet giving details of a university, company, etc.

prosper *v.* be successful. **—prosperity** *n.* success and wealth. **—prosperous** *adj.*

THESAURUS

propitious bright, encouraging, favourable, fortunate, happy, lucky, opportune, rosy, timely

proportion 1. ratio 2. agreement, balance, congruity, harmony, symmetry 3. amount, division, fraction, measure, part, percentage, quota, segment, share 4. *Plural* breadth, bulk, capacity, dimensions, expanse, extent, range, scope, size, volume

proportional, proportionate balanced, compatible, consistent, corresponding, equitable, even, in proportion, just

proposal bid, design, motion, offer, overture, plan, programme, project, scheme, suggestion, tender

propose 1. advance, present, proffer, propound, submit, suggest, tender 2. introduce, invite, name, nominate, present, recommend 3. aim, design, intend, mean, plan, purpose, scheme 4. offer marriage, pay suit

proposition motion, plan, project, scheme, suggestion

proprietor, proprietress landlady, landlord, landowner, owner, titleholder

propriety courtesy, decorum, etiquette, politeness, seemliness

prosaic boring, dry, dull, everyday, flat, humdrum, matter-of-fact, mundane, ordinary, pedestrian, routine, stale, tame, trite

proscribe 1. ban, censure, condemn, damn, doom, embargo, forbid, interdict, prohibit, reject 2. banish, deport, exclude, exile, expatriate, expel, ostracize, outlaw

prosecute 1. *Law* arraign, indict, litigate, sue, summon, try 2. carry on, conduct, direct, discharge, manage, perform, practise

prospect *n.* 1. anticipation, calculation, expectation, future, hope, odds, opening, outlook, plan, promise, proposal, thought 2. landscape, outlook, panorama, perspective, scene, sight, spectacle, view, vision, vista 3. *Sometimes plural* chance, likelihood, possibility ~*v.* 4. explore, search, seek, survey

prospective anticipated, awaited, coming, destined, eventual, expected, future, imminent, intended, likely, looked-for, possible, potential

prospectus catalogue, list, outline, plan, programme, scheme, syllabus, synopsis

prosper advance, bloom, flourish, flower, progress, succeed, thrive

prosperity affluence, ease, fortune, luxury, plenty, prosperousness, riches, success, wealth, well-being

DICTIONARY

prostate *n.* gland in male mammals that surrounds the neck of the bladder.

prosthesis [pross-**theess**-iss] *n., pl.* **-ses** [-seez]. artificial body part, such as a limb or breast. —**prosthetic** *adj.*

prostitute *n.* person who offers sexual intercourse in return for payment. —*v.* make a prostitute of; offer (oneself or one's talents) for unworthy purposes. —**prostitution** *n.*

prostrate *adj.* lying face downwards; physically or emotionally exhausted. —*v.* lie face downwards; exhaust physically or emotionally. —**prostration** *n.*

protagonist *n.* leading character in a play or a story; supporter of a cause.

protea [**pro**-tee-a] *n.* African shrub with showy flowers.

protean [pro-**tee**-an] *adj.* constantly changing.

protect *v.* defend from trouble, harm, or loss. —**protection** *n.* —**protectionism** *n.* policy of protecting industries by taxing competing imports. —**protectionist** *n.* —**protective** *adj.* giving protection, e.g. *protective clothing;* tending or wishing to protect someone. —**protector** *n.* person or thing that protects; regent. —**protectorate** *n.* territory largely controlled by a stronger state; (period of) rule of a regent.

protégé [**pro**-ti-zhay] *n.* person who is protected and helped by another. —**protégée** *n. fem.*

protein *n.* any of a group of complex organic compounds that are essential for life.

pro tempore *adv., adj.* (often shortened to **pro tem**) for the time being.

protest *n.* declaration or demonstration of ob-

jection. —*v.* object, disagree; assert formally. —**protestation** *n.* strong declaration.

Protestant *adj.* of or relating to any of the Christian churches that split from the Roman Catholic Church in the sixteenth century. —*n.* member of a Protestant church. —**Protestantism** *n.*

proto-, prot- *combining form* first. —**protohuman** *n., adj.*

protocol *n.* rules of behaviour for formal occasions.

proton *n.* positively charged particle in the nucleus of an atom.

protoplasm *n.* substance forming the living contents of a cell.

prototype *n.* original or model after which something is copied.

protozoan [pro-toe-**zoe**-an] *n., pl.* **-zoa.** microscopic one-celled creature.

protract *v.* lengthen or extend. —**protracted** *adj.* —**protraction** *n.* —**protractor** *n.* instrument for measuring angles.

protrude *v.* stick out, project. —**protrusion** *n.*

protuberant *adj.* swelling out, bulging. —**protuberance** *n.*

proud *adj.* feeling pleasure and satisfaction; feeling honoured; thinking oneself superior to other people; dignified. —**proudly** *adv.* —**proud flesh** flesh growing around a healing wound.

prove *v.* **proving, proved, proved** *or* **proven.** establish the validity of; demonstrate, test; be found to be. —**proven** *adj.* known from experience to work.

provenance [**prov**-in-anss] *n.* place of origin.

THESAURUS

prosperous 1. blooming, booming, fortunate, lucky, prospering, successful, thriving 2. affluent, opulent, rich, wealthy, well-off

prostitute 1. *n.* call girl, courtesan, harlot, trollop, whore 2. *v.* cheapen, debase, degrade, demean, devalue, pervert, profane

prostrate *adj.* 1. abject, flat, prone 2. dejected, depressed, desolate, exhausted, inconsolable, overcome, spent, worn out ~*v.* 3. crush, depress, disarm, overthrow, paralyse, reduce, ruin

protagonist hero, heroine, lead, principal

protect cover, defend, foster, guard, harbour, keep, safeguard, save, screen, secure, shelter, shield, support

protection care, charge, custody, defence, safeguard, safety, security

protective defensive, fatherly, maternal, motherly, paternal, possessive, vigilant, warm, watchful

protector bodyguard, champion, counsel, defender, guardian, patron

protégé, protégée charge, student, ward

protest 1. *n.* complaint, dissent, objection, outcry, remonstrance 2. *v.* complain, demonstrate, demur, disagree, disapprove, object, oppose

protocol conventions, customs, decorum, etiquette, manners, propriety

prototype example, first, model, original, pattern, precedent, standard, type

proud 1. content, glad, gratified, pleased, satisfied, well-pleased 2. arrogant, boastful, conceited, disdainful, haughty, imperious, lordly, overbearing, self-satisfied, snobbish, supercilious, vain

prove 1. authenticate, confirm, demonstrate, determine, establish, justify, show, substantiate, verify 2. analyse, assay, check, examine, experiment, test, try 3. end up, result, turn out

DICTIONARY

provender *n. Old-fashioned* fodder.

proverb *n.* short saying that expresses a truth or gives a warning. —**proverbial** *adj.*

provide *v.* make available; (foll. by *for*) take precautions (against); support financially. —**provider** *n.* —**provided that** on condition that.

providence *n.* God or nature seen as a protective force that arranges people's lives. —**provident** *adj.* thrifty; showing foresight. —**providential** *adj.* lucky. —**providentially** *adv.*

province *n.* area governed as a unit of a country or empire; area of learning, activity, etc. —*pl.* any part of a country outside the capital. —**provincial** *adj.* of a province or the provinces; unsophisticated and narrow-minded. —*n.* unsophisticated person; person from a province or the provinces. —**provincialism** *n.* narrow-mindedness and lack of sophistication.

provision *n.* act of supplying something; something supplied; *Law* condition incorporated in a document. —*pl.* food. —*v.* supply with food. —**provisional** *adj.* temporary; conditional. —**provisionally** *adv.*

proviso [pro-**vize**-oh] *n., pl.* **-sos, -soes.** condition, stipulation.

provoke *v.* deliberately anger; cause (an adverse reaction). —**provocation** *n.* —**provocative** *adj.*

provost *n.* head of certain university colleges; chief councillor of a Scottish town. —**provost marshal** head of military police.

prow *n.* bow of a vessel.

prowess *n.* superior skill or ability; bravery, fearlessness.

prowl *v.* move stealthily around a place as if in search of prey or plunder. —*n.* prowling. —**prowler** *n.*

proximate *adj.* nearest, next; close; immediately preceding or following in a series. —**proximity** *n.*

proxy *n., pl.* **proxies.** person authorized to act on behalf of someone else; authority to act on behalf of someone else.

prude *n.* person who is excessively modest, prim, or proper. —**prudish** *adj.* —**prudery** *n.*

prudent *adj.* cautious, discreet, and sensible. —**prudence** *n.* —**prudential** *adj. Old-fashioned* prudent.

prune[1] *n.* dried plum.

prune[2] *v.* cut out dead parts or excessive branches from (a tree or plant); shorten, reduce.

prurient *adj.* excessively interested in sexual matters. —**prurience** *n.*

pry *v.* **prying, pried.** make an impertinent or uninvited inquiry into a private matter.

THESAURUS

proverb adage, dictum, maxim, saw, saying

proverbial axiomatic, conventional, current, famed, famous, legendary, notorious, traditional, typical, well-known

provide 1. cater, equip, furnish, outfit, stock up, supply 2. add, afford, bring, give, impart, lend, present, produce, render, serve, yield 3. *With* **for** *or* **against** anticipate, forearm, plan ahead, plan for, prepare for 4. *With* **for** keep, maintain, support, sustain, take care of

providence destiny, fate, fortune

provident careful, cautious, discreet, far-seeing, forearmed, frugal, prudent, shrewd, thrifty, vigilant, well-prepared, wise

province 1. colony, department, district, division, region, section, tract, zone 2. *Fig.* area, business, capacity, charge, concern, duty, field, function, line, orbit, part, post, responsibility, role, sphere

provision 1. catering, equipping, furnishing, providing, supplying 2. *Fig.* agreement, clause, condition, demand, requirement, stipulation, term

provisional conditional, contingent, interim, limited, qualified, temporary, tentative

provisions comestibles, eatables, fare, food, foodstuff, rations, stores, supplies, victuals

proviso clause, condition, qualification, requirement, rider, stipulation

provocation 1. cause, grounds, incitement, motivation, reason, stimulus 2. affront, annoyance, challenge, dare, grievance, insult, offence, taunt

provocative annoying, goading, insulting, offensive, provoking, stimulating

provoke 1. anger, annoy, chafe, enrage, exasperate, gall, incense, infuriate, insult, irk, irritate, madden, offend, pique, rile, vex 2. call forth, cause, draw forth, elicit, evoke, excite, fire, incite, inspire, kindle, move, occasion, produce, promote, prompt, rouse, stimulate, stir

prowess accomplishment, adeptness, aptitude, expertise, genius, mastery, skill, talent

proximity closeness, nearness, vicinity

proxy agent, delegate, deputy, factor, representative, substitute

prudence care, caution, common sense, discretion, judgment, vigilance, wariness, wisdom

prudent careful, cautious, discerning, discreet, judicious, politic, sensible, shrewd, vigilant, wary, wise

DICTIONARY

PS postscript.

psalm *n.* sacred song. —**psalmist** *n.* writer of psalms. —**psalmody** *n.* singing of sacred music.

Psalter *n.* book containing (a version of) psalms from the Bible. —**psaltery** *n.* ancient instrument played by plucking strings.

PSBR public sector borrowing requirement.

psephology [sef-**fol**-a-jee] *n.* statistical study of elections.

pseud *n. Informal* pretentious person.

pseudo-, pseud- *combining form* false, pretending, or unauthentic, e.g. *pseudo-intellectual.*

pseudonym *n.* fictitious name adopted, esp. by an author. —**pseudonymous** *adj.*

psittacosis *n.* disease of parrots that can be transmitted to humans.

psych up *v.* prepare (oneself) mentally for a contest or task.

psyche *n.* human mind or soul.

psychedelic *adj.* denoting a drug that causes hallucinations; having vivid colours and complex patterns similar to those experienced during hallucinations.

psychiatry *n.* branch of medicine concerned with mental disorders. —**psychiatric** *adj.* —**psychiatrist** *n.*

psychic *adj.* (also **psychical**) having mental powers which cannot be explained by natural laws; relating to the mind. —*n.* person with psychic powers.

psycho *n. Informal* short for PSYCHOPATH.

psychoanalysis *n.* method of treating mental and emotional disorders by discussion and analysis of one's thoughts and feelings. —**psychoanalyse** *v.* —**psychoanalyst** *n.*

psychology *n., pl.* **-gies.** study of human and animal behaviour; *Informal* person's mental make-up. —**psychological** *adj.* of psychology; of or affecting the mind. —**psychologist** *n.*

psychopath *n.* person afflicted with a personality disorder causing him or her to commit antisocial or violent acts. —**psychopathic** *adj.*

psychosis *n., pl.* **-choses.** severe mental disorder in which the sufferer's contact with reality becomes distorted. —**psychotic** *adj., n.*

psychosomatic *adj.* (of a physical disorder) thought to have psychological causes.

psychotherapy *n.* treatment of nervous disorders by psychological methods. —**psychotherapeutic** *adj.* —**psychotherapist** *n.*

pt part; point; port.

Pt *Chem.* platinum.

PT *Old-fashioned* physical training.

pt. pint.

PTA Parent-Teacher Association.

ptarmigan [**tar**-mig-an] *n.* bird of the grouse family which turns white in winter.

pterodactyl [terr-roe-**dak**-til] *n.* extinct flying reptile with batlike wings.

PTO please turn over.

ptomaine [**toe**-main] *n.* any of a group of poisonous alkaloids found in decaying matter.

Pu *Chem.* plutonium.

pub *n.* building with a bar licensed to sell alcoholic drinks.

puberty [**pew**-ber-tee] *n.* sexual maturity. —**pubertal** *adj.*

pubic [**pew**-bik] *adj.* of the lower abdomen.

public *n.* the community, people in general. —*adj.* of or concerning the people as a whole; for use by everyone; well-known; performed or made openly. —**publicly** *adv.* —**publican** *n.* person who owns or runs a pub. —**public house** pub. —**public relations** promotion of a favourable opinion towards an organization among the public. —**public school** private fee-paying school in England. —**public-spirited** *adj* having or showing an active interest in the good of the community.

THESAURUS

prune clip, cut, dock, reduce, shape, shorten, snip, trim

pry interfere, intrude, meddle, peep, peer, poke

psalm chant, hymn

pseudo *adj.* artificial, bogus, fake, false, imitation, mock, pretended, sham, spurious

pseudonym alias, assumed name, incognito, pen name

psyche anima, individuality, mind, personality, self, soul, spirit, subconscious, true being

psychiatrist analyst, psychoanalyst, psychologist

psychic extrasensory, mystic, occult, supernatural, telepathic

psychological 1. cerebral, intellectual, mental 2. emotional, imaginary, irrational, subconscious

psychology 1. behaviourism 2. *Inf.* attitude, way of thinking

psychopath lunatic, madman, maniac

pub *or* **public house** bar, inn, tavern

puberty adolescence, teenage, teens

public *adj.* 1. civic, common, general, national, popular, social, state, universal, widespread 2. accessible, communal, open, unrestricted 3.

DICTIONARY

publicity *n.* process or information used to arouse public attention; public interest aroused. **—publicize** *v.* advertise. **—publicist** *n.* person who publicizes something, such as a press agent or journalist.

publish *v.* produce and issue (printed matter) for sale; announce formally or in public. **—publication** *n.* **—publisher** *n.*

puce *adj.* purplish-brown.

puck[1] *n.* small rubber disc used in ice hockey.

puck[2] *n.* mischievous or evil spirit. **—puckish** *adj.*

pucker *v.* gather into wrinkles. **—*n.*** wrinkle or crease.

pudding *n.* dessert, esp. a cooked one served hot; savoury dish with pastry or batter, e.g. *steak-and-kidney pudding;* sausage-like mass of meat, e.g. *black pudding.*

puddle *n.* small pool of water, esp. of rain.

puerile *adj.* silly and childish.

puerperium [pure-**peer**-ee-um] *n.* period following childbirth. **—puerperal** [pure-per-al] *adj.*

puff *n.* (sound of) a short blast of breath, wind, etc.; instance of breathing in and out; act of inhaling cigarette smoke. **—*v.*** blow or breathe in short quick draughts; take draws at (a cigarette); send out in small clouds; swell. **—out of puff** out of breath. **—puffy** *adj.* **—puffball** *n.* ball-shaped fungus. **—puff pastry** light flaky pastry.

puffin *n.* black-and-white sea bird with a large brightly-coloured beak.

pug *n.* small snub-nosed dog. **—pug nose** short stubby upturned nose.

pugilism [pew-jil-iz-zum] *n.* boxing. **—pugilist** *n.* **—pugilistic** *adj.*

pugnacious *adj.* ready and eager to fight. **—pugnacity** *n.*

puissant [pew-**iss**-sant] *adj. Poetic* powerful. **—puissance** *n.* showjumping competition that tests a horse's ability to jump large obstacles.

puke *Slang* **—*v.*** vomit. **—*n.*** act of vomiting; vomited matter.

pulchritude *n. Lit.* beauty.

pule *v.* whine; whimper.

pull *v.* exert force on (an object) to move it towards the source of the force; move in a specified direction; strain or stretch; remove or extract; attract. **—*n.*** pulling; force used in pulling; act of taking in drink or smoke; *Informal* power, influence. **—pull in** *v.* (of a vehicle or driver) draw in to the side of the road or stop; reach a destination; attract in large numbers; *Slang* arrest. **—pull off** *v. Informal* succeed in performing. **—pull out** *v.* (of a vehicle or driver) move away from the side of the road or move out to overtake; (of a train) depart; withdraw; remove by pulling. **—pull up** *v.* (of a vehicle or driver) stop; remove by the roots; reprimand.

pullet *n.* young hen.

pulley *n.* wheel with a grooved rim in which a belt, chain, or piece of rope runs in order to lift weights by a downward pull.

Pullman *n., pl.* **-mans.** luxurious railway coach.

pullover *n.* sweater that is pulled on over the head.

pulmonary *adj.* of the lungs.

pulp *n.* soft moist plant tissue, such as the material used to make paper; flesh of a fruit; any soft soggy mass; poor-quality books and magazines. **—*v.*** reduce to pulp.

THESAURUS

acknowledged, exposed, known, notorious, obvious, open, overt, patent, plain **4.** important, prominent, respected, well-known ~*n.* **5.** citizens, community, electorate, everyone, nation, people, populace, society, voters

publication brochure, handbill, issue, leaflet, magazine, newspaper, pamphlet, periodical

publicity attention, boost, press, promotion

publicize advertise, broadcast, make known, play up, promote, puff, push, spotlight

publish 1. issue, print, produce, put out **2.** advertise, announce, broadcast, circulate, declare, disclose, divulge, impart, leak, proclaim, promulgate, reveal, spread

puerile babyish, childish, foolish, immature, inane, juvenile, naive, petty, silly, trivial, weak

puff *n.* **1.** blast, breath, draught, gust, whiff ~*v.* **2.** blow, breathe, exhale, gasp, gulp, pant,

wheeze **3.** drag (*Sl.*), draw, inhale, pull at *or* on, smoke, suck **4.** *Usually with* **up** bloat, dilate, distend, expand, inflate, swell

pugilist boxer, fighter

pugnacious aggressive, bellicose, belligerent, choleric, combative, hot-tempered, irascible, irritable, petulant, quarrelsome

pull *v.* **1.** drag, draw, haul, jerk, tow, trail, tug, yank **2.** cull, extract, gather, pick, pluck, remove, uproot, weed **3.** dislocate, rend, rip, sprain, strain, stretch, tear, wrench **4.** *Inf.* attract, draw, entice, lure, magnetize ~*n.* **5.** jerk, tug, twitch, yank **6.** attraction, effort, exertion, force, influence, lure, magnetism, power **7.** influence, muscle, weight

pull out depart, evacuate, leave, quit, retreat, withdraw

pull up 1. brake, halt, stop **2.** admonish, reprimand, reprove

DICTIONARY

pulpit *n.* raised platform for a preacher.

pulsar *n.* small dense star which emits regular bursts of radio waves.

pulse[1] *n.* regular beating of blood through the arteries at each heartbeat which can be felt at the wrists and elsewhere; any regular beat or vibration. —**pulsate** *v.* throb, quiver. —**pulsation** *n.*

pulse[2] *n.* edible seed of a pod-bearing plant such as a bean or pea.

pulverize *v.* reduce to fine pieces; destroy completely. —**pulverization** *n.*

puma *n.* large American cat with a greyish-brown coat.

pumice [**pumm**-iss] *n.* light porous stone used for scouring.

pummel *v.* -**melling**, -**melled.** strike repeatedly with or as if with the fists.

pump[1] *n.* machine used to force a liquid or gas to move in a particular direction. —*v.* raise or drive with a pump; supply in large amounts; extract information from; operate or work in the manner of a pump.

pump[2] *n.* light flat-soled shoe.

pumpkin *n.* large round fruit with an orange rind, soft flesh, and many seeds.

pun *n.* use of words to exploit double meanings for humorous effect. —*v.* **punning, punned.** make puns. —**punster** *n.* person fond of making puns.

punch[1] *v.* strike at with a clenched fist. —*n.* blow with a clenched fist; *Informal* effectiveness or vigour. —**punchy** *adj.* forceful. —**punch-drunk** *adj.* dazed by or as if by repeated blows to the head.

punch[2] *n.* tool or machine for shaping, piercing, or engraving. —*v.* pierce, cut, stamp, shape, or drive with a punch.

punch[3] *n.* drink made from a mixture of wine, spirits, fruit, sugar, and spices.

punctilious *adj.* paying great attention to correctness in etiquette; careful about small details.

punctual *adj.* arriving or taking place at the correct time. —**punctuality** *n.* —**punctually** *adv.*

punctuate *v.* put punctuation marks in; interrupt at frequent intervals. —**punctuation** *n.* (use of) marks such as commas, colons, etc. in writing, to assist in making the sense clear.

puncture *n.* small hole made by a sharp object, esp. in a tyre. —*v.* pierce a hole in.

pundit *n.* expert who speaks publicly on a subject.

pungent *adj.* having a strong sharp bitter flavour. —**pungency** *n.*

punish *v.* cause (someone) to suffer or undergo a penalty for some wrongdoing. —**punishing** *adj.* harsh or difficult. —**punishment** *n.* —**punitive** [**pew**-nit-tiv] *adj.* relating to punishment.

punk *n.* anti-Establishment youth movement and style of rock music of the late 1970s; follower of this music; worthless person.

punnet *n.* small basket for fruit.

punt[1] *n.* open flat-bottomed boat propelled by a pole. —*v.* travel in a punt.

punt[2] *Sport* —*v.* kick (a ball) before it touches the ground when dropped from the hands. —*n.* such a kick.

punt[3] *n.* monetary unit of the Irish Republic.

punter *n.* person who bets; any member of the public.

THESAURUS

pulp *n.* 1. flesh, soft part 2. mash, mush, paste ~*v.* 3. crush, mash, squash

pulse 1. *n.* beat, beating, rhythm, stroke, throb, vibration 2. *v.* beat, throb, tick, vibrate

pump *v.* 1. drive, force, inject, pour, push, send, supply 2. interrogate, probe, quiz

pun double entendre, quip, witticism

punch[1] *v.* 1. box, hit, slam, smash, strike ~*n.* 2. blow, hit, knock, thump 3. *Inf.* bite, drive, forcefulness, impact, point, verve, vigour

punch[2] *v.* bore, cut, drill, pierce, pink, prick, puncture, stamp

punctilious careful, ceremonious, exact, finicky, formal, fussy, nice, proper, scrupulous

punctual early, exact, precise, prompt, strict, timely

punctuality promptitude, promptness, readiness, regularity

punctuate 1. break, interrupt, pepper, sprinkle 2. emphasize, mark, stress, underline

puncture *n.* 1. break, cut, damage, hole, leak, nick, opening, slit 2. flat, flat tyre ~*v.* 3. bore, cut, nick, penetrate, perforate, pierce, prick, rupture

pungent acid, acrid, bitter, hot, peppery, piquant, seasoned, sharp, sour, spicy, strong, tart

punish beat, castigate, chasten, chastise, correct, discipline, flog, penalize, scourge, sentence, whip

punishment chastening, chastisement, correction, discipline, penalty, penance, retribution, sanction

punter backer, better, gambler

puny diminutive, dwarfish, feeble, frail, little, sickly, stunted, tiny, underfed, weak, weakly

DICTIONARY

puny *adj.* **-nier, -niest.** small and feeble.

pup *n.* young of certain animals, such as dogs and seals.

pupa [pew-pa] *n., pl.* **-pae, -pas.** insect at the stage of development between a larva and an adult. **—pupal** *adj.*

pupil[1] *n.* person who is taught by a teacher.

pupil[2] *n.* round dark opening in the centre of the eye.

puppet *n.* small doll or figure moved by strings or by the operator's hand; person or country controlled by another. **—puppeteer** *n.*

puppy *n., pl.* **-pies.** young dog.

purblind *adj.* partly or nearly blind.

purchase *v.* obtain by payment. **—***n.* buying; what is bought; leverage, grip. **—purchaser** *n.*

purdah *n.* Muslim and Hindu custom of keeping women in seclusion, with clothing that conceals them completely when they go out.

pure *adj.* unmixed, untainted; faultless; innocent; complete, e.g. *pure delight;* concerned with theory only, e.g. *pure mathematics.* **—purely** *adv.* **—purity** *n.* **—purify** *v.* make or become pure. **—purification** *n.* **—purist** *n.* person obsessed with strict obedience to the traditions of a subject.

purée [pure-ray] *n.* pulp of cooked food. **—***v.* **-reing, -réed.** make into a purée.

purgatory *n.* place or state of temporary suffering; **(P-)** *RC Church* place where souls of the dead undergo punishment for their sins before being admitted to Heaven. **—purgatorial** *adj.*

purge *v.* rid (a thing or place) of unwanted (things or people). **—***n.* purging. **—purgation** *n.* **—purgative** *adj., n.* (medicine) designed to cause defecation.

Puritan *n. Hist.* member of the English Protestant group who wanted simpler church ceremonies; **(p-)** person with strict moral and religious principles. **—puritanical** *adj.* **—puritanism** *n.*

purl *n.* stitch made by knitting a plain stitch backwards. **—***v.* knit in purl.

purlieus [per-lyooz] *pl. n. Lit.* outskirts.

purloin *v.* steal.

purple *adj.* of a colour between red and blue.

purport *v.* claim (to be or do something). **—***n.* apparent meaning, significance.

purpose *n.* reason for which something is done or exists; determination; practical advantage or use, e.g. *use the time to good purpose.* **—***v. Old-fashioned* intend. **—purposely** *adv.* (also **on purpose**) intentionally.

purr *n.* low vibrant sound that a cat makes when pleased. **—***v.* make this sound.

purse *n.* small bag for money; *US* handbag; financial resources; prize money. **—***v.* draw (one's lips) together into a small round shape. **—purser** *n.* ship's officer who keeps the accounts.

pursue *v.* chase; follow (a goal); engage in; continue to discuss or ask about (something). **—pursuer** *n.* **—pursuit** *n.* pursuing; occupation. **—pursuance** *n.* carrying out.

THESAURUS

pupil beginner, disciple, learner, novice, scholar, schoolboy, schoolgirl, student

puppet 1. doll, marionette 2. *Fig.* creature, dupe, instrument, mouthpiece, pawn, stooge, tool

purchase 1. *v.* acquire, buy, come by, gain, get, invest in, obtain, pay for, pick up, procure, secure 2. *n.* asset, buy, gain, investment, possession, property

pure 1. authentic, clear, flawless, genuine, natural, neat, perfect, real, simple, straight, true, unalloyed, unmixed 2. clean, germ-free, immaculate, sanitary, spotless, sterile, sterilized, unadulterated, uncontaminated, unpolluted, untainted, wholesome 3. blameless, chaste, honest, innocent, maidenly, modest, true, virgin, virtuous

purely absolutely, completely, entirely, exclusively, just, merely, only, simply, solely, wholly

purge 1. *v.* dismiss, eject, eradicate, expel, exterminate, kill liquidate, oust, remove 2. *n.*

cleanup, crushing, ejection, elimination, eradication, liquidation, removal, suppression, witch hunt

purify 1. clarify, clean, cleanse, disinfect, filter, fumigate, refine, wash 2. absolve, cleanse, exonerate, lustrate, redeem, sanctify, shrive

purist formalist, pedant, stickler

puritan fanatic, moralist, prude, rigorist, zealot

purpose *n.* 1. aim, design, idea, intention, object, point, reason 2. determination, firmness, persistence, resolution, resolve, tenacity, will 3. **on purpose** deliberately, designedly, intentionally, knowingly ~*v.* 4. aim, aspire, contemplate, decide, design, determine, intend, mean, meditate, plan, propose, resolve

purposely consciously, deliberately, expressly, intentionally, knowingly, wilfully, with intent

purse 1. pouch, wallet 2. exchequer, funds, means, money, resources, treasury, wealth 3. award, gift, present, prize, reward

pursue 1. accompany, attend, chase, dog, follow, harass, harry, haunt, hound, hunt, hunt

DICTIONARY

purulent [**pure**-yoo-lent] *adj.* of or containing pus. —**purulence** *n.*

purvey *v.* supply (provisions). —**purveyance** *n.* —**purveyor** *n.*

purview *n.* scope or range of activity or outlook.

pus *n.* yellowish matter produced by infected tissue.

push *v.* move or try to move by steady force; drive or spur (oneself or another person) to do something; *Informal* sell (drugs) illegally. —*n.* pushing; special effort. —**the push** *Slang* dismissal from a job; ending of a relationship. —**pusher** *n.* person who sells illegal drugs. —**pushy** *adj.* too assertive or ambitious. —**pushchair** *n.* collapsible chair-shaped carriage for a baby.

pusillanimous *adj.* cowardly. —**pusillanimity** *n.*

puss, pussy *n., pl.* **pusses, pussies.** cat.

pussyfoot *v. Informal* behave too cautiously.

pustule *n.* pimple containing pus. —**pustular** *adj.*

put *v.* **putting, put.** cause to be (in a position, state, or place); express; throw (the shot) in the shot put. —*n.* throw in putting the shot. —**put across** *v.* express successfully. —**put off** *v.* postpone; disconcert; repel. —**put up** *v.* erect; accommodate; nominate. —**put-upon** *adj.* taken advantage of.

putative [**pew**-tat-iv] *adj.* reputed, supposed.

putrid *adj.* rotten and foul-smelling. —**putrefy** *v.* rot and produce an offensive smell. —**putrefaction** *n.* —**putrescent** *adj.* becoming putrid; rotting.

putsch *n.* sudden violent attempt to remove a government from power.

putt *Golf* —*n.* stroke on the green with a putter to roll the ball into or near the hole. —*v.* strike (the ball) in this way. —**putter** *n.* golf club with a short shaft for putting.

puttee *n.* strip of cloth worn wound around the leg from the ankle to the knee.

putty *n.* paste used to fix glass into frames and fill cracks in woodwork.

puzzle *v.* perplex and confuse or be perplexed or confused. —*n.* problem that cannot be easily solved; toy, game, or question that requires skill or ingenuity to solve. —**puzzlement** *n.* —**puzzling** *adj.*

PVC polyvinyl chloride.

py(a)emia *n.* blood poisoning.

Pygmy *n., pl.* **-mies.** member of one of the dwarf peoples of Equatorial Africa. —*adj.* (**p-**) very small.

pyjamas *pl. n.* loose-fitting trousers and top worn in bed.

pylon *n.* steel tower-like structure supporting electrical cables.

pyorrh(o)ea [pire-**ree**-a] *n.* disease of the gums and tooth sockets which causes bleeding of the gums and the formation of pus.

pyramid *n.* solid figure with a flat base and triangular sides sloping upwards to a point; structure of this shape, esp. an ancient Egyptian one. —**pyramidal** *adj.*

pyre *n.* pile of wood for burning a dead body on.

Pyrex *n.* ® heat-resistant glassware.

pyrites [pie-**rite**-eez] *n.* sulphide of a metal, esp. iron pyrites.

pyromania *n.* uncontrollable urge to set things on fire. —**pyromaniac** *n.*

THESAURUS

down, plague, run after, shadow, stalk, tail, track 2. desire, purpose, seek, strive for, try for, work towards 3. adhere to, carry on, continue, cultivate, maintain, persist in, proceed

pursuit 1. chase, hunt, inquiry, quest, search, seeking, trail, trailing 2. activity, hobby, interest, line, occupation, pastime, pleasure

push *v.* 1. depress, drive, press, propel, ram, shove, thrust 2. elbow, jostle, move, shoulder, shove, squeeze, thrust 3. encourage, expedite, hurry, impel, incite, persuade, press, spur, urge ~*n.* 4. butt, jolt, nudge, poke, prod, shove, thrust 5. *Inf.* ambition, determination, drive, dynamism, energy, enterprise, initiative, vigour 6. *Inf.* advance, assault, attack, charge, effort, offensive, thrust

put 1. bring, deposit, establish, fix, lay, place, position, rest, set, settle, situate 2. advance, forward, offer, posit, present, propose, submit,

tender 3. cast, fling, heave, hurl, lob, pitch, throw, toss

put across convey, explain, spell out

put off 1. defer, delay, postpone, reschedule 2. abash, confuse, discomfit, disconcert, dismay, distress, nonplus, perturb, unsettle

put up 1. build, construct, erect, fabricate, raise 2. accommodate, board, entertain, house, lodge 3. float, nominate, offer, present, propose, recommend, submit

puzzle *v.* 1. baffle, bewilder, confound, confuse, mystify, perplex, stump 2. brood, muse, ponder, study, think hard, wonder ~*n.* 3. conundrum, enigma, mystery, paradox, poser, problem, question, riddle

puzzling abstruse, baffling, bewildering, enigmatic, hard, incomprehensible, involved, knotty, mystifying, perplexing

DICTIONARY

pyrotechnics *n.* art of making fireworks; firework display. —**pyrotechnic** *adj.*

Pyrrhic victory [**pir**-ik] *n.* victory in which the victor's losses are as great as those of the defeated.

python *n.* large nonpoisonous snake that crushes its prey.

Q

QC Queen's Counsel.

QED which was to be shown or proved.

QM Quartermaster.

qr. quarter; quire.

qt. quart.

qua [kwah] *prep.* in the capacity of.

quack[1] *v.* (of a duck) utter a harsh guttural sound. —*n.* sound made by a duck.

quack[2] *n.* unqualified person who claims medical knowledge; *Informal* doctor.

quad *n.* short for QUADRUPLET or QUADRANGLE. —*adj.* short for QUADRAPHONIC.

quadrangle *n.* rectangular courtyard with buildings on all four sides; geometric figure consisting of four points connected by four lines. —**quadrangular** *adj.*

quadrant *n.* quarter of a circle; quarter of a circle's circumference; instrument for measuring the altitude of the stars.

quadraphonic *adj.* using four independent channels to reproduce or record sound.

quadratic *Maths* —*n.* equation in which the variable is raised to the power of two, but nowhere raised to a higher power. —*adj.* of the second power.

quadrennial *adj.* occurring every four years; lasting four years.

quadr(i)- *combining form* four, e.g. *quadrilateral.*

quadrilateral *adj.* having four sides. —*n.* polygon with four sides.

quadrille *n.* square dance for four couples.

quadruped [kwod-roo-ped] *n.* any animal with four legs.

quadruple *v.* multiply by four. —*adj.* four times as much or as many; consisting of four parts.

quadruplet *n.* one of four offspring born at one birth.

quaff [kwoff] *v.* drink heartily or in one draught.

quagmire [kwog-mire] *n.* soft wet area of land.

quail[1] *n.* small game bird of the partridge family.

quail[2] *v.* shrink back with fear.

quaint *adj.* attractively unusual, esp. in an old-fashioned style. —**quaintly** *adv.* —**quaintness** *n.*

quake *v.* shake or tremble with or as if with fear.

Quaker *n.* member of a Christian sect, the Society of Friends. —**Quakerism** *n.*

qualify *v.* **-fying, -fied.** provide or be provided with the abilities necessary for a task, office, or duty; moderate or restrict (something, esp. a statement). —**qualified** *adj.* —**qualification** *n.* quality or skill needed for a particular activity; condition that modifies or limits; act of qualifying.

quality *n., pl.* **-ties.** degree or standard of excellence; distinguishing characteristic or attribute; basic character or nature of something. —**qualitative** *adj.* of or relating to quality.

qualm [kwahm] *n.* pang of conscience; sudden sensation of misgiving.

quandary *n., pl.* **-ries.** difficult situation or dilemma.

THESAURUS

quack *n.* charlatan, fake, fraud, humbug, impostor, mountebank, pretender

quagmire bog, fen, marsh, mire, quicksand, slough, swamp

quail blanch, blench, cower, cringe, droop, faint, falter, flinch, quake, recoil, shake, shrink

quaint bizarre, curious, droll, eccentric, fanciful, odd, old-fashioned, peculiar, queer, singular, strange, unusual, whimsical

quake move, quiver, rock, shake, shiver, shudder, throb, totter, tremble, vibrate, waver

qualification 1. ability, aptitude, capability, capacity, eligibility, fitness, skill, suitability 2. allowance, caveat, condition, exception, limitation, modification, requirement, reservation, stipulation

qualified 1. able, adept, capable, certificated, competent, efficient, equipped, experienced, expert, fit, practised, proficient, skilful, talented, trained 2. bounded, conditional, confined, equivocal, guarded, limited, modified, provisional, reserved, restricted

qualify 1. certify, commission, condition, empower, endow, equip, fit, ground, permit, prepare, ready, sanction, train 2. abate, adapt, assuage, diminish, ease, lessen, limit, moderate, reduce, regulate, restrain, restrict, soften, temper, vary

quality 1. aspect, attribute, condition, feature, mark, property, trait 2. description, essence, kind, make, nature, sort 3. calibre, distinction, excellence, grade, merit, position, rank, standing, status, superiority, value, worth

quandary difficulty, dilemma, doubt, impasse, perplexity, plight, puzzle, strait, uncertainty

DICTIONARY

quango *n., pl.* **-gos.** partly independent official body, set up by a government.

quanta *n.* plural of QUANTUM.

quantify *v.* **-fying, -fied.** discover or express the quantity of. —**quantifiable** *adj.* —**quantification** *n.*

quantity *n., pl.* **-ties.** specified or definite amount or number; aspect of anything that can be measured, weighed, or counted. —**quantitative** *adj.* of or relating to quantity. —**quantity surveyor** person who estimates the cost of the materials and labour necessary for a construction job.

quantum *n., pl.* **-ta.** desired or required amount. —**quantum theory** physics theory based on the idea that energy of electrons is discharged in discrete quanta.

quarantine *n.* period of isolation of people or animals to prevent the spread of disease. —*v.* isolate in or as if in quarantine.

quark *n. Physics* particle thought to be the fundamental unit of matter.

quarrel *n.* angry disagreement; cause of dispute. —*v.* **-relling, -relled.** have a disagreement or dispute. —**quarrelsome** *adj.*

quarry[1] *n., pl.* **-ries.** place where stone is dug from the surface of the earth. —*v.* **-rying, -ried.** extract (stone) from a quarry.

quarry[2] *n., pl.* **-ries.** person or animal that is being hunted.

quart *n.* unit of liquid measure equal to two pints.

quarter *n.* one of four equal parts of something; fourth part of a year; *Informal* unit of weight equal to 4 ounces; region or district of a town or city; *US* 25-cent piece; mercy or pity, as shown towards a defeated opponent. —*pl.* lodgings. —*v.* divide into four equal parts; billet or be billeted in lodgings. —**quarterly** *adj.* occurring, due, or issued at intervals of three months. —*n.* magazine issued every three months. —*adv.* once every three months. —**quarter day** any of the

four days in the year when certain payments become due. —**quarterdeck** *n. Naut.* rear part of the upper deck of a ship. —**quarterfinal** *n.* round before the semifinal in a competition. —**quartermaster** *n.* military officer responsible for accommodation, food, and equipment.

quartet *n.* group of four performers; music for such a group.

quarto *n., pl.* **-tos.** book size in which the sheets are folded into four leaves.

quartz *n.* hard glossy mineral, used in making very accurate clocks and watches.

quasar [kway-zar] *n.* extremely distant starlike object that emits powerful radio waves.

quash *v.* annul or make void; subdue forcefully and completely.

quasi- [kway-zie-] *combining form* almost but not really, e.g. *quasi-religious, a quasi-scholar.*

quatrain *n.* stanza or poem of four lines.

quaver *v.* (of a voice) quiver or tremble. —*n. Music* note half the length of a crotchet; tremulous sound or note.

quay [kee] *n.* wharf built parallel to the shore.

queasy *adj.* **-sier, -siest.** having the feeling that one is about to vomit; feeling or causing uneasiness. —**queasily** *adv.* —**queasiness** *n.*

queen *n.* female sovereign who is the official ruler or head of state; wife of a king; woman, place, or thing considered to be the best of her or its kind; *Slang* effeminate male homosexual; only fertile female in a colony of bees, wasps, or ants; the most powerful piece in chess. —**queen it** *Informal* behave in an overbearing manner. —**queenly** *adj.* —**Queen's Counsel** barrister or advocate appointed Counsel to the Crown.

queer *adj.* not normal or usual; faint, giddy, or queasy; *Offens.* homosexual. —*n. Offens.* homosexual. —**queer someone's pitch** *Informal* spoil someone's chances of something.

THESAURUS

quantity allotment, amount, lot, number, part, sum, total

quarrel 1. *n.* affray, argument, brawl, breach, controversy, disagreement, discord, dispute, dissension, feud, fight, row, squabble, strife, tiff, tumult, vendetta 2. *v.* argue, bicker, brawl, clash, differ, disagree, dispute, fight, row, wrangle

quarrelsome argumentative, combative, cross, disputatious, fractious, irascible, irritable, peevish, petulant, querulous

quarry aim, game, goal, objective, prey, prize, victim

quarter *n.* 1. area, district, locality, neighbourhood, part, place, point, position, province, region, side, spot, station, territory 2. favour, forgiveness, leniency, mercy, pity ~*v.* 3. accommodate, billet, board, house, install, lodge, place, post, station

quarters abode, barracks, billet, chambers, domicile, dwelling, lodging, post, residence, rooms, shelter, station

quash annul, cancel, invalidate, nullify, overrule, overthrow, rescind, reverse, revoke

quaver *v.* flicker, flutter, quake, shake, shudder, thrill, tremble, trill, vibrate, waver

DICTIONARY

quell v. suppress; overcome.

quench v. satisfy (one's thirst); put out or extinguish.

quern n. stone hand mill for grinding corn.

querulous [kwer-yoo-luss] adj. complaining or peevish. —**querulously** adv.

query n., pl. **-ries**. question, esp. one raising doubt; question mark. —v. **-rying, -ried.** express uncertainty, doubt, or an objection concerning (something).

quest n. long and difficult search. —v. (foll. by for or after) go in search of.

question n. form of words addressed to a person in order to obtain an answer; point at issue; difficulty or uncertainty. —v. put a question or questions to (a person); express uncertainty about. —**in question** under discussion. —**out of the question** impossible. —**questionable** adj. of disputable value or authority. —**questionably** adv. —**questionnaire** n. set of questions on a form, used to collect information from people. —**question mark** punctuation mark (?) written at the end of questions.

queue n. line of people or vehicles waiting for something. —v. **queueing** or **queuing, queued.** (often foll. by up) form or remain in a line while waiting.

quibble v. make trivial objections. —n. trivial objection.

quiche [keesh] n. savoury flan with an egg custard filling to which vegetables etc. are added.

quick adj. lasting or taking a short time; alert and responsive; easily excited or aroused. —n. area of sensitive flesh under a nail. —adv. Informal in a rapid manner. —**cut someone to the quick** hurt someone's feelings deeply. —**quickly** adv. —**quicken** v. make or become faster or more lively. —**quicklime** n. white solid used in the manufacture of glass and steel. —**quicksand** n. deep mass of loose wet sand that sucks anything on top of it into it. —**quicksilver** n. mercury. —**quickstep** n. fast modern ballroom dance.

quid n., pl. **quid.** Brit. slang pound (sterling).

quid pro quo n. one thing, esp. an advantage or object, given in exchange for another.

quiescent [kwee-ess-ent] adj. quiet, inactive, or dormant. —**quiescence** n.

quiet adj. with little noise; calm or tranquil; untroubled. —n. quietness. —v. make or become quiet. —**on the quiet** without other people knowing, secretly. —**quietly** adv. —**quietness** n. —**quieten** v. (often foll. by down) make or become quiet. —**quietude** n. quietness, peace, or tranquillity.

THESAURUS

queen consort, monarch, ruler, sovereign

queer adj. 1. abnormal, curious, droll, extraordinary, funny, odd, peculiar, remarkable, singular, strange, uncanny, uncommon, unnatural, weird 2. doubtful, dubious, irregular, mysterious, suspicious 3. crazy, eccentric, irrational, mad, odd, touched

quench check, crush, douse, end, extinguish, put out, smother, stifle, suppress

querulous captious, carping, complaining, critical, cross, dissatisfied, fretful, grumbling, irascible, irritable, peevish, petulant, plaintive, sour, testy, touchy

query 1. v. challenge, disbelieve, dispute, distrust, doubt, mistrust, suspect 2. n. demand, doubt, hesitation, inquiry, objection, problem, question, suspicion

question v. 1. ask, cross-examine, enquire, examine, interrogate, interview, probe, quiz 2. challenge, disbelieve, dispute, doubt, mistrust, oppose, query, suspect ~n. 3. inquiry, investigation 4. argument, contention, controversy, debate, difficulty, dispute, doubt, misgiving, problem, query 5. issue, motion, point, proposal, proposition, subject, theme, topic

questionable controversial, debatable, doubt-

ful, equivocal, moot, problematical, suspect, uncertain, unreliable

queue chain, file, line, order, sequence, series, string, train

quibble 1. v. carp, cavil, evade, pretend, shift 2. n. cavil, complaint, criticism, evasion, nicety, objection, pretence, quirk, shift, subterfuge, subtlety

quick 1. active, brief, brisk, express, fast, fleet, hasty, headlong, hurried, prompt, rapid, speedy, swift 2. agile, alert, animated, energetic, flying, keen, lively, nimble, spirited, spry, vivacious 3. able, acute, adept, adroit, apt, astute, bright, clever, deft, discerning, intelligent, perceptive, quick-witted, receptive, sharp, shrewd, skilful, smart

quicken 1. accelerate, expedite, hasten, hurry, impel, speed 2. arouse, excite, incite, inspire, revive, stimulate

quickly abruptly, briskly, fast, hastily, hurriedly, promptly, rapidly, soon, speedily, swiftly

quiet adj. 1. dumb, hushed, inaudible, low, peaceful, silent, soft, soundless 2. calm, contented, gentle, mild, pacific, peaceful, placid, restful, serene, smooth, tranquil ~n. 3. calm-

DICTIONARY

quietism *n.* passivity and calmness of mind towards external events. —**quietist** *n., adj.*

quiff *n.* tuft of hair brushed up above the forehead.

quill *n.* pen made from the feather of a bird's wing or tail; stiff hollow spine of a hedgehog or porcupine.

quilt *n.* padded covering for a bed. —**quilted** *adj.* consisting of two layers of fabric with a layer of soft material between them.

quin *n.* short for QUINTUPLET.

quince *n.* acid-tasting pear-shaped fruit.

quinine *n.* bitter drug used as a tonic and formerly to treat malaria.

quinquennial *adj.* occurring every five years; lasting five years.

quinsy *n.* inflammation of the throat or tonsils.

quintessence *n.* most perfect representation of a quality or state. —**quintessential** *adj.*

quintet *n.* group of five performers; music for such a group.

quintuplet *n.* one of five offspring born at one birth.

quip *n.* witty saying. —*v.* **quipping, quipped.** make a quip.

quire *n.* set of 24 or 25 sheets of paper.

quirk *n.* peculiarity of character; unexpected twist or turn, e.g. *a quirk of fate.* —**quirky** *adj.*

quisling *n.* traitor who aids an occupying enemy force.

quit *v.* **quitting, quit.** depart from; give up (a job); *Chiefly US* stop (doing something). —**quitter** *n.* person who lacks perseverance. —**quits** *adj. Informal* on an equal footing.

quite *adv.* absolutely, e.g. *you're quite right;* somewhat, e.g. *she's quite pretty;* in actuality, truly. —*interj.* expression of agreement.

quiver[1] *v.* shake with a tremulous movement. —*n.* shaking or trembling.

quiver[2] *n.* case for arrows.

quixotic [kwik-**sot**-ik] *adj.* romantic and unrealistic. —**quixotically** *adv.*

quiz *n., pl.* **quizzes.** entertainment in which the knowledge of the players is tested by a series of questions. —*v.* **quizzing, quizzed.** investigate by close questioning. —**quizzical** *adj.* questioning and mocking, e.g. *a quizzical look.* —**quizzically** *adv.*

quod *n. Brit. slang* jail.

quoit *n.* large ring used in the game of quoits. —*pl.* game in which quoits are tossed at a stake in the ground in attempts to encircle it.

quorum *n.* minimum number of people required to be present at a meeting before any transactions can take place. —**quorate** *adj.* having or being a quorum.

quota *n.* share that is due from, due to, or allocated to a group or person; prescribed number or quantity allowed, required, or admitted.

quote *v.* repeat (words) exactly from (an earlier work, speech, or conversation); state (a price) for goods or a job of work. —*n. Informal* quotation. —**quotable** *adj.* —**quotation** *n.* written or spoken passage repeated exactly in a later work, speech, or conversation; act of quoting; estimate of costs submitted by a contractor to a prospective client.

quoth *v. Obs.* said.

quotidian *adj.* daily; commonplace.

quotient *n.* result of the division of one number or quantity by another.

q.v. (used to refer a reader to another item in the same book) which (word, item, etc.) see.

qwerty *n.* standard English language typewriter or computer keyboard.

THESAURUS

ness, ease, peace, repose, rest, serenity, silence, tranquillity

quieten allay, appease, blunt, calm, compose, deaden, dull, hush, lull, muffle, mute, quell, quiet, silence, soothe, stifle, still, stop, subdue

quietly 1. inaudibly, mutely, noiselessly, privately, secretly, silently, softly 2. calmly, contentedly, meekly, mildly, patiently, placidly, serenely

quietness calm, hush, peace, repose, rest, serenity, silence, stillness, tranquillity

quip *n.* gibe, jest, joke, pleasantry, repartee, retort, witticism

quit 1. abandon, decamp, depart, desert, exit, go, leave, resign, retire, surrender, withdraw 2.

cease, discontinue, drop, end, halt, stop, suspend

quite 1. completely, entirely, fully, largely, totally, wholly 2. fairly, rather, somewhat

quiver *v.* oscillate, palpitate, pulsate, shiver, shudder, tremble, vibrate

quiz 1. *n.* questioning, test 2. *v.* ask, examine, investigate, question

quota allowance, assignment, part, portion, ration, share, slice

quotation 1. cutting, excerpt, extract, passage, reference 2. *Commerce* charge, cost, estimate, figure, price, rate, tender

quote attest, cite, detail, instance, name, proclaim, recall, recite, recollect, refer to, repeat, retell

R

R Queen; King; River; *Chess* rook.

r radius; ratio; right.

RA Royal Academy; Royal Artillery.

Ra *Chem.* radium.

rabbi [rab-bye] *n., pl.* **-bis.** Jewish spiritual leader. **—rabbinical** *adj.*

rabbit *n.* small burrowing mammal with long ears. **—go rabbiting** hunt rabbits. **—rabbit on** *v. Informal* talk too much.

rabble *n.* disorderly crowd of noisy people.

rabid *adj.* fanatical; having rabies. **—rabidly** *adv.*

rabies [ray-beez] *n.* acute infectious viral disease transmitted by dogs and certain other animals.

RAC Royal Automobile Club.

raccoon *n.* small N American mammal with a long striped tail.

race¹ *n.* contest of speed. *—pl.* meeting for horse racing. *—v.* compete with in a race; run swiftly; (of an engine) run faster than normal. **—racer** *n.* **—racecourse** *n.* **—racehorse** *n.* **—racetrack** *n.*

race² *n.* group of people of common ancestry with distinguishing physical features, such as skin colour. **—racial** *adj.* **—racism, racialism** *n.* hostile attitude or behaviour to members of other races, based on a belief in the innate superiority of one's own race. **—racist, racialist** *adj., n.*

raceme [rass-eem] *n.* cluster of flowers along a central stem, as in the foxglove.

rack¹ *n.* framework for holding particular articles, such as coats or luggage; straight bar with teeth on its edge, to work with a cogwheel; *Hist.* instrument of torture that stretched the victim's body. *—v.* cause great suffering to. **—rack one's brains** try very hard to remember.

rack² *n.* **—go to rack and ruin** be destroyed.

racket¹ *n.* noisy disturbance, din; occupation by which money is made illegally. **—racketeer** *n.* person making illegal profits.

racket², racquet *n.* bat with strings stretched in an oval frame, used in tennis etc. **—rackets** *n.* ball game played in a paved walled court.

raconteur [rak-on-tur] *n.* skilled storyteller.

racy *adj.* **racier, raciest.** slightly shocking; spirited or lively. **—racily** *adv.* **—raciness** *n.*

radar *n.* device for tracking distant objects by bouncing high-frequency radio pulses off them.

radial *adj.* emanating from a common central point; of a radius; (also **radial-ply**) (of a tyre) having flexible sidewalls strengthened with radial cords.

radiate *v.* emit or be emitted as radiation; spread out from a centre. **—radiant** *adj.* looking happy; shining; emitting radiation. **—radiance** *n.* **—radiation** *n.* transmission of heat or light from one body to another; particles or rays emitted in nuclear decay; process of radiating. **—radiator** *n.* arrangement of pipes containing hot water or steam to heat a room; tubes containing water as cooling apparatus for a car engine.

radical *adj.* fundamental; thorough; advocating fundamental change. *—n.* person advocating fundamental (political) change; number expressed as the root of another. **—radically** *adv.* **—radicalism** *n.*

THESAURUS

rabble crowd, herd, horde, mob, swarm, throng

rabid berserk, crazed, frantic, furious, mad, raging, violent, wild

race¹ 1. *n.* chase, contest, dash, pursuit, rivalry 2. *v.* career, compete, contest, dart, dash, fly, gallop, hurry, run, speed, tear

race² blood, breed, clan, family, folk, house, issue, kin, kindred, line, nation, offspring, people, progeny, stock, tribe, type

rack *n.* 1. frame, framework, stand, structure 2. agony, anguish, misery, pain, pang, persecution, suffering, torment, torture ~*v.* 3. afflict, agonize, crucify, harass, harrow, oppress, pain, torment, torture

racket 1. clamour, din, fuss, noise, outcry, row, shouting, tumult, uproar 2. fraud, scheme

racy animated, buoyant, energetic, entertaining, exciting, heady, lively, sparkling, spirited

radiance 1. brightness, brilliance, glare, gleam, glitter, glow, light, lustre, shine 2. delight, gaiety, happiness, joy, pleasure, rapture, warmth

radiant bright, brilliant, gleaming, glittering, glorious, glowing, luminous, resplendent, shining

radiate 1. diffuse, emit, gleam, pour, scatter, send out, shed, shine, spread 2. diverge, issue

radical *adj.* 1. basic, deep-seated, essential, innate, native, natural, profound 2. complete, entire, excessive, extreme, extremist, fanatical, severe, sweeping, thorough, violent ~*n.* 3. extremist, fanatic, militant

DICTIONARY

radicle *n.* small or developing root.

radii *n.* a plural of RADIUS.

radio *n., pl.* **-dios.** use of electromagnetic waves for broadcasting, communication, etc.; device for receiving and amplifying radio signals; sound broadcasting. —*v.* transmit (a message) by radio.

radio- *combining form* of rays, radiation, or radium.

radioactive *adj.* emitting radiation as a result of nuclear decay. —**radioactivity** *n.*

radiography [ray-dee-**og**-ra-fee] *n.* production of an image on a film or plate by radiation. —**radiographer** *n.*

radiology [ray-dee-**ol**-a-jee] *n.* science of using x-rays in medicine. —**radiologist** *n.*

radiotherapy *n.* treatment of disease, esp. cancer, by radiation. —**radiotherapist** *n.*

radish *n.* small hot-flavoured root vegetable eaten raw in salads.

radium *n.* radioactive metallic element.

radius *n., pl.* **radii** *or* **radiuses.** (length of) a straight line from the centre to the circumference of a circle; outer of two bones in the forearm.

radon [ray-don] *n.* radioactive gaseous element.

RAF Royal Air Force.

raffia *n.* prepared palm fibre for weaving mats etc.

raffish *adj.* disreputable.

raffle *n.* lottery with an article as a prize. —*v.* offer as a prize in a raffle.

raft *n.* floating platform of logs, planks, etc.

rafter *n.* one of the main beams of a roof.

rag[1] *n.* fragment of cloth; torn piece; *Informal* newspaper. —*pl.* tattered clothing. —**ragged** [rag-gid] *adj.* torn; dressed in shabby or torn clothes; lacking smoothness. —**ragtime** *n.* style of jazz piano music.

rag[2] *v.* **ragging, ragged.** tease; play practical jokes on. —*n.* carnival with processions etc., organized by students to raise money for charities.

ragamuffin *n.* ragged dirty child.

rage *n.* violent anger or passion. —*v.* speak or act with fury; proceed violently and without check, e.g. *a storm was raging.* —**all the rage** very popular.

raglan *adj.* (of a sleeve) joined to a garment by diagonal seams from the neck to the underarm.

ragout [rag-**goo**] *n.* richly seasoned stew of meat and vegetables.

raid *n.* sudden surprise attack or search. —*v.* make a raid on. —**raider** *n.*

rail[1] *n.* horizontal bar, esp. as part of a fence or track; railway. —**railing** *n.* fence made of rails supported by posts. —**railway**, *US* **railroad** *n.* track of iron rails on which trains run; company operating a railway.

rail[2] *v.* (foll. by *at* or *against*) complain bitterly or loudly. —**raillery** *n.* teasing or joking.

rail[3] *n.* small marsh bird.

raiment *n. Obs.* clothing.

rain *n.* water falling in drops from the clouds. —*v.* fall or pour down as rain. —**rainy** *adj.* —**rainbow** *n.* arch of colours in the sky. —**raincoat** *n.* water-resistant overcoat. —**rainfall** *n.* amount of rain. —**rainforest** *n.* dense forest in the tropics.

raise *v.* lift up; set upright; build; increase in amount or intensity; bring up (a family); put forward for consideration; collect or levy; end, e.g. *raise a siege.*

raisin *n.* dried grape.

raison d'être [ray-zon **det**-ra] *n. French* reason or justification for existence.

Raj *n.* —**the Raj** former British rule in India.

rajah *n.* Indian prince or ruler.

rake[1] *n.* tool with a long handle and a crosspiece with teeth, used for smoothing earth or gathering leaves, hay, etc. —*v.* gather or smooth with a rake; search (through); sweep (with gunfire). —**rake it in** *Informal* make a large amount of money. —**rake-off** *n. Slang* share of profits, esp. illegal. —**rake up** *v.* revive memories of (a forgotten unpleasant event).

rake[2] *n.* dissolute or immoral man. —**rakish** *adj.*

THESAURUS

rage 1. *n.* anger, frenzy, fury, ire, madness, obsession, rampage, violence, wrath 2. *v.* chafe, fret, fume, rave, seethe, storm

ragged mean, poor, rent, shabby, threadbare, torn, unkempt, worn-out

raid 1. *n.* attack, foray, incursion, inroad, invasion, sally, seizure, sortie 2. *v.* assault, attack, foray, invade, pillage, plunder, rifle, sack

raider attacker, forager (*Military*), invader, marauder, plunderer, reiver (*Dialect*), robber, thief

railing balustrade, barrier, fence, paling, rails

rain 1. *n.* deluge, downpour, drizzle, fall, showers 2. *v.* drizzle, fall, pour, shower, teem

raise 1. build, elevate, erect, exalt, heave, hoist, lift, promote, rear, uplift 2. advance, aggravate, amplify, boost, enhance, enlarge, heighten, increase, inflate, intensify, magnify,

DICTIONARY

rakish [ray-kish] *adj.* dashing or jaunty.

rally *v.* **rallying, rallied.** bring or come together after dispersal or for a common cause; regain health or strength, revive. —*n., pl.* **-lies.** large gathering of people for a (political) meeting; car-driving competition on public roads; *Tennis* lively exchange of strokes.

RAM *Computers* random access memory.

ram *n.* male sheep; hydraulic machine. —*v.* **ramming, rammed.** force or drive; strike against with force; cram or stuff.

Ramadan *n.* 9th Muslim month; strict fasting observed during this time.

ramble *v.* walk without a definite route; talk incoherently. —*n.* walk, esp. in the country. —**rambler** *n.* climbing rose; person who rambles.

ramekin [ram-ik-in] *n.* small ovenproof dish for a single serving of food.

ramify *v.* **-ifying, -ified.** become complex; spread in branches, subdivide. —**ramification** *n.* consequence.

ramp *n.* slope joining two level surfaces.

rampage *v.* dash about violently. —**on the rampage** behaving violently or destructively.

rampant *adj.* unrestrained in growth or spread, rife; (of a heraldic beast) on its hind legs.

rampart *n.* mound or wall for defence.

ramshackle *adj.* tumbledown, rickety, or makeshift.

ran *v.* past tense of RUN.

ranch *n.* large cattle farm in the American West. —**rancher** *n.*

rancid *adj.* (of butter, bacon, etc.) stale and having an offensive smell. —**rancidity** *n.*

rancour *n.* deep bitter hate. —**rancorous** *adj.*

rand *n.* monetary unit of S Africa.

random *adj.* made or done by chance or without plan. —**at random** haphazard(ly).

randy *adj.* **randier, randiest.** *Slang* sexually aroused.

rang *v.* past tense of RING[2].

range *n.* limits of effectiveness or variation; whole set of related things; distance that a missile or plane can travel; distance of a mark shot at; place for shooting practice or rocket testing; chain of mountains; kitchen stove. —*v.* vary between one point and another; cover or extend over; roam. —**ranger** *n.* official in charge of a nature reserve etc.; (R-) member of the senior branch of Guides. —**rangefinder** *n.* instrument for finding how far away an object is.

rangy [rain-jee] *adj.* **rangier, rangiest.** having long slender limbs.

rank[1] *n.* status; relative place or position; social class; order; row or line. —*v.* have a specific rank or position; arrange in rows or lines. —**rank and file** ordinary people or members. —**the ranks** common soldiers.

rank[2] *adj.* smelling offensively strong; complete or absolute, e.g. *rank favouritism;* growing too thickly. —**rankly** *adv.*

THESAURUS

strengthen 3. advance, broach, introduce, moot, suggest 4. collect, form, gather, get, levy, mass, muster, obtain, rally, recruit

rake[1] *v.* 1. collect, gather, remove 2. harrow, hoe, scour, scrape, scratch

rake[2] *n.* lecher, libertine, playboy, profligate, roué

rally *v.* 1. reassemble, re-form, regroup, reorganize, unite ~*n.* 2. reunion, stand ~*v.* 3. assemble, collect, convene, gather, marshal, mobilize, organize, round up, summon, unite ~*n.* 4. convention, convocation, gathering, meeting, muster ~*v.* 5. improve, pick up, recover, recuperate, revive

ram butt, crash, dash, drive, force, hit, impact, smash, strike

ramble *v.* 1. drift, range, roam, rove, saunter, straggle, stray, stroll, walk, wander 2. chatter, digress, maunder, wander, wander ~*n.* 3. excursion, hike, saunter, stroll, tour, trip, walk

rambler hiker, rover, walker, wanderer, wayfarer

ramification complication, consequence, development, result, sequel, upshot

rampant aggressive, flagrant, outrageous, raging, riotous, unbridled, wanton, wild

rampart bastion, bulwark, defence, fence, fort, guard, security, wall

ramshackle crumbling, decrepit, derelict, flimsy, rickety, shaky, unsafe, unsteady

random accidental, aimless, casual, chance, fortuitous, haphazard, hit or miss, incidental, spot

range 1. *n.* area, bounds, distance, extent, field, latitude, limits, orbit, province, radius, reach, scope, span, sphere, sweep 2. *v.* cruise, explore, ramble, roam, rove, stray, stroll, sweep, wander

rank[1] *n.* 1. caste, class, degree, dignity, division, grade, level, order, position, quality, sort, station, status, type 2. column, file, group, line, range, row, series, tier ~*v.* 3. align, arrange, array, class, classify, grade, locate, marshal, order, range, sort

rank[2] 1. dense, lush, productive, profuse, vigorous 2. bad, fetid, foul, fusty, musty, off, putrid, rancid

DICTIONARY

rankle *v.* continue to cause resentment or bitterness.

ransack *v.* search thoroughly; pillage, plunder.

ransom *n.* money demanded in return for the release of someone who has been kidnapped.

rant *v.* talk in a loud and excited way. —**ranter** *n.*

ranunculus *n., pl.* **-luses, -li.** genus of plants including the buttercup.

rap *n.* quick slight blow; rhythmic monologue performed to music. —*v.* **rapping, rapped.** give a rap to; utter (a command) abruptly; perform rhythmic monologue with musical backing. —**take the rap** *Slang* suffer punishment for something whether guilty or not. —**rapper** *n.*

rapacious *adj.* greedy or grasping. —**rapacity** *n.*

rape[1] *v.* force to submit to sexual intercourse. —*n.* act of raping; any violation or abuse. —**rapist** *n.*

rape[2] *n.* plant with oil-yielding seeds, also used as fodder.

rapid *adj.* quick, swift. —**rapids** *pl. n.* stretch of a river with a fast turbulent current. —**rapidly** *adv.* —**rapidity** *n.*

rapier [ray-pyer] *n.* fine-bladed sword.

rapport [rap-**pore**] *n.* harmony or agreement.

rapprochement [rap-**prosh**-mong] *n.* re-establishment of friendly relations, esp. between nations.

rapt *adj.* engrossed or spellbound. —**rapture** *n.* ecstasy. —**rapturous** *adj.*

raptorial *adj.* predatory; of birds of prey.

rare[1] *adj.* uncommon; infrequent; of uncommonly high quality; (of air at high altitudes) having low density, thin. —**rarely** *adv.* seldom. —**rarity** *n.*

rare[2] *adj.* (of meat) lightly cooked.

rarebit *n.* savoury cheese dish.

rarefied [**rare**-if-ide] *adj.* highly specialized, exalted; (of air) thin.

raring *adj.* —**raring to go** enthusiastic, willing, or ready.

rascal *n.* rogue; naughty (young) person. —**rascally** *adj.*

rash[1] *adj.* hasty, reckless, or incautious. —**rashly** *adv.*

rash[2] *n.* skin eruption; outbreak of (unpleasant) occurrences.

rasher *n.* thin slice of bacon.

rasp *n.* harsh grating noise; coarse file. —*v.* speak in a grating voice; make a scraping noise.

raspberry *n.* red juicy edible berry; plant which bears it; *Informal* spluttering noise made with the tongue and lips, to show contempt.

Rastafarian *n., adj.* (member) of a Jamaican cult regarding Haile Selassie as God (often shortened to **Rasta**).

rat *n.* small rodent; *Informal* contemptible person, esp. a deserter or informer. —*v.* **ratting, ratted.** *Informal* inform (on); hunt rats. —**ratty** *adj. Slang* bad-tempered, irritable. —**rat race** continual hectic competitive activity.

ratafia [rat-a-**fee**-a] *n.* liqueur made from fruit; almond-flavoured biscuit.

ratatouille [rat-a-**twee**] *n.* vegetable casserole of tomatoes, aubergines, etc.

ratchet *n.* set of teeth on a bar or wheel allowing motion in one direction only.

rate *n.* degree of speed or progress; proportion between two things; charge. —*pl.* local tax on

THESAURUS

rankle anger, annoy, chafe, gall, irk

ransack 1. explore, rake, scour, search 2. despoil, gut, loot, pillage, plunder, raid, ravage, rifle, sack, strip

ransom money, payment, payoff, price

rant bluster, cry, declaim, rave, roar, shout, yell

rape *n.* 1. outrage, violation 2. abuse, desecration, maltreatment, violation ~*v.* 3. outrage, ravish, violate

rapid brisk, express, fast, fleet, flying, hasty, hurried, prompt, quick, swift

rapidly briskly, fast, hastily, promptly, quickly, speedily, swiftly

rapt absorbed, engrossed, enthralled, gripped, held, intent, spellbound

rapture bliss, delight, ecstasy, exaltation, happiness, joy, spell, transport

rapturous blissful, delighted, exalted, happy, joyful, transported

rare 1. few, infrequent, scarce, singular, sparse, strange, uncommon, unusual 2. choice, extreme, fine, great, peerless, superb

rarely hardly, little, seldom

rarity 1. curio, find, gem, pearl, treasure 2. infrequency, shortage

rascal blackguard, devil, disgrace, imp, miscreant, rake, reprobate, rogue, scamp, scoundrel, villain, wastrel, wretch

rash[1] brash, careless, foolhardy, hasty, headlong, heedless, hot-headed, ill-advised, impetuous, imprudent, impulsive, incautious, reckless

rash[2] 1. eruption, outbreak 2. flood, outbreak, plague, series, spate, wave

DICTIONARY

business (and formerly also domestic) property. —*v.* consider or value; estimate the value of. —**at any rate** in any case. —**rat(e)able** *adj.* able to be rated; (of property) liable to payment of rates. —**ratepayer** *n.*

rather *adv.* to some extent; preferably; more willingly.

ratify *v.* -**ifying**, -**ified.** give formal approval to. —**ratification** *n.*

rating *n.* valuation or assessment; classification; noncommissioned sailor. —*pl.* size of the audience for a TV programme.

ratio *n., pl.* -**tios.** relationship between two numbers or amounts expressed as a proportion.

ratiocinate [rat-ee-**oss**-in-nate] *v.* reason or think out. —**ratiocination** *n.*

ration *n.* fixed allowance of food etc. —*v.* limit to a certain amount per person.

rational *adj.* reasonable, sensible; capable of reasoning. —**rationally** *adv.* —**rationality** *n.* —**rationale** [rash-a-**nahl**] *n.* reason for an action or decision. —**rationalism** *n.* philosophy that regards reason as the only basis for beliefs or actions. —**rationalist** *n.* —**rationalize** *v.* justify by plausible reasoning; reorganize to improve efficiency or profitability. —**rationalization** *n.*

rattan *n.* climbing palm with jointed stems; cane from this.

rattle *v.* give out a succession of short sharp sounds; clatter; shake briskly causing sharp sounds; *Informal* confuse or fluster. —*n.* short sharp sound; instrument for making it. —**rattlesnake** *n.* poisonous snake with loose horny segments on the tail that make a rattling sound.

raucous *adj.* hoarse or harsh.

raunchy *adj.* **raunchier, raunchiest.** *Slang* earthy, sexy.

ravage *v. Lit.* lay waste or plunder. —**ravages** *pl. n.* destruction.

rave *v.* talk wildly in delirium or with enthusiasm. —**raving** *adj.* delirious; *Informal* exceptional, e.g. *a raving beauty.*

ravel *v.* -**elling**, -**elled.** tangle or become entangled.

raven *n.* black bird like a crow. —*adj.* (of hair) shiny black.

ravenous *adj.* very hungry.

ravine [rav-**veen**] *n.* narrow steep-sided valley worn by a stream.

ravioli *pl. n.* small squares of pasta with a savoury filling.

ravish *v.* enrapture; *Lit.* rape. —**ravishing** *adj.* lovely or entrancing.

raw *adj.* uncooked; not manufactured or refined; inexperienced, e.g. *raw recruits;* chilly. —**raw deal** unfair or dishonest treatment. —**rawhide** *n.* untanned hide.

ray[1] *n.* single line or narrow beam of light; any of a set of radiating lines.

ray[2] *n.* large sea fish with a whiplike tail.

rayon *n.* (fabric made of) a synthetic fibre.

THESAURUS

rate *n.* 1. degree, proportion, ratio, scale, standard 2. charge, cost, dues, duty, fee, figure, hire, price, tariff, tax 3. measure, pace, speed, tempo, time 4. **at any rate** anyhow, anyway, nevertheless ~*v.* 5. appraise, assess, class, consider, count, estimate, evaluate, grade, measure, rank, reckon, regard, value, weigh

rather 1. a bit, a little, fairly, moderately, quite, relatively, slightly, somewhat, to some degree, to some extent 2. instead, preferably, sooner

ratify affirm, approve, bind, confirm, corroborate, endorse, establish, sanction, sign, uphold

rating class, degree, estimate, grade, order, placing, position, rank, rate, status

ratio fraction, percentage, proportion, rate, relation

ration 1. *n.* allotment, allowance, dole, helping, measure, part, portion, provision, quota, share 2. *v.* budget, conserve, control, limit, restrict, save

rational enlightened, intelligent, logical, lucid, realistic, reasonable, sane, sensible, sound, wise

rationalize excuse, justify, vindicate

rattle *v.* 1. bang, clatter 2. bounce, jar, jolt, shake, vibrate 3. disconcert, frighten, scare, shake, upset

raucous grating, harsh, hoarse, husky, loud, noisy, rasping, rough, strident

ravage demolish, despoil, destroy, devastate, loot, pillage, plunder, ransack, ruin, sack, spoil

ravenous famished, starved

ravine canyon, defile, gorge, gully, pass

raving crazed, delirious, frantic, frenzied, furious, hysterical, insane, irrational, mad, rabid, raging, wild

raw 1. fresh, natural, uncooked, undressed, unprepared 2. basic, coarse, crude, green, natural, organic, rough, unprocessed, unrefined, unripe 3. callow, green, immature, inexperienced, new 4. biting, bitter, bleak, chill, cold, damp, harsh

ray bar, beam, flash, gleam, shaft

raze demolish, destroy, flatten, level, remove, ruin

DICTIONARY

raze v. destroy (buildings or a town) completely.

razor n. sharp instrument for shaving. —**razorbill** n. N Atlantic auk.

razzle-dazzle, razzmatazz n. Slang showy activity; spree.

RC Roman Catholic; Red Cross.

Rd Road.

RE religious education.

re prep. with reference to, concerning.

re- prefix again, e.g. re-enter, retrial.

reach v. arrive at; extend to; succeed in touching; make contact or communication with. —n. distance that one can reach; range of influence; stretch of a river between two bends. —**reachable** adj.

react v. act in response or opposition (to). —**reaction** n. physical or emotional response to a stimulus; any action resisting another; opposition to change; chemical or nuclear change, combination, or decomposition. —**reactionary** n., adj. (person) opposed to change, esp. in politics. —**reactance** n. Electricity resistance in a coil due to the current reacting on itself. —**reactive** adj. chemically active. —**reactor** n. apparatus in which a nuclear reaction is maintained and controlled to produce nuclear energy.

read v. reading, read. look at and understand or take in (written or printed matter); look at and say aloud; study; understand (an indicating instrument); (of an instrument) register. —**reading** n. —**reader** n. person who reads; senior university lecturer; textbook. —**readership** n. readers of a publication collectively. —**readable** adj. enjoyable to read; legible. —**readability** n.

readjust v. adapt to a new situation. —**readjustment** n.

ready adj. **readier, readiest.** prepared for use or action; willing; prompt. —**readily** adv. —**readiness** n. —**ready-made** adj. for immediate use by any customer.

reagent [ree-age-ent] n. chemical substance that reacts with another, used to detect the presence of the other.

real adj. existing in fact; happening; actual; genuine; (of property) consisting of land and houses. —**really** adv. very; truly. —interj. indeed! —**reality** n. real existence. —**real ale** beer allowed to ferment in the barrel. —**real estate** landed property.

realistic adj. seeing and accepting things as they really are; practical. —**realistically** adv. —**realism** n. —**realist** n.

realize v. become aware or grasp the significance of; achieve (a plan, hopes, etc.); convert into money. —**realization** n.

THESAURUS

reach v. 1. contact, extend to, grasp, stretch to, touch 2. arrive at, attain, drop, fall, move, rise, sink ~n. 3. ambit, capacity, command, compass, distance, extension, extent, grasp, influence, jurisdiction, mastery, power, range, scope, spread, stretch, sweep

react 1. answer, reply, respond 2. act, behave, function, operate, proceed, work

reaction 1. answer, feedback, reply, response 2. recoil

reactionary 1. adj. blimpish, conservative 2. n. die-hard, obscurantist, rightist

read 1. look at, peruse, pore over, scan, study 2. announce, declaim, deliver, recite, speak, utter 3. comprehend, construe, decipher, discover, interpret, see, understand 4. display, indicate, record, register, show

readily 1. eagerly, freely, gladly, promptly, quickly, willingly 2. easily, effortlessly, quickly, smoothly, speedily, unhesitatingly

readiness 1. fitness, maturity 2. aptness, eagerness, inclination, keenness, willingness 3. adroitness, dexterity, ease, facility, promptness

reading 1. inspection, perusal, review, scrutiny, study 2. lecture, lesson, recital, rendering, sermon 3. grasp, impression, interpretation, treatment, version 4. education, erudition, knowledge, learning, scholarship

ready 1. arranged, completed, fit, organized, prepared, primed, ripe, set 2. agreeable, apt, disposed, eager, glad, happy, inclined, keen, prone, willing 3. acute, adroit, alert, apt, astute, bright, clever, deft, expert, handy, perceptive, prompt, quick, rapid, sharp, skilful, smart

real absolute, actual, authentic, certain, factual, genuine, honest, intrinsic, positive, right, rightful, sincere, true, unfeigned, valid, veritable

realistic common-sense, level-headed, matter-of-fact, practical, real, sensible, sober

reality actuality, fact, realism, truth, validity, verity

realization 1. awareness, cognizance, conception, grasp, imagination, perception, recognition, understanding 2. completion, fulfilment

realize 1. appreciate, comprehend, conceive, grasp, imagine, recognize, understand 2. accomplish, bring off, complete, consummate, do, effect, fulfil, perform

really actually, categorically, certainly, genuinely, indeed, positively, surely, truly

DICTIONARY

realm *n.* kingdom; sphere of interest.

ream *n.* twenty quires of paper, generally 500 sheets. —*pl. Informal* large quantity (of written matter).

reap *v.* cut and gather (harvest); receive as the result of a previous activity. —**reaper** *n.*

reappear *v.* appear again. —**reappearance** *n.*

rear[1] *n.* back part; part of an army, procession, etc. behind the others. —**bring up the rear** come last. —**rearmost** *adj.* —**rear admiral** high-ranking naval officer. —**rearguard** *n.* troops protecting the rear of an army.

rear[2] *v.* care for and educate (children); breed (animals); (of a horse) rise on its hind feet.

rearrange *v.* organize differently, alter. —**rearrangement** *n.*

reason *n.* ground or motive; faculty of rational thought; sanity. —*v.* think logically in forming conclusions; (usu. foll. by *with*) persuade by logical argument into doing something. —**reasonable** *adj.* sensible; not excessive; suitable; logical. —**reasonably** *adv.*

reassess *v.* reconsider the value or importance of.

reassure *v.* restore confidence to. —**reassurance** *n.*

rebate *n.* discount or refund.

rebel *v.* **-belling, -belled.** revolt against the ruling power; reject accepted conventions. —*n.* person who rebels. —**rebellion** *n.* organized open resistance to authority; rejection of conventions. —**rebellious** *adj.*

rebore, reboring *n.* boring of a cylinder to restore its true shape.

rebound *v.* spring back; misfire so as to hurt the perpetrator of a plan or deed. —**on the rebound** *Informal* while recovering from rejection.

rebuff *v.* reject or snub. —*n.* blunt refusal, snub.

rebuke *v.* scold sternly. —*n.* stern scolding.

rebus [ree-buss] *n., pl.* **-buses.** puzzle consisting of pictures and symbols representing words or syllables.

rebut *v.* **-butting, -butted.** refute or disprove. —**rebuttal** *n.*

recalcitrant *adj.* wilfully disobedient. —**recalcitrance** *n.*

recall *v.* recollect or remember; order to return; annul or cancel. —*n.* order to return; ability to remember.

recant *v.* withdraw (a statement or belief) publicly. —**recantation** *n.*

recap *Informal* —*v.* **-capping, -capped.** recapitulate. —*n.* recapitulation.

recapitulate *v.* state again briefly, repeat. —**recapitulation** *n.*

THESAURUS

reap acquire, collect, cut, derive, gain, garner, gather, get, harvest, win

rear[1] back, end, rearguard, stern, tail, tail end

rear[2] breed, cultivate, educate, foster, grow, nurse, nurture, raise, train

reason *n.* 1. brains, intellect, judgment, logic, mentality, mind, sanity, sense(s), soundness, understanding 2. aim, basis, cause, design, end, goal, grounds, impetus, incentive, inducement, intention, motive, object, occasion, purpose, target, warrant ~*v.* 3. conclude, deduce, infer, make out, ratiocinate, resolve, solve, think, work out

reasonable 1. arguable, believable, credible, intelligent, logical, plausible, practical, sane, sensible, sober, sound, tenable, wise 2. average, equitable, fair, fit, honest, inexpensive, just, moderate, modest, proper, right, tolerable

reassure comfort, encourage, hearten, inspirit, restore confidence to

rebel *v.* 1. mutiny, resist, revolt 2. defy, disobey, dissent ~*n.* 3. insurgent, revolutionary, revolutionist, secessionist 4. apostate, dissenter, heretic, schismatic

rebellion 1. mutiny, resistance, revolt, revolution, rising, uprising 2. defiance, dissent, heresy, schism

rebellious 1. defiant, disloyal, disobedient, disorderly, insurgent, mutinous, rebel, revolutionary, unruly 2. difficult, refractory, resistant

rebound *v.* 1. bounce, recoil, return 2. backfire, boomerang, misfire, recoil

rebuff 1. *v.* cold-shoulder, cut, decline, deny, discourage, refuse, reject, repulse, resist, slight, snub, spurn 2. *n.* check, defeat, denial, discouragement, opposition, refusal, rejection, repulse, slight, snub

rebuke 1. *v.* admonish, blame, castigate, censure, chide, lecture, reprehend, reproach, reprove, scold, upbraid 2. *n.* blame, censure, lecture, reprimand, reproach, reproof

recall *v.* 1. evoke, recollect, remember 2. annul, cancel, countermand, repeal, retract, revoke, withdraw ~*n.* 3. memory, remembrance

recant deny, disclaim, disown, recall, repudiate, retract, revoke, withdraw

recapitulate outline, recount, repeat, restate, review, summarize

DICTIONARY

recapture v. experience again; capture again.

recce *Slang* —v. **-ceing, -ced** or **-ceed.** reconnoitre. —n. reconnaissance.

recede v. become distant; (of the hair) stop growing at the front.

receipt n. written acknowledgment of money or goods received; receiving or being received.

receive v. take, accept, or get; experience; greet (guests). —**received** adj. generally accepted. —**receiver** n. equipment in a telephone, radio, or television that converts electrical signals into sound; person who handles stolen goods knowing they have been stolen; person appointed by court to manage property of a bankrupt. —**receivership** n.

recent adj. having happened lately; new. —**recently** adv.

receptacle n. object used to contain something.

reception n. area for receiving guests, clients, etc.; formal party; manner of receiving; welcome; (in broadcasting) quality of signals received. —**receptionist** n. person who receives guests, clients, etc.

receptive adj. willing to receive new ideas, suggestions, etc. —**receptivity** n.

recess n. niche or alcove; secret hidden place; holiday between sessions of work. —**recessed** adj. hidden or placed in a recess.

recession n. period of reduction in trade. —**recessive** adj. receding.

recherché [rish-**air**-shay] adj. of studied elegance; choice or rare.

recidivist n. person who relapses into crime.

recipe n. directions for cooking a dish; method for achieving something.

recipient n. person who receives something.

reciprocal [ris-**sip**-pro-kal] adj. mutual; given or done in return. —**reciprocally** adv. —**reciprocity** n.

reciprocate v. give or feel in return; (of a machine part) move backwards and forwards. —**reciprocation** n.

recite v. repeat aloud, esp. to an audience. —**recital** [ris-**site**-al] n. musical performance; act of reciting. —**recitation** n. recital, usu. from memory, of poetry or prose. —**recitative** [ress-it-a-**teev**] n. musical narration.

reckless adj. heedless of danger. —**recklessly** adv. —**recklessness** n.

reckon v. expect; consider or think; make calculations, count. —**reckoner** n. —**reckoning** n.

reclaim v. regain possession of; make fit for cultivation. —**reclamation** n.

recline v. rest in a leaning position. —**reclining** adj.

recluse n. person avoiding society; hermit. —**reclusive** adj.

THESAURUS

recede 1. abate, ebb, fall back, regress, retire, retreat, return, subside, withdraw 2. decline, dwindle, fade, lessen, shrink, sink, wane

receipt 1. stub, voucher 2. acceptance, delivery, receiving, reception

receive 1. accept, acquire, collect, derive, get, obtain, pick up, take 2. bear, encounter, experience, suffer, sustain, undergo 3. accommodate, admit, entertain, greet, meet, take in, welcome

recent current, fresh, late, latter, modern, new, novel, young

receptacle container, holder

reception 1. acknowledgment, greeting, reaction, response, treatment, welcome 2. function, levee, party, soirée

receptive alert, bright, perceptive, responsive, sensitive

recess 1. alcove, bay, corner, hollow, niche, nook, oriel 2. break, closure, holiday, interval, respite, rest, vacation

recession decline, depression, slump

recipe 1. ingredients, instructions 2. formula, method, prescription, procedure, process, technique

reciprocate barter, exchange, reply, requite, respond, return, swap, trade

recital account, narrative, performance, reading, rehearsal, rendering, statement, story, tale, telling

recitation lecture, passage, piece, reading, recital

recite declaim, deliver, describe, detail, itemize, narrate, perform, recount, repeat, speak, tell

reckless careless, hasty, headlong, heedless, imprudent, indiscreet, mindless, precipitate, rash, thoughtless, wild

reckon 1. add up, compute, count, figure, number, tally, total 2. account, appraise, consider, count, deem, esteem, gauge, hold, judge, rate, regard 3. assume, believe, imagine, suppose, surmise, think

reckoning addition, calculation, count, estimate, working

reclaim recapture, recover, redeem, reform, regain, reinstate

recline lean, loll, lounge, repose, rest, sprawl

recluse anchoress, anchorite, ascetic, hermit, monk, solitary

DICTIONARY

recognize *v.* identify as (a person or thing) already known; accept as true or existing; treat as valid; notice, show appreciation of. **—recognition** *n.* **—recognizable** *adj.* **—recognizance** [rik-**og**-nizz-anss] *n.* undertaking before a court to observe some condition.

recoil *v.* jerk or spring back; draw back in horror; (of an action) go wrong so as to hurt the perpetrator. **—n.** backward jerk; recoiling.

recollect *v.* call back to mind, remember. **—recollection** *n.*

recommend *v.* advise or counsel; praise or commend; make acceptable. **—recommendation** *n.*

recompense *v.* pay or reward; compensate or make up for. **—n.** compensation; reward or remuneration.

reconcile *v.* harmonize (conflicting beliefs etc.); bring back into friendship; accept or cause to accept (an unpleasant situation) **—reconcilable** *adj.* **—reconciliation** *n.*

recondite *adj.* difficult to understand, abstruse.

recondition *v.* restore to good condition or working order.

reconnaissance [rik-**kon**-iss-anss] *n.* survey for military or engineering purposes.

reconnoitre [rek-a-**noy**-ter] *v.* make a reconnaissance of.

reconsider *v.* think about again, consider changing.

reconstitute *v.* restore (food) to its former state, esp. by the addition of water to a concentrate. **—reconstitution** *n.*

reconstruct *v.* use evidence to re-create; rebuild. **—reconstruction** *n.*

record *n.* document or other thing that preserves information; disc with indentations which a record player transforms into sound; best recorded achievement; known facts about a person's past. **—v.** put in writing; preserve (sound, TV programmes, etc.) on plastic disc, magnetic tape, etc., for reproduction on a playback device; show or register. **—off the record** not for publication. **—recorder** *n.* person or machine that records, esp. a video, cassette, or tape recorder; type of flute, blown at one end; judge in certain courts. **—recording** *n.* **—record player** instrument for reproducing sound on records.

re-count *v.* count again. **—n.** second or subsequent count, esp. of votes.

recount *v.* tell in detail.

recoup [rik-**koop**] *v.* regain or make good (a loss); recompense or compensate.

recourse *n.* (resorting to) a source of help; *Law* right of action or appeal.

recover *v.* become healthy again; get back (a loss or expense). **—recovery** *n.* **—recoverable** *adj.*

THESAURUS

recognition 1. discovery, recall, remembrance 2. acceptance, admission, allowance, appreciation, avowal, confession, notice, perception, respect

recognize 1. identify, know, notice, place, recall, recollect, remember, spot 2. accept, admit, allow, avow, concede, confess, grant, own, perceive, realize, respect, see, understand

recoil *v.* 1. jerk back, kick, react, rebound, spring back 2. draw back, falter, quail, shrink 3. backfire, misfire, rebound ~*n.* 4. backlash, kick, reaction, rebound, repercussion

recollect place, recall, remember, summon up

recollection impression, memory, recall, reminiscence

recommend advance, advise, advocate, counsel, enjoin, exhort, propose, put forward, suggest, urge

recommendation 1. advice, counsel, proposal 2. advocacy, approval, blessing, endorsement, praise, reference, sanction, testimonial

reconcile 1. accept, resign, submit, yield 2. appease, conciliate, propitiate, reunite 3. ad-

just, compose, harmonize, rectify, resolve, settle, square

reconciliation conciliation, reunion, understanding

recondite arcane, concealed, dark, deep, difficult, hidden, mysterious, obscure, occult, profound, secret

reconnaissance exploration, observation, patrol, scan, survey

reconnoitre explore, inspect, investigate, observe, patrol, scan, scout, spy out, survey

reconsider reassess, rethink, review, revise

reconstruct 1. rebuild, recreate, re-establish, regenerate, remodel, renovate, reorganize, restore 2. build up, deduce

record *n.* 1. account, chronicle, diary, entry, file, journal, log, memoir, minute, register, report 2. background, career, history, performance 3. album, disc, recording, release, single 4. **off the record** confidential, private, unofficial ~*v.* 5. document, enrol, enter, inscribe, log, minute, note, register, report, transcribe

recorder archivist, chronicler, clerk, diarist, historian, scorer, scribe

DICTIONARY

recreant *n. Old-fashioned* cowardly or disloyal person.

re-create *v.* make happen or exist again.

recreation *n.* agreeable or refreshing occupation, relaxation or amusement. —**recreational** *adj.*

recrimination *n.* mutual blame. —**recriminatory** *adj.*

recruit *n.* newly enlisted soldier; new member or supporter. —*v.* enlist (new soldiers, members, etc.). —**recruitment** *n.*

rectangle *n.* oblong four-sided figure with four right angles. —**rectangular** *adj.*

rectify *v.* **-fying, -fied.** put right, correct; purify by distillation; *Electricity* convert (alternating current) into direct current. —**rectification** *n.* —**rectifier** *n.*

rectilinear [rek-tee-**lin**-ee-er] *adj.* in a straight line; characterized by straight lines.

rectitude *n.* moral correctness.

recto *n., pl.* **-tos.** right-hand page of a book; front of a sheet of paper.

rector *n.* clergyman in charge of a parish; head of certain academic institutions. —**rectory** *n.* rector's house.

rectum *n., pl.* **-ta.** final section of the large intestine. —**rectal** *adj.*

recumbent *adj.* lying down.

recuperate *v.* recover from illness. —**recuperation** *n.* —**recuperative** *adj.*

recur *v.* **-curring, -curred.** happen again. —**recurrence** *n.* repetition. —**recurrent** *adj.*

recusant [rek-yew-zant] *n. Hist.* person who refused to obey the Church of England; person refusing to obey authority.

recycle *v.* reprocess (used materials) for further use.

red *adj.* **redder, reddest.** of a colour varying from crimson to orange and seen in blood, fire, etc.; flushed in the face from anger, shame, etc. —*n.* red colour; (**R-**) *Informal* communist. —**in the red** *Informal* in debt. —**see red** *Informal* be angry. —**redness** *n.* —**redden** *v.* make or become red. —**reddish** *adj.* —**red-blooded** *adj. Informal* vigorous; virile. —**redbrick** *adj.* (of a university) founded in the late 19th or early 20th century. —**red carpet** very special welcome for an important guest. —**redcoat** *n. Hist.* British soldier. —**Red Cross** international organization providing help for victims of war or natural disasters. —**red-handed** *adj. Informal* (caught) in the act of doing something wrong or illegal. —**red herring** something which diverts attention from the main issue. —**red-hot** *adj.* glowing red; extremely hot; very keen. —**Red Indian** *Offens.* N American Indian. —**red light** traffic signal to stop; danger signal. —**red meat** dark meat, esp. beef or lamb. —**red tape** excessive adherence to official rules.

redeem *v.* buy back; pay off (a loan or debt); free from sin; reinstate (oneself) in someone's good opinion; make up for. —**the Redeemer** Jesus Christ. —**redeemable** *adj.* —**redemption** *n.* —**redemptive** *adj.*

redeploy *v.* assign to a new position or task.

redevelop *v.* rebuild or renovate (an area or building). —**redevelopment** *n.*

redolent *adj.* smelling strongly (of); reminiscent (of). —**redolence** *n.*

redouble *v.* increase, multiply, or intensify.

THESAURUS

recording disc, record, tape, video

recount depict, detail, enumerate, narrate, portray, recite, rehearse, relate, repeat, report, tell

recover 1. recapture, reclaim, redeem, regain, repair, repossess, restore, retrieve 2. convalesce, get better, get well, heal, improve, mend, rally, recuperate, revive

recovery 1. healing, improvement, mending, rally, revival 2. betterment, improvement, rally, restoration, revival, upturn

recreation amusement, diversion, enjoyment, exercise, fun, hobby, pastime, play, pleasure, relaxation, relief, sport

recruit 1. *v.* draft, enlist, enrol, impress, levy, mobilize, muster, raise 2. *n.* apprentice, beginner, convert, helper, initiate, learner, novice, trainee

rectify adjust, amend, correct, emend, fix, improve, mend, redress, reform, remedy, repair, right, square

rectitude decency, goodness, honesty, honour, integrity, justice, morality, principle, probity, uprightness, virtue

recuperate convalesce, improve, mend, recover

recur come again, happen again, persist, reappear, repeat, return, revert

recurrent continued, frequent, habitual, periodic

red 1. cardinal, carmine, cherry, coral, crimson, rose, ruby, scarlet, vermilion, wine 2. bay, chestnut, flaming, foxy, reddish, sandy, titian 3. blushing, florid, flushed, rubicund

redeem 1. reclaim, recover, regain, repossess, repurchase, retrieve, win back 2. acquit, carry out, discharge, fulfil, keep, meet, perform, satisfy 3. deliver, emancipate, free, liberate, ransom

DICTIONARY

redoubt *n.* small fort defending a hilltop or pass.

redoubtable *adj.* formidable.

redound *v.* cause advantage or disadvantage (to).

redox *n.* chemical reaction in which one substance is reduced and the other is oxidized.

redress *v.* make amends for. —*n.* compensation or amends.

reduce *v.* bring down, lower; lessen, weaken; bring by force or necessity to some state or action; slim; simplify; make (sauce) more concentrated; *Chem.* separate (a substance) from others with which it is combined. —**reducible** *adj.* —**reduction** *n.*

redundant *adj.* (of a worker) no longer needed; superfluous. —**redundancy** *n.*

reed *n.* tall grass that grows in swamps and shallow water; tall straight stem of this plant; *Music* vibrating cane or metal strip in certain wind instruments. —**reedy** *adj.* full of reeds; harsh and thin in tone.

reef[1] *n.* ridge of rock or coral near the surface of the sea; vein of ore.

reef[2] *n.* part of a sail which can be rolled up to reduce its area. —*v.* take in a reef of. —**reefer** *n.* short thick jacket worn esp. by sailors; *Old-fashioned slang* hand-rolled cigarette containing cannabis. —**reef knot** two overhand knots turned opposite ways.

reek *n.* strong (unpleasant) smell. —*v.* smell strongly; (foll. by *of*) be full (of).

reel[1] *n.* cylindrical object on which film, tape, thread, or wire is wound; winding apparatus, as of a fishing rod. —*v.* wind on a reel; draw in by means of a reel. —**reel off** *v.* recite or write fluently or quickly.

reel[2] *v.* stagger, sway, or whirl.

reel[3] *n.* lively Scottish dance.

reeve *n. Hist.* manorial steward or official.

ref *n. Informal* referee in sport.

refectory *n., pl.* **-tories.** room for meals in a college etc.

refer *v.* **-ferring, -ferred.** (foll. by *to*) relate or allude (to); send (to) for information; be relevant (to); submit (to) for decision. —**referral** *n.* —**reference** *n.* act of referring; citation or direction in a book; appeal to the judgment of another; testimonial; person to whom inquiries as to character etc. may be made. —**with reference to** concerning.

referee *n.* umpire in sports, esp. football or boxing; person willing to testify to someone's character etc.; arbitrator. —*v.* **-eeing, -eed.** act as referee of.

referendum *n., pl.* **-dums, -da.** submitting of a question to the electorate.

refill *v.* fill again. —*n.* subsequent filling; replacement supply of something in a permanent container.

refine *v.* purify; improve. —**refined** *adj.* cultured or polite; purified. —**refinement** *n.* subtlety; improvement or elaboration; fineness of taste or manners. —**refinery** *n.* place where sugar, oil, etc. is refined. —**refiner** *n.*

reflation *n.* (steps taken to produce) an increase in the economic activity of a country etc. —**reflate** *v.* —**reflationary** *adj.*

reflect *v.* throw back, esp. rays of light, heat, etc.; form an image of; show; bring credit or discredit upon; consider at length. —**reflection**

THESAURUS

reduce 1. abate, abridge, curtail, decrease, dilute, diminish, impair, lessen, lower, moderate, shorten, truncate, weaken 2. bring, conquer, drive, force, master, overpower, subdue, vanquish 3. cheapen, cut, discount, lower, slash 4. break, degrade, downgrade, humble

redundant excessive, superfluous, supernumerary, surplus, unwanted

reek 1. *v.* smell, stink 2. *n.* odour, smell, stench, stink

reel 1. lurch, pitch, rock, roll, stagger, sway 2. revolve, spin, swim, swirl, twirl, whirl

refer 1. advert, allude, cite, hint, invoke, mention 2. direct, guide, point, recommend, send 3. apply, consult, go, turn to 4. apply, belong, be relevant to, concern, pertain, relate

referee 1. *n.* arbiter, arbitrator, judge, umpire 2. *v.* adjudicate, arbitrate, judge, umpire

reference 1. allusion, mention, note, quotation, remark 2. bearing, concern, connection, consideration, regard, relation, respect 3. character, recommendation, testimonial

referendum plebiscite, public vote

refine 1. clarify, cleanse, distil, filter, process, purify, rarefy 2. civilize, cultivate, elevate, hone, improve, perfect, polish, temper

refined 1. civilized, courtly, cultivated, elegant, gracious, ladylike, polished, polite, urbane 2. delicate, discerning, exact, fastidious, fine, nice, precise, punctilious, sensitive, sublime, subtle

refinement 1. fine point, nicety, nuance, subtlety 2. civility, courtesy, courtliness, cultivation, culture, discrimination, finish, gentility, graciousness, polish

DICTIONARY

n. act of reflecting; return of rays of heat, light, etc. from a surface; image of an object given back by a mirror etc.; conscious thought or meditation; attribution of discredit or blame. **—reflective** *adj.* quiet, contemplative; capable of reflecting images. **—reflector** *n.* polished surface for reflecting light etc.

reflex *n.* involuntary response to a stimulus or situation. **—***adj.* (of a muscular action) involuntary; reflected; (of an angle) more than 180°. **—reflexive** *adj. Grammar* denoting a verb whose subject is the same as its object, e.g. *to dress oneself.*

reflexology *n.* foot massage as a therapy in alternative medicine.

reform *v.* improve; abandon evil practices. **—***n.* improvement. **—reformer** *n.* **—reformation** [ref-fer-**may**-shun] *n.* a reforming; (**R-**) religious movement in 16th-century Europe that resulted in the establishment of the Protestant Churches. **—reformatory** *n.* (formerly) institution for reforming juvenile offenders.

refract *v.* change the course of (light etc.) passing from one medium to another. **—refraction** *n.* **—refractive** *adj.* **—refractor** *n.*

refractory *adj.* unmanageable or rebellious; *Med.* resistant to treatment; resistant to heat.

refrain[1] *v.* (foll. by *from*) keep oneself from doing.

refrain[2] *n.* frequently repeated part of a song.

refrangible *adj.* that can be refracted. **—refrangibility** *n.*

refresh *v.* revive or reinvigorate, as through

food, drink, or rest; stimulate (the memory). **—refresher** *n.* **—refreshing** *adj.* **—refreshment** *n.* something that refreshes, esp. food or drink.

refrigerate *v.* freeze; cool. **—refrigeration** *n.* **—refrigerator** *n.* apparatus in which food and drinks are kept cool.

refuge *n.* (source of) shelter or protection. **—refugee** *n.* person who seeks refuge, esp. in a foreign country.

refulgent *adj.* shining, radiant. **—refulgence** *n.*

refund *v.* pay back. **—***n.* return of money; amount returned.

refurbish *v.* renovate and brighten up.

refuse[1] *v.* decline, deny, or reject. **—refusal** *n.* denial of anything demanded or offered.

refuse[2] *n.* rubbish or useless matter.

refute *v.* disprove. **—refutable** *adj.* **—refutation** *n.*

regain *v.* get back or recover; reach again.

regal *adj.* of or like a king or queen. **—regally** *adv.* **—regality** *n.* **—regalia** *pl. n.* ceremonial emblems of royalty, an order, etc.

regale *v.* (foll. by *with*) attempt to entertain (someone) with (stories).

regard *v.* look at; consider; relate to; heed. **—***n.* look; attention; particular respect; esteem. **—***pl.* expression of goodwill. **—as regards, regarding** in respect of, concerning. **—regardless** *adj.* heedless. **—***adv.* in spite of everything.

regatta *n.* meeting for yacht or boat races.

regenerate *v.* (cause to) undergo spiritual,

THESAURUS

reflect 1. echo, mirror, reproduce, return, throw back 2. cogitate, consider, meditate, muse, ponder, ruminate, think, wonder

reflection 1. echo, image 2. cogitation, consideration, idea, meditation, musing, observation, opinion, pondering, study, thinking, view

reform 1. *v.* amend, correct, emend, improve, mend, rebuild, reclaim, regenerate, remodel, renovate, repair, restore 2. *n.* amendment, betterment, improvement, rehabilitation

refrain *v.* abstain, avoid, cease, desist, forbear, renounce, stop

refresh 1. brace, cheer, cool, enliven, freshen, reinvigorate, revitalize, revive, revivify, stimulate 2. prompt, renew, stimulate

refreshing bracing, cooling, fresh, invigorating, new, novel, original, stimulating

refreshment 1. enlivenment, freshening, renewal, repair, revival, stimulation 2. drinks, snacks, titbits

refuge asylum, harbour, haven, hide-out, resort, retreat, shelter

refugee émigré, escapee, exile, fugitive, runaway

refund 1. *v.* pay back, reimburse, repay, restore, return 2. *n.* repayment, return

refusal denial, rebuff, rejection, repudiation

refuse *v.* decline, deny, reject, repel, repudiate, withhold

regain recapture, recoup, recover, repossess, retake, retrieve

regard *v.* 1. behold, eye, mark, notice, observe, remark, view, watch 2. adjudge, believe, consider, deem, esteem, hold, imagine, rate, see, suppose, think, treat, value, view 3. attend, heed, listen to, mind, note, respect ~*n.* 4. attention, heed, mind, notice 5. affection, care, concern, deference, esteem, honour, love, note, repute, respect, store, sympathy, thought

regardless 1. *adj.* heedless, inconsiderate, indifferent, neglectful, rash, reckless, remiss, unmindful 2. *adv.* anyway, nevertheless, nonetheless

DICTIONARY

moral, or physical renewal; reproduce or re-create. —**regeneration** n. —**regenerative** adj.

regent n. ruler of a kingdom during the absence, childhood, or illness of its monarch. —adj. ruling as a regent, e.g. prince regent. —**regency** n. status or period of office of a regent.

reggae n. style of Jamaican popular music with a strong beat.

regicide n. person who kills a king; killing of a king.

regime [ray-**zheem**] n. system of government; particular administration.

regimen n. prescribed system of diet etc.; rule.

regiment n. organized body of troops as a unit of the army. —v. discipline, organize (too) rigidly. —**regimental** adj. —**regimentals** pl. n. military uniform. —**regimentation** n.

region n. administrative division of a country; an area considered as a unit but with no definite boundaries; part of the body. —**regional** adj.

register n. (book containing) an official list or record of things; range of a voice or instrument. —v. show or be shown on a meter or the face; enter in a register, record, or set down in writing. —**registration** n. —**registration number** numbers and letters displayed on a vehicle to identify it. —**registrar** n. keeper of official records; senior hospital doctor, junior to a consultant. —**register office**, Informal **registry office** place where births, marriages, and deaths are recorded.

Regius professor [**reej**-yuss] n. professor appointed by the Crown to a university chair founded by a royal patron.

regress v. revert to a former worse condition. —**regression** n. act of regressing; Psychol. using an earlier (inappropriate) mode of behaviour. —**regressive** adj.

regret v. -**gretting**, -**gretted**. feel sorry about; express apology or distress. —n. feeling of repentance, guilt, or sorrow. —**regretful** adj. —**regrettable** adj.

regular adj. normal; habitual; done or occurring according to a rule; periodical; straight or level; symmetrical or even; employed continuously in the armed forces. —n. regular soldier; Informal regular customer. —**regularity** n. —**regularize** v.

regulate v. control, esp. by rules; adjust slightly. —**regulation** n. rule; regulating. —**regulator** n. device that automatically controls pressure, temperature, etc.

regurgitate v. vomit; (of some birds and animals) bring back (partly digested food) into the mouth; reproduce (ideas, facts, etc.) without understanding them. —**regurgitation** n.

rehabilitate v. help (a person) to readjust to society after illness, imprisonment, etc.; restore to a former position or rank; restore the good reputation of. —**rehabilitation** n.

rehash v. rework or reuse. —n. old materials presented in a new form.

rehearse v. practise (a play, concert, etc.); repeat aloud. —**rehearsal** n.

rehouse v. provide with a new (and better) home.

reign n. period of a sovereign's rule. —v. rule (a country); be supreme.

THESAURUS

regime government, leadership, management, reign, rule, system

region area, country, district, expanse, land, locality, part, place, quarter, section, sector, territory, tract, zone

regional district, local, parochial, provincial, sectional, zonal

register n. 1. archives, catalogue, chronicle, diary, file, ledger, list, log, record, roll, roster, schedule ~v. 2. catalogue, chronicle, enlist, enrol, enter, inscribe, list, note, record, take down 3. betray, display, exhibit, express, indicate, manifest, mark, read, record, reflect, reveal, say, show

regret 1. v. bemoan, bewail, deplore, grieve, lament, miss, mourn, repent, rue 2. n. bitterness, compunction, contrition, disappointment, penitence, remorse, repentance, ruefulness, sorrow

regrettable disappointing, distressing, lamentable, pitiable, sad, shameful, unfortunate

regular 1. common, customary, daily, everyday, habitual, normal, ordinary, routine, typical, usual 2. consistent, constant, even, fixed, ordered, periodic, set, stated, steady, systematic, uniform 3. balanced, even, flat, level, smooth, straight, symmetrical, uniform

regulate adjust, arrange, balance, conduct, control, direct, fit, govern, guide, handle, manage, monitor, order, rule, run, settle, supervise, tune

regulation n. 1. adjustment, control, direction, government, management, supervision 2. decree, dictate, direction, edict, law, order, precept, procedure, requirement, rule, statute

rehearsal drill, practice, preparation, reading

rehearse act, drill, practise, prepare, ready, recite, repeat, run through, study, train, try out

reign 1. n. command, control, dominion, empire, influence, monarchy, power, rule, sway 2. v. administer, command, govern, influence, rule

DICTIONARY

reimburse v. refund, pay back. —**reimbursement** n.

rein n. (usu. pl.) narrow strap attached to a bit to guide a horse; means of control. —v. check or manage with reins; control.

reincarnation n. rebirth of a soul in successive bodies; one of a series of such transmigrations. —**reincarnate** v.

reindeer n. deer of arctic regions with large branched antlers.

reinforce v. strengthen with new support, material, or force; strengthen with additional troops, ships, etc. —**reinforcement** n.

reinstate v. restore or re-establish. —**reinstatement** n.

reiterate v. repeat again and again. —**reiteration** n.

reject v. refuse to accept or believe; discard as useless; rebuff (a person). —n. person or thing rejected as not up to standard. —**rejection** n.

rejig v. -**jigging**, -**jigged**. re-equip (a factory or plant); rearrange.

rejoice v. feel or express great happiness.

rejoin v. reply; join again.

rejoinder n. answer, retort.

rejuvenate v. restore youth or vitality to. —**rejuvenation** n.

relapse v. fall back into bad habits, illness, etc. —n. return of bad habits, illness, etc.

relate v. tell (a story) or describe (an event); establish a relation between; have reference or relation to; (foll. by to) form a sympathetic relationship (with). —**related** adj.

relation n. connection by blood or marriage; relative; connection between things; act of relating (a story). —pl. social or political dealings; family; Euphemistic sexual intercourse. —**relationship** n. dealings and feelings between people or countries; emotional or sexual affair; connection between two things; association by blood or marriage, kinship.

relative adj. dependent on relation to something else, not absolute; having reference or relation (to); Grammar referring to a word or clause earlier in the sentence. —n. person connected by blood or marriage; Grammar relative pronoun or clause. —**relatively** adv. —**relativity** n. state of being relative; subject of two theories of Albert Einstein, dealing with relationships of space, time, and motion, and acceleration and gravity.

relax v. make or become looser, less tense, or less rigid; ease up from effort or attention, rest; become more friendly; be less strict about. —**relaxing** adj. —**relaxation** n.

relay n. fresh set of people or animals relieving

THESAURUS

rein n. brake, bridle, check, control, curb, harness, hold, restraint

reinforce bolster, emphasize, fortify, harden, increase, prop, stiffen, strengthen, stress, support, toughen, underline

reinforcement 1. enlargement, fortification, increase, strengthening, supplement 2. brace, buttress, prop, shore, stay, support

reinstate recall, rehabilitate, replace, restore, return

reject 1. v. decline, deny, despise, discard, jettison, rebuff, refuse, renounce, repel, scrap, spurn, throw away or out, turn down, veto 2. n. castoff, discard, failure, second

rejection dismissal, exclusion, rebuff, refusal, repudiation, veto

rejoice celebrate, delight, exult, glory, joy, revel, triumph

relapse v. 1. degenerate, fail, lapse, regress, revert, weaken 2. deteriorate, fade, fail, sicken, sink, weaken, worsen ~n. 3. lapse, regression, retrogression, reversion 4. deterioration, weakening, worsening

relate 1. describe, detail, narrate, present, recite, rehearse, report, tell 2. associate, connect, coordinate, couple, join, link 3. apply, concern, pertain, refer

related 1. affiliated, akin, associated, connected, interconnected, joint, linked 2. akin, kin, kindred

relation n. 1. affinity, kindred, kinship 2. kin, kinsman, relative 3. bearing, bond, comparison, connection, link, pertinence, reference, regard, similarity

relations 1. affairs, connections, contact, interaction, intercourse, liaison, meetings, rapport, terms 2. clan, family, kin, kindred, tribe

relationship affair, bond, conjunction, connection, exchange, kinship, liaison, link, proportion, similarity, tie-up

relative adj. 1. allied, connected, contingent, dependent, reciprocal, related, respective 2. applicable, apposite, appropriate, appurtenant, apropos, germane, pertinent, relevant ~n. 3. kinsman

relatively comparatively, rather, somewhat

relax 1. abate, ease, ebb, lessen, let up, loosen, lower, moderate, reduce, relieve, slacken, weaken 2. calm, laze, soften, unwind

relaxation enjoyment, fun, leisure, pleasure, recreation, refreshment, rest

DICTIONARY

others; *Electricity* device for making or breaking a local circuit; broadcasting station receiving and retransmitting programmes. —*v*. **-laying, -layed.** pass on (a message). —**relay race** race between teams of which each runner races part of the distance.

release *v*. set free; let go or fall; permit public showing of (a film etc.); emit heat, energy, etc. —*n*. setting free; written discharge; statement to the press; catch or handle; newly issued film, record, etc.

relegate *v*. put in a less important position, demote. —**relegation** *n*.

relent *v*. give up a harsh intention, become less severe. —**relentless** *adj*. merciless; unremitting.

relevant *adj*. to do with the matter in hand. —**relevance** *n*.

reliable *adj*. see RELY.

reliance *n*. see RELY.

relic *n*. something that has survived from the past; body or possession of a saint, regarded as holy. —*pl*. remains or traces. —**relict** *n*. *Obs.* widow.

relief *n*. gladness at the end or removal of pain, distress, etc.; money or food given to victims of disaster, poverty, etc.; release from monotony or duty; person who relieves another; freeing of a besieged city etc.; projection of a carved design from the surface; distinctness or prominence, e.g. *stand out in bold relief.* —**relieve** *v*. bring relief to. —**relieve oneself** urinate or defecate.

—**relief map** map showing the shape and height of land by shading.

religion *n*. system of belief in and worship of a supernatural power or god. —**religious** *adj*. of religion; pious or devout; scrupulous or conscientious. —**religiously** *adv*.

relinquish *v*. give up or abandon. —**relinquishment** *n*.

reliquary [rel-lik-wer-ee] *n., pl*. **-ries.** case or shrine for holy relics.

relish *v*. enjoy, like very much. —*n*. liking or gusto; appetizing savoury food, such as pickle; zestful quality or flavour.

relocate *v*. move to a new place to live or work. —**relocation** *n*.

reluctant *adj*. unwilling or disinclined. —**reluctantly** *adv*. —**reluctance** *n*.

rely *v*. **-lying, -lied.** depend (on); trust. —**reliable** *adj*. able to be trusted, dependable. —**reliably** *adv*. —**reliability** *n*. —**reliance** *n*. dependence, confidence, or trust. —**reliant** *adj*.

remain *v*. stay, be left behind; continue; be left (over); be left to be done, said, etc. —**remains** *pl. n*. relics, esp. of ancient buildings; dead body. —**remainder** *n*. part which is left; amount left over after subtraction or division. —*v*. offer (copies of a poorly selling book) at reduced prices.

THESAURUS

relay *n*. 1. relief, shift, turn 2. dispatch, message, transmission ~*v*. 3. broadcast, carry, hand on, pass on, send, spread, transmit

release *v*. 1. deliver, discharge, drop, extricate, free, liberate, loose, set free, unchain, undo, unfasten, unfetter, unloose, untie 2. circulate, distribute, issue, launch, present, publish, put out, unveil ~*n*. 3. acquittal, delivery, discharge, freedom, liberty, relief

relent be merciful, capitulate, forbear, melt, soften, unbend, yield

relentless cruel, fierce, grim, hard, harsh, pitiless, remorseless

relevant admissible, apposite, appropriate, apt, fitting, material, pertinent, proper, related, significant, suited

reliable dependable, faithful, honest, predictable, regular, responsible, safe, sound, stable, sure, true

relic fragment, keepsake, memento, remnant, scrap, token, trace, vestige

relief 1. balm, comfort, cure, deliverance, ease, mitigation, release, remedy, solace 2. aid, as-

sistance, help, succour, support 3. break, diversion, remission, respite, rest

relieve 1. alleviate, appease, assuage, calm, comfort, console, cure, dull, ease, mitigate, mollify, relax, soften, solace, soothe 2. aid, assist, help, succour, support, sustain 3. stand in for, substitute for

religious devotional, devout, faithful, godly, holy, pious, pure, reverent, righteous, sacred, spiritual

relish *v*. 1. delight in, enjoy, fancy, like, prefer, savour, taste ~*n*. 2. appreciation, enjoyment, fancy, fondness, gusto, liking, love, partiality, penchant, stomach, taste, zest 3. condiment, sauce, seasoning 4. flavour, savour, smack, spice, tang, taste, trace

reluctance aversion, dislike, distaste, hesitancy, loathing, repugnance

reluctant disinclined, grudging, hesitant, loath, slow, unwilling

rely bank, bet, count, depend, lean, reckon, trust

remain abide, cling, continue, delay, dwell, en-

DICTIONARY

remand v. send back into custody. —**on remand** in custody. —**remand centre** place where accused people are detained awaiting trial.

remark v. make casual comment (on); say; observe or notice. —n. observation or comment. —**remarkable** adj. worthy of note or attention; striking or unusual. —**remarkably** adv.

remedy n., pl. **-dies.** means of curing pain or disease; means of solving a problem. —v. **-edying, -edied.** put right. —**remedial** adj. intended to correct a specific disability, handicap, etc.

remember v. retain in or recall to one's memory; have in mind. —**remembrance** n. memory; token or souvenir; honouring of the memory of a person or event.

remind v. cause to remember; put in mind (of). —**reminder** n. something that recalls the past; note to remind a person of something not done.

reminisce v. talk or write of past times, experiences, etc. —**reminiscence** n. remembering; thing recollected. —pl. memoirs. —**reminiscent** adj. reminding or suggestive (of).

remiss adj. negligent or careless.

remission n. reduction in the length of a prison term; pardon or forgiveness; easing of intensity, as of an illness.

remit v. **-mitting, -mitted.** send (money) for goods, services, etc., esp. by post; cancel (a punishment or debt); refer (a decision) to a higher authority or later date. —n. area of competence or authority. —**remittance** n. sending of money; money sent.

remnant n. small piece, esp. of fabric, left over; surviving trace.

remonstrate v. argue in protest. —**remonstrance** n.

remorse n. feeling of sorrow and regret for something one did. —**remorseful** adj. —**remorsefully** adv. —**remorseless** adj. pitiless; persistent. —**remorselessly** adv.

remote adj. far away, distant; aloof; slight or faint. —**remotely** adv. —**remote control** control of an apparatus from a distance by an electrical device.

remould v. renovate (a worn tyre). —n. renovated tyre.

remove v. take away or off; dismiss from office; get rid of. —n. degree of difference. —**removable** adj. —**removal** n. removing, esp. changing residence.

THESAURUS

dure, last, linger, persist, prevail, rest, stand, stay, survive, tarry, wait

remainder balance, excess, leavings, residue, residuum, rest, surplus, trace

remains balance, crumbs, debris, dregs, fragments, leavings, leftovers, oddments, pieces, relics, remnants, residue, rest, scraps, traces, vestiges

remark v. 1. comment, declare, mention, observe, pass comment, reflect, say, state 2. espy, heed, mark, note, notice, observe, perceive, regard, see ~n. 3. comment, declaration, reflection, statement, thought, utterance, word

remarkable distinguished, extraordinary, famous, impressive, notable, outstanding, phenomenal, pre-eminent, rare, signal, singular, strange, striking, surprising, uncommon, unusual, wonderful

remedy 1. n. cure, medicine, nostrum, panacea, relief, treatment 2. v. alleviate, assuage, control, cure, ease, heal, help, relieve, restore, soothe, treat

remember call up, commemorate, recall, recognize, recollect, reminisce, retain

remind call up, prompt

reminiscence anecdote, memoir, recall, review

reminiscent remindful, similar, suggestive

remiss careless, dilatory, forgetful, heedless, inattentive, lax, negligent, slack, tardy, thoughtless, unmindful

remission 1. absolution, amnesty, discharge, excuse, exemption, exoneration, forgiveness, pardon, release, reprieve 2. alleviation, lull, moderation, reduction, relaxation, respite, suspension

remit v. 1. dispatch, forward, mail, post, send, transmit 2. cancel, desist, forbear, halt, repeal, rescind, stop

remittance allowance, fee, payment

remnant balance, bit, end, fragment, leftovers, piece, remainder, remains, residue, rest, scrap, shred, vestige

remorse anguish, compassion, compunction, contrition, grief, guilt, pity, regret, shame

remorseless 1. inexorable, relentless 2. callous, cruel, hard, harsh, inhumane, merciless, pitiless

remote 1. distant, far, inaccessible, isolated, secluded 2. abstracted, aloof, cold, detached, distant, removed, reserved, standoffish, withdrawn

removal 1. dislodgment, dismissal, dispossession, ejection, elimination, eradication, expulsion, extraction, stripping, subtraction, taking off, uprooting, withdrawal 2. departure, move, relocation, transfer

remove 1. abolish, delete, depose, detach, dis~

DICTIONARY

remunerate *v.* reward or pay. —**remuneration** *n.* —**remunerative** *adj.*

renaissance *n.* revival or rebirth, esp. (**R-**) the revival of learning in the 14th–16th centuries.

renal [ree-nal] *adj.* of the kidneys.

renascent *adj.* becoming active or vigorous again. —**renascence** *n.*

rend *v.* **rending, rent.** tear or wrench apart; (of a sound) break (the silence) violently.

render *v.* submit or present (a bill); give or provide (aid, a service, etc.); cause to become; portray or represent; melt down (fat); cover with plaster.

rendezvous [ron-day-voo] *n., pl.* **-vous.** appointment; meeting place. —*v.* meet as arranged.

rendition *n.* performance; translation.

renegade *n.* person who deserts a cause.

renege [rin-nayg] *v.* (usu. foll. by *on*) go back on (a promise etc.).

renew *v.* begin again; reaffirm; make valid again; grow again; restore to a former state; replace (a worn part). —**renewable** *adj.* —**renewal** *n.*

rennet *n.* substance for curdling milk to make cheese.

renounce *v.* give up (a belief, habit, etc.) voluntarily; give up (a title or claim) formally. —**renunciation** *n.*

renovate *v.* restore to good condition. —**renovation** *n.*

renown *n.* widespread good reputation. —**renowned** *adj.* famous.

rent[1] *n.* regular payment for use of land, a building, machine, etc. —*v.* give or have use of in return for rent. —**rental** *n.* sum payable as rent.

rent[2] *n.* tear or fissure. —*v.* past of REND.

renunciation *n.* see RENOUNCE.

reorganize *v.* organize in a new and more efficient way. —**reorganization** *n.*

rep[1] *adj., n.* short for REPERTORY (COMPANY).

rep[2] *n.* short for REPRESENTATIVE.

repair[1] *v.* restore to good condition, mend. —*n.* repaired part; state or condition, e.g. *in good repair.* —**repairable** *adj.* —**reparation** *n.* something done or given as compensation.

repair[2] *v.* go (to).

repartee *n.* witty retort; interchange of witty retorts.

repast *n.* meal.

repatriate *v.* send (someone) back to his or her own country. —**repatriation** *n.*

repay *v.* pay back, refund; make a return for. —**repayable** *adj.* —**repayment** *n.*

repeal *v.* cancel (a law) officially. —*n.* act of repealing.

repeat *v.* say or do again; happen again, recur. —*n.* act or instance of repeating; programme broadcast again. —**repeatedly** *adv.* —**repeater** *n.* firearm that may be discharged many times without reloading.

THESAURUS

charge, dismiss, displace, doff, efface, eject, eliminate, erase, expel, extract, move, oust, purge, relegate, shed, transfer, transport, unseat, withdraw 2. depart, move away, quit, relocate, shift, transfer, vacate

remuneration earnings, emolument, fee, income, payment, profit, reparation, retainer, return, reward, salary, stipend, wages

remunerative lucrative, paying, profitable, rich, worthwhile

renaissance, renascence reappearance, reawakening, rebirth, renewal, restoration, revival

render 1. deliver, furnish, give, pay, present, provide, show, submit, supply, tender, turn over, yield 2. exchange, give, return, swap, trade 3. act, depict, do, give, interpret, perform, play, portray, present, represent

renew continue, extend, mend, modernize, overhaul, reaffirm, recreate, refit, refurbish, rejuvenate, renovate, reopen, repair, repeat, replace, restock, restore, resume, transform

renounce abjure, abstain from, cast off, decline, deny, discard, disown, forgo, forsake, forswear,

quit, recant, reject, relinquish, repudiate, resign, spurn, waive

renovate modernize, overhaul, recondition, refit, reform, renew, repair, restore

renowned celebrated, distinguished, eminent, esteemed, famous, notable, noted, well-known

rent[1] 1. *n.* fee, hire, lease, payment, rental, tariff 2. *v.* charter, hire, lease, let

rent[2] gash, hole, opening, rip, slash, slit, split, tear

repair 1. *v.* fix, heal, mend, patch, patch up, recover, rectify, redress, renew, renovate, restore 2. *n.* darn, mend, overhaul, patch

reparation atonement, damages, redress, repair, restitution, satisfaction

repartee badinage, banter, sally, wit, wordplay

repay 1. compensate, refund, reimburse, requite, restore, square 2. avenge, reciprocate, retaliate, revenge

repeal 1. *v.* abolish, annul, cancel, invalidate, nullify, recall, reverse, revoke, withdraw 2. *n.* annulment, invalidation, rescindment, withdrawal

DICTIONARY

repel *v.* **-pelling, -pelled.** be disgusting to; drive back, ward off; resist. —**repellent** *adj.* distasteful; resisting water etc. —*n.* something that repels, esp. a chemical to repel insects.

repent *v.* feel regret for (a deed or omission). —**repentance** *n.* —**repentant** *adj.*

repercussion *n.* indirect effect, often unpleasant.

repertoire *n.* stock of plays, songs, etc. that a player or company can give.

repertory *n., pl.* **-ries.** repertoire. —**repertory company** permanent theatre company producing a succession of plays.

repetition *n.* act of repeating; thing repeated. —**repetitive, repetitious** *adj.* full of repetition.

rephrase *v.* express in different words.

repine *v.* fret or complain.

replace *v.* substitute for; put back. —**replacement** *n.*

replay *n.* (also **action replay**) immediate re-showing on TV of an incident in sport, esp. in slow motion; second sports match, esp. one following an earlier draw. —*v.* play (a match, recording, etc.) again.

replenish *v.* fill up again, resupply. —**replenishment** *n.*

replete *adj.* filled or gorged.

replica *n.* exact copy. —**replicate** *v.* make or be a copy of.

reply *v.* **-plying, -plied.** answer or respond. —*n., pl.* **-plies.** answer or response.

report *n.* account or statement; written statement of a child's progress at school; rumour; bang. —*v.* announce or relate; give an account of; make a report (on); make a formal complaint about; present oneself (to); be responsible (to). —**reportedly** *adv.* according to rumour. —**reporter** *n.* person who gathers news for a newspaper, TV, etc.

repose *n.* peace; composure; sleep. —*v.* lie or lay at rest.

repository *n., pl.* **-ries.** place where valuables are deposited for safekeeping, store.

repossess *v.* (of a lender) take back property from a customer who is behind with payments. —**repossession** *n.*

reprehend *v.* find fault with. —**reprehensible** *adj.* open to criticism, unworthy.

represent *v.* stand for; act as a delegate for; symbolize; make out to be; portray, as in art. —**representation** *n.* —**representative** *n.* person chosen to stand for a group; (travelling) salesperson. —*adj.* typical.

THESAURUS

repeat 1. *v.* echo, iterate, quote, recite, rehearse, reiterate, relate, renew, replay, reproduce, restate, retell 2. *n.* duplicate, echo, reiteration, repetition, replay, reproduction, reshowing

repeatedly frequently, many times, often

repel 1. check, confront, decline, fight, oppose, parry, rebuff, refuse, reject, repulse, resist 2. disgust, nauseate, offend, revolt, sicken

repent atone, deplore, regret, relent, rue, sorrow

repentant ashamed, chastened, contrite, rueful, sorry

repercussion backlash, consequence, echo, rebound, recoil, result

repetition echo, recital, recurrence, rehearsal, reiteration, relation, renewal, repeat, replication, restatement, return, tautology

replace follow, oust, re-establish, reinstate, restore, substitute, succeed, supersede, supplant, supply

replacement double, proxy, substitute, successor, surrogate, understudy

replenish fill, furnish, provide, refill, reload, replace, restore, supply, top up

replica carbon copy, copy, duplicate, facsimile, imitation, model, reproduction

reply 1. *v.* answer, counter, echo, react, reciprocate, rejoin, respond, retaliate, retort, return 2. *n.* answer, counter, echo, reaction, rejoinder, response, retort, return

report *n.* 1. account, announcement, article, declaration, description, detail, dispatch, message, news, note, paper, piece, statement, story, tale, tidings, word, write-up 2. gossip, hearsay, rumour, talk 3. bang, blast, boom, crack, crash, detonation, discharge, explosion, noise, sound ~*v.* 4. air, broadcast, circulate, cover, declare, describe, detail, document, inform of, mention, narrate, note, pass on, proclaim, publish, recite, record, recount, relate, relay, state, tell 5. appear, arrive, come, turn up

reporter correspondent, journalist, newspaperman, pressman, writer

repose 1. ease, peace, quietness, relaxation, respite, rest, sleep, slumber, stillness, tranquillity 2. calmness, composure, dignity, poise, serenity, tranquillity

reprehensible bad, culpable, delinquent, disgraceful, errant, ignoble, remiss, shameful, unworthy

represent 1. act for, be, betoken, express, mean, serve as, speak for, stand for, symbolize 2. embody, epitomize, exemplify, personify, symbolize, typify 3. denote, depict, describe,

DICTIONARY

repress v. keep (feelings) in check; subjugate. —**repression** n. —**repressive** adj.

reprieve v. postpone the execution of (a condemned person); give temporary relief to. —n. postponement or cancellation of a punishment; temporary relief.

reprimand v. blame (someone) officially for a fault. —n. official blame.

reprint v. print further copies of (a book). —n. reprinted copy.

reprisal n. retaliation.

reproach v. blame or rebuke. —n. scolding or blame. —**reproachful** adj. —**reproachfully** adv.

reprobate [rep-roh-bate] adj., n. depraved or disreputable (person). —**reprobation** n. disapproval or blame.

reproduce v. produce a copy of; bring new individuals into existence; re-create. —**reproducible** adj. —**reproduction** n. process of reproducing; thing that is reproduced; facsimile, as of a painting etc.; quality of sound from an audio system. —**reproductive** adj.

reprove v. speak severely to (someone) about a fault. —**reproof** n. severe blaming of someone for a fault.

reptile n. cold-blooded air-breathing vertebrate with horny scales or plates, such as a snake or tortoise. —**reptilian** adj.

republic n. form of government in which the people or their elected representatives possess the supreme power. —**Republican** n., adj. (member or supporter) of the Republican Party, one of the two main political parties in the US. —**Republicanism** n.

repudiate [rip-pew-dee-ate] v. reject the authority or validity of; disown. —**repudiation** n.

repugnant adj. offensive or distasteful. —**repugnance** n.

repulse v. be disgusting to; drive (an army) back; rebuff or reject. —n. driving back; rejection; rebuff. —**repulsion** n. distaste or aversion; Physics force separating two objects. —**repulsive** adj. loathsome, disgusting.

reputation n. estimation in which a person is held. —**reputable** [rep-yoo-tab-bl] adj. of good reputation, respectable. —**repute** n. reputation. —**reputed** adj. supposed. —**reputedly** adv.

request n. asking; thing asked for. —v. ask.

Requiem [rek-wee-em] n. Mass for the dead; music for this.

require v. want or need; demand. —**requirement** n. essential condition; specific need or want.

THESAURUS

evoke, outline, picture, portray, render, reproduce, show, sketch

representation account, description, illustration, image, likeness, model, picture, portrait, portrayal, relation, sketch

representative n. 1. agent, rep, salesman, traveller 2. agent, councillor, delegate, deputy, member, proxy ~adj. 3. archetypal, characteristic, illustrative, symbolic, typical

repress chasten, check, control, crush, curb, inhibit, master, muffle, overcome, overpower, quash, quell, restrain, silence, smother, stifle, subdue, suppress, swallow

repression constraint, control, despotism, domination, restraint, subjugation, suppression, tyranny

reprieve 1. v. abate, allay, alleviate, mitigate, palliate, relieve, respite 2. n. amnesty, deferment, pardon, postponement, remission, suspension

reprimand 1. n. blame, censure, rebuke, reprehension, reproach, reproof, row 2. v. blame, censure, check, chide, rebuke, reproach, scold, upbraid

reproach 1. v. blame, censure, chide, condemn, criticize, discredit, find fault with, rebuke, reprimand, reprove, scold, upbraid 2. n. abuse,

blemish, censure, contempt, disgrace, disrepute, scorn, shame, slight, slur, stain, stigma

reproduce 1. copy, echo, imitate, match, mirror, print, recreate, repeat 2. breed, multiply, proliferate, propagate, spawn

reproduction 1. generation, increase, multiplication 2. copy, duplicate, facsimile, imitation, picture, print, replica

reproof blame, censure, condemnation, criticism, rebuke, reprimand, scolding

repudiate deny, desert, discard, disclaim, disown, forsake, reject, renounce, rescind

repulsive abominable, disagreeable, distasteful, foul, hateful, hideous, objectionable, odious, revolting, sickening, ugly, vile

reputable creditable, excellent, good, honourable, legitimate, reliable, respectable, trustworthy, upright, worthy

reputation credit, esteem, fame, honour, name, opinion, stature

reputed alleged, believed, considered, deemed, estimated, held, reckoned, regarded, said, supposed

reputedly allegedly, apparently, ostensibly, seemingly, supposedly

request 1. v. ask (for), beg, beseech, demand, desire, entreat, petition, pray, seek, solicit 2.

DICTIONARY

requisite [rek-wizz-it] *adj.* necessary, essential. —*n.* an essential.

requisition *n.* formal demand, such as for materials or supplies. —*v.* demand (supplies).

requite *v.* return to someone (the same treatment or feeling as received). —**requital** *n.*

reredos [rear-doss] *n.* ornamental screen behind an altar.

rescind *v.* annul or repeal.

rescue *v.* -cuing, -cued. deliver from danger or trouble, save. —*n.* rescuing. —**rescuer** *n.*

research *n.* systematic investigation to discover facts or collect information. —*v.* carry out investigations. —**researcher** *n.*

resemble *v.* be or look like. —**resemblance** *n.*

resent *v.* feel indignant or bitter about. —**resentful** *adj.* —**resentment** *n.*

reservation *n.* seat etc. that has been reserved; doubt; exception or limitation; area of land reserved for use by a particular group.

reserve *v.* set aside, keep for future use; obtain by arranging beforehand, book; retain. —*n.* something, esp. money or troops, kept for emergencies; area of land reserved for a particular purpose; concealment of feelings or friendliness; *Sport* substitute. —**reserved** *adj.* not showing one's feelings, lacking friendliness. —**reservist** *n.* member of a military reserve.

reservoir *n.* natural or artificial lake storing water for community supplies; store or supply of something.

reshuffle *n.* reorganization. —*v.* reorganize.

reside *v.* dwell permanently. —**residence** *n.* home or house. —**resident** *adj.*, *n.* —**residential** *adj.* (of part of a town) consisting mainly of houses; providing living accommodation.

residue *n.* what is left, remainder. —**residual** *adj.*

resign *v.* give up office, a job, etc.; reconcile (oneself) to. —**resigned** *adj.* content to endure. —**resignation** *n.* resigning; passive endurance of difficulties.

resilient *adj.* able to return to normal shape after stretching etc.; (of a person) recovering quickly from a shock etc. —**resilience** *n.*

resin [rezz-in] *n.* sticky substance from plants, esp. pines; similar synthetic substance. —**resinous** *adj.*

THESAURUS

n. appeal, asking, begging, call, demand, desire, petition, prayer, suit

require 1. crave, desire, lack, miss, need, want, wish 2. ask, beg, bid, command, compel, constrain, demand, direct, enjoin, exact, insist upon, oblige, order

requirement demand, essential, lack, must, need, precondition, stipulation, want

requisite called for, essential, indispensable, necessary, needed, needful, obligatory, vital

requisition 1. *n.* call, demand, request, summons 2. *v.* demand, request

rescue 1. *v.* deliver, free, get out, liberate, recover, redeem, release, salvage, save 2. *n.* deliverance, liberation, recovery, release, relief, salvage, saving

research 1. *n.* examination, exploration, probe, study 2. *v.* analyse, examine, experiment, explore, investigate, probe, scrutinize, study

resemblance comparison, correspondence, facsimile, image, kinship, likeness, semblance

resemble duplicate, echo, look like, remind one of, take after

resent begrudge, dislike, grudge, take exception to

resentful angry, bitter, incensed, indignant, irate, jealous, piqued

resentment anger, bitterness, displeasure, fury, grudge, hurt, ire, malice, pique, rage, umbrage, wrath

reservation 1. condition, doubt, scepticism, scruple, stipulation 2. enclave, homeland, preserve, sanctuary, territory, tract

reserve *v.* 1. hoard, hold, husband, keep, preserve, put by, retain, save, stockpile, store, withhold 2. book, engage, prearrange, retain, secure ~*n.* 3. backlog, cache, capital, fund, hoard, reservoir, savings, stock, store, supply 4. park, preserve, reservation, sanctuary, tract 5. coolness, formality, restraint, reticence, shyness, silence

reserved cautious, cold, cool, demure, modest, restrained, reticent, secretive, shy, silent

reservoir basin, lake, pond, tank

reside abide, dwell, inhabit, live, lodge, remain, settle, sojourn, stay

residence domicile, dwelling, habitation, home, house, lodging, place, quarters

resident citizen, inhabitant, local, lodger, occupant, tenant

resign abandon, abdicate, cede, forgo, forsake, hand over, leave, quit, relinquish, renounce, surrender, turn over, vacate, yield

resignation 1. abdication, departure, notice, retirement, surrender 2. acquiescence, compliance, endurance, fortitude, passivity, patience, submission, sufferance

resigned compliant, long-suffering, patient, stoical, subdued

DICTIONARY

resist *v.* withstand or oppose; refrain from despite temptation; be proof against. —**resistance** *n.* act of resisting; opposition; *Electricity* opposition offered by a circuit to the passage of a current through it. —**resistant** *adj.* —**resistible** *adj.* —**resistivity** *n.* measure of electrical resistance. —**resistor** *n.* component of an electrical circuit producing resistance.

resit *v.* retake (an exam). —*n.* exam that has to be retaken.

resolute *adj.* firm in purpose. —**resolutely** *adv.* —**resolution** *n.* resolving; firmness; thing resolved upon; decision of a court or vote of an assembly.

resolve *v.* make up one's mind; decide with an effort of will; form (a resolution) by a vote; separate the component parts of; make clear, settle. —**resolved** *adj.* determined.

resonance *n.* echoing, esp. with a deep sound; sound produced in one object by sound waves coming from another object. —**resonant** *adj.* —**resonate** *v.* —**resonator** *n.*

resort *v.* have recourse (to) for help etc. —*n.* place for holidays; recourse.

resound [riz-**zownd**] *v.* echo or ring with sound. —**resounding** *adj.* echoing; clear and emphatic.

resource *n.* ingenuity; thing resorted to for support; expedient. —*pl.* sources of economic wealth; stock that can be drawn on, funds. —**resourceful** *adj.* —**resourcefully** *adv.* —**resourcefulness** *n.*

respect *n.* deference or esteem; point or aspect; reference or relation, e.g. *with respect to*; consideration. —*v.* treat with esteem; show consideration for. —**respecter** *n.* —**respectful** *adj.* —**respecting** *prep.* concerning.

respectable *adj.* worthy of respect; fairly good. —**respectably** *adv.* —**respectability** *n.*

respective *adj.* relating separately to each of those in question. —**respectively** *adv.*

respiration [ress-per-**ray**-shun] *n.* breathing. —**respirator** *n.* apparatus worn over the mouth and breathed through as protection against dust, poison gas, etc., or to provide artificial respiration. —**respiratory** *adj.* —**respire** *v.* breathe.

respite *n.* pause, interval of rest; delay.

resplendent *adj.* brilliant or splendid; shining. —**resplendence** *n.*

respond *v.* answer; act in answer to any stimulus; react favourably. —**respondent** *n. Law* defendant. —**response** *n.* answer; reaction to a stimulus. —**responsive** *adj.* readily reacting to some influence. —**responsiveness** *n.*

THESAURUS

resist battle, check, combat, confront, curb, defy, dispute, hinder, oppose, refuse, repel, thwart, weather, withstand

resistance battle, contention, defiance, fight, hindrance, impediment, obstruction, opposition, refusal, struggle

resolute bold, constant, determined, dogged, firm, fixed, obstinate, relentless, set, staunch, steadfast, stubborn, unbending, undaunted, unflinching, unshakable

resolution 1. boldness, courage, dedication, determination, doggedness, earnestness, firmness, fortitude, purpose, resolve, sincerity, steadfastness, tenacity, willpower 2. aim, decision, declaration, intent, intention, judgment, motion, purpose, resolve, verdict

resolve *v.* 1. agree, conclude, decide, determine, fix, intend, purpose, settle, undertake 2. answer, fathom, work out 3. analyse, break down, clear, disintegrate

resort 1. *v.* employ, exercise, look to, turn to, use, utilize 2. *n.* haunt, refuge, retreat, spot, tourist centre

resound echo, re-echo, resonate, reverberate, ring

resource 1. ability, capability, cleverness, ingenuity, initiative, talent 2. hoard, reserve, source, stockpile, supply 3. course, device, expedient, means, resort

resourceful able, bright, capable, clever, creative, ingenious, inventive, quick-witted, sharp, talented

resources assets, capital, funds, holdings, money, property, reserves, riches, supplies, wealth

respect *n.* 1. admiration, consideration, deference, esteem, honour, recognition, regard, veneration 2. aspect, detail, feature, matter, particular, point, sense, way 3. bearing, connection, reference, regard, relation ~4. admire, adore, appreciate, defer to, esteem, honour, look up to, recognize, regard, value, venerate 5. abide by, adhere to, attend, follow, heed, honour, notice, obey, observe, regard

respectable 1. decent, decorous, dignified, estimable, good, honest, proper, upright, venerable, worthy 2. ample, appreciable, decent, fair, goodly, presentable, reasonable, sizable, substantial, tolerable

respective individual, own, particular, personal, relevant, several, specific

respite break, cessation, halt, interval, lull, pause, recess, relaxation, relief, rest

respond answer, counter, react, reciprocate, rejoin, reply, retort, return

DICTIONARY

responsible *adj.* having control and authority; reporting or accountable (to); sensible and dependable; involving responsibility. **—responsibly** *adv.* **—responsibility** *n., pl.* **-ties.** state of being responsible; person or thing for which one is responsible.

rest[1] *n.* repose; freedom from exertion etc.; an object used for support; pause, esp. in music. *—v.* take a rest; give a rest (to); be supported; place on a support. **—restful** *adj.* **—restless** *adj.*

rest[2] *n.* what is left; others. *—v.* remain, continue to be.

restaurant *n.* commercial establishment serving meals. **—restaurateur** [rest-er-a-**tur**] *n.* person who owns or runs a restaurant.

restitution *n.* giving back; reparation or compensation.

restive *adj.* restless or impatient.

restore *v.* return (a building, painting, etc.) to its original condition; re-establish; give back, return; cause to recover health or spirits. **—restoration** *n.* **—restorative** [rest-**or**-a-tiv] *adj.* restoring. *—n.* food or medicine to strengthen etc. **—restorer** *n.*

restrain *v.* hold (someone) back from action; control or restrict. **—restraint** *n.* restraining; control, esp. self-control. **—restrained** *adj.* not displaying emotion.

restrict *v.* confine to certain limits. **—restriction** *n.* **—restrictive** *adj.*

result *n.* outcome or consequence; number obtained from a calculation; score; exam mark or grade. *—v.* (foll. by *from*) be the outcome or consequence (of); (foll. by *in*) end (in). **—resultant** *adj.* arising as a result.

résumé [**rez**-yoo-may] *n.* summary.

resume *v.* begin again; occupy or take again. **—resumption** *n.*

resurgence *n.* rising again to vigour. **—resurgent** *adj.*

resurrect *v.* restore to life; use once more (something discarded etc.), revive. **—resurrection** *n.* rising again (esp. from the dead); revival.

THESAURUS

response answer, feedback, reaction, rejoinder, reply, retort, return, riposte

responsibility 1. answerability, care, charge, duty, liability, obligation, onus, trust 2. authority, importance, power

responsible 1. in charge, in control 2. accountable, answerable, bound, chargeable, duty-bound, liable, subject 3. executive, high, important

rest[1] *n.* 1. calm, doze, leisure, nap, relaxation, relief, repose, siesta, sleep, slumber, stillness, tranquillity 2. break, cessation, halt, holiday, interlude, intermission, interval, lull, pause, stop, time off, vacation 3. base, holder, prop, shelf, stand, support, trestle ~*v.* 4. doze, nap, relax, sit down, sleep, slumber 5. lay, lean, lie, prop, recline, repose, sit, stand

rest[2] balance, excess, others, remainder, remnants, residue, rump, surplus

restful calm, calming, pacific, peaceful, placid, quiet, relaxed, serene, sleepy, tranquil

restive agitated, edgy, fidgety, fretful, impatient, jumpy, nervous, uneasy, unquiet, unruly

restless 1. active, bustling, hurried, irresolute, nomadic, roving, transient, turbulent, unsettled, unstable, unsteady, wandering 2. agitated, disturbed, edgy, fidgety, fitful, fretful, jumpy, nervous, restive, sleepless, troubled, uneasy, unquiet

restoration 1. recovery, refreshment, rehabilitation, renewal, renovation, repair, revival 2. recovery, replacement, restitution, return

restore 1. fix, mend, recover, refurbish, renew, renovate, repair, retouch, touch up 2. build up, refresh, revitalize, revive, strengthen 3. give back, hand back, recover, reinstate, replace, return, send back

restrain bridle, check, confine, contain, control, curb, curtail, debar, govern, hamper, hinder, hold, hold back, inhibit, keep, limit, prevent, repress, restrict, subdue, suppress

restrained calm, controlled, mild, moderate, muted, reticent, soft, steady

restraint 1. compulsion, constraint, control, curtailment, grip, hindrance, hold, inhibition, moderation, self-control, self-discipline, suppression 2. ban, bridle, check, curb, embargo, interdict, limit, limitation, rein

restrict bound, confine, contain, hamper, handicap, hem in, impede, inhibit, limit, regulate, restrain

restriction check, condition, containment, control, handicap, inhibition, limitation, regulation, restraint, rule

result 1. *n.* consequence, decision, development, effect, end, event, fruit, issue, outcome, product, reaction, sequel, upshot 2. *v.* appear, arise, derive, develop, emanate, ensue, flow, follow, happen, issue, spring, stem, turn out

resume begin again, carry on, continue, go on, proceed, reopen, restart

resumption continuation, re-establishment, renewal, reopening, restart, resurgence

resurrect bring back, reintroduce, renew, revive

DICTIONARY

resuscitate [ris-**suss**-it-tate] *v.* restore to consciousness. —**resuscitation** *n.*

retail *n.* selling of goods to the public. —*adv.* by retail. —*v.* sell or be sold retail; recount in detail. —**retailer** *n.*

retain *v.* keep; engage the services of. —**retainer** *n.* fee to retain someone's services; old-established servant of a family. —**retention** *n.* retaining. —**retentive** *adj.* capable of retaining or remembering.

retaliate *v.* repay (an injury or wrong) in kind. —**retaliation** *n.* —**retaliatory** *adj.*

retard *v.* delay or slow (progress or development). —**retarded** *adj.* underdeveloped, esp. mentally. —**retardation** *n.*

retch *v.* try to vomit.

rethink *v.* consider again, esp. with a view to changing one's tactics.

reticent *adj.* uncommunicative, reserved. —**reticence** *n.*

reticulate *adj.* made or arranged like a net. —**reticulation** *n.*

retina *n., pl.* **-nas, -nae.** light-sensitive membrane at the back of the eye.

retinue *n.* band of attendants.

retire *v.* (cause to) give up office or work, esp. through age; go away or withdraw; go to bed. —**retired** *adj.* having retired from work etc. —**retirement** *n.* —**retiring** *adj.* shy.

retort[1] *v.* reply quickly, wittily, or angrily. —*n.* quick, witty, or angry reply.

retort[2] *n.* glass container with a bent neck used for distilling.

retouch *v.* restore or improve by new touches, esp. of paint.

retrace *v.* go back over (a route etc.) again.

retract *v.* withdraw (a statement etc.); draw in or back. —**retractable, retractile** *adj.* able to be retracted. —**retraction** *n.*

retread *v., n.* same as REMOULD.

retreat *v.* move back from a position, withdraw. —*n.* act of or military signal for retiring or withdrawal; place to which anyone retires, refuge.

retrench *v.* reduce expenditure, cut back. —**retrenchment** *n.*

retrial *n.* second trial of a case or defendant in a court of law.

retribution *n.* punishment or vengeance for evil deeds. —**retributive** *adj.*

retrieve *v.* fetch back again; restore to a better state; recover (information) from a computer. —**retrievable** *adj.* —**retrieval** *n.* —**retriever** *n.* dog trained to retrieve shot game.

retroactive *adj.* effective from a date in the past.

retroflex *adj.* bent or curved backwards.

retrograde *adj.* tending towards an earlier worse condition. —**retrogression** *n.* —**retrogressive** *adj.*

retrorocket *n.* small rocket engine used to slow a spacecraft.

retrospect *n.* —**in retrospect** when looking back on the past. —**retrospective** *adj.* looking back in time; applying from a date in the past. —*n.* exhibition of an artist's life's work.

THESAURUS

resurrection reappearance, rebirth, renaissance, renewal, restoration, resurgence, resuscitation, return, revival

resuscitate renew, rescue, restore, resurrect, revive, save

retain 1. absorb, contain, grasp, grip, hold, hold back, keep, maintain, preserve, reserve, restrain, save 2. employ, engage, hire, pay, reserve

retainer 1. attendant, domestic, flunky, footman, lackey, servant, supporter, valet, vassal 2. advance, deposit, fee

retaliate give tit for tat, make reprisal, reciprocate, strike back, take revenge

retaliation counterblow, reciprocation, repayment, reprisal, retribution, revenge, vengeance

reticence reserve, restraint, silence

reticent mum, quiet, reserved, secretive, silent

retire 1. give up work, stop working 2. depart, exit, go away, leave, remove, withdraw 3. go to bed, go to sleep

retirement obscurity, privacy, retreat, seclusion, solitude, withdrawal

retiring coy, demure, diffident, humble, meek, modest, quiet, reserved, reticent, shy, timid, timorous, unassertive, unassuming

retract 1. pull back, sheathe 2. cancel, deny, disavow, disclaim, disown, recall, recant, repeal, repudiate, reverse, revoke, take back, unsay, withdraw

retreat *v.* 1. depart, draw back, ebb, fall back, go back, leave, pull back, recede, recoil, retire, shrink, turn tail, withdraw ~*n.* 2. ebb, flight, retirement, withdrawal 3. den, haunt, haven, refuge, resort, retirement, sanctuary, seclusion

retribution compensation, justice, reckoning, redress, repayment, reprisal, requital, retaliation, revenge, reward, satisfaction, vengeance

retrieve recall, recapture, recoup, recover, redeem, regain, repair, rescue, restore, salvage, save, win back

DICTIONARY

retroussé [rit-**troo**-say] *adj.* (of a nose) turned upwards.

retsina *n.* resinous Greek wine.

return *v.* go or come back; give, put, or send back; reply; elect. —*n.* returning; being returned; profit; official report, as of taxable income; return ticket. —**returnable** *adj.* —**returning officer** person in charge of an election. —**return ticket** ticket allowing a passenger to travel to a place and back.

reunion *n.* gathering of people who have been apart. —**reunite** *v.* bring or come together again after a separation.

reuse *v.* use again. —**reusable** *adj.*

rev *Informal* —*n.* revolution (of an engine). —*v.* **revving, revved.** (foll. by *up*) increase the speed of revolution of (an engine).

Rev., Revd. Reverend.

revalue *v.* adjust the exchange value of (a currency) upwards. —**revaluation** *n.*

revamp *v.* renovate or restore.

reveal *v.* make known; expose or show. —**revelation** *n.*

reveille [riv-**val**-ee] *n.* morning bugle call to waken soldiers.

revel *v.* **-elling, -elled.** take pleasure (in); make merry. —*n.* (*usu. pl.*) merrymaking. —**reveller** *n.* —**revelry** *n.* festivity.

revenge *n.* retaliation for wrong done. —*v.* avenge (oneself or another); make retaliation for. —**revengeful** *adj.*

revenue *n.* income, esp. of a state, as taxes.

reverberate *v.* echo or resound. —**reverberation** *n.*

revere *v.* be in awe of and respect greatly. —**reverence** *n.* awe mingled with respect and esteem. —**reverend** *adj.* (**R-** esp. as a prefix to a clergyman's name) worthy of reverence. —**reverent** *adj.* showing reverence. —**reverently** *adv.* —**reverential** *adj.* marked by reverence.

reverie *n.* absent-minded daydream.

revers [riv-**veer**] *n.* turned back part of a garment, such as the lapel.

reverse *v.* turn upside down or the other way round; change completely; move (a vehicle) backwards. —*n.* opposite or contrary; back side, obverse; defeat; reverse gear. —*adj.* opposite or contrary. —**reversal** *n.* —**reversible** *adj.* —**reverse gear** mechanism enabling a vehicle to move backwards.

revert *v.* return to a former state; come back to a subject; (of property) return to its former

THESAURUS

return *v.* 1. come back, go back, reappear, rebound, recur, repair, retreat, revert, turn back 2. convey, give back, put back, re-establish, reinstate, remit, render, replace, restore, send, take back, transmit 3. give back, pay back, refund, reimburse, repay, requite 4. choose, elect, pick, vote in ~*n.* 5. homecoming, rebound, recoil, recurrence, retreat, reversion 6. reinstatement, replacement, restoration 7. advantage, benefit, gain, income, interest, proceeds, profit, revenue, takings, yield 8. account, form, list, report, statement, summary

reveal 1. betray, broadcast, disclose, divulge, give away, give out, impart, leak, let on, let out, let slip, proclaim, publish, tell 2. bare, display, exhibit, manifest, open, show, uncover, unearth, unmask, unveil

revel *v.* 1. *With* **in** delight, gloat, indulge, joy, lap up, luxuriate, rejoice, relish, savour, wallow 2. carouse, celebrate ~*n.* 3. *Often plural* carousal, celebration, debauch, festivity, gala, jollification, party, spree

revelation disclosure, discovery, display, exhibition, exposition, giveaway, leak, news, publication, telling

reveller carouser, partygoer

revelry celebration, debauch, festivity, fun, jollification, party, spree

revenge 1. *n.* reprisal, retaliation, retribution, satisfaction 2. *v.* avenge, repay, requite, retaliate

revenue gain, income, proceeds, profits, receipts, returns, rewards, yield

reverberate echo, rebound, recoil, re-echo, resound, ring, vibrate

revere adore, defer to, exalt, honour, respect, reverence, venerate, worship

reverence admiration, adoration, awe, deference, devotion, homage, honour, respect, worship

reverent adoring, awed, deferential, devout, humble, loving, meek, pious, respectful, solemn

reverse *v.* 1. invert, transpose, turn back, turn over, turn round, turn upside down, upend 2. alter, annul, cancel, change, countermand, invalidate, overrule, overturn, quash, repeal, rescind, retract, revoke, undo, upset 3. back, go backwards, move backwards, retreat ~*n.* 4. contrary, converse, inverse, opposite 5. adversity, affliction, blow, check, defeat, failure, hardship, mishap, repulse, reversal, setback, trial ~*adj.* 6. backward, contrary, inverted, opposite

DICTIONARY

owner. —**reversion** n. (of property) rightful passing to the owner, designated heir, etc.

revetment n. facing of stone, sandbags, etc. for a wall.

review v. hold or write a review of; examine, reconsider, or look back on; inspect formally. —n. critical assessment of a book, concert, etc.; periodical with critical articles; general survey; inspection of troops. —**reviewer** n. writer of reviews.

revile v. be abusively scornful of.

revise v. look over and correct; restudy (work) in preparation for an examination; change or alter. —**revision** n.

revive v. bring or come back to life, vigour, use, etc. —**revival** n. reviving or renewal; movement seeking to restore religious faith. —**revivalism** n. —**revivalist** n.

revoke v. cancel (a will, agreement, etc.). —**revocation** n.

revolt n. uprising against authority. —v. rise in rebellion; cause to feel disgust. —**revolting** adj. disgusting, horrible.

revolution n. overthrow of a government by the governed; great change; complete rotation; spinning round. —**revolutionary** adj., n. —**revolutionize** v. change considerably.

revolve v. turn round, rotate; (foll. by around) be centred (on). —**revolver** n. repeating pistol.

revue n. theatrical entertainment with topical sketches and songs.

revulsion n. strong disgust.

reward n. something given in return for a service; sum of money offered for finding a criminal or missing property. —v. pay or give something to (someone) for a service, information, etc. —**rewarding** adj. giving personal satisfaction, worthwhile.

rewind v. run (a tape or film) back to an earlier point in order to replay.

rewire v. provide (a house, engine, etc.) with new wiring.

rewrite v. write again in a different way. —n. something rewritten.

rhapsody n., pl. **-dies.** freely structured emotional piece of music; expression of ecstatic enthusiasm. —**rhapsodic** adj. —**rhapsodize** v. speak or write with extravagant enthusiasm.

rhea [ree-a] n. S American three-toed ostrich.

rheostat n. instrument for varying the resistance of an electric circuit.

rhesus [ree-suss] n. small long-tailed monkey of

THESAURUS

review v. 1. reassess, reconsider, re-examine, rethink, revise, think over 2. recall, recollect, remember, summon up 3. assess, criticize, examine, inspect, judge, study, weigh ~n. 4. examination, report, scrutiny, study, survey 5. commentary, criticism, critique, evaluation, judgment, notice, study 6. journal, magazine, periodical 7. *Military* display, inspection, march past, parade, procession

reviewer commentator, critic, essayist, judge

revise alter, amend, change, correct, edit, emend, review, rework, rewrite, update

revision 1. amendment, change, correction, emendation, modification, review, rewriting 2. homework, rereading, studying

revival reawakening, rebirth, recrudescence, renaissance, renewal, restoration, resurgence, resuscitation

revive awaken, bring round, cheer, comfort, invigorate, quicken, rally, reanimate, recover, refresh, rekindle, renew, renovate, restore, resuscitate, rouse

revoke abrogate, annul, call back, cancel, countermand, disclaim, invalidate, negate, nullify, quash, recall, recant, renounce, repeal, repudiate, rescind, retract, reverse, withdraw

revolt n. 1. insurgency, insurrection, rebellion, revolution, rising, uprising ~v. 2. defect, mu-

tiny, rebel, resist, rise 3. disgust, nauseate, offend, repel, sicken

revolting abhorrent, disgusting, foul, horrible, nasty, nauseating, obnoxious, obscene, offensive, repugnant, repulsive, shocking, sickening

revolution n. 1. coup, insurgency, mutiny, rebellion, revolt, rising, uprising 2. innovation, reformation, shift, transformation, upheaval 3. circle, circuit, cycle, gyration, lap, orbit, rotation, round, spin, turn, wheel, whirl

revolutionary n. 1. insurgent, mutineer, rebel, revolutionist ~adj. 2. extremist, insurgent, radical, rebel, subversive 3. different, drastic, experimental, fundamental, innovative, new, novel, progressive, radical

revolve circle, gyrate, orbit, rotate, spin, turn, twist, wheel, whirl

revulsion abhorrence, abomination, aversion, disgust, distaste, loathing, repugnance

reward 1. n. benefit, bonus, bounty, gain, honour, merit, payment, premium, prize, profit, return, wages 2. v. honour, pay, recompense, repay

rewarding edifying, enriching, fulfilling, gainful, gratifying, pleasing, productive, profitable, satisfying, valuable

DICTIONARY

S Asia. **—rhesus factor, Rh factor** feature distinguishing different types of human blood.

rhetoric [ret-a-rik] *n.* art of effective speaking or writing; artificial or exaggerated language. **—rhetorical** [rit-**tor**-ik-kal] *adj.* (of a question) not requiring an answer. **—rhetorically** *adv.*

rheumatism *n.* painful inflammation of joints or muscles. **—rheumatic** *n., adj.* (person) affected by rheumatism. **—rheumaticky** *adj. Informal* affected by rheumatism. **—rheumatoid** *adj.* of or like rheumatism.

Rh factor *n.* see RHESUS.

rhinestone *n.* imitation diamond.

rhino *n.* short for RHINOCEROS.

rhinoceros *n., pl.* **-oses, -os.** large thick-skinned animal with one or two horns on its nose.

rhizome *n.* thick underground stem producing new plants.

rhodium *n.* hard metal like platinum.

rhododendron *n.* evergreen flowering shrub.

rhombus *n., pl.* **-buses, -bi.** parallelogram with sides of equal length but no right angles, diamond-shaped figure. **—rhomboid** *n.* parallelogram with adjacent sides of unequal length.

rhubarb *n.* garden plant of which the fleshy stalks are cooked as fruit.

rhyme *n.* sameness of the final sounds at the ends of lines of verse, or in words; word or syllable identical in sound to another; verse marked by rhyme. —*v.* make a rhyme.

rhythm *n.* measured beat esp. of words, music, etc. **—rhythmic(al)** *adj.* **—rhythmically** *adv.* **—rhythm and blues** popular music, orig. Black American, influenced by the blues.

rib¹ *n.* one of the curved bones forming the framework of the upper part of the body; cut of meat including the rib(s); curved supporting part, as in the hull of a boat; raised series of rows in knitting. —*v.* **ribbing, ribbed.** provide or mark with ribs; knit to form a rib pattern. **—ribbed**

adj. **—ribbing** *n.* **—ribcage** *n.* bony structure of ribs enclosing the lungs.

rib² *v.* **ribbing, ribbed.** *Informal* tease or ridicule. **—ribbing** *n.*

ribald *adj.* humorously or mockingly rude or obscene. **—ribaldry** *n.*

ribbon *n.* narrow band of fabric used for trimming, tying, etc.; any long strip, for example an inked tape in a typewriter.

riboflavin [rye-boe-**flay**-vin] *n.* form of vitamin B.

rice *n.* cereal plant grown on wet ground in warm countries; its seeds as food.

rich *adj.* owning a lot of money or property, wealthy; fertile; abounding; valuable; (of food) containing much fat or sugar; mellow; amusing. **—riches** *pl. n.* wealth. **—richly** *adv.* elaborately; fully. **—richness** *n.*

rick¹ *n.* stack of hay etc.

rick² *v.,* *n.* sprain or wrench.

rickets *n.* disease of children marked by softening of the bones, bow legs, etc., caused by vitamin D deficiency.

rickety *adj.* shaky or unstable.

rickshaw *n.* light two-wheeled man-drawn Asian vehicle.

ricochet [rik-osh-ay] *v.* (of a bullet) rebound from a solid surface. —*n.* such a rebound.

rid *v.* **ridding, rid.** clear or relieve (of). **—get rid of** free oneself of (something undesirable). **—good riddance** relief at getting rid of something or someone.

ridden *v.* past participle of RIDE. —*adj.* afflicted or affected by the thing specified, e.g. *disease-ridden.*

riddle¹ *n.* question made puzzling to test one's ingenuity; puzzling person or thing.

riddle² *v.* pierce with many holes. —*n.* coarse sieve for gravel etc. **—riddled with** full of.

ride *v.* **riding, rode, ridden.** sit on and control or

THESAURUS

rhetoric 1. eloquence, oratory 2. bombast, hyperbole, rant, verbosity, wordiness

rhyme 1. *n.* ode, poem, poetry, song, verse 2. *v.* harmonize, sound like

rhythm accent, beat, cadence, flow, lilt, metre, movement, pattern, pulse, swing, tempo, time

ribald bawdy, blue, broad, coarse, earthy, filthy, gross, indecent, licentious, naughty, obscene, racy, rude, scurrilous, vulgar

rich 1. affluent, moneyed, opulent, prosperous, wealthy, well-off 2. full, productive, well-stocked, well-supplied 3. abounding, abundant, ample, copious, exuberant, fertile, fruitful, full, lush, luxurious, plentiful, productive,

prolific 4. costly, elaborate, elegant, expensive, exquisite, fine, gorgeous, lavish, palatial, precious, priceless, splendid, superb, valuable 5. creamy, delicious, juicy, luscious, savoury, spicy, succulent, sweet, tasty

riches affluence, assets, fortune, gold, money, plenty, property, resources, substance, treasure, wealth

rid 1. clear, deliver, disburden, disencumber, free, make free, purge, relieve, unburden 2. **get rid of** dump, eject, eliminate, expel, jettison, remove, unload

riddle brain-teaser (*Inf.*), conundrum, enigma, mystery, poser, problem, puzzle

DICTIONARY

propel (a horse, bicycle, etc.); go on horseback or in a vehicle; be carried on or across; travel over; lie at anchor. —*n.* journey on a horse etc., or in a vehicle; type of movement experienced in a vehicle. —**rider** *n.* person who rides; supplementary clause added to a document. —**ride up** *v.* (of a garment) move up from the proper position.

ridge *n.* long narrow hill; long narrow raised part on a surface; line where two sloping surfaces meet; elongated area of high pressure. —**ridged** *adj.*

ridiculous *adj.* deserving to be laughed at, absurd. —**ridicule** *n.* treatment of a person or thing as ridiculous. —*v.* laugh at, make fun of.

riding *n.* former administrative district of Yorkshire.

riesling *n.* type of white wine.

rife *adj.* widespread or common. —**rife with** full of.

riff *n. Jazz, rock* short repeated melodic figure.

riffle *v.* flick through (pages etc.) quickly.

riffraff *n.* rabble, disreputable people.

rifle[1] *n.* firearm with a long barrel.

rifle[2] *v.* search and rob; ransack.

rift *n.* break in friendly relations; crack, split, or cleft. —**rift valley** long narrow valley resulting from subsidence between faults.

rig *v.* **rigging, rigged.** arrange in a dishonest way; (often foll. by *up*) set up, esp. as a makeshift; equip; provide (a ship) with spars, ropes,

etc. —*n.* apparatus for drilling for oil and gas; way a ship's masts and sails are arranged; (also **rigout**) *Informal* outfit of clothes. —**rigging** *n.* ship's spars and ropes.

right *adj.* just; in accordance with truth and duty; true; correct; proper; of the side that faces east when the front is turned to the north; (also **right-wing**) *Politics* conservative or reactionary; straight; upright; of the outer side of a fabric. —*v.* bring or come back to a vertical position; do justice to. —*n.* claim, title, etc. allowed or due; what is just or due; conservative political party. —*adv.* straight; properly; very; on or to the right side. —**in the right** morally or legally correct. —**right away** immediately. —**rightly** *adv.* —**rightful** *adj.* —**rightist** *n., adj.* (person) on the political right. —**right angle** angle of 90°. —**right-handed** *adj.* using or for the right hand. —**right-hand man** person's most valuable assistant. —**right of way** *Law* right to pass over someone's land; path used.

righteous [rye-chuss] *adj.* upright, godly, or virtuous; morally justified. —**righteousness** *n.*

rigid *adj.* inflexible or strict; unyielding or stiff. —**rigidly** *adv.* —**rigidity** *n.*

rigmarole *n.* meaningless string of words; long complicated procedure.

rigor mortis *n.* stiffening of the body after death.

rigour *n.* harshness, severity, or strictness; hardship. —**rigorous** *adj.* harsh, severe, or stern.

rile *v.* anger or annoy.

THESAURUS

ride *v.* 1. control, handle, manage, sit on 2. float, go, journey, move, progress, sit, travel ~*n.* 3. drive, jaunt, journey, lift, outing, trip

ridicule 1. *n.* banter, chaff, derision, gibe, irony, jeer, laughter, mockery, raillery, sarcasm, satire 2. *v.* banter, caricature, chaff, deride, humiliate, jeer, lampoon, mock, parody, pooh-pooh, satirize, scoff, sneer, taunt

ridiculous absurd, comical, derisory, farcical, foolish, funny, incredible, laughable, outrageous, risible, silly, stupid

rift 1. breach, break, chink, cleft, crack, crevice, fault, fissure, flaw, gap, space, split 2. breach, disagreement, division, quarrel, schism, separation, split

rig *v.* 1. equip, fit out, furnish, provision, supply, turn out 2. arrange, engineer, fake, falsify, gerrymander, juggle, manipulate ~*n.* 3. apparatus, equipment, fittings, fixtures, gear, machinery, outfit, tackle

right *adj.* 1. equitable, ethical, fair, good, honest, just, lawful, moral, proper, true, virtuous 2. accurate, admissible, authentic, correct, ex-

act, factual, genuine, precise, sound, true, unerring, valid 3. appropriate, becoming, convenient, deserved, desirable, done, due, favourable, fit, ideal, proper, propitious, seemly, suitable 4. conservative, reactionary ~*adv.* 5. appropriately, aptly, fittingly, properly, satisfactorily, suitably 6. directly, promptly, quickly, straight ~*n.* 7. business, claim, due, freedom, interest, liberty, licence, permission, power, prerogative, privilege, title 8. equity, good, goodness, honour, integrity, justice, lawfulness, legality, morality, propriety, reason, truth, virtue ~*v.* 9. correct, fix, rectify, redress, repair, settle, sort out

rigid austere, exact, fixed, harsh, inflexible, rigorous, set, severe, stern, stiff, strict, unalterable, uncompromising

rigorous 1. challenging, demanding, exacting, firm, hard, harsh, inflexible, severe, stern, strict, tough 2. bad, bleak, extreme, harsh, inclement, severe

rigour austerity, hardship, inflexibility, ordeal, sternness, suffering, trial

DICTIONARY

rill *n.* small stream.

rim *n.* edge or border; outer ring of a wheel. —**rimmed** *adj.*

rime *n. Lit.* hoarfrost.

rind *n.* outer coating of fruits, cheese, or bacon.

ring[1] *n.* circle of gold etc., esp. for a finger; any circular band, coil, or rim; circle of people; enclosed area, esp. a circle for a circus or a roped-in square for boxing; group operating (illegal) control of a market. —*v.* put a ring round; mark (a bird) with a ring; kill (a tree) by cutting the bark round the trunk. —**ringer** *n. Slang* person or thing apparently identical to another (also **dead ringer**). —**ringlet** *n.* curly lock of hair. —**ringleader** *n.* instigator of a mutiny, riot, etc. —**ring road** main road that bypasses a town (centre). —**ringside** *n.* row of seats nearest a boxing or circus ring. —**ringworm** *n.* fungal skin disease in circular patches.

ring[2] *v.* **ringing, rang, rung.** give out a clear resonant sound, as a bell; resound; cause (a bell) to sound; (also **ring up**) telephone. —*n.* ringing; telephone call. —**ring off** *v.* end a telephone call.

rink *n.* sheet of ice for skating or curling; floor for roller skating.

rinkhals *n.* S African ring-necked cobra.

rinse *v.* remove soap from (washed clothes, hair, etc.) by applying clean water; wash lightly. —*n.* rinsing; liquid to tint hair.

riot *n.* disorderly unruly disturbance; loud revelry; *Slang* very amusing person or thing; profusion. —*v.* take part in a riot. —**read the riot act** reprimand severely. —**run riot** behave without restraint; grow profusely. —**riotous** *adj.* unruly or rebellious; unrestrained.

RIP rest in peace.

rip *v.* **ripping, ripped.** tear violently; tear away; *Informal* rush. —*n.* split or tear. —**let rip** act or speak without restraint. —**ripcord** *n.* cord pulled to open a parachute. —**rip off** *v. Slang* cheat by overcharging. —**rip-off** *n. Slang* cheat or swindle. —**rip-roaring** *adj. Informal* boisterous and exciting.

riparian [rip-**pair**-ee-an] *adj.* of or on the banks of a river.

ripe *adj.* ready to be reaped, eaten, etc.; matured; ready or suitable. —**ripen** *v.* grow ripe; mature.

riposte [rip-**posst**] *n.* verbal retort; counterattack. —*v.* make a riposte.

ripple *n.* slight wave, ruffling of a surface; sound like ripples of water. —*v.* flow or form into little waves (on); (of sounds) rise and fall gently.

rise *v.* **rising, rose, risen.** get up; move upwards; (of the sun or moon) appear above the horizon; reach a higher level; (of an amount or price) increase; rebel; (of a court) adjourn; have its source. —*n.* rising; upward slope; increase, esp. of wages. —**get, take a rise out of** *Slang* provoke an angry reaction from. —**give rise to** cause. —**riser** *n.* person who rises, esp. from bed; vertical part of a step. —**rising** *n.* revolt. —*adj.* increasing in rank or maturity.

risible [**riz**-zib-bl] *adj.* causing laughter, ridiculous.

risk *n.* chance of disaster or loss; person or thing considered as a potential hazard. —*v.* act in spite of the possibility of (injury or loss); expose to danger or loss. —**risky** *adj.* full of risk, dangerous. —**riskily** *adv.*

risotto *n., pl.* **-tos.** dish of rice cooked in stock with vegetables, meat, etc.

THESAURUS

rim border, brim, brink, edge, lip, margin, verge

ring[1] *n.* 1. band, circle, circuit, halo, hoop, loop, round 2. arena, circus, enclosure, rink 3. association, band, cartel, clique, combine, coterie, gang, group, mob, syndicate ~*v.* 4. encircle, enclose, gird, girdle, hem in, surround

ring[2] *v.* 1. chime, clang, peal, reverberate, sound, toll 2. call, phone, telephone ~*n.* 3. chime, knell, peal 4. call, phone call

riot *n.* 1. anarchy, confusion, disorder, fray, lawlessness, quarrel, row, strife, tumult, turbulence, turmoil, uproar 2. carousal, excess, festivity, frolic, revelry, romp 3. display, flourish, show, splash 4. **run riot a.** go wild, rampage **b.** grow profusely, luxuriate ~*v.* 5. carouse, cut loose, frolic, revel, romp

riotous 1. disorderly, lawless, rampageous, rebellious, refractory, rowdy, unruly, violent 2. loud, noisy, unrestrained, wild

ripe 1. mature, mellow, ready, seasoned 2. favourable, ideal, opportune, right, suitable, timely

ripen burgeon, develop, mature, prepare, season

rise *v.* 1. get up, stand up, surface 2. ascend, climb, enlarge, go up, grow, improve, increase, intensify, lift, mount, soar, swell, wax 3. appear, crop up, emanate, emerge, eventuate, flow, happen, issue, occur, originate, spring 4. mutiny, rebel, resist, revolt 5. ascend, climb, get steeper, go uphill, mount, slope upwards ~*n.* 6. advance, climb, improvement, increase, upsurge, upturn 7. advancement, climb, progress, promotion 8. ascent, incline, upward slope 9. increment, pay increase

risk 1. *n.* chance, danger, gamble, hazard, jeopardy, peril, speculation, uncertainty, venture 2. *v.* chance, dare, endanger, gamble, hazard, imperil, jeopardize, venture

DICTIONARY

risqué [risk-ay] *adj.* bordering on indecency.

rissole *n.* cake of minced meat, coated with breadcrumbs and fried.

rite *n.* formal practice or custom, esp. religious. —**ritual** *n.* prescribed order of rites; regular repeated action or behaviour. —*adj.* concerning rites. —**ritually** *adv.* —**ritualistic** *adj.* like a ritual.

ritzy *adj.* **ritzier, ritziest.** *Slang* luxurious or elegant.

rival *n.* person or thing that competes with or equals another for favour, success, etc. —*adj.* in the position of a rival. —*v.* **-valling, -valled.** (try to) equal. —**rivalry** *n.* keen competition.

riven *adj.* split.

river *n.* large natural stream of water; copious flow.

rivet [riv-vit] *n.* bolt for fastening metal plates, the end being put through holes and then beaten flat. —*v.* **riveting, riveted.** cause to be fixed, as in fascination; fasten with rivets. —**riveter** *n.* —**riveting** *adj.* very interesting and exciting.

rivulet *n.* small stream.

RN Royal Navy.

RNA ribonucleic acid: substance in living cells essential for the synthesis of protein.

roach *n.* freshwater fish.

road *n.* way prepared for passengers, vehicles, etc.; way or course, e.g. *the road to fame;* street. —**on the road** travelling. —**roadie** *n. Informal* person who transports and sets up equipment for a band. —**roadblock** *n.* barricade across a road to stop traffic for inspection etc. —**road hog** *Informal* selfish aggressive driver. —**roadhouse** *n.* pub or restaurant on a country road. —**road metal** broken stones used in building roads. —**roadside** *n., adj.* —**road test** test of a vehicle

etc. in actual use. —**roadway** *n.* the part of a road used by vehicles. —**roadworks** *pl. n.* repairs to a road, esp. blocking part of the road. —**roadworthy** *adj.* (of a vehicle) mechanically sound.

roam *v.* wander about.

roan *adj.* (of a horse) having a brown or black coat sprinkled with white hairs. —*n.* roan horse.

roar *v.* make or utter a loud deep hoarse sound like that of a lion; shout (something) as in anger; laugh loudly. —*n.* such a sound. —**roaring** *adj. Informal* brisk and profitable. —*adv.* noisily.

roast *v.* cook by dry heat, as in an oven; make or be very hot. —*n.* roasted joint of meat. —*adj.* roasted. —**roasting** *Informal* —*adj.* extremely hot. —*n.* severe criticism or scolding.

rob *v.* **robbing, robbed.** steal from; deprive. —**robber** *n.* —**robbery** *n.*

robe *n.* long loose outer garment. —*v.* put a robe on.

robin *n.* small brown bird with a red breast.

robot *n.* automated machine, esp. one performing functions in a human manner; person of machine-like efficiency; *S Afr.* traffic lights. —**robotic** *adj.* —**robotics** *n.* science of designing and using robots.

robust *adj.* very strong and healthy. —**robustly** *adv.* —**robustness** *n.*

roc *n.* monstrous bird of Arabian mythology.

rock[1] *n.* hard mineral substance that makes up part of the earth's crust, stone; large rugged mass of stone; hard sweet in sticks. —**on the rocks** (of a marriage) about to end; (of an alcoholic drink) served with ice. —**rocky** *adj.* having many rocks. —**rockery** *n.* mould of stones in a garden for (alpine) plants. —**rock bottom** lowest possible level. —**rock cake** small fruit cake with a rough surface.

THESAURUS

rite act, ceremonial, custom, form, liturgy, mystery, observance, practice, procedure, sacrament, service, solemnity, usage

rival 1. *n.* adversary, challenger, competitor, contender, contestant, opponent 2. *adj.* competing, conflicting, opposed 3. *v.* come up to, compare with, compete, contend, equal, match, oppose, vie with

rivalry antagonism, competition, conflict, contention, contest, duel, opposition

road avenue, course, highway, lane, motorway, path, pathway, roadway, route, street, thoroughfare, track, way

roam prowl, ramble, range, rove, stray, stroll, travel, walk, wander

roar *v.* 1. bawl, bay, bellow, clamour, crash, cry, howl, rumble, shout, yell 2. guffaw, hoot ~*n.*

3. bellow, clamour, crash, cry, howl, outcry, rumble, shout, thunder, yell

rob burgle, cheat, defraud, despoil, dispossess, gyp (*Sl.*), hold up, loot, pillage, plunder, raid, ransack, rifle, sack, strip, swindle

robber bandit, brigand, burglar, cheat, fraud, highwayman, pirate, plunderer, raider, stealer, thief

robbery burglary, fraud, hold-up, larceny, pillage, plunder, raid, rapine, stealing, swindle, theft

robe 1. *n.* costume, gown, habit 2. *v.* attire, clothe, drape, dress, garb

robust athletic, brawny, fit, hale, hardy, healthy, hearty, lusty, muscular, powerful, rude, rugged, sinewy, sound, staunch, stout, strong, sturdy, tough, vigorous, well

DICTIONARY

rock² *v.* (cause to) sway to and fro. —*n.* style of pop music with a heavy beat. —**rocky** *adj.* shaky or unstable. —**rock and roll** style of pop music blending rhythm and blues and country music.

rocker *n.* curved piece of wood etc. on which something may rock; rocking chair. —**off one's rocker** *Informal* insane.

rocket *n.* self-propelling device powered by the burning of explosive contents (used as a firework, weapon, etc.); vehicle propelled by a rocket engine, as a weapon or carrying a spacecraft. —*v.* **rocketing, rocketed.** move fast, esp. upwards, as a rocket. —**rocketry** *n.*

rococo [rok-**koe**-koe] *adj.* (of furniture, architecture, etc.) having much elaborate decoration in an early 18th-century French style.

rod *n.* slender straight bar, stick; cane.

rode *v.* past tense of RIDE.

rodent *n.* animal with teeth specialized for gnawing, such as a rat.

rodeo *n., pl.* **-deos.** display of skill by cowboys, such as bareback riding.

roe¹ *n.* small species of deer.

roe² *n.* mass of eggs in a fish.

roentgen [**ront**-gan] *n.* unit measuring a radiation dose.

rogue *n.* dishonest or unprincipled person; mischief-loving person. —*adj.* (of a wild beast) having a savage temper and living apart from the herd. —**roguery** *n.* —**roguish** *adj.*

roister *v.* make merry noisily or boisterously. —**roisterer** *n.*

role, rôle *n.* actor's part; task or function.

roll *v.* move by turning over and over; wind round; smooth out with a roller; move or sweep along; undulate; (of a ship or aircraft) turn from side to side about a line from nose to tail. —*n.* act of rolling over or from side to side; piece of paper etc. rolled up; list or register; small round-

ed individually baked piece of bread; swaying unsteady movement or gait; continuous sound, as of drums, thunder, etc. —**roll call** calling out of a list of names, as in a school or the army, to check who is present. —**rolled gold** metal coated with a thin layer of gold. —**rolling pin** cylindrical roller for pastry. —**rolling stock** locomotives, carriages, etc. of a railway. —**rolling stone** restless, wandering person. —**roll-on/roll-off** *adj.* denoting a ship which vehicles can be driven straight onto or off. —**roll-top** *adj.* (of a desk) having a flexible lid sliding in grooves. —**roll up** *v. Informal* appear or arrive. —**roll-up** *n. Informal* cigarette made by the smoker from loose tobacco and cigarette paper.

roller *n.* rotating cylinder used for smoothing or supporting a thing to be moved, spreading paint, etc.; long wave of the sea. —**roller coaster** (at a funfair) narrow railway with steep slopes. —**roller skate** skate with wheels.

rollicking *adj.* boisterously carefree.

roly-poly *adj.* round or plump.

ROM *Computers* read only memory.

Roman *adj.* of Rome or the Church of Rome. —**Roman Catholic** member of that section of the Christian Church that acknowledges the supremacy of the Pope. —**Roman numerals** the letters I, V, X, L, C, D, M, used to represent numbers. —**roman type** plain upright letters in printing.

Romance *adj.* (of a language) developed from Latin, such as French or Spanish.

romance *n.* love affair; mysterious or exciting quality; novel or film dealing with love, esp. sentimentally; story with scenes remote from ordinary life. —*v.* exaggerate or fantasize. —**romancer** *n.*

Romanesque *adj., n.* (in) a style of architecture of 9th–12th centuries characterized by round arches.

THESAURUS

rock¹ boulder, stone

rock² lurch, pitch, reel, roll, sway, swing, toss

rocky craggy, rough, rugged, stony

rod bar, baton, birch, cane, mace, pole, sceptre, shaft, staff, stick, wand

rogue charlatan, cheat, fraud, rascal, reprobate, scamp, scoundrel, swindler, villain

role 1. character, part, portrayal, representation 2. capacity, duty, function, job, part, position, post, task

roll *v.* 1. elapse, flow, go round, gyrate, pass, pivot, reel, revolve, rock, rotate, run, spin, swivel, trundle, turn, twirl, wheel, whirl 2. bind, coil, curl, enfold, entwine, envelop, furl, swathe, twist, wind, wrap 3. flatten, level,

press, smooth, spread 4. billow, lurch, reel, rock, sway, swing, toss, tumble, wallow, welter ~*n.* 5. cycle, reel, revolution, rotation, run, spin, turn, twirl, wheel, whirl 6. annals, catalogue, census, chronicle, directory, index, inventory, list, record, register, schedule, scroll, table 7. boom, growl, grumble, resonance, reverberation, roar, rumble, thunder

romance 1. affair, amour, attachment, intrigue, liaison, passion, relationship 2. charm, colour, excitement, fascination, glamour, mystery, sentiment 3. fantasy, fiction, idyll, legend, melodrama, novel, story, tale

DICTIONARY

romantic *adj.* of or dealing with love; idealistic but impractical; (of literature, music, etc.) displaying passion and imagination rather than order and form. —*n.* romantic person or artist. —**romantically** *adv.* —**romanticism** *n.* —**romanticist** *n.* —**romanticize** *v.*

Romany *n., pl.* **-nies**, *adj.* Gypsy.

romp *v.* play wildly and joyfully. —*n.* spell of romping. —**romp home** win easily. —**rompers** *pl. n.* child's overalls.

rondavel *n. S Afr.* circular building, often thatched.

rondeau *n., pl.* **-deaux**. short poem with the opening words used as a refrain.

rondo *n., pl.* **-dos**. piece of music with a leading theme continually returned to.

rood *n. Christianity* the Cross; crucifix. —**rood screen** (in a church) screen separating the nave from the choir.

roof *n., pl.* **roofs**. outside upper covering of a building, car, etc. —*v.* put a roof on.

rook[1] *n.* bird of the crow family. —*v. Old-fashioned slang* swindle. —**rookery** *n.* colony of rooks.

rook[2] *n.* piece in chess.

rookie *n. Informal* recruit, esp. in the army.

room *n.* space; space enough; division of a house; scope or opportunity. —*pl.* lodgings. —**roomy** *adj.* spacious.

roost *n.* perch for fowls. —*v.* perch. —**rooster** *n. US* domestic cock.

root *n.* part of a plant that grows down into the earth obtaining nourishment; plant with an edible root, such as a carrot; source or origin; part of a tooth, hair, etc. below the skin; form of a word from which other words and forms are derived; *Maths* factor of a quantity which, when multiplied by itself the number of times indicat-

ed, gives the quantity. —*pl.* person's sense of belonging. —*v.* establish a root and start to grow; dig or burrow. —**rootless** *adj.* having no sense of belonging. —**root for** *v. Informal* cheer on. —**root out** *v.* get rid of completely. —**root up** *v.* pull up by the roots.

rope *n.* thick cord. —**know the ropes** be thoroughly familiar with an activity. —**rope in** *v.* persuade to join in.

ropy *adj.* **ropier, ropiest.** *Informal* inferior or inadequate; *Informal* not well. —**ropiness** *n.*

rorqual *n.* whalebone whale with a dorsal fin.

rosary *n., pl.* **-saries**. series of prayers; string of beads for counting these prayers.

rosé [roe-zay] *n.* pink wine.

rose[1] *n.* shrub or climbing plant with prickly stems and fragrant flowers; the flower; perforated flat nozzle for a hose; pink colour. —*adj.* pink. —**roseate** [roe-zee-ate] *adj.* rose-coloured. —**rosy** *adj.* flushed; hopeful or promising. —**rose-coloured** *adj.* unjustifiably optimistic. —**rose window** circular window with spokes branching from the centre. —**rosewood** *n.* fragrant wood.

rose[2] *v.* past tense of RISE.

rosehip *n.* berry-like fruit of a rose plant.

rosemary *n.* fragrant flowering shrub; its leaves as a herb.

rosette *n.* rose-shaped ornament, esp. a circular bunch of ribbons.

rosin [rozz-in] *n.* resin.

roster *n.* list of people and their turns of duty.

rostrum *n., pl.* **-trums, -tra**. platform or stage.

rot *v.* **rotting, rotted.** decompose or decay; slowly deteriorate physically or mentally. —*n.* decay; *Informal* nonsense.

rota *n.* list of people who take it in turn to do a particular task.

rotary *adj.* revolving; operated by rotation.

THESAURUS

romantic *adj.* 1. amorous, fond, loving, passionate, sentimental, tender 2. colourful, exciting, exotic, fascinating, glamorous, mysterious, nostalgic, picturesque 3. dreamy, high-flown, idealistic, quixotic, utopian, visionary, whimsical ~*n.* 4. dreamer, idealist, sentimentalist, visionary

room 1. area, capacity, compass, expanse, extent, leeway, margin, play, range, scope, space, territory, volume 2. apartment, chamber, office 3. chance, occasion, scope

root *n.* 1. rhizome, stem, tuber 2. base, bottom, cause, core, crux, derivation, foundation, fundamental, germ, heart, nucleus, occasion, origin, seat, seed, source 3. *Plural* birthplace, cradle, family, heritage, home, origins ~*v.* 4.

anchor, embed, entrench, establish, fasten, fix, ground, implant, moor, set, stick

rope *n.* cable, cord, hawser, line, strand

rope in engage, enlist, inveigle, involve, persuade

roster agenda, catalogue, list, register, roll, rota, scroll, table

rosy 1. blooming, blushing, fresh, glowing, reddish, roseate, rubicund, ruddy 2. auspicious, bright, cheerful, encouraging, favourable, hopeful, optimistic, promising, sunny

rot *v.* 1. corrupt, crumble, decay, decompose, deteriorate, go bad, moulder, perish, putrefy, spoil, taint 2. decline, deteriorate, waste away ~*n.* 3. blight, canker, corruption, decay, mould, putrefaction

DICTIONARY

rotate *v.* (cause to) move round a centre or on a pivot; (cause to) follow a set sequence.

rote *n.* mechanical repetition. —**by rote** by memory.

rotisserie *n.* (electrically driven) rotating spit for cooking meat.

rotor *n.* revolving portion of a dynamo, motor, or turbine.

rotten *adj.* decomposed; *Informal* very bad; corrupt.

rotter *n.* *Slang* despicable person.

Rottweiler [**rawt**-vile-er] *n.* large sturdy dog with a smooth black and tan coat and usu. a docked tail.

rotund [roe-**tund**] *adj.* round and plump; sonorous. —**rotundity** *n.*

rotunda *n.* circular building or room, esp. with a dome.

rouble [roo-bl] *n.* monetary unit of Russia.

roué [**roo**-ay] *n.* man given to immoral living.

rouge *n.* red cosmetic used to colour the cheeks.

rough *adj.* not smooth, uneven or irregular; violent, stormy, or boisterous; rude; lacking refinement; approximate; in preliminary form. —*v.* make rough; plan out approximately. —*n.* rough state or area. —**rough it** live without the usual comforts etc. —**roughen** *v.* —**roughly** *adv.* —**roughness** *n.* —**roughage** *n.* indigestible constituents of food which aid digestion. —**rough-and-ready** *adj.* hastily prepared but adequate. —**rough-and-tumble** *n.* playful fight. —**rough-hewn** *adj.* roughly shaped. —**roughhouse** *n.* *Slang* fight.

roughcast *n.* mixture of plaster and small stones for outside walls. —*v.* coat with this.

roughshod *adv.* —**ride roughshod over** act with total disregard for.

roulette *n.* gambling game played with a revolving wheel and a ball.

round *adj.* spherical, cylindrical, circular, or curved; complete or whole, e.g. *round numbers;* plump. —*adv.* with a circular or circuitous course. —*n.* thing round in shape; recurrent duties; customary course, as of a milkman; stage in a competition; game (of golf); one of several periods in a boxing match etc.; bullet or shell for a gun; part song in which singers join at equal intervals; circular movement; set of sandwiches. —*prep.* surrounding or encircling; on or outside the perimeter of; on all sides of. —*v.* make or become round; move round. —**roundly** *adv.* thoroughly. —**rounders** *n.* bat-and-ball team game. —**round robin** petition signed with names in a circle to conceal the order. —**round-the-clock** *adj.* throughout the day and night. —**round trip** journey out and back again, esp. by a different route. —**round up** *v.* gather (people or animals) together. —**roundup** *n.*

roundabout *n.* road junction at which traffic passes round a central island; revolving circular platform on which people ride for amusement. —*adj.* not straightforward.

roundel *n.* small disc; rondeau. —**roundelay** *n.* simple song with a refrain.

Roundhead *n.* supporter of Parliament against Charles I in the English Civil War.

rouse *v.* wake up; provoke or excite. —**rousing** *adj.* lively, vigorous.

THESAURUS

rotate go round, gyrate, pivot, reel, revolve, spin, swivel, turn, wheel

rotten 1. bad, corrupt, crumbling, decayed, decomposed, festering, fetid, foul, mouldy, perished, putrid, rank, sour, stinking, tainted, unsound 2. corrupt, deceitful, degenerate, dishonest, disloyal, faithless, immoral, perfidious, treacherous, venal, vicious 3. bad, deplorable, disappointing, regrettable, unfortunate, unlucky

rotter bad lot, blackguard, swine

rotund chubby, corpulent, fat, heavy, plump, podgy, portly, stout, tubby

rough *adj.* 1. broken, bumpy, craggy, irregular, jagged, rocky, stony, uneven 2. boisterous, choppy, squally, stormy, turbulent, wild 3. bearish, bluff, blunt, brusque, churlish, coarse, curt, discourteous, ill-bred, ill-mannered, impolite, loutish, rude, uncivil, uncouth, uncultured, unmannerly, unrefined

4. cruel, curt, drastic, extreme, hard, harsh, nasty, rowdy, severe, sharp, tough, unjust, unpleasant, violent 5. basic, crude, cursory, hasty, imperfect, incomplete, quick, raw, rudimentary, shapeless, sketchy, unpolished 6. estimated, foggy, general, hazy, imprecise, inexact, sketchy, vague

round *adj.* 1. circular, curved, cylindrical, disc-shaped, globular, rotund, rounded, spherical 2. ample, fleshy, full, full-fleshed, plump, rotund ~*n.* 3. ball, band, circle, disc, globe, orb, ring, sphere 4. bout, cycle, sequence, series, session, succession 5. division, lap, level, period, session, stage, turn 6. ambit, beat, circuit, compass, course, routine, schedule, series, tour, turn 7. bullet, discharge, shell, shot ~*v.* 8. bypass, circle, encircle, flank, go round, skirt, turn

roundabout *adj.* circuitous, devious, discursive, evasive, indirect, oblique, tortuous

DICTIONARY

roustabout *n.* labourer on an oil rig.

rout *n.* overwhelming defeat; disorderly retreat. —*v.* defeat and put to flight. —**rout out** *v.* search for; drive out.

route *n.* road; chosen way. —**routemarch** *n.* long training march.

routine *n.* usual or regular method of procedure; set sequence. —*adj.* ordinary; regular.

roux [roo] *n.* fat and flour cooked together as a basis for sauces.

rove *v.* wander. —**rover** *n.* person who roves; pirate.

row[1] *n.* straight line of people or things. —**in a row** in succession.

row[2] *v.* propel (a boat) by oars. —*n.* spell of rowing. —**rowing boat.**

row[3] *Informal* —*n.* dispute; disturbance; reprimand. —*v.* quarrel noisily.

rowan *n.* tree producing bright red berries, mountain ash.

rowdy *adj.* **-dier, -diest.** disorderly, noisy, and rough. —*n., pl.* **-dies.** person like this.

rowel [rhymes with **towel**] *n.* small spiked wheel on a spur.

rowlock *n.* device on the gunwale of a boat that holds an oar in place.

royal *adj.* of, befitting, or supported by a king or queen; splendid. —*n. Informal* member of a royal family. —**royally** *adv.* —**royalist** *n.* supporter of monarchy. —**royalty** *n.* royal people; rank or power; payment to author, musician, inventor, etc. —**royal blue** bright blue.

RPI retail price index.

rpm revolutions per minute.

RSI repetitive strain injury.

RSPCA Royal Society for the Prevention of Cruelty to Animals.

RSVP please reply.

rub *v.* **rubbing, rubbed.** apply pressure and friction to (something) with a circular or backwards-and-forwards movement; clean, polish, or dry by rubbing; remove by rubbing; chafe or fray through rubbing. —*n.* act of rubbing. —**rub it in** emphasize an unpleasant fact. —**rub out** *v.* remove with a rubber.

rubato *Music* with expressive flexibility of tempo.

rubber[1] *n.* strong waterproof elastic material, orig. made from the dried sap of a tropical tree, now usually synthetic; piece of rubber used for erasing mistakes. —*adj.* made of or producing rubber. —**rubberize** *v.* coat or treat with rubber. —**rubbery** *adj.* like rubber, soft or elastic. —**rubberneck** *v. US* stare with unthinking curiosity. —**rubber stamp** device for imprinting the date, a name, etc.; automatic authorization.

rubber[2] *n.* match consisting of three games of bridge, whist, etc.

rubbish *n.* waste matter; anything worthless; nonsense. —**rubbishy** *adj.*

rubble *n.* fragments of broken stone, brick, etc.

rubella [roo-**bell**-a] *n.* same as GERMAN MEASLES.

rubicund [**roo**-bik-kund] *adj.* ruddy.

rubric [**roo**-brik] *n.* heading or explanation inserted in a text.

ruby *n., pl.* **-bies.** red precious gemstone. —*adj.* deep red.

THESAURUS

round up collect, drive, gather, group, herd, marshal, muster, rally

rouse 1. awaken, call, rise, wake, wake up 2. agitate, anger, animate, disturb, excite, incite, inflame, instigate, move, provoke, startle, stimulate, stir, whip up

rout 1. *n.* beating, debacle, defeat, drubbing, headlong flight, overthrow, ruin, shambles, thrashing 2. *v.* beat, chase, conquer, crush, defeat, destroy, dispel, overpower, overthrow, scatter, thrash

route beat, circuit, course, direction, itinerary, journey, passage, path, road, round, run, way

routine 1. *n.* custom, formula, groove, method, order, pattern, practice, programme, usage, way 2. *adj.* customary, everyday, familiar, habitual, normal, ordinary, standard, typical, usual, workaday

row[1] bank, column, file, line, queue, range, rank, sequence, series, string, tier

row[2] 1. *n.* brawl, dispute, disturbance, fray, fuss, noise, quarrel, racket, rumpus, squabble, tiff, trouble, tumult, uproar 2. *v.* argue, brawl, dispute, fight, wrangle

rowdy disorderly, loud, noisy, rough, unruly, uproarious, wild

royal 1. imperial, kingly, princely, queenly, regal, sovereign 2. august, grand, impressive, majestic, splendid, stately, superb, superior

rub *v.* 1. caress, chafe, clean, fray, grate, massage, polish, scour, scrape, shine, smooth, stroke, wipe 2. apply, put, smear, spread ~*n.* 3. caress, massage, polish, shine, stroke, wipe

rubbish 1. debris, dregs, dross, garbage, junk, litter, lumber, offal, refuse, scrap, trash, waste 2. bunkum, drivel, gibberish, nonsense, piffle (*Inf.*), rot, tommyrot, twaddle

rub out cancel, delete, efface, erase, expunge, obliterate, remove, wipe out

DICTIONARY

ruck[1] *n.* rough crowd of common people; *Rugby* loose scrummage.

ruck[2] *n., v.* wrinkle or crease.

rucksack *n.* large pack carried on the back.

ructions *pl. n. Informal* noisy uproar.

rudder *n.* vertical hinged piece at the stern of a boat or at the rear of an aircraft, for steering.

ruddy *adj.* **-dier, -diest.** of a fresh healthy red colour.

rude *adj.* impolite or insulting; coarse, vulgar, or obscene; roughly made; robust; unexpected and unpleasant. —**rudely** *adv.* —**rudeness** *n.*

rudiments *pl. n.* simplest and most basic stages of a subject. —**rudimentary** *adj.* basic, elementary.

rue[1] *v.* **ruing, rued.** feel regret for. —**rueful** *adj.* regretful or sorry. —**ruefully** *adv.*

rue[2] *n.* plant with evergreen bitter leaves.

ruff *n.* starched and frilled collar; natural collar of feathers, fur, etc. on certain birds and animals.

ruffian *n.* violent lawless person.

ruffle *v.* disturb the calm of; annoy, irritate. —*n.* frill or pleat.

rug *n.* small carpet; thick woollen blanket.

rugby *n.* form of football played with an oval ball, which may be handled by the players.

rugged [**rug**-gid] *adj.* rough; uneven and jagged; strong-featured; tough and sturdy.

rugger *n. Informal* rugby.

ruin *n.* broken-down unused building(s); destruction or decay; loss of wealth, position, etc. —*v.* reduce to ruins; spoil; impoverish. —**ruination** *n.* act of ruining; state of being ruined; cause of ruin. —**ruinous** *adj.* causing ruin; more expensive than is reasonable. —**ruinously** *adv.*

rule *n.* statement of what is allowed, for example in a game or procedure; what is usual; government, authority, or control; measuring device with a straight edge. —*v.* govern; restrain; give a formal decision; be pre-eminent; mark with straight line(s). —**as a rule** usually. —**ruler** *n.* person who governs; measuring device with a straight edge. —**ruling** *n.* formal decision. —**rule of thumb** practical but imprecise approach. —**rule out** *v.* exclude.

rum *n.* alcoholic drink distilled from sugar cane.

rumba *n.* lively ballroom dance of Cuban origin.

rumble[1] *v.* (of traffic etc.) make a low continuous noise. —*n.* such a noise.

rumble[2] *v. Informal* discover the (disreputable) truth about.

THESAURUS

rude 1. abrupt, abusive, blunt, brusque, cheeky, churlish, curt, discourteous, ill-mannered, impertinent, impolite, impudent, insolent, insulting, offhand, short, unmannerly 2. boorish, brutish, coarse, crude, graceless, gross, illiterate, loutish, low, oafish, obscene, rough, savage, uncivilised, uncouth, uncultured, vulgar 3. artless, crude, inartistic, inelegant, makeshift, primitive, raw, rough, simple 4. abrupt, harsh, sharp, startling, sudden, unpleasant, violent

rudimentary basic, early, fundamental, immature, initial, primitive, vestigial

rudiments basics, beginnings, elements, essentials, first principles, foundation, fundamentals

ruffian brute, bully, hooligan, miscreant, rascal, rogue, rowdy, scoundrel, thug, tough, villain, wretch

ruffle 1. derange, disarrange, discompose, disorder, rumple, tousle, wrinkle 2. agitate, annoy, confuse, disquiet, disturb, fluster, harass, irritate, nettle, perturb, put out, stir, torment, trouble, unsettle, upset, vex, worry

rugged 1. broken, bumpy, craggy, difficult, jagged, ragged, rocky, rough, stark, uneven 2. furrowed, lined, rough-hewn, weathered, worn, wrinkled

ruin 1. *n.* bankruptcy, breakdown, collapse, crash, damage, decay, defeat, destruction, devastation, disrepair, dissolution, downfall, failure, fall, havoc, overthrow, wreckage 2. *v.* bankrupt, break, bring down, crush, defeat, demolish, destroy, devastate, impoverish, lay waste, overthrow, overturn, overwhelm, pauperize, raze, shatter, smash, wreck

rule *n.* 1. axiom, canon, decree, direction, guideline, law, maxim, order, ordinance, precept, principle, regulation, standard 2. ascendancy, authority, command, control, direction, domination, empire, government, influence, leadership, mastery, power, regime, reign, supremacy, sway 3. condition, convention, custom, form, habit, practice, procedure, routine, wont ~*v.* 4. administer, command, control, direct, dominate, govern, guide, hold sway, lead, manage, preside over, regulate, reign 5. decide, decree, determine, establish, find, judge, lay down, pronounce, resolve, settle

ruler 1. commander, controller, emperor, empress, governor, king, leader, lord, monarch, potentate, prince, princess, queen, sovereign 2. measure, rule, straight edge, yardstick

ruling *n.* adjudication, decision, decree, finding, judgment, pronouncement, resolution, verdict

DICTIONARY

rumbustious *adj.* boisterous or unruly.

ruminate *v.* ponder or meditate; chew the cud. —**ruminant** *adj., n.* cud-chewing (animal, such as a cow, sheep, or deer). —**rumination** *n.* quiet meditation and reflection. —**ruminative** *adj.*

rummage *v.* search untidily and at length. —*n.* untidy search through a collection of things.

rummy *n.* card game in which players try to collect sets or sequences.

rumour *n.* gossip or common talk; unproved statement. —**be rumoured** be circulated as a rumour.

rump *n.* buttocks; rear of an animal.

rumple *v.* make untidy, crumpled, or dishevelled.

rumpus *n., pl.* **-puses.** noisy commotion.

run *v.* **running, ran, run.** move with a more rapid gait than walking; go quickly (across); flow; compete in a race, election, etc.; continue (for a specified period); function; travel according to schedule; melt; spread; (of stitches) unravel; expose oneself to (a risk); (of a newspaper) publish (a story); smuggle (goods, esp. arms); manage or be in charge of. —*n.* ride in a car; act or spell of running; rush; tendency or trend, e.g. *the run of the market;* continuous period, e.g. *a run of good luck;* sequence; heavy demand; enclosure for domestic fowls; series of unravelled stitches, ladder; score of one at cricket; steep snow-covered course for skiing. —**run away** *v.* make one's escape, flee. —**run down** *v.* be rude about; stop working; reduce in number or size.

—**rundown** *n.* —**run-down** *adj.* exhausted. —**run into** *v.* meet. —**run-of-the-mill** *adj.* ordinary. —**run out** *v.* be completely used up. —**run up** *v.* incur (a debt).

rune *n.* any character of the earliest Germanic alphabet. —**runic** *adj.*

rung[1] *n.* crossbar on a ladder.

rung[2] *v.* past participle of RING[2].

runnel *n.* small brook or rivulet.

runner *n.* competitor in a race; messenger; part underneath an ice skate etc., on which it slides; slender horizontal stem of a plant, such as a strawberry, running along the ground and forming new roots at intervals; long strip of carpet or decorative cloth. —**runner-up** *n.* person who comes second in a competition.

running *adj.* continuous; consecutive; (of water) flowing. —*n.* act of moving or flowing quickly; management of a business etc. —**in** *or* **out of the running** having or not having a good chance in a competition.

runny *adj.* **-nier, -niest.** tending to flow; exuding moisture.

runt *n.* smallest animal in a litter; *Offens.* undersized person.

runway *n.* hard level roadway where aircraft take off and land.

rupee *n.* monetary unit of India and Pakistan.

rupture *n.* breaking, breach; hernia. —*v.* break, burst, or sever.

rural *adj.* in or of the countryside.

THESAURUS

rumour buzz, canard, gossip, hearsay, news, report, story, talk, tidings, whisper, word

run *v.* 1. bolt, career, dart, dash, gallop, hare (*Brit. inf.*), hasten, hie, hotfoot, hurry, jog, race, rush, scamper, scramble, scud, scurry, speed, sprint 2. function, go, operate, perform, tick, work 3. administer, carry on, conduct, control, coordinate, direct, head, lead, manage, operate, oversee, own, regulate, supervise 4. continue, extend, go, last, lie, proceed, range, reach, stretch 5. dissolve, fuse, go soft, liquefy, melt 6. ladder, tear, unravel 7. be current, circulate, climb, creep, go round, spread, trail 8. display, feature, print, publish 9. challenge, compete, contend, stand, take part 10. bootleg, ship, smuggle, sneak, traffic ~*n.* 11. dash, gallop, jog, race, rush, sprint, spurt 12. drive, excursion, jaunt, journey, lift, outing, ride, round 13. course, cycle, passage, period, round, season, sequence, series, spell, stretch, string 14. ladder, rip, snag, tear 15. coop, enclosure, pen

run away abscond, bolt, clear out, decamp, escape, flee, take flight, take off

run down 1. curtail, cut, cut back, decrease, drop, reduce, trim 2. belittle, criticize adversely, decry, defame, disparage, revile

run-down below par, debilitated, drained, enervated, exhausted, unhealthy, weak, weary, worn-out

run into be beset by, bump into, chance upon, come across, come upon, encounter, meet

running *adj.* 1. constant, continuous, incessant, perpetual, together, unbroken, uninterrupted 2. flowing, moving, streaming ~*n.* 3. charge, conduct, control, direction, leadership, management, organization, regulation, supervision

run-of-the-mill average, common, fair, mediocre, middling, ordinary, passable, tolerable, undistinguished

run out cease, close, dry up, end, expire, fail, finish, terminate

rupture 1. *n.* breach, break, burst, cleavage, cleft, crack, rent, split, tear 2. *v.* break, burst,

DICTIONARY

rusbank *n. S Afr.* wooden bench or settle.

ruse [rooz] *n.* stratagem or trick.

rush[1] *v.* move or do very quickly; force (someone) to act hastily; make a sudden attack upon (a person or place). —*n.* sudden quick or violent movement. —*pl.* first unedited prints of a scene for a film. —*adj.* done with speed, hasty. —**rush hour** period at the beginning and end of the working day, when many people are travelling to or from work.

rush[2] *n.* marsh plant with a slender pithy stem. —**rushy** *adj.* full of rushes.

rusk *n.* hard brown crisp biscuit, used esp. for feeding babies.

russet *adj.* reddish-brown. —*n.* the colour; apple with rough reddish-brown skin.

rust *n.* reddish-brown coating formed on iron etc. that has been exposed to moisture; disease of plants with rust-coloured spots. —*adj.* reddish-brown. —*v.* become coated with rust. —**rusty** *adj.* coated with rust; of a rust colour; out of practice. —**rustproof** *adj.*

rustic *adj.* of or resembling country people; rural; crude, awkward, or uncouth; (of furniture) made of untrimmed branches. —*n.* person from the country. —**rusticity** *n.*

rusticate *v.* banish temporarily from university as a punishment. —**rustication** *n.*

rustle[1] *v.* make a low whispering sound, as of dry leaves. —*n.* this sound.

rustle[2] *v. US* steal (cattle). —**rustler** *n. US* cattle thief. —**rustle up** *v.* prepare at short notice.

rut[1] *n.* furrow made by wheels; dull settled habits or way of living.

rut[2] *n.* recurrent period of sexual excitability in male deer. —*v.* **rutting, rutted.** be in a period of sexual excitability.

ruthless *adj.* pitiless, merciless. —**ruthlessly** *adv.* —**ruthlessness** *n.*

rye *n.* kind of grain used for fodder and bread; *US* whiskey made from rye.

rye-grass *n.* any of several kinds of grass cultivated for fodder.

THESAURUS

cleave, crack, fracture, rend, separate, sever, split, tear

rural agricultural, country, pastoral, rustic, sylvan

ruse artifice, blind, device, dodge, hoax, imposture, ploy, sham, stratagem, subterfuge, trick, wile

rush 1. *v.* bolt, career, dart, dash, fly, hasten, hurry, press, push, quicken, race, run, scramble, scurry, shoot, speed, sprint, tear 2. *n.* charge, dash, expedition, haste, hurry, race, scramble, speed, surge, swiftness, urgency

rust *n.* 1. corrosion, oxidation 2. blight, mildew, mould, must, rot ~*v.* 3. corrode, oxidize

rustic *adj.* 1. country, pastoral, rural, sylvan 2. artless, homespun, plain, simple, unaffected, unpolished, unrefined 3. awkward, boorish, churlish, clownish, coarse, crude, loutish, rough, uncouth ~*n.* 4. boor, bumpkin, clod, countryman, peasant, yokel

rustle 1. *v.* crackle, whisper 2. *n.* crackle, rustling, whisper

rut 1. furrow, gouge, groove, indentation, score, track, wheelmark 2. dead end, groove, habit, pattern, routine, system

ruthless brutal, callous, cruel, ferocious, fierce, hard, harsh, heartless, inexorable, inhuman, merciless, pitiless, relentless, savage, severe, stern, unmerciful

S

S Saint; South(ern); *Chem.* sulphur.

s second(s); singular.

SA Salvation Army; South Africa.

Sabbath *n.* day of worship and rest: Saturday for Jews, Sunday for Christians. —**sabbatical** *adj., n.* (denoting) leave for study.

sable *n.* dark fur from a small weasel-like Arctic animal. —*adj.* black.

sabot [sab-oh] *n.* wooden shoe, clog.

sabotage *n.* intentional damage done to machinery, systems, etc. —*v.* damage intentionally. —**saboteur** *n.* person who commits sabotage.

sabre *n.* curved cavalry sword.

sac *n.* pouchlike structure in an animal or plant.

saccharin(e) *n.* artificial sweetener. —*adj.* excessively sweet.

sacerdotal *adj.* of priests.

sachet *n.* small envelope or bag containing a single portion.

sack *n.* large bag made of coarse material; plundering of a captured town; *Informal* dismissal; *Slang* bed. —*v.* plunder (a captured town); *Informal* dismiss. —**sackcloth** *n.* coarse fabric used for sacks, formerly worn as a penance.

sacrament *n.* ceremony of the Christian Church, esp. Communion. —**sacramental** *adj.*

sacred *adj.* holy; set apart, reserved; connected with religion.

sacrifice *n.* giving something up; thing given up; making of an offering to a god; thing offered. —*v.* offer as a sacrifice; give (something) up. —**sacrificial** *adj.*

sacrilege *n.* misuse or desecration of something sacred. —**sacrilegious** *adj.*

sacristan *n.* person in charge of the contents of a church. —**sacristy** *n.* room in a church where sacred objects are kept.

sacrosanct *adj.* regarded as sacred, inviolable.

sacrum [say-krum] *n., pl.* **-cra.** compound bone at the base of the spine.

sad *adj.* **sadder, saddest.** sorrowful, unhappy; deplorably bad. —**sadden** *v.* make sad. —**sadly** *adv.* —**sadness** *n.*

saddle *n.* rider's seat on a horse or bicycle; joint of meat. —*v.* put a saddle on (a horse); burden (with a responsibility). —**saddler** *n.* maker or seller of saddles.

sadism [say-dizz-um] *n.* gaining of (sexual) pleasure from inflicting pain. —**sadist** *n.* —**sadistic** *adj.* —**sadistically** *adv.*

sadomasochism *n.* combination of sadism and masochism. —**sadomasochist** *n.*

s.a.e. stamped addressed envelope.

safari *n., pl.* **-ris.** expedition to hunt or observe wild animals, esp. in Africa. —**safari park** park where lions, elephants, etc. are kept uncaged so that people can see them from cars.

safe *adj.* secure, protected; uninjured, out of danger; not involving risk. —*n.* strong lockable container. —**safely** *adv.* —**safe-conduct** *n.* permit allowing travel through a dangerous area. —**safe deposit** place where valuables can be stored safely. —**safekeeping** *n.* protection.

safeguard *n.* protection. —*v.* protect.

THESAURUS

sabotage 1. *v.* damage, destroy, disable, disrupt, subvert, undermine, vandalize, wreck 2. *n.* damage, destruction, disruption, subversion, treachery, treason, wrecking

sack[1] *v.* discharge, dismiss

sack[2] *v.* demolish, despoil, destroy, devastate, loot, maraud, pillage, plunder, raid, ravage, rifle, rob, ruin, spoil, strip

sacred 1. blessed, divine, hallowed, holy, revered, sanctified, venerable 2. inviolable, protected, sacrosanct, secure 3. holy, religious, solemn

sacrifice 1. *v.* give up, immolate, lose, offer, surrender 2. *n.* destruction, loss, oblation, renunciation, surrender

sacrilege blasphemy, heresy, impiety, irreverence, mockery, profanation, violation

sad 1. blue, depressed, disconsolate, dismal, doleful, down, gloomy, glum, grieved, lugubri-ous, melancholy, mournful, pensive, sombre, unhappy, wistful, woebegone 2. bad, dismal, lamentable, miserable, regrettable, serious, shabby, sorry, unfortunate, unhappy, wretched

sadden cast down, dash, deject, depress, distress, grieve

saddle *v.* burden, charge, encumber, load

sadistic barbarous, brutal, cruel, ruthless, vicious

sadness bleakness, depression, gloominess, grief, melancholy, misery, mournfulness, poignancy, sorrow, unhappiness

safe *adj.* 1. guarded, intact, protected, secure, undamaged, unharmed, unhurt 2. harmless, pure, tame, wholesome ~*n.* 3. coffer, repository, safe-deposit box, strongbox, vault

safeguard 1. *v.* defend, preserve, protect,

DICTIONARY

safety *n., pl.* **-ties.** state of being safe. **—safety net** net to catch performers on a trapeze or high wire if they fall. **—safety pin** pin with a spring fastening and a guard over the point when closed. **—safety valve** valve that allows steam etc. to escape if pressure becomes excessive.

saffron *n.* orange-coloured flavouring obtained from a crocus. **—adj.** orange.

sag *v.* **sagging, sagged.** sink in the middle; tire; (of clothes) hang loosely. **—n.** droop.

saga [**sah**-ga] *n.* legend of Norse heroes; any long story.

sagacious *adj.* wise. **—sagaciously** *adv.* **—sagacity** *n.*

sage[1] *n.* aromatic herb with grey-green leaves.

sage[2] *n.* very wise man. **—adj.** *Lit.* wise. **—sagely** *adv.*

sago *n.* starchy cereal from the powdered pith of the **sago palm.**

said *v.* past of SAY.

sail *n.* sheet of fabric stretched to catch the wind for propelling a sailing boat; journey by boat; arm of a windmill. **—v.** travel by water; move smoothly; begin a voyage. **—sailor** *n.* member of a ship's crew. **—sailboard** *n.* board with a mast and single sail, used for windsurfing.

saint *n. Christianity* person venerated after death as specially holy; exceptionally good person. **—saintly** *adj.* **—saintliness** *n.*

saithe *n.* dark-coloured edible sea fish.

sake[1] *n.* benefit; purpose. **—for the sake of** for the purpose of; to please or benefit (someone).

sake[2], **saki** [**sah**-kee] *n.* Japanese alcoholic drink made from fermented rice.

salaam [sal-**ahm**] *n.* low bow of greeting among Muslims.

salacious *adj.* excessively concerned with sex.

salad *n.* dish of raw vegetables, eaten as a meal or part of a meal.

salamander *n.* type of lizard; mythical reptile supposed to live in fire.

salami *n.* highly spiced sausage.

salary *n., pl.* **-ries.** fixed regular payment, usu. monthly, to an employee. **—salaried** *adj.*

sale *n.* exchange of goods for money; selling of goods at unusually low prices; auction. **—saleable** *adj.* fit or likely to be sold. **—salesman, saleswoman** *n.* person who sells goods. **—salesmanship** *n.* skill in selling.

salient [**say**-lee-ent] *adj.* prominent, noticeable. **—n.** *Mil.* projecting part of a front line.

saline [**say**-line] *adj.* containing salt. **—salinity** *n.*

saliva [sal-**lie**-va] *n.* liquid that forms in the mouth, spittle. **—salivary** *adj.* **—salivate** *v.* produce saliva.

sallow[1] *adj.* of an unhealthy pale or yellowish colour.

sallow[2] *n.* tree or shrub related to the willow.

sally *n., pl.* **-lies.** sudden brief attack by troops; witty remark. **—v.** **-lying, -lied.** (foll. by *forth*) rush out; go out.

salmon *n.* large fish with orange-pink flesh valued as food. **—adj.** orange-pink.

salmonella *n., pl.* **-lae.** bacterium causing food poisoning.

salon *n.* commercial premises of a hairdresser, beautician, etc.; elegant reception room for guests.

saloon *n.* car with a fixed roof; large public room, as on a ship; *US* bar serving alcoholic drinks. **—saloon bar** more expensive bar in a pub.

salsify *n.* plant with a long white edible root.

salt *n.* white crystalline substance used to season food; chemical compound of acid and metal. **—v.** season with salt. **—old salt** experienced sailor. **—with a pinch, grain of salt** allowing for exaggeration. **—worth one's salt** efficient. **—salty**

THESAURUS

screen, shield 2. *n.* aegis, armour, bulwark, convoy, defence, escort, security, shield, surety

safety assurance, cover, immunity, protection, refuge, sanctuary, security, shelter

sage 1. *adj.* acute, canny, discerning, learned, politic, prudent, sensible, wise 2. *n.* authority, elder, expert, master, philosopher, savant, wise man

sail *v.* 1. embark, set sail 2. captain, cruise, navigate, pilot, skipper, steer, voyage 3. drift, float, fly, glide, scud, shoot, skim, skirr, soar, sweep, wing

sailor marine, mariner, navigator, salt, sea dog, seafarer, seaman

saintly beatific, blessed, devout, god-fearing, godly, holy, pious, righteous, virtuous, worthy

sake account, behalf, consideration, gain, good, interest, profit, regard, respect, welfare

salary earnings, emolument, income, pay, remuneration, stipend

sale 1. deal, disposal, transaction 2. demand, market, outlet, purchasers

sally *v.* erupt, go forth, issue, rush, set out, surge

salt *n.* flavour, relish, savour, seasoning, taste

DICTIONARY

adj. —**saltcellar** *n.* small container for salt at table.

saltpetre *n.* compound used in gunpowder and as a preservative.

salubrious *adj.* favourable to health. —**salubrity** *n.*

Saluki *n.* tall hound with a silky coat.

salutary *adj.* producing a beneficial result.

salute *n.* motion of the arm as a formal military sign of respect; firing of guns as a military greeting of honour. —*v.* greet with a salute; make a salute; acknowledge with praise. —**salutation** *n.* greeting by words or actions.

salvage *n.* saving of a ship or other property from destruction; property so saved. —*v.* save from destruction or waste.

salvation *n.* fact or state of being saved from harm or the consequences of sin.

salve *n.* healing or soothing ointment. —*v.* soothe or appease, e.g. *salve one's conscience.*

salver *n.* (silver) tray on which something is presented.

salvia *n.* plant with blue or red flowers.

salvo *n., pl.* **-vos, -voes.** simultaneous discharge of guns etc.; burst of applause or questions.

sal volatile [sal vol-**at**-ill-ee] *n.* preparation of ammonia, used to revive a person who feels faint.

SAM surface-to-air missile.

Samaritan *n.* person who helps people in distress.

samba *n., pl.* **-bas.** lively Brazilian dance.

same *adj.* identical, not different, unchanged; just mentioned. —**sameness** *n.*

samovar *n.* Russian tea urn.

Samoyed *n.* dog with a thick white coat and tightly curled tail.

sampan *n.* small boat with oars used in China.

samphire *n.* plant found on rocks by the seashore.

sample *n.* part taken as representative of a whole. —*v.* take and test a sample of. —**sampler** *n.* piece of embroidery showing the embroiderer's skill. —**sampling** *n.*

samurai *n., pl.* **-rai.** member of an ancient Japanese warrior caste.

sanatorium *n., pl.* **-riums, -ria.** institution for invalids or convalescents; room for sick pupils at a boarding school.

sanctify *v.* **-fying, -fied.** make holy. —**sanctification** *n.*

sanctimonious *adj.* making a show of piety.

sanction *n.* (usu. *pl.*) permission, authorization; coercive measure or penalty. —*v.* allow, authorize.

sanctity *n.* sacredness, inviolability.

sanctuary *n., pl.* **-aries.** place of safety for a fugitive; place where animals or birds can live undisturbed; holy place; part of a church nearest the altar.

sanctum *n., pl.* **-tums, -ta.** sacred place; person's private room.

sand *n.* substance consisting of small grains of rock, esp. on a beach or in a desert. —*pl.* stretches of sand forming a beach or desert. —*v.* smooth with sandpaper. —**sander** *n.* power tool for smoothing surfaces. —**sandy** *adj.* covered with sand; (of hair) reddish-fair. —**sandbag** *n.* bag filled with sand, used as protection against gunfire, floodwater, etc. —**sandblast** *v., n.* (clean with) a jet of sand blown from a nozzle under pressure. —**sandpaper** *n.* paper coated with sand for smoothing a surface. —**sandpiper** *n.* shore bird with a long bill and slender legs. —**sandstone** *n.* rock composed of sand. —**sandstorm** *n.* desert wind that whips up clouds of sand.

sandal *n.* light shoe consisting of a sole attached by straps.

sandalwood *n.* sweet-scented wood.

sandwich *n.* two slices of bread with a layer of food between. —*v.* insert between two other things. —**sandwich board** pair of boards hung

THESAURUS

salutation address, greeting, salute, welcome

salute *v.* 1. acknowledge, address, greet, hail, kiss, welcome 2. acknowledge, honour, recognize ~*n.* 3. address, greeting, obeisance, recognition, salutation, tribute

salvage *v.* glean, recover, redeem, rescue, restore, retrieve, save

salvation deliverance, escape, preservation, redemption, rescue, saving

same *adj.* 1. aforementioned, aforesaid 2. corresponding, duplicate, equal, identical, twin

sample 1. *n.* example, illustration, instance, model, pattern, sign 2. *v.* experience, inspect, taste, test, try

sanctimonious canting, false, hypocritical, pious, self-satisfied, smug, unctuous

sanction *n.* 1. approval, authority, backing, confirmation, countenance, endorsement, ratification, support 2. *Often plural* ban, boycott, embargo, penalty ~*v.* 3. allow, approve, authorize, back, endorse, permit, support

sanctuary 1. altar, church, shrine, temple 2. asylum, haven, protection, refuge, retreat, shelter

DICTIONARY

over a person's shoulders to display advertisements in front and behind.

sane *adj.* of sound mind; sensible, rational. **—sanity** *n.*

sang *v.* past tense of SING.

sang-froid [sahng **frwah**] *n.* composure, self-possession.

sanguinary *adj.* accompanied by bloodshed; bloodthirsty.

sanguine *adj.* cheerful, optimistic.

sanitary *adj.* promoting health by getting rid of dirt and germs. **—sanitation** *n.* sanitary measures, esp. drainage or sewerage.

sank *v.* past tense of SINK.

Sanskrit *n.* ancient language of India.

sap[1] *n.* moisture that circulates in plants; energy; *Informal* gullible person.

sap[2] *v.* **sapping, sapped.** undermine; weaken. **—***n.* trench dug to undermine an enemy position. **—sapper** *n.* soldier in an engineering unit.

sapient [**say**-pee-ent] *adj. Lit.* wise, shrewd. **—sapience** *n.*

sapling *n.* young tree.

sapphire *n.* blue precious stone. **—***adj.* deep blue.

saraband(e) *n.* slow stately Spanish dance.

Saracen *n. Hist.* Arab or Muslim who opposed the Crusades.

sarcasm *n.* (use of) bitter or wounding ironic language. **—sarcastic** *adj.* **—sarcastically** *adv.*

sarcophagus *n., pl.* **-gi, -guses.** stone coffin.

sardine *n.* small fish of the herring family, usu. preserved in tightly packed tins.

sardonic *adj.* mocking or scornful. **—sardonically** *adv.*

sargassum, sargasso *n.* type of floating seaweed.

sari, saree *n.* long piece of cloth draped

around the body and over one shoulder, worn by Hindu women.

sarong *n.* long piece of cloth tucked around the waist or under the armpits, worn esp. in Malaysia.

sarsaparilla *n.* soft drink, orig. made from the root of a tropical American plant.

sartorial *adj.* of men's clothes or tailoring.

SAS Special Air Service.

sash[1] *n.* decorative strip of cloth worn round the waist or over one shoulder.

sash[2] *n.* wooden frame containing the panes of a window. **—sash window** window consisting of two sashes that can be opened by sliding one over the other.

sassafras *n.* American tree with aromatic bark used medicinally.

Sassenach *n. Scot.* English person.

sat *v.* past of SIT.

Satan *n.* the Devil. **—satanic** *adj.* of Satan; supremely evil. **—Satanism** *n.* worship of Satan.

satchel *n.* bag, usu. with a shoulder strap, for carrying school books.

sate *v.* satisfy (a desire or appetite) fully.

satellite *n.* man-made device orbiting in space; heavenly body that orbits another; country that is dependent on a more powerful one.

satiate [**say**-she-ate] *v.* satisfy fully; surfeit. **—satiety** [sat-**tie**-a-tee] *n.* feeling of having had too much.

satin *n.* silky fabric with a glossy surface on one side. **—satiny** *adj.* of or like satin. **—satinwood** *n.* tropical tree yielding hard wood.

satire *n.* use of ridicule to expose vice or folly; poem or other work that does this. **—satirical** *adj.* **—satirist** *n.* **—satirize** *v.* ridicule by means of satire.

THESAURUS

sane 1. lucid, mentally sound, normal, rational 2. balanced, judicious, level-headed, moderate, reasonable, sensible, sober, sound

sanguine assured, buoyant, cheerful, confident, hopeful, lively, optimistic, spirited

sanitary clean, germ-free, healthy, hygienic, wholesome

sanity 1. normality, rationality, reason, stability 2. good sense, level-headedness, rationality, sense

sap[1] *n.* 1. essence, lifeblood, vital fluid 2. *Inf.* fool, idiot, noddy, simpleton

sap[2] *v.* bleed, drain, erode, exhaust, rob, undermine, weaken, wear down

sarcasm bitterness, contempt, cynicism, derision, irony, mockery, satire

sarcastic biting, caustic, cutting, cynical, derisive, disparaging, ironical, mocking, mordant, sardonic, satirical, sharp, taunting

sardonic bitter, cynical, derisive, dry, ironical, jeering, malicious, mocking, mordant, sarcastic, wry

satanic black, devilish, diabolic, evil, fiendish, hellish, inhuman, malevolent, malignant, wicked

satellite moon, sputnik

satiate 1. cloy, glut, gorge, jade, nauseate, overfill, stuff 2. sate, slake, surfeit

DICTIONARY

satisfy v. -fying, -fied. please, content; provide amply for (a need or desire); convince, persuade. —**satisfaction** n. —**satisfactory** adj.

satsuma n. kind of small orange.

saturate v. soak thoroughly; cause to absorb the maximum amount of something. —**saturation** n.

Saturday n. seventh day of the week.

Saturn n. Roman god; one of the planets. —**saturnine** adj. gloomy in temperament or appearance. —**saturnalia** n. wild revelry.

satyr n. woodland god, part man, part goat; lustful man.

sauce n. liquid added to food to enhance flavour; Informal impudence. —**saucy** adj. impudent; pert, jaunty. —**saucily** adv. —**saucepan** n. cooking pot with a long handle.

saucer n. small round dish put under a cup.

sauerkraut n. shredded cabbage fermented in brine.

sauna n. Finnish-style steam bath.

saunter v. walk in a leisurely manner, stroll. —n. leisurely walk.

saurian adj. of or like a lizard.

sausage n. minced meat in an edible tube-shaped skin. —**sausage roll** skinless sausage covered in pastry.

sauté [so-tay] v. fry quickly in a little fat.

savage adj. wild, untamed; cruel and violent; uncivilized, primitive. —n. uncivilized person. —v. attack ferociously. —**savagely** adv. —**savagery** n.

savanna(h) n. extensive open grassy plain in Africa.

savant n. learned person.

save v. rescue or preserve from harm, protect; keep for the future; set aside (money); Sport prevent the scoring of (a goal). —n. Sport act of preventing a goal. —**saver** n. —**saving** adj., n. —**savings** pl. n. money put by for future use.

saveloy n. spicy smoked sausage.

saviour n. person who rescues another; (S-) Christ.

savoir-faire [sav-wah fair] n. French ability to do and say the right thing in any situation.

savory n. aromatic herb used in cooking.

savour n. characteristic taste or odour; slight but distinctive quality. —v. (foll. by of) have a flavour or suggestion of; enjoy, relish. —**savoury** adj. salty or spicy; not sweet. —n. savoury dish served before or after a meal.

THESAURUS

satire burlesque, irony, lampoon, parody, raillery, ridicule, sarcasm

satirical biting, bitter, burlesque, caustic, cutting, cynical, incisive, ironical, mocking, mordant, pungent

satisfaction 1. comfort, content, contentment, ease, enjoyment, happiness, pleasure, pride, repletion, well-being 2. assuaging, fulfilment, gratification, resolution, settlement 3. amends, compensation, damages, justice, redress, reparation, restitution, settlement, vindication

satisfactory acceptable, adequate, all right, average, competent, fair, passable, sufficient, suitable

satisfied at ease, complacent, content, convinced, happy, pacified, positive, smug, sure

satisfy 1. appease, assuage, content, fill, gratify, indulge, mollify, pacify, please, quench, sate, slake, surfeit 2. answer, do, fulfil, meet, qualify, serve, suffice 3. assure, convince, persuade, quiet, reassure

saturate drench, imbue, soak, souse, steep, suffuse, waterlog

sauce impertinence, impudence, insolence, rudeness

saucy disrespectful, flippant, forward, impertinent, impudent, insolent, pert, rude

saunter 1. v. amble, dally, linger, meander, ramble, roam, rove, stroll, tarry, wander 2. n. airing, amble, constitutional, promenade, ramble, stroll, turn, walk

savage adj. 1. rough, rugged, untamed, wild 2. barbarous, beastly, bloody, brutal, brutish, cruel, devilish, ferocious, fierce, harsh, murderous, pitiless, ruthless, vicious 3. primitive, rude, unspoilt ~n. 4. aboriginal, barbarian, heathen, native, primitive ~v. 5. attack, lacerate, mangle, maul

savagery brutality, cruelty, ferocity, fierceness, inhumanity, viciousness

save 1. deliver, free, liberate, recover, redeem, rescue, salvage, set free 2. collect, economize, gather, hoard, hold, husband, keep, lay by, put by, reserve, retrench, salt away, set aside, store, treasure up 3. conserve, guard, keep safe, look after, preserve, protect, screen, shield

saving 1. adj. qualifying, redeeming 2. n. bargain, discount, economy, reduction

saviour defender, deliverer, guardian, liberator, preserver, protector, rescuer, salvation

savour n. 1. flavour, piquancy, relish, smack, smell, tang, taste 2. distinctive quality, flavour, interest, salt, spice, zest ~v. 3. appreciate, enjoy, like, luxuriate in, partake, relish

DICTIONARY

savoy *n.* variety of cabbage.

savvy *Slang* —*v.* **-vying, -vied.** understand. —*n.* understanding, intelligence.

saw¹ *n.* cutting tool with a toothed metal blade. —*v.* **sawing, sawed, sawed** *or* **sawn.** cut with a saw; move (something) back and forth. —**sawyer** *n.* person who saws timber for a living. —**sawdust** *n.* fine wood fragments made in sawing. —**sawfish** *n.* fish with a long toothed snout. —**sawmill** *n.* mill where timber is sawn into planks.

saw² *v.* past tense of SEE.

saw³ *n.* wise saying, proverb.

sax *n. Informal* short for SAXOPHONE.

saxifrage *n.* alpine rock plant with small flowers.

Saxon *n.* member of the W Germanic people who settled widely in Europe in the early Middle Ages. —*adj.* of the Saxons.

saxophone *n.* brass wind instrument with keys and a curved body. —**saxophonist** *n.*

say *v.* **saying, said.** speak or utter; express (an idea) in words; suppose as an example or possibility; give as one's opinion. —*n.* right or chance to speak; share in a decision. —**saying** *n.* maxim, proverb.

scab *n.* crust formed over a wound; *Offens.* blackleg. —**scabby** *adj.* covered with scabs; *Informal* despicable.

scabbard *n.* sheath for a sword or dagger.

scabies [skay-beez] *n.* itchy skin disease.

scabious [skay-bee-uss] *n.* plant with globular blue flower heads.

scabrous [skay-bruss] *adj.* indecent; rough and scaly.

scaffold *n.* temporary platform for workmen; gallows. —**scaffolding** *n.* (materials for building) scaffolds.

scalar *n., adj.* (variable quantity) having magnitude but no direction.

scald *v.* burn with hot liquid or steam; sterilize with boiling water; heat (liquid) almost to boiling point. —*n.* injury by scalding.

scale¹ *n.* one of the thin overlapping plates covering fishes and reptiles; thin flake; coating which forms in kettles etc. due to hard water; tartar formed on the teeth. —*v.* remove scales from; come off in scales. —**scaly** *adj.*

scale² *n.* (often *pl.*) weighing instrument.

scale³ *n.* graduated table or sequence of marks at regular intervals, used as a reference in making measurements; fixed series of notes in music; ratio of size between a thing and a representation of it; relative degree or extent. —*v.* climb. —**scale up** *or* **down** *v.* increase *or* decrease proportionately in size.

scalene *adj.* (of a triangle) with three unequal sides.

scallop *n.* edible shellfish; one of a series of small curves along an edge. —**scalloped** *adj.* decorated with small curves along the edge.

scallywag *n. Informal* scamp, rascal.

scalp *n.* skin and hair on top of the head. —*v.* cut off the scalp of.

scalpel *n.* small surgical knife.

scamp *n.* mischievous child. —*v.* do carelessly.

scamper *v.* run about hurriedly or in play. —*n.* scampering.

scampi *pl. n.* large prawns.

scan *v.* **scanning, scanned.** scrutinize carefully; glance over quickly; examine or search (an area) by passing a radar or sonar beam over it; (of verse) conform to metrical rules. —*n.* scanning. —**scanner** *n.* electronic device used for scanning. —**scansion** *n.* metrical scanning of verse.

scandal *n.* disgraceful action or event; malicious gossip. —**scandalize** *v.* shock by scandal. —**scandalous** *adj.*

THESAURUS

savoury agreeable, dainty, delectable, delicious, good, luscious, palatable, piquant, rich, spicy, tasty

saw adage, aphorism, axiom, byword, dictum, maxim, proverb, saying

say *v.* 1. add, affirm, announce, assert, declare, maintain, mention, pronounce, remark, speak, state, utter, voice 2. deliver, do, orate, perform, read, recite, rehearse, render, repeat 3. assume, conjecture, estimate, guess, imagine, judge, presume, suppose, surmise 4. communicate, convey, express, imply ~*n.* 5. authority, influence, power, sway, weight

saying adage, aphorism, axiom, byword, dictum, maxim, proverb, saw

scale *n.* 1. gradation, graduation, hierarchy, ladder, progression, ranking, register, sequence, series, spectrum, spread, steps 2. proportion, ratio 3. degree, extent, range, reach, scope, way ~*v.* 4. ascend, climb, escalade, mount, surmount

scamp devil, imp, monkey, rascal, rogue, wretch

scamper dart, dash, fly, hasten, hurry, romp, run, scoot, sprint

scan check, examine, glance over, investigate,

DICTIONARY

scant *adj.* barely sufficient, meagre.

scanty *adj.* **scantier, scantiest.** barely sufficient or not sufficient. —**scantily** *adv.* —**scantiness** *n.*

scapegoat *n.* person made to bear the blame for others.

scapula *n., pl.* **-lae, -las.** shoulder blade. —**scapular** *adj.* of the scapula.

scar *n.* mark left by a healed wound; permanent emotional damage left by an unpleasant experience. —*v.* **scarring, scarred.** mark or become marked with a scar.

scarab *n.* sacred beetle of ancient Egypt.

scarce *adj.* not common, rarely found; insufficient to meet demand. —**make oneself scarce** *Informal* go away. —**scarcely** *adv.* only just; not quite; definitely or probably not. —**scarcity** *n.*

scare *v.* frighten or be frightened. —*n.* fright, sudden panic. —**scary** *adj. Informal* frightening. —**scarecrow** *n.* figure dressed in old clothes, set up to scare birds away from crops; raggedly dressed person. —**scaremonger** *n.* person who spreads alarming rumours.

scarf[1] *n.* piece of material worn round the neck, head, or shoulders.

scarf[2] *n.* joint between two pieces of timber made by notching the ends and fastening them together. —*v.* join in this way.

scarify *v.* **-fying, -fied.** scratch or cut slightly all over; break up and loosen (topsoil); criticize mercilessly. —**scarification** *n.*

scarlet *adj., n.* brilliant red. —**scarlet fever** infectious fever with a scarlet rash.

scarp *n.* steep slope.

scarper *v. Slang* run away.

scat[1] *v.* **scatting, scatted.** *Informal* go away.

scat[2] *n.* jazz singing using improvised vocal sounds instead of words.

scathing *adj.* harshly critical.

scatter *v.* throw about in various directions; put here and there; disperse. —**scatterbrain** *n.* empty-headed person.

scatty *adj.* **-tier, -tiest.** *Informal* empty-headed.

scavenge *v.* search for (anything usable) among discarded material. —**scavenger** *n.* person who scavenges; animal that feeds on decaying matter.

scenario *n., pl.* **-rios.** summary of the plot of a play or film; imagined sequence of future events.

scene *n.* place of action of a real or imaginary event; subdivision of a play or film in which the action is continuous; view of a place; display of emotion; *Informal* specific activity or interest, e.g. *the fashion scene.* —**behind the scenes** backstage; in secret. —**scenery** *n.* natural features of a landscape; painted backcloths or screens used on stage to represent the scene of action. —**scenic** *adj.* picturesque.

scent *n.* pleasant smell; smell left in passing, by which an animal can be traced; series of clues;

THESAURUS

run over, scour, scrutinize, search, skim, survey, sweep

scandal 1. crime, disgrace, embarrassment, offence, sin, wrongdoing 2. abuse, aspersion, backbiting, dirt, gossip, rumours, slander, talk, tattle

scandalous 1. atrocious, disgraceful, disreputable, infamous, monstrous, odious, outrageous, shameful, shocking, unseemly 2. defamatory, gossiping, libellous, scurrilous, untrue

scant bare, deficient, inadequate, insufficient, limited, little, minimal

scanty bare, deficient, inadequate, meagre, narrow, poor, restricted, short, skimpy, slender, sparing, thin

scar 1. *n.* blemish, injury, mark 2. *v.* brand, damage, disfigure, mark

scarce deficient, few, infrequent, insufficient, rare, uncommon, unusual, wanting

scarcely 1. barely, hardly 2. definitely not, hardly

scarcity dearth, deficiency, insufficiency, lack, paucity, rareness, shortage, want

scare 1. *v.* alarm, dismay, frighten, intimidate, panic, shock, startle, terrify 2. *n.* alarm, alert, fright, panic, shock, start, terror

scathing biting, caustic, critical, cutting, harsh, mordant, sarcastic, scornful, trenchant

scatter 1. diffuse, disseminate, fling, litter, shower, sow, spread, sprinkle, strew 2. disband, dispel, disperse, dissipate

scenario outline, résumé, rundown, scheme, sketch, summary, synopsis

scene 1. backdrop, location, set, setting 2. act, division, episode, incident, part, stage 3. commotion, exhibition, fuss, performance, row, tantrum, to-do, upset 4. landscape, panorama, prospect, view, vista

scenery 1. landscape, surroundings, terrain, view, vista 2. *Theatre* backdrop, décor, flats, set, setting, stage set

scent *n.* 1. aroma, bouquet, fragrance, odour, perfume, smell 2. spoor, track, trail ~*v.* 3. detect, discern, nose out, recognize, sense, smell, sniff

DICTIONARY

perfume. —*v.* detect by smell; suspect; fill with fragrance.

sceptic [**skep**-tik] *n.* person who habitually doubts generally accepted beliefs. —**sceptical** *adj.* —**sceptically** *adv.* —**scepticism** *n.*

sceptre *n.* ornamental rod symbolizing royal power.

schedule *n.* plan of procedure for a project; timetable; list. —*v.* plan to occur at a certain time.

schema *n., pl.* **-mata.** overall plan or diagram. —**schematic** *adj.* presented as a plan or diagram. —**schematize** *v.* arrange in a scheme.

scheme *n.* systematic plan; secret plot. —*v.* plan in an underhand manner. —**scheming** *adj., n.*

scherzo [**skairt**-so] *n., pl.* **-zos, -zi.** brisk lively piece of music.

schism [**skizz**-um] *n.* (group resulting from) division in an organization. —**schismatic** *adj., n.*

schist [**skist**] *n.* crystalline rock which splits into layers.

schizoid *adj.* abnormally introverted; *Informal* contradictory. —*n.* schizoid person.

schizophrenia *n.* mental disorder involving deterioration of or confusion about the personality; *Informal* contradictory behaviour or attitudes. —**schizophrenic** *adj., n.*

schmaltz *n.* excessive sentimentality. —**schmaltzy** *adj.*

schnapps *n.* strong alcoholic spirit.

schnitzel *n.* thin slice of meat, esp. veal.

scholar *n.* learned person; pupil; student receiving a scholarship. —**scholarly** *adj.* learned.

—**scholarship** *n.* learning; financial aid given to a student because of academic merit. —**scholastic** *adj.* of schools or scholars.

school[1] *n.* place where children are taught or instruction is given in a subject; group of artists, thinkers, etc. with shared principles or methods. —*v.* educate; discipline, train.

school[2] *n.* shoal of fish, whales, etc.

schooner *n.* sailing ship rigged fore-and-aft; large glass.

sciatica *n.* severe pain in the large nerve in the back of the leg. —**sciatic** *adj.* of the hip; of or afflicted with sciatica.

science *n.* systematic study and knowledge of natural or physical phenomena. —**scientific** *adj.* of science; systematic. —**scientifically** *adv.* —**scientist** *n.* person who studies or practises a science. —**science fiction** stories making imaginative use of scientific knowledge. —**science park** area where scientific research and commercial development are carried on in cooperation.

scimitar *n.* curved oriental sword.

scintillating *adj.* animated or witty.

scion [**sy**-on] *n.* descendant or heir; shoot of a plant for grafting.

scissors *pl. n.* cutting instrument with two crossed pivoted blades.

sclerosis *n., pl.* **-ses.** abnormal hardening of body tissues.

scoff[1] *v.* express derision.

scoff[2] *v. Slang* eat rapidly.

scold *v.* find fault with, reprimand. —*n.* person who scolds. —**scolding** *n.*

THESAURUS

sceptic agnostic, cynic, disbeliever, doubter

sceptical cynical, doubtful, dubious, hesitating, incredulous, quizzical, scoffing

schedule 1. *n.* agenda, calendar, catalogue, inventory, list, plan, programme, timetable 2. *v.* appoint, arrange, be due, book, organize, plan, programme, time

scheme *n.* 1. contrivance, design, device, plan, programme, project, proposal, strategy, system, tactics, theory 2. conspiracy, intrigue, manoeuvre, plot, ploy, ruse, shift, stratagem, subterfuge ~*v.* 3. collude, conspire, intrigue, machinate, manoeuvre, plot

scholar 1. academic, intellectual, savant 2. disciple, learner, pupil, schoolboy, schoolgirl, student

scholarship 1. accomplishments, attainments, book-learning, education, erudition, knowledge, learning, lore 2. bursary, exhibition, fellowship

school *n.* 1. academy, college, department, discipline, faculty, institution, seminary 2. adherents, circle, class, clique, denomination, devotees, disciples, faction, followers, group, pupils, sect, set ~*v.* 3. coach, discipline, drill, educate, indoctrinate, instruct, prepare, prime, train, tutor, verse

scientific accurate, controlled, exact, mathematical, precise, systematic

scoff belittle, deride, despise, flout, gibe, jeer, mock, pooh-pooh, revile, ridicule, scorn, sneer, taunt, twit

scold 1. *v.* berate, blame, castigate, censure, chide, lecture, nag, rate, rebuke, reprimand, reproach, reprove, vituperate 2. *n.* nag, shrew, termagant

scolding lecture, piece of one's mind (*Inf.*), rebuke, row

DICTIONARY

sconce n. bracket on a wall for holding candles or lights.

scone n. small plain cake baked in an oven or on a griddle.

scoop n. shovel-like tool for ladling or hollowing out; news story reported in one newspaper before all its rivals. —v. take up or hollow out with or as if with a scoop; beat (rival newspapers) in reporting a news item.

scoot v. Slang leave or move quickly. —**scooter** n. child's vehicle propelled by pushing on the ground with one foot; light motorcycle.

scope n. range of activity; opportunity for using abilities.

scorch v. burn on the surface; parch or shrivel from heat. —n. slight burn. —**scorcher** n. Informal very hot day.

score n. points gained in a game or competition; twenty; written version of a piece of music showing parts for each musician; mark or cut; grievance, e.g. settle old scores. —pl. lots. —v. gain points in a game; mark or cut; (foll. by out) cross out; arrange music (for); keep a record of points; achieve a success.

scorn n. contempt, derision. —v. despise; reject with contempt. —**scornful** adj. —**scornfully** adv.

scorpion n. small lobster-shaped animal with a sting at the end of a jointed tail.

Scot n. person from Scotland. —**Scottish** adj. (also **Scots**) of Scotland, its people, or their languages. —**Scotch** n. whisky distilled in Scotland. —**Scotsman, Scotswoman** n.

scotch v. put an end to.

scot-free adj. without harm or punishment.

scoundrel n. Old-fashioned villainous person.

scour[1] v. clean or polish by rubbing with something rough; clear or flush out. —**scourer** n. small rough nylon pad used for cleaning pots and pans.

scour[2] v. search thoroughly and energetically.

scourge n. person or thing causing severe suffering; whip. —v. cause severe suffering to; whip.

scout n. person sent out to reconnoitre; (**S-**) member of the **Scout Association,** an organization for boys which aims to develop character and promotes outdoor activities. —v. act as a scout; reconnoitre. —**Scouter** n. leader of a troop of Scouts.

scow n. unpowered barge.

scowl v., n. (have) an angry or sullen expression.

scrabble v. scrape at with the hands, feet, or claws.

scrag n. lean end of a neck of mutton. —**scraggy** adj. thin, bony.

scram v. **scramming, scrammed.** (of a nuclear reactor) shut or be shut down in an emergency; Informal go away hastily. —n. emergency shutdown of a nuclear reactor.

scramble v. climb or crawl hastily or awkwardly; struggle with others (for); mix up; cook (eggs beaten up with milk); render (transmitted

THESAURUS

scoop n. 1. dipper, ladle, spoon 2. exclusive, exposé, revelation, sensation ~v. 3. bail, dig, dip, empty, excavate, gouge, hollow, ladle, scrape, shovel

scope area, capacity, compass, extent, freedom, latitude, liberty, opportunity, orbit, outlook, purview, range, reach, room, space, span, sphere

scorch blacken, blister, burn, char, parch, roast, sear, shrivel, singe, wither

score n. 1. grade, mark, outcome, points, record, result, total 2. grievance, grudge, injury, injustice, wrong ~v. 3. achieve, amass, gain, make, win 4. count, keep count, record, register, tally 5. cut, deface, gouge, graze, indent, mar, mark, nick, notch, scrape, scratch, slash 6. With out cancel, cross out, delete, obliterate, strike out 7. Music adapt, arrange, orchestrate, set 8. triumph

scorn 1. n. contempt, derision, disdain, disparagement, mockery, sarcasm, slight, sneer 2. v. be above, contemn, deride, disdain, flout, reject, scoff at, slight, spurn

scornful contemptuous, defiant, derisive, disdainful, haughty, insolent, insulting, mocking, sarcastic, sardonic, scathing, slighting, sneering

scoundrel blackguard, cheat, good-for-nothing, heel (Sl.), incorrigible, miscreant, rascal, reprobate, rogue, scamp, vagabond, villain, wretch

scour[1] abrade, buff, clean, flush, polish, purge, scrub, wash

scour[2] beat, comb, hunt, rake, ransack, search

scourge n. 1. affliction, bane, curse, infliction, misfortune, pest, plague, punishment, terror, torment, visitation 2. cat, lash, strap, switch, thong, whip ~v. 3. beat, belt, cane, chastise, flog, horsewhip, lash, leather, punish, thrash, trounce, whale, whip

scout 1. v. investigate, observe, probe, reconnoitre, spy, survey, watch 2. n. escort, lookout, outrider, precursor, reconnoitrer, vanguard

scowl 1. v. frown, glower, lower 2. n. black look, frown, glower

DICTIONARY

speech) unintelligible by an electronic device; (of an aircraft or aircrew) take off hurriedly in an emergency. —*n.* scrambling; rough climb; disorderly struggle; motorcycle race over rough ground. —**scrambler** *n.* electronic device that renders transmitted speech unintelligible.

scrap *n.* small piece; waste metal collected for reprocessing; *Informal* fight or quarrel. —*pl.* leftover food. —*v.* **scrapping, scrapped.** discard as useless; *Informal* fight or quarrel. —**scrappy** *adj.* fragmentary, disjointed. —**scrapbook** *n.* book with blank pages in which newspaper cuttings or pictures are stuck.

scrape *v.* rub with something rough or sharp; clean or smooth thus; rub with a harsh noise; economize. —*n.* act or sound of scraping; mark or wound caused by scraping; *Informal* awkward situation. —**scraper** *n.* —**scrape thorough** *v.* succeed in or obtain with difficulty.

scratch *v.* mark or cut with claws, nails, or anything rough or sharp; scrape (skin) with nails or claws to relieve itching; withdraw from a race or competition. —*n.* wound, mark, or sound made by scratching. —*adj.* put together at short notice. —**from scratch** from the very beginning. —**up to scratch** up to standard. —**scratchy** *adj.*

scrawl *v.* write carelessly or hastily. —*n.* scribbled writing.

scrawny *adj.* **scrawnier, scrawniest.** thin and bony.

scream *v.* utter a piercing cry, esp. of fear or pain; utter with a scream. —*n.* shrill piercing cry; *Informal* very funny person or thing.

scree *n.* slope of loose shifting stones.

screech *v., n.* (utter) a shrill cry.

screed *n.* long tedious piece of writing.

screen *n.* movable structure used to shelter, divide, or conceal something; surface of a television set, VDU, etc., on which an image is formed; white surface on which photographs are projected. —*v.* shelter or conceal with or as if with a screen; show (a film); examine (a person or group) to determine suitability for a task or to detect the presence of disease or weapons. —**the screen** cinema generally.

screw *n.* metal pin with a spiral ridge along its length, twisted into materials to fasten them together; *Slang* a prison guard. —*v.* turn (a screw); fasten with screw(s); twist; *Informal* extort. —**screwy** *adj.* *Informal* crazy or eccentric. —**screwdriver** *n.* tool for turning screws. —**screw up** *v.* *Informal* bungle; distort.

scribble *v.* write hastily or illegibly; make meaningless or illegible marks. —*n.* something scribbled.

scribe *n.* person who copied manuscripts before the invention of printing; *Bible* scholar of the Jewish Law. —**scribal** *adj.*

scrimmage *n.* rough or disorderly struggle.

scrimp *v.* be very economical.

scrip *n.* certificate representing a claim to stocks or shares.

script *n.* text of a film, play, or TV programme; particular system of writing, e.g. *Arabic script;* handwriting.

scripture *n.* sacred writings of a religion. —**scriptural** *adj.*

scrofula *n.* tuberculosis of the lymphatic glands. —**scrofulous** *adj.*

scroll *n.* roll of parchment or paper; ornamental

THESAURUS

scramble *v.* 1. climb, crawl, push, struggle, swarm 2. contend, hasten, jostle, push, run, rush, strive, vie ~*n.* 3. climb, trek 4. commo~ tion, competition, confusion, hassle (*Inf.*), hustle, melee, muddle, race, rush, struggle, tussle

scrap[1] *n.* 1. atom, bit, bite, crumb, fragment, grain, morsel, mouthful, part, particle, piece, portion, snatch, snippet, trace 2. junk, off cuts, waste 3. *Plural* bits, leavings, leftovers, remains, scrapings ~*v.* 4. abandon, demolish, discard, drop, jettison, shed, write off

scrap[2] battle, brawl, dispute, fight, quarrel, row, tiff, wrangle

scrape *v.* 1. bark, graze, rub, scratch, scuff, skin 2. grate, grind, rasp, scratch, squeak 3. clean, erase, file, remove, rub, scour 4. pinch, save, scrimp, skimp, stint

scratch 1. *v.* claw, cut, damage, etch, grate, graze, incise, mark, rub, score, scrape 2. *n.*

blemish, gash, graze, laceration, mark, scrape 3. *adj.* haphazard, impromptu, improvised, rough

scream *v.* 1. bawl, cry, screech, shriek, shrill, squeal, yell 2. clash, jar, shriek ~*n.* 3. howl, outcry, screech, shriek, wail, yell, yelp

screen *v.* 1. cloak, conceal, cover, hide, mask, shade, shroud, veil 2. defend, guard, protect, shelter, shield 3. evaluate, examine, filter, gauge, grade, process, scan, sieve, sift, sort, vet 4. present, put on, show ~*n.* 5. awning, cano~ py, cloak, concealment, cover, guard, hedge, mantle, shade, shelter, shield, shroud 6. mesh, net, partition, room divider

screw *v.* 1. tighten, turn, twist 2. coerce, con~ strain, force, pressurize, squeeze

scribe clerk, copyist, secretary, writer

script 1. handwriting, letters, longhand, writing 2. book, copy, dialogue, libretto, lines, text, words

DICTIONARY

carving shaped like this. —*v.* move (text) up or down on a VDU screen.

scrotum *n., pl.* **-ta, -tums.** pouch of skin containing the testicles.

scrounge *v. Informal* get by cadging or begging. —**scrounger** *n.*

scrub[1] *v.* **scrubbing, scrubbed.** clean by rubbing, often with a hard brush and water; *Informal* delete or cancel. —*n.* scrubbing.

scrub[2] *n.* stunted trees; area of land covered with scrub. —**scrubby** *adj.* covered with scrub; stunted; *Informal* shabby.

scruff *n.* nape (of the neck).

scruffy *adj.* **scruffier, scruffiest.** unkempt or shabby.

scrum, scrummage *n. Rugby* restarting of play in which opposing packs of forwards push against each other to gain possession of the ball; disorderly struggle.

scrumptious *adj. Informal* delicious.

scruple *n.* doubt produced by one's conscience or morals. —*v.* have doubts on moral grounds. —**scrupulous** *adj.* very conscientious; very careful or precise. —**scrupulously** *adv.*

scrutiny *n., pl.* **-nies.** close examination. —**scrutinize** *v.* examine closely.

scuba diving *n.* sport of swimming under water using cylinders containing compressed air attached to breathing apparatus.

scud *v.* **scudding, scudded.** move along swiftly.

scuff *v.* drag (the feet) while walking; scrape (one's shoes) by doing so. —*n.* mark caused by scuffing.

scuffle *v.* fight in a disorderly manner; move by shuffling. —*n.* disorderly struggle; scuffling sound.

scull *n.* small oar. —*v.* row (a boat) using a scull.

scullery *n., pl.* **-leries.** small room where washing-up and other kitchen work is done.

sculpture *n.* art of making figures or designs in wood, stone, etc.; product of this art. —*v.* (also **sculpt**) represent in sculpture. —**sculptor, sculptress** *n.* —**sculptural** *adj.*

scum *n.* impure or waste matter on the surface of a liquid; worthless people. —**scummy** *adj.*

scupper *v. Informal* defeat or ruin.

scurf *n.* flaky skin on the scalp. —**scurfy** *adj.*

scurrilous *adj.* untrue and defamatory. —**scurrility** *n.*

scurry *v.* **-rying, -ried.** move hastily. —*n.* act or sound of scurrying.

scurvy *n.* disease caused by lack of vitamin C.

scut *n.* short tail of the hare, rabbit, or deer.

scuttle[1] *n.* fireside container for coal.

scuttle[2] *v.* run with short quick steps. —*n.* hurried run.

scuttle[3] *v.* make a hole in (a ship) to sink it.

scythe *n.* long-handled tool with a curved blade for cutting grass. —*v.* cut with a scythe.

SE southeast(ern).

sea *n.* mass of salt water covering three quarters of the earth's surface; particular area of this; turbulence or swell; vast expanse. —**at sea** in a ship on the ocean; confused or bewildered. —**sea anemone** sea animal with suckers like petals. —**seaboard** *n.* coast. —**sea dog** experienced sailor. —**seafaring** *adj.* working or travelling by sea. —**seafood** *n.* edible saltwater fish or shellfish. —**sea gull** gull. —**sea horse** small sea fish with a plated body and horselike head. —**sea level** average level of the sea's surface in relation to the land. —**sea lion** kind of large seal. —**seaman** *n.* sailor. —**seaplane** *n.* aircraft designed to take off from and land on water. —**seasick** *adj.* suffering from nausea caused by the motion of a ship. —**seasickness** *n.* —**seaside** *n.* area, esp. a holiday resort, on the coast. —**sea urchin** sea animal with a round spiky shell. —**seaweed** *n.* plant growing in the sea. —**seaworthy** *adj.* (of a ship) in fit condition for a sea voyage.

THESAURUS

scrounge beg, cadge, sponge

scrounger cadger, parasite, sponger

scrub *v.* 1. clean, cleanse, rub, scour 2. *Inf.* abolish, call off, cancel, delete, drop, forget about, give up

scruffy disreputable, frowzy, mangy, ragged, run-down, seedy, shabby, slovenly, sluttish, squalid, tattered, untidy

scrupulous careful, exact, fastidious, honourable, meticulous, minute, nice, precise, principled, punctilious, rigorous, strict, upright

scrutinize dissect, examine, explore, inspect,

investigate, peruse, probe, scan, search, sift, study

scrutiny analysis, examination, exploration, inquiry, inspection, investigation, perusal, search, sifting

scuffle 1. *v.* clash, contend, fight, grapple, jostle, struggle, tussle 2. *n.* brawl, commotion, disturbance, fight, fray, tussle

sculpture *v.* carve, chisel, cut, form, hew, model, mould, sculpt, shape

scum 1. dross, film, froth 2. rabble, riffraff

scurrilous abusive, coarse, foul, gross, indecent,

DICTIONARY

seal[1] *n.* piece of wax, lead, etc. with a special design impressed upon it, attached to a letter or document as a mark of authentication; device or material used to close an opening tightly. —*v.* affix a seal to or stamp with a seal; close with or as if with a seal; make airtight or watertight; decide (one's fate) irrevocably. —**sealant** *n.* any substance used for sealing. —**seal off** *v.* enclose or isolate (a place) completely.

seal[2] *n.* amphibious mammal with flippers as limbs. —**sealskin** *n.*

seam *n.* line where two edges are joined, as by stitching; thin layer of coal or ore. —*v.* mark with furrows or wrinkles. —**seamless** *adj.* —**seamy** *adj.* sordid.

seamstress *n.* woman who sews.

seance [say-anss] *n.* meeting at which spiritualists attempt to communicate with the dead.

sear *v.* scorch, burn the surface of; cause to wither.

search *v.* examine closely in order to find something. —*n.* searching. —**searching** *adj.* keen or thorough, e.g. *a searching look.* —**searchlight** *n.* powerful light with a beam that can be shone in any direction.

season *n.* one of four divisions of the year, each of which has characteristic weather conditions; period during which a thing happens or is plentiful; fitting or proper time. —*v.* flavour with salt, herbs, etc.; dry (timber) till ready for use. —**seasonable** *adj.* appropriate for the season; timely or opportune. —**seasonal** *adj.* depending on or varying with the seasons. —**seasoned** *adj.* experienced. —**seasoning** *n.* salt, herbs, etc. added

to food to enhance flavour. —**season ticket** ticket for a series of journeys or events within a specified period.

seat *n.* thing designed or used for sitting on; place to sit in a theatre, esp. one that requires a ticket; buttocks; membership of a legislative or administrative body; country house. —*v.* cause to sit; provide seating for. —**seat belt** belt worn in a car or aircraft to prevent a person being thrown forward in a crash.

sebaceous *adj.* of, like, or secreting fat or oil.

secateurs *pl. n.* small pruning shears.

secede *v.* withdraw formally from a political alliance or federation. —**secession** *n.*

seclude *v.* keep (a person) from contact with others. —**secluded** *adj.* private, sheltered. —**seclusion** *n.*

second[1] *adj.* coming directly after the first; alternate, additional; inferior. —*n.* person or thing coming second; sixtieth part of a minute; moment; attendant in a duel or boxing match. —*pl.* inferior goods. —*v.* express formal support for (a motion proposed in a meeting). —**secondly** *adv.* —**second-class** *adj.* inferior; cheaper, slower, or less comfortable than first-class. —**second-hand** *adj.* bought after use by another. —**second nature** something so habitual that it seems part of one's character. —**second sight** supposed ability to predict events. —**second thoughts** revised opinion on a matter already considered. —**second wind** renewed ability to continue effort.

second[2] [si-kawnd] *v.* transfer (a person) temporarily to another job. —**secondment** *n.*

THESAURUS

infamous, low, obscene, ribald, scandalous, slanderous, vulgar

sea *n.* 1. main, ocean, the deep, the waves 2. expanse, mass, multitude, plethora, profusion, sheet 3. **at sea** adrift, astray, baffled, bewildered, confused, lost, mystified, puzzled, upset

seal *v.* 1. close, enclose, fasten, plug, secure, shut, stop, stopper, waterproof 2. clinch, conclude, consummate, finalize, settle 3. *With* **off** isolate, quarantine, segregate ~*n.* 4. assurance, imprimatur, insignia, notification, stamp

search 1. *v.* check, comb, examine, explore, ferret, inquire, inspect, investigate, look, probe, pry, ransack, rummage through, scour, scrutinize, seek, sift 2. *n.* examination, exploration, hunt, inquiry, inspection, investigation, pursuit, quest, rummage, scrutiny

season 1. *n.* division, interval, juncture, occasion, opportunity, period, spell, term, time 2.

v. colour, enliven, flavour, lace, pep up, salt, spice

seasoned experienced, hardened, mature, old, practised, veteran

seat *n.* 1. bench, chair, pew, settle, stall, stool 2. abode, ancestral hall, house, mansion, residence 3. chair, constituency, membership, place ~*v.* 4. accommodate, cater for, contain, hold, sit, take 5. fix, install, locate, place, set, settle, sit

secluded cloistered, cut off, isolated, lonely, private, reclusive, remote, retired, sheltered, solitary

second[1] *adj.* 1. following, next, subsequent, succeeding 2. additional, alternative, extra, further, other 3. inferior, lesser, lower, subordinate, supporting ~*v.* 4. aid, approve, assist, back, endorse, forward, further, help, promote, support

second[2] *n.* flash, instant, minute, moment, trice, twinkling

DICTIONARY

secondary *adj.* coming after or derived from what is primary or first; of less importance; relating to the education of people between the ages of 11 and 18.

secret *adj.* kept from the knowledge of others. —*n.* something kept secret; mystery; underlying explanation, e.g. *the secret of my success.* —**in secret** without other people knowing. —**secretly** *adv.* —**secrecy** *n.* —**secretive** *adj.* inclined to keep things secret. —**secretiveness** *n.*

secretariat *n.* administrative office or staff of a legislative body.

secretary *n., pl.* -**ries.** person who deals with correspondence and general clerical work; head of a state department, e.g. *Home Secretary.* —**secretarial** *adj.* —**Secretary of State** head of a major government department.

secrete *v.* hide or conceal; (of an organ, gland, etc.) produce and release (a substance). —**secretion** *n.* —**secretory** [sek-reet-or-ee] *adj.*

sect *n.* subdivision of a religious or political group, esp. one with extreme beliefs. —**sectarian** *adj.* of a sect; narrow-minded.

section *n.* part cut off; part or subdivision of something; distinct part of a country or community; cutting; drawing of something as if cut through. —*v.* cut or divide into sections. —**sectional** *adj.*

sector *n.* part or subdivision; part of a circle enclosed by two radii and the arc which they cut off.

secular *adj.* worldly, as opposed to sacred; not connected with religion or the church.

secure *adj.* free from danger; free from anxiety; firmly fixed; reliable. —*v.* obtain; make safe; make firm; guarantee payment of (a loan) by giving something as security. —**securely** *adv.* —**security** *n.* state of being secure; precautions against theft, espionage, or other danger; something given or pledged to guarantee payment of a loan; certificate of ownership of a share, stock, or bond.

sedan *n.* US saloon car. —**sedan chair** *Hist.* enclosed chair for one person, carried on poles by two bearers.

sedate[1] *adj.* calm and dignified; sober or decorous. —**sedately** *adv.*

sedate[2] *v.* give a sedative drug to. —**sedation** *n.* —**sedative** *adj.* having a soothing or calming effect. —*n.* sedative drug.

sedentary [sed-en-tree] *adj.* done sitting down, involving little exercise.

sedge *n.* coarse grasslike plant growing on wet ground.

sediment *n.* matter which settles to the bottom of a liquid; material deposited by water, ice, or wind. —**sedimentary** *adj.*

THESAURUS

secondary 1. derived, indirect, resultant 2. contingent, inferior, lesser, lower, minor, subordinate, unimportant

second-hand *adj.* nearly new, used

secrecy 1. concealment, mystery, privacy, retirement, seclusion, silence, solitude 2. furtiveness, secretiveness, stealth

secret *adj.* 1. backstairs, close, concealed, covered, disguised, furtive, hidden, reticent, underground, undisclosed, unknown, unseen 2. hidden, private, retired, secluded, unknown —*n.* 3. code, confidence, enigma, formula, key, mystery, recipe

secretive close, cryptic, deep, enigmatic, reserved, reticent, withdrawn

secretly confidentially, furtively, privately, quietly, stealthily, surreptitiously, unobserved

sectarian bigoted, doctrinaire, exclusive, factional, hidebound, insular, limited, parochial, partisan, rigid

section component, division, fraction, instalment, part, passage, piece, portion, sample, segment, slice

sector area, district, division, part, quarter, region, subdivision, zone

secular civil, earthly, laic, lay, profane, state, temporal, worldly

secure *adj.* 1. immune, protected, safe, sheltered, unassailable, unharmed 2. dependable, fast, fastened, firm, fixed, immovable, stable, steady, tight 3. assured, certain, easy, reassured, sure 4. absolute, conclusive, definite, reliable, solid, steadfast, well-founded —*v.* 5. acquire, gain, get, obtain, procure 6. attach, batten down, bolt, chain, fasten, fix, lash, lock, lock up, moor, padlock, rivet, tie up

security 1. asylum, care, cover, custody, preservation, refuge, retreat, safety 2. defence, protection, surveillance 3. assurance, certainty, confidence, conviction, positiveness, reliance, sureness 4. collateral, gage, guarantee, hostage, insurance, pawn, pledge, surety

sedate calm, collected, composed, cool, deliberate, dignified, earnest, grave, placid, proper, quiet, seemly, serene, serious, sober, solemn, staid, tranquil

sedative 1. *adj.* anodyne, calming, relaxing, soothing 2. *n.* anodyne, narcotic, opiate, tranquillizer

sedition agitation, subversion, treason

DICTIONARY

sedition *n.* speech or action encouraging rebellion against the government. —**seditious** *adj.*

seduce *v.* persuade into sexual intercourse; tempt into wrongdoing. —**seducer, seductress** *n.* —**seduction** *n.* —**seductive** *adj.*

sedulous *adj.* diligent or persevering. —**sedulously** *adv.*

see[1] *v.* **seeing, saw, seen.** perceive with the eyes or mind; watch; find out; make sure (of something); consider or decide; have experience of; meet or visit; interview; frequent the company of; accompany. —**seeing** *conj.* in view of the fact that.

see[2] *n.* diocese of a bishop.

seed *n.* mature fertilized grain of a plant; such grains used for sowing; origin; *Obs.* offspring; *Sport* seeded player. —*v.* sow with seed; remove seeds from; arrange (the draw of a sports tournament) so that the outstanding competitors will not meet in the early rounds. —**go, run to seed** (of plants) produce or shed seeds after flowering; lose vigour or usefulness. —**seedling** *n.* young plant raised from a seed. —**seedy** *adj.* shabby; *Informal* unwell.

seek *v.* **seeking, sought.** try to find or obtain; try (to do something).

seem *v.* appear to be. —**seeming** *adj.* apparent but not real. —**seemingly** *adv.*

seemly *adj.* **-lier, -liest.** proper or fitting. —**seemliness** *n.*

seen *v.* past participle of SEE.

seep *v.* trickle through slowly, ooze. —**seepage** *n.*

seer *n.* prophet.

seersucker *n.* light cotton fabric with a slightly crinkled surface.

seesaw *n.* plank balanced in the middle so that two people seated on either end ride up and down alternately. —*v.* move up and down.

seethe *v.* **seething, seethed.** be very agitated; (of a liquid) boil or foam.

segment *n.* one of several sections into which something may be divided. —*v.* divide into segments. —**segmentation** *n.*

segregate *v.* set apart. —**segregation** *n.*

seine [sane] *n.* large fishing net that hangs vertically from floats.

seismic *adj.* relating to earthquakes. —**seismology** *n.* study of earthquakes. —**seismologic, seismological** *adj.* —**seismologist** *n.* —**seismograph, seismometer** *n.* instrument that records the strength of earthquakes.

seize *v.* take hold of forcibly or quickly; take immediate advantage of; (usu. foll. by *up*) (of mechanical parts) stick tightly through overheating. —**seizure** *n.* seizing or being seized; sudden violent attack of an illness.

seldom *adv.* not often, rarely.

select *v.* pick out or choose. —*adj.* chosen in preference to others; restricted to a particular group, exclusive. —**selection** *n.* selecting; things that have been selected; range from which something may be selected. —**selective** *adj.* chosen or choosing carefully. —**selectively** *adv.* —**selectivity** *n.* —**selector** *n.*

THESAURUS

seduce 1. betray, corrupt, deflower, deprave, dishonour 2. allure, attract, beguile, deceive, decoy, ensnare, entice, lure, mislead, tempt

seductive alluring, attractive, bewitching, enticing, inviting, irresistible, provocative, ravishing, specious, tempting

see *v.* 1. behold, descry, discern, distinguish, espy, glimpse, heed, identify, look, mark, note, notice, observe, perceive, recognize, regard, sight, spot, view, witness 2. ascertain, determine, discover, find out, investigate, learn 3. ensure, guarantee, mind, take care 4. consider, decide, deliberate, judge, reflect 5. confer with, consult, encounter, interview, meet, receive, run into, speak to, visit 6. accompany, attend, escort, lead, show, usher, walk

seed 1. egg, embryo, germ, grain, kernel, ovum 2. beginning, germ, inkling, nucleus, source, start, suspicion

seedy decaying, dilapidated, faded, grubby, mangy, old, run-down, shabby, sleazy, slovenly, squalid, unkempt, worn

seeing *conj.* as, inasmuch as, since

seek 1. follow, hunt, inquire, pursue, search for 2. aim, aspire to, attempt, endeavour, essay, strive, try

seem appear, assume, look, pretend

seemly becoming, befitting, decent, decorous, fit, fitting, nice, proper, suitable, suited

seesaw *v.* alternate, fluctuate, oscillate, pitch, swing, teeter

seethe 1. boil, bubble, churn, ferment, fizz, foam, froth 2. fume, rage, simmer, storm

segregate discriminate against, dissociate, isolate, separate, set apart

seize 1. clutch, fasten, grab, grasp, grip, lay hands on, snatch, take 2. abduct, annex, arrest, capture, commandeer, confiscate, impound

seizure 1. arrest, capture, commandeering, grabbing, taking 2. attack, convulsion, fit, paroxysm, spasm

DICTIONARY

selenium n. nonmetallic element with photo-electric properties.

self n., pl. **selves.** distinct individuality or identity of a person or thing; one's basic nature; one's own welfare or interests. —**selfish** adj. caring too much about oneself and not enough about others. —**selfishly** adv. —**selfishness** n. —**selfless** adj. unselfish.

self- combining form used with many main words to mean: of oneself or itself; by, to, in, due to, for, or from the self; automatic(ally). —**self-assured** adj. confident. —**self-catering** adj. (of accommodation) for people who provide their own food. —**self-certification** n. completion of a form by a worker stating that absence was due to sickness. —**self-coloured** adj. having only a single colour. —**self-conscious** adj. embarrassed at being the object of others' attention. —**self-contained** adj. containing everything needed, complete; (of a flat) having its own facilities. —**self-determination** n. the right of a nation to decide its own form of government. —**self-evident** adj. obvious without proof. —**self-interest** n. one's own advantage. —**self-made** adj. having achieved wealth or status by one's own efforts. —**self-possessed** adj. having control of one's emotions, calm. —**self-raising** adj. (of flour) containing a raising agent. —**self-righteous** adj. thinking oneself more virtuous than others. —**selfsame** adj. the very same. —**self-seeking** adj., n. seeking to promote only one's own interests. —**self-service** adj. denoting a shop, café, or garage where customers serve themselves and then pay a cashier. —**self-styled** adj. using a title or name that one has taken without right. —**self-sufficient** adj. able to provide for oneself without help. —**self-willed** adj. stubbornly determined to get one's own way.

sell v. **selling, sold.** exchange (something) for money; stock, deal in; (of goods) be sold; (foll. by for) have a specified price; Informal persuade (someone) to accept (something). —n. manner of selling. —**seller** n. —**sell out** v. dispose of (something) completely by selling; Informal betray. —**sellout** n. performance of a show etc. for which all the tickets are sold; Informal betrayal.

Sellotape n. ® type of adhesive tape. —v. stick with Sellotape.

selvage, selvedge n. edge of cloth, woven so as to prevent unravelling.

selves n. plural of **self.**

semantic adj. relating to the meaning of words. —**semantics** pl. n. study of linguistic meaning.

semaphore n. system of signalling by holding two flags in different positions to represent letters of the alphabet.

semblance n. outward or superficial appearance.

semen n. sperm-carrying fluid produced by male animals.

semester n. US either of two divisions of the academic year.

semi n. Informal semidetached house.

semi- prefix used with many main words to mean: half, e.g. semicircle; partly or almost, e.g. semiprofessional.

semibreve n. musical note four beats long.

semicolon n. the punctuation mark (;).

semiconductor n. substance with an electrical conductivity that increases with temperature.

semidetached adj. (of a house) joined to another on one side.

semifinal n. match or round before the final. —**semifinalist** n.

seminal adj. capable of developing; original and influential; of semen or seed.

THESAURUS

seldom infrequently, not often, occasionally, rarely

select 1. v. choose, pick, prefer, sort out 2. adj. choice, excellent, first-rate, hand-picked, picked, preferable, prime, rare, selected, special, superior

selection 1. choice, choosing, option, pick, preference 2. assortment, choice, collection, line-up, medley, range, variety

selective careful, discerning, discriminating, particular

self-conscious affected, awkward, bashful, diffident, embarrassed, ill at ease, insecure, nervous, sheepish

self-evident clear, incontrovertible, obvious, undeniable

selfish egoistic, egotistical, greedy, mean, mercenary, narrow, self-seeking, ungenerous

self-possessed collected, confident, cool, poised, self-assured, unruffled

self-righteous complacent, pious, priggish, sanctimonious, self-satisfied, smug, superior

sell 1. barter, exchange, trade 2. deal in, handle, market, peddle, retail, stock, trade in, traffic in, vend

seller agent, dealer, merchant, rep, retailer, salesman, shopkeeper, tradesman, vendor

sell out 1. dispose of, get rid of, sell up 2. betray, fail, give away, play false, rat on

DICTIONARY

seminar n. meeting of a group of students for discussion.

seminary n., pl. -ries. college for priests.

semiprecious adj. (of gemstones) having less value than precious stones.

semiquaver n. musical note half the length of a quaver.

Semite n. member of the group of peoples including Jews and Arabs. —**Semitic** adj.

semitone n. smallest interval between two notes in Western music.

semolina n. hard grains of wheat left after the milling of flour, used to make puddings and pasta.

SEN State Enrolled Nurse.

Senate n. upper house of some parliaments; governing body of some universities. —**senator** n. member of a Senate. —**senatorial** adj.

send v. sending, sent. cause (a person or thing) to go to or be taken or transmitted to a place; bring into a specified state or condition. —**send-off** n. demonstration of good wishes at a person's departure. —**send up** v. Informal make fun of by imitating. —**send-up** n. Informal imitation.

senile adj. mentally or physically weak because of old age. —**senility** n.

senior adj. superior in rank or standing; older; of or for older pupils. —n. senior person. —**seniority** n.

senna n. tropical plant; its dried leaves or pods used as a laxative.

señor [sen-**nyor**] n., pl. -**ores.** Spanish term of address equivalent to sir or Mr. —**señora** [sen-**nyor**-a] n. Spanish term of address equivalent to madam or Mrs. —**señorita** [sen-nyor-**ee**-ta] n. Spanish term of address equivalent to madam or Miss.

sensation n. ability to feel things physically; physical feeling; general feeling or awareness; state of excitement; exciting person or thing. —**sensational** adj. causing intense shock, anger, or excitement; Informal very good. —**sensationalism** n. deliberate use of sensational language or subject matter. —**sensationalist** adj., n.

sense n. any of the faculties of perception or feeling (sight, hearing, touch, taste, or smell); ability to perceive; feeling perceived through one of the senses; awareness; (sometimes pl.) sound practical judgment or intelligence; specific meaning. —v. perceive. —**senseless** adj.

sensible adj. having or showing good sense; (foll. by of) aware; practical, e.g. sensible shoes. —**sensibly** adv. —**sensibility** n. ability to experience deep feelings.

sensitive adj. responsive to external stimuli; easily hurt or offended; (of an instrument) responsive to slight changes; (of a subject) liable to arouse controversy or strong feelings. —**sensitively** adv. —**sensitivity** n. —**sensitize** v. make sensitive.

sensor n. device that detects or measures the presence of something, such as radiation.

sensory adj. of the senses or sensation.

THESAURUS

send consign, convey, direct, dispatch, forward, remit, transmit

sendoff departure, farewell, leave-taking, start, valediction

senile decrepit, doting, failing, imbecile

senior adj. elder, higher ranking, older, superior

seniority eldership, precedence, priority, rank, superiority

sensation 1. consciousness, feeling, impression, perception, sense, tingle 2. agitation, commotion, excitement, furore, scandal, stir, surprise, thrill

sensational amazing, astounding, dramatic, electrifying, exciting, lurid, melodramatic, revealing, shocking, spectacular, staggering, startling, thrilling

sense n. 1. faculty, feeling, sensation 2. atmosphere, aura, awareness, consciousness, feel, impression, perception, premonition, presentiment 3. definition, drift, gist, implication, import, interpretation, meaning, message, nuance, purport, significance, substance 4. Sometimes plural brains (Inf.), cleverness, discernment, discrimination, intelligence, judgment, mother wit, quickness, reason, sagacity, tact, understanding, wisdom ~v. 5. appreciate, discern, divine, feel, grasp, notice, observe, perceive, pick up, realize, suspect, understand

senseless 1. absurd, crazy, fatuous, foolish, halfwitted, idiotic, illogical, inane, incongruous, inconsistent, irrational, ludicrous, mad, mindless, nonsensical, pointless, ridiculous, silly, simple, stupid, unreasonable, unwise 2. cold, insensate, numb, out, stunned, unconscious

sensible canny, discreet, down-to-earth, farsighted, intelligent, judicious, practical, prudent, rational, realistic, sage, sane, shrewd, sober, sound, wise

sensitive 1. acute, delicate, fine, keen, perceptive, precise, reactive, responsive, susceptible 2. delicate, irritable, temperamental, tender, touchy

DICTIONARY

sensual *adj.* giving pleasure to the body and senses rather than the mind; having a strong liking for physical pleasures. —**sensually** *adv.* —**sensuality** *n.* —**sensualism** *n.* —**sensualist** *n.*

sensuous *adj.* pleasing to the senses. —**sensuously** *adv.*

sent *v.* past of SEND.

sentence *n.* sequence of words capable of standing alone as a statement, question, or command; punishment passed on a criminal. —*v.* pass sentence on (a convicted person).

sententious *adj.* trying to sound wise; pompously moralizing. —**sententiously** *adv.* —**sententiousness** *n.*

sentient [**sen**-tee-ent] *adj.* capable of feeling. —**sentience** *n.*

sentiment *n.* thought, opinion, or attitude; feeling expressed in words; exaggerated or mawkish emotion. —**sentimental** *adj.* excessively romantic or nostalgic. —**sentimentalism** *n.* —**sentimentality** *n.* —**sentimentalize** *v.* make sentimental.

sentinel *n.* sentry.

sentry *n., pl.* **-tries.** soldier on watch.

sepal *n.* leaflike division of the calyx of a flower.

separate *v.* divide up into parts; distinguish between; (of a married couple) stop living together. —*adj.* set apart; not the same, different; not shared, individual. —**separately** *adv.* —**separation** *n.* separating or being separated; *Law* living apart of a married couple without divorce. —**separable** *adj.* —**separatist** *n.* person who advocates the separation of a group from an organization or country. —**separatism** *n.*

sepia *adj., n.* reddish-brown (pigment).

sepsis *n.* poisoning caused by pus-forming bacteria.

Sept. September.

September *n.* ninth month of the year.

septet *n.* group of seven performers; music for such a group.

septic *adj.* (of a wound) infected; of or caused by harmful bacteria. —**septic tank** tank in which sewage is decomposed by the action of bacteria.

septicaemia [sep-tis-**see**-mee-a] *n.* blood poisoning.

septuagenarian *n., adj.* (person) between seventy and seventy-nine years old.

sepulchre [**sep**-pull-ker] *n.* tomb or burial vault. —**sepulchral** [sip-**pulk**-ral] *adj.* gloomy.

sequel *n.* novel, play, or film that continues the story of an earlier one; consequence.

sequence *n.* arrangement of two or more things in successive order; the successive order of two or more things; section of a film showing a single uninterrupted episode. —**sequential** *adj.*

sequester *v.* separate; seclude.

sequestrate *v.* confiscate (property) until its owner's debts are paid or a court order is complied with. —**sequestration** *n.*

sequin *n.* small ornamental metal disc on a garment. —**sequined** *adj.*

sequoia *n.* giant Californian coniferous tree.

seraglio [sir-**ah**-lee-oh] *n., pl.* **-raglios.** harem of a Muslim palace; Turkish sultan's palace.

THESAURUS

sensual 1. animal, bodily, carnal, fleshly, luxurious, physical, voluptuous 2. erotic, lascivious, lecherous, lewd, lustful, sexual, unchaste

sensuous epicurean, gratifying, hedonistic, lush, rich, sybaritic

sentence 1. *n.* condemnation, decision, decree, doom, judgment, order, ruling, verdict 2. *v.* condemn, doom, penalize

sentiment 1. emotion, sensibility, tenderness 2. *Often plural* attitude, belief, feeling, idea, judgment, opinion, persuasion, view, way of thinking 3. emotionalism, romanticism

sentimental dewy-eyed, emotional, impressionable, maudlin, nostalgic, overemotional, pathetic, romantic, simpering, soft-hearted, tearful, tender, touching

sentimentality bathos, nostalgia, romanticism, tenderness

separate *v.* 1. come away, detach, disconnect, disjoin, divide, remove, sever, split, sunder, uncouple 2. isolate, segregate, single out, sort out 3. bifurcate, break up, disunite, diverge, divorce, estrange, part, split up ~*adj.* 4. detached, disconnected, discrete, disjointed, divided, divorced, isolated 5. alone, apart, distinct, independent, individual, particular, single, solitary

separately alone, apart, independently, individually, personally, severally, singly

separation 1. break, disconnection, dissociation, disunion, division, gap, segregation, severance 2. break-up, divorce, farewell, parting, rift, split

sepulchre burial place, grave, tomb

sequel conclusion, continuation, development, end, follow-up, issue, outcome, result, upshot

sequence arrangement, chain, course, cycle, order, procession, progression, series, succession

seraphic angelic, beatific, blissful, celestial, divine, heavenly, holy, pure

DICTIONARY

seraph *n.* member of the highest order of angels. —**seraphic** *adj.*

serenade *n.* music played or sung to a woman by a lover. —*v.* sing or play a serenade to (someone).

serendipity *n.* gift of making fortunate discoveries by accident.

serene *adj.* calm, peaceful. —**serenely** *adv.* —**serenity** *n.*

serf *n.* medieval farm labourer who could not leave the land he worked on. —**serfdom** *n.*

serge *n.* strong woollen fabric.

sergeant *n.* noncommissioned officer in the army; police officer ranking between constable and inspector. —**sergeant at arms** parliamentary or court officer with ceremonial duties. —**sergeant major** highest rank of noncommissioned officer in the army.

serial *n.* story or play produced in successive instalments. —*adj.* of or forming a series; published or presented as a serial. —**serialize** *v.* publish or present as a serial.

seriatim [seer-ree-**ah**-tim] *adv.* one after another.

series *n., pl.* -**ries.** group or succession of related things, usu. arranged in order; set of radio or TV programmes about the same subject or characters.

serious *adj.* giving cause for concern; concerned with important matters; not cheerful, grave; sincere, not joking. —**seriously** *adv.* —**seriousness** *n.*

sermon *n.* speech on a religious or moral subject by a clergyman in a church service; long moralizing speech. —**sermonize** *v.* make a long moralizing speech.

serpent *n.* snake. —**serpentine** *adj.* twisting like a snake.

serrated *adj.* having a notched or sawlike edge. —**serration** *n.*

serried *adj.* in close formation.

serum [**seer**-um] *n.* watery fluid left after blood has clotted; this fluid from the blood of immunized animals used for inoculation or vaccination.

serval *n.* feline African mammal.

servant *n.* person employed to do household work for another.

serve *v.* work for (a person, community, or cause); perform official duties; attend to (customers); provide with food or drink; present (food or drink); provide with a service; be a member of the armed forces; spend (time) in prison; be useful or suitable; *Tennis etc.* put (the ball) into play; deliver (a legal document) to (a person). —*n. Tennis etc.* act of serving the ball.

service *n.* serving; system that provides something needed by the public; overhaul of a machine or vehicle; availability for use; department of public employment and its employees; set of dishes etc. for serving a meal; formal religious ceremony; *Tennis etc.* act, manner, or right of serving the ball. —*pl.* armed forces. —*v.* provide a service or services to; overhaul (a machine or vehicle). —**serviceable** *adj.* useful or helpful; able or ready to be used. —**service area** area beside a motorway with garage, restaurant, and toilet facilities. —**service flat** flat where domestic services are provided. —**serviceman** *n.* member of the armed forces. —**service road** narrow road giving access to houses and shops. —**service station** garage selling fuel for motor vehicles.

serviette *n.* table napkin.

THESAURUS

serene calm, composed, peaceful, placid, tranquil, undisturbed, unruffled, untroubled

series chain, course, line, order, progression, run, sequence, set, string, succession, train

serious 1. grave, pensive, sedate, sober, solemn, stern, thoughtful, unsmiling 2. deliberate, determined, earnest, genuine, honest, in earnest, resolute, sincere 3. crucial, deep, difficult, fateful, grim, important, momentous, pressing, significant, urgent, weighty, worrying 4. acute, alarming, critical, dangerous, grave, severe

seriously 1. earnestly, gravely, sincerely, solemnly, thoughtfully 2. acutely, badly, critically, dangerously, distressingly, gravely, grievously, severely, sorely

sermon 1. address, homily 2. harangue, lecture

servant attendant, domestic, help, helper, maid, retainer, slave, vassal

serve 1. aid, assist, help, minister to, oblige, succour, wait on, work for 2. act, attend, complete, discharge, do, fulfil, observe, officiate, pass, perform 3. answer, be acceptable, be adequate, content, do, function as, satisfy, suffice, suit 4. arrange, deal, deliver, dish up, distribute, handle, present, provide, set out, supply

service *n.* 1. advantage, assistance, avail, benefit, help, supply, usefulness, utility 2. check, maintenance, overhaul 3. business, duty, employ, labour, office, work 4. ceremony, function, observance, rite, worship ~*v.* 5. check, fine tune, go over, maintain, overhaul, recondition, repair, tune (up)

DICTIONARY

servile *adj.* too eager to obey people, fawning; suitable for a slave. —**servility** *n.*

servitude *n.* bondage or slavery.

servomechanism *n.* device which converts a small force into a larger force, used esp. in steering mechanisms.

sesame [sess-am-ee] *n.* plant cultivated for its seeds and oil, which are used in cooking.

session *n.* meeting of a court, parliament, or council; series or period of such meetings; period spent in an activity; academic term or year.

set *v.* **setting, set.** put in a specified position or state; make ready; make or become firm or rigid; put (a broken bone) or (of a broken bone) be put into a normal position for healing; establish, arrange; prescribe, assign; put to music; arrange (hair) while wet, so that it dries in position; (of the sun) go down. —*adj.* fixed or established beforehand; rigid or inflexible; conventional or stereotyped; determined (to do something); ready. —*n.* number of things or people grouped or belonging together; *Maths* group of numbers or objects that satisfy a given condition or share a property; television or radio receiver; scenery used in a play or film; *Tennis etc.* group of games in a match. —**setback** *n.* anything that delays progress. —**set square** flat right-angled triangular instrument used for drawing triangles. —**set theory** branch of mathematics concerned with the properties of sets. —**set up** *v.* arrange or establish. —**setup** *n.* way in which anything is organized or arranged.

set(t) *n.* badger's burrow.

settee *n.* couch.

setter *n.* long-haired gun dog.

setting *n.* background or surroundings; time and place where a film, book, etc. is supposed to have taken place; music written for the words of a text; decorative metalwork in which a gem is set; plates and cutlery for a single place at table; descending below the horizon of the sun; position or level to which the controls of a machine can be adjusted.

settle[1] *v.* arrange or put in order; establish or become established as a resident; colonize; make quiet, calm, or stable; come to rest; dispose of, conclude; end (a dispute); pay (a bill); bestow (property) legally. —**settlement** *n.* act of settling; place newly colonized; property bestowed legally; subsidence (of a building). —**settler** *n.* colonist.

settle[2] *n.* long wooden bench with high back and arms.

seven *adj., n.* one more than six. —**seventh** *adj., n.* (of) number seven in a series. —**seventeen** *adj., n.* ten and seven. —**seventeenth** *adj., n.* —**seventy** *adj., n.* ten times seven. —**seventieth** *adj., n.*

sever *v.* separate, divide; cut off. —**severance** *n.* —**severance pay** compensation paid by a firm to an employee for loss of employment.

several *adj.* some, a few; various, separate. —*pron.* indefinite small number. —**severally** *adv.* separately.

THESAURUS

session assembly, conference, discussion, hearing, meeting, period, sitting, term

set[1] *v.* 1. aim, apply, direct, fasten, fix, lay, locate, lodge, mount, park, place, plant, put, rest, seat, situate, station, stick, turn 2. allocate, appoint, arrange, assign, conclude, decide determine, establish, fix, name, ordain, regulate, resolve, schedule, settle, specify 3. arrange, lay, make ready, prepare, spread 4. adjust, rectify, regulate, synchronize 5. cake, congeal, crystallize, harden, solidify, stiffen, thicken 6. allot, decree, impose, ordain, prescribe, specify 7. decline, dip, disappear, go down, sink, subside, vanish ~*n.* 8. scene, scenery, setting ~*adj.* 9. agreed, appointed, arranged, customary, decided, definite, firm, fixed, prescribed, regular, scheduled, settled, usual 10. entrenched, firm, hard and fast, hardened, hidebound, immovable, inflexible, rigid, strict, stubborn

set[2] *n.* 1. band, circle, class, clique, company, coterie, crowd, faction, gang, group, sect 2.

assortment, batch, collection, compendium, kit, outfit, series

setback blow, check, defeat, disappointment, hitch, hold-up, misfortune, rebuff, reverse, upset

setting backdrop, background, context, location, perspective, scene, scenery, site, surroundings

settle 1. adjust, dispose, order, regulate, straighten out, work out 2. choose, clear up, complete, conclude, decide, dispose of, reconcile, resolve 3. calm, compose, lull, pacify, quell, quiet, quieten, reassure, relax, relieve, sedate, soothe 4. alight, descend, land, light 5. dwell, inhabit, live, move to, reside 6. colonize, found, people, pioneer, plant, populate 7. clear, discharge, pay, quit

settlement 1. agreement, arrangement, conclusion, confirmation, disposition, resolution 2. clearance, clearing, defrayal, discharge, payment 3. colony, community, encampment, hamlet, outpost, peopling

DICTIONARY

severe *adj.* strict or harsh; very intense or unpleasant; strictly restrained in appearance. —**severely** *adv.* —**severity** *n.*

sew *v.* sewing, sewed, sewn *or* sewed. join with thread repeatedly passed through with a needle; make or fasten by sewing.

sewage *n.* waste matter or excrement carried away in sewers. —**sewer** *n.* drain to remove waste water and sewage. —**sewerage** *n.* system of sewers.

sewn *v.* a past participle of SEW.

sex *n.* state of being male or female; male or female category; sexual intercourse; sexual feelings or behaviour. —*v.* ascertain the sex of. —**sexy** *adj.* sexually exciting or attractive; *Informal* exciting or trendy. —**sexism** *n.* discrimination on the basis of a person's sex. —**sexist** *adj.,* *n.* —**sexual** *adj.* —**sexually** *adv.* —**sexuality** *n.* —**sexual intercourse** sexual act in which the male's penis is inserted into the female's vagina.

sexagenarian *n., adj.* (person) between sixty and sixty-nine years old.

sextant *n.* navigator's instrument for measuring angles, as between the sun and horizon, to calculate one's position.

sextet *n.* group of six performers; music for such a group.

sexton *n.* official in charge of a church and churchyard.

SF science fiction.

shabby *adj.* -**bier,** -**biest.** worn or dilapidated in appearance; mean or unworthy, e.g. *shabby treatment.* —**shabbily** *adv.* —**shabbiness** *n.*

shack *n.* rough hut. —**shack up with** *v.* *Slang* live with (one's lover).

shackle *n.* one of a pair of metal rings joined by a chain, for securing a person's wrists or ankles. —*v.* fasten with shackles; hamper.

shad *n.* herring-like fish.

shade *n.* relative darkness; place sheltered from sun; depth of colour; slight amount; *Lit.* ghost; screen or cover used to protect from a direct source of light. —*pl. Slang* sunglasses. —*v.* screen from light; darken; represent (darker areas) in drawing; change slightly or by degrees. —**shady** *adj.* situated in or giving shade; of doubtful honesty or legality.

shadow *n.* dark shape cast on a surface when something stands between a light and the surface; patch of shade; slight trace; threatening influence; inseparable companion. —*v.* cast a shadow over; follow secretly. —**shadowy** *adj.* —**shadow-boxing** *n.* boxing against an imaginary opponent for practice. —**Shadow Cabinet** members of the main opposition party in Parliament who would be ministers if their party were in power.

shaft *n.* long narrow straight handle of a tool or weapon; ray of light; revolving rod that transmits power in a machine; vertical passageway, as for a lift; one of the bars between which an animal is harnessed to a vehicle.

THESAURUS

settler colonist, immigrant, pioneer, planter

set up arrange, begin, compose, establish, found, initiate, institute, organize, prearrange, prepare

several *adj.* different, disparate, distinct, diverse, individual, many, particular, respective, single, some, sundry, various

severe 1. austere, cruel, hard, harsh, oppressive, pitiless, relentless, rigid, strict, unrelenting 2. cold, dour, flinty, forbidding, grave, grim, serious, sober, stern, strait-laced, unsmiling 3. acute, bitter, critical, dangerous, extreme, fierce, inclement, intense, violent 4. ascetic, austere, chaste, classic, forbidding, plain, restrained, simple, unadorned, unfussy

severely 1. harshly, sternly, strictly 2. acutely, badly, critically, dangerously, extremely, hard, sorely

sex 1. gender 2. *Inf.* coition, coitus, copulation, (sexual) intercourse, intimacy lovemaking 3. desire, libido, reproduction

shabby 1. dilapidated, faded, frayed, mean, neglected, poor, ragged, run-down, seedy, tattered, tatty, threadbare, worn-out 2. cheap, contemptible, despicable, dirty, dishonourable, ignoble, low, mean, shameful, shoddy, unworthy

shade *n.* 1. dimness, dusk, gloom, obscurity, screen, shadow 2. blind, canopy, cover, covering, curtain, screen, shield, veil 3. colour, hue, stain, tinge, tint, tone 4. ghost, phantom, shadow, spectre, spirit ~*v.* 5. cloud, conceal, cover, darken, dim, hide, mute, obscure, protect, screen, shadow, shield, veil

shadow *n.* 1. cover, darkness, dimness, dusk, gloaming, gloom, protection, shade, shelter 2. hint, suggestion, suspicion, trace 3. blight, cloud, gloom, sadness ~*v.* 4. darken, overhang, screen, shade, shield 5. dog, follow, stalk, trail

shadowy dark, dim, dusky, gloomy, indistinct, murky, obscure, shaded

shady 1. cool, dim, leafy, shaded 2. *Inf.* crooked, disreputable, dubious, shifty, slippery, suspect

shaft 1. handle, pole, rod, shank, stem 2. beam, gleam, ray, streak

DICTIONARY

shag[1] *n.* coarse shredded tobacco. —*adj.* (of a carpet) having a long pile. —**shaggy** *adj.* covered with rough hair or wool; tousled, unkempt. —**shagginess** *n.* —**shaggy-dog story** long anecdote with a humorous twist at the end.

shag[2] *n.* cormorant.

shagreen *n.* rough grainy untanned leather; sharkskin.

shah *n.* formerly, ruler of Iran.

shake *v.* **shaking, shook, shaken.** move quickly up and down or back and forth; make unsteady; tremble; grasp (someone's hand) in greeting or agreement; shock or upset. —*n.* shaking; vibration; *Informal* short period of time. —**shaky** *adj.* unsteady; uncertain or questionable. —**shakily** *adv.*

shale *n.* flaky sedimentary rock.

shall *v., past tense* **should.** used as an auxiliary to make the future tense or to indicate intention, obligation, or inevitability.

shallot [shal-**lot**] *n.* kind of small onion.

shallow *adj.* not deep; lacking depth of character or intellect. —**shallows** *pl. n.* area of shallow water. —**shallowness** *n.*

sham *n.* thing or person that is not genuine. —*adj.* not real or genuine. —*v.* **shamming, shammed.** fake, feign.

shamble *v.* walk in a shuffling awkward way.

shambles *n.* disorderly event or place.

shame *n.* painful emotion caused by awareness of having done something dishonourable or foolish; capacity to feel shame; cause of shame; cause for regret. —*v.* cause to feel shame; dis-

grace; compel by shame, e.g. *she was shamed into helping.* —**shameful** *adj.* causing or deserving shame. —**shamefully** *adv.* —**shameless** *adj.* with no sense of shame. —**shamefaced** *adj.* looking ashamed.

shammy *n., pl.* **-mies.** *Informal* piece of chamois leather.

shampoo *n.* liquid soap for washing hair, carpets, or upholstery; process of shampooing. —*v.* wash with shampoo.

shamrock *n.* clover leaf, esp. as the Irish emblem.

shandy *n., pl.* **-dies.** drink made of beer and lemonade.

shanghai *v.* force or trick (someone) into doing something.

shank *n.* lower leg; shaft or stem.

shan't shall not.

shantung *n.* soft Chinese silk with a knobbly surface.

shanty[1] *n., pl.* **-ties.** shack or crude dwelling. —**shantytown** *n.* slum consisting of shanties.

shanty[2] *n., pl.* **-ties.** sailor's traditional song.

shape *n.* outward form of an object; way in which something is organized; pattern or mould; condition or state. —*v.* form or mould; devise or develop. —**shapeless** *adj.* —**shapely** *adj.* having an attractive shape.

shard *n.* broken piece of pottery.

share[1] *n.* part of something that belongs to or is contributed by a person; one of the equal parts into which the capital stock of a public company is divided. —*v.* give or take a share of (some-

---

THESAURUS

shake *v.* 1. bump, jar, quake, rock, shiver, shudder, sway, totter, tremble, vibrate, waver 2. brandish, flourish, wave 3. discompose, distress, disturb, frighten, intimidate, move, shock, unnerve, upset ~*n.* 4. agitation, convulsion, disturbance, jerk, quaking, shiver, shock, shudder, trembling, tremor, vibration

shaky 1. faltering, insecure, precarious, quivery, rickety, trembling, unstable, unsteady, weak 2. dubious, suspect, uncertain

shallow empty, flimsy, foolish, frivolous, idle, ignorant, puerile, simple, slight, superficial, surface, trivial, unintelligent

sham *n.* 1. feint, forgery, fraud, hoax, humbug, imitation, impostor, pretence 2. *adj.* artificial, bogus, counterfeit, false, feigned, imitation, mock, pretended, simulated, spurious, synthetic 3. *v.* affect, assume, fake, feign, imitate, pretend, put on, simulate

shame *n.* 1. blot, derision, disgrace, disrepute, infamy, obloquy, odium, reproach, scandal,

smear 2. abashment, chagrin, compunction, humiliation, ignominy ~*v.* 3. abash, confound, disconcert, embarrass, humble, reproach, ridicule 4. blot, debase, defile, degrade, dishonour, smear, stain

shameful 1. base, degrading, disgraceful, ignominious, indecent, low, mean, scandalous, unbecoming, wicked 2. degrading, humiliating, shaming

shameless audacious, brash, brazen, corrupt, depraved, dissolute, flagrant, hardened, immodest, improper, impudent, indecent, insolent, profligate, unabashed, unprincipled, wanton

shape *n.* 1. build, configuration, contours, cut, figure, form, lines, make, outline, profile, silhouette 2. frame, model, mould, pattern 3. aspect, form, guise, likeness, semblance 4. condition, fettle, health, kilter, state, trim ~*v.* 5. create, fashion, form, make, model, mould, produce 6. adapt, define, develop, devise, frame, guide, plan, prepare, regulate

DICTIONARY

thing); join with others in doing or using (something). **—shareholder** n.

share[2] n. blade of a plough.

shark n. large usu. predatory sea fish; person who cheats others.

sharkskin n. stiff glossy fabric.

sharp adj. having a keen cutting edge or fine point; not gradual; clearly defined; mentally acute; clever but underhand; shrill; bitter or sour in taste; (of a note) being one semitone above natural pitch; (of an instrument or voice) out of tune by being too high in pitch. **—**adv. promptly. **—**n. Music symbol raising a note one semitone above natural pitch; note raised in this way. **—sharply** adv. **—sharpness** n. **—sharpen** v. make or become sharp or sharper. **—sharpener** n. **—sharpshooter** n. marksman.

shatter v. break into pieces; destroy completely; upset (someone) greatly.

shave v. **shaving, shaved, shaved** or **shaven**. remove (hair) from (the face, head, or body) with a razor or shaver; pare away; touch lightly in passing; reduce. **—**n. shaving. **—close shave** Informal narrow escape. **—shaver** n. electric razor. **—shavings** pl. n. parings.

shawl n. piece of cloth worn over a woman's head or shoulders or wrapped around a baby.

she pron. female person or animal previously mentioned; something regarded as female, such as a car, ship, or nation.

sheaf n., pl. **sheaves**. bundle of papers; tied bundle of reaped corn.

shear v. **shearing, sheared, sheared** or **shorn**. clip hair or wool from; cut through. **—shears** pl. n. large scissors or a cutting tool shaped like these. **—shearer** n.

sheath n. close-fitting cover, esp. for a knife or sword; condom. **—sheathe** v. put into a sheath.

shebeen n. Irish, Scot., & S Afr. place where alcoholic drink is sold illegally.

shed[1] n. building used for storage or shelter or as a workshop.

shed[2] v. **shedding, shed**. pour forth (tears); cast off (skin); lose (hair).

sheen n. glistening brightness on the surface of something.

sheep n., pl. **sheep**. ruminant animal bred for wool and meat. **—sheep-dip** n. liquid disinfectant in which sheep are immersed. **—sheepdog** n. dog used for herding sheep. **—sheepskin** n. skin of a sheep with the fleece still on, used for clothing or rugs.

sheepish adj. embarrassed because of feeling foolish. **—sheepishly** adv.

sheer[1] adj. absolute, complete, e.g. sheer folly; (of material) so fine as to be transparent; perpendicular, steep.

sheer[2] v. change course suddenly.

sheet[1] n. large piece of cloth used as an inner bedcover; broad thin piece of any material; large expanse.

sheet[2] n. rope for controlling the position of a sail. **—sheet anchor** strong anchor for use in an emergency; person or thing relied on.

sheik(h) [shake] n. Arab chief. **—sheik(h)-dom** n.

sheila n. Aust. slang girl or woman.

shekel n. monetary unit of Israel. **—**pl. Informal money.

shelf n., pl. **shelves**. board fixed horizontally for holding things; ledge. **—shelf life** time a packaged product will remain fresh.

shell n. hard outer covering of an egg, nut, or certain animals; explosive projectile fired from a large gun; external frame of something. **—**v. take the shell from; fire at with artillery shells. **—shellfish** n. aquatic mollusc or crustacean. **—shell out** v. Informal pay out or hand over

---

THESAURUS

share 1. v. assign, distribute, divide, partake, participate, receive, split 2. n. allotment, allowance, contribution, division, due, lot, part, portion, quota, ration

sharp adj. 1. acute, jagged, keen, pointed, serrated, spiky 2. abrupt, distinct, extreme, marked, sudden 3. alert, apt, astute, bright, clever, knowing, observant, perceptive, quick, ready, subtle 4. clear, clear-cut, crisp, distinct, well-defined 5. acerbic, acid, acrid, burning, hot, piquant, pungent, sour, tart, vinegary ~adv. 6. exactly, on time, precisely, promptly, punctually

sharpen edge, grind, strop, whet

shatter 1. break, burst, crack, crush, demolish,

explode, pulverize, shiver, smash, split 2. blast, blight, demolish, destroy, disable, exhaust, impair, overturn, ruin, torpedo, wreck 3. crush, devastate

sheer 1. abrupt, precipitous, steep 2. arrant, complete, downright, pure, rank, total, unalloyed, unqualified, utter

sheet 1. coat, film, folio, layer, leaf, overlay, pane, panel, piece, plate, slab, surface, veneer 2. area, blanket, covering, expanse, stretch, sweep

shell n. 1. case, husk, pod ~v. 2. husk 3. attack, blitz, bomb, bombard, strike ~n. 4. frame, framework, hull, structure

DICTIONARY

(money). —**shell shock** nervous disorder caused by exposure to battle conditions.

shellac *n.* resin used in varnishes. —*v.* **-lacking, -lacked.** coat with shellac.

shelter *n.* structure providing protection from danger or the weather; protection. —*v.* give shelter to; take shelter.

shelve *v.* put aside or postpone; slope. —**shelving** *n.* (material for) shelves.

shenanigans *pl. n. Informal* mischief or nonsense; trickery.

shepherd *n.* person who tends sheep. —*v.* guide or watch over (people). —**shepherdess** *n. fem.* —**shepherd's pie** baked dish of mince covered with mashed potato.

sherbet *n.* fruit-flavoured fizzy powder.

sheriff *n.* in the U.S., chief law enforcement officer of a county; in England and Wales, chief executive officer of the Crown in a county; in Scotland, chief judge of a district.

Sherpa *n.* member of a people of Tibet and Nepal.

sherry *n., pl.* **-ries.** pale or dark brown fortified wine.

shibboleth *n.* slogan or principle, usu. considered outworn, characteristic of a particular group.

shield *n.* piece of armour carried on the arm to protect the body from blows or missiles; anything that protects; sports trophy in the shape of a shield. —*v.* protect.

shift *v.* move; transfer (blame or responsibility); remove or be removed. —*n.* shifting; group of workers who work during a specified period; period of time during which they work; loose-fitting straight underskirt or dress. —**shiftless** *adj.* lacking in ambition or initiative. —**shifty** *adj.* evasive or untrustworthy. —**shiftiness** *n.*

shillelagh [shil-**lay**-lee] *n.* (in Ireland) a cudgel.

shilling *n.* former British coin, replaced by the 5p piece.

shillyshally *v.* **-lying, -lied.** *Informal* be indecisive.

shimmer *v., n.* (shine with) a faint unsteady light.

shin *n.* front of the lower leg. —*v.* **shinning, shinned.** climb by using the hands or arms and legs. —**shinbone** *n.* tibia.

shindig *n. Informal* noisy party; brawl.

shine *v.* **shining, shone.** give out or reflect light; aim (a light); polish; excel. —*n.* brightness or lustre. —**take a shine to** *Informal* take a liking to (someone). —**shiny** *adj.* —**shiner** *n. Informal* black eye.

shingle¹ *n.* wooden roof tile. —*v.* cover (a roof) with shingles.

shingle² *n.* coarse gravel found on beaches.

shingles *n.* disease causing a rash of small blisters along a nerve.

Shinto *n.* Japanese religion in which ancestors and nature spirits are worshipped. —**Shintoism** *n.*

shinty *n.* game like hockey.

ship *n.* large seagoing vessel. —*v.* **shipping, shipped.** send or transport by carrier, esp. a ship; bring or go aboard a ship. —**shipment** *n.* act of shipping cargo; consignment of goods shipped. —**shipping** *n.* freight transport business; ships collectively. —**shipshape** *adj.* orderly or neat. —**shipwreck** *n.* destruction of a ship through storm or collision. —*v.* cause to undergo shipwreck. —**shipyard** *n.* place where ships are built.

shire *n.* county.

shire horse *n.* large powerful breed of horse.

shirk *v.* avoid (duty or work). —**shirker** *n.*

shirt *n.* garment for the upper part of the body.

shirty *adj.* **-tier, -tiest.** *Slang* annoyed.

THESAURUS

shelter 1. *v.* cover, defend, guard, harbour, hide, protect, safeguard, shield 2. *n.* asylum, cover, defence, guard, haven, protection, refuge, retreat, safety, sanctuary, screen, security, umbrella

shelve defer, freeze, mothball, pigeonhole, postpone

shield *n.* 1. buckler 2. aegis, bulwark, cover, defence, guard, protection, safeguard, screen, shelter ~*v.* 3. cover, defend, guard, protect, safeguard, screen, shelter

shift 1. *v.* alter, budge, change, displace, move, relocate, remove, reposition, swerve, switch, transfer, transpose, vary, veer 2. *n.* alteration,

change, fluctuation, move, removal, shifting, switch, transfer, veering

shimmer dance, gleam, glisten, twinkle

shine *v.* 1. beam, flash, glare, gleam, glisten, glitter, glow, radiate, sparkle, twinkle 2. be conspicuous, excel, stand out, star ~*n.* 3. brightness, glare, gleam, light, radiance, shimmer, sparkle

shining 1. beaming, bright, brilliant, gleaming, glistening, radiant, resplendent, shimmering, sparkling 2. *Fig.* brilliant, celebrated, conspicuous, distinguished, eminent, glorious, leading, splendid

shirk avoid, dodge, evade, shun, sidestep

DICTIONARY

shiver[1] *v.* tremble, as from cold or fear. —*n.* shivering.

shiver[2] *v.* splinter into pieces.

shoal[1] *n.* large number of fish swimming together.

shoal[2] *n.* stretch of shallow water; sandbank.

shock[1] *v.* horrify, disgust, or astonish. —*n.* sudden violent emotional disturbance; sudden violent blow or impact; something causing this; state of bodily collapse caused by physical or mental shock; pain and muscular spasm caused by an electric current passing through the body. —**shocker** *n.* —**shocking** *adj.* causing horror, disgust, or astonishment; *Informal* very bad.

shock[2] *n.* bushy mass (of hair).

shod *v.* past of SHOE.

shoddy *adj.* **-dier, -diest.** of poor quality.

shoe *n.* outer covering for the foot, ending below the ankle; horseshoe. —*v.* **shoeing, shod.** fit with a shoe or shoes. —**shoehorn** *n.* smooth curved implement inserted at the heel of a shoe to ease the foot into it. —**shoestring** *n.* —**on a shoestring** using a very small amount of money.

shone *v.* past of SHINE.

shoo *interj.* go away! —*v.* drive away as by saying 'shoo'.

shook *v.* past tense of SHAKE.

shoot *v.* **shooting, shot.** hit, wound, or kill with a missile fired from a weapon; fire (a missile from) a weapon; send out or move rapidly; hunt; (of a plant) sprout; photograph or film; *Sport* take a shot at goal. —*n.* new branch or sprout of a plant; hunting expedition. —**shooting star** meteor. —**shooting stick** stick with a spike at one end and a folding seat at the other.

shop *n.* place for sale of goods and services; workshop. —*v.* **shopping, shopped.** visit a shop or shops to buy goods; *Slang* inform against (someone). —**talk shop** discuss one's work, esp. on a social occasion. —**shop around** *v.* visit various shops to compare goods and prices. —**shop floor** production area of a factory; workers in a factory. —**shoplifter** *n.* person who steals from a shop. —**shopsoiled** *adj.* soiled or faded from being displayed in a shop. —**shop steward** trade-union official elected to represent his or her fellow workers.

shore[1] *n.* edge of a sea or lake.

shore[2] *v.* (foll. by *up*) prop or support.

shorn *v.* a past participle of SHEAR.

short *adj.* not long; not tall; not lasting long, brief; deficient, e.g. *short of cash;* abrupt, rude; (of a drink) consisting chiefly of a spirit; (of pastry) crumbly. —*adv.* abruptly. —*n.* drink of spirits; short film; *Informal* short circuit. —*pl.* short trousers. —**shortage** *n.* deficiency. —**shorten** *v.* make or become shorter. —**shortly** *adv.* soon; rudely. —**shortbread, shortcake** *n.* crumbly biscuit made with butter. —**short-change** *v.* give (someone) less than the correct amount of change; *Slang* swindle. —**short circuit** faulty or accidental connection in a circuit, which deflects current through a path of low resistance. —**shortcoming** *n.* failing or defect. —**short cut** quicker route or method. —**shortfall** *n.* deficit. —**shorthand** *n.* system of rapid writing using symbols to represent words. —**short-handed** *adj.* not having enough workers. —**short list** selected list of candidates for a job or prize, from which the final choice will be made. —**short-list** *v.* put on a short list. —**short shrift** brief and unsympathetic treatment. —**short-sighted** *adj.* unable to see faraway things clearly; lacking in foresight.

THESAURUS

shock 1. *v.* agitate, astound, disgust, disquiet, horrify, jar, jolt, nauseate, numb, offend, outrage, revolt, shake, sicken, stagger, stun, stupefy, unsettle 2. *n.* blow, bombshell, breakdown, collapse, distress, disturbance, stupor, trauma, upset

shocking appalling, atrocious, detestable, disgraceful, disquieting, dreadful, foul, frightful, ghastly, hideous, horrible, monstrous, odious, offensive, outrageous, revolting, scandalous, sickening, unspeakable

shoddy inferior, poor, second-rate, slipshod, tawdry, trashy

shoot[1] *v.* 1. bag, hit, kill, open fire, pick off 2. discharge, emit, fire, fling, hurl, launch, project, propel 3. bolt, charge, dart, dash, flash, fly, hurtle, race, rush, speed, spring, streak, tear, whisk

shoot[2] 1. *n.* branch, bud, slip, sprig, sprout, twig 2. *v.* bud, germinate, sprout

shore beach, coast, sands, seashore, waterside

short *adj.* 1. brief, compressed, concise, curtailed, laconic, pithy, succinct, summary, terse 2. dumpy, little, low, petite, small, squat 3. brief, fleeting, momentary 4. deficient, lacking, limited, meagre, poor, scant, scanty, scarce, slender, slim, tight, wanting ~*adv.* 5. abruptly, by surprise, suddenly, unaware

shortage dearth, deficit, failure, lack, paucity, poverty, scarcity, want

shortcoming defect, failing, fault, flaw, frailty, imperfection, weakness

shorten abbreviate, curtail, cut, decrease, diminish, dock, lessen, reduce, trim, turn up

DICTIONARY

—**short wave** radio wave with a wavelength of less than 60 metres.

shot *n.* shooting; small lead pellets used in a shotgun; person with specified skill in shooting; *Slang* attempt; *Sport* act or instance of hitting, kicking, or throwing the ball; photograph; uninterrupted film sequence; *Informal* drink of spirits. —*adj.* woven so that the colour varies according to the angle of light. —*v.* past of SHOOT. —**shotgun** *n.* gun for firing a charge of shot at short range.

shot put *n.* athletic event in which contestants hurl a heavy metal ball as far as possible. —**shot-putter** *n.*

should *v.* past tense of SHALL: used as an auxiliary to make the subjunctive mood or to indicate obligation or possibility.

shoulder *n.* part of the body to which an arm, foreleg, or wing is attached; cut of meat including the upper foreleg; part of a garment which covers the shoulder; side of a road. —*v.* bear (a burden or responsibility); put on one's shoulder; push with one's shoulder. —**shoulder blade** large flat triangular bone at the shoulder.

shouldn't should not.

shout *n.* loud cry. —*v.* cry out loudly. —**shout down** *v.* silence (someone) by shouting.

shove *v.* push roughly; *Informal* put. —*n.* rough push. —**shove off** *v. Informal* go away.

shovel *n.* tool for lifting or moving loose material. —*v.* **-elling, -elled.** lift or move as with a shovel.

show *v.* **showing, showed, shown** *or* **showed.** make, be, or become noticeable or visible; exhibit or display; indicate; instruct by demonstration; prove; guide; reveal or display (an emo-

tion). —*n.* public exhibition; theatrical or other entertainment; mere display or pretence. —**showy** *adj.* gaudy; ostentatious. —**showily** *adv.* —**show business** the entertainment industry. —**showcase** *n.* glass case used to display objects; situation in which something is displayed to best advantage. —**showdown** *n.* confrontation that settles a dispute. —**showjumping** *n.* competitive sport of riding horses to demonstrate skill in jumping. —**showman** *n.* man skilled at presenting anything spectacularly. —**showmanship** *n.* —**show off** *v.* exhibit to invite admiration; *Informal* behave flamboyantly in order to attract attention. —**show-off** *n. Informal* person who shows off. —**showpiece** *n.* excellent specimen shown for display or as an example. —**showroom** *n.* room in which goods for sale are on display. —**show up** *v.* reveal or be revealed clearly; expose the faults or defects of; *Informal* embarrass; *Informal* arrive.

shower *n.* kind of bath in which a person stands while being sprayed with water; wash in this; short period of rain, hail, or snow; sudden abundant fall of objects, eg *shower of sparks.* —*v.* wash in a shower; bestow (things) or present (someone) with things liberally. —**showery** *adj.*

shown *v.* a past participle of SHOW.

shrank *v.* a past tense of SHRINK.

shrapnel *n.* artillery shell filled with pellets which scatter on explosion; fragments from this.

shred *n.* long narrow strip torn from something; small amount. —*v.* **shredding, shredded** *or* **shred.** tear to shreds.

shrew *n.* small mouselike animal; bad-tempered nagging woman. —**shrewish** *adj.*

shrewd *adj.* clever and perceptive. —**shrewdly** *adv.* —**shrewdness** *n.*

THESAURUS

shot *n.* 1. discharge, lob, pot shot, throw 2. ball, bullet, lead, pellet, projectile, slug 3. marksman, shooter 4. *Inf.* attempt, chance, effort, endeavour, essay, go, guess, opportunity, stab, surmise, try, turn

shoulder *v.* 1. accept, assume, bear, be responsible for, carry, take on 2. elbow, jostle, press, push, shove, thrust

shout 1. *n.* bellow, call, cry, roar, scream, yell 2. *v.* bawl, bay, bellow, call (out), cry (out), roar, scream, yell

shove *v.* crowd, drive, elbow, impel, jostle, press, propel, push, thrust

show *v.* 1. appear, disclose, display, divulge, evidence, exhibit, indicate, manifest, present, register, reveal 2. assert, clarify, demonstrate, explain, instruct, present, prove, teach 3. attend, conduct, escort, guide, lead ~*n.* 4. array,

demonstration, display, exhibition, fair, pageant, parade, sight, spectacle, view 5. affectation, air, appearance, display, illusion, likeness, ostentation, parade, pose, pretence, pretext, profession

showdown clash, climax, crisis

shower 1. *n.* barrage, deluge, rain, stream, torrent, volley 2. *v.* deluge, heap, lavish, load, pour, rain, spray, sprinkle

showman entertainer, impresario, performer, publicist

show off 1. advertise, display, exhibit, flaunt, parade, spread out 2. boast, brag, swagger

show up 1. expose, lay bare, pinpoint, reveal, unmask 2. appear, stand out 3. *Inf.* embarrass, let down, mortify, shame 4. *Inf.* appear, arrive, come, turn up

shrewd acute, artful, astute, canny, clever,

DICTIONARY

shriek *n.* shrill cry. —*v.* utter (with) a shriek.

shrike *n.* songbird with a heavy hooked bill.

shrill *adj.* (of a sound) sharp and high-pitched. —**shrillness** *n.* —**shrilly** *adv.*

shrimp *n.* small edible shellfish; *Informal* small person. —**shrimping** *n.* fishing for shrimps.

shrine *n.* place of worship associated with a sacred person or object.

shrink *v.* **shrinking, shrank** *or* **shrunk, shrunk** *or* **shrunken.** become or make smaller; recoil or withdraw. —*n. Slang* psychiatrist. —**shrinkage** *n.* decrease in size, value, or weight.

shrive *v.* **shriving, shrived** *or* **shrove, shriven.** *Old-fashioned* give absolution to after hearing confession.

shrivel *v.* **-elling, -elled.** shrink and wither.

shroud *n.* piece of cloth used to wrap a dead body; anything which conceals. —*v.* conceal.

Shrovetide *n.* the three days preceding Lent. —**Shrove Tuesday** day before Ash Wednesday.

shrub *n.* woody plant smaller than a tree. —**shrubbery** *n.* area planted with shrubs.

shrug *v.* **shrugging, shrugged.** raise and then drop (the shoulders) as a sign of indifference, ignorance, or doubt. —*n.* shrugging. —**shrug off** *v.* dismiss as unimportant.

shrunk *v.* a past of SHRINK.

shrunken *v.* a past participle of SHRINK.

shudder *v.* shake or tremble violently, esp. with horror. —*n.* shaking or trembling.

shuffle *v.* walk without lifting the feet; rearrange; jumble together. —*n.* shuffling; rearrangement.

shun *v.* **shunning, shunned.** avoid.

shunt *v.* move (objects or people) to a different position; move (a train) from one track to another.

shush *interj.* be quiet!

shut *v.* **shutting, shut.** bring together or fold, close; prevent access to. —**shutter** *n.* hinged doorlike cover for closing off a window; device in a camera letting in the light required to expose a film. —**shut down** *v.* close or stop (a factory, machine, or business). —**shutdown** *n.*

shuttle *n.* vehicle going to and fro over a short distance; instrument which passes the weft thread between the warp threads in weaving. —*v.* travel by or as if by shuttle.

shuttlecock *n.* small light cone with feathers stuck in one end, struck to and fro in badminton.

shy[1] *adj.* not at ease in company; timid; (foll. by *of*) cautious or wary. —*v.* **shying, shied.** start back in fear; (foll. by *away from*) avoid (doing something) through fear or lack of confidence. —**shyly** *adv.* —**shyness** *n.*

shy[2] *v.* **shying, shied.** throw. —*n., pl.* **shies.** throw.

Si *Chem.* silicon.

SI *French* Système International (d'Unités), international metric system of units of measurement.

Siamese *adj.* of Siam, former name of Thailand. —**Siamese cat** breed of cat with cream fur, dark ears and face, and blue eyes. —**Siamese twins** twins born joined to each other at some part of the body.

sibilant *adj.* hissing. —*n.* consonant pronounced with a hissing sound.

sibling *n.* brother or sister.

sibyl *n.* (in ancient Greece and Rome) prophetess. —**sibylline** *adj.*

sic *Latin* thus: used to indicate that an odd spelling or reading is in fact accurate.

sick *adj.* vomiting or likely to vomit; physically or mentally unwell; *Informal* amused by something sadistic or morbid; (foll. by *of*) *Informal* disgusted (by) or weary (of). —**sickness** *n.* —**sicken** *v.* make nauseated or disgusted; become ill. —**sickly** *adj.* unhealthy, weak; causing revulsion or nausea. —**sickbay** *n.* place for sick people, such as that on a ship.

THESAURUS

crafty, cunning, discerning, far-seeing, intelligent, keen, knowing, perceptive, perspicacious, sharp, sly, smart, wily

shrewdness acumen, discernment, grasp, judgment, perspicacity, sagacity, sharpness, smartness

shrill acute, high, penetrating, piercing, piping, screeching, sharp

shrink 1. contract, decrease, diminish, dwindle, lessen, narrow, shorten, shrivel, wither, wrinkle 2. cower, cringe, draw back, flinch, hang back, quail, recoil, retire, wince, withdraw

shrivel desiccate, dwindle, shrink, wilt, wither, wizen, wrinkle

shudder 1. *v.* convulse, quake, quiver, shake, shiver, tremble 2. *n.* quiver, spasm, tremor

shuffle 1. drag, scrape, shamble 2. confuse, disarrange, disorder, intermix, mix, rearrange, shift

shun avoid, elude, eschew, evade

shut bar, close, draw to, fasten, push to, seal, secure, slam

shut down cease, close, discontinue, halt, stop

shy bashful, cautious, chary, coy, diffident,

DICTIONARY

sickle *n.* tool with a curved blade for cutting grass or grain.

side *n.* line or surface that borders anything; either surface of a flat object; either of two halves into which something can be divided; area immediately next to a person or thing; region; aspect or part; one of two opposing groups or teams; line of descent through one parent; *Slang* conceit. —*adj.* at or on the side; subordinate. —**on the side** as an extra; unofficially. —**siding** *n.* short stretch of railway track on which trains or wagons are shunted from the main line. —**sideboard** *n.* piece of furniture for holding plates, cutlery, etc. in a dining room. —*pl.* (also **sideburns**) man's side whiskers. —**side-effect** *n.* additional undesirable effect. —**sidekick** *n. Informal* close friend or associate. —**sidelight** *n.* either of two small lights on the front of a vehicle. —**sideline** *n.* subsidiary interest or source of income; *Sport* line marking the boundary of a playing area. —**sidelong** *adj.* sideways; oblique. —*adv.* obliquely. —**side-saddle** *n.* saddle designed to allow a woman rider to sit with both legs on the same side of the horse. —**sidestep** *v.* dodge (an issue); avoid by stepping sideways. —**sidetrack** *v.* divert from the main topic. —**sidewalk** *n. US* pavement. —**sideways** *adv.* to or from the side; obliquely. —**side with** *v.* support (one side in a dispute).

sidereal [side-eer-ee-al] *adj.* of or determined with reference to the stars.

sidle *v.* move in a furtive manner.

SIDS sudden infant death syndrome, cot death.

siege *n.* surrounding and blockading of a place.

sienna *n.* reddish- or yellowish-brown pigment made from natural earth.

sierra *n.* range of mountains in Spain or America with jagged peaks.

siesta *n.* afternoon nap, taken in hot countries.

sieve [siv] *n.* utensil with mesh through which a substance is sifted or strained. —*v.* sift or strain through a sieve.

sift *v.* remove the coarser particles from a substance with a sieve; examine (information or evidence) to select what is important.

sigh *n.* long audible breath expressing sadness, tiredness, relief, or longing. —*v.* utter a sigh.

sight *n.* ability to see; instance of seeing; range of vision; thing seen; thing worth seeing; *Informal* unsightly thing; device for guiding the eye while using a gun or optical instrument; *Informal* a lot. —*v.* catch sight of. —**sightless** *adj.* blind. —**sight-read** *v.* play or sing printed music without previous preparation. —**sightseeing** *n.* visiting places of interest. —**sightseer** *n.*

sign *n.* indication of something not immediately or outwardly observable; notice displayed to advertise, inform, or warn; gesture, mark, or symbol conveying a meaning; omen. —*v.* make a sign or gesture; write (one's name) on (a document or letter) to show its authenticity or one's agreement. —**sign on** *v.* register as unemployed; sign a document committing oneself to a job, course, etc. —**signpost** *n.* post bearing a sign that shows the way.

THESAURUS

hesitant, modest, nervous, reserved, reticent, retiring, shrinking, suspicious, timid, wary

sick 1. ill, nauseated, qualmish, queasy 2. ailing, diseased, feeble, indisposed, unwell, weak 3. *Inf.* black, ghoulish, macabre, morbid, sadistic

sicken 1. disgust, nauseate, repel, revolt 2. contract, fall ill, take sick

sickly 1. ailing, bloodless, delicate, faint, feeble, infirm, languid, peaky, pining, unhealthy, wan, weak 2. cloying, mawkish, nauseating

sickness 1. nausea, vomiting 2. affliction, ailment, bug (*Inf.*), complaint, disease, disorder, illness, indisposition, infirmity, malady

side *n.* 1. border, boundary, division, edge, limit, margin, part, perimeter, rim, sector, verge 2. aspect, face, facet, flank, hand, part, surface, view 3. camp, cause, faction, party, sect, team 4. *Brit. sl.* airs, arrogance, insolence, pretentiousness ~*adj.* 5. lateral 6. ancillary, incidental, indirect, lesser, marginal, minor, secondary, subsidiary

sidetrack deflect, distract, divert

sideways *adv.* edgeways, laterally

siesta catnap, doze, nap, rest, sleep

sift 1. filter, part, riddle, separate, sieve 2. analyse, examine, fathom, investigate, probe, screen, scrutinize

sigh *v.* breathe, complain, grieve, lament, moan, sorrow

sight *n.* 1. eye, eyes, seeing, vision 2. appearance, ken, perception, view, viewing 3. display, exhibition, pageant, scene, show, spectacle, vista ~*v.* 4. behold, discern, distinguish, make out, observe, perceive, see, spot

sign *n.* 1. clue, evidence, gesture, hint, indication, mark, note, proof, signal, suggestion, symptom, token, trace, vestige 2. board, notice, placard, warning 3. badge, cipher, device, emblem, ensign, figure, logo, mark, symbol 4. augury, auspice, foreboding, omen, portent, warning ~*v.* 5. autograph, endorse, initial, inscribe, subscribe 6. beckon, gesticulate, gesture, indicate, signal, use sign language, wave

DICTIONARY

signal *n.* sign or gesture to convey information; sequence of electrical impulses or radio waves transmitted or received. —*adj.* remarkable or striking. —*v.* **-nalling, -nalled.** make a signal; convey (information) by signal. —**signally** *adv.* —**signal box** building from which railway signals are operated. —**signalman** *n.* railwayman in charge of signals and points.

signatory [sig-na-tree] *n., pl.* **-ries.** one of the parties who sign a document.

signature *n.* person's name written by himself or herself in signing something; sign at the start of a piece of music to show the key or tempo. —**signature tune** tune used to introduce a particular television or radio programme.

signet *n.* small seal used to authenticate documents. —**signet ring** finger ring bearing a signet.

significant *adj.* important; having or expressing a meaning. —**significantly** *adv.* —**significance** *n.*

signify *v.* **-fying, -fied.** indicate or suggest; be a symbol or sign for; be important. —**signification** *n.* meaning.

signor [see-nyor] *n.* Italian term of address equivalent to *Sir* or *Mr.* —**signora** [see-nyor-a] *n.* Italian term of address equivalent to *madam* or *Mrs.* —**signorina** [see-nyor-ee-na] *n.* Italian term of address equivalent to *madam* or *Miss.*

Sikh [seek] *n.* member of an Indian religion having only one God.

silage [sile-ij] *n.* fodder crop harvested while green and partially fermented in a silo.

silence *n.* absence of noise or speech. —*v.* make silent; put a stop to. —**silent** *adj.* —**silently** *adv.* —**silencer** *n.* device to reduce the noise of an engine exhaust or gun.

silhouette *n.* outline of a dark shape seen against a light background. —*v.* show in silhouette.

silica *n.* hard glossy mineral found as quartz and in sandstone. —**silicosis** *n.* lung disease caused by inhaling silica dust.

silicon *n.* brittle nonmetallic element widely used in chemistry and industry. —**silicone** *n.* tough synthetic substance made from silicon and used in lubricants, paints, and resins. —**silicon chip** tiny wafer of silicon processed to form an integrated circuit.

silk *n.* fibre made by the larva (**silkworm**) of a certain moth; thread or fabric made from this. —**silky, silken** *adj.* of or like silk.

sill *n.* ledge at the bottom of a window.

silly *adj.* **-lier, -liest.** foolish. —**silliness** *n.*

silo *n., pl.* **-los.** pit or airtight tower for storing silage; underground structure in which nuclear missiles are kept ready for launching.

silt *n.* mud deposited by moving water. —*v.* (foll. by *up*) fill or be choked with silt.

silvan *adj.* same as SYLVAN.

silver *n.* white precious metal; coins or articles made of silver. —*adj.* made of or of the colour of silver. —**silver birch** tree with silvery-white bark. —**silverfish** *n.* small wingless silver-coloured insect. —**silverside** *n.* cut of beef from below the rump and above the leg. —**silver wedding** twenty-fifth wedding anniversary.

simian *adj., n.* (of or like) a monkey or ape.

THESAURUS

signal 1. *n.* beacon, cue, gesture, indication, indicator, mark, sign, token 2. *v.* beckon, gesticulate, gesture, indicate, motion, nod, sign, wave

significance 1. force, import, meaning, message, point, purport, sense 2. consequence, importance, matter, moment, relevance, weight

significant 1. eloquent, expressive, indicative, knowing, meaning, suggestive 2. critical, important, material, momentous, noteworthy, serious, vital, weighty

signify betoken, connote, convey, denote, evidence, exhibit, express, imply, indicate, intimate, matter, mean, portend, proclaim, represent, show, stand for, suggest, symbolize

silence *n.* 1. calm, hush, lull, peace, quiet, stillness 2. dumbness, muteness, reticence, taciturnity ~*v.* 3. cut off, cut short, deaden, extinguish, gag, muffle, quell, quieten, stifle, still, subdue, suppress

silent 1. hushed, muted, quiet, soundless, still 2. dumb, mum, mute, speechless, taciturn, tongue-tied, voiceless, wordless

silently dumbly, mutely, noiselessly, quietly, soundlessly, speechlessly

silhouette 1. *n.* form, outline, profile, shape 2. *v.* etch, outline, stand out

silky silken, sleek, smooth, velvety

silly absurd, asinine, brainless, childish, fatuous, foolhardy, foolish, frivolous, giddy, idiotic, immature, inane, irresponsible, meaningless, pointless, puerile, ridiculous, stupid

similar alike, comparable, in agreement, resembling, uniform

similarity affinity, agreement, analogy, closeness, correspondence, likeness, relation, resemblance

similarly correspondingly, likewise

DICTIONARY

similar *adj.* alike but not identical. —**similarity** *n.* —**similarly** *adv.*

simile [sim-ill-ee] *n.* figure of speech comparing one thing to another, using 'as' or 'like'.

similitude *n.* similarity, likeness.

simmer *v.* cook gently at just below boiling point; be in a state of suppressed rage. —**simmer down** *v.* calm down.

simnel cake *n.* fruit cake covered with marzipan.

simper *v.* smile in a silly or affected way; utter (something) with a simper. —*n.* simpering smile.

simple *adj.* easy to understand or do; plain or unpretentious; not combined or complex; sincere or frank; feeble-minded. —**simply** *adv.* —**simplicity** *n.* —**simplify** *v.* -**fying, -fied.** make less complicated. —**simplification** *n.* —**simplistic** *adj.* oversimplified or oversimplifying. —**simpleton** *n.* foolish or half-witted person.

simulate *v.* make a pretence of; have the appearance of; imitate the conditions of (a particular situation). —**simulation** *n.* —**simulator** *n.*

simultaneous *adj.* occurring at the same time. —**simultaneity** *n.* —**simultaneously** *adv.*

sin *n.* breaking of a religious or moral law; offence against a principle or standard. —*v.* **sinning, sinned.** commit a sin. —**sinful** *adj.* being a sin; guilty of sin. —**sinfully** *adv.* —**sinner** *n.*

since *prep.* during the period of time after. —*conj.* from the time when; for the reason that. —*adv.* from that time.

sincere *adj.* without pretence or deceit. —**sincerely** *adv.* —**sincerity** *n.*

sine *n.* (in trigonometry) ratio of the length of the opposite side to that of the hypotenuse in a right-angled triangle.

sinecure [sin-ee-cure] *n.* paid job with minimal duties.

sine die [sin-ay dee-ay] *adv. Latin* with no date fixed for future action.

sine qua non [sin-ay kwah non] *n. Latin* essential requirement.

sinew *n.* tough fibrous tissue joining muscle to bone; muscles or strength. —**sinewy** *adj.*

sing *v.* **singing, sang, sung.** make musical sounds with the voice; perform (a song); make a humming or whistling sound. —**singer** *n.* —**singing telegram** service in which a messenger presents greetings to a person by singing. —**singsong** *n.* informal singing session. —*adj.* (of the voice) repeatedly rising and falling in pitch.

singe *v.* **singeing, singed.** burn the surface of. —*n.* superficial burn.

single *adj.* one only; distinct from others of the same kind; unmarried; designed for one user; formed of only one part; (of a ticket) valid for an outward journey only. —*n.* single thing; thing intended for one person; record with one short song or tune on each side; single ticket. —*pl.* game between two players. —*v.* (foll. by *out*) pick out from others. —**singly** *adv.* —**single file** (of people or things) arranged in one line. —**single-handed** *adj.* without assistance. —**single-minded** *adj.* having one aim only.

THESAURUS

simple 1. clear, easy, intelligible, lucid, plain, uncomplicated, understandable, uninvolved 2. classic, clean, natural, plain, unfussy 3. elementary, pure, single, uncombined, unmixed 4. artless, childlike, frank, guileless, innocent, naive, natural, sincere, unsophisticated 5. brainless, dense, feeble, foolish, moronic, obtuse, shallow, silly, slow, stupid, thick

simpleton blockhead, dolt, dunce, fool, idiot, moron

simplicity 1. clarity, clearness, ease 2. modesty, naturalness, plainness, purity, restraint 3. artlessness, candour, directness, innocence, naivety, openness

simplify abridge, disentangle, facilitate, streamline

simply 1. clearly, directly, easily, modestly, naturally, plainly, unaffectedly, unpretentiously, without any elaboration 2. just, merely, only, purely, solely

sin 1. *n.* crime, error, evil, guilt, iniquity, mis-

deed, offence, trespass, unrighteousness, wickedness, wrong 2. *v.* err, fall, lapse, offend, transgress

sincere artless, candid, earnest, frank, genuine, guileless, heartfelt, honest, natural, open, real, serious, true, unaffected

sincerely earnestly, genuinely, honestly, really, seriously, truly

sincerity candour, frankness, genuineness, good faith, honesty, probity, seriousness, truth

sinful bad, corrupt, criminal, erring, guilty, immoral, iniquitous, ungodly, unholy, unrighteous, wicked

sing carol, chant, chirp, croon, pipe, trill, warble, yodel

singer chorister, crooner, minstrel, songster, vocalist

single 1. distinct, individual, lone, one, only, separate, sole, solitary, unique 2. free, unattached, unmarried, unwed 3. exclusive, individual, separate, unblended, undivided, unmixed, unshared

DICTIONARY

singlet *n.* sleeveless vest.

singular *adj.* (of a word or form) denoting one person or thing; remarkable, unusual. —*n.* singular form of a word. —**singularity** *n.* —**singularly** *adv.*

sinister *adj.* threatening or suggesting evil or harm.

sink *v.* **sinking, sank** *or* **sunk, sunk** *or* **sunken.** submerge (in liquid); descend or cause to descend; decline in value or amount; become weaker in health; dig or drill (a hole or shaft); invest (money); *Golf, snooker* hit (a ball) into a hole or pocket. —*n.* fixed basin with a water supply and drainage pipe. —**sinker** *n.* weight for a fishing line. —**sink in** *v.* penetrate the mind. —**sinking fund** money set aside regularly to repay a long-term debt.

Sino- *combining form* Chinese.

sinuous *adj.* curving; lithe. —**sinuously** *adv.*

sinus [**sine**-uss] *n.* hollow space in a bone, esp. an air passage opening into the nose.

sip *v.* **sipping, sipped.** drink in small mouthfuls. —*n.* amount sipped.

siphon *n.* bent tube which uses air pressure to draw liquid from a container. —*v.* draw off thus; redirect (resources).

sir *n.* polite term of address for a man; (**S-**) title of a knight or baronet.

sire *n.* male parent of a horse or other domestic animal; respectful term of address to a king. —*v.* father.

siren *n.* device making a loud wailing noise as a warning; dangerously alluring woman.

sirloin *n.* prime cut of loin of beef.

sirocco *n., pl.* **-cos.** hot wind blowing from N Africa into S Europe.

sisal [**size**-al] *n.* (fibre of) plant used in making ropes.

siskin *n.* yellow-and-black finch.

sissy *n., pl.* **-sies.** weak or cowardly person.

sister *n.* girl or woman with the same parents as another person; senior nurse; nun; female fellow-member of a group. —*adj.* closely related, similar. —**sisterhood** *n.* state of being a sister; group of women united by common aims or beliefs. —**sisterly** *adj.* —**sister-in-law** *n., pl.* **sisters-in-law.** sister of one's husband or wife; one's brother's wife.

sit *v.* **sitting, sat.** rest one's body upright on the buttocks; cause to sit; perch; (of a bird) incubate (eggs) by sitting on them; be situated; pose for a portrait; occupy an official position; (of an official body) hold a session; take (an examination). —**sit-in** *n.* protest in which demonstrators occupy a place and refuse to move. —**sitting room** room in a house where people sit and relax.

sitar *n.* Indian stringed musical instrument.

sitcom *n. Informal* situation comedy.

site *n.* place where something is, was, or is intended to be located. —*v.* provide with a site.

situate *v.* place. —**situation** *n.* location and surroundings; state of affairs; position of employment. —**situation comedy** radio or television series involving the same characters in various situations.

six *adj., n.* one more than five. —**sixth** *adj., n.* (of) number six in a series. —**sixteen** *adj., n.* six and ten. —**sixteenth** *adj., n.* —**sixty** *adj., n.* six times ten. —**sixtieth** *adj., n.*

size[1] *n.* dimensions, bigness; one of a series of standard measurements of goods. —*v.* arrange according to size. —**siz(e)able** *adj.* quite large. —**size up** *v. Informal* assess.

size[2] *n.* gluey substance used as a sealer.

THESAURUS

single-minded dedicated, determined, dogged, fixed, steadfast, stubborn, tireless

singular 1. eminent, exceptional, noteworthy, outstanding, prodigious, rare, remarkable, uncommon, unique, unparalleled 2. curious, eccentric, odd, out-of-the-way, peculiar, puzzling, queer, strange, unusual 3. individual, separate, single, sole

sinister dire, disquieting, evil, malignant, menacing, ominous, threatening

sink *v.* 1. decline, descend, dip, disappear, droop, drop, drown, ebb, engulf, fall, founder, lower, merge, plunge, sag, slope, submerge, subside 2. decay, decline, depreciate, die, diminish, dwindle, fade, fail, flag, lessen, weaken, worsen 3. bore, dig, drill, drive, excavate, lay

sip 1. *v.* sample, sup, taste 2. *n.* drop, swallow, taste, thimbleful

siren charmer, Circe, seductress, temptress, witch

sit 1. perch, rest, settle 2. assemble, convene, deliberate, meet, officiate, preside

site 1. *n.* ground, location, place, plot, position, spot 2. *v.* install, locate, place, position, set, situate

situation 1. location, place, position, seat, setting, site, spot 2. case, circumstances, condition, plight, state 3. employment, job, office, place, position, post

size amount, bulk, dimensions, extent, immensity, mass, proportions, range, vastness, volume

DICTIONARY

sizzle *v.* make a hissing sound like frying fat.

skate[1] *n.* boot with a steel blade or sets of wheels attached to the sole for gliding over ice or a hard surface. —*v.* glide on or as if on skates. —**skateboard** *n.* board mounted on small wheels for riding on while standing up. —**skate over, round** *v.* avoid discussing or dealing with (a matter) fully.

skate[2] *n.* large marine flatfish.

skedaddle *v. Informal* run off.

skein *n.* yarn wound in a loose coil; flock of geese in flight.

skeleton *n.* framework of bones inside a person's or animal's body; essential framework of a structure. —*adj.* reduced to a minimum. —**skeletal** *adj.* —**skeleton key** key which can open many different locks.

skerry *n., pl.* **-ries.** rocky island or reef.

sketch *n.* rough drawing; brief description; short humorous play. —*v.* make a sketch (of). —**sketchy** *adj.* incomplete or inadequate.

skew *v.* make slanting or crooked. —*adj.* slanting or crooked. —**skewwhiff** *adj. Informal* slanting or crooked.

skewbald *adj.* (of a horse) marked with patches of white and another colour.

skewer *n.* pin to hold meat together during cooking. —*v.* fasten with a skewer.

ski *n.* one of a pair of long runners fastened to boots for gliding over snow or water. —*v.* **skiing, skied** *or* **ski'd.** travel on skis. —**skier** *n.*

skid *v.* **skidding, skidded.** (of a moving vehicle) slide sideways uncontrollably. —*n.* skidding.

skiff *n.* small boat.

skill *n.* special ability or expertise; something requiring special training or expertise. —**skilful** *adj.* having or showing skill. —**skilfully** *adv.* —**skilled** *adj.*

skillet *n.* small frying pan or shallow cooking pot.

skim *v.* **skimming, skimmed.** remove floating matter from the surface of (a liquid); glide smoothly over; read quickly. —**skim(med) milk** milk from which the cream has been removed.

skimp *v.* not invest enough time, money, material, etc. —**skimpy** *adj.* scanty or insufficient.

skin *n.* outer covering of the body; complexion; outer layer or covering; film on a liquid; animal skin used as a material or container. —*v.* **skinning, skinned.** remove the skin of. —**skinless** *adj.* —**skinny** *adj.* thin. —**skin-deep** *adj.* superficial. —**skin diving** underwater swimming using flippers and light breathing apparatus. —**skindiver** *n.* —**skinflint** *n.* miser. —**skinhead** *n.* youth with very short hair.

skint *adj. Slang* having no money.

skip[1] *v.* **skipping, skipped.** leap lightly from one foot to the other; jump over a rope as it is swung under one; *Informal* pass over, omit. —*n.* skipping.

skip[2] *n.* large open container for builders' rubbish.

skipper *n., v.* captain.

skirl *n.* sound of bagpipes.

skirmish *n.* brief or minor fight or argument. —*v.* take part in a skirmish.

skirt *n.* woman's garment hanging from the waist; part of a dress or coat below the waist; cut of beef from the flank. —*v.* border; go round; avoid dealing with (an issue). —**skirting (board)** narrow board round the bottom of an interior wall.

skit *n.* brief satirical sketch.

skittish *adj.* playful or lively.

skittle *n.* bottle-shaped object used as a target in some games. —*pl.* game in which players try to knock over skittles by rolling a ball at them.

THESAURUS

skeleton *Fig.* bones, draft, framework, outline, sketch

sketch 1. *v.* delineate, depict, draft, draw, outline, paint, plot, portray, represent, rough out 2. *n.* delineation, design, draft, drawing, outline, plan

sketchy bitty, crude, cursory, inadequate, incomplete, outline, perfunctory, rough, scrappy, skimpy, slight, superficial, vague

skilful able, adept, adroit, apt, clever, experienced, expert, handy, masterly, practised, professional, proficient, quick, ready, skilled, trained

skill ability, adroitness, aptitude, art, cleverness, competence, dexterity, expertise, facil-ity, finesse, handiness, ingenuity, knack, readiness, talent, technique

skilled able, experienced, expert, masterly, practised, professional, proficient, skilful, trained

skin *n.* 1. hide, pelt 2. casing, coating, crust, film, husk, outside, peel, rind ~*v.* 3. bark, flay, graze, peel, scrape

skinny emaciated, lean, thin, undernourished

skip *v.* 1. bob, caper, dance, flit, frisk, gambol, hop, prance, trip 2. eschew

skirmish 1. *n.* affair, battle, brush, clash, combat, conflict, contest, encounter, engagement, fracas, incident, spat, tussle 2. *v.* clash, collide

skirt *v.* border, edge, flank

DICTIONARY

skive v. Informal evade work or responsibility.

skivvy n., pl. **-vies.** female servant who does menial work.

skua n. large predatory gull.

skulduggery n. Informal trickery.

skulk v. move stealthily; lurk.

skull n. bony framework of the head. —**skullcap** n. close-fitting brimless cap.

skunk n. small black-and-white N American mammal which emits an evil-smelling fluid when attacked; Slang despicable person.

sky n., pl. **skies.** upper atmosphere as seen from the earth. —**skydiving** n. sport of jumping from an aircraft and performing manoeuvres before opening one's parachute. —**skylark** n. lark that sings while soaring at a great height. —**skylight** n. window in a roof or ceiling. —**skyscraper** n. very tall building.

slab n. broad flat piece.

slack[1] adj. not tight; negligent; not busy. —n. slack part. —pl. informal trousers. —v. neglect one's work or duty. —**slackness** n. —**slacken** v. make or become slack. —**slacker** n.

slack[2] n. coal dust or small pieces of coal.

slag n. waste left after metal is smelted. —v. **slagging, slagged.** Slang criticize.

slain v. past participle of SLAY.

slake v. satisfy (thirst or desire); combine (quicklime) with water.

slalom n. skiing or canoeing race over a winding course.

slam v. **slamming, slammed.** shut, put down, or hit violently and noisily; Informal criticize harshly. —n. act or sound of slamming. —**grand slam** winning of all of a group of competitions.

slander n. false and malicious statement about a person; crime of making such a statement. —v. utter slander about. —**slanderous** adj.

slang n. very informal language. —**slangy** adj. —**slanging match** abusive argument.

slant v. lean at an angle, slope; present (information) in a biased way. —n. slope; point of view, esp. a biased one. —**slanting** adj.

slap n. blow with the open hand or a flat object. —v. **slapping, slapped.** strike with the open hand or a flat object; Informal place forcefully or carelessly. —**slapdash** adj. careless and hasty. —**slap-happy** adj. Informal cheerfully careless. —**slapstick** n. boisterous knockabout comedy. —**slap-up** adj. (of a meal) large and luxurious.

slash v. gash; cut with a sweeping stroke; reduce drastically. —n. gash; sweeping stroke.

slat n. narrow strip of wood or metal.

slate n. rock which splits easily into thin layers; piece of this for covering a roof or, formerly, for writing on. —v. criticize severely.

slattern n. Old-fashioned slovenly woman. —**slatternly** adj.

slaughter v. kill (animals) for food; kill (people) savagely or indiscriminately. —n. slaughtering. —**slaughterhouse** n. place where animals are killed for food.

slave n. person owned by another for whom he or she has to work; person dominated by another or by a habit; drudge. —v. work like a slave. —**slaver** n. person or ship engaged in the slave trade. —**slavery** n. state or condition of being a slave; practice of owning slaves. —**slavish** adj. of or like a slave; imitative. —**slave-driver** n. person who makes others work very hard.

THESAURUS

slab chunk, lump, piece, portion, slice, wedge

slack adj. 1. baggy, easy, flexible, lax, limp, loose, relaxed 2. easy-going, idle, inactive, inattentive, lax, lazy, neglectful, negligent, permissive, remiss, tardy 3. dull, inactive, quiet, slow, slow-moving, sluggish ~n. 4. excess, leeway, play, room ~v. 5. dodge, flag, idle, neglect, relax, shirk

slacken abate, decrease, diminish, drop off, lessen, loosen, moderate, reduce, relax, release

slacker dodger, idler, loafer, passenger, shirker

slam bang, crash, dash, fling, hurl, smash, throw, thump

slander 1. n. calumny, libel, misrepresentation, scandal, smear 2. v. calumniate, decry, defame, detract, disparage, libel, malign, muckrake, slur, smear, traduce, vilify

slant v. 1. bend, bevel, cant, incline, lean, list, shelve, slope, tilt ~n. 2. camber, gradient,

incline, pitch, rake, ramp, slope, tilt ~v. 3. angle, bias, colour, distort, twist, weight ~n. 4. angle, bias, emphasis, leaning, onesidedness, prejudice, viewpoint

slanting angled, aslant, bent, canted, diagonal, inclined, oblique, sideways, sloping, tilted, tilting

slap 1. n. bang, blow, cuff, smack, spank, whack 2. v. bang, clap, cuff, hit, spank, strike, whack

slapdash careless, clumsy, hasty, hurried, messy, perfunctory, slipshod, slovenly, untidy

slash 1. v. cut, gash, hack, lacerate, rend, rip, score, slit 2. n. cut, gash, incision, laceration, rent, rip, slit

slate v. berate, blame, censure, criticize, scold, slang

slaughter 1. n. bloodshed, butchery, carnage, extermination, killing, massacre, murder,

DICTIONARY

slaver *v.* dribble saliva from the mouth.

slay *v.* **slaying, slew, slain.** kill.

sleazy *adj.* **-zier, -ziest.** sordid. —**sleaziness** *n.*

sledge[1] *n.* carriage on runners for sliding on snow; light wooden frame for sliding over snow. —*v.* travel by sledge.

sledge[2], **sledgehammer** *n.* heavy hammer with a long handle.

sleek *adj.* glossy, smooth, and shiny.

sleep *n.* state of rest characterized by unconsciousness; period of this. —*v.* **sleeping, slept.** be in or as if in a state of sleep; have sleeping accommodation for (a specified number). —**sleeper** *n.* person who sleeps; beam supporting the rails of a railway; railway car fitted for sleeping in; ring worn in a pierced ear to stop the hole from closing up. —**sleepy** *adj.* —**sleepily** *adv.* —**sleepiness** *n.* —**sleepless** *adj.* —**sleeping bag** padded bag for sleeping in. —**sleeping sickness** African disease spread by the tsetse fly. —**sleep with, together** *v.* have sexual intercourse (with).

sleet *n.* rain and snow or hail falling together.

sleeve *n.* part of a garment which covers the arm; tubelike cover; gramophone record cover. —**up one's sleeve** secretly ready. —**sleeveless** *adj.*

sleigh *n.* sledge.

sleight of hand [slite] *n.* skilful use of the hands when performing conjuring tricks.

slender *adj.* slim; small in amount.

slept *v.* past of SLEEP.

sleuth [slooth] *n.* detective.

slew[1] *v.* past tense of SLAY.

slew[2] *v.* twist or swing round.

slice *n.* thin flat piece cut from something; share; kitchen tool with a broad flat blade; *Sport* hitting of a ball so that it travels obliquely. —*v.* cut into slices; *Sport* hit (a ball) with a slice.

slick *adj.* persuasive and glib; skilfully devised or carried out; well-made and attractive, but superficial. —*v.* make smooth or sleek. —*n.* patch of oil on water.

slide *v.* **sliding, slid.** slip smoothly along (a surface); pass unobtrusively. —*n.* sliding; surface or structure for sliding on or down; piece of glass holding an object to be viewed under a microscope; photographic transparency; ornamental hair clip. —**slide rule** mathematical instrument formerly used for rapid calculations. —**sliding scale** variable scale according to which things such as wages fluctuate in response to changes in other factors.

slight *adj.* small in quantity or extent; not important; slim and delicate. —*v., n.* snub. —**slightly** *adv.*

slim *adj.* **slimmer, slimmest.** not heavy or stout, thin; slight. —*v.* **slimming, slimmed.** make or become slim by diet and exercise. —**slimmer** *n.*

slime *n.* unpleasant thick slippery substance. —**slimy** *adj.* of, like, or covered with slime; ingratiating.

THESAURUS

slaying 2. *v.* butcher, destroy, kill, liquidate, massacre, murder, slay

slave 1. *n.* drudge, serf, servant, skivvy, vassal, villein 2. *v.* drudge, slog, toil

slavery bondage, captivity, serfdom, servitude, thrall

slavish abject, base, cringing, despicable, fawning, low, mean, menial, obsequious, servile

slay assassinate, butcher, destroy, dispatch, eliminate, exterminate, kill, massacre, murder, slaughter

sleek glossy, lustrous, shiny, smooth, well-fed, well-groomed

sleep 1. *v.* catnap, doze, drowse, slumber, snore 2. *n.* dormancy, doze, nap, repose, rest, siesta, slumber(s)

sleepless restless, wakeful

sleepy 1. drowsy, dull, heavy, inactive, lethargic, sluggish, torpid 2. dull, hypnotic, inactive, slow, somnolent

slender 1. lean, narrow, slight, slim, willowy 2. inadequate, insufficient, little, meagre, scanty, small, spare

slice 1. *n.* cut, helping, piece, portion, segment, share, sliver, wedge 2. *v.* carve, cut, divide, sever

slick 1. glib, plausible, polished, smooth, specious 2. adroit, deft, dextrous, polished, sharp, skilful

slide *v.* coast, glide, skim, slip, slither, veer

slight *adj.* 1. feeble, insignificant, meagre, minor, modest, paltry, scanty, small, superficial, trivial, unimportant, weak 2. delicate, feeble, fragile, lightly-built, slim, small, spare ~*v.* 3. affront, disdain, disparage, ignore, insult, neglect, scorn, snub ~*n.* 4. affront, contempt, discourtesy, disdain, disrespect, insult, neglect, rebuff, snub

slightly a little, somewhat

slim *adj.* 1. lean, narrow, slender, slight, sylphlike, thin, trim 2. faint, poor, remote, slender, slight ~*v.* 3. diet, reduce

slimy 1. clammy, glutinous, miry, muddy, viscous 2. creeping, obsequious, oily, servile, sycophantic, unctuous

DICTIONARY

sling¹ *n.* bandage hung from the neck to support an injured hand or arm; strap with a string at each end for throwing a stone; rope or strap for lifting something. —*v.* **slinging, slung.** throw; carry, hang, or throw with or as if with a sling.

sling² *n.* sweetened drink with a spirit base, e.g. gin sling.

slink *v.* **slinking, slunk.** move furtively or guiltily. —**slinky** *adj.* (of clothes) figure-hugging; sinuously graceful.

slip¹ *v.* **slipping, slipped.** lose balance by sliding; move smoothly, easily, or quietly; (foll. by *on* or *off*) put on or take off easily or quickly; pass out of (the mind). —*n.* slipping; mistake; petticoat; small piece (of paper). —**give someone the slip** escape from someone. —**slippy** *adj. Informal* slippery. —**slipknot** *n.* knot tied so that it will slip along the rope round which it is made. —**slipped disc** painful condition in which one of the discs connecting the bones of the spine becomes displaced. —**slip road** narrow road giving access to a motorway. —**slipshod** *adj.* (of an action) careless. —**slipstream** *n.* stream of air forced backwards by a fast-moving object. —**slip up** *v.* make a mistake. —**slipway** *n.* launching slope on which ships are built or repaired.

slip² *n.* clay mixed with water used for decorating pottery.

slipper *n.* light shoe for indoor wear.

slippery *adj.* so smooth or wet as to cause slipping or be difficult to hold; (of a person) untrustworthy.

slit *v.* **slitting, slit.** make a long straight cut in. —*n.* long narrow cut or opening.

slither *v.* slide unsteadily.

sliver [sliv-ver] *n.* small thin piece.

slob *n. Informal* lazy and untidy person. —**slobbish** *adj.*

slobber *v.* dribble or drool. —**slobbery** *adj.*

sloe *n.* sour blue-black fruit.

slog *v.* **slogging, slogged.** work hard and steadily; make one's way with difficulty; hit hard. —*n.* long and exhausting work or walk.

slogan *n.* catchword or phrase used in politics or advertising.

sloop *n.* small single-masted ship.

slop *v.* **slopping, slopped.** splash or spill. —*n.* spilt liquid; liquid food. —*pl.* liquid refuse and waste food used to feed animals. —**sloppy** *adj.* careless or untidy; gushingly sentimental.

slope *v.* slant. —*n.* sloping surface; degree of inclination. —**slope off** *v. Informal* go furtively.

slosh *n.* splashing sound. —*v.* splash carelessly; *Slang* hit hard. —**sloshed** *adj. Slang* drunk.

slot *n.* narrow opening for inserting something; *Informal* place in a series or scheme. —*v.* **slotting, slotted.** make a slot or slots in; fit into a slot. —**slot machine** automatic machine worked by placing a coin in a slot.

sloth [rhymes with **both**] *n.* slow-moving animal of tropical America; laziness. —**slothful** *adj.* lazy or idle.

slouch *v.* sit, stand, or move with a drooping posture. —*n.* drooping posture; *Informal* incompetent or lazy person.

slough¹ [rhymes with **now**] *n.* bog.

slough² [sluff] *v.* (of a snake) shed (its skin) or (of a skin) be shed. —**slough off** *v.* get rid of (something unwanted or unnecessary).

sloven *n.* habitually dirty or untidy person. —**slovenly** *adj.* dirty or untidy; careless.

slow *adj.* taking a longer time than is usual or expected; not fast; (of a clock or watch) showing a time earlier than the correct one; stupid. —*v.* reduce the speed (of). —**slowly** *adv.* —**slowness** *n.* —**slowcoach** *n. Informal* person who moves or works slowly.

THESAURUS

slip *v.* 1. glide, skate, slide, slither 2. fall, skid 3. *Sometimes with* **up** blunder, err, miscalculate, mistake ~*n.* 4. blunder, error, failure, fault, indiscretion, mistake, omission, oversight 5. **give (someone) the slip** dodge, elude, evade, lose (someone), outwit

slippery 1. glassy, greasy, icy, perilous, smooth, unsafe, unsteady 2. crafty, cunning, devious, dishonest, evasive, false, tricky, two-faced, unpredictable, unreliable

slipshod careless, loose, slapdash, slovenly, untidy

slit 1. *v.* cut (open), gash, knife, lance, pierce, rip, slash 2. *n.* cut, gash, incision, opening, rent, split, tear

slogan catchword, jingle, motto

slope 1. *v.* drop away, fall, incline, lean, pitch, rise, slant, tilt 2. *n.* descent, gradient, incline, ramp, rise, scarp, slant, tilt

sloppy *Inf.* careless, clumsy, inattentive, messy, slipshod, slovenly, unkempt, untidy, weak

slot 1. aperture, channel, groove, hole, slit 2. *Inf.* opening, place, position, space, time, vacancy

sloth idleness, inactivity, inertia, laziness, slackness, sluggishness, torpor

slovenly careless, disorderly, loose, negligent, slack, slapdash, slipshod, untidy

slow 1. dawdling, deliberate, easy, laggard, lazy, leaden, leisurely, measured, ponderous, slug~

DICTIONARY

slowworm *n.* small legless lizard.

sludge *n.* thick mud; sewage.

slug[1] *n.* land snail with no shell; bullet. —**sluggish** *adj.* slow-moving, lacking energy. —**sluggishly** *adv.* —**sluggishness** *n.* —**sluggard** *n.* lazy person.

slug[2] *v.* **slugging, slugged.** hit hard. —*n.* heavy blow; *Informal* mouthful of an alcoholic drink.

sluice *n.* channel carrying off water; sliding gate used to control the flow of water in this; water controlled by a sluice. —*v.* pour a stream of water over or through.

slum *n.* squalid overcrowded house or area. —*v.* **slumming, slummed.** temporarily and deliberately experience poorer places or conditions than usual.

slumber *v., n. Lit.* sleep.

slump *v.* sink or fall heavily; (of prices or demand) decline suddenly. —*n.* sudden decline in prices or demand; time of substantial unemployment.

slung *v.* past of SLING[1].

slunk *v.* past of SLINK.

slur *v.* **slurring, slurred.** pronounce or utter (words) indistinctly; *Music* sing or play (notes) smoothly without a break. —*n.* slurring of words; remark intended to discredit someone; *Music* slurring of notes; curved line indicating notes to be slurred.

slurp *Informal* —*v.* eat or drink noisily. —*n.* slurping sound.

slurry *n., pl.* **-ries.** muddy liquid mixture.

slush *n.* watery muddy substance; sloppy senti-

mental talk or writing. —**slushy** *adj.* —**slush fund** fund for financing bribery or corruption.

slut *n.* dirty or immoral woman. —**sluttish** *adj.*

sly *adj.* **slyer, slyest** *or* **slier, sliest.** crafty; secretive and cunning; roguish. —*n.* —**on the sly** secretly. —**slyly** *adv.* —**slyness** *n.*

smack[1] *v.* slap sharply; open and close (the lips) loudly in enjoyment or anticipation. —*n.* sharp slap; slapping sound; loud kiss. —*adv. Informal* squarely or directly, e.g. *smack in the middle.* —**smacker** *n. Slang* loud kiss.

smack[2] *n.* slight flavour or trace; *Slang* heroin. —*v.* have a slight flavour or trace (of).

smack[3] *n.* small single-masted fishing boat.

small *adj.* not large in size, number, or amount; unimportant; mean or petty. —*n.* narrow part of the lower back. —*pl. Informal* underwear. —**smallness** *n.* —**smallholding** *n.* small area of farming land. —**small hours** hours just after midnight. —**small-minded** *adj.* intolerant, petty. —**smallpox** *n.* contagious disease with blisters that leave scars. —**small talk** light social conversation. —**small-time** *adj.* insignificant or minor.

smarmy *adj.* **smarmier, smarmiest.** *Informal* unpleasantly suave or flattering.

smart *adj.* well-kept and neat; astute; witty; impertinent; fashionable; brisk. —*v.* feel or cause stinging pain. —*n.* stinging pain. —**smart aleck** *Informal* irritatingly clever person. —**smarten** *v.* make or become smart. —**smartly** *adv.* —**smartness** *n.*

smash *v.* break violently and noisily; throw (against) violently; collide forcefully; destroy. —*n.* act or sound of smashing; violent collision of

THESAURUS

gish, unhurried 2. backward, behind, delayed, dilatory, late, long-delayed, tardy 3. gradual, lingering, prolonged, protracted 4. bovine, dense, dim, dull, dull-witted, obtuse, retarded, stupid, thick, unresponsive

slowly gradually, leisurely, ploddingly, steadily, unhurriedly

sluggish dull, heavy, inactive, indolent, inert, lethargic, lifeless, listless, slothful, slow, torpid

slumber doze, nap, repose, sleep

slump 1. *v.* collapse, crash, deteriorate, fall, fall off, plunge, sink, slip 2. *n.* collapse, crash, decline, depression, downturn, failure, fall, low, recession, reverse, trough

slur *n.* affront, aspersion, blot, discredit, disgrace, innuendo, insinuation, insult, reproach, smear, stain, stigma

sly 1. *adj.* artful, astute, clever, crafty, cunning, devious, furtive, guileful, scheming, secret,

shifty, stealthy, subtle, underhand, wily 2. *n.* **on the sly** covertly, privately, secretly, surreptitiously, underhandedly, under the counter (*Inf.*)

small 1. diminutive, immature, little, mini, miniature, minute, petite, puny, slight, tiny, undersized, wee, young 2. insignificant, lesser, minor, negligible, paltry, petty, trifling, trivial 3. base, grudging, illiberal, mean, narrow, petty, selfish

small-minded bigoted, envious, grudging, hidebound, intolerant, mean, petty, rigid, ungenerous

smart[1] *adj.* 1. acute, adept, agile, apt, astute, bright, brisk, canny, clever, ingenious, intelligent, keen, nimble, quick, ready, sharp, shrewd 2. chic, elegant, fine, modish, neat, snappy, spruce, stylish, trim 3. effective, impertinent, pointed, ready, saucy, witty

smart[2] *v.* burn, hurt, pain, sting, throb, tingle

DICTIONARY

vehicles; *Informal* popular success; *Sport* powerful overhead shot. **—smasher** *n. Informal* attractive person or thing. **—smashing** *adj. Informal* excellent.

smattering *n.* slight knowledge.

smear *v.* spread with a greasy or sticky substance; rub so as to produce a dirty mark or smudge; slander. **—n.** dirty mark or smudge; slander; *Med.* sample of a secretion smeared on to a slide for examination under a microscope.

smell *v.* **smelling, smelt** *or* **smelled.** perceive (a scent or odour) by means of the nose; have or give off a smell; detect by instinct. **—n.** odour or scent; smelling; ability to perceive odours by the nose. **—smelly** *adj.* having a nasty smell. **—smelling salts** preparation of ammonia used to revive a person who feels faint.

smelt[1] *v.* extract (a metal) from (an ore) by heating. **—smelter** *n.*

smelt[2] *n.* small fish of the salmon family.

smelt[3] *v.* a past of SMELL.

smile *n.* turning up of the corners of the mouth to show pleasure, amusement, or friendliness. **—v.** give a smile. **—smile on, upon** *v.* regard favourably.

smirch *v., n.* disgrace.

smirk *n.* smug smile. **—v.** give a smirk.

smite *v.* **smiting, smote, smitten.** *Old-fashioned* strike hard; affect severely.

smith *n.* worker in metal. **—smithy** *n.* blacksmith's workshop.

smithereens *pl. n.* shattered fragments.

smitten *v.* past participle of SMITE.

smock *n.* loose overall; woman's loose blouse-like garment. **—v.** gather (material) by sewing in a honeycomb pattern. **—smocking** *n.*

smog *n.* mixture of smoke and fog.

smoke *n.* cloudy mass that rises from something burning; spell of smoking tobacco. **—v.** give off smoke; inhale and expel smoke of (a cigar, cigarette, or pipe); do this habitually; cure (meat, fish, or cheese) by treating with smoke. **—smokeless** *adj.* **—smoker** *n.* **—smoky** *adj.* **—smoke screen** something said or done to hide the truth.

smooch *Informal* **—v.** kiss and cuddle. **—n.** smooching.

smooth *adj.* even in surface, texture, or consistency; without obstructions or difficulties; charming and polite but possibly insincere; free from jolts; not harsh in taste. **—v.** make smooth; calm. **—smoothly** *adv.*

smorgasbord *n.* buffet meal of assorted dishes.

smote *v.* past tense of SMITE.

smother *v.* suffocate or stifle; cover thickly; suppress.

smoulder *v.* burn slowly with smoke but no flame; (of feelings) exist in a suppressed state.

smudge *v.* make or become smeared or soiled. **—n.** dirty mark; blurred form. **—smudgy** *adj.*

smug *adj.* **smugger, smuggest.** self-satisfied. **—smugly** *adv.* **—smugness** *n.*

smuggle *v.* import or export (goods) secretly and illegally; take somewhere secretly. **—smuggler** *n.*

smut *n.* speck of soot; mark left by this; obscene jokes, pictures, etc. **—smutty** *adj.*

Sn *Chem.* tin.

snack *n.* light quick meal. **—snack bar** place where snacks are sold.

snaffle *n.* jointed bit for a horse. **—v.** *Slang* steal.

snag *n.* difficulty or disadvantage; sharp projecting point; hole in fabric caused by a sharp object. **—v.** **snagging, snagged.** catch or tear on a point.

THESAURUS

smash *v.* 1. break, collide, crash, crush, demolish, pulverize, shatter, shiver ~*n.* 2. accident, collision, crash ~*v.* 3. defeat, destroy, lay waste, overthrow, ruin, wreck

smear *v.* 1. bedaub, bedim, blur, coat, cover, daub, dirty, patch, plaster, smudge, soil, spread over, stain, sully ~*n.* 2. blot, blotch, daub, smudge, splotch, streak ~*v.* 3. asperse, blacken, sully, tarnish, traduce, vilify ~*n.* 4. calumny, libel, slander, vilification

smell *n.* 1. aroma, bouquet, fragrance, odour, perfume, scent, whiff ~*v.* 2 nose, scent, sniff 3. reek, stink

smooth *adj.* 1. even, flat, flush, horizontal, level, plain, plane 2. glossy, polished, shiny, silky, sleek, soft, velvety 3. agreeable, bland, mellow, mild, pleasant, soothing 4. facile, glib, persuasive, silky, slick, suave, unctuous, urbane 5. easy, effortless, flowing, fluent, regular, rhythmic, steady, uniform, well-ordered ~*v.* 6. flatten, iron, level, plane, polish, press 7. allay, appease, assuage, calm, ease, facilitate, mitigate, mollify, palliate, soften

smother 1. choke, snuff, stifle, strangle, suffocate 2. conceal, hide, muffle, repress, stifle, suppress

smoulder *Fig.* be resentful, boil, burn, fester, fume, rage, seethe, simmer

smug complacent, conceited, priggish, superior

smuggler bootlegger, gentleman, runner, wrecker

DICTIONARY

snail *n.* slow-moving mollusc with a spiral shell. **—snail's pace** very slow speed.

snake *n.* long thin scaly limbless reptile. **—***v.* move in a winding course like a snake. **—snake in the grass** treacherous person. **—snaky** *adj.* twisted or winding.

snap *v.* **snapping, snapped.** break suddenly; (cause to) make a sharp cracking sound; bite (at) suddenly; move suddenly; speak sharply and angrily; take a snapshot of. **—***n.* act or sound of snapping; fastener that closes with a snapping sound; *Informal* snapshot; sudden brief spell of cold weather; card game in which the word 'snap' is called when two similar cards are put down. **—***adj.* made on the spur of the moment. **—snapper** *n.* fish of the perch family. **—snappy** *adj.* irritable; *Slang* quick; *Slang* smart and fashionable. **—snapdragon** *n.* plant with flowers that can open and shut like a mouth. **—snapshot** *n.* informal photograph. **—snap up** *v.* take eagerly and quickly.

snare *n.* trap with a noose. **—***v.* catch in or as if in a snare.

snarl *v.* (of an animal) growl with bared teeth; speak or utter fiercely; make tangled. **—***n.* act or sound of snarling; tangled mass. **—snarl-up** *n.* *Informal* confused situation such as a traffic jam.

snatch *v.* seize or try to seize suddenly; take (food, rest, etc.) hurriedly. **—***n.* snatching; fragment.

snazzy *adj.* **-zier, -ziest.** *Informal* stylish and flashy.

sneak *v.* move furtively; bring, take, or put furtively; *Informal* tell tales. **—***n.* cowardly or underhand person; *Informal* telltale. **—sneaking** *adj.* secret; slight but persistent. **—sneaky** *adj.*

sneakers *pl. n. US* canvas shoes with rubber soles.

sneer *n.* contemptuous expression or remark. **—***v.* show contempt by a sneer.

sneeze *v.* expel air from the nose suddenly, involuntarily, and noisily. **—***n.* act or sound of sneezing.

snib *n.* catch of a door or window.

snicker *n., v.* same as SNIGGER.

snide *adj.* maliciously derogatory.

sniff *v.* inhale through the nose in short audible breaths; smell by sniffing. **—***n.* act or sound of sniffing. **—sniffle** *v.* sniff repeatedly, as when suffering from a cold. **—***n.* slight cold. **—sniff at** *v.* express contempt for. **—sniffer dog** police dog trained to detect drugs or explosives by smell.

snifter *n.* *Informal* small quantity of alcoholic drink.

snigger *n.* sly disrespectful laugh, esp. one partly stifled. **—***v.* utter a snigger.

snip *v.* **snipping, snipped.** cut in small quick strokes with scissors or shears. **—***n.* act or sound of snipping; *Informal* bargain. **—snippet** *n.* small piece.

snipe *n.* wading bird with a long straight bill. **—***v.* (foll. by *at*) shoot at (a person) from cover; make critical remarks about. **—sniper** *n.*

snitch *Informal* **—***v.* act as an informer; steal. **—***n.* informer.

snivel *v.* **-elling, -elled.** cry in a whining way.

snob *n.* person who judges others by social rank; person who feels smugly superior in his or her tastes or interests. **—snobbery** *n.* **—snobbish** *adj.*

snood *n.* pouch, often of net, loosely holding a woman's hair at the back.

THESAURUS

snack bite, break, light meal, nibble, refreshment(s), titbit

snag catch, difficulty, disadvantage, drawback, hitch, inconvenience, obstacle, problem, stumbling block

snap *v.* 1. break, crack, separate 2. bite, catch, grip, nip, seize, snatch 3. bark, flare out, flash, growl, lash out at, retort, snarl 4. click, crackle, pop ~*adj.* 5. abrupt, immediate, instant, sudden

snap up grab, grasp, seize

snare 1. *v.* catch, entrap, net, seize, trap, wire 2. *n.* catch, gin net, noose, pitfall

snarl *v.* complain, growl, grumble, mumble, murmur

snatch 1. *v.* clutch, gain, grab, grasp, grip, pluck, pull, rescue, seize, take, win, wrench, wrest 2. *n.* bit, fragment, part, piece, smattering, snippet, spell

sneak *v.* 1. cower, lurk, pad, sidle, skulk, slink, slip, smuggle, spirit, steal 2. *Inf.* inform on, tell tales ~*n.* 3. informer, telltale

sneaking 1. hidden, private, secret, unconfessed, unexpressed, unvoiced 2. nagging, persistent, uncomfortable, worrying

sneer 1. *v.* deride, disdain, gibe, jeer, laugh, mock, ridicule, scoff, scorn, sniff at, snigger 2. *n.* derision, disdain, gibe, jeer, mockery, ridicule, scorn, snigger

sniff *v.* breathe, inhale, smell, snuff, snuffle

snigger giggle, laugh, sneer, titter

snip *v.* 1. clip, crop, cut, nick, notch, shave, trim ~*n.* 2. bit, clipping, fragment, piece, scrap, shred 3. *Inf.* bargain, giveaway

snobbery airs, condescension, pretension, pride

snobbish arrogant, condescending, patronizing, pretentious, superior

DICTIONARY

snook *n.* —**cock a snook at** show contempt for.

snooker *n.* game played on a billiard table. —*v.* leave (a snooker opponent) in a position such that another ball blocks the target ball; *Informal* put (someone) in a position where he or she can do nothing.

snoop *Informal* —*v.* pry. —*n.* snooping. —**snooper** *n.*

snooty *adj.* **snootier, snootiest.** *Informal* haughty.

snooze *Informal* —*v.* take a brief light sleep. —*n.* brief light sleep.

snore *v.* make snorting sounds while sleeping. —*n.* sound of snoring.

snorkel *n.* tube allowing a swimmer to breathe while face down on the surface of the water. —*v.* **-kelling, -kelled.** swim using a snorkel.

snort *v.* exhale noisily through the nostrils; express contempt or anger by snorting. —*n.* act or sound of snorting.

snot *n. Taboo* mucus from the nose.

snout *n.* animal's projecting nose and jaws.

snow *n.* frozen vapour falling from the sky in flakes; *Slang* cocaine. —*v.* fall as or like snow. —**be snowed under** be overwhelmed, esp. with paperwork. —**snowy** *adj.* —**snowball** *n.* snow pressed into a ball for throwing. —*v.* increase rapidly. —**snowdrift** *n.* bank of deep snow. —**snowdrop** *n.* small white bell-shaped spring flower. —**snowflake** *n.* single crystal of snow. —**snow line** (on a mountain) height above which there is permanent snow. —**snowman** *n.* figure shaped out of snow. —**snowplough** *n.* vehicle for clearing away snow. —**snowshoes** *pl. n.* racket-shaped shoes for travelling on snow.

snub *v.* **snubbing, snubbed.** insult deliberately. —*n.* deliberate insult. —*adj.* (of a nose) short and blunt. —**snub-nosed** *adj.*

snuff¹ *n.* powdered tobacco for sniffing up the nostrils.

snuff² *v.* extinguish (a candle). —**snuff it** *Informal* die.

snuffle *v.* breathe noisily or with difficulty.

snug *adj.* **snugger, snuggest.** warm and comfortable; comfortably close-fitting. —**snugly** *adv.*

snuggle *v.* nestle into a person or thing for warmth or from affection.

so *adv.* to such an extent; in such a manner; very; also; thereupon. —*conj.* in order that; with the result that; therefore. —*interj.* exclamation of surprise, triumph, or realization. —**so-and-so** *n. Informal* person whose name is not specified; unpleasant person or thing. —**so-called** *adj.* called (in the speaker's opinion, wrongly) by that name. —**so long** goodbye. —**so that** in order that.

soak *v.* make wet; put or lie in liquid so as to become thoroughly wet; (of liquid) penetrate. —*n.* soaking; *Slang* drunkard. —**soaking** *n., adj.* —**soak up** *v.* absorb.

soap *n.* compound of alkali and fat, used with water as a cleaning agent; *Informal* soap opera. —*v.* apply soap to. —**soapy** *adj.* —**soap opera** radio or television serial dealing with domestic themes.

soapstone *n.* soft mineral used for making table tops and ornaments.

soar *v.* rise or fly upwards; increase suddenly.

sob *v.* **sobbing, sobbed.** weep with convulsive gasps; utter with sobs. —*n.* act or sound of sobbing. —**sob story** tale of personal distress told to arouse sympathy.

sober *adj.* not drunk; serious; (of colours) plain and dull. —*v.* make or become sober. —**soberly** *adv.* —**sobriety** *n.* state of being sober.

sobriquet [so-brik-ay] *n.* nickname.

soccer *n.* football played by two teams of eleven kicking a spherical ball.

sociable *adj.* friendly or companionable; (of an occasion) providing companionship. —**sociability** *n.* —**sociably** *adv.*

THESAURUS

snooze 1. *v.* catnap, doze, nap 2. *n.* catnap, doze, nap, siesta

snub 1. *v.* cold-shoulder, humble, humiliate, mortify, rebuff, shame, slight 2. *n.* affront, insult

snug comfortable, cosy, homely, intimate, sheltered, warm

soak bathe, damp, drench, immerse, infuse, moisten, penetrate, permeate, saturate, steep, wet

soaking drenched, dripping, saturated, soaked, sodden, sopping, streaming, waterlogged, wringing wet

sob *v.* boohoo, cry, howl, snivel, weep

sober 1. abstemious, abstinent, moderate, temperate 2. calm, cold, composed, cool, dispassionate, grave, lucid, peaceful, practical, rational, realistic, reasonable, sedate, serene, serious, solemn, sound, staid, steady, unexcited, unruffled 3. dark, drab, plain, quiet, severe, sombre, subdued

sociable affable, approachable, companionable, convivial, cordial, familiar, friendly, genial, gregarious, outgoing, social, warm

DICTIONARY

social *adj.* living in a community; of society or its organization; sociable. —*n.* convivial gathering. —**socially** *adv.* —**socialize** *v.* meet others socially. —**socialite** *n.* member of fashionable society. —**social security** state provision for the unemployed, aged, or sick. —**social services** welfare services provided by the local authorities. —**social work** work which involves helping people with serious financial or family problems.

socialism *n.* political system which advocates public ownership of industries, resources, and transport. —**socialist** *n., adj.* —**socialistic** *adj.*

society *n., pl.* **-ties.** human beings considered as a group; organized community; structure and institutions of such a community; organized group with common aims and interests; upperclass or fashionable people collectively; companionship.

sociology *n.* study of human societies. —**sociological** *adj.* —**sociologist** *n.*

sock[1] *n.* cloth covering for the foot.

sock[2] *Slang* —*v.* hit hard. —*n.* hard blow.

socket *n.* hole or recess into which something fits.

sod *n.* (piece of) turf; *Slang* obnoxious person.

soda *n.* compound of sodium; soda water. —**soda water** fizzy drink made from water charged with carbon dioxide.

sodden *adj.* soaked.

sodium *n.* silver-white metallic element. —**sodium bicarbonate** white soluble compound used in baking powder.

sodomy *n.* anal intercourse. —**sodomite** *n.* person who practises sodomy.

sofa *n.* couch.

soft *adj.* not hard, rough, or harsh; (of a breeze or climate) mild; (too) lenient; easily influenced or imposed upon; feeble or silly; not robust; *Informal* easy; (of water) containing few mineral salts; (of drugs) not liable to cause addiction. —**softly** *adv.* —**soften** *v.* make or become soft or softer. —**soft drink** nonalcoholic drink. —**soft furnishings** curtains, rugs, lampshades, and furniture covers. —**soft option** easiest alternative. —**soft-pedal** *v.* deliberately avoid emphasizing something. —**soft-soap** *v. Informal* flatter. —**software** *n.* computer programs. —**softwood** *n.* wood of a coniferous tree.

soggy *adj.* **-gier, -giest.** soaked; moist and heavy. —**sogginess** *n.*

soigné, *fem.* soignée [swah-nyay] *adj.* well-groomed, elegant.

soil[1] *n.* top layer of earth; country or territory.

soil[2] *v.* make or become dirty; disgrace.

soiree [swah-ray] *n.* evening party or gathering.

sojourn [soj-urn] *v.* stay temporarily. —*n.* temporary stay.

solace [sol-iss] *n., v.* comfort in distress.

solar *adj.* of the sun; using the energy of the sun. —**solar plexus** network of nerves at the pit of the stomach; this part of the stomach. —**solar system** the sun and the heavenly bodies that go round it.

solarium *n., pl.* **-laria, -lariums.** place with beds and ultraviolet lights used for acquiring an artificial suntan.

sold *v.* past of SELL.

solder *n.* soft alloy used to join two metal surfaces. —*v.* join with solder. —**soldering iron** tool for melting and applying solder.

soldier *n.* member of an army. —*v.* serve in an

THESAURUS

social 1. *adj.* collective, common, communal, community, general, group, organized, public 2. *n.* gathering, get-together (*Inf.*)

society 1. civilization, culture, mankind, people, the community, the public 2. companionship, company, fellowship, friendship 3. association, circle, club, fellowship, fraternity, group, guild, institute, league, sisterhood, union 4. beau monde, elite, gentry, high society, upper classes

soft 1. cushioned, elastic, gelatinous, pulpy, spongy, squashy, swampy, yielding 2. bendable, elastic, flexible, plastic, pliable, supple 3. downy, feathery, fleecy, flowing, fluid, rounded, silky, smooth, velvety 4. balmy, bland, caressing, delicate, diffuse, dim, dulcet, faint, gentle, light, low, mellow, mild, murmured, muted, pale, pastel, pleasing, qui-

et, restful, shaded, subdued, sweet, temperate, twilight, whispered 5. compassionate, gentle, kind, pitying, sensitive, sentimental, sympathetic, tender 6. effeminate, flabby, flaccid, limp, pampered, podgy, weak

soften abate, allay, appease, calm, cushion, ease, lessen, lighten, lower, melt, mitigate, moderate, mollify, muffle, palliate, quell, relax, soothe, still, subdue, temper

soil[1] *n.* clay, dirt, dust, earth, ground, loam

soil[2] *v.* befoul, begrime, defile, dirty, foul, muddy, pollute, smear, spatter, spot, stain, sully, tarnish

solace 1. *n.* comfort, consolation, relief 2. *v.* allay, alleviate, comfort, console, mitigate, soften, soothe

soldier fighter, man-at-arms, redcoat, serviceman, trooper, warrior

DICTIONARY

army. **—soldierly** *adj.* **—soldier on** *v.* persist doggedly.

sole[1] *adj.* one and only; not shared, exclusive. **—solely** *adv.* only, completely; entirely; alone.

sole[2] *n.* underside of the foot; underside of a shoe. **—***v.* provide (a shoe) with a sole.

sole[3] *n.* small edible flatfish.

solecism [sol-iss-izz-um] *n.* minor grammatical mistake; breach of etiquette.

solemn *adj.* serious, deeply sincere; formal. **—solemnly** *adv.* **—solemnity** *n.* **—solemnize** *v.* celebrate or perform (a ceremony); make solemn. **—solemnization** *n.*

solenoid [sole-in-oid] *n.* coil of wire magnetized by passing a current through it.

sol-fa *n.* system of syllables used as names for the notes of a scale.

solicit *v.* -iting, -ited. request; (of a prostitute) offer (a person) sex for money. **—solicitation** *n.*

solicitor *n.* lawyer who advises clients and prepares documents and cases.

solicitous *adj.* anxious about someone's welfare. **—solicitude** *n.*

solid *adj.* (of a substance) keeping its shape; strong or substantial; not liquid or gas; not hollow; of the same substance throughout; sound or reliable; having three dimensions. **—***n.* three-dimensional shape; solid substance. **—solidly** *adv.* **—solidify** *v.* make or become solid or firm. **—solidity** *n.*

solidarity *n.* agreement in aims or interests, total unity.

soliloquy *n., pl.* -quies. speech made by a person while alone, esp. in a play. **—soliloquize** *v.* utter a soliloquy.

solipsism *n.* doctrine that the self is the only thing known to exist. **—solipsist** *n.*

solitaire *n.* game for one person played with pegs set in a board; gem set by itself.

solitary *adj.* alone, single; (of a place) lonely. **—solitude** *n.* state of being solitary.

solo *n., pl.* -los. music for one performer; any act done without assistance. **—***adj.* done alone. **—***adv.* by oneself, alone. **—soloist** *n.*

solstice *n.* either the shortest (in winter) or longest (in summer) day of the year.

soluble *adj.* able to be dissolved; able to be solved. **—solubility** *n.*

solution *n.* answer to a problem; act of solving a problem; liquid with something dissolved in it; process of dissolving.

solve *v.* find the answer to (a problem). **—solvable** *adj.*

solvent *adj.* able to meet financial obligations. **—***n.* liquid capable of dissolving other substances. **—solvency** *n.* **—solvent abuse** deliberate inhaling of intoxicating fumes from certain solvents.

sombre *adj.* dark, gloomy.

sombrero *n., pl.* -ros. wide-brimmed Mexican hat.

some *adj.* unknown or unspecified; unknown or unspecified quantity or number of; considerable number or amount of; *Informal* remarkable. **—***pron.* certain unknown or unspecified people or things; unknown or unspecified number or quantity. **—somebody** *pron.* some person. **—***n.*

THESAURUS

sole alone, individual, one, single, singular, solitary

solecism blunder, gaffe, gaucherie, impropriety, lapse, mistake

solely alone, completely, entirely, exclusively, merely, only, singly

solemn 1. earnest, glum, grave, portentous, sedate, serious, sober, staid, thoughtful 2. august, ceremonial, dignified, formal, grand, grave, imposing, impressive, momentous, stately

solicit ask, beg, canvass, crave, entreat, implore, importune, petition, pray, seek, supplicate

solicitous anxious, attentive, careful, caring, eager, troubled, uneasy, worried, zealous

solid *adj.* 1. compact, concrete, dense, firm, hard, massed, stable, strong, sturdy, unshakable 2. genuine, good, pure, real, reliable, sound

solidarity accord, camaraderie, cohesion, concordance, harmony, soundness, stability, team spirit, unanimity, unity

solidify cake, coagulate, cohere, congeal, harden, jell, set

solitary 1. desolate, hidden, lonely, remote, retired, secluded, unvisited 2. alone, lone, single, sole

solitude isolation, loneliness, privacy, retirement, seclusion

solution 1. answer, elucidation, explanation, key, resolution, result, solving, unfolding 2. blend, compound, mix, mixture, solvent dissolution, liquefaction, melting

solve answer, clear up, crack, decipher, disentangle, elucidate, explain, expound, interpret, resolve, unfold

sombre dark, dim, dismal, doleful, drab, dull, dusky, gloomy, grave, joyless, mournful, obscure, sad, sepulchral, shadowy, shady, sober

DICTIONARY

important person. —**somehow** adv. in some unspecified way. —**someone** pron. somebody. —**something** pron. unknown or unspecified thing or amount; impressive or important thing. —**sometime** adv. at some unspecified time. —adj. former. —**sometimes** adv. from time to time, now and then. —**somewhat** adv. to some extent, rather. —**somewhere** adv. in, to, or at some unspecified or unknown place.

somersault n. leap or roll in which the trunk and legs are turned over the head. —v. perform a somersault.

somnambulist n. person who walks in his or her sleep. —**somnambulism** n.

somnolent adj. drowsy. —**somnolence** n.

son n. male offspring. —**son-in-law** n., pl. **sons-in-law.** daughter's husband.

sonar n. device for detecting underwater objects by the reflection of sound waves.

sonata n. piece of music in several movements for one instrument with or without piano. —**sonatina** n. short sonata.

son et lumière [sawn eh **loo**-mee-er] n. French night-time entertainment with lighting and sound effects, telling the story of the place where it is staged.

song n. music for the voice; tuneful sound made by certain birds; singing. —**for a song** very cheaply. —**songster, songstress** n. singer. —**songbird** n. any bird with a musical call.

sonic adj. of or producing sound. —**sonic boom** loud bang caused by an aircraft flying faster than sound.

sonnet n. fourteen-line poem with a fixed rhyme scheme.

sonorous adj. (of sound) deep or resonant. —**sonorously** adv. —**sonority** n.

soon adv. in a short time. —**sooner** adv. rather, e.g. I'd sooner go alone. —**sooner or later** eventually.

soot n. black powder formed by the incomplete burning of an organic substance. —**sooty** adj.

soothe v. make calm; relieve (pain etc.).

soothsayer n. seer or prophet.

sop n. concession to pacify someone. —v. **sopping, sopped.** mop up or absorb (liquid). —**sopping** adj. completely soaked. —**soppy** adj. Informal oversentimental.

sophist n. person who uses clever but invalid arguments. —**sophism, sophistry** n. clever but invalid argument.

sophisticate v. make less natural or innocent; make more complex or refined. —n. sophisticated person. —**sophisticated** adj. having or appealing to refined or cultured tastes and habits; complex and refined. —**sophistication** n.

sophomore n. US student in second year at college.

soporific adj. causing sleep. —n. drug that causes sleep.

soprano n., pl. **-pranos.** (singer with) the highest female or boy's voice; highest pitched of a family of instruments.

sorbet n. flavoured water ice.

sorcerer n. magician. —**sorceress** n. fem. —**sorcery** n. witchcraft or magic.

sordid adj. dirty, squalid; base, vile; selfish and grasping. —**sordidly** adv. —**sordidness** n.

sore adj. painful; causing annoyance; resentful; (of need) urgent. —adv. Obs. greatly. —n. painful

THESAURUS

somebody n. celebrity, dignitary, household name, luminary, name, notable, personage, star, superstar

sometimes at times, occasionally

somnolent dozy, drowsy, half-awake, sleepy, soporific, torpid

song air, anthem, ballad, carol, chant, chorus, ditty, hymn, lay, lyric, melody, number, psalm, shanty, strain, tune

soon before long, in the near future, shortly

soothe allay, alleviate, appease, assuage, calm, compose, ease, hush, lull, mitigate, mollify, pacify, quiet, relieve, settle, soften, still, tranquillize

sophisticated 1. cosmopolitan, cultivated, cultured, refined, seasoned, urbane, worldly 2. advanced, complex, complicated, delicate, elaborate, intricate, refined, subtle

soporific 1. adj. sedative, sleepy, somnolent, tranquillizing 2. n. anaesthetic, hypnotic, opiate, tranquillizer

sorcerer enchanter, magician, sorceress, warlock, witch, wizard

sordid 1. dirty, filthy, foul, mean, seedy, slovenly, squalid, unclean, wretched 2. base, debauched, degenerate, low, shabby, shameful, vicious, vile 3. avaricious, corrupt, covetous, grasping, miserly, niggardly, selfish, venal

sore 1. angry, burning, inflamed, irritated, painful, raw, sensitive, smarting, tender 2. annoying, severe, sharp, troublesome 3. acute, critical, desperate, dire, extreme, pressing, urgent 4. afflicted, angry, hurt, irked, irritated, pained, resentful, stung, upset, vexed

DICTIONARY

area on the body. **—sorely** *adv.* greatly; grievously. **—soreness** *n.*

sorghum *n.* kind of grass cultivated for grain.

sorrel *n.* bitter-tasting plant; reddish-brown colour; horse of this colour.

sorrow *n.* grief or sadness; cause of sorrow. *—v.* grieve. **—sorrowful** *adj.* **—sorrowfully** *adv.*

sorry *adj.* **-rier, -riest.** feeling pity or regret; pitiful or wretched.

sort *n.* group all sharing certain qualities or characteristics; *Informal* type of character. *—v.* arrange according to kind; mend or fix. **—out of sorts** slightly unwell or bad-tempered.

sortie *n.* sally by besieged forces; operational flight made by military aircraft.

SOS *n.* international code signal of distress; call for help.

so-so *adj. Informal* mediocre.

sot *n.* habitual drunkard.

sotto voce [sot-toe **voe**-chay] *adv.* in an undertone.

soubriquet [so-brik-ay] *n.* same as SOBRIQUET.

soufflé [soo-flay] *n.* light fluffy dish made with beaten egg whites and other ingredients.

sough [rhymes with **now**] *v.* (of the wind) make a sighing sound.

sought [sawt] *v.* past of SEEK.

souk [sook] *n.* open-air marketplace in Muslim countries.

soul *n.* spiritual and immortal part of a human being; essential part or fundamental nature; deep and sincere feelings; person regarded as typifying some quality; person; (also **soul music**) type of Black music combining blues, pop, and gospel. **—soulful** *adj.* full of emotion. **—soulless** *adj.* lacking human qualities, mechanical; (of a person) lacking sensitivity.

sound¹ *n.* something heard, noise. *—v.* make or cause to make a sound; seem to be as specified; pronounce. **—sound barrier** *Informal* sudden increase in air resistance against an object as it approaches the speed of sound. **—soundproof** *adj.* not penetrable by sound. *—v.* make soundproof. **—sound track** recorded sound accompaniment to a film.

sound² *adj.* in good condition; firm, substantial; showing good judgment; ethically correct; financially reliable; thorough; (of sleep) deep. **—soundly** *adv.*

sound³ *v.* find the depth of (water etc.); ascertain the views of; examine with a probe. **—soundings** *pl. n.* measurements of depth taken by sounding. **—sounding board** person or group used to test a new idea.

sound⁴ *n.* channel or strait.

soup *n.* liquid food made from meat, vegetables, etc. **—soupy** *adj.* **—soup kitchen** place where food and drink is served to needy people. **—soup up** *v.* modify (an engine) to increase its power.

soupçon [soop-sonn] *n.* small amount.

sour *adj.* sharp-tasting; (of milk) gone bad; (of a person's temperament) sullen. *—v.* make or become sour. **—sourly** *adv.* **—sourness** *n.* **—sourpuss** *n. Informal* sullen person.

THESAURUS

sorrow 1. *n.* anguish, distress, grief, heartache, misery, mourning, regret, sadness, unhappiness, woe 2. *v.* agonize, bemoan, bewail, grieve, lament, moan, mourn, weep

sorrowful dejected, depressed, distressing, grievous, lamentable, lugubrious, melancholy, miserable, mournful, painful, piteous, rueful, sad, sorry, tearful, unhappy, woebegone, woeful, wretched

sorry 1. contrite, penitent, regretful, remorseful, repentant, shamefaced 2. moved, pitying, sympathetic 3. abject, base, deplorable, dismal, distressing, mean, miserable, paltry, pathetic, piteous, pitiable, pitiful, poor, sad, shabby, vile, wretched

sort 1. *n.* brand, breed, category, character, class, denomination, description, family, genus, group, ilk, kind, make, nature, order, quality, race, species, stamp, style, type, variety 2. *v.* arrange, assort, catalogue, categorize, choose, class, classify, divide, file, grade, group, order, rank, select, separate, systematize

soul 1. essence, intellect, life, mind, psyche, reason, spirit 2. being, body, creature, individual, man, mortal, person, woman 3. essence, personification, quintessence, type

sound¹ *n.* 1. din, noise, report, reverberation, tone, voice *~v.* 2. echo, resound, reverberate 3. appear, look, seem 4. announce, articulate, declare, enunciate, express, pronounce, signal, utter

sound² *adj.* 1. complete, entire, firm, fit, hale, healthy, intact, perfect, robust, solid, sturdy, substantial, unhurt, uninjured, vigorous, whole 2. correct, fair, just, logical, orthodox, proper, prudent, rational, reasonable, reliable, responsible, right, sensible, true, trustworthy, valid, well-founded, wise 3. established, orthodox, proven, recognized, reliable, reputable, safe, secure, solid, solvent, stable, tried-and-true

sound³ *v.* fathom, plumb, probe

sour 1. acetic, acid, bitter, pungent, sharp, tart 2. acrid, churlish, crabbed, cynical, disagree-

DICTIONARY

source *n.* origin or starting point; spring where a river or stream begins; person, book, etc. providing information.

souse *v.* plunge (something) into liquid; drench; pickle.

soutane [soo-**tan**] *n.* Roman Catholic priest's cassock.

south *n.* direction towards the South Pole, opposite north; area lying in or towards the south. —*adj.* to or in the south; (of a wind) from the south. —*adv.* in, to, or towards the south. —**southerly** *adj.* —**southern** *adj.* —**southerner** *n.* person from the south of a country or area. —**southward** *adj., adv.* —**southwards** *adv.* —**southpaw** *n. Informal* left-handed person, esp. a boxer.

souvenir *n.* keepsake, memento.

sou'wester *n.* seaman's waterproof hat covering the head and back of the neck.

sovereign *n.* king or queen; former British gold coin worth one pound. —*adj.* supreme in rank or authority; excellent; (of a state) independent. —**sovereignty** *n.*

soviet *n.* elected council at various levels of government in the USSR. —*adj.* of the USSR.

sow¹ *v.* **sowing, sowed, sown** *or* **sowed.** scatter or plant (seed) in or on (the ground); implant or introduce.

sow² *n.* female adult pig.

soya *n.* plant whose edible bean (**soya bean**) is used for food and as a source of oil. —**soy(a) sauce** sauce made from fermented soya beans, used in Chinese cookery.

sozzled *adj. Slang* drunk.

spa *n.* resort with a mineral-water spring.

space *n.* unlimited expanse in which all objects exist and move; interval; blank portion; unoccupied area; the universe beyond the earth's atmosphere. —*v.* place at intervals. —**spacious** *adj.* having a large capacity or area. —**spacecraft, spaceship** *n.* vehicle for travel beyond the earth's atmosphere. —**space shuttle** manned reusable vehicle for repeated space flights. —**spacesuit** *n.* sealed pressurized suit worn by an astronaut.

spade¹ *n.* tool for digging. —**spadework** *n.* hard preparatory work.

spade² *n.* playing card of the suit marked with black leaf-shaped symbols.

spaghetti *n.* pasta in the form of long strings.

span *n.* space between two points; complete extent; distance from thumb to little finger of the expanded hand. —*v.* **spanning, spanned.** stretch or extend across.

spangle *n.* small shiny metallic ornament. —*v.* decorate with spangles.

spaniel *n.* dog with long ears and silky hair.

spank *v.* slap with the open hand, esp. on the buttocks. —*n.* such a slap. —**spanking** *n.* series of spanks. —*adj. Informal* quick; outstandingly fine or smart.

spanner *n.* tool for gripping and turning a nut or bolt.

spar¹ *n.* pole used as a ship's mast, boom, or yard.

spar² *v.* **sparring, sparred.** box using light blows for practice; argue (with someone).

spare *v.* refrain from punishing or harming; protect (someone) from (something unpleasant); afford to give. —*adj.* extra; in reserve; (of a person) thin. —*n.* duplicate kept in case of damage or loss. —**to spare** in addition to what is needed. —**sparing** *adj.* economical. —**spare ribs** pork ribs with most of the meat trimmed off.

THESAURUS

able, discontented, embittered, grudging, ill-natured, jaundiced, peevish, tart, ungenerous, waspish

source 1. author, begetter, beginning, cause, derivation, origin, rise, spring, wellspring 2. authority, informant

souse drench, dunk, immerse, marinate (*Cookery*), pickle, soak, steep

souvenir keepsake, memento, relic, reminder

sovereign *n.* 1. chief, emperor, empress, king, monarch, potentate, prince, queen, ruler, shah, tsar ~*adj.* 2. absolute, chief, dominant, imperial, kingly, predominant, principal, regal, royal, ruling, supreme 3. effectual, efficacious, efficient, excellent

sow broadcast, disseminate, implant, lodge, plant, scatter, seed

space 1. capacity, expanse, extent, leeway, margin, play, room, scope, volume 2. blank, distance, gap, interval, omission 3. duration, interval, period, span, time, while

spacious ample, broad, comfortable, commodious, expansive, extensive, huge, large, roomy, sizable, vast

span 1. *n.* amount, distance, extent, length, reach, spread, stretch 2. *v.* bridge, cover, cross, link, traverse, vault

spank *v.* cuff, slap, smack

spar *v.* argue, bicker, dispute, skirmish, squabble, wrangle, wrestle

spare *adj.* 1. additional, emergency, extra, free, leftover, odd, over, superfluous, surplus, unoccupied, unused, unwanted 2. gaunt, lank, lean, meagre, slender, slight, slim, wiry ~*v.* 3.

DICTIONARY

spark n. fiery particle thrown out from a fire or caused by friction; flash of light produced by an electrical discharge; trace or hint (of a particular quality). —v. give off sparks; initiate. —**spark plug, sparking plug** device in an engine that ignites the fuel by producing an electric spark.

sparkle v. glitter with many points of light; be vivacious or witty. —n. sparkling points of light; vivacity or wit. —**sparkler** n. hand-held firework that emits sparks. —**sparkling** adj. (of wine or mineral water) slightly fizzy.

sparrow n. small brownish bird. —**sparrowhawk** n. small hawk.

sparse adj. thinly scattered. —**sparsely** adv. —**sparseness** n.

spartan adj. strict and austere.

spasm n. involuntary muscular contraction; sudden burst of activity or feeling. —**spasmodic** adj. occurring in spasms. —**spasmodically** adv.

spastic n. person with cerebral palsy. —adj. suffering from cerebral palsy; affected by spasms.

spat[1] v. past of SPIT[1].

spat[2] n. slight quarrel.

spat[3] n. old-fashioned short gaiter.

spate n. sudden outpouring or flood.

spathe n. large sheathlike leaf enclosing a flower cluster.

spatial adj. of or in space.

spatter v. scatter or be scattered in drops over (something). —n. spattering sound; something spattered.

spatula n. utensil with a broad flat blade for spreading or stirring.

spawn n. jelly-like mass of eggs of fish, frogs, or molluscs. —v. (of fish, frogs, or molluscs) lay eggs; generate.

spay v. remove the ovaries from (a female animal).

speak v. **speaking, spoke, spoken.** say words, talk; communicate or express in words; give a speech or lecture; know how to talk in (a specified language). —**speaker** n. person who speaks, esp. at a formal occasion; loudspeaker; (**S-**) official chairman of a body.

spear n. weapon consisting of a long shaft with a sharp point; slender shoot. —v. pierce with or as if with a spear. —**spearhead** n. leading force in an attack or campaign. —v. lead (an attack or campaign).

spearmint n. type of mint.

spec n. —**on spec** Informal as a risk or gamble.

special adj. distinguished from others of its kind; for a specific purpose; exceptional; particular. —**specially** adv. —**specialist** n. expert in a particular activity or subject. —**speciality** n. special interest or skill; product specialized in. —**specialize** v. be a specialist. —**specialization** n.

specie n. coins as distinct from paper money.

species n., pl. **-cies.** group of plants or animals that are related closely enough to interbreed naturally.

specific adj. particular, definite. —n. drug used to treat a particular disease. —pl. particular details. —**specifically** adv. —**specification** n. detailed description of something to be made or done. —**specify** v. refer to or state specifically. —**specific gravity** ratio of the density of a substance to that of water.

specimen n. individual or part typifying a whole.

THESAURUS

afford, allow, bestow, dispense with, give, grant, part with, relinquish 4. be merciful to, have mercy on, leave, pardon, refrain from, release, relieve from, save from

sparing careful, chary, economical, frugal, prudent, saving, thrifty

spark 1. flare, flash, flicker, gleam, glint, spit 2. atom, hint, jot, scrap, trace, vestige

sparkle v. 1. beam, dance, flash, gleam, glint, glisten, glitter, glow, shimmer, shine, spark, twinkle, wink ~n. 2. brilliance, dazzle, flash, flicker, gleam, glint, radiance, spark, twinkle 3. dash, élan, gaiety, life, spirit, vitality

spartan abstemious, ascetic, austere, bleak, disciplined, extreme, frugal, plain, rigorous, severe, stern, strict

spasm 1. contraction, convulsion, paroxysm, twitch 2. access, burst, eruption, fit, frenzy, outburst, seizure

speak 1. articulate, converse, discourse, express, pronounce, say, state, talk, tell, utter, voice 2. address, argue, declaim, descant, discourse, harangue, lecture, plead, speechify

speaker lecturer, orator, public speaker, spokesman

special 1. distinguished, especial, exceptional, extraordinary, festive, gala, important, memorable, significant, uncommon, unique, unusual 2. appropriate, certain, distinctive, individual, particular, peculiar, precise 3. chief, main, major, particular, primary

species breed, category, class, description, group, kind, sort, type, variety

specific definite, exact, explicit, express, limited, particular, precise, unequivocal

DICTIONARY

specious [spee-shuss] *adj.* apparently true, but actually false.

speck *n.* small spot or particle. —**speckle** *n.* small spot. —*v.* mark with speckles.

specs *pl. n. Informal* short for SPECTACLES.

spectacle *n.* strange, interesting, or ridiculous sight; impressive public show. —*pl.* pair of glasses for correcting faulty vision. —**spectacular** *adj.* impressive. —*n.* spectacular public show. —**spectacularly** *adv.*

spectate *v.* watch. —**spectator** *n.* person viewing anything, onlooker.

spectre *n.* ghost; menacing mental image. —**spectral** *adj.*

spectrum *n., pl.* **-tra.** range of different colours, radio waves, etc. in order of their wavelengths; entire range of anything. —**spectroscope** *n.* instrument for producing or examining spectra.

speculate *v.* guess, conjecture; buy property, shares, etc. in the hope of selling them at a profit. —**speculation** *n.* —**speculative** *adj.* —**speculator** *n.*

speculum *n., pl.* **-la, -lums.** medical instrument for examining body cavities.

sped *v.* a past of SPEED.

speech *n.* act, power, or manner of speaking; talk given to an audience; language or dialect. —**speechify** *v.* make speeches, esp. boringly. —**speechless** *adj.* unable to speak because of great emotion.

speed *n.* swiftness; rate at which something moves or acts; *Slang* amphetamine. —*v.* **speeding, sped** or **speeded.** go quickly; drive faster than the legal limit. —**speedy** *adj.* rapid; prompt.

—**speedily** *adv.* —**speedboat** *n.* light fast motorboat. —**speedometer** *n.* instrument to show the speed of a vehicle. —**speed up** *v.* accelerate. —**speedway** *n.* track for motorcycle racing. —**speedwell** *n.* plant with small blue flowers.

speleology *n.* study and exploration of caves. —**speleological** *adj.* —**speleologist** *n.*

spell[1] *v.* **spelling, spelt** or **spelled.** give in correct order the letters that form (a word); (of letters) make up (a word); indicate. —**spelling** *n.* way a word is spelt; person's ability to spell. —**spell out** *v.* make explicit.

spell[2] *n.* formula of words supposed to have magic power; effect of a spell; fascination. —**spellbound** *adj.* entranced.

spell[3] *n.* period of time of weather or activity.

spelt *v.* a past of SPELL[1].

spend *v.* **spending, spent.** pay out (money); use or pass (time); use up completely. —**spendthrift** *n.* person who spends money wastefully.

sperm *n.* male reproductive cell; semen. —**spermicide** *n.* substance that kills sperm. —**sperm whale** large toothed whale.

spermaceti [sper-ma-**set**-ee] *n.* waxy solid obtained from the sperm whale.

spermatozoon [sper-ma-toe-**zoe**-on] *n., pl.* **-zoa.** sperm.

spew *v.* vomit; send out in a stream.

sphagnum *n.* moss found in bogs.

sphere *n.* perfectly round solid object; field of activity. —**spherical** *adj.*

THESAURUS

specify cite, define, designate, detail, enumerate, indicate, mention, name, particularize

specimen copy, example, exemplification, exhibit, individual, instance, model, pattern, proof, sample, type

spectacle 1. display, event, pageant, parade, performance, show, sight 2. curiosity, laughing stock, marvel, scene, sight, wonder

spectacular daring, dazzling, dramatic, grand, impressive, magnificent, marked, remarkable, splendid, staggering, striking

spectator beholder, bystander, eyewitness, looker-on, observer, onlooker, viewer, watcher, witness

speculate 1. conjecture, consider, meditate, muse, scheme, suppose, surmise, theorize, wonder 2. gamble, hazard, risk

speech 1. communication, conversation, dialogue, discussion, intercourse, talk 2. address, discourse, harangue, homily, lecture, oration

speechless dumb, inarticulate, mum, mute, silent, wordless

speed 1. *n.* celerity, expedition, fleetness, haste, hurry, pace, quickness, rapidity, rush, swiftness, velocity 2. *v.* career, dispatch, expedite, flash, gallop, hasten, hurry, quicken, race, rush, sprint, tear, urge, zoom

speedy expeditious, express, fast, fleet, hasty, headlong, hurried, immediate, nimble, precipitate, prompt, quick, rapid, summary, swift, winged

spell[1] *n.* charm, incantation, sorcery, witchery

spell[2] *n.* bout, course, interval, period, season, stint, stretch, term, time, turn

spelling orthography

spell out clarify, elucidate, specify

spend 1. disburse, expend 2. consume, deplete, dispense, drain, empty, exhaust, run through, squander, use up, waste 3. fill, occupy, pass, while away

DICTIONARY

sphincter *n.* ring of muscle which controls the opening and closing of a hollow organ.

Sphinx *n.* statue in Egypt with a lion's body and human head; (**s-**) enigmatic person.

spice *n.* aromatic substance used as flavouring; something that adds zest or interest. —*v.* flavour with spices. —**spicy** *adj.* flavoured with spices; *Informal* slightly scandalous.

spick-and-span *adj.* neat and clean.

spider *n.* small eight-legged creature which spins a web to catch insects for food. —**spidery** *adj.*

spiel *n.* glib plausible talk.

spigot *n.* stopper for, or tap fitted to, a cask.

spike *n.* sharp point; sharp pointed metal object. —*v.* put spikes on; pierce or fasten with a spike; add alcohol to (a drink). —**spike someone's guns** thwart someone. —**spiky** *adj.*

spill[1] *v.* **spilling, spilt** *or* **spilled.** pour from or as if from a container. —*n.* fall; amount spilt. —**spill the beans** *Informal* give away a secret. —**spillage** *n.*

spill[2] *n.* thin strip of wood or paper for lighting pipes or fires.

spin *v.* **spinning, spun.** revolve or cause to revolve rapidly; draw out and twist (fibres) into thread. —*n.* revolving motion; continuous spiral descent of an aircraft; *Informal* short drive for pleasure. —**spin a yarn** tell an improbable story. —**spinner** *n.* —**spin-dry** *v.* dry (clothes) in a spin-dryer. —**spin-dryer** *n.* machine in which washed clothes are spun in a perforated drum to remove excess water. —**spin-off** *n.* incidental benefit. —**spin out** *v.* prolong.

spina bifida *n.* condition in which part of the spinal cord protrudes through a gap in the backbone, often causing paralysis.

spinach *n.* dark green leafy vegetable.

spindle *n.* rotating rod that acts as an axle; weighted rod rotated for spinning thread by hand. —**spindly** *adj.* long, slender, and frail.

spindrift *n.* spray blown along the surface of the sea.

spine *n.* backbone; sharp point on an animal or plant; edge of a book, record sleeve, etc. on which the title is printed. —**spinal** *adj.* of the spine. —**spineless** *adj.* lacking courage. —**spiny** *adj.* covered with spines.

spinet *n.* small harpsichord.

spinnaker *n.* large sail on a racing yacht.

spinney *n.* small wood.

spinster *n.* unmarried woman.

spiral *n.* continuous curve formed by a point winding about a central axis at an ever-increasing distance from it; steadily accelerating increase or decrease. —*v.* **-ralling, -ralled.** move in a spiral; increase or decrease with steady acceleration. —*adj.* having the form of a spiral.

spire *n.* pointed part of a steeple.

spirit *n.* force giving life to a body; temperament or disposition; liveliness; courage; prevailing feeling; essential meaning as opposed to literal interpretation; ghost. —*pl.* emotional state; strong alcoholic drink. —*v.* **-iting, -ited.** carry away mysteriously. —**spirited** *adj.* lively. —**spirituous** *adj.* alcoholic. —**spirit level** glass tube containing a bubble in liquid, used to check whether a surface is level.

spiritual *adj.* relating to the spirit; relating to sacred things. —*n.* type of religious folk song originating among Black slaves in America. —**spiritually** *adv.* —**spirituality** *n.* —**spiritualism** *n.* belief that the spirits of the dead can communicate with the living. —**spiritualist** *n.*

THESAURUS

spent consumed, expended, finished, gone, used up

sphere 1. ball, circle, globe, orb 2. capacity, compass, domain, field, function, pale, province, range, rank, realm, scope, station, territory

spherical globe-shaped, rotund, round

spice 1. relish, savour, seasoning 2. colour, excitement, gusto, pep, piquancy, tang, zest

spike 1. *n.* barb, point, prong, spine 2. *v.* impale, spear, spit, stick

spill discharge, disgorge, overflow, overturn, scatter, shed, slop over, spill *or* run over, throw off, upset

spin 1. *v.* pirouette, reel, revolve, rotate, turn,

twirl, twist, wheel, whirl 2. *n.* gyration, revolution, roll, twist, whirl

spin out amplify, delay, drag out, draw out, extend, lengthen, prolong

spiral *adj.* circular, coiled, corkscrew, scrolled, winding

spirit *n.* 1. air, breath, life, soul, vital spark 2. attitude, character, complexion, disposition, essence, humour, outlook, quality, temper, temperament 3. ardour, backbone, courage, energy, enterprise, enthusiasm, fire, force, grit, life, liveliness, mettle, resolution, sparkle, vigour, warmth, zest 4. atmosphere, feeling, gist, humour, tenor, tone 5. essence, intent, intention, meaning, purport, purpose, sense, substance 6. *Plural* feelings, humour, mood, morale 7. apparition, ghost, phantom,

DICTIONARY

spit[1] *v.* **spitting, spat.** eject (saliva or food) from the mouth; throw out particles explosively; rain slightly; utter (words) in a violent manner. —*n.* saliva. —**spitting image** *Informal* person who looks very like another. —**spittle** *n.* fluid produced in the mouth, saliva. —**spittoon** *n.* bowl to spit into.

spit[2] *n.* sharp rod on which meat is skewered for roasting; long strip of land projecting into the sea.

spite *n.* deliberate nastiness. —*v.* annoy or hurt from spite. —**in spite of** in defiance of. —**spiteful** *adj.* —**spitefully** *adv.*

spitfire *n.* person with a fiery temper.

spiv *n. Slang* smartly dressed man who makes a living by shady dealings.

splash *v.* scatter (liquid) or (of liquid) be scattered in drops; scatter liquid on (something); print (a story or photograph) prominently in a newspaper. —*n.* splashing sound; patch (of colour or light); extravagant display; small amount of liquid added to a drink. —**splash out** *v. Informal* spend extravagantly.

splatter *v., n.* splash.

splay *v.* spread out; slant outwards. —*adj.* splayed.

spleen *n.* abdominal organ which filters bacteria from the blood; bad temper. —**splenetic** *adj.* spiteful or irritable.

splendid *adj.* excellent; brilliant in appearance. —**splendidly** *adv.* —**splendour** *n.*

splice *v.* join by interweaving or overlapping ends. —**get spliced** *Slang* get married.

splint *n.* rigid support for a broken bone.

splinter *n.* thin sharp piece broken off, esp. from wood. —*v.* break into fragments. —**splinter group** group that has broken away from an organization.

split *v.* **splitting, split.** break into separate pieces; separate; share. —*n.* crack or division caused by splitting. —*pl.* act of sitting with the legs outstretched in opposite directions. —**split second** very short period of time.

splotch, splodge *n., v.* splash, daub.

splurge *v.* spend money extravagantly. —*n.* bout of extravagance.

splutter *v.* make hissing spitting sounds; utter with spitting sounds. —*n.* spluttering.

spoil *v.* **spoiling, spoilt** or **spoiled.** damage; harm the character of (a child) by giving it all it wants; rot, go bad. —**spoils** *pl. n.* booty. —**spoiling for** eager for. —**spoilsport** *n.* person who spoils the enjoyment of others.

spoke[1] *v.* past tense of SPEAK.

spoke[2] *n.* bar joining the hub of a wheel to the rim.

spoken *v.* past participle of SPEAK.

spokesman, spokeswoman, spokes-

THESAURUS

spectre, sprite, vision ~*v.* 8. abduct, abstract, carry, convey, purloin, remove, seize, steal, whisk

spiritual devotional, divine, ghostly, holy, pure, religious, sacred

spit 1. *v.* eject, expectorate, hiss, splutter, throw out 2. *n.* dribble, drool, saliva, slaver, spittle

spite 1. animosity, gall, grudge, hate, hatred, malice, pique, rancour, spitefulness, spleen, venom 2. **in spite of** despite, notwithstanding, regardless of

spiteful barbed, cruel, ill-natured, malevolent, malicious, venomous, vindictive

splash *v.* 1. shower, slop, spatter, spray, spread, sprinkle, squirt, strew, wet 2. broadcast, flaunt, headline, plaster, publicize, tout, trumpet ~*n.* 3. burst, dash, patch, spattering, splodge, touch 4. *Inf.* display, effect, impact, sensation, splurge, stir

splendid 1. excellent, fine, glorious, great (*Inf.*), marvellous, wonderful 2. beaming, bright, brilliant, glittering, glowing, lustrous, radiant, refulgent

splendour brightness, brilliance, dazzle, display, glory, grandeur, lustre, magnificence,

majesty, pomp, radiance, renown, resplendence, richness, show, solemnity, spectacle, sumptuousness

splinter 1. *n.* chip, flake, fragment, needle, shaving 2. *v.* disintegrate, fracture, shatter, shiver, split

split *v.* 1. branch, break, burst, cleave, crack, disband, disunite, diverge, fork, gape, open, part, rend, rip, separate, slash, slit, snap, splinter 2. allocate, allot, apportion, distribute, divide, halve, parcel out, partition, share out, slice up ~*n.* 3. breach, crack, damage, division, fissure, gap, rent, rip, slash, slit, tear 4. breach, break, break-up, difference, discord, dissension, disunion, division, estrangement, partition, rift, rupture, schism

spoil 1. blemish, damage, deface, destroy, disfigure, harm, impair, injure, mar, mess up, ruin, upset, wreck 2. coddle, cosset, indulge, mollycoddle, overindulge, pamper 3. addle, curdle, decay, go bad, mildew, putrefy, rot, turn

spoken expressed, oral, phonetic, put into words, said, told, unwritten, uttered, verbal, viva voce, voiced

DICTIONARY

person *n.* person chosen to speak on behalf of a group.

spoliation *n.* plundering.

sponge *n.* sea animal with a porous absorbent skeleton; skeleton of a sponge, or a substance like it, used for cleaning; type of light cake. —*v.* wipe with a sponge; live at the expense of others. —**sponger** *n. Slang* person who sponges on others. —**spongy** *adj.*

sponsor *n.* person who promotes something; person who agrees to give money to a charity on completion of a specified activity by another; godparent. —*v.* act as a sponsor for. —**sponsorship** *n.*

spontaneous *adj.* voluntary and unpremeditated; occurring through natural processes without outside influence. —**spontaneously** *adv.* —**spontaneity** *n.*

spoof *n.* mildly satirical parody.

spook *n. Informal* ghost. —**spooky** *adj.*

spool *n.* cylinder round which something can be wound.

spoon *n.* shallow bowl attached to a handle for eating, stirring, or serving food. —*v.* lift with a spoon. —**spoonful** *n.* —**spoon-feed** *v.* feed with a spoon; give (someone) too much help.

spoonerism *n.* accidental changing over of the initial sounds of a pair of words, such as *half-warmed fish* for *half-formed wish.*

spoor *n.* trail of an animal.

sporadic *adj.* intermittent, scattered. —**sporadically** *adv.*

spore *n.* minute reproductive body of some plants.

sporran *n.* pouch worn in front of a kilt.

sport *n.* activity for pleasure, competition, or exercise; such activities collectively; enjoyment; playful joking; person who reacts cheerfully. —*v.* wear proudly. —**sporting** *adj.* of sport; having a

sportsmanlike attitude. —**sporting chance** reasonable chance of success. —**sporty** *adj.* —**sportive** *adj.* playful. —**sports car** fast low-built car, usu. open-topped. —**sports jacket** man's casual jacket. —**sportsman, sportswoman** *n.* person who plays sports; person who plays fair and is good-humoured when losing. —**sportsmanlike** *adj.* —**sportsmanship** *n.*

spot *n.* small mark on a surface; pimple; location; *Informal* awkward situation; *Informal* small quantity. —*v.* **spotting, spotted.** notice; watch for and take note of; mark with spots. —**on the spot** at the place in question; immediately; in an awkward predicament. —**spotless** *adj.* absolutely clean. —**spotlessly** *adv.* —**spotty** *adj.* with spots. —**spot check** random examination. —**spotlight** *n.* powerful light illuminating a small area; centre of attention. —**spot-on** *adj. Informal* absolutely accurate.

spouse *n.* husband or wife.

spout *n.* projecting tube or lip for pouring liquids; stream or jet of liquid. —*v.* pour out in a stream or jet; *Slang* utter (a stream of words) lengthily.

sprain *v.* injure (a joint) by a sudden twist. —*n.* such an injury.

sprang *v.* a past tense of SPRING.

sprat *n.* small sea fish.

sprawl *v.* lie or sit with the limbs spread out; spread out in a straggling manner. —*n.* sprawling arrangement.

spray[1] *n.* (device for producing) fine drops of liquid. —*v.* scatter in fine drops; cover with a spray. —**spray gun** device for spraying paint etc.

spray[2] *n.* branch with buds, leaves, flowers, or berries; ornament like this.

THESAURUS

spongy absorbent, cushioned, cushiony, elastic, light, porous, springy

sponsor 1. *n.* backer, godparent, patron, promoter 2. *v.* back, finance, fund, guarantee, patronize, promote, subsidize

spontaneous free, impulsive, instinctive, natural, unforced, unprompted, voluntary, willing

sporadic intermittent, irregular, isolated, occasional, random, scattered, spasmodic

sport *n.* 1. amusement, diversion, exercise, game, pastime, play, recreation 2. badinage, banter, frolic, fun, jest, joking, merriment, mirth, teasing 3. buffoon, butt, derision, game, mockery, plaything, ridicule ~*v.* 4. *Inf.* display, exhibit, wear

spot *n.* 1. blemish, blot, blotch, daub, flaw, mark, pimple, smudge, speck, stain, taint 2. location, place, point, position, scene, site 3. *Inf.* difficulty, mess, plight, predicament, quandary, trouble ~*v.* 4. detect, discern, espy, identify, observe, recognize, see, sight 5. besmirch, blot, dirty, dot, fleck, mark, soil, spatter, speckle, splodge, stain, sully, taint, tarnish

spotted dappled, dotted, flecked, mottled, pied, specked

spouse consort, helpmate, husband, mate, partner, wife

spout *v.* discharge, emit, erupt, gush, jet, shoot, spray, spurt, squirt, stream, surge

DICTIONARY

spread v. **spreading, spread.** open out or be displayed to the fullest extent; extend over a larger expanse; apply as a coating; send or be sent in all directions. —n. spreading; extent; *Informal* ample meal; soft food which can be spread. —**spread-eagled** adj. with arms and legs outstretched.

spree n. session of overindulgence, usu. in drinking or spending money.

sprig n. twig or shoot.

sprightly adj. **-lier, -liest.** lively and brisk. —**sprightliness** n.

spring v. **springing, sprang** or **sprung, sprung.** move suddenly upwards or forwards in a single motion, jump; develop unexpectedly; originate (from); *Informal* arrange the escape of (someone) from prison. —n. season between winter and summer; coil which can be compressed, stretched, or bent and returns to its original shape when released; natural pool forming the source of a stream; jump; elasticity. —**springy** adj. elastic. —**springboard** n. flexible board used to gain height or momentum in diving or gymnastics. —**spring-clean** v. clean (a house) thoroughly. —**spring tide** high tide at new or full moon.

springbok n. S African antelope.

springer n. small spaniel.

sprinkle v. scatter (liquid or powder) in tiny drops or particles over (something). —**sprinkler** n. —**sprinkling** n. small quantity or number.

sprint v. run a short distance at top speed. —n. short race run at top speed; fast run. —**sprinter** n.

sprit n. small spar set diagonally across a sail to extend it. —**spritsail** n. sail extended by a sprit.

sprite n. elf.

sprocket n. wheel with teeth on the rim, that drives or is driven by a chain.

sprout v. put forth shoots; begin to grow or develop. —n. shoot; short for BRUSSELS SPROUT.

spruce[1] n. kind of fir.

spruce[2] adj. neat and smart. —**spruce up** v. make neat and smart.

sprung v. a past tense and the past participle of SPRING.

spry adj. **spryer, spryest** or **sprier, spriest.** active or nimble.

spud n. *Informal* potato.

spume n., v. froth.

spun v. past of SPIN.

spunk n. *Informal* courage, spirit. —**spunky** adj.

spur n. spiked wheel on the heel of a rider's boot used to urge on a horse; stimulus or incentive; projection. —v. **spurring, spurred.** urge on, incite (someone). —**on the spur of the moment** on impulse.

spurge n. plant with milky sap.

spurious adj. not genuine.

spurn v. reject with scorn.

spurt v. gush or cause to gush out in a jet. —n.

THESAURUS

sprawl v. flop, loll, lounge, ramble, slouch, slump, spread, straggle, trail

spray[1] 1. v. diffuse, scatter, shower, sprinkle 2. n. aerosol, atomizer, sprinkler

spray[2] n. bough, branch, corsage, shoot, sprig

spread v. 1. bloat, broaden, dilate, expand, extend, open, sprawl, stretch, swell, unfold, unfurl, unroll, widen 2. multiply, mushroom, proliferate ~n. 3. advance, development, diffusion, dispersion, escalation, expansion, increase, transmission 4. compass, extent, period, reach, span, stretch, sweep, term

spree bacchanalia, bender (*Inf.*), binge (*Inf.*), carouse, debauch, fling, jag (*Sl.*), junketing, orgy, revel

sprightly active, agile, airy, alert, blithe, brisk, cheerful, gay, jaunty, joyous, lively, nimble, perky, playful, spirited, spry

spring v. 1. bounce, bound, hop, jump, leap, rebound, recoil, vault 2. arise, come, derive, descend, emanate, emerge, grow, issue, originate, proceed, start, stem 3. appear, develop, mushroom, shoot up ~n. 4. bound, buck, hop,

jump, leap, vault 5. buoyancy, elasticity, flexibility, recoil, resilience

sprinkle dredge, dust, pepper, powder, scatter, shower, spray, strew

sprout v. bud, develop, grow, push, shoot, spring

spruce dainty, dapper, elegant, neat, smart, trim, well-groomed

spry active, agile, alert, brisk, nimble, quick, ready, sprightly, supple

spur v. 1. animate, drive, goad, impel, incite, press, prick, prod, prompt, stimulate, urge ~n. 2. goad, prick 3. impetus, impulse, incentive, incitement, inducement, motive, stimulus

spurious artificial, bogus, deceitful, fake, false, forged, imitation, mock, pretended, sham, specious, unauthentic

spurn despise, disdain, rebuff, reject, repulse, scorn, slight, snub

spurt v. burst, erupt, gush, jet, shoot, spew, squirt, surge

DICTIONARY

short sudden burst of activity or speed; sudden gush.

sputnik *n.* early Soviet artificial satellite.

sputter *v., n.* splutter.

sputum *n., pl.* **-ta.** spittle, usu. mixed with mucus.

spy *n., pl.* **spies.** person employed to obtain secret information; person who secretly watches others. —*v.* **spying, spied.** act as a spy; catch sight of.

Sq. Square.

squabble *v., n.* (engage in) a petty or noisy quarrel.

squad *n.* small group of people working or training together.

squadron *n.* division of an air force, fleet, or cavalry regiment.

squalid *adj.* dirty and unpleasant; morally sordid. —**squalor** *n.* disgusting dirt and filth.

squall *n.* sudden strong wind; harsh cry. —*v.* cry noisily, yell.

squander *v.* waste (money or resources).

square *n.* geometric figure with four equal sides and four right angles; open area in a town in this shape; product of a number multiplied by itself. —*adj.* square in shape; denoting a measure of area; straight or level; fair and honest; with all accounts or debts settled. —*v.* make square; multiply (a number) by itself; be or cause to be consistent. —*adv.* squarely, directly. —**squarely** *adv.* in a direct way; in an honest and frank manner. —**square dance** formation dance in which the couples form squares. —**square meal** substantial meal. —**square root** number of which a given number is the square. —**square**

up to *v.* prepare to confront (a person or problem).

squash *v.* crush flat; suppress; humiliate with a crushing retort; push into a confined space. —*n.* sweet fruit drink diluted with water; crowd of people in a confined space; (also **squash rackets**) game played in an enclosed court with a rubber ball and long-handled rackets; marrow-like vegetable. —**squashy** *adj.*

squat *v.* **squatting, squatted.** crouch with the knees bent and the weight on the feet; occupy unused premises to which one has no legal right. —*n.* place where squatters live. —*adj.* short and broad. —**squatter** *n.* illegal occupier of unused premises.

squaw *n. Offens.* native American woman.

squawk *n.* loud harsh cry. —*v.* utter a squawk.

squeak *n.* short shrill cry or sound. —*v.* make or utter a squeak. —**narrow squeak** *Informal* narrow escape. —**squeaky** *adj.*

squeal *n.* long shrill cry or sound. —*v.* make or utter a squeal; *Slang* inform on someone to the police.

squeamish *adj.* easily sickened or shocked.

squeegee *n.* tool with a rubber blade for clearing water from a surface.

squeeze *v.* grip or press firmly; crush or press to extract liquid; push into a confined space; hug; obtain (something) by force or great effort. —*n.* squeezing; amount extracted by squeezing; hug; crush of people in a confined space; restriction on borrowing.

squelch *v.* make a wet sucking sound, as by walking through mud. —*n.* squelching sound.

squib *n.* small firework that hisses before exploding.

THESAURUS

spy 1. *n.* mole, undercover agent 2. *v.* descry, espy, glimpse, notice, observe, spot

squabble 1. *v.* argue, bicker, brawl, clash, dispute, fight, quarrel, row, wrangle 2. *n.* argument, disagreement, dispute, fight, row, tiff

squad band, company, crew, force, gang, group, team, troop

squalid decayed, dirty, fetid, filthy, foul, low, nasty, repulsive, seedy, sleazy, slovenly, slummy, sordid, unclean

squalor decay, filth, foulness, meanness, squalidness, wretchedness

squander consume, dissipate, expend, fritter away, lavish, misspend, misuse, scatter, spend, waste

square *Fig. adj.* aboveboard, decent, ethical, fair, genuine, honest, just, straight, upright

squash *v.* 1. compress, crush, distort, flatten,

mash, pound, press, pulp, smash 2. annihilate, crush, humiliate, quash, quell, silence, suppress

squeak *v.* peep, pipe, shrill, squeal, whine, yelp

squeal 1. *n.* scream, screech, shriek, wail, yell, yelp, yowl 2. *v.* scream, screech, shout, shriek, shrill, wail, yelp

squeamish 1. delicate, fastidious, particular, prudish, scrupulous, strait-laced 2. queasy, queer, sick

squeeze *v.* 1. clutch, compress, crush, grip, nip, pinch, press, squash, wring 2. cram, crowd, force, jam, jostle, pack, press, ram, stuff, thrust, wedge 3. clasp, cuddle, embrace, enfold, hug 4. extort, milk, oppress, pressurize, wrest ~*n.* 5. clasp, embrace, handclasp, hold, hug 6. congestion, crowd, crush, jam, press, squash

DICTIONARY

squid *n.* sea creature with a torpedo-shaped body and ten tentacles.

squiggle *n.* wavy line. —**squiggly** *adj.*

squint *v.* have eyes which face in different directions; glance sideways. —*n.* squinting condition of the eye; *Informal* glance. —*adj.* crooked.

squire *n.* country gentleman, usu. the main landowner in a community; *Hist.* knight's apprentice.

squirm *v.* wriggle, writhe; feel embarrassed. —*n.* wriggling movement.

squirrel *n.* small bushy-tailed tree-living animal.

squirt *v.* force (a liquid) or (of a liquid) be forced out of a narrow opening; squirt liquid at. —*n.* jet of liquid; *Informal* small or insignificant person.

squish *v., n.* (make) a soft squelching sound. —**squishy** *adj.*

Sr *Chem.* strontium.

Sr. Senior; Señor.

SRN State Registered Nurse.

SS Schutzstaffel: Nazi paramilitary security force; steamship.

St. Saint; Street.

st. stone (weight).

stab *v.* **stabbing, stabbed.** pierce with something pointed; jab (at). —*n.* stabbing; sudden unpleasant sensation; *Informal* attempt.

stabilize *v.* make or become stable. —**stabilization** *n.* —**stabilizer** *n.* device for stabilizing a child's bicycle, an aircraft, or a ship.

stable[1] *n.* building in which horses are kept; establishment that breeds and trains racehorses; establishment that manages or trains several entertainers or athletes. —*v.* put or keep (a horse) in a stable.

stable[2] *adj.* firmly fixed or established; firm in character; *Science* not subject to decay or decomposition. —**stability** *n.*

staccato [stak-**ah**-toe] *adj., adv. Music* with the notes sharply separated. —*adj.* consisting of short abrupt sounds.

stack *n.* ordered pile; large amount; chimney. —*v.* pile in a stack; control (aircraft waiting to land) so that they fly at different altitudes.

stadium *n., pl.* **-diums, -dia.** sports arena with tiered seats for spectators.

staff[1] *n.* people employed in an organization; stick used as a weapon, support, etc. —*v.* supply with personnel.

staff[2] *n., pl.* **staves.** set of five horizontal lines on which music is written.

stag *n.* adult male deer. —**stag beetle** beetle with large branched jaws. —**stag party, night** party for men only.

stage *n.* step or period of development; platform in a theatre where actors perform; portion of a journey; separate unit of a rocket that can be jettisoned. —*v.* put (a play) on stage; organize and carry out (an event). —**the stage** theatre as a profession. —**stagy** *adj.* overtheatrical. —**stage-coach** *n.* large horse-drawn vehicle formerly used to carry passengers and mail. —**stage fright** nervousness felt by a person about to face an audience. —**stage whisper** loud whisper intended to be heard by an audience.

stagger *v.* walk unsteadily; astound; arrange in alternating positions or periods. —*n.* staggering. —**staggering** *adj.*

stagnant *adj.* (of water or air) stale from not moving; not growing or developing. —**stagnate** *v.* be stagnant. —**stagnation** *n.*

staid *adj.* sedate, serious, and rather dull.

stain *v.* discolour, mark; colour with a penetrating pigment. —*n.* discoloration or mark; moral blemish or slur; penetrating liquid used to colour things. —**stainless** *adj.* —**stainless steel** steel alloy that does not rust.

THESAURUS

stab *v.* 1. cut, gore, injure, jab, knife, pierce, spear, stick, thrust, transfix, wound ~*n.* 2. gash, incision, jab, puncture, rent, thrust, wound 3. ache, pang, prick, twinge 4. attempt, endeavour, essay, try

stability constancy, firmness, solidity, steadfastness, steadiness, strength

stable abiding, constant, durable, enduring, established, fast, firm, fixed, invariable, lasting, permanent, reliable, secure, sound, steadfast, steady, strong, sturdy, sure, well-founded

stack 1. *n.* heap, hoard, load, mass, mound, mountain, pile 2. *v.* amass, assemble, bank up, heap up, load, pile

staff *n.* 1. employees, officers, organization,
personnel, teachers, team, workers, work force 2. cane, pole, prop, rod, stave, wand

stage division, lap, leg, length, level, period, phase, point, step

stagger 1. falter, hesitate, lurch, reel, sway, vacillate, waver, wobble 2. amaze, astonish, astound, confound, nonplus, overwhelm, shake, shock, stun, stupefy, surprise 3. alternate, overlap, step, zigzag

stagnant brackish, quiet, sluggish, stale, standing, still

stagnate decay, decline, fester, idle, languish, rot, rust

staid calm, composed, grave, quiet, sedate, serious, sober, steady

DICTIONARY

stairs *pl. n.* flight of steps between floors, usu. indoors. **—staircase, stairway** *n.* flight of stairs with a handrail or banisters.

stake *n.* pointed stick or post driven into the ground as a support or marker; money wagered; an interest, usu. financial, held in something. **—***v.* support or mark out with stakes; wager, risk. **—at stake** being risked. **—stake a claim to** claim a right to. **—stake out** *v. Slang* (of police) keep (a place) under surveillance.

stalactite *n.* lime deposit hanging from the roof of a cave.

stalagmite *n.* lime deposit sticking up from the floor of a cave.

stale *adj.* not fresh; uninteresting from overuse; lacking energy or ideas through overwork or monotony. **—staleness** *n.*

stalemate *n. Chess* position in which any of a player's moves would put his king in check, resulting in a draw; deadlock, impasse.

stalk[1] *n.* plant's stem.

stalk[2] *v.* follow or approach stealthily; walk in a stiff or haughty manner. **—stalking-horse** *n.* pretext.

stall *n.* small stand for the display and sale of goods; ground-floor seat in a theatre or cinema; one of a row of seats in a church for the choir or clergy; compartment in a stable; small room or compartment. **—***v.* stop (a motor vehicle or engine) or (of a motor vehicle or engine) stop accidentally; (of an aircraft) begin to drop because the speed is too low; employ delaying tactics.

stallion *n.* uncastrated male horse.

stalwart [**stawl**-wart] *adj.* strong and sturdy; dependable. **—***n.* stalwart person.

stamen *n.* pollen-producing part of a flower.

stamina *n.* enduring energy and strength.

stammer *v.* speak or say with involuntary pauses or repetition of syllables. **—***n.* tendency to stammer.

stamp *v.* stick a postage stamp on; impress (a pattern or mark) on; bring (one's foot) down forcefully; walk with heavy footsteps; characterize. **—***n.* (also **postage stamp**) piece of gummed paper stuck to an envelope or parcel to show that the postage has been paid; instrument for stamping a pattern or mark; pattern or mark stamped; act of stamping the foot; characteristic feature. **—stamping ground** favourite meeting place. **—stamp out** *v.* suppress by force.

stampede *n.* sudden rush of frightened animals or of a crowd. **—***v.* (cause to) take part in a stampede.

stance *n.* manner of standing; attitude.

stanch [**stahnch**] *v.* same as STAUNCH[2].

stanchion *n.* upright bar used as a support.

stand *v.* **standing, stood.** be in, rise to, or place in an upright position; be situated; be in a specified state or position; remain unchanged or valid; tolerate; offer oneself as a candidate; *Informal* treat to. **—***n.* stall for the sale of goods; structure for spectators at a sports ground; firmly held opinion; *US* witness box; rack or piece of furniture on which things may be placed. **—standing** *n.* reputation or status; duration. **—***adj.* permanent, lasting. **—stand for** *v.* represent or mean; *Informal* tolerate. **—stand in** *v.* act as a substitute. **—stand-in** *n.* substitute. **—stand-offish** *adj.* reserved or haughty. **—stand up for** *v.* support or defend.

THESAURUS

stain *v.* 1. blemish, blot, colour, dirty, discolour, dye, mark, soil, spot, tarnish, tinge ~*n.* 2. blemish, blot, dye, spot, tint 3. blemish, disgrace, dishonour, infamy, reproach, shame, slur, stigma

stake *n.* 1. ante, bet, chance, hazard, peril, pledge, risk, venture, wager 2. claim, concern, interest, investment, involvement, share ~*v.* 3. bet, chance, gamble, hazard, imperil, pledge, put on, risk, venture, wager

stale decayed, dry, faded, fetid, flat, fusty, hard, insipid, musty, old, sour, tasteless

stalk *v.* follow, haunt, hunt, pursue, shadow, track

stalwart athletic, brawny, dependable, lusty, manly, muscular, redoubtable, robust, rugged, sinewy, staunch, stout, strong, sturdy, valiant, vigorous

stamina energy, force, power, resilience, resistance, strength, vigour

stammer *v.* falter, hesitate, pause, splutter, stumble, stutter

stamp *v.* 1. beat, crush, trample 2. engrave, fix, impress, imprint, inscribe, mark, mould, print ~*n.* 3. brand, cast, earmark, hallmark, imprint, mark, mould, signature 4. breed, cast, character, cut, description, fashion, form, kind, sort, type

stampede *n.* charge, flight, rout, rush

stamp out crush, destroy, eliminate, eradicate, extinguish, extirpate, quell, quench, scotch, suppress

stance 1. bearing, carriage, deportment, posture 2. attitude, position, stand, standpoint, viewpoint

stand *v.* 1. be upright, erect, mount, place,

DICTIONARY

standard *n.* level of quality; example against which others are judged or measured; moral principle; distinctive flag; upright pole. —*adj.* usual, regular, or average; accepted as correct; of recognized authority. —**standardize** *v.* cause to conform to a standard. —**standardization** *n.* —**standard lamp** lamp attached to an upright pole on a base.

standpipe *n.* tap attached to a water main to provide a public water supply.

standpoint *n.* point of view.

standstill *n.* complete halt.

stank *v.* a past tense of STINK.

stanza *n.* verse of a poem.

staple¹ *n.* U-shaped piece of metal used to fasten papers or secure things. —*v.* fasten with staples. —**stapler** *n.* small device for fastening papers together.

staple² *adj.* of prime importance, principal. —*n.* main constituent of anything.

star *n.* hot gaseous mass in space, visible in the night sky as a point of light; star-shaped mark used to indicate excellence; asterisk; celebrity in the entertainment or sports world. —*pl.* astrological forecast, horoscope. —*v.* **starring, starred.** mark with a star or stars; feature or be featured as a star. —*adj.* leading, famous. —**stardom** *n.* status of a star in the entertainment or sports world. —**starry** *adj.* full of or like stars. —**starry-eyed** *adj.* full of naive optimism. —**starfish** *n.* star-shaped sea creature.

starboard *n.* right-hand side of a ship, when facing forward. —*adj.* of or on this side.

starch *n.* carbohydrate forming the main food element in bread, potatoes, etc., and used mixed with water for stiffening fabric. —*v.* stiffen (fabric) with starch. —**starchy** *adj.* containing starch; stiff and formal.

stare *v.* look or gaze fixedly (at). —*n.* fixed gaze.

stark *adj.* desolate, bare; without elaboration; absolute. —*adv.* completely.

starling *n.* songbird with glossy black speckled feathers.

start *v.* take the first step, begin; set or be set in motion; establish or set up; make a sudden involuntary movement from fright. —*n.* first part of something; place or time of starting; advantage or lead in a competitive activity; starting movement from fright. —**starter** *n.* first course of a meal; device for starting a car's engine; person who signals the start of a race.

startle *v.* slightly surprise or frighten.

starve *v.* die or suffer or cause to die or suffer from hunger; deprive of something needed. —**starvation** *n.*

stash *v. Informal* store in a secret place.

state *n.* condition of a person or thing; *Informal* excited or agitated condition; pomp; (often S-) sovereign political power or its territory; (often S-) the government. —*adj.* of or concerning the State; involving ceremony. —*v.* express in words. —**stately** *adj.* dignified or grand. —**statement** *n.* something stated; printed financial account. —**stateroom** *n.* private cabin on a ship; large room in a palace, used for ceremonial occasions. —**statesman, stateswoman** *n.* experienced and respected political leader. —**statesmanship** *n.*

THESAURUS

position, put, rank, rise, set 2. belong, be valid, continue, exist, halt, hold, obtain, pause, prevail, remain, rest, stay, stop 3. abide, allow, bear, brook, countenance, endure, experience, handle, stomach, suffer, support, sustain, take, tolerate, undergo, weather, withstand ~*n.* 4. halt, rest, stay, stop 5. attitude, determination, opinion, position, stance

standard 1. *n.* average, canon, criterion, example, grade, guide, measure, model, norm, pattern, principle, requirement, rule, sample, specification, type 2. *adj.* accepted, average, basic, customary, normal, orthodox, prevailing, regular, set, staple, stock, typical, usual

standardize assimilate, institutionalize, mass-produce, regiment

standing *n.* condition, credit, eminence, estimation, footing, position, rank, reputation, repute, station, status

standpoint angle, position, post, stance, station

stand up for champion, defend, support, uphold

star 1. *n.* celebrity, idol, lead, luminary, name 2. *adj.* brilliant, celebrated, leading, major, principal, prominent, well-known

stare *v.* gape, gawk, gaze, look, watch

start *v.* 1. appear, arise, begin, commence, depart, issue, leave, originate, set off, set out 2. activate, initiate, instigate, open, originate, turn on 3. begin, create, establish, father, found, inaugurate, initiate, institute, introduce, launch, pioneer, set up 4. blench, flinch, jerk, jump, recoil, shy, twitch ~*n.* 5. beginning, birth, dawn, foundation, inception, initiation, onset, opening, outset 6. advantage, edge, lead 7. jar, jump, spasm, twitch

startle agitate, alarm, amaze, frighten, scare, shock, surprise

state¹ *v.* 1. affirm, articulate, assert, aver, declare, explain, expound, express, present, propound, put, report, say, specify, voice ~*n.* 2.

DICTIONARY

static *adj.* stationary or inactive; (of a force) acting but producing no movement. —*n.* crackling sound or speckled picture caused by interference in radio or television reception; (also **static electricity**) electric sparks produced by friction. —**statics** *n.* branch of mechanics dealing with the forces producing a state of equilibrium.

station *n.* place where trains stop for passengers; headquarters of the police or a fire brigade; building with special equipment for a particular purpose, e.g. *power station;* television or radio channel; position in society. —*v.* assign (someone) to a particular place. —**station wagon** *US* estate car.

stationary *adj.* not moving.

stationery *n.* writing materials such as paper and pens. —**stationer** *n.* dealer in stationery.

statistic *n.* numerical fact collected and classified systematically. —**statistics** *n.* science of classifying and interpreting numerical information. —**statistical** *adj.* —**statistically** *adv.* —**statistician** *n.* person who compiles and studies statistics.

statue *n.* large sculpture of a human or animal figure. —**statuary** *n.* statues collectively. —**statuesque** [stat-yoo-**esk**] *adj.* (of a woman) tall and well-proportioned. —**statuette** *n.* small statue.

stature *n.* person's height; intellectual or moral greatness.

status *n.* social position; prestige; person's legal standing. —**status quo** existing state of affairs.

statute *n.* written law. —**statutory** *adj.* required or authorized by law.

staunch[1] *adj.* loyal, firm.

staunch[2], **stanch** *v.* stop (a flow of blood).

stave *n.* one of the strips of wood forming a barrel; *Music* same as STAFF. —*v.* **staving, staved** *or* **stove.** burst a hole in. —**stave off** *v.* ward off.

stay[1] *v.* remain in a place or condition; reside temporarily; endure. —*n.* period of staying in a place; postponement. —**staying power** stamina.

stay[2] *n.* rope or wire supporting a ship's mast. —*pl.* corset.

STD sexually transmitted disease; subscriber trunk dialling.

stead *n.* —**in someone's stead** in someone's place. —**stand someone in good stead** be useful to someone.

steadfast *adj.* firm, determined. —**steadfastly** *adv.*

steady *adj.* **steadier, steadiest.** not shaky or wavering; sensible and dependable; regular or continuous. —*v.* **steadying, steadied.** make steady. —*adv.* in a steady manner. —**steadily** *adv.* —**steadiness** *n.*

THESAURUS

case, category, circumstances, condition, mode, pass, plight, position, shape, situation 3. ceremony, dignity, display, glory, grandeur, majesty, pomp, splendour, style

state[2] *n.* commonwealth, country, federation, government, kingdom, land, nation, republic, territory

stately august, dignified, elegant, grand, imperial, lofty, majestic, measured, noble, pompous, regal, royal, solemn

statement account, communiqué, declaration, explanation, proclamation, recital, relation, report

static changeless, constant, fixed, immobile, inert, motionless, stagnant, stationary, still, unmoving, unvarying

station *n.* 1. base, depot, headquarters, location, place, position, post, seat, situation 2. appointment, business, calling, employment, grade, occupation, position, post, rank, situation, sphere, standing, status ~*v.* 3. assign, establish, fix, garrison, install, locate, post, set

stationary fixed, inert, moored, motionless, parked, standing, static, stock-still

status condition, consequence, degree, distinction, eminence, grade, position, prestige, rank, standing

stay 1. *v.* abide, continue, delay, halt, hover, linger, loiter, pause, remain, reside, settle, stand, stop, tarry, wait 2. *n.* holiday, sojourn, stop, stopover, visit

steadfast constant, dedicated, dependable, faithful, fast, firm, fixed, intent, loyal, persevering, reliable, resolute, stable, staunch, steady, unswerving, unwavering

steady *adj.* 1. firm, fixed, safe, stable, substantial, uniform 2. balanced, calm, dependable, equable, imperturbable, level-headed, reliable, sensible, serene, settled, sober, staid, steadfast 3. ceaseless, confirmed, consistent, constant, continuous, even, faithful, habitual, incessant, nonstop, persistent, regular, rhythmic, unbroken, uninterrupted, unvarying ~*v.* 4. balance, brace, secure, stabilize, support

steal 1. appropriate, embezzle, filch, misappropriate, pilfer, plagiarize, poach, purloin, shoplift, take, thieve 2. creep, flit, insinuate oneself, slink, slip, sneak, tiptoe

DICTIONARY

steak *n.* thick slice of meat, esp. beef; slice of fish.

steal *v.* **stealing, stole, stolen.** take unlawfully or without permission; move stealthily.

stealth *n.* secret or underhand behaviour. **—stealthy** *adj.* **—stealthily** *adv.*

steam *n.* vapour into which water changes when boiled; power, energy, or speed. *—v.* give off steam; (of a vehicle) move by steam power; cook or treat with steam. **—steamer** *n.* steam-propelled ship; container used to cook food in steam. **—steam engine** engine worked by steam. **—steamroller** *n.* steam-powered vehicle with heavy rollers, used to level road surfaces. *—v.* use overpowering force to make (someone) do what one wants.

steatite [stee-a-tite] *n.* same as SOAPSTONE.

steed *n. Lit.* horse.

steel *n.* hard malleable alloy of iron and carbon; steel rod used for sharpening knives; hardness of character or attitude. *—v.* make (oneself) hard and unfeeling. **—steely** *adj.*

steep[1] *adj.* sloping sharply; *Informal* (of a price) unreasonably high. **—steeply** *adv.* **—steepness** *n.*

steep[2] *v.* soak or be soaked in liquid. **—steeped in** filled with, e.g. *steeped in history.*

steeple *n.* church tower with a spire. **—steeplejack** *n.* person who repairs steeples and chimneys.

steeplechase *n.* horse race with obstacles to jump; track race with hurdles and a water jump.

steer[1] *v.* direct the course of (a vehicle or ship); direct (one's course). **—steerage** *n.* cheapest accommodation on a passenger ship. **—steering wheel** wheel turned by the driver of a vehicle in order to steer it.

steer[2] *n.* castrated male ox.

stein [stine] *n.* earthenware beer mug.

stellar *adj.* of stars.

stem[1] *n.* long thin central part of a plant; long slender part, as of a wineglass; part of a word to which inflections are added. *—v.* **stemming, stemmed. —stem from** *v.* originate from.

stem[2] *v.* **stemming, stemmed.** stop (the flow of something).

stench *n.* foul smell.

stencil *n.* thin sheet with cut-out pattern through which ink or paint passes to form the pattern on the surface below; pattern made thus. *—v.* **-cilling, -cilled.** make (a pattern) with a stencil.

stenography *n.* shorthand. **—stenographer** *n. US* shorthand typist.

stentorian *adj.* (of a voice) very loud.

step *v.* **stepping, stepped.** move and set down the foot, as when walking; walk a short distance. *—n.* stepping; distance covered by a step; sound made by stepping; foot movement in a dance; one of a sequence of actions taken in order to achieve a goal; degree in a series or scale; flat surface for placing the foot on when going up or down. *—pl.* stepladder. **—step in** *v.* intervene. **—stepladder** *n.* folding portable ladder with supporting frame. **—stepping stone** one of a series of stones for stepping on in crossing a stream; means of progress towards a goal. **—step up** *v.* increase (something) by steps.

step- *combining form* denoting a relationship created by the remarriage of a parent, e.g. *stepmother.*

steppe *n.* wide grassy treeless plain.

stereo *adj.* short for STEREOPHONIC. *—n.* stereophonic record player; stereophonic sound.

stereophonic *adj.* using two separate loudspeakers to give the effect of naturally distributed sound.

stereoscopic *adj.* having a three-dimensional effect.

stereotype *n.* standardized idea of a type of person or thing. *—v.* form a stereotype of.

sterile *adj.* free from germs; unable to produce offspring; lacking inspiration or vitality. **—steril-**

THESAURUS

stealth secrecy, slyness, surreptitiousness, unobtrusiveness

stealthy clandestine, furtive, secret, secretive, sly, sneaking, surreptitious

steep *adj.* 1. abrupt, headlong, precipitous, sheer 2. *Inf.* exorbitant, extortionate, extreme, high, unreasonable

steer conduct, control, direct, govern, guide, pilot

stem[1] *n.* axis, branch, shoot, stalk, stock, trunk

stem[2] *v.* check, contain, curb, dam, oppose, stop, withstand

step *n.* 1. footfall, footprint, footstep, gait, impression, pace, print, stride, trace, track, walk 2. act, action, deed, expedient, means, measure, move 3. degree, level, rank, remove ~*v.* 4. move, pace, tread, walk

stereotype 1. *n.* formula, mould, pattern 2. *v.* categorize, dub, standardize, typecast

sterile 1. bare, barren, dry, empty, fruitless, unfruitful, unproductive, unprofitable 2. aseptic, disinfected, germ-free, sterilized

DICTIONARY

ity *n.* **—sterilize** *v.* make sterile. **—sterilization** *n.*

sterling *n.* British money system. **—adj.** genuine; reliable.

stern[1] *adj.* severe, strict. **—sternly** *adv.* **—sternness** *n.*

stern[2] *n.* rear part of a ship.

sternum *n., pl.* **-na, -nums.** breast bone.

steroid *n.* organic compound containing a carbon ring system, such as many hormones.

stertorous *adj.* (of breathing) laboured and noisy.

stethoscope *n.* medical instrument for listening to sounds made inside the body.

stetson *n.* tall broad-brimmed hat, worn mainly by cowboys.

stevedore *n.* person who loads and unloads ships.

stew *n.* food cooked slowly in a closed pot; *Informal* troubled or worried state. **—v.** cook slowly in a closed pot.

steward *n.* person who looks after passengers on a ship or aircraft; official who helps at a public event such as a race; person who administers another's property. **—stewardess** *n. fem.*

stick[1] *n.* long thin piece of wood; such a piece of wood shaped for a special purpose, e.g. *hockey stick;* something like a stick, e.g. *stick of celery; Slang* verbal abuse, criticism.

stick[2] *v.* **sticking, stuck.** push (a pointed object) into (something); fasten or be fastened by or as if by pins or glue; (foll. by *out*) extend beyond something else, protrude; *Informal* put; come to a standstill; jam; remain for a long time; *Slang* tolerate, abide. **—sticker** *n.* adhesive label or

sign. **—sticky** *adj.* covered with an adhesive substance; (of weather) warm and humid; *Informal* difficult, unpleasant. **—stick-in-the-mud** *n.* person who does not like anything new. **—stick-up** *n. Slang* robbery at gunpoint. **—stick up for** *v. Informal* support or defend.

stickleback *n.* small fish with sharp spines on its back.

stickler *n.* person who insists on something, e.g. *stickler for accuracy.*

stiff *adj.* not easily bent or moved; firm in consistency; unrelaxed or awkward; severe, e.g. *stiff punishment;* strong, e.g. *a stiff drink.* **—n.** *Slang* corpse. **—stiffly** *adv.* **—stiffness** *n.* **—stiffen** *v.* make or become stiff. **—stiff-necked** *adj.* haughtily stubborn.

stifle *v.* suffocate; suppress.

stigma *n.* mark of social disgrace; part of a plant that receives pollen. **—stigmata** *pl. n.* marks resembling the wounds of the crucified Christ. **—stigmatize** *v.* mark as being shameful.

stile *n.* set of steps allowing people to climb a fence.

stiletto *n., pl.* **-tos.** small slender dagger; (also **stiletto heel**) high narrow heel on a woman's shoe.

still[1] *adv.* now or in the future as before; up to this or that time; even or yet, e.g. *still more insults;* quietly or without movement. **—adj.** motionless; silent and calm, undisturbed; (of a drink) not fizzy. **—v.** make still. **—n.** photograph from a film scene. **—stillness** *n.* **—stillborn** *adj.* born dead. **—still life** painting of inanimate objects.

still[2] *n.* apparatus for distilling alcoholic drinks.

THESAURUS

stern austere, bitter, cruel, flinty, forbidding, frowning, grim, hard, harsh, inflexible, relentless, rigid, serious, severe, strict, unyielding

stick[1] baton, birch, cane, pole, rod, staff, stake, switch, twig, wand

stick[2] *v.* 1. adhere, affix, attach, bind, bond, cement, cleave, cling, fasten, fix, fuse, glue, hold, hold on, join, paste, weld 2. dig, gore, insert, jab, penetrate, pierce, pin, poke, prod, puncture, spear, stab, thrust, transfix 3. *With out* bulge, extend, jut, obtrude, poke, project, protrude, show 4. catch, clog, jam, lodge, snag, stop 5. linger, persist, remain, stay 6. **stick up for** *Inf.* champion, defend, support, uphold

sticky 1. adhesive, clinging, gluey, glutinous, gummy, syrupy, tacky, tenacious, viscous 2. *Inf.* awkward, delicate, difficult, embarrassing, nasty, painful, thorny, tricky, unpleasant

stiff 1. firm, hard, inelastic, inflexible, rigid,

solid, taut, tense, tight, unbending, unyielding 2. artificial, austere, chilly, cold, constrained, forced, formal, laboured, mannered, pompous, priggish, prim, standoffish, uneasy, wooden 3. awkward, clumsy, crude, graceless, inelegant, jerky, ungainly, ungraceful, unsupple

stiffen brace, congeal, harden, jell, reinforce, set, solidify, starch, tauten, tense, thicken

stifle 1. choke, smother, strangle, suffocate 2. check, curb, extinguish, hush, muffle, prevent, repress, restrain, silence, smother, stop, suppress

still 1. *adj.* calm, hushed, inert, motionless, peaceful, placid, quiet, restful, serene, silent, smooth, stationary, tranquil, undisturbed 2. *v.* allay, alleviate, appease, calm, hush, lull, pacify, quieten, settle, silence, smooth, soothe, subdue, tranquillize 3. *conj.* but, however, nevertheless, notwithstanding, yet

DICTIONARY

stilted *adj.* stiff and formal in manner.

stilts *pl. n.* pair of poles with footrests for walking raised from the ground; long posts supporting a building above ground level.

stimulus *n., pl.* **-li.** something that rouses a person or thing to activity. —**stimulant** *n.* something, such as a drug, that acts as a stimulus. —**stimulate** *v.* act as a stimulus (on). —**stimulation** *n.*

sting *v.* **stinging, stung.** (of certain animals or plants) wound by injecting with poison; feel or cause to feel sharp physical or mental pain; *Slang* cheat (someone) by overcharging. —*n.* wound or pain caused by or as if by stinging; mental pain; sharp pointed organ of certain animals or plants by which poison can be injected.

stingy *adj.* **-gier, -giest.** mean or miserly. —**stinginess** *n.*

stink *v.* **stinking, stank** *or* **stunk, stunk.** give off a strong unpleasant smell; *Slang* be very unpleasant. —*n.* strong unpleasant smell; *Slang* unpleasant fuss.

stint *v.* (foll. by *on*) be miserly with (something). —*n.* allotted amount of work.

stipend [sty-pend] *n.* regular allowance or salary, esp. that paid to a clergyman. —**stipendiary** *adj.* receiving a stipend.

stipple *v.* paint, draw, or engrave using dots. —**stippling** *n.*

stipulate *v.* specify as a condition of an agreement. —**stipulation** *n.*

stir *v.* **stirring, stirred.** mix up (a liquid) by moving a spoon etc. around in it; move; excite or stimulate (a person) emotionally. —*n.* a stirring; strong reaction, usu. of excitement.

stirrup *n.* metal loop attached to a saddle for supporting a rider's foot.

stitch *n.* link made by drawing thread through material with a needle; loop of yarn formed round a needle or hook in knitting or crochet; sharp pain in the side. —*v.* sew. —**in stitches** *Informal* laughing uncontrollably. —**not a stitch** *Informal* no clothes at all.

stoat *n.* small mammal of the weasel family, with brown fur that turns white in winter.

stock *n.* total amount of goods available for sale in a shop; supply stored for future use; financial shares in, or capital of, a company; lineage; livestock; handle of a rifle; liquid produced by boiling meat, fish, bones, or vegetables; fragrant flowering plant; standing or status. —*pl. Hist.* instrument of punishment consisting of a wooden frame with holes into which the hands and feet of the victim were locked. —*adj.* kept in stock, standard; hackneyed. —*v.* keep for sale or future use; supply (a farm) with livestock or (a lake etc.) with fish. —**stockist** *n.* dealer who stocks a particular product. —**stocky** *adj.* (of a person) broad and sturdy. —**stockbroker** *n.* person who buys and sells stocks and shares for customers. —**stock car** car modified for a form of racing in which the cars often collide. —**stock exchange, market** institution for the buying and

THESAURUS

stimulant excitant, restorative, reviver, tonic

stimulate animate, arouse, encourage, fan, fire, goad, impel, incite, instigate, prompt, provoke, quicken, rouse, spur, urge

stimulus encouragement, goad, incentive, inducement, provocation, spur

sting burn, hurt, pain, smart, tingle, wound

stint period, quota, share, shift, spell, stretch, term, time, tour, turn

stipulate agree, contract, covenant, engage, guarantee, lay down, pledge, postulate, promise, require, settle, specify

stipulation agreement, clause, condition, contract, engagement, provision, qualification, requirement, restriction, settlement, specification, term

stir *v.* 1. agitate, beat, disturb, flutter, mix, move, quiver, rustle, shake, tremble 2. arouse, awaken, excite, incite, inflame, prompt, provoke, quicken, raise, spur, stimulate, urge 3. bestir, be up and about (*Inf.*), budge, hasten,

mill about, move ~*n.* 4. activity, ado, agitation, bustle, commotion, disorder, excitement, ferment, flurry, fuss, movement, to-do, tumult, uproar

stirring dramatic, emotive, exciting, heady, impassioned, inspiring, lively, moving, rousing, spirited, stimulating, thrilling

stock *n.* 1. array, assets, choice, commodities, fund, goods, hoard, inventory, range, reserve, selection, stockpile, store, supply, variety, wares 2. *Animals* beasts, cattle, flocks, herds, horses, livestock, sheep 3. *Money* capital, funds, investment, property ~*adj.* 4. banal, basic, conventional, customary, formal, ordinary, overused, regular, routine, set, standard, staple, traditional, trite, usual, worn-out ~*v.* 5. deal in, handle, keep, sell, supply, trade in 6. amass, buy up, gather, hoard, replenish, save, supply

DICTIONARY

selling of shares. —**stockpile** v. acquire and store a large quantity of (something) for future use. —n. accumulated store. —**stock-still** adj. motionless. —**stocktaking** n. counting and valuing of the goods in a shop.

stockade n. enclosure or barrier made of stakes.

stockinet n. machine-knitted elastic fabric.

stocking n. close-fitting covering for the foot and leg. —**stocking stitch** alternate rows of plain and purl in knitting.

stodgy adj. **stodgier, stodgiest.** (of food) heavy and starchy; (of a person) serious and boring. —**stodge** n. heavy starchy food.

stoep [stoop] n. S Afr. veranda.

stoic [stow-ik] n. person who suffers hardship without showing his or her feelings. —adj. (also **stoical**) suffering hardship without showing one's feelings. —**stoically** adv. —**stoicism** [stow-iss-izz-um] n.

stoke v. feed and tend a (fire or furnace). —**stoker** n.

stole[1] v. past tense of STEAL.

stole[2] n. long scarf or shawl.

stolen v. past participle of STEAL.

stolid adj. showing little emotion or interest. —**stolidity** n. —**stolidly** adv.

stomach n. organ in the body which digests food; front of the body around the waist; desire or inclination. —v. put up with.

stomp v. US informal tread heavily.

stone n. material of which rocks are made; piece of this; gem; hard central part of a fruit; hard deposit formed in the kidney or bladder; unit of weight equal to 14 pounds. —v. throw stones at; remove stones from (a fruit). —**stoned** adj. Slang under the influence of alcohol or drugs. —**stony** adj. of or like stone; unfeeling or hard. —**stonily** adv. —**Stone Age** prehistoric

period when tools were made of stone. —**stone-cold** adj. completely cold. —**stone-deaf** adj. completely deaf. —**stonewall** v. obstruct or hinder discussion. —**stoneware** n. hard kind of pottery fired at a very high temperature. —**stony-broke** adj. Slang completely penniless.

stood v. past of STAND.

stooge n. actor who feeds lines to a comedian or acts as the butt of his jokes; Slang person taken advantage of by a superior.

stool n. chair without arms or back; piece of excrement.

stool pigeon n. informer for the police.

stoop v. bend (the body) forward and downward; carry oneself habitually in this way; degrade oneself. —n. stooping posture.

stop v. **stopping, stopped.** bring to or come to a halt; cease or cause to cease from doing (something); prevent or restrain; withhold; block or plug; stay or rest. —n. place where something stops; stopping or being stopped; full stop; knob on an organ that is pulled out to allow a set of pipes to sound. —**stoppage** n. —**stoppage time** same as INJURY TIME. —**stopper** n. plug for closing a bottle etc. —**stopcock** n. valve to control or stop the flow of fluid in a pipe. —**stopgap** n. temporary substitute. —**stopover** n. short break in a journey. —**stop press** news item put into a newspaper after printing has been started. —**stopwatch** n. watch which can be stopped instantly for exact timing of a sporting event.

store v. collect and keep (things) for future use; put (furniture etc.) in a warehouse for safekeeping; stock (goods); Computers enter or retain (data). —n. shop; supply kept for future use; storage place, such as a warehouse. —pl. stock of provisions. —**in store** forthcoming or imminent. —**set great store by** value greatly. —**storage** n. storing; space for storing. —**storage heater** electric device that can accumulate and radiate heat generated by off-peak electricity.

THESAURUS

stoicism acceptance, calmness, dispassion, fatalism, fortitude, impassivity, indifference, patience, resignation, stolidity

stolid apathetic, doltish, dull, heavy, obtuse, slow, stupid, unemotional, wooden

stomach n. 1. belly, pot, tummy (Inf.) 2. appetite, desire, inclination, mind, relish, taste ~v. 3. abide, bear, endure, suffer, swallow, take, tolerate

stony Fig. blank, callous, chilly, expressionless, frigid, hard, heartless, hostile, icy, indifferent, merciless, pitiless, unforgiving, unresponsive

stoop v. bend, bow, crouch, descend, duck, hunch, incline, kneel, lean, squat

stop v. 1. cease, conclude, cut short, desist, discontinue, draw up, end, finish, halt, leave off, pause, put an end to, quit, refrain, run down, shut down, stall, terminate 2. arrest, bar, block, break, check, close, frustrate, hinder, hold back, impede, intercept, interrupt, obstruct, plug, prevent, repress, restrain, seal, silence, staunch, stem, suspend 3. lodge, put up, rest, sojourn, stay, tarry ~n. 4. cessation, conclusion, end, finish, halt, standstill 5. break, rest, sojourn, stay, visit 6. bar, block, break, check, control, hindrance, impediment, plug 7. depot, destination, halt, stage, station, termination, terminus

stoppage arrest, close, closure, cutoff, deduc-

DICTIONARY

storey *n.* floor or level of a building.

stork *n.* large wading bird.

storm *n.* violent weather with wind, rain, or snow; strongly expressed reaction. —*v.* rush violently or angrily; rage; attack or capture (a place) suddenly. —**stormy** *adj.* characterized by storms; involving violent emotions.

story *n., pl.* **-ries.** description of a series of events told or written for entertainment; plot of a book or film; newspaper report; *Informal* lie.

stoup [stoop] *n.* small basin for holy water.

stout *adj.* fat; thick and strong; brave and resolute. —*n.* strong dark beer. —**stoutly** *adv.* —**stoutness** *n.*

stove[i] *n.* apparatus for cooking or heating.

stove[2] *v.* a past of STAVE.

stow *v.* pack or store. —**stow away** *v.* hide as a stowaway. —**stowaway** *n.* person who hides on a ship or aircraft in order to travel free.

straddle *v.* have one leg or part on each side of (something).

strafe *v.* attack (an enemy) with machine guns from the air.

straggle *v.* go or spread in a rambling or irregular way. —**straggler** *n.* —**straggly** *adj.*

straight *adj.* not curved or crooked; level or upright; orderly; honest or frank; in continuous succession; (of spirits) undiluted; *Theatre* serious; *Slang* heterosexual; *Slang* conventional. —*n.* straight part. —*adv.* in a straight line; immediately; in a level or upright position. —**go straight** *Informal* reform after being a criminal. —**straighten** *v.* —**straightaway** *adv.* immediately. —**straight face** serious facial expression concealing a desire to laugh. —**straightforward** *adj.* (of a task) easy; honest, frank.

strain[1] *v.* cause (something) to be used or tested beyond its limits; make an intense effort; injure by overexertion; sieve. —*n.* force exerted by straining; injury from overexertion; great demand on strength or resources; tension or tiredness; melody or theme. —**strained** *adj.* not re-

---

THESAURUS

tion, halt, hindrance, shutdown, standstill, stopping

store *v.* 1. deposit, garner, hoard, husband, keep, put aside, put by, put in storage, reserve, salt away, save, stockpile ~*n.* 2. accumulation, cache, fund, hoard, lot, mine, plenty, plethora, provision, quantity, reserve, stock, supply, wealth 3. emporium, market, mart, outlet, shop, supermarket 4. depository, repository, storeroom, warehouse

storm *n.* 1. blast, blizzard, cyclone, gale, gust, hurricane, squall, tempest, tornado, whirlwind 2. *Fig.* agitation, anger, clamour, commotion, disturbance, furore, outburst, outcry, passion, roar, row, rumpus, stir, strife, tumult, turmoil, violence ~*v.* 3. assail, assault, beset, charge, rush 4. bluster, complain, (*Inf.*), fume, rage, rant, rave, scold, thunder 5. flounce, fly, rush, stalk, stamp

stormy blustery, boisterous, dirty, foul, gusty, raging, rough, squally, turbulent, wild, windy

story 1. account, anecdote, history, legend, narrative, novel, recital, record, relation, romance, tale, version, yarn 2. article, feature, news, news item, report, scoop

stout 1. big, bulky, burly, fat, fleshy, heavy, overweight, plump, portly, rotund, substantial, tubby 2. able-bodied, athletic, brawny, hardy, hulking, lusty, robust, stalwart, strapping, strong, sturdy, tough, vigorous 3. bold, brave, courageous, fearless, gallant, manly, plucky, resolute, valiant

straggle drift, lag, loiter, ramble, range, roam, rove, stray, wander

straight *adj.* 1. aligned, erect, even, horizontal, level, plumb, right, smooth, square, true, upright, vertical 2. above board, accurate, authentic, decent, equitable, fair, honest, honourable, just, reliable, respectable, trustworthy, upright 3. arranged, in order, neat, orderly, organized, put to rights, shipshape, sorted out, tidy 4. consecutive, continuous, nonstop, running, solid, successive, sustained, through 5. neat, pure, unadulterated, undiluted, unmixed ~*adv.* 6. at once, directly, immediately, instantly

straightaway at once, directly, immediately, instantly, now, right away

straightforward 1. candid, direct, forthright, genuine, guileless, honest, open, sincere, truthful 2. clear-cut, easy, elementary, routine, simple, uncomplicated

strain[1] *v.* 1. distend, extend, stretch, tauten, tighten 2. drive, exert, fatigue, injure, overtax, overwork, pull, sprain, tax, tear, tire, twist, weaken, wrench 3. endeavour, labour, strive, struggle 4. filter, percolate, purify, riddle, screen, seep, separate, sieve, sift ~*n.* 5. effort, exertion, force, injury, pull, sprain, struggle, tautness, tension, wrench 6. anxiety, burden, pressure, stress, tension

strain[2] *n.* ancestry, blood, descent, extraction, family, race, stock

strained artificial, awkward, difficult, embarrassed, false, forced, laboured, put on, stiff, tense, uneasy, unnatural

DICTIONARY

laxed, tense; not natural, forced. —**strainer** *n.* sieve.

strain² *n.* breed or race; trace or streak.

strait *n.* narrow channel connecting two areas of sea. —*pl.* position of acute difficulty. —**straitjacket** *n.* strong jacket with long sleeves used to bind the arms of a violent person. —**strait-laced** *adj.* prudish or puritanical.

straitened *adj.* —**in straitened circumstances** not having much money.

strand¹ *v.* run aground; leave in difficulties. —*n. Poetic* shore.

strand² *n.* single thread of string, wire, etc.

strange *adj.* odd or unusual; not familiar; inexperienced (in) or unaccustomed (to). —**strangely** *adv.* —**strangeness** *n.* —**stranger** *n.* person who is not known or is new to a place or experience.

strangle *v.* kill by squeezing the throat; prevent the development of. —**strangler** *n.* —**strangulation** *n.* strangling. —**stranglehold** *n.* strangling grip in wrestling; powerful control.

strap *n.* strip of flexible material for lifting, fastening, or holding in place. —*v.* **strapping, strapped.** fasten with a strap or straps. —**strapping** *adj.* tall and sturdy.

strata *n.* plural of STRATUM.

stratagem *n.* clever plan, trick.

strategy *n., pl.* **-gies.** overall plan; art of planning in war. —**strategic** [strat-ee-jik] *adj.* advantageous; (of weapons) aimed at an enemy's homeland. —**strategically** *adv.* —**strategist** *n.*

strathspey *n.* Scottish dance with gliding steps.

stratosphere *n.* atmospheric layer between about 15 and 50 km above the earth.

stratum [strah-tum] *n., pl.* **strata.** layer, esp. of rock; social class. —**stratify** *v.* divide into strata. —**stratification** *n.*

straw *n.* dried stalks of grain; single stalk of straw; long thin tube used to suck up liquid into the mouth. —**straw poll** unofficial poll taken to determine general opinion.

strawberry *n.* sweet fleshy red fruit with small seeds on the outside. —**strawberry mark** red birthmark.

stray *v.* wander; digress. —*adj.* having strayed; scattered, random. —*n.* stray animal.

streak *n.* long band of contrasting colour or substance; quality or characteristic; short stretch (of good or bad luck). —*v.* mark with streaks; move rapidly; *Informal* run naked in public. —**streaker** *n.* —**streaky** *adj.*

stream *n.* small river; steady flow, as of liquid, speech, or people; schoolchildren grouped together because of similar ability. —*v.* flow steadily; move in unbroken succession; float in the air; group (pupils) in streams. —**streamer** *n.* strip of coloured paper that unrolls when tossed; long narrow flag.

streamline *v.* give (a car, plane, etc.) a smooth even shape to offer least resistance to the flow of air or water; make more efficient by simplifying.

street *n.* public road, usu. lined with buildings. —**streetcar** *n. US* tram. —**streetwalker** *n.* prostitute. —**streetwise** *adj.* knowing how to survive in big cities.

strength *n.* quality of being strong; quality or

THESAURUS

strait-laced moralistic, narrow, prim, proper, prudish, puritanical, strict

straits *n. Sometimes singular* 1. crisis, difficulty, dilemma, distress, emergency, extremity, hardship, mess, pass, plight, predicament 2. channel, narrows, sound

strand *n.* fibre, filament, length, lock, rope, string, thread, tress, twist

strange 1. abnormal, bizarre, curious, eccentric, exceptional, extraordinary, fantastic, funny, marvellous, mystifying, odd, peculiar, queer, rare, remarkable, singular, uncanny, unheard of, weird, wonderful 2. alien, exotic, foreign, new, novel, remote, unfamiliar, unknown, untried

stranger alien, foreigner, guest, incomer, newcomer, outlander, visitor

strangle 1. asphyxiate, choke, smother, suffocate, throttle 2. inhibit, repress, stifle, suppress

strap 1. *n.* belt, leash, thong, tie 2. *v.* bind, buckle, fasten, lash, secure, tie

stratagem artifice, device, dodge, feint, intrigue, plan, plot, ploy, ruse, scheme, trick

strategy approach, grand design, plan, policy, procedure, programme

stray *v.* 1. deviate, digress, diverge, ramble 2. drift, err, meander, range, roam, rove, straggle, wander ~*adj.* 3. abandoned, homeless, lost, roaming, vagrant

streak *n.* 1. band, layer, line, slash, strip, stripe, stroke, vein 2. dash, element, strain, touch, trace, vein ~*v.* 3. dart, flash, fly, hurtle, speed, sprint, sweep, tear, whistle, zoom

stream 1. *n.* beck, brook, burn, course, current, drift, flow, rill, river, run, rush, surge, tide, torrent, tributary 2. *v.* cascade, course, emit, flood, flow, glide, gush, issue, pour, run, shed, spill, spout

street avenue, lane, road, roadway, row, terrace

DICTIONARY

ability considered an advantage; degree of intensity; total number of people in a group. —**on the strength of** on the basis of. —**strengthen** v.

strenuous adj. requiring great energy or effort. —**strenuously** adv.

streptococcus [strep-toe-**kok**-uss] n., pl. -**cocci.** bacterium occurring in chains, many species of which cause disease.

streptomycin n. antibiotic drug.

stress n. emphasis; tension or strain; stronger sound in saying a word or syllable; *Physics* force producing strain. —v. emphasize; subject to stress; put stress on (a word or syllable).

stretch v. extend or be extended; be able to be stretched; extend the limbs or body; strain (resources or abilities) to the utmost. —n. stretching; continuous expanse; period; ability to be stretched; *Informal* term of imprisonment. —**stretchy** adj. —**stretcher** n. frame covered with canvas, on which an injured person is carried.

strew v. **strewing, strewed, strewed** or **strewn.** scatter (things) over a surface.

striation n. scratch or groove; pattern of scratches or grooves. —**striated** adj.

stricken adj. seriously affected by disease, grief, pain, etc.

strict adj. stern or severe; adhering closely to specified rules; complete, absolute. —**strictly** adv. —**strictness** n.

stricture n. severe criticism.

stride v. **striding, strode, stridden.** walk with long steps. —n. long step; regular pace. —pl. progress.

strident adj. loud and harsh. —**stridently** adv. —**stridency** n.

strife n. conflict, quarrelling.

strike v. **striking, struck.** cease work as a protest; hit; attack suddenly; afflict; enter the mind of; agree (a bargain); ignite (a match) by friction; (of a clock) indicate (a time) by sounding a bell; discover (gold, oil, etc.); make (a coin) by stamping it; take up (a posture). —n. striking. —**strike camp** dismantle and pack up tents. —**strike home** have the desired effect. —**striker** n. striking worker; attacking footballer. —**striking** adj. noteworthy; impressive. —**strike off, out** v. cross out. —**strike up** v. begin (a conversation or friendship); begin to play music.

string n. thin cord used for tying; set of objects threaded on a string; series of things or events; stretched wire or cord on a musical instrument that produces sound when vibrated. —pl. restrictions or conditions; section of an orchestra consisting of stringed instruments. —v. **stringing, strung.** provide with a string or strings; thread on a string. —**pull strings** use one's influence. —**stringed** adj. (of a musical instrument) having strings that are plucked or played with a bow. —**stringy** adj. like string; (of meat) fibrous. —**string along** v. *Informal* accompany; deceive

THESAURUS

strength 1. backbone, brawn, courage, firmness, fortitude, health, might, muscle, robustness, sinew, stamina, stoutness, sturdiness, toughness 2. effectiveness, efficacy, energy, force, intensity, potency, power, resolution, spirit, vehemence, vigour 3. advantage, anchor, asset, mainstay, security

strengthen 1. brace up, consolidate, encourage, fortify, harden, hearten, invigorate, nerve, nourish, restore, stiffen, toughen 2. bolster, brace, build up, buttress, confirm, enhance, establish, harden, heighten, increase, intensify, justify, reinforce, steel, support

strenuous 1. arduous, demanding, hard, laborious, taxing, toilsome, tough, unrelaxing, uphill 2. active, bold, determined, eager, earnest, energetic, persistent, resolute, spirited, strong, tireless, zealous

stress n. 1. emphasis, force, importance, significance, urgency, weight 2. anxiety, burden, pressure, strain, tension, trauma, worry 3. accent, accentuation, beat, emphasis ~v. 4. accentuate, dwell on, emphasize, harp on, point up, repeat, rub in, underline

stretch v. 1. cover, extend, put forth, reach, spread, unfold, unroll 2. distend, draw out, elongate, expand, inflate, lengthen, pull, rack, strain, swell, tighten ~n. 3. area, distance, expanse, extent, spread, sweep, tract

strict 1. austere, authoritarian, firm, harsh, rigid, rigorous, severe, stern, stringent 2. accurate, close, exact, faithful, meticulous, particular, precise, religious, scrupulous, true 3. absolute, total, utter

strife battle, clash, combat, conflict, contention, contest, discord, friction, quarrel, rivalry, row, struggle, warfare

strike v. 1. beat, box, buffet, chastise, cuff, hammer, hit, knock, punish, slap, smack, smite, thump 2. affect, come to, hit, impress, occur to, reach, seem 3. affect, assail, assault, attack, devastate, hit, invade, set upon, smite 4. down tools, mutiny, revolt, walk out

striking conspicuous, dazzling, extraordinary, forcible, impressive, memorable, noticeable, outstanding

string n. 1. cord, fibre, twine 2. chain, file, line, procession, row, sequence, series, strand, succession

DICTIONARY

over a period of time. —**string up** v. *Informal* kill by hanging.

stringent [strin-jent] *adj.* strictly controlled or enforced. —**stringently** *adv.* —**stringency** *n.*

strip v. **stripping, stripped.** take (the covering or clothes) off; take a title or possession away from (someone); dismantle (an engine). —*n.* long narrow piece; clothes a football team plays in. —**stripper** *n.* person who performs a striptease. —**strip cartoon** sequence of drawings telling a story. —**striptease** *n.* entertainment in which a performer undresses to music.

stripe *n.* long narrow band of contrasting colour or substance; chevron on a uniform to indicate rank. —**striped, stripy** *adj.*

stripling *n.* youth.

strive v. **striving, strove, striven.** make a great effort.

strobe *n.* short for STROBOSCOPE.

stroboscope *n.* instrument producing a very bright flashing light.

strode v. past tense of STRIDE.

stroke v. touch or caress lightly with the hand. —*n.* light touch or caress with the hand; rupture of a blood vessel in the brain; mark made by a pen or paintbrush; style or method of swimming; blow; action or occurrence of the kind specified, e.g. *a stroke of luck;* chime of a clock.

stroll v. walk in a leisurely manner. —*n.* leisurely walk.

strong *adj.* having physical power; not easily broken; having an extreme or drastic effect, e.g. *strong discipline;* great in degree or intensity; having moral force; (of a drink) containing a lot of alcohol; having a specified number, e.g. *twenty strong.* —**strongly** *adv.* —**stronghold** *n.* fortress; area of predominance of a particular belief. —**strongroom** *n.* room designed for the safe-keeping of valuables.

strontium *n.* silvery-white metallic element. —**strontium-90** *n.* radioactive isotope present in the fallout of nuclear explosions.

strop *n.* leather strap for sharpening razors.

stroppy *adj.* **-pier, -piest.** *Slang* angry or awkward.

strove v. past tense of STRIVE.

struck v. past of STRIKE.

structure *n.* complex construction; manner or basis of construction or organization. —*v.* give a structure to. —**structural** *adj.* —**structuralism** *n.* approach to literature, social sciences, etc., which sees changes in the subject as caused and organized by a hidden set of universal rules. —**structuralist** *n., adj.*

strudel *n.* thin sheet of filled dough rolled up and baked, usu. with an apple filling.

struggle v. work, strive, or make one's way with difficulty; move about violently in an attempt to get free; fight (with someone). —*n.* striving; fight.

strum v. **strumming, strummed.** play (a guitar or banjo) by sweeping the thumb or a plectrum across the strings.

THESAURUS

strip[1] v. 1. bare, denude, deprive, despoil, divest, empty, gut, loot, peel, pillage, plunder, ransack, rob, sack, skin, spoil 2. disrobe, unclothe, undress

strip[2] n. band, belt, bit, fillet, piece, ribbon, shred, slip, tongue

striped banded, barred, striated, stripy

strive attempt, compete, contend, endeavour, fight, labour, strain, struggle, toil, try, try hard

stroke n. 1. achievement, blow, feat, flourish, hit, knock, move, pat, rap, thump 2. apoplexy, attack, collapse, fit, seizure, shock ~v. 3. caress, fondle, pat, pet, rub

stroll 1. v. amble, ramble, saunter, wander 2. n. airing, constitutional, excursion, promenade, ramble, turn, walk

strong 1. athletic, brawny, burly, capable, hale, hardy, healthy, muscular, powerful, robust, sound, stalwart, stout, strapping, sturdy, tough, virile 2. brave, courageous, determined, forceful, high-powered, plucky, resilient, resolute, steadfast, stouthearted, tenacious, tough, unyielding 3. acute, dedicated, deep, eager, fervent, fierce, firm, intense, keen, severe, staunch, vehement, violent, zealous 4. clear, compelling, convincing, distinct, effective, formidable, great, marked, persuasive, potent, redoubtable, sound, telling, unmistakable, urgent, weighty, well-founded 5. drastic, extreme, forceful, severe 6. durable, hard-wearing, heavy-duty, reinforced, sturdy, substantial, well-built

stronghold bastion, bulwark, castle, citadel, fort, fortress, keep

structure n. 1. arrangement, conformation, design, fabric, form, formation, make, make-up, organization 2. building, construction, edifice, erection, pile ~v. 3. arrange, assemble, build up, design, organize, shape

struggle v. 1. exert oneself, labour, strain, strive, toil, work ~n. 2. effort, exertion, labour, pains, scramble, toil, work ~v. 3. battle, compete, contend, fight, grapple, scuffle, wrestle ~n. 4. battle, brush, clash, combat, conflict, contest, encounter, skirmish, strife, tussle

DICTIONARY

strumpet n. *Old-fashioned* prostitute.

strung v. past of STRING.

strut v. **strutting, strutted.** walk pompously, swagger. —n. bar supporting a structure; strutting walk.

strychnine [strik-neen] n. very poisonous drug used in small quantities as a stimulant.

stub n. short piece left after use; counterfoil of a cheque or ticket. —v. **stubbing, stubbed.** strike (the toe) painfully against an object; put out (a cigarette) by pressing the end against a surface. —**stubby** adj. short and broad.

stubble n. short stalks of grain left in a field after reaping; short growth of hair on the chin of a man who has not shaved recently. —**stubbly** adj.

stubborn adj. refusing to agree or give in; difficult to deal with. —**stubbornly** adv. —**stubbornness** n.

stucco n. plaster used for coating or decorating walls. —**stuccoed** adj.

stuck v. past of STICK². —**stuck-up** adj. *Informal* conceited or snobbish.

stud¹ n. small piece of metal attached to a surface for decoration; disc-like removable fastener for clothes; one of several small round objects fixed to the sole of a football boot to give better grip. —v. **studding, studded.** set with studs.

stud² n. male animal, esp. a stallion, kept for breeding; (also **stud farm**) place where horses are bred; *Slang* virile or sexually active man.

student n. person who studies a subject, esp. at university.

studio n., pl. **-dios.** workroom of an artist or photographer; room or building in which televi-

sion or radio programmes, records, or films are made. —**studio flat** one-room flat with a small kitchen and bathroom.

study v. **studying, studied.** be engaged in learning (a subject); investigate by observation and research; scrutinize. —n., pl. **studies.** act or process of studying; room for studying in; book or paper produced as a result of study; sketch done as practice or preparation; musical composition designed to improve playing technique. —**studied** adj. carefully practised or planned. —**studious** [styoo-dee-uss] adj. fond of study; careful and deliberate. —**studiously** adv.

stuff v. pack, cram, or fill completely; fill (food) with a seasoned mixture; fill (an animal's skin) with material to restore the shape of the live animal; fill with padding. —n. substance or material; collection of unnamed things. —**stuff oneself** *Informal* eat large quantities. —**stuffing** n. seasoned mixture with which food is stuffed; padding.

stuffy adj. **stuffier, stuffiest.** lacking fresh air; *Informal* dull or conventional.

stultify v. **-fying, -fied.** dull the mind of (someone) by boring routine.

stumble v. trip and nearly fall; walk with frequent stumbling; make frequent mistakes in speech. —n. stumbling. —**stumble across** v. discover accidentally. —**stumbling block** obstacle or difficulty.

stump n. base of a tree left when the main trunk has been cut away; part of a thing left after a larger part has been removed; *Cricket* one of the three upright sticks forming the wicket. —v. baffle; *Cricket* dismiss (a batsman) by breaking his wicket with the ball; walk with heavy steps. —**stumpy** adj. short and stubby.

THESAURUS

stubborn cross-grained, dogged, dour, fixed, headstrong, inflexible, intractable, obdurate, obstinate, persistent, pig-headed, recalcitrant, self-willed, tenacious, unbending, unshakable, unyielding, wilful

student apprentice, disciple, learner, observer, pupil, scholar, undergraduate

studied conscious, deliberate, intentional, planned, premeditated, wilful

studious academic, assiduous, attentive, bookish, careful, diligent, eager, earnest, meditative, reflective, scholarly, serious, thoughtful

study v. 1. cogitate, consider, contemplate, examine, learn, meditate, ponder, pore over, read, read up 2. analyse, deliberate, examine, investigate, peruse, research, scrutinize, survey ~n. 3. application, learning, lessons, reading, research, school work, thought 4.

analysis, attention, contemplation, inquiry, investigation, review, scrutiny, survey

stuff v. 1. cram, crowd, fill, force, jam, load, pack, pad, push, ram, shove, squeeze, stow, wedge 2. gorge, guzzle, overindulge, sate ~n. 3. belongings, effects, equipment, gear, impedimenta, junk, kit, luggage, objects, tackle, things, trappings 4. cloth, fabric, material, raw material, textile 5. essence, matter, pith, staple, substance

stuffy 1. airless, close, frowsty, heavy, muggy, oppressive, stale, stifling, sultry, unventilated 2. deadly, dreary, dull, fusty, pompous, priggish, prim, staid, stilted, stodgy

stumble fall, falter, flounder, hesitate, lurch, reel, slip, stagger, trip

stump v. baffle, bewilder, confound, confuse, foil, mystify, outwit, perplex, puzzle, stop

DICTIONARY

—stump up *v. Informal* give (the money required).

stun *v.* **stunning, stunned.** knock senseless; shock or overwhelm. **—stunning** *adj.* very attractive or impressive.

stung *v.* past of STING.

stunk *v.* a past of STINK.

stunt[1] *v.* prevent or impede the growth of. **—stunted** *adj.*

stunt[2] *n.* acrobatic or dangerous action; anything spectacular done to gain publicity.

stupefy *v.* **-fying, -fied.** make insensitive or lethargic; astound. **—stupefaction** *n.*

stupendous *adj.* astonishing; huge. **—stupendously** *adv.*

stupid *adj.* lacking intelligence; silly; in a stupor. **—stupidity** *n.* **—stupidly** *adv.*

stupor *n.* dazed or unconscious state.

sturdy *adj.* **-dier, -diest.** healthy and robust; strongly built. **—sturdily** *adv.* **—sturdiness** *n.*

sturgeon *n.* fish from which caviar is obtained.

stutter *v.* speak with repetition of initial consonants. **—n.** tendency to stutter.

sty[1] *n., pl.* **sties.** pen for pigs.

sty[2]**, stye** *n., pl.* **sties, styes.** inflammation at the base of an eyelash.

style *n.* manner of writing, speaking, or doing something; shape or design; elegance, refinement; prevailing fashion. **—v.** shape or design; name or call. **—stylish** *adj.* smart, elegant, and fashionable. **—stylishly** *adv.* **—stylist** *n.* hair-dresser; designer; person who writes with great attention to style. **—stylistic** *adj.* of literary or artistic style. **—stylize** *v.* cause to conform to an established stylistic form. **—styling mousse** foamy substance applied to hair before styling to hold the style.

stylus *n.* needle-like device on a record player that rests in the groove of the record and picks up the sound signals.

stymie *v.* **-mieing, -mied.** hinder or thwart.

styptic *n., adj.* (drug) used to stop bleeding.

suave [swahv] *adj.* smooth and sophisticated in manner. **—suavely** *adv.* **—suavity** *n.*

sub *n.* subeditor; submarine; subscription; substitute; *Informal* advance payment of wages or salary. **—v. subbing, subbed.** act as a substitute; grant advance payment to; act as a subeditor.

sub- *prefix* used with many main words to mean: under or beneath, e.g. *submarine;* subordinate, e.g. *sublieutenant;* falling short of, e.g. *subnormal;* forming a subdivision, e.g. *subheading.*

subaltern *n.* army officer below the rank of captain.

subatomic *adj.* of or being one of the particles which make up an atom.

subcommittee *n.* small committee formed from some members of a larger committee.

subconscious *adj.* happening or existing without one's awareness. **—n.** *Psychoanalysis* that part of the mind of which one is not aware but

THESAURUS

stun *Fig.* astonish, astound, bewilder, confound, confuse, knock out, overcome, overpower, shock, stagger, stupefy

stunning beautiful, brilliant, dazzling, gorgeous, impressive, lovely, marvellous, sensational, spectacular, striking, wonderful

stunt *n.* act, deed, exploit, feat, feature, trick

stupefy amaze, astound, bewilder, daze, numb, shock, stagger, stun

stupendous amazing, astounding, breathtaking, colossal, enormous, gigantic, huge, marvellous, overwhelming, phenomenal, prodigious, staggering, superb, surprising, vast, wonderful

stupid 1. brainless, deficient, dense, dim, dull, foolish, gullible, half-witted, moronic, naive, obtuse, simple, simple-minded, slow, slow-witted, sluggish, stolid, thick, unintelligent, witless 2. futile, idiotic, inane, indiscreet, laughable, ludicrous, mindless, pointless, puerile, rash, senseless, unintelligent 3. dazed, groggy, insensate, semiconscious, senseless, stunned, stupefied

stupidity 1. brainlessness, denseness, dimness, dullness, imbecility, obtuseness, puerility, simplicity, slowness, thickness 2. absurdity, fatuity, folly, idiocy, inanity, ineptitude, lunacy, madness, silliness

sturdy athletic, brawny, determined, durable, firm, flourishing, hardy, hearty, muscular, powerful, resolute, robust, secure, solid, staunch, steadfast, substantial, vigorous, well-built, well-made

style *n.* 1. cut, design, form, hand, manner 2. fashion, mode, rage, trend, vogue 3. approach, custom, manner, method, mode, way 4. chic, dash, elegance, flair, grace, panache, polish, refinement, smartness, sophistication, taste, urbanity ~*v.* 5. adapt, arrange, cut, design, dress, fashion, shape, tailor 6. address, call, denominate, designate, dub, entitle, label, name, term

stylish chic, dapper, fashionable, modish, polished, smart, urbane, voguish

subconscious *adj.* hidden, inner, intuitive, latent, repressed, subliminal

DICTIONARY

which can influence one's behaviour. —**subconsciously** adv.

subcontinent n. large land mass that is a distinct part of a continent.

subcontract n. secondary contract by which the main contractor for a job puts work out to others. —v. put out (work) on a subcontract. —**subcontractor** n.

subcutaneous [sub-cute-**ayn**-ee-uss] adj. under the skin.

subdivide v. divide (a part of something) into smaller parts. —**subdivision** n.

subdue v. -**duing**, -**dued**. overcome; make less intense.

subeditor n. person who checks and edits text for a newspaper or magazine.

subject n. person or thing being dealt with or studied; Grammar word or phrase that represents the person or thing performing the action of the verb in a sentence; person under the rule of a monarch or government. —adj. being under the rule of a monarch or government. —v. (foll. by to) cause to undergo. —**subject to** liable to; conditional upon. —**subjection** n. —**subjective** adj. based on personal feelings or prejudices. —**subjectively** adv.

sub judice [sub **joo**-diss-ee] adj. Latin under judicial consideration.

subjugate v. bring (a group of people) under one's control. —**subjugation** n.

subjunctive Grammar —n. mood of verbs used when the content of the clause is doubted, supposed, or wished. —adj. in or of that mood.

sublet v. -**letting**, -**let**. rent out (property rented from someone else).

sublimate v. Psychol. direct the energy of (a primitive impulse) into socially acceptable activities. —**sublimation** n.

sublime adj. of high moral, intellectual, or spiritual value; unparalleled, supreme. —v. Chem. change from a solid to a vapour without first melting. —**sublimely** adv.

subliminal adj. relating to mental processes of which the individual is not aware.

sub-machine-gun n. portable machine-gun with a short barrel.

submarine n. vessel which can operate below the surface of the sea. —adj. below the surface of the sea.

submerge v. put or go below the surface of water or other liquid. —**submersion** n.

submit v. -**mitting**, -**mitted**. surrender; be (voluntarily) subjected to a process or treatment; put forward for consideration. —**submission** n. submitting; something submitted for consideration; state of being submissive. —**submissive** adj. meek and obedient.

subordinate adj. of lesser rank or importance. —n. subordinate person or thing. —v. make or treat as subordinate. —**subordination** n.

suborn v. bribe or incite (a person) to commit a wrongful act.

subpoena [sub-**pee**-na] n. writ requiring a person to appear before a lawcourt. —v. summon (someone) with a subpoena.

subscribe v. pay (a subscription); give support or approval (to). —**subscriber** n. —**subscription** n. payment for issues of a publication over a period; money contributed to a charity etc.; membership fees paid to a society.

THESAURUS

subdue 1. break, conquer, control, crush, defeat, discipline, humble, master, overcome, overpower, overrun, quell, tame, trample, vanquish 2. check, control, mellow, moderate, repress, soften, suppress, tone down

subject n. 1. affair, business, issue, matter, object, point, question, substance, theme, topic 2. case, client, participant, patient, victim 3. citizen, dependant, liegeman, national, vassal ~adj. 4. answerable, bound by, captive, dependent, inferior, obedient, satellite, subordinate ~v. 5. expose, lay open, submit, treat

subjective biased, emotional, intuitive, personal, prejudiced

sublime elevated, eminent, exalted, glorious, grand, great, high, imposing, lofty, magnificent, majestic, noble

submerge deluge, dip, drown, duck, engulf, flood, immerse, overflow, overwhelm, plunge, sink, swamp

submission 1. assent, capitulation, surrender, yielding 2. compliance, deference, docility, meekness, obedience, passivity, resignation 3. argument, contention, proposal 4. entry, presentation, tendering

submit 1. accede, bend, bow, capitulate, comply, defer, endure, give in, stoop, succumb, surrender, tolerate, yield 2. commit, hand in, present, proffer, refer, table, tender

subordinate adj. 1. dependent, inferior, junior, lesser, lower, minor, secondary, subject 2. ancillary, auxiliary, subsidiary, supplementary ~n. 3. aide, assistant, attendant, inferior, junior, second, underling

subscribe contribute, donate, give, offer, pledge, promise

subscription donation, dues, gift, membership fee, offering

DICTIONARY

subsection *n.* division of a section.

subsequent *adj.* occurring after, succeeding. —**subsequently** *adv.*

subservient *adj.* submissive, servile. —**subservience** *n.*

subside *v.* become less intense; sink to a lower level. —**subsidence** *n.* act or process of subsiding.

subsidiary *adj.* of lesser importance; subordinate. —*n., pl.* **-aries.** subsidiary person or thing.

subsidize *v.* help financially. —**subsidy** *n.* financial aid.

subsist *v.* manage to live. —**subsistence** *n.*

subsonic *adj.* moving at a speed less than that of sound.

substance *n.* solid, powder, liquid, or paste; physical composition of something; essential meaning of something; solid or meaningful quality; wealth. —**substantial** *adj.* of considerable size or value; (of food or a meal) sufficient and nourishing; solid or strong; real. —**substantially** *adv.* —**substantiate** *v.* support (a story) with evidence. —**substantiation** *n.* —**substantive** *adj.* of or being the essential element of a thing. —*n.* noun.

substitute *v.* take the place of or put in place of another. —*n.* person or thing taking the place of (another). —**substitution** *n.*

subsume *v.* incorporate (an idea, case, etc.) under a comprehensive classification.

subterfuge *n.* trick used to achieve an objective.

subterranean *adj.* underground.

subtitle *n.* secondary title of a book. —*pl.* printed translation at the bottom of the picture in a film with foreign dialogue. —*v.* provide with a subtitle or subtitles.

subtle *adj.* not immediately obvious; having or requiring ingenuity. —**subtly** *adv.* —**subtlety** *n.*

subtract *v.* take (one number or quantity) from another. —**subtraction** *n.*

subtropical *adj.* of the regions bordering on the tropics.

suburb *n.* residential area on the outskirts of a city. —**suburban** *adj.* of or inhabiting a suburb; narrow or unadventurous in outlook. —**suburbia** *n.* suburbs and their inhabitants.

subvention *n.* subsidy.

subvert *v.* overthrow the authority of. —**subversion** *n.* —**subversive** *adj.*

subway *n.* passage under a road or railway; *Scot. & US* underground railway.

succeed *v.* accomplish an aim; turn out satisfactorily; come next in order after (something); take over a position from (someone). —**success** *n.* favourable outcome of an attempt; attainment of wealth, fame, or position; successful person or thing. —**successful** *adj.* having success. —**successfully** *adv.* —**succession** *n.* series of people or things following one another in order; act or

---

THESAURUS

subsequent after, ensuing, following, later, succeeding, successive

subsequently afterwards, consequently, later

subside abate, decrease, diminish, dwindle, ease, ebb, lessen, melt away, moderate, peter out, quieten, recede, slacken, wane

subsidiary aiding, ancillary, assistant, auxiliary, helpful, lesser, minor, secondary, subordinate, supplementary, useful

subsidize finance, fund, promote, sponsor, support, underwrite

subsidy aid, allowance, assistance, contribution, grant, help, support

subsist be, continue, endure, exist, last, live, remain, survive

subsistence existence, food, keep, living, maintenance, provision, rations, support, survival, sustenance, upkeep

substance 1. body, fabric, material, stuff, texture 2. burden, essence, gist, import, matter, meaning, pith, significance, subject, theme 3. actuality, concreteness, entity, force, reality 4. affluence, assets, estate, means, property, resources, wealth

substantial ample, big, generous, goodly, important, large, significant, sizable, worthwhile

substantiate authenticate, confirm, establish, prove, support, verify

substitute 1. *v.* change, exchange, interchange, replace, switch 2. *n.* agent, deputy, equivalent, expedient, locum, makeshift, proxy, relief, replacement, representative, reserve, stand-by, stopgap, sub, supply

subterfuge artifice, deception, dodge, evasion, excuse, ploy, pretence, quibble, ruse, shift, stall, stratagem, trick

subtle 1. deep, delicate, ingenious, nice, profound, refined, sophisticated 2. delicate, faint, implied, indirect, slight

subtlety acumen, cleverness, delicacy, intricacy, nicety, refinement, sagacity, skill, sophistication

subtract deduct, detract, diminish, remove, take from, take off

suburb environs, neighbourhood, outskirts, precincts, residential areas, suburbia

subversive destructive, overthrowing, riotous, seditious, underground

DICTIONARY

right by which one person succeeds another in a position. —**successive** *adj.* consecutive. —**successively** *adv.* —**successor** *n.* person who succeeds someone in a position.

succinct *adj.* brief and clear. —**succinctly** *adv.*

succour *v., n.* help in distress.

succulent *adj.* juicy and delicious; (of a plant) having thick fleshy leaves. —*n.* succulent plant. —**succulence** *n.*

succumb *v.* (foll. by *to*) give way (to something overpowering); die of (an illness).

such *adj.* of the kind specified; so great, so much. —*pron.* such things. —**such-and-such** *adj.* specific, but not known or named. —**suchlike** *adj. Informal* of the kind specified.

suck *v.* draw (liquid or air) into the mouth; take (something) into the mouth and moisten, dissolve, or roll it around with the tongue; (foll. by *in*) draw in by irresistible force. —*n.* sucking. —**sucker** *n. Slang* person who is easily deceived or swindled; organ or device which adheres by suction; shoot coming from a plant's root or the base of its main stem. —**suck up to** *v. Informal* flatter (someone) for one's own profit.

suckle *v.* feed at the breast. —**suckling** *n.* unweaned baby or young animal.

sucrose [soo-kroze] *n.* chemical name for sugar.

suction *n.* sucking; force produced by drawing air out of a space to make a vacuum that will suck in a substance from another space.

sudden *adj.* done or occurring quickly and unexpectedly. —*n.* —**all of a sudden** quickly and unexpectedly. —**suddenly** *adv.* —**suddenness** *n.*

—**sudden death** *Sport* period of extra time in which the first competitor to score wins.

sudorific [syoo-dor-**if**-ik] *n., adj.* (drug) causing sweating.

suds *pl. n.* froth of soap and water, lather.

sue *v.* **suing, sued.** start legal proceedings against.

suede *n.* leather with a velvety finish on one side.

suet *n.* hard fat obtained from sheep and cattle, used in cooking.

suffer *v.* undergo or be subjected to; tolerate. —**sufferer** *n.* —**suffering** *n.* —**sufferance** *n.* —**on sufferance** tolerated with reluctance.

suffice [suf-**fice**] *v.* be enough for a purpose. —**sufficiency** *n.* adequate amount. —**sufficient** *adj.* enough, adequate. —**sufficiently** *adv.*

suffix *n.* letter or letters added to the end of a word to form another word.

suffocate *v.* kill or be killed by deprivation of oxygen; feel or cause to feel discomfort from heat and lack of air. —**suffocation** *n.*

suffragan *n.* bishop appointed to assist an archbishop or another bishop.

suffrage *n.* right to vote in public elections. —**suffragette** *n.* (in Britain in the early 20th century) a woman who campaigned militantly for the right to vote.

suffuse *v.* spread through or over (something). —**suffusion** *n.*

sugar *n.* sweet crystalline carbohydrate found in many plants and used to sweeten food and drinks. —*v.* sweeten or cover with sugar. —**sugary** *adj.* —**sugar beet** beet cultivated for the

THESAURUS

succeed 1. flourish, make good, prosper, thrive, triumph, work 2. come next, ensue, follow, result, supervene

success 1. ascendancy, fame, fortune, happiness, luck, prosperity, triumph 2. celebrity, market leader, sensation, somebody, star, winner

successful acknowledged, booming, favourable, flourishing, fortunate, fruitful, lucky, lucrative, paying, profitable, prosperous, rewarding, thriving, top, unbeaten, victorious, wealthy

successfully favourably, victoriously, well

succession 1. chain, course, cycle, flow, order, progression, run, sequence, series, train 2. accession, assumption, elevation, inheritance, taking over

successive consecutive, following, sequent

succinct brief, compact, concise, condensed, laconic, pithy, summary, terse

succour 1. *v.* aid, assist, comfort, encourage, foster, help, nurse, relieve, render assistance to, support 2. *n.* aid, assistance, comfort, help, relief, support

succulent juicy, luscious, lush, rich

succumb capitulate, die, fall, submit, surrender, yield

sudden abrupt, hasty, hurried, quick, rapid, rash, swift, unexpected

suddenly abruptly, unexpectedly, without warning

sue charge, indict, prosecute, summon

suffer bear, endure, experience, feel, support, sustain, tolerate, undergo

suffering *n.* agony, anguish, discomfort, distress, hardship, misery, ordeal, pain, torment

suffice answer, content, do, satisfy, serve

sufficient adequate, competent, enough

DICTIONARY

sugar obtained from its roots. —**sugar cane** tropical grass cultivated for the sugar obtained from its canes. —**sugar daddy** *Slang* elderly man who gives a young woman money and gifts in return for sexual favours.

suggest *v.* put forward (an idea) for consideration; bring to mind by the association of ideas; give a hint of. —**suggestible** *adj.* easily influenced. —**suggestion** *n.* suggesting; thing suggested; hint or indication. —**suggestive** *adj.* suggesting something indecent; conveying a hint (of). —**suggestively** *adv.*

suicide *n.* killing oneself intentionally; person who kills himself intentionally; self-inflicted ruin of one's own prospects or interests. —**suicidal** *adj.* liable to commit suicide. —**suicidally** *adv.*

suit *n.* set of clothes designed to be worn together; outfit worn for a specific purpose; one of the four sets into which a pack of cards is divided; lawsuit. —*v.* be appropriate for; be acceptable to. —**suitable** *adj.* appropriate or proper. —**suitably** *adv.* —**suitability** *n.* —**suitcase** *n.* portable travelling case for clothing.

suite *n.* set of connected rooms in a hotel; matching set of furniture; set of musical pieces in the same key.

suitor *n. Old-fashioned* man who is courting a woman.

sulk *v.* be silent and sullen because of resentment or bad temper. —*n.* resentful or sullen mood. —**sulky** *adj.* —**sulkily** *adv.* —**sulkiness** *n.*

sullen *adj.* unwilling to talk or be sociable; dark and dismal. —**sullenly** *adv.* —**sullenness** *n.*

sully *v.* **-lying, -lied.** make dirty; ruin (someone's reputation).

sulphate *n.* salt or ester of sulphuric acid.

sulphide *n.* compound of sulphur with another element.

sulphite *n.* salt or ester of sulphurous acid.

sulphonamide [sulf-on-a-mide] *n.* any of a class of drugs that prevent the growth of bacteria.

sulphur *n.* pale yellow nonmetallic element. —**sulphuric, sulphurous** *adj.* of or containing sulphur.

sultan *n.* sovereign of a Muslim country. —**sultana** *n.* kind of raisin; sultan's wife, mother, or daughter. —**sultanate** *n.* territory of a sultan.

sultry *adj.* **-trier, -triest.** (of weather or climate) hot and humid; passionate, sensual.

sum *n.* result of addition, total; problem in arithmetic; quantity of money. —**sum total** complete or final total. —**sum up** *v.* **summing, summed.** summarize; form a quick opinion of.

summary *n., pl.* **-ries.** brief account giving the main points of something. —*adj.* done quickly, without formalities. —**summarily** *adv.* —**summarize** *v.* make or be a summary of (something). —**summation** *n.* summary; adding up.

summer *n.* warmest season of the year, between spring and autumn. —**summery** *adj.* —**summertime** *n.* period or season of summer. —**summer time** time shown by clocks put forward in summer to give extra daylight in the evenings.

THESAURUS

suggest 1. advise, move, propose, recommend 2. connote, evoke 3. hint, imply, indicate, insinuate, intimate

suggestion 1. motion, plan, proposal, proposition 2. breath, hint, indication, intimation, trace, whisper

suit *v.* 1. agree, answer, become, befit, conform to, do, gratify, harmonize, match, please, satisfy, tally 2. accommodate, adapt, adjust, fashion, fit, modify, proportion, tailor ~*n.* 3. *Law* action, case, cause, lawsuit, proceeding, prosecution, trial 4. clothing, costume, dress, ensemble, habit, outfit

suitability aptness, fitness, rightness, timeliness

suitable applicable, apposite, appropriate, apt, becoming, befitting, convenient, due, fit, fitting, opportune, pertinent, proper, relevant, right, satisfactory

suite apartment, rooms, series, set

sulk brood, look sullen, pout

sulky aloof, churlish, cross, ill-humoured, moody, morose, perverse, petulant, querulous, resentful, sullen, vexed

sullen brooding, cheerless, cross, dismal, dull, gloomy, heavy, moody, morose, obstinate, silent, sombre, sour, surly, unsociable

sultry close, hot, humid, oppressive, sticky, stifling, stuffy

sum aggregate, amount, quantity, score, tally, total, whole

summarily arbitrarily, immediately, promptly, speedily, swiftly

summarize abridge, condense, encapsulate, epitomize, outline, précis, review, sum up

summary abridgment, abstract, digest, epitome, extract, outline, précis, résumé, review, rundown, synopsis

summit acme, apex, crown, head, height, peak, pinnacle, top, zenith

DICTIONARY

summit *n.* highest point; top of a mountain or hill; conference between heads of state.

summon *v.* order (someone) to come; send for (someone) to appear in court; call upon (someone) to do something; gather (one's courage, strength, etc.). —**summons** *n.* command summoning someone; order requiring someone to appear in court. —*v.* order (someone) to appear in court.

sumo *n.* Japanese style of wrestling.

sump *n.* receptacle in an internal-combustion engine into which oil can drain; hollow into which liquid drains.

sumptuous *adj.* lavish, magnificent. —**sumptuously** *adv.* —**sumptuousness** *n.*

sun *n.* star around which the earth and other planets revolve; any star around which planets revolve; heat and light from the sun. —*v.* **sunning, sunned.** expose (oneself) to the sun's rays. —**sunless** *adj.* —**sunny** *adj.* full of or exposed to sunlight; cheerful. —**sunbathe** *v.* lie in the sunshine in order to get a suntan. —**sunbeam** *n.* ray of sun. —**sunburn** *n.* painful reddening of the skin caused by overexposure to the sun. —**sunburnt, sunburned** *adj.* —**sundial** *n.* device showing the time by means of a pointer that casts a shadow on a marked dial. —**sundown** *n.* US sunset. —**sunflower** *n.* tall plant with large golden flowers. —**sunrise** *n.* daily appearance of the sun above the horizon; time of this. —**sunset** *n.* daily disappearance of the sun below the horizon; time of this. —**sunshine** *n.* light and warmth from the sun. —**sunspot** *n.* dark patch appearing temporarily on the sun's surface. —**sunstroke** *n.* illness caused by prolonged exposure to intensely hot sunlight. —**suntan** *n.* browning of the skin caused by exposure to the sun. —**sun-up** *n.* US sunrise.

sundae *n.* ice cream topped with fruit etc.

Sunday *n.* first day of the week and the Chris-tian day of worship. —**Sunday school** school for teaching children about Christianity.

sunder *v.* break or tear apart.

sundry *adj.* several, various. —**sundries** *pl. n.* miscellaneous unspecified items. —**all and sundry** everybody.

sung *v.* past participle of SING.

sunk *v.* a past of SINK.

sunken *v.* a past participle of SINK.

sup *v.* **supping, supped.** take (liquid) by sips; *Obs.* take supper.

super *adj. Informal* excellent.

super- *prefix* used with many main words to mean: above or over, e.g. *superimpose;* outstanding, e.g. *superstar;* of greater size or extent, e.g. *supermarket.*

superannuation *n.* regular payment by an employee into a pension fund; pension paid from this. —**superannuated** *adj.* discharged with a pension, owing to old age or illness.

superb *adj.* excellent, impressive, or splendid. —**superbly** *adv.*

supercharged *adj.* (of an engine) having a supercharger. —**supercharger** *n.* device that increases the power of an internal-combustion engine by forcing extra air into it.

supercilious *adj.* showing arrogant pride or scorn. —**superciliousness** *n.*

superconductor *n.* substance which has almost no electrical resistance at very low temperatures. —**superconductivity** *n.*

superficial *adj.* of or on the surface; not careful or thorough; (of a person) without depth of character, shallow. —**superficially** *adv.* —**superficiality** *n.*

superfluous [soo-per-flew-uss] *adj.* more than is needed. —**superfluity** *n.*

superhuman *adj.* beyond normal human ability or experience.

THESAURUS

summon arouse, bid, call, cite, convene, convoke, invite, rally, rouse

sumptuous costly, dear, gorgeous, grand, lavish, luxurious, opulent, rich, splendid, superb

sum up 1. close, conclude, recapitulate, review, summarize 2. estimate

sundry assorted, different, miscellaneous, several, some, varied, various

sunny 1. bright, brilliant, clear, fine, radiant, summery, sunlit, unclouded 2. *Fig.* beaming, blithe, buoyant, cheerful, genial, happy, joyful, pleasant

sunrise cockcrow, dawn, daybreak, daylight

sunset dusk, eventide, gloaming, nightfall, sundown

superb admirable, choice, excellent, exquisite, fine, first-rate, gorgeous, grand, magnificent, marvellous, splendid, superior, unrivalled

supercilious arrogant, contemptuous, disdainful, haughty, imperious, insolent, lofty, lordly, overbearing, patronizing, proud, scornful

superficial 1. exterior, external, on the surface, peripheral, shallow, skin-deep, slight, surface 2. casual, cursory, desultory, hasty, hurried, perfunctory, sketchy, slapdash

superficially apparently, externally, ostensibly

superfluous excess, extra, left over, needless, redundant, remaining, residuary, spare, supererogatory, supernumerary, surplus, uncalled-for, unnecessary, unrequired

DICTIONARY

superimpose *v.* place (something) on or over something else.

superintend *v.* supervise (a person or activity). **—superintendence** *n.* **—superintendent** *n.* senior police officer; supervisor.

superior *adj.* greater in quality, quantity, or merit; higher in position or rank; believing oneself to be better than others. *—n.* person of greater rank or status. **—superiority** *n.*

superlative [soo-per-lat-iv] *adj.* of outstanding quality; *Grammar* denoting the form of an adjective or adverb indicating *most. —n. Grammar* superlative form of a word.

superman *n.* man of apparently superhuman powers.

supermarket *n.* large self-service store selling food and household goods.

supernatural *adj.* of or relating to things beyond the laws of nature. *—n.* **-the supernatural** supernatural forces, occurrences, and beings collectively.

supernova *n., pl.* **-vae, -vas.** star that explodes and briefly becomes exceptionally bright.

supernumerary *adj.* exceeding the required or regular number. *—n., pl.* **-ries.** supernumerary person or thing.

superphosphate *n.* chemical fertilizer containing phosphates.

superpower *n.* extremely powerful nation.

superscript *adj.* (of a character) printed or written above the line. *—n.* superscript character.

supersede *v.* replace, supplant.

supersonic *adj.* of or travelling at a speed greater than the speed of sound.

superstition *n.* belief in omens, ghosts, etc.; idea or practice based on this. **—superstitious** *adj.*

superstructure *n.* structure erected on something else; part of a ship above the main deck.

supervene *v.* occur as an unexpected development. **—supervention** *n.*

supervise *v.* watch over to direct or check. **—supervision** *n.* **—supervisor** *n.* **—supervisory** *adj.*

supine [soo-pine] *adj.* lying flat on one's back.

supper *n.* light evening meal.

supplant *v.* take the place of, oust.

supple *adj.* (of a person) moving and bending easily and gracefully; bending easily without damage. **—suppleness** *n.* **—supply** *adv.*

supplement *n.* thing added to complete something or make up for a lack; magazine inserted into a newspaper; section added to a publication to supply further information. *—v.* provide or be a supplement to (something). **—supplementary** *adj.*

supplication *n.* humble request. **—supplicant** *n.* person who makes a humble request.

supply *v.* **-plying, -plied.** provide with something required; make available. *—n., pl.* **-plies.** supplying; amount available. *—pl.* food or equipment. **—supplier** *n.*

THESAURUS

superhuman heroic, prodigious, stupendous, valiant

superintend administer, control, direct, inspect, manage, overlook, oversee, run, supervise

superintendent chief, controller, director, governor, inspector, manager, overseer, supervisor

superior *adj.* 1. better, grander, greater, higher, paramount, preferred, surpassing, unrivalled 2. choice, de luxe, distinguished, excellent, exceptional, exclusive, fine, first-class, first-rate, good 3. airy, condescending, disdainful, haughty, lofty, lordly, patronizing, pretentious, snobbish ~*n.* 4. boss (*Inf.*), chief, director, manager, principal, senior, supervisor

superiority advantage, ascendancy, excellence, lead, preponderance, supremacy

superlative *adj.* excellent, greatest, highest, matchless, outstanding, peerless, supreme, surpassing, transcendent, unparalleled, unrivalled, unsurpassed

supernatural dark, ghostly, hidden, miraculous, mysterious, mystic, occult, paranormal, phantom, psychic, spectral, supranatural, uncanny, unearthly

supervise administer, conduct, control, direct, handle, inspect, look after, manage, oversee, run, superintend

supervision administration, care, charge, control, direction, guidance, management, oversight

supervisor administrator, chief, foreman, manager, overseer, steward

supplant displace, oust, remove, replace, undermine, unseat

supple bending, elastic, flexible, limber, lithe, plastic, pliable, pliant

supplement 1. *n.* addition, codicil, extra, insert, postscript, pull-out, sequel 2. *v.* add, augment, complement, extend, fill out, reinforce, top up

supplementary additional, ancillary, auxiliary, extra, secondary

DICTIONARY

support *v.* bear the weight of; provide the necessities of life for; give practical or emotional help to; take an active interest in (a sports team, political principle, etc.); help to prove (a theory etc.). —*n.* supporting; means of support. —**supporter** *n.* person who supports a team, principle, etc. —**supportive** *adj.*

suppose *v.* presume to be true; consider as a proposal for the sake of discussion. —**supposed** *adj.* presumed to be true without proof; doubtful. —**supposed to** expected or required to, e.g. *you were supposed to phone me;* permitted to, e.g. *we're not supposed to swim here.* —**supposedly** *adv.* —**supposition** *n.* supposing; something supposed.

suppository *n., pl.* **-ries.** solid medication inserted into the rectum or vagina and left to melt.

suppress *v.* put an end to; restrain (an emotion or response); prevent publication of (information). —**suppression** *n.*

suppurate *v.* (of a wound etc.) produce pus. —**suppuration** *n.*

supreme *adj.* highest in authority, rank, or degree. —**supremely** *adv.* extremely. —**su-**

premacy *n.* supreme power; state of being supreme. —**supremo** *n. Informal* person in overall authority.

surcharge *n.* additional charge.

surd *n. Maths* number that cannot be expressed in whole numbers.

sure *adj.* free from uncertainty or doubt; reliable; inevitable. —*adv., interj. Informal* certainly. —**surely** *adv.* it must be true that. —**surefooted** *adj.* unlikely to slip or stumble.

surety *n., pl.* **-ties.** person who takes responsibility, or thing given as a guarantee, for the fulfilment of another's obligation.

surf *n.* foam caused by waves breaking on the shore. —*v.* take part in surfing. —**surfing** *n.* sport of riding towards the shore on a surfboard on the crest of a wave. —**surfer** *n.* —**surfboard** *n.* board used in surfing.

surface *n.* outside or top of an object; material covering the surface of an object; superficial appearance. —*v.* rise to the surface; put a surface on.

surfeit *n.* excessive amount.

THESAURUS

supply *v.* 1. afford, contribute, endow, fill, furnish, give, grant, outfit, produce, provide, replenish, satisfy, stock, store, yield ~*n.* 2. cache, fund, hoard, quantity, reserve, reservoir, source, stock, store 3. *Usually plural* equipment, food, foodstuff, materials, necessities, provisions, rations, stores

support *v.* 1. bear, brace, buttress, carry, hold, prop, reinforce, sustain, underpin, uphold 2. buoy up, cherish, finance, foster, fund, keep, maintain, nourish, provide for, strengthen, sustain, underwrite 3. aid, assist, back, champion, defend, forward, help, promote, second, side with, uphold ~*n.* 4. back, brace, foundation, lining, pillar, post, prop, shore, stay, underpinning 5. aid, approval, assistance, backing, blessing, comfort, encouragement, friendship, help, loyalty, patronage, protection, relief, succour, sustenance 6. keep, subsistence, sustenance, upkeep 7. backbone, backer, comforter, mainstay, prop, second, stay, supporter

supporter adherent, advocate, champion, fan, follower, friend, helper, patron, sponsor, well-wisher

suppose *v.* 1. assume, conjecture, expect, imagine, infer, judge, opine, presume, surmise, granted, think 2. believe, conceive, conclude, conjecture, consider, fancy, imagine, pretend

supposition conjecture, doubt, guess, hypothesis, idea, presumption, speculation, surmise, theory

suppress 1. beat down, check, conquer, crush, extinguish, overpower, overthrow, quash, quell, quench, stop, subdue, trample on 2. censor, conceal, contain, curb, muffle, muzzle, repress, restrain, silence, smother, stifle, withhold

supremacy ascendancy, dominance, lordship, mastery, predominance, primacy, sovereignty, sway

supreme cardinal, chief, crowning, extreme, final, first, foremost, greatest, head, highest, leading, matchless, paramount, peerless, pre-eminent, prevailing, prime, principal, sovereign, superlative, surpassing, top, ultimate, utmost

sure 1. assured, certain, clear, confident, convinced, decided, definite, persuaded, positive, satisfied 2. accurate, dependable, effective, foolproof, honest, indisputable, infallible, precise, reliable, trustworthy, trusty, undeniable, undoubted, unerring, unfailing 3. assured, bound, guaranteed, inescapable, inevitable, irrevocable

surely certainly, definitely, doubtlessly, inevitably, undoubtedly, unquestionably

surface 1. *n.* covering, exterior, face, outside, plane, side, skin, top, veneer 2. *v.* appear, come to light, come up, crop up (*Inf.*), emerge, materialize, rise, transpire

surfeit *n.* excess, glut, plethora, superfluity

DICTIONARY

surge n. sudden powerful increase; strong rolling movement of the sea. —v. increase suddenly; move forward strongly.

surgeon n. doctor who specializes in surgery. —**surgery** n. treatment in which the patient's body is cut open in order to treat the affected part; place where, or time when, a doctor, dentist, MP, etc. can be consulted. —**surgical** adj. —**surgically** adv.

surly adj. -**lier**, -**liest**. ill-tempered and rude. —**surliness** n.

surmise v., n. guess, conjecture.

surmount v. overcome (a problem); be on top of (something). —**surmountable** adj.

surname n. family name.

surpass v. be greater than or superior to.

surplice n. loose white robe worn by clergymen and choristers.

surplus n. amount left over in excess of what is required.

surprise n. unexpected event; amazement and wonder. —v. cause to feel amazement or wonder; come upon, attack, or catch suddenly and unexpectedly. —**take someone by surprise** catch someone unprepared.

surrealism n. movement in art and literature involving the combination of incongruous images, as in a dream. —**surreal** adj. —**surrealist** n., adj. —**surrealistic** adj.

surrender v. give (something) up to another; give oneself up; yield (to a temptation or influence). —n. surrendering.

surreptitious adj. done secretly or stealthily. —**surreptitiously** adv.

surrogate n. substitute. —**surrogate mother** woman who gives birth to a child on behalf of a couple who cannot have children.

surround v. be, come, or place all around (a person or thing). —n. border or edging. —**surroundings** pl. n. conditions, scenery, etc. around a person, place, or thing.

surtax n. extra tax on incomes above a certain level.

surveillance n. close observation.

survey v. view or consider in a general way; make a map of (an area); inspect (a building) to assess its condition and value; find out the incomes, opinions, etc. of (a group of people). —n. surveying; report produced by a survey. —**surveyor** n.

survive v. continue to live or exist after (a difficult experience); live after the death of (another). —**survival** n. condition of having survived; thing that has survived from an earlier time. —**survivor** n.

susceptible adj. liable to be influenced or affected by. —**susceptibility** n.

suspect v. believe (someone) to be guilty without having any proof; think (something) to be false or questionable; believe (something) to be the case. —adj. not to be trusted. —n. person who is suspected.

THESAURUS

surge billow, eddy, gush, heave, rise, roll, rush, swell, swirl, tower, undulate, well forth

surly churlish, crabbed, cross, crusty, gruff, morose, perverse, sulky, sullen, testy, uncivil, ungracious

surmise 1. v. conclude, conjecture, consider, deduce, fancy, guess, imagine, infer, opine, presume, speculate, suppose, suspect 2. n. conclusion, conjecture, deduction, guess, idea, inference, notion, speculation, supposition, suspicion

surmount conquer, exceed, master, overcome, pass, surpass, vanquish

surpass beat, best, eclipse, exceed, excel, outdo, outshine, outstrip, override, transcend

surplus n. balance, excess, remainder, residue, surfeit

surprise v. 1. amaze, astonish, astound, bewilder, confuse, disconcert, stagger, stun 2. discover, spring upon, startle ~n. 3. amazement, astonishment, incredulity, wonder 4. bombshell, jolt, revelation, shock

surrender v. 1. abandon, cede, concede, forego, part with, relinquish, renounce, resign, waive, yield 2. capitulate, give in, give way, quit, submit, succumb, yield ~n. 3. capitulation, delivery, renunciation, resignation, submission

surreptitious covert, fraudulent, furtive, secret, sly, stealthy, underhand, veiled

surround encircle, enclose, encompass, envelop, environ, girdle, ring

surroundings background, environs, location, milieu, setting

surveillance care, control, direction, inspection, scrutiny, supervision, vigilance, watch

survey v. 1. contemplate, examine, inspect, observe, research, review, scan, scrutinize, study, view 2. appraise, assess, estimate, measure, plan, plot, prospect, size up, triangulate ~n. 3. examination, inquiry, inspection, overview, perusal, random sample, review, scrutiny, study

DICTIONARY

suspend v. hang from a high place; cause to remain floating or hanging; cause to cease temporarily; remove (someone) temporarily from a job or team. —**suspenders** pl. n. straps for holding up stockings; US braces.

suspense n. state of uncertainty while awaiting news, an event, etc.

suspension n. suspending or being suspended; system of springs and shock absorbers supporting the body of a vehicle; mixture of fine particles of a solid in a fluid. —**suspension bridge** bridge hanging from cables attached to towers at each end.

suspicion n. feeling of not trusting a person or thing; belief that something is true without definite proof; slight trace. —**suspicious** adj. feeling or causing suspicion. —**suspiciously** adv.

suss out v. Slang work out using one's intuition.

sustain v. maintain or prolong; suffer (an injury or loss); keep up the vitality or strength of; support. —**sustenance** n. food.

suture [soo-cher] n. stitch joining the edges of a wound.

suzerain n. state or sovereign with limited authority over another self-governing state. —**suzerainty** n.

svelte adj. attractively or gracefully slim.

SW southwest(ern).

swab n. small piece of cotton wool used to apply medication, clean a wound, etc. —v. **swabbing, swabbed.** clean (a wound) with a swab; clean (the deck of a ship) with a mop.

swaddle v. wrap (a baby) in swaddling clothes. —**swaddling clothes** long strips of cloth formerly wrapped round a newborn baby.

swag n. Slang stolen property; Aust. informal bundle of belongings carried by a swagman. —**swagman** n. Aust. tramp who carries his belongings in a bundle on his back.

swagger v. walk or behave arrogantly. —n. arrogant walk or manner.

swain n. Poetic suitor; country youth.

swallow[1] v. cause to pass down one's throat; make a gulping movement in the throat, as when nervous; Informal believe (something) gullibly; refrain from showing (a feeling); engulf or absorb. —n. swallowing; amount swallowed.

swallow[2] n. small migratory bird with long pointed wings and a forked tail.

swam v. past tense of SWIM.

swamp n. watery area of land, bog. —v. cause (a boat) to fill with water and sink; overwhelm. —**swampy** adj.

swan n. large usu. white water bird with a long graceful neck. —v. **swanning, swanned.** Informal wander about idly. —**swan song** person's last performance before retirement or death.

swank Slang —v. show off or boast. —n. showing off or boasting. —**swanky** adj. Slang expensive and showy, stylish.

swap v. **swapping, swapped.** exchange (something) for something else. —n. exchange.

sward n. stretch of short grass.

swarm[1] n. large group of bees or other insects; large crowd. —v. move in a swarm; (of a place) be crowded or overrun.

swarm[2] v. (foll. by up) climb (a ladder or rope) by gripping with the hands and feet.

THESAURUS

survive be extant, endure, exist, last, live, live on, outlast, outlive, remain alive, subsist

suspect v. 1. distrust, doubt, mistrust 2. believe, conclude, conjecture, consider, fancy, feel, guess, speculate, suppose, surmise ~adj. 3. doubtful, dubious, questionable

suspend 1. attach, dangle, hang, swing 2. arrest, cease, cut short, debar, defer, delay, discontinue, interrupt, postpone, put off, shelve, stay, withhold

suspense anxiety, apprehension, doubt, expectation, indecision, insecurity, irresolution, tension, uncertainty, wavering

suspicion 1. distrust, doubt, jealousy, misgiving, mistrust, qualm, scepticism, wariness 2. conjecture, guess, hunch, idea, impression, notion, supposition, surmise 3. glimmer, hint, shade, shadow, soupçon, strain, streak, suggestion, tinge, touch, trace

suspicious 1. doubtful, jealous, sceptical, unbelieving, wary 2. doubtful, dubious, funny, irregular, queer, questionable

sustain 1. bear, carry, support, uphold 2. bear, endure, experience, feel, suffer, withstand 3. aid, assist, comfort, foster, help, keep alive, nourish, nurture, relieve 4. approve, confirm, continue, maintain, prolong, protract, ratify

sustenance comestibles, eatables, food, nourishment, rations, refreshments, victuals

swagger 1. v. bluster, boast, brag, bully, hector, parade, prance, strut 2. n. arrogance, bluster, display, pomposity, show

swallow absorb, consume, devour, drink, eat, gulp, ingest, swill, wash down

swamp 1. n. bog, fen, marsh, mire, morass, quagmire, slough 2. v. capsize, drench, engulf, flood, inundate, overwhelm, sink, submerge, upset, waterlog

DICTIONARY

swarthy *adj.* **-thier, -thiest.** dark-complexioned.

swashbuckler *n.* daredevil adventurer. **—swashbuckling** *adj.*

swastika *n.* symbol in the shape of a cross with the arms bent at right angles, used as the emblem of Nazi Germany.

swat *v.* **swatting, swatted.** hit sharply. **—***n.* sharp blow.

swatch *n.* sample of cloth.

swath [swawth] *n.* the width of one sweep of a scythe or mower.

swathe *v.* wrap in bandages or layers of cloth. **—***n.* same as SWATH.

sway *v.* swing to and fro or from side to side; waver or cause to waver in opinion. **—***n.* power or influence; swaying motion.

swear *v.* **swearing, swore, sworn.** use obscene or blasphemous language; state earnestly; state or promise on oath. **—swear by** *v.* have complete confidence in. **—swear in** *v.* cause to take an oath. **—swearword** *n.* word considered obscene or blasphemous.

sweat *n.* salty liquid given off through the pores of the skin; *Slang* drudgery or hard labour. **—***v.* have sweat coming through the pores; be anxious; toil. **—sweaty** *adj.* **—sweatband** *n.* strip of cloth tied around the forehead or wrist to absorb sweat. **—sweatshirt** *n.* long-sleeved cotton jersey. **—sweatshop** *n.* place where employees work long hours in poor conditions for low pay.

sweater *n.* (woollen) garment for the upper part of the body.

swede *n.* kind of turnip.

sweep *v.* **sweeping, swept.** remove dirt from (a floor) with a broom; move smoothly and quickly; spread rapidly; move majestically; carry away suddenly or forcefully; stretch in a long wide curve. **—***n.* sweeping; sweeping motion; wide expanse; person who cleans chimneys; sweepstake. **—sweeping** *adj.* indiscriminate; wide-ranging. **—sweepstake** *n.* lottery in which the stakes of the participants make up the prize.

sweet *adj.* tasting of or like sugar; agreeable to the senses or mind; kind and charming. **—***n.* shaped piece of food consisting mainly of sugar; dessert. **—sweetly** *adv.* **—sweetness** *n.* **—sweeten** *v.* **—sweetener** *n.* sweetening agent that does not contain sugar; *Slang* bribe. **—sweetbread** *n.* animal's pancreas used as food. **—sweetbrier** *n.* wild rose. **—sweet corn** type of maize with sweet yellow kernels, eaten as a vegetable. **—sweetheart** *n.* lover. **—sweetmeat** *n.* *Old-fashioned* sweet delicacy such as a small cake. **—sweet pea** climbing plant with bright fragrant flowers. **—sweet potato** tropical root vegetable with yellow flesh. **—sweet-talk** *v.* *Informal* coax or flatter. **—sweet tooth** strong liking for sweet foods. **—sweet william** garden plant with flat clusters of scented flowers.

swell *v.* **swelling, swelled, swollen** *or* **swelled.** expand or increase; be puffed up with pride or other emotion; (of a sound) become gradually louder. **—***n.* swelling or being swollen; movement of waves in the sea; *Old-fashioned slang* fashionable person. **—***adj.* *US slang* excellent or

---

THESAURUS

swap *v.* bandy, barter, exchange, interchange, switch, trade, traffic

swarm *n.* 1. army, bevy, crowd, drove, flock, herd, horde, host, mass, multitude, myriad, shoal, throng ~*v.* 2. crowd, flock, mass, stream, throng 3. abound, bristle, crawl, teem

swarthy black, brown, dark, dusky

swashbuckling bold, dashing, gallant, spirited, swaggering

sway *v.* 1. bend, incline, lean, lurch, oscillate, rock, roll, swing, wave 2. affect, control, direct, dominate, govern, guide, induce, influence, persuade ~*n.* 3. ascendency, authority, command, control, influence, jurisdiction, power, predominance, rule, sovereignty

swear 1. affirm, assert, attest, avow, declare, depose, promise, testify, vow, warrant 2. blaspheme, curse, imprecate

sweat *n.* 1. perspiration 2. *Inf.* chore, drudgery, effort, labour ~*v.* 3. glow, perspire 4. *Inf.* agonize, chafe, fret, suffer, torture oneself, worry

sweep *v.* 1. brush, clean, clear, remove 2. career, fly, glance, glide, hurtle, pass, sail, scud, skim, tear, zoom ~*n.* 3. arc, bend, curve, move, stroke, swing 4. compass, extent, range, scope, stretch

sweet *adj.* 1. cloying, honeyed, luscious, melting, sweetened 2. affectionate, agreeable, amiable, appealing, beautiful, charming, engaging, fair, gentle, kind, lovable, tender, unselfish, winning 3. aromatic, balmy, clean, fragrant, fresh, new, pure, wholesome ~*n.* 4. confectionery

sweeten 1. honey, sugar 2. alleviate, appease, pacify, soothe

sweetheart admirer, beau, beloved, boyfriend, darling, dear, girlfriend, love, lover, suitor

swell 1. *v.* balloon, belly, billow, bloat, bulge, dilate, distend, enlarge, expand, extend, fatten, grow, increase, protrude, rise, tumefy, well up 2. *n.* billow, rise, surge, wave

swelling *n.* bruise, bulge, bump, dilation, enlargement, inflammation, lump, protuberance

DICTIONARY

fine. **—swelling** n. enlargement of part of the body, caused by injury or infection.

swelter v. be oppressed by heat.

swept v. past of SWEEP.

swerve v. turn aside from a course sharply or suddenly. —n. swerving.

swift adj. moving or able to move quickly. —n. fast-flying bird with pointed wings. **—swiftly** adv. **—swiftness** n.

swig n. large mouthful of drink. —v. **swigging, swigged.** drink in large mouthfuls.

swill v. drink greedily; rinse (something) in large amounts of water. —n. sloppy mixture containing waste food, fed to pigs; deep drink; rinsing.

swim v. **swimming, swam, swum.** move along in water by movements of the limbs; be covered or flooded with liquid; reel, e.g. *her head was swimming.* —n. act or period of swimming. **—swimmer** n. **—swimmingly** adv. successfully and effortlessly. **—swimming pool** (building containing an) artificial pond for swimming in.

swindle v. cheat (someone) out of money. —n. instance of swindling. **—swindler** n.

swine n. contemptible person; pig. **—swinish** adj.

swing v. **swinging, swung.** move to and fro, sway; move in a curve; hit out with a sweeping motion; (of an opinion or mood) change sharply; *Slang* be hanged. —n. swinging; suspended seat on which a child can swing to and fro; style of popular dance music played by big bands in the 1930s.

swingeing [swin-jing] adj. punishing, severe.

swipe v. strike (at) with a sweeping blow; *Slang* steal. —n. sweeping blow.

swirl v. turn with a whirling motion. —n. whirling motion; twisting shape.

swish v. move with a whistling or hissing sound. —n. whistling or hissing sound. —adj. *Informal* fashionable, smart.

Swiss adj. of Switzerland or its people. —n., pl.

Swiss. person from Switzerland. **—swiss roll** sponge cake spread with jam or cream and rolled up.

switch n. device for opening and closing an electric circuit; abrupt change; exchange or swap; flexible rod or twig. —v. change abruptly; exchange or swap. **—switchback** n. road or railway with many sharp hills or bends. **—switchboard** n. installation in a telephone exchange or office where telephone calls are connected. **—switch on** *or* **off** v. turn (a device) on *or* off by means of a switch.

swivel n. coupling device that allows an attached object to turn freely. —v. **-elling, -elled.** turn on or as if on a swivel.

swizzle stick n. small ornamental stick used to stir a cocktail.

swollen v. a past participle of SWELL.

swoon v., n. faint.

swoop v. sweep down or pounce on suddenly. —n. swooping.

swop v. **swopping, swopped.** same as SWAP. —n. same as SWAP.

sword n. weapon with a long sharp blade. **—swordfish** n. large fish with a very long upper jaw. **—swordsman** n. person skilled in the use of a sword.

swore v. past tense of SWEAR.

sworn v. past participle of SWEAR. —adj. bound by or as if by an oath, e.g. *sworn enemies.*

swot *Informal* —v. **swotting, swotted.** study hard. —n. person who studies hard.

swum v. past participle of SWIM.

swung v. past of SWING.

sybarite [sib-bar-ite] n. lover of luxury. **—sybaritic** adj.

sycamore n. tree with five-pointed leaves and two-winged fruits.

sycophant n. person who uses flattery to win favour from people with power or influence. **—sycophantic** adj. **—sycophancy** n.

THESAURUS

swerve v. bend, deflect, deviate, diverge, incline, shift, stray, swing, turn, turn aside, veer, wander, wind

swift abrupt, express, fast, fleet, flying, hurried, nimble, prompt, quick, rapid, ready, short, speedy, sudden, winged

swindle 1. v. cheat, deceive, defraud, dupe, fleece, overcharge, trick 2. n. deceit, deception, fraud, knavery, racket, roguery, trickery

swindler charlatan, cheat, fraud, impostor, mountebank, rascal, rogue, shark, trickster

swing v. 1. dangle, hang, suspend 2. fluctuate,

oscillate, rock, sway, vary, veer, vibrate, wave ~n. 3. fluctuation, stroke, sway, vibration

swirl v. churn, eddy, spin, surge, twist

switch 1. v. change, deflect, deviate, divert, exchange, shift, substitute, trade 2. n. alteration, change, exchange, reversal, shift, substitution

swollen bloated, distended, enlarged, inflamed, tumid

swoop 1. v. descend, dive, pounce, rush, stoop, sweep 2. n. drop, lunge, pounce, rush

DICTIONARY

syllable *n.* part of a word pronounced as a unit. —**syllabic** *adj.*

syllabub *n.* dessert of beaten cream, sugar, and wine.

syllabus *n.* list of subjects for a course of study.

syllogism *n.* form of logical reasoning consisting of two premises and a conclusion. —**syllogistic** *adj.*

sylph *n.* imaginary being supposed to inhabit the air; slender graceful girl or woman. —**sylphlike** *adj.*

sylvan *adj. Lit.* relating to woods and trees.

symbiosis *n.* close association of two species living together to their mutual benefit. —**symbiotic** *adj.*

symbol *n.* sign or thing that stands for something else. —**symbolic** *adj.* —**symbolically** *adv.* —**symbolism** *n.* representation of something by symbols; movement in art and literature using symbols to express abstract and mystical ideas. —**symbolist** *n., adj.* —**symbolize** *v.* be a symbol of; represent with a symbol.

symmetry *n.* state of having two halves that are mirror images of each other. —**symmetrical** *adj.* —**symmetrically** *adv.*

sympathy *n., pl.* **-thies.** compassion for someone's pain or distress; agreement with someone's feelings or interests. —**sympathetic** *adj.* feeling or showing sympathy; likeable or appealing. —**sympathetically** *adv.* —**sympathize** *v.* feel or express sympathy. —**sympathizer** *n.*

symphony *n., pl.* **-nies.** composition for orchestra, with several movements. —**symphonic** *adj.*

symposium *n., pl.* **-siums, -sia.** conference for discussion of a particular topic.

symptom *n.* sign indicating the presence of an illness; sign that something is wrong. —**symptomatic** *adj.*

synagogue *n.* Jewish place of worship and religious instruction.

sync(h) *n. Informal* synchronization.

synchromesh *adj.* (of a gearbox) having a device that synchronizes the speeds of gears before they engage.

synchronize *v.* (of two or more people) perform (an action) at the same time; match (the soundtrack and action of a film) precisely; set (watches) to show the same time. —**synchronization** *n.* —**synchronous, synchronic** *adj.* happening or existing at the same time.

syncline *n.* downward fold of rock strata in the earth's surface.

syncopate *v. Music* stress the weak beats in (a rhythm) instead of the strong ones. —**syncopation** *n.*

syncope [**sing**-kop-ee] *n. Med.* a faint.

syndicate *n.* group of people or firms undertaking a joint business project; agency that sells material to several newspapers. —*v.* form a syndicate; publish (material) in several newspapers. —**syndication** *n.*

syndrome *n.* combination of symptoms indicating a particular disease; set of characteristics indicating a particular problem.

synod *n.* church council.

synonym *n.* word with the same meaning as another. —**synonymous** *adj.*

synopsis *n., pl.* **-ses.** summary or outline.

syntax *n. Grammar* way in which words are arranged to form phrases and sentences. —**syntactic** *adj.* —**syntactically** *adv.*

synthesis *n., pl.* **-ses.** combination of objects or ideas into a whole; artificial production of a substance. —**synthesize** *v.* produce by synthesis. —**synthesizer** *n.* electronic musical instrument producing a range of sounds. —**synthetic** *adj.* (of a substance) made artificially; not genuine, insincere. —**synthetically** *adv.*

syphilis *n.* serious sexually transmitted disease. —**syphilitic** *adj.*

syphon *n., v.* same as SIPHON.

syringa *n.* same as MOCK ORANGE or LILAC.

syringe *n.* device for withdrawing or injecting fluids, consisting of a hollow cylinder, a piston,

---

THESAURUS

syllabus course of study, curriculum

symbol badge, emblem, figure, image, representation, sign, token, type

symmetrical balanced, proportional, regular

symmetry agreement, balance, evenness, harmony, order, proportion

sympathetic 1. caring, compassionate, concerned, condoling, feeling, interested, kind, kindly, pitying, responsive, supportive, tender, warm 2. agreeable, appreciative, compatible, congenial, friendly, responsive

sympathize 1. commiserate, condole, feel for, pity 2. agree, understand

sympathizer partisan, supporter, well-wisher

sympathy 1. compassion, pity, tenderness, understanding 2. affinity, agreement, congeniality, harmony, rapport, union, warmth

symptom expression, indication, mark, note, sign, token, warning

synthesis 1. amalgamation, combination, integration, welding 2. amalgam, blend, combination, composite, compound, fusion, union

synthetic artificial, fake, man-made, mock

DICTIONARY

and a hollow needle. —*v.* wash out or inject with a syringe.

syrup *n.* solution of sugar in water; thick sweet liquid; excessive sentimentality. —**syrupy** *adj.*

system *n.* method or set of methods; scheme of classification or arrangement; network or assembly of parts that form a whole. —**systematic** *adj.* —**systematically** *adv.* —**systematize** *v.* organize using a system. —**systematization** *n.* —**systemic** *adj.* affecting the entire animal or body.

systole [**siss**-tol-ee] *n.* regular contraction of the heart as it pumps blood. —**systolic** *adj.*

THESAURUS

system 1. arrangement, classification, coordination, organization, scheme, structure 2. method, practice, procedure, routine, technique, theory, usage 3. method, orderliness, regularity

systematic efficient, methodical, orderly, organized, precise

T

t tonne.

T n. —**to a T** in every detail; perfectly.

t. ton.

TA Territorial Army.

ta interj. Informal thank you.

tab n. small flap or projecting label. —**keep tabs on** Informal watch closely.

tabard n. short sleeveless tunic.

Tabasco n. ® very hot red pepper sauce.

tabby n., pl. -bies, adj. (cat) with dark stripes on a lighter background.

tabernacle n. portable shrine of the Israelites; RC Church receptacle for the consecrated Host; Christian place of worship not called a church.

tabla n., pl. -blas, -bla. one of a pair of Indian drums played with the hands.

table n. piece of furniture with a flat top supported by legs; arrangement of information in columns. —v. submit (a motion) for discussion by a meeting; US suspend discussion of (a proposal). —**tableland** n. high plateau. —**tablespoon** n. large spoon for serving food. —**table tennis** game like tennis played on a table with small bats and a light ball.

tableau [tab-loh] n., pl. -leaux, -leaus. silent motionless group arranged to represent some scene.

table d'hôte [tah-bla dote] n., pl. tables d'hôte, adj. (meal) having a set number of dishes at a fixed price.

tablet n. pill of compressed medicinal substance; flattish cake of soap etc.; inscribed slab of stone etc.

tabloid n. small-sized newspaper with many photographs and a concise, usu. sensational style.

taboo n., pl. -boos. prohibition resulting from religious or social conventions. —adj. forbidden by a taboo.

tabular adj. arranged in a table. —**tabulate** v. arrange (information) in a table. —**tabulation** n.

tachograph n. device for recording the speed and distance travelled by a motor vehicle.

tachometer n. device for measuring speed, esp. that of a revolving shaft.

tacit [tass-it] adj. implied but not spoken. —**tacitly** adv.

taciturn [tass-it-turn] adj. habitually uncommunicative. —**taciturnity** n.

tack[1] n. short nail with a large head; long loose stitch. —v. fasten with tacks; stitch with tacks; append.

tack[2] n. course of a ship sailing obliquely into the wind; course of action. —v. sail into the wind on a zigzag course.

tack[3] n. riding harness for horses.

tackle n. set of ropes and pulleys for lifting heavy weights; equipment for a particular activity; Sport act of tackling an opposing player. —v. undertake (a task); confront (an opponent); Sport attempt to get the ball from (an opposing player).

tacky[1] adj. tackier, tackiest. slightly sticky. —**tackiness** n.

tacky[2] adj. tackier, tackiest. Informal vulgar and tasteless; shabby.

tact n. skill in avoiding giving offence. —**tactful** adj. —**tactfully** adv. —**tactless** adj. —**tactlessly** adv.

THESAURUS

table n. 1. bench, board, counter, slab, stand 2. agenda, chart, diagram, graph, index, list, plan, record, register, roll, schedule ~v. 3. enter, move, propose, put forward, submit, suggest

taboo 1. adj. banned, forbidden, outlawed, prohibited, proscribed, unmentionable, unthinkable 2. n. anathema, ban, prohibition, proscription, restriction

tacit implicit, implied, inferred, silent, understood, unspoken, unstated

taciturn aloof, cold, distant, dumb, mute, quiet, reserved, reticent, silent, unforthcoming

tack n. 1. nail, pin, staple 2. approach, bearing, course, direction, heading, line, method, path, tactic, way ~v. 3. affix, attach, fasten, fix, nail, pin, staple 4. baste, stitch

tackle n. 1. apparatus, equipment, gear, outfit, rigging, tools, trappings 2. block, challenge, stop ~v. 3. attempt, begin, embark upon, engage in, essay, undertake 4. block, bring down, grab, grasp, halt, seize, stop, throw

tact address, delicacy, diplomacy, discretion, judgment, perception, skill

tactful careful, considerate, delicate, diplomatic, discreet, judicious, polite, sensitive, subtle, thoughtful

tactic 1. approach, course, device, line, means, method, move, ploy, policy, scheme, trick, way 2. Plural campaign, plans, strategy

tactical artful, clever, cunning, politic, shrewd, skilful, smart

DICTIONARY

tactics *pl. n.* art of directing military forces in battle; methods or plans to achieve an end. —**tactical** *adj.* —**tactician** *n.*

tactile *adj.* of or having the sense of touch.

tadpole *n.* limbless tailed larva of a frog or toad.

taffeta *n.* shiny silk or rayon fabric.

taffrail *n.* rail at the stern of a ship.

tag[1] *n.* label bearing information; pointed end of a cord or lace; trite quotation. —*v.* **tagging, tagged.** attach a tag to. —**tag along** *v.* accompany someone, esp. if uninvited.

tag[2] *n.* children's game where the person being chased becomes the chaser upon being touched. —*v.* **tagging, tagged.** touch and catch in this game.

tagliatelle *n.* pasta in long narrow strips.

tail *n.* rear part of an animal's body, usu. forming a flexible appendage; rear or last part or parts of something; *Informal* person employed to follow and spy on another. —*pl.* side of a coin without a portrait of a head on it; *Informal* tail coat. —*v. Informal* follow (someone) secretly. —*adj.* at the rear. —**turn tail** run away. —**tailless** *adj.* —**tailback** *n.* queue of traffic stretching back from an obstruction. —**tailboard** *n.* removable or hinged rear board on a lorry etc. —**tail coat** man's coat with a long back split into two below the waist. —**tail off, away** *v.* diminish gradually. —**tailplane** *n.* small stabilizing wing at the rear of an aircraft. —**tailspin** *n.* uncontrolled spinning dive of an aircraft. —**tailwind** *n.* wind coming from the rear.

tailor *n.* person who makes men's clothes. —*v.* adapt to suit a purpose. —**tailor-made** *adj.* made by a tailor; perfect for a purpose.

taint *v.* spoil with a small amount of decay, contamination, or other bad quality. —*n.* something that taints.

take *v.* **taking, took, taken.** remove from a place; get possession of, esp. dishonestly; carry or accompany; capture; require (time, resources, or ability); use; assume; write down; accept; subtract or deduct. —*n.* one of a series of recordings from which the best will be used. —**take place** happen. —**taking** *adj.* charming. —**takings** *pl. n.* money received by a shop. —**take after** *v.* look or behave like (a parent etc.). —**take away** *v.* subtract. —**takeaway** *n.* shop or restaurant selling meals for eating elsewhere; meal bought at a takeaway. —**take in** *v.* understand; make (clothing) smaller; deceive or swindle. —**take off** *v.* (of an aircraft) leave the ground; *Informal* depart; *Informal* parody. —**take-off** *n.* —**take up** *v.* occupy or fill (space or time); adopt the study or activity of; accept (an offer); shorten (a garment).

talc *n.* soft mineral of magnesium silicate; talcum powder. —**talcum powder** powder, usu. scented, used to dry or perfume the body.

tale *n.* story; malicious piece of gossip.

THESAURUS

tactless careless, clumsy, gauche, harsh, impolite, inconsiderate, indiscreet, insensitive, maladroit, rough, rude, sharp, thoughtless, unfeeling, unkind

tail 1. *n.* conclusion, end, extremity, train 2. *v. Inf.* follow, shadow, stalk, track, trail

tail off *or* **away** decrease, drop, dwindle, fade, fall away, wane

tailor 1. *n.* clothier, dressmaker, outfitter, seamstress 2. *v.* adapt, adjust, alter, convert, cut, fashion, fit, modify, mould, shape, style, suit

taint 1. *v.* contaminate, corrupt, dirty, foul, infect, pollute, spoil 2. *n.* blemish, blot, defect, disgrace, dishonour, fault, flaw, shame, smear, spot, stain, stigma

take 1. abduct, acquire, arrest, capture, catch, clutch, entrap, get, grasp, grip, have, obtain, receive, secure, seize, win 2. abstract, appropriate, filch, pocket, purloin, steal 3. accept, adopt, assume, undertake 4. assume, believe, consider, deem, hold, perceive, presume, receive, regard, understand 5. bear, bring, carry, cart, convey, ferry, fetch, haul, transport 6. accompany, bring, conduct, convoy, escort, guide, lead, usher 7. deduct, eliminate, remove, subtract

take in 1. absorb, assimilate, comprehend, digest, grasp, understand 2. cheat, deceive, dupe, fool, hoodwink, mislead, swindle, trick

take off 1. take to the air 2. *Inf.* beat it (*Sl.*), decamp, depart, disappear, go, hit the road (*Sl.*), leave, set out, split (*Sl.*), strike out 3. *Inf.* caricature, imitate, lampoon, mimic, mock, parody, satirize

take-off 1. departure, launch, liftoff 2. *Inf.* caricature, imitation, lampoon, mocking, parody, satire, travesty

take up 1. adopt, assume, engage in, start 2. absorb, consume, cover, fill, occupy

taking 1. *adj.* attractive, charming, compelling, delightful, enchanting, intriguing, pleasing, winning 2. *n. Plural* earnings, gain, gate, income, proceeds, profits, receipts, returns, yield

tale 1. account, anecdote, fable, fiction, legend, novel, relation, report, romance, saga, story 2. fabrication, falsehood, fib, lie, rigmarole, rumour, untruth

DICTIONARY

talent *n.* natural ability; ancient unit of weight or money. —**talented** *adj.*

talisman *n., pl.* **-mans.** object believed to have magic power. —**talismanic** *adj.*

talk *v.* express ideas or feelings by means of speech; utter; discuss, e.g. *let's talk business;* reveal information; (be able to) speak in a specified language. —**talker** *n.* —**talkative** *adj.* fond of talking. —**talk back** *v.* answer impudently. —**talking-to** *n. Informal* reproof.

tall *adj.* higher than average; of a specified height. —**tall order** difficult task. —**tall story** unlikely and probably untrue tale.

tallboy *n.* high chest of drawers.

tallow *n.* hard animal fat used to make candles.

tally *v.* **-lying, -lied.** (of two things) correspond. —*n., pl.* **-lies.** record of a debt or score.

tally-ho *interj.* huntsman's cry when the quarry is sighted.

Talmud *n.* body of Jewish law. —**Talmudic** *adj.*

talon *n.* bird's hooked claw.

tamarind *n.* tropical tree; its acid fruit.

tamarisk *n.* evergreen shrub with slender branches and feathery flower clusters.

tambourine *n.* percussion instrument like a small drum with jingling metal discs attached.

tame *adj.* (of animals) brought under human control; (of animals) not afraid of people; meek or submissive; uninteresting. —*v.* make tame. —**tamely** *adv.* —**tamer** *n.*

Tamil *n.* member of a people of Sri Lanka and S India; their language.

tam-o'-shanter *n.* brimless wool cap with a bobble in the centre.

tamp *v.* pack down by repeated blows.

tamper *v.* (foll. by *with*) interfere.

tampon *n.* absorbent plug of cotton wool inserted into the vagina during menstruation.

tan *v.* **tanning, tanned.** (of skin) go brown from exposure to sunlight; convert (a hide) into leather. —*n.* brown colour of tanned skin. —*adj.* yellowish-brown. —**tannery** *n.* place where hides are tanned. —**tanner** *n.*

tandem *n.* bicycle for two riders, one behind the other. —**in tandem** together.

tandoor *n.* Indian clay oven. —**tandoori** *adj.* cooked in a tandoor.

tang *n.* strong taste or smell; trace or hint. —**tangy** *adj.*

tangent *n.* line that touches a curve without intersecting it; (in trigonometry) ratio of the length of the opposite side to that of the adjacent side of a right-angled triangle. —**go off at a tangent** suddenly take a completely different line of thought or action. —**tangential** *adj.* of a tangent; of superficial relevance only. —**tangentially** *adv.*

tangerine *n.* small orange-like fruit of an Asian citrus tree.

tangible *adj.* able to be touched; clear and definite. —**tangibly** *adv.* —**tangibility** *n.*

tangle *n.* confused mass or situation. —*v.* twist together in a tangle; (often foll. by *with*) come into conflict.

tango *n., pl.* **-gos.** S American dance. —*v.* dance a tango.

tank *n.* container for liquids or gases; armoured fighting vehicle moving on tracks. —**tanker** *n.* ship or lorry for carrying liquid in bulk.

tankard *n.* large beer-mug, often with a hinged lid.

tannic acid, tannin *n.* vegetable substance used in tanning.

THESAURUS

talent ability, aptitude, bent, capacity, endowment, faculty, flair, genius, gift

talented able, artistic, brilliant, gifted, well-endowed

talk *v.* 1. chat, chatter, converse, gossip, natter, prate, say, speak, utter 2. confer, have a confab (*Inf.*), hold discussions, negotiate, parley 3. crack, inform

talking-to criticism, lecture, rebuke, reprimand, reproach, reproof, row, scolding

tall big, giant, high, lanky, lofty, soaring

tally 1. *v.* accord, agree, coincide, concur, conform, fit, match, square, suit 2. *n.* count, mark, reckoning, record, score, total

tame *adj.* 1. broken, cultivated, disciplined, docile, gentle, obedient 2. compliant, docile, meek, subdued, unresisting 3. bland, boring,

dull, flat, insipid, prosaic, tedious ~*v.* 4. break in, domesticate, pacify, train 5. break the spirit of, conquer, curb, discipline, enslave, humble, master, repress, subjugate, suppress

tamper alter, interfere, intrude, meddle, muck about (*Brit. sl.*), poke one's nose into (*Inf.*), tinker

tangible actual, concrete, definite, evident, manifest, material, objective, perceptible, physical, positive, real, solid, substantial, touchable

tangle *n.* 1. coil, confusion, knot, mass, mat, mesh, snarl, twist, web 2. complication, imbroglio, labyrinth, maze, mess, mix-up ~*v.* 3. coil, confuse, jam, kink, knot, mat, mesh, snarl, twist

DICTIONARY

Tannoy *n.* ® type of public-address system.

tansy *n., pl.* **-sies.** yellow-flowered plant.

tantalize *v.* torment by showing but withholding something desired. —**tantalizing** *adj.* —**tantalizingly** *adv.*

tantalus *n.* case in which bottles can be locked with their contents visible.

tantamount *adj.* (foll. by *to*) equivalent in effect to.

tantrum *n.* childish outburst of temper.

tap[1] *v.* **tapping, tapped.** knock lightly and usu. repeatedly. —*n.* light knock. —**tap dance** dance in which the feet beat out an elaborate rhythm.

tap[2] *n.* valve to control the flow of liquid from a pipe or cask. —*v.* **tapping, tapped.** listen in on (a telephone) secretly by making an illegal connection; fit a tap to (a pipe etc.); draw off with or as if with a tap. —**on tap** *Informal* readily available; (of beer etc.) drawn from a cask.

tape *n.* narrow long strip of material; string stretched across a race track to mark the finish; recording made on magnetized tape. —*v.* bind or fasten with tape; record on magnetized tape. —**have a person** *or* **situation taped** *Informal* have full understanding and control of a person *or* situation. —**tape measure** tape marked off in centimetres or inches for measuring. —**tape recorder** device for recording and reproducing sound on magnetized tape. —**tapeworm** *n.* long flat parasitic worm living in the intestines of vertebrates.

taper *v.* become narrower towards one end. —*n.* long thin candle; narrowing. —**taper off** *v.* become gradually less.

tapestry *n., pl.* **-tries.** fabric decorated with coloured woven designs.

tapioca *n.* beadlike starch made from cassava root, used in puddings.

tapir [**tape**-er] *n.* piglike mammal of tropical America and SE Asia, with a long snout.

tappet *n.* short steel rod in an engine, transferring motion from one part to another.

taproot *n.* main root of a plant, growing straight down.

tar *n.* thick black liquid distilled from coal etc. —*v.* **tarring, tarred.** coat with tar.

taramasalata *n.* creamy pink pâté made from fish roe.

tarantella *n.* lively Italian dance; music for this.

tarantula *n., pl.* **-las, -lae.** large poisonous hairy spider.

tardy *adj.* **-dier, -diest.** slow or late. —**tardily** *adv.* —**tardiness** *n.*

tare[1] *n.* weight of the wrapping or container of goods; unladen weight of a vehicle.

tare[2] *n.* type of vetch; *Bible* weed.

target *n.* object or person a missile is aimed at; goal or objective; object of criticism. —*v.* **-geting, -geted.** aim or direct.

tariff *n.* tax levied on imports; list of fixed prices.

Tarmac *n.* ® mixture of tar, bitumen, and crushed stones used for roads etc.; (**t**-) airport runway.

tarn *n.* small mountain lake.

tarnish *v.* make or become stained or less bright; damage or taint. —*n.* discoloration or blemish.

tarot [**tarr**-oh] *n.* special pack of cards used mainly in fortune-telling. —**tarot card**

tarpaulin *n.* (sheet of) heavy waterproof fabric.

tarragon *n.* aromatic herb.

tarry *v.* **-rying, -ried.** *Old-fashioned* linger or delay; stay briefly.

tarsier *n.* monkey-like mammal of the E Indies.

tarsus *n., pl.* **-si.** bones of the heel and ankle collectively.

tart[1] *n.* pie or flan with a sweet filling.

tart[2] *adj.* sharp or bitter. —**tartly** *adv.* —**tartness** *n.*

THESAURUS

tantalize baffle, balk, entice, frustrate, provoke, taunt, tease, thwart, torment, torture

tantamount equal, equivalent, synonymous

tantrum fit, ill humour, outburst, storm, temper

tap[1] 1. *v.* beat, drum, knock, pat, rap, strike, touch 2. *n.* beat, knock, light blow, pat, rap, touch

tap[2] *n.* 1. spigot, spout, stopcock, valve 2. bung, plug, stopper ~*v.* 3. bleed, broach, drain, open, pierce, unplug

tape *n.* 1. band, ribbon, strip ~*v.* 2. bind, seal, secure 3. record, video

taper come to a point, narrow, thin

target 1. aim, bull's-eye, end, goal, intention, mark, object, objective 2. butt, quarry, scapegoat, victim

tariff 1. duty, excise, impost, levy, rate, tax, toll 2. charges, menu, schedule

tarnish befoul, blacken, blemish, blot, darken, dim, dull, rust, soil, spot, stain, sully, taint

tart[1] 1. pastry, pie 2. harlot, loose woman, prostitute, slut, strumpet, trollop, whore

tart[2] acid, bitter, pungent, sharp, sour, tangy

DICTIONARY

tart[3] *n. Informal* sexually provocative or promiscuous woman. —**tart up** *v. Informal* dress or decorate in a smart or flashy way.

tartan *n.* design of straight lines crossing at right angles, esp. one associated with a Scottish clan; cloth with such a pattern.

tartar[1] *n.* hard deposit on the teeth; deposit formed during the fermentation of wine.

tartar[2] *n.* fearsome or formidable person.

tartrazine [tar-traz-zeen] *n.* artificial yellow dye used in food etc.

task *n.* (difficult or unpleasant) piece of work to be done. —**take to task** criticize or scold. —**task force** (military) group formed to carry out a specific task. —**taskmaster** *n.* person who enforces hard work.

tassel *n.* decorative fringed knot of threads. —**tasselled** *adj.*

taste *n.* sense by which the flavour of a substance is distinguished in the mouth; distinctive flavour; brief experience of something; small amount tasted; liking; ability to appreciate what is beautiful or excellent. —*v.* distinguish the taste of (a substance); take a small amount of (something) into the mouth; have a specific taste; experience briefly. —**tasteful** *adj.* having or showing good taste. —**tastefully** *adv.* —**tasteless** *adj.* bland or insipid; showing bad taste. —**tastelessly** *adv.* —**tasty** *adj.* pleasantly flavoured. —**taste bud** small organ on the tongue which perceives flavours.

tat *n.* tatty or tasteless article(s).

tattered *adj.* ragged or torn. —**tatters** *pl. n.* ragged pieces.

tattle *n., v.* gossip or chatter.

tattoo[1] *v.* **-tooing, -tooed.** make (a pattern) on the skin by pricking and staining it with indelible inks. —*n.* pattern so made. —**tattooist** *n.*

tattoo[2] *n.* military display or pageant; drumming or tapping.

tatty *adj.* **-tier, -tiest.** shabby or worn out. —**tattiness** *n.*

taught *v.* past of TEACH.

taunt *v.* tease with jeers. —*n.* jeering remark.

taupe *adj.* brownish-grey.

taut *adj.* drawn tight; showing nervous strain. —**tauten** *v.* make or become taut.

tautology *n., pl.* **-gies.** use of words which merely repeat something already stated. —**tautological** *adj.*

tavern *n. Old-fashioned* pub.

tawdry *adj.* **-drier, -driest.** cheap, showy, and of poor quality. —**tawdriness** *n.*

tawny *adj.* yellowish-brown.

tax *n.* compulsory payment levied by a government on income, property, etc. to raise revenue; heavy demand on something. —*v.* levy a tax on; make heavy demands on. —**taxable** *adj.* —**taxation** *n.* levying of taxes. —**taxpayer** *n.* —**tax return** statement of personal income for tax purposes.

taxi *n.* (also **taxicab**) car with a driver that may be hired to take people to any specified destination. —*v.* **taxiing, taxied.** (of an aircraft) run

---

THESAURUS

task *n.* assignment, charge, chore, duty, employment, enterprise, exercise, job, labour, mission, toil, work

taste *n.* 1. flavour, relish, savour, smack, tang 2. bit, bite, dash, drop, morsel, mouthful, nip, sample, sip, swallow, titbit, touch 3. appetite, bent, desire, fancy, inclination, leaning, liking, palate, penchant, preference, relish 4. appreciation, cultivation, culture, discernment, discrimination, elegance, grace, judgment, perception, polish, refinement, style ~*v.* 5. differentiate, discern, distinguish, perceive 6. assay, nibble, relish, sample, savour, sip, test, try 7. experience, feel, know, undergo

tasteful artistic, beautiful, charming, cultivated, delicate, elegant, exquisite, fastidious, graceful, handsome, harmonious, polished, refined, restrained, smart, stylish

tasteless 1. bland, boring, dull, flat, insipid, mild, stale, tame, thin, uninteresting, vapid, weak 2. cheap, coarse, crass, crude, flashy, garish, gaudy, graceless, gross, improper, inelegant, low, rude, tawdry, uncouth, vulgar

tasty appetizing, delectable, delicious, flavourful, luscious, palatable, sapid, savoury

taunt 1. *v.* deride, flout, gibe, insult, jeer, mock, revile, ridicule, tease, torment, upbraid 2. *n.* barb, censure, cut, derision, dig, gibe, insult, jeer, reproach, ridicule, sarcasm

taut flexed, rigid, strained, stretched, tense, tight

tawdry cheap, flashy, gaudy, meretricious, raffish, showy, tasteless, tinsel, vulgar

tax *n.* 1. assessment, charge, customs, duty, excise, impost, levy, rate, tariff, tithe, toll, tribute 2. burden, demand, drain, load, pressure, strain, weight ~*v.* 3. assess, charge, demand, exact, impose, rate 4. burden, drain, enervate, exhaust, load, overburden, push, sap, strain, stretch, task, try, weaken, weary

DICTIONARY

along the ground before taking off or after landing. —**taximeter** *n.* meter in a taxi that registers the fare. —**taxi rank** place where taxis wait to be hired.

taxidermy *n.* art of stuffing and mounting animal skins to give them a lifelike appearance. —**taxidermist** *n.*

taxonomy *n.* classification of plants and animals into groups. —**taxonomic** *adj.* —**taxonomist** *n.*

TB tuberculosis.

tbs., tbsp. tablespoon(ful).

tea *n.* dried leaves of an Asian bush; drink made by infusing these leaves in boiling water; drink made like tea from other plants; main evening meal; light afternoon meal of tea, cakes, etc. —**tea bag** small porous bag of tea leaves. —**tea cosy** covering for a teapot to keep the tea warm. —**teapot** *n.* container with a lid, spout, and handle for making and serving tea. —**teaspoon** *n.* small spoon for stirring tea. —**tea towel** towel for drying dishes.

teach *v.* **teaching, taught.** tell or show (someone) how to do something; cause to learn or understand; give lessons in (a subject). —**teacher** *n.* —**teaching** *n.*

teak *n.* very hard wood of an E Indian tree.

teal *n.* kind of small duck.

team *n.* group of people forming one side in a game; group of people or animals working together. —**teamster** *n. US* lorry driver. —**team up** *v.* make or join a team. —**teamwork** *n.* cooperative work by a team.

tear¹, **teardrop** *n.* drop of fluid appearing in and falling from the eye. —**in tears** weeping. —**tearful** *adj.* weeping or about to weep. —**tear gas** gas that stings the eyes and causes temporary blindness. —**tear-jerker** *n. Informal* excessively sentimental film or book.

tear² *v.* **tearing, tore, torn.** rip a hole in; rip apart; become ripped; rush. —*n.* hole or split. —**tearaway** *n.* wild or unruly person.

tease *v.* make fun of (someone) in a provoking or playful way; separate the fibres of. —*n.* person who teases. —**teasing** *adj., n.*

teasel, teazel, teazle *n.* plant with prickly leaves and flowers.

teat *n.* rubber nipple of a feeding bottle; nipple of a breast or udder.

tech *n. Informal* technical college.

technical *adj.* of or specializing in industrial, practical, or mechanical arts and applied sciences; skilled in technical subjects; relating to a particular field; according to the letter of the law; showing technique, e.g. *technical brilliance.* —**technically** *adv.* —**technicality** *n.* petty point based on a strict application of rules. —**technician** *n.* person skilled in a particular technical field. —**technical college** higher educational institution with courses in art and technical subjects.

Technicolor *n.* ® system of colour photography used for the cinema.

technique *n.* method or skill used for a particular task; technical proficiency.

technocracy *n., pl.* **-cies.** government by technical experts. —**technocrat** *n.*

technology *n., pl.* **-gies.** application of practical or mechanical sciences to industry or commerce; sciences applied thus. —**technological** *adj.* —**technologist** *n.*

tectonics *pl. n.* study of the earth's crust and the forces affecting it.

teddy *n., pl.* **-dies.** teddy bear; combined camisole and knickers. —**teddy bear** soft toy bear.

tedious *adj.* causing fatigue or boredom. —**tediously** *adv.* —**tedium** *n.* monotony.

THESAURUS

teach advise, coach, direct, drill, educate, enlighten, guide, impart, implant, inculcate, inform, instil, instruct, school, show, train, tutor

teacher coach, don, educator, guide, instructor, lecturer, master, mentor, mistress, pedagogue, professor, schoolmaster, schoolmistress, trainer, tutor

team 1. *n.* band, body, bunch, company, crew, gang, group, set, side, squad, troupe 2. *v. Often with* **up** cooperate, couple, join, link, unite, work together, yoke

tear *v.* 1. claw, divide, mangle, rend, rip, rive, run, scratch, sever, shred, split, sunder 2. bolt, career, charge, dart, dash, fly, gallop, hurry, race, run, rush, shoot, speed, sprint 3. grab,

pluck, pull, rip, seize, snatch ~*n.* 4. hole, mutilation, rent, rip, run, rupture, scratch, split

tearful crying, sobbing, weeping, whimpering

tease annoy, badger, bait, bedevil, chaff, gibe, goad, mock, needle, pester, provoke, rag, ridicule, taunt, torment, vex

technique 1. course, fashion, means, method, mode, procedure, style, system, way 2. address, art, artistry, craft, execution, facility, knack, proficiency, skill, touch

tedious banal, boring, drab, dreary, dull, irksome, laborious, lifeless, monotonous, prosaic, soporific, tiring, unexciting, uninteresting, vapid, wearisome

tedium banality, boredom, drabness, dreari-

DICTIONARY

tee *n.* small peg supporting a golf ball when teeing off; area of a golf course from which the first stroke of a hole is made. —**tee off** *v.* make the first stroke of a hole in golf.

teem *v.* abound in; rain heavily.

teenage *adj.* of the period of life between the ages of 13 and 19. —**teenager** *n.* person aged between 13 and 19.

teens *pl. n.* period of being a teenager.

teepee *n.* same as TEPEE.

tee-shirt *n.* same as T-SHIRT.

teeter *v.* wobble or move unsteadily.

teeth *n.* plural of TOOTH.

teethe *v.* (of a baby) grow his or her first teeth. —**teething troubles** problems during the early stages of something.

teetotal *adj.* drinking no alcohol. —**teetotaller** *n.*

TEFL Teaching of English as a Foreign Language.

Teflon *n.* ® substance used for nonstick coatings on saucepans etc.

tele- *prefix* at or over a distance, e.g. *telescope;* involving television or telephone, e.g. *telesales.*

telecommunications *pl. n.* communications using telephone, radio, television, etc.

telegram *n.* message sent by telegraph.

telegraph *n.* system for sending messages over a distance along a cable. —*v.* communicate by telegraph. —**telegraphic** *adj.* —**telegraphist** *n.* person who works a telegraph. —**telegraphy** *n.* science or use of a telegraph.

telekinesis *n.* movement of objects by thought or willpower.

telemeter *n.* device for recording or measuring a distant event and transmitting the data to a receiver. —**telemetry** *n.* —**telemetric** *adj.*

teleology *n.* belief that all things have a predetermined purpose. —**teleological** *adj.*

telepathy *n.* direct communication between minds. —**telepathic** *adj.* —**telepathically** *adv.*

telephone *n.* device for transmitting sound over a distance along wires. —*v.* call or talk to (a person) by telephone. —**telephony** *n.* —**telephonic** *adj.* —**telephonist** *n.* person operating a telephone switchboard.

telephoto lens *n.* camera lens producing a magnified image of a distant object.

teleprinter *n.* apparatus like a typewriter for sending and receiving typed messages by wire.

Teleprompter *n.* ® device under a television camera enabling a speaker to read the script while appearing to look at the camera.

telesales *pl. n.* selling of a product or service by telephone.

telescope *n.* optical instrument for magnifying distant objects. —*v.* shorten by the sliding of each part over the next; shorten by crushing. —**telescopic** *adj.*

teletext *n.* system which shows information and news on subscribers' television screens.

television *n.* system of producing a moving image and accompanying sound on a distant screen; device for receiving broadcast signals and converting them into sound and pictures; content of television programmes. —**televise** *v.* broadcast on television. —**televisual** *adj.*

telex *n.* international communication service using teleprinters; message sent by telex. —*v.* transmit by telex.

tell *v.* **telling, told.** make known in words; order or instruct; give an account of; discern or distinguish; have an effect; *Informal* reveal secrets. —**teller** *n.* narrator; bank cashier; person who counts votes. —**telling** *adj.* having a marked effect. —**tell off** *v.* reprimand. —**telling-off** *n.* —**telltale** *n.* person who reveals secrets. —*adj.* revealing.

tellurian *adj.* of the earth.

telly *n., pl.* **-lies.** *Informal* television.

temerity [tim-**merr**-it-tee] *n.* boldness or audacity.

temp *Informal* —*n.* temporary employee, esp. a secretary. —*v.* work as a temp.

temp. temperature; temporary.

THESAURUS

ness, dullness, monotony, routine, tedious~ness

teem abound, bear, brim, bristle, overflow, swarm

telegraph 1. *n.* cable, radiogram, telegram 2. *v.* cable, send, telex, transmit

telepathy mind-reading, sixth sense

telephone 1. *n.* handset, line, phone 2. *v.* call, call up, dial, phone, ring (*Brit.*)

telescope *n.* 1. glass, spyglass ~*v.* 2. crush,

squash 3. compress, condense, curtail, cut, shorten, shrink, trim, truncate

tell 1. announce, communicate, confess, disclose, divulge, express, impart, inform, mention, notify, proclaim, reveal, say, speak, state, utter 2. bid, call upon, command, direct, enjoin, instruct, order, require, summon 3. depict, describe, narrate, portray, recount, rehearse, relate, report 4. discern, distinguish, identify

DICTIONARY

temper *n.* outburst of anger; tendency to become angry; calm mental condition, e.g. *I lost my temper;* frame of mind. *—v.* make less extreme; strengthen or toughen (metal).

tempera *n.* painting medium of pigment and egg yolk.

temperament *n.* person's character or disposition. **—temperamental** *adj.* having changeable moods; of temperament; *Informal* erratic and unreliable. **—temperamentally** *adv.*

temperate *adj.* (of climate) not extreme; self-restrained or moderate. **—temperance** *n.* moderation; abstinence from alcohol.

temperature *n.* degree of heat or cold; *Informal* abnormally high body temperature.

tempest *n.* violent storm. **—tempestuous** *adj.* violent or stormy. **—tempestuously** *adv.*

template *n.* pattern used to cut out shapes accurately.

temple[1] *n.* building for worship.

temple[2] *n.* region on either side of the forehead.

tempo *n., pl.* **-pos, -pi.** speed of a piece of music; rate or pace.

temporal *adj.* of time; secular rather than spiritual; of the temple(s) of the head.

temporary *adj.* lasting only for a short time. **—temporarily** *adv.*

temporize *v.* gain time by negotiation or evasiveness; adapt to circumstances. **—temporization** *n.*

tempt *v.* (try to) entice (a person) to do something wrong; risk provoking, e.g. *you're tempting fate.* **—tempter, (***fem.***) temptress** *n.* **—tempting** *adj.* attractive or inviting. **—temptation** *n.* tempting; tempting thing.

ten *adj., n.* one more than nine. **—tenth** *adj., n.* (of) number ten in a series. **—tenner** *n. Informal* ten-pound note.

tenable *adj.* able to be held or maintained.

tenacious *adj.* holding fast; stubborn. **—tenacity** *n.*

tenant *n.* person who rents land or a building. **—tenancy** *n.*

tench *n., pl.* **tench.** freshwater game fish.

tend[1] *v.* be inclined; go in the direction of. **—tendency** *n.* inclination to act in a certain way. **—tendentious** *adj.* biased, not impartial.

tend[2] *v.* take care of.

tender[1] *adj.* not tough; gentle and affectionate; vulnerable or sensitive. **—tenderly** *adv.* **—ten-**

THESAURUS

temper *n.* 1. attitude, disposition, humour, mind, mood, nature, vein 2. fury, passion, rage, tantrum 3. anger, annoyance, heat, irritability, passion, peevishness, petulance, surliness 4. calm, calmness, composure, equanimity, moderation, tranquillity ~*v.* 5. abate, admix, allay, assuage, calm, lessen, moderate, restrain, soften, soothe

temperament bent, character, complexion, constitution, humour, make-up, mettle, nature, outlook, personality, quality, soul, spirit

temperamental 1. capricious, emotional, erratic, excitable, fiery, impatient, irritable, moody, passionate, sensitive, touchy, volatile 2. erratic, inconsistent, unreliable

temperance 1. forbearance, moderation, restraint, self-control, self-restraint 2. abstinence, prohibition, sobriety, teetotalism

temperate 1. agreeable, balmy, calm, cool, fair, gentle, mild, pleasant, soft 2. calm, dispassionate, equable, mild, moderate, reasonable, sensible, stable

temple church, sanctuary, shrine

temporarily briefly, fleetingly, momentarily, pro tem

temporary brief, ephemeral, fleeting, impermanent, interim, momentary, passing, provisional, transient

tempt 1. allure, attract, coax, decoy, draw, entice, inveigle, invite, lure, seduce, woo 2. bait, dare, provoke, risk, test, try

temptation allurement, appeal, attraction, bait, blandishments, coaxing, decoy, draw, inducement, invitation, lure, pull, seduction, snare, tantalization

tempting alluring, attractive, enticing, inviting, seductive, tantalizing

tenacious 1. clinging, fast, firm, forceful, iron, strong, tight 2. adamant, determined, dogged, firm, inflexible, obstinate, persistent, resolute, staunch, stubborn, sure, unyielding

tenacity 1. firmness, force, power, strength 2. application, determination, diligence, doggedness, firmness, intransigence, obstinacy, persistence, resolution, resolve, stubborness

tenancy holding, lease, occupancy, possession, residence

tenant holder, inhabitant, leaseholder, lessee, occupier, resident

tend[1] gravitate, incline, lean, trend

tend[2] attend, control, cultivate, feed, guard, handle, keep, maintain, manage, nurse, protect, wait on, watch, watch over

tendency bent, inclination, leaning, partiality, penchant, predilection, predisposition, propensity

DICTIONARY

derness *n.* —**tenderize** *v.* soften (meat) by pounding or treatment with a special substance. —**tenderizer** *n.*

tender[2] *v.* offer; make a tender. —*n.* formal offer to supply goods or services at a stated cost. —**legal tender** currency that must, by law, be accepted as payment.

tender[3] *n.* small boat that brings supplies to a larger ship in a port; carriage for fuel and water attached to a steam locomotive.

tendon *n.* sinew attaching a muscle to a bone.

tendril *n.* slender stem by which a climbing plant clings.

tenement *n.* building divided into several flats.

tenet [ten-nit] *n.* doctrine or belief.

tennis *n.* game in which players use rackets to hit a ball back and forth over a net.

tenon *n.* projecting end on a piece of wood fitting into a slot in another.

tenor *n.* (singer with) the second highest male voice; general meaning. —*adj.* (of a voice or instrument) between alto and baritone.

tenpin bowling *n.* game in which players try to knock over ten skittles by rolling a ball at them.

tense[1] *n.* form of a verb showing the time of action.

tense[2] *adj.* stretched tight; emotionally strained. —*v.* make or become tense. —**tensile** *adj.* of tension. —**tension** *n.* degree of stretching; emotional strain; hostility or suspense; *Electricity* voltage.

tent *n.* portable canvas shelter.

tentacle *n.* flexible organ of many invertebrates, used for grasping, feeding, etc.

tentative *adj.* provisional or experimental; cautious or hesitant. —**tentatively** *adv.*

tenterhooks *pl. n.* —**on tenterhooks** in anxious suspense.

tenuous *adj.* slight or flimsy. —**tenuously** *adv.* —**tenuousness** *n.*

tenure *n.* (period of) the holding of an office or position.

tepee [tee-pee] *n.* N American Indian cone-shaped tent.

tepid *adj.* slightly warm; half-hearted.

tequila *n.* Mexican alcoholic drink.

tercentenary *adj., n., pl.* **-naries.** (of) a three hundredth anniversary.

term *n.* word or expression; fixed period; period of the year when a school etc. is open or a lawcourt holds sessions. —*pl.* conditions; mutual relationship. —*v.* name or designate.

terminal *adj.* at or being an end; (of an illness) ending in death. —*n.* terminating point or place; point where current enters or leaves an electrical device; keyboard and VDU having input and output links with a computer; place where people or vehicles begin or end a journey. —**terminally** *adv.*

terminate *v.* bring or come to an end. —**termination** *n.*

terminology *n., pl.* **-gies.** technical terms relating to a subject. —**terminological** *adj.*

terminus *n., pl.* **-ni, -nuses.** final point; railway or bus station at the end of a line.

termite *n.* white antlike insect destructive to timber.

THESAURUS

tender[1] 1. delicate, feeble, fragile, frail, soft, weak 2. green, immature, new, raw, sensitive, unripe, vulnerable, young 3. affectionate, amorous, benevolent, caring, compassionate, fond, gentle, humane, kind, loving, merciful, pitiful, sympathetic, warm

tender[2] 1. *v.* extend, give, offer, present, proffer, propose, submit, suggest, volunteer 2. *n.* bid, estimate, offer, proffer, proposal

tenderness 1. feebleness, fragility, softness, weakness 2. callowness, greenness, immaturity, newness, youth 3. affection, attachment, care, compassion, fondness, gentleness, liking, love, mercy, pity, sympathy

tense 1. rigid, strained, stretched, taut, tight 2. edgy, fidgety, jumpy, keyed up, nervous, restless, strained, wrought up

tension 1. pressure, stiffness, stress, tautness,

tightness 2. anxiety, hostility, pressure, strain, stress, unease

tentative 1. experimental, indefinite, provisional, speculative, unsettled 2. cautious, diffident, doubtful, faltering, hesitant, timid, uncertain, unsure

tepid 1. lukewarm, warmish 2. apathetic, cool, indifferent, lukewarm

term *n.* 1. denomination, designation, expression, name, phrase, title, word 2. period, season, space, span, spell, time 3. course, session ~*v.* 4. call, denominate, designate, dub, entitle, label, name, style

terminate cease, close, complete, conclude, cut off, discontinue, end, expire, finish, issue, lapse, result, run out, stop, wind up

termination cessation, close, conclusion, discontinuation, effect, end, ending, expiry, finale, finish, issue, result

DICTIONARY

tern *n.* gull-like sea bird.

ternary *adj.* consisting of three parts.

Terpsichorean *adj.* of dancing.

terra firma *n.* dry land or solid ground.

terrace *n.* row of houses built as one block; paved area next to a building; level tier cut out of a hill. —*pl.* (also **terracing**) tiered area in a stadium where spectators stand. —*v.* form into or provide with a terrace.

terracotta *adj., n.* (made of) brownish-red unglazed pottery. —*adj.* brownish-red.

terrain *n.* area of ground, esp. with reference to its physical character.

terrapin *n.* kind of aquatic tortoise.

terrarium *n., pl.* **-rariums, -raria.** enclosed container for small plants or animals.

terrazzo *n., pl.* **-zos.** floor of marble chips set in mortar and polished.

terrestrial *adj.* of the earth; of or living on land.

terrible *adj.* very serious; *Informal* very bad; causing fear. —**terribly** *adv.*

terrier *n.* any of various breeds of small active dog.

terrific *adj.* great or intense; *Informal* excellent.

terrify *v.* **-fying, -fied.** fill with fear. —**terrifying** *adj.*

terrine [terr-**reen**] *n.* pâté or similar food; earthenware dish with a lid.

territory *n., pl.* **-ries.** district; area under the control of a particular government; area inhabited and defended by an animal; area of knowledge. —**territorial** *adj.* —**Territorial Army** reserve army.

terror *n.* great fear; terrifying person or thing; *Informal* troublesome person or thing. —**terrorism** *n.* use of violence and intimidation to achieve political ends. —**terrorist** *n., adj.* —**terrorize** *v.* force or oppress by fear or violence.

terry *n.* fabric with the loops in its pile uncut.

terse *adj.* concise; curt. —**tersely** *adv.*

tertiary [**tur**-shar-ee] *adj.* third in degree, order, etc.

Terylene *n.* ® synthetic polyester yarn or fabric.

tessellated *adj.* paved or inlaid with a mosaic of small tiles. —**tessera** *n., pl.* **-serae.** small square tile used in mosaics.

test *v.* try out to ascertain the worth, capability, or endurance of; carry out an examination on. —*n.* critical examination; method or standard of judgment; test match. —**testing** *adj.* —**test case** lawsuit that establishes a precedent. —**test match** one of a series of international cricket or rugby matches. —**test tube** narrow cylindrical glass vessel used in scientific experiments. —**test-tube baby** baby conceived outside the mother's body.

testament *n. Law* will; proof or tribute. —**testamentary** *adj.*

testate *adj.* having left a valid will. —**testacy** *n.* —**testator** [test-**tay**-tor], (*fem.*) **testatrix** [test-**tay**-triks] *n.* maker of a will.

testicle *n.* either of the two male reproductive glands.

testify *v.* **-fying, -fied.** give evidence under oath; (foll. by *to*) be evidence (of).

THESAURUS

terminology argot, cant, jargon, language, phraseology, terms, vocabulary

terminus 1. close, end, extremity, goal, limit, target, termination 2. depot, garage, station

terms conditions, particulars, provisions, qualifications, specifications, stipulations

terrible 1. bad, dangerous, extreme, serious, severe 2. awful, bad, dire, dreadful, frightful, hideous, loathsome, odious, offensive, poor, repulsive, revolting, unpleasant, vile 3. awful, dreadful, fearful, frightful, gruesome, harrowing, horrible, horrifying, monstrous, shocking

terrific 1. awful, dreadful, enormous, extreme, fearful, fierce, great, harsh, huge, intense, severe, tremendous 2. amazing, breathtaking, excellent, fine, marvellous, outstanding, superb, wonderful

terrified alarmed, appalled, awed, dismayed, horrified, intimidated, petrified, scared, shocked, terror-stricken

terrify alarm, appal, awe, dismay, frighten, horrify, intimidate, petrify, scare, shock, terrorize

territory area, country, district, land, province, region, state, tract, zone

terror alarm, anxiety, awe, dismay, dread, fear, fright, horror, intimidation, panic, shock

terrorize 1. browbeat, bully, intimidate, menace, oppress, threaten 2. alarm, awe, dismay, frighten, horrify, intimidate, petrify, scare, shock, terrify

terse 1. brief, clipped, compact, concise, crisp, incisive, laconic, neat, pithy, short, succinct, summary 2. abrupt, brusque, curt, short, snappy

test 1. *v.* analyse, assess, check, experiment, investigate, prove, try, verify 2. *n.* analysis, assessment, attempt, catechism, check, evaluation, examination, investigation, ordeal, proof, trial

testify affirm, assert, attest, witness, certify,

DICTIONARY

testimony *n., pl.* **-nies.** declaration of truth or fact; evidence given under oath. **—testimonial** *n.* recommendation of the worth of a person or thing; tribute for services or achievement.

testis *n., pl.* **-tes.** testicle.

testy *adj.* **-tier, -tiest.** irritable or touchy. **—testily** *adv.* **—testiness** *n.*

tetanus *n.* acute infectious disease producing muscular spasms and convulsions.

tête-à-tête *n., pl.* **-têtes, -tête.** private conversation.

tether *n.* rope or chain for tying an animal to a spot. **—v.** tie up with rope. **—at the end of one's tether** at the limit of one's endurance.

tetrahedron [tet-ra-**heed**-ron] *n., pl.* **-drons, -dra.** *Geom.* solid figure with four faces.

tetralogy *n., pl.* **-gies.** series of four related works.

Teutonic [tew-**tonn**-ik] *adj.* of or like the (ancient) Germans.

text *n.* main body of a book as distinct from illustrations etc.; passage of the Bible as the subject of a sermon; novel or play needed for a course. **—textual** *adj.* **—textbook** *n.* standard book on a particular subject. **—adj.** perfect, e.g. *a textbook landing.*

textile *n.* fabric or cloth, esp. woven.

texture *n.* structure, feel, or consistency. **—textured** *adj.* **—textural** *adj.*

thalidomide [thal-**lid**-oh-mide] *n.* drug formerly used as a sedative, but found to cause abnormalities in developing fetuses.

thallium *n.* highly toxic metallic element.

than *conj.* used to introduce the second element of a comparison.

thane *n. Hist.* Anglo-Saxon or medieval Scottish nobleman.

thank *v.* express gratitude to; hold responsible. **—thanks** *pl. n.* words of gratitude. **—interj.** (also **thank you**) polite expression of gratitude. **—thanks to** because of. **—thankful** *adj.* grateful. **—thankless** *adj.* unrewarding or unappreciated.

—Thanksgiving Day autumn public holiday in Canada and the US.

that *det., pron.* used to refer to something already mentioned or familiar, or further away. **—conj.** used to introduce a clause. **—pron.** used to introduce a relative clause.

thatch *n.* roofing material of reeds or straw. **—v.** roof (a house) with reeds or straw. **—thatcher** *n.*

thaw *v.* make or become unfrozen; become more relaxed or friendly. **—n.** thawing; weather causing snow or ice to melt.

the *det.* the definite article.

theatre *n.* place where plays etc. are performed; drama and acting in general; hospital operating room. **—theatrical** *adj.* of the theatre; exaggerated or affected. **—theatricals** *pl. n.* (amateur) dramatic performances. **—theatrically** *adv.* **—theatricality** *n.*

thee *pron. Obs.* objective form of THOU.

theft *n.* stealing.

their *det.* of or associated with them. **—theirs** *pron.* (thing or person) belonging to them.

theism [**thee**-iz-zum] *n.* belief in the creation of the universe by one God. **—theist** *n., adj.* **—theistic** *adj.*

them *pron.* refers to people or things other than the speaker or those addressed. **—themselves** *pron.* emphatic and reflexive form of THEY and THEM.

theme *n.* main idea or subject being discussed; recurring melodic figure in music. **—thematic** *adj.* **—theme park** leisure area based on a single theme.

then *adv.* at that time; after that; that being so.

thence *adv.* from that place or time; therefore.

theocracy *n., pl.* **-cies.** government by a god or priests. **—theocratic** *adj.*

theodolite [thee-**odd**-oh-lite] *n.* surveying instrument for measuring angles.

theology *n., pl.* **-gies.** study of religions and religious beliefs. **—theologian** *n.* **—theological** *adj.* **—theologically** *adv.*

THESAURUS

corroborate, declare, evince, show, state, swear, vouch, witness

testimonial certificate, commendation, endorsement, reference, tribute

testimony affidavit, attestation, avowal, corroboration, deposition, evidence, profession, statement, submission, witness

text 1. body, matter 2. wording, words

texture character, consistency, fabric, feel, grain, make, quality, structure, surface, tissue, weave

thanks appreciation, credit, gratefulness, gratitude, recognition, thanksgiving

thaw defrost, melt, soften, warm

theatrical affected, artificial, ceremonious, dramatic, exaggerated, histrionic, mannered, overdone, pompous, showy, stagy, stilted, unreal

theft fraud, larceny, pilfering, robbery, stealing, swindling

theme argument, idea, keynote, matter, subject, text, thesis, topic

DICTIONARY

theorem *n.* proposition that can be proved by reasoning.

theory *n., pl.* **-ries.** set of ideas to explain something; abstract knowledge or reasoning; idea or opinion; ideal or hypothetical situation. —**theoretical** *adj.* based on theory rather than practice or fact. —**theoretically** *adv.* —**theorist** *n.* —**theorize** *v.* form theories, speculate.

theosophy *n.* religious or philosophical system claiming to be based on intuitive insight into the divine nature. —**theosophical** *adj.*

therapy *n., pl.* **-pies.** curing treatment. —**therapist** *n.* —**therapeutic** [ther-rap-**pew**-tik] *adj.* curing. —**therapeutics** *n.* art of curing.

there *adv.* in or to that place; in that respect. —**thereby** *adv.* by that means. —**therefore** *adv.* consequently, that being so. —**thereupon** *adv.* immediately after that.

therm *n.* unit of heat. —**thermal** *adj.* of heat; hot or warm; (of clothing) retaining heat. —*n.* rising current of warm air.

thermionic valve *n.* electronic valve in which electrons are emitted from a heated rather than a cold cathode.

thermocouple *n.* device for measuring heat, consisting of two wires of different metals joined at both ends.

thermodynamics *pl. n.* scientific study of the relationship between heat and other forms of energy.

thermometer *n.* instrument for measuring temperature.

thermonuclear *adj.* involving nuclear fusion.

thermoplastic *adj.* (of a plastic) softening when heated and resetting on cooling.

Thermos *n.* ® vacuum flask.

thermosetting *adj.* (of a plastic) remaining hard when heated.

thermostat *n.* device for automatically regulating temperature. —**thermostatic** *adj.* —**thermostatically** *adv.*

thesaurus [thiss-**sore**-uss] *n., pl.* **-ri, -ruses.** book containing lists of synonyms and related words.

these *det., pron.* plural of THIS.

thesis *n., pl.* **theses.** written work submitted for a degree; doctrine maintained in argument.

Thespian *adj.* of the theatre. —*n.* actor or actress.

they *pl. pron.* refers to: people or things other than the speaker or people addressed; people in general; *Informal* he or she.

thiamine *n.* vitamin found in the outer coat of rice and other grains.

thick *adj.* of great or specified extent from one side to the other; having a dense consistency; full of; *Informal* stupid or insensitive; (of a voice) throaty; *Informal* friendly. —**a bit thick** *Informal* unfair or unreasonable. —**the thick** busiest or most intense part. —**thickly** *adv.* —**thickness** *n.* state of being thick; dimension through an object; layer. —**thicken** *v.* make or become thick or thicker. —**thickset** *adj.* stocky in build; set closely together.

thicket *n.* dense growth of small trees.

thief *n., pl.* **thieves.** person who steals. —**thieve** *v.* steal. —**thieving** *adj., n.*

thigh *n.* upper part of the human leg.

thimble *n.* cap protecting the end of the finger when sewing.

thin *adj.* **thinner, thinnest.** not thick; slim or lean; sparse or meagre; of low density; poor or unconvincing. —*v.* **thinning, thinned.** make or become thin. —**thinness** *n.*

THESAURUS

theoretical abstract, academic, ideal, impractical, pure, speculative

theorize conjecture, formulate, guess, project, speculate, suppose

theory 1. assumption, guess, hypothesis, speculation, surmise, thesis 2. philosophy, plan, proposal

therapeutic corrective, curative, good, healing, remedial, salutary, sanative

therefore accordingly, consequently, ergo, so, then, thus, whence

thick 1. broad, deep, fat, solid, wide 2. close, clotted, compact, crowded, deep, dense, heavy, opaque 3. bristling, bursting, chock-a-block, chock-full, covered, crawling, frequent, full, numerous, packed, replete, swarming, teem-

ing 4. brainless, dense, dull, obtuse, slow, stupid, thickheaded 5. distorted, guttural, hoarse, husky, inarticulate, indistinct, throaty 6. close, devoted, familiar, friendly, inseparable, intimate

thicken cake, clot, condense, congeal, deepen, gel, jell, set

thief bandit, burglar, cheat, embezzler, housebreaker, pickpocket, plunderer, robber, shoplifter, stealer, swindler

thieve cheat, embezzle, filch, misappropriate, peculate, pilfer, plunder, poach, purloin, rob, steal, swindle

thin *adj.* 1. fine, narrow, threadlike 2. delicate, filmy, fine, flimsy, gossamer, sheer, unsubstantial 3. bony, lank, lanky, lean, light, mea-

DICTIONARY

thine det., pron. Obs. (something) of or associated with you (thou).

thing n. material object; object, fact, or idea considered as a separate entity; Informal obsession. —pl. possessions, clothes, etc.

think v. thinking, thought. consider, judge, or believe; make use of the mind; be considerate enough or remember to do something. —**thinker** n. —**thinking** adj., n. —**think-tank** n. group of experts studying specific problems. —**think up** v. invent or devise.

third adj. of number three in a series; rated or graded below the second level. —n. one of three equal parts. —**third degree** violent interrogation. —**third party** (applying to) a person involved by chance or only incidentally in legal proceedings, an accident, etc. —**Third World** developing countries of Africa, Asia, and Latin America.

thirst n. desire to drink; craving or yearning. —v. feel thirst. —**thirsty** adj. —**thirstily** adv.

thirteen adj., n. three plus ten. —**thirteenth** adj., n.

thirty adj., n. three times ten. —**thirtieth** adj., n.

this det., pron. used to refer to a thing or person nearby or just mentioned; used to refer to the present time, e.g. this morning.

thistle n. prickly plant with dense flower heads.

thither adv. Obs. to or towards that place.

thong n. thin strip of leather etc.

thorax n., pl. thoraxes, thoraces. part of the body between the neck and the abdomen. —**thoracic** adj.

thorium n. radioactive metallic element.

thorn n. prickle on a plant; bush with thorns. —**thorn in one's side, flesh** source of irritation. —**thorny** adj.

thorough adj. careful or methodical; complete. —**thoroughly** adv. —**thoroughness** n. —**thoroughbred** n., adj. (animal) of pure breed. —**thoroughfare** n. way through from one place to another.

those det., pron. plural of THAT.

thou pron. Obs. singular form of YOU.

though conj. despite the fact that. —adv. nevertheless.

thought v. past of THINK. —n. thinking; concept or idea; ideas typical of a time or place; consideration; intention or expectation. —**thoughtful** adj. considerate; showing careful thought; pen-

THESAURUS

gre, skinny, slender, slight, slim, spare 4. deficient, meagre, scanty, scarce, scattered, skimpy, sparse, wispy 5. diluted, runny, watery, weak 6. feeble, flimsy, inadequate, lame, poor, scant, scanty, shallow, slight, superficial, weak

thing 1. affair, article, body, concept, entity, fact, matter, object, part, portion, substance 2. apparatus, contrivance, device, gadget, implement, instrument, machine, means, mechanism, tool 3. Plural baggage, belongings, clothes, effects, equipment, goods, luggage, possessions, stuff

think 1. believe, conceive, conclude, consider, deem, esteem, estimate, hold, imagine, judge, reckon, regard, suppose, surmise 2. brood, cerebrate, cogitate, consider, deliberate, meditate, muse, ponder, reason, reflect, revolve 3. recall, recollect, remember

thinking adj. contemplative, cultured, intelligent, philosophical, rational, reasoning, reflective, thoughtful

thirst n. 1. drought, dryness, thirstiness 2. appetite, craving, longing, passion, yearning

thirsty arid, dry, parched

thorny 1. bristly, pointed, prickly, sharp, spinous 2. awkward, difficult, hard, irksome, ticklish, tough, trying, worrying

thorough 1. assiduous, careful, complete, conscientious, efficient, exhaustive, full, intensive, painstaking, scrupulous, sweeping 2. absolute, arrant, complete, downright, entire, perfect, pure, sheer, total, unqualified, utter

thoroughly 1. carefully, completely, efficiently, exhaustively, fully, painstakingly, scrupulously, sweepingly, throughout 2. absolutely, completely, downright, entirely, perfectly, quite, totally, to the full, utterly

though allowing, even if, granted, notwithstanding, while

thought 1. cogitation, consideration, contemplation, deliberation, introspection, meditation, musing, reflection, regard 2. assessment, belief, concept, conclusion, conviction, idea, judgment, opinion, thinking, view 3. attention, heed, regard, scrutiny, study 4. aim, design, idea, intention, notion, object, plan, purpose 5. dream, expectation, hope, prospect

thoughtful 1. attentive, caring, considerate, helpful, kind, kindly, solicitous, unselfish 2. contemplative, deliberative, meditative, musing, pensive, rapt, reflective, ruminative, serious, studious, wistful

thoughtless 1. impolite, insensitive, rude, selfish, tactless, uncaring, unkind 2. careless, foolish, heedless, inattentive, mindless, neglectful, rash, reckless, remiss, silly, stupid, unthinking

DICTIONARY

sive or reflective. —**thoughtless** *adj.* inconsiderate.

thousand *adj., n.* ten hundred; large but unspecifed number. —**thousandth** *adj., n.* (of) number one thousand in a series.

thrall, thraldom *n.* state of being in the power of another person.

thrash *v.* beat, esp. with a stick or whip; defeat soundly; move about wildly; thresh. —**thrashing** *n.* severe beating. —**thrash out** *v.* solve by thorough argument.

thread *n.* fine strand or yarn; spiral ridge on a screw, nut, or bolt; unifying theme. —*v.* pass thread through; fit (a film, tape, etc.) into a machine; pick (one's way etc.). —**threadbare** *adj.* (of fabric) with the nap worn off; hackneyed; shabby.

threat *n.* declaration of intent to harm; dangerous person or thing. —**threaten** *v.* make or be a threat to; be a menacing indication of.

three *adj., n.* one more than two.—**threefold** *adj., adv.* (having) three times as many or as much. —**threesome** *n.* group of three. —**three-dimensional, 3-D** *adj.* having three dimensions. —**three-ply** *adj.* (of wood) having three layers; (of wool) having three strands.

threnody *n., pl.* **-dies.** lament for the dead.

thresh *v.* beat (wheat etc.) to separate the grain from the husks and straw; move about wildly.

threshold *n.* bar forming the bottom of a doorway; entrance; starting point; point at which a stimulus produces a response.

threw *v.* past tense of THROW.

thrice *adv. Lit.* three times.

thrift *n.* wisdom and caution with money; low-growing plant with pink flowers. —**thrifty** *adj.* —**thriftily** *adv.* —**thriftiness** *n.* —**thriftless** *adj.*

thrill *n.* sudden feeling of excitement. —*v.* (cause to) feel a thrill. —**thrilling** *adj.* —**thriller** *n.* book, film, etc. with an atmosphere of mystery or suspense.

thrive *v.* **thriving, thrived** *or* **throve, thrived** *or* **thriven.** grow well; flourish or prosper.

throat *n.* front of the neck; passage from the mouth and nose to the stomach and lungs. —**throaty** *adj.* (of the voice) hoarse.

throb *v.* **throbbing, throbbed.** pulsate repeatedly; vibrate rhythmically. —*n.* throbbing.

throes *pl. n.* violent pangs or pains. —**in the throes of** *Informal* struggling with difficulty with.

thrombosis *n., pl.* **-ses.** forming of a clot in a blood vessel or the heart.

throne *n.* ceremonial seat of a monarch or bishop; sovereign power.

throng *n., v.* crowd.

throstle *n.* song-thrush.

throttle *n.* device controlling the amount of fuel entering an engine. —*v.* strangle.

through *prep.* from end to end or side to side of; because of; during. —*adj.* finished; (of transport) going directly to a place; (on a telephone line) connected. —**through and through** completely. —**throughout** *adv., prep.* in every part (of). —**throughput** *n.* amount of material processed.

throve *v.* past tense of THRIVE.

throw *v.* **throwing, threw, thrown.** hurl through the air; move or put suddenly or carelessly; bring into a specified state, esp. suddenly; direct (a look, light, etc.); give (a party); project (the

THESAURUS

thrash 1. beat, belt, birch, cane, drub, flog, leather, punish, scourge, spank, whip 2. beat, clobber (*Brit. sl.*), crush, defeat, drub, maul, overwhelm, rout, trounce

thrash out debate, discuss, resolve, settle

thread 1. *n.* cotton, fibre, line, strand, string, yarn 2. *v.* ease, inch, loop, pass, string, wind

threat 1. menace, warning 2. foreboding, omen, portent, presage

threaten 1. endanger, jeopardize 2. forebode, foreshadow, impend, portend, presage, warn 3. browbeat, bully, cow, intimidate, menace

threshold 1. door, doorway, entrance, sill 2. beginning, brink, dawn, opening, outset, start, verge

thrift carefulness, economy, parsimony, prudence, saving

thrill 1. *n.* adventure, glow, pleasure, sensation, tingle, titillation 2. *v.* arouse, electrify, excite, flush, glow, move, stimulate, stir, tingle

thrilling exciting, gripping, rousing, sensational, stimulating, stirring

thrive advance, bloom, boom, develop, flourish, grow, increase, prosper, succeed, wax

throb 1. *v.* beat, pound, pulsate, thump, vibrate 2. *n.* beat, pounding, pulse, thump, thumping, vibration

throng 1. *n.* crowd, crush, horde, host, jam, mass, mob, multitude, pack, press, swarm 2. *v.* bunch, converge, cram, crowd, fill, flock, hem in, herd, jam, pack, press, troop

throttle *v.* choke, strangle

through *prep.* 1. between, by, past 2. because of, by means of, by way of, using, via 3. during, in, in the middle of, throughout ~*adj.* 4. completed, done, ended, finished

throughout everywhere, the whole time

DICTIONARY

voice) so that it seems to come from elsewhere; shape (pottery) on a wheel; move (a switch, lever, etc.); *Informal* baffle or disconcert. —*n.* throwing; distance thrown. —**throwaway** *adj.* designed to be discarded after use; done or said casually. —**throwback** *n.* person or thing that reverts to an earlier type. —**throw up** *v.* vomit.

thrush[1] *n.* brown songbird.

thrush[2] *n.* fungal disease of the mouth or vagina.

thrust *v.* **thrusting, thrust.** push forcefully; stab. —*n.* lunge or stab; force or power; intellectual or emotional drive.

thud *n.* dull heavy sound. —*v.* **thudding, thudded.** make such a sound.

thug *n.* violent criminal. —**thuggery** *n.* —**thuggish** *adj.*

thumb *n.* short thick finger set apart from the others. —*v.* touch or handle with the thumb; flick through (a book or magazine); signal with the thumb for a lift in a vehicle.

thump *n.* (sound of) a dull heavy blow. —*v.* strike heavily.

thunder *n.* loud noise accompanying lightning. —*v.* rumble with thunder; shout; move fast, heavily, and noisily. —**thunderous** *adj.* —**thundery** *adj.* —**thunderbolt** *n.* lightning flash; something sudden and unexpected. —**thunderclap** *n.* peal of thunder. —**thunderstruck** *adj.* amazed.

Thursday *n.* fifth day of the week.

thus *adv.* in this way; therefore.

thwack *v., n.* whack.

thwart *v.* foil or frustrate. —*n.* seat across a boat.

thy *det. Obs.* of or associated with you (thou). —**thyself** *pron. Obs.* emphatic form of THOU.

thyme [time] *n.* aromatic herb.

thymus *n., pl.* **-muses, -mi.** small gland at the base of the neck.

thyroid *adj., n.* (of) a gland in the neck controlling body growth.

Ti *Chem.* titanium.

tiara *n.* semicircular jewelled headdress.

tibia *n., pl.* **tibiae, tibias.** inner bone of the lower leg. —**tibial** *adj.*

tic *n.* spasmodic muscular twitch.

tick[1] *n.* mark (√) used to check off or indicate the correctness of something; recurrent tapping sound, as of a clock; *Informal* moment. —*v.* mark with a tick; make a ticking sound. —**tick off** *v.* mark off; reprimand. —**tick over** *v.* (of an engine) idle; function smoothly. —**ticktack** *n.* bookmakers' sign language.

tick[2] *n.* tiny bloodsucking parasitic animal.

tick[3] *n. Informal* credit or account.

ticket *n.* card or paper entitling the holder to admission, travel, etc.; label; official notification of a parking or traffic offence; declared policy of a political party. —*v.* **-eting, -eted.** attach or issue a ticket to.

ticking *n.* strong cotton fabric used for mattress covers.

tickle *v.* touch or stroke (a person) to produce laughter; please or amuse; itch or tingle. —*n.* tickling. —**ticklish** *adj.* sensitive to tickling; requiring care or tact.

tiddler *n. Informal* very small fish. —**tiddly** *adj.* tiny; *Informal* slightly drunk.

tiddlywinks *pl. n.* game in which players try to flip small plastic discs into a cup.

tide *n.* rise and fall of the sea caused by the gravitational pull of the sun and moon; current caused by this; widespread feeling or tendency. —**tidal** *adj.* —**tidal wave** huge wave produced by an earthquake. —**tide over** *v.* help (someone) temporarily.

THESAURUS

throw 1. *v.* cast, heave, hurl, launch, pitch, project, propel, put, send, shy, sling, toss 2. *n.* cast, fling, heave, pitch, put, shy, sling, toss

thrust *v.* 1. drive, force, impel, jam, plunge, poke, press, prod, propel, push, ram, shove, urge 2. jab, lunge, pierce, stab, stick ~*n.* 3. drive, lunge, poke, prod, push, shove, stab 4. impetus, momentum

thud *n./v.* clump, crash, knock, smack, thump

thug assassin, bandit, gangster, hooligan, killer, murderer, robber, ruffian, tough

thump 1. *n.* bang, blow, crash, knock, rap, smack, thud, whack 2. *v.* bang, batter, beat, crash, hit, knock, pound, rap, smack, strike, thrash, throb, thud

thunder 1. *n.* boom, crash, detonation, explo-

sion, pealing, rumble, rumbling 2. *v.* blast, boom, clap, crack, crash, peal, resound, reverberate, roar, rumble

thunderstruck aghast, amazed, astonished, astounded, nonplussed, petrified, shocked, staggered

thus 1. like this, so 2. accordingly, consequently, ergo, hence, then, therefore

tick[1] *n.* 1. clack, click, tap 2. dash, mark, stroke ~*v.* 3. clack, click, tap 4. choose, indicate, mark, select

tick[2] account, credit

ticket 1. card, coupon, pass, slip, token, voucher 2. card, label, marker, slip, sticker, tab, tag

ticklish critical, delicate, risky, sensitive, thorny, touchy, tricky, unsteady

DICTIONARY

tidings *pl. n.* news.

tidy *adj.* **-dier, -diest.** neat and orderly; *Informal* considerable. —*v.* **-dying, -died.** put in order. —**tidily** *adv.* —**tidiness** *n.*

tie *v.* **tying, tied.** fasten or be fastened with string, rope, etc.; make (a knot or bow) in (something); restrict or limit; score the same as another competitor. —*n.* bond or fastening; long narrow piece of material worn knotted round the neck; drawn game or contest. —**tied** *adj.* (of a pub) allowed to sell only the beer of a particular brewery; (of a cottage etc.) rented to the tenant only as long as he or she is employed by the owner.

tier *n.* row, layer, or level.

tiff *n.* petty quarrel.

tiger *n.* large yellow-and-black striped Asian cat. —**tigress** *n.* female tiger; fierce woman.

tight *adj.* stretched or drawn taut; closely fitting; secure or firm; cramped; *Informal* mean; *Informal* drunk; (of a match or game) very close. —**tights** *pl. n.* one-piece clinging garment covering the body from the waist to the feet. —**tightly** *adv.* —**tighten** *v.* make or become tight or tighter. —**tightrope** *n.* rope stretched taut on which acrobats perform.

tike *n. Informal* same as TYKE.

tilde *n.* accent (˜) used in Spanish to indicate that the letter 'n' is to be pronounced in a particular way.

tile *n.* flat piece of ceramic, plastic, etc. used to cover a roof, floor, or wall. —*v.* cover with tiles. —**tiled** *adj.* —**tiling** *n.* tiles collectively.

till¹ *prep., conj.* until.

till² *v.* cultivate (land). —**tillage** *n.* —**tiller** *n.*

till³ *n.* drawer for money, usu. in a cash register.

tiller *n.* lever to move a rudder of a boat.

tilt *v.* slant at an angle; compete against in a jousting contest; aim or thrust with a lance. —*n.* slope; *Hist.* jousting contest. —**at full tilt** at full speed or force.

timber *n.* wood as a building material; trees collectively; wooden beam in the frame of a house, boat, etc. —**timbered** *adj.* —**timber line** height above which trees will not grow.

timbre [**tam**-bra] *n.* distinctive quality of sound of a voice or instrument.

time *n.* past, present, and future as a continuous whole; specific point in time; unspecified interval; period with specific features; instance; occasion; tempo; *Slang* imprisonment. —*v.* note the time taken by; choose a time for. —**timeless** *adj.* unaffected by time; eternal. —**timely** *adj.* at the appropriate time. —**time-honoured** *adj.* sanctioned by custom. —**time-lag** *n.* period between cause and effect. —**timepiece** *n.* watch or clock. —**timeserver** *n.* person who changes his or her views to gain support or favour. —**time sharing** system of part ownership of a holiday property for a specified period each year; system enabling users at different terminals of a computer to use it at the same time. —**timetable** *n.* plan showing the times when something takes place,

---

THESAURUS

tick off 1. check off, mark off 2. censure, chide, lecture, reprimand, scold, upbraid

tide course, current, ebb, flow

tidings advice, greetings, message, news, report, word

tidy 1. *adj.* clean, methodical, neat, ordered, shipshape, spruce, trim, well-ordered 2. *v.* clean, groom, neaten, order, straighten

tie *v.* 1. attach, bind, connect, fasten, join, lash, link, moor, rope, secure, tether, unite 2. bind, confine, hamper, hinder, hold, limit, restrain 3. be even, draw, equal, match ~*n.* 4. band, bond, cord, fastening, fetter, joint, knot, link, rope, string 5. dead heat, deadlock, draw, stalemate

tier bank, file, layer, level, line, order, rank, row, series

tight 1. close, compact, constricted, cramped, fast, firm, fixed, narrow, rigid, secure, snug, stiff, stretched, taut, tense 2. impervious, proof, sealed, sound 3. close, grasping, mean, miserly, sparing, stingy 4. close, even, near, well-matched 5. drunk, intoxicated, tipsy

tighten close, cramp, fasten, fix, narrow, screw, secure, stretch, tense

till¹ cultivate, dig, plough, work

till² cash box, cash register

tilt *v.* 1. cant, lean, list, slant, slope, tip 2. attack, clash, contend, duel, encounter, fight, joust, spar ~*n.* 3. angle, cant, incline, list, pitch, slant, slope

timber beams, boards, forest, logs, planks, trees, wood

time *n.* 1. age, date, epoch, era, generation, hour, interval, period, season, space, span, spell, stretch, term 2. allotted span, day, duration, life, season 3. *Mus.* beat, measure, metre, rhythm, tempo ~*v.* 4. clock, control, count, judge, measure, regulate, set

timely convenient, judicious, opportune, prompt, punctual, seasonable, suitable

timetable calendar, curriculum, diary, list, programme, schedule

DICTIONARY

the departure and arrival times of trains or buses, etc.

timid *adj.* easily frightened; shy, not bold. —**timidly** *adv.* —**timidity** *n.* —**timorous** [tim-mor-uss] *adj.* timid.

timpani [tim-pan-ee] *pl. n.* set of kettledrums. —**timpanist** *n.*

tin *n.* soft metallic element; airtight metal container. —**tinned** *adj.* (of food) preserved by being sealed in a tin. —**tinny** *adj.* (of sound) thin and metallic. —**tinpot** *adj. Informal* worthless or unimportant.

tincture *n.* medicinal extract in a solution of alcohol.

tinder *n.* dry easily-burning material used to start a fire. —**tinderbox** *n.*

tine *n.* prong of a fork or antler.

ting *n.* high metallic sound, as of a small bell.

tinge *n.* slight tint; trace. —*v.* **tingeing** *or* **tinging, tinged.** give a slight tint or trace to.

tingle *v., n.* (feel) a prickling or stinging sensation.

tinker *n.* travelling mender of pots and pans; *Scot. & Irish* Gypsy; tinkering. —*v.* fiddle with (an engine etc.) in an attempt to repair it.

tinkle *v.* ring with a high tinny sound like a small bell. —*n.* tinkling.

tinsel *n.* decorative metallic strips or threads; anything cheap and gaudy.

tint *n.* (pale) shade of a colour; dye for the hair; trace. —*v.* give a tint to.

tiny *adj.* **tinier, tiniest.** very small.

tip[1] *n.* narrow or pointed end of anything; small piece forming an end. —*v.* **tipping, tipped.** put a tip on.

tip[2] *n.* money given in return for service; helpful hint or warning; piece of inside information. —*v.* **tipping, tipped.** give a tip to. —**tipster** *n.* person who sells tips about races.

tip[3] *v.* **tipping, tipped.** tilt or overturn; dump (rubbish). —*n.* rubbish dump.

tippet *n.* piece of fur worn as a scarf.

tipple *v.* drink (alcohol) habitually, esp. in small quantities. —*n.* drink. —**tippler** *n.*

tipsy *adj.* **-sier, -siest.** slightly drunk.

tiptoe *v.* **-toeing, -toed.** walk quietly with the heels off the ground.

tiptop *adj.* of the highest quality or condition.

tirade *n.* long angry speech.

tire *v.* reduce the energy of, as by exertion; weary or bore. —**tired** *adj.* weary; hackneyed or stale. —**tiring** *adj.* —**tireless** *adj.* not tiring easily. —**tiresome** *adj.* boring and irritating.

tiro *n., pl.* **-ros.** same as TYRO.

tissue *n.* substance of an animal body or plant; piece of thin soft paper used as a handkerchief etc.; interwoven series, e.g. *a tissue of lies.*

tit[1] *n.* any of various small songbirds.

tit[2] *n. Slang* female breast.

titanic *adj.* huge.

titanium *n.* strong light metallic element used to make alloys.

titbit *n.* tasty piece of food; pleasing scrap of scandal.

tit for tat *n.* equivalent given in retaliation.

tithe *Hist.* —*n.* one tenth of one's income or produce paid to the church as a tax. —*v.* charge a tithe.

Titian [tish-an] *adj.* (of hair) reddish-gold.

THESAURUS

timid afraid, bashful, cowardly, coy, diffident, fearful, irresolute, modest, nervous, retiring, shy

tinge *n.* 1. cast, colour, dye, shade, stain, wash 2. bit, dash, drop, pinch, smack, sprinkling, touch, trace ~*v.* 3. colour, dye, imbue, shade, stain, suffuse

tinker *v.* dabble, meddle, play, potter, toy

tint *n.* 1. cast, colour, hue, shade, tone 2. dye, rinse, stain, wash ~*v.* 3. colour, dye, rinse, stain

tiny diminutive, insignificant, little, minute, negligible, petite, slight, small, trifling, wee

tip[1] apex, cap, crown, end, head, peak, point, top

tip[2] *n.* 1. gift 2. clue, forecast, hint, pointer, suggestion, warning, word ~*v.* 3. remunerate, reward

tip[3] *v.* 1. cant, capsize, incline, lean, list, slant,

spill, upset 2. dump, empty, pour out, unload ~*n.* 3. refuse heap, rubbish heap

tire 1. drain, droop, exhaust, fail, flag, jade, sink, weary 2. annoy, bore, harass, irk, irritate, weary

tired drained, drowsy, exhausted, fatigued, sleepy, spent, weary, worn out

tireless determined, energetic, industrious, resolute, vigorous

tiresome dull, exasperating, flat, irksome, laborious, tedious, trying, vexatious, wearing, wearisome

tiring arduous, exacting, fatiguing, strenuous, tough, wearing

titillate arouse, excite, interest, provoke, stimulate, tantalize, tease, thrill, tickle, turn on (*Sl.*)

DICTIONARY

titillate v. excite or stimulate pleasurably. —**titillating** adj. —**titillation** n.

titivate v. smarten up. —**titivation** n.

title n. name of a book, film, etc.; name signifying rank or position; formal designation, such as *Mrs.*; *Sport* championship; *Law* legal right of possession. —**titled** adj. aristocratic. —**title deed** legal document of ownership.

titter v. laugh in a suppressed way. —n. suppressed laugh.

tittle-tattle n., v. gossip.

titular adj. of a title; in name only.

tizzy n., pl. -**zies**. *Informal* confused or agitated state.

TNT n. trinitrotoluene, a powerful explosive.

to prep. towards; as far as; used to mark the indirect object or infinitive of a verb; used to indicate equality or comparison; before the hour of. —adv. to a closed position, e.g. *pull the door to*. —**to and fro** back and forth.

to-do n., pl. -**dos**. *Informal* fuss or commotion.

toad n. animal like a large frog. —**toady** n., pl. **toadies**. ingratiating person. —v. **toadying, toadied**. be ingratiating. —**toad-in-the-hole** n. sausages baked in batter. —**toadstool** n. poisonous fungus like a mushroom.

toast n. slice of bread browned by heat; tribute or proposal of health or success marked by people raising glasses and drinking together; person or thing so honoured. —v. brown bread by heat; drink a toast to; warm or be warmed. —**toaster** n. electrical device for toasting bread.

tobacco n., pl. -**cos, -coes**. plant with large leaves dried for smoking. —**tobacconist** n. person or shop selling tobacco, cigarettes, etc.

toboggan n. narrow sledge for sliding over snow. —v. -**ganing, -ganed**. ride a toboggan.

toby jug n. mug in the form of a stout seated man.

toccata [tok-**kah**-ta] n. rapid piece of music for a keyboard instrument.

tocsin n. alarm signal or bell.

today n. this day; the present age. —adv. on this day; nowadays.

toddle v. walk with short unsteady steps. —**toddler** n. child beginning to walk.

toddy n., pl. -**dies**. sweetened drink of spirits and hot water.

toe n. digit of the foot; part of a shoe or sock covering the toes. —v. **toeing, toed**. touch or kick with the toe. —**toe the line** conform.

toff n. *Slang* well-dressed or upper-class person.

toffee n. chewy sweet made of boiled sugar.

tofu n. soft food made from soya-bean curd.

tog n. unit for measuring the insulating power of duvets. —pl. *Informal* clothes.

toga [**toe**-ga] n. garment worn by citizens of ancient Rome.

together adv. in company; simultaneously. —adj. *Informal* organized.

toggle n. small bar-shaped button inserted through a loop for fastening; switch used to turn a machine or computer function on or off.

toil n. hard work. —v. work hard; progress with difficulty. —**toilsome** adj. requiring hard work.

toilet n. (room with) a bowl connected to a drain for receiving and disposing of urine and faeces; washing and dressing. —**toiletry** n. object or cosmetic used to clean or groom oneself. —**toilet water** light perfume.

token n. sign or symbol; memento; disc used as money in a slot machine; voucher exchangeable for goods of a specified value. —adj. nominal or slight. —**tokenism** n. policy of making only a token effort, esp. to comply with a law.

told v. past of TELL.

THESAURUS

title n. 1. caption, heading, label, legend, name, style 2. designation, epithet, name, nickname, pseudonym, sobriquet, term 3. championship, crown, laurels 4. claim, entitlement, ownership, privilege, right

toady 1. n. hanger-on, jackal, lackey, parasite, sycophant, yes man 2. v. crawl, creep, cringe, flatter, grovel

toast n. 1. drink, health, pledge, salute, tribute 2. darling, favourite, heroine ~v. 3. drink to

together 1. closely, in concert, in unison, jointly, mutually 2. concurrently, en masse, in unison, simultaneously

toil 1. n. drudgery, effort, exertion, hard work, industry, labour, pains, slog, sweat, travail 2.

v. drudge, grub, labour, slave, slog, strive, struggle, work

toilet 1. bathroom, closet, convenience, latrine, lavatory, loo, outhouse, privy, urinal, washroom, W.C. 2. ablutions, bathing, dressing, grooming, toilette

token n. 1. badge, clue, earnest, evidence, index, mark, note, proof, sign, symbol, warning 2. keepsake, memento, remembrance, reminder, souvenir ~adj. 3. hollow, nominal, superficial, symbolic

tolerable 1. acceptable, bearable, endurable, supportable 2. acceptable, adequate, average, fair, indifferent, mediocre, middling, ordinary, unexceptional

DICTIONARY

tolerate *v.* put up with; permit. **—toleration** *n.*
—tolerable *adj.* bearable; *Informal* quite good.
—tolerably *adv.* **—tolerance** *n.* acceptance of
other people's rights to their own opinions or
actions; ability to endure something. **—tolerant**
adj. **—tolerantly** *adv.*

toll[1] *v.* ring (a bell) slowly and regularly, esp. to
announce a death. **—***n.* tolling.

toll[2] *n.* charge for the use of a bridge or road;
total loss or damage from a disaster.

tom *n.* male cat.

tomahawk *n.* fighting axe of the N American
Indians.

tomato *n., pl.* **-toes.** red fruit used in salads and
as a vegetable.

tomb *n.* grave; monument over a grave.
—tombstone *n.* gravestone.

tombola *n.* lottery with tickets drawn from a
revolving drum.

tomboy *n.* girl who acts or dresses like a boy.

tome *n.* large heavy book.

tomfoolery *n.* foolish behaviour.

Tommy gun *n.* light sub-machine-gun.

tomorrow *adv., n.* (on) the day after today; (in)
the future.

tom-tom *n.* drum beaten with the hands.

ton *n.* unit of weight equal to 2240 lbs or 1016 kg
(**long ton**) or, in the US, 2000 lbs or 907 kg (**short
ton**). **—tonnage** *n.* weight capacity of a ship.
—metric ton same as TONNE.

tone *n.* sound with reference to its pitch, volume, etc.; *US music* note; *Music* (also **whole
tone**) interval of two semitones; quality of a
colour; general character; healthy bodily condi-

tion. **—***v.* give tone to; harmonize (with). **—tonal**
adj. Music written in a key. **—tonality** *n.* **—toneless** *adj.* **—tone-deaf** *adj.* unable to perceive
subtle differences in pitch. **—tone down** *v.* make
or become more moderate.

tongs *pl. n.* large pincers for grasping and
lifting.

tongue *n.* muscular organ in the mouth, used in
speaking and tasting; animal tongue as food;
language; flap of leather on a shoe; thin projecting strip.

tonic *n.* medicine to improve body tone; *Music*
first note of a scale. **—***adj.* invigorating. **—tonic
(water)** *n.* mineral water containing quinine.

tonight *adv., n.* (in or during) the night or
evening of this day.

tonne [tunn] *n.* unit of weight equal to 1000 kg.

tonsil *n.* small gland in the throat. **—tonsillecto-
my** *n.* surgical removal of the tonsils. **—tonsilli-
tis** *n.* inflammation of the tonsils.

tonsure *n.* shaving of all or the top of the head
as a religious or monastic practice; part shaved.
—tonsured *adj.*

too *adv.* also, as well; to excess; extremely.

took *v.* past tense of TAKE.

tool *n.* implement used by hand; person used by
another to perform unpleasant or dishonourable
tasks. **—***v.* work on with a tool; equip with tools.

toot *n.* short hooting sound. **—***v.* (cause to) make
such a sound.

tooth *n., pl.* **teeth.** bonelike projection in the
jaws of most vertebrates for biting and chewing;
toothlike prong or point. **—sweet tooth** liking for
sweet food. **—toothless** *adj.* **—toothpaste** *n.*

THESAURUS

tolerance 1. charity, magnanimity, patience,
sufferance, sympathy 2. endurance, fortitude,
hardness, resilience, resistance, stamina,
toughness

tolerant 1. charitable, fair, forbearing, liberal,
open-minded, patient, unbigoted, unprejudiced 2. indulgent, lax, lenient, permissive,
soft

tolerate abide, accept, admit, allow, bear,
brook, condone, endure, permit, pocket, receive, sanction, stand, stomach, suffer, swallow, take, undergo, wink at

toleration condonation, endurance, indulgence,
sufferance

toll[1] 1. *v.* chime, clang, knell, peal, ring, sound,
strike 2. *n.* chime, clang, knell, peal, ring

toll[2] 1. charge, customs, demand, duty, fee,
impost, levy, payment, rate, tariff, tax, tribute
2. cost, damage, inroad, loss, penalty

tomb crypt, grave, sepulchre, vault

tombstone gravestone, marker, memorial,
monument

tone *n.* 1. accent, emphasis, force, modulation,
pitch, strength, stress, timbre, volume 2. air,
approach, aspect, attitude, character, drift,
effect, feel, frame, grain, manner, mood, note,
quality, spirit, style, temper, vein 3. cast,
colour, hue, shade, tinge, tint ~*v.* 4. blend, go
well with, harmonize, match, suit

tongue 1. dialect, idiom, language, speech, talk,
vernacular 2. articulation, utterance, voice

tonic boost, cordial, fillip, refresher, stimulant

too 1. also, as well, besides, further, likewise,
moreover, to boot 2. excessively, extremely,
unduly

tool *n.* 1. appliance, contrivance, device, gadget,
implement, instrument, machine, utensil 2.
cat's-paw, creature, hireling, jackal, minion,
pawn, puppet

DICTIONARY

paste used to clean the teeth. —**toothpick** *n*. small stick for removing scraps of food from between the teeth.

top[1] *n*. highest point or part; lid or cap; highest rank; garment for the upper part of the body. —*adj*. at or of the top. —*v*. **topping, topped.** form a top on; be at the top of; exceed or surpass. —**topping** *n*. sauce or garnish for food. —**topless** *adj*. (of a costume or woman) with no covering for the breasts. —**topmost** *adj*. highest or best. —**top brass** most important officers or leaders. —**top-dress** *v*. spread fertilizer on the surface of the land. —**top-dressing** *n*. —**top hat** man's tall cylindrical hat. —**top-heavy** *adj*. unstable through being overloaded at the top. —**top-notch** *adj*. excellent, first-class. —**topsoil** *n*. surface layer of soil.

top[2] *n*. toy which spins on a pointed base.

topaz [toe-pazz] *n*. semiprecious stone in various colours.

tope *n*. small European shark.

topee, topi [toe-pee] *n*. lightweight pith hat.

topiary [tope-yar-ee] *n*. art of trimming trees and bushes into decorative shapes. —**topiarist** *n*.

topic *n*. subject of a conversation, book, etc. —**topical** *adj*. relating to current events. —**topicality** *n*.

topography *n., pl.* **-phies.** (science of describing) the surface features of a place. —**topographer** *n*. —**topographic** *adj*.

topology *n*. geometry of the properties of a shape which are unaffected by continuous distortion. —**topological** *adj*.

topple *v*. (cause to) fall over; overthrow (a government etc.).

topsy-turvy *adj*. upside down; in confusion.

toque [toke] *n*. small round hat.

tor *n*. high rocky hill.

Torah *n*. body of traditional Jewish teaching.

torch *n*. small portable battery-powered lamp; burning brand carried as a light.

tore *v*. past tense of TEAR[2].

toreador [torr-ee-a-dor] *n*. bullfighter.

torment *v*. cause (someone) great suffering; tease cruelly. —*n*. great suffering; source of suffering. —**tormentor** *n*.

torn *v*. past participle of TEAR[2].

tornado *n., pl.* **-does, -dos.** violent whirlwind.

torpedo *n., pl.* **-does.** self-propelled underwater missile. —*v*. **-doing, -doed.** attack or destroy with or as if with torpedoes.

torpid *adj*. sluggish and inactive. —**torpidity** *n*. —**torpor** *n*. torpid state.

torque [tork] *n*. force causing rotation; Celtic necklace or armband of twisted metal.

torrent *n*. rushing stream; downpour. —**torrential** *adj*.

torrid *adj*. very hot and dry; highly emotional.

torsion *n*. twisting.

torso *n., pl.* **-sos.** trunk of the human body; statue of a nude human trunk.

tort *n. Law* civil wrong or injury for which damages may be claimed.

tortilla *n*. thin Mexican pancake.

tortoise *n*. slow-moving land reptile with a dome-shaped shell. —**tortoiseshell** *n*. mottled brown shell of a turtle, used for making ornaments. —*adj*. having brown, orange, and black markings.

tortuous *adj*. winding or twisting; not straightforward.

torture *v*. cause (someone) severe pain or mental anguish. —*n*. severe physical or mental pain; torturing. —**torturer** *n*.

THESAURUS

top *n*. 1. apex, crest, crown, head, height, meridian, peak, pinnacle, summit, vertex, zenith 2. cap, cork, cover, lid 3. head, lead ~*adj*. 4. best, chief, crowning, dominant, elite, finest, first, greatest, head, highest, lead, prime, principal, ruling, sovereign, superior, topmost, upper ~*v*. 5. be first, command, head, lead, rule 6. beat, best, better, outdo, surpass, transcend

topic issue, matter, point, subject, text, theme, thesis

topical current, popular

topmost foremost, highest, leading, loftiest, supreme, top, upper, uppermost

topsy-turvy chaotic, confused, disorderly, inside-out, jumbled, messy, untidy

torment *v*. 1. afflict, agonize, distress, harrow, pain, rack, torture 2. annoy, bedevil, bother, harass, persecute, pester, provoke, trouble ~*n*. 3. agony, anguish, distress, hell, misery, pain, suffering, torture 4. affliction, bother, nuisance, persecution, pest, plague, scourge, trouble, vexation, worry

tornado cyclone, gale, squall, storm, tempest, typhoon, whirlwind

torrent cascade, deluge, flood, flow, gush, rush, spate, stream, tide

tortuous bent, crooked, curved, indirect, sinuous, twisted, twisting, winding

torture 1. *v*. afflict, agonize, distress, lacerate, martyr, pain, persecute, torment 2. *n*. affliction, agony, anguish, distress, hell, martyrdom, misery, pain, persecution, suffering, torment

DICTIONARY

Tory *n., pl.* **Tories.** member of the Conservative Party. —*adj.* of Tories. —**Toryism** *n.*

toss *v.* throw lightly; fling or be flung about; (of a horse) throw (its rider); coat (food) by gentle stirring or mixing; throw up (a coin) to decide between alternatives by guessing which side will land uppermost. —*n.* tossing. —**toss up** *v.* toss a coin. —**toss-up** *n.* even chance or risk.

tot[1] *n.* small child; small drink of spirits.

tot[2] *v.* **totting, totted.** —**tot up** add (numbers) together.

total *n.* whole, esp. a sum of parts. —*adj.* complete; of or being a total. —*v.* **totalling, totalled.** amount to; add up. —**totally** *adv.* —**totality** *n.* —**totalizator** *n.* machine operating a betting system in which money is paid out to the winners in proportion to their stakes.

totalitarian *adj.* of a dictatorial one-party government. —**totalitarianism** *n.*

tote[1] *n.* short for TOTALIZATOR.

tote[2] *v.* haul or carry.

totem *n.* tribal badge or emblem. —**totem pole** post carved or painted with totems by American Indians.

totter *v.* move unsteadily; be about to fall.

toucan *n.* large-billed tropical American bird.

touch *n.* sense by which an object's qualities are perceived when they come into contact with part of the body; gentle tap, push, or caress; small amount; characteristic style; detail. —*v.* come into contact with; tap, feel, or stroke; affect; move emotionally; eat or drink; refer to in passing; equal or match; *Slang* ask for money.

—**touch and go** risky or critical. —**touched** *adj.* emotionally moved; slightly mad. —**touching** *adj.* emotionally moving. —**touchy** *adj.* easily offended. —**touch down** *v.* (of an aircraft) land. —**touchline** *n.* side line of the pitch in some games. —**touchstone** *n.* criterion. —**touch-type** *v.* type without looking at the keyboard.

touché [too-shay] *interj.* acknowledgment that a fencing blow or remark has been successful.

tough *adj.* strong or resilient; difficult to chew or cut; hardy and fit; rough and violent; difficult; firm and determined; *Informal* unlucky or unfair. —*n. Informal* rough violent person. —**toughness** *n.* —**toughen** *v.* make or become tough or tougher.

toupée [too-pay] *n.* wig.

tour *n.* journey visiting places of interest along the way; trip to perform or play in different places. —*v.* make a tour (of). —**tourism** *n.* tourist travel as an industry. —**tourist** *n.* person travelling for pleasure. —**touristy** *adj.* full of tourists or tourist attractions.

tour de force *n., pl.* **tours de force.** *French* brilliant stroke or achievement.

tournament *n.* sporting competition with several stages to decide the overall winner; *Hist.* (also **tourney**) contest between knights on horseback.

tourniquet [tour-nick-kay] *n.* something twisted round a limb to stop bleeding.

tousled *adj.* ruffled and untidy.

tout [rhymes with **shout**] *v.* solicit custom in a persistent manner; obtain and sell information

---

THESAURUS

toss *v.* 1. cast, fling, hurl, launch, pitch, project, propel, shy, sling, throw 2. agitate, disturb, jolt, rock, roll, shake, thrash, tumble ~*n.* 3. cast, fling, pitch, shy, throw

total 1. *n.* all, amount, entirety, mass, sum, whole 2. *adj.* all-out, complete, consummate, downright, entire, full, gross, integral, outright, perfect, sheer, thorough, unqualified, utter, whole 3. *v.* add up, amount to, reach, reckon

touch *n.* 1. feel, feeling 2. blow, brush, caress, contact, hit, pat, push, stroke, tap 3. bit, dash, detail, drop, hint, jot, pinch, smack, smattering, speck, spot, taste, trace, whiff 4. approach, manner, method, style, way ~*v.* 5. brush, caress, contact, feel, finger, fondle, graze, handle, hit, pat, push, strike, stroke, tap 6. abut, adjoin, border, brush, contact, converge, graze, meet 7. affect, disturb, impress, influence, inspire, mark, melt, move, soften, stir, strike, upset 8. come near, compare with, equal, match, rival

touching affecting, melting, moving, piteous, pitiful, poignant, sad, stirring, tender

tough *adj.* 1. durable, firm, hard, leathery, resistant, rigid, rugged, solid, stiff, strong, sturdy 2. brawny, fit, hardy, resilient, seasoned, stalwart, stout, strong, sturdy, vigorous 3. rough, ruffianly, ruthless, vicious, violent 4. callous, firm, merciless, obstinate, resolute, severe, stern, strict, unbending 5. difficult, hard, irksome, knotty, strenuous, thorny, troublesome, uphill 6. hard luck, regrettable ~*n.* 7. brute, hooligan, rowdy, ruffian, thug

tour *n.* 1. excursion, journey, outing, progress, trip 2. circuit, course, round ~*v.* 3. explore, holiday in, journey, sightsee, visit

tourist holiday-maker, sightseer, traveller, tripper, voyager

tournament contest, event, match, meeting, series

DICTIONARY

about racehorses. —n. person who sells tickets for a popular event at inflated prices.

tow[1] v. drag, esp. by means of a rope. —n. towing. —**in tow** following closely behind. —**on tow** being towed. —**towbar** n. metal bar on a car for towing vehicles. —**towpath** n. path beside a canal or river, originally for horses towing boats.

tow[2] n. fibre of hemp or flax. —**tow-headed** adj. with blond hair.

towards, toward prep. in the direction of; with regard to; as a contribution to.

towel n. cloth for drying things. —**towelling** n. material used for making towels.

tower n. tall structure, often forming part of a larger building. —v. be very tall; loom (over). —**tower of strength** person who supports or comforts.

town n. group of buildings larger than a village; central part of this; people of a town. —**township** n. small town; (in S Africa) urban settlement for Black or Coloured people only. —**town hall** large building used for council meetings, concerts, etc.

toxaemia [tox-**seem**-ya] n. blood poisoning; high blood pressure in pregnancy.

toxic adj. poisonous; caused by poison. —**toxicity** n. —**toxicology** n. study of poisons. —**toxin** n. poison of bacterial origin.

toy n. something designed to be played with. —adj. very small. —**toy with** v. play or fiddle with.

trace[1] n. track left by something; indication; minute quantity. —v. follow the course of; track down and find; copy exactly by drawing on a thin sheet of transparent paper set on top of the original. —**traceable** adj. —**tracer** n. projectile which leaves a visible trail. —**tracing** n. traced copy. —**tracery** n. pattern of interlacing lines. —**trace element** chemical element occurring in very small amounts in soil etc.

trace[2] n. strap by which a horse pulls a vehicle. —**kick over the traces** escape or defy control.

trachea [track-**kee**-a] n., pl. **tracheae.** windpipe. —**tracheotomy** [track-ee-**ot**-a-mee] n. surgical incision into the trachea.

track n. mark or trail left by the passage of anything; rough road or path; railway line; course of action or thought; endless band round the wheels of a tank, bulldozer, etc.; course for racing; separate section on a record, tape, or CD. —v. follow the trail or path of. —**track down** v. hunt for and find. —**track event** athletic sport held on a track. —**track record** past accomplishments of a person or organization. —**tracksuit** n. warm loose-fitting suit worn by athletes etc., esp. during training.

tract[1] n. wide area; Anat. system of organs with a particular function.

tract[2] n. pamphlet, esp. a religious one.

tractable adj. easy to manage or control.

traction n. pulling, esp. by engine power; Med. application of a steady pull on an injured limb by weights and pulleys; grip of the wheels of a vehicle on the ground. —**traction engine** old-fashioned steam-powered vehicle for pulling heavy loads.

tractor n. motor vehicle with large rear wheels for pulling farm machinery.

trade n. buying, selling, or exchange of goods; person's job or craft; (people engaged in) a particular industry or business. —v. buy and sell; exchange; engage in trade. —**trader** n. —**trading** n. —**trade-in** n. used article given in part payment for a new one. —**trademark, tradename** n. (legally registered) name or symbol used by a firm to distinguish its goods. —**trade-off** n. exchange made as a compromise. —**tradesman** n. skilled worker; shopkeeper. —**trade union** society of workers for the protec-

---

THESAURUS

tow v. drag, haul, lug, pull, trail, tug

towards 1. for, to 2. about, concerning, for, regarding

tower 1. n. belfry, column, pillar, skyscraper, steeple, turret 2. v. ascend, dominate, exceed, loom, mount, overlook, rear, rise, soar, top

toy 1. n. doll, game, plaything 2. v. flirt, play, sport, trifle, wanton

trace n. 1. evidence, mark, record, relic, remnant, sign, survival, token 2. bit, dash, drop, hint, shadow, suggestion, touch, trifle, whiff ~v. 3. detect, determine, discover, find, follow, pursue, seek, shadow, stalk, track, trail, unearth 4. chart, copy, draw, map, outline, record, show, sketch

track n. 1. footmark, footprint, footstep, mark, path, scent, slot, trace, trail, wake 2. course, flight path, line, path, pathway, road, track, way 3. line, rail, rails ~v. 4. chase, dog, follow, pursue, shadow, stalk, trace, trail

tract area, district, estate, extent, lot, plot, quarter, region, stretch, zone

trade n. 1. barter, business, commerce, dealing, exchange, traffic, truck 2. business, calling, craft, job, line, occupation, profession, pursuit, skill ~v. 3. bargain, barter, deal, exchange, peddle, traffic, transact, truck 4. barter, exchange, swap, switch

tradesman 1. dealer, merchant, seller, shopkeeper, vendor 2. craftsman, workman

DICTIONARY

tion of their interests. —**trade wind** wind blowing steadily towards the equator.

tradition *n.* unwritten body of beliefs, customs, etc. handed down from generation to generation; custom or practice of long standing. —**traditional** *adj.* —**traditionally** *adv.*

traduce *v.* slander.

traffic *n.* vehicles coming and going on a road; (illicit) trade. —*v.* **-ficking, -ficked.** trade, usu. illicitly. —**trafficker** *n.* —**traffic lights** set of coloured lights at a junction to control the traffic flow. —**traffic warden** person employed to control the movement and parking of traffic.

tragedy *n., pl.* **-dies.** shocking or sad event; serious play, film, etc. in which the hero is destroyed by a personal failing in adverse circumstances. —**tragedian** [traj-**jee**-dee-an] *n.* actor in or writer of tragedies. —**tragedienne** [traj-jee-dee-**enn**] *n.* actress in tragedies. —**tragic** *adj.* of or like a tragedy. —**tragically** *adv.* —**tragicomedy** *n.* play with both tragic and comic elements.

trail *v.* drag along the ground; follow the tracks of; lag behind; (of plants) grow along the ground or hang loosely. —*n.* track or trace; path, track, or road. —**trailer** *n.* vehicle designed to be towed by another vehicle; extract from a film or programme used to advertise it.

train *v.* instruct in a skill; cause (an animal) to perform or (a plant) to grow in a particular way; aim (a gun etc.); exercise in preparation for a

sports event. —*n.* line of railway coaches or wagons drawn by an engine; sequence or series; long trailing back section of a dress; body of attendants. —**trainer** *n.* —**trainee** *n.* person being trained.

traipse *v. Informal* walk wearily.

trait *n.* characteristic feature.

traitor *n.* person guilty of treason or treachery. —**traitorous** *adj.*

trajectory *n., pl.* **-ries.** line of flight, esp. of a projectile.

tram *n.* public transport vehicle powered by an overhead wire and running on rails laid in the road. —**tramlines** *pl. n.* track for trams.

trammel *v.* **-elling, -elled.** hinder or restrain.

tramp *v.* travel on foot, hike; walk heavily. —*n.* homeless person who travels on foot; hike; sound of tramping; cargo ship available for hire; *US* promiscuous woman.

trample *v.* tread on and crush.

trampoline *n.* tough canvas sheet attached to a frame by springs, used by acrobats etc. —*v.* bounce on a trampoline.

trance *n.* unconscious or dazed state; state of ecstasy or total absorption.

tranquil *adj.* calm and quiet. —**tranquilly** *adv.* —**tranquillity** *n.* —**tranquillize** *v.* make calm. —**tranquillizer** *n.* drug which reduces anxiety or tension.

trans- *prefix* across, through, or beyond.

THESAURUS

tradition custom, customs, folklore, habit, institution, ritual, usage

traditional accustomed, ancestral, conventional, customary, established, fixed, folk, historic, old, oral, unwritten, usual

traffic *n.* 1. freight, movement, passengers, transport, vehicles 2. barter, business, commerce, dealing, doings, exchange, relations, trade, truck ~*v.* 3. bargain, barter, deal, exchange, market, peddle, trade, truck

tragedy adversity, affliction, calamity, disaster, misfortune

tragic appalling, awful, catastrophic, deadly, dire, disastrous, doleful, dreadful, fatal, grievous, ill-fated, ill-starred, miserable, pathetic, ruinous, sad, shocking, sorrowful, unfortunate, woeful, wretched

trail *v.* 1. drag, draw, haul, pull, stream, tow 2. chase, follow, hunt, pursue, shadow, stalk, trace, track 3. dawdle, follow, lag, linger, loiter, straggle ~*n.* 4. footsteps, mark, path, scent, spoor, trace, track, wake 5. beaten track, footpath, path, road, route, track, way

train *v.* 1. coach, drill, educate, guide, instruct,

prepare, rear, school, teach, tutor 2. aim, direct, focus, level, point ~*n.* 3. chain, course, order, series, set, string 4. caravan, column, convoy, file, procession 5. appendage, tail, trail 6. court, entourage, followers, retinue, staff, suite

trainer coach

trait attribute, feature, mannerism, quality, quirk

traitor betrayer, deceiver, deserter, informer, quisling, rebel, renegade, turncoat

trajectory course, flight, flight path, line, path, route, track

tramp *v.* 1. hike, march, range, roam, rove, slog, trek, walk 2. march, plod, stamp, toil, trudge ~*n.* 3. vagabond, vagrant 4. hike, march, ramble, slog, trek

trample crush, squash, stamp, tread

trance daze, dream, muse, rapture, reverie, spell, stupor

tranquil calm, composed, cool, pacific, peaceful, placid, quiet, restful, sedate, serene, still

tranquillizer bromide, opiate, sedative

DICTIONARY

transact v. conduct or negotiate (a business deal). **—transaction** n. transacting; business deal transacted.

transatlantic adj. on, from, or to the other side of the Atlantic.

transceiver n. combined radio transmitter and receiver.

transcend v. rise above; be superior to. **—transcendence** n. **—transcendent** adj. **—transcendental** adj. based on intuition rather than experience; supernatural or mystical. **—transcendentalism** n.

transcribe v. copy out; write down (something said); record for a later broadcast; arrange (music) for a different instrument. **—transcript** n. copy.

transducer n. device that converts one form of energy to another.

transept n. either of the two shorter wings of a cross-shaped church.

transfer v. **-ferring, -ferred.** move or send from one person or place to another. **—**n. transferring; design which can be transferred from one surface to another. **—transfe(r)rable** adj. **—transference** n. transferring.

transfigure v. change in appearance. **—transfiguration** n.

transfix v. astound or stun; pierce through.

transform v. change the shape or character of. **—transformation** n. **—transformer** n. device for changing the voltage of an alternating current.

transfusion n. injection of blood into the blood vessels of a patient. **—transfuse** v. give a transfusion to; permeate or infuse.

transgress v. break (a moral law). **—transgression** n. **—transgressor** n.

transient adj. lasting only for a short time. **—transience** n.

transistor n. semiconducting device used to amplify electric currents; portable radio using transistors. **—transistorized** adj.

transit n. going from one place to another. **—transition** n. change from one state to another. **—transitional** adj. **—transitive** adj. (of a verb) requiring a direct object. **—transitory** adj. not lasting long.

translate v. turn from one language into another. **—translation** n. **—translator** n.

transliterate v. convert to the letters of a different alphabet. **—transliteration** n.

translucent adj. letting light pass through, but not transparent. **—translucence** n.

transmigrate v. (of a soul) pass into another body. **—transmigration** n.

transmit v. **-mitting, -mitted.** pass (something) from one person or place to another; send out (signals) by radio waves; broadcast (a radio or television programme). **—transmission** n. transmitting; shafts and gears through which power passes from a vehicle's engine to its wheels. **—transmittable** adj. **—transmitter** n.

transmogrify v. **-fying, -fied.** Informal change completely.

transmute v. change the form or nature of. **—transmutation** n.

transom n. horizontal bar across a window; bar separating a door from the window over it.

THESAURUS

transact accomplish, conduct, discharge, do, enact, handle, manage, perform, prosecute, settle

transaction action, affair, bargain, business, coup, deal, event, matter, occurrence, proceeding, undertaking

transcribe 1. engross, note, reproduce, rewrite, transfer 2. record, tape

transcript copy, duplicate, manuscript, note, record, reproduction, version

transfer 1. v. carry, change, convey, displace, move, remove, shift, translate, transport, turn over 2. n. change, handover, move, removal, shift, transposition

transform alter, change, make over, reconstruct, remodel, renew, translate

transformation change, conversion, revolution

transgress break, defy, disobey, encroach, err, exceed, infringe, lapse, misbehave, offend, overstep, sin, violate

transgressor criminal, culprit, felon, miscreant, offender, sinner, villain, wrongdoer

transient brief, fleeting, flying, fugitive, momentary, passing, short, temporary

transit n. carriage, crossing, motion, passage, shipment, travel

transition change, conversion, flux, passage, passing, shift, transit, upheaval

transitional changing, fluid, passing, unsettled

transitory brief, ephemeral, fleeting, flying, fugacious, momentary, passing, short, temporary, transient

translate convert, decode, render, transcribe

translation decoding, gloss, paraphrase, rendering, version

transmission 1. carriage, conveyance, sending, shipment, spread, transfer, transport 2. broadcasting, relaying, sending, showing 3. broadcast, programme

transmit 1. bear, carry, convey, diffuse, dis-

DICTIONARY

transparent *adj.* able to be seen through, clear; easily understood or recognized. —**transparently** *adv.* —**transparency** *n.* transparent quality; colour photograph on transparent film, viewed by means of a projector.

transpire *v.* become known; *Informal* happen; give off water vapour through pores. —**transpiration** *n.*

transplant *v.* remove and transfer (a plant) to another place; transfer (an organ or tissue) surgically from one part or body to another. —*n.* surgical transplanting; thing transplanted. —**transplantation** *n.*

transport *v.* convey from one place to another; *Hist.* exile (a criminal) to a penal colony; enrapture. —*n.* business or system of transporting; vehicle used in transport; ecstasy or rapture. —**transportation** *n.* —**transporter** *n.* large goods vehicle.

transpose *v.* interchange two things; put (music) into a different key. —**transposition** *n.*

transsexual *n.* person who has had a sex-change operation.

transubstantiation *n. Christianity* doctrine that the bread and wine consecrated in the Eucharist changes into the substance of Christ's body.

transuranic [tranz-yoor-**ran**-ik] *adj.* (of an element) having an atomic number greater than that of uranium.

transverse *adj.* crossing from side to side.

transvestite *n.* person who seeks sexual pleas-ure by wearing the clothes of the opposite sex. —**transvestism** *n.*

trap *n.* device for catching animals; plan for tricking or catching a person; bend in a pipe containing liquid to prevent the escape of gas; stall in which greyhounds are enclosed before a race; *Hist.* two-wheeled carriage; *Slang* mouth. —*v.* **trapping, trapped.** catch; trick. —**trapper** *n.* person who traps animals for their fur. —**trapdoor** *n.* door in a floor or roof.

trapeze *n.* horizontal bar suspended from two ropes, used by circus acrobats.

trapezium *n., pl.* **-ziums, -zia.** quadrilateral with two parallel sides of unequal length. —**trapezoid** [**trap**-piz-zoid] *n.* quadrilateral with no sides parallel; *US* trapezium.

trappings *pl. n.* equipment or ornaments.

Trappist *n.* member of an order of Christian monks who observe strict silence.

trash *n.* anything worthless; *US* rubbish. —**trashy** *adj.*

trauma [**traw**-ma] *n.* emotional shock; injury or wound. —**traumatic** *adj.* —**traumatize** *v.*

travail *v., n. Lit.* labour or toil.

travel *v.* **-elling, -elled.** go from one place to another, through an area, or for a specified distance. —*n.* travelling, esp. as a tourist. —*pl.* (account of) travelling. —**traveller** *n.* —**travelogue** *n.* film or talk about someone's travels.

traverse *v.* move over or back and forth over; move sideways. —*n.* traversing; path or road across.

THESAURUS

patch, forward, impart, remit, send, spread, transport 2. broadcast, radio, relay, send

transparency 1. clarity, limpidity, pellucidity, pellucidness, sheerness, translucency 2. photograph, slide

transparent 1. clear, diaphanous, filmy, limpid, lucent, lucid, translucent 2. apparent, dis~ tinct, easy, evident, explicit, manifest, obvi~ ous, patent, plain, recognizable, visible

transpire 1. *Inf.* arise, befall, chance, happen, occur, turn up 2. come out

transport *v.* 1. bear, bring, carry, convey, fetch, haul, move, remove, run, ship, take, transfer 2. banish, deport, exile 3. captivate, delight, electrify, enchant, enrapture, move, ravish ~*v.* 4. conveyance, vehicle 5. carriage, convey~ ance, removal, shipment, shipping 6. en~ chantment, euphoria, heaven, rapture 7. bliss, delight, ecstasy, ravishment

transpose alter, change, exchange, move, relo~ cate, reorder, shift, substitute, swap (*Inf.*), switch, transfer

trap *n.* 1. ambush, net, noose, pitfall, snare, springe 2. ambush, artifice, device, ruse ~*v.* 3. catch, corner, enmesh, ensnare, snare, take 4. ambush, beguile, deceive, dupe, inveigle, trick

trappings adornments, dress, equipment, fin~ ery, fittings, fixtures, gear, livery, panoply

trash 1. balderdash, drivel, foolish talk, hog~ wash, inanity, nonsense, rot, rubbish, tripe (*Inf.*), trumpery, twaddle 2. dregs, dross, gar~ bage, junk, litter, offscourings, refuse, rubbish

trashy cheap, flimsy, meretricious, tawdry, tin~ sel, worthless

travel cross, go, journey, move, proceed, pro~ gress, ramble, roam, rove, tour, traverse, voy~ age, walk, wander

traveller explorer, gypsy, hiker, migrant, no~ mad, passenger, tourist, tripper, voyager, wanderer, wayfarer

travelling *adj.* itinerant, migrant, mobile, rest~ less, roaming, roving, unsettled, wandering

traverse bridge, cover, cross, negotiate, pass over, ply, range, roam, span, wander

DICTIONARY

travesty *n., pl.* **-ties.** grotesque imitation or mockery. —*v.* **-tying, -tied.** make or be a travesty of.

trawl *n.* net dragged at deep levels behind a fishing boat. —*v.* fish with such a net. —**trawler** *n.* trawling boat.

tray *n.* flat board, usu. with a rim, for carrying things; open receptacle for office correspondence.

treachery *n., pl.* **-eries.** wilful betrayal. —**treacherous** *adj.* disloyal; unreliable or dangerous. —**treacherously** *adv.*

treacle *n.* thick dark syrup produced when sugar is refined. —**treacly** *adj.*

tread *v.* **treading, trod, trodden** *or* **trod.** set one's foot on; crush by walking on. —*n.* way of walking or dancing; treading; upper surface of a step; part of a tyre that touches the ground. —**treadmill** *n. Hist.* cylinder turned by treading on steps projecting from it; dreary routine.

treadle [**tred**-dl] *n.* lever worked by the foot to turn a wheel.

treason *n.* betrayal of one's sovereign or country; treachery or disloyalty. —**treasonable, treasonous** *adj.*

treasure *n.* collection of wealth, esp. gold or jewels; valued person or thing. —*v.* prize or cherish. —**treasurer** *n.* official in charge of funds. —**treasury** *n.* storage place for treasure; government department in charge of finance.

—**treasure-trove** *n.* treasure found with no evidence of ownership.

treat *n.* pleasure, entertainment, etc. given or paid for by someone else. —*v.* deal with or regard in a certain manner; give medical treatment to; subject to a chemical or industrial process; provide (someone) with (something) as a treat. —**treatment** *n.* way of treating a person or thing; medical care.

treatise [**treat**-izz] *n.* formal piece of writing on a particular subject.

treaty *n., pl.* **-ties.** signed contract between states.

treble *adj.* threefold, triple; *Music* high-pitched. —*n.* (singer with or part for) a soprano voice. —*v.* increase threefold. —**trebly** *adv.*

tree *n.* large perennial plant with a woody trunk. —**treeless** *adj.* —**tree surgery** repair of damaged trees. —**tree surgeon**

trefoil [**tref**-foil] *n.* plant, such as clover, with a three-lobed leaf; carved ornament like this.

trek *n.* long difficult journey, esp. on foot; *S Afr.* migration by ox wagon. —*v.* **trekking, trekked.** make such a journey.

trellis *n.* framework of horizontal and vertical strips of wood.

tremble *v.* shake or quiver; feel fear or anxiety. —*n.* trembling. —**trembling** *adj.*

tremendous *adj.* huge; *Informal* great in quality or amount. —**tremendously** *adv.*

THESAURUS

travesty 1. *n.* caricature, lampoon, mockery, parody, sham 2. *v.* burlesque, caricature, deride, distort, mock, parody, ridicule, sham

treacherous 1. deceitful, disloyal, faithless, false, perfidious, treasonable, unfaithful, unreliable, untrue 2. dangerous, hazardous, icy, perilous, risky, slippery, tricky, unsafe, unstable

treachery betrayal, disloyalty, duplicity, infidelity, perfidy, treason

tread *v.* 1. hike, march, pace, plod, stamp, step, stride, tramp, walk 2. squash, trample ~*n.* 3. footstep, gait, pace, step, stride, walk

treason disloyalty, mutiny, perfidy, sedition, treachery

treasure *n.* 1. cash, fortune, funds, gold, jewels, money, riches, valuables, wealth 2. darling, gem, jewel, paragon, pearl, precious, prize ~*v.* 3. adore, cherish, esteem, idolize, love, prize, revere, value, venerate, worship

treasury 1. bank, cache, hoard, store, vault 2. assets, capital, coffers, exchequer, finances, funds, money, resources, revenues

treat *n.* 1. banquet, entertainment, feast, gift,

party 2. delight, enjoyment, fun, joy, pleasure, satisfaction, surprise, thrill ~*v.* 3. consider, deal with, handle, manage, regard, use 4. attend to, care for, doctor, nurse 5. buy for, feast, give, lay on, pay for, provide, regale

treatise dissertation, essay, monograph, pamphlet, paper, study, thesis, tract, work, writing

treatment 1. care, cure, healing, medicine, remedy, surgery 2. conduct, dealing, handling, manipulation, reception, usage

treaty agreement, alliance, bond, compact, concordat, contract, convention, covenant, entente, pact

trek 1. *n.* hike, journey, march, slog, tramp 2. *v.* footslog, hike, journey, march, plod, range, roam, rove, slog, tramp

tremble 1. *v.* quake, quiver, rock, shake, shiver, shudder, teeter, totter, vibrate 2. *n.* quake, quiver, shake, shiver, shudder, tremor, vibration

tremendous 1. awesome, awful, colossal, dreadful, enormous, fearful, frightful, great, huge, immense, monstrous, stupendous, towering, vast 2. amazing, excellent, exceptional, great, incredible, marvellous, wonderful

DICTIONARY

tremolo *n., pl.* **-los.** *Music* quivering effect in singing or playing.

tremor *n.* involuntary shaking; minor earthquake.

tremulous *adj.* trembling, as from fear or excitement.

trench *n.* long narrow ditch, esp. one used as a shelter in war. —**trench coat** double-breasted waterproof coat.

trenchant *adj.* incisive; effective.

trencher *n. Hist.* wooden plate for serving food. —**trencherman** *n.* hearty eater.

trend *n.* general tendency or direction; fashion. —**trendy** *adj., n. Informal* consciously fashionable (person). —**trendiness** *n.*

trepidation *n.* fear or anxiety.

trespass *v.* go onto another's property without permission. —*n.* trespassing; *Old-fashioned* sin or wrongdoing. —**trespasser** *n.* —**trespass on** *v.* take unfair advantage of (someone's friendship, patience, etc.).

tress *n.* long lock of hair.

trestle *n.* board fixed on pairs of spreading legs, used as a support.

trews *pl. n.* close-fitting tartan trousers.

tri- *prefix* three.

triad *n.* group of three; (**T-**) Chinese criminal secret society.

trial *n.* trying or testing; *Law* investigation of a case before a judge; thing or person straining endurance or patience. —*pl.* sporting competition for individuals.

triangle *n.* geometric figure with three sides;

triangular percussion instrument; situation involving three people. —**triangular** *adj.*

tribe *n.* group of clans or families believed to have a common ancestor. —**tribal** *adj.* —**tribalism** *n.* loyalty to a tribe.

tribulation *n.* great distress.

tribune *n.* person who upholds public rights; people's representative in ancient Rome. —**tribunal** *n.* lawcourt; board appointed to inquire into a specific matter.

tributary *n., pl.* **-taries.** stream or river flowing into a larger one. —*adj.* (of a stream or river) flowing into a larger one.

tribute *n.* sign of respect or admiration; tax paid by one state to another.

trice *n.* —**in a trice** instantly.

triceps *n.* muscle at the back of the upper arm.

trichology [trick-**ol**-a-jee] *n.* study and treatment of hair and its diseases. —**trichologist** *n.*

trick *n.* deceitful or cunning action or plan; joke or prank; feat of skill or cunning; knack; mannerism; cards played in one round. —*v.* cheat or deceive. —**trickery** *n.* —**trickster** *n.* —**tricky** *adj.* difficult, needing careful handling; crafty.

trickle *v.* (cause to) flow in a thin stream or drops; move gradually. —*n.* gradual flow.

tricolour [**trick**-kol-lor] *n.* three-coloured striped flag.

tricycle *n.* three-wheeled cycle.

trident *n.* three-pronged spear.

triennial *adj.* happening every three years.

trifle *n.* insignificant thing; small amount; des-

THESAURUS

trench channel, cut, ditch, drain, furrow, gutter, pit, trough

trenchant acerbic, acid, acute, biting, caustic, cutting, incisive, keen, mordant, pungent, severe, sharp, tart

trend 1. bias, course, current, drift, flow, leaning, tendency 2. craze, fashion, look, mode, rage, style, thing, vogue

trespass 1. *v.* encroach, infringe, intrude, poach 2. *n.* encroachment, infringement, poaching

trial *n.* 1. audition, check, examination, experience, experiment, probation, proof, test, testing 2. contest, hearing, litigation, tribunal 3. attempt, effort, endeavour, go, stab, try, venture 4. adversity, affliction, burden, grief, hardship, load, misery, ordeal, pain, suffering, tribulation, trouble, woe 5. bane, bother, irritation, nuisance, pest, vexation

tribe blood, clan, class, division, family, house, people, race, seed, stock

tribulation adversity, affliction, blow, burden,

care, curse, distress, grief, misery, misfortune, ordeal, pain, sorrow, suffering, trial, trouble, vexation, woe, worry

tribunal bar, bench, court, hearing, trial

tribute 1. acknowledgment, applause, compliment, esteem, gift, honour, praise, recognition, respect 2. charge, customs, duty, excise, homage, impost, offering, payment, ransom, subsidy, tax, toll

trick *n.* 1. artifice, deceit, deception, device, dodge, feint, fraud, gimmick, hoax, imposture, ploy, ruse, stratagem, swindle, trap, wile 2. antic, caper, device, feat, frolic, gambol, jape, joke, juggle, prank, stunt 3. art, command, craft, device, expertise, gift, knack, secret, skill, technique ~*v.* 4. cheat, deceive, delude, dupe, fool, hoax, mislead, trap

trickle 1. *v.* crawl, creep, drip, drop, exude, ooze, run, seep, stream 2. *n.* dribble, drip, seepage

tricky complicated, delicate, difficult, risky, ticklish

DICTIONARY

sert of sponge cake, custard, etc. —v. (usu. foll. by *with*) toy with. —**trifling** *adj.* insignificant.

trigger *n.* small lever releasing a catch on a gun or machine; action that sets off a course of events. —v. (usu. foll. by *off*) set (an action or process) in motion. —**trigger-happy** *adj.* too quick to use guns.

trigonometry *n.* branch of mathematics dealing with relations of the sides and angles of triangles. —**trigonometrical** *adj.*

trike *n. Informal* tricycle.

trilateral *adj.* having three sides.

trilby *n., pl.* -**bies.** man's soft felt hat.

trill *n.* rapid alternation between two notes; shrill warbling sound made by some birds. —v. play or sing a trill.

trillion *n. Brit.* one million million million, 10^{18}; *US* one million million, 10^{12}.

trilobite [**trile**-oh-bite] *n.* small prehistoric sea animal.

trilogy [**trill**-a-jee] *n., pl.* -**gies.** series of three related books, plays, etc.

trim *adj.* **trimmer, trimmest.** neat and smart; slender; in good condition. —v. **trimming, trimmed.** cut or prune into good shape; decorate with lace, ribbons, etc.; adjust the balance of (a ship or aircraft) by shifting the cargo etc. —n. decoration; upholstery and decorative facings in a car; trim state; haircut that neatens the existing style. —**trimming** *n.* decoration. —*pl.* usual accompaniments, e.g. *turkey with all the trimmings.*

trimaran [**trime**-a-ran] *n.* three-hulled boat.

trinitrotoluene *n.* full name of TNT.

trinity *n., pl.* -**ties.** group of three; (**T**-) *Christianity* union of three persons, Father, Son, and Holy Spirit, in one God.

trinket *n.* small or worthless ornament or piece of jewellery.

trio *n., pl.* **trios.** group of three; piece of music for three performers.

trip *n.* journey to a place and back, esp. for pleasure; stumble; switch on a mechanism; *Informal* hallucinogenic drug experience. —v. **tripping, tripped.** (cause to) stumble; (often foll. by *up*) catch (someone) in a mistake; move or tread lightly; operate (a switch); *Informal* take a hallucinogenic drug. —**tripper** *n.* tourist.

tripe *n.* stomach of a cow used as food; *Informal* nonsense.

triple *adj.* having three parts; three times as great or as many. —v. increase threefold. —**triplet** *n.* one of three babies born at one birth. —**triple jump** athletics event in which competitors make a hop, a step, and a jump as a continuous movement.

triplicate *adj.* triple. —n. one of three copies. —**in triplicate** in three copies.

tripod [**tripe**-pod] *n.* three-legged stand, stool, etc.

tripos [**tripe**-poss] *n.* final examinations for the degree of BA at Cambridge University.

triptych [**trip**-tick] *n.* painting or carving on three hinged panels, often forming an altarpiece.

trite *adj.* hackneyed or banal.

tritium *n.* radioactive isotope of hydrogen.

triumph *n.* (happiness caused by) victory or success. —v. be victorious or successful; rejoice over a victory. —**triumphal** *adj.* celebrating a triumph. —**triumphant** *adj.* feeling or showing triumph.

THESAURUS

trifle *n.* 1. gewgaw, nothing, plaything, toy, triviality 2. bit, dash, drop, jot, little, pinch, spot, touch, trace ~*v.* 3. amuse oneself, coquet, dally, dawdle, flirt, idle, palter, play, toy, wanton, waste

trigger *v.* activate, cause, elicit, generate, produce, prompt, start

trim *adj.* 1. compact, dapper, neat, nice, orderly, smart, spruce, tidy, well turned-out 2. fit, shapely, sleek, slender, slim, streamlined, willowy ~*v.* 3. barber, clip, crop, curtail, cut, dock, lop, pare, prune, shave, shear, tidy 4. adorn, array, bedeck, decorate, dress, embellish, embroider, garnish, ornament 5. adjust, arrange, balance, distribute, order, prepare, settle

trimming 1. adornment, braid, decoration, edging, embellishment, frill, fringe, piping 2. *Plu-*

ral accessories, extras, frills, garnish, ornaments, trappings

trinity threesome, trilogy, trio, triple, triumvirate

trinket bagatelle, ornament, toy, trifle

trio threesome, trinity, triplet, triptych, triumvirate, triune

trip *n.* 1. errand, excursion, expedition, foray, jaunt, journey, outing, ramble, run, tour, travel, voyage 2. blunder, error, fall, indiscretion ~*v.* 3. blunder, err, fall, lapse, miscalculate, misstep, slip, stumble, tumble 4. catch out, confuse, disconcert, trap, unsettle

tripe claptrap, drivel, garbage, inanity, nonsense, rot, rubbish, trash, twaddle

triple *adj.* threefold, three-way

tripper journeyer, sightseer, tourist

DICTIONARY

triumvirate [try-**umm**-vir-rit] *n.* group of three people in joint control.

trivet [**triv**-vit] *n.* metal stand for a pot or kettle.

trivial *adj.* of little importance; everyday, trite. —**trivially** *adv.* —**trivia** *pl. n.* trivial things or details. —**triviality** *n.* —**trivialize** *v.* make (something) seem less important or complex than it is.

trod *v.* past tense and a past participle of TREAD.

trodden *v.* a past participle of TREAD.

troglodyte *n.* cave dweller.

troika *n.* Russian vehicle drawn by three horses abreast; group of three people in authority.

troll *n.* giant or dwarf in Scandinavian folklore.

trolley *n.* small wheeled table for food and drink; wheeled cart for moving goods. —**trolleybus** *n.* bus powered by electricity from an overhead wire but not running on rails.

trollop *n.* promiscuous or slovenly woman.

trombone *n.* brass musical instrument with a sliding tube. —**trombonist** *n.*

troop *n.* large group; artillery or cavalry unit; Scout company. —*pl.* soldiers. —*v.* move in a crowd. —**trooper** *n.* cavalry soldier.

trope *n.* figure of speech.

trophy *n., pl.* **-phies.** cup, shield, etc. given as a prize; memento of success.

tropic *n.* either of two lines of latitude at 23½° N (**tropic of Cancer**) or 23½° S (**tropic of Capricorn**). —*pl.* part of the earth's surface between these lines. —**tropical** *adj.* of or in the tropics; (of climate) very hot.

trot *v.* **trotting, trotted.** move or cause (a horse) to move at a medium pace, lifting the feet in diagonal pairs; (of a person) move at a steady brisk pace. —*n.* trotting. —**trotter** *n.* pig's foot. —**trot out** *v.* repeat (old ideas etc.) without fresh thought.

troth [rhymes with **growth**] *n.* pledge of fidelity, esp. a betrothal.

troubadour [**troo**-bad-oor] *n.* medieval travelling poet and singer.

trouble *n.* (cause of) distress or anxiety; disease or malfunctioning; care or effort. —*v.* (cause to) worry; cause inconvenience to; exert oneself. —**troubled** *adj.* —**troublesome** *adj.* —**troubleshooter** *n.* person employed to locate and deal with faults or problems.

trough [troff] *n.* long open container, esp. for animals' food or water; narrow channel between two waves or ridges; *Meteorol.* area of low pressure.

trounce *v.* defeat utterly.

troupe [troop] *n.* company of performers. —**trouper** *n.*

trousers *pl. n.* two-legged outer garment with legs reaching usu. to the ankles. —**trouser** *adj.* of trousers.

trousseau [**troo**-so] *n., pl.* **-seaux, -seaus.** bride's collection of clothing etc. for her marriage.

trout *n.* game fish related to the salmon.

THESAURUS

trite banal, commonplace, dull, hack, ordinary, pedestrian, routine, stale, stock, tired, worn

triumph *n.* 1. elation, joy, pride, rejoicing 2. accomplishment, achievement, attainment, conquest, coup, feat, mastery, success, victory ~*v.* 3. celebrate, exult, gloat, glory, rejoice, revel

triumphant celebratory, conquering, dominant, elated, exultant, glorious, proud, rejoicing, successful, victorious

trivial commonplace, everyday, frivolous, incidental, inconsequential, inconsiderable, insignificant, little, meaningless, minor, negligible, paltry, petty, puny, slight, small, trifling, trite, unimportant, valueless, worthless

troop *n.* 1. band, body, company, contingent, crowd, drove, flock, gang, gathering, group, herd, horde, multitude, squad, swarm, team, unit 2. *Plural* armed forces, army, men, military, soldiers ~*v.* 3. crowd, flock, march, parade, stream, swarm

trophy award, booty, cup, laurels, prize, souvenir, spoils

tropical hot, humid, lush, steamy, stifling, sultry, torrid

trot 1. *v.* canter, jog, lope, run, scamper 2. *n.* brisk pace, canter, jog, lope

trouble *n.* 1. annoyance, anxiety, disquiet, distress, grief, irritation, misfortune, pain, sorrow, suffering, torment, vexation, woe, worry 2. ailment, complaint, defect, disease, disorder, failure, illness, upset 3. bother, concern, danger, difficulty, dilemma, mess, nuisance, pest, problem 4. attention, bother, care, effort, exertion, inconvenience, labour, pains, struggle, thought, work ~*v.* 5. afflict, annoy, bother, disconcert, disquiet, distress, disturb, fret, grieve, harass, pain, perplex, perturb, pester, plague, sadden, torment, upset, vex, worry 6. bother, burden, disturb, incommode, inconvenience, put out 7. make an effort, take pains

troublesome annoying, bothersome, difficult, harassing, hard, irritating, oppressive, taxing, tiresome, upsetting, wearisome

trounce beat, crush, drub, overwhelm, rout, thrash

DICTIONARY

trowel *n.* hand tool with a flat wide blade for spreading mortar, lifting plants, etc.

troy (weight) *n.* system of weights used for gold, silver, and jewels.

truant *n.* pupil who stays away from school without permission. —**play truant** stay away from school without permission. —**truancy** *n.*

truce *n.* temporary agreement to stop fighting.

truck[1] *n.* railway goods wagon; *US* lorry. —**trucker** *n. US* lorry driver.

truck[2] *n.* —**have no truck with** refuse to be involved with.

truckle *v.* (usu. foll. by *to*) yield weakly.

truculent [truck-yew-lent] *adj.* aggressively defiant. —**truculence** *n.*

trudge *v.* walk heavily or wearily. —*n.* long tiring walk.

true *adj.* **truer, truest.** in accordance with facts; faithful; exact; genuine. —**truly** *adv.* —**truism** *n.* self-evident truth. —**truth** *n.* state of being true; something true. —**truthful** *adj.* honest; exact. —**truthfully** *adv.*

truffle *n.* edible underground fungus; sweet flavoured with chocolate.

trug *n.* long shallow basket used by gardeners.

trump[1] *n., adj.* (card) of the suit temporarily outranking the others. —*v.* play a trump card on (another card). —*pl. n.* trump suit. —**turn up trumps** turn out unexpectedly well. —**trump up** *v.* invent or concoct.

trump[2] *n. Lit.* (sound of) a trumpet.

trumpet *n.* valved brass instrument with a flared tube. —*v.* **-peting, -peted.** (of an elephant) cry loudly; proclaim loudly. —**trumpeter** *n.*

truncate *v.* cut short.

truncheon *n.* small club carried by a policeman.

trundle *v.* move heavily on wheels.

trunk *n.* main stem of a tree; person's body excluding the head and limbs; large case or box for clothes etc.; elephant's long nose; *US* car boot. —*pl.* man's swimming shorts. —**trunk call** long-distance telephone call. —**trunk road** main road.

truss *v.* tie or bind up. —*n.* device for holding a hernia in place; framework supporting a roof, bridge, etc.

trust *n.* confidence in the truth, reliability, etc. of a person or thing; obligation arising from responsibility; charge or care; arrangement in which one person administers property, money, etc. on another's behalf; property held for another; group of companies joined to control a market. —*v.* believe in and rely on; expect or hope; consign to someone's care. —**trustee** *n.* person holding property on another's behalf. —**trusteeship** *n.* —**trustful, trusting** *adj.* inclined to trust. —**trustworthy** *adj.* reliable or honest. —**trusty** *adj.* faithful or reliable.

truth *n.* see TRUE.

THESAURUS

truancy absence, malingering

truant absentee, delinquent, deserter, malingerer, shirker

truce armistice, break, ceasefire, cessation, interval, lull, peace, respite, rest, stay, treaty

truculent aggressive, bellicose, combative, contentious, cross, defiant, fierce, hostile, obstreperous, pugnacious, sullen, violent

trudge 1. *v.* hike, lumber, march, plod, slog, stump, tramp, trek 2. *n.* footslog, haul, hike, march, slog, tramp, trek

true *adj.* 1. accurate, actual, authentic, bona fide, correct, exact, factual, genuine, natural, precise, pure, real, right, valid, veracious, veritable 2. confirmed, constant, dedicated, devoted, dutiful, faithful, fast, firm, honest, loyal, pure, sincere, staunch, steady, trusty, upright 3. accurate, correct, exact, perfect, precise, proper, unerring

truly 1. accurately, correctly, factually, precisely, really, rightly 2. constantly, devotedly, loyally, sincerely, with dedication, with devotion 3. exceptionally, greatly, indeed, really, very

trumpet 1. *n.* bugle, horn 2. *v.* advertise, announce, broadcast, extol, proclaim, publish, sound loudly

truncate clip, crop, curtail, cut, lop, pare, prune, shorten, trim

trunk 1. bole, stalk, stem, stock 2. body, torso 3. proboscis, snout 4. bin, box, case, chest, coffer, crate, locker

trust *n.* 1. belief, certainty, confidence, credit, faith, hope, reliance 2. duty, obligation, responsibility 3. care, charge, custody, guard, protection, trusteeship ~*v.* 4. assume, believe, expect, hope, presume, suppose, surmise 5. believe, rely upon, swear by 6. assign, command, commit, confide, consign, delegate, entrust, give

trustworthy dependable, honest, honourable, mature, reliable, responsible, righteous, sensible, steadfast, true, truthful, upright

truth 1. accuracy, exactness, fact, genuineness, legitimacy, precision, reality, veracity 2. candour, dedication, devotion, dutifulness, faith, fidelity, honesty, integrity, loyalty, uprightness 3. axiom, fact, law, maxim, reality, truism

DICTIONARY

try *v.* **trying, tried.** make an effort or attempt; test or sample; put strain on, e.g. *he tries my patience;* investigate (a case); examine (a person) in a lawcourt. —*n., pl.* **tries.** attempt or effort; *Rugby* score gained by touching the ball down over the opponent's goal line. —**try it on** *Informal* try to deceive or fool someone. —**trying** *adj.* difficult or annoying.

tryst *n. Old-fashioned* arrangement to meet.

tsar [zahr] *n. Hist.* Russian emperor.

tsetse [tset-see] *n.* bloodsucking African fly whose bite transmits disease.

T-shirt *n.* short-sleeved casual shirt or top.

tsp. teaspoon.

T-square *n.* T-shaped ruler.

tsunami *n., pl.* **-mis, -mi.** tidal wave.

TT teetotal.

tub *n.* open, usu. round container; bath. —**tubby** *adj.* (of a person) short and fat.

tuba [tube-a] *n.* valved low-pitched brass instrument.

tube *n.* hollow cylinder; flexible cylinder with a cap to hold pastes. —**the tube** underground railway, esp. the one in London. —**tubing** [tube-ing] *n.* length of tube; system of tubes. —**tubular** [tube-yew-lar] *adj.* of or like a tube.

tuber [tube-er] *n.* fleshy underground root of a plant such as a potato. —**tuberous** [tube-er-uss] *adj.*

tubercle [tube-er-kl] *n.* small rounded swelling.

tuberculosis [tube-berk-yew-lohss-iss] *n.* infectious disease causing tubercles, esp. in the lungs. —**tubercular** [tube-berk-yew-lar] *adj.* of tuberculosis. —**tuberculin** *n.* extract from a bacillus used to test for tuberculosis.

TUC Trades Union Congress.

tuck *v.* push or fold into a small space; stitch in folds. —*n.* stitched fold; *Informal* food. —**tuck away** *v.* store in a safe place.

Tudor *adj.* of the English royal house ruling from 1485–1603; in an architectural style characterized by half-timbered buildings.

Tuesday *n.* third day of the week.

tufa [tew-fa] *n.* porous rock formed as a deposit from springs.

tuffet *n.* small mound or seat.

tuft *n.* bunch of feathers, grass, hair, etc. held or growing together at the base.

tug *v.* **tugging, tugged.** pull hard. —*n.* hard pull; small ship used to tow other vessels. —**tug of war** contest in which two teams pull against one another on a rope.

tuition *n.* instruction, esp. received individually or in a small group.

tulip *n.* plant with bright cup-shaped flowers.

tulle [tewl] *n.* fine net fabric of silk etc.

tumble *v.* (cause to) fall, esp. awkwardly or violently; roll or twist, esp. in play; rumple. —*n.* fall; somersault. —**tumbler** *n.* stemless drinking glass; acrobat; spring catch in a lock. —**tumble-down** *adj.* dilapidated. —**tumble dryer, tumbler dryer** machine that dries laundry by rotating it in warm air. —**tumble to** *v. Informal* realize, understand.

tumbrel, tumbril *n.* farm cart used during the French Revolution to take prisoners to the guillotine.

tumescent [tew-mess-ent] *adj.* swollen or becoming swollen. —**tumescence** *n.*

tummy *n., pl.* **-mies.** *Informal* stomach.

tumour [tew-mer] *n.* abnormal growth in or on the body.

tumult [tew-mult] *n.* uproar or commotion. —**tumultuous** [tew-mull-tew-uss] *adj.*

tumulus [tew-mew-luss] *n., pl.* **-li.** burial mound.

tun *n.* large beer cask.

tuna [tune-a] *n.* large marine food fish.

tundra *n.* vast treeless Arctic region with permanently frozen subsoil.

tune *n.* (pleasing) sequence of musical notes; correct musical pitch, e.g. *she sang out of tune.*

THESAURUS

truthful accurate, candid, correct, exact, faithful, honest, literal, precise, realistic, reliable, sincere, veritable

try *v.* 1. aim, attempt, endeavour, essay, seek, strive, struggle, undertake 2. appraise, evaluate, examine, inspect, prove, sample, taste, test 3. afflict, annoy, irk, irritate, pain, strain, tax, tire, trouble, upset, vex, weary 4. adjudge, adjudicate, examine, hear ~*n.* 5. attempt, effort, endeavour, essay, go, stab

tuck *v.* 1. fold, gather, insert, push ~*n.* 2. fold, gather, pinch, pleat 3. food, victuals

tug 1. *v.* drag, draw, haul, heave, jerk, lug, pull, tow, wrench, yank 2. *n.* drag, haul, heave, jerk, pull, tow, yank

tuition education, instruction, lessons, schooling, teaching, training

tumble 1. *v.* drop, fall, flop, pitch, plummet, roll, stumble, topple, toss, trip up 2. *n.* collapse, drop, fall, flop, plunge, roll, spill, stumble, toss, trip

tumult ado, agitation, bedlam, brawl, commotion, din, disorder, excitement, fracas, outbreak, quarrel, racket, riot, row, stir, strife, turmoil, unrest, uproar

DICTIONARY

—*v.* adjust (a musical instrument) so that it is in tune; adjust (a machine) to obtain the desired performance. —**tuneful** *adj.* —**tunefully** *adv.* —**tuneless** *adj.* —**tuner** *n.* —**tune in** *v.* adjust (a radio or television) to receive (a station or programme).

tungsten *n.* greyish-white metal.

tunic *n.* close-fitting jacket forming part of some uniforms; loose knee-length garment.

tunnel *n.* underground passage. —*v.* **-nelling, -nelled.** make a tunnel (through).

tunny *n., pl.* **-nies, -ny.** same as TUNA.

tup *n.* male sheep.

turban *n.* Muslim or Sikh man's headcovering made by winding cloth round the head.

turbid *adj.* muddy, not clear. —**turbidity** *n.*

turbine *n.* machine or generator driven by gas, water, etc. turning blades.

turbo- *combining form* of or powered by a turbine.

turbot *n.* large European flatfish.

turbulence *n.* confusion, movement, or agitation; atmospheric instability causing gusty air currents. —**turbulent** *adj.*

tureen *n.* serving dish for soup.

turf *n., pl.* **turfs, turves.** short thick even grass; square of this with roots and soil attached. —*v.* cover with turf. —**the turf** horse racing; racecourse. —**turf accountant** bookmaker. —**turf out** *v. Informal* throw out.

turgid [tur-jid] *adj.* swollen and thick; (of language) pompous. —**turgidity** *n.*

turkey *n.* large bird bred for food.

Turkish *adj.* of Turkey, its people, or their language. —*n.* Turkish language. —**Turkish bath**

steam bath. —**Turkish delight** jelly-like sweet coated with icing sugar.

turmeric *n.* yellow spice obtained from the root of an Asian plant.

turmoil *n.* agitation or confusion.

turn *v.* move around an axis, rotate; change the position or direction (of); (usu. foll. by *into*) change in nature or character; become sour; shape on a lathe; go round (a corner); reach or pass in age, time, etc., e.g. *she has just turned twenty.* —*n.* turning; direction or drift; opportunity to do something as part of an agreed succession; period or spell; short theatrical performance. —**good** *or* **bad turn** helpful or unhelpful act. —**turner** *n.* —**turning** *n.* road or path leading off a main route. —**turning point** moment when a decisive change occurs. —**turncoat** *n.* person who deserts one party or cause to join another. —**turn down** *v.* refuse or reject; reduce the volume or brightness (of). —**turn in** *v.* go to bed; hand in. —**turn off** *v.* stop (something) working by using a knob etc. —**turn on** *v.* start (something) working by using a knob etc.; become aggressive towards; *Informal* excite, esp. sexually. —**turnout** *n.* number of people appearing at a gathering; outfit. —**turnover** *n.* total sales made by a business over a certain period; rate at which staff leave and are replaced; small pastry. —**turnpike** *n.* road where a toll is collected at barriers. —**turnstile** *n.* revolving gate for admitting one person at a time. —**turntable** *n.* revolving platform. —**turn up** *v.* arrive or appear; find or be found; increase the volume or brightness (of). —**turn-up** *n.* turned-up fold at the bottom of a trouser leg; *Informal* unexpected event.

turnip *n.* root vegetable with orange or white flesh.

THESAURUS

tune *n.* 1. air, melody, motif, song, strain, theme 2. concert, concord, euphony, harmony, pitch, unison ~*v.* 3. adapt, adjust, attune, pitch, regulate

tunnel 1. *n.* burrow, channel, hole, passage, shaft, subway 2. *v.* burrow, dig, excavate, mine, undermine

turbulence agitation, commotion, confusion, disorder, roughness, storm, turmoil, unrest

turbulent agitated, boiling, choppy, disordered, foaming, furious, raging, rough, unsettled, unstable

turf 1. clod, divot, grass, green, sod, sward 2. **the turf** racing, the flat

turmoil agitation, bedlam, bustle, chaos, confusion, disorder, flurry, noise, row, stir, strife, trouble, tumult, uproar, violence

turn *v.* 1. circle, gyrate, pivot, revolve, roll,

rotate, spin, swivel, twirl, twist, wheel, whirl 2. go back, move, return, reverse, shift, switch, veer, wheel 3. arc, come round, corner, negotiate, pass 4. adapt, alter, become, change, convert, divert, fashion, fit, form, mould, mutate, remodel, shape, transfigure, transform 5. curdle, go sour, spoil, taint 6. construct, deliver, execute, fashion, frame, make, mould, perform, shape, write ~*n.* 7. bend, change, circle, curve, cycle, gyration, pivot, reversal, spin, swing, twist, whirl 8. bias, direction, drift, heading, tendency, trend 9. bend, curve, departure, deviation, shift 10. chance, fling, go, opportunity, period, round, shift, spell, stint, time, try

turning point change, crisis, crossroads, crux

turn off cut out, kill, put out, shut down, stop, switch off, turn out, unplug

DICTIONARY

turpentine n. (oil made from) the resin of certain trees. **—turps** n. turpentine oil.

turpitude n. depravity.

turquoise n. blue-green precious stone. —adj. blue-green.

turret n. small tower; revolving gun tower on a warship or tank.

turtle n. sea tortoise. **—turn turtle** capsize. **—turtledove** n. small wild dove. **—turtleneck** n. (sweater with) a round high close-fitting neck.

tusk n. long pointed tooth of an elephant, walrus, etc.

tussle n., v. fight or scuffle.

tussock n. tuft of grass.

tutelage [tew-till-lij] n. tuition; guardianship. **—tutelary** [tew-till-lar-ee] adj.

tutor n. person teaching individuals or small groups. —v. act as a tutor to. **—tutorial** n. period of instruction with a tutor.

tutu n. short stiff skirt worn by ballerinas.

tuxedo n., pl. **-dos.** US dinner jacket.

TV television.

twaddle n. nonsense.

twain n., det. Obs. two.

twang n. sharp ringing sound; nasal speech. —v. (cause to) make a twang.

tweak v. pinch or twist sharply. —n. tweaking.

twee adj. Informal too sentimental, sweet, or pretty.

tweed n. thick woollen cloth. —pl. suit of tweed. **—tweedy** adj.

tweet n., v. chirp. **—tweeter** n. loudspeaker reproducing high-frequency sounds.

tweezers pl. n. small pincer-like tool.

twelve adj., n. two more than ten. **—twelfth** adj., n. (of) number twelve in a series.

twenty adj., n. two times ten. **—twentieth** adj., n.

twerp n. Informal silly person.

twice adv. two times.

twiddle v. (foll. by with) fiddle (with), twirl. **—twiddle one's thumbs** be bored, have nothing to do.

twig[1] n. small branch or shoot.

twig[2] v. **twigging, twigged.** Informal realize or understand.

twilight n. soft dim light just after sunset.

twill n. fabric woven to produce parallel ridges.

twin n. one of a pair, esp. of two children born at one birth. —v. **twinning, twinned.** pair or be paired.

twine v. twist or coil round. —n. string or cord.

twinge n. sudden sharp pain or pang.

twinkle v. shine brightly but intermittently. —n. flickering brightness. **—in the twinkling of an eye** in a very short time.

twirl v. turn or twist around quickly; twiddle, esp. idly.

twirp n. Informal same as TWERP.

twist v. turn out of the natural position; wind or twine; distort or pervert. —n. twisting; twisted thing; unexpected development in the plot of a film, book, etc.; bend or curve; distortion. **—twisted** adj. (of a person) cruel or perverted. **—twister** n. Informal swindler. **—twisty** adj.

twit[1] v. **twitting, twitted.** taunt, esp. in jest.

twit[2] n. Informal foolish person.

twitch v. move spasmodically; pull sharply. —n. nervous muscular spasm; sharp pull.

THESAURUS

turn on 1. activate, ignite, start 2. assail, assault, attack

turn up 1. appear, arrive, attend, come 2. appear, disclose, discover, expose, find, pop up, reveal, transpire, unearth

tussle 1. v. battle, brawl, contend, fight, grapple, scuffle, struggle, vie, wrestle 2. n. battle, bout, brawl, competition, conflict, contest, fight, fracas, fray, scuffle, struggle

tutor 1. n. coach, governor, guardian, guide, instructor, lecturer, master, mentor, schoolmaster, teacher 2. v. coach, direct, edify, educate, guide, instruct, lecture, school, teach, train

twilight n. dusk, evening, half-light, sundown, sunset

twin n. counterpart, double, fellow, likeness, match, mate

twine 1. n. cord, string, yarn 2. v. bend, coil, curl, encircle, loop, meander, spiral, surround, twist wind, wrap

twirl v. gyrate, revolve, rotate, spin, turn, twist, wheel, whirl, wind

twist v. 1. coil, curl, entwine, screw, spin, swivel, weave, wind, wrap, wreathe, wring 2. contort, distort ~n. 3. coil, curl, spin, swivel, twine, wind 4. braid, coil, curl, plug, quid, roll 5. change, slant, surprise, turn, variation 6. arc, bend, convolution, curve, meander, turn, zigzag 7. defect, distortion, flaw, imperfection, kink, warp

twit ass, clown, fool, halfwit, idiot, nitwit, simpleton

twitch 1. v. blink, jerk, pluck, pull, snatch, tug, yank 2. n. blink, flutter, jerk, jump, pull, spasm, tic, twinge

DICTIONARY

twitter v. (of birds) utter chirping sounds. —n. chirping.

two adj., n. one more than one. —**two-edged** adj. (of a remark) having both a favourable and an unfavourable interpretation. —**two-faced** adj. deceitful, hypocritical. —**two-time** v. Informal deceive (a lover) by having an affair with someone else.

tycoon n. powerful wealthy businessman.

tyke n. Informal small cheeky child; small mongrel dog.

tympani [tim-pan-ee] n. same as TIMPANI.

type n. class or category; Informal person, esp. of a specified kind; block with a raised character used for printing; printed text. —v. print with a typewriter; typify; classify. —**typist** n. person who types with a typewriter. —**typecast** v. continually cast (an actor or actress) in similar roles. —**typewriter** n. machine which prints a character when the appropriate key is pressed.

typhoid (**fever**) n. acute infectious feverish disease.

typhoon n. violent tropical storm.

typhus n. infectious feverish disease.

typical adj. true to type, characteristic. —**typically** adv.

typify v. -**fying**, -**fied**. be typical of.

typography n. art or style of printing. —**typographical** adj. —**typographer** n.

tyrant n. oppressive or cruel ruler; person who exercises authority tyrannically. —**tyrannical** adj. like a tyrant, oppressive. —**tyrannically** adv. —**tyrannize** v. exert power (over) oppressively or cruelly. —**tyrannous** adj. —**tyranny** n. tyrannical rule.

tyre n. rubber ring, usu. inflated, over the rim of a vehicle's wheel to grip the road.

tyro n., pl. -**ros**. novice or beginner.

THESAURUS

tycoon baron, capitalist, financier, industrialist, magnate, mogul, potentate

type 1. category, class, form, group, ilk, kind, order, sort, species, strain, variety 2. case, face, fount, print, printing

typhoon cyclone, squall, storm

typical average, characteristic, classic, essential, indicative, model, normal, orthodox, representative, standard, stock, usual

typify embody, epitomize, exemplify, illustrate, personify, symbolize

tyrannical arbitrary, autocratic, cruel, despotic, dictatorial, domineering, high-handed, imperious, inhuman, oppressive, overbearing, overweening, severe, unjust, unreasonable

tyranny authoritarianism, autocracy, coercion, cruelty, despotism, dictatorship, imperiousness, oppression, unreasonableness

tyrant autocrat, despot, dictator, oppressor, slave-driver

tyro apprentice, beginner, initiate, learner, novice, novitiate, pupil, student, trainee

U

ubiquitous [yew-**bik**-wit-uss] *adj.* being or seeming to be everywhere at once. **—ubiquity** *n.*

udder *n.* large baglike milk-producing gland of cows, sheep, or goats.

UFO unidentified flying object.

ugly *adj.* **uglier, ugliest.** of unpleasant appearance; ominous or menacing. **—ugliness** *n.*

UHF ultrahigh frequency.

UHT ultra-heat-treated (milk or cream).

UK United Kingdom.

ukulele [yew-kal-**lay**-lee] *n.* small guitar with four strings.

ulcer *n.* open sore on the surface of the skin or mucous membrane. **—ulcerate** *v.* make or become ulcerous. **—ulceration** *n.* **—ulcerous** *adj.* of, like, or characterized by ulcers.

ulna *n., pl.* **-nae, -nas.** inner and longer of the two bones of the human forearm. **—ulnar** *adj.*

ulterior [ult-**ear**-ee-or] *adj.* lying beyond what is revealed or seen, e.g. *ulterior motives.*

ultimate *adj.* final in a series or process; highest or most significant. **—ultimately** *adv.* **—ultimatum** [ult-im-**may**-tum] *n.* final communication stating that action will be taken unless certain conditions are met.

ultra- *prefix* beyond a specified extent, range, or limit, e.g. *ultrasonic;* extremely, e.g. *ultramodern.*

ultrahigh frequency *n.* radio frequency between 3000 and 300 megahertz.

ultramarine *adj.* vivid blue.

ultrasonic *adj.* of or producing sound waves with a higher frequency than the human ear can hear. **—ultrasonically** *adv.*

ultraviolet *adj., n.* (of) light beyond the limit of visibility at the violet end of the spectrum.

ululate [**yewl**-yew-late] *v.* howl or wail. **—ululation** *n.*

umber *adj.* dark brown to greenish-brown.

umbilical [um-**bill**-ik-al] *adj.* of the navel. **—umbilical cord** long flexible tube of blood vessels that connects a fetus with the placenta.

umbrage *n.* displeasure or resentment. **—take umbrage** feel offended or upset.

umbrella *n.* portable device used for protection against rain, consisting of a folding frame covered in material attached to a central rod; single organization, idea, etc. that contains or covers many different organizations.

umpire *n.* official who rules on the playing of a game. **—***v.* act as umpire in (a game).

umpteen *det. Informal* very many. **—umpteenth** *n., adj.*

UN United Nations.

un- *prefix* not, e.g. *uncertain;* denoting reversal of an action, e.g. *untie;* denoting removal from, e.g. *unthrone.*

unable *adj.* (foll. by *to*) lacking the necessary power, ability, or authority to (do something).

unaccountable *adj.* that cannot be explained; (foll. by *to*) not answerable to. **—unaccountably** *adv.*

unadopted *adj.* (of a road) maintained by local residents rather than by a local authority.

unadulterated *adj.* with nothing added, pure.

unanimous [yew-**nan**-im-uss] *adj.* in complete agreement; agreed by all. **—unanimity** *n.*

unarmed *adj.* without weapons.

unassuming *adj.* modest or unpretentious.

unaware *adj.* not aware or conscious. **—unawares** *adv.* by surprise; without knowing.

THESAURUS

ubiquitous ever-present, everywhere, pervasive

ugly 1. hard-featured, misshapen, plain, unattractive, unprepossessing, unsightly 2. disagreeable, distasteful, frightful, hideous, horrid, monstrous, repugnant, repulsive, shocking, unpleasant, vile 3. dangerous, menacing, ominous, sinister

ulterior concealed, covert, hidden, secret, selfish, unexpressed

ultimate 1. decisive, end, eventual, extreme, final, furthest, last 2. extreme, greatest, highest, paramount, superlative, supreme, topmost, utmost

umbrage anger, displeasure, grudge, huff, offence, pique, resentment

umpire 1. *n.* arbiter, arbitrator, judge, moderator, referee 2. *v.* adjudicate, judge, referee

unable impotent, incapable, ineffectual, powerless, unfit, unfitted, unqualified

unanimous agreed, common, concerted, harmonious, like-minded, of one mind, united

unarmed defenceless, exposed, helpless, open, weak

unassuming diffident, humble, modest, quiet, reserved, retiring, simple

unaware heedless, ignorant, unconscious, uninformed, unsuspecting

unawares 1. by surprise, off guard, suddenly, unexpectedly 2. accidentally, inadvertently,

DICTIONARY

unbalanced *adj.* mentally deranged; biased or one-sided.

unbearable *adj.* not able to be endured. —**unbearably** *adv.*

unbeknown *adv.* (foll. by *to*) without the knowledge of (a person).

unbend *v. Informal* relax (the mind) or (of the mind) become relaxed. —**unbending** *adj.* unwilling to change one's beliefs or attitudes.

unbidden *adj.* not ordered or asked.

unborn *adj.* not yet born.

unbosom *v.* relieve (oneself) of (secrets or feelings) by telling someone.

unbridled *adj.* (of feelings or behaviour) not controlled in any way.

unburden *v.* relieve (one's mind or oneself) of a worry by confiding in someone.

uncalled-for *adj.* not fair or justified.

uncanny *adj.* weird or mysterious. —**uncannily** *adv.* —**uncanniness** *n.*

unceremonious *adj.* without ceremony; abrupt or rude. —**unceremoniously** *adv.*

uncertain *adj.* not able to be accurately known or predicted; not able to be depended upon; changeable. —**uncertainty** *n.*

un-Christian *adj.* not in accordance with Christian principles.

uncle *n.* brother of one's father or mother; husband of one's aunt.

unclean *adj.* lacking moral, spiritual, or physical cleanliness.

uncomfortable *adj.* not physically relaxed; anxious or uneasy.

uncommon *adj.* beyond normal experience; in excess of what is normal. —**uncommonly** *adv.*

uncompromising *adj.* not prepared to compromise.

unconcerned *adj.* lacking in concern or involvement. —**unconcernedly** *adv.*

unconditional *adj.* without conditions or limitations.

unconscionable *adj.* having no principles, unscrupulous; excessive in amount or degree.

unconscious *adj.* lacking normal awareness through the senses; not aware of one's actions or behaviour. —**unconsciously** *adv.* —**unconsciousness** *n.*

uncooperative *adj.* not willing to cooperate, unhelpful.

uncouth *adj.* lacking in good manners, refinement, or grace.

uncover *v.* remove the cap, top, etc. from; reveal or disclose.

unction *n.* act of anointing with oil in sacra-

THESAURUS

unwittingly

unbalanced crazy, demented, deranged, eccentric, insane, irrational, lunatic, mad, unsound

unbearable insufferable, intolerable, unacceptable

unbending 1. aloof, distant, inflexible, rigid, stiff 2. firm, intractable, resolute, severe, strict, stubborn, tough, uncompromising

unborn awaited, embryonic, expected

unbridled excessive, licentious, riotous, unchecked, unrestrained, unruly, violent, wanton

unburden confess, confide, disclose, reveal

uncalled-for gratuitous, needless, undeserved, unnecessary, unwarranted

uncanny eerie, mysterious, queer, strange, supernatural, unnatural, weird

uncertain 1. doubtful, indefinite, indistinct, questionable, risky, speculative 2. dubious, hazy, irresolute, unclear, unconfirmed, undecided, unsettled, unsure, vague

uncertainty ambiguity, confusion, doubt, hesitancy, indecision, perplexity, quandary, scepticism, unpredictability

unclean corrupt, defiled, dirty, evil, filthy, foul, impure, polluted, soiled, stained

uncomfortable 1. awkward, cramped, hard, painful, rough 2. awkward, confused, disquieted, distressed, disturbed, troubled, uneasy

uncommon 1. curious, novel, odd, peculiar, queer, rare, scarce, strange, unusual 2. distinctive, extraordinary, inimitable, notable, outstanding, rare, remarkable, special

uncommonly 1. hardly ever, infrequently, occasionally, rarely, seldom 2. extremely, particularly, unusually, very

uncompromising firm, inexorable, inflexible, intransigent, strict, stubborn, unbending

unconcerned aloof, cool, detached, dispassionate, distant, unmoved

unconditional absolute, complete, entire, full, outright, positive, unlimited, unreserved

unconscious 1. insensible, numb, out, senseless, stunned 2. heedless, ignorant, oblivious, unaware, unknowing 3. accidental, unintentional, unwitting

uncouth awkward, boorish, clownish, clumsy, coarse, crude, graceless, gross, loutish, rough, rude, uncultivated, vulgar

uncover 1. bare, open, show, strip, unwrap 2. disclose, make known, reveal, unearth, unmask

DICTIONARY

mental ceremonies. —**unctuous** *adj.* pretending to be kind and concerned.

undeceive *v.* reveal the truth to (someone previously misled or deceived).

undecided *adj.* not having made up one's mind; (of an issue or problem) not agreed or decided upon.

undeniable *adj.* indisputably true. —**undeniably** *adv.*

under *prep.* on, to, or beneath the underside or base of; less than; subject to the supervision, control, or influence of; subject to (conditions). —*adv.* to a position underneath.

under- *prefix* below, e.g. *underground;* insufficient or insufficiently, e.g. *underrate.*

underage *adj.* below the required or standard age.

underarm *Sport* —*adj.* denoting a style of throwing, bowling, or serving in which the hand is swung below shoulder level. —*adv.* in an underarm style.

undercarriage *n.* landing gear of an aircraft; framework supporting the body of a vehicle.

undercoat *n.* coat of paint applied before the final coat.

undercover *adj.* done or acting in secret.

undercurrent *n.* current that is not apparent at the surface; underlying opinion or emotion.

undercut *v.* charge less than (a competitor) to obtain trade.

underdog *n.* person or team unlikely to win in a competition.

underdone *adj.* not cooked enough.

underestimate *v.* make too low an estimate of; not think highly enough of.

underfelt *n.* thick felt laid under a carpet to increase insulation.

underfoot *adv.* under the feet.

undergarment *n.* any piece of underwear.

undergo *v.* experience, endure, or sustain.

undergraduate *n.* person studying in a university for a first degree.

underground *adj.* occurring, situated, used, or going below ground level; secret. —*n.* electric passenger railway operated in underground tunnels; movement dedicated to overthrowing a government or occupation forces.

undergrowth *n.* small trees and bushes growing beneath taller trees in a wood or forest.

underhand *adj.* sly, deceitful, and secretive.

underlie *v.* lie or be placed under; be the foundation, cause, or basis of. —**underlying** *adj.* fundamental or basic.

underline *v.* draw a line under; state forcibly, emphasize.

underling *n.* subordinate.

undermine *v.* weaken gradually; (of the sea or wind) wear away the base of (cliffs).

underneath *prep., adv.* under or beneath. —*adj., n.* lower (part or surface).

underpants *pl. n.* man's undergarment for the lower part of the body.

underpass *n.* section of a road that passes under another road or a railway line.

underpin *v.* give strength or support to.

THESAURUS

undecided 1. dithering, hesitant, irresolute, torn, uncertain, uncommitted, unsure 2. indefinite, moot, open, pending, tentative, unsettled, vague

undeniable certain, clear, evident, indisputable, manifest, obvious, patent, proven, sound, sure

under *prep.* 1. below, beneath, underneath 2. governed by, secondary to, subject to, subservient to ~*adv.* 3. below, beneath, down, lower

undercover concealed, confidential, covert, hidden, intelligence, private, secret, spy

undercurrent 1. rip, riptide, undertow 2. aura, drift, feeling, flavour, hint, murmur, sense, suggestion, tendency, tinge, trend, undertone

underestimate belittle, hold cheap, minimize, miscalculate, underrate, undervalue

undergo bear, endure, experience, stand, suffer, sustain, withstand

underground *adj.* 1. buried, covered, subterra-

nean 2. clandestine, concealed, covert, hidden, secret ~*n.* 3. the metro, the subway, the tube

undergrowth bracken, briars, brush, scrub, underwood

underhand crafty, deceitful, devious, dishonest, fraudulent, furtive, secret, sly, sneaky, stealthy, treacherous, unscrupulous

underline 1. mark, underscore 2. accentuate, emphasize, highlight, stress

underlying basic, elementary, intrinsic, primary, prime

undermine 1. erode, excavate, mine, tunnel 2. disable, impair, sabotage, sap, subvert, threaten, weaken

underprivileged deprived, destitute, impoverished, needy, poor

underrate belittle, discount, underestimate, undervalue

DICTIONARY

underprivileged adj. lacking the rights and advantages of other members of society.

underrate v. underestimate. —**underrated** adj.

underseal n. coating of tar etc. applied to the underside of a motor vehicle to retard corrosion.

underside n. bottom or lower surface.

understand v. know and comprehend the nature or meaning of; realize or grasp (something); assume, infer, or believe. —**understandable** adj. —**understandably** adv. —**understanding** n. ability to learn, judge, or make decisions; personal interpretation of a subject; mutual agreement, usu. an informal or private one. —adj. kind and sympathetic.

understate v. describe or represent (something) in restrained terms; state that (something, such as a number) is less than it is. —**understatement** n.

understudy n. actor who studies a part in order to be able to replace the usual actor if necessary. —v. act as an understudy for.

undertake v. agree or commit oneself to (something) or (to do something); promise. —**undertaking** n. task or enterprise; agreement to do something.

undertaker n. person whose profession is to prepare corpses for burial and organize funerals.

undertone n. quiet tone of voice; underlying quality or feeling.

undertow n. strong undercurrent flowing in a different direction from the surface current.

underwear n. clothing worn under the outer garments and next to the skin.

underworld n. criminals and their associates; Greek & Roman myth regions below the earth's surface regarded as the abode of the dead.

underwrite v. accept financial responsibility for (a commercial project); sign and issue (an insurance policy), thus accepting liability. —**underwriter** n.

undesirable adj. not desirable or pleasant, objectionable. —**undesirably** adv.

undo v. open, unwrap; reverse the effects of; cause the downfall of. —**undoing** n. cause of someone's downfall. —**undone** adj.

undoubted adj. certain or indisputable. —**undoubtedly** adv.

undue adj. greater than is reasonable, excessive. —**unduly** adv.

undulate v. move in waves. —**undulation** n.

undying adj. never ending, eternal.

unearth v. dig up out of the earth; reveal or discover.

unearthly adj. ghostly or eerie; ridiculous or unreasonable, e.g. an unearthly hour. —**unearthliness** n.

THESAURUS

understand 1. appreciate, apprehend, comprehend, conceive, discern, fathom, follow, get, grasp, know, make out, penetrate, perceive, realize, recognize, see, take in 2. assume, believe, conclude, gather, hear, learn, presume, suppose, think 3. accept, appreciate

understanding n. 1. appreciation, awareness, discernment, grasp, insight, judgment, knowledge, perception, sense 2. belief, conclusion, idea, judgment, notion, opinion, view 3. accord, agreement, pact ~adj. 4. compassionate, considerate, discerning, forgiving, kind, patient, perceptive, responsive, sensitive, tolerant

understudy n. double, replacement, reserve, sub, substitute

undertake agree, bargain, contract, covenant, engage, guarantee, pledge, promise, stipulate

undertaking 1. affair, attempt, business, effort, enterprise, game, operation, project, task, venture 2. assurance, pledge, promise, word, vow, word

undertone 1. murmur, whisper 2. feeling, flavour, hint, tinge, touch, trace

underwear lingerie, underclothes, undies

underworld 1. criminals, gangsters 2. Hades, hell, the inferno

underwrite 1. back, finance, fund, guarantee, insure, sponsor, subsidize 2. endorse, initial, sign, subscribe

undesirable disliked, distasteful, dreaded, offensive, unacceptable, unattractive, unsavoury, unsuitable

undo 1. disentangle, loose, open, unbutton, unfasten, untie, unwrap 2. annul, cancel, neutralize, nullify, offset, reverse 3. defeat, destroy, impoverish, mar, overturn, quash, ruin, shatter, undermine, upset, wreck

undoing collapse, defeat, disgrace, downfall, overthrow, overturn, reversal, ruin, shame

undone left, neglected, omitted, unfinished, unfulfilled, unperformed

undoubted certain, definite, evident, obvious, sure

undoubtedly assuredly, certainly, definitely, surely

undue excessive, extreme, improper, needless, overmuch, undeserved, unseemly

DICTIONARY

uneasy *adj.* (of a person) anxious or apprehensive; (of a condition) precarious or uncomfortable. —**unease** *n.* —**uneasily** *adv.* —**uneasiness** *n.*

unemployed *adj.* out of work. —**unemployment** *n.*

unequivocal *adj.* completely clear in meaning. —**unequivocally** *adv.*

unerring *adj.* never mistaken, consistently accurate.

unexceptionable *adj.* beyond criticism or objection.

unfailing *adj.* continuous or reliable. —**unfailingly** *adv.*

unfair *adj.* not right, fair, or just. —**unfairly** *adv.* —**unfairness** *n.*

unfaithful *adj.* guilty of adultery; not true to a promise or vow. —**unfaithfulness** *n.*

unfeeling *adj.* without sympathy.

unfit *adj.* (foll. by *for*) unqualified or unsuitable; in poor physical condition.

unflappable *adj. Informal* hard to upset. —**unflappability** *n.*

unfold *v.* open or spread out from a folded state; reveal or be revealed.

unforgettable *adj.* impossible to forget, memorable.

unfortunate *adj.* unlucky, unsuccessful, or unhappy; regrettable or unsuitable. —**unfortunately** *adv.*

unfrock *v.* deprive (a priest in holy orders) of his priesthood.

ungainly *adj.* **-lier, -liest.** lacking grace when moving. —**ungainliness** *n.*

ungodly *adj.* wicked or sinful; *Informal* unreasonable or outrageous. —**ungodliness** *n.*

ungrateful *adj.* not grateful or thankful. —**ungratefully** *adv.* —**ungratefulness** *n.*

unguarded *adj.* not protected; incautious or careless.

unguent [ung-gwent] *n.* ointment.

unhand *v. Old-fashioned or lit.* release from one's grasp.

unhappy *adj.* sad or depressed; unfortunate or wretched. —**unhappily** *adv.* —**unhappiness** *n.*

unhealthy *adj.* characterized by ill health, sick;

THESAURUS

unduly excessively, overmuch, unnecessarily, unreasonably

unearth 1. dig up, dredge up, excavate, exhume 2. discover, expose, find, reveal, uncover

unearthly 1. eerie, ghostly, haunted, phantom, spectral, strange, uncanny, weird 2. absurd, ridiculous, strange

uneasiness agitation, alarm, anxiety, disquiet, doubt, misgiving, qualms, suspicion, worry

uneasy 1. agitated, anxious, disturbed, edgy, impatient, nervous, perturbed, restive, restless, troubled, upset, worried 2. awkward, insecure, precarious, shaky, strained, tense, uncomfortable

unemployed idle, jobless, laid off, redundant, workless

unfailing 1. bottomless, boundless, ceaseless, continuous, endless, persistent, unflagging, unlimited 2. certain, constant, faithful, loyal, reliable, staunch, sure, true

unfair biased, bigoted, one-sided, partial, partisan, prejudiced, unjust

unfaithful 1. deceitful, disloyal, false, perfidious, recreant (*Archaic*), traitorous, treacherous, treasonable, untrustworthy 2. adulterous, faithless, fickle, inconstant

unfit 1. inadequate, incapable, no good, not equal to, not up to, unprepared, unqualified, untrained, useless 2. inadequate, ineffective, unsuitable, unsuited, useless 3. decrepit, feeble, flabby, unhealthy

unfold 1. disentangle, expand, flatten, open, straighten, undo, unfurl, unravel, unroll, unwrap 2. *Fig.* clarify, describe, disclose, divulge, explain, illustrate, present, reveal, show, uncover

unforgettable exceptional, impressive, memorable, notable

unfortunate 1. cursed, doomed, hapless, luckless, poor, unhappy, unlucky, unsuccessful, wretched 2. ill-advised, infelicitous, lamentable, regrettable, unbecoming, unsuitable

ungainly awkward, clumsy, gawky, inelegant, lumbering, slouching, uncouth

ungodly corrupt, depraved, godless, immoral, impious, irreligious, profane, sinful, vile, wicked

ungrateful heedless, selfish, unappreciative

unguarded 1. careless, foolhardy, heedless, impolitic, imprudent, rash, thoughtless, unthinking, unwary 2. defenceless, undefended, unprotected, vulnerable

unhappy 1. blue, dejected, depressed, dispirited, down, downcast, gloomy, miserable, mournful, sad, sorrowful 2. cursed, hapless, ill-fated, ill-omened, luckless, wretched

unhealthy 1. ailing, delicate, feeble, frail, infirm, invalid, sick, unwell, weak 2. detrimental, harmful, insanitary, noisome, unwholesome

DICTIONARY

of, causing, or due to ill health; morbid, unnatural. —**unhealthiness** n.

unhinge v. derange or unbalance (a person or his or her mind).

uni- combining form of, consisting of, or having only one, e.g. unisexual.

unicorn n. imaginary horselike creature with one horn growing from its forehead.

uniform n. special identifying set of clothes for the members of an organization, such as soldiers. —adj. unvarying; alike or like. —**uniformly** adv. —**uniformity** n.

unify v. -fying, -fied. make or become one. —**unification** n.

unilateral adj. made or done by only one person or group. —**unilateralism** n.

unimpeachable adj. completely honest and reliable.

union n. uniting or being united; association or confederation of individuals or groups for a common purpose; short for TRADE UNION. —**unionist** n. member or supporter of a trade union. —**unionize** v. organize (workers) into a trade union. —**unionization** n. —**Union Jack** national flag of the United Kingdom.

unique [yoo-**neek**] adj. being the only one of a particular type; without equal or like. —**uniquely** adv.

unisex adj. designed for use by both sexes.

unison n. complete agreement; Music singing or playing the same notes together at the same time.

unit n. single undivided entity or whole; group or individual regarded as a basic element of a larger whole; fixed quantity etc., used as a standard of measurement. —**unitary** adj. —**unit trust** Brit. investment trust that issues units for public sale and invests the money in many different businesses.

Unitarian n. person who believes that God is one being and rejects the Trinity. —**Unitarianism** n.

unite v. make or become an integrated whole; (cause to) enter into an association or alliance. —**unity** n. state of being one; mutual agreement.

universe n. whole of all existing matter, energy, and space; the world. —**universal** adj. of or typical of the whole of mankind or of nature; existing everywhere. —**universality** n. —**universally** adv.

university n., pl. -ties. institution of higher education having the authority to award degrees.

unkempt adj. (of the hair) not combed; slovenly or untidy.

unknown adj. not known; not famous. —n. unknown person, quantity, or thing.

unleaded adj. (of petrol) containing less tetraethyl lead, in order to reduce environmental pollution.

unless conj. except under the circumstances that.

unlike adj. dissimilar or different. —prep. not like or typical of. —**unlikely** adj. improbable. —**unlikeliness** n.

THESAURUS

uniform n. 1. costume, dress, garb, habit, livery, outfit, regalia, suit ~adj. 2. consistent, constant, even, regular, smooth, unchanging 3. alike, equal, like, same, similar

union 1. amalgamation, blend, combination, conjunction, fusion, junction, mixture, uniting 2. alliance, association, coalition, confederacy, federation, league 3. accord, agreement, concord, harmony, unison, unity

unique 1. lone, only, single, solitary 2. incomparable, inimitable, matchless, peerless, unequalled, unmatched, unrivalled

unison accord, accordance, agreement, concert, concord, harmony

unit 1. assembly, detachment, entity, group, section, whole 2. component, constituent, element, item, member, module, part, portion, section, segment

unite 1. amalgamate, blend, combine, consolidate, couple, fuse, join, link, marry, merge, unify, wed 2. ally, band, close ranks, cooperate, league, pool

unity 1. entity, integrity, singleness, undividedness, union, wholeness 2. accord, agreement, concord, consensus, harmony, peace, solidarity

universal common, entire, general, total, unlimited, whole, widespread, worldwide

universally always, everywhere, invariably, uniformly

universe cosmos, creation, nature

unknown 1. alien, concealed, dark, hidden, mysterious, new, secret, strange, unrevealed, untold 2. anonymous, nameless, uncharted, undiscovered, unidentified, unnamed 3. humble, obscure, unfamiliar

unlike different, dissimilar, distinct, diverse, ill-matched, incompatible, opposite, unequal, unrelated

unlikely doubtful, faint, improbable, remote, slight

unload discharge, dump, empty, relieve, unpack

DICTIONARY

unload *v.* remove (cargo) from (a ship, lorry, or plane); get rid of; remove the ammunition from (a firearm).

unmask *v.* remove the mask or disguise from; (cause to) appear in true character.

unmentionable *adj.* unsuitable as a topic of conversation.

unmistak(e)able *adj.* not ambiguous, clear. —**unmistak(e)- ably** *adv.*

unmitigated *adj.* not reduced or lessened in severity etc.; total and complete.

unmoved *adj.* not affected by emotion, indifferent.

unnatural *adj.* contrary to nature; not in accordance with accepted standards of behaviour.

unnerve *v.* cause to lose courage, confidence, or self-control.

unnumbered *adj.* countless; not counted or given a number.

unorthodox *adj.* not conventional in belief, behaviour, etc.

unpack *v.* remove the contents of (a suitcase, trunk, etc.); take (something) out of a packed container.

unparalleled *adj.* not equalled, supreme.

unpick *v.* undo (the stitches) of (a piece of sewing).

unpleasant *adj.* not pleasant or agreeable. —**unpleasantly** *adv.* —**unpleasantness** *n.*

unprintable *adj.* unsuitable for printing for reasons of obscenity or libel.

unprofessional *adj.* contrary to the accepted code of a profession; not belonging to a profession. —**unprofessionally** *adv.*

unqualified *adj.* lacking the necessary qualifications; not modified.

unravel *v.* -elling, -elled. reduce (something knitted or woven) to separate strands; become unravelled; explain or solve.

unremitting *adj.* never slackening or stopping.

unrest *n.* rebellious state of discontent.

unrivalled *adj.* having no equal.

unroll *v.* open out or unwind (something rolled or coiled) or (of something rolled or coiled) become opened out or unwound.

unruly *adj.* -lier, -liest. given to disobedience or indiscipline.

unsavoury *adj.* distasteful or objectionable.

unscathed *adj.* not harmed or injured.

unscrupulous *adj.* unprincipled or without scruples.

unseat *v.* throw or displace from a seat or saddle; depose from an office or position.

unsettled *adj.* lacking order or stability; dis-

THESAURUS

unmask bare, disclose, discover, expose, reveal, uncover, unveil

unmentionable disgraceful, forbidden, indecent, scandalous, shameful, shocking, taboo, unspeakable

unmistakable certain, clear, decided, distinct, evident, indisputable, manifest, obvious, plain, positive, sure, unequivocal

unmitigated 1. grim, harsh, intense, persistent, unbroken, undiminished, unrelieved 2. absolute, arrant, complete, downright, outright, perfect, rank, sheer, thorough, utter

unmoved cold, impassive, indifferent, unimpressed, unresponsive, untouched

unnatural 1. abnormal, anomalous, irregular, odd, perverse, perverted, unusual 2. extraordinary, freakish, queer, strange, unaccountable, uncanny

unnerve confound, demoralize, disarm, discourage, dishearten, dismay, fluster, frighten, intimidate, shake, upset

unorthodox abnormal, irregular, unusual, unwonted

unpleasant bad, disagreeable, displeasing, distasteful, nasty, repulsive, unattractive

unprofessional 1. improper, lax, negligent, un-

ethical, unseemly, unworthy 2. amateurish, inefficient, untrained

unqualified 1. ill-equipped, incapable, incompetent, ineligible, unfit, unprepared 2. downright, outright, unreserved

unravel disentangle, free, separate, undo, unwind

unrest agitation, discontent, discord, dissension, protest, rebellion, sedition, strife, tumult

unrivalled beyond compare, incomparable, matchless, peerless, supreme, unmatched, unparalleled, unsurpassed, without equal

unruly disobedient, fractious, lawless, mutinous, rebellious, riotous, rowdy, turbulent, wayward, wild, wilful

unsavoury distasteful, nasty, obnoxious, offensive, repellent, repulsive, revolting, unpleasant

unscrupulous corrupt, dishonest, immoral, improper, knavish, roguish, unethical, unprincipled

unsettled 1. disorderly, shaky, unstable, unsteady 2. changing, inconstant, uncertain, variable 3. agitated, anxious, confused, disturbed, flustered, restive, restless, shaken, tense, unnerved

DICTIONARY

turbed and restless; constantly changing or moving from place to place.

unsightly *adj.* unpleasant to look at.

unsocial *adj.* antisocial; falling outside the normal working day, e.g. *unsocial hours*.

unsound *adj.* unhealthy or unstable; not based on truth or fact.

unstable *adj.* lacking stability or firmness; having abrupt changes of mood or behaviour.

unstudied *adj.* natural or spontaneous.

unsuitable *adj.* not right or appropriate for a particular purpose. —**unsuitably** *adv.*

unswerving *adj.* not turning aside.

unthinkable *adj.* out of the question, inconceivable.

untidy *adj.* not neat, slovenly. —**untidily** *adv.* —**untidiness** *n.*

untie *v.* open or free (something that is tied); free from constraint.

until *conj.* up to the time that. —*prep.* in or throughout the period before. —**not until** not before (a time or event).

untimely *adj.* occurring before the expected or normal time; inappropriate to the occasion or time. —**untimeliness** *n.*

unto *prep. Old-fashioned* to.

untold *adj.* incapable of description; incalculably great in number or quantity.

untouchable *adj.* above reproach or suspicion; unable to be touched. —*n.* member of the lowest Hindu caste in India.

untoward *adj.* causing misfortune or annoyance.

untruth *n.* statement that is not true, lie.

unusual *adj.* uncommon or extraordinary. —**unusually** *adv.*

unutterable *adj.* incapable of being expressed in words. —**unutterably** *adv.*

unvarnished *adj.* not elaborated upon.

unwieldy *adj.* too heavy, large, or awkward to be easily handled.

unwind *v.* (cause to) slacken, undo, or unravel; make or become relaxed.

unwitting *adj.* not knowing or conscious; not intentional. —**unwittingly** *adv.*

unwonted *adj.* out of the ordinary.

unworthy *adj.* not deserving or worthy; (foll. by *of*) beneath the level considered befitting (to); lacking merit or value.

unwrap *v.* remove the wrapping from (something) or (of something wrapped) have the covering removed.

unwritten *adj.* not printed or in writing; operating only through custom.

up *prep.* indicating movement to a higher position; at a higher or further level or position in or on. —*adv.* to an upward, higher, or erect position; indicating readiness for an activity, e.g. *up and about;* indicating intensity or completion of an action; to the place referred to or where the speaker is. —*adj.* of a high or higher position; out of bed. —*v.* **upping, upped.** increase or raise; *Informal* do something suddenly, e.g. *he upped and left.* —**up against** having to cope with. —**ups**

THESAURUS

unsightly disagreeable, hideous, horrid, repulsive, ugly, unattractive

unsound 1. ailing, defective, delicate, diseased, frail, ill, unhealthy, unstable, unwell, weak 2. defective, fallacious, false, flawed, illogical, shaky, specious, weak

unsuitable improper, inapt, ineligible, unacceptable, unbecoming, unfitting, unseemly, unsuited

unthinkable 1. absurd, impossible, unlikely, unreasonable 2. implausible, inconceivable, incredible, unimaginable

untidy chaotic, cluttered, disorderly, littered, messy, rumpled, slipshod, slovenly, unkempt

untie free, loosen, release, unbind, undo, unfasten, unknot, unlace

untimely awkward, early, inappropriate, inauspicious, inconvenient, inopportune, premature, unfortunate, unsuitable

untoward annoying, disastrous, inconvenient, irritating, troublesome, unfortunate

untruth deceit, falsehood, fib, fiction, lie, story, tale, trick

unusual bizarre, curious, different, extraordinary, odd, queer, rare, remarkable, singular, strange, surprising, uncommon, unexpected, unfamiliar

unwieldy 1. awkward, cumbersome, inconvenient, unmanageable 2. bulky, clumsy, hefty, massive, ponderous

unwind 1. slacken, uncoil, undo, unreel, unroll, untwine, untwist 2. relax, take it easy

unwitting 1. ignorant, innocent, unaware, unknowing, unsuspecting 2. accidental, chance, involuntary, unintended, unmeant, unplanned

unworthy base, contemptible, degrading, discreditable, disgraceful, dishonourable, disreputable, ignoble, shameful

unwritten 1. oral, vocal 2. accepted, customary, tacit, understood

DICTIONARY

and downs alternating periods of good and bad luck. **—what's up?** *Informal* what is the matter?; what is happening? **—upward** *adj.* directed or moving towards a higher place or level. *—adv.* (also **upwards**) from a lower to a higher place, level, or condition.

upbeat *n. Music* unaccented beat. *—adj. Informal* cheerful and optimistic.

upbraid *v.* scold or reproach.

upbringing *n.* education of a person during the formative years.

update *v.* bring up to date.

upend *v.* turn or set or be turned or set on end.

upfront *adj.* open and frank. *—adv., adj.* (of money) paid out at the beginning of a business arrangement.

upgrade *v.* promote (a person or job) to a higher rank.

upheaval *n.* strong, sudden, or violent disturbance.

uphill *adj.* sloping or leading upwards; requiring a great deal of effort. *—adv.* up a slope.

uphold *v.* maintain or defend against opposition; give moral support to. **—upholder** *n.*

upholster *v.* fit (a chair or sofa) with padding, springs, and covering. **—upholsterer** *n.* **—upholstery** *n.* act of upholstering; soft covering on a chair or sofa.

upkeep *n.* act, process, or cost of keeping something in good repair.

upland *n.* area of high or relatively high ground. *—adj.* of or in an upland.

uplift *v.* raise or lift up; raise morally or spiritually. *—n.* act, process, or result of lifting up. **—uplifting** *adj.*

upon *prep.* on; up and on.

upper *adj.* higher or highest in physical position, wealth, rank, or status. *—n.* part of a shoe above the sole. **—uppermost** *adj.* highest in position, power, or importance. *—adv.* in or into the highest place or position. **—upper-case** *adj.* denoting capital letters as used in printed or typed matter. **—upper class** highest social class. **—upper-class** *adj.* **—upper crust** *Informal* upper class. **—upper hand** position of control.

uppish, uppity *adj. Informal* snobbish, arrogant, or presumptuous.

upright *adj.* vertical or erect; honest or just. *—adv.* vertically. *—n.* vertical support, such as a post. **—uprightness** *n.*

uprising *n.* rebellion or revolt.

uproar *n.* disturbance characterized by loud noise and confusion. **—uproarious** *adj.* very funny; (of laughter) loud and boisterous. **—uproariously** *adv.*

uproot *v.* pull up by or as if by the roots; displace (a person or people) from their native or usual surroundings.

upset *v.* tip over; disturb the normal state or stability of; disturb mentally or emotionally; make physically ill. *—n.* unexpected defeat or reversal; disturbance or disorder of the emotions, mind, or body. *—adj.* emotionally or physically disturbed or distressed. **—upsetting** *adj.*

upshot *n.* final result or conclusion.

THESAURUS

upbringing breeding, care, cultivation, education, tending, training

upgrade advance, better, elevate, enhance, improve, promote, raise

upheaval disorder, disruption, eruption, revolution, turmoil

uphill *adj.* 1. ascending, climbing, mounting, rising 2. arduous, difficult, exhausting, gruelling, hard, laborious, strenuous, taxing, tough

uphold advocate, aid, back, champion, defend, encourage, endorse, justify, maintain, promote, support, sustain

upkeep 1. keep, maintenance, repair, running, subsistence 2. expenditure, outlay, overheads

uplift *v.* 1. elevate, hoist, lift up, raise 2. advance, better, civilize, cultivate, edify, improve, inspire, raise, refine, upgrade *~n.* 3. edification, enhancement, enlightenment, enrichment, improvement, refinement

upper 1. high, higher, loftier, top, topmost 2. elevated, eminent, greater, important, superior

upper hand advantage, ascendancy, dominion, edge, mastery, supremacy, sway

uppermost 1. highest, loftiest, top, topmost 2. chief, dominant, greatest, leading, main, principal, supreme

upright 1. erect, straight, vertical 2. conscientious, ethical, faithful, good, honest, just, principled, righteous, true, virtuous

uproar brawl, clamour, commotion, confusion, din, furore, mayhem, noise, outcry, racket, riot, turbulence, turmoil

upset *v.* 1. capsize, overturn, spill 2. change, disorder, disturb, spoil 3. agitate, bother, discompose, disconcert, dismay, distress, disturb, fluster, grieve, ruffle, trouble *~n.* 4. defeat, reverse, surprise 5. complaint, disorder, illness, malady, sickness 6. agitation, bother, discomposure, disquiet, distress, disturbance, shock, trouble, worry *~adj.* 7. disor-

DICTIONARY

upside down *adj.* turned over completely; *Informal* confused or jumbled. —*adv.* in an inverted fashion; in a chaotic manner.

upstage *adj.* at the back half of the stage. —*v. Informal* draw attention to oneself from (someone else).

upstairs *adv.* up the stairs. —*n.* upper floor. —*adj.* situated on an upper floor.

upstanding *adj.* of good character.

upstart *n.* person who has risen suddenly to a position of power and behaves arrogantly.

upstream *adv., adj.* in or towards the higher part of a stream.

upsurge *n.* rapid rise or swell.

uptake *n.* —**quick** *or* **slow on the uptake** *Informal* quick *or* slow to understand or learn.

uptight *adj. Informal* nervously tense, irritable, or angry.

up-to-date *adj.* modern or fashionable.

upturn *n.* upward trend or improvement; upheaval.

uranium [yew-**rain**-ee-um] *n.* radioactive silvery-white metallic element, used chiefly as a source of nuclear energy.

Uranus *n.* Greek god of the sky; seventh planet from the sun.

urban *adj.* of or living in a city or town. —**urbanize** *v.* make (a rural area) more industrialized and urban. —**urbanization** *n.*

urbane *adj.* characterized by courtesy, elegance, and sophistication. —**urbanity** *n.*

urchin *n.* mischievous child.

urethra [yew-**reeth**-ra] *n., pl.* **-thrae, -thras.** canal that carries urine from the bladder out of the body.

urge *n.* strong impulse, inner drive, or yearning. —*v.* plead with or press (a person to do something); advocate earnestly; force or drive onwards. —**urgent** *adj.* requiring speedy action or attention. —**urgency** *n.* —**urgently** *adv.*

urine *n.* pale yellow fluid excreted by the kidneys to the bladder and passed as waste from the body. —**uric** *adj.* —**urinal** *n.* (place with) sanitary fitting(s) used by men for urination. —**urinary** *adj.* —**urinate** *v.* discharge urine. —**urination** *n.*

urn *n.* vase used as a container for the ashes of the dead; large metal container with a tap, used for making and holding tea or coffee.

ursine *adj.* of or like a bear.

us *pl. pron.* objective case of WE.

US, USA United States (of America).

use *v.* put into service or action; behave towards in a particular way, usu. selfishly; consume or expend. —*n.* using or being used; ability or permission to use; usefulness or advantage; purpose for which something is used. —**user** *n.* —**user-friendly** *adj.* easy to familiarize oneself with, understand, and use. —**usable** *adj.* able to be used. —**usability** *n.* —**usage** *n.* act or a manner of using; constant use, custom, or habit. —**used** *adj.* second-hand. —**used to** *adj.* accustomed to. —*v.* used as an auxiliary to express past habitual or accustomed actions, e.g. *I used to live there.* —**useful** *adj.* —**usefully** *adv.* —**usefulness** *n.* —**useless** *adj.* —**uselessly** *adv.* —**uselessness** *n.*

THESAURUS

dered, disturbed, gippy (*Sl.*), ill, queasy, sick 8. agitated, bothered, confused, dismayed, distressed, disturbed, frantic, grieved, hurt, ruffled, troubled, worried

upshot culmination, end, end result, event, finale, issue, outcome, result

upside down 1. inverted, overturned, upturned 2. confused, disordered, muddled, topsy-turvy

upstart arriviste, nobody

up-to-date current, fashionable, in, modern, newest, stylish

urban city, civic, metropolitan, municipal, town

urbane civil, civilized, courteous, cultured, debonair, elegant, polished, refined, smooth, suave

urchin brat, gamin, ragamuffin, waif

urge *v.* 1. beg, beseech, entreat, exhort, implore, plead, press, solicit 2. advise, advocate, champion, counsel, recommend, support 3. compel, drive, encourage, force, goad, hasten,

impel, incite, induce, instigate, press, propel, push, spur, stimulate ~*n.* 4. desire, drive, fancy, impulse, itch, longing, wish, yearning

urgency extremity, gravity, hurry, importance, importunity, necessity, need, pressure, stress

urgent compelling, critical, crucial, immediate, imperative, important, instant, pressing

usable available, current, functional, practical, serviceable, utilizable, valid, working

usage 1. control, employment, management, operation, running, treatment 2. convention, custom, form, habit, method, mode, practice, procedure, regime, routine, rule, tradition

use *v.* 1. apply, employ, exercise, operate, ply, practise, utilize, wield, work 2. exploit, handle, manipulate, treat 3. consume, exhaust, expend, run through, spend, waste ~*n.* 4. application, employment, exercise, handling, operation, practice, service, usage 5. advantage, application, avail, benefit, good, help,

DICTIONARY

usher *n.* official who shows people to their seats, as in a church. —*v.* conduct or escort. —**usherette** *n.* woman assistant in a cinema who shows people to their seats.

USSR Union of Soviet Socialist Republics.

usual *adj.* of the most normal, frequent, or regular type. —**usually** *adv.*

usurp [yewz-**zurp**] *v.* seize (a position or power) without authority. —**usurpation** *n.* —**usurper** *n.*

usury *n., pl.* **-ries.** practice of lending money at an extremely high rate of interest. —**usurer** [**yewz**-yoor-er] *n.*

utensil *n.* tool or container for practical use.

uterus [**yew**-ter-russ] *n.* womb. —**uterine** *adj.*

utilitarian *adj.* of utilitarianism; useful rather than beautiful. —**utilitarianism** *n.* doctrine that the right action is that which brings about the greatest good for the greatest number of people.

utility *n., pl.* **-ties.** usefulness; public service, such as electricity. —*adj.* designed for use rather than beauty. —**utilize** *v.* make practical use of. —**utilization** *n.*

utmost *adj., n.* (of the) greatest possible degree or amount.

Utopia [yew-**tope**-ee-a] *n.* any real or imaginary society, place, or state considered to be perfect or ideal. —**Utopian** *adj.*

utter[1] *v.* express (something) audibly. —**utterance** *n.* something uttered; act or power of uttering.

utter[2] *adj.* total or absolute. —**utterly** *adv.*

uttermost *adj., n.* same as UTMOST.

U-turn *n.* turn, made by a vehicle, in the shape of a U, resulting in a reversal of direction; complete change in policy.

UV ultraviolet.

uvula [**yew**-view-la] *n., pl.* **-las, -lae.** small fleshy part of the soft palate that hangs in the back of the throat. —**uvular** *adj.*

uxorious [ux-**or**-ee-uss] *adj.* excessively fond of or dependent on one's wife.

THESAURUS

point, profit, service, value, worth 6. custom, habit, practice, way, wont

used cast-off, second-hand, shopsoiled, worn

useful advantageous, effective, fruitful, helpful, practical, profitable, salutary, valuable, worthwhile

useless 1. disadvantageous, fruitless, futile, hopeless, idle, ineffective, pointless, profitless, unavailing, unproductive, unworkable, vain, valueless, worthless 2. *Inf.* hopeless, ineffectual, inept, stupid, weak

usher 1. *n.* attendant, doorkeeper, escort, guide 2. *v.* conduct, direct, escort, guide, lead, pilot, steer

usual common, constant, customary, everyday, expected, familiar, fixed, general, habitual, normal, ordinary, regular, routine, standard, stock, typical

usually commonly, generally, habitually, mainly, mostly, normally, ordinarily, regularly, routinely

utility avail, benefit, convenience, efficacy, fitness, point, practicality, profit, service

utmost 1. *adj.* chief, extreme, greatest, highest, maximum, paramount, pre-eminent, supreme 2. *n.* best, greatest, hardest, highest

utter[1] *v.* 1. articulate, express, pronounce, say, speak, voice 2. declare, divulge, proclaim, promulgate, publish, reveal, state

utter[2] *adj.* absolute, complete, downright, entire, perfect, sheer, stark, total, unqualified

utterly absolutely, entirely, extremely, fully, perfectly, thoroughly, totally

V

V volt.

v. versus; very.

vacant *adj.* (of a toilet, room, etc.) unoccupied; without interest or understanding. **—vacantly** *adv.* **—vacancy** *n., pl.* **-cies.** unfilled job; unoccupied room in a guesthouse; state of being unoccupied.

vacate *v.* leave (a place or job). **—vacation** *n.* time when universities and law courts are closed; *US* holiday.

vaccinate *v.* inoculate with a vaccine. **—vaccination** *n.* **—vaccine** *n.* substance designed to cause a mild form of a disease to make a person immune to the disease itself.

vacillate [**vass**-ill-late] *v.* waver in one's opinions. **—vacillation** *n.*

vacuous *adj.* not expressing intelligent thought. **—vacuity** *n.*

vacuum *n., pl.* **vacuums, vacua.** empty space from which all or most air or gas has been removed. **—v.** clean with a vacuum cleaner. **—vacuum cleaner** electrical appliance for removing dust by suction. **—vacuum flask** double-walled flask with a vacuum between the walls that keeps drinks hot or cold. **—vacuum-packed** *adj.* contained in packaging from which the air has been removed.

vagabond *n.* person with no fixed home, esp. a beggar.

vagaries [**vaig**-a-reez] *pl. n.* unpredictable changes.

vagina [vaj-**jine**-a] *n., pl.* **-nas, -nae.** in female mammals, passage from the womb to the external genitals. **—vaginal** *adj.*

vagrant [**vaig**-rant] *n.* person with no settled home. **—adj.** wandering. **—vagrancy** *n.*

vague *adj.* not clearly explained; unable to be seen or heard clearly; absent-minded. **—vaguely** *adv.*

vain *adj.* excessively proud, esp. of one's appearance; bound to fail, futile. **—in vain** unsuccessfully.

vainglorious *adj. Lit.* boastful. **—vainglory** *n.*

valance [**val**-lenss] *n.* piece of drapery round the edge of a bed.

vale *n. Lit.* valley.

valediction [val-lid-**dik**-shun] *n.* farewell speech. **—valedictory** *adj.*

valence [**vale**-ence] *n.* molecular bonding between atoms.

valency *n., pl.* **-cies.** power of an atom to make molecular bonds.

valentine *n.* (person to whom one sends) a romantic card on Saint Valentine's Day, 14th February.

valerian *n.* herb used as a sedative.

valet *n.* man's personal male servant.

valetudinarian [val-lit-yew-din-**air**-ee-an] *n.* person with a long-term illness; hypochondriac.

valiant *adj.* brave or courageous.

valid *adj.* soundly reasoned; having legal force. **—validate** *v.* make valid. **—validation** *n.* **—validity** *n.*

valise [val-**leez**] *n. Old-fashioned* travelling bag.

Valium *n.* ® drug used as a tranquillizer.

valley *n.* low area between hills, usu. with a river running through it.

valour *n. Lit.* bravery. **—valorous** *adj.*

value *n.* importance, usefulness; monetary worth. **—pl.** moral principles. **—v.** **valuing, valued.** assess the value of; have a high regard for. **—valuable** *adj.* having great worth. **—valuables** *pl. n.* valuable personal property. **—valuation** *n.*

THESAURUS

vacancy 1. job, opportunity, position, post, room, situation 2. abstraction, inanity, inattentiveness

vacant 1. available, empty, free, idle, unemployed, unfilled, untenanted, void 2. abstracted, blank, dreamy, idle, inane

vacuum emptiness, gap, space, void

vague dim, doubtful, hazy, ill-defined, imprecise, indefinite, indistinct, lax, loose, obscure, shadowy, uncertain, unclear, unknown, unspecified, woolly

vain 1. arrogant, egotistical, overweening, proud, swaggering, vainglorious 2. abortive, empty,

fruitless, futile, hollow, idle, pointless, senseless, unimportant, unproductive, unprofitable, useless, worthless 3. **in vain** bootless, ineffectual(ly), unsuccessfully, wasted

valiant bold, brave, doughty, heroic, plucky, stouthearted, worthy

valid authentic, bona fide, genuine, lawful, legal, legitimate, official

valley coomb, cwm (*Welsh*), dale, dell, depression, dingle, glen, hollow, strath (*Scot.*), vale

valuable *adj.* 1. costly, dear, precious 2. cherished, esteemed, helpful, important, prized, serviceable, treasured, useful, valued, worthy

DICTIONARY

assessment of worth. —**valueless** *adj.* —**valuer** *n.* —**value-added tax** *Brit.* see VAT. —**value judgment** opinion based on personal belief.

valve *n.* device to control the movement of fluid through a pipe; *Anat.* flap in a part of the body allowing blood to flow in one direction only; *Physics* tube containing a vacuum, allowing current to flow from a cathode to an anode. —**valvular** *adj.*

vamoose *v. Slang* go away.

vamp[1] *n. Informal* woman who seduces men to her own advantage.

vamp[2] *v.* (foll. by *up*) renovate; improvise an accompaniment to (a tune).

vampire *n.* (in folklore) a corpse that rises at night to drink the blood of the living. —**vampire bat** tropical bat that feeds on blood.

van[1] *n.* motor vehicle for transporting goods; *Brit.* railway carriage for goods in which the guard travels.

van[2] *n.* short for VANGUARD.

vanadium *n.* metallic element, used in steel.

vandal *n.* person who deliberately damages property. —**vandalism** *n.* —**vandalize** *v.*

vane *n.* flat blade on a rotary device such as a weathercock or propeller.

vanguard *n.* unit of soldiers leading an army; most advanced group or position in a movement or activity.

vanilla *n.* seed pod of a tropical climbing orchid, used for flavouring.

vanish *v.* disappear suddenly or mysteriously; cease to exist.

vanity *n., pl.* -**ties.** (display of) excessive pride.

vanquish *v. Lit.* defeat (someone) utterly. —**vanquishable** *adj.* —**vanquisher** *n.*

vantage *n.* advantage. —**vantage point** position that gives one an overall view.

vapid *adj.* lacking character, dull. —**vapidity** *n.*

vapour *n.* moisture suspended in air as steam or mist; gaseous form of something that is liquid or solid at room temperature. —**vaporize** *v.* —**vaporizer** *n.* —**vaporous** *adj.*

variable *adj.* not always the same, changeable. —*n. Maths* expression with a range of values. —**variability** *n.*

variant *adj.* different or alternative. —*n.* alternative form. —**at variance** in disagreement.

variation *n.* extent to which something varies; *Music* repetition in different forms of a basic theme. —**variational** *adj.*

varicose veins *pl. n.* knotted and swollen veins, esp. in the legs.

variegated *adj.* having patches or streaks of different colours. —**variegation** *n.*

variety *n., pl.* -**ties.** state of being various; different things of the same kind; sort or kind; light entertainment composed of unrelated acts.

various *adj.* of several kinds. —**variously** *adv.*

varlet *n. Obs.* rascal.

varnish *n.* solution of oil and resin, put on a surface to make it hard and glossy. —*v.* apply varnish to.

vary *v.* **varying, varied.** change; cause differences in. —**varied** *adj.*

vascular *adj. Biol.* relating to vessels.

vas deferens *n., pl.* **vasa deferentia.** *Anat.* sperm-carrying duct in each testicle.

vase *n.* ornamental jar, esp. for flowers.

vasectomy *n., pl.* -**mies.** (operation for) the removal of part of the vas deferens, as a contraceptive method.

Vaseline *n.* ® thick oily cream made from petroleum, used in skin care.

vassal *n. Hist.* man given land in return for allegiance to his lord. —**vassalage** *n.*

vast *adj.* extremely large. —**vastly** *adv.* —**vastness** *n.*

THESAURUS

value *n.* 1. cost, rate 2. advantage, benefit, desirability, help, importance, merit, profit, use, worth 3. *Plural* ethics, standards, principles ~*v.* 4. account, assess, estimate, price, rate, survey 5. cherish, esteem, prize, regard highly, respect, treasure

vanguard forefront, front rank, leaders, spearhead, trendsetters, van

vanish disappear, evaporate, exit, fade

vanity airs, arrogance, conceit, egotism, ostentation, pride, vainglory

vapour breath, fog, fumes, haze, mist, smoke, steam

variable changeable, fickle, fitful, inconstant, mercurial, shifting, unstable, unsteady

variation alteration, change, departure, deviation, difference, diversity, innovation, novelty

varied assorted, different, miscellaneous, mixed, motley, sundry, various

variety 1. change, difference, diversity, variation 2. array, assortment, collection, medley, mixture, range 3. brand, breed, category, class, kind, make, order, sort. species, strain, type

various assorted, different, disparate, distinct, diverse, many, miscellaneous, several, sundry

varnish *v.* adorn, decorate, gild, glaze, gloss, polish

DICTIONARY

VAT *Brit.* value-added tax: tax on the difference between the cost of materials and the selling price.

vat *n.* large container for liquids.

Vatican *n.* the Pope's palace.

vaudeville *n. US* variety entertainment in a theatre.

vault[1] *n.* secure room for storing valuables; underground burial chamber. —**vaulted** *adj.* having an arched roof.

vault[2] *v.* jump over (something) by resting one's hand(s) on it. —*n.* such a jump.

vaunt *v.* describe or display (success or possessions) boastfully. —**vaunted** *adj.*

VC Vice Chancellor; Victoria Cross.

VCR video cassette recorder.

VD venereal disease.

VDU visual display unit.

veal *n.* calf meat.

vector *n. Maths* quantity that has size and direction, such as force; animal, usu. an insect, that carries disease.

veer *v.* change direction suddenly.

vegan [vee-gan] *n.* person who eats no meat, eggs, or dairy products. —*adj.* suitable for a vegan. —**veganism** *n.*

vegetable *n.* edible plant; *Informal* severely brain-damaged person. —*adj.* of or like plants or vegetables.

vegetarian *n.* person who eats no meat. —*adj.* suitable for a vegetarian. —**vegetarianism** *n.*

vegetate *v.* live a dull uncreative life.

vegetation *n.* plant life of a given place.

vehement *adj.* expressing strong feelings. —**vehemence** *n.* —**vehemently** *adv.*

vehicle *n.* machine, esp. with an engine and wheels, for carrying people or objects; means of communicating something. —**vehicular** *adj.*

veil *n.* piece of thin cloth covering the head or face; something that masks the truth, e.g. *a veil of secrecy.* —*v.* cover with a veil. —**take the veil** become a nun. —**veiled** *adj.* disguised.

vein *n.* tube that takes blood to the heart; line in a leaf or an insect's wing; layer of ore or mineral in rock; streak in marble; feature of someone's writing or speech, e.g. *a vein of humour;* mood, e.g. *in a lighter vein.* —**veined** *adj.*

Velcro *n.* ® fastening consisting of one piece of fabric with tiny hooked threads and another with a coarse surface that adheres to it.

veld(t) *n.* high grassland in Southern Africa.

vellum *n.* fine calfskin parchment; type of smooth paper.

velocity [vel-loss-it-ee] *n., pl.* **-ties.** speed of movement in a given direction.

velour(s) [vel-loor] *n.* velvety fabric.

velvet *n.* fabric with a thick pile. —**velvety** *adj.* soft and smooth. —**velveteen** *n.* cotton velvet.

venal [vee-nal] *adj.* easily bribed; characterized by bribery. —**venally** *adv.* —**venality** *n.*

vend *v.* sell. —**vendor** *n.* —**vending machine** machine that dispenses goods when coins are inserted.

vendetta *n.* prolonged quarrel between families, esp. one involving revenge killings.

veneer *n.* thin layer of wood etc. covering a cheaper material; superficial appearance, e.g. *a veneer of sophistication.*

venerable *adj.* worthy of deep respect. —**venerate** *v.* hold (a person) in deep respect. —**veneration** *n.*

THESAURUS

vary alter, change, depart, diverge, diversify, fluctuate, modify, reorder, transform

vast boundless, enormous, extensive, great, huge, immense, limitless, massive, monstrous, prodigious, sweeping, tremendous, unbounded, unlimited

vault[1] *n.* 1. cellar, crypt 2. depository, strongroom

vault[2] *v.* bound, clear, hurdle, jump, leap, spring

veer be deflected, change, change course, change direction, sheer, shift, swerve, tack, turn

vegetate idle, languish, moulder, stagnate

vehemence eagerness, emphasis, energy, enthusiasm, fervour, fire, force, forcefulness, heat, intensity, keenness, passion, vigour, warmth, zeal

vehement ardent, eager, earnest, emphatic, fervent, fierce, forceful, forcible, impetuous, intense, passionate, strong, violent

veil 1. *v.* cloak, conceal, cover, dim, disguise, hide, mantle, mask, obscure, screen, shield 2. *n.* blind, cloak, cover, curtain, disguise, film, mask, screen, shade, shroud

vein 1. course, current, seam, streak, stripe 2. dash, hint, strain, streak, thread, trait 3. bent, faculty, humour, mode, mood, note, style, temper, tenor, tone, turn

vendetta feud, quarrel

veneer *n. Fig.* appearance, façade, front, gloss, guise, pretence

venerable august, esteemed, grave, honoured, sage, sedate, wise

venerate adore, esteem, honour, respect, worship

DICTIONARY

venereal disease [ven-**ear**-ee-al] *n.* disease transmitted sexually.

Venetian blind *n.* window blind made of horizontal slats that turn to let in more or less light.

vengeance *n.* revenge. —**vengeful** *adj.* wanting revenge. —**vengefully** *adv.*

venial [**veen**-ee-al] *adj.* (of a sin or fault) easily forgiven. —**veniality** *n.*

venison *n.* deer meat.

venom *n.* poison produced by snakes etc.; malice or spite. —**venomous** *adj.*

venous [**vee**-nuss] *adj. Anat.* of veins.

vent[1] *n.* outlet releasing fumes or fluid. —*v.* express (an emotion) freely.

vent[2] *n.* vertical slit in a jacket.

ventilate *v.* let fresh air into; discuss (a complaint) openly. —**ventilation** *n.* —**ventilator** *n.*

ventral *adj.* relating to the front of the body.

ventricle *n. Anat.* one of the four cavities of the heart or brain.

ventriloquist *n.* entertainer who can speak without moving his or her lips, so that a voice seems to come from elsewhere. —**ventriloquism** *n.*

venture *n.* risky undertaking, esp. in business. —*v.* do something risky; dare to express (an opinion); go to an unknown place. —**venturesome** *adj.*

venue *n.* place where an organized gathering is held.

Venus *n.* planet second nearest to the sun; Roman goddess of love. —**Venus('s) flytrap** plant that traps and digests insects between hinged leaves.

veracious *adj.* habitually truthful. —**veracity** *n.*

veranda(h) *n.* open porch attached to a house.

verb *n.* word that expresses the idea of action, happening, or being. —**verbal** *adj.* spoken; of a verb. —**verbally** *adv.* —**verbalize** *v.* express (something) in words.

verbatim [verb-**bait**-im] *adv., adj.* word for word.

verbena *n.* plant with sweet-smelling flowers.

verbiage *n.* excessive use of words.

verbose [verb-**bohss**] *adj.* long-winded. —**verbosity** *n.*

verdant *adj. Lit.* covered in green vegetation.

verdict *n.* decision of a jury; opinion formed after examining the facts.

verdigris [**ver**-dig-riss] *n.* green film on copper, brass, or bronze.

verdure *n. Lit.* flourishing green vegetation.

verge *n.* grass border along a road. —**on the verge of** having almost reached (a point or condition). —**verge on** *v.* be near to (a condition).

verger *n. C of E* church caretaker.

verify *v.* -**ifying**, -**ified.** check the truth or accuracy of. —**verifiable** *adj.* —**verification** *n.*

verily *adv. Obs.* in truth.

verisimilitude *n.* appearance of being real.

veritable *adj.* rightly called, without exaggeration, e.g. *a veritable feast*. —**veritably** *adv.*

verity *n., pl.* -**ties.** true statement or principle.

vermicelli [ver-me-**chell**-ee] *n.* fine strands of pasta; tiny strands of chocolate.

vermiform *adj.* shaped like a worm. —**vermiform appendix** *Anat.* same as APPENDIX.

vermilion *adj.* orange-red.

vermin *pl. n.* animals, esp. insects and rodents, that spread disease or cause damage. —**verminous** *adj.*

vermouth [**ver**-muth] *n.* wine flavoured with herbs.

vernacular [ver-**nak**-yew-lar] *n.* most widely spoken language of a particular people or place.

vernal *adj.* occurring in spring.

vernier [**ver**-nee-er] *n.* movable scale on a graduated measuring instrument for taking readings in fractions.

THESAURUS

vengeance avenging, reprisal, retaliation, retribution

venom 1. bane, poison, toxin 2. acrimony, bitterness, grudge, hate, malice, rancour, spite, spleen, virulence

vent 1. *n.* aperture, duct, hole, outlet, split 2. *v.* air, discharge, emit, empty, express, release, utter, voice

ventilate *Fig.* air, broadcast, debate, discuss, examine, scrutinize, sift

venture *v.* 1. chance, hazard, imperil, risk, speculate, stake, wager 2. advance, dare, haz-

ard, presume, volunteer ~*n.* 3. chance, endeavour, enterprise, fling, gamble, hazard, project, risk

verbal literal, oral, spoken

verbatim exactly, precisely, word for word

verdict conclusion, decision, finding, judgment, opinion, sentence

verification authentication, confirmation, proof

verify attest, authenticate, check, confirm, prove, support, validate

vernacular *n.* argot, cant, dialect, idiom, parlance, patois, speech

DICTIONARY

veronica *n.* plant with small flowers.

verruca [ver-**roo**-ka] *n., pl.* **-cae, -cas.** wart, usu. on the foot.

versatile *adj.* having many skills or uses. —**versatility** *n.*

verse *n.* group of lines in a song or poem; poetry as distinct from prose; subdivision of a book of the Bible. —**versed in** knowledgeable about. —**versify** *v.* write in verse. —**versification** *n.*

version *n.* form of something, such as a piece of writing, with some differences from other forms; account of an incident from a particular point of view.

verso *n., pl.* **-sos.** left-hand page of a book; back of a sheet of paper.

versus *prep. Sport & Law* against; in contrast with.

vertebra [ver-tib-ra] *n., pl.* **vertebrae** [ver-tib-ree]. one of the bones that form the spine. —**vertebral** *adj.* —**vertebrate** *n., adj.* (animal) having a spine.

vertex *n. Maths* point on a geometric figure where the sides form an angle; highest point of a triangle.

vertical *adj.* straight up and down. —*n.* vertical direction.

vertigo *n.* dizziness when looking down from a high place. —**vertiginous** *adj.*

vervain *n.* plant with spikes of blue, purple, or white flowers.

verve *n.* enthusiasm or liveliness.

very *adv.* more than usually, extremely. —*adj.* absolute, exact, e.g. *the very top, the very man.*

vesicle *n. Biol.* sac or small cavity, esp. one containing fluid.

vespers *pl. n. RC Church* (service of) evening prayer.

vessel *n. Lit.* container, esp. for liquids; ship; *Biol.* tubular structure in animals and plants that carries body fluids, such as blood or sap.

vest *n. Brit.* undergarment worn on the top half of the body; *US* waistcoat. —*v.* (foll. by *in* or *with*) give (authority) to (someone). —**vested interest** interest someone has in a matter because he or she might benefit from it.

vestibule *n.* entrance hall.

vestige [vest-ij] *n.* small amount or trace. —**vestigial** [vest-**ij**-ee-al] *adj.*

vestments *pl. n.* priest's robes.

vestry *n., pl.* **-tries.** room in a church used as an office by the priest or minister.

vet[1] *n.* short for VETERINARY SURGEON. —*v.* **vetting, vetted.** check the suitability of (a candidate).

vet[2] *n. US* military veteran.

vetch *n.* climbing plant with a beanlike fruit used as fodder.

veteran *n.* person with long experience in a particular activity, esp. military service. —*adj.* long-serving.

veterinary *adj.* concerning animal health. —**veterinary surgeon** medical specialist who treats sick animals.

veto [vee-toe] *n., pl.* **-toes.** official power to cancel a proposal. —*v.* **-toing, -toed.** enforce a veto against.

vex *v.* frustrate, annoy. —**vexation** *n.* something annoying; being annoyed. —**vexatious** *adj.* —**vexed question** much debated subject.

VHF very high frequency: radio frequency band between 30 and 300 MHz.

VHS Video Home System: format for recording on video.

via *prep.* by way of.

THESAURUS

versatile adaptable, flexible, functional, handy, protean, resourceful, variable

version account, exercise, portrayal, reading, rendering, side, translation

vertical erect, on end, upright

vertigo dizziness, giddiness

verve animation, dash, élan, energy, force, gusto, life, liveliness, sparkle, spirit, vigour, vitality, zeal

very absolutely, acutely, decidedly, deeply, eminently, exceedingly, extremely, greatly, highly, noticeably, particularly, really, remarkably, truly, unusually, wonderfully

vessel 1. boat, craft, ship 2. container, pot, receptacle, utensil

vest *v. With* in *or* with authorize, upon, bestow, confer, consign, empower, endow, entrust, furnish, lodge, place, settle

vet *v.* appraise, check, examine, investigate, look over, pass under review, review, scan, scrutinize

veteran 1. *n.* master, trouper 2. *adj.* adept, expert, old, proficient, seasoned

veto 1. *v.* ban, forbid, negative, prohibit, reject, rule out, turn down 2. *n.* ban, embargo, interdict, prohibition

vex afflict, agitate, annoy, bother, displease, distress, disturb, exasperate, harass, irritate, molest, offend, perplex, pester, plague, provoke, put out, rile, tease, torment, trouble, upset, worry

DICTIONARY

viable *adj.* able to be put into practice; *Biol.* able to live and grow independently. —**viability** *n.*

viaduct *n.* bridge over a valley.

vial *n.* same as PHIAL.

viands *pl. n. Obs.* food.

vibes *pl. n. Informal* emotional reactions between people, atmosphere of a place; short for VIBRAPHONE.

vibrant [**vibe**-rant] *adj.* vigorous in appearance, energetic; (of a voice) resonant; (of a colour) strong and bright.

vibraphone *n.* musical instrument with metal bars that resonate electronically when hit.

vibrate *v.* move back and forth rapidly; (cause to) resonate. —**vibration** *n.* —**vibrator** *n.* device that produces vibratory motion, used for massage or as a sex aid. —**vibratory** *adj.*

vibrato *Music* rapid fluctuation in the pitch of a note.

vicar *n.* C of E clergyman in charge of a parish. —**vicarage** *n.* vicar's house.

vicarious [vick-**air**-ee-uss] *adj.* felt indirectly by imagining what another person experiences; delegated. —**vicariously** *adv.*

vice[1] *n.* immoral personal quality; criminal immorality, esp. involving sex; minor imperfection in someone's character.

vice[2] *n.* tool with a screw mechanism for holding an object while working on it.

vice[3] *adj.* serving in place of.

vice chancellor *n.* chief executive of a university.

vice versa [**vie**-see **ver**-sa] *adv. Latin* conversely, the other way round.

viceroy *n.* governor of a colony who represents the monarch. —**viceregal** *adj.*

vicinity [viss-**in**-it-ee] *n.* surrounding area.

vicious *adj.* cruel and violent. —**viciously** *adv.* —**vicious circle** sequence of problems and solutions which always leads back to the original problem.

vicissitudes [viss-**iss**-it-yewds] *pl. n.* changes in fortune.

victim *n.* person or thing harmed or killed; person or animal killed as a sacrifice. —**victimize** *v.* punish unfairly; discriminate against. —**victimization** *n.*

victor *n.* person who has defeated an opponent, esp. in war or in sport. —**victorious** *adj.* —**victory** *n.* winning of a battle or contest.

Victoria Cross *n. Brit.* highest award for bravery.

Victorian *adj.* of or in the reign of Queen Victoria (1837-1901); characterized by prudery or hypocrisy. —*n.* person who lived during Victoria's reign.

victuals [**vit**-als] *pl. n. Old-fashioned* food. —**victual** *v.* **victualling, victualled.** supply with or obtain victuals. —**victualler** *n.*

vicuna [vik-**koo**-nya] *n.* S American animal like the llama; fine cloth made from its wool.

video *n.* short for VIDEO CASSETTE (RECORDER). —*v.* **videoing, videoed.** record (a TV programme or event) on video. —*adj.* relating to or used in producing television images. —**video cassette** cassette containing video tape. —**video cassette recorder** tape recorder for recording and playing back TV programmes and films. —**video nasty** horrific or pornographic film, usu. made for video. —**video tape** magnetic tape used to record video-frequency signals in TV production; magnetic tape used to record programmes when they are broadcast. —**videotape** *v.* record (a TV programme) on video tape. —**video tape recorder** tape recorder for vision signals, used in TV production. —**videotex** *v.* same as VIEWDATA. —**videotext** *n.* means of representing on a TV screen information that is held in a computer.

vie *v.* **vying, vied.** compete (with someone).

view *n.* everything that can be seen from a given place; picture of this; opinion. —*v.* think of (something) in a particular way. —**in view of** taking into consideration. —**on view** exhibited to the public. —**viewer** *n.* person who watches

---

THESAURUS

vibrant 1. oscillating, pulsating, quivering, trembling 2. alive, animated, colourful, dynamic, sensitive, sparkling, spirited, vivacious, vivid

vibrate fluctuate, pulsate, quiver, shake, shiver, sway, swing, throb, tremble

vibration oscillation, pulse, quiver, resonance, shaking, throb, trembling, tremor

vice corruption, depravity, evil, evildoing, immorality, iniquity, sin, wickedness

vicious abandoned, atrocious, bad, corrupt,

cruel, dangerous, degraded, depraved, fiendish, foul, immoral, monstrous, savage, sinful, vile, violent, wicked, worthless, wrong

victim casualty, fatality, martyr, sacrifice, scapegoat, sufferer

victimize persecute, pick on

victor champion, conqueror, first, winner

victorious champion, first, successful, triumphant, winning

victory conquest, laurels, mastery, success, superiority, triumph, win

DICTIONARY

television; hand-held device for looking at photographic slides. **—viewfinder** *n.* window on a camera showing what will appear in a photograph.

viewdata *n.* videotext service linking users to a computer by telephone.

vigil [vij-ill] *n.* night-time period of staying awake to look after a sick person, pray, etc. **—vigilant** *adj.* watchful in case of danger. **—vigilance** *n.*

vigilante [vij-ill-**ant**-ee] *n.* person, esp. as one of a group, who takes it upon himself or herself to enforce the law.

vignette [vin-yet] *n.* concise description of the typical features of something; small decorative illustration in a book.

vigour *n.* physical or mental energy. **—vigorous** *adj.* **—vigorously** *adv.*

Viking *n. Hist.* seafaring raider and settler from Scandinavia.

vile *adj.* very wicked; disgusting. **—vilely** *adv.* **—vileness** *n.*

vilify [vill-if-fie] *v.* **-ifying, -ified.** unjustly attack the character of. **—vilification** *n.*

villa *n.* large house with gardens; holiday home, usu. in the Mediterranean.

village *n.* small group of houses in a country area; rural community. **—villager** *n.*

villain *n.* wicked person; main wicked character in a play. **—villainous** *adj.* **—villainy** *n.*

villein [vill-an] *n. Hist.* peasant bound in service to his lord.

vinaigrette *n.* salad dressing of oil and vinegar.

vindicate *v.* clear (someone) of guilt; justify (someone) whose behaviour has been challenged. **—vindication** *n.*

vindictive *adj.* maliciously seeking revenge. **—vindictiveness** *n.* **—vindictively** *adv.*

vine *n.* climbing plant, esp. one producing grapes. **—vineyard** [vinn-yard] *n.* plantation of grape vines, esp. for making wine.

vinegar *n.* acid liquid made from wine, beer, or cider. **—vinegary** *adj.*

vino [vee-noh] *n. Informal* wine.

vintage *n.* wine from a particular harvest of grapes. **—adj.** best and most typical. **—vintage car** car built between 1919 and 1930.

vintner *n.* dealer in wine.

vinyl [vine-ill] *n.* type of plastic, used in mock leather and records.

viol [vie-oll] *n.* early stringed instrument preceding the violin.

viola[1] [vee-**oh**-la] *n.* stringed instrument lower in pitch than a violin.

viola[2] [vie-ol-la] *n.* variety of pansy.

violate *v.* break (a law or agreement); disturb (someone's privacy); treat (a sacred place) disrespectfully; rape. **—violation** *n.* **—violator** *n.*

violent *adj.* using or marked by physical strength that is harmful or destructive; aggressively intense; using excessive force. **—violence** *n.* **—violently** *adv.*

THESAURUS

view *n.* 1. aspect, outlook, panorama, picture, prospect, scene, vista 2. sight, vision 3. attitude, belief, feeling, impression, notion, opinion, sentiment, thought ~*v.* 4. consider, deem, judge, regard, think about

viewer observer, onlooker, spectator, watcher

vigilant alert, attentive, careful, cautious, sleepless, unsleeping, wakeful, watchful

vigorous active, brisk, effective, energetic, flourishing, forceful, hale, hardy, healthy, intense, lively, lusty, powerful, robust, sound, spirited, strong, virile, vital

vigour activity, animation, dash, dynamism, energy, force, gusto, health, liveliness, might, power, soundness, spirit, strength, verve, virility, vitality

vile 1. bad, base, coarse, contemptible, corrupt, debased, degenerate, degrading, depraved, disgraceful, evil, ignoble, impure, loathsome, low, mean, miserable, perverted, shocking, sinful, ugly, vicious, vulgar, wicked, worthless, wretched 2. disgusting, foul, horrid, loath-

some, nasty, repellent, repugnant, repulsive, sickening

villain blackguard, criminal, miscreant, profligate, reprobate, rogue, scoundrel, wretch

villainous bad, base, criminal, cruel, debased, evil, fiendish, hateful, infamous, mean, ruffianly, sinful, thievish, vicious, vile, wicked

vindicate absolve, acquit, clear, defend, exculpate, excuse, exonerate, justify, rehabilitate

vindication apology, defence, excuse, justification, plea, support

vindictive malicious, malignant, rancorous, resentful, revengeful, spiteful, vengeful

vintage 1. *n.* crop, era, harvest, origin, year 2. *adj.* best, choice, mature, prime, rare, ripe, select, superior

violate 1. break, disobey, disregard, infract, infringe, transgress 2. abuse, assault, debauch, defile, desecrate, dishonour, invade, outrage, pollute

violence 1. bloodshed, brutality, cruelty, ferocity, fighting, force, frenzy, fury, passion, sav-

DICTIONARY

violet *n.* plant with bluish-purple flowers. —*adj.* bluish-purple.

violin *n.* small four-stringed musical instrument played with a bow. —**violinist** *n.*

violoncello [vie-oll-on-**chell**-oh] *n., pl.* **-los.** same as CELLO.

VIP very important person.

viper *n.* poisonous snake.

virago [vir-**rah**-go] *n., pl.* **-goes, -gos.** aggressive woman.

viral [**vie**-ral] *adj.* of or caused by a virus.

virgin *n.* person, esp. a woman, who has not had sexual intercourse. —*adj.* not having had sexual intercourse; not yet exploited or explored. —**virginal** *adj.* like a virgin. —*n.* rectangular keyboard instrument like a small harpsichord. —**virginity** *n.*

virile *adj.* having the traditional male characteristics of physical strength and a high sex drive. —**virility** *n.*

virology *n.* study of viruses.

virtual *adj.* having the effect but not the form of. —**virtually** *adv.* practically, almost.

virtue *n.* moral goodness; positive moral quality; merit. —**by virtue of** by reason of. —**virtuous** *adj.* morally good. —**virtuously** *adv.*

virtuoso *n., pl.* **-sos, -si.** person with impressive musical skill. —**virtuosity** *n.*

virulent [**vir**-yew-lent] *adj.* very infectious; violently harmful.

virus *n.* microorganism that causes disease in animals and plants; *Computers* program that propagates itself, via disks and electronic networks, to cause disruption.

visa *n.* permission to enter a country, granted by its government and shown by a stamp on one's passport.

visage [**viz**-zij] *n. Lit.* face.

vis-à-vis [veez-ah-**vee**] *prep.* in relation to, regarding.

viscera [**viss**-er-a] *pl. n.* large abdominal organs. —**visceral** *adj.* instinctive; of or relating to the viscera.

viscid [**viss**-id] *adj.* sticky. —**viscidity** *n.*

viscose *n.* synthetic fabric made from cellulose.

viscount [**vie**-count] *n.* British nobleman ranking between an earl and a baron. —**viscountcy** *n.*

viscountess [**vie**-count-iss] *n.* wife or widow of a viscount; woman holding the rank of viscount in her own right.

viscous *adj.* thick and sticky. —**viscosity** *n.*

visible *adj.* able to be seen; able to be perceived by the mind. —**visibly** *adv.* —**visibility** *n.* range or clarity of vision.

vision *n.* ability to see; mental image of something; foresight; hallucination. —**visionary** *adj.* showing foresight; idealistic but impractical. —*n.* visionary person.

visit *v.* **-iting, -ited.** go or come to see; stay temporarily with; (foll. by *upon*) *Lit.* afflict. —*n.* instance of visiting; official call. —**visitor** *n.* —**visitation** *n.* formal visit or inspection; catastrophe seen as divine punishment.

THESAURUS

agery, wildness 2. power, raging, storminess, tumult, wildness

violent 1. berserk, brutal, cruel, fiery, forcible, furious, headstrong, impetuous, passionate, powerful, raging, riotous, rough, savage, strong, ungovernable, vehement, vicious, wild 2. devastating, powerful, raging, ruinous, strong, tempestuous, turbulent, wild

virgin 1. *n.* girl, vestal 2. *adj.* chaste, fresh, immaculate, maidenly, modest, new, pure, undefiled, untouched, unused, vestal

virtual essential, implicit, implied, indirect

virtually as good as, effectually, in effect, nearly, practically

virtue 1. excellence, goodness, incorruptibility, integrity, justice, morality, probity, rectitude, uprightness, worth 2. advantage, asset, attribute, credit, merit, strength 3. chastity, honour, innocence, purity, virginity

virtuoso *n.* artist, genius, maestro, master

virtuous 1. blameless, excellent, exemplary, good, honest, incorruptible, moral, pure, righteous, upright, worthy 2. celibate, chaste, innocent, pure, spotless, virginal

virulent 1. deadly, infective, lethal, poisonous, septic 2. bitter, hostile, malevolent, malicious, resentful, vicious, vindictive

visible apparent, clear, detectable, discernible, distinguishable, evident, manifest, noticeable, observable, obvious, perceivable, plain, unconcealed

vision 1. eyes, eyesight, perception, seeing, sight, view 2. discernment, foresight, imagination, insight, intuition 3. concept, daydream, dream, fantasy, idea, image 4. apparition, delusion, ghost, illusion, mirage, revelation, spectre, wraith

visionary 1. *adj.* idealistic, romantic 2. *n.* dreamer, idealist, mystic, prophet, seer

visit *v.* 1. inspect, stay with 2. afflict, assail, attack, befall, haunt, smite ~*n.* 3. call, sojourn, stay, stop

DICTIONARY

visor [vize-or] *n.* part of a helmet that moves up and down over the face; eyeshade, esp. in a car; peak on a cap.

vista *n.* (beautiful) extensive view.

visual *adj.* done by or used in seeing; designed to be looked at. —**visualize** *v.* form a mental image of. —**visualization** *n.* —**visual display unit** device with a screen for displaying data held in a computer.

vital *adj.* essential or highly important; lively; necessary to maintain life. —**vitals** *pl. n.* body organs. —**vitally** *adv.* —**vitality** *n.* physical or mental energy. —**vital statistics** statistics of births, deaths, and marriages; *Informal* woman's bust, waist, and hip measurements.

vitamin *n.* one of a group of substances that are essential in the diet for specific body processes.

vitiate [vish-ee-ate] *v.* spoil the effectiveness of. —**vitiation** *n.*

viticulture *n.* cultivation of grape vines.

vitreous *adj.* like or made from glass. —**vitreous humour** gelatinous substance that fills the eyeball.

vitrify *v.* -**ified**, -**ifying**. change or be changed into glass or a glassy substance. —**vitrification** *n.*

vitriol *n.* language expressing bitterness and hatred; sulphuric acid. —**vitriolic** *adj.*

vituperative [vite-**tyew**-pra-tiv] *adj.* bitterly abusive. —**vituperation** *n.*

viva[1] *interj.* long live (a person or thing).

viva[2] *n.* examination in the form of an interview.

vivace [viv-**vah**-chee] *Music* in a lively manner.

vivacious *adj.* full of energy and enthusiasm. —**vivacity** *n.*

vivarium *n., pl.* -**iums, -ia.** place where animals are kept in natural conditions.

viva voce [vive-a **voh**-chee] *adv.* in spoken words. —*n.* same as VIVA[2].

vivid *adj.* very bright; conveying images that are true to life. —**vividly** *adv.* —**vividness** *n.*

viviparous [viv-**vip**-a-russ] *adj.* producing live offspring.

vivisection *n.* performing surgical experiments on living animals. —**vivisectionist** *n.*

vixen *n.* female fox; *Informal* spiteful woman. —**vixenish** *adj.*

viz. (introducing specified items) namely.

vizier [viz-**zeer**] *n.* (formerly) Muslim high official.

vizor *n.* same as VISOR.

vocabulary *n., pl.* -**aries.** all the words that a person knows; all the words in a language; specialist terms used in a given subject; list of words in another language with their translation.

vocal *adj.* relating to the voice; outspoken. —**vocals** *pl. n.* singing part of a piece of pop music. —**vocally** *adv.* —**vocalist** *n.* singer. —**vocalize** *v.* express with or use the voice. —**vocalization** *n.* —**vocal cords** membranes in the larynx that vibrate to produce sound.

vocation *n.* occupation that someone feels called to; profession or trade. —**vocational** *adj.* directed towards a particular profession or trade.

vociferous *adj.* characterized by noisy shouting.

vodka *n.* (Russian) spirit distilled from potatoes or grain.

vogue *n.* popular style; period of popularity.

THESAURUS

visitation 1. examination, inspection, visit 2. bane, blight, calamity, disaster, ordeal, trial

visitor caller, company, guest, visitant

visual 1. optic, optical 2. discernible, observable, perceptible, visible

visualize envisage, imagine, picture

vital 1. basic, cardinal, essential, indispensable, requisite 2. critical, crucial, decisive, important, key, significant, urgent 3. animated, dynamic, energetic, forceful, lively, spirited, vivacious, zestful

vitality animation, energy, life, liveliness, sparkle, stamina, strength, vigour, vivacity

vivacious cheerful, ebullient, frolicsome, gay, jolly, light-hearted, lively, merry, spirited, sprightly, vital

vivid 1. bright, brilliant, clear, glowing, intense, rich 2. distinct, graphic, lifelike, memorable, powerful, sharp, stirring, strong, telling

vocabulary dictionary, glossary, language, lexicon, wordbook, words

vocal *adj.* 1. articulate, oral, said, spoken, uttered, voiced 2. blunt, clamorous, eloquent, expressive, forthright, frank, noisy, outspoken, strident

vocation business, calling, career, employment, job, mission, office, post, profession, pursuit, role, trade

vociferous clamant, loud, noisy, shouting, strident, vehement

vogue 1. craze, custom, fashion, mode, style, trend, way 2. acceptance, currency, favour, popularity, prevalence, usage, use

DICTIONARY

voice *n.* (quality of) sound made when speaking or singing; expression of opinion by a person or group; property of verbs that makes them active or passive. —*v.* express verbally. —**voiceless** *adj.* —**voice-over** *n.* film commentary spoken by someone off-camera.

void *adj.* not legally binding; empty. —*n.* empty space. —*v.* make invalid; empty.

voile [voyl] *n.* light semitransparent fabric.

vol. volume.

volatile [**voll**-a-tile] *adj.* evaporating quickly; liable to sudden change, esp. in behaviour. —**volatility** *n.*

vol-au-vent [**voll**-oh-von] *n.* small puff-pastry case with a savoury filling.

volcano *n., pl.* **-noes, -nos.** mountain with a vent through which lava is ejected. —**volcanic** *adj.*

vole *n.* small rodent.

volition *n.* faculty of exercising the will. —**of one's own volition** through one's own choice.

volley *n.* simultaneous discharge of ammunition; burst of questions or critical comments; *Sport* stroke or kick at a moving ball before it hits the ground. —*v.* discharge (ammunition) in a volley; hit or kick (a ball) in a volley. —**volleyball** *n.* team game where a ball is hit with the hands over a high net.

volt *n.* unit of electric potential. —**voltaic** *adj.* same as GALVANIC. —**voltage** *n.* electric potential difference expressed in volts. —**voltmeter** *n.* instrument for measuring voltage.

volte-face [volt-**fass**] *n.* reversal of opinion.

voluble *adj.* talking easily and at length. —**volubility** *n.* —**volubly** *adv.*

volume *n.* size of the space occupied by some-

thing; amount; loudness of sound; control on a radio or TV for adjusting this; book, esp. one of a series. —**voluminous** *adj.* (of clothes) large and roomy; (of writings) extensive. —**volumetric** *adj.* relating to measurement by volume.

voluntary *adj.* done by choice; done or maintained without payment; controlled by the will. —*n., pl.* **-taries.** organ solo in a church service. —**voluntarily** *adv.*

volunteer *n.* person who offers voluntarily to do something, esp. military service. —*v.* offer one's services; offer the services of (another person); give (information) willingly.

voluptuous *adj.* (of a woman) sexually alluring through fullness of figure; sensually pleasurable. —**voluptuary** *n., pl.* **-aries.** person devoted to sensual pleasures.

volute *n.* spiral or twisting turn, form, or object.

vomit *v.* **-iting, -ited.** eject (the contents of the stomach) through the mouth. —*n.* matter vomited.

voodoo(ism) *n.* religion involving ancestor worship and witchcraft.

voracious *adj.* craving great quantities of food; insatiably eager. —**voraciously** *adv.* —**voracity** *n.*

vortex *n., pl.* **-texes, -tices.** whirlpool; whirling motion.

vote *n.* choice made by a participant in a shared decision, esp. in electing a candidate; right to this choice; total number of votes cast; collective voting power of a given group, e.g. *the Black vote.* —*v.* make a choice by a vote; authorize (something) by vote. —**voter** *n.*

votive *adj.* done or given to fulfil a vow.

vouch *v.* (foll. by *for*) give one's personal assur-

THESAURUS

voice *n.* 1. language, sound, tone, utterance, words 2. decision, expression, part, say, view, vote, will, wish ~*v.* 3. air, articulate, assert, declare, divulge, enunciate, express, utter

void *adj.* 1. bare, clear, drained, empty, free, unfilled, unoccupied, vacant 2. dead, invalid, useless, vain, worthless ~*n.* 3. blank, emptiness, gap, lack, opening, space, vacuum, want ~*v.* 4. discharge, drain, eject, emit, empty, evacuate

volatile airy, changeable, erratic, explosive, fickle, flighty, gay, giddy, inconstant, lively, mercurial, sprightly, unsettled, unstable, unsteady, up and down (*Inf.*), variable

volley *n.* barrage, blast, burst, discharge, explosion, hail, salvo, shower

volume 1. aggregate, amount, body, bulk, capacity, mass, quantity, total 2. book, publication, tome, treatise

voluntarily freely, willingly

voluntary free, gratuitous, honorary, intentional, optional, spontaneous, unforced, unpaid, willing

volunteer *v.* advance, offer, present, proffer, propose, suggest, tender

vomit *v.* be sick, disgorge, eject, emit, heave, regurgitate, retch

voracious avid, devouring, gluttonous, greedy, hungry, omnivorous, ravenous, uncontrolled

vote 1. *n.* ballot, franchise, plebiscite, poll, referendum, suffrage 2. *v.* ballot, elect, opt, return

vouch *Usually with* **for** affirm, answer for, assert, back, certify, confirm, guarantee, support, uphold

DICTIONARY

ance about; (foll. by *for*) be proof of. —**voucher** *n.* ticket used instead of money to buy specified goods; record of a financial transaction, receipt.

vouchsafe *v. Old-fashioned* give, entrust; agree graciously.

vow *n.* solemn promise, esp. to a god or saint. —*v.* promise solemnly.

vowel *n.* speech sound made without obstructing the flow of breath; letter representing this.

vox pop *n.* interviews with members of the public on TV or radio.

vox populi *n.* public opinion.

voyage *n.* long journey by sea or in space. —*v.* make a voyage. —**voyager** *n.*

voyeur *n.* person who derives pleasure from watching people undressing or having sex.

vs versus.

V-sign *n.* offensive gesture made by sticking up the index and middle fingers with the palm inwards; similar gesture, with the palm outwards, meaning victory or peace.

VSO Voluntary Service Overseas.

VTR video tape recorder.

vulcanize *v.* strengthen (rubber) by treating it with sulphur. —**vulcanization** *n.* —**vulcanite** *n.* vulcanized rubber.

vulgar *adj.* showing lack of good taste, decency, or refinement. —**vulgarly** *adv.* —**vulgarity** *n.* —**vulgarian** *n.* vulgar (rich) person. —**vulgarism** *n.* coarse word or phrase. —**vulgar fraction** simple fraction.

Vulgate *n.* fourth-century Latin version of the Bible.

vulnerable *adj.* unprotected from physical or emotional hurt; unable to defend oneself. —**vulnerability** *n.*

vulpine *adj.* of or like a fox.

vulture *n.* large bird that feeds on the flesh of dead animals.

vulva *n.* woman's external genitals.

vying present participle of VIE.

THESAURUS

vow 1. *v.* affirm, dedicate, devote, pledge, promise, swear 2. *n.* oath, pledge, promise

voyage *n.* crossing, cruise, journey, passage, travels, trip

vulgar boorish, coarse, common, crude, dirty, flashy, gaudy, gross, ill-bred, impolite, improper, indecent, indelicate, low, nasty, naughty, ribald, rude, suggestive, tasteless, tawdry, unmannerly, unrefined

vulgarity bad taste, coarseness, crudeness, grossness, indelicacy, ribaldry, rudeness, tawdriness

vulnerable assailable, defenceless, exposed, sensitive, susceptible, tender, weak, wide open

W

W *Chem.* tungsten; watt; Wednesday; west(ern).

wacky *adj.* **wackier, wackiest.** *Informal* eccentric or funny. **—wackiness** *n.*

wad *n.* small mass of soft material; roll or bundle. **—v. wadding, wadded.** make into a wad; pad or stuff with wadding. **—wadding** *n.* soft material used for padding or stuffing.

waddle *v.* walk with short swaying steps. **—n.** swaying walk.

wade *v.* walk with difficulty through water or mud; proceed with difficulty. **—wader** *n.* long-legged water bird. **—pl.** angler's long waterproof boots.

wadi [**wod**-dee] *n., pl.* **-dies.** in N Africa and Arabia, a watercourse which is dry except in the wet season.

wafer *n.* thin crisp biscuit; thin disc of unleavened bread used at Communion; thin slice.

waffle[1] *Informal* **—v.** speak or write in a vague wordy way. **—n.** vague wordy talk or writing.

waffle[2] *n.* square crisp pancake with a grid-like pattern.

waft *v.* drift or carry gently through air or water. **—n.** something wafted.

wag *v.* **wagging, wagged.** move rapidly from side to side. **—n.** wagging; *Informal* humorous witty person. **—waggish** *adj.* **—wagtail** *n.* small long-tailed bird.

wage *n.* (*often pl.*) payment for work done, esp. when paid weekly. **—v.** engage in (an activity).

wager *n., v.* bet on the outcome of something.

waggle *v.* wag. **—waggly** *adj.*

wag(g)on *n.* four-wheeled vehicle for heavy loads; railway freight truck. **—wag(g)oner** *n.*

waif *n.* homeless child.

wail *v.* cry out in pain or misery. **—n.** mournful cry.

wain *n. Poetic* farm wagon.

wainscot, wainscot(t)ing *n.* wooden lining of the lower part of the walls of a room.

waist *n.* part of the body between the ribs and hips; narrow middle part. **—waistcoat** *n.* sleeveless garment which buttons up the front, worn under a jacket. **—waistline** *n.* (size of) the waist of a person or garment.

wait *v.* remain inactive in expectation (of something); be ready (for something); delay or be delayed; serve in a restaurant etc. **—n.** waiting. **—waiter** *n.* man who serves in a restaurant etc. **—waitress** *n. fem.*

waive *v.* refrain from enforcing (a law, right, etc.). **—waiver** *n.* (written statement of) this act.

wake[1] *v.* **waking, woke, woken.** rouse from sleep or inactivity. **—n.** vigil beside a corpse the night before burial. **—waken** *v.* wake. **—wakeful** *adj.*

wake[2] *n.* track left by a moving ship. **—in the wake of** following close behind.

walk *v.* move on foot with at least one foot always on the ground; pass through or over on foot; escort or accompany on foot. **—n.** walking; distance walked; manner of walking; place or route for walking. **—walk of life** occupation or career. **—walker** *n.* **—walkabout** *n.* informal walk among the public by royalty etc. **—walkie-**

THESAURUS

wade ford, paddle, splash

waft *v.* bear, carry, convey, drift, float, ride, transport

wag 1. *v.* bob, flutter, nod, quiver, rock, shake, stir, wave 2. *n.* bob, flutter, nod, oscillation, quiver, shake, toss, wave

wage *n. Also* **wages** allowance, compensation, earnings, emolument, fee, hire, pay, payment, remuneration, reward, stipend

wager 1. *n.* bet, gamble, pledge, stake 2. *v.* bet, chance, gamble, hazard, lay, pledge, punt, risk, stake

waif foundling, orphan, stray

wail 1. *v.* bemoan, cry, deplore, grieve, howl, lament, weep 2. *n.* complaint, cry, grief, howl, lament, moan, weeping

wait 1. *v.* abide, dally, delay, hang fire, hold

back, linger, pause, remain, rest, stay, tarry 2. *n.* delay, halt, interval, pause, rest, stay

waiter, waitress attendant, server, steward, stewardess

waive abandon, defer, forgo, give up, postpone, put off, relinquish, remit, renounce, resign, surrender

wake[1] *v.* 1. arise, bestir, get up, rouse, stir 2. activate, animate, arouse, awaken, enliven, excite, fire, galvanize, kindle, provoke, quicken, stimulate, stir up

wake[2] backwash, path, track, trail, train, wash, waves

wakeful 1. insomniac, restless, sleepless 2. alert, alive, attentive, heedful, observant, unsleeping, vigilant, wary, watchful

waken activate, arouse, enliven, fire, galvanize, get up, kindle, quicken, rouse, stimulate, stir

DICTIONARY

talkie *n.* portable radio transmitter and receiver. —**walking stick** stick used as a support when walking. —**walk into** *v.* meet with unwittingly. —**Walkman** *n.* ® small portable cassette player with headphones. —**walkout** *n.* strike; act of leaving as a protest. —**walkover** *n.* easy victory.

wall *n.* structure of brick, stone, etc. used to enclose, divide, or support; something having the function or effect of a wall. —*v.* enclose or seal with a wall or walls. —**wallflower** *n.* fragrant garden plant; at a dance, a woman who remains seated for lack of a partner. —**wallpaper** *n.* decorative paper to cover interior walls.

wallaby *n., pl.* **-bies.** marsupial like a small kangaroo.

wallet *n.* small folding case for paper money, documents, etc.

walleyed *adj.* having eyes with an abnormal amount of white showing.

wallop *Informal* —*v.* **-loping, -loped.** hit hard. —*n.* hard blow. —**walloping** *Informal* —*n.* thrashing. —*adj.* large or great.

wallow *v.* roll in liquid or mud; revel in an emotion. —*n.* wallowing.

wally *n., pl.* **-lies.** *Slang* stupid person.

walnut *n.* edible nut with a wrinkled shell; tree it grows on; its wood.

walrus *n., pl.* **-ruses, -rus.** large sea mammal with long tusks.

waltz *n.* ballroom dance; music for this. —*v.* dance a waltz; move in a relaxed confident way.

wampum [**wom**-pum] *n.* shells woven together, formerly used by N American Indians for money and ornament.

wan [rhymes with **swan**] *adj.* **wanner, wannest.** pale and sickly looking.

wand *n.* thin rod, esp. one used in doing magic.

wander *v.* move about without a definite destination or aim; go astray, deviate. —*n.* wandering. —**wanderer** *n.* —**wanderlust** *n.* great desire to travel.

wane *v.* decrease gradually in size or strength; (of the moon) decrease in size. —**on the wane** in decline.

wangle *v. Informal* get by devious methods.

want *v.* desire; lack. —*n.* wanting; thing wanted; lack; poverty. —**wanted** *adj.* sought by the police. —**wanting** *adj.* lacking; not good enough.

wanton *adj.* dissolute or immoral; without motive; unrestrained.

wapiti [**wop**-pit-tee] *n., pl.* **-tis.** large N American and NZ deer.

war *n.* fighting between nations; conflict or contest. —*adj.* of, like, or caused by war. —*v.* **warring, warred.** make war. —**warring** *adj.* —**warlike** *adj.* of, for, or fond of war. —**war crime** crime, such as killing, committed during a war in violation of accepted conventions. —**war**

THESAURUS

walk *v.* 1. advance, go, hike, move, pace, promenade, saunter, step, stride, stroll, tramp, trek, trudge 2. accompany, convoy, escort, take ~*n.* 3. hike, march, promenade, ramble, saunter, stroll, tramp, trek, trudge, turn 4. carriage, gait, pace, step, stride 5. alley, avenue, footpath, lane, path, pathway, pavement, promenade, sidewalk, trail

walker hiker, pedestrian, rambler

walkout protest, stoppage, strike

wall 1. divider, enclosure, panel, partition, screen 2. barricade, embankment, fortification, parapet, rampart 3. barrier, block, fence, hedge, impediment, obstacle

wallet case, holder, notecase, pouch, purse

wallow 1. lie, splash around, tumble, welter 2. bask, delight, glory, luxuriate, relish, revel

wan anaemic, ashen, colourless, ghastly, livid, pale, pallid, pasty, sickly

wand baton, rod, sprig, stick, twig

wander *v.* 1. cruise, drift, meander, peregrinate, ramble, range, roam, rove, straggle, stray, stroll 2. depart, digress, diverge, err, lapse, veer ~*n.* 3. cruise, excursion, meander, ramble

wanderer drifter, gypsy, itinerant, nomad,

rambler, ranger, rover, stroller, traveller, vagabond, voyager

wane 1. *v.* abate, decline, decrease, dim, drop, dwindle, ebb, fade, fail, lessen, sink, subside, weaken, wind down, wither 2. *n.* **on the wane** declining, dropping, dwindling, ebbing, fading, subsiding, weakening, withering

want *v.* 1. covet, crave, desire, need, require, wish, yearn for 2. be short of, be without, call for, demand, lack, miss, need, require ~*n.* 3. appetite, craving, demand, desire, fancy, hankering, hunger, longing, need, thirst, wish 4. absence, dearth, default, deficiency, famine, lack, scarcity, shortage 5. destitution, need, penury, poverty

wanting 1. absent, incomplete, lacking, less, missing, short, shy 2. defective, faulty, imperfect, patchy, poor, sketchy, substandard, unsound

wanton *adj.* 1. abandoned, dissolute, fast, immoral, lewd, libertine, licentious, loose, shameless, unchaste 2. cruel, evil, gratuitous, malicious, motiveless, needless, senseless, spiteful, unjustified, unprovoked, vicious, wicked, wilful

DICTIONARY

criminal —**warfare** n. fighting or hostilities. —**warhead** n. explosive front part of a missile. —**warmonger** n. person who encourages war. —**warship** n. ship designed and equipped for naval combat.

warble v. sing with trills. —**warbler** n. any of various small songbirds.

ward n. room in a hospital for patients needing a similar kind of care; electoral division of a town; child under the care of a guardian or court. —**warder** n. prison officer. —**wardress** n. fem. —**ward off** v. avert or repel. —**wardroom** n. officers' quarters on a warship.

warden n. person in charge of a building and its occupants; official responsible for the enforcement of regulations. —**wardenship** n.

wardrobe n. cupboard for hanging clothes in; person's collection of clothes; costumes of a theatrical company.

ware n. articles of a specified type or material, e.g. *silverware*. —*pl*. goods for sale. —**warehouse** n. building for storing goods prior to sale or distribution.

warlock n. sorcerer.

warm adj. moderately hot; providing warmth; affectionate; enthusiastic; (of a colour) predominantly yellow or red. —v. make or become warm. —**warmly** adv. —**warmth** n. mild heat; cordiality; intensity of emotion. —**warm up** v. make or become warmer; do preliminary exercises before a race or more strenuous exercise; make or become more lively. —**warm-up** n.

warn v. make aware of possible danger or harm; caution or scold; inform (someone) in advance. —**warning** n. something that warns; scolding or caution. —**warn off** v. advise (someone) not to become involved with.

warp v. twist out of shape; pervert. —n. state of being warped; lengthwise threads on a loom.

warrant n. (document giving) official authorization. —v. guarantee; give authority or power to. —**warranty** n. (document giving) a guarantee. —**warrant officer** officer in certain armed services with a rank between a commissioned and noncommissioned officer.

warren n. series of burrows in which rabbits live; overcrowded building or part of a town.

warrior n. person who fights in a war.

wart n. small hard growth on the skin. —**wart hog** kind of African wild pig.

wary [ware-ree] adj. **warier, wariest**. watchful or cautious. —**warily** adv. —**wariness** n.

THESAURUS

war 1. n. battle, bloodshed, combat, conflict, contest, enmity, fighting, hostilities, strife, struggle, warfare 2. v. battle, clash, combat, contend, contest, fight, struggle

ward 1. area, district, division, precinct, quarter, zone 2. charge, minor, protégé, pupil 3. care, charge, custody, keeping, protection

warden administrator, caretaker, curator, guardian, janitor, keeper, ranger, steward, warder, watchman

warder, wardress custodian, gaoler, guard, jailer, keeper, prison officer

ward off avert, avoid, block, deflect, forestall, parry, repel, thwart

wardrobe 1. closet, clothes cupboard 2. apparel, attire, clothes, outfit

warehouse depository, depot, stockroom, store, storehouse

wares commodities, goods, merchandise, produce, stock, stuff

warfare arms, battle, blows, combat, conflict, contest, discord, fighting, hostilities, strategy, strife, struggle, war

warily carefully, cautiously, gingerly, guardedly, suspiciously, vigilantly, watchfully

warlike aggressive, belligerent, combative, hawkish, hostile, jingoistic, martial, militaristic, pugnacious, warmongering

warm adj. 1. balmy, heated, pleasant, sunny 2. affable, affectionate, amiable, amorous, cheerful, cordial, friendly, genial, happy, hearty, kindly, loving, pleasant, tender 3. ardent, earnest, effusive, emotional, enthusiastic, fervent, glowing, heated, keen, lively, passionate, spirited, vigorous, violent ~v. 4. heat, melt, thaw 5. animate, awaken, excite, interest, rouse, stimulate, stir

warmonger belligerent, hawk, militarist

warmth 1. heat, warmness 2. animation, ardour, eagerness, enthusiasm, excitement, fervour, fire, heat, intensity, passion, spirit, vigour, violence, zeal, zest 3. affability, affection, cordiality, happiness, heartiness, kindliness, love, tenderness

warn admonish, advise, alert, caution, forewarn, inform, notify, summon, tip off

warning n. admonition, advice, alarm, alert, caution, hint, notice, notification, omen, premonition, sign, signal, threat, tip, token

warrant n. 1. assurance, authority, authorization, commission, guarantee, licence, permission, permit, pledge, sanction, security ~v. 2. affirm, assure, attest, avouch, certify, declare, guarantee, pledge, underwrite, uphold 3. approve, authorize, commission, demand, empower, entitle, excuse, justify, license, permit, require, sanction

DICTIONARY

was *v.* first and third person singular past tense of BE.

wash *v.* clean (oneself, clothes, etc.) with water and usu. soap; be washable; flow or sweep over or against; *Informal* be believable or acceptable, e.g. *that excuse won't wash.* —*n.* washing; clothes washed at one time; thin coat of paint; trail of water left by a moving ship. —**washable** *adj.* —**washer** *n.* ring put under a nut or bolt or in a tap as a seal. —**washing** *n.* clothes to be washed. —**washing-up** *n.* (washing of) dishes and cutlery needing to be cleaned after a meal. —**wash away** *v.* carry or be carried off by moving water. —**washout** *n. Informal* complete failure. —**wash up** *v.* wash dishes and cutlery after a meal.

wasp *n.* stinging insect with a slender black-and-yellow body. —**waspish** *adj.* bad-tempered.

waste *v.* use pointlessly or thoughtlessly; fail to take advantage of; (cause to) decline in health or strength. —*n.* wasting; anything wasted; waste material. —*pl.* desert. —*adj.* rejected as worthless or surplus to requirements; not cultivated or inhabited. —**wastage** *n.* loss by wear or waste; reduction in size of a workforce by not filling vacancies. —**wasteful** *adj.* extravagant. —**wastefully** *adv.* —**waster, wastrel** *n.* layabout.

watch *v.* look at closely; wait expectantly (for); guard or supervise. —*n.* portable timepiece for the wrist or pocket; (period of) watching; sailor's spell of duty. —**watchable** *adj.* —**watcher** *n.* —**watchful** *adj.* vigilant or alert. —**watchfully**

adv. —**watchdog** *n.* dog kept to guard property; person or group guarding against inefficiency or illegality. —**watchman** *n.* man employed to guard a building or property. —**watchword** *n.* password; slogan.

water *n.* clear colourless tasteless liquid that falls as rain and forms rivers etc.; body of water, such as a sea or lake; level of the tide; urine. —*v.* put water on or into; (of the eyes) fill with tears; (of the mouth) salivate. —**watery** *adj.* —**water bed** waterproof mattress filled with water. —**water buffalo** oxlike Asian animal. —**water closet** (room containing) a toilet flushed by water. —**watercolour** *n.* paint thinned with water; painting done in this. —**watercourse** *n.* stream or river. —**watercress** *n.* edible plant growing in clear ponds and streams. —**water down** *v.* dilute, make less strong. —**waterfall** *n.* place where the waters of a river drop vertically. —**waterfront** *n.* part of a town alongside a body of water. —**water ice** ice cream made from frozen fruit-flavoured syrup. —**water lily** water plant with large floating leaves. —**watermark** *n.* faint translucent design in a sheet of paper. —**watermelon** *n.* melon with green skin and red flesh. —**water polo** team game played by swimmers with a ball. —**waterproof** *adj.* not letting water through. —*v.* make waterproof. —*n.* waterproof garment. —**watershed** *n.* line separating two river systems; dividing line. —**water-skiing** *n.* sport of riding over water on skis towed by a speedboat. —**watertight** *adj.* not letting water through; with no loopholes or weak points.

THESAURUS

warrior combatant, fighter, soldier

wary alert, attentive, careful, cautious, chary, distrustful, guarded, heedful, prudent, suspicious, vigilant, watchful

wash *v.* 1. bath, bathe, clean, cleanse, launder, moisten, rinse, scrub, shower, wet 2. *With away* carry off, erode, move, sweep away, wash off 3. *Inf.* be convincing, hold water ~*n.* 4. ablution, bath, cleaning, rinse, scrub, shampoo, shower, washing 5. flow, roll, surge, sweep, swell, wave

washout disappointment, disaster, failure, fiasco, mess

waste *v.* 1. dissipate, lavish, misuse, squander 2. consume, corrode, crumble, decay, decline, disable, drain, dwindle, exhaust, fade, gnaw, perish, sink, undermine, wane, wither 3. despoil, destroy, pillage, rape, ravage, raze, ruin, sack, spoil ~*n.* 4. extravagance, loss, misapplication, misuse, prodigality, squandering, wastefulness 5. desolation, destruction, devastation, havoc, ravage, ruin 6. debris, dregs, dross, garbage, leavings, litter, offal, refuse,

rubbish, scrap, trash 7. desert, solitude, void, wilderness ~*adj.* 8. superfluous, unused, worthless 9. bare, barren, desolate, dismal, dreary, empty, unproductive, wild

wasteful extravagant, lavish, prodigal, ruinous, spendthrift, thriftless, uneconomical

watch *v.* 1. contemplate, eye, look, mark, note, observe, regard, see, stare at, view 2. attend, be watchful, look out, take heed, wait 3. guard, keep, look after, mind, protect, tend ~*n.* 4. chronometer, clock, timepiece 5. eye, heed, lookout, notice, surveillance, vigil, vigilance

watchdog 1. guard dog 2. custodian, inspector, monitor, protector, scrutineer

watcher lookout, observer, onlooker, spectator, spy, viewer, witness

watchful alert, attentive, guarded, heedful, observant, suspicious, vigilant, wary, wide awake

watchman caretaker, custodian, guard, security man

water 1. *n.* aqua, H_2O 2. *v.* dampen, drench,

DICTIONARY

watt [wott] *n.* unit of power. —**wattage** *n.* electrical power expressed in watts.

wattle [wott-tl] *n.* branches woven over sticks to make a fence; fold of skin hanging from the neck of certain birds.

wave *v.* move the hand to and fro as a greeting or signal; move or flap to and fro. —*n.* moving ridge on water; curve(s) in the hair; gesture of waving; vibration carrying energy through a medium; prolonged spell of something. —**wavy** *adj.* —**wavelength** *n.* distance between the same points of two successive waves.

waver *v.* hesitate or be irresolute; be or become unsteady. —**waverer** *n.*

wax[1] *n.* solid shiny fatty or oily substance used for sealing, making candles, etc.; similar substance made by bees; waxy secretion of the ear. —*v.* coat or polish with wax. —**waxen** *adj.* made of or like wax. —**waxy** *adj.* —**waxwing** *n.* small songbird. —**waxwork** *n.* lifelike wax model of a (famous) person. —*pl.* place exhibiting these.

wax[2] *v.* increase in size or strength; (of the moon) get gradually larger.

way *n.* manner or method; route or direction; track or path; room for movement or activity, e.g. *you're in the way;* distance; passage or journey; characteristic manner; *Informal* state or condition. —**wayward** *adj.* erratic, selfish, or stubborn. —**waywardness** *n.* —**wayfarer** *n.* traveller. —**waylay** *v.* lie in wait for and accost or attack. —**wayside** *adj., n.* (situated by) the side of a road.

WC water closet.

we *pron.* (used as the subject of a verb) the speaker or writer and one or more others; people in general; formal word for *I* used by editors and monarchs.

weak *adj.* lacking strength; liable to give way; lacking flavour; unconvincing. —**weaken** *v.* make or become weak. —**weakling** *n.* feeble person or animal. —**weakly** *adj.* weak or sickly. —*adv.* feebly. —**weakness** *n.*

weal *n.* raised mark left on the skin by a blow.

THESAURUS

flood, hose, irrigate, moisten, soak, souse, spray, sprinkle

waterfall cascade, cataract, chute, fall

watertight 1. sound, waterproof 2. airtight, firm, flawless, foolproof, impregnable, sound, unassailable

watery damp, fluid, humid, liquid, marshy, moist, soggy, squelchy, wet

wave *v.* 1. brandish, flourish, flutter, oscillate, quiver, ripple, shake, stir, sway, swing, undulate, wag, wield 2. beckon, direct, gesture, indicate, sign, signal ~*n.* 3. billow, breaker, ridge, ripple, roller, sea surf, swell 4. current, drift, flood, movement, outbreak, rash, rush, stream, surge, sweep, tendency, trend, upsurge

waver 1. dither, falter, hesitate, seesaw, vacillate 2. flicker, fluctuate, quiver, reel, shake, sway, undulate, vary, wave, weave, wobble

wax *v.* develop, dilate, enlarge, expand, grow, increase, magnify, mount, rise, swell

way 1. approach, fashion, manner, means, method, mode, plan, practice, procedure, process, scheme, system, technique 2. access, avenue, channel, course, direction, lane, path, road, route, street, track, trail 3. elbowroom, opening, room, space 4. distance, journey, length, stretch, trail 5. advance, approach, journey, march, passage, progress 6. characteristic, conduct, custom, habit, manner, nature, personality, practice, style, trait, usage, wont

wayfarer globetrotter, itinerant, nomad, rover, traveller, voyager, walker, wanderer

wayward capricious, contrary, cross-grained, disobedient, erratic, fickle, flighty, headstrong, incorrigible, mulish, obdurate, obstinate, perverse, rebellious, self-willed, stubborn, ungovernable, unpredictable, unruly, wilful

weak 1. anaemic, debilitated, decrepit, delicate, effete, exhausted, faint, feeble, fragile, frail, infirm, puny, shaky, sickly, spent, tender, unsteady, wasted 2. cowardly, impotent, indecisive, ineffectual, infirm, irresolute, powerless, soft, spineless 3. feeble, flimsy, hollow, inconclusive, invalid, lame, pathetic, shallow, slight, unsatisfactory 4. defenceless, exposed, helpless, unprotected, unsafe, untenable, vulnerable, wide open 5. diluted, insipid, runny, tasteless, thin, watery

weaken 1. abate, depress, diminish, droop, dwindle, enervate, fade, fail, flag, impair, invalidate, lessen, lower, moderate, reduce, sap, temper, tire, undermine, wane 2. cut, debase, dilute, thin

weakness faintness, feebleness, frailty, impotence, infirmity, powerlessness, vulnerability

wealth 1. affluence, assets, capital, cash, estate, fortune, funds, goods, means, money, opulence, possessions, property, resources, riches, substance 2. abundance, bounty, fullness, plenty, profusion, richness, store

wealthy affluent, comfortable, moneyed, opulent, prosperous, rich, well-off

DICTIONARY

wealth *n.* riches; abundance. —**wealthy** *adj.* —**wealthiness** *n.*

wean *v.* accustom to food other than mother's milk; coax away from.

weapon *n.* object used in fighting; anything used to get the better of an opponent. —**weaponry** *n.* weapons collectively.

wear *v.* **wearing, wore, worn.** have on the body as clothing or ornament; show as one's expression; (cause to) deteriorate by constant use or action; endure constant use; *Informal* tolerate. —*n.* wearing; things to wear, e.g. *leisure wear;* damage caused by use; ability to endure constant use. —**wearer** *n.* —**wear off** *v.* gradually decrease in intensity. —**wear on** *v.* (of time) pass slowly.

weary *adj.* **-rier, -riest.** tired or exhausted; tiring. —*v.* **-rying, -ried.** make or become weary. —**wearily** *adv.* —**weariness** *n.* —**wearisome** *adj.* tedious.

weasel *n.* small carnivorous mammal with a long body and short legs.

weather *n.* day-to-day meteorological conditions of a place. —*v.* (cause to) be affected by the weather; come safely through. —**under the weather** *Informal* slightly ill. —**weather-beaten** *adj.* worn, damaged, or (of skin) tanned by exposure to the weather. —**weathercock, weathervane** *n.* vane revolving to show which way the wind is blowing.

weave *v.* **weaving, wove** *or* **weaved, woven** *or* **weaved.** make (fabric) by interlacing (yarn) on a loom; compose (a story); move from side to side while going forwards. —**weaver** *n.*

web *n.* net spun by a spider; skin between the toes of a duck, frog, etc. —**webbed** *adj.* —**webbing** *n.* strong fabric woven in strips.

wed *v.* **wedding, wedded** *or* **wed.** marry; unite closely. —**wedding** *n.* act or ceremony of marriage. —**wedlock** *n.* marriage.

wedge *n.* piece of material thick at one end and thin at the other. —*v.* fasten or split with a wedge; squeeze into a narrow space.

Wednesday *n.* fourth day of the week.

wee *adj.* small.

weed *n.* plant growing where undesired; *Informal* thin ineffectual person. —*v.* clear of weeds. —**weedy** *adj.* —**weed out** *v.* remove or eliminate (what is unwanted).

weeds *pl. n. Obs.* widow's mourning clothes.

week *n.* period of seven days, esp. one beginning on a Sunday; hours or days of work in a week. —**weekly** *adj., adv.* happening, done, etc. once a week. —*n., pl.* **-lies.** periodical published once a week. —**weekday** *n.* any day of the week except Saturday or Sunday. —**weekend** *n.* Saturday and Sunday.

weep *v.* **weeping, wept.** shed tears; grieve or lament; ooze liquid. —**weepy** *adj.* —**weeping willow** willow with drooping branches.

weevil *n.* small beetle which eats grain etc.

weft *n.* cross threads in weaving.

weigh *v.* measure the weight of; have a specified weight; consider carefully; be influential; be burdensome. —**weigh anchor** raise a ship's anchor or (of a ship) have its anchor raised. —**weighbridge** *n.* machine for weighing vehicles by means of a metal plate set into the road.

THESAURUS

wear *v.* 1. bear, carry, clothe oneself, don, have on, put on, sport 2. display, exhibit, fly, show 3. abrade, consume, corrode, deteriorate, erode, fray, grind, impair, rub, use, wash away, waste 4. bear up, endure, hold up, last, stand up ~*n.* 5. employment, mileage (*Inf.*), service, use, utility 6. apparel, attire, clothes, costume, dress, garments, gear, habit, outfit 7. abrasion, attrition, damage, depreciation, erosion, friction, use

weariness drowsiness, exhaustion, fatigue, lassitude, lethargy, prostration, tiredness

wearisome annoying, boring, bothersome, burdensome, dull, exhausting, fatiguing, irksome, oppressive, prosaic, tedious, troublesome, trying, wearing

wear off abate, decrease, diminish, dwindle, ebb, fade, subside, wane, weaken

weary *adj.* 1. dead beat (*Inf.*), drained, drowsy, exhausted, fatigued, flagging, jaded, sleepy, spent, tired, wearied, worn out 2. arduous, irksome, laborious, taxing, wearing ~*v.* 3. burden, drain, droop, enervate, fade, fail, fatigue, sap, tax, tire, wear out 4. annoy, become bored, bore, exasperate, irk, jade, plague, sicken, vex

weather *n.* 1. climate, conditions 2. **under the weather** ailing, ill, indisposed, off-colour, sick ~*v.* 3. expose, harden, season, toughen 4. brave, endure, overcome, pull through, resist, stand, suffer, surmount, survive, withstand

weave 1. blend, braid, entwine, fuse, intermingle, intertwine, introduce, knit, merge, plait, twist, unite 2. build, construct, contrive, create, fabricate, make, spin 3. wind, zigzag

wed espouse, join, make one, marry, unite

wedding marriage, nuptials, wedlock

wedge 1. *n.* block, chock, chunk, lump 2. *v.* block, cram, force, jam, lodge, pack, split, squeeze, stuff, thrust

DICTIONARY

weight *n.* heaviness of an object; object of known mass used for weighing; unit of measurement of weight; heavy object; importance or influence. —*v.* add weight to; burden. —**weighting** *n.* extra allowance paid in special circumstances. —**weightless** *adj.* —**weightlessness** *n.* —**weighty** *adj.* heavy; important; causing worry. —**weightily** *adv.*

weir *n.* river dam.

weird *adj.* unearthly or eerie; strange or bizarre. —**weirdo** *n. Informal* peculiar person.

welch *v.* same as WELSH.

welcome *adj.* received gladly; freely permitted. —*n.* kindly greeting. —*v.* -**coming, -comed.** greet with pleasure; receive gladly.

weld *v.* join (pieces of metal or plastic) by softening with heat; unite closely. —*n.* welded joint. —**welder** *n.*

welfare *n.* wellbeing; help given to people in need. —**welfare state** system in which the government takes responsibility for the wellbeing of its citizens.

well[1] *adv.* **better, best.** satisfactorily; skilfully; completely; prosperously; suitably; intimately; favourably; considerably. —*adj.* in good health; satisfactory. —*interj.* exclamation of surprise, interrogation, etc. —**wellbeing** *n.* state of being well, happy, or prosperous. —**well-disposed** *adj.* inclined to be friendly or sympathetic. —**well-**

meaning *adj.* having good intentions. —**well-spoken** *adj.* speaking in a polite or articulate way.

well[2] *n.* hole sunk into the earth to reach water, oil, or gas; deep open shaft. —*v.* flow upwards or outwards.

wellies *pl. n. Informal* wellingtons.

wellingtons *pl. n.* high waterproof rubber boots.

Welsh *adj.* of Wales. —*n.* language or people of Wales. —**Welsh rabbit, rarebit** dish of melted cheese on toast.

welsh *v.* fail to pay a debt or fulfil an obligation.

welt *n.* raised or strengthened seam; weal. —*v.* provide with a welt.

welter *n.* jumbled mass.

welterweight *n.* boxer weighing up to 147lb (professional) or 67kg (amateur).

wen *n.* cyst on the scalp.

wench *n. Facetious* young woman.

wend *v.* go or travel.

went *v.* past tense of GO.

wept *v.* past of WEEP.

we're we are.

were *v.* form of the past tense of BE used after *we, you, they,* or a plural noun; subjunctive of BE.

weren't were not.

THESAURUS

weep bemoan, bewail, complain, cry, lament, moan, mourn, snivel, sob, ululate, whimper

weigh 1. consider, contemplate, evaluate, examine, ponder, study 2. count, cut any ice (*Inf.*), have influence, impress, matter, tell 3. burden, oppress, prey

weight *n.* 1. burden, gravity, heaviness, load, mass, pressure, tonnage 2. ballast, load, mass 3. burden, load, millstone, pressure, strain 4. authority, consequence, consideration, emphasis, impact, importance, influence, moment, power, substance, value ~*v.* 5. ballast, charge, freight, load 6. burden, encumber, handicap, impede, oppress, overburden

weighty 1. burdensome, dense, heavy, massive, ponderous 2. considerable, critical, crucial, forcible, grave, important, momentous, serious, significant, solemn, substantial 3. crushing, demanding, difficult, exacting, onerous, oppressive, taxing, worrying

weird bizarre, eerie, freakish, ghostly, grotesque, mysterious, odd, queer, strange, uncanny, unearthly, unnatural

welcome *adj.* 1. acceptable, agreeable, delightful, desirable, gratifying, pleasant, pleasing, pleasurable, refreshing, wanted 2. free, invited

~*n.* 3. acceptance, greeting, hospitality, reception, salutation ~*v.* 4. embrace, greet, hail, meet, receive

welfare advantage, benefit, good, happiness, health, interest, profit, prosperity, success, wellbeing

well[1] *adv.* 1. agreeably, capitally, happily, nicely, pleasantly, satisfactorily, smoothly, splendidly, successfully 2. ably, adeptly, adequately, admirably, correctly, effectively, efficiently, expertly, proficiently, properly, skilfully 3. comfortably, flourishingly, prosperously 4. correctly, easily, fairly, fittingly, justly, properly, readily, rightly, suitably 5. closely, completely, deeply, fully, intimately, personally, profoundly, thoroughly 6. approvingly, favourably, glowingly, graciously, highly, kindly, warmly 7. abundantly, amply, completely, considerably, fully, greatly, heartily, highly, substantially, sufficiently, thoroughly, very much ~*adj.* 8. able-bodied, fit, hale, healthy, hearty, robust, sound, strong

well[2] *n.* 1. pool, source, spring 2. bore, hole, pit, shaft ~*v.* 3. flow, gush, jet, ooze, pour, rise, run, seep, spout, spring, spurt, stream, surge, trickle

DICTIONARY

werewolf n. (in folklore) person who can turn into a wolf.

west n. (direction towards) the point on the horizon where the sun sets; region lying in this direction; (**W-**) western Europe and the U.S. —adj. in, going towards, facing, or (of the wind) blowing from the west. —adv. in or to the west. —**westerly** adj. in, towards, or (of the wind) blowing from the west. —**western** adj. of or in the west. —n. film or story about cowboys in the western U.S. —**westerner** n. —**westernize** v. adapt to the customs and culture of the West. —**westward** adj., adv. —**westwards** adv.

wet adj. **wetter, wettest.** covered or soaked with water or another liquid; not yet dry, e.g. wet paint; Informal (of a person) feeble or foolish. —n. moisture or rain; Informal feeble or foolish person. —v. **wetting, wet** or **wetted.** make wet. —**wet blanket** Informal person who has a depressing effect on others. —**wetland** n. area of marshy land. —**wet nurse** woman employed to breast-feed another's child. —**wet suit** close-fitting rubber suit worn by divers etc.

wether n. castrated ram.

whack v. strike with a resounding blow. —n. such a blow; Informal share; Informal attempt. —**whacked** adj. exhausted. —**whacking** adj. Informal huge.

whale n. large fish-shaped sea mammal. —**a whale of a** Informal very large or fine example of (something). —**whaling** n. hunting of whales. —**whaler** n. —**whalebone** n. horny substance hanging from the upper jaw of toothless whales.

wharf n., pl. **wharves, wharfs.** platform at a harbour for loading and unloading ships. —**wharfage** n. accommodation at or charge for use of a wharf.

what det. which thing; that which; request for a statement to be repeated. —adv. in which way, how much, e.g. what do you care? —interj. exclamation of surprise, anger, etc. —**what for?** why? —**whatever** pron. everything or anything that; no matter what. —**whatnot** n. Informal similar unspecified things. —**whatsoever** adj. at all.

wheat n. grain used in making flour, bread, and pasta; plant producing this. —**wheaten** adj. —**wheatear** n. small songbird. —**wheatmeal** adj., n. (made with) brown, but not wholemeal, flour.

wheedle v. coax or cajole.

wheel n. disc that revolves on an axle; pivoting movement. —v. push or pull (something with wheels); turn as if on an axis; turn round suddenly. —**wheeling and dealing** use of shrewd and sometimes unscrupulous methods to achieve success. —**wheeler-dealer** n. —**wheelbarrow** n. shallow box for carrying loads, with a wheel at the front and two handles. —**wheelbase** n. distance between a vehicle's front and back axles. —**wheelchair** n. chair mounted on wheels for use by people who cannot walk. —**wheel clamp** immobilizing device fixed to one wheel of an illegally parked car.

wheeze v. breathe with a hoarse whistling noise. —n. wheezing sound. —**wheezy** adj.

whelk n. edible snail-like shellfish.

whelp n. pup or cub; Offens. youth. —v. produce whelps.

when adv. at what time. —conj. at the time that; although; considering the fact that. —pron. at which time. —**whenever** adv., conj. at whatever time.

whence adv., conj. Obs. from what place or source.

where adv. in, at, or to what place. —pron. in, or to which place. —conj. in the place at which. —**whereabouts** adv. at what place. —n. present position. —**whereas** conj. but on the other hand; considering that. —**whereby** conj. by which. —**wherefore** Obs. —adv. why. —conj. consequently. —**whereupon** conj. at which point. —**wherever** adv. at whatever place. —**wherewithal** n. necessary funds, resources, etc.

wherry n., pl. **-ries.** barge; light rowing boat.

whet v. **whetting, whetted.** sharpen (a tool); increase (appetite or desire). —**whetstone** n. stone for sharpening tools.

whether conj. used to introduce an indirect question or a clause expressing doubt or choice.

whey [way] n. watery liquid that separates from the curd when milk is clotted.

which det., pron. used to request or refer to a

THESAURUS

wet 1. adj. damp, dank, dripping, humid, moist, saturated, soaking, sodden, soggy, sopping, waterlogged 2. n. dampness, humidity, liquid, moisture 3. v. damp, dip, douse, drench, irrigate, moisten, saturate, soak, splash, spray, sprinkle, steep

wharf dock, jetty, pier, quay

wheedle cajole, charm, coax, court, draw, entice, flatter, persuade

wheel 1. n. circle, pivot, revolution, roll, rotation, spin, turn, twirl, whirl 2. v. circle, orbit, revolve, roll, rotate, spin, swing, swivel, turn, twirl, whirl

wheeze 1. v. cough, gasp, hiss, rasp, whistle 2. n. cough, gasp, hiss, rasp, whistle

whereabouts location, position, site, situation

whet edge, file, grind, hone, sharpen, strop

DICTIONARY

choice from different possibilities. —*pron.* person or thing referred to. —**whichever** *det., pron.* any out of several; no matter which.

whiff *n.* puff of air or odour; trace or hint.

Whig *n.* member of a British political party of the 18th–19th centuries that sought limited reform.

while *conj.* in the time that; despite the fact that; whereas. —*n.* period of time. —**whilst** *conj.* while. —**while away** *v.* pass (time) idly but pleasantly.

whim *n.* sudden fancy. —**whims**(e)**y** *n.* capricious idea; light or fanciful humour. —**whimsical** *adj.* fanciful; full of whims. —**whimsicality** *n.*

whimper *v.* cry in a soft whining way. —*n.* soft plaintive whine.

whin *n.* gorse.

whine *n.* high-pitched plaintive cry; peevish complaint. —*v.* make such a sound. —**whining** *n., adj.*

whinge *v.* complain. —*n.* complaint.

whinny *v.* **-nying, -nied.** neigh softly. —*n.* soft neigh.

whip *v.* **whipping, whipped.** strike with a whip, strap, or cane; *Informal* pull, remove, or move quickly; rouse into a particular condition; urge by or as if by whipping; beat (esp. eggs or cream) to a froth; *Informal* steal. —*n.* cord attached to a handle, used for beating animals or people; call made on members of Parliament to attend for important divisions; politician responsible for organizing and disciplining fellow party members; whipped dessert. —**whiplash injury** neck injury caused by a sudden jerk to the unsupported head. —**whip-round** *n. Informal* collection of money.

whippet *n.* racing dog like a small greyhound.

whirl *v.* spin or revolve; be dizzy or confused; drive or move at high speed. —*n.* whirling movement; confusion or giddiness; bustling activity.

—**whirlpool** *n.* strong circular current of water.
—**whirlwind** *n.* column of air whirling violently upwards in a spiral. —*adj.* much quicker than normal.

whir(r) *n.* prolonged soft buzz. —*v.* **whirring, whirred.** (cause to) make a whir.

whisk *v.* brush away lightly; move or remove quickly; beat (esp. eggs or cream) to a froth. —*n.* light brush; egg-beating utensil.

whisker *n.* any of the long stiff hairs on the face of a cat or other mammal. —*pl.* hair growing on a man's cheeks. —**by a whisker** *Informal* only just.

whisky *n., pl.* **-kies.** spirit distilled from fermented cereals. —**whiskey** *n.* Irish or American whisky.

whisper *v.* speak softly, without vibration of the vocal cords; rustle. —*n.* soft voice; something whispered; rustling; *Informal* rumour.

whist *n.* card game.

whistle *v.* produce a shrill sound by forcing breath through pursed lips; make a similar sound; signal by a whistle. —*n.* instrument blown to make a whistling sound; whistling sound. —**blow the whistle on** *Informal* inform on or put a stop to. —**whistling** *n., adj.*

whit *n.* —**not a whit** not the slightest amount.

white *adj.* of the colour of snow; pale; light in colour; (of coffee) served with milk. —*n.* colour of snow; white part; clear fluid round the yolk of an egg; (**W-**) member of the race of people with light-coloured skin. —**whiten** *v.* make or become white or whiter. —**whiteness** *n.* —**whitish** *adj.* —**whitebait** *n.* small edible fish. —**white-collar** *adj.* denoting nonmanual salaried workers. —**white elephant** useless or unwanted possession. —**white flag** signal of surrender or truce. —**white goods** large domestic appliances such as cookers and fridges. —**white-hot** *adj.* very hot. —**white lie** minor unimportant lie. —**White**

THESAURUS

whiff *n.* aroma, blast, breath, draught, gust, hint, odour, puff, scent, smell, sniff

whim caprice, conceit, craze, fancy, humour, impulse, notion, quirk, urge, vagary

whimper 1. *v.* cry, moan, snivel, sob, weep 2. *n.* moan, snivel, sob, whine

whine *n.* 1. cry, moan, sob, wail 2. complaint, grouse, grumble, moan ~*v.* 3. carp, complain, cry, grouse, grumble, moan, sob, wail

whip *v.* 1. beat, cane, castigate, flog, lash, punish, scourge, spank, strap, switch, thrash 2. exhibit, flash, jerk, produce, pull, remove, seize, show, snatch, whisk 3. beat, whisk ~*n.* 4. birch, cane, crop, horsewhip, lash, rawhide, scourge, switch, thong

whirl *v.* 1. circle, pirouette, pivot, reel, revolve, roll, rotate, spin, swirl, turn, twirl, twist, wheel 2. reel, spin ~*n.* 3. circle, pirouette, reel, revolution, roll, rotation, spin, swirl, turn, twist, wheel 4. confusion, daze, dither, flurry, giddiness, spin

whirlwind 1. *n.* tornado, waterspout 2. *adj.* hasty, headlong, lightning, quick, rapid, rash, short, speedy, swift

whisper *v.* 1. breathe, murmur 2. hiss, murmur, rustle, sigh ~*n.* 3. low voice, murmur, undertone 4. hiss, murmur, rustle, sigh, sighing 5. breath, fraction, hint, shadow, suggestion, suspicion, tinge, trace, whiff 6. gossip, innuendo, insinuation, report, rumour

DICTIONARY

Paper report by the government, outlining its policy on a matter. —**whitewash** *n.* substance for whitening walls. —*v.* cover with whitewash; *Informal* conceal or gloss over faults.

whither *adv. Obs.* to what place.

whiting [white-ing] *n.* edible sea fish.

Whitsun *n.* week following **Whit Sunday**, the seventh Sunday after Easter.

whittle *v.* cut or carve (wood) with a knife. —**whittle down, away** *v.* reduce or wear away gradually.

whiz(z) *v.* **whizzing, whizzed.** make a loud buzzing sound; *Informal* move quickly. —*n., pl.* **whizzes.** loud buzzing sound; *Informal* person skilful at something.

who *pron.* which or what person; used to refer to a person or people already mentioned. —**whoever** *pron.* any person who; no matter who.

whodunnit [hoo-**dun**-nit] *n. Informal* detective story, play, or film.

whole *adj.* containing all the elements or parts; uninjured or undamaged; healthy; (of a number) not containing a fraction. —*n.* complete thing or system. —**on the whole** taking everything into consideration. —**wholly** *adv.* —**wholesome** *adj.* physically or morally beneficial. —**wholehearted** *adj.* sincere or enthusiastic. —**wholemeal** *adj.* (of flour) made from the whole wheat grain; made from wholemeal flour. —**wholesale** *n.* sale of goods in large quantities to retailers. —*adj., adv.* dealing by wholesale; extensive(ly). —**wholesaler** *n.*

whom *pron.* objective case of WHO.

whoop *n., v.* shout or cry to express excitement.

whoopee *interj. Informal* cry of joy.

whooping cough *n.* infectious disease marked by convulsive coughing and noisy breathing.

whopper *n. Informal* anything unusually large; huge lie. —**whopping** *adj.*

whore [hore] *n.* prostitute.

whorl *n.* ring of leaves or petals; one turn of a spiral; something coiled.

whose *det.* of who or which.

why *adv.* for what reason. —*pron.* because of which.

wick *n.* cord through a lamp or candle which carries fuel to the flame.

wicked *adj.* morally bad; mischievous. —**wickedly** *adv.* —**wickedness** *n.*

wicker *adj.* made of woven cane. —**wickerwork** *n.*

wicket *n.* set of three cricket stumps and two bails; cricket pitch; small gate.

wide *adj.* large from side to side; spacious or extensive; having a specified width; far from the target; opened fully. —*adv.* over an extensive area; to the full extent; far from the target. —**widely** *adv.* —**widen** *v.* make or become wider. —**width** *n.* distance from side to side; quality of being wide. —**widespread** *adj.* extending over a wide area.

widgeon *n.* same as WIGEON.

widow *n.* woman whose husband is dead and who has not remarried. —*v.* make a widow of. —**widowhood** *n.* —**widower** *n.* man whose wife is dead and who has not remarried.

THESAURUS

white 1. ashen, bloodless, grey, pale, pasty, wan 2. grey, grizzled, hoary, silver, snowy

whiten blanch, bleach, blench, fade, pale

whitewash *v.* conceal, extenuate, suppress

whole *adj.* 1. complete, entire, full, integral, total, uncut 2. faultless, flawless, good, intact, mint, perfect, sound, unbroken, unimpaired, uninjured, unscathed, untouched 3. ablebodied, better, cured, fit, hale, healed, healthy, recovered, robust, sound, strong, well ~*n.* 4. aggregate, all, everything, lot, sum total, total 5. ensemble, entirety, entity, fullness, piece, totality, unit, unity

wholehearted committed, dedicated, determined, devoted, earnest, enthusiastic, genuine, real, sincere, true, unreserved, unstinting, warm, zealous

wholesale 1. *adj.* broad, extensive, far-reaching, indiscriminate, mass, sweeping 2. *adv.* comprehensively, extensively

wicked 1. abandoned, amoral, atrocious, bad,

corrupt, debased, dissolute, evil, fiendish, flagitious, foul, guilty, heinous, immoral, iniquitous, irreligious, nefarious, scandalous, shameful, sinful, unrighteous, vicious, vile, villainous, worthless 2. arch, impish, mischievous, naughty, rascally, roguish

wide *adj.* 1. ample, broad, comprehensive, encyclopedic, expanded, expansive, general, immense, inclusive, large, sweeping, vast 2. away, distant, off, remote 3. dilated, distended, expanded, outspread, outstretched 4. ample, baggy, commodious, full, loose, roomy, spacious ~*adv.* 5. completely, fully 6. astray, nowhere near, off course, out

widen broaden, dilate, enlarge, expand, extend, spread, stretch

widespread broad, common, extensive, general, popular, prevalent, rife, sweeping, universal, wholesale

width breadth, compass, diameter, extent, girth, range, reach, scope, span

DICTIONARY

wield v. hold and use (a weapon); have and use (power).

wife n., pl. **wives.** man's partner in marriage.

wig n. artificial head of hair. —**wigged** adj.

wigeon n. duck found in marshland.

wiggle v. move jerkily from side to side. —n. wiggling movement. —**wiggly** adj.

wight n. Obs. person.

wigwam n. N American Indian's tent.

wild adj. (of animals) not tamed or domesticated; (of plants) not cultivated; not civilized; lacking restraint or control; violent or stormy; random; Informal furious; Informal excited. —**wilds** pl. n. desolate or uninhabited place. —**wildly** adv. —**wildness** n. —**wildcat** n. European wild animal like a large domestic cat. —adj. (of a strike) sudden and unofficial. —**wild-goose chase** futile search or undertaking. —**wildlife** n. wild animals and plants collectively.

wildebeest n. gnu.

wilderness n. uninhabited uncultivated region.

wildfire n. —**spread like wildfire** spread quickly and uncontrollably.

wile n. trick or ploy. —**wily** adj. crafty or sly.

wilful adj. headstrong or obstinate; intentional. —**wilfully** adv. —**wilfulness** n.

will[1] v. past **would.** used as an auxiliary to form the future tense or to indicate intention, ability, or expectation.

will[2] n. faculty of deciding what one will do; directions written for disposal of one's property after death; desire or wish; attitude towards others, e.g. ill will. —v. use one's will in an attempt to do (something); bequeath (property) by a will; wish or desire. —**willing** adj. ready or inclined (to do something); done or given readily. —**willingly** adv. —**willingness** n. —**willpower** n. ability to control oneself and one's actions.

will-o'-the-wisp n. pale light sometimes seen over marshes at night; elusive person or thing.

willow n. tree with thin flexible branches; its wood. —**willowy** adj. slender and graceful.

willy-nilly adv. whether desired or not.

wilt v. (cause to) become limp or lose strength.

wimp n. Informal feeble ineffectual person.

wimple n. garment framing the face, worn by medieval women and now by nuns.

win v. **winning, won.** come first in (a competition, fight, etc.); gain (a prize) in a competition; get by effort. —n. victory, esp. in a game. —**winner** n. —**winning** adj. charming. —**winnings** pl. n. sum won, esp. in gambling. —**win over** v. gain the support or consent of (someone).

wince v. draw back, as from pain. —n. wincing.

winceyette n. cotton fabric with a raised nap.

winch n. machine for lifting or hauling using a

THESAURUS

wield 1. brandish, employ, flourish, handle, manage, manipulate, ply, swing, use 2. apply, command, control, exercise, exert, have, hold, maintain, manage, possess, utilize

wife bride, helpmate, mate, partner, spouse

wild adj. 1. ferocious, fierce, savage, untamed 2. desert, desolate, empty, trackless, uncivilized, uncultivated, unpopulated 3. barbaric, brut~ ish, ferocious, fierce, primitive, rude, savage, uncivilized 4. boisterous, chaotic, disorderly, lawless, noisy, riotous, rough, turbulent, un~ disciplined, unrestrained, unruly, uproarious, violent, wayward 5. berserk, crazy, delirious, demented, excited, frantic, frenzied, hysteri~ cal, irrational, mad, maniacal, rabid, raving

wilderness desert, jungle, waste

wile artfulness, artifice, cheating, craft, crafti~ ness, cunning, fraud, guile, slyness, trickery

wilful 1. determined, dogged, headstrong, in~ flexible, obstinate, persistent, perverse, self-willed, stubborn, unyielding 2. conscious, de~ liberate, intentional, purposeful, voluntary, willed

will n. 1. choice, decision, discretion, option 2. declaration, testament 3. choice, decision, de~

cree, desire, fancy, mind, pleasure, wish 4. aim, determination, intention, purpose, reso~ lution, resolve 5. attitude, disposition, feeling ~v. 6. bid, cause, command, decree, deter~ mine, direct, effect, ordain, order, resolve 7. choose, desire, elect, opt, prefer, see fit, want, wish 8. bequeath, confer, give, leave, pass on, transfer

willing agreeable, amenable, consenting, con~ tent, desirous, disposed, eager, enthusiastic, favourable, game, happy, inclined, pleased, prepared, ready

willingly cheerfully, eagerly, freely, gladly, hap~ pily, readily, voluntarily

willingness agreement, consent, desire, enthu~ siasm, favour, good will, inclination, volition, will, wish

willpower determination, drive, grit, resolution, resolve, self-control

win v. 1. be victorious, come first, conquer, overcome, prevail, succeed, triumph 2. ac~ complish, achieve, acquire, attain, catch, col~ lect, earn, gain, get, net, obtain, procure, re~ ceive, secure ~n. 3. Inf. conquest, success, triumph, victory

DICTIONARY

cable wound round a drum. —*v.* lift or haul using a winch.

wind¹ *n.* current of air; hint or suggestion; idle talk; breath; flatulence; scent borne by the air. —*v.* render short of breath; get the scent of. —**windy** *adj.* —**windward** *adj., n.* (of or in) the direction from which the wind is blowing. —**windfall** *n.* unexpected good luck; fallen fruit. —**wind instrument** musical instrument played by blowing. —**windmill** *n.* machine for grinding or pumping driven by sails turned by the wind. —**windpipe** *n.* tube linking the throat and the lungs. —**windscreen** *n.* front window of a motor vehicle. —**windsock** *n.* cloth cone on a mast at an airfield to indicate wind direction. —**windsurfing** *n.* sport of riding on water using a surfboard propelled and steered by a sail.

wind² *v.* **winding, wound.** coil or wrap around; tighten the spring of (a clock or watch); move in a twisting course. —*n.* winding; single turn or bend. —**wind up** *v.* bring to or reach an end; tighten the spring of (a clock or watch); *Informal* make tense or agitated.

windlass *n.* winch worked by a crank.

window *n.* opening in a wall to let in light or air; glass pane or panes fitted in such an opening; display area behind the window of a shop. —**window-dressing** *n.* arrangement of goods in a shop window; attempt to make something more attractive than it really is. —**window-shopping** *n.* looking at goods in shop windows without intending to buy.

wine *n.* alcoholic drink made from fermented grapes; similar drink made from other fruits. —**wine and dine** entertain or be entertained with fine food and drink.

wing *n.* one of the limbs or organs of a bird, insect, or bat that are used for flying; one of the winglike supporting parts of an aircraft; projecting side part of a building; part of a car body surrounding the wheels; *Sport* (player on) either side of the pitch; faction of a political party. —*pl.* sides of a stage. —*v.* go very fast; wound slightly in the wing or arm. —**winged** *adj.* —**winger** *n. Sport* player positioned on a wing.

wink *v.* close and open (an eye) rapidly as a signal; twinkle. —*n.* winking; smallest amount of sleep.

winkle *n.* shellfish with a cone-shaped shell. —**winkle out** *v. Informal* extract or prise out.

winnow *v.* separate (chaff) from (grain); examine to select desirable elements.

winsome *adj.* charming or winning.

winter *n.* coldest season. —*v.* spend the winter. —**wintry** *adj.* of or like winter; cold or unfriendly. —**winter sports** open-air sports held on snow or ice.

wipe *v.* clean or dry by rubbing; erase (a tape). —*n.* wiping. —**wiper** *n.* (also **windscreen wiper**) device that automatically wipes rain etc. from a windscreen. —**wipe out** *v.* destroy completely; *Slang* kill.

wire *n.* thin flexible strand of metal; length of this used to carry electric current; fencing made of wire; telegram. —*v.* provide with wires; send by telegraph. —**wiring** *n.* system of wires. —**wiry** *adj.* like wire; lean and tough. —**wirehaired** *adj.* (of a dog) having a stiff wiry coat.

wireless *n. Old-fashioned* same as RADIO.

THESAURUS

wind¹ *n.* 1. air, blast, breath, breeze, draught, gust, zephyr 2. bluster, empty talk, humbug, talk 3. breath, puff, respiration

wind² *v.* 1. coil, curl, furl, loop, reel, roll, spiral, twine, twist, wreathe 2. bend, curve, deviate, meander, ramble, turn, twist, zigzag ~*n.* 3. bend, curve, meander, turn, twist, zigzag

windfall bonanza, find, godsend

winding 1. *n.* bend, convolution, curve, meander, turn, twist, undulation 2. *adj.* anfractuous, bending, circuitous, convoluted, crooked, curving, flexuous, indirect, meandering, roundabout, serpentine, sinuous, spiral, tortuous, turning, twisting

wind up close, conclude, end, finalize, finish, liquidate, settle, terminate

windy blustery, breezy, gusty, squally, stormy, wild, windswept

wing *n.* 1. arm, branch, circle, clique, coterie, faction, group, section, set, side 2. annexe, extension ~*v.* 3. fleet, fly, hasten, hurry, race, speed, zoom 4. clip, hit, nick, wound

wink *v.* 1. bat, blink, flutter 2. flash, gleam, sparkle, twinkle ~*n.* 3. blink, flutter 4. flash, gleam, glimmering, sparkle, twinkle

winner champion, conqueror, first, master, victor

winning alluring, amiable, bewitching, captivating, charming, delightful, disarming, endearing, engaging, fetching, lovely, pleasing, sweet, taking

winnow comb, divide, fan, part, screen, select, separate, sift

wintry 1. chilly, cold, harsh, icy, snowy 2. bleak, cheerless, cold, desolate, dismal

wipe *v.* 1. brush, clean, dry, dust, mop, rub, sponge, swab 2. erase, remove ~*n.* 3. brush, lick, rub, swab

DICTIONARY

wise[1] *adj.* having wisdom; sensible. —**wisely** *adv.* —**wisdom** *n.* good sense and judgment; accumulated knowledge. —**wisdom tooth** any of the four large molar teeth cut usu. after the age of twenty. —**wiseacre** *n.* person who wishes to seem wise. —**wisecrack** *Informal* —*n.* flippant or sardonic remark. —*v.* make a wisecrack.

wise[2] *n. Obs.* manner.

wish *v.* want or desire; feel or express a hope about someone's wellbeing, success, etc. —*n.* expression of a desire; thing desired. —**wishful** *adj.* too optimistic. —**wishbone** *n.* V-shaped bone above the breastbone of a fowl.

wishy-washy *adj. Informal* insipid or bland.

wisp *n.* light delicate streak; twisted bundle or tuft; anything slender and delicate. —**wispy** *adj.*

wisteria *n.* climbing shrub with blue or purple flowers.

wistful *adj.* sadly longing. —**wistfully** *adv.*

wit *n.* ability to use words or ideas in a clever and amusing way; person with this ability; speech or writing showing wit; (*sometimes pl.*) practical intelligence. —**witty** *adj.* —**wittily** *adv.* —**witticism** *n.* witty remark. —**wittingly** *adv.* intentionally. —**witless** *adj.* foolish.

witch *n.* person, usu. female, who practises (black) magic; ugly wicked woman; fascinating woman. —**witchcraft** *n.* use of magic. —**witch doctor** in certain societies, a man appearing to cure or cause injury or disease by magic. —**witch-hunt** *n.* campaign against people with unpopular views.

with *prep.* by means of; in the company of; possessing; in relation to; in a manner characterized by; because of; understanding or agreeing with. —**within** *prep., adv.* in or inside. —**without** *prep.* not having, accompanied by, or using; *Obs.* outside.

withdraw *v.* -drawing, -drew, -drawn. take or move out or away. —**withdrawal** *n.* —**withdrawn** *adj.* unsociable.

wither *v.* wilt or dry up. —**withering** *adj.* (of a look or remark) scornful.

withers *pl. n.* ridge between a horse's shoulder blades.

withhold *v.* -holding, -held. refrain from giving.

withstand *v.* -standing, -stood. oppose or resist successfully.

witness *n.* person who has seen something happen; evidence or testimony; person giving evidence in court. —*v.* see at first hand; give evidence; sign (a document) to certify that it is genuine.

THESAURUS

wipe out annihilate, destroy, eradicate, erase, massacre, obliterate

wisdom astuteness, discernment, enlightenment, erudition, foresight, insight, intelligence, judgment, knowledge, learning, prudence, reason, sagacity, sapience, sense

wise aware, clever, discerning, enlightened, erudite, informed, intelligent, judicious, knowing, perceptive, politic, prudent, rational, reasonable, sage, sapient, sensible, shrewd, sound, well-advised, well-informed

wisecrack barb, jest, jibe, joke, quip, smart remark, witticism

wish 1. *v.* aspire, covet, crave, desiderate, desire, hanker, hope, hunger, long, need, thirst, want, yearn 2. *n.* aspiration, desire, hankering, hope, hunger, liking, longing, thirst, urge, want, whim, will, yearning

wistful contemplative, dreaming, forlorn, longing, meditative, melancholy, mournful, musing, pensive, reflective, sad, yearning

wit 1. badinage, banter, fun, humour, levity, pleasantry, raillery, repartee 2. comedian, humorist, joker, wag 3. acumen, brains, cleverness, comprehension, discernment, ingenuity, insight, intellect, judgment, mind, perception, reason, sense, understanding, wisdom

witch enchantress, magician, occultist, sorceress

witchcraft enchantment, incantation, magic, sorcery, spell, wizardry

withdraw 1. extract, remove 2. absent oneself, back out, depart, disengage, drop out, go, leave, pull back, pull out, retire, retreat, secede

withdrawal 1. extraction, removal 2. departure, exit, exodus, retirement, retreat, secession

withdrawn aloof, detached, distant, introverted, quiet, reserved, retiring, shy, silent, taciturn

wither blast, blight, decay, decline, disintegrate, droop, dry, fade, languish, perish, shrink, wane, waste, wilt

withering blasting, devastating, hurtful, scornful, snubbing

withhold check, conceal, deduct, hide, hold back, keep, keep back, refuse, repress, reserve, resist, restrain, retain, suppress

witness *n.* 1. beholder, observer, onlooker, spectator, viewer, watcher 2. deponent, testifier ~*v.* 3. attend, be present at, mark, note, notice, observe, perceive, see, view, watch 4. attest, bear out, confirm

wits acumen, astuteness, faculties, ingenuity,

DICTIONARY

wives *n.* plural of WIFE.

wizard *n.* magician; person with outstanding skill in a particular field. —**wizardry** *n.*

wizened [wiz-zend] *adj.* shrivelled or wrinkled.

woad *n.* blue dye obtained from a plant.

wobble *v.* move unsteadily; shake. —*n.* unsteady movement; shake. —**wobbly** *adj.*

wodge *n. Informal* thick lump or chunk.

woe *n.* grief. —**woeful** *adj.* miserable; causing woe; pitiful. —**woefully** *adv.* —**woebegone** *adj.* looking miserable.

wok *n.* bowl-shaped Chinese cooking pan, used esp. for frying.

woke *v.* past tense of WAKE[1]. —**woken** *v.* past participle of WAKE[1].

wold *n.* open downs.

wolf *n., pl.* **wolves.** wild predatory canine mammal. —*v.* eat ravenously. —**cry wolf** raise a false alarm. —**wolf whistle** whistle by a man indicating that he thinks a woman is attractive.

wolfram *n.* tungsten.

wolverine *n.* carnivorous mammal of Arctic regions.

woman *n., pl.* **women.** adult human female; women collectively. —**womanhood** *n.* —**womanish** *adj.* effeminate. —**womanly** *adj.* having qualities traditionally associated with a woman. —**womanize** *v.* (of a man) indulge in casual affairs with women. —**womanizer** *n.* —**Women's Liberation** (also **women's lib**) movement for the removal of social and economic inequalities between women and men.

womb *n.* hollow organ in female mammals where babies are conceived and develop.

wombat *n.* small heavily-built burrowing Aust. marsupial.

won *v.* past of WIN.

wonder *n.* emotion caused by an amazing or unusual thing; wonderful thing. —*v.* be curious about; feel wonder. —*adj.* spectacularly successful, e.g. *a wonder drug.* —**wonderful** *adj.* remarkable; very fine. —**wonderfully** *adv.* —**wonderment** *n.* —**wondrous** *adj. Old-fashioned* wonderful; strange.

wonky *adj.* **-kier, -kiest.** *Informal* shaky or unsteady; not working properly.

won't will not.

wont [rhymes with **don't**] *n.* custom. —*adj.* accustomed.

woo *v.* seek to marry; seek zealously; try to persuade. —**wooer** *n.*

wood *n.* substance trees are made of; timber; firewood; (*also pl.*) area where trees grow. —**wooded** *adj.* covered with trees. —**wooden** *adj.* made of wood; without expression. —**woody** *adj.* —**woodbine** *n.* honeysuckle. —**woodcock** *n.* game bird. —**woodcut** *n.* engraved block of wood; print made from this. —**woodland** *n.* forest. —**woodlouse** *n.* small insect-like creature with many legs. —**woodpecker** *n.* bird which searches tree trunks for insects. —**wood pigeon** large Eurasian pigeon. —**woodwind** *adj., n.* (of) a type of wind instrument made of wood. —**woodworm** *n.* insect larva that bores into wood.

woof *n.* cross threads in weaving.

woofer *n.* loudspeaker for reproducing low-frequency sounds.

wool *n.* soft hair of sheep, goats, etc.; yarn spun from this. —**woollen** *adj.* —**woolly** *adj.* of or like wool; vague or muddled. —*n.* knitted woollen garment. —**woolgathering** *n.* daydreaming. —**Woolsack** *n.* Lord Chancellor's seat in the British House of Lords.

THESAURUS

intelligence, judgement, reason, sense, understanding

witty amusing, brilliant, clever, droll, epigrammatic, facetious, fanciful, funny, gay, humorous, ingenious, jocular, lively, original, piquant, sparkling, waggish, whimsical

wizard 1. conjurer, enchanter, magician, necromancer, sorcerer, witch 2. adept, expert, genius, maestro, master, prodigy, star, virtuoso

wizened dried up, gnarled, lined, shrivelled, shrunken, withered, wrinkled

woe adversity, affliction, agony, anguish, burden, curse, depression, disaster, distress, gloom, grief, hardship, melancholy, misery, pain, sadness, sorrow, suffering, trial, tribulation, trouble, wretchedness

woman female, girl, lady, lass, lassie, maid, maiden, miss, she

wonder *n.* 1. admiration, astonishment, awe, bewilderment, curiosity, fascination, surprise 2. curiosity, marvel, miracle, portent, prodigy, rarity, sight, spectacle ~*v.* 3. ask oneself, conjecture, inquire, meditate, ponder, puzzle, query, question, speculate, think 4. boggle, gape, gawk, marvel, stare

wonderful 1. amazing, astounding, extraordinary, marvellous, miraculous, odd, peculiar, remarkable, staggering, startling, strange, surprising 2. admirable, brilliant, excellent, magnificent, outstanding, sensational, stupendous, superb, terrific, tremendous

woo chase, court, pursue

wooden 1. timber 2. blank, colourless, deadpan, dull, emotionless, lifeless, vacant

wool fleece, hair, yarn

woolly *adj.* 1. fleecy, woollen 2. blurred, cloud-

DICTIONARY

woozy *adj.* **woozier, wooziest.** *Informal* weak, dizzy, and confused.

word *n.* smallest single meaningful unit of speech or writing; chat or discussion; brief remark; message; promise; command. —*v.* express in words. —**wordy** *adj.* using too many words. —**wordiness** *n.* —**wording** *n.* choice and arrangement of words. —**word processor** keyboard, microprocessor, and VDU for electronic organization and storage of text. —**word processing** *n.*

wore *v.* past tense of WEAR.

work *n.* physical or mental effort directed to making or doing something; paid employment; duty or task; something made or done; decoration of a specified kind, e.g. *needlework.* —*pl.* factory; total of a writer's or artist's achievements; *Informal* full treatment; mechanism of a machine. —*v.* (cause to) do work; be employed; (cause to) operate; cultivate (land); manipulate, shape, or process; (cause to) reach a specified condition; accomplish. —*adj.* of or for work. —**work to rule** adhere strictly to all working regulations to reduce the rate of work as a protest. —**work-to-rule** *n.* —**workable** *adj.* —**worker** *n.* —**workaholic** *n.* person addicted to work. —**workhouse** *n. Hist.* institution where the poor were given food and lodgings in return for work. —**working class** social class consisting of wage earners, esp. manual workers. —**working-class** *adj.* —**working party** committee investigating a specific problem. —**workman** *n.* manual worker. —**workmanship** *n.* skill of a workman; skill exhibited in a finished product. —**worktop** *n.* surface in a kitchen, used for food preparation.

world *n.* the planet earth; mankind; society; sphere of existence. —*adj.* of the whole world. —**worldly** *adj.* not spiritual; concerned with material things; wise in the ways of the world.

worm *n.* small limbless invertebrate animal; shaft with a spiral thread forming part of a gear system; *Informal* wretched or spineless person. —*pl.* illness caused by parasitic worms in the intestines. —*v.* crawl; insinuate (oneself); extract (information) craftily; rid of worms. —**wormy** *adj.* —**wormcast** *n.* coil of earth excreted by a burrowing worm. —**worm-eaten** *adj.* eaten into by worms.

wormwood *n.* bitter plant.

worn *v.* past participle of WEAR.

worry *v.* **-rying, -ried.** (cause to) be anxious or

THESAURUS

ed, confused, foggy, fuzzy, hazy, ill-defined, indefinite, indistinct, muddled, nebulous, unclear, vague

word *n.* 1. chat, colloquy, consultation, discussion 2. comment, declaration, expression, remark, utterance 3. expression, name, term 4. account, advice, bulletin, dispatch, information, intelligence, message, news, notice, report, tidings 5. command, order, signal 6. affirmation, assertion, assurance, guarantee, oath, parole, pledge, promise, solemn oath, undertaking, vow 7. bidding, command, commandment, decree, edict, mandate, order ~*v.* 8. couch, express, phrase, put, say, state, utter

wordy diffuse, discursive, garrulous, long-winded, loquacious, prolix, rambling, verbose, windy

work *n.* 1. drudgery, effort, exertion, industry, labour, slog, sweat, toil 2. business, calling, craft, duty, employment, job, line, occupation, office, profession, pursuit, trade 3. assignment, chore, commission, duty, job, stint, task, undertaking 4. achievement, composition, creation, handiwork, opus, performance, piece, production 5. art, craft, skill, workmanship ~*v.* 6. drudge, labour, slave, sweat, toil 7. be employed, have a job 8. act, control, direct, drive, handle, manage, manipulate, move, operate, ply, use, wield 9. function, go, operate, perform, run 10. cultivate, dig, farm, till

worker artisan, craftsman, employee, hand, labourer, tradesman

workman artisan, craftsman, employee, hand, labourer, mechanic, tradesman

works 1. factory, mill, plant, shop 2. canon, output, productions, writings 3. actions, acts, deeds, doings 4. action, machinery, mechanism, movement, parts

world 1. earth, globe 2. everybody, everyone, humanity, man, mankind, men 3. area, domain, environment, field, kingdom, province, realm, sphere, system

worldly 1. carnal, earthly, fleshly, lay, mundane, physical, profane, secular, temporal, terrestrial 2. avaricious, covetous, grasping, greedy, materialistic, selfish 3. blasé, experienced, knowing, politic, sophisticated, urbane

worried afraid, anxious, bothered, concerned, distraught, distressed, fearful, frightened, nervous, overwrought, perturbed, tense, tormented, troubled, uneasy, upset

worry 1. *v.* agonize, annoy, bother, brood, disquiet, distress, disturb, fret, harass, harry, importune, irritate, perturb, pester, plague, tantalize, tease, torment, trouble, unsettle, upset, vex 2. *n.* annoyance, care, irritation, pest, plague, problem, torment, trial, trouble, vexation

DICTIONARY

uneasy; annoy or bother; (of a dog) bite repeatedly. —*n., pl.* **-ries.** (cause of) anxiety or concern. —**worried** *adj.* —**worrying** *adj., n.*

worse *adj., adv.* comparative of BAD or BADLY. —*n.* worse thing. —**worst** *adj., adv.* superlative of BAD or BADLY. —*n.* worst thing. —**worsen** *v.* make or grow worse.

worship *v.* **-shipping, -shipped.** show religious devotion to; love and admire. —*n.* worshipping; (**W-**) title for a mayor or magistrate. —**worshipper** *n.* —**worshipful** *adj.* worshipping; (in titles) honourable.

worsted [wooss-tid] *n.* type of woollen yarn or fabric. —*adj.* made of worsted.

wort [wurt] *n.* infusion of malt used to make beer.

worth *adj.* meriting or justifying; having a value of. —*n.* excellence; value or price; amount to be had for a given sum. —**worthless** *adj.* —**worthy** *adj.* deserving; having value or merit. —*n. Informal* notable person. —**worthily** *adv.* —**worthiness** *n.* —**worthwhile** *adj.* worth the time or effort involved.

would *v.* used as an auxiliary to form the past tense or subjunctive mood of WILL[1], express a request, or describe a habitual past action. —**would-be** *adj.* wishing or pretending to be.

wouldn't would not.

wound[1] *n.* injury caused by violence; injury to the feelings. —*v.* inflict a wound on.

wound[2] *v.* past of WIND[2].

wove *v.* a past tense of WEAVE. —**woven** *v.* a past participle of WEAVE.

wow *interj.* exclamation of astonishment. —*n. Informal* astonishing person or thing.

wpm words per minute.

wrack *n.* seaweed.

wraith *n.* apparition of a person seen shortly before his or her death; ghost.

wrangle *v.* argue noisily. —*n.* noisy argument.

wrap *v.* **wrapping, wrapped.** fold (something) round (a person or thing) so as to cover. —*n.* garment wrapped round the shoulders. —**wrapper** *n.* cover; loose dressing gown. —**wrapping** *n.* material used to wrap. —**wrap up** *v.* fold paper round; put warm clothes on; *Informal* finish or settle (a matter).

wrasse *n.* colourful sea fish.

wrath [roth] *n.* intense anger. —**wrathful** *adj.*

wreak *v.* inflict (vengeance); cause (chaos).

wreath *n.* twisted ring or band of flowers or leaves used as a memorial or tribute. —**wreathe** *v.* form into a wreath; encircle; twist round.

wreck *n.* accidental destruction of a ship at sea; wrecked ship; remains of something destroyed; person in very poor condition. —*v.* cause the wreck of. —**wrecker** *n.* —**wreckage** *n.* wrecked remains.

THESAURUS

worsen aggravate, decline, degenerate, deteriorate, exacerbate, get worse, go downhill (*Inf.*), go from bad to worse, sink

worship 1. *v.* adore, adulate, deify, exalt, glorify, honour, laud, love, praise, respect, revere, venerate 2. *n.* adoration, devotion, exaltation, glorification, glory, homage, honour, love, praise, regard, respect, reverence

worth 1. aid, assistance, avail, benefit, credit, estimation, excellence, goodness, help, importance, merit, quality, usefulness, value, virtue 2. cost, price, rate, value

worthless 1. futile, ineffectual, insignificant, meaningless, paltry, pointless, poor, rubbishy, trashy, trifling, trivial, unavailing, unimportant, unusable, useless 2. abandoned, base, depraved, despicable, ignoble, useless, vile

worthwhile beneficial, constructive, gainful, good, helpful, productive, profitable, useful, valuable

worthy 1. *adj.* admirable, commendable, creditable, decent, deserving, estimable, excellent, good, honest, laudable, meritorious, reliable, reputable, respectable, righteous, upright, valuable 2. *n.* dignitary, luminary, notable

wound *n.* 1. cut, gash, harm, hurt, injury, lesion, slash 2. anguish, distress, grief, heartbreak, injury, insult, offence, pain, pang, shock, slight, torment, torture ~*v.* 3. cut, damage, gash, harm, hit, hurt, injure, irritate, lacerate, pierce, slash, wing 4. annoy, distress, grieve, hurt, offend, pain, shock, sting

wrangle 1. *v.* argue, bicker, brawl, contend, disagree, dispute, quarrel, row, scrap 2. *n.* brawl, clash, contest, dispute, quarrel, row, squabble, tiff

wrap *v.* absorb, bind, cloak, cover, encase, enclose, enfold, envelop, fold, muffle, pack, package, sheathe, shroud, surround, swathe, wind

wrapper case, cover, envelope, jacket, paper, sheath, sleeve

wrath anger, displeasure, fury, indignation, ire, passion, rage, temper

wreath band, chaplet, coronet, crown, festoon, garland, loop, ring

wreathe adorn, coil, crown, enfold, entwine, festoon, intertwine, surround, twine, twist, wind, wrap

wreck *v.* 1. break, demolish, destroy, devastate,

DICTIONARY

wren *n.* small brown songbird.

Wren *n. Informal* member of the Women's Royal Naval Service.

wrench *v.* twist or pull forcefully; sprain. —*n.* forceful twist or pull; sprain; difficult or painful parting; adjustable spanner.

wrest *v.* take by force; twist violently.

wrestle *v.* fight, esp. as a sport, by grappling with and trying to throw down an opponent; struggle hard with. —**wrestler** *n.* —**wrestling** *n.*

wretch *n.* despicable person; pitiful person. —**wretched** [retch-id] *adj.* miserable or unhappy; worthless. —**wretchedly** *adv.* —**wretchedness** *n.*

wrier *adj.* a comparative of WRY. —**wriest** *adj.* a superlative of WRY.

wriggle *v.* move with a twisting action; manoeuvre oneself by devious means. —*n.* wriggling movement.

wright *n.* maker, e.g. *playwright.*

wring *v.* wringing, wrung. twist, esp. to squeeze liquid out of; clasp and twist (the hands); obtain by forceful means.

wrinkle *n.* slight crease, esp. one in the skin due to age. —*v.* make or become wrinkled. —**wrinkly** *adj.*

wrist *n.* joint between the hand and the arm. —**wristwatch** *n.* watch worn on the wrist.

writ *n.* written legal command.

write *v.* writing, wrote, written. mark paper etc. with symbols or words; set down in words; communicate by letter; be the author or composer of. —**writing** *n.* —**writer** *n.* author; person who has written something specified. —**write-off** *n. Informal* something damaged beyond repair. —**write-up** *n.* published account of something.

writhe *v.* twist or squirm in or as if in pain; be very embarrassed.

wrong *adj.* incorrect or mistaken; immoral or bad; not intended or suitable; not working properly. —*n.* something immoral or unjust. —*v.* treat unjustly; malign. —**wrongly** *adv.* —**wrongful** *adj.* —**wrongfully** *adv.* —**wrongdoer** *n.* person who acts immorally or illegally.

wrote *v.* past tense of WRITE.

THESAURUS

mar, ravage, ruin, shatter, smash, spoil 2. founder, shipwreck, strand ~*n.* 3. derelict, hulk

wreckage debris, fragments, hulk, pieces, remains, rubble, ruin, wrack

wrench *v.* 1. force, jerk, pull, rip, tear, tug, twist, wrest, wring, yank 2. distort, rick, sprain, strain ~*n.* 3. jerk, pull, rip, tug, twist, yank 4. sprain, strain, twist 5. ache, blow, pain, pang, shock, upheaval

wrestle battle, combat, contend, fight, grapple, strive, struggle

wretch 1. outcast, profligate, rascal, rogue, ruffian, scoundrel, vagabond, villain 2. poor thing, unfortunate

wretched 1. abject, cheerless, comfortless, dejected, deplorable, depressed, distressed, downcast, forlorn, gloomy, hapless, hopeless, miserable, pitiful, poor, sorry, unhappy, woebegone, woeful 2. calamitous, deplorable, inferior, miserable, paltry, pathetic, poor, sorry

wriggle *v.* 1. squirm, turn, twist, wag, writhe 2. crawl, slink, snake, worm, zigzag 3. crawl, dodge, sneak, worm ~*n.* 4. jerk, squirm, turn, twist, wag

wring coerce, extort, extract, force, screw, squeeze, twist, wrench, wrest

wrinkle 1. *n.* crease, crow's-foot, crumple, fold, furrow, gather, line, pucker, rumple 2. *v.* crease, crumple, fold, furrow, gather, line, ruck

writ decree, document, summons

write compose, copy, create, draft, inscribe, pen, record, scribble, tell, transcribe

writer author, columnist, essayist, hack, novelist, penman, scribbler, scribe

writhe contort, distort, jerk, squirm, struggle, thrash, thresh, toss, twist, wiggle, wriggle

writing 1. calligraphy, hand, handwriting, print, scrawl, scribble, script 2. book, composition, document, letter, opus, publication, work

wrong *adj.* 1. erroneous, fallacious, false, faulty, inaccurate, incorrect, mistaken, out, unsound, untrue 2. bad, criminal, crooked, dishonest, evil, illegal, illicit, immoral, sinful, unfair, unjust, unlawful, wicked, wrongful 3. funny, improper, inapt, incorrect, not done, unacceptable, undesirable, unfitting, unhappy, unseemly, unsuitable 4. amiss, askew, awry, defective, faulty ~*n.* 5. abuse, crime, error, grievance, infraction, infringement, injury, injustice, misdeed, offence, sin, sinfulness, transgression, trespass, wickedness ~*v.* 6. abuse, cheat, discredit, harm, hurt, ill-use, injure, malign, maltreat, mistreat, oppress

wrongdoer criminal, culprit, evildoer, lawbreaker, miscreant, offender, sinner, transgressor

wrongful blameworthy, criminal, dishonest, dishonourable, evil, felonious, illegal, illegitimate, illicit, immoral, improper, reprehensible, unethical, unfair, unjust, unlawful, wicked

DICTIONARY

wrought [rawt] *v. Lit.* past of WORK. —*adj.* (of metals) shaped by hammering or beating. —**wrought iron** pure form of iron used for decorative work.

wrung *v.* past of WRING.

wry *adj.* **wrier, wriest** *or* **wryer, wryest.** dryly humorous; (of a facial expression) contorted. —**wryly** *adv.*

wt. weight.

wych-elm *n.* elm with large rough leaves.

wynd *n. Scot.* narrow lane or alley.

THESAURUS

wry 1. askew, aslant, crooked, deformed, distorted, twisted, uneven, warped 2. droll, dry, ironic, mocking, sardonic

X

X indicating an error, a choice, or a kiss; indicating an unknown, unspecified, or variable factor, number, person, or thing; Roman numeral for ten.

Xe *Chem.* xenon.

xenon *n.* colourless odourless gas found in very small quantities in the air.

xenophobia [zen-oh-**fobe**-ee-a] *n.* fear or hatred of people from other countries.

Xerox [**zeer**-ox] *n.* ® machine for copying printed material; ® copy made by a Xerox machine. —*v.* copy (a document) using such a machine.

Xmas [**eks**-mass] *n.* Christmas.

x-ray *n.* stream of radiation that can pass through some solid materials; picture made by sending x-rays through someone's body to examine internal organs. —*v.* photograph, treat, or examine using x-rays.

xylem [**zy**-lem] *n.* plant tissue that conducts water and minerals from the roots to all other parts.

xylophone [**zile**-oh-fone] *n.* musical instrument made of a row of wooden bars played with hammers.

Y

yacht [yott] *n.* large boat with sails or an engine used for racing or pleasure cruising. —**yachting** *n.* —**yachtsman, yachtswoman** *n.*

yak[1] *n.* Tibetan ox with long shaggy hair.

yak[2] *v.* **yakking, yakked.** *Slang* talk continuously about unimportant matters.

yam *n.* sweet potato.

yank *v.* pull or jerk suddenly. —*n.* sudden pull or jerk.

Yank(ee) *adj., n. Slang* (of) a person from the United States.

yap *v.* **yapping, yapped.** bark with a high-pitched sound; *Informal* talk continuously. —*n.* high-pitched bark.

yard[1] *n.* unit of length equal to 36 inches or about 91.4 centimetres. —**yardstick** *n.* standard against which to judge other people or things.

yard[2] *n.* enclosed area, usu. next to a building and often used for a particular purpose, e.g. *builder's yard.*

yarmulke [yar-mull-ka] *n.* skullcap worn by Jewish men.

yarn *n.* thread used for knitting or making cloth; *Informal* long involved story. —**spin a yarn** *Informal* tell a long involved story.

yarrow *n.* wild plant with flat clusters of white flowers.

yashmak *n.* veil worn by a Muslim woman to cover her face in public.

yaw *v.* (of an aircraft or ship) turn to one side or from side to side while moving.

yawl *n.* two-masted sailing boat.

yawn *v.* open the mouth wide and take in air deeply, often when sleepy or bored; (of an opening) be large and wide. —*n.* act of yawning. —**yawning** *adj.*

yaws *n.* infectious tropical skin disease.

yd. yard.

ye [yee] *pron. Obs.* you.

year *n.* time taken for the earth to make one revolution around the sun, about 365 days; twelve months from January 1 to December 31. —**yearly** *adj., adv.* (happening) every year or once a year. —**yearling** *n.* animal between one and two years old.

yearn *v.* (foll. by *for*) want (something) very much. —**yearning** *n., adj.*

yeast *n.* fungus used to make bread rise and to ferment alcoholic drinks. —**yeasty** *adj.*

yell *v.* shout or scream in a loud or piercing way. —*n.* loud cry of pain, anger, or fear.

yellow *n.* the colour of gold, a lemon, etc. —*adj.* of this colour; *Informal* cowardly. —*v.* make or become yellow. —**yellow fever** serious infectious tropical disease. —**yellowhammer** *n.* European songbird with a yellow head and body. —**Yellow Pages** *pl. n.* ® telephone directory which lists businesses under the headings of the type of business or service they provide.

yelp *v., n.* (give) a short, sudden cry.

yen[1] *n., pl.* **yen.** main unit of currency in Japan.

yen[2] *n. Informal* longing or desire.

yeoman [yo-man] *n., pl.* **-men.** *Hist.* farmer owning and farming his own land. —**yeoman of the guard** member of the ceremonial bodyguard of the British monarchy.

yes *interj.* expresses consent, agreement, or approval; used to answer when one is addressed. —**yes man** person who always agrees with his or her superior.

yesterday *adv., n.* (on) the day before today; (in) the recent past.

yet *adv.* up until then or now; still. —*conj.* nevertheless, still.

yeti *n.* same as ABOMINABLE SNOWMAN.

yew *n.* evergreen tree with needle-like leaves and red berries.

Yiddish *adj., n.* (of or in) a language of German

THESAURUS

yank *v./n.* hitch, jerk, pull, snatch, tug, wrench

yardstick criterion, gauge, measure, standard

yarn *n.* 1. fibre, thread 2. *Inf.* anecdote, cock-and-bull story (*Inf.*), fable, story, tale, tall story

yawning cavernous, chasmal, gaping, vast, wide, wide-open

yearly annual, annually, every year, once a year, per annum

yearn ache, covet, crave, desire, hanker, have a

yen for (*Inf.*), hunger, itch, languish, long, lust, pant, pine

yell 1. *v.* bawl, holler (*Inf.*), howl, scream, shout, shriek, squeal 2. *n.* cry, howl, scream, screech, shriek

yes man bootlicker (*Inf.*), bosses' lackey, company man, crawler (*Sl.*), creature, minion, sycophant, timeserver, toady

yet 1. so far, thus far 2. however, still

DICTIONARY

origin spoken by many Jews in Europe and elsewhere.

yield *v.* produce or bear; give up control of, surrender; give in. —*n.* amount produced. —**yielding** *adj.* submissive; soft or flexible.

YMCA Young Men's Christian Association.

yob(bo) *n. Slang* bad-mannered aggressive youth.

yodel *v.* **-delling, -delled.** sing with abrupt changes between a normal and a falsetto voice. —*n.* act or sound of yodelling.

yoga *n.* Hindu method of exercise and discipline aiming at spiritual, mental, and physical well-being. —**yogi** *n.* person who practises yoga.

yoghurt, yogurt, *or* **yoghourt** *n.* slightly sour custard-like food made from milk that has had bacteria added to it, often sweetened and flavoured with fruit.

yoke *n.* wooden bar put across the necks of two animals to hold them together; frame fitting over a person's shoulders for carrying buckets; *Lit.* oppressive force, e.g. *the yoke of the tyrant;* fitted part of a garment to which a fuller part is attached. —*v.* put a yoke on; unite or link.

yokel *n. Offens.* person who lives in the country and is usu. simple and old-fashioned.

yolk *n.* yellow part of an egg that provides food for the developing embryo.

Yom Kippur *n.* annual Jewish religious holiday.

yonder *adv.* over there.

yonks *pl. n. Informal* very long time.

yore *n. Lit.* the distant past.

Yorkshire pudding *n.* baked batter made from flour, milk, and eggs and often eaten with roast beef.

you *pron.* refers to: the person or people addressed; an unspecified person or people in general.

young *adj.* in an early stage of life or growth. —*n.* offspring, esp. young animals; young people in general. —**youngster** *n.* young person.

your *det.* of, belonging to, or associated with you; of, belonging to, or associated with an unspecified person or people in general. —**yours** *pron.* something belonging to you. —**yourself** *pron.*

youth *n.* time of being young; boy or young man; young people as a group. —**youthful** *adj.* —**youthfulness** *n.* —**youth Club** club that provides leisure activities for young people. —**youth hostel** inexpensive lodging place for young people travelling cheaply.

yowl *v., n.* (produce) a loud mournful cry.

yo-yo *n., pl.* **-yos.** toy consisting of a spool attached to a string, by which it is repeatedly spun out and reeled in.

YTS Youth Training Scheme.

yucca *n.* tropical plant with spikes of white leaves.

yucky, Yukky *adj.* **yuckier, yuckiest** *or* **yukkier, yukkiest.** *Slang.* disgusting, nasty.

Yule *n. Lit.* Christmas or the Christmas season.

Yuppie *n.* young highly-paid professional person, esp. one who has a fashionable way of life. —*adj.* typical of or reflecting the values of Yuppies.

YWCA Young Women's Christian Association.

THESAURUS

yield *v.* 1. afford, bear, earn, furnish, generate, give, net, pay, produce, provide, return, supply ~*n.* 2. crop, earnings, harvest, output, produce, profit, return, takings ~*v.* 3. bow, capitulate, cede, give way, part with, relinquish, resign, submit, succumb, surrender 4. accede, agree, allow, bow, comply, concede, consent, grant, permit

yielding 1. accommodating, acquiescent, biddable, compliant, docile, easy, flexible, obedient, pliant, submissive, tractable 2. elastic, pliable, quaggy, resilient, soft, spongy, springy, supple, unresisting

yoke *n.* 1. bond, chain, coupling, link, tie 2. bondage, burden, enslavement, oppression, service, servitude, slavery, thraldom ~*v.* 3. bracket, connect, couple, harness, hitch, join, link, tie, unite

yokel boor, countryman, peasant, rustic

young *adj.* adolescent, green, growing, immature, infant, junior, little, youthful

youngster boy, cub, girl, juvenile, lad, lass, teenager, urchin

youth 1. boyhood, girlhood, immaturity 2. adolescent, boy, kid (*Inf.*), lad, stripling, teenager, youngster

youthful 1. boyish, childish, immature, juvenile, puerile, young 2. active, fresh, spry, vigorous

Z

zany [zane-ee] *adj.* **zanier, zaniest.** comical in an endearing way.

zap *v.* **zapping, zapped.** *Slang* kill (by shooting); change television channels rapidly by remote control; move quickly.

zeal *n.* great enthusiasm or eagerness. **—zealot** [zel-lot] *n.* fanatic or extreme enthusiast. **—zealous** [zel-luss] *adj.* extremely eager or enthusiastic. **—zealously** *adv.*

zebra *n.* black-and-white striped African animal of the horse family. **—zebra crossing** pedestrian crossing marked by black and white stripes on the road.

zebu [zee-boo] *n.* Asian ox with a humped back and long horns.

Zen *n.* Japanese form of Buddhism that concentrates on learning through meditation and intuition.

zenith *n.* highest point of success or power; point in the sky directly above an observer.

zephyr [zef-fer] *n.* soft gentle breeze.

zeppelin *n. Hist.* large cylindrical airship.

zero *n., pl.* **-ros, -roes.** (symbol representing) the number 0; point on a scale of measurement from which the graduations commence; lowest point; nothing, nil. **—adj.** having no measurable quantity or size. **—zero in on** *v.* aim at; *Informal* concentrate on.

zest *n.* enjoyment or excitement; interest, flavour, or charm; peel of an orange or lemon.

zigzag *n.* line or course having sharp turns in alternating directions. **—v. -zagging, -zagged.** move in a zigzag. **—adj.** formed in or proceeding in a zigzag. **—adv.** in a zigzag manner.

zinc *n.* bluish-white metallic element used in alloys and to coat metal.

zing *n. Informal* quality in something that makes it lively or interesting.

zinnia *n.* garden plant with solitary heads of brightly coloured flowers.

Zionism *n.* movement to found and support a Jewish homeland in Israel. **—Zionist** *n., adj.*

zip *n.* fastener with two rows of teeth that are closed or opened by a small clip pulled between them; short whizzing sound; *Informal* energy, vigour. **—v. zipping, zipped.** fasten with a zip; move with a sharp whizzing sound.

zircon *n.* mineral used as a gemstone and in industry.

zither *n.* musical instrument consisting of strings stretched over a flat box and plucked to produce musical notes.

Zn *Chem.* zinc.

zodiac *n.* imaginary belt in the sky within which the sun, moon, and planets appear to move, divided into twelve equal areas, called signs of the zodiac, each named after a constellation.

zombi(e) *n.* person who appears to be lifeless, apathetic, or totally lacking in independent judgment; corpse brought back to life by witchcraft.

zone *n.* area with particular features or properties; one of the divisions of the earth's surface according to temperature. **—v.** divide into zones. **—zonal** *adj.*

zoo *n., pl.* **zoos.** place where live animals are kept for show.

zoology *n.* study of animals. **—zoologist** *n.* **—zoological** *adj.* **—zoological garden** zoo.

zoom *v.* move or rise very rapidly; make or move with a buzzing or humming sound. **—zoom lens** lens that can make the details of a picture larger or smaller while keeping the picture in focus.

Zulu *n.* member of a tall Black people of southern Africa; language of this people.

THESAURUS

zeal ardour, devotion, enthusiasm, fervency, fervour, fire, gusto, keenness, militancy, passion, spirit, verve, warmth, zest

zealot bigot, enthusiast, extremist, fanatic, maniac, militant

zealous afire, ardent, burning, devoted, eager, earnest, enthusiastic, fanatical, fervent, fervid, impassioned, keen, militant, passionate, rabid, spirited

zenith apex, climax, height, high point, meridian, peak, pinnacle, summit, top, vertex

zero naught, nil, nothing, nought

zest 1. appetite, delectation, enjoyment, gusto, keenness, relish, zeal, zing (*Inf.*) 2. charm, flavour, interest, kick (*Inf.*), piquancy, pungency, relish, savour, smack, spice, tang, taste

zip 1. *n. Fig.* brio, drive, energy, get-up-and-go (*Inf.*), go (*Inf.*), gusto, life, liveliness, oomph (*Inf.*), pep, pizazz (*Sl.*), punch (*Inf.*), sparkle, spirit, verve, vigour, vim (*Sl.*), vitality, zest, zing (*Inf.*) 2. *v.* dash, flash, fly, hurry, rush, shoot, speed, tear, whiz (*Inf.*), zoom

zone area, belt, district, region, section, sector, sphere

SUPPLEMENTS

CLASSICAL AND FOREIGN WORDS AND PHRASES

Abbreviations - L. Latin; G. Greek; F. French; It. Italian; Ger. German.

à bas [F.] down with.

ab initio [L.] from the beginning.

ab ovo [L.] from the beginning.

absit omen [L.] may there be no ill omen.

accouchement [F.] childbirth, confinement.

à cheval [F.] on horseback, astride.

à deux [F.] of, for two persons.

ad hoc [L.] for this special object.

ad hominem [L.] to the man.

ad infinitum [L.] to infinity.

ad interim [L.] in the meanwhile.

ad majorem Dei gloriam [L.] for the greater glory of God.

ad nauseam [L.] to the point of disgust.

ad referendum [L.] for consideration.

ad rem [L.] to the point.

adsum [L.] I am here; present!

ad valorem [L.] according to value.

affaire d'amour [F.] a love affair.

affaire d'honneur [F.] an affair of honour, a duel.

affaire du coeur [F.] an affair of the heart.

a fortiori [L.] with stronger reason.

agent provocateur [F.] a police or secret service spy.

aide mémoire [F.] memorandum; summary.

à la carte [F.] picking from the bill of fare; *see* **table d'hote**.

à la française [F.] in the French style.

à la mode [F.] in the fashion.

al dente [It.] cooked so as to be firm when eaten.

al fresco [It.] in the open air.

alma mater [L.] benign mother; the term is used by former students in referring to their university.

alter ego [L.] another self, a close friend.

alto relievo [It.] high relief.

amende honorable [F.] apology.

amor patriae [L.] love of country.

amour propre [F.] self-esteem.

ancien régime [F.] the old order.

anglice [L.] in English.

anno Domini [L.] in the year of our Lord.

anno regni [L.] in the year of the reign.

anno urbis conditae [L.] (**A.U.C.**) in the year from the time of the building of the City (Rome).

annus mirabilis [L.] year of wonder.

ante meridiem [L.] before noon.

aperçu [F.] summary; insight.

à propos [F.] to the point.

arrière-pensée [F.] mental reservation.

arrivederci [It.] goodbye.

au contraire [F.] on the contrary.

au courant [F.] fully acquainted (with).

au fait [F.] fully informed; expert.

au fond [F.] fundamentally; essentially.

au naturel [F.] naked; uncooked or plainly cooked.

au revoir [F.] good-bye, till we meet again.

auf wiedersehen [Ger.] good-bye, till we meet again.

auto da fé [Portuguese] act of faith, the public burning of heretics.

beau geste [F.] noble or gracious act.

beau idéal [F.] ideal excellence, imagined state of perfection.

beau monde [F.] fashionable world.

bel esprit [F.] a man of wit.

bête noire [F.] an object of special detestation, pet aversion.

billet doux [F.] a love-letter.

blitzkrieg [Ger.] lightning war.

CLASSICAL AND FOREIGN WORDS AND PHRASES

bona fide [L.] in good faith.
bonhomie [F.] good nature.
bonjour [F.] good-morning, good-day.
bon marché [F.] cheaply.
bonne bouche [F.] titbit.
bonsoir [F.] good-evening, good-night.
bon ton [F.] good breeding.

carpe diem [L.] enjoy the present day.
carte blanche [F.] full powers.
casus belli [L.] something which involves war.
cause célèbre [F.] famous lawsuit or controversy.
ça va sans dire [F.] that is a matter of course.
caveat emptor [L.] let the buyer beware.
cave canem [L.] beware of the dog.
c'est la vie [F.] that's life.
chacun à son gout [F.] every one to his taste.
ceteris paribus [L.] other things being equal.
chef-d'oeuvre [F.] masterpiece.
cherchez la femme [F.] look for the woman; there is a woman at the bottom of the business.
che sarà, sarà [It.] what will be, will be.
ciao [It.] hello, goodbye.
ci-devant [F.] former.
cogito, ergo sum [L.] I think, therefore I am.
comme il faut [F.] as it should be.
compos mentis [L.] sane.
compte rendu [F.] a report.
con amore [It.] with love, earnestly.
concierge [F.] a porter or doorkeeper.
coram populo [L.] in the presence of the people, openly.

corpus delicti [L.] the substance of the offence; the body of the victim of murder.
corrigenda [L.] things to be corrected.
coup d'état [F.] a stroke of policy, a sudden decisive political move, an abuse of authority.
coup de foudre [F.] sudden amazing event.
coup de grâce [F.] a finishing blow.
coup de théâtre [F.] a theatrical effect, a sudden change in a situation.
cui bono? [L.] for whose benefit is it? (i.e. the crime - in a law-case).
cum grano salis [L.] with a grain of salt, with reservation.

de facto [L.] actually, in fact.
Dei gratia [L.] by the grace of God.
de jure [L.] in law, by right.
de mortuis nil nisi bonum [L.] say nothing but good about the dead.
de novo [L.] anew.
Deo gratias [L.] thanks to God.
Deo volente [L.] (**D.V.**) God willing.
de profundis [L.] out of the depths. (The first words of the Latin version of Psalm 130.)
de rigueur [F.] indispensable, obligatory.
dernier cri [F.] latest fashion.
de trop [F.] superfluous, intrusive.
deus ex machina [L.] literally, a god out of the (theatrical) machine, i.e. a too obvious device in the plot of a play or story.
dies non [L.] a day on which judges do not sit.
Dieu et mon droit [F.] God and my right; motto of the British crown.
disjecta membra [L.] the scattered remains.

CLASSICAL AND FOREIGN WORDS AND PHRASES

distingué [F.] of distinguished appearance.

distrait [F.] absent-minded.

dolce far niente [It.] pleasant idleness.

double entendre [F.] double meaning.

douceur [F.] a tip, a bribe.

dramatis personae [L.] the characters in a drama.

ecce homo! [L.] behold the man! (Spoken by Pilate; St. John, c.19, v.5.)

embarras de richesses [F.] perplexing wealth.

emeritus [L.] retired from office.

éminence grise [F.] person who wields power unofficially or behind the scenes.

en famille [F.] with one's family; at home; informally.

enfant terrible [F.] literally, "a terrible child."

en fête [F.] on holiday, in a state of festivity.

en masse [F.] in a body.

en passant [F.] in passing, by the way.

en rapport [F.] in sympathy with.

en règle [F.] in due order.

en route [F.] on the way; march!

entente cordiale [F.] friendly understanding between two nations.

entre nous [F.] between ourselves.

e pluribus unum [L.] one out of many. (Motto of the U.S.A.)

erratum (*pl.* **errata**) [L.] error.

esprit de corps [F.] team-spirit.

eureka! (**heureka**) [G.] I have found it! (The exclamation of Archimedes.)

ex cathedra [L.] from the chair of office, hence, authoritatively.

exeat [L.] literally, "let him go out"; formal leave of absence.

exempli gratia [L.] (**e.g.**) for example.

exeunt omnes [L.] all go out.

exit [L.] goes out.

ex libris [L.] from the books ... (followed by the name of the owner).

ex officio [L.] by virtue of his office.

ex parte [L.] on one side, partisan.

facile princeps [L.] an easy first.

fait accompli [F.] a thing done.

faute de mieux [F.] for lack of anything better.

faux pas [F.] a false step, a mistake.

felo de se [L.] a suicide, literally, a "felon of himself."

femme fatale [F.] seductive woman.

festina lente [L.] hasten slowly.

fête champêtre [F.] a rural festival.

feu de joie [F.] a bonfire; gun salute.

fiat lux [L.] let there be light.

fidei defensor [L.] defender of the faith.

fille de joie [F.] prostitute.

fin de siècle [F.] end of the 19th century; decadent.

finis [L.] the end.

flagrante delicto [L.] in the very act, red-handed.

folie de grandeur [F.] delusions of grandeur.

fons et origo [L.] the source and origin.

gaudeamus igitur [L.] let us then rejoice.

gendarme [F.] one of the *gendarmerie*, a body of armed police in France.

haute couture [F.] high fashion.

haute cuisine [F.] high-class cooking.

hic jacet [L.] here lies.

CLASSICAL AND FOREIGN WORDS AND PHRASES

honi soit qui mal y pense [Old F.] shame to him who thinks ill of it.

horribile dictu [L.] horrible to relate.

hors de combat [F.] out of condition to fight.

ibidem (abbreviated as **ib;** or **ibid;**) [L.] in the same place.

ich dien [Ger.] I serve.

idée fixe [F.] an obsession, monomania.

id est [L.] (usually **i.e.**) that is.

idem [L.] the same.

ignis fatuus [L.] a will-o'-the-wisp.

imprimatur [L.] literally, "let it be printed", a licence to print, sanction.

in camera [L.] in a (judge's private) room.

in extremis [L.] at the point of death.

infra dignitatem [L.] (**infra dig.**) below one's dignity.

in loco parentis [L.] in the place of a parent.

in medias res [L.] into the midst of things.

in memoriam [L.] to the memory of.

in perpetuum [L.] for ever.

in re [L.] in the matter of.

in situ [L.] in its original position.

in statu quo [L.] in the former state.

inter alia [L.] among other things.

in toto [L.] entirely.

in vino veritas [L.] in wine the truth (comes out).

ipse dixit [L.] "he himself said it"; his unsupported word.

ipsissima verba [L.] the very words.

ipso facto [L.] by the fact itself.

je ne sais quoi [F.] "I don't know what", a something or other.

jeu d'esprit [F.] a witticism.

joie de vivre [F.] joy of living; ebullience.

laissez faire [F.] policy of inaction.

lapsus linguae [L.] a slip of the tongue.

lares et penates [L.] household gods.

leitmotif [Ger.] a theme used to indicate a person, idea, etc. in opera, etc.

lèse-majesté [F.] high treason.

l'état, c'est moi [F.] I am the state. (Saying of Louis XIV.)

lettre de cachet [F.] a sealed letter; a royal warrant for imprisonment.

locum tenens [L.] "one occupying the place", a deputy or substitute.

magnum opus [L.] a great work.

mal à propos [F.] ill-timed.

mal de mer [F.] sea-sickness.

malentendu [F.] a misunderstanding.

manqué [F.] potential; would-be.

mariage de convenance [F.] a marriage from motives of interest rather than love.

mauvaise honte [F.] false modesty, bashfulness.

mauvais quart d'heure [F.] a brief unpleasant experience.

mea culpa [L.] by my fault.

memento mori [L.] remember death.

ménage à trois [F.] sexual arrangement involving a married couple and the lover of one of them.

mens sana in corpore sano [L.] a sound mind in a sound body.

mésalliance [F.] marriage with someone of lower social status.

meum et tuum [L.] mine and thine.

mirabile dictu [L.] wonderful to relate.

mise en scène [F.] scenic setting.

modus operandi [L.] manner of working.

mot juste [F.] the exact right word.

moue [F.] a disdainful or pouting look.

multum in parvo [L.] much in little.

mutatis mutandis [L.] with the necessary changes.

née [F.] "born", her maiden name being; e.g. *Mrs. Brown née Smith.*

nemine contradicente [L.] (often as **nem.con.**) without opposition.

nemo me impune lacessit [L.] no one hurts me with impunity.

ne plus ultra [L.] nothing further; the uttermost point.

nihil obstat [L.] there is no obstacle.

nil desperandum [L.] despair of nothing.

noblesse oblige [F.] nobility imposes obligations.

nolens volens [L.] whether he will or not.

noli me tangere [L.] don't touch me.

nom de guerre [F.] an assumed name. (**nom de plume** is hardly used in French.)

non compos mentis [L.] insane.

non sequitur [L.] it does not follow.

nota bene [L.] (**N.B.**) note well.

nous avons changé tout cela [F.] we have changed all that.

nouveau riche [F.] one newly enriched, an upstart.

nulli secundus [L.] second to none.

obiit [L.] he (or she) died.

obiter dictum [L.] (*pl.* **obiter dicta**) something said by the way.

on dit [F.] they say; a rumour.

ora pro nobis [L.] pray for us.

O tempora! O mores! [L.] literally, "O the times! O the manners!"; what dreadful times and doings.

pace [L.] by leave of.

par avion [F.] by aeroplane (of mail sent by air).

par excellence [F.] pre-eminently.

pari passu [L.] with equal pace; together.

passim [L.] here and there, everywhere.

pax vobiscum [L.] peace be with you.

peccavi [L.] I have sinned.

per ardua ad astra [L.] through difficulties to the stars.

persona non grata [L.] unacceptable or unwelcome person.

post hoc, ergo propter hoc [L.] after this, therefore because of this (a fallacy in reasoning.)

pour encourager les autres [F.] in order to encourage the others.

prima facie [L.] at a first view.

primus inter pares [L.] first among equals.

pro patria [L.] for one's country.

pro tempore [L.] for the time being.

quis custodiet ipsos custodes? [L.] who will guard the guards?

qui vive? [F.] who goes there?

quod erat demonstrandum [L.] (**Q.E.D.**) which was to be proved.

quot homines, tot sententiae [L.] as many men as there are opinions.

quo vadis? [L.] whither goest thou?

rara avis [L.] a rare bird, something prodigious.

reductio ad absurdum [L.] a reducing to the absurd.

répondez s'il vous plait [F.] (**R.S.V.P.**) please reply.

requiescat in pace [L.] (**R.I.P.**) may he (or she) rest in peace.

rus in urbe [L.] the country in the town.

sans peur et sans reproche [F.] without fear and without reproach.

sans souci [F.] without care.

sauve qui peut [F.] save himself who can - the cry of disorderly retreat.

semper fidelis [L.] always faithful.

seriatim [L.] in order.

sic [L.] thus. Often used to call attention to some quoted mistake.

sic transit gloria mundi [L.] so passes the glory of the world.

sine die [L.] without date, indefinitely postponed.

si monumentum requiris, circumspice [L.] if you seek (his) monument, look around you. (The inscription on the architect Wren's tomb in St. Paul's.)

sine qua non [L.] an indispensable condition.

soi-disant [F.] so-called; self-styled.

status quo [L.] "the state in which", the pre-existing state of affairs.

stet [L.] let it stand.

Sturm und Drang [Ger.] storm and stress.

sub judice [L.] under consideration.

sub rosa [L.] "under the rose", secretly.

sub voce [L.] under that heading.

sursum corda [L.] lift up your hearts (to God).

table d'hôte [F.] general guest-table, meal at a fixed price.

tant mieux [F.] so much the better.

tant pis [F.] so much the worse.

tempore [L.] in the time of.

tempus fugit [L.] time flies.

terra firma [L.] solid earth.

terra incognita [L.] unexplored land or area of study.

tour de force [F.] a feat of strength or skill.

tout de suite [F.] at once.

tout ensemble [F.] the whole taken together, the general effect.

tout le monde [F.] all the world, everyone.

ubique [L.] everywhere.

ultima Thule [L.] the utmost boundary or limit.

ultra vires [L.] beyond one's powers.

vade in pace [L.] go in peace.

vade mecum [L.] go with me; a constant companion, work of reference.

vale [L.] farewell.

veni, vidi, vici [L.] I came, I saw, I conquered.

ventre à terre [F.] belly to the ground; at high speed.

verbum sapienti satis [L.] (**verb. sap.**) a word is enough for a wise man.

via media [L.] a middle course.

videlicet [L.] (**viz.**) namely, to wit.

volente Deo [L.] God willing.

Weltschmerz [Ger.] world-weariness; sentimental pessimism.

Zeitgeist [Ger.] the spirit of the times.

GROUP NAMES AND COLLECTIVE NOUNS

barren of mules
bevy of quails
bevy of roes
brace or lease of bucks
brood or covey of grouse
brood of hens or chickens
building or clamour of rooks
bunch, company or knob of
   wigeon (in the water)
bunch, knob or spring of teal
cast of hawks
cete of badgers
charm of goldfinches
chattering of choughs
clowder of cats
colony of gulls (breeding)
covert of coots
covey of partridges
cowardice of curs
desert of lapwings
dopping of sheldrakes
down or husk of hares
drove or herd of cattle (kine)
exaltation of larks
fall of woodcocks
field or string of racehorses
flight of wigeon (in the air)
flight or dule of doves
flight of swallows
flight of dunlins
flight, rush, bunch or knob of
pochards
flock or flight of pigeons
flock of sheep
flock of swifts
flock or gaggle of geese
flock, congregation, flight or
   volery of birds
gaggle of geese (on the ground)

gang of elk
haras (stud) of horses
herd of antelopes
herd of buffaloes
herd, sedge or siege of cranes
herd of curlews
herd of deer
herd of giraffes
herd or tribe of goats
herd or pod of seals
herd or bevy of swans
herd of ponies
herd of swine
hill of ruffs
host of sparrows
kindle of kittens
labour of moles
leap of leopards
litter of cubs
litter of pups or pigs
litter of whelps
murmuration of starlings
muster of peacocks
nest of rabbits
nye or nide of pheasants
pace or herd of asses
pack of grouse
pack, mute or cry of hounds
pack, rout or herd of wolves
paddling of ducks
plump, sord or sute of wild fowl
pod of whiting
pride or troop of lions
rag of colts
richesse of martens
run of poultry
school or run of whales
school or gam of porpoises
sedge or siege of bitterns

GROUP NAMES AND COLLECTIVE NOUNS

sedge or siege of herons
shoal or glean of herrings
shoal, draught, haul, run or
   catch of fish
shrewdness of apes
skein of geese (in flight)
skulk of foxes
sloth of bears
sord or sute of mallards
sounder of boars
sounder or dryft of swine
stand or wing of plovers

stud of mares
swarm of insects
swarm or grist of bees, or flies
swarm or cloud of gnats
tok of capercailzies
team of ducks (in flight)
troop of kangaroos
troop of monkeys
walk or wisp of snipe
watch of nightingales
yoke, drove, team or herd
   of oxen

BEVERAGE MEASURES

BEER MEASURES

1 nip = 1/4 pint
1 small = 1/2 pint
1 large = 1 pint
1 flagon = 1 quart
1 anker = 10 gallons
1 firkin = 9 gallons
1 kilderkin = 2 firkins
1 barrel = 2 kilderkins
1 hogshead = 1 1/2 barrels
1 butt = 2 hogsheads
1 tun = 2 butts
      216 gallons

US SPIRITS MEASURES

1 pony = 1/2 jigger
1 jigger = 1 1/2 shot
1 shot = 1 fl oz
1 pint = 16 shots
1 fifth = 25.6 shots
     1.6 pints
     0.8 quart
     0.758 litre
1 quart = 32 shots
     1 1/4 fifths
1 magnum of wine = 2 quarts
         2 1/2 bottles

HANDY MEASURES

small jigger = 1 fl oz
small wine glass = 2 fl oz
cocktail glass = 1/4 pint
sherry glass = 1/4 pint
large wine glass = 1/4 pint
tumbler = 1/2 pint

WINE MEASURES

10 gallons = 1 anker
1 hogshead = 63 gallons
2 hogsheads = 1 pipe
2 pipes = 1 tun
1 puncheon = 84 gallons
1 butt (sherry) = 110 gallons

CHEMICAL ELEMENTS

actinium
aluminium
americium
antimony
argon
arsenic
astatine
barium
berkelium
beryllium
bismuth
boron
bromine
cadmium
caesium
calcium
californium
carbon
cerium
chlorine
chromium
cobalt
copper
curium
dysprosium
einsteinium
erbium
europium
fermium
fluorine
francium
gadolinium
gallium
germanium
gold

hafnium
hahnium
helium
holmium
hydrogen
indium
iodine
iridium
iron
krypton
lanthanum
lawrencium
lead
lithium
lutetium
magnesium
manganese
mendelevium
mercury
molybdenum
neodymium
neon
neptunium
nickel
niobium
nitrogen
nobelium
osmium
oxygen
palladium
phosphorus
platinum
plutonium
polonium
potassium

praseodymium
proactinium
promethium
radium
radon
rhenium
rhodium
rubidium
ruthenium
rutherfordium
samarium
scandium
selenium
silicon
silver
sodium
strontium
sulphur
tantalum
technetium
tellurium
terbium
thallium
thorium
thulium
tin
titanium
tungsten
uranium
vanadium
xenon
ytterbium
yttrium
zinc
zirconium

BOOKS OF THE BIBLE
(including the Apocrypha)

Acts of the Apostles	Haggai	Micah
Amos	Hebrews	Nahum
Baruch	Hosea	Nehemiah
Chronicles	Isaiah	Numbers
Colossians	James	Obadiah
Corinthians	Jeremiah	Peter
Daniel	Job	Philemon
Daniel and	Joel	Philippians
Susanna	John	Proverbs
Daniel, Bel, and	Jonah	Psalms
the Snake	Joshua	Revelations
Deuteronomy	Jude	Romans
Ecclesiastes	Judges	Ruth
Ecclesiasticus	Judith	Samuel
Ephesians	Kings	Solomon
Esdras	Lamentations	Song of Songs
Esther	Leviticus	Song of the Three
Exodus	Luke	Thessalonians
Ezekiel	Maccabees	Timothy
Ezra	Malachi	Titus
Galatians	Manasseh	Tobit
Genesis	Mark	Zechariah
Habbakuk	Matthew	Zephaniah

WEDDING ANNIVERSARIES

YEAR	TRADITIONAL	MODERN
1st	Paper	Clocks
2nd	Cotton	China
3rd	Leather	Crystal, glass
4th	Linen (silk)	Electrical appliances
5th	Wood	Silverware
6th	Iron	Wood
7th	Wool (copper)	Desk sets
8th	Bronze	Linen, lace
9th	Pottery (china)	Leather
10th	Tin (aluminium)	Diamond jewellery
11th	Steel	Fashion jewellery, accessories
12th	Silk	Pearls or coloured gems
13th	Lace	Textile, furs
14th	Ivory	Gold jewellery
15th	Crystal	Watches
20th	China	Platinum
25th	Silver	Sterling silver jubilee
30th	Pearl	Diamond
35th	Coral (jade)	Jade
40th	Ruby	Ruby
45th	Sapphire	Sapphire
50th	Gold	Gold
55th	Emerald	Emerald
60th	Diamond	Diamond

THE SOLAR SYSTEM

The Planets

Planet	Equatorial diameter (kilometres)	Mass (earth masses = 5.974 x 10^24 kg)	Mean distance from sun (millions of kilometres)	Sidereal period
Mercury	4878	0.06	57.91	87.97 days
Venus	12 104	0.82	108.21	224.70 days
Earth	12 756	1.000	149.60	365.26 days
Mars	6787	0.11	227.94	686.980 days
Jupiter	142 800	317.83	778.34	11.86 years
Saturn	120 000	95.17	1427.01	29.46 years
Uranus	50 800	14.50	2869.6	84.01 years
Neptune	48 600	17.20	4496.7	164.79 years
Pluto	3000?	0.002	5907	247.70 years

Planetary Satellites

Planet & satellite	Diameter (km)	Distance from primary (1000km)	Year of discovery
EARTH			
Moon	3 476	384.40	–
MARS			
Phobos	22	9.38	1877
Deimos	13	23.46	1877
JUPITER			
Metis	40	128	1979
Adrastea	20	129	1979
Amalthea	190	181	1892
Thebe	100	222	1979
Io	3 630	422	1610
Europa	3 140	671	1610
Ganymede	5 260	1 070	1610
Callisto	4 800	1 883	1610
Leda	15	11 094	1974
Himalia	185	11 480	1904
Lysithea	35	11 720	1938
Elara	75	11 737	1905
Ananke	30	21 200	1951
Carme	40	22 600	1938
Pasiphae	50	23 500	1908
Sinope	35	23 700	1914

Planetary Satellites

Planet & satellite	Diameter (km)	Distance from primary (1000km)	Year of discovery
SATURN			
Atlas	30	138	1980
Prometheus	105	139	1980
Pandora	90	142	1980
Janus	90	151	1966
Epimetheus	120	151	1966
Mimas	390	186	1789
Enceladus	500	238	1789
Tethys	1 060	295	1684
Telesto	30	295	1980
Calypso	25	295	1980
Dione	1120	377	1684
Helene	30	377	1980
Rhea	1 530	527	1672
Titan	5 150	1 222	1655
Hyperion	290	1 481	1848
Iapetus	1 460	3 561	1671
Phoebe	220	12 952	1898
URANUS			
Cordelia	40	50	1986
Ophelia	50	54	1986
Bianca	50	59	1986
Cressida	60	62	1986
Desdemona	60	63	1986
Juliet	80	64	1986
Portia	90	66	1986
Rosalind	60	70	1986
Belinda	50	75	1986
Puck	170	86	1985
Miranda	480	129	1948
Ariel	1 160	191	1851
Umbriel	1 190	266	1851
Titania	1 610	436	1787
Oberon	1 550	584	1787
NEPTUNE			
1989 N6	50	48	1989
1989 N5	90	50	1989
1989 N3	140	53	1989
1989 N4	160	62	1989
1989 N2	200	74	1989
1989 N1	420	118	1989
Triton	2 720	354	1846
Nereid	340	5 511	1949
PLUTO			
Charon	1 200	19	1978

SI UNITS

Base and supplementary SI units

Physical quantity	SI unit	Symbol
length	metre	m
mass	kilogram	kg
time	second	s
electric current	ampere	A
thermodynamic temperature	kelvin	K
luminous intensity	candela	cd
amount of substance	mole	mol
plane angle (supplementary unit)	radian	rad
solid angle (supplementary unit)	steradian	sr

Derived SI units with special names

Physical quantity	SI unit	Symbol
frequency	hertz	Hz
energy	joule	J
force	newton	N
power	watt	W
pressure	pascal	Pa
electric charge	coulomb	C
electric potential difference	volt	V
electric resistance	ohm	Ω
electric conductance	siemens	S
electric capacitance	farad	F
magnetic flux	weber	Wb
inductance	henry	H
magnetic flux density (magnetic induction)	tesla	T
luminous flux	lumen	lm
illuminance	lux	lx
absorbed dose	gray	Gy
activity	becquerel	Bq
dose equivalent	sievert	Sv

Decimal multiples and submultiples used with SI units

Submultiple	Prefix	Symbol	Multiple	Prefix	Symbol
10^{-1}	deci–	d	10	deca–	da
10^{-2}	cent–	c	10^2	hecto–	h
10^{-3}	milli–	m	10^3	kilo–	k
10^{-6}	micro–	μ	10^6	mega–	M
10^{-9}	nano–	n	10^9	giga–	G
10^{-12}	pico–	p	10^{12}	tera–	T
10^{-15}	femto–	f	10^{15}	peta–	P
10^{-18}	atto–	a	10^{18}	exa–	E

PUNCTUATION AND THE USE OF CAPITAL LETTERS

apostrophe   The sign ('), used to indicate possession. In the singular -'s is used (e.g. *day's end*); in the plural the apostrophe is added to the end of the word (e.g. *the neighbours' dog*). Plurals that do not end in -s also take -'s (e.g. *sheep's eyes*). Except for a few traditional exceptions (like *Jesus', Keats'*) proper names ending in -s take -'s at the end (e.g. *Thomas's, the Jones's*).

brackets   These serve to isolate part of a sentence which could be omitted and still leave an intelligible statement. Punctuation of the rest of the sentence should run as if the bracketed portion were not there, e.g. *That house over there (with the blue door) is ours.* Square brackets are used where the writer inserts his own information into a quotation, e.g. *I knew Pitt [the Younger] as a boy.*

capital letters   These are used at the beginning of a sentence or quoted speech, and for proper names and titles of people and organizations, e.g. *Mr Robertson, Dr Smith, South America, British Rail.* They are not used when speaking of a general topic like *the pay of miners, the manufacture of cosmetics.* If an initial *the* is included in a title it has a capital,
e.g. *We went to see The Tempest.*

colons and semicolons   The function of these is to provide more of a break than a comma, and less than a full stop. The colon is used to make an abrupt break between two related statements, e.g. *Take it or leave it: the choice is yours.* It is also used to introduce a list, quotation, or summary and may be followed by a dash if the following matter begins on a separate line. Semicolons can be used instead of conjunctions to link two sentences or parts of them, e.g. *Two of the lights were working; two were out.*

commas   1. These make divisions or slight pauses in sentences, e.g. *She stormed out, slamming the door behind her.*
2. Commas are used to divide units in a series of nouns, adjectives, or phrases, e.g. *The cupboard was full of pots, pans and crockery.* In such a series the last comma (i.e. before 'and' or 'or') is optional. It is not usual to place a comma between the last of a series of adjectives and the noun, e.g. *It was a long, hot, humid day.*
3. Commas also serve to mark off a word or phrase in a sentence which can stand grammatically complete on its own, as can dashes and brackets.

PUNCTUATION AND THE USE OF CAPITAL LETTERS

Commas give the lightest degree of separation, dashes produce a jerky effect, and brackets cut off part of a sentence most firmly, e.g. *He hurried home, taking a short cut, but still arrived too late. It's a long time – over two years – since last we met. They both went to Athens (unaware of each other's plans) and stayed in the same hotel.*
4. When two phrases are linked by a conjunction a comma is used if there is a contrast, e.g. *She was dark, but her brother was fair.*
5. When addressing a person, commas are used before and after the person's name or title, e.g. *Well, Mrs Smith, how are you today?*

exclamation marks   These should only be used after genuine exclamations and not after ordinary statements.

full stops (periods)   Normally, these appear only at the end of a complete sentence containing a main verb, except in reported speech and where a passage takes the form of an argument, e.g. *You may think you can get away with it. Not a chance.* Full stops are also used after abbreviations and initial letters standing for the whole word (as in *fig., a.m., R.C.*) but they are often omitted after abbreviations which include the first and last letters of a word (*Dr, Mr, ft*) and in much-used titles like *BBC, USA, TUC.* As usage is currently in a state of flux the above should be taken only as a guide to common practice.

hyphens   Compound words, like *lay-by* or *manor house*, or words with a prefix, like *unpick*, may or may not contain a hyphen. It is generally used when the compound is new and dropped as it becomes familiar. When a compound adjective comes before a noun it should be hyphenated to stress that the constituent parts are not to be used independently, e.g. *He has a half-Italian wife.*

Inverted commas (quotation marks, quotes)   1. These are used for direct quotation, not for indirect speech. It is usual to have a comma before and after a quotation if the sentence is resumed, e.g. *He said, "Follow me", and set off down the street.*
2. Single quotation marks can be used in indicate a title or quotation within a speech, e.g. *"I loved 'War and Peace', " she said, "but it took so long to read."*

question marks   These are used at the end of direct questions, but not after reported ones.

TYPES OF CALENDAR

The number of days in a year varies among cultures and from year to year.

GREGORIAN

The Gregorian calendar is a 16th-century adaptation of the Julian calendar devised in the 1st century BC. The year in this calendar is based on the solar year, which lasts about 365 1/4 days. In this system, years whose number is not divisible by 4 have 365 days, as do centennial years unless the figures before the noughts are divisible by 4. All other years have 366 days; these are leap years.

Below are the names of the months and number of days for a non-leap year.

January 31	April 30	July 31	October 31
February 28*	May 31	August 31	November 30
March 31	June 30	September 30	December 31

* 29 in leap years

JEWISH

A year in the Jewish calendar has 13 months if its number, when divided by 19, leaves 0, 3, 6, 8, 11, 14 or 17; otherwise, it has 12 months. The year is based on the lunar year, but its number of months varies to keep broadly in line with the solar cycle. Its precise number of days is fixed with reference to particular festivals that must not fall on certain days of the week.

Below are the names of the months and number of days in each for the year 5471, a 12-month year (1980 AD in Gregorian).

Tishri 30	Tevet 29	Nisan 30	Tammuz 29
Cheshvan 29*	Shevat 30	Iyar 29	Av 30
Kislev 29*	Adar 29	Sivan 30	Elul 29

* 30 in some years.

In 13-month years, the month Veadar, with 29 days, falls between Adar and Nisan.

MUSLIM

A year in the Muslim calendar has 355 days if its number, when divided by 30, leaves 2, 5, 7, 10, 13, 16, 18, 21, 24, 26 or 29; otherwise it has 354 days. As in the Jewish calendar, years are based on the lunar cycle.

Below are the names of the months and number of days in each for the Muslim year 1401 (1980 AD in Gregorian).

Muharram 30	Rabi'II 29	Rajab 30	Shawwal 29
Safar 29	Jumada I 30	Sha'ban 29	Dhu 1-Qa'dah 30
Rabi'I 30	Jumada II 29	Ramadan 30	Dhu 1-Hijja 30*

* 29 in some years.

Collins English Dictionaries and English Language Reference:

a selection

Collins English Dictionary
1824 pages • 180,000 references
Includes encyclopedic material

Collins Concise Dictionary
1656 pages • 125,000 references
Includes encyclopedic material

Collins Paperback Dictionary
1024 pages • 63,000 references

Collins Pocket Dictionary
576 pages • 44,000 references

Collins English Dictionary and Thesaurus
1408 pages • 105,000 references
325,000 synonyms and antonyms
All key words in colour

Collins English Thesaurus in A-Z Form
828 pages • 325,000 synonyms and antonyms
All entry words in colour

Collins Paperback Thesaurus in A-Z Form
720 pages • 300,000 synonyms and antonyms